DTT	dithiothreitol		HBV	hepatitis B virus
EACA	epsilon aminocaproic acid		Hct	hematocrit
EBAA	Eye Bank Association of America		HCV	hepatitis C virus
EBV	Epstein-Barr virus		HDFN	hemolytic disease of the fetus and newborn
ECMO	extracorporeal membrane oxygenation		HDV	hepatitis D virus
EDTA	ethylenediaminetetraacetic acid		HES	hydroxyethyl starch
EIA	enzyme immunoassay		HEV	hepatitis E virus
ELAT	enzyme-linked antiglobulin test		HIV	human immunodeficiency virus
ELBW	extremely low birthweight		HPC	hematopoietic progenitor cell
ELISA	enzyme-linked immunosorbent assay		HTLV-I	human T-cell lymphotropic virus type I
EPO	erythropoietin		HTR	hemolytic transfusion reaction
ESR	erythrocyte sedimentation rate		HUS	hemolytic uremic syndrome
FACT	Foundation for the Accreditation of Cellular Therapy		IAT	indirect antiglobulin test
FDA	Food and Drug Administration		Ig	immunoglobulin
FFP	Fresh Frozen Plasma		IGIV	Immunoglobulin Intravenous
FMH	fetomaternal hemorrhage		IHA	immune hemolytic anemia
FNHTR	febrile nonhemolytic transfusion reaction		IL-1α	interleukin 1 alpha
			IL-1ß	interleukin 1 beta
FTA-ABS	fluorescent treponemal antibody absorption test		IL-2	interleukin 2
			IPT	intraperitoneal transfusion
5-FU	5-fluorouracil		IS	immediate spin
G-CSF	granulocyte colony-stimulating factors		ISBT	International Society of Blood Transfusion
GalNAc	N-acetylgalactosamine		ISCT	International Society for Cellular Therapy
GM-CSF	granulocyte macrophage colony-stimulating factors		ITP	idiopathic thrombocytopenic purpura
GMP	good manufacturing practice		IUT	intrauterine transfusion
Gp	glycoprotein		IVT	intravascular transfusion
GPA	glycophorin A		JCAHO	Joint Commission on Accreditation of Healthcare Organizations
GPB	glycophorin B		L/S	lecithin to sphingomyelin
GPC	glycophorin C		LDH	lactate dehydrogenase
GPD	glycophorin D		LDL	low-density lipoproteins
GVHD	graft-vs-host disease		LISS	low ionic strength saline
Gy	Gray		LT-CIC	long-term culture-initiating cells
HAM	HTLV-associated myelopathy		MAC	membrane attack complex
HAV	hepatitis A virus		2-ME	2-mercaptoethanol
HAZMAT	hazardous material		MF	mixed field
Hb	hemoglobin		MHC	major histocompatibility complex
HBc	hepatitis B core antigen		MLC	mixed lymphocyte (leukocyte) culture
HBIG	hepatitis B immunoglobulin			
HBsAg	hepatitis B surface antigen			

(cont'd)

MLR	mixed lymphocyte (leukocyte) reaction	RBCs	Red Blood Cells (blood donor unit)
MoAb	monoclonal antibody	RCA	regulators of complement activation
mRNA	messenger ribonucleic acid	RES	reticuloendothelial system
MSBOS	maximum surgical blood order schedule	RFLP	restriction fragment length polymorphism
MSDS	material safety data sheets	Rh	Rhesus factor
NAIT	neonatal alloimmune thrombocytopenia	RhIG	Rh Immune Globulin
NAT	nucleic acid testing	RIBA	recombinant immunoblot assay
NIH	National Institutes of Health	RNA	ribonucleic acid
NK	natural killer	RPGN	rapidly progressive glomerulonephritis
NMDP	National Marrow Donor Program	RPR	rapid plasma reagin (serologic test for syphilis)
NRC	Nuclear Regulatory Commission	RR	repeatedly reactive or relative risk
NT	not tested	RT	room temperature or reverse transcriptase
OSHA	Occupational Safety and Health Administration	SBO	standard blood order
p	probability	SCF	stem cell factor
PAD	preoperative autologous (blood) donation	SGP	sialoglycoprotein
PBPC	peripheral blood progenitor cell	SOP	standard operating procedure
PBS	phosphate-buffered saline	SPA	staphylococcal protein A
PCH	paroxysmal cold hemoglobinuria	SSO	sequence-specific oligonucleotide
PCR	polymerase chain reaction	STS	serologic test for syphilis
PEG	polyethylene glycol	TA	transfusion-associated
PHA	phytohemagglutinin	TCR	T-cell receptor
PI	paternity index	TNF-α	tumor necrosis factor alpha
PPE	personal protective equipment	TPE	therapeutic plasma exchange
PPF	plasma protein fraction	TRALI	transfusion-related acute lung injury
PPTA	Plasma Protein Therapeutics Association	tRNA	transfer ribonucleic acid
PRA	panel reactive antibody	TTP	thrombotic thrombocytopenic purpura
PT	prothrombin time or proficiency test	UNOS	United Network for Organ Sharing
PTP	posttransfusion purpura	VLBW	very low birthweight
PUBS	percutaneous umbilical blood sampling	vWD	von Willebrand disease
PVC	polyvinyl chloride	vWF	von Willebrand factor
QA	quality assessment or quality assurance	WAIHA	warm autoimmune hemolytic anemia
QC	quality control	WB	Whole Blood or Western blot
QSE	quality system essential	XM	crossmatch

TECHNICAL MANUAL

FIFTEENTH EDITION

**Advancing Transfusion and
Cellular Therapies Worldwide**

Other related publications available from the AABB:

Technical Manual and Standards for Blood Banks and
Transfusion Services on CD-ROM

Transfusion Therapy: Clinical Principles and Practice, 2nd Edition
Edited by Paul D. Mintz, MD

Transfusion Medicine Self-Assessment and Review
By Pam S. Helekar, MD; Douglas P. Blackall, MD; Jeffrey L. Winters, MD;
and Darrell J. Triulzi, MD

Blood Transfusion Therapy: A Physician's Handbook, 8th Edition
Edited by Jerry Gottschall, MD

Practical Guide to Transfusion Medicine
By Marian Petrides, MD, and Gary Stack, MD, PhD

Transfusion Medicine Interactive: A Case Study Approach CD-ROM
By Marian Petrides, MD; Roby Rogers, MD; and Nora Ratcliffe, MD

To purchase books, please call our sales department at (866)222-2498 (within the United States) or (301)215-6499 (outside the United States); fax orders to (301)907-6895 or email orders to sales@aabb.org. View the AABB Publications Catalog and order books on the AABB Web site at www.aabb.org. For other book services, including chapter reprints and large quantity sales, ask for the Senior Sales Associate.

Technical Manual

15th Edition

aaBB

AABB
8101 Glenbrook Road
Bethesda, Maryland 20814-2749

ISBN No. 1-56395-196-7
Printed in the United States

Cataloging-in-Publication Data

Technical manual / editor, Mark E. Brecher. —15th ed.
        p. ; cm.
   Including bibliographic references and index.
ISBN 1-56395-196-7
1. Blood Banks—Handbooks, manuals, etc. I. Brecher, Mark E. II. AABB.
[DNLM: 1. Blood Banks—laboratory manuals. 2. Blood Transfusion—
laboratory manuals. WH 25 T2548 2005]
RM172.T43 2005
615'.39—dc23
DNLM/DLC

Technical Manual Program Unit

Chair and Editor

Mark E. Brecher, MD

Associate Editors

Regina M. Leger, MSQA, MT(ASCP)SBB, CQMgr(ASQ)
Jeanne V. Linden, MD, MPH
Susan D. Roseff, MD

Members/Authors

Martha Rae Combs, MT(ASCP)SBB
Gregory Denomme, PhD, FCSMLS(D)
Brenda J. Grossman, MD, MPH
N. Rebecca Haley, MD, MT(ASCP)SBB
Teresa Harris, MT(ASCP)SBB, CQIA(ASQ)
Betsy W. Jett, MT(ASCP), CQA(ASQ)CQMgr
Regina M. Leger, MSQA, MT(ASCP)SBB, CQMgr(ASQ)
Jeanne V. Linden, MD, MPH
Janice G. McFarland, MD
James T. Perkins, MD
Susan D. Roseff, MD
Joseph Sweeney, MD
Darrell J. Triulzi, MD

Liaisons

Gilliam B. Conley, MA, MT(ASCP)SBB
Michael C. Libby, MSc, MT(ASCP)SBB

Acknowledgments

The Technical Manual Program Unit extends special thanks to those volunteers who provided peer review and made other contributions:

James P. AuBuchon, MD

Lucia M. Berte, MA, MT(ASCP)SBB, DLM, CQA(ASQ)CQMgr

Arthur Bracey, MD

Linda Braddy, MT(ASCP)SBB

Donald R. Branch, MT(ASCP)SBB, PhD

Ritchard Cable, MD

Sally Caglioti, MT(ASCP)SBB

Loni Calhoun, MT(ASCP)SBB

Tony S. Casina, MT(ASCP)SBB

Geoff Daniels, PhD, MRcPath

Robertson Davenport, MD

Richard J. Davey, MD

Walter Dzik, MD

Ted Eastlund, MD

Anne F. Eder, MD, PhD

Ronald O. Gilcher, MD, FACP

Lawrence T. Goodnough, MD

Linda Hahn, MT(ASCP)SBB, MPM

Heather Hume, MD

Mark A. Janzen, PhD

Susan T. Johnson, MSTM, MT(ASCP)SBB

W. John Judd, FIBMS, MIBiol

Michael H. Kanter, MD

Louis M. Katz, MD

Debra Kessler, RN, MS

Thomas Kickler, MD

Karen E. King, MD

Joanne Kosanke, MT(ASCP)SBB

Thomas A. Lane, MD

Alan H. Lazarus, PhD

German F. Leparc, MD

Douglas M. Lublin, MD, PhD

Dawn Michelle, MT(ASCP)SBB

Kenneth Moise, Jr., MD

S. Breanndan Moore, MD

Tania Motschman, MS, MT(ASCP)SBB, CQA(ASQ)

Marilyn K. Moulds, MT(ASCP)SBB

Nancy C. Mullis, MT(ASCP)SBB

Scott Murphy, MD

Patricia Pisciotto, MD

Mark A. Popovsky, MD

Marion E. Reid, PhD, FIBMS

Jennifer F. Rhamy, MBA, MA, MT(ASCP), SBB, HP

Scott D. Rowley, MD

Arell S. Shapiro, MD

R. Sue Shirey, MS, MT(ASCP)SBB

Bruce Spiess, MD, FAHA

Jerry E. Squires, MD, PhD

Marilyn J. Telen, MD

Susan Veneman, MT(ASCP)SBB

Phyllis S. Walker, MS, MT(ASCP)SBB

Dan A. Waxman, MD

Robert Weinstein, MD

Connie M. Westhoff, PhD, MT(ASCP)SBB

Members of AABB committees who reviewed manuscripts as part of committee resource charges

The staff of the Armed Services Blood Program Office

The staff of the US Food and Drug Administration, Center for Biologics Evaluation and Research

The staff of the Transplantation and Transfusion Service, McClendon Clinical Laboratories, UNC Hospitals

Special thanks are due to Laurie Munk, Janet McGrath, Nina Hutchinson, Jay Pennington, Frank McNeirney, Kay Gregory, MT(ASCP)SBB, and Allene Carr-Greer, MT(ASCP)SBB of the AABB National Office for providing support to the Program Unit during preparation of this edition.

Introduction

The 15th edition of the AABB *Technical Manual* is the first in the second half century of this publication. The original *Technical Manual* (then called *Technical Methods and Procedures*) was published in 1953 and the 14th edition marked the 50th anniversary of this publication.

Over the years, this text has grown and matured, until today it is a major textbook used by students (medical technology and residents) and practicing health-care professionals (technologists, nurses, and physicians) around the world. Selected editions or excerpts have been translated into French, Hungarian, Italian, Japanese, Spanish, Polish, and Russian. It is one of only two AABB publications that are referenced by name in the AABB *Standards for Blood Banks and Transfusion Services* (the other being the *Circular of Information for the Use of Human Blood Components*). All branches of the US Armed Services have adopted the AABB *Technical Manual* as their respective official manuals for blood banking and transfusion medicine activities.

The *Technical Manual* serves a diverse readership and is used as a technical reference, a source for developing policies and procedures, and an educational tool. The *Technical Manual* is often the first reference consulted in many laboratories; thus, it is intended to provide the background information to allow both students and experienced individuals to rapidly familiarize themselves with the rationale and scientific basis of the AABB standards and current standards of practice. As in previous editions, the authors and editors have tried to provide both breadth and depth, including substantial theoretical and clinical material as well as technical details. Due to space limitations, the *Technical Manual* cannot provide all of the advanced information on any specific topic. However, it is hoped that sufficient information is provided to answer the majority of queries for which individuals consult the text, or at a minimum, to direct someone toward additional pertinent references.

Readers should be aware that, unlike most textbooks in the field, this book is subjected to extensive peer review (by experts in specific subject areas, AABB committees, and regulatory bodies such as the Food and Drug Administration). As such, this text is relatively unique, and represents a major effort on the part of the AABB to provide an authoritative and balanced reference source.

As in previous recent editions, the content is necessarily limited in order to retain the size of the *Technical Manual* to that of a textbook that can be easily handled. Nevertheless, readers will find extensive new and updated information, including expanded coverage of quality approaches, apheresis indications, cellular nomenclature, molecular diagnostics, hematopoietic progenitor cell processing, and transfusion-transmitted diseases.

Techniques and policies outlined in the *Technical Manual* are, to the best of the Technical Manual Program Unit's ability, in conformance with AABB *Standards*. They are not to be considered the only permissible way in which requirements of *Standards* can be met. Other methods, not included, may give equally acceptable results. If discrepancy occurs between techniques or suggestions in the *Technical Manual* and the requirements of *Standards*, authority resides in *Standards*. Despite the best efforts of both the Program Unit and the extensive number of outside reviewers, errors may remain in the text. As with previous editions, the Program Unit welcomes suggestions, criticisms, or questions about the current edition.

I would like to thank the members of the Technical Manual Program Unit for their dedication and long hours of work that went into updating this edition. I would also like to thank all the AABB committees, the expert reviewers, and the readers who have offered numerous helpful suggestions that helped to make this edition possible. I would particularly like to thank my three associate editors—Gina Leger, Jeanne Linden, and Sue Roseff—who have provided countless invaluable hours in the preparation of this edition. Finally I would like to thank Laurie Munk, AABB Publications Director, whose tireless efforts on behalf of the *Technical Manual* never cease to amaze me, and who has made the publication of this book a pleasure.

This edition is my third and final *Technical Manual*. I served as associate editor for the 13th edition and chief editor for the 14th and 15th editions. It has been an honor to help shepherd these editions to fruition and it is my hope that the AABB *Technical Manual* will continue to be one of the AABB's premier publications for decades to come.

Mark E. Brecher, MD
Chief Editor
Chapel Hill, NC

Contents

Quality Issues

Blood Donation and Collection

Immunologic and Genetic Principles

Blood Groups

Serologic Principles and Transfusion Medicine

Clinical Considerations in Transfusion Practice

Methods

Appendices

Chapter 1

Quality Systems

A PRIMARY GOAL OF blood centers and transfusion services is to promote high standards of quality in all aspects of production, patient care, and service. This commitment to quality is reflected in standards of practice set forth by the AABB.[1(p1)] A quality system includes the organizational structure, responsibilities, policies, processes, procedures, and resources established by the executive management to achieve quality.[1(p1)] A glossary of quality terms used in this chapter is included in Appendix 1-1.

The establishment of a formal quality assurance program is required by regulation under the Centers for Medicare and Medicaid Services (CMS)[2] Clinical Laboratory Improvement Amendments (CLIA) and the Food and Drug Administration (FDA)[3-5] current good manufacturing practice (cGMP). The FDA regulations in 21 CFR 211.22 require an independent quality control or quality assurance unit that has responsibil-

ity for the overall quality of the finished product and authority to control the processes that may affect this product.[4] (See *Code of Federal Regulations* quality-related citations in Appendix 1-2.) Professional and accrediting organizations, such as the AABB,[1] Joint Commission on Accreditation of Healthcare Organizations (JCAHO),[6] College of American Pathologists (CAP),[7] and the Clinical and Laboratory Standards Institute (formerly NCCLS),[8] have also established requirements and guidelines to address quality issues. The International Organization for Standardization (ISO) quality management standards (ISO 9001) are generic to any industry and describe the key elements of a quality system.[9] In addition, the Health Care Criteria for Performance Excellence[10] published by the Baldrige National Quality Program provide an excellent framework for implementing quality on an organizational level. The AABB defines the minimum elements that must be addressed in a blood bank or transfusion service quality system in its Quality System Essentials (QSEs).[11] The AABB QSEs were developed to be compatible with ISO 9001 standards and the FDA Guideline for Quality Assurance in Blood Establishments.[5] Table 1-1 shows a comparison of the AABB QSEs and ISO 9001:2000 requirements.

Quality Control, Quality Assurance, and Quality Management

The purpose of *quality control* (QC) is to provide feedback to operational staff about the state of a process that is in progress. It tells staff whether to continue (everything is acceptable), or whether to stop until a problem has been resolved (something is found to be out of control). Product QC is performed to determine whether the product or service meets specifications. Historically, blood banks and transfusion services have employed many QC measures as standard practice in their operations. Examples include reagent QC, clerical checks, visual inspections, and measurements such as temperature readings on refrigerators and volume or cell counts performed on finished blood components.

Quality assurance activities are not tied to the actual performance of a process. They include retrospective review and analysis of operational performance data to determine if the overall process is in a state of control and to detect shifts or trends that require attention. Quality assurance provides information to process managers regarding levels of performance that can be used in setting priorities for process improvement. Examples in blood banking include record reviews, monitoring of quality indicators, and internal assessments.

Quality management considers interrelated processes in the context of the organization and its relations with customers and suppliers. It addresses the leadership role of executive management in creating a commitment to quality throughout the organization, the understanding of suppliers and customers as partners in quality, the management of human and other resources, and quality planning. The quality systems approach described in this chapter encompasses all of these activities. It ensures the application of quality principles throughout the organization and reflects the changing focus of quality efforts from detection to prevention.

Quality Concepts

Juran's Quality Trilogy

Juran's Quality Trilogy is one example of a quality management approach. This model centers around three fundamental processes for the management of quality in any organization: planning, control, and improvement.[12(p2.5)]

The *planning* process for a new product or service includes activities to identify requirements, to develop product and process specifications to meet those requirements, and to design the process. During the planning phase, the facility must perform the following steps:

1. Establish quality goals for the project.
2. Identify the customers.
3. Determine customer needs and expectations.
4. Develop product and service specifications to meet customer, operational, regulatory, and accreditation requirements.

Table 1-1. Comparison of the AABB Quality System Essentials and the ISO 9001 Categories*

AABB Quality System Essentials	ISO 9001:2000
Organization	4.1 General requirements 5.1 Management commitment 5.2 Customer focus 5.3 Quality policy 5.4 Planning 5.5 Responsibility, authority, and communication 5.6 Management review
Resources	6.1 Provision of resources 6.2 Human resources
Equipment	6.3 Infrastructure 7.6 Control of monitoring and measuring devices
Supplier and Customer Issues	7.2 Customer-related processes 7.4 Purchasing
Process Control	7.1 Planning of product realization 7.3 Design and development 7.5 Production and service provision
Documents and Records	4.2 Documentation requirements
Deviations, Nonconformances, and Complications	8.3 Control of nonconforming product
Assessments: Internal and External	8.2 Monitoring and measuring 8.4 Analysis of data
Process Improvement	8.1 General 8.4 Analysis of data 8.5 Improvement
Facilities and Safety	6.3 Infrastructure 6.4 Work environment

*This table represents only one way of comparing the two systems.

5. Develop operational processes for production and delivery, including written procedures and resources requirements.
6. Develop process controls and validate the process in the operational setting.

The results of the planning process are referred to as design output.[9]

Once implemented, the *control* process provides a feedback loop for operations that includes the following:

1. Evaluation of actual performance.
2. Comparison of performance to goals.
3. Action to correct any discrepancy between the two.

It addresses control of inputs, production, and delivery of products and services to meet specifications. Process controls should put operational staff in a state of self-control such that they can recognize when things are going wrong, and either make appropriate adjustments to ensure the quality of the product or stop the process. An important goal in quality management is to establish a set of controls that ensure process and product quality but that are not excessive. Controls that do not add value should be eliminated in order to conserve limited resources and to allow staff to focus attention on those controls that are critical to the operation. Statistical tools, such as process capability measurement and control charts, allow the facility to evaluate process performance during the planning stage and in operations. These tools help determine whether a process is stable (ie, in statistical control) and whether it is capable of meeting product and service specifications.[12(p22.19)]

Quality *improvement* is intended to attain higher levels of performance, either by creating new or better features that add value, or by removing existing deficiencies in the process, product, or service. Opportunities to improve may be related to deficiencies in the initial planning process; unforeseen factors that are discovered upon implementation; shifts in customer needs; or changes in starting materials, environmental factors, and other variables that affect the process. Improvements must be based on data-driven analysis; an ongoing program of measurement and assessment is fundamental to this process.

Process Approach

In its most generic form, a process includes all of the resources and activities that transform an input into an output. An understanding of how to manage and control processes in the blood bank or transfusion service is based on the simple equation:

$$INPUT \rightarrow PROCESS \rightarrow OUTPUT$$

For example, a key process for donor centers is donor selection. The "input" includes 1) the individual who presents for donation and 2) all of the resources required for the donor health screening. Through a series of activities including verification of eligibility (based on results of prior donations, mini-physical, and health history questionnaire), an individual is deemed an "eligible donor." The "output" is either an eligible donor who can continue to the next process (blood collection) or an ineligible donor who is deferred. When the selection process results in a deferred donor, the resources (inputs) associated with that process are wasted and contribute to the cost of quality. One way that donor centers attempt to minimize this cost is to educate potential donors before the health screening so that those who are not eligible do not enter the selection process.

Strategies for managing a process should consider all of its components, including its interrelated activities, inputs, outputs, and resources. Supplier qualification, formal agreements, supply verification, and inventory control are strategies for ensuring that the inputs to a process meet specifications. Personnel training and competency assessment, equipment maintenance and control, management of documents and records, and implementation of appropriate in-process controls provide assurance that the process will operate as intended. End-product testing and inspection, customer feedback, and outcome measurement provide information to help evaluate the quality of the product and to improve the process as a whole. These output measurements and quality indicators are used to evaluate the effectiveness of the process and process controls.

In order to manage a system of processes effectively, the facility must understand how its processes interact and any cause-and-effect relationships between them. In the donor selection example, the consequences of accepting a donor who is not eligible reach into almost every other process in the facility. One example would be a donor with a history of high-risk behavior that is not identified during the selection process. The donated product may test positive for one of the viral marker assays, triggering follow-up testing, look-back investigations, and donor deferral and notification procedures. Components must be quarantined and their discard documented. Staff involved in collecting and processing the product are at risk of exposure to infectious agents. Part of quality planning is to identify those relationships so that quick and appropriate corrective action can be taken if process controls fail. It is important to remember that operational processes include not only product manufacture or service creation, but also the delivery of a product or service. Delivery generally involves interaction with the customer. The quality of this transaction is critical to customer satisfaction and should not be overlooked in the design and ongoing assessment of the quality system.

Service vs Production

Quality principles apply equally to a broad spectrum of activities, from those involved in processing and production, to those involving the interactions between individuals in the delivery of a service. However, different strategies may be appropriate when there are differing expectations related to customer satisfaction. Although the emphasis in a production process is to minimize variation in order to create a product that consistently meets specifications, service processes require a certain degree of flexibility to address customer needs and circumstances at the time of the transaction. In production, personnel need to know how to maintain uniformity in the day-to-day operation. In service, personnel need to be able to adapt the service in a way that meets customer expectations but does not compromise quality. To do this, personnel must have sufficient knowledge and understanding of interrelated processes to use independent judgment appropriately, or they must have ready access to higher level decision-makers. When designing quality systems for production processes, it is useful to think of the process as the driver, with people providing the oversight and support needed to keep it running smoothly and effectively. In service, people are the focus; the underlying process provides a foundation that enables staff to deliver safe and effective services that meet the needs of the customers in almost any situation.

Quality Management as an Evolving Science

It is important to remember that quality management is an evolving science. The principles and tools in use today will change as research provides new knowledge of organizational behavior, as technology provides new solutions, and as the field of transfusion medicine presents new challenges. Periodic assessments of the quality management systems will help identify practices that are no longer effective or that could be improved through the use of new technology or new tools.

Practical Application of Quality Principles

The remainder of this chapter discusses the elements of a quality system and practical application of quality principles to the blood bank and transfusion service environment. These basic elements include:

- Organizational management
- Human resources
- Customer and supplier relations
- Equipment management
- Process management
- Documents and records
- Deviations and nonconforming products and services
- Monitoring and assessment
- Process improvement
- Work environment

Organizational Management

The facility should be organized in a manner that promotes effective implementation and management of its quality system. The structure of the organization must be documented and the responsibilities for the provision of blood, components, products, and services must be clearly defined. These should include a description of the relationships and avenues of communication between organizational units and those responsible for key quality functions. Each facility may define its structure in any format that suits its operations. Organizational trees or charts that show the structure and relationships are helpful.

The facility must define in writing the authority and responsibilities of management to establish and maintain the quality system. These include oversight of operations and regulatory and accreditation compliance as well as periodic review and assessment of quality system effectiveness. Executive management support for quality system goals, objectives, and policies is critical to the success of the program. Management must participate in the review and approval of quality and technical policies, processes, and procedures.

The individual designated to oversee the facility's quality functions must report directly to management. This person has the responsibility to coordinate, monitor, and facilitate quality system activities and has the authority to recommend and initiate corrective action when appropriate.[5] The designated individual need not perform all of the quality functions personally. Ideally, this person should be independent of the operational functions of the donor center or transfusion service. In small facilities, however, this may not always be possible. Depending on the size and scope of the organization, the designated oversight person may work in a department (eg, transfusion service), may have responsibilities covering several areas (eg, laboratory-wide), may have a staff of workers (eg, quality unit), or may be part of an organization-wide unit (eg, hospital quality management). Individuals with dual quality and operational responsibilities should not provide quality oversight for operational work they have performed (21 CFR 211.194).

Quality oversight functions may include the following[5]:

- Review and approval of standard operating procedures (SOPs) and training plans.
- Review and approval of validation plans and results.
- Review and approval of document control and record-keeping systems.
- Audit of operational functions.
- Development of criteria for evaluating systems.
- Review and approval of suppliers.
- Review and approval of product specifications, ie, requirements to be met by the products used in the manufacturing, distribution, or transfusion of blood and components.
- Review of reports of adverse reactions, deviations in the manufacturing process, nonconforming products and services, and customer complaints.
- Participation in decisions to determine blood and component suitability for use, distribution, or recall.
- Review and approval of corrective action plans.
- Surveillance of problems (eg, error reports, inspection deficiencies, customer complaints) and the effectiveness of corrective actions implemented to solve these problems.
- Use of information resources to identify trends and potential problems before a situation worsens and products or patients are affected.
- Preparation of periodic (as specified by the organization) reports of quality issues, trends, findings, and corrective and preventive actions.

Quality oversight functions may be shared among existing staff, departments, and facilities, or, in some instances, may be contracted to an outside firm. The goal is to provide as much of an independent evaluation of the facility's quality activities as pos-

sible. Policies, processes, and procedures must exist to define the roles and responsibilities of all individuals in the development and maintenance of these quality goals. Quality system policies and processes should be applicable across the entire facility. A blood bank or transfusion service need not develop its own quality policies if it is part of a larger entity whose quality management system addresses all of the minimum requirements. The quality system must address all matters related to compliance with federal, state, and local regulations and accreditation standards applicable to the organization.

Human Resources

This element of the quality system is aimed at management of personnel, including selection, orientation, training, competency assessment, and staffing.

Selection

Each blood bank, transfusion service, or donor center must have a process to provide adequate numbers of qualified personnel to perform, verify, and manage all activities within the facility.[1(p3),3] Qualification requirements are determined based on job responsibilities. The selection process should consider the applicant's qualifications for a particular position as determined by education, training, experience, certifications, and/or licensure. For laboratory testing staff, the standards for personnel qualifications must be compatible with the regulatory requirements established under CLIA.[2] Job descriptions are required for all personnel involved in processes and procedures that affect the quality of blood, components, tissues, and services. Effective job descriptions clearly define the qualifications, responsibilities, and reporting relationships of the position.

Orientation, Training, and Competency Assessment

Once hired, employees must be oriented to their position and to the organization's policies and procedures. The orientation program should include facility-specific requirements and an introduction to policies that address issues such as safety, quality, computers, security, and confidentiality. The job-related portion of the orientation program covers the operational issues specific to the work area. Training must be provided for each procedure for which employees have responsibility. The ultimate result of the orientation and training program is to deem new employees competent to work independently in performing the duties and responsibilities defined in their job descriptions. Time frames should be established to accomplish this goal. Before the introduction of a new test or service, existing personnel must be trained to perform their newly assigned duties and must be deemed competent. During orientation and training, the employee should be given the opportunity to ask questions and seek additional help or clarification. All aspects of the training must be documented and the facility trainer or designated facility management representative and the employee should mutually agree upon the determination of competence.

FDA cGMP training is required for staff involved in the manufacture of blood and blood components.[4] It should provide staff with an understanding of the regulatory basis for the facility's policies and procedures as well as train them in facility-specific application of the cGMP requirements as described in their own written operating procedures. This training must be provided at periodic intervals to ensure that staff remain familiar with regulatory requirements.

To ensure that skills are maintained, the facility must have regularly scheduled competence evaluations of all staff whose activities affect the quality of blood, components, tissues, or services.[2,6] Depending upon the nature of the job duties, such assessments may include: written evaluations; direct observation of activities; review of work records or reports, computer records, and QC records; testing of unknown samples; and evaluation of the employee's problem-solving skills.[5]

A formal competency plan that includes a schedule of assessments, defined minimum acceptable performance, and remedial measures is one way to ensure appropriate and consistent competence assessments. Assessments need not be targeted at each individual test or procedure performed by the employee; instead, they can be grouped together to assess like techniques or methods. Written tests can be used effectively to evaluate problem-solving skills and to rapidly cover many topics by asking one or more questions for each area to be assessed. For testing personnel, CMS requires that employees who perform testing be assessed semiannually during the first year and annually thereafter.[2]

The quality oversight personnel should assist in the development, review, and approval of training programs, including the criteria for retraining.[5] Quality oversight personnel also monitor the effectiveness of the training program and competence evaluations and make recommendations for changes as needed. In addition, JCAHO requires the analysis of aggregate competency assessment data for the purpose of identifying staff learning needs.[6]

Staffing

Management should have a staffing plan that describes the number and qualifications of personnel needed to perform the functions of the facility safely and effectively. JCAHO requires that hospitals evaluate staffing effectiveness by looking at human resource indicators (eg, overtime, staff injuries, staff satisfaction) in conjunction with operational performance indicators (eg, adverse events, patient's complaints).[6] The results of this evaluation should feed into the facility's human resource planning process along with projections based on new or changing operational needs.

Customer and Supplier Relations

Materials, supplies, and services used as inputs to a process are considered "critical" if they affect the quality of products and services being produced. Examples of critical supplies are blood components, blood bags, test kits, and reagents. Examples of critical services are infectious disease testing, blood component irradiation, transportation, equipment calibration, and preventive maintenance services. The suppliers of these materials and services may be internal (eg, other departments within the same organization) or external (outside vendors). Supplies and services used in the collection, testing, processing, preservation, storage, distribution, transport, and administration of blood, components, and tissue that have the potential to affect quality should be qualified before use and obtained from suppliers who can meet the facility's requirements.[1(pp8,9)] The quality system must include a process to evaluate the suppliers' abilities to meet these requirements. Three important elements are supplier qualification; agreements; and receipt, inspection, and testing of incoming supplies.

Supplier Qualification

Critical supplies and services must be qualified on the basis of defined require-ments. Similarly, the supplier should be qualified to ensure a reliable source of materials. The facility should clearly define requirements or expectations for the suppliers and share this information with staff and the supplier. The ability of suppliers to consistently meet specifications for a supply or service should be evaluated along with performance relative to availability, delivery, and support. Examples of factors that could be considered to qualify suppliers are:

- Licensure, certification, or accreditation.
- Supply or product requirements.
- Review of supplier-relevant quality documents.
- Results of audits or inspections.
- Review of quality summary reports.
- Review of customer complaints.
- Review of experience with supplier.
- Cost of materials or services.
- Delivery arrangements.
- Financial security, market position, and customer satisfaction.
- Support after the sale.

A list of approved suppliers should be maintained, including both primary suppliers and suitable alternatives for contingency planning. Critical supplies and services should be purchased only from those suppliers who have been qualified. Once qualified, periodic evaluation of the supplier's performance helps to ensure its continued ability to meet requirements. Tracking the supplier's ability to meet expectations gives the facility valuable information about the stability of the supplier's processes and its commitment to quality. Documented failures of supplies or suppliers to meet defined requirements should result in immediate action by the facility. These actions include notifying the supplier, quality oversight personnel, and management with contracting authority, if applicable. Supplies may need to be replaced or quarantined until all quality issues have been resolved.

Agreements

Contracts and agreements define expectations and reflect concurrence of the parties involved.[1(p8)] Periodic review of agreements ensures that expectations of all parties continue to be met. Changes must be mutually agreed upon and incorporated as needed.

Blood banks and transfusion services should maintain written contracts or agreements with outside suppliers of critical materials and services such as blood components, irradiation, compatibility testing, or infectious disease marker testing. The outside supplier may be another department within the same facility that is managed independently, or it may be another facility (eg, contract manufacturer). The contracting facility assumes responsibility for the manufacture of the product; ensuring the safety, purity, and potency of the product; and ensuring that the contract manufacturer complies with all applicable product standards and regulations. Both the contracting facility and the contractor are legally responsible for the work performed by the contractor.

It is important for the blood bank or transfusion service to participate in the evaluation and selection of suppliers. They should review contracts and agreements to ensure that all aspects of critical materials and services are addressed. Examples of issues that could be addressed in an agreement or a contract include: responsibility for a product or blood sample during shipment; the responsibility of the supplier to promptly notify the facility when changes that could affect the safety of blood, components, or patients have been made to the materials or services; and the responsibility of the supplier to notify the facility when information that a product may not be considered safe is discovered, such as during look-back procedures.

Receipt, Inspection, and Testing of Incoming Supplies

Before acceptance and use, critical materials, such as reagents and blood components, must be inspected and tested (if necessary) to ensure that they meet specifications for their intended use.[1(pp8,9),4] It is essential that supplies used in the collection, processing, preservation, testing, storage, distribution, transport, and administration of blood and components also meet FDA requirements.

The facility must define acceptance criteria for critical supplies (21 CFR 210.3) and develop procedures to control materials that do not meet specifications to prevent their inadvertent use. Corrective action may include returning the material to the vendor or destroying it. Receipt and inspection records provide the facility with a means to trace materials that have been used in a particular process and also provide information for ongoing supplier qualification.

Equipment Management

Equipment that must operate within defined specifications to ensure the quality of blood, components, tissues, and services is referred to as "critical" equipment in the quality system.[1(p4)] Critical equipment may include instruments, measuring devices, and computer systems (hardware and software). Activities designed to ensure that equipment performs as intended include qualification, calibration, maintenance, and monitoring. Calibration, functional and safety checks, and preventive maintenance must be scheduled and performed according to the manufacturer's recommendations and regulatory requirements of the FDA[3] and CMS.[2] Written procedures for the use and control of equipment must comply with the manufacturer's recommendations unless an alternative method has been validated by the facility and approved by the appropriate regulatory and accrediting agencies.

When selecting new equipment, it is important to consider not only the performance of equipment as it will be used in the facility, but also any supplier issues regarding ongoing service and support. There should be a written plan for installation, operational, and performance qualification. After installation, there must be documentation of any problems and the follow-up actions taken. Recalibration and requalification may be necessary if repairs are made that affect the critical operating functions of the equipment. Recalibration and requalification should also be considered when existing equipment is relocated.

The facility must develop a mechanism to uniquely identify and track all critical equipment, including equipment software versions, if applicable. The unique identifier may be the manufacturer's serial number or a facility's unique identification number. Maintaining a list of all critical equipment helps in the control function of scheduling and performing functional and safety checks, calibrations, preventive maintenance, and repair. The equipment listing can be used to ensure that all appropriate actions have been performed and recorded. Evaluation and analysis of equipment calibration, maintenance, and repair data will assist the facility in assessing the suitability of the equipment. They will also allow for better control in managing defective equipment and in identifying equipment that may need replacement. When equipment is found to be operating outside acceptable parameters, the potential effects on the quality of products or test results must be evaluated and documented.

Process Management

Written, approved policies, processes, and procedures must exist for all critical functions performed in the facility and must be carried out under controlled conditions. Each facility should have a systematic approach for identifying, planning, and implementing policies, processes, and procedures that affect the quality of blood, components, tissues, and services. These documents must be reviewed by management personnel with direct authority over the process and by quality oversight personnel before implementation. Changes must be documented, validated, reviewed, and approved. Additional information on policies, processes, and procedures can be found in the Documents and Records section.

Once a process has been implemented, the facility must have a mechanism to ensure that procedures are performed as defined and that critical equipment, reagents, and supplies are used in conformance with manufacturers' written instructions and facility requirements. Table 1-2 lists elements that constitute sound process control. A facility using reagents, supplies, or critical equipment in a manner that is different from the manufacturer's directions must have validated such use and may be required to request FDA approval to operate at variance to 21 CFR 606.65(e) if the activity is covered under regulations for blood and blood components (21 CFR 640.120). If a facility believes that changes to the manufacturer's directions would be appropriate, it should encourage the manufacturer to make such changes in the labeling (ie, package insert or user manual).

Process Validation

Validation is used to demonstrate that a process is capable of achieving planned results.[9] It is critical to validate processes

Table 1-2. Elements of a Sound Process Control System

- Systematic approach to developing policies, processes, or procedures and controlling changes.
- Validation of policies, processes, and procedures.
- Development and use of standard operating procedures.
- Equipment qualification processes.
- Staff training and competence assessment.
- Acceptance testing for new or revised computer software involved in blood bank procedures.
- Establishment of quality control, calibration, and preventive maintenance schedules.
- Monitoring of quality control, calibration, preventive maintenance, and repairs.
- Monitoring and control of production processes.
- Processes to determine that supplier qualifications and product specifications are maintained.
- Participation in proficiency testing appropriate for each testing system in place.
- Processes to control nonconforming materials, blood, components, and products.

in situations where it is not feasible to measure or inspect each finished product or service in order to fully verify conformance with specifications. However, even when effective end-product testing can be achieved, it is advisable to validate important processes to generate information that can be used to optimize performance. Prospective validation is used for new or revised processes. Retrospective validation may be used for processes that are already in operation but were not adequately validated before implementation. Concurrent validation is used when required data cannot be obtained without performance of a "live" process. If concurrent validation is used, data are reviewed at predefined intervals before final approval for full implementation occurs. Modifications to a validated process may warrant revalidation, depending on the nature and extent of the change. It is up to the facility to determine the need for revalidation based on its understanding of how the proposed changes may affect the process.

Validation Plan

Validation must be planned if it is to be effective. Development of a validation plan is best accomplished after obtaining an adequate understanding of the system, or framework, within which the process will occur. Many facilities develop a template for the written validation plan to ensure that all aspects are adequately addressed. Although no single format for a validation plan is required, the following elements are common to most:

- System description
- Purpose/objectives
- Risk assessment
- Responsibilities
- Validation procedures
- Acceptance criteria
- Approval signatures
- Supporting documentation

The validation plan must be reviewed and approved by quality oversight personnel. Staff responsible for carrying out the validation activities must be trained in the process before the plan is implemented. The results and conclusions of these activities may be appended to the approved validation plan or recorded in a separate document. This documentation typically contains the following elements:

- Expected and observed results
- Interpretation of results as acceptable or unacceptable
- Corrective action and resolution of unexpected results
- Conclusions and limitations
- Approval signatures
- Supporting documentation
- Implementation time line

When a validation process does not produce the expected outcome, its data and corrective actions must be documented as well. The responsible quality oversight personnel should have final review and approval of the validation plan, results, and corrective actions and determine whether new or modified processes and equipment may be implemented, or implemented with specified limitations.

Equipment Validation

Validation of new equipment used in a process should include installation qualification, operational qualification, and performance qualification.[13]

- Installation qualification demonstrates that the instrument is properly installed in environmental conditions that meet the manufacturer's specifications.
- Operational qualification demonstrates that the installed equipment operates as intended. It focuses on the capability of the equipment to operate within the established limits and specifications supplied by the manufacturer.
- Performance qualification demonstrates that the equipment performs as expected for its intended use in

the processes established by the facility and that the output meets specifications. It evaluates the adequacy of equipment for use in a specific process that employs the facility's own personnel, procedures, and supplies in a normal working environment.

Computer System Validation

The FDA considers computerized systems to include: "hardware, software, peripheral devices, personnel, and documentation."[14] End-user validation of computer systems and the interfaces between systems should be conducted in the environment where it will be used. Testing performed by the vendor or supplier of computer software is not a substitute for computer validation at the facility. End-user acceptance testing may repeat some of the validation performed by the developer, such as load or stress testing and verification of security, safety, and control features, in order to evaluate performance under actual operating conditions. In addition, the end user must evaluate the ability of personnel to use the computer system as intended within the context of actual work processes. Staff must be able to successfully navigate the hardware and software interface and respond appropriately to messages, warnings, and other functions. Depending upon the nature of the computer functionality, changes to the computer system may result in changes to how a process is performed. If this occurs, process revalidation must also be performed. As with process validation, quality oversight personnel should review and approve validation plans, results, and corrective actions and determine whether implementation may proceed with or without limitations. Facilities that develop their own software should refer to

FDA guidance regarding general principles of software validation for additional information.[15]

Quality Control

QC testing is performed to ensure the proper functioning of materials, equipment, and methods during operations. QC performance expectations and acceptable ranges must be defined and readily available to staff so that they will recognize unacceptable results and trends and respond appropriately. The frequency for QC testing is determined by the facility in accordance with the applicable CMS, FDA, AABB, state, and manufacturer's requirements. QC results must be documented concurrently with performance.[3] Records of QC testing must include identification of personnel, identification of reagent (including lot number, expiration dates, etc), identification of equipment, testing date and time (when applicable), results, interpretation, and reviews. Unacceptable QC results must be investigated and corrective action implemented, if indicated, before repeating the QC procedure or continuing the operational process. Specific examples of suggested quality control intervals for blood banks and transfusion services are included in Appendix 10 at the end of the book, and information regarding methods of quality control are found in the methods section devoted to QC.

Documents and Records

Documentation provides a framework for understanding and communication throughout the organization. Documents describe the way that processes are intended to work, how they interact, where they must be controlled, what their requirements are, and how to implement them. Records provide evidence that the process was performed as intended and information needed to assess the quality of products and services. Together, documents and records are used by quality oversight personnel to evaluate the effectiveness of a facility's policies, processes, and procedures. An example of quality system documentation is provided in ISO 9001 and includes the following items[9]:

1. The quality policy and objectives.
2. A description of the interactions between processes.
3. Documented procedures for the control of documents, control of records, control of a nonconforming product, corrective action, preventive action, and internal quality audits.
4. Records related to the quality system, operational performance, and product/service conformance.
5. All other documents needed by the organization to ensure the effective planning, operation, and control of its processes.

Written policies, process descriptions, procedures, work instructions, labels, forms, and records are all part of the facility's documentation system. They may be paper-based or electronic. Documents provide a description or instructions of what is supposed to happen; records provide evidence of what did happen. A document management system provides assurance that documents are comprehensive, current, and available, and that records are accurate and complete. A well-structured document management system links policies, process descriptions, procedures, forms, and records together in an organized and workable system.

Documents

Documents should be developed in a format that conveys information clearly and provides staff with instructions and forms.

The Clinical and Laboratory Standards Institute offers guidance regarding general levels of documentation[8] as well as detailed instructions on how to write procedures.[16] General types of documentation are described below.

Policies. Policies communicate the highest level goals, objectives, and intent of the organization. The rest of the organization's documentation will interpret and provide instruction regarding implementation of these policies.

Processes. Process documents describe a sequence of actions and identify responsibilities, decision points, requirements, and acceptance criteria. Table 1-3 lists examples of process documents that might be in place to support a quality system. Process diagrams or flowcharts are often used for this level of documentation. It is helpful to show process control points on the diagram as well as flow of information and handoffs between departments or work groups.

Procedures and Work Instructions. These documents provide step-by-step directions on how to perform job tasks and procedures. Procedures and work instructions should include enough detail to perform the task correctly, but not so much as to make them difficult to read. The use of standardized formats will help staff know where to find specific elements and facilitates implementation and control.[1(p66)] Procedures may also be incorporated by reference, such as those from a manufacturer's manual. Relevant procedures must be available to staff in each area where the corresponding job tasks are performed.[1(p66),3]

Forms. Forms provide a template for capturing data either on paper or electronically. These documents specify the data requirements called for in SOPs and processes. Forms should be carefully designed for ease of use, to minimize the likelihood of errors, and to facilitate retrieval of information. They should include instructions for use when it is not immediately evident what information should be recorded or how to record it. For quantitative data, the form should indicate units of measure. Computer data entry and review screens are a type of form. Forms must be designed to effectively capture outcomes and support process traceability.

Labels. Blood component labels are a critical material subject to the requirements of a document management system. Many facilities maintain a master set of labels that can be used as reference to verify that only current approved stock is in use. New label stock must be verified as accurate before it is put into inventory; comparison against a master label provides a mechanism for accomplishing this. Change control procedures must be established for the use of on-demand label printers to prevent nonconforming modification of label format or content.

Each facility must have a defined process for developing and maintaining documents. It should include: basic elements required for document formats; procedures for review and approval of new or revised documents; a method for keeping documents current; control of document distribution; and a process for archiving, protecting, and retrieving obsolete documents. Training must be provided to staff responsible for the content of new or revised documents. Document management systems include established processes to:

1. Verify the adequacy of the document before approval and issue.
2. Periodically review, modify, and re-approve as needed to keep documents current.
3. Identify changes and revision status.
4. Ensure that documents are legible, identifiable, and readily available.
5. Prevent unintended use of outdated or obsolete documents.
6. Protect documents from unintended damage or destruction.

Table 1-3. Examples of Quality System Process Documents

Organization	■ Management review process
Resources	■ Personnel hiring process ■ Training process ■ Competence assessment process
Equipment	■ Equipment management process ■ Installation qualification process
Supplier and Customer Issues	■ Supplier qualification process ■ Contract review process ■ Process for qualification of critical materials ■ Ordering and inventory control of critical materials ■ Receipt, inspection, and testing of incoming critical materials
Process Control	■ Change control process ■ Validation process ■ Process for acceptance testing of computer software ■ Process for handling proficiency testing ■ Process for handling, storage, distribution, and transport of blood components
Documents and Records	■ Process for creation and approval of documents ■ Document management process ■ Records management process
Deviations, Nonconformances, and Complications	■ Event management process ■ Process for handling customer complaints ■ Process for notification of external sources
Assessments	■ Internal audit process ■ Process for quality monitoring ■ Process for handling external assessments
Process Improvement	■ Corrective and preventive action processes
Facilities and Safety	■ Process for handling disasters ■ Employee safety management process

External documents that are incorporated by reference become part of the document management system and must be identified and controlled. The facility must have a mechanism to detect changes to external documents in its system, such as a manufacturer's package inserts or user manuals, so that corresponding changes to procedures and forms can be made. When new or revised policies, process descriptions, procedures, or forms are added to or replaced in the facility's manual, the documents must be marked with the effective date. One copy of retired documents must be retained as defined by existing and applicable standards and regulations.

A master list of all current policies, process descriptions, procedures, forms, and labels is useful for maintaining document control. It should include the document title, the individual or work group responsible for maintaining it, the revision date and number (if one is assigned), and the area where it is used. It should also identify the number and location of controlled copies in circulation. Copies of documents that will be used in the workplace should be identified and controlled to ensure that none are overlooked when changes are implemented.

Records

Records provide evidence that critical steps in a procedure have been performed appropriately and that products and services conform to specified requirements. Review of records is an important tool to help evaluate the effectiveness of the quality system. Records must be created concurrently with the performance of each significant step and clearly indicate the identity of individuals who performed each step and when it occurred.[3] The quality system must include a process for managing records that addresses the following items:

- Creation and identification of records
- Protection from accidental or unauthorized modification or destruction
- Verification of completeness, accuracy, and legibility
- Storage and retrieval
- Creation of copies or backups
- Retention periods
- Confidentiality

Record-keeping systems must allow for ready retrieval within time frames established by the facility and must permit traceability of blood components as required by federal regulations.[3] Specific requirements for records to be maintained by blood banks and transfusion services are included in the AABB *Standards for Blood Banks and Transfusion Services*[1(pp69-80)] and in 21 CFR 606.160.

When forms are used for capturing data or recording steps or test results, the forms become records. Data must be recorded in a format that is clear and consistent. The facility must define a process and time frames for the record review to ensure accuracy, completeness, and appropriate follow-up. It must determine how reports and records are to be archived and define their retention period. When copies of records are retained, the facility must verify that the copy contains complete, legible, and accessible content of the original record before the original is destroyed.

If records are maintained electronically, adequate backup must exist in case of system failure. Electronic records must be readable for the entire length of their retention period. Obsolete computer software, necessary to reconstruct or trace records, must be archived appropriately. If the equipment or software used to access archived data cannot be maintained, the records should be converted to another format or copied to another medium to permit continued access. Converted data must be verified against the original to ensure completeness and accuracy. Electronic media such as magnetic tapes, optical disks, and online computer data storage are widely used for archiving documents. Records kept in this manner must meet FDA requirements for electronic record-keeping.[17] Microfilm or microfiche may be used to archive written records. The medium selected should be appropriate for the retention requirements.

Privacy of patient and donor information must be addressed in the quality system with established policies and procedures to maintain the security and confidentiality of records. Computer systems must be designed with security features to prevent unauthorized access and use. This system may include levels of security defined by job responsibility and administered by the use of security codes and passwords.

Each facility should have a policy for altering or correcting records. A common practice is to indicate the date, the change, the identity of the person making the change, and evidence of review by a responsible person. The original recording must not be obliterated in written records; it may be crossed out with a single line, but it should remain legible. Electronic records must permit tracking of both original and corrected data and include the date and user identification of the person making the change. There should be a process for controlling changes.[1(p10)] A method for referencing changes to records, linked to the original records, and a system for reviewing changes for completeness and accuracy are essential. Audit trails for changed data in computerized systems are required by the FDA.[17]

The following are issues that might be considered when planning record storage:

- Storage of records in a manner that protects them from damage and from accidental or unauthorized destruction or modification.

- Degree of accessibility of records in proportion to frequency of their use.
- Method and location of record storage related to the volume of records and the amount of available storage space.
- Availability of properly functioning equipment, computer hardware, and software to view archived records.
- Documentation that microfiched records legitimately replace original documents that may be stored elsewhere or destroyed.
- Retention of original color-coded records when only black-and-white reproductions are available.

Considerations for electronic records include:

- A method of verifying the accuracy of data entry.
- Prevention of unintended deletion of data or access by unauthorized persons.
- Adequate protection against inadvertent data loss (eg, when a storage device is full).
- Validated safeguards to ensure that a record can be edited by only one person at a time.
- Security and access of confidential data.

A backup disk or tape should be maintained in the event of unexpected loss of information from the storage medium. Backup or archived computer records and databases must be stored off-site.[1(p68)] The storage facility should be secure and maintain appropriate conditions, in accordance with the manufacturer's recommendations and instructions. An archival copy of the computer operating system and applications software should be stored in the same manner.

The facility should develop and maintain alternative systems to ensure information access if computerized data are not available. The backup and recovery procedures for computer downtime must be defined, with validation documentation to show that the backup system works properly. The associated processes must be checked periodically to ensure that the backup system remains effective. Special consideration should be given to staff competence and readiness to use the backup system.

To link relevant personnel to recorded data, the facility must maintain a record of names, inclusive dates of employment, signatures, and identifying initials or identification codes of personnel authorized to create, sign, initial, or review reports and records. Magnetically coded employee badges and other computer-related identifying methods are generally accepted in lieu of written signatures provided they meet electronic record-keeping requirements.

Deviations and Nonconforming Products or Services

The quality system must include a process for detecting, investigating, and responding to events that result in deviations from accepted policies, processes, and procedures or in failures to meet requirements, as defined by the donor center or transfusion service, AABB standards, or applicable regulations.[1(p81),3] This includes the discovery of nonconforming products and services as well as adverse reactions to blood donation and transfusion.[1(pp81-85),2] The facility should define how to:

■ Document and classify occurrences.

■ Determine the effect, if any, on the quality of products or services.

■ Evaluate the impact on interrelated activities.

■ Implement corrective action, including notification and recall, as appropriate.

■ Analyze the event to understand root causes.

■ Implement preventive actions as appropriate on the basis of root-cause analysis.

■ Report to external agencies, when required.

Facility personnel should be trained to recognize and report such occurrences. Depending upon the severity of the event and risk to patients, donors, and products, as well as the likelihood of recurrence, investigation into contributing factors and underlying cause(s) may be warranted. The cGMP regulations require an investigation and documentation of the results if a specific event could adversely affect patient safety or the safety, purity, potency, or efficacy of blood or components.[2,3] Tools and approaches for performing root-cause analysis and implementing corrective action are discussed in the section addressing process improvement. A summary of the event, investigation, and any follow-up must be documented. Table 1-4 outlines suggested components of an internal event report.

Fatalities related to blood collection or transfusion must be reported as soon as possible to the FDA Center for Biologics Evaluation and Research (CBER) [21 CFR 606.170(b)]. Instructions for reporting to CBER are available in published guidance[20] and at http://www.fda.gov/cber/transfusion.htm. A written follow-up report is submitted within 7 days of the fatality and should include a description of any new procedures implemented to avoid recurrence. AABB Association Bulletin #04-06 provides additional information, including a form to be used for reporting donor fatalities.[21]

Regardless of their licensure and registration status with the FDA, all donor centers, blood banks, and transfusion services must promptly report biologic product deviations (previously known as errors and

Table 1-4. Components of an Internal Event Report[18,19]

WHO	■ Identity of reporting individual(s) ■ Identity of individuals involved (by job title) in committing, compounding, discovering, investigating, and initiating any immediate action ■ Patient or donor identification ■ Reviewer(s) of report
WHAT	■ Brief description of event ■ Effects on and outcome to patient, donor, or blood component ■ Name of component and unit identification number ■ Manufacturer, lot number, and expiration date of applicable reagents and supplies ■ Immediate action taken
WHEN	■ Date of report ■ Date and time of event occurrence ■ Date and time of discovery ■ Collection and shipping dates of blood component(s)
WHERE	■ Physical location of event ■ Where in process detected ■ Where in process initiated
WHY/HOW	■ Explanation of how event occurred ■ Contributing factors ■ Root cause(s)
FOLLOW-UP	■ External reports or notifications (eg, FDA*, manufacturer, or patient's physician) ■ Corrective actions ■ Implementation dates ■ Effectiveness of actions taken

*The following are *some* examples identified by the FDA as reportable events if components or products *are released for distribution*:
– Arm preparation not performed or done incorrectly
– Units from donors who are (or should have been) either temporarily or permanently deferred because of their medical history or a history of repeatedly reactive viral marker tests
– Shipment of unit with repeatedly reactive viral markers
– ABO/Rh or infectious disease testing not done in accordance with the manufacturer's package insert
– Units from donors for whom test results were improperly interpreted because of testing errors related to the improper use of equipment
– Units released before completion of all tests (except as emergency release)
– Sample used for compatibility testing that contains the incorrect identification
– Testing error that results in the release of an incorrect unit
– Incorrectly labeled blood components (eg, ABO, expiration date)
– Incorrect crossmatch label or tag
– Storage of biological products at the incorrect temperature
– Microbial contamination of blood components when the contamination is attributed to an error in manufacturing

accidents) and information relevant to these events to the FDA[3,22] using Form FDA-3486 when the event:

- Is associated with manufacturing (ie, testing, processing, packing, labeling, storing, holding, or distributing).
- Represents a deviation from current good manufacturing practice, applicable regulations or standards, or established specifications, or is unexpected or unforeseen.
- May affect the safety, purity, or potency of the product.
- Occurs while the facility had control of or was responsible for the product.
- Involves a product that has left the control of the facility (ie, distributed).

There must also be a mechanism to report medical device adverse events to the FDA.[23] The JCAHO encourages reporting of sentinel events, including hemolytic transfusion reactions involving the administration of blood or components having major blood group incompatibilities.[6]

Each facility should track reported events and look for trends. The use of classification schemes may facilitate trend analysis and typically involves one or more of the following categories: the nature of the event, the process (or procedure) in which the event occurred, event severity, and causes. If several events within a relatively short period involve a particular process or procedure, that process or procedure should be further investigated. The most useful schemes involve use of multiple categories for each event, which allow data to be sorted in a variety of ways so that patterns can emerge (see example in Table 1-5). Such sorting can result in identification of situations that require closer monitoring or of problems needing corrective action. The extent of monitoring and length of time to monitor processes will depend on the frequency of the occurrence and the critical aspects of the occurrences. Reporting and monitoring of events are essential problem identification methods for process improvement activities in a quality management system.

Occasionally, the blood bank or transfusion service may need to deviate from approved procedures in order to meet the unique medical needs of a particular patient. When this situation arises, a medically indicated exception is planned and approved in advance by the facility's medical director. The rationale and nature of the planned exception must be documented. Careful consideration should be given to maintaining a controlled process and to verifying the safety and quality of the resulting product or service. Any additional risk to the patient must be disclosed.

Table 1-5. Example of Event Classification

Event: A unit of Red Blood Cells from a directed donor was issued to an incorrect patient.

- Classification of event
    Type of event – patient
    Procedure involved – issuing products
    Process involved – blood administration
    Product involved – Red Blood Cells
    Other factors – directed donor
- Investigation revealed
    Proximate cause – two patients with similar names had crossmatched blood available
    Root cause – inadequate procedure for verification of patient identification during issue

Monitoring and Assessment

The quality system should describe how the facility monitors and evaluates its processes. The AABB *Standards*[1(p93)] defines assessment as a systematic, independent examination that is performed at defined intervals and at sufficient frequency to determine whether actual activities comply with planned activities, are implemented effectively, and achieve objectives. Evaluations typically include comparison of actual results to expected results. Depending on the focus, this can include evaluation of process outputs (eg, results), the activities that make up a process as well as its outputs, or a group of related processes and outputs (ie, the system). Types of assessments include external assessments, internal assessments, quality assessments, peer review, and self-assessments.

Internal Assessments

Internal assessments may include evaluation of quality indicator data, targeted audits of a single process, or system audits that are broader in scope and cover a set of interrelated processes. These assessments should be planned and scheduled. The details of who performs the assessments and how they are performed should be addressed. Assessments should cover the quality system and major operating systems found in the blood bank, transfusion service, or donor center.

In addition, there must be a process for responding to the issues raised as a result of the assessment, including review processes and time frames. The results should be documented and submitted to management personnel with authority over the process assessed as well as to executive management. Management should develop corrective and preventive action plans with input from operational staff and quality oversight personnel for any deficiencies noted in the assessment. Quality oversight personnel should track progress toward implementation of corrective and preventive actions and monitor them for effectiveness.

In order to make the best use of these assessments, there must be a process to track, trend, and analyze the problems identified so that opportunities for improvement can be recognized.[1(pp86,87)] Early detection of trends makes it possible to develop preventive actions before patient safety or blood components are adversely affected. Evaluation summaries provide information useful in correcting individual or group performance problems and ensuring adequacy of test methods and equipment. In addition to review of assessment results, executive management must review any associated corrective or preventive action.

Quality Indicators

Quality indicators are specific performance measurements designed to monitor one or more processes during a defined time and are useful for evaluating service demands, production, adequacy of personnel, inventory control, and process stability. These indicators can be process-based or outcome-based. Process-based indicators measure the degree to which a process can be consistently performed. An example of a process-based indicator is measurement of turnaround time from blood component ordering until transfusion. Outcome-based indicators are often used to measure what does or does not happen after a process is or is not performed. Counting incorrect test result reports is an example of such an indicator. For each indicator, thresholds are set that represent warning limits and/or action limits. These thresholds can be determined from regulatory or accreditation requirements, benchmarking, or internally derived data.

Tools frequently used for displaying quality indicator data are run charts and control charts. In a run chart, time is plotted on the x-axis and values on the y-axis. In control charts, the mean of the data and upper and lower control limits, which have been calculated from the data, are added to the chart. Single points outside the upper and lower control limits result from special causes. Statistical rules for interpreting consecutive points outside 1 standard deviation (SD), 2 SD, and 3 SD should be used to recognize a process that is out of control; the root cause should be determined and corrective action should be initiated if indicated.

Blood Utilization Assessment

The activities of blood usage review committees in the transfusion setting are an example of internal assessment. Guidelines are available from the AABB for both adult and pediatric utilization review.[24-26] Peer review of transfusion practices, required by the AABB, is also required by the JCAHO[6] for hospital accreditation, by the CMS[2] for hospitals to qualify for Medicare reimbursement, and by some states for Medicaid reimbursement.

Transfusion audits provide a review of policies and practices to ensure safe and appropriate transfusions and are based on measurable, predetermined performance criteria. Transfusion services should investigate an adequate sampling of cases (eg, 5% of the number of cases occurring within a defined time frame or 30 cases, whichever is larger). Audits assess the facility's performance and effectiveness in:

- Blood ordering practices for all categories of blood and components.
- Minimizing wastage of blood components.
- Distribution, handling, use, and administration of blood components.
- Evaluating all confirmed transfusion reactions.
- Meeting patients' transfusion needs.
- Informing patients and physicians in a timely and confidential manner of possible infectious disease transmission.

One method of assessing the blood administration process is to observe a predetermined number of transfusions by following the unit of blood as it is issued for transfusion and as it is transfused.[25]

Assessments of transfusion safety policy and practice may include a review of transfusion reactions and transfusion-transmitted diseases. The review committee may monitor policies and practices for notifying recipients of recalled products (look-back notification) and donors of abnormal test results. Other assessments important in transfusion practice include the review of policies for informed consent, indication for transfusion, release of directed donor units, and outpatient or home transfusion. Additional assessments should include, where appropriate: therapeutic apheresis, use of cell-saver devices, procurement and storage of hematopoietic progenitor cells, perioperative autologous blood collection, procurement and storage of tissue, and evaluation of evolving technologies and products. Appendix 1-4 lists blood utilization assessment examples.

External Assessments

External assessments include inspections, surveys, audits, and assessments performed by those not affiliated with the organization, such as the FDA, AABB, CAP, or JCAHO. Participation in an external assessment program provides an independent, objective view of the facility's performance. External assessors often bring broad-based experience and knowledge of best practices that can be shared. In the preparation phase of scheduled assessments, there is typically some data gathering and information to submit to the organization performing the assessment. Coordinated scheduling and planning will help ensure that adequate time is allotted for each area to be covered and that adequate staff are available to answer questions and assist in the assessment activities. During the assessment phase, it is important to know who is responsible for the assessors or inspectors during the time they are in the facility. Clear descriptions of what information can be given to these individuals, and in what form, will help the facility through the assessment or inspection process. After the assessment, identified issues must be addressed. Usually a written response is submitted.

Proficiency Testing for Laboratories

Proficiency testing (PT) is one means for determining that test systems (including methods, supplies, and equipment) are performing as expected. As a condition for certification, the CMS requires laboratories to participate successfully in an approved PT program for each specialty and analyte that they routinely test. When no approved PT program exists for a particular analyte, the laboratory must have another means to verify the accuracy of the test procedure at least twice annually.[2] Proficiency testing must be performed using routine work processes and conditions if it is to provide meaningful information. Handling and testing of PT samples should be the same as those for patient or donor specimens. Supervisory review of the summary evaluation report must be documented along with investigation and corrective action for results that are unacceptable.

Quality oversight personnel should monitor the proficiency testing program and verify that test systems are maintained in a state of control and that appropriate corrective action is taken when indicated.

Process Improvement

Continuous improvement is a fundamental goal in any quality management system. In transfusion medicine, this goal is tied to patient safety goals and expectations for the highest quality health care. The importance of identifying, investigating, correcting, and preventing problems cannot be overstated. The process of developing corrective and preventive action plans includes identification of problems and their causes, and identification and evaluation of solutions to prevent future problems. It must include a mechanism for data collection and analysis, as well as follow-up to evaluate the effectiveness of the actions taken. Statistical tools and their applications may be found in publications from the AABB and the American Society for Quality.[27,28] The JCAHO standards for performance improvement are outlined in Table 1-6.[6]

Corrective action is defined as the action taken to eliminate the causes of an existing nonconformance or other undesirable situation in order to prevent recurrence.[1(p94)] Preventive action is defined as the action taken to eliminate the causes of a potential nonconformance or other undesirable situation in order to prevent occurrence.[1(p97)] Corrective action can be thought of as a reactive approach to reported problems that includes a preventive component, whereas preventive action can be thought of as a proactive approach resulting from the analysis of data and information. In contrast, remedial action is defined as the action taken to alleviate the symptoms of existing nonconformances or any other undesirable

Table 1-6. Applicable JCAHO Performance Improvement Standards[6]

- Data are collected to measure the performance of potentially high-risk processes, including blood utilization.

- Performance data are systematically aggregated and analyzed to determine current performance levels, patterns, and trends over time.

- Undesirable patterns and trends in performance are evaluated. All confirmed transfusion reactions are analyzed.

- There is a defined process for identification and management of serious adverse events. Root-cause analysis and corrective action are documented.

- Information from data analysis is used to improve performance and patient safety and minimize the risk of serious adverse events.

- The facility defines and implements a program to proactively identify opportunities for improvement. Preventive actions are implemented and monitored for effectiveness.

situation.[27,28] Remedial action addresses only the visible indicator of a problem, not the actual cause (see comparisons in Table 1-7). Effective corrective and preventive actions cannot be implemented until the underlying cause is determined and the process is evaluated in relationship to other processes. Pending such evaluation, it may be desirable to implement interim remedial action.

Identification of Problems and Their Causes

Sources of information for process improvement activities include the following: blood product and other deviations; nonconforming products and services; customer complaints; QC records; proficiency testing; internal audits; quality in-

dicators; and external assessments. Active monitoring programs may be set up to help identify problem areas. These programs should be representative of the facility processes, consistent with organizational goals, and reflect customer needs. Preparation of an annual facility quality report, in which data from all these sources are collated and analyzed, can be a valuable tool to identify issues for performance improvement.

Once identified, problems must be analyzed to determine their scope, potential effects on the quality and operational systems, relative frequency, and the extent of variation. This analysis is important to avoid tampering with processes that are showing normal variation or problems with little impact.

Table 1-7. Comparison of Remedial, Corrective, and Preventive Action[29]

Action	Problem	Approach	Outcome
Remedial	Existent	Reactive	Alleviates symptoms
Corrective	Existent	Reactive	Prevents recurrence
Preventive	Nonexistent	Proactive	Prevents occurrence

Identifying underlying causes for an undesirable condition or problem can be accomplished by an individual or a group. The more complex the problem and the more involved the process, the greater the need to enlist a team of individuals and to formalize the analysis. The three most commonly used tools for identifying underlying causes in an objective manner are process flowcharting, use of the "repetitive why," and the cause-and-effect diagram. A process flowchart gives a detailed picture of the multiple activities and important decision points within the process. By examining this picture, problem-prone areas may be identified. The "repetitive why" is used to work backward through the process. One repeatedly asks the question "why did this happen?" until: 1) no new information can be gleaned, 2) the causal path cannot be followed because of missing information, or 3) further investigation is impractical,

impossible, or outside the boundaries of the organization. Use of the "repetitive why" prevents the mistake of interpreting an effect as a cause.

The cause-and-effect diagram, also known as the Ishikawa or fish-bone diagram, employs a specialized form of brainstorming that breaks down problems into "bite-size" pieces. An example of a cause-and-effect diagram is shown in Fig 1-1. It is a method designed to focus ideas around the component parts of a process, as well as give a pictorial representation of the ideas that are generated and their interactions. When using the cause-and-effect diagram, one looks at equipment, materials, methods, environment, and human factors. These tools identify both active and latent failures. Active failures are those that have an immediate adverse effect. Latent failures are those more global actions and decisions with potential for damage that may lie dormant

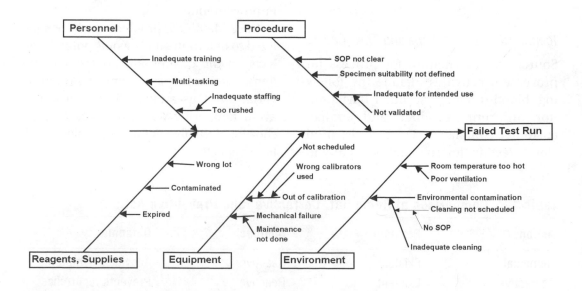

Figure 1-1. Example of a cause-and-effect diagram (SOP = standard operating procedure).

and become evident only when triggered by the presence of localized factors. The key to successfully determining root cause is not to stop too soon or get caught in the trap of placing blame on an individual.

Most problems, particularly those that are complex, have several root causes. A method that can be of use when this occurs is the Pareto analysis. A chart of causes, laid out in order of decreasing frequency, is prepared. Those that occur most frequently are considered the "vital few"; the rest are considered the "trivial many." This method offers direction about where to dedicate resources for maximal impact. An example of a Pareto chart is shown in Fig 1-2.

Identification and Evaluation of Solutions

Potential solutions to problems are identified during the creative phase of process improvement. Brainstorming and process flowcharting can be particularly helpful in this phase. Possible solutions should be evaluated relative to organizational constraints and narrowed down to those most reasonable. Individuals who perform the process are usually the most knowledgeable about what will work. They should be included when possible solutions are being considered. Individuals with knowledge of the interrelationships of processes and the more "global" view of the organization should also be included. Solutions may fail if representatives with these perspectives are not involved.

Potential solutions should be tested before full implementation, with a clear plan relative to methods, objectives, timelines, decision points, and algorithms for all possible results of the trial. Large-scale solutions can be tried on a limited basis and expanded if successful; smaller scale solutions can be implemented pending an effectiveness evaluation. Nonetheless, data should be collected to evaluate the effec-

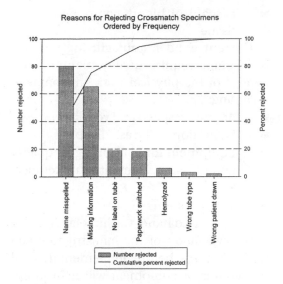

Figure 1-2. Example of a Pareto chart.

tiveness of the proposed change. Data can be collected by the methods used initially to identify the problems or by methods specially designed for the trial. Once solutions have been successfully tested, full implementation can occur. Following implementation, data should be collected, on at least a periodic basis, to ensure adequate control of the process.

Work Environment

The facility must provide a safe workplace with adequate environmental controls and emergency procedures for the safety of the employees, donors, patients, and all other inhabitants or visitors.[1(p88)] Procedures must be in place to address:

- General safety
- Disaster preparedness
- Biological safety (blood-borne pathogens)
- Chemical safety
- Fire safety
- Radiation safety, if applicable

■ Discard of blood, components, and tissue

Current good manufacturing practice regulations require quality planning and control of the physical work environment, including:

■ Adequate space and ventilation
■ Sanitation and trash disposal
■ Equipment for controlling air quality and pressure, humidity, and temperature
■ Water systems
■ Toilet and hand-washing facilities

An evaluation of the infrastructure and its limitations before implementation of procedures or equipment will help to ensure maximum efficiency and safety. A more thorough discussion of facilities and safety can be found in Chapter 2.

References

1. Silva MA, ed. Standards for blood banks and transfusion services. 23rd ed. Bethesda, MD: AABB, 2005.

2. Code of federal regulations. Title 42 CFR Part 493. Washington, DC: US Government Printing Office, 2004 (revised annually).

3. Code of federal regulations. Title 21 CFR Parts 606, 610, 630, and 640. Washington, DC: US Government Printing Office, 2004 (revised annually).

4. Code of federal regulations. Title 21 CFR Parts 210 and 211. Washington, DC: US Government Printing Office, 2004 (revised annually).

5. Food and Drug Administration. Guideline for quality assurance in blood establishments. Docket #91N-0450. (July 11, 1995) Rockville, MD: CBER Office of Communication, Training, and Manufacturers Assistance, 1995.

6. Hospital accreditation standards. Oakbrook Terrace, IL: Joint Commission Resources, Inc., 2004.

7. College of American Pathologists Laboratory Accreditation Program checklists. Chicago, IL: College of American Pathologists, 2003.

8. A quality system model for health care; NCCLS approved guideline (HS1-A). Wayne, PA: National Committee for Clinical Laboratory Standards, 2002.

9. ANSI/ISO/ASQ Q9000-2000 series—quality management standards. Milwaukee, WI: ASQ Quality Press, 2000.

10. Baldrige National Quality Program. Health care criteria for performance excellence. Gaithersburg, MD: National Institute of Standards and Technology, 2004 (revised annually).

11. Quality program implementation. Association Bulletin 97-4. Bethesda, MD: AABB, 1997.

12. Juran JM, Godfrey AB. Juran's quality handbook. 5th ed. New York: McGraw-Hill, 1999.

13. Food and Drug Administration. Guidance on general principles of process validation. (May 1, 1987) Rockville, MD: CBER Office of Communication, Training, and Manufacturers Assistance, 1987.

14. Food and Drug Administration. Glossary of computerized system and software development terminology. (August 1995) Rockville, MD: Division of Field Investigations, Office of Regional Operations, Office of Regulatory Affairs, 1995.

15. Food and Drug Administration. Guidance for industry: General principles of software validation: Final guidance for industry and FDA staff. (January 11, 2002) Rockville, MD: CBER Office of Communication, Training, and Manufacturers Assistance, 2002.

16. Clinical laboratory technical procedure manuals. NCCLS approved guideline. 4th ed. (GP2-A4). Wayne, PA: National Committee for Clinical Laboratory Standards, 2002.

17. Code of federal regulations. Title 21 CFR Part 11. Washington, DC: US Government Printing Office, 2004 (revised annually).

18. Motschman TL, Santrach PJ, Moore SB. Error/incident management and its practical application. In: Duckett JB, Woods LL, Santrach PJ, eds. Quality in action. Bethesda, MD: AABB, 1996:37-67.

19. Food and Drug Administration. Biological products: Reporting of biological product deviations in manufacturing. Docket No. 97N-0242. (November 7, 2000) Fed Regist 2000;65:66621-35.

20. Food and Drug Administration. Guidance for industry: Notifying FDA of fatalities related to blood collection or transfusion. (September 22, 2003) Rockville, MD: CBER Office of Communication, Training, and Manufacturers Assistance, 2003.

21. Reporting donor fatalities. Association Bulletin #04-06. Bethesda, MD: AABB, 2004.

22. Food and Drug Administration. Draft guidance for industry: Biological product deviation reporting for blood and plasma establishments. (August 10, 2001) Rockville, MD:

CBER Office of Communication, Training, and Manufacturers Assistance, 2001.

23. Code of federal regulations. Title 21 CFR Part 803. Washington, DC: US Government Printing Office, 2004 (revised annually).

24. Shulman IA, Lohr K, Derdiarian AK, et al. Monitoring transfusionist practices: A strategy for improving transfusion safety. Transfusion 1994;34:11-15.

25. Becker J, Blackall D, Evans C, et al for the Scientific Section Coordinating Committee. Guidelines for blood utilization review. Bethesda, MD: AABB, 2001.

26. Strauss RG, Blanchette VS, Hume H. National acceptability of American Association of Blood Banks Hemotherapy Committee guidelines for auditing pediatric transfusion practices. Transfusion 1993;33:168-71.

27. Anderson TD. Tools for statistical process control. In: Ziebell LW, Kavemeier K, eds. Quality control: A component of process control in blood banking and transfusion medicine. Bethesda, MD: AABB Press, 1999:13-48.

28. Russell JP, Regel T. After the quality audit. 2nd ed. Milwaukee, WI: ASQ Quality Press, 2000.

29. Motschman T. Corrective versus preventive action. AABB News 1999;21(8):5,33.

Appendix 1-1. Glossary of Commonly Used Quality Terms

Calibration	Comparison of measurements performed by an instrument to those made by a more accurate instrument or standard for the purpose of detecting, reporting, and eliminating errors in measurement.
Change control	Established procedures for planning, documenting, communicating, and executing changes to infrastructure, processes, products, or services. This includes the submission, analysis, decision making, approval, implementation, and postimplementation review of the change. Formal change control provides a measure of stability and safety and avoids arbitrary changes that might affect quality.
Control chart	A graphic tool used to determine whether the distribution of data values generated by a process is stable over time. A control chart plots a statistic vs time and helps to determine whether a process is in control or out of control according to defined criteria, eg, a shift from a central line or a trend toward upper or lower acceptance limits.
Design output	Documents, records, and evidence in any format used to verify that design goals have been met. Design output should identify characteristics of a product or service that are crucial to safety and function and to meeting regulatory requirements. It should contain or make reference to acceptance criteria. Examples of design output include standard operating procedures, specifications for supplies, reagents and equipment, identification of quality control requirements, and the results of verification and validation activities.
End-product test and inspection	Verification through observation, examination, and/or testing that the finished product or service conforms to specified requirements.
Process capability	Ability of a controlled process to produce a service or product that fulfills requirements. Also, a statistical measure of the inherent process variability for a given characteristic relative to design specifications. The most widely accepted formula for process capability is six sigma.
Process control	Activities intended to minimize variation within a process in order to produce a predictable output that meets specifications.
Qualification	Demonstration that an entity is capable of fulfilling specified requirements. Verification of attributes that must be met or complied with in order for a person or thing to be considered fit to perform a particular function. For example, equipment may be qualified for an intended use by verifying performance characteristics such as linearity, sensitivity, or ease of use. An employee may be qualified based on technical, academic, and practical knowledge and skills developed through training, education, and on-the-job performance.
Quality assurance	Activities involving quality planning, control, assessment, reporting, and improvement necessary to ensure that a product or service meets defined quality standards and requirements.

Appendix 1-1. Glossary of Commonly Used Quality Terms (cont'd)

Quality control	Operational techniques and activities used to monitor and eliminate causes of unsatisfactory performance at any stage of a process.
Quality indicators	Measurable aspects of processes or outcomes that provide an indication of the condition or direction of performance over time. Used to monitor progress toward stated quality goals and objectives.
Quality management	The organizational structure, processes, and procedures necessary to ensure that the overall intentions and direction of an organization's quality program are met and that the quality of the product or service is ensured. Quality management includes strategic planning, allocation of resources, and other systematic activities such as quality planning, implementation, and evaluation.
Requirement	A stated or obligatory need or expectation that can be measured or observed and is necessary to ensure quality, safety, effectiveness, or customer satisfaction. Requirements can include things that the system or product must do, characteristics it must have, and levels of performance it must attain.
Specification	Description of a set of requirements to be satisfied by a product, material, or process indicating, if appropriate, the procedures to be used to determine whether the requirements are satisfied. Specifications are often in the form of written descriptions, drawings, professional standards, and other descriptive references.
Validation	Demonstration through objective evidence that the requirements for a particular application or intended use have been met. Validation provides assurance that new or changed processes and procedures are capable of consistently meeting specified requirements before implementation.
Verification	Confirmation, by examination of objective evidence, that specified requirements have been met.

Appendix 1-2. Code of Federal Regulations Quality-Related References

21 CFR Citation	Topic
606.20	Personnel
606.40	Facilities
606.60	Equipment quality control
606.65	Supplies, reagents
606.100	Standard operating procedures
606.140	Laboratory controls
606.160	Records
606.170	Adverse reactions
606.171	Biological product deviations
211.22	Quality control/quality assurance unit responsibilities
211.25	Personnel qualifications
211.28	Personnel responsibilities
211.160	Laboratory controls
211.192	Production record review
211.194	Laboratory records and reviews

Appendix 1-3. Statistical Tables for Binomial Distribution* Used to Determine Adequate Sample Size and Level of Confidence for Validation of Pass/Fail Data

Confidence Levels (%) for Percent Conforming

Sample Size	No. of Failures	Requirement for % Conforming		Sample Size	No. of Failures	Requirement for % Conforming	
		90%	95%			90%	95%
		% Confidence				% Confidence	
10	0	65.1	–	50	0	99.5	92.3
	1	26.4	–		1	96.6	72.1
20	0	87.8	64.2		2	88.8	45.9
	1	60.8	26.4		3	75.0	–
	2	32.3	–		4	56.9	–
30	0	95.8	78.5		5	38.4	–
	1	81.6	44.6	60	0	99.8	95.4
	2	58.9	–		1	98.6	80.8
	3	35.3	–		2	94.7	58.3
40	0	98.5	87.1		3	86.3	35.3
	1	91.9	60.1		4	72.9	–
	2	77.7	32.3		5	56.3	–
	3	57.7	–		6	39.4	–
	4	37.1	–				

This table answers the question, *"How confident am I that [90 or 95]% of all products manufactured will meet specifications if I have tested __ number of samples and found __ number to be nonconforming (failures)?"*

*Data from Reliability Analysis Center, http://rac.alionscience.com/Toolbox/.

(cont'd)

Appendix 1-3. Statistical Tables for Binomial Distribution* Used to Determine Adequate Sample Size and Level of Confidence for Validation of Pass/Fail Data (cont'd)

Minimum Sample Size for Percent Conforming

	Requirement for Percent Conforming								
	90%			95%			99%		
	Confidence Level			Confidence Level			Confidence Level		
	90%	95%	99%	90%	95%	99%	90%	95%	99%
No. of Failures	Sample Size			Sample Size			Sample Size		
0	22	29	45	46	59	90	230	299	459
1	39	47	65	77	94	130	388	467	662
2	53	63	83	106	125	166	526	625	838
3	66	76	98	133	180	198	664	773	1002
4	78	90	113	159	208	228	789	913	1157
5	91	103	128	184	235	258	926	1049	1307
6	104	116	142	209	260	288	1051	1186	1453
7	116	129	158	234	286	317	1175	1312	
8	128	143	170	258	310	344	1297	1441	
9	140	154	184	282	336	370	1418		
10	152	167	197	306	361	397			

This table answers the question, *"How many samples do I need to test with ___ number of failures if I want to have [90, 95, or 99] % confidence that [90, 95, or 99]% of all products will meet specifications?"*

*Data from Reliability Analysis Center, http://rac.alionscience.com/Toolbox/.

Appendix 1-3. Statistical Tables for Binomial Distribution* Used to Determine Adequate Sample Size and Level of Confidence for Validation of Pass/Fail Data (cont'd)

Example of Minimum Sample Size and Number of Failures Allowed to Meet AABB Requirements for Product Validation and Quality Control

Product	Requirement[1]	Sample Size[2]	Number of Failures	% Confidence Level
Platelets Pheresis	**At least 90%** of units sampled contain $\geq 3 \times 10^{11}$ platelets and have a pH ≥ 6.2 at the end of allowable storage.	10 10	0 1	65 26
Platelets Pheresis, Leukocytes Reduced	**At a minimum, 95%** of units sampled shall contain a residual leukocyte count $<5 \times 10^6$.	20 20	0 1	64 26
Red Blood Cells Pheresis	**At least 95%** of units sampled shall have >50 g of hemoglobin (or 150 mL red cell volume) per unit.	20 20	0 1	64 26
Granulocytes Pheresis	Prepared by a method known to yield a minimum of 1.0×10^{10} granulocytes **in at least 75%** of the units tested.	4 4	0 1	68 26

1. From Silva MA, ed. Standards for blood banks and transfusion services. 23rd ed. Bethesda, MD: AABB, 2005. Although the AABB *Standards* does not require a specific confidence level, the facility may use this as a way to assess the degree of certainty that each product manufactured will meet specifications.
2. Period of time used to define a population for sampling is determined by the facility. (NOTE: The longer the period, the more difficult it may be to identify causes of failure, and the more products already in distribution that may be involved in a recall.)

*Data from Reliability Analysis Center, http://rac.alionscience.com/Toolbox/.

Appendix 1-4. Assessment Examples: Blood Utilization[1,2]

A blood usage review committee should consider the following areas of practice and develop specific measurements for monitoring blood transfusion processes. Some measurements provide data for several processes.

Ordering of Appropriate Blood Components

1.	Preanalytical errors	Errors in specimen collection, verbal orders, transfusion orders.
2.	Units transfused	Figures for each type of blood component and special preparation. Use of autologous and directed donor collections. Analyze by clinical service or by prescriber.
3.	Patients transfused	Total number of patients receiving each of the components or products listed in item 2.
4.	Units transfused per patient transfused	Average number of units of each component or product given to patients receiving that component. May be useful to analyze by diagnosis or surgical/medical procedure.
5.	Special components prepared and transfused	Number and relative percent of leukocyte-reduced, irradiated, cytomegalovirus-negative units; aliquots prepared and transfused; outpatient and home transfusions.
6.	Units returned unused	Number and percent of units issued and later returned unused. Analyze by ward, by clinical service, or by prescriber.
7.	Crossmatch-to-transfusion (C:T) ratio	Number of units crossmatched divided by the number of units transfused. Analysis could be by institutional total, by emergency vs routine requests, or by clinical service, surgical procedure, or prescriber, as needed.
8.	Transfusion guidelines	Verification that guidelines are current, appropriate for the patient population being treated, and readily available to physicians.

Distributing, Handling, and Dispensing Blood Components

1.	Turnaround time	Interval between the time a transfusion request is received and time the unit is available for transfusion and/or is transported to the patient's bedside. May analyze by emergency, routine, or operative requests.
2.	Emergency requests	Number and percent may be analyzed by clinical service, prescriber, diagnosis, or time (week, day, shift).
3.	Uncrossmatched units	Number and percent of units issued uncrossmatched or with abbreviated pretransfusion testing. May analyze by clinical service, or prescriber.
4.	Age distribution of units	Age of units in inventory and crossmatched by ABO and Rh type, age of units when received from the supplier, age at the time of transfusion, age when returned to the supplier.

Appendix 1-4. Assessment Examples: Blood Utilization[1,2] (cont'd)

5. Surgical cancellations due to unavailability of blood

Number and percent of cases delayed due to the unavailability of blood; number of hours or days of delay, analyzed by surgical procedure and by cause (eg, antibody problem in an individual patient, general shortage, or shortage of a particular ABO or Rh type).

6. Significant type switches due to unavailability of blood

Number of Rh-negative patients given Rh-positive red cells or platelets; transfusions with ABO-incompatible plasma.

7. Outdate rate

Number of units outdated (expired unused) divided by the number of units received; should be monitored for all blood components and derivatives. Analysis by ABO and Rh type may prove informative.

8. Wastage rates

Number of units wasted due to breakage, improper preparation, improper handling or storage; units prepared for a patient but not used; number of units that failed to meet inspection requirements.

9. Adequacy of service from the blood supplier

Number of orders placed that could be filled as requested; average time between the order and receipt of emergency delivery; number of orders associated with an error such as improper unit received or units improperly shipped.

10. Compatibility testing requirements

Adequacy, currency, and appropriateness of policies and procedures.

11. Quality control policies and procedures

Percent of records of temperature, equipment, component preparation, or testing that are incomplete or have deviations.

Administration of Blood and Components

1. Blood issue/delivery errors

Number of wrong units issued; number of units delivered to wrong patient-care area or improperly transported.

2. Blood administration policies and procedures

Adherence to facility-specific requirements when monitoring patients for signs and symptoms of adverse reactions. Availability of copies of current policies and procedures and of current *Circular of Information for the Use of Human Blood and Blood Components*.

3. Blood administration audits

Summary of on-site performance reviews, to include number of deviations by category (eg, identification of patient and donor unit, documentation and completeness of medical record). May include audit for documentation of transfusion order and indication for transfusion or informed consent.

4. Transfusion equipment

Review of quality control documentation for equipment, including blood warmers, infusion pumps, special filters or administration sets; documentation in the medical record that devices were used; number of situations where their use was inappropriate.

(cont'd)

Appendix 1-4. Assessment Examples: Blood Utilization[1,2] (cont'd)

5.	Special transfusion situations	Review of compliance with policies for out-of-hospital transfusions and perioperative and postoperative collection of autologous blood.

Monitoring Transfusion Results

1.	Compliance with transfusion guidelines	Number and percent of inappropriate transfusions, as determined by the blood usage review committee; analysis of reasons for inappropriate transfusion.
2.	Transfusion reactions	Number and percent of reported transfusion reactions; turnaround time for complete investigation; documentation of transfusion service and committee review; documentation in the medical record.
3.	Transfusion-transmitted disease	Number of cases by infectious agent; turnaround time of investigation; completeness of review and recording.
4.	Look-back investigations	Number of cases by infectious agent; turnaround time of investigation; completeness of case-finding, notification, review, and recording.
5.	Review of policies and procedures	Adequacy, currency, and appropriateness of policies and procedures for detection and reporting of adverse effects of transfusion.

Management Data

1.	Workload and productivity	Evaluation of activities and efficiency of the laboratory; may be analyzed by day of week and by shift. Hours worked per unit transfused or patient transfused may be more valuable as an efficiency measure than data obtained from traditional productivity calculations.
2.	Event reports	Number of events dealing with laboratory processes (eg, labeling, preparation, testing, issue); procedural events in blood administration; errors, accidents, and recalls by blood supplier(s).
3.	Staff training and competency	Documentation of training and continuing competency of laboratory and nursing staff to perform transfusion-related procedures and policies.

1.   Comprehensive accreditation manual for hospitals: The official handbook. Oakbrook Terrace, IL: Joint Commission Resources, Inc., 2002.
2.   Becker J, Blackall D, Evans C, et al for the Scientific Section Coordinating Committee. Guidelines for blood utilization review. Bethesda, MD: AABB, 2001.

Chapter 2

2

Facilities and Safety

FACILITY DESIGN AND maintenance are critical to ensure that operational needs are met and that
the work environment is safe for both
staff and visitors. The layout of the physical space; management of utilities such as
water and air ventilation; flow of personnel, materials, and waste; and ergonomic
factors should all be considered in the facility management plan.

In addition to providing adequate facilities, the organization must develop and
implement a safety program that defines
policies and procedures for safe work
practices. This includes hazard communication, use of protective equipment, training, and competency assessment in accordance with regulations for emergency and
disaster preparedness, chemical hygiene,
blood-borne pathogens, and radiation
safety when applicable. All employees are
responsible for protecting their own safety

and the safety of others by adhering to policies set forth in the facility safety program.

The AABB requires accredited blood
banks and transfusion services to plan, implement, and maintain a program to minimize risks to the health and safety of donors, patients, volunteers, and employees
from biological, chemical, and radiological
hazards.[1(p88)] Other professional and accrediting organizations have similar or more detailed safety program requirements, including the College of American Pathologists
(CAP), the Clinical and Laboratory Standards Institute (formerly NCCLS), and the
Joint Commission on Accreditation of
Healthcare Organizations (JCAHO).[2-5]

Several federal agencies have issued regulations and recommendations to protect
the safety of workers and the public. Those
relevant to health-care settings are listed in
Appendix 2-1. The contents of these regulations and guidelines are discussed in more

detail in each section of this chapter. Blood banks and transfusion services should consult with state and local agencies as well to identify any additional safety requirements. Trade and professional organizations also provide safety recommendations that are relevant to blood banks and transfusion services. These organizations are also listed in Appendix 2-1.

Facilities
Facility Design and Workflow

Proper design and maintenance of facilities and organization of work can reduce or eliminate many potential hazards. Design, maintenance, and organization also affect efficiency, productivity, error rates, employee and customer satisfaction, and the quality of products and services. State and local building codes should be consulted in the design planning stages for architectural safety regarding space, furnishings, and storage.

During the design phase for a new space, the location and flow of personnel, materials, and equipment should be considered in the context of the processes to be performed. Adequate space must be allotted for personnel movement, location of supplies and large equipment, and private or "distraction-free" zones for certain manufacturing tasks (eg, donor interviewing, record review, and blood component labeling). The facility must be able to accommodate designated "clean" and "dirty" spaces and provide for controlled movement of materials and waste in and out of these areas so as to avoid contamination. Chemical fume hoods and biological safety cabinets should be located away from drafts and high-traffic areas. The number and location of eyewashes and emergency showers must also be considered. Water sources for reagent preparation must be considered. Staff handling hazardous materials must have ready access to hand-washing sinks. For certain pieces of heavy equipment, such as irradiators, load-bearing capacity must be taken into account.

Laboratories must be designed with adequate illumination, electrical power, and conveniently located outlets. Emergency backup power sources, such as uninterruptible power supplies and backup generators, should be considered to ensure that loss of blood products does not occur during power failures. The National Electrical Code[6] is routinely used as a national guideline for the design of essential electrical distribution systems, with modifications approved by the local building authority having jurisdiction.

Appropriate systems for heating, ventilation, and air conditioning must be used. Environmental monitoring systems should be considered for laboratories that require positive or negative air pressure differentials to be maintained, or where air filtration systems are used to control particle levels. The nationally accepted specifications for ventilation are published by the American Society of Heating, Refrigerating, and Air-Conditioning Engineers, Inc.[7]

Housekeeping

The workplace should be kept clean and free of clutter. Work surfaces and equipment should be regularly cleaned and disinfected. Items that may accumulate dust and debris should not be stored above clean supplies or work surfaces. Exits and fire safety equipment must not be blocked or obstructed in any way. Receptacles and disposal guidelines for nonhazardous solid waste, biohazardous, chemical, and radiation waste should be clearly delineated. Housekeeping responsibilities, methods, and schedules should be defined for every work area. Written procedures, initial training, continuing education of personnel, and ongoing monitoring of housekeeping effectiveness are essential to safe operations.

Restricted Areas

Hazardous areas should be clearly and uniformly identified with warning signs in accordance with federal Occupational Safety and Health Administration (OSHA) and Nuclear Regulatory Commission (NRC) standards so that personnel entering or working around them are aware of existing biological, chemical, or radiation dangers.[8-11] Staff not normally assigned to these areas should receive adequate training to avoid endangering themselves. Risk areas can be stratified. For example, "high-risk" areas might include chemical fume hoods, biological safety cabinets, and storage areas for volatile chemicals or radioisotopes. Technical work areas could be considered "moderate risk" and restricted to laboratory personnel. Administrative and clerical areas could be considered "low risk" and not restricted.

Whenever possible, functions not requiring special precautions should be separated from those performed in restricted areas. Every effort should be made to prevent the contamination of designated "clean" areas and common equipment. Work area telephones can be equipped with speakers to eliminate the need to pick up the receiver. Computer keyboards and telephones can be covered with plastic. They should be cleaned on a regular basis and when visibly soiled. Employees should remove their personal protective barriers such as gloves and laboratory coats and wash their hands with soap and water when leaving a "contaminated" area.

Concerns for safety dictate that there be no casual visitors in areas where laboratory hazards may be encountered.[12] Children,

especially, should not be allowed in areas where they could be exposed to hazards and should be closely supervised in those areas where their presence is permitted. Facilities should consider establishing specific safety guidelines for visitors with business in restricted areas and documenting that this information was received and understood.

Mobile Sites

Mobile blood collection operations can present special problems. An individual trained in safety principles should make an advance visit to the collection site to ensure that hazards are minimized. All mobile personnel should be trained to recognize unsafe conditions and understand infection control policies and procedures, but responsibility for site safety should be assigned to a senior-level employee.

Hand-washing access is essential at all collection sites. Carpeted or difficult-to-clean surfaces may be protected with an absorbent overlay with waterproof backing to protect from possible blood spills. Portable screens and ropes are helpful in directing traffic flow to maintain safe work areas. Food service areas should be physically separated from areas for blood collection and storage. Blood-contaminated waste must be either returned to a central location for disposal or packaged and decontaminated using thermal (autoclave, incinerator) or chemical disinfectant in accordance with local regulations for medical wastes. Trained staff must perform this decontamination with particular attention paid to cleanup of mobile sites after blood collection.

Ergonomics

Consideration in physical design should be given to ergonomics and accommodations for individuals covered under the Americans with Disabilities Act (42 U.S.C.

§ 12101-12213, 1990). Several factors may contribute to employee fatigue, musculoskeletal disorder syndromes, or injury, including the following[13]:

■ *Awkward postures*—positions that place stress on the body such as reaching overhead, twisting, bending, kneeling, or squatting.

■ *Repetition*—performing the same motions continuously or frequently.

■ *Force*—the amount of physical effort used to perform work.

■ *Pressure points*—pressing the body against hard or sharp surfaces.

■ *Vibration*—continuous or high-intensity hand-arm or whole-body vibration.

■ *Other factors*—extreme high or low temperatures; lighting too dark or too bright.

Both the total time per work shift and the length of uninterrupted periods of work can be significant in contributing to problems. Actions to correct problems associated with ergonomics may include:

■ Engineering improvements to reduce or eliminate the underlying cause, such as making changes to equipment, workstations, or materials.

■ Administrative improvements, such as providing variety in tasks; adjusting work schedules and work pace; providing recovery or relaxation time; modifying work practices; ensuring regular housekeeping and maintenance of work spaces, tools, and equipment; and encouraging exercise.

■ Provision of safety gear such as gloves, knee and elbow pads, footwear, and other items that employees wear to protect themselves against injury.

Safety Program

An effective safety program starts with a well-thought-out safety plan. This plan identifies the applicable regulatory requirements and describes how they will be met. In general, institutions are required to:

■ Provide a workplace free of recognized hazards.

■ Evaluate all procedures for potential exposure risks.

■ Evaluate each employment position for potential exposure risks.

■ Identify hazardous areas or materials with appropriate labels and signs.

■ Educate staff, document training, and monitor compliance.

■ Apply Standard Precautions (including Universal and Blood and Body Fluid Precautions) to the handling of blood, body fluids, and tissues.

■ Dispose of hazardous waste appropriately.

■ Report incidents and accidents and provide treatment and follow-up.

■ Provide ongoing review of safety policies, procedures, operations, and equipment.

■ Develop facility policies for disaster preparedness and response.

Safety programs should consider the needs of all persons affected by the work environment. Most obvious is the safety of technical staff, but potential risks for blood donors, ancillary personnel, volunteers, visitors, housekeeping staff, and maintenance and repair workers must also be evaluated. Appropriate provisions must be applied if these individuals cannot be excluded from risk areas.

Laboratories should appoint a safety officer who can provide general guidance and expertise.[3] This individual might develop the safety program, oversee orientation and training, perform safety audits, survey work sites, recommend changes, and serve on or direct the activities of safety committees. It is recommended that facilities using hazardous chemicals and radioactive materials appoint a chemical hygiene officer and radiation safety officer to oversee chemical and radiation protection programs.[8,11] A general safety officer with sufficient expertise may fill these roles, or separate officers may be appointed and program oversight given to a safety committee.

There are five basic elements that must be addressed for each type of hazard covered in the safety program:

1. Training.
2. Hazard identification and communication.
3. Engineering controls and personal protective equipment.
4. Safe work practices, including waste disposal.
5. Emergency response plan.

In addition, management controls should be implemented to ensure that these elements are in place and effective. Management is responsible for:

1. Developing and communicating the written plan.
2. Ensuring implementation and providing adequate resources.
3. Providing access to employee health services related to prevention strategies and treatment of exposures.
4. Monitoring compliance and effectiveness.
5. Evaluating and improving the safety plan.

Basic Elements of a Safety Program

Training

Employees must understand the hazards in their workplace and the appropriate precautions to take in order to manage them safely. The mandate for employee training programs is based on good general practice as well as OSHA requirements.[9-11] All persons must be trained to protect themselves appropriately before beginning work with hazardous materials. Supervisors or their designees are responsible for documenting the employee's understanding of and ability to apply safety precautions before independent work is permitted. Safety training must precede even temporary work assignments if significant potential for exposure exists. Staff who do not demonstrate the requisite understanding and skills must undergo retraining. These requirements apply not only to laboratory staff, but also to housekeeping and other personnel who may come into contact with hazardous substances or waste. Table 2-1 lists topics to cover in work safety training programs.

Hazard Identification and Communication

Employees must know when they are working with hazardous substances and must know where they are located in the workplace. Employers are required to provide information about workplace hazards to their employees to help reduce the risk of occupational illnesses and injuries. This is done by means of signage, labels on containers, written information, and training programs.

Engineering Controls and Personal Protective Equipment

Whenever possible, the physical workspace should be designed to eliminate the potential for exposure. When this is not possible, protective gear must be provided to protect the employee. Engineering controls are physical plant controls or equipment such as sprinkler systems, chemical fume hoods, and needleless systems that isolate or remove the hazard from the workplace. Personal protective equipment (PPE) is specialized clothing or equipment worn by an employee for protection against a hazard, such as gloves,

Table 2-1. Topics to Cover in a Work Safety Training Program

Work safety training programs should ensure that all personnel:

- Have access to a copy of pertinent regulatory texts and an explanation of the contents.
- Understand the employer's exposure control plan and how to obtain a copy of the written plan.
- Understand how hepatitis and human immunodeficiency virus (HIV) are transmitted and how often; be familiar with the symptoms and consequences of hepatitis B virus (HBV), hepatitis C virus (HCV), and HIV infection.
- Know that they are offered vaccination against HBV.
- Recognize tasks that pose infectious risks and distinguish them from other duties.
- Know what protective clothing and equipment are appropriate for the procedures they will perform and how to use them.
- Know and understand the limitations of protective clothing and equipment (eg, different types of gloves are recommended based on the permeability of the hazardous material to be used). Employers and staff should be forewarned against a false sense of security.
- Know where protective clothing and equipment are kept.
- Are familiar with and understand all requirements for work practices specified in standard operating procedures (SOPs) for the tasks they perform, including the meaning of signs and labels.
- Know how to remove, handle, decontaminate, and dispose of contaminated material.
- Know the appropriate actions to take and the personnel to contact if exposed to blood or other biological, chemical, or radiological hazards.
- Know the corrective actions to take in the event of spills or personal exposure to fluids, tissues, and contaminated sharps, the appropriate reporting procedures, and the medical monitoring recommended when parenteral exposure may have occurred.
- Know their right for access to medical treatment and medical records.

---

masks, and laboratory coats. General guidance on the use of engineering controls and PPE is included in Appendix 2-2.

Safe Work Practices

Employees must be trained to know how to work with hazardous materials in a way that protects themselves, their co-workers, and the environment. Safe work practices are defined as tasks performed in a manner that reduces the likelihood of exposure to workplace hazards. General recommendations for safe work practices are included in Appendix 2-2.

Emergency Response Plan

When engineering and work practice controls fail, employees must know how to respond. The purpose of advance planning is to control the hazardous situation as quickly and safely as possible. Regular testing of the emergency response plan will identify areas for improvement and will also build confidence in staff to respond effectively in a real situation. OSHA requires a written plan for facilities with more than 10 employees. Verbal communication of the plan is acceptable for 10 or fewer employees.[14]

Management Controls

Supervisory personnel must monitor safety practices in their areas of responsibility. Continuing attention to safety issues should be addressed in routine staff meetings and training sessions. Periodic audits performed by a safety professional help increase safety awareness. Management should seek staff input into the design and improvement of the facility's safety plan.

The safety program, with its policies, guidelines, and supporting references to regulatory documents, should be detailed in a safety manual and made available to all personnel at risk. This manual, along with operational procedures manuals, should be reviewed at least annually and updated as technology evolves and new information becomes available. Work sites and safety equipment also should be inspected regularly to ensure compliance and response readiness. Checklists are helpful in documenting these audits and assessing safety preparedness. Checklist items and essential elements for safety and environmental management audits can be obtained from other sources[2,3,15] or can be developed internally.

Employee Health Services

Hepatitis Prophylaxis

All employees routinely exposed to blood must be offered hepatitis B virus (HBV) vaccine if they do not already have HBV-protective antibodies (ie, anti-HBs). OSHA requires that the vaccine be offered at no cost to the employee, and if the employee refuses the vaccine, that the refusal be documented.[10]

Monitoring Programs

The employer must provide a system for monitoring exposure to certain substances as defined in the OSHA standard if there is reason to believe that exposure levels routinely exceed the action level.[16]

Medical First Aid and Follow-up

When requested by a worker who has sustained known or suspected blood exposure, monitoring for HBV, hepatitis C virus (HCV), and human immunodeficiency virus (HIV) antibodies should be provided with appropriate counseling. Informed consent is required for this voluntary testing; rejection of offered testing must be documented. The usual schedule would include immediate tests on the worker and on the source of the potentially infectious material, with follow-up of the worker at intervals after exposure.[9,10] All aspects of accident follow-up should be appropriately documented.

The Centers for Disease Control and Prevention (CDC) has published recommendations for both pre- and postexposure prophylaxis if the contaminating material is HBV-positive or if this information is unknown.[17] Hepatitis B Immune Globulin is usually given concurrently with hepatitis B vaccine in cases of penetrating injuries. When administered in accordance with the manufacturer's directions, both products are very safe and carry no documented risk for infection with HBV, HCV, or HIV. Postexposure prophylaxis for HIV is continually evolving; policies are generally based on Public Health Service recommendations[17] and current standards of practice.

Reporting Accidents and Injuries

When an injury occurs, as much relevant information as possible should be documented (see Table 2-2). In addition, the supervisor should complete any accident reports and investigation forms required by the institution's insurer and worker's compensation agencies. Medical records for individual employees should be pre-

Table 2-2. Information to Be Included in Injury Reports

- Name and address of the injured person.
- Time of the injury (hour, day, month, year).
- Specified place where the injury occurred.
- Details of the injured person's activities at the time of injury.
- Nature of the injury (eg, bruise, laceration, burn, etc).
- Part of the body injured (eg, head, arm, leg, etc).
- Nature of the known or potential agent, in cases of exposure to pathologic organisms or other hazardous materials.
- Nature of medical attention or first aid applied in the workplace.
- Date the injured person stopped work.
- Date the injured person returned to work.
- Estimated cost of damage to property or to equipment.
- Injured person's statement of the events leading to the injury.
- Statements from witnesses.
- Cause of the injury.
- Corrective action taken or recommendations for corrective action.

served for the duration of employment plus 30 years, with few exceptions.[17]

OSHA requires health service employers with 11 or more workers to maintain records of occupational injuries and illnesses that require care that exceeds the capabilities of a person trained in first aid.[18] Records of first aid provided by a nonphysician for minor injuries such as cuts or burns do not have to be retained. Initial documentation must be completed within 6 days of the incident. All logs, summaries, and supplemental records must be preserved for at least 5 years beyond the calendar year of occurrence. Employers must report fatalities and injuries resulting in the hospitalization of three or more employees to OSHA within 8 hours of the accident.[18]

Latex Allergies

With the increased use of gloves, there has been a rise in the number of health-care workers with latex allergies. Adverse reactions associated with latex and/or powdered gloves include contact dermatitis, allergic dermatitis, urticaria, and anaphylaxis. Medical devices that contain latex must bear a caution label. The National Institute for Occupational Safety and Health offers the following recommendations[19]:

- Make nonlatex gloves available as an alternative to latex. Encourage use of nonlatex gloves for activities and work environments where there is minimal risk of exposure to infectious materials.

- If latex gloves are used, provide reduced protein, powder-free gloves. (Note: This is not a requirement, but a recommendation to reduce exposure.)

- Use good housekeeping practices to remove latex-containing dust from the workplace.

- Use work practices that reduce the chance of reaction, such as hand washing and avoiding oil-based hand lotions.
- Provide workers with education programs and training materials about latex allergy.
- Periodically screen high-risk workers for latex allergy symptoms.
- Evaluate current prevention strategies.
- If symptoms of latex allergy develop, avoid direct contact with latex and consult a physician about allergy precautions.

Fire Prevention

Fire prevention relies on a combination of facility design based on the National Fire Protection Association (NFPA) Life Safety Code,[20] defined processes to maintain fire protection systems in good working order, and fire safe work practices. The Life Safety Code includes both active and passive fire protection systems (eg, alarms, smoke detectors, sprinklers, egress lights and corridors, and fire-rated barriers).

Training

Fire safety training is recommended at the start of employment and at least annually thereafter. Training should emphasize prevention and an employee's awareness of the work environment, including how to recognize and report unsafe conditions, how to report fires, the locations of the nearest alarm and fire containment equipment and their use, and evacuation policies and routes.

All staff are required to participate in fire drills at least annually by the CAP and the JCAHO.[2,4] In areas where patients are housed or treated, the JCAHO requires quarterly drills on each shift. Staff partici-

pation and understanding should be documented.

Hazard Identification and Communication

Emergency exits must be clearly marked with an "EXIT" sign. Additional signage must be posted along the route of egress to show the direction of travel if it is not immediately apparent. All flammable materials should be labeled with appropriate hazard warnings and flammable storage cabinets should be clearly marked.

Engineering Controls and Personal Protective Equipment

Laboratories storing large volumes of flammable chemicals are usually built with 2-hour fire separation walls, or with 1-hour separation if there is an automatic fire extinguishing system.[3] Permanent exit routes must be designed to provide free and unobstructed egress from all parts of the facility to an area of safety. Secondary exits may be required for areas larger than 1000 square feet; consult local safety authority having jurisdiction such as the local fire marshal and the NFPA. Fire detection and alarm systems should be provided in accordance with federal, state, and local regulations.

Safe Work Practices

All fire equipment should be inspected on a regular basis to ensure good working order. Fire extinguishers should be made readily available and staff should be trained to use them properly. Nothing should be stored along emergency exit routes that would obstruct evacuation efforts. Exit doors cannot be locked from the inside. Housekeeping and inventory management plans should be designed to control the accumulations of flammable and combustible materials stored in the facility. In areas where sprinkler systems are installed, all items should be stored at least 18 inches below the sprinkler head. Local fire codes may require greater clearance.

Emergency Response Plan

The fire emergency response plan should encompass both facility-wide and area-specific situations. It should describe reporting and alarm systems; location and use of emergency equipment; roles and responsibilities for staff during the response; "defend in place" strategies; and conditions for evacuation, evacuation procedures, and routes of egress.[4,14] When a fire occurs, the general sequence for immediate response should be to 1) rescue anyone in immediate danger, 2) activate the fire alarm system and alert others in the area, 3) confine the fire by closing doors and shutting off fans or other oxygen sources if possible, and 4) extinguish the fire with a portable extinguisher if the fire is small, or evacuate if it is too large to manage.

Electrical Safety

Electrical hazards, including fire and shock, may arise from use of faulty electrical equipment, damaged receptacles, connectors or cords, or unsafe work practices. Proper use of electrical equipment, periodic inspection and maintenance, and hazard recognition training are essential to help prevent accidents that may result in electric shock or electrocution. The severity of shock depends on the path that the electrical current takes through the body, the amount of current flowing through the body, and the length of time that it is flowing through the body. Even low-voltage exposures can lead to serious injury.[21]

Training

Safety training should be designed to make employees aware of electrical hazards associated with receptacles and connectors and help them recognize potential problems such as broken receptacles and connectors, improper electrical connections, damaged cords, and inadequate grounding.

Hazard Identification and Communication

The safety plan should address the proper use of receptacles and connectors. Equipment that does not meet safety standards should be marked to prevent accidental use.

Engineering Controls and Personal Protective Equipment

OSHA requires that electrical systems and equipment be constructed and installed in a way that minimizes the potential for workplace hazards. When purchasing equipment, the facility should verify that it bears the mark of an OSHA-approved independent testing laboratory such as Underwriters Laboratories (UL).[22] Adequate working space should be provided around equipment to allow easy access for safe operation and maintenance. Ground-fault circuit interrupters should be installed in damp or wet areas.

Safe Work Practices

Electrical safety practices are focused around 1) proper use of electrical equipment and 2) proper maintenance and repair. Staff should not plug or unplug equipment from an electrical source when their hands are wet. Overloading circuits with too many devices may cause the current to heat the wires to a very high temperature and generate a fire. Damaged receptacles and faulty electrical equipment must be tagged and removed from service until they have been repaired and checked for safety. Flexible cords should be secured to prevent tripping and should be protected from damage from heavy or sharp objects. Slack in flexible cords should be kept to prevent tension on electrical terminals and cords should be checked for cut, broken, or cracked insulation. Extension cords should not be used in lieu of permanent wiring.

Emergency Response Plan

When it is not possible to decrease the power or disconnect equipment, the power supply should be shut off from the circuit breaker. If it is not possible to interrupt the power supply, a nonconductive material such as dry wood should be used to pry a victim from the source of current.[21] Victims must not be touched directly. Emergency first aid for victims of electrical shock must be sought. Water-based fire extinguishers are not to be used on electrical fires.

Biosafety

The blood bank or transfusion service must define and enforce measures to minimize the risk of exposure to biohazardous materials in the workplace. Requirements published by OSHA (Bloodborne Pathogen Standard)[10] and recommendations published by the US Department of Health and Human Services[9,12] provide the basis for an effective biosafety plan.

Bloodborne Pathogen Standard

The OSHA Bloodborne Pathogen Standard is intended to protect employees in all occupations where there is a risk of exposure to blood and other potentially infectious materials. It requires that the facility develop an Exposure Control Plan and describes appropriate engineering controls, personal protective equipment, and work practice controls to minimize the risk of exposure. It also requires employers to provide hepatitis B vaccination for staff with occupational exposure, to provide medical follow-up in case of accidental exposure, and to keep records related to accidents and exposures.

Standard Precautions

Standard Precautions represent the most current recommendations by CDC to reduce the risk of transmission of bloodborne and other pathogens in hospitals. Published in 1996 in the *Guidelines for Isolation Precautions in Hospitals,*[9] they build on earlier recommendations, including Body Substance Isolation (1987), Universal Precautions (1986), and Blood and Body Fluid Precautions (1983). The Bloodborne Pathogen Standard refers to the use of Universal Precautions; however, OSHA recognizes the more recent guidelines from the CDC and, in Directive CPL 2-2.69, allows hospitals to use acceptable alternatives, including Standard Precautions, as long as all other requirements in the standard are met.[23]

Standard Precautions apply to all patient care activities regardless of diagnosis where there is a risk of exposure to 1) blood; 2) all body fluids, secretions, and excretions, *except sweat*; 3) nonintact skin; and 4) mucous membranes.

Biosafety Levels

Recommendations for biosafety in laboratories are based on the potential hazards for specific infectious agents and the activities performed.[12] They include guidance on both engineering controls and safe work practices. The four biosafety levels are designated in ascending order, with increasing protection for personnel, the environment, and the community.

Biosafety Level 1 (BSL-1) involves work with agents of no known or of minimal potential hazard to laboratory personnel and the environment. Activities are usually conducted on open surfaces and no containment equipment is needed.

Biosafety Level 2 (BSL-2) work involves agents of moderate potential hazard to personnel and the environment, usually from contact-associated exposure. Most blood bank laboratory activities are considered BSL-2. Precautions described in this section will focus on BSL-2 requirements. Laboratories should consult the CDC or National Institutes of Health (NIH) guidelines for precautions appropriate for higher levels of containment.

Biosafety Level 3 (BSL-3) includes work with indigenous or exotic agents that may cause serious or potentially lethal disease as a result of exposure to aerosols (eg, *Mycobacterium tuberculosis*) or by other routes that would result in grave consequences to the infected host (eg, HIV). Recommendations for work at BSL-3 are designed to contain biohazardous aerosols and minimize the risk of surface contamination.

Biosafety Level 4 (BSL-4) applies to work with dangerous or exotic agents that pose high individual risk of life-threatening disease from aerosols (eg, agents of hemorrhagic fevers, filoviruses). BSL-4 is not applicable to routine blood-bank-related activities.

Training

OSHA requires annual training for all employees whose tasks carry risk of infectious exposure.[10,23] Training programs must be tailored to the target group, both in level and content. General background knowledge of biohazards, understanding of control procedures, or work experience cannot meet the requirement for specific training, although assessment of such knowledge is a first step in planning program content. Workplace volunteers require at least as much safety training as paid staff performing similar functions.

Hazard Identification and Communication

The facility's Exposure Control Plan communicates the risks present in the workplace and describes controls to minimize exposure. BSL-2 through BSL-4 facilities must have a biohazard sign posted at the entrance when infectious agents are in use. It serves to notify personnel and visitors about the agents used, a point of contact for the area, and any special protective equipment or work practices required.

Biohazard warning labels must be placed on containers of regulated waste; refrigerators and freezers containing blood or other potentially infectious material; and other containers used to store, transport, or ship blood or other potentially infectious materials. Blood components that are labeled to identify their contents and have been released for transfusion or other clinical use are exempted.

Engineering Controls and Personal Protective Equipment

OSHA requires that hazards be controlled by engineering or work practices whenever possible. Engineering controls for BSL-2 laboratories include limited access to the laboratory when work is in progress and biological safety cabinets or other containment equipment for work that may involve infectious aerosols or splashes. Hand-washing sinks and eyewash stations must be available. The work space should be designed so that it can be easily cleaned and bench-tops should be impervious to water and resistant to chemicals and solvents.

Biological safety cabinets (BSCs) are primary containment devices for handling moderate- and high-risk organisms. There are three types—Class I, II, and III—with Class III providing the highest protection to the worker. A comparison of the features and applications for the three classes of cabinets is provided in Table 2-3.[24] BSCs are not required for Standard Precautions, but centrifugation of open blood samples or manipulation of units known to be positive for HBsAg or HIV are examples of blood bank procedures for which a BSC could be useful. The effectiveness of the BSC is a function of directional airflow inward and downward, through a high-efficiency filter. Efficacy is reduced by anything that disrupts the airflow pattern, eg, arms moving rapidly in and out of the BSC, rapid movements behind the employee using the BSC, downdrafts from ventilation systems, or open laboratory doors. Care should be taken not to block the front intake and rear exhaust grills. Performance should be certified annually.[25]

Injuries from contaminated needles and other sharps continued to be a major concern in health-care settings even after the Bloodborne Pathogens Standard went into effect. In 2001, OSHA revised the standard to include reference to engineered sharps injury protections and needleless systems.[26] It requires that employers implement appropriate new control technologies and safer medical devices in their Exposure Control Plan and that they solicit input from their employees to identify, evaluate, and select engineering and work practice controls. Examples of safer devices are needleless systems and self-sheathing needles in which the sheath is an integral part of the device.

Decontamination

Reusable equipment and work surfaces that may be contaminated with blood re-quire daily cleaning and decontamination. Obvious spills on equipment or work surfaces should be cleaned up immediately; routine wipe-downs with disinfectant should occur at the end of each shift or on a regular basis that provides equivalent safety. Equipment that is exposed to blood or other potentially infectious material must be decontaminated before servicing or shipping. When decontamination of all or a portion of the equipment is not feasible, a biohazard label stating which portions remain contaminated should be attached before servicing or shipping.

Choice of Disinfectants

The Environmental Protection Agency (EPA) maintains a list of chemical products that have been shown to be effective antimicrobial disinfectants.[27] (See http://www.epa.gov/oppad001/chemreginex.htm for a current list.) The Association for Professionals in Infection Control and Epidemiology also publishes a guideline to assist health-care professionals in their decisions involving judicious selection and proper use of specific disinfectants.[28] For facilities covered under the Bloodborne Pathogens Rule, OSHA allows the use of EPA-registered tuberculocidal disinfectants, EPA-registered disinfectants that are effective against both HIV and HBV, and/or a diluted bleach solution to decontaminate work surfaces.[23]

Before selecting a product, workers should consider several factors. Among them are the type of material or surface to be treated, the hazardous properties of the chemical such as corrosiveness, and the level of disinfection required. After selecting a product, procedures need to be written to ensure effective and consistent cleaning and treatment of work surfaces. Some factors to consider for effective de-

Table 2-3. Comparison of Class I, II, and III Biological Safety Cabinets*

	Main Features	Intended Use	Common Applications
Class I	Unfiltered room air is drawn into the cabinet. Inward airflow protects personnel from exposure to materials inside the cabinet. Exhaust is HEPA filtered to protect the environment. Maintains airflow at a minimum velocity of 75 linear feet per minute (lfpm) across the front opening (face velocity).	Personal and environmental protection	To enclose equipment (eg, centrifuges) or procedures that may generate aerosols
Class II (General-applies to all types of Class II cabinets)	Uses laminar flow (air moving at a constant velocity in one direction along parallel lines). Room air is drawn into the front grille. HEPA filtered air is forced downward in a laminar flow to minimize cross-contamination of materials in the cabinet. Exhaust is HEPA filtered.	Personal, environmental, and product protection	Work with microorganisms assigned to biosafety levels 1, 2, or 3 Handling of products where prevention of contamination is critical, such as cell culture propagation or manipulation of blood components in an open system
Class II, A	75% of air is recirculated after passing through a HEPA filter. Face velocity = 75 lfpm.	See Class II, general	See Class II, general
Class II, B1	70% of air exits through the rear grille, is HEPA filtered, and then discharged from the building. The other 30% is drawn into the front grille, HEPA filtered, and recirculated. Face velocity = 100 lfpm.	See Class II, general	Allows for safe manipulation of small quantities of hazardous chemicals and biologics

Class	Description	Protection	Comments
Class II, B2	100% of air is exhausted; none is recirculated. A supply blower draws air from the room or outside and passes it through a HEPA filter to provide the downward laminar flow. Face velocity = 100 lfpm.	See Class II, general	Provides both chemical and biological containment. More expensive to operate because of the volume of conditioned room air being exhausted.
Class II, B3	Similar in design to Type A, but the system is ducted and includes a negative pressure system to keep any possible contamination within the cabinet. Face velocity = 100 lfpm.	See Class II, general	Allows for safe manipulation of small quantities of hazardous chemicals and biologics
Class III	Cabinet is airtight. Materials are handled with rubber gloves attached to the front of the cabinet. Supply air is HEPA filtered. Exhaust air is double HEPA filtered or may have one filter and an air incinerator. Materials are brought in and out of the cabinet either through a dunk tank or a double-door pass-through box that can be decontaminated. Cabinet is kept under negative pressure.	Maximum protection to personnel and environment.	Work with biosafety level 4 microorganisms

*Data from the US Department of Health and Human Services.[24]

contamination include the contact time, the type of microorganisms, the presence of organic matter, and the concentration of the chemical agent. Workers should review the basic information on decontamination and follow the manufacturer's instructions.

Storage

Hazardous materials must be segregated and areas for different types of storage must be clearly demarcated. Blood must be protected from unnecessary exposure to other materials and vice versa. If transfusion products cannot be stored in a separate refrigerator from reagents, specimens, and unrelated materials, areas within the refrigerator must be clearly labeled, and extra care must be taken to reduce the likelihood of spills and other accidents. Storage areas must be kept clean and orderly; food or drink is never allowed where biohazardous materials are stored.

Personal Protective Equipment

Where hazards cannot be eliminated, OSHA requires employers to provide appropriate PPE and clothing, and to clean, launder, or dispose of PPE at no cost to their employees.[10] Standard PPE and clothing include uniforms, laboratory coats, gloves, face shields, masks, and safety goggles. Indications and guidelines for their use are discussed in Appendix 2-2.

Safe Work Practices

Safe work practices appropriate for Standard Precautions include the following:

- Wash hands after touching blood, body fluids, secretions, excretions, and contaminated items, whether or not gloves are worn.
- Wear gloves when touching blood, body fluids, secretions, excretions, and contaminated items, and change them between tasks.
- Wear a mask and eye protection or a face shield during activities that are likely to generate splashes or sprays of blood, body fluids, secretions, and excretions.
- Wear a gown during activities that are likely to generate splashes or sprays of blood, body fluids, secretions, or excretions.
- Handle soiled patient-care equipment in a manner that prevents exposures; ensure that reusable equipment is not used for another patient until it has been cleaned and reprocessed appropriately; and ensure that single-use items are discarded properly.
- Ensure that adequate procedures are defined and followed for the routine care, cleaning, and disinfection of environmental surfaces and equipment.
- Handle soiled linen in a manner that prevents exposures.
- Handle needles, scalpels, and other sharp instruments or devices in a manner that minimizes the risk of exposure.
- Use mouthpieces, resuscitation bags, or other ventilation devices as an alternative to mouth-to-mouth resuscitation methods.
- Place in a private room those patients who are at risk of contaminating the environment or who are not able to maintain appropriate hygiene (eg, tuberculosis).

Laboratory Biosafety Precautions

Several factors need to be considered when assessing the risk of blood exposures among laboratory personnel. Some factors include the number of specimens processed, personnel behaviors, laboratory techniques, and type of equipment.[29] The laboratory director may wish to institute BSL-3 practices for procedures that are considered to be higher risk than BSL-2. When there is doubt whether an activity is BSL-2 or BSL-3, the safety precautions for BSL-3 should be followed. BSL-2 precautions that are applicable to the laboratory setting are summarized in Appendix 2-3.

Considerations for the Donor Room

The Bloodborne Pathogen Standard acknowledges a difference between hospital patients and healthy donors, in whom the prevalence of infectious disease markers is significantly lower. The employer in a volunteer blood donation facility may determine that routine use of gloves is not required for phlebotomy as long as[10]:

- The policy is periodically reevaluated.
- Gloves are made available to those who want to use them, and use is not discouraged.
- Gloves are required when an employee has cuts, scratches, or breaks in skin; when there is a likelihood that contamination will occur; while drawing autologous units; while performing therapeutic procedures; and during training in phlebotomy.

Procedures used in the donation of blood should be assessed for risks of biohazardous exposures and risks inherent in working with a donor or patient. Some procedures are more likely to cause injury than others, such as using lancets for finger puncture, handling capillary tubes, crushing vials for arm cleaning, handling any unsheathed needle, cleaning scissors, and giving cardiopulmonary resuscitation.

In some instances, it may be necessary to collect blood from donors known to pose a high risk of infectivity (eg, collection of autologous blood or Source Plasma for the production of other products such as vaccines). The Food and Drug Administration (FDA) provides guidance for collecting blood from such "high-risk" donors.[30] The most recent regulations and guidelines should be consulted for changes or additions.

Emergency Response Plan

Blood Spills

Every facility handling blood should be prepared for spills in advance. Table 2-4 lists steps to be taken when a spill occurs. Cleanup is easier when preparation includes the following elements:

- Design work areas so that cleanup is relatively simple.
- Prepare a spill kit or cart that contains all necessary supplies and equipment with instructions for their use. Place it near areas where spills are anticipated.
- Assign responsibility for kit/cart maintenance, spill handling, record-keeping, and review of significant incidents.
- Train personnel in cleanup procedures and reporting of significant incidents.

Biohazardous Waste

Medical waste is defined as any waste (solid, semisolid, or liquid) generated in the diagnosis, treatment, or immunization of human beings or animals in related research, production, or testing of biologics. Infectious waste includes disposable equipment, articles, or substances that may harbor or transmit pathogenic organisms or their toxins. In general, infectious waste should either be incinerated or decontaminated before disposal in a sanitary landfill. Blood and components, suctioned fluids, excretions, and secretions may be carefully poured down a drain connected to a sanitary sewer if state law allows. Sanitary sewers may also

Table 2-4. Blood Spill Cleanup

- Contain the spill if possible.
- Evacuate the area for 30 minutes if an aerosol has been created.
- Post warnings to keep the area clear.
- Remove clothing if it is contaminated.
- If the spill occurs in the centrifuge, turn the power off immediately and leave the cover closed for 30 minutes. The use of overwraps helps prevent aerosolization and helps contain the spill.
- Wear appropriate protective clothing and gloves. If sharp objects are involved, gloves must be puncture-resistant, and a broom or other instrument should be used during cleanup to avoid injury.
- Use absorbent material to mop up most of the liquid contents.
- Clean the spill area with detergent.
- Flood the area with disinfectant and use it as described in the manufacturer's instructions. Allow adequate contact time with the disinfectant.
- Wipe up residual disinfectant if necessary.
- Dispose of all materials safely in accordance with biohazard guidelines. All blood-contaminated items must be autoclaved or incinerated.

be used to dispose of other potentially infectious wastes that can be ground and flushed into the sewer. State and local health departments should be consulted about laws and regulations on disposal of biological waste into the sewer.

Laboratories should clearly define what will be considered hazardous waste. For example, in the blood bank items contaminated with liquid or semiliquid blood are biohazardous. Items contaminated with dried blood are considered hazardous if there is potential for the dried material to flake off during handling. Contaminated sharps are always considered hazardous because of the risk for percutaneous injury. However, items such as used gloves, swabs, plastic pipettes with excess liquid removed, or gauze contaminated with small droplets of blood may be considered nonhazardous if the material is dried and will not be released into the environment during handling.

Guidelines for Biohazardous Waste Disposal. Employees must be trained before handling or disposing of biohazardous waste, even if it is packaged. The following disposal guidelines are recommended[31]:

- Identify biohazardous waste consistently; red seamless plastic bags (at least 2 mil thick) or containers carrying the biohazard symbol are recommended.

- Place bags in a protective container with closure upward to avoid breakage and leakage during storage or transport.

- When transported over public roads, the waste must be prepared and shipped according to US Department of Transportation regulations.

- Discard sharps (eg, needles, broken glass, glass slides, wafers from sterile connecting devices) in rigid, puncture-proof, leakproof containers.

- Put liquids only in leakproof, unbreakable containers.

- Do not compact waste materials.

Storage areas for infectious material must be secured to reduce accident risk. Infectious waste must never be placed in the public trash collection system. Most facilities hire private carriers to decontaminate and dispose of infectious or hazardous waste. Contracts with these companies should include disclosure of the risks of handling the waste by the facility, and an acknowledgment by the carrier that all federal, state, and local laws for biohazardous (medical) waste transport, treatment, and disposal are known and followed.

Treating Infectious or Medical Waste. Facilities that incinerate hazardous waste must comply with EPA standards of performance for new stationary sources and emission guidelines for existing sources.[32] In this regulation, a hospital/medical/infectious waste incinerator (HMIWI) is any device that combusts any amount of hospital waste or medical/infectious waste.

Decontamination of biohazardous waste by autoclaving is another common method for decontamination/inactivation of blood samples and blood components. The following elements are considered in determining processing time for autoclaving:

- Size of load being autoclaved.

- Type of packaging of item(s) being autoclaved.

- Density of items being autoclaved.

- Number of items in single autoclave load.

- Placement of items in the autoclave, to allow for steam penetration.

It is useful to place a biological indicator in the center of loads that vary in size and contents to evaluate optimal steam penetration times. The EPA provides detailed information about choosing and operating such equipment.[31]

Longer treatment times are needed for sterilization, but decontamination requires a minimum of 1 hour. A general rule is to process 1 hour for every 10 pounds of waste being processed. Usually, decontaminated laboratory wastes can be disposed of as nonhazardous solid wastes. Staff should check with the local solid waste authority to ensure that the facility is in compliance with the regulations for their area. Waste containing broken glass or other sharp items should be disposed of in a method consistent with policies for the disposal of other sharp or potentially dangerous materials.

Chemical Safety

One of the most effective preventive measures a facility can take to reduce hazardous chemical exposure is to evaluate the use of alternative nonhazardous chemicals whenever possible. A review of ordering practices of hazardous chemicals can result in the purchase of smaller quantities of hazardous chemicals, thus reducing the risk of storing excess chemicals and later dealing with the disposal of these chemicals.

OSHA requires that facilities using hazardous chemicals develop a written Chemical Hygiene Plan (CHP) and that the plan be accessible to all employees. The CHP should outline procedures, equipment, personal protective equipment, and work practices that are capable of protecting employees from hazardous chemicals used in the facility.[11,16] This plan must also provide assurance that equipment and protective devices are functioning properly and that criteria to determine implementation and maintenance of all aspects of the plan are in control. Employees must be informed of all chemical hazards in the workplace and be trained to recognize chemical hazards, to protect themselves when working with these chemicals, and where to find information on particular hazardous chemicals. Appendix 2-4 provides an example of a hazardous chemical data safety sheet that may be used in the CHP. Safety audits and annual reviews of the CHP are important control steps to help ensure that safety practices comply with the policies set forth in the CHP and that the CHP is up to date.

Establishing a clear definition of what constitutes hazardous chemicals is sometimes difficult. Generally, hazardous chemicals are those that pose a significant health risk if an employee is exposed to them or pose a significant physical risk, such as fire or explosion, if handled or stored improperly. Categories of health and physical hazards are listed in Tables 2-5 and 2-6. Appendix 2-5 lists examples of hazardous chemicals that may be found in the blood bank.

The facility should identify a qualified chemical hygiene officer to be responsible for determining guidelines for hazardous materials.[16] The chemical hygiene officer is also accountable for monitoring and documenting accidents and initiating process change as needed.

Training

Initial training is required for all employees who may be exposed to hazardous chemicals—before they begin work in an area where hazards exist. If an individual has received prior training, it may not be necessary to retrain them, depending on the employer's evaluation of the new employee's level of knowledge. New employee training is likely to be necessary regarding such specifics as the location of the relevant Material Safety Data Sheets (MSDS), details of chemical labeling, the personal protective equipment to be used, and site-specific emergency procedures.

Training must be provided whenever a new physical or health hazard is introduced into the workplace, but not for each new chemical that falls within a particular hazard class.[11] For example, if a new solvent is brought into the workplace and it has haz-

Table 2-5. Categories of Health Hazards

Hazard	Definition
Carcinogens	Cancer-producing substances
Irritants	Agents causing irritations (edema, burning, etc) to skin or mucous membranes upon contact
Corrosives	Agents causing destruction of human tissue at the site of contact
Toxic or highly toxic agents	Substances causing serious biologic effects following inhalation, ingestion, or skin contact with relatively small amounts
Reproductive toxins	Chemicals that affect reproductive capabilities, including chromosomal damages and effects on fetuses
Other toxins	Hepatotoxins, nephrotoxins, neurotoxins, agents that act on the hematopoietic systems, and agents that damage the lungs, skin, eyes, or mucous membranes

Table 2-6. Categories of Physical Hazards

Hazard	Definition
Combustible or flammable chemicals	Chemicals that can burn (includes combustible and flammable liquids, solids, aerosols, and gases)
Compressed gases	A gas or mixture of gases in a container under pressure
Explosives	Unstable or reactive chemicals that undergo violent chemical change at normal temperatures and pressure
Unstable (reactive) chemicals	Chemicals that could be self-reactive under conditions of shocks, pressure, or temperature
Water-reactive chemicals	Chemicals that react with water to release a gas that is either flammable or presents a health hazard

ards similar to existing chemicals for which training has already been conducted, then the employer need only make employees aware of the new solvent's hazard category (eg, corrosive, irritant). However, if the newly introduced solvent is a suspected carcinogen and carcinogenic hazard training has not been provided before, then new training must be conducted for employees with potential exposure. Retraining is advisable as often as necessary to ensure that employees understand the hazards, particularly the chronic and specific target-organ health hazards, linked to the materials with which they work.

Hazard Identification and Communication

Hazard Communication

Employers must prepare a comprehensive hazard communication program for all areas using hazardous chemicals to complement the CHP and to "ensure that the hazards of all chemicals produced or imported are evaluated, and that information concerning their hazards is transmitted to employers and employees."[11] The program should include labeling hazardous chemicals, when and how to post warning labels for chemicals, managing MSDS re-

ports for hazardous chemicals in the facilities, and employee training.

Safety materials made available to employees should include:

- The facility's written CHP.
- The facility's written program for hazard communication.
- Identification of work areas where hazardous chemicals are located.
- Required list of hazardous chemicals and their MSDS. (It is the responsibility of the facility to determine which chemicals may present a hazard to employees. This determination should be based on the quantity of chemical used; the physical properties, potency, and toxicity of the chemical; the manner in which the chemical is used; and the means available to control the release of, or exposure to, the chemical.)

Hazardous Chemical Labeling and Signs

The Hazard Communication Standard requires manufacturers of chemicals and hazardous materials to provide the user with basic information about the hazards of these materials through product labeling and Material Safety Data Sheets.[11] Employers are required to provide the following to employees who are expected to work with these hazardous materials: information about the hazards of the materials, how to read the labeling, how to interpret symbols and signs on the labels, and how to read and use the MSDS. Table 2-7 lists the elements to be included in an MSDS.

At a minimum, hazardous chemical container labels must include the name of the chemical, the name and address of the manufacturer, hazard warnings, labels, signs, placards, and other forms of warning to provide visual reminders of specific hazards. The label may refer to the MSDS for additional information. Labels applied by the manufacturer must remain on containers. The user may add storage requirements and dates of receipt, opening, and expiration. If chemicals are aliquotted into secondary containers, the secondary container must be labeled with the name of the chemical and appropriate hazard warnings. Additional information such as precautionary measures, concentration if applicable, and date of preparation are helpful but not mandatory. It is a safe practice to label all containers with the content, even water.

Transfer containers used for temporary storage need not be labeled if the person performing the transfer retains control and intends them for immediate use. Information regarding acceptable standards for hazard communication labeling is provided by the NFPA[33] and the National Paint and Coatings Association.[34]

Signs meeting OSHA requirements must be posted in areas where hazardous chemicals are used. Decisions on where to post warning signs are based on the manufacturer's recommendations on the chemical hazards, the quantity of the chemical in the room or laboratory, and the potency and toxicity of the chemical.

Material Safety Data Sheets

The MSDS identifies the physical and chemical properties of a hazardous chemical (eg, flash point, vapor pressure), its physical and health hazards (eg, potential for fire, explosion, signs and symptoms of exposure), and precautions for safe handling and use. Specific instructions in an individual MSDS take precedence over

Table 2-7. Required Elements of a Material Safety Data Sheet

- Identity of product as it appears on label
- Chemical and common name(s) of all hazardous ingredients
- Physical/chemical characteristics
- Fire and explosion hazard data
- Reactivity data
- Health hazard data, including primary route(s) of entry and exposure limits
- Precautions for safe handling and use
- Exposure control measures
- Emergency and first aid procedures
- Manufacturer information, MSDS revision date

generic information in the Hazardous Materials (HAZMAT) program.

Employers must maintain copies of the required MSDS in the workplace for each hazardous chemical and must ensure that they are readily accessible during each work shift to employees when they are in their work areas. When household consumer products are used in the workplace in the same manner that a consumer would use them, ie, where the duration and frequency of use (and therefore exposure) are not greater than those the typical consumer would experience, OSHA does not require that an MSDS be provided to purchasers. However, if exposure to such products exceeds that normally found in consumer applications, then employees have a right to know about the properties of such hazardous chemicals. OSHA does not require or encourage employers to maintain an MSDS for nonhazardous chemicals.

Engineering Controls and Personal Protective Equipment

Guidelines for laboratory areas in which hazardous chemicals are used or stored must be established. Physical facilities, especially ventilation, must be adequate for the nature and volume of work conducted. Chemicals must be stored according to chemical compatibility (eg, corrosives, flammables, oxidizers, etc) and in minimal volumes. Bulk chemicals should be kept outside work areas. NFPA standards and others provide guidelines for proper storage.[3,33,35]

Chemical fume hoods are recommended for use with organic solvents, volatile liquids, and dry chemicals with a significant inhalation hazard.[3] Although constructed with safety glass, most fume hood sashes are not designed as safety shields. Hoods should be positioned in an area where there is minimal foot traffic to avoid disrupting the airflow and compromising the containment field.

Personal protective equipment that may be provided depending on the hazardous chemicals used includes chemical resistant gloves and aprons, shatterproof safety goggles, and respirators.

Emergency showers should be available to areas where caustic, corrosive, toxic, flammable, or combustible chemicals are used.[3,36] There should be unobstructed access, within 10 seconds, from the areas where hazardous chemicals are used. Safety showers should be periodically flushed and tested for function, and associated floor drains should be checked to ensure that drain traps remain filled with water.

Safe Work Practices

Hazardous material should not be stored or transported in open containers. Containers and their lids or seals should be designed to prevent spills or leakage in all reasonably anticipated conditions. Containers should be able to safely store the maximum anticipated volume and should be easy to clean. Surfaces should be kept clean and dry at all times. When working with a chemical fume hood, all materials should be kept at a distance of at least six inches behind the face opening; the vertical sliding sash should be positioned at the height specified on the certification sticker. The airfoil, baffles and rear ventilation slot must not be blocked. Appendix 2-6 lists specific chemicals and suggestions on how to work with them safely.

Emergency Response

The time to prepare for a chemical spill is before a spill occurs. A comprehensive employee training program should provide the employee with all tools necessary to act responsibly at the time of a chemical spill. The employee should know response procedures, be able to assess the severity of a chemical spill, know or be able to quickly look up the basic physical characteristics of the chemicals, and know where to find emergency response phone numbers. The employee should be able to: assess, stop, and confine the spill; either clean up the spill or call for a spill clean-up team; and follow up on the report of the spill. The employee must know when to ask for assistance, when to isolate the area, and where to find cleanup materials.

Chemical spills in the workplace can be categorized as follows[37]:

- *Incidental releases* are spills that are limited in quantity and toxicity and pose no significant safety or health hazard to the employee. They may be safely cleaned up by the employees familiar with the hazards of the chemical involved in the spill. Waste from the cleanup may be classified as hazardous and must be disposed of in the proper fashion. Appendix 2-7 describes appropriate responses to incidental spills.

- *Releases that may be incidental or may require an emergency response* are spills that may pose an exposure risk to the employees depending upon the circumstances. Considerations such as the hazardous substance properties, the circumstances of release, and mitigating factors play a role in determining the appropriate response. The facility's emergency response plan should provide guidance in how to determine whether the spill is incidental or requires an emergency response.

- *Emergency response releases* are spills that pose a threat to health and safety regardless of the circumstances surrounding their release.

The spill may require evacuation of the immediate area. The response typically comes from outside the immediate release area by personnel trained as emergency responders. These spills include but are not limited to: immediate danger to life or health, serious threat of fire or explosion, and high levels of toxic substances.

Appendix 2-8 addresses the management of hazardous chemical spills. Spill cleanup kits or carts tailored to the specific hazards present should be available in each area. These may contain the following: rubber gloves and aprons, shoe covers, goggles, suitable aspirators, general absorbents, neutralizing agents, broom, dust pan, appropriate trash bags or cans for waste disposal, and cleanup directions. Chemical absorbents such as clay absorbents or spill blankets can be used for cleaning up a number of chemicals and thus may be easier for the employee to use in spill situations.

With any spill of a hazardous chemical, but especially with a carcinogenic agent, it is essential to refer to the MSDS and to contact a designated supervisor or designee trained to handle these spills and hazardous waste disposal.[3] Facility environmental health and safety personnel also can offer assistance. The employer must assess the extent of the employee's exposure. After an exposure, the employee must be given an opportunity for medical consultation to determine the need for a medical examination.

Another source of a workplace hazard is the unexpected release of hazardous vapors into the environment. OSHA has set limits for exposure to hazardous vapors from toxic and hazardous substances.[38] The potential risk associated with the chemical is determined by the manufacturer and listed on the MSDS. See Table 2-8 for a listing of the limits of exposure.

Table 2-8. Regulatory Limits for Exposure to Toxic and Hazardous Vapors[32]

Limit	Definition
Permissible exposure limit	The maximum concentration of vapors in parts per million (ppm) that an employee may be exposed to in an 8-hour day/40-hour work week.
Short-term exposure limit	The maximum allowable concentration of vapors that an employee may be exposed to in a 15-minute period, with a maximum of four exposures per day allowed with at least 1 hour between each.
Ceiling limit	The maximum concentration of vapors that may not be exceeded instantaneously at any time.

Chemical Waste Disposal

Most laboratory chemical waste is considered hazardous and is regulated by the EPA through the Resource Conservation and Recovery Act (42 U.S.C. § 6901 et seq, 1976). This regulation specifies that hazardous waste can only be legally disposed of at an EPA-approved disposal facility. Disposal of chemical waste into a sanitary sewer is regulated by the Clean Water Act (33 U.S.C. § 1251 et seq, 1977), and most states have strict regulations concerning disposal of chemicals in the water system. Federal and applicable state regulations should be consulted when setting up and reviewing facility waste disposal policies.

Radiation Safety

Radiation can be defined as energy in the form of waves or particles emitted and propagated through space or a material medium. Gamma rays are electromagnetic radiation, whereas alpha and beta emitters are examples of particulate radiation. The presence of radiation in the blood bank, either from radioisotopes used in laboratory testing or from self-contained blood irradiators, requires additional precautions and training.[3,39]

Radiation Measurement Units

The measurement unit quantifying the amount of energy absorbed per unit mass of tissue is the Gray (Gy) or rad (radiation absorbed dose); 1 Gy equals 100 rads.

Dose equivalency measurements are more useful than simple energy measurements because they take into account the effectiveness of the different types of radiation to cause biologic effects. The ability of radiation to cause damage is assigned a number called a quality factor (QF). For example, exposure to a given amount of alpha particles (QF = 20) is far more damaging than exposure to an equivalent amount of gamma rays (QF = 1). The common unit of measurement for dose equivalency is the rem (rad equivalent man). To obtain dose from a particular type of radiation in rem, multiply the number of rad by the quality factor (rad × QF = rem). Because the quality factor for gamma rays, x-rays, and most beta particles is 1, the dose in rad is equal to the dose in rem for these types of radiation.

Biologic Effects of Radiation

Any harm to tissue begins with the absorption of radiation energy and subsequent disruption of chemical bonds. Molecules and atoms become ionized and/or excited by absorbing this energy. The "direct action" path leads to radiolysis or formation of free radicals that, in turn, alter the structure and function of molecules in the cell.

Molecular alterations can cause cellular or chromosomal changes, depending upon the amount and type of radiation energy absorbed. Cellular changes can manifest as a visible somatic effect, eg, erythema. Changes at the chromosome level may manifest as leukemia or other cancers, or possibly as germ cell defects that are transmitted to future generations.

The type of radiation, the part of the body exposed, the total absorbed dose, and the dose rate influence biologic damage. The total absorbed dose is the cumulative amount of radiation absorbed in the tissue. The greater the dose, the greater the potential for biologic damage. Exposure can be acute or chronic. The low levels of ionizing radiation likely to occur in blood banks should not pose any detrimental risk.[40-43]

Regulations

The NRC controls use of radioactive materials by establishing licensure requirements. States and municipalities may also have requirements for inspection and/or licensure. The type of license for using radioisotopes or irradiators will depend on the scope and magnitude of the use of radioactivity. Facilities should contact the NRC and appropriate state agencies for license requirements and application as soon as such activities are proposed.

NRC-licensed establishments must have a qualified radiation safety officer who is responsible for establishing personnel protection requirements and for proper disposal and handling of radioactive materials. Specific radiation safety policies and procedures should address dose limits, employee

training, warning signs and labels, shipping and handling guidelines, radiation monitoring, and exposure management. Emergency procedures must be clearly defined and readily available to staff.

Exposure Limits

The NRC sets standards for protection against radiation hazards arising from licensed activities, including dose limits.[8] These limits, or maximum permissible dose equivalents, are a measure of the radiation risk over time and serve as standards for exposure. The occupational total effective-dose-equivalent limit is 5 rem/year. The shallow dose equivalent (skin) is 50 rem/year, the extremity dose equivalent limit is 50 rem/year, and the eye dose equivalent limit is 15 rem/year.[8,41] Dose limits to an embryo/fetus must not exceed 0.5 rem during the pregnancy.[8,41,44]

Employers are expected not only to maintain radiation exposure below allowable limits, but also to keep exposure levels as far below these limits as can reasonably be achieved.

Radiation Monitoring

Monitoring is essential for early detection and prevention of problems due to radiation exposure. It is used to evaluate the environment, work practices, and procedures, and to comply with regulations and NRC licensing requirements. Monitoring is accomplished with the use of dosimeters, bioassay, survey meters, and wipe tests.[3]

Dosimeters, such as film or thermoluminescent badges and/or rings, measure personnel radiation doses. The need for dosimeters depends on the amount and type of radioactive materials in use; the facility radiation safety officer will determine individual dosimeter needs. Film badges must be changed at least quarterly and in some instances monthly, protected from high temperature and humidity, and stored at work away from sources of radiation.

Bioassay, such as thyroid and whole body counting or urinalysis, may be used to determine if there is radioactivity inside the body and, if so, how much. If necessary, bioassays are usually performed quarterly and after an incident where accidental intake may have occurred.

Survey meters are sensitive to low levels of gamma or particulate radiation and provide a quantitative assessment of radiation hazard. They can be used to monitor storage areas for radioactive materials or wastes, testing areas during or after completion of a procedure, and packages or containers of radioactive materials. Survey meters must be calibrated annually by an authorized NRC licensee. Selection of appropriate meters should be discussed with the radiation safety officer.

In areas where radioactive materials are handled, work surfaces, equipment, and floors that may be contaminated should be checked regularly with a wipe test. In the wipe test, a moistened absorbent material (the wipe) is passed over the surface and then counted for radiation. Kits are available for this purpose. In most clinical laboratories, exposure levels of radiation are well below the limits set by federal and state regulations.

Training

Personnel who handle radioactive materials or work with blood irradiators must receive radiation safety training before beginning work. This training should cover an explanation of the presence and potential hazards of radioactive materials found in the employee's specific work area, general health protection issues, emergency procedures, and radiation warning signs and labels in use. Instruction in the following is also suggested:

- NRC regulations and license conditions.
- The importance of observing license conditions and regulations and reporting violations or conditions of unnecessary exposure.
- Precautions to minimize exposure.
- Interpretation of results of monitoring devices.
- Requirements for pregnant workers.
- Employees' rights.
- Documentation and record-keeping requirements.

The need for refresher training is determined by the license agreement between the NRC and the facility.

Engineering Controls and Personal Protective Equipment

Although self-contained blood irradiators present little risk to laboratory staff and film badges are not required for routine operation, blood establishments with irradiation programs must be licensed by the NRC.[41]

The manufacturer of the blood irradiator usually accepts responsibility for radiation safety requirements during transportation, installation, and validation of the unit as part of the purchase contract. The radiation safety officer can help oversee the installation and validation processes and confirm that appropriate training, monitoring systems, procedures, and maintenance protocols are in place before use and reflect the manufacturer's recommendations. Suspected malfunctions must be reported immediately to defined facility authorities so that appropriate actions can be initiated.

Blood irradiators should be located in secure areas with limited access so that only trained individuals have access. Fire protection for the unit must also be considered. Automatic fire detection and control systems should be readily available in the immediate area. Blood components that have been irradiated are not radioactive and pose no threat to staff or the general public.

Safe Work Practices

Each laboratory should establish policies and procedures for the safe use of radioactive materials. They should include requirements for following general laboratory safety principles, appropriate storage of radioactive solutions, and proper disposal of radioactive wastes. Radiation safety can be improved with the following:

- Minimize time of exposure by working as efficiently as possible.
- Maximize distance from the source of the radiation by staying as far from the source as possible.
- Maximize shielding (eg, by using a self-shielded irradiator or by wearing lead aprons when working with certain radioactive materials). These requirements are usually stipulated in the license conditions.
- Use good housekeeping practices to minimize spread of radioactivity to uncontrolled areas.

Emergency Response Plan

Radioactive contamination is the dispersal of radioactive material into or onto areas where it is not intended; for example, the floor, work areas, equipment, personnel clothing, or skin. The NRC regulations state that gamma or beta radioactive contamination cannot exceed 2200 $dpm/100 \, cm^2$ in the posted (restricted) area or 220 $dpm/100 \, cm^2$ in an unrestricted area such as corridors; for alpha emitters, these values are 220 $dpm/100 \, cm^2$ and 22 $dpm/100 \, cm^2$, respectively.[45]

If a spill occurs, contaminated skin surfaces must be washed several times and the radiation safety officer must be notified immediately for further guidance. Others must not be allowed to enter the area until emergency response personnel arrive.

Waste Management

Policies for the disposal of radioactive waste, whether liquid or solid, should be established, with input from the radiation safety officer and the disposal contractor, if an approved company is used.

Liquid radioactive waste may be collected into large sturdy bottles labeled with an appropriate radiation waste tag. The rules for separation by chemical compatibility apply. Bottles must be carefully stored to protect against spillage or breakage. Dry or solid waste may be sealed in a plastic bag and tagged as radiation waste. The isotope, activity of the isotope, and date that the activity was measured should be placed on the bag. Radiation waste must never be discharged into the drain system without prior approval of the radiation safety officer.

Shipping Hazardous Materials

Local surface transport of blood specimens, components, and biohazardous materials from one facility (or part thereof) to another may be made by a local approved courier service. The safe transport of these materials requires that they be packaged in such a way that the possibility of leakage or other release from the package under normal conditions of transport does not occur. See Method 1.1 for detailed shipping instructions for diagnostic specimens and infectious substances.

Waste Management

Those responsible for safety must be concerned with protecting the environment, as well as staff. Every effort should be made to establish facility-wide programs to reduce solid wastes, including nonhazardous and especially hazardous wastes (ie, biohazardous, chemical, and radiation wastes). A hazardous waste reduction program instituted at the point of use of the material achieves several goals. It reduces the institutional risk for occupational exposures to hazardous agents and "cradle to grave" liability for disposal as well as enhances compliance with environmental requirements to reduce pollution generated from daily operations of the laboratory.[31,46,47] These requirements necessitate that a facility minimize pollution of the environment by the "three R's" (reduce, reuse, and recycle). Seeking suitable alternatives to the use of materials that create hazardous waste and separating hazardous waste from nonhazardous waste can reduce the volume of hazardous waste and decrease costs for its disposal.

A goal of waste management should be to reduce to a minimum the volume of hazardous material. Noninfectious waste should always be separated from infectious waste. Changes in techniques or materials, which reduce the volume of infectious waste or render it less hazardous, should be carefully considered and employees should be encouraged to identify safer alternatives wherever possible.

Facilities should check with state and local health and environmental authorities for current requirements for storage and disposal of a particular multihazardous waste before creating that waste. If the multihazardous waste cannot be avoided, the volume generated should be minimized. In some states, copper sulfate contaminated with blood is considered a multi-hazardous waste. The disposal of this waste poses several problems with transportation from draw sites to a central facility to disposal of the final containers. State and local health departments must be involved in the review of transportation and disposal practices where this is an issue, and procedures must be developed in accordance with their regulations as well as those of the US Department of Transportation.

Disaster Planning

Blood banks and transfusion services should establish action plans for uncommon but potential dangers (eg, floods; hurricanes; tornadoes; earthquakes; fires; explosions; biological, chemical, or radiation emergencies; structural collapse; hostage situations; bomb threats and other acts of terrorism; or other events in which mass casualties might occur). These events require a plan to ensure the safety of patients, visitors, workers, and the blood supply. Such disasters may involve the facility alone, the surrounding area, or both, and can be categorized by severity level: minor impact on normal operations; moderate to substantial reduction in operations; or severe, prolonged loss of operations. The JCAHO requires a plan to address four phases of activities: mitigation, preparedness, response, and recovery.[4] Policies and procedures may address:

■ Notification procedures.
■ Ongoing communication (ie, command center).
■ Evacuation or relocation.
■ Isolation or containment.
■ Personal safety and protection.
■ Provision of additional staffing.

Typically, in a disaster situation, the first person who becomes aware of the disaster takes immediate action and notifies others, either through an alarm activation system (eg, fire alarm) or by notifying an individual in authority, who then implements the initial response steps and contacts the facility's disaster coordinator. Emergency telephone numbers should be prominently posted. Employees should be trained in the facility's disaster response policies. Because the likelihood of being involved in an actual disaster is minimal, drills should be conducted to ensure appropriate responses and prepare staff to act quickly. Every disaster is a unique occurrence. Modifications must be made as necessary; flexibility is important. Once the disaster is under control and recovery is under way, actions should be evaluated and modifications made to the disaster plan as needed. However, the single most effective protection a facility has against unexpected danger is the awareness that safety-minded employees have for their surroundings.

References

1. Silva MA, ed. Standards for blood banks and transfusion services. 23rd ed. Bethesda, MD: AABB, 2005:88.
2. Laboratory Accreditation Program Laboratory general checklist. Chicago, IL: College of American Pathologists Commission on Laboratory Accreditation, 2002.
3. Clinical laboratory safety; approved guideline. NCCLS document GP17-A. National Committee for Clinical Laboratory Standards. Wayne, PA: NCCLS, 1996.
4. 2003 Hospital accreditation standards. Oakbrook Terrace, IL: Joint Commission on Accreditation of Healthcare Organizations, 2003.
5. 2002-2003 Standards for pathology and laboratory services. Oakbrook Terrace, IL: Joint Commission on Accreditation of Healthcare Organizations, 2002.
6. NFPA 70 - National electrical code. Quincy, MA: National Fire Protection Association, 2002.
7. ANSI/ASHRAE Standard 62-1999. Ventilation for acceptable indoor air quality. Atlanta, GA: American Society of Heating, Refrigerating, and Air-Conditioning Engineers, Inc., 1999.
8. Code of federal regulations. Standards for protection against radiation. Title 10 CFR Part 20. Washington, DC: US Government Printing Office, 2004 (revised annually).
9. Garner JS, for the CDC Hospital Infection Control Practices Advisory Committee. Guidelines for isolation precautions in hospitals. Infect Control Hosp Epidemiol 1996;17:53-80.
10. Code of federal regulations. Occupational exposure to bloodborne pathogens, final rule. Title 29 CFR Part 1910.1030. Washington, DC: US Government Printing Office, 2004 (revised annually).
11. Code of federal regulations. Hazard communication standard. Title 29 CFR Part 1910.1200. Washington, DC: US Government Printing Office, 2004 (revised annually).
12. Richmond JY, McKinney RW, eds. Biosafety in microbiological and biomedical laboratories. 4th ed. Washington, DC: US Government Printing Office, 1999.
13. Bernard B, ed. Musculoskeletal disorders and workplace factors: A critical review of epidemiologic evidence for work-related musculoskeletal disorders of the neck, upper extremity, and low back. NIOSH Publication 97-141. Cincinnati, OH: US Department of Health and Human Services, Public Health Service, Centers for Disease Control and Prevention, National Institute for Occupational Safety and Health, 1997.
14. Code of federal regulations. Emergency action plans. Title 29 CFR Part 1910.38. Washington, DC: US Government Printing Office, 2004 (revised annually).
15. Wagner KD, ed. Environmental management in healthcare facilities. Philadelphia: WB Saunders, 1998.
16. Code of federal regulations. Occupational exposure to hazardous chemicals in laboratories. Title 29 CFR Part 1910.1450. Washington, DC: US Government Printing Office, 2004 (revised annually).
17. Centers for Disease Control. Public Health Service guidelines for the management of occupational exposures to HBV, HCV, and HIV and recommendations for post-exposure prophylaxis. MMWR Morb Mortal Wkly Rep 2001;50:1-52.
18. Code of federal regulations. Access to employee exposure and medical records. Title 29 CFR Part 1910.1020. Washington, DC: US Government Printing Office, 2004 (revised annually).
19. National Institute for Occupational Safety and Health. NIOSH Alert: Preventing allergic reactions to natural rubber latex in the workplace. (June 1997) NIOSH Publication No. 97-135. Washington, DC: National Institute for

Occupational Safety and Health, 1997. [Available at http://www.cdc.gov/niosh/latexalt.html.]

20. NFPA 101: Code for safety to life from fire in buildings and structures. Quincy, MA: National Fire Protection Association, 2000.

21. Fowler TW, Miles KK. Electrical safety: Safety and health for electrical trades student manual. (January 2002) NIOSH Publication No. 2002-123. Washington, DC: National Institute for Occupational Safety and Health, 2002.

22. Occupational Safety and Health Administration. OSHA technical manual: TED 1-0.15A. Washington, DC: US Department of Labor, 1999.

23. Occupational Safety and Health Administration. Enforcement procedures for the occupational exposure to bloodborne pathogens, Directive CPL 2-2.69. Washington, DC: US Department of Labor, 2001.

24. US Department of Health and Human Services, CDC, and NIH. Primary containment for biohazards: Selection, installation and use of biological safety cabinets. (September, 1995) Bethesda, MD: National Institutes of Health, 1995. [Available at http://www.niehs.nih.gov/odhsb/biosafe/bsc/bsc.htm.]

25. Richmond JY. Safe practices and procedures for working with human specimens in biomedical research laboratories. J Clin Immunoassay 1988;11:115-9.

26. Code of federal regulations. Occupational exposure to bloodborne pathogens; needlestick and other sharps injuries; final rule. Title 29 CFR Part 1910.1030. Fed Regist 2001;66:5317-25.

27. Environmental Protection Agency. Registered hospital disinfectants and sterilants (TS767C). Washington, DC: Antimicrobial Program Branch, 1992.

28. Rutala WA. APIC guideline for selection and use of disinfectants. Am J Infect Control 1996; 24:313-42.

29. Evans MR, Henderson DK, Bennett JE. Potential for laboratory exposures to biohazardous agents found in blood. Am J Public Health 1990;80:423-7.

30. Food and Drug Administration. Memorandum: Guideline for collection of blood products from donors with positive tests for infectious disease markers ("high risk" donors). (October 26, 1989) Rockville, MD: CBER Office of Communication, Training, and Manufacturers Assistance, 1989.

31. Environmental Protection Agency. EPA guide for infectious waste management. EPA/530-SW-86-014. NTIS #PB86-199130. Washington, DC: National Technical Information Service, 1986.

32. Code of federal regulations. Standards of performance for new stationary sources and emission guidelines for existing sources: Hospital/medical/infectious waste incinerators. Title 40 CFR Part 60. Washington, DC: US Government Printing Office, 2004 (revised annually).

33. NFPA 704—standard for the identification of the hazards of materials for emergency response. Quincy, MA: National Fire Protection Association, 2001.

34. HMIS implementation manual. 3rd ed. Neenah, WI: JJ Keller and Associates, Inc., 2001.

35. Lisella FS, Thomasston SW. Chemical safety in the microbiology laboratory. In: Fleming DO, Richardson JH, Tulis JJ, Vesley D, eds. Laboratory safety, principles and practices. 2nd ed. Washington, DC: American Society for Microbiology Press, 1995:247-54.

36. American National Standards Institute. American national standards for emergency eyewash and shower equipment. ANSI Z358.1-1998. New York, NY: ANSI, 1998.

37. Occupational Safety and Health Administration. Inspection procedures for the hazardous waste operations and emergency response standard, 29 CFR 1910.120 and 1926.65, paragraph (q): Emergency response to hazardous substance releases. OSHA directive CPL 2-2.59A. Washington, DC: US Government Printing Office, 1998.

38. Code of federal regulations. Air contaminants: Toxic and hazardous substances. Title 29 CFR Part 1910.1000. Washington, DC: US Government Printing Office, 2004 (revised annually).

39. Cook SS. Selection and installation of self-contained irradiators. In: Butch S, Tiehen A, eds. Blood irradiation: A user's guide. Bethesda, MD: AABB Press, 1996:19-40.

40. Beir V. Health effects of exposure to low levels of ionizing radiation. Washington, DC: National Academy Press, 1990:1-8.

41. Regulatory Guide 8.29: Instruction concerning risks from occupational radiation exposure. Washington, DC: Nuclear Regulatory Commission, 1996.

42. NCRP Report No. 115: Risk estimates for radiation protection: Recommendations of the National Council on Radiation Protection and Measurements. Bethesda, MD: National Council on Radiation Protection and Measurements, 1993.

43. NCRP Report No. 105: Radiation protection for medical and allied health personnel: Recommendations of the National Council on Radiation Protection and Measurements. Bethesda, MD: National Council on Radiation Protection and Measurements, 1989.

44. NRC Regulatory Guide 8.13: Instruction concerning prenatal radiation exposure. Washington, DC: Nuclear Regulatory Commission, 1999.

45. NRC Regulatory Guide 8.23: Radiation surveys at medical institutions. Washington, DC: Nuclear Regulatory Commission, 1981.

46. United States Code. Pollution Prevention Act. 42 U.S.C. § 13101 and 13102 et seq. Washington, DC: US Government Printing Office, 1990.

47. Clinical laboratory waste management. Approved Standard Doc GP5-A. Wayne, PA: National Committee for Clinical Laboratory Standards, 1993.

Suggested Reading

CDC Office of Biosafety. Radiation safety manual. Atlanta, GA: Centers for Disease Control, 1992.

Disaster operations handbook: Coordinating the nation's blood supply during disasters and biological events. Bethesda, MD: AABB, 2003.

Disaster plan development procedure manual. In: Developing a disaster plan. Bethesda, MD: AABB, 1998.

Handbook of compressed gases. 3rd ed. Compressed Gas Association. New York: Chapman and Hall, 1990.

Heinsohn PA, Jacobs RR, Concoby BA, eds. Biosafety reference manual. 2nd ed. Fairfax, VA: American Industrial Hygiene Association Biosafety Committee, 1995.

Liberman DF, ed. Biohazards management handbook. 2nd ed. New York: Marcel Dekker, Inc, 1995.

NIH guide to waste disposal. Bethesda, MD: National Institutes of Health, 2003. [Available at http://www.nih.gov/od/ors/ds/wasteguide.]

Prudent practices for handling hazardous chemicals in laboratories. Washington, DC: National Academy Press, 1981.

Risk management and safety procedure manual. In: Developing a disaster plan. Bethesda, MD: AABB, 1998.

Vesley D, Lauer JL. Decontamination, sterilization, disinfection and antisepsis. In: Fleming DO, Richardson JH, Tulis JJ, Vesley D, eds. Laboratory safety, principles and practices. 2nd ed. Washington, DC: American Society for Microbiology Press, 1995:219-37.

Appendix 2-1. Safety Regulations and Recommendations Applicable to Health-Care Settings

Agency/Organization	Reference	Title
Federal Regulations and Recommendations		
Nuclear Regulatory Commission (NRC)	10 CFR 20	Standards for Protection Against Radiation
	Guide 8.29	Instruction Concerning Risks from Occupational Radiation Exposure
Department of Labor, Occupational Safety and Health Administration (OSHA)	29 CFR 1910.1030	Occupational Exposure to Bloodborne Pathogens
	29 CFR 1910.1096	Ionizing Radiation
	29 CFR 1910.1200	Hazard Communication Standard
	29 CFR 1910.1450	Occupational Exposure to Hazardous Chemicals in Laboratories
Department of Transportation (DOT)	49 CFR 171-180	Hazardous Materials Regulations
Environmental Protection Agency (EPA)		EPA Guide for Infectious Waste Management
Centers for Disease Control and Prevention (CDC)		Guideline for Isolation Precautions in Hospitals
Food and Drug Administration (FDA)	21 CFR 606.40, 606.60, and 606.65	Current Good Manufacturing Practice for Blood and Blood Components
		Guideline for Collection of Blood Products from Donors with Positive Tests for Infectious Disease Markers
	21 CFR 801.437	User Labeling for Devices that Contain Natural Rubber

(cont'd)

Appendix 2-1. Safety Regulations and Recommendations Applicable to Health-Care Settings (cont'd)

Agency/Organization	Reference	Title
Trade and Professional Organizations		
National Fire Protection Association (NFPA)	NFPA 70	National Electrical Code
	NFPA 70E	Electrical Safety Requirements for Employee Workplaces
	NFPA 101	Code for Safety to Life from Fire in Buildings and Structures
	NFPA 704	Standard for the Identification of the Hazards of Materials for Emergency Response
National Paint and Coatings Association		Hazardous Materials Identification System (HMIS) Implementation Manual
International Air Traffic Association (IATA)		Dangerous Goods Regulations

Appendix 2-2. General Guidelines for Safe Work Practices, Personal Protective Equipment, and Engineering Controls

Uniforms and Laboratory Coats

Closed laboratory coats or full aprons over long-sleeved uniforms or gowns should be worn when personnel are exposed to blood, corrosive chemicals, or carcinogens. The material of required coverings should be appropriate for the type and amount of hazard exposure. Plastic disposable aprons may be worn over cotton coats when there is a high probability of large spills or splashing of blood and body fluids; nitrile rubber aprons may be preferred when pouring caustic chemicals.

Protective coverings should be removed before leaving the work area and should be discarded or stored away from heat sources and clean clothing. Contaminated clothing should be removed promptly, placed in a suitable container, and laundered or discarded as potentially infectious. Home laundering of garments worn in Biosafety Level 2 areas (see below) is not permitted because unpredictable methods of transportation and handling can spread contamination, and home laundering techniques may not be effective.[1]

Gloves

Gloves or equivalent barriers should be used whenever tasks are likely to involve exposure to hazardous materials. Latex or vinyl gloves are adequate for handling most blood specimens and chemicals (see latex allergy issues below).

Types of Gloves

Glove type varies with the task:
- Sterile gloves: for procedures involving contact with normally sterile areas of the body.
- Examination gloves: for procedures involving contact with mucous membranes, unless otherwise indicated, and for other patient care or diagnostic procedures that do not require the use of sterile gloves.
- Rubber utility gloves: for housekeeping chores involving potential blood contact, for instrument cleaning and decontamination procedures, for handling concentrated acids and organic solvents. Utility gloves may be decontaminated and reused but should be discarded if they show signs of deterioration (peeling, cracks, discoloration) or if they develop punctures or tears.
- Insulated gloves: for handling hot or frozen material.

Indications for Use

The following guidelines should be used to determine when gloves are necessary[1]:
- For donor phlebotomy when the health-care worker has cuts, scratches, or other breaks in his or her skin.
- For phlebotomy of autologous donors or patients (eg, therapeutic apheresis procedures, intraoperative red cell collection).
- For persons who are receiving training in phlebotomy.
- When handling "open" blood containers or specimens.
- When collecting or handling blood or specimens from patients or from donors known to be infected with a blood-borne pathogen.
- When examining mucous membranes or open skin lesions.
- When handling corrosive chemicals and radioactive materials.

(cont'd)

Appendix 2-2. General Guidelines for Safe Work Practices, Personal Protective Equipment, and Engineering Controls (cont'd)

- When cleaning up spills or handling waste materials.
- When likelihood of exposure cannot be assessed because of lack of experience with a procedure or situation.

The Occupational Safety and Health Administration (OSHA) does not require routine use of gloves by phlebotomists working with healthy prescreened donors or the changing of unsoiled gloves between donors if gloves are worn.[1,2] Experience has shown that the phlebotomy process is low risk because donors have low rates of infectious disease markers. Also, exposure to blood is rare during routine phlebotomy, and other alternatives can be utilized to provide barrier protection, such as using a folded gauze pad to control any blood flow when the needle is removed from the donor's arm.

The employer whose policies and procedures do not require routine gloving should periodically reevaluate the potential need for gloves. Employees should never be discouraged from using gloves, and gloves should always be available.

Guidelines on Use

Guidelines for the safe use of gloves include the following[3,4]:
- Securely bandage or cover open skin lesions on hands and arms before putting on gloves.
- Change gloves immediately if they are torn, punctured, or contaminated; after handling high-risk samples; or after performing a physical examination, eg, on an apheresis donor.
- Remove gloves by keeping their outside surfaces in contact only with outside and by turning the glove inside out while taking it off.
- Use gloves only where needed and avoid touching clean surfaces such as telephones, door knobs, or computer terminals with gloves.
- Change gloves between patient contacts. Unsoiled gloves need not be changed between donors.
- Wash hands with soap or other suitable disinfectant after removing gloves.
- Do not wash or disinfect surgical or examination gloves for reuse. Washing with surfactants may cause "wicking" (ie, the enhanced penetration of liquids through undetected holes in the glove). Disinfecting agents may cause deterioration of gloves.
- Use only water-based hand lotions with gloves, if needed; oil-based products cause minute cracks in latex.

Face Shields, Masks, and Safety Goggles

Where there is a risk of blood or chemical splashes, the eyes and the mucous membranes of the mouth and nose should be protected.[5] Permanent shields, fixed as a part of equipment or bench design, are preferred, eg, splash barriers attached to tubing sealers or centrifuge cabinets. All barriers should be cleaned and disinfected on a regular schedule.

Safety glasses alone provide impact protection from projectiles but do not adequately protect eyes from biohazardous or chemical splashes. Full-face shields or masks and safety goggles are recommended when permanent shields cannot be used. Many designs are commercially available; eliciting staff input on comfort and selection can improve compliance on use.

Appendix 2-2. General Guidelines for Safe Work Practices, Personal Protective Equipment, and Engineering Controls (cont'd)

Masks should be worn whenever there is danger from inhalation. Simple, disposable dust masks are adequate for handling dry chemicals, but respirators with organic vapor filters are preferred for areas where noxious fumes are produced, eg, for cleaning up spills of noxious materials. Respirators should be fitted to their specific wearers and checked annually.

Hand Washing

Frequent effective hand washing is the first line of defense in infection control. Blood-borne pathogens generally do not penetrate intact skin, so immediate removal reduces the likelihood of transfer to a mucous membrane or broken skin area or of transmission to others. Thorough washing of hands (and arms) also reduces the risks from exposure to hazardous chemicals and radioactive materials.

Hands should always be washed before leaving a restricted work area, before using a biosafety cabinet, between medical examinations, immediately after becoming soiled with blood or hazardous materials, after removing gloves, and after using the toilet. Washing hands thoroughly before touching contact lenses or applying cosmetics is essential.

OSHA allows the use of waterless antiseptic solutions for hand washing as an interim method.[2] These solutions are useful for mobile donor collections or in areas where water is not readily available for cleanup purposes. If such methods are used, however, hands must be washed with soap and running water as soon as feasible thereafter. Because there is no listing or registration of acceptable hand wipe products similar to the one the Environmental Protection Agency maintains for surface disinfectants, consumers should request data from the manufacturer to support advertising claims.

Eye Washes

Laboratory areas that contain hazardous chemicals must be equipped with eye wash stations.[3,6] Unobstructed access, within 10 seconds from the location of chemical use, must be provided for these stations. Eye washes must operate so that both of the user's hands are free to hold open the eyes. Procedures and indications for use must be posted and routine function checks must be performed. Testing eye wash fountains weekly helps ensure proper function and flushes out the stagnant water. Portable eye wash systems are allowed only if they can deliver flushing fluid to the eyes at a rate of at least 1.5 liters per minute for 15 minutes. They should be monitored routinely to ensure the purity of their contents.

Employees should be trained in the proper use of eye wash devices, although prevention, through consistent and appropriate use of safety glasses or shields, is preferred. If a splash occurs, the employee should be directed to keep the eyelids open and use the eye wash according to procedures, or go to the nearest sink and direct a steady, tepid stream of water into the eyes. Solutions other than water should be used only upon a physician's direction.

After adequate flushing (many facilities recommend 15 minutes), follow-up medical care should be sought, especially if pain or redness develops. Whether eye washing is effective in preventing infection has not been demonstrated but it is considered desirable when accidents occur.

(cont'd)

Appendix 2-2. General Guidelines for Safe Work Practices, Personal Protective Equipment, and Engineering Controls (cont'd)

1. Code of federal regulations. Occupational exposure to bloodborne pathogens, final rule. Title 29 CFR Part 1910.1030. Fed Regist 1991;56(235):64175-82.
2. Occupational Safety and Health Administration. Enforcement procedures for the occupational exposure to bloodborne pathogens. OSHA Instruction CPL2-2.44D. Washington, DC: US Government Printing Office, 1999.
3. Clinical and Laboratory Standards Institute. Clinical laboratory safety; approved guideline. NCCLS document GP17-A. Wayne, PA: CLSI, 1996.
4. Food and Drug Administration. Medical glove powder report. (September 1997) Rockville, MD: Center for Devices and Radiological Health, 1997. [Available at http://www.fda.gov/cdrh/glvpwd.html.]
5. Inspection checklist: General laboratory. Chicago, IL: College of American Pathologists, 2001.
6. American National Standards Institute. American national standards for emergency eyewash and shower equipment. ANSI Z358.1-1998. New York: ANSI, 1998.

Appendix 2-3. Biosafety Level 2 Precautions

Biosafety Level 2 precautions as applied in the blood establishment setting include at least the following[1,2]:

■ High-risk activities are appropriately segregated from lower risk activities, and the boundaries are clearly defined.

■ Bench tops are easily cleaned and are decontaminated daily with a hospital disinfectant approved by the Environmental Protection Agency.

■ Laboratory rooms have closable doors and sinks. An air system with no recirculation is preferred, but not required.

■ Workers are required to perform procedures that create aerosols (eg, opening evacuated tubes, centrifuging, mixing, or sonicating) in a biologic safety cabinet or equivalent, or to wear masks and goggles in addition to gloves and gowns during such procedures. (Note: Open tubes of blood should not be centrifuged. If whole units of blood or plasma are centrifuged, overwrapping is recommended to contain leaks.)

■ Gowns and gloves are used routinely and in accordance with general safety guidelines. Face shields or their equivalent are used where there is a risk from splashing.

■ Mouth pipetting is prohibited.

■ No eating, drinking, smoking, application of cosmetics, or manipulation of contact lenses occurs in the work area. All food and drink are stored outside the restricted area, and laboratory glassware is never used for food or drink. Personnel are instructed to avoid touching their face, ears, mouth, eyes, or nose with their hands or other objects, such as pencils and telephones.

■ Needles and syringes are used and disposed of in a safe manner. Needles are never bent, broken, sheared, replaced in sheath, or detached from syringe before being placed in puncture-proof, leakproof containers for controlled disposal. Procedures are designed to minimize exposure to sharp objects.

■ All blood specimens are placed in well-constructed containers with secure lids to prevent leaking during transport. Blood is packaged for shipment in accordance with regulatory agency requirements for etiologic agents or clinical specimens, as appropriate.

■ Infectious waste is not compacted and is decontaminated before its disposal in leakproof containers. Proper packaging includes double, seamless, tear-resistant, orange or red bags enclosed in protective cartons. Both the carton and the bag inside display the biohazard symbol. Throughout delivery to an incinerator or autoclave, waste is handled only by suitably trained persons. If a waste management contractor is used, the agreement should clearly define respective responsibilities of the staff and the contractor.

■ Equipment to be repaired or submitted for preventive maintenance, if potentially contaminated with blood, must be decontaminated before its release to a repair technician.

■ Accidental exposure to suspected or actual hazardous material is reported to the laboratory director or responsible person immediately.

1. Clinical and Laboratory Standards Institute. Clinical laboratory safety; approved guideline. NCCLS document GP17-A. Wayne, PA: CLSI, 1996.
2. Fleming DO. Laboratory biosafety practices. In: Fleming DO, Richardson JH, Tulis JJ, Vesley D, eds. Laboratory safety, principles and practices. 2nd ed. Washington, DC: American Society for Microbiology Press, 1995:203-18.

Appendix 2-4. Sample Hazardous Chemical Data Sheet

The following information should be a part of the procedures for use of hazardous chemicals.

Facility Identification : _____

Laboratory Name : _____

Room Number : _____

Name of Chemical : _____

Synonyms : _____

Chemical Abstract No.

  (Case #) : _____

Common Name : _____

Primary Hazard   Carcinogen: _____

    Reproductive toxin: _____

    High acute toxicity: _____

    Other health hazard: _____

    Safety hazard: _____

    MSDS or other reference available: _____

    Is prior approval required for use of the chemical; if so,

    by whom? _____

General and Special Precautions:

  Signs Required (Warning signs indicating presence of hazardous chemicals/operations):

_____

  Storage (Secondary containment, temperature-sensitive, incompatibilities, water-reactive, etc): _____

_____

  Special Controls and Location (Fume hood, glove box, etc): _____

_____

Appendix 2-4. Sample Hazardous Chemical Data Sheet (cont'd)

Special Equipment and Location (Vacuum line filter, liquid or other traps, special shielding):

_____

Personal Protective Equipment (Glove type, eye protection, special clothing, etc): _____

_____

Emergency Procedures:

Spill or release: _____

Fire:_____

Decontamination procedures: _____

Disposal procedures: _____

_____

_____

Appendix 2-5. Sample List of Hazardous Chemicals in the Blood Bank

Chemical	Hazard
Ammonium chloride	Irritant
Bromelin	Irritant, sensitizer
Calcium chloride	Irritant
Carbon dioxide, frozen (dry ice)	Corrosive
Carbonyl iron powder	Oxidizer
Chloroform	Toxic, suspected carcinogen
Chloroquine	Irritant, corrosive
Chromium-111 chloride hexahydrate	Toxic, irritant, sensitizer
Citric acid	Irritant
Copper sulfate (cupric sulfate)	Toxic, irritant
Dichloromethane	Toxic, irritant
Digitonin	Toxic
Dimethyl sulfoxide (DMSO)	Irritant
Dry ice (carbon dioxide, frozen)	Corrosive
Ethidium bromide	Carcinogen, irritant
Ethylenediaminetetraacetic acid (EDTA)	Irritant
Ethyl ether	Highly flammable and explosive, toxic, irritant
Ficin (powder)	Irritant, sensitizer
Formaldehyde solution (34.9%)	Suspected carcinogen, combustible, toxic
Glycerol	Irritant
Hydrochloric acid	Highly toxic, corrosive
Imidazole	Irritant
Isopropyl (rubbing) alcohol	Flammable, irritant
Liquid nitrogen	Corrosive
Lyphogel	Corrosive
2-Mercaptoethanol	Toxic, stench
Mercury	Toxic
Mineral oil	Irritant, carcinogen, combustible
Papain	Irritant, sensitizer
Polybrene	Toxic
Potassium hydroxide	Corrosive, toxic
Saponin	Irritant
Sodium azide	Toxic, irritant, explosive when heated
Sodium ethylmercurithiosalicylate (thimerosal)	Highly toxic, irritant
Sodium hydrosulfite	Toxic, irritant
Sodium hydroxide	Corrosive, toxic
Sodium hypochlorite (bleach)	Corrosive

Appendix 2-5. Sample List of Hazardous Chemicals in the Blood Bank (cont'd)

Chemical	Hazard
Sodium phosphate	Irritant, hygroscopic
Sulfosalicylic acid	Toxic, corrosive
Trichloroacetic acid (TCA)	Corrosive, toxic
Trypsin	Irritant, sensitizer
Xylene	Highly flammable, toxic, irritant

Appendix 2-6. Specific Chemical Categories and How to Work Safely with These Chemicals

Chemical Category	Hazard	Precautions	Special Treatment
Acids, alkalis, and corrosive compounds	Irritation Severe burns Tissue damage	During transport, protect large containers with plastic or rubber bucket carriers During pouring, wear eye protection and chemical-resistant-rated gloves and gowns as recommended Always ADD ACID TO WATER, never water to acid When working with large jugs, have one hand on the neck and the other at the base, and position them away from the face	Store concentrated acids in acid safety cabinets Limit volumes of concentrated acids to 1 liter Post cautions for materials in the area Report changes in appearance (perchloric acid may be explosive if it becomes yellowish or brown) to chemical safety officer
Acrylamide	Neurotoxic Carcinogenic Adsorbed through the skin	Wear chemically rated gloves Wash hands immediately after exposure	Store in a chemical cabinet
Compressed gases	Explosive	Label as to contents Leave valve safety covers on until use Open valves slowly for use Label empty tanks	Transport using hand trucks or dollies Place cylinders in a stand or secure them to prevent falling Store in well-ventilated separate rooms Oxygen should not be stored close to combustible gas or solvents Check connections for leaks with soapy water
Liquid nitrogen	Freeze injury Severe burns to skin or eyes	Use heavy insulated gloves and goggles when working with liquid nitrogen	The tanks should be securely supported to avoid being tipped over The final container of liquid nitrogen (freezing unit) must be securely supported to avoid tipping over

Appendix 2-6. Specific Chemical Categories and How to Work Safely with These Chemicals (cont'd)

Chemical Category	Hazard	Precautions	Special Treatment
Flammable solvents	Classified according to flash point—see MSDS Classified according to volatility	Use extreme caution when handling Post NO SMOKING signs in working area Have a fire extinguisher and solvent cleanup kit in the room Pour volatile solvents under suitable hood Use eye protection when pouring and chemical-resistant neoprene gloves No flame or other source of possible ignition should be in or near areas where flammable solvents are being poured Label as FLAMMABLE	Make every attempt to replace hazardous materials with less hazardous materials Store containers larger than 1 gallon in a flammable solvent storage room or in a fire safety cabinet Ground metal containers by connecting the can to a water pipe or ground connection; if recipient container is also metal, it should be electrically connected to the delivery container while pouring

Appendix 2-7. Incidental Spill Response*

Chemicals	Hazards	PPE	Control Materials
Acids Acetic Hydrochloric Nitric Perchloric Sulfuric Photographic chemicals (acid)	Severe irritant if inhaled Contact causes burns to skin and eyes Corrosive Fire or contact with metal may produce irritating or poisonous gas Nitric, perchloric, and sulfuric acids are water-reactive oxidizers	Acid-resistant gloves Apron and coveralls Goggles and face shield Acid-resistant foot covers	Acid neutralizers/absorbent Absorbent boom Leakproof containers Absorbent pillow Mat (cover drain) Shovel or paddle
Bases and caustics Potassium hydroxide Sodium hydroxide Photographic chemicals (basic)	Corrosive Fire may produce irritating or poisonous gas	Gloves; impervious apron or coveralls Goggles or face shield; impervious foot covers	Base control/neutralizer Absorbent pillow Absorbent boom Drain mat Leakproof container Shovel/paddle
Chlorine Bleach Sodium hypochlorite	Inhalation can cause respiratory irritation Liquid contact can produce irritation of the eyes or skin Toxicity due to alkalinity, possible chlorine gas generation, and oxidant properties	Gloves (double set 4H undergloves and butyl or nitrile overgloves); impervious apron or coveralls Goggles or face shield Impervious foot covers (neoprene boots for emergency response releases) Self-contained breathing apparatus (emergency response releases)	Chlorine control powder Absorbent pillow Absorbent Absorbent boom Drain mat Vapor barrier Leakproof container Shovel or paddle

Material	Hazards	Personal Protective Equipment	Spill Cleanup
Cryogenic gases Carbon dioxide Nitrous oxide Liquid nitrogen	Contact with liquid nitrogen can produce frostbite Asphyxiation (displaces oxygen) Anesthetic effects (nitrous oxide)	Full face shield or goggles; neoprene boots; gloves (insulated to protect from the cold)	Hand truck (to transport cylinder outdoors if necessary) Soap solution (to check for leaks) Putty (to stop minor pipe and line leaks)
Flammable gases Acetylene Oxygen gases Butane Propane	Simple asphyxiate (displaces air) Anesthetic potential Extreme fire and explosion hazard Release can create an oxygen-deficient atmosphere	Face shield and goggles; neoprene boots; double set of gloves; coveralls with hood and feet	Hand truck (to transport cylinder outdoors if needed) Soap solution (to check for leaks)
Flammable liquids Acetone Xylene Methyl alcohol toluene Ethyl alcohol Other alcohols	Vapors harmful if inhaled (central nervous system depressants) Harmful via skin absorption Extreme flammability Liquid evaporates to form flammable vapors	Gloves (double 4H undergloves and butyl or nitrile overgloves); impervious apron or coveralls; goggles or face shield; impervious foot covers	Absorbent Absorbent boom Absorbent pillow Shovel or paddle (nonmetal, nonsparking) Drain mat Leakproof containers
Formaldehyde and glutaraldehyde 4% formaldehyde 37% formaldehyde 10% formalin 2% glutaraldehyde	Harmful if inhaled or absorbed through skin; Irritation to skin, eyes, and respiratory tract Formaldelyde is a suspected human carcinogen Keep away from heat, sparks, and flame (37% formaldehyde)	Gloves (double set 4H undergloves and butyl or nitrile overgloves); impervious apron or coveralls; goggles; impervious foot covers	Aldehyde neutralizer/absorbent Absorbent boom Absorbent pillow Shovel or pallet (nonsparking) Drain mat Leakproof container

(cont'd)

Appendix 2-7. Incidental Spill Response* (cont'd)

Chemicals	Hazards	PPE	Control Materials
Mercury Cantor tubes Thermometers Barometers Sphygmomanometers Mercuric chloride	Mercury and mercury vapors are rapidly absorbed in respiratory tract, GI tract, skin Short-term exposure may cause erosion of respiratory/GI tracts, nausea, vomiting, bloody diarrhea, shock, headache, metallic taste Inhalation of high concentrations can cause pneumonitis, chest pain, dyspnea, coughing stomatitis, gingivitis, and salivation Avoid evaporation of mercury from tiny globules by quick and thorough cleaning	Gloves (double set 4H underglove and butyl or nitrile overglove); impervious apron or coveralls; goggles; impervious foot covers	Mercury vacuum or spill kit Scoop Aspirator Hazardous waste containers Mercury indicator powder Absorbent Spatula Disposable towels Sponge with amalgam Vapor suppressor

*This list of physical and health hazards is not intended as a substitute for the specific MSDS information. In the case of a spill or if any questions arise, always refer to the chemical-specific MSDS for more complete information. GI = gastrointestinal; MSDS = material safety data sheet; PPE = personal protective equipment.

Appendix 2-8. Managing Hazardous Chemical Spills

Actions	Instructions for Hazardous Liquids, Gases, and Mercury
De-energize	Liquids: For 37% formaldehyde, de-energize and remove all sources of ignition within 10 feet of spilled hazardous material. For flammable liquids, remove all sources of ignition. Gases: Remove all sources of heat and ignition within 50 feet for flammable gases. Remove all sources of heat and ignition for nitrous oxide release.
Isolate, evacuate, and secure the area	Isolate the spill area and evacuate everyone from the area surrounding the spill except those responsible for cleaning up the spill. (For mercury, evacuate within 10 feet for small spills, 20 feet for large spills.) Secure area.
Have the appropriate PPE	See Appendix 2-2 for recommended PPE.
Contain the spill	Liquids or mercury: Stop the source of spill if possible. Gases: Assess the scene; consider the circumstances of the release (quantity, location, ventilation). If circumstances indicate it is an emergency response release, make appropriate notifications; if release is determined to be incidental, contact supplier for assistance.
Confine the spill	Liquids: Confine spill to initial spill area using appropriate control equipment and material. For flammable liquids, dike off all drains. Gases: Follow supplier's suggestions or request outside assistance. Mercury: Use appropriate materials to confine the spill (see Appendix 2-2). Expel mercury from aspirator bulb into leakproof container, if applicable.
Neutralize the spill	Liquids: Apply appropriate control materials to neutralize the chemical—see Appendix 2-2. Mercury: Use mercury spill kit if needed.
Spill area cleanup	Liquids: Scoop up solidified material, booms, pillows, and any other materials. Put used materials into a leakproof container. Label container with name of hazardous material. Wipe up residual material. Wipe spill area surface three times with detergent solution. Rinse areas with clean water. Collect supplies used (goggles, shovels, etc) and remove gross contamination; place into separate container for equipment to be washed and decontaminated. Gases: Follow supplier's suggestions or request outside assistance. Mercury: Vacuum spill using a mercury vacuum or scoop up mercury paste after neutralization and collect it in designated container. Use sponge and detergent to wipe and clean spill surface three times to remove absorbent. Collect all contaminated disposal equipment and put into hazardous waste container. Collect supplies and remove gross contamination; place them into a separate container for equipment that will be thoroughly washed and decontaminated.

(cont'd)

Appendix 2-8. Managing Hazardous Chemical Spills (cont'd)

Actions	Instructions for Hazardous Liquids, Gases, and Mercury
Disposal	Liquids: For material that was neutralized, dispose of it as solid waste. Follow facility's procedures for disposal. For flammable liquids, check with facility safety officer for appropriate waste determination. Gases: The manufacturer or supplier will instruct facility on disposal if applicable. Mercury: Label with appropriate hazardous waste label and DOT diamond label.
Report	Follow appropriate spill documentation and reporting procedures. Investigate the spill; perform root cause analysis if needed. Act on opportunities for improving safety.

DOT = Department of Transportation; PPE = personal protective equipment.

Chapter 3

Blood Utilization Management

THE GOAL OF BLOOD utilization management is to ensure effective use of limited blood resources. It includes the policies and practices related to inventory management and blood usage review. Although regional blood centers and transfusion services approach utilization management from different perspectives, they share the common goal of providing appropriate, high-quality blood products with minimum waste. This chapter reviews the elements of utilization management, emphasizing the transfusion service.

Minimum and Ideal Inventory Levels

Transfusion services should establish both minimum and ideal inventory levels. Inventory levels should be evaluated periodically and adjusted if needed. Important indicators of performance include, but are not limited to, outdate rates, the frequency of emergency blood shipments, and delays in scheduling elective surgery. Inventory levels should also be reevaluated whenever a significant change is planned or observed. Examples of significant change may include adding more beds; performing new surgical procedures; or changing practices in oncology, transplantation, neonatology, or cardiac surgery.

Determining Inventory Levels

The ideal inventory level provides adequate supplies of blood for routine and emergency situations and minimizes outdating. Forecasting is an attempt to predict future blood product use from data collected about past usage. The optimal number of units to keep in inventory can be estimated using mathematical formulas, computer simulations, or empirical calculations. Three less complicated methods of estimating minimum inventory are described below. When the minimum inventory level has been calculated, a buffer margin for emergencies should be added to obtain an ideal inventory level.

Average Weekly Use Estimate

This method gives an estimate of the average weekly blood usage of each ABO group and Rh type.

1. Collect weekly blood and product usage data over a 26-week period.
2. Record usage by ABO group and Rh type for each week.
3. Disregard the single highest usage for each type to correct for unusual week-to-week variation (eg, a large volume used for an emergency).
4. Total the number of units of each ABO group and Rh type, omitting the highest week in each column.
5. Divide each total by 25 (total number of weeks minus the highest week). This gives an estimate of the average weekly blood usage of each ABO group and Rh type.

Average Daily Use Estimate

Facilities that transfuse on a daily basis may calculate daily blood usage by the following method.

1. Determine the total use over several months.
2. Divide the total use by the number of days in the period covered.
3. Determine the percentage of each of the blood types used during one or more representative months.
4. Multiply the average blood use per day by the percentage of blood use by type.
5. Determine the minimum inventory level by multiplying the daily use by the number of days of blood supply

required to be on hand (this may be 3, 5, or 7 days depending on the blood supplier's delivery schedule).

A transfusion service may find the average daily use calculation more helpful when blood shipments are made once or more per day.

Moving Average Method

The moving average method can be useful in facilities with any level of activity.

1. Determine the preferred recording period (such as day or week).
2. Add the number of units used in each period to obtain the total use.
3. Divide the total number of units by the number of recording periods.
4. Delete old data as new data are added.

This method tends to minimize variation from one period to another.

Factors that Affect Outdating

Benchmark data on component outdating have been published by the National Blood Data Resource Center (NBDRC).[1] The data from this report showed that approximately 2,190,000 total components outdated in 2001, a 6.6% decrease from 1999. Whole-blood-derived platelet concentrates accounted for more than half of the outdated components (49%), or 1,074,000 units. Outdated allogeneic RBCs (directed and nondirected) accounted for 26.8% of all outdated components, or 588,000 units. The outdate rate for each component is shown in Table 3-1. Outdating continues to be a problem, particularly for autologous units and platelets. The outdate rate is affected by many factors other than inventory level (eg, the size of the hospital, the extent of services provided, the shelf life of the products, the shipping distance and frequency, and ordering policies).

Table 3-1. Blood Component Units Processed, Transfused, and Outdated in United States in 2001[1]

Component	Units Processed	Units Transfused	Units Outdated	Percent Outdated
RBCs (allogeneic, nondirected)	14,259,000	13,361,000	576,000	4.0
RBCs (autologous)	619,000	359,000	263,000	42.5
RBCs (directed)	169,000	95,000	12,000	7.1
Platelets (whole-blood-derived)	4,164,000	2,614,000	1,074,000	25.8
Platelets Pheresis	1,456,000	1,264,000	160,000	11.0
FFP	4,437,000	3,926,000	77,000	1.7
Cryoprecipitated AHF	1,068,000	898,000	28,000	2.6

FFP = Fresh Frozen Plasma; RBCs = Red Blood Cells.

In addition to establishing both minimum and ideal inventory levels, maximum inventory levels may assist staff in determining when to arrange for return or transfer of in-date products to avoid outdating. Both transfusion services and donor centers should establish record-keeping systems that allow personnel to determine the number of units ordered and the number of units received or shipped. The responsibility for ordering may be centralized, and orders should be based on established policies for minimal and maximal levels.

Standing orders can simplify inventory planning for both transfusion services and blood centers. Blood centers may send a predetermined number of units on a regular schedule or may keep the transfusion service inventory at established levels by replacing all units reported as transfused.

Optimal inventory management requires distribution and transfusion of the oldest blood first and this requires clearly written policies on blood storage and blood selec-tion. Technologists generally find it easier to select, crossmatch, and issue the oldest units first when inventories are arranged by expiration date.

Policies on blood selection must be flexible, to allow use of fresher blood when indicated (eg, for infants). Generally, however, oldest units are crossmatched for patients most likely to need transfusion.

Improving Transfusion Service Blood Ordering Practices

The shelf life decreases each time a unit is held or crossmatched for a patient who does not use it. When physicians order more blood than needed, it is unavailable for other patients, which may increase the outdate rate. Providing testing guidelines, such as type and screen (T/S) policies and maximum surgical blood order schedules (MSBOS),[2] as well as monitoring cross-match-to-transfusion (C:T) ratios may be helpful. A C:T ratio greater than 2.0 usually indicates excessive crossmatch requests. In some situations, it may be useful to determine C:T ratios by service to identify areas with the highest ratio.

Some institutions define those procedures that normally do not use blood in a "type and screen" guideline. Both the T/S guideline and the MSBOS use data about past surgical blood use to recommend a T/S order or a maximum number of units that should be ordered initially for common elective surgical procedures. With the MSBOS, physicians may order the number of units believed to be appropriate for the patient since the MSBOS is intended to be a guideline for appropriate patient care. Some institutions have modified the MSBOS concept into a "standard" blood order (SBO) system for surgical procedures.[3]

Ordering guidelines such as those in Table 3-2 are derived by reviewing a facility's blood use over a suitable period. Conclusions can then be drawn about the likelihood of transfusion and probable blood use for each surgical procedure. A T/S order is a recommended SBO for procedures that require on average less than 0.5 unit of blood per patient per procedure. An SBO often represents the average number of units transfused for each procedure, whereas the MSBOS often defines the number of units needed to meet the needs of 80% to 90% of patients undergoing a specific surgical procedure.[3]

An institution's guidelines must reflect local patterns of surgical practice and patient population. These may be compared to published guidelines to ensure that local practice does not markedly deviate from generally accepted standards of care. (Transfusion audits are discussed in Chapter 1.) Once the T/S, MSBOS, SBO, or other

Table 3-2. Example of a Maximum Surgical Blood Order Schedule

Procedure	Units*
General Surgery	
Breast biopsy	T/S
Colon resection	2
Exploratory laparotomy	T/S
Gastrectomy	2
Laryngectomy	2
Mastectomy, radical	T/S
Pancreatectomy	4
Splenectomy	2
Thyroidectomy	T/S
Cardiac-Thoracic	
Aneurism resection	6
Redo coronary artery bypass graft	4
Primary coronary artery bypass graft	2
Lobectomy	T/S
Lung biopsy	T/S
Vascular	
Aortic bypass with graft	4
Endarterectomy	T/S
Femoral-popliteal bypass with graft	2
Orthopedics	
Arthroscopy	T/S
Laminectomy	T/S
Spinal fusion	3
Total hip replacement	3
Total knee replacement	T/S
OB-GYN	
Abdomino-perineal repair	T/S
Cesarean section	T/S
Dilation and curettage	T/S
Hysterectomy, abdominal/ laparoscopic	T/S
Hysterectomy, radical	2
Urology	
Bladder, transurethral resection	T/S
Nephrectomy, radical	3
Radical prostatectomy, perineal	2
Prostatectomy, transurethral	T/S
Renal transplant	2

*Numbers may vary with institutional practice.

schedule is accepted, inventory levels often can be reduced. Ordering guidelines should be periodically reviewed to keep pace with changing methods and practices. A change in the C:T ratio might signal a significant modification in clinical practice.

The T/S, MSBOS, or SBO systems are intended for typical circumstances. Surgeons or anesthesiologists may individualize specific requests and override the system to accommodate special needs. The transfusion service must give special consideration to patients with a positive antibody screen. The antibody should be identified and, if it is potentially clinically significant, an appropriate number of antigen-negative units should be identified (eg, two, if the original order was a type and screen).

Facilities using the immediate spin or computer crossmatch can provide additional crossmatched units more rapidly if required. This capability can allow such facilities to adjust their T/S, MSBOS, and SBO schedules accordingly. More procedures can be safely handled as type and screens and fewer crossmatched units may be necessary.

Routine vs Emergency Orders

Transfusion services should establish procedures that define ideal stocking levels for each blood type and critical levels at which emergency orders are indicated. Transfusion service staff should have institutional policies identifying the following:

■ *Who* monitors inventory levels?
■ *Who* is responsible for placing orders?
■ *When* and *how* are orders to be placed (by telephone or facsimile)?
■ *How* are orders documented?

The addresses and telephone numbers of approved blood suppliers and any needed courier or cab services should be immediately available. Transfusion services need to establish guidelines for handling blood

shortages and unexpected emergencies. Equally important is specifying the actions to take if transfusion requests cannot immediately be met.

Transfusion services should develop policies defining the following:

■ When ABO-compatible units may be given instead of ABO-identical units.
■ When Rh-positive units may be given to Rh-negative recipients.
■ When units crossmatched for a surgical procedure may be released before the standard interval.
■ If units may be crossmatched for more than one patient at a time.
■ What resources are available for transfer of inventory.
■ Mechanisms to notify physicians of critical blood shortages.
■ When cancellation of elective procedures should be considered.
■ Methods to notify staff and patients of surgery cancellations.

Inventory Counts and Inspection

On-hand units may be counted once or several times a day to determine ordering needs; computerized facilities may prefer to take inventory electronically. Individual units must be visually inspected for signs of contamination or atypical appearance before issue or shipping. Units that do not meet inspection criteria must be quarantined for further evaluation.

An organizational format for storage should be established and followed. Unprocessed or incompletely processed units, autologous units, and unsuitable units must be clearly segregated (quarantined) from routine stock.[4(p15)] Most institutions organize their blood inventory by status (quarantined, retype unconfirmed, retype confirmed, available, crossmatched, etc), by product, by ABO group and Rh type, and, within these categories, by expiration date.

Attention to detail in placing blood into storage is necessary because a placement error could be critical if a quarantined unit is issued or a group O Rh-positive unit, incorrectly placed among group O Rh-negative units, is issued without careful checking in an emergency situation.

Special Product Concerns

Platelets

Few articles address the management of platelet inventory. Optimal levels are difficult to determine because demand is episodic and the shelf life is short. Often, the effective shelf life is 3 days because, of the allowable 5 days after phlebotomy, day 1 may be taken for testing and day 2 for shipment. Planning is further complicated by requests for special products, such as leukocyte-reduced, crossmatched, HLA-matched, or cytomegalovirus (CMV)-seronegative platelets.

Platelet inventory management requires good communication and cooperation among patient care providers, transfusion services, and blood centers. Information about patients' diagnoses and expected transfusion schedules helps the blood center plan how many platelets to prepare and which donors to recruit for plateletpheresis.

Transfusion services with low platelet use usually order platelets only when they receive a specific request. If the transfusion service staff follows daily platelet counts and special transfusion requirements of known platelet users, they can often anticipate needs and place orders in advance. Transfusion services with high use may find it helpful to maintain platelets in inventory. Transfusion services should define selection and transfusion guidelines for ABO group, Rh type, irradiation, CMV serologic testing, and leukocyte reduction of platelet products. The formulas described in the beginning of the chapter may be used to estimate ideal inventory ranges.

Platelet usage often increases the day after a holiday because elective procedures and oncology transfusions will have been postponed. Planning ahead to stock platelets helps meet postholiday demand.

Frozen Plasma Products

Because plasma components can be stored frozen up to 1 year, these inventories are easier to manage. Optimal inventory levels are determined by assessing statistics on patient populations and usage patterns. Production goals and schedules can then be established. Most centers find it best to maintain consistent production levels throughout the year, to achieve evenly distributed expiration dates.

Some facilities prefer to freeze plasma from group AB and A donors because these units will be ABO-compatible with most potential recipients. Plasma can be collected by apheresis to increase general stock and provide for special needs.

Cryoprecipitated AHF is a labor-intensive product to prepare and supplies cannot easily be increased to meet large acute needs. It is prudent to maintain inventories at close-to-maximum levels.

Autologous and Directed Units

If autologous and directed donor units constitute an increasing fraction of inventory, their management becomes a significant and controversial issue both for the intended recipients and for institutions. An extended discussion of autologous blood collection and transfusion methods can be found in Chapter 5.

Autologous and directed units should be stored in separate designated areas in the blood refrigerator. Such units are often arranged alphabetically by the intended recipient's last name. Available units must be clearly identified and monitored to ensure issue in the proper sequence. Autologous blood should always be used first, followed by directed donor blood, and, finally, allogeneic units from general stock. Policies about the reservation period for directed donor units and possible release to other recipients should be established at both the transfusion service and donor center and should be made known to laboratory staff, to potential recipients, and to their physicians.

Special Inventories

Donor centers and transfusion services are faced with requests for specialty products such as CMV-reduced-risk units, HLA-matched platelets, antigen-matched red cells, or irradiated components. The appropriate use of these products is discussed in other chapters. Depending on how and when they were prepared, these products may have shortened expiration dates.

If demand and inventory levels are very high, a transfusion service may need to keep separate inventories of these products to make them easier to locate and monitor. These special units can be rotated into general stock as they near their outdate because they can be given safely to others.

References

1.   Comprehensive report on blood collection and transfusion in the United States in 2001. Bethesda, MD: National Blood Data Resource Center, 2003.

2.   Friedman BA, Oberman HA, Chadwick AR, et al. The maximum surgical blood order schedule and surgical blood use in the United States. Transfusion 1976;16:380-7.

3.   Devine P, Linden JV, Hoffstadter L, et al. Blood donor-, apheresis-, and transfusion-related activities: Results of the 1991 American Association of Blood Banks Institutional Membership Questionnaire. Transfusion 1993;33:779-82.

4.   Silva MA, ed. Standards for blood banks and transfusion services. 23rd ed. Bethesda, MD: AABB, 2005:15.

Chapter 4

Allogeneic Donor Selection and Blood Collection

BLOOD CENTERS AND transfusion services depend on volunteer donors to provide the blood necessary to meet the needs of the patients they serve. To attract volunteer donors and encourage their continued participation, it is essential that conditions surrounding blood donation be as pleasant, safe, and convenient as possible. To protect donors and recipients, donors are questioned about their medical history and are given a miniphysical examination to help blood center staff determine whether they are eligible donors. The phlebotomy is conducted carefully to minimize any potential donor reactions or bacterial contamination of the unit.

Blood Donation Process

The donor area should be attractive, accessible, and open at hours convenient for donors. It must be well lighted, comfortably ventilated, orderly, and clean. Personnel should be friendly, understanding, professional, and well trained. The area must provide adequate space for private and accurate examinations of individuals to determine their eligibility as blood donors, and for the withdrawal of blood from donors with minimum risk of contamination or exposure to activities and equipment unrelated to blood collection.

Registration

The information obtained from the donor during registration must fully identify the donor and link the donor to existing records.[1(p13)] Some facilities require photographic identification. Current information must be obtained and recorded for each donation. Selected portions of donation records must be kept indefinitely and must make it possible to notify the donor of any information that needs to be conveyed.[1(p69)] The following information should be included:

1. Date and time of donation.
2. Name: Last, first (and middle initial if available).
3. Address: Residence and/or business.
4. Telephone: Residence and/or business.
5. Gender.
6. Age or date of birth. Blood donors must be at least 17 years of age or the age stipulated by applicable state law.
7. A record of reasons for previous deferrals, if any. Persons who have been placed on a deferral or surveillance list must be identified before any unit drawn from them is made available for release. Ideally, a donor deferral registry should be available to identify ineligible donors before blood is drawn. If such a registry is not available, there must be a procedure to review prior donation records and/or deferral registries before releasing the components from quarantine.[2]

The following information may also be useful:

1. Additional identification such as social security or driver's license number or any other name used by the donor on a previous donation. The Social Security Act specifically allows the use of the social security number for this purpose. These data are required for information retrieval in some computerized systems. Identification of other names used by a donor is particularly important to ensure that the appropriate donor file is accessed or that a deferral status is accurate.
2. Name of patient or group to be acknowledged.
3. Race. Although not required, this information can be particularly useful when blood of a specific phenotype is needed for patients who have un-expected antibodies. Care should be taken to be sure that minority populations understand the medical importance and scientific applications of this information.[3,4]

4. Unique characteristics of the donor. Certain information about the donor may enable the blood bank to make optimal use of the donation. For example, blood from donors who are seronegative for cytomegalovirus (CMV), or who are group O, Rh negative, is often designated for neonatal patients. The blood center may specify that blood from these individuals be drawn routinely into collection bags suitable for pediatric transfusion. Individuals known to have clinically significant antibodies may be identified so that their blood can be processed into components that contain only minimal amounts of plasma.
5. A record of special communications to a donor, special drawing of blood samples for studies, etc.
6. If the donation is directed to a specific patient, information about when and where the intended recipient will be hospitalized should be obtained. An order from the intended recipient's physician should be provided to the blood center staff. The intended recipient's date of birth, social security number, or other identifiers may be required by the transfusion service. If the donor is a blood relative of the intended recipient, this information must be noted so that cellular components can be irradiated.[1(p43)]

Information Provided to the Prospective Donor

All donors must be given educational materials informing them of significant risk of the procedure, the clinical signs and symptoms associated with human immunodeficiency virus (HIV) infection and AIDS, high-risk activities for transmission, and the importance of refraining from donating blood if they have engaged in these activities or experienced associated signs or symptoms. Before donating, the prospective donors must document that they have read the material and have been given the opportunity to ask questions about the information. This information must include a list of activities defined by the Food and Drug Administration (FDA) that increase the risk of exposure to HIV. A description of HIV-associated clinical signs and symptoms, including the following, must be provided[5]:

1. Unexplained weight loss.
2. Night sweats.
3. Blue or purple spots on or under the skin or on mucous membranes.
4. Swollen lymph nodes lasting more than 1 month.
5. White spots or unusual sores in the mouth.
6. Temperature greater than 100.5 F for more than 10 days.
7. Persistent cough and shortness of breath.
8. Persistent diarrhea.

The donor should be provided with information about the tests to be done on his or her blood, the existence of registries of ineligible donors, and regulations or local standard operating procedures (SOPs) that require notification to government agencies of the donor's infectious disease status. The requirement to report positive test results may differ from state to state; they may include HIV, syphilis, and hepatitis testing. Prospective donors must also be informed if there are routine circumstances in which some tests for disease markers are not to be performed.[1(p15)] The donor should be told that he or she will be notified when abnormal test results are recorded and the donor has been placed on a deferral list. When applicable, the donor must also be informed that his or her blood is to be tested with an investigational test such as a nucleic acid amplification test. The possibility that testing may fail to identify infective individuals in an early seronegative stage of infection should be included as well.[6] The same educational material can be used to warn the prospective donor of possible reactions and provide suggestions for postphlebotomy care.

This information should be presented in a way that the donor will understand.[5] Provisions should be made for the hearing- or vision-impaired, and interpreters should be available for donors not fluent in English. The use of interpreters known to the donor should be discouraged. If such a practice is necessary, a signed confidentiality statement should be obtained. In some locations, it may be helpful to have brochures in more than one language. It is also helpful to provide more detailed information for first-time donors. Information about alternative sites or other mechanisms to obtain HIV tests should be available to all prospective donors.

Donor Selection

The donor screening process is one of the most important steps in protecting the safety of the blood supply. The process is intended to identify elements of the medical history and behavior or events that put a person at risk for transmissible disease or at personal medical risk. It is, therefore, imperative that proper guidelines and procedures be followed to make the donor screening process effective.

A qualified physician must determine the eligibility of donors. The responsibility may be delegated to a designee working under the physician's direction after appropriate training.[7] Donor selection criteria are established through regulations, recommendations, and standards of practice. When a donor's condition is not covered or addressed by any of these, a qualified physician should determine the eligibility.

Donor selection is based on a medical history and a limited physical examination done on the day of donation to determine if giving blood will harm the donor or if transfusion of the unit will harm a recipient.[1(p17)] The medical history questions (including questions pertaining to risk behavior associated with HIV infections) may be asked by a qualified interviewer or donors may complete their own record, which must then be reviewed with the donor and initialed by a trained knowledgeable staff member of the donor service according to local SOPs, state, and FDA approval.[5,8] Some donor centers have instituted an FDA-approved computer-generated questionnaire.

The interview and physical examination must be performed in a manner that ensures adequate auditory and visual privacy, allays apprehensions, and provides time for any necessary discussion or explanation. Details explaining a donor's answers that require further investigation should be documented by the staff on the donor form. Results of observations made when a physical examination is given and when tests are performed must be recorded concurrently.

Donors must understand the information that is presented to them in order to make an informed decision to donate their blood. Effective communication is vital for conveying important information and eliminating ineligible donors from the donor pool. Of equal importance is the training of donor center staff. Screening can be effective only if the staff members are proficient in their jobs and understand thoroughly the technical information required to perform the job. Good interpersonal and public relations skills are essential for job competency. Because donor center staff are in constant contact with donors, knowledgeable personnel and effective communication contribute to positive public perception and to the success of donor screening programs.

Medical History

While the medical history is obtained, some very specific questions are necessary to ensure that, to the greatest extent possible, it is safe for the donor to donate and for the blood to be transfused. The interviewer should review and evaluate all responses to determine eligibility for donation and document the decision. To be sure that all the appropriate questions are asked and that donors are given a consistent message, use of the most recent FDA-approved AABB donor history questionnaire is recommended. The most recent FDA-approved version is found on the AABB Web site. (See Appendices 4-1 through 4-3, which were current at the time of this writing.)

One area of the medical history—medications and drugs taken by the donor—often requires further investigation. New prescription drugs and over-the-counter medications enter the marketplace daily, and donors may report use of a drug not specifically noted in the facility's SOP manual. Although there is consensus on those drugs that are always or never a cause for deferral, many drugs fall into a category over which disagreement exists. In these cases, the reason for taking the drug (rather than the drug itself) is usually the cause for deferral. Appendix 4-4 lists drugs that many blood banks do consider acceptable without approval from a donor center physician. Prospective donors who have taken isotretinoin (Accutane) or finasteride (Proscar or Propecia) within the 30 days preceding donation; dutasteride (Avodart) within the 6 months preceding donation; acitretin (Soriatane) within the 3 years preceding donation; or etretinate (Tegison) at any time must be deferred.[1(p62)] The Armed Services Blood Program Office makes its drug deferral list available to the public.[9]

Deferring or rejecting potential donors often leaves those persons with negative feelings about themselves as well as the blood donation process. Donors who are deferred must be given a full explanation of the reason and be informed whether or when they can return to donate. It may be prudent to document this notification.

Confidential Unit Exclusion

Donors may be given the opportunity to indicate confidentially whether their blood is or is not suitable for transfusion to others. This should be done by a mechanism that allows the donor to avoid face-to-face admission of risk behaviors.

The donor must be given instructions to the effect that he or she may call the blood bank after the donation and ask that the unit collected not be used. A mechanism should exist to allow retrieval of the unit without obtaining the donor's identity (eg, use of Whole Blood number).

If the donor indicates that blood collected should not be used for transfusion, he or she should be informed that the blood will be subjected to testing and that there will be notification of any positive results. Counseling or referral must be provided for positive HIV test results, or if any other medically significant test results have been detected.

Physical Examination

The following variables must be evaluated for each donor. The donor center physician must approve exceptions to routinely acceptable findings. For special donor categories, the medical director may provide policies and procedures to guide decisions. Other donors may require individual evaluation.

1. General appearance: If the donor looks ill, or is excessively nervous, it is best to defer the donation.

2. Weight: No more than 10.5 mL of whole blood per kilogram of body weight shall be collected at a donation.[1(p61)] This amount shall include samples for testing. If it is necessary to draw a smaller amount than appropriate for a standard collection container, then the amount of anticoagulant in the container must be adjusted appropriately. The formula in Table 4-1 may be used to determine the amount of anticoagulant to remove. The volume of blood drawn must be measured carefully and accurately.

3. Temperature: The donor's temperature must not exceed 37.5 C (99.5 F) if measured orally, or its equivalent if measured by another method. Lower

---

Table 4-1. Calculations for Drawing Donors Weighing Less than 50 kg (110 lb)

A. Volume to draw* = (Donor's weight in kg/50) × 450 mL

B. Amount of anticoagulant† needed = (A/100) × 14

C. Amount of anticoagulant to remove from collection bag = 63 mL − B

*Approximately 12% of total blood volume.
†CPD or CPDA-1 solutions for which the desired anticoagulant:blood ratio is 1.4:10.

than normal temperatures are usually of no significance in healthy individuals; however, they should be repeated for confirmation.

4. Pulse: The pulse rate should be counted for at least 15 seconds. It should exhibit no pathologic irregularity, and the frequency should be between 50 and 100 beats per minute. If a prospective donor is a known athlete with high exercise tolerance, a pulse rate below 50 may be noted and should be acceptable. A donor center physician should evaluate marked abnormalities of pulse and recommend acceptance, deferral, or referral for additional evaluation.

5. Blood pressure: The blood pressure should be no higher than 180 mm Hg systolic and 100 mm Hg diastolic. Prospective donors whose blood pressure is above these values should not be drawn without individual evaluation by a qualified physician.

6. Hemoglobin or packed cell volume (hematocrit): Before donation, the hemoglobin or hematocrit must be determined from a sample of blood obtained at the time of donation. Although this screening test is intended to prevent collection of blood from a donor with anemia, it does not ensure that the donor has an adequate store of iron. Table 4-2 gives the lower limits of hemoglobin for accepting allogeneic donors. Individuals with unusually high hemoglobin or hematocrit levels may need to be evaluated by a physician because the elevated levels may reflect pulmonary, hematologic, or other abnormalities. Methods to evaluate hemoglobin concentration include 1) specific gravity determined by copper sulfate (see Method 6.1), 2) spectrophotometric measurement of hemoglobin or determination of the hematocrit, or 3) alternate accepted methods to rule out erroneous results that may lead to rejection of a donor. Earlobe puncture is not an acceptable source for a blood sample. [1(p61),10]

7. Skin lesions: The skin at the site of venipuncture must be free of lesions. Both arms must be examined for signs of repeated parenteral entry, especially multiple needle puncture marks and/or sclerotic veins as seen with drug use. Such evidence is reason for indefinite exclusion of a prospective donor. Mild skin disorders or the rash of poison ivy should not be cause for deferral unless unusually extensive and/or present in the antecubital area. Individuals with boils, purulent wounds, or severe skin infections anywhere on the

Table 4-2. Minimum Levels of Hemoglobin, Hematocrit, and Red Cell Density for Accepting an Allogeneic Blood Donor

Donor Test Method	Minimal Acceptable Value[1]
Hemoglobin	12.5 g/dL
Hematocrit	38%
Copper sulfate	1.053 sp gr

body should be deferred, as should anyone with purplish-red or hemorrhagic nodules or indurated plaques suggestive of Kaposi's sarcoma.

The record of the physical examination and the medical history must identify and contain the examiner's initials or signature. Any reasons for deferral must be recorded and explained to the donor. A mechanism must exist to notify the donor of clinically significant abnormal findings in the physical examination, medical history, or post-donation laboratory testing.[11] Abnormalities found before donation may be explained verbally by qualified personnel. Test results obtained after donation that preclude further donation may be reported in person, by telephone, or by letter. Donors should be asked to report any illness developing within a few days after donation and, especially, to report a positive HIV test or the occurrence of hepatitis or AIDS that develops within 12 months after donation.

Donor Consent

Written consent that allows donor center personnel to collect and use blood from the prospective donor is required.[1(p15)] The consent form is part of the donor record and must be completed before donation. The procedure must be explained in terms that donors can understand, and there must be an opportunity for the prospective donor to ask questions. The signed donor record or consent form should also indicate that the donor has read and understood the information about infectious diseases transmissible by transfusion and has given accurate and truthful answers to the medical history questions. Wording equivalent in meaning to the following is suggested:

"I have read and understand the information provided to me regarding the spread of the AIDS virus (HIV) by blood and plasma. If I am potentially at risk for spreading the virus known to cause AIDS, I agree not to donate blood or plasma for transfusion to another person or for further manufacture. I understand that my blood will be tested for HIV and other disease markers; however, there may be unforeseen circumstances when infectious disease testing may not be performed. If this testing indicates that I should no longer donate blood or plasma because of the risk of transmitting an infectious disease, my name will be entered on a list of permanently deferred donors. I understand that I will be notified of a positive laboratory test result(s). If, instead, the results of the testing are not clearly negative or positive, my blood will not be used and my name may be placed on a deferral list."

If units are occasionally used for reasons other than transfusion, such as research, then the informed consent should address such occasions.

Special Donor Categories

Exceptions to the usual eligibility requirements may be made for special donor categories:

1. Autologous donors: The indications for collection and variations from usual donor procedures are discussed in Chapter 5.
2. Hemapheresis: Special requirements and recommendations for cytapheresis donors or for donors in a plasmapheresis program are detailed in Chapter 6.
3. Recipient-specific "designated" donations: Under certain circumstances, it may be important to use blood or components from a specific donor for a specific patient. Examples include the patient with an antibody to a high-incidence antigen or a combination of antibodies that makes

it difficult to find compatible blood; the infant with neonatal alloimmune thrombocytopenia whose mother can provide platelets; the patient awaiting a kidney transplant from a living donor; or the multitransfused patient whose family members can provide components.

The repeated use of a single donor to supply components needed for a single patient is allowed, provided it is requested by the patient's physician and approved by the donor center physician. The donor must meet all the usual requirements for donation, except that the frequency of donation can be as often as every 3 days, as long as the predonation hemoglobin level meets or exceeds the minimum value for routine allogeneic blood donation.

The blood must be processed according to AABB *Standards for Blood Banks and Transfusion Services*.[1(pp24-32)] Special tags identifying the donor unit number and the intended recipient must be affixed to the blood or component bag, and all such units must be segregated from the normal inventory. A protocol for handling such units must be included in the SOP manual.

4. Directed donors: The public's concern about the safety of transfusion has generated demands from potential recipients to choose the donors to be used for their transfusions. Several states have laws establishing this as an acceptable procedure that must be offered by a donor service in nonemergency situations, if requested by a potential blood recipient or ordered by a physician. Despite logistic and philosophic problems associated with these "directed" donations, most blood centers and

hospitals provide this service. The selection and testing of directed donors should be the same as for other allogeneic donors, although special exemptions to the 56-day (or 112 days for double red cell donation) waiting period between donations may be made. Federal regulations state that a person may serve as a source of Whole Blood more than once in 8 weeks only if at the time of donation the donor is examined and certified by a physician to be in good health.[12] To avoid misunderstandings, it is important to establish SOPs that define the interval required between collection of the blood and its availability to the recipient; the policy about determining ABO group before collection; and the policy for releasing units for use by other patients.

Collection of Blood

Blood is to be collected only by trained personnel working under the direction of a qualified licensed physician. Blood collection must be by aseptic methods, using a sterile closed system. If more than one skin puncture is needed, a new container and donor set must be used for each additional venipuncture unless the SOP allows the use of an FDA-approved device to attach a new needle while preserving sterility. The phlebotomist must sign or initial the donor record, even if the phlebotomy did not result in the collection of a full unit.

Blood Containers

Blood must be collected into an FDA-approved container that is pyrogen-free and sterile and contains sufficient anticoagulant for the quantity of blood to be collected. The container label must state the type and amount of anticoagulant and the approximate amount of blood collected.

Blood bags may be supplied in packages containing more than one bag. The manufacturer's directions should be followed for the length of time unused bags may be stored in packages that have been opened.

Identification

Identification is essential in each step from donor registration to final disposition of each component. A numeric or alphanumeric system must be used that identifies, and relates to, the source donor, the donor record, the specimens used for testing, the collection container, and all components prepared from the unit. Extreme caution is necessary to avoid any mix-up or duplication of numbers. All records and labels should be checked before use for printing errors. If duplicate numbers are found, they must be removed and may be investigated to ascertain the reason for the duplication (eg, supplier error, etc). A record must be kept of all voided numbers.

Before beginning the collection, the phlebotomist should:
1. Identify the donor record (at least by name) with the donor and ask the donor to state or spell his or her name.
2. Attach numbered labels to the donor record and ensure that it matches the blood collection container, attached satellite bags, and tubes for donor blood samples. Attaching the numbers at the donor chair, rather than during the examination procedures, helps reduce the likelihood of identification errors.
3. Be sure that the processing tubes are correctly numbered and that they accompany the container during the collection of blood. Tubes may be attached in any convenient manner to the primary bag or integral tubing.
4. Recheck all numbers.

Preparation of the Venipuncture Site

Blood should be drawn from a large firm vein in an area (usually the antecubital space) that is free of skin lesions. Both arms must be inspected for evidence of drug use, skin disease, or scarring. A tourniquet or a blood pressure cuff inflated to 40 to 60 mm Hg makes the veins more prominent. Having the donor open and close the hand a few times is also helpful. Once the vein is selected, the pressure device should be released before the skin site is prepared.

There is no way to make the venipuncture site completely aseptic, but surgical cleanliness can be achieved to provide the best assurance of an uncontaminated unit. Several acceptable procedures exist (see Method 6.2). After the skin has been prepared, it must not be touched again to repalpate the vein. The entire site preparation must be repeated if the cleansed skin is touched.

Phlebotomy and Collection of Samples

A technique for drawing a donor unit and collecting samples for testing appears in Method 6.3. The unit should be collected from a single venipuncture after the pressure device has again been inflated. During collection, the blood should be mixed with the anticoagulant. The amount of blood collected should be monitored carefully so that the total, including samples, does not exceed 10.5 mL per kilogram of donor weight per donation.[1(p61)] When the appropriate amount has been collected, segments and specimen tubes must be filled. The needle and any blood-contaminated waste must be disposed of safely in accordance with universal precaution guidelines. The needle must not be recapped unless a safety recapping device is used. Disposal of the needle must be in a puncture-proof container. After collection, there must be verification that the identifiers on the unit, the donor history, and the tubes are the same. Gloves must be available for use during phlebotomy and must be worn by phlebotomists when collecting autologous blood and when individuals are in training.

Care of the Donor After Phlebotomy

After removing the needle from the vein, the phlebotomist should:

1. Apply firm pressure with sterile gauze over the point of entry of the needle into vein. (The donor may be instructed to continue application of pressure for several minutes.) Check arm and apply a bandage only after all bleeding stops.

2. Have donor remain reclining on the bed or in the donor chair for a few minutes under close observation by staff.

3. Allow the donor to sit up under observation until his or her condition appears satisfactory. The donor should be observed in the upright position before release to the observation/refreshment area. Staff should monitor donors in this area. The period of observation and provision of refreshment should be specified in the SOP manual.

4. Give the donor instructions about postphlebotomy care. The medical director may wish to include some or all of the following recommendations or instructions:

   a. Eat and drink something before leaving the donor site.

   b. Do not leave until released by a staff member.

   c. Drink more fluids than usual in the next 4 hours.

   d. Avoid consuming alcohol until something has been eaten.

   e. Do not smoke for 30 minutes.

   f. If there is bleeding from the phlebotomy site, raise arm and apply pressure to the site.

   g. If fainting or dizziness occurs, either lie down or sit with the head between the knees.

   h. If any symptoms persist, either telephone or return to the donor center or see a doctor.

   i. Resume all normal activities if asymptomatic. Donors who work in certain occupations (eg, construction workers, operators of machinery) or persons working at heights should be cautioned that dizziness or faintness may occur if they return to work immediately after giving blood.

   j. Remove bandage after a few hours.

   k. Maintain high fluid intake for several days to restore blood volume.

5. Thank the donor for an important contribution and encourage repeat donation after the proper interval. All personnel on duty throughout the donor area, volunteer or paid, should be friendly and qualified to observe for signs of a reaction such as lack of concentration, pallor, rapid breathing, or excessive perspiration. Donor room personnel should be trained and competent to interpret instructions, answer questions, and accept responsibility for releasing the donor in good condition.

6. Note on the donor record any adverse reactions that occurred. If the donor leaves the area before being released, note this on the record.

Adverse Donor Reactions

Most donors tolerate giving blood very well, but adverse reactions occur occasionally. Personnel must be trained to recognize adverse reactions and to provide initial treatment.

Donor room personnel should be trained in cardiopulmonary resuscitation (CPR). Special equipment to handle emergency situations must be available.

Syncope (fainting or vasovagal syndrome) may be caused by the sight of blood, by watching others give blood, or by individual or group excitement; it may also happen for unexplained reasons. Whether caused by psychologic factors or by neurophysiologic response to blood donation, the symptoms may include weakness, sweating, dizziness, pallor, loss of consciousness, convulsions, and involuntary passage of feces or urine. On occasion, the skin feels cold and blood pressure falls. Sometimes, the systolic blood pressure levels fall as low as 50 mm Hg or cannot be heard with the stethoscope. The pulse rate often slows significantly. This can be useful in distinguishing between vasovagal attack and cardiogenic or hypovolemic shock, in which cases the pulse rate rises. This distinction, although characteristic, is far from absolute.

Rapid breathing or hyperventilation may cause the anxious or excited donor to lose excessive amounts of carbon dioxide. This may cause generalized sensations of suffocation or anxiety, or localized problems such as tingling or twitching.

The donor center physician must provide written instructions for handling donor reactions, including a procedure for obtaining emergency medical help. Sample instructions might be as follows:

1. General.
   a. Remove the tourniquet and withdraw the needle from the arm if signs of a reaction occur during the phlebotomy.
   b. If possible, remove any donor who experiences an adverse reaction to an area where he or she can be attended in privacy.
   c. Apply the measures suggested below and, if they do not lead to rapid recovery, call the blood bank physician or the physician designated for such purposes.
2. Fainting.
   a. Apply cold compresses to the donor's forehead or the back of the neck.
   b. Place the donor on his or her back, with their legs raised above the level of the head.
   c. Loosen tight clothing.
   d. Be sure the donor has an adequate airway.
   e. Monitor blood pressure, pulse, and respiration periodically until the donor recovers.

   Note: Some donors who experience prolonged hypotension may respond to an infusion of normal saline. The decision to initiate such therapy should be made by the donor center physician either on a case-by-case basis or in a policy stated in the facility's SOP manual.
3. Nausea and vomiting.
   a. Make the donor as comfortable as possible.
   b. Instruct the donor who is nauseated to breathe slowly and deeply.
   c. Apply cold compresses to the donor's forehead and/or back of neck.
   d. Turn the donor's head to the side.
   e. Provide a suitable receptacle if the donor vomits and have cleansing tissues or a damp towel ready. Be sure the donor's head

is turned to the side because of the danger of aspiration.

   f.   After vomiting has ended, give the donor some water to rinse out his or her mouth.

4.   Twitching or muscular spasms. Extremely nervous donors may hyperventilate, causing faint muscular twitching or tetanic spasm of their hands or face. Donor room personnel should watch closely for these symptoms during and immediately after the phlebotomy.

   a.   Divert the donor's attention by engaging in conversation, to interrupt the hyperventilation pattern.

   b.   Have the donor cough if he or she is symptomatic. **Do not give oxygen.**

5.   Hematoma during or after phlebotomy.

   a.   Remove the tourniquet and the needle from the donor's arm.

   b.   Place three or four sterile gauze squares over the venipuncture site and apply firm digital pressure for 7 to 10 minutes, with the donor's arm held above the heart level. An alternative is to apply a tight bandage, which should be removed after 7 to 10 minutes to allow inspection.

   c.   Apply ice to the area for 5 minutes, if desired.

   d.   Should an arterial puncture be suspected, immediately withdraw needle and apply firm pressure for 10 minutes. Apply pressure dressing afterwards. Check for the presence of a radial pulse. If pulse is not palpable or is weak, call a donor center physician.

6.   Convulsions.

   a.   Call for help immediately. Prevent the donor from injuring himself or herself. During severe seizures, some people exhibit great muscular power and are difficult to restrain. If possible, hold the donor on the chair or bed; if not possible, place the donor on the floor. Try to prevent injury to the donor and to yourself.

   b.   Be sure the donor has an adequate airway. A padded device should separate the jaws *after convulsion has ceased.*

   c.   Notify the donor center physician.

7.   Serious cardiac difficulties.

   a.   Call for medical aid and/or an emergency care unit immediately.

   b.   If the donor is in cardiac arrest, begin CPR immediately and continue it until help arrives.

The nature and treatment of all reactions should be recorded on the donor's record or a special incident report form. This should include a notation of whether the donor should be accepted for future donations.

The medical director should decide what emergency supplies and drugs should be in the donor area. The distance to the nearest emergency room or emergency care unit heavily influences decisions about necessary supplies and drugs. Most donor centers maintain some or all of the following:

1.   Emesis basin or equivalent.

2.   Towels.

3.   Oropharyngeal airway, plastic or hard rubber.

4.   Oxygen and mask.

5.   Emergency drugs: Drugs are seldom required to treat a donor's reaction. If the donor center physician wishes to have any drugs available, the kind and amount to be kept on hand must be specified in writing. In addition, the medical director must provide written policies stating when and by

whom any of the above medical supplies or drugs may be used.

References

1.   Silva MA, ed. Standards for blood banks and transfusion services. 23rd ed. Bethesda, MD: AABB, 2005.
2.   Code of federal regulations. Title 21 CFR 606.160(e). Washington, DC: US Government Printing Office, 2004 (revised annually).
3.   Beattie KM, Shafer AW. Broadening the base of a rare donor program by targeting minority populations. Transfusion 1986;26:401-4.
4.   Vichinsky EP, Earles A, Johnson RA, et al. Alloimmunization in sickle cell anemia and transfusion of racially unmatched blood. N Engl J Med 1990;322:1617-21.
5.   Food and Drug Administration. Memorandum: Revised recommendations for the prevention of human immunodeficiency virus (HIV) transmission by blood and blood products. (April 23, 1992) Rockville, MD: CBER Office of Communication, Training, and Manufacturers Assistance, 1992.
6.   Centers for Disease Control. Update: Universal precautions for prevention of transmission of human immunodeficiency virus, hepatitis B virus, and other bloodborne pathogens in health-care settings. JAMA 1988;260:528-31.
7.   Code of federal regulations. Title 21 CFR 640.4(a). Washington, DC: US Government Printing Office, 2004 (revised annually).
8.   Food and Drug Administration. Guidance for Industry: Streamlining the donor interview process: Recommendations for self-administered questionnaires. (July 3, 2003) Rockville, MD: CBER Office of Communication, Training, and Manufacturers Assistance, 2003.
9.   Armed Services Blood Program Office. Drugs and medications. [Available at http://www.tricare.osd.mil/asbpo/library/policies/downloads/medication_list.doc.]
10. Newman B. Blood donor suitability and allogeneic whole blood donation. Transfus Med Rev 2001;15:234-44.
11. Food and Drug Administration. General requirements for blood, blood components, and blood derivatives; donor notification. Title 21 CFR 630.6. Fed Regist 2001;66:31165-77.
12. Code of federal regulations. Title 21 CFR 640.3(f). Washington, DC: US Government Printing Office, 2004 (revised annually).

Suggested Reading

Code of federal regulations. Title 21 CFR 640.3. Washington, DC: US Government Printing Office, 2004 (revised annually). [History of viral hepatitis before the 11th birthday.]

Food and Drug Administration. Memorandum: Revised recommendations for the prevention of human immunodeficiency virus (HIV) transmission by blood and blood products. (April 23, 1992) Rockville, MD: CBER Office of Communication, Training, and Manufacturers Assistance, 1992.

Food and Drug Administration. Guidance for industry: Revised preventive measures to reduce the possible risk of transmission of Creutzfeldt-Jakob disease (CJD) and new variant Creutzfeldt-Jakob disease (nvCJD) by blood and blood products. (January 9, 2002) Rockville, MD: CBER Office of Communication, Training, and Manufacturers Assistance, 2002.

Infectious disease testing for blood transfusions. NIH Consensus Statement 13:1, January 1995. Bethesda, MD: National Institutes of Health, 1995.

Kasprisin C, Laird-Fryer B, eds. Blood donor collection practices. Bethesda, MD: AABB, 1993.

Linder J, ed. Practical solutions to practical problems in transfusion medicine and tissue banking. [Supplement 1 to Am J Clin Pathol 1997;107(4).] Chicago, IL: American Society of Clinical Pathologists, 1997.

Schmuñis GA. *Trypanosoma cruzi*, the etiologic agent of Chagas' disease: Status in the blood supply in endemic and nonendemic countries. Transfusion 1991;31:547-57.

Smith KJ, Simon TL. Recruitment and evaluation of blood and plasma donors. In: Rossi EC, Simon TL, Moss GS, eds. Principles of transfusion medicine. 2nd ed. Baltimore, MD: Williams and Wilkins, 1995:871-9.

Tan L, Williams MA, Khan MK, et al. Risk of transmission of bovine spongiform encephalopathy to humans in the United States. JAMA 1999;281:2330-8.

Appendix 4-1. Full-Length Donor History Questionnaire*

	Yes	No	
Are you			
1. Feeling healthy and well today?	☐	☐	
2. Currently taking an antibiotic?	☐	☐	
3. Currently taking any other medication for an infection?	☐	☐	
Please read the Medication Deferral List.			
4. Are you now taking or have you ever taken any medications on the Medication Deferral List?	☐	☐	
5. Have you read the educational materials and had your questions answered?	☐	☐	
In the past 48 hours			
6. Have you taken aspirin or anything that has aspirin in it?	☐	☐	
In the past week			
7. Have you had a headache and fever at the same time?	☐	☐	
In the past 6 weeks			
8. Female donors: Have you been pregnant or are you pregnant now? (Males: check "I am male.")	☐	☐	☐ I am male
In the past 8 weeks have you			
9. Donated blood, platelets or plasma?	☐	☐	
10. Had any vaccinations or other shots?	☐	☐	
11. Had contact with someone who had a smallpox vaccination?	☐	☐	
In the past 16 weeks			
12. Have you donated a double unit of red cells using an apheresis machine?	☐	☐	
In the past 12 months have you			
13. Had a blood transfusion?	☐	☐	
14. Had a transplant such as organ, tissue, or bone marrow?	☐	☐	
15. Had a graft such as bone or skin?	☐	☐	
16. Come into contact with someone else's blood?	☐	☐	
17. Had an accidental needle-stick?	☐	☐	
18. Had sexual contact with anyone who has HIV/AIDS or has had a positive test for the HIV/AIDS virus?	☐	☐	
19. Had sexual contact with a prostitute or anyone else who takes money or drugs or other payment for sex?	☐	☐	
20. Had sexual contact with anyone who has ever used needles to take drugs or steroids, or anything not prescribed by their doctor?	☐	☐	
21. Had sexual contact with anyone who has hemophilia or has used clotting factor concentrates?	☐	☐	
22. Female donors: Had sexual contact with a male who has ever had sexual contact with another male? (Males: check "I am male.")	☐	☐	☐ I am male

v. DHQ-1.0   eff. April 2004

Appendix 4-1. Full-Length Donor History Questionnaire (cont'd)*

	Yes	No
23. Had sexual contact with a person who has hepatitis?	☐	☐
24. Lived with a person who has hepatitis?	☐	☐
25. Had a tattoo?	☐	☐
26. Had ear or body piercing?	☐	☐
27. Had or been treated for syphilis or gonorrhea?	☐	☐
28. Been in juvenile detention, lockup, jail, or prison for more than 72 hours?	☐	☐
In the past three years have you		
29. Been outside the United States or Canada?	☐	☐
From 1980 through 1996,		
30. Did you spend time that adds up to three (3) months or more in the United Kingdom? (Review list of countries in the UK)	☐	☐
31. Were you a member of the U.S. military, a civilian military employee, or a dependent of a member of the U.S. military?	☐	☐
From 1980 to the present, did you		
32. Spend time that adds up to five (5) years or more in Europe? (Review list of countries in Europe.)	☐	☐
33. Receive a blood transfusion in the United Kingdom ? (Review list of countries in the UK.)	☐	☐
From 1977 to the present, have you		
34. Received money, drugs, or other payment for sex?	☐	☐
35. Male donors: had sexual contact with another male, even once? (Females: check "I am female.")	☐	☐
Have you EVER		
36. Had a positive test for the HIV/AIDS virus?	☐	☐
37. Used needles to take drugs, steroids, or anything <u>not</u> prescribed by your doctor?	☐	☐
38. Used clotting factor concentrates?	☐	☐
39. Had hepatitis?	☐	☐
40. Had malaria?	☐	☐
41. Had Chagas' disease?	☐	☐
42. Had babesiosis?	☐	☐
43. Received a dura mater (or brain covering) graft?	☐	☐
44. Had any type of cancer, including leukemia?	☐	☐
45. Had any problems with your heart or lungs?	☐	☐
46. Had a bleeding condition or a blood disease?	☐	☐
47. Had sexual contact with anyone who was born in or lived in Africa?	☐	☐
48. Been in Africa?	☐	☐
49. Have any of your relatives had Creutzfeldt-Jakob disease?	☐	☐

(For question 35: ☐ I am female)

Appendix 4-1. Full-Length Donor History Questionnaire (cont'd)*

Additional Questions	Yes	No

v. DHQ-1.0   eff. April 2004

Appendix 4-2. Medication Deferral List*

Please tell us if you are now taking or if you have <u>EVER</u> taken any of these medications:

- ❑   **Proscar© (finasteride)** – usually given for prostate gland enlargement

- ❑   **Avodart© (dutasteride)** – usually given for prostate enlargement

- ❑   **Propecia© (finasteride)** – usually given for baldness

- ❑   **Accutane© (isotretinoin)** – usually given for severe acne

- ❑   **Soriatane© (acitretin)** – usually given for severe psoriasis

- ❑   **Tegison© (etretinate)** – usually given for severe psoriasis

- ❑   **Growth Hormone from Human Pituitary Glands** – used only until 1985, usually for children with delayed or impaired growth

- ❑   **Insulin from Cows (Bovine, or Beef, Insulin)** – used to treat diabetes

- ❑   **Hepatitis B Immune Globulin** – given following an exposure to hepatitis B.
      NOTE: This is different from the hepatitis B vaccine which is a series of 3 injections given over a 6 month period to prevent future infection from exposures to hepatitis B.

IF YOU WOULD LIKE TO KNOW WHY THESE MEDICINES AFFECT YOU AS A BLOOD DONOR, PLEASE KEEP READING:

- If you have taken or are taking <u>**Proscar, Avodart, Propecia, Accutane, Soriatane, or Tegison**</u>, these medications can cause birth defects. Your donated blood could contain high enough levels to damage the unborn baby if transfused to a pregnant woman. Once the medication has been cleared from your blood, you may donate again. Following the last dose, the deferral period is one month Proscar, Propecia and Accutane, six months for Avodart and three years for Soriatane. Tegison is an indefinite deferral.

- <u>**Growth hormone from human pituitary glands**</u> was prescribed until 1985 for children with delayed or impaired growth. The hormone was obtained from human pituitary glands, which are found in the brain. Some people who took this hormone developed a rare nervous system condition called Creutzfeldt-Jakob Disease (CJD, for short). CJD has not been associated with growth hormone preparations available since 1985.

- <u>**Insulin from cows (bovine, or beef, insulin)**</u> is an injected material used to treat diabetes. If this insulin was imported into the US from countries in which "Mad Cow Disease" has been found, it could contain material from infected cattle. There is concern that "Mad Cow Disease" may be transmitted by transfusion.

- <u>**Hepatitis B Immune Globulin (HBIG)**</u> is an injected material used to prevent infection following an exposure to hepatitis B. HBIG does not prevent hepatitis B infection in every case, therefore persons who have received HBIG must wait 12 months to donate blood to be sure they were not infected since hepatitis B can be transmitted through transfusion to a patient.

v. Med-1.0   eff. April 2004

Appendix 4-3. Blood Donor Education Materials*

Blood Donor Educational Materials:
MAKING YOUR BLOOD DONATION SAFE

Thank you for coming in today! This information sheet explains how **YOU** can help us make the donation process safe for yourself and patients who might receive your blood. **PLEASE READ THIS INFORMATION BEFORE YOU DONATE! If you have any questions now or anytime during the screening process, please ask blood center staff.**

ACCURACY AND HONESTY ARE ESSENTIAL!
Your **complete honesty** in answering all questions is very important for the safety of patients who receive your blood. **All information you provide is confidential.**

DONATION PROCESS:
To determine if you are eligible to donate we will:
-Ask questions about health, travel, and medicines
-Ask questions to see if you might be at risk for hepatitis, HIV, or AIDs
- Take your blood pressure, temperature and pulse
- Take a small blood sample to make sure you are not anemic
If you are able to donate we will:
- Cleanse your arm with an antiseptic. **(If you are allergic to Iodine, please tell us!)**
-Use a new, sterile, disposable needle to collect your blood

DONOR ELIGIBILITY – SPECIFIC INFORMATION
Why we ask questions about sexual contact:
Sexual contact may cause contagious diseases like HIV to get into the bloodstream and be spread through transfusions to someone else.
Definition of "sexual contact":
The words "have sexual contact with" and "sex" are used in some of the questions we will ask you, and apply to any of the activities below, whether or not a condom or other protection was used:
1. Vaginal sex (contact between penis and vagina)
2. Oral sex (mouth or tongue on someone's vagina, penis, or anus)
3. Anal sex (contact between penis and anus)

HIV/AIDS RISK BEHAVIORS AND SYMPTOMS
AIDS is caused by HIV. HIV is spread mainly through sexual contact with an infected person OR by sharing needles or syringes used for injecting drugs.

DO NOT DONATE IF YOU:
   -**Have AIDS or have ever had a positive HIV test**
   -Have ever used needles to take drugs, steroids, or anything not prescribed by your doctor
   - Are a male who has had sexual contact with another male, even once, since 1977
   - Have ever taken money, drugs or other payment for sex since 1977
   - Have had sexual contact in the past 12 months with anyone described above
   - Have had syphilis or gonorrhea in the past 12 months
   - In the last 12 months have been in juvenile detention, lockup, jail or prison for more than 72 hours
   -Have any of the following conditions that can be signs or symptoms of HIV/AIDS:
      •Unexplained weight loss or night sweats
      •Blue or purple spots in your mouth or skin
      •Swollen lymph nodes for more than one month
      •White spots or unusual sores in your mouth
      •Cough that won't go away or shortness of breath
      •Diarrhea that won't go away
      •Fever of more than 100.5 °F for more than 10 days

Remember that you CAN give HIV to someone else through blood transfusions even if you feel well and have a negative HIV test. This is because tests cannot detect infections for a period of time after a person is exposed to HIV. **If you think you may be at risk for HIV/AIDS or want an HIV/AIDS test, please ask for information about other testing facilities.** *PLEASE DO NOT DONATE TO GET AN HIV TEST!*

Travel to or birth in other countries
Blood donor tests may not be available for some contagious diseases that are found only in certain countries. If you were born in, have lived in, or visited certain countries, you may not be eligible to donate.

What happens after your donation:
To protect patients, your blood is tested for hepatitis B and C, HIV, certain other viruses, and syphilis. If your blood tests positive it will not be given to a patient. You will be notified about test results that may disqualify you from donating in the future. **Please do not donate to get tested for HIV, hepatitis, or any other infections!**

Thank you for donating blood today!
(Donor Center Name)
(Telephone Number)

v. Edu-1.0   eff. April 2004

Appendix 4-4. Some Drugs Commonly Accepted in Blood Donors

In many blood centers, blood donation may be allowed by individuals who have taken the following drugs:

- Tetracyclines and other antibiotics taken to treat acne.
- Topical steroid preparations for skin lesions not at the venipuncture site.
- Blood pressure medications, taken chronically and successfully so that pressure is at or below allowable limits. The prospective donor taking antihypertensive drugs should be free from side effects, especially episodes of postural hypotension, and should be free of any cardiovascular symptoms.
- Over-the-counter bronchodilators and decongestants.
- Oral hypoglycemic agents in well-controlled diabetics without any vascular complications of the disease.
- Tranquilizers, under most conditions. A physician should evaluate the donor to distinguish between tranquilizers and antipsychotic medications.
- Hypnotics used at bedtime.
- Marijuana (unless currently under the influence), oral contraceptives, mild analgesics, vitamins, replacement hormones, or weight reduction pills.

Note: Acceptance of donors must always be with the approval of the blood bank's medical director.

Chapter 5

Autologous Blood Donation and Transfusion

AUTOLOGOUS BLOOD TRANSFU-
sion is an alternative therapy for
many patients anticipating transfusion. Different categories of autologous
transfusion are:

1. Preoperative collection (blood is drawn
   and stored before anticipated need).
2. Perioperative collection and administration.
   a. Acute normovolemic hemodi-
      lution (blood is collected at the
      start of surgery and then in-
      fused during or at the end of
      the procedure).
   b. Intraoperative collection (shed
      blood is recovered from the
      surgical field or circulatory de-
      vice and then infused).
   c. Postoperative collection (blood
      is collected from drainage de-
      vices and reinfused to the pa-
      tient).

Each type of autologous transfusion
practice offers potential benefits and risks

depending on the type of surgery, condition
of the patient, and technology available.
Each facility must analyze its own transfusion practices, transfusion practices of
other similarly situated institutions, and its
own capabilities to determine the appropriate services to be offered.

However, it is generally accepted that,
when feasible, the patient should have the
option to use his or her own blood. The US
Supreme Court has ruled that asymptomatic infection with HIV is a disability protected under the Americans with Disabilities Act.[1] Therefore, if institutions offer
autologous services to any patient, they
should consider offering such services to
HIV-positive patients.[2] Patients who are
likely to require transfusion therapy and
who also meet the donation criteria should
be told about the options for autologous
transfusion therapies. Patients considering
autologous transfusion therapy should be
informed about the risks and benefits of both
the autologous donation and the auto-

logous transfusion process. Specific issues unique to the use of autologous transfusion in the anticipated surgical procedure should be identified, including the possibility of administrative error. In addition, patients need information about any special fees for autologous services, the level of infectious disease testing that will be performed, and the possibility that additional, allogeneic, units may be used.

Preoperative Autologous Blood Collection

Frequently cited advantages and disadvantages of preoperative autologous blood donation (PAD) are summarized in Table 5-1. Candidates for preoperative collection are stable patients scheduled for surgical procedures in which blood transfusion is likely. For procedures that are unlikely to require transfusion (ie, a maximal surgical blood ordering schedule does not suggest that crossmatched blood be available), the use of preoperative blood collection is not recommended.

In selected patient subgroups, preoperative collection of autologous blood can significantly reduce exposure to allogeneic blood. PAD collections should be considered for patients likely to receive transfusion, such as patients undergoing major orthopedic procedures, vascular surgery, and cardiac or thoracic surgery.[3,4] The most common surgical procedures for which autologous blood is donated are total joint replacements.[4] Autologous blood should not be collected for procedures that seldom (less than 10% of cases) require transfusion, such as cholecystectomy, herniorrhaphy, vaginal hysterectomy, and uncomplicated obstetric delivery.[5]

Special Patient Categories

In special circumstances, preoperative autologous blood collection can be performed for patients who would not ordinarily be considered for allogeneic donation. The availability of medical support is important in assessing patient eligibility. With suitable volume modification, parental cooperation, and attention to preparation and reassurance, pediatric patients

Table 5-1. Autologous Blood Donation

Advantages	Disadvantages
1. Prevents transfusion-transmitted disease.	1. Does not eliminate risk of bacterial contamination.
2. Prevents red cell alloimmunization.	2. Does not eliminate risk of ABO incompatibility error.
3. Supplements the blood supply.	3. Is more costly than allogeneic blood.
4. Provides compatible blood for patients with alloantibodies.	4. Results in wastage of blood that is not transfused.
5. Prevents some adverse transfusion reactions.	5. Increased incidence of adverse reactions to autologous donation.
6. Provides reassurance to patients concerned about blood risks.	6. Subjects patients to perioperative anemia and increased likelihood of transfusion.

can participate in preoperative collection programs.[6] The successful use of autologous blood in a patient with sickle cell disease has been reported,[7] and it may be particularly useful for a sickle cell patient with multiple alloantibodies; however, the patient may derive greater benefit from allogeneic transfusions that provide hemoglobin A. Red cells containing hemoglobin S require special handling during the cryopreservation process.[8]

Patients with significant cardiac disease are considered poor risks for autologous blood donation. Despite reports of safety in small numbers of patients who underwent autologous blood donation,[9] the risks that are associated with autologous blood donation[10] in these patients are probably greater than the current estimated risks of allogeneic transfusion.[11,12] Table 5-2 summarizes the contraindications to a patient's participation in an autologous blood donation program.[13]

The collection of autologous blood from women during routine pregnancy is unwarranted,[14] because blood is so seldom needed. Many centers give serious consideration to autologous collection for women with alloantibodies to multiple or high-incidence antigens, placenta previa, or other conditions placing them at high risk for ante- or intrapartum hemorrhage.[5] A policy should be developed for situations in which maternal red cells are considered for transfusion to the infant.

Voluntary Standards

AABB *Standards for Blood Banks and Transfusion Services* offers uniform standards to be followed in determining patient eligibility; collecting, testing, and labeling the unit; and pretransfusion testing.[15(pp18,39,51)] These AABB standards apply to preoperative autologous blood collection. *Standards for Perioperative Autologous Blood Collection and Administration* have been established to enhance the quality and safety of perioperative autologous transfusion activities (intra- and postoperative blood recovery, perioperative autologous component production, and intraoperative acute normovolemic hemodilution).[16]

Compliance Considerations

Food and Drug Administration (FDA) requirements have evolved over time. The FDA first issued guidance for autologous blood and blood components in March of 1989.[17] This guidance was clarified in a second memorandum issued in February of 1990.[18] Much of the information in previous guidance has been superseded by regulations. The FDA included requirements regarding autologous blood in regulations issued June 11, 2001.[19,20]

Testing

The FDA requires tests for evidence of infection resulting from the following com-

Table 5-2. Contraindications to Participation in Autologous Blood Donation Programs

1. Evidence of infection and risk of bacteremia.
2. Scheduled surgery to correct aortic stenosis.
3. Unstable angina.
4. Uncontrolled seizure disorder.
5. Myocardial infarction or cerebrovascular accident within 6 months of donation.
6. Patients with significant cardiac or pulmonary disease who have not yet been cleared for surgery by their treating physician.
7. High-grade left main coronary artery disease.
8. Cyanotic heart disease.
9. Uncontrolled hypertension.

municable diseases: HIV-1, HIV-2, HBV, HCV, HTLV-I, and HTLV-II (21 CFR 610.40) and a serologic test for syphilis [21 CFR 610.40(a)(1) and 610.40(I)]. Such tests include nucleic acid tests for HCV and HIV.[21] Testing of autologous donations is not required unless the donations are to be used for allogeneic transfusion [21 CFR 610.40(d)(1)]. Autologous donations that are to be shipped to another facility that does allow autologous units to be used for allogeneic transfusion must be tested [21 CFR 610.40(d)(2)]. For autologous donations shipped to another establishment that does *not* allow autologous donations to be used for allogeneic transfusion, the first donation in each 30-day period must be tested [21 CFR 610.40(d)(3)].[15(p34)]

Autologous donations found to be reactive by a required screening test must be retested whenever a supplemental (additional, more specific) test has been approved by the FDA. At a minimum, the first reactive donation in each 30-day period must be tested unless a record exists for a positive supplemental test result for that donor [21 CFR 610.40(e)(1,2)]. Both the AABB *Standards*[15(p34)] and the FDA requirements [21 CFR 630.6(d)] state that the patient and the patient's physicians must be notified of any medically significant abnormalities.

Donor Deferral

If an autologous donor has a reactive screening test for a communicable disease agent or a reactive screening test for syphilis (21 CFR 610.41), the donor must be deferred from making future allogeneic donations. Within 8 weeks, the patient and referring physician must be notified of the reason for deferral, including the results of supplemental testing and, where appropriate, the types of donation that the autologous donor should not make in the future (21 CFR 630.6).

Special Labeling Considerations

Each autologous unit must be labeled "Autologous Donor." Another special label, "BIOHAZARD," is required for any unit that is reactive in the current collection or reactive in the last 30 days. Autologous units that are untested must be labeled "DONOR UNTESTED." If the autologous unit tested negative within the last 30 days, it must be labeled "DONOR TESTED WITHIN THE LAST 30 DAYS" [21 CFR 610.40(d)(4)].

Shipping

Blood or components (including reactive donations) intended for autologous use may be shipped provided that the units have been tested as required and are labeled appropriately [21 CFR 610.40(d)]. If distributed on a common carrier not under the direct control of the collection facility, the transportation of the product must meet provisions for shipping an infectious agent.[22]

Establishing a Preoperative Autologous Blood Collection Program

Each blood center or hospital that decides to conduct an autologous blood collection program must establish its own policies, processes, and procedures. Guidelines exist for establishing a new program, monitoring utilization, or improving an existing one.[13,23,24]

Physician Responsibility

A successful autologous program requires cooperation and communication among all the physicians involved. Responsibility for the health and safety of the patient during the collection process rests with the medical director of the collecting facility; during the transfusion, responsibility rests with the patient's physician and the medical director of the transfusion service. The patient's physician initiates the request for autologous services, which must be approved by the transfusion service physician. There should be a transfusion medicine physician available to help assess patients whose medical history suggests a risk for complications if a donor reaction occurs during blood collection.

Supplemental Iron

The patient should be advised about taking supplemental iron. Ideally, supplemental iron is prescribed by the requesting physician before the first blood collection, in time to allow maximum iron intake. Iron-restricted erythropoiesis is one of the limiting factors in collecting multiple units of blood over a short interval. Oral iron is commonly provided but may be insufficient to maintain iron stores.[25] The dose and administration schedule should be adjusted to minimize gastrointestinal side effects.

Collection

The collection of autologous blood has many elements in common with collection from regular volunteer donors, but numerous special considerations exist. Requests for autologous blood collection are made in writing by the patient's physician; a request form (which may be a simple prescription or a form designed for the purpose) is kept by the collecting facility. The request should include the patient's name, a unique identification number, the number of units and kind of component requested, the date of scheduled surgery, the nature of the surgical procedure, and the physician's signature.

It is important to establish guidelines for the appropriate number of units to be collected. A sufficient number of units should be drawn, whenever possible, so that the patient can minimize exposure to allogeneic blood. However, excessive collection and/or collection close to the date of surgery increases the patient's likelihood of requiring transfusion. A hospital's surgical blood order schedule can provide estimates of transfusion levels for specific procedures. Two-unit collections via an automated red cell apheresis system may be an option. The collection of units for liquid blood storage should be scheduled as far in advance of surgery as possible, in order to allow compensatory erythropoiesis to minimize anemia.

A schedule for blood collections should be established with the patient. A weekly schedule is often used. Table 5-3 details the value of beginning autologous blood donation early in the known preoperative interval, in order to allow optimal compensatory erythropoiesis (shown here as equivalent RBC units).[26] Ordinarily, the last collection should occur no sooner than 72 hours before the scheduled surgery and preferably longer, to allow time for adequate volume repletion. Programs should notify the requesting physician of the total number of units donated when the requested number of units cannot be collected. Each program should establish a policy regarding rescheduling of surgery beyond the expiration date of autologous units and whether discarding or freezing the unit are options.

Donor Screening

Because of the special circumstances regarding autologous blood transfusion, rigid criteria for donor selection are not required. In situations where requirements for allogeneic donor selection or collection are not applied, alternative requirements must be established by the medical director and recorded in the procedures manual. The hemoglobin concentration of the donor should be no less

Table 5-3. Timing and Red Cell Regeneration During Preoperative Autologous Donation[26]

Time from Donation to Surgery (days)	No. of Patients	Mean RBC Units Regenerated	5% CI of Mean
6-13	39	0.52	0.25-0.79
14-20	127	0.54	0.40-0.68
21-27	128	0.75	0.61-0.90
28-34	48	1.16	0.96-1.36
35-41	30	1.93	1.64-2.2

than 11.0 g/dL and the hematocrit, if substituted, should be no less than 33%. Individual deviations from the alternate requirements must be approved by the blood bank medical director, usually in consultation with the donor-patient's physician.

Medical Interview

The medical interview should be structured to meet the special needs of autologous donors. For example, more attention should be given to questions about medications, associated medical illnesses, and cardiovascular risk factors.[10] Questions should elicit any possibility of intermittent bacteremia. Because crossover is not routinely permitted, a substantially shortened set of interview questions can be used for autologous donations; for example, questions related to donor risks for transfusion-transmitted diseases are not necessary.

Volume Collected

For autologous donors weighing >50 kg, the 450-mL collection bag is usually used instead of the 500-mL bag, in case the donor cannot give a full unit. If a low-volume (300-405 mL) unit is collected, the red cells are suitable for storage and subsequent autologous transfusion. The plasma from low-volume units cannot be transfused because of the abnormal anticoagulant/plasma ratio. Under-collected units (<300 mL) may be suitable for autologous use with approval of the medical director. For patients weighing <50 kg, there should be a proportional reduction in the volume of blood collected. Regardless of donor weight, the volume collected should not exceed 10.5 mL/kg of the donor's estimated body weight, including the samples for testing.

Serologic Testing

The collecting facility must determine ABO and Rh type on all units. Transfusing facilities must retest ABO and Rh type on units drawn at other facilities, unless the collecting facility tests segments from the unit according to AABB *Standards*.[15(p37)]

Testing for ABO and Rh type must be performed on a properly labeled blood sample from the patient. An antibody screen should be performed to provide for the possible need for allogeneic blood.

Labeling

Units should be clearly labeled with the patient's name and an identifying number, the expiration date of the unit, and, if available, the name of the facility where the patient is to be transfused. The unit should be clearly marked "For Autologous Use Only" if intended for autologous use only. If components have been prepared, the container of each component must be similarly labeled. A biohazard label must be applied when indicated by FDA requirements (see Compliance Considerations). Labeling requirements for autologous units are detailed in the AABB *Standards,*[15(p51)] which parallels the FDA regulations.

Storage

Collection should be scheduled to allow for the longest possible shelf life for collected units. This increases flexibility for the patient and the collecting facility and allows time for the patient to rebuild red cell mass during the interval between blood collection and surgery. Liquid storage is feasible for up to 6 weeks. Some programs store autologous units as Whole Blood for 35 days rather than as RBCs; Whole Blood is simpler to store, and the risk of volume overload subsequent to transfusion is low. The collection of autologous units more than 6 weeks before scheduled surgery has been described, but requires that the red cells be frozen. Although this provides more time for the donor to recover lost red cell mass, freezing and thawing add to the cost of the program, reduce the volume of red cells through processing losses, and complicate blood availability during the perioperative period.

Transfusion of Autologous Units

Autologous transfusion programs should have a system to ensure that if autologous blood is available, it be issued and used before allogeneic components are given. A special "autologous" label may be used with numbering to ensure that the oldest units are issued first. Anesthesiologists, surgeons, and physicians should be educated about the importance of selecting autologous components before allogeneic units are given, and a policy should be in place regarding the issue of autologous, allogeneic, and/or directed units to the operating room.

Records

AABB standards for the proper issue and return of unused autologous units are the same as for allogeneic units.[15(pp45,71)] Records must be maintained that identify the unit and all components made from it, from collection and processing through their eventual disposition.

Adverse Reactions

The investigation of suspected adverse transfusion events should be the same for autologous and allogeneic units. Autologous transfusions have a lower risk of infectious and immune complications but carry a similar risk of bacterial contamination, volume overload, and misadministration compared with volunteer allogeneic units. For these reasons, autologous blood should not be transfused without a clear indication for transfusion.

Continuous Quality Improvement

Several quality improvement issues have been identified for PAD practices.[5] The most important indicator for autologous blood practice is how effectively it reduces allogeneic transfusions to participating patients. The "wastage" rate of autologous units for surgical procedures can also be monitored. However, even for procedures such as joint replacement or radical prostatectomy, a well-designed program may result in 50% of collected units being unused (Fig 5-1).[5,27] Nevertheless, as much as 25% of autologous blood is collected for procedures that seldom require transfusion, such as vaginal hysterectomies and normal vaginal deliveries. Up to 90% of units collected for these procedures are wasted.[14] The additional costs associated

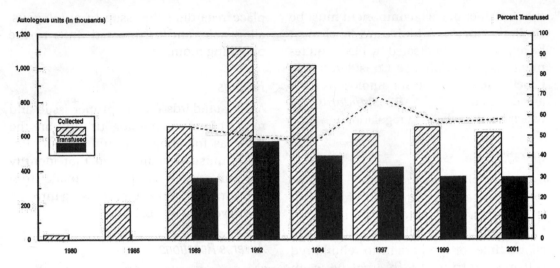

Percent of Total RBCs that Were PAD RBCs

	1980	1986	1989	1992	1994	1997	1999	2001
Collected	0.3	1.5	4.8	8.5	7.8	4.9	4.7	4.0
Transfused		<1.0	3.1	5.0	4.3	3.7	3.0	2.6

Figure 5-1. Autologous RBC collection and transfusion data from 1980 to 2001 in the United States illustrate the rise and fall of interest in PAD. The dashed line in the chart indicates the percent (right axis) of collected PAD units transfused. (Modified with permission from Brecher and Goodnough.[27])

with the collection of autologous units, along with advances in the safety of allogeneic blood, have altered the cost-effectiveness of PAD in many situations.[28] Such cost-effectiveness analyses do not consider an immunomodulatory effect of avoiding allogeneic leukocytes, which remains controversial.[29,30]

Criteria can be established to monitor the appropriateness of autologous transfusions. These criteria may be the same as, or different from, those established for allogeneic units.[24] As with allogeneic blood, transfusion of preoperatively donated autologous blood carries the same risks associated with administrative error or bacterial contamination. Autologous programs should be monitored for unavailability of autologous blood when needed, the transfusion of allogeneic blood before autologous blood, and identification errors.

Evolving Issues in Preoperative Autologous Services

Selection of Patients

Attempts to stratify patients into groups at high and low risk for needing transfusion based on the baseline level of hemoglobin and on the type of procedure show some promise. In a Canadian study using a point score system, 80% of patients undergoing orthopedic procedures were identified to be at low risk (<10%) for transfusion, so autologous blood procurement for these patients would not be recommended.[31] However, one problem with algorithms that consider the estimated blood loss and preoperative hematocrit is that blood losses are difficult to measure[32,33] or predict because specific surgical procedures performed even by the same surgeon can be accompanied by a wide range of blood losses.

The Role of Aggressive Phlebotomy and the Use of Erythropoietin

The efficacy of PAD is dependent on the degree to which the patient's erythropoiesis increases the production of red cells.[25,34-36] The endogenous erythropoietin response and compensatory erythropoiesis are suboptimal under "standard" conditions of one blood unit donated weekly. Weekly PAD is accompanied by an 11% (with no oral iron supplementation) to 19% (with oral iron supplementation) expansion in red cell volume over a 3-week period, which is not sufficient to prevent increasing anemia in patients undergoing PAD.[34,35] If the erythropoietic response to autologous blood phlebotomy is not able to maintain the patient's hematocrit level during the donation interval, the donation of autologous blood may be harmful.[37] This outcome was confirmed in a study of patients undergoing hysterectomies,[38] in which it was shown that PAD resulted in perioperative anemia and an increased likelihood of any blood transfusion. A published mathematical model[37] illustrates the relationship between anticipated surgical blood losses, the level of hematocrit that the physician may want to maintain perioperatively, and the need for autologous blood donation for individual patients (Fig 5-2). Models such as this may be helpful in designing autologous procurement programs or monitoring their value through quality assurance.

In contrast to autologous blood donation under "standard" conditions, studies of "aggressive" autologous blood phlebotomy (twice weekly for 3 weeks, beginning 25 to 35 days before surgery) have demonstrated that endogenous erythropoietin levels do increase, along with enhanced erythropoie-

sis representing 19% to 26% red cell volume expansion.[39-41] Exogenous (pharmacologic) erythropoietin therapy to further stimulate erythropoiesis (up to 50% red cell volume expansion[39-41]) during autologous phlebotomy has been approved in Canada and Japan but not in the United States.[42]

Transfusion Trigger

Disagreement exists about the proper hemoglobin/hematocrit level ("transfusion trigger") at which autologous blood should be given.[23] Autologous blood transfusion is not without risks to the recipient; these include misidentification of patients or units, bacterial contamination of stored units, and volume overload. The case can be made that autologous and allogeneic blood transfusion triggers should be similar because the additional mortality risks of allogeneic blood now approach the risks of mortality from administrative errors associated with both autologous and allogeneic blood.[43] Data from a well-designed clinical trial indicate that even critical care patients can tolerate substantial anemia (to hemoglobin ranges of 7 to 9 g/dL) with no apparent benefit from more aggressive transfusion therapy.[44]

Cost-Effectiveness

Although autologous blood collections have become popular, the costs associated with their collection are usually higher than those associated with the collection of allogeneic blood. The continued need for autologous blood programs has been questioned because of the reduced risk of allogeneic blood transfusions and pressure to reduce health-care costs.[27] Table 5-4 lists suggestions for improving the efficiency of hospital-based autologous blood programs without sacrificing safety.[45]

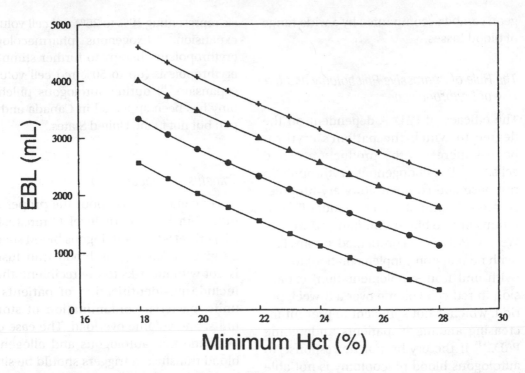

Figure 5-2. Relationship of estimated blood loss (EBL) and minimum (nadir) hematocrit during hospitalization at various initial hematocrit levels (30%,35%,40%,45%) in a surgical patient with a whole blood volume of 5000 mL. ■ = 30%; ● = 35%; ▲ = 40%; + = 45%.(Reprinted with permission from Cohen and Brecher.[37])

Preoperative Collection of Components

Some workers believe that preoperative or intraoperative collection of platelet-rich plasma during cardiopulmonary bypass surgery may improve hemostasis and decrease allogeneic exposures, but others have found no benefit.[46] Preoperative collection of autologous platelets, especially in cardiac surgery, is often impractical because patients may be taking antiplatelet drugs; surgery is often scheduled on an emergency basis; and relatively low numbers of platelets are harvested.

Recently, autologous platelet collection using commercial point-of-care collection systems has been advocated to produce a platelet gel for topical use.[47] Platelet gel is created by adding calcium chloride and thrombin to a platelet concentrate. The platelet gel serves as a rich source of platelet-derived growth factors, which have been reported in small studies to enhance tissue repair and wound healing.[48,49] Larger randomized clinical trials are needed to establish the clinical efficacy of this product. Platelet gel is not FDA-approved yet.

Acute Normovolemic Hemodilution

Acute normovolemic hemodilution (ANH) is the removal of whole blood from a patient, with concurrent restoration of the circulating blood volume with an acellular fluid shortly before an anticipated significant surgical blood loss. To minimize the manual labor associated with hemodilution, the blood should be collected in standard blood bags containing anticoag-

Table 5-4. Suggestions for Making Autologous Blood Transfusion Protocols Cost-Effective

1. Use standardized indications for preoperative autologous blood collection and transfusion.
2. Streamline the autologous blood donor interview.
3. Discontinue serologic tests for infectious disease markers following autologous blood collections.
4. Simplify the donation process for uncomplicated patients.
5. Limit the use of frozen blood.
6. Store autologous whole blood, rather than components.
7. Use standardized indications and appropriate technology for intraoperative and postoperative autologous blood recovery.
8. Share intraoperative blood recovery resources among institutions.
9. Cautiously adopt new research applications for autologous blood techniques.

ulant on a tilt-rocker with automatic cut-off via volume sensors. Then, the blood is stored at room temperature and reinfused during surgery after major blood loss has ceased, or sooner if indicated. Simultaneous infusions of crystalloid (3 mL crystalloid for each 1 mL of blood withdrawn) and colloid (dextrans, starches, gelatin, albumin, 1 mL for each 1 mL of blood withdrawn) have been recommended.[50]

Subsequent intraoperative fluid management is based on the usual surgical requirements. Blood units are reinfused in the reverse order of collection. The first unit collected, and therefore the last unit transfused, has the highest hematocrit and concentration of coagulation factors and platelets. Although this technique has been primarily developed and used in Europe, increasing interest in the United States has led to data that show promise as an alternative method of autologous blood procurement.[51] Augmented hemodilution (replacement of ANH collected or surgical blood lost in part by oxygen therapeutics) has the advantage of not being limited by anemia. Its use is restricted to the investigational setting until these solutions are approved by the FDA.

Physiologic Considerations

Conserved Red Cell Mass

The chief benefit of ANH is the reduction of red cell losses when whole blood is shed perioperatively at lower hematocrit levels after ANH has been completed.[52] Mathematical modeling has suggested that severe ANH to preoperative hematocrit levels of less than 20%, accompanied by substantial blood losses, would be required before the red cell volume "saved" by ANH would become clinically important.[53] However, the equivalent of one blood unit[54] can be "saved" by ANH,[55] which approaches the red cell volume expansion generated by PAD under standard conditions (Table 5-3).

Improved Oxygenation

Withdrawal of whole blood and replacement with crystalloid or colloid solution decrease arterial oxygen content, but compensatory hemodynamic mechanisms and the existence of surplus oxygen-delivery capacity make ANH safe. A sudden decrease in red cell concentration lowers blood viscosity, thereby decreasing peripheral resistance and increasing cardiac output. If cardiac output can effectively compensate, oxygen delivery to the tissues at a hematocrit of 25% to 30% is as good as, but no better than, oxygen delivery at a hematocrit of 30% to 35%.[56]

Preservation of Hemostasis

Because blood collected by ANH is stored at room temperature and is usually returned to the patient within 8 hours of collection, there is little deterioration of platelets or coagulation factors. The hemostatic value of blood collected by ANH is of questionable benefit for orthopedic or urologic surgery because plasma and platelets are rarely indicated in this setting. Its value in protecting plasma and platelets from the acquired coagulopathy of extracorporeal circulation in cardiac surgery is better established.[46,57]

Clinical Studies

Prospective randomized studies in radical prostatectomy,[58] knee replacement,[59] and hip replacement[60] suggest that ANH can be considered equivalent to PAD as a method of autologous blood procurement. Additional, selected clinical trials of ANH are summarized in Table 5-5.[61-67] Reviews[68,69] and commentaries[70] on the merits of ANH have been published. However, a recently published meta-analysis of 42 clinical trials of ANH found only a modest benefit with unproven safety.[71] When ANH and reinfusion are accomplished in the operating room by on-site personnel, the procurement and administration costs are minimized. Blood obtained during ANH does not require the commitment of the patient's time, transportation, costs, and loss of work time that can be associated with PAD. The wastage of PAD units (approximately 50% of units collected) also is eliminated with ANH. Additionally, autologous blood units procured by ANH require no inventory or testing costs. Because the blood never leaves the patient's room, ANH minimizes the possibility of an administrative or a clerical error that could lead to an ABO-incompatible blood transfusion and death, as well as bacterial contamination associated with prolonged storage at 4 C.

Practical Considerations

The following considerations are important in establishing an ANH program:

1. Decisions about ANH should be based on the surgical procedure and on the patient's preoperative blood volume and hematocrit, target hemodilution hematocrit, and other physiologic variables.

2. The institution's policy and procedures and the mechanisms for educating staff should be established and periodically reviewed.

3. There should be careful monitoring of the patient's circulating volume and perfusion status during the procedure.

4. Blood must be collected in an aseptic manner, ordinarily into standard blood collection bags with citrate anticoagulant.

5. Units must be properly labeled and stored. The label must contain, at a minimum, the patient's full name, medical record number, date, and time of collection, and the statement "For Autologous Use Only." Room temperature storage should not exceed 8 hours. Units maintained at room temperature should be reinfused in the reverse order of collection to provide the maximum number of functional platelets and coagulation factors in the last units infused. If more time elapses between collection and transfusion,

Table 5-5. Selected Clinical Trials of Acute Normovolemic Hemodilution (ANH)

Surgery	Estimated Blood Loss (mL)			Postoperative Hematocrit (%)			Allogeneic RBC-Containing Units or Liters Transfused			Reference
	Control	ANH	p Value	Control	ANH	p Value	Control	ANH	p Value	
Vascular	2250	2458	NS	NR	33.0	NR	6.0	2.6	<0.01	61
Liver resection	1479	1284	NS	37.9	33.8	<0.01	3.8	0.4	<0.001	62
Hip arthroplasty	1800	2000	NS	38.4	32.4	NS	(2.1)	(0.9)	NR	63
Spinal fusion	5490	1700	<0.005	NR	28.7	NR	8.6	<1.0	<0.001	64
Colectomy	NR	NR	NR	37.0	35.0	NR	2.4	0	NR	65
Prostate	1246	1106	NS	35.5	31.8	<0.001	0.16	0	NS	66
Prostate	1717	1710	NS	29.5	27.9	<0.5	0.30	0.13	NS	67

Modified from Brecher and Rosenfeld.[53] NR = not reported; NS = not significant.

the blood should be stored in a monitored refrigerator. ANH blood collected from an open system (eg, from a central venous line or an arterial catheter) may be stored for up to 8 hours at room temperature or 24 hours in a monitored refrigerator. Policies, procedures, and guidelines must be developed for ANH by an experienced group of anesthesiologists in conjunction with the operating room's nursing staff and the hospital's blood bank and transfusion services.[68] These will include indications for ANH, monitoring requirements, endpoints for blood withdrawal and transfusion, types and amounts of replacement fluids (ie,

colloid/crystalloid ratios), and full adherence to AABB guidelines. Some practical considerations are listed in Table 5-6. Suggested criteria for patient selection are listed in Table 5-7.

Intraoperative Blood Collection

The term intraoperative blood collection or recovery describes the technique of collecting and reinfusing blood lost by a patient during surgery. The oxygen-transport properties of recovered red cells are equivalent to stored allogeneic red cells. The survival of recovered blood cells appears to be at least comparable to that of

Table 5-6. Practical Considerations for Acute Normovolemic Hemodilution (ANH)

- There must be a physician responsible for the perioperative blood recovery program. Responsibilities shall include compliance with AABB standards,[16] the establishment of written policies and procedures, and periodic review of those policies and procedures.
- The blood bank or transfusion service should participate in the development of policies and procedures related to the perioperative blood recovery program.
- Blood collected perioperatively shall not be transfused to other patients.
- Methods for perioperative blood collection and reinfusion shall be safe and aseptic and ensure accurate identification of all blood and components collected. The equipment used shall be pyrogen-free, shall include a filter capable of retaining particles potentially harmful to the recipient, and must preclude air embolism. If the blood is warmed before infusion, warming protocols apply.
- A complete written protocol of all perioperative collection procedures should be maintained, including selection of anticoagulants and solutions used for processing, labeling of collected blood or components, and procedures for the prevention and treatment of adverse reactions.
- All facilities regularly collecting blood by perioperative procedures should establish a program of quality control and quality assurance. Written procedures should include criteria for acceptable performance. Records of results should be reviewed and retained. Quality control measurements should address the safety and quality of the blood or components collected for the recipient.
- Units collected for ANH shall be stored under one of the following conditions before the start of transfusion:
  — At room temperature, for up to 8 hours
  — At 1 to 6 C for up to 24 hours, provided that storage at 1 to 6 C is begun within 8 hours of initiating the collection.

Table 5-7. Criteria for Selection of Patients for Acute Normovolemic Hemodilution

1. Likelihood of transfusion exceeds 10% (ie, blood requested for crossmatch according to maximum surgical blood order schedule).
2. Preoperative hemoglobin level of at least 12 g/dL.
3. Absence of clinically significant coronary, pulmonary, renal, or liver disease.
4. Absence of severe hypertension.
5. Absence of infection and risk of bacteremia.

---

transfused allogeneic red cells.[72] Intraoperative collection is contraindicated when certain procoagulant materials (eg, topical collagen) are applied to the surgical field because systemic activation of coagulation may result. Microaggregate filters (40 microns) are used most often because recovered blood may contain tissue debris, small blood clots, or bone fragments.

Cell washing devices can provide the equivalent of 12 units of banked blood per hour to a massively bleeding patient.[72] Data regarding adverse events of reinfusion of recovered blood have been published.[73] Air embolus is a potentially serious problem. Three fatalities from air embolus were reported over a 5-year interval to the New York State Department of Public Health, for an overall fatality risk of one in 30,000.[43] Hemolysis of recovered blood can occur during suctioning from the surface instead of from deep pools of shed blood. For this reason, manufacturers' guidelines recommend a maximum vacuum setting of no more than 150 torr. One study found that vacuum settings as high as 300 torr could be used when necessary, without causing excessive hemolysis.[74] The clinical importance of free hemoglobin in the concentrations usually seen has not been established, although excessive free hemoglobin may indicate inadequate washing. Positive bacterial cultures from recovered blood are sometimes observed; however, clinical infection is rare.[75]

Most programs use machines that collect shed blood, wash it, and concentrate the red cells. This process typically results in 225-mL units of saline-suspended red cells with a hematocrit of 50% to 60%. Patients exhibit a level of plasma-free hemoglobin that is usually higher than after allogeneic transfusion. Sodium and chloride concentrations are the same as in the saline wash solution, and potassium concentration is low. The infusate contains minimal coagulation factors and platelets.

Clinical Studies

As with PAD and ANH, collection and recovery of intraoperative autologous blood should undergo scrutiny with regard to both safety and efficacy. Controlled studies in cardiothoracic surgery have reported conflicting results when transfusion requirements and clinical outcome were followed.[75,76] Although the collection of a minimum of one blood unit equivalent is possible for less expensive (with unwashed blood) methods, it is generally agreed that at least two blood unit equivalents need to be recovered using a cell-recovery instrument (with washed blood) in order to achieve cost-effectiveness.[77] The value of intraoperative blood collection has been best defined for vascular surgeries with large blood losses, such as aortic aneurysm repair and liver transplantation.[78] However, a prospective randomized trial[79] of intraoperative recovery and reinfusion in patients undergoing aortic aneurysm repair showed no benefit in the reduction of allogeneic blood exposure. A mathematical model of cell recovery suggests that when it is combined with normovolemic anemia, the need for allogeneic transfusion can be avoided—even with large blood loss, eg, 5 to 10 liters.[80] The value of this technology may rest on cost savings and blood inventory considerations in patients with substantial blood losses.

Medical Controversies

Collection devices that neither concentrate nor wash shed blood before reinfusion increase the risk of adverse effects. Shed blood has undergone varying degrees of coagulation/fibrinolysis and hemolysis, and infusion of large volumes of washed or unwashed blood has been described in association with disseminated intravascular coagulation.[81] Factors that affect the degree of coagulation and clot lysis include:

1. Whether the patient had received systemic anticoagulation.
2. The amount and type of anticoagulant used.
3. The extent of contact between blood and serosal surfaces.
4. The extent of contact between blood and artificial surfaces.
5. The degree of turbulence during collection.

In general, blood collected at low flow rates or during slow bleeding from patients who are not systemically anticoagulated will have undergone coagulation and fibrinolysis and will not contribute to hemostasis upon reinfusion.

The high suction pressure and surface skimming during aspiration and the turbulence or mechanical compression that occurs in roller pumps and plastic tubing make some degree of hemolysis inevitable. High concentrations of free hemoglobin may be nephrotoxic to patients with impaired renal function. Many programs limit the quantity of recovered blood that may be reinfused without processing.

Practical Considerations

Collection and recovery services require the coordinated efforts of surgeons, anesthesiologists, transfusion medicine specialists, and specific personnel trained in the use of special equipment. Equipment options may include:

1. Devices that collect recovered blood for direct reinfusion.
2. Devices that collect recovered blood, which is then concentrated and washed in a separate cell washer.
3. High-speed machines that automatically concentrate and wash recovered red cells.

Some hospitals develop their own programs, whereas others contract with outside services. Each hospital's needs should dictate whether blood collection and recovery are used and how they are achieved.

Processing Before Reinfusion

Several devices automatically process recovered blood before reinfusion. Vacuum suction and simultaneous anticoagulation are used for collection. To minimize hemolysis, the vacuum level should ordinarily not exceed 150 torr, although higher levels of suction may occasionally be needed during periods of rapid bleeding. Either citrate (ACD) or heparin may be used as an anticoagulant. Blood is held in a reservoir until centrifuged and washed with a volume of saline that varies between 500 and 1500 mL. If not infused immediately, the unit must be labeled with the patient's name and identification number, the date and time collection was initiated, and the statement "For Autologous Use Only."

An alternative approach is to collect blood in a canister system designed for direct reinfusion and then concentrate and wash the recovered red cells in a blood bank cell washer. Intraoperatively collected and recovered blood must be handled in the transfusion service laboratory like any other autologous unit. The unit should be reinfused through a filter.

Direct Reinfusion

Systems are available that collect recovered blood and return it directly. These systems generally consist of a suction catheter attached to a disposable collection bag or rigid plastic canister, to which anticoagulant (citrate or heparin) may have been added. Blood is suctioned into the holding canister before being reinfused through a microaggregate filter. Low-vacuum suction and minimal hemolysis are preferred in nonwashed systems.

Requirements and Recommendations

The AABB requires a process that includes patient and storage bag identification and time collected with expiration date.[16(p10)] Units collected intraoperatively should be labeled with the patient's first and last name, hospital identification number, the date and time of collection and expiration, and the statement "For Autologous Use Only."[16(p10)]

Conditions for storage and expiration of autologous components collected in the operating room are listed in Table 5-8.[16(p14)] If the blood leaves the patient for washing or storage in a remote location, there must be appropriate procedures to ensure proper labeling of the blood according to AABB standards.[16(pp9,10)]

Hospitals with collection and recovery programs should establish written policies and procedures that are regularly reviewed by a physician who has been assigned responsibility for the program. Transfusion medicine specialists should play an active role in design, implementation, and operation of the program. Written policies must be in place for the proper collection, labeling, and storage of intraoperative autologous blood. Equipment and techniques for collection and infusion must ensure that the blood is aseptic. Quality management should include evaluation of the appropriate use of blood collection and recovery services and adequate training of personnel. Written protocols, procedure logs, machine maintenance, procedures for handling adverse events, and documentation are recommended.[24]

Postoperative Blood Collection

Postoperative blood collection denotes the recovery of blood from surgical drains followed by reinfusion, with or without processing. In some programs, postoperative shed blood is collected into sterile canisters and reinfused, without processing, through a microaggregate filter. Recovered blood is dilute, partially hemolyzed and defibrinated, and may contain high concentrations of cytokines. For these reasons, most programs set an upper limit on the volume (eg, 1400 mL) of unprocessed blood that can be reinfused. If transfusion of blood has not begun within 6 hours of initiating the collection, the blood must be discarded. Hospitals should establish written policies, procedures, labeling requirements, quality assurance, and review consistent with AABB standards.[16(p2)]

Table 5-8. Handling, Storage, and Expiration of Intraoperative Blood Collections

Collection Type	Storage Temperature	Expiration	Special Conditions
Acute normovolemic hemodilution	Room temperature	8 hours from start of collection	None
	1-6 C	24 hours from start of collection	Storage at 1-6 C shall begin within 8 hours of start of collection
Intraoperative blood recovered with processing	Room temperature	4 hours from end of collection	None
	1-6 C	24 hours from start of collection	Storage at 1-6 C shall begin within 4 hours of start of collection
Intraoperative blood recovered without processing	Room temperature or 1-6 C	4 hours from end of collection	None
Shed blood under postoperative or posttraumatic conditions with or without processing	N/A	6 hours from start of collection	None
Non-red-cell component preparation	Room temperature	Shall be used before leaving the operating room	None

Clinical Studies

The evolution of cardiac surgery has been accompanied by a broad experience in postoperative conservation of blood. Postoperative autologous blood transfusion is practiced widely, but not uniformly. Prospective and controlled trials have disagreed over the efficacy of postoperative blood recovery in cardiac surgery patients; at least three such studies have demonstrated lack of efficacy,[82-84] but at least two studies have shown benefit.[85,86] The disparity of the results in these studies may be explained, in part, by differences in transfusion practices. Modification of physician transfusion practices may have been an uncredited intervention in these blood conservation studies.

In the postoperative orthopedic surgical setting, several reports have similarly described the successful recovery and reinfusion of washed[87] and unwashed[88,89] wound drainage from patients undergoing arthroplasty. Red cells recovered in this setting appear to have normal survival in the circulation.[90] The volume of reinfused drainage blood has been reported to be as much as 3000 mL and averages more than 1100 mL in patients undergoing cementless knee replacement.[89] Because the red cell content of the fluid collected is low (hematocrit levels of 20%), the volume of red cells reinfused is often small.[91] A prospective randomized study of postoperative recovery and reinfusion in patients undergoing total knee or hip replacement found no differences in perioperative hemoglobin levels or allogeneic blood transfusions between patients who did or did not have joint drainage devices.[92] The safety of reinfused unwashed orthopedic wound drainage has been controversial. Theoretical concerns have been expressed regarding infusion of potentially harmful materials in recovered blood, including free hemoglobin, red cell stroma, marrow fat, toxic irritants, tissue or methacrylate debris, fibrin degradation products, activated coagulation factors, and complement. Although two small studies have reported complications,[93,94] several larger studies have reported no serious adverse effects when drainage was passed through a standard 40-micron blood filter.[88,89,95]

Patient Selection

The potential for decreasing exposure to allogeneic blood among orthopedic patients undergoing postoperative blood collection (whether washed or unwashed) is greatest for cementless bilateral total knee replacement, revision hip or knee replacement, and long segment spinal fusion. As in the case of intraoperative recovery, blood loss must be sufficient to warrant the additional cost of processing technology.[96,97] As in the selection of patients who can benefit from PAD and ANH, prospective identification of patients who can benefit from intra- and postoperative autologous blood recovery is possible if anticipated surgical blood losses and the perioperative "transfusion trigger" are taken into account (Fig 5-2).

References

1. Pub. Law No. 101-336, 104 Stat. 327 (1990). Codified at 42 USC §12101-213.
2. The ADA, HIV, and autologous blood donation. Association Bulletin 98-5. Bethesda, MD: AABB, 1998.
3. Goodnough LT. Preoperative autologous donation. In: Spence RK, ed. Problems in general surgery. Philadelphia: Lippincott Williams & Wilkins, 2000;17:25-31.
4. Bierbaum BE, Callaghan JJ, Galante JO, Rubash HE. An analysis of blood management in patients having total hip or knee arthroplasty. J Bone J Surg 1999;81A:2-10.
5. Renner SW, Howanitz PJ, Bachner P. Preoperative autologous blood donation in 612 hospitals. Arch Pathol Lab Med 1992;116:613-9.
6. Silvergleid AJ. Safety and effectiveness of predeposit autologous transfusions in preteen and adolescent children. JAMA 1987;257:3403-4.
7. Chaplin H, Mischeaux JR, Inkster MD, Sherman LA. Frozen storage of 11 units of sickle cell red cells for autologous transfusion of a single patient. Transfusion 1986;26:341-5.
8. Meryman HT, Hornblower M. Freezing and deglycerolizing sickle trait red blood cells. Transfusion 1976;16:627-32.
9. Mann M, Sacks HJ, Goldfinger D. Safety of autologous blood donation prior to elective surgery for a variety of potentially high risk patients. Transfusion 1983;23:229-32.
10. Popovsky MA, Whitaker B, Arnold NL. Severe outcomes of allogeneic and autologous blood donation: Frequency and characterization. Transfusion 1995;35:734-7.
11. Goodnough LT, Brecher ME, Kanter MH, AuBuchon JP. Transfusion medicine. First of two parts. Blood transfusion. N Engl J Med 1999;340:438-47.
12. Dodd RY, Notari EP, Stramer SL. Current prevalence and incidence of infectious disease markers and estimated window-period risk in the American Red Cross blood donor populations. Transfusion 2002;42:975-9.
13. Thomas MJG, Gillon J, Desmond MJ. Preoperative autologous blood donation. Transfusion 1996;36:633-9.
14. Sayers MH. Controversies in transfusion medicine. Autologous blood donation in pregnancy: Con. Transfusion 1990;30:172-4.
15. Silva MA, ed. Standards for blood banks and transfusion services. 23rd ed. Bethesda, MD: AABB, 2005.
16. Santrach P, ed. Standards for perioperative autologous blood collection and administration. 1st ed. Bethesda, MD: AABB, 2001.

17. Food and Drug Administration. Memorandum: Guidance for autologous blood and blood components. (March 15, 1989) Rockville, MD: CBER Office of Communication, Training, and Manufacturers Assistance, 1989.

18. Food and Drug Administration. Memorandum: Autologous blood collection and processing procedures. (February 12, 1990) Rockville, MD: CBER Office of Communication, Training, and Manufacturers Assistance, 1990.

19. Food and Drug Administration. General requirements for blood, blood components, and blood derivatives; donor notification. 21 CFR 630.6. Fed Regist 2001;66(112):31165-77.

20. Food and Drug Administration. Requirements for testing human blood donors for evidence of infection due to communicable disease agents. 21 CFR 610.40. Fed Regist 2001; 66(112):31146-65.

21. Food and Drug Administration. Guidance for industry: Use of nucleic acid tests on pooled and individual samples from donors of whole blood and blood components (including Source Plasma and Source Leukocytes) to adequately and appropriately reduce the risk of transmission of HIV-1 and HCV. (October 21, 2004) Rockville, MD: CBER Office of Communication, Training, and Manufacturers Assistance, 2004.

22. Code of federal regulations. Title 42 CFR Part 72.3. Washington, DC: US Government Printing Office, 2004 (revised annually).

23. National Heart, Lung, and Blood Institute Autologous Transfusion Symposium Working Group. Autologous transfusion: Current trends and research issues. Transfusion 1995;35:525-31.

24. Becker J, Blackall D, Evans C, et al for the Scientific Section Coordinating Committee. Guidelines for blood utilization review. Bethesda, MD: AABB, 2001:20-4.

25. Goodnough LT, Skikne B, Brugnara C. Erythropoietin, iron, and erythropoiesis. Blood 2000;96:823-33.

26. Toy P, Ahn D, Bacchetti P. When should the first of two autologous donations be made? (abstract) Transfusion 1994;34(Suppl):14S.

27. Brecher ME, Goodnough LT. The rise and fall of preoperative autologous blood donation (editorial). Transfusion 2001;41:1459-62.

28. Etchason J, Petz L, Keeler E, et al. The cost-effectiveness of preoperative autologous blood donations. N Engl J Med 1995;332:719-24.

29. Vamvakas EC. Meta-analysis of randomized controlled trials comparing the risk of postoperative infection between recipients of allogeneic and autologous blood. Vox Sang 2002;83:339-46.

30. Vanderlinde E, Heal JM, Blumberg N. Autologous transfusion. Br Med J 2002;324:772-5.

31. Larocque BJ, Gilbert K, Brien WF. Prospective validation of a point score system for predicting blood transfusion following hip or knee replacement. Transfusion 1998;38:932-7.

32. Brecher MA, Monk TG, Goodnough LT. A standardized method for calculating blood loss. Transfusion 1997;37:1070-4.

33. Rosencher N. Orthopedic surgery transfusion hemoglobin overview (OSTHEO) study. Transfusion 2003;43:459-69.

34. Kasper SM, Gerlich W, Buzello W. Preoperative red cell production in patients undergoing weekly autologous blood donation. Transfusion 1997;37:1058-62.

35. Kasper SM, Lazansky H, Stark C, et al. Efficacy of oral iron supplementation is not enhanced by additional intravenous iron during autologous blood donation. Transfusion 1998;38:764-70.

36. Weisbach V, Skoda P, Rippel R, et al. Oral or intravenous iron as an adjunct to autologous blood donation in elective surgery: A randomized, controlled study. Transfusion 1999; 39:465-72.

37. Cohen JA, Brecher ME. Preoperative autologous blood donation: Benefit or detriment? A mathematical analysis. Transfusion 1995;35:640-4.

38. Kanter MH, Van Maanen D, Anders KH, et al. Preoperative autologous blood donation before elective hysterectomy. JAMA 1996;276: 798-801.

39. Goodnough LT, Rudnick S, Price TH, et al. Increased preoperative collection of autologous blood with recombinant human erythropoietin therapy. N Engl J Med 1989;321:1163-8.

40. Goodnough LT, Price TH, Rudnick S, Soegiarso RW. Preoperative red blood cell production in patients undergoing aggressive autologous blood phlebotomy with and without erythropoietin therapy. Transfusion 1992;32:441-5.

41. Goodnough LT, Price TH, Friedman KD, et al. A phase III trial of recombinant human erythropoietin therapy in non-anemic orthopedic patients subjected to aggressive autologous blood phlebotomy: Dose, response, toxicity, efficacy. Transfusion 1994;34:66-71.

42. Goodnough LT, Monk TG, Andriole GL. Erythropoietin therapy. N Engl J Med 1997;336: 933-8.

43. Linden JV, Wagner K, Voytovich AE, Sheehan J. Transfusion errors in New York State: An analysis of 10 years' experience. Transfusion 2000;40:1207-13.

44. Hébert PC, Wells G, Blajchman MA, et al. A multicenter, randomized, controlled clinical trial of transfusion requirements in critical care. N Engl J Med 1999;340:409-17.

45. Kruskall MS, Yomtovian R, Dzik WH, et al. On improving the cost effectiveness of autologous blood transfusion practices. Transfusion 1994;34:259-64.

46. Triulzi DJ, Gilmor GD, Ness PM, et al. Efficacy of autologous fresh whole blood or platelet-rich plasma in adult cardiac surgery. Transfusion 1995;35:627-34.

47. Kevy SV, Jacobson MS. Comparison of methods for point of care preparation of autologous platelet gel. J Extra Corpor Technol 2004;36:28-35.

48. Crovetti G, Martinelli G, Issi M, et al. Platelet gel for healing cutaneous chronic wounds. Transfus Apheresis Sci 2004;30:145-51.

49. Mazzucco L, Medici D, Serra M, et al. The use of autologous platelet gel to treat difficult to heal wounds: A pilot study. Transfusion 2004; 44:1013-8.

50. Goodnough LT, Brecher ME, Monk TG. Acute normovolemic hemodilution in surgery. Hematology 1992;2:413-20.

51. Goodnough LT, Brecher ME, Kanter MH, AuBuchon JP. Transfusion medicine. Second of two parts. Blood conservation. N Engl J Med 1999;340:525-33.

52. Messmer K, Kreimeier M, Intagliett A. Present state of intentional hemodilution. Eur Surg Res 1986;18:254-63.

53. Brecher ME, Rosenfeld M. Mathematical and computer modeling of acute normovolemic hemodilution. Transfusion 1994;34:176-9.

54. Goodnough LT, Bravo J, Hsueh Y, et al. Red blood cell volume in autologous and homologous units: Implications for risk/benefit assessment for autologous blood "crossover" and directed blood transfusion. Transfusion 1989;29:821-2.

55. Goodnough LT, Grishaber JE, Monk TG, Catalona WJ. Acute normovolemic hemodilution in patients undergoing radical suprapubic prostatectomy: A case study analysis. Anesth Analg 1994;78:932-7.

56. Weiskopf RB. Mathematical analysis of isovolemic hemodilution indicates that it can decrease the need for allogeneic blood transfusion. Transfusion 1995;35:37-41.

57. Petry AF, Jost T, Sievers H. Reduction of homologous blood requirements by blood pooling at the onset of cardiopulmonary bypass. J Thorac Cardiovasc Surg 1994;1097:1210-14.

58. Monk TG, Goodnough LT, Brecher ME, et al. A prospective, randomized trial of three blood conservation strategies for radical prostatectomy. Anesthesiology 1999;91:24-33.

59. Goodnough LT, Merkel K, Monk TG, Despotis GJ. A randomized trial of acute normovolemic hemodilution compared to preopera-tive autologous blood donation in total knee arthroplasty. Vox Sang 1999;77:11-16.

60. Goodnough LT, Despotis GJ, Merkel K, Monk TG. A randomized trial of acute normovolemic hemodilution compared to preoperative autologous blood donation in total hip arthroplasty. Transfusion 2000;40:1054-7.

61. Davies MJ, Cronin KD, Domanique C. Haemodilution for major vascular surgery using 3.5% polygeline (Haemaccel). Anaesth Intensive Care 1982;10:265-70.

62. Sejourne P, Poirier A, Meakins JL, et al. Effects of haemodilution on transfusion requirements in liver resection. Lancet 1989;ii:1380-2.

63. Rosenberg B, Wulff K. Regional lung function following hip arthroplasty and preoperative normovolemic hemodilution. Acta Anaesthesiol Scand 1979;23:242-7.

64. Kafer ER, Isley MR, Hansen T, et al. Automated acute normovolemic hemodilution reduces blood transfusion requirements for spinal fusion (abstract). Anesth Analg 1986; 65(Suppl):S76.

65. Rose D, Coustoftides T. Intraoperative normovolemic hemodilution. J Surg Res 1981;31:375-81.

66. Ness PM, Bourke DL, Walsh PC. A randomized trial of perioperative hemodilution versus transfusion of preoperatively deposited autologous blood in elective surgery. Transfusion 1991;31:226-30.

67. Monk TG, Goodnough LT, Birkmeyer JD, et al. Acute normovolemic hemodilution is a cost-effective alternative to preoperative autologous blood donation by patients undergoing radical retropubic prostatectomy. Transfusion 1995;35:559-65.

68. Shander A. Acute normovolemic hemodilution. In: Spence RK, ed. Problems in general surgery. Philadelphia: Lippincott Williams & Wilkins, 1999;17:32-40.

69. Monk TG, Goodnough LT, Brecher ME, et al. Acute normovolemic hemodilution can replace preoperative autologous blood donation as a standard of care for autologous blood procurement in radical prostatectomy. Anesth Analg 1997;85:953-8.

70. Goodnough LT, Monk TG, Brecher ME. Acute normovolemic hemodilution should replace preoperative autologous blood donation before elective surgery. Transfusion 1998;38: 473-7.

71. Segal JB, Blasco-Colmenares E, Norris EJ, Guallar E. Preoperative acute normovolemic hemodilution: A meta-analysis. Transfusion 2004;44:632-44.

72. Williamson KR, Taswell HF. Intraoperative blood salvage: A review. Transfusion 1991;31: 662-75.

73. Domen RE. Adverse reactions associated with autologous blood transfusion: Evaluation and incidence at a large academic hospital. Transfusion 1998;38:296-300.

74. Gregoretti S. Suction-induced hemolysis at various vacuum pressures: Implications for intraoperative blood salvage. Transfusion 1996;36:57-60.

75. Bell K, Stott K, Sinclair CJ, et al. A controlled trial of intra-operative autologous transfusion in cardiothoracic surgery measuring effect on transfusion requirements and clinical outcome. Transfus Med 1992;2:295-300.

76. Tempe DK, Banjerjee A, Virmani S, et al. Comparison of the effects of a cell saver and low dose aprotinin on blood loss and homologous blood use in patients undergoing valve surgery. J Cardiothorac Vasc Anesth 2001;15:326-30.

77. Bovill DF, Moulton CW, Jackson WS, et al. The efficacy of intraoperative autologous transfusion in major orthopaedic surgery: A regression analysis. Orthopedics 1986;9:1403-7.

78. Goodnough LT, Monk TG, Sicard G, et al. Intraoperative salvage in patients undergoing elective abdominal aortic aneurysm repair. An analysis of costs and benefits. J Vasc Surg 1996;24:213-8.

79. Claggett GP, Valentine RJ, Jackson MR, et al. A randomized trial of intraoperative transfusion during aortic surgery. J Vasc Surg 1999;29:22-31.

80. Waters JH, Karafa MT. A mathematical model of cell salvage efficiency. Anesth Analg 2002;95:1312-7.

81. de Haan J, Boonstra P, Monnink S, et al. Retransfusion of suctioned blood during cardiopulmonary bypass impairs hemostasis. Ann Thorac Surg 1995;59:901-7.

82. Ward HB, Smith RA, Candis KP, et al. A prospective, randomized trial of autotransfusion after routine cardiac surgery. Ann Thorac Surg 1993;56:137-41.

83. Thurer RL, Lytle BW, Cosgrove DM, Loop FD. Autotransfusion following cardiac operations: A randomized, prospective study. Ann Thorac Surg 1979;27:500-6.

84. Roberts SP, Early GL, Brown B, et al. Autotransfusion of unwashed mediastinal shed blood fails to decrease banked blood requirements in patients undergoing aorta coronary bypass surgery. Am J Surg 1991;162:477-80.

85. Schaff HV, Hauer JM, Bell WR, et al. Autotransfusion of shed mediastinal blood after cardiac surgery. A prospective study. J Thorac Cardiovasc Surg 1978;75:632-41.

86. Eng J, Kay PH, Murday AJ, et al. Post-operative autologous transfusion in cardiac surgery. A prospective, randomized study. Eur J Cardiothorac Surg 1990;4:595-600.

87. Semkiw LB, Schurman OJ, Goodman SB, Woolson ST. Postoperative blood salvage using the cell saver after total joint arthroplasty. J Bone Joint Surg (Am) 1989;71A:823-7.

88. Faris PM, Ritter MA, Keating EM, Valeri CR. Unwashed filtered shed blood collected after knee and hip arthroplasties. J Bone Joint Surg (Am) 1991;73A:1169-77.

89. Martin JW, Whiteside LA, Milliano MT, Reedy ME. Postoperative blood retrieval and transfusion in cementless total knee arthroplasty. J Arthroplasty 1992;7:205-10.

90. Umlas J, Jacobson MS, Kevy SV. Survival and half-life of red cells salvaged after hip and knee replacement surgery. Transfusion 1993;33:591-3.

91. Umlas J, Foster RR, Dalal SA, et al. Red cell loss following orthopedic surgery: The case against postoperative blood salvage. Transfusion 1994;34:402-6.

92. Ritter MA, Keating EM, Faris PM. Closed wound drainage in total hip or knee replacement: A prospective, randomized study. J Bone J Surg 1994;76:35-8.

93. Clements DH, Sculco TP, Burke SW, et al. Salvage and reinfusion of postoperative sanguineous wound drainage. J Bone Joint Surg (Am)1992;74A:646-51.

94. Woda R, Tetzlaff JE. Upper airway oedema following autologous blood transfusion from a wound drainage system. Can J Anesth 1992;39:290-2.

95. Blevins FT, Shaw B, Valeri RC, et al. Reinfusion of shed blood after orthopedic procedures in children and adolescents. J Bone Joint Surg (Am) 1993;75A:363-71.

96. Goodnough LT, Verbrugge D, Marcus RE. The relationship between hematocrit, blood lost, and blood transfused in total knee replacement: Implications for postoperative blood salvage and reinfusion. Am J Knee Surg 1995;8:83-7.

97. Jackson BR, Umlas J, AuBuchon JP. The cost-effectiveness of postoperative recovery of RBCs in preventing transfusion-associated virus transmission after joint arthroplasty. Transfusion 2000;40:1063-6.

Chapter 6

Apheresis

APHERESIS, FROM THE Greek *pheresis* meaning "to take away," involves the selective removal of blood constituents from blood donors or patients.

The AABB provides standards[1] for voluntary compliance for apheresis activities. The Food and Drug Administration (FDA) has established specific requirements that are set forth in the *Code of Federal Regulations*[2] for apheresis activities. The American Society for Apheresis (ASFA)[3] has published additional guidelines and recommendations. In addition, hemapheresis practitioner (HP) and apheresis technician (AT) certifications are available through the American Society of Clinical Pathology Board of Registry. All personnel involved with apheresis activities should be familiar with these sources and should have documentation that they are qualified by training and experience to perform apheresis.

Separation Techniques

Automated blood processing devices are used for both component preparation and therapeutic applications of apheresis. Manual apheresis, in which whole blood is collected in multiple bags and centrifuged offline, requires great care to ensure that the bags are labeled correctly and are returned to the correct donor. With the currently available automated technology, this process is seldom used.

Separation by Centrifugation

In most apheresis instruments, centrifugal force separates blood into components on the basis of differences in density. A measured amount of anticoagulant solution is added to the whole blood as it is drawn from the donor or patient. The blood is pumped into a rotating bowl, chamber, or tubular rotor in which layering of com-

6

ponents occurs on the basis of their densities. The desired fraction is diverted and the remaining elements are returned to the donor (or patient) by intermittent or continuous flow.

All systems require prepackaged disposable sets of sterile bags, tubing, and centrifugal devices unique to the instrument. Each system has a mechanism to allow the separation device to rotate without twisting the attached tubing. In the intermittent flow method, the centrifuge container is alternately filled and emptied. Most instruments in use today employ a method that involves the continuous flow of blood through a separation chamber. Depending on the procedure and device used, the apheresis procedure time varies from 30 minutes to several hours.

Each manufacturer supplies detailed information and operational protocols. Each facility must have, in a manual readily available to nursing and technical personnel, detailed descriptions of each type of procedure performed, specific for each type of blood processor.[4]

Separation by Adsorption

Selective removal of a pathologic material has theoretical advantages over the removal of all plasma constituents. Centrifugal devices can be adapted to protocols that selectively remove specific soluble plasma constituents by exploiting the principles of affinity chromatography.[5] Selective removal of low-density lipoproteins (LDLs) in patients with familial hypercholesterolemia has been accomplished using both immunoaffinity (anti-LDL) and chemical affinity (eg, dextran sulfate) columns.[6] Adsorbents such as staphylococcal protein A (SPA), monoclonal antibodies, blood group substances, DNA-collodion, and polymers with aggregated IgG attached can extract antibodies, protein antigens, and immune complexes. Returning the depleted plasma along with the cellular components reduces or eliminates the need for replacement fluids. Immunoadsorption can be performed online, or the plasma can be separated from the cellular components, passed through an offline column, and then reinfused.

Component Collection

Whenever components intended for transfusion are collected by apheresis, the donor must give informed consent. Although apheresis collection and preparation processes are different from those used for whole-blood-derived components, storage conditions, transportation requirements, and some quality control steps are the same. See Chapter 8 for more detailed information. The facility must maintain written protocols for all procedures used and must keep records for each procedure as required by AABB *Standards for Blood Banks and Transfusion Services.*[1(p2)]

Platelets Pheresis

Plateletpheresis is used to obtain platelets from random volunteer donors, from patients' family members, or from donors with matched HLA or platelet antigen phenotypes. Because large numbers of platelets can be obtained from a single individual, collection by apheresis reduces the number of donor exposures for patients. AABB *Standards* requires the component to contain at least 3×10^{11} platelets in 90% of sampled units.[1(p31)] When a high yield is obtained, the original apheresis unit may be divided into multiple units, each of which must meet minimum standards independently. Some instruments are programmed to calculate the yield from the donor's hematocrit, platelet count, height, and weight. For alloimmunized patients who are refractory to random allogeneic platelets (see Chapters 16 and 21), platelets from an apheresis donor selected on the basis of a compatible platelet crossmatch or matched for HLA antigens may be the only way to achieve a satisfactory post-transfusion platelet increment. Within the United States, the use of apheresis platelets has been steadily increasing over the last 25 years. Currently, it is estimated that 77% of therapeutic platelet doses are transfused as apheresis platelets.[7]

Donor Selection and Monitoring

Plateletpheresis donors may donate more frequently than whole blood donors but must meet all other donor criteria. The interval between donations should be at least 2 days, and donors should not undergo plateletpheresis more than twice in a week or more than 24 times in a year.[1(pp19,20)] If the donor donates a unit of Whole Blood or if it becomes impossible to return the donor's red cells during plateletpheresis, at least 8 weeks should elapse before a subsequent plateletpheresis procedure, unless the extracorporeal red cell volume is less than 100 mL.[1(p20)] Platelets may be collected from donors who do not meet these requirements if the component is expected to be of particular value to a specific intended recipient, and if a physician certifies in writing that the donor's health will not be compromised (eg, an HLA-matched donor). Donors who have taken aspirin-containing medications within 36 hours of donation are usually deferred because the platelets obtained by apheresis are often the single source of platelets given to a patient. Vasovagal and hypovolemic reactions are rare in apheresis donors, but paresthesias and other reactions to the citrate anticoagulant are common (see Complications, later in this chapter). Serious reactions occur less often among apheresis donors than among whole blood donors.

Plateletpheresis donors should meet usual donor requirements, including hemoglobin or hematocrit level. A platelet count is not required before the first apheresis collection or if 4 weeks or more have elapsed since the last procedure. If the donation interval is less than 4 weeks, the donor's platelet count should be above 150,000/μL before subsequent plateletpheresis occurs. AABB *Standards* permits documentation of the platelet count from a sample collected immediately before the procedure or from a sample obtained either before or after the previous procedure.[1(p21)] Exceptions to these laboratory criteria should be approved in writing by the apheresis physician. The FDA specifies that the total volume of plasma collected should be no more than 500 mL (or 600 mL for donors weighing more than 175 pounds).[8] The platelet count of each unit should be kept on record but need not be written on the product label.[8]

Some plateletpheresis programs collect plasma for use as Fresh Frozen Plasma (FFP) in a separate bag during platelet collection. Apheresis can also be used to collect plasma for FFP without platelets, ie, plasmapheresis. The FDA has provided guidance with regard to the volume of plasma that is allowed to be collected using automated devices.[9] A total serum or plasma protein determination and a quantitative determination of IgG and IgM (or a serum protein electrophoresis) must be determined at 4-month intervals for donors undergoing large-volume plasma collection, if the total annual volume of plasma collected exceeds 12 liters (14.4 L for donors weighing more than 175 pounds) or if the donor is a frequent (more often than every 4 weeks) plasma donor.[10] AABB *Standards* requires that the donor's intravascular volume deficit must be less than 10.5 mL per kilogram of body weight at all times.[1(p24)]

Laboratory Testing

Tests for ABO group and Rh type, unexpected alloantibodies, and markers for transfusion-transmitted diseases must be performed by the collecting facility in the same manner as for other blood components. Each unit must be tested unless the donor is undergoing repeated procedures to support a single patient, in which case testing for disease markers need be repeated only at 30-day intervals.[1(p34)]

If red cells are visible in a product, the hematocrit should be determined. FDA guidelines require that if the component contains more than 2 mL of red cells, a sample of donor blood for compatibility testing be attached to the container.[8] In some instances, it may be desirable for the donor plasma to be ABO-compatible with the recipient's red cells—for example, if the recipient is a child or an ABO-mismatched allogeneic progenitor cell transplant recipient. In order to be considered leukocyte-reduced, apheresis platelets must contain less than 5×10^6 leukocytes and must meet the specifications of the apheresis device manufacturer. Chapter 8 describes additional quality control measures that apply to all platelet components.

Records

Complete records (see Chapter 1) must be kept for each procedure. All adverse reactions should be documented along with the results of their investigation and follow-up. Records of all laboratory findings and collection data must be periodically reviewed by a knowledgeable physician and found to be within acceptable limits. FDA guidelines require review at least once every 4 months.[8] Facilities must have policies and procedures in place to ensure that donor red cell loss during each procedure does not exceed acceptable limits.

Plasma

Apheresis can be used to collect plasma as FFP or for Source Plasma for subsequent manufacturing. FDA requirements for plasma collection are different from those for whole blood or plateletpheresis; personnel who perform serial plasmapheresis must be familiar with both AABB standards and FDA requirements. If plasma is intended for transfusion, testing requirements are the same as those for red cell components. Plasma collected for manufacture of plasma derivatives is subject to different requirements for infectious disease testing.

A distinction is made between "occasional plasmapheresis," in which the donor undergoes plasmapheresis no more often than once in 4 weeks, and "serial plasmapheresis," in which donation is more frequent than every 4 weeks. For donors in an occasional plasmapheresis program, donor selection and monitoring are the same as for whole blood donation. For serial plasmapheresis using either automated instruments or manual techniques, the following principles apply:

1. Donors must provide informed consent. They must be observed closely during the procedure and emergency medical care must be available.

2. Red cell losses related to the procedure, including samples collected for testing, must not exceed 25 mL per week, so that no more than 200 mL of red cells are removed in 8 weeks. If the donor's red cells cannot be returned during an apheresis procedure, hemapheresis or whole blood donation should be deferred for 8 weeks.

3. In manual plasma collection systems, there must be a mechanism to ensure safe reinfusion of the autologous red cells. Before the blood container

is separated from the donor for processing, there should be two separate, independent means of identification, so that both the donor and the phlebotomist can ascertain that the contents are those of the donor. Often, the donor's signature is one identifier, along with a unique identification number.

4. In manual procedures for donors weighing 50 to 80 kg (110-176 lb), no more than 500 mL of whole blood should be removed at one time, or 1000 mL during the session or within a 48-hour period. The limits for donors who weigh more than 80 kg are 600 mL and 1200 mL, respectively. For automated procedures, the allowable volume has been determined for each instrument by the FDA.[9]

5. At least 48 hours should elapse between successive procedures; ordinarily, donors should not undergo more than two procedures within a 7-day period. Exceptions are permissible when plasma is expected to have special therapeutic value for a single recipient.

6. At the time of initial plasmapheresis and at 4-month intervals thereafter for donors undergoing plasmapheresis more often than once every 4 weeks, serum or plasma must be tested for total protein and serum protein electrophoresis or quantitative immunoglobulins. Results must be within normal limits.[2]

7. A qualified, licensed physician, knowledgeable in all aspects of hemapheresis, must be responsible for the program.

Red Cells

Both AABB standards and FDA-approved protocols address the removal of two allogeneic or autologous Red Blood Cell units every 16 weeks by an automated apheresis method. Saline infusion is used to minimize volume depletion, and the procedure is limited to persons who are larger and have higher hematocrits than current minimum standards for whole blood donors (for males: weight 130 lb, height 5'1"; for females: weight 150 lb, height 5'5"; hematocrit 40% for both genders).[11]

Granulocytes

The indications for granulocyte transfusion are controversial (see Chapter 21). A meta-analysis of randomized controlled trials of granulocyte transfusion indicates that effectiveness depends on an adequate dose ($>1 \times 10^{10}$ granulocytes/day) and crossmatch compatibility (no recipient antibodies to granulocyte antigens).[12] There is renewed interest in granulocyte transfusion therapy for adults because much larger cell doses can be delivered when cells are collected from donors who receive colony-stimulating factors.[13] Some success with granulocyte transfusions has been observed in the treatment of septic infants,[14] possibly because the usual dose is relatively larger in these tiny recipients and because HLA alloimmunization is absent.

Drugs Administered for Leukapheresis

A daily dose of at least 1×10^{10} granulocytes is necessary to achieve a therapeutic effect.[15] Collection of this number of cells requires administration of drugs or other adjuvants to the donor. The donor's consent should include specific permission for any drugs or sedimenting agents to be used.

Hydroxyethyl Starch. A common sedimenting agent, hydroxyethyl starch (HES), causes red cells to aggregate and thereby sediment more completely. Sedimenting agents enhance granulocyte harvest and result in minimal red cell content. Because HES can be detected in donors for as long as a year after infusion, AABB *Standards* requires facilities performing granulocyte collections to have a process to control the maximal cumulative dose of any sedimenting agent administered to the donor within a given interval.[1(p24)] Because HES is a colloid, it acts as a volume expander, and donors who have received HES may experience headaches or peripheral edema because of expanded circulatory volume.

Corticosteroids. Corticosteroids can double the number of circulating granulocytes by mobilizing them from the marginal pool. A protocol using 60 mg of oral prednisone as a single or divided dose before donation gives superior granulocyte harvests with minimal systemic steroid activity.[16] Alternatively, 8 mg of oral dexamethasone may be used. Before administration of corticosteroids, donors should be questioned about any history or symptoms of hypertension, diabetes, cataracts,[17] and peptic ulcer.

Growth Factors. Recombinant hematopoietic growth factors—specifically, granulocyte colony-stimulating factor (G-CSF)—can effectively increase granulocyte yields. Hematopoietic growth factors alone can result in collection of up to 4 to 8×10^{10} granulocytes per apheresis procedure.[13] Typical doses of G-CSF employed are 5 to 10 μg/kg given 8 to 12 hours before collection.[18] Preliminary evidence suggests that in-vivo recovery and survival of these granulocytes are excellent and that growth factors are well tolerated by donors.[13]

Laboratory Testing

Testing for ABO and Rh, alloantibodies, and infectious disease markers on a sample drawn at the time of phlebotomy are required. Red cell content in granulocyte concentrates is inevitable; the red cells should be ABO-compatible with the recipient's plasma and, if more than 2 mL are present, the component should be crossmatched. Ideally, D-negative recipients should receive granulocyte concentrates from D-negative donors. Leukocyte (HLA) matching is recommended in alloimmunized patients.

Storage and Infusion

Because granulocyte function deteriorates during storage, concentrates should be transfused as soon as possible after preparation. AABB *Standards* prescribes a storage temperature of 20 to 24 C, for no longer than 24 hours.[1(p57)] Agitation during storage is probably undesirable. Irradiation is required before administration to immunodeficient recipients and will probably be indicated for nearly all recipients because of their primary disease. Infusion through a microaggregate or leukocyte reduction filter is contraindicated.

Hematopoietic Progenitor Cells

Cytapheresis for collection of hematopoietic progenitor cells is useful for obtaining progenitor cells for marrow reconstitution in patients with cancer, leukemia in remission, and various lymphomas (see Chapter 25). Cytapheresis procedures can also be used to collect donor lymphocytes for infusion as an immune therapy in these patients (see Chapter 25). The AABB has published *Standards for Cellular Therapy Product Services.*[19] Additional requirements are reviewed in Chapter 25.

Therapeutic Apheresis

Therapeutic apheresis has been used to treat many different diseases. Cells, plasma, or plasma constituents may be removed from the circulation and replaced by normal plasma, crystalloid, or colloid solutions of starch or albumin. The term "therapeutic apheresis" is used for the general procedure and the term "therapeutic plasma exchange" (TPE) is used for procedures in which the goal is the removal of plasma, regardless of the solution used as replacement.

The theoretical basis for therapeutic apheresis is to reduce the patient's load of a pathologic substance to levels that will allow clinical improvement. In some conditions, replacement with normal plasma is intended to supply an essential substance that is absent. In the absence of the need to replace plasma constituents, colloidal solutions and/or saline should be used as replacement fluids. Other possible outcomes of therapeutic apheresis include alteration of the antigen-to-antibody ratio, modification of mediators of inflammation or immunity, and clearance of immune complexes. Some perceived benefit may result from a placebo effect. Despite difficulties in documentation, there is general agreement that therapeutic apheresis is effective treatment for the conditions listed in Table 6-1 as Category I or Category II.[3,20-22]

General Considerations

Appropriate use of therapeutic apheresis requires considerable medical knowledge and judgment. The patient should be evaluated for treatment by his or her personal physician and by the apheresis physician. Close consultation between these physicians is important, especially if the patient is small or elderly, has poor vascular access or cardiovascular instability, or has a condition for which apheresis is of uncertain benefit. The apheresis physician should make the final determination about appropriateness of the procedure and eligibility of the patient (see Table 6-1).[3,20-22] When therapeutic apheresis is anticipated, those involved with the pa-

tient's care should establish a treatment plan and the goal of therapy. The endpoint may be an agreed-upon objective outcome or a predetermined duration for the therapy, whichever is achieved first. It is helpful to document these mutually acceptable goals in the patient's medical record. The nature of the procedure, its expected benefits, its possible risks, and the available alternatives should be explained to the patient by a knowledgeable individual, and the patient's consent should be documented. The procedure should be performed only in a setting where there is ready access to care for untoward reactions, including equipment, medications, and personnel trained in managing serious reactions.

Vascular Access

For most adults needing a limited number of procedures, the antecubital veins are suitable for removal and return of blood. For critically ill adults and for children, indwelling central or peripheral venous catheters are typically used. Especially effective are rigid-wall, large-bore, double-lumen catheters placed in the subclavian, femoral, or internal jugular vein. Catheters of the type used for temporary hemodialysis allow both removal and return of blood at high flow rates. Central catheters can be maintained for weeks if multiple procedures are necessary. Tunnel catheters can be used when long-term apheresis is anticipated.

Removal of Pathologic Substances

During TPE, plasma that contains the pathologic substance is removed and a replacement fluid is infused. The efficiency with which material is removed can be estimated by calculating the patient's plasma volume and using Fig 6-1. This estimate depends on the following assump-

Table 6-1. Indication Categories for Therapeutic Apheresis[20]

Disease	Procedure	Indication Category
Renal and metabolic diseases		
Antiglomerular basement membrane antibody disease	Plasma exchange	I
Rapidly progressive glomerulonephritis	Plasma exchange	II
Hemolytic uremic syndrome	Plasma exchange	III
Renal transplantation		
Rejection	Plasma exchange	IV
Sensitization	Plasma exchange	III
Recurrent focal glomerulosclerosis	Plasma exchange	III
Heart transplant rejection	Plasma exchange	III
	Photopheresis	III
Acute hepatic failure	Plasma exchange	III
Familial hypercholesterolemia	Selective adsorption	I
	Plasma exchange	II
Overdose or poisoning	Plasma exchange	III
Phytanic acid storage disease	Plasma exchange	I
Autoimmmune and rheumatic diseases		
Cryoglobulinemia	Plasma exchange	II
Idiopathic thrombocytopenic purpura	Immunoadsorption	II
Raynaud's phenomenon	Plasma exchange	III
Vasculitis	Plasma exchange	III
Autoimmune hemolytic anemia	Plasma exchange	III
Rheumatoid arthritis	Immunoadsorption	II
	Lymphoplasmapheresis	II
	Plasma exchange	IV
Scleroderma or progressive systemic sclerosis	Plasma exchange	III
Systemic lupus erythematosus	Plasma exchange	III
Lupus nephritis	Plasma exchange	IV
Psoriasis	Plasma exchange	IV
Hematolic diseases		
ABO-mismatched marrow transplant	RBC removal (marrow)	I
	Plasma exchange (recipient)	II

Table 6-1. Indication Categories for Therapeutic Apheresis[20] (cont'd)

Disease	Procedure	Indication Category
Erythrocytosis or polycythemia vera	Phlebotomy	I
	Erythrocytapheresis	II
Leukocytosis and thrombocytosis	Cytapheresis	I
Thrombotic thrombocytopenia purpura	Plasma exchange	I
Posttransfusion purpura	Plasma exchange	I
Sickle cell diseases	RBC exchange	I
Myeloma, paraproteins, or hyperviscosity	Plasma exchange	II
Myeloma or acute renal failure	Plasma exchange	II
Coagulation factor inhibitors	Plasma exchange	II
Aplastic anemia or pure RBC aplasia	Plasma exchange	III
Cutaneous T-cell lymphoma	Photopheresis	I
	Leukapheresis	III
Hemolytic disease of the fetus and newborn	Plasma exchange	III
Platelet alloimmunization and refractoriness	Plasma exchange	III
	Immunoadsorption	III
Malaria or babesiosis	RBC exchange	III
AIDS	Plasma exchange	IV
Neurologic disorders		
Chronic inflammatory demyelinating polyradiculoneuropathy	Plasma exchange	I
Acute inflammatory demyelinating polyradiculoneuropathy	Plasma exchange	I
Lambert-Eaton myasthenia syndrome	Plasma exchange	II
Multiple sclerosis		
Relapsing	Plasma exchange	III
Progressive	Plasma exchange	III
	Lymphocytapheresis	III
Myasthenia gravis	Plasma exchange	I
Acute central nervous system inflammatory demyelinating disease	Plasma exchange	II
Paraneoplastic neurologic syndromes	Plasma exchange	III
	Immunoadsorption	III

(cont'd)

Table 6-1. Indication Categories for Therapeutic Apheresis[20] (cont'd)

Disease	Procedure	Indication Category
Demyelinating polyneuropathy with IgG and IgA	Plasma exchange	I
	Immunoadsorption	III
Sydenham's chorea	Plasma exchange	II
Polyneuropathy with IgM (with or without Waldenstrom's)	Plasma exchange	II
	Immunoadsorption	III
Cryoglobulinemia with polyneuropathy	Plasma exchange	II
Multiple myeloma with polyneuropathy	Plasma exchange	III
POEMS syndrome	Plasma exchange	III
Systemic (AL) amyloidosis	Plasma exchange	IV
Polymyositis or dermatomyositis	Plasma exchange	III
	Leukapheresis	IV
Inclusion-body myositis	Plasma exchange	III
	Leukapheresis	IV
Rasmussen's encephalitis	Plasma exchange	III
Stiff-person syndrome	Plasma exchange	III
PANDAS	Plasma exchange	II
Amyotrophic lateral sclerosis	Plasma exchange	IV

POEMS = polyneuropathy, organomegaly, endocrinopathy, monoclonal gammopathy, and skin lesions; PANDAS = pediatric autoimmune neuropsychiatric disorders; Category I = standard acceptable therapy; Category II = sufficient evidence to suggest efficacy usually as adjunctive therapy; Category III = inconclusive evidence of efficacy or uncertain risk/benefit ratio; Category IV = lack of efficacy in controlled trials.

tions: 1) the patient's blood volume does not change; 2) mixing occurs immediately; and 3) there is relatively little production or mobilization of the pathologic material to be removed during the procedure. As seen in Fig 6-1, removal is greatest early in the procedure and diminishes progressively during the exchange. Exchange is usually limited to 1 or 1.5 plasma volumes, or approximately 40 to 60 mL plasma exchanged per kg of body weight in patients with normal hematocrit and average body size. This maximizes the efficacy per procedure but may make it necessary to repeat the process. Rarely are two or more plasma volumes exchanged in one procedure. Although larger volume exchange causes greater initial diminution of the pathologic substance, overall it is less efficient and requires considerably more time. Larger volume exchanges can increase the risk of coagulopathy, citrate toxicity, or electrolyte imbalance, depending on the replacement fluid.

The rates at which a pathologic substance is synthesized and distributed between intravascular and extravascular com-

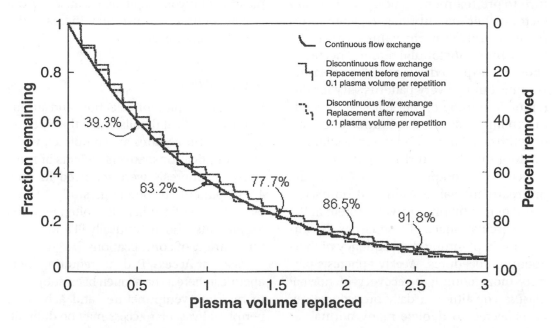

Figure 6-1. The relationship between the volume of plasma exchange and the patient's original plasma remaining.

partments affect the outcome of TPE. For example, the abnormal IgM of Waldenstrom's macroglobulinemia is synthesized slowly and remains almost entirely (about 75%) intravascular, making apheresis particularly effective in removing it.[23] In addition, a relatively small change in intravascular protein concentration may result in a large change in blood viscosity. In contrast, efforts to prevent hydrops fetalis with intensive TPE to lower the mother's level of IgG anti-D have been less successful. This is due in part to the fact that about 55% of IgG is in the extravascular fluid. In addition, rapid reduction of IgG may cause antibody synthesis to increase rapidly and "rebound" over pretreatment levels.[24] Rebound synthesis may also complicate TPE treatment of autoimmune diseases. Immuno-suppressive agents such as cyclophosphamide, azathioprine, or prednisone may be administered to blunt the autoantibody rebound response to apheresis.

Plasma removed during TPE should be handled carefully and disposed of properly. Such plasma cannot be used for subsequent manufacture of transfusable plasma derivatives.

Removal of Normal Plasma Constituents

When the quantity of plasma removed during TPE exceeds 1.5 times the plasma volume, different rates of removal and reconstitution are observed for different constituents.[25] In the case of fibrinogen, the third component of complement (C3), and immune complexes, 75% to 85% of the original substance is removed after a 1.5 plasma-volume procedure. Pretreatment levels are restored in 3 to 4 days. The concentrations of electrolytes, uric acid, Factor VIII, and other proteins are less affected by a plasma exchange. A 10% or more decrease in platelet count generally occurs, with 2 to 4 days needed for a return to pretreatment values.[26] Coagulation factors other than fibrinogen generally return to pretreatment values within 24 hours. Immunoglobulin removal occurs at about the expected rate of 65% per plasma volume, but recovery patterns vary for different immunoglobulin classes, depending on intravascular distribution and rates of synthesis. (Table 11-3 describes immunoglobulin characteristics.) Plasma IgG levels return to approximately 60% of the pretreatment value within 48 hours because of reequilibration with protein in the extravascular space. These issues are important in planning the frequency of therapeutic procedures. Weekly apheresis permits more complete recovery of normal plasma constituents; daily procedures can be expected to deplete many normal, as well as abnormal, constituents. Additionally, intensive apheresis reduces the concentration of potentially diagnostic plasma constituents, so blood for testing should be drawn before TPE.

Replacement Fluids

Available replacement solutions include: crystalloids, albumin solutions, plasma (FFP, cryosupernatant plasma, or Plasma Frozen within 24 Hours of Collection), and HES.[27] Table 6-2 presents advantages and disadvantages of each. A combination is often used, the relative proportions being determined by the physician on the basis of the patient's disease and physical condition, the planned frequency of procedures, and cost. Acute treatment of immediately life-threatening conditions usually requires a series of daily plasma exchange procedures, often producing a significant reduction of coagulation factors. Monitoring the platelet count, prothrombin time, activated partial thromboplastin time, and fibrinogen level helps determine the need for supplemental platelets, plasma, or cryoprecipitate. Because plasma contains citrate, its use may increase the risk of citrate toxicity.

Complications

With careful patient selection and attention to technical details, most therapeutic apheresis procedures are completed without complications. Adverse effects of therapeutic apheresis were reported in only 4% of patients in one large study.[28] However, therapeutic apheresis is often required for patients who are critically ill and at risk for a variety of complications.

Vascular Access. Patients requiring therapeutic apheresis have often been subjected to multiple venipunctures and achieving peripheral vascular access may be difficult. Frequently, special venous access, such as placement of an indwelling double-lumen apheresis/dialysis catheter, is required. Venous access devices may cause further vascular damage, sometimes resulting in thrombosis. Infrequently, they may result in severe complications such as pneumothorax or perforation of the heart or great vessels.[28] Other complications include arterial puncture, deep hematomas, and arteriovenous fistula formation. Bacterial colonization often complicates long-term placement and may lead to catheter-associated sepsis, especially in patients who are receiving steroids or other immunosuppressants. Inadvertent disconnection of catheters may produce hemorrhage or air embolism.

Alteration of Pharmacodynamics. TPE can lower blood levels of drugs, especially those that bind to albumin. Apheresis reduces plasma levels of antibiotics and anticonvulsants, but few clinical data exist to suggest adverse patient outcomes due to apheresis-associated lowering of drug levels. Nevertheless, the pharmacokinetics of all drugs being given to a patient should be

Table 6-2. Comparison of Replacement Fluids

Replacement Solution	Advantages	Disadvantages
Crystalloids	Low cost Hypoallergenic No viral risk	2-3 volumes required Hypo-oncotic No coagulation factors No immunoglobulins
Albumin	Iso-oncotic No contaminating "inflammatory mediators" No viral risk	High cost No coagulation factors No immunoglobulins
Hydroxyethyl starch	Moderate cost Iso-oncotic No contaminating "inflammatory mediators"	No coagulation factors Long-term residual levels of HES Contraindicated with renal failure Possible coagulopathy

Plasma	Maintains normal levels of:
	    immunoglobulins
	    complement
	    antithrombin
	    other proteins
		Viral transmission risk
		Citrate load
		ABO incompatibility risk
		Allergic reactions
		Sensitization

considered before starting apheresis and dosage schedules adjusted if necessary. It is prudent to withhold the administration of drugs scheduled to be given during or up to an hour before apheresis until after the procedure has finished. Removal of plasma cholinesterase may complicate the administration of paralyzing agents such as succinylcholine in the immediate post-exchange period.

Hypocalcemia. Most patients and donors with normal parathyroid and liver function maintain calcium homeostasis during apheresis. However, symptoms of hypocalcemia related to citrate toxicity are the most common adverse effect reported in 3.0% of therapeutic apheresis procedures in one large study.[28] Symptoms of reduced plasma levels of ionized calcium (perioral paresthesias, tingling, a feeling of vibrations) reflect the rate at which citrate anticoagulant is returned, ionized and bound calcium are removed, and ionized calcium is bound to "calcium-stripped" albumin replacement. Hyperventilation, hypothermia, hypomagnesemia, and the use of plasma as a replacement solution exacerbate citrate toxicity. Hypocalcemia can usually be controlled by reducing the proportion of citrate or slowing the reinfusion rate. If untreated, symptoms may progress to muscle twitching, chills, pressure in the chest, nausea, vomiting, and hypotension. Low ionized calcium concentrations can induce severe cardiac arrhythmias. Asking the patient to report any vibrations or tingling sensations can help determine the appropriate reinfusion rate. Extra precautions must be taken in patients who are unable to communicate or who may metabolize citrate poorly (eg, those with liver failure). Hypocalcemic toxicity can usually be managed by administering oral calcium carbonate or intravenous calcium.[22,23,29]

Circulatory Effects. Hypovolemia and subsequent hypotension may occur during apheresis, especially when the volume of extracorporeal blood exceeds 15% of the total blood volume. Hypotension tends to occur in ill children, the elderly, neurology patients, anemic patients, and those treated with intermittent-flow devices that have large extracorporeal volumes. Continuous-flow devices typically do not require large extracorporeal volumes but can produce hypovolemia if return flow is inadvertently diverted to a waste collection bag, either through operator oversight or mechanical or software failures. Hypovolemia may also be secondary to inadequate volume or protein replacement. During all procedures, it is essential to maintain careful and continuous records of the volumes removed and returned. The use of antihypertensive medications, especially angiotensin-converting enzyme (ACE) inhibitors combined with albumin replacement, may also contribute to hypotensive reactions (see Chapter 27). Patients taking agents that inhibit ACE have experienced severe hypotensive episodes when treated with SPA columns and with other immunosorbents.[30] Patients should not receive these medications for 72 hours before undergoing immunoabsorption treatment. Because infusion of cold fluids through a central venous catheter may induce arrhythmias, some apheresis programs use blood warmers for selected patients.

Infections. Plasma is the only commonly used replacement solution with the risk of transmitting infectious viruses. Bacterial colonization and infection related to repeated apheresis usually arise from within the vascular catheter. Intensive apheresis regimens decrease levels of immunoglobulins and the opsonic components of complement. In addition, immunosuppressive drugs used to prevent rebound antibody production may further compromise defense mechanisms.

Mechanical Hemolysis and Equipment Failures. Collapsed or kinked tubing, malfunctioning pinch valves, or improper threading of tubing may damage donor or patient red cells in the extracorporeal circuit. Machine-related hemolysis was observed in 0.07% of over 195,000 apheresis procedures performed in the United Kingdom.[31] Similar rates of hemolysis, 0.06% and 0.01%, were reported in response to uniform questionnaires regarding therapeutic and donor apheresis procedures, respectively.[32,33]

Hemolysis can also occur with incompatible replacement fluids such as D5W (eg, D5W used to dilute 25% albumin) or ABO-discrepant plasma. The operator should carefully observe plasma collection lines for pink discoloration suggestive of hemolysis. Other types of equipment failure, such as problems with the rotating seal, leaks in the plastic, and roller pump failure, are rare.[34]

Allergic Reactions and Respiratory Distress. Respiratory difficulty during or immediately following apheresis can have many causes: pulmonary edema, massive pulmonary embolism, air embolism, obstruction of the pulmonary microvasculature, anaphylactic reactions, and transfusion-related acute lung injury.[35] Hemothorax or hemopericardium due to vascular erosion by a central venous catheter is typically unsuspected yet may be fatal.[36,37] Pulmonary edema that results from volume overload or cardiac failure is usually associated with dyspnea, an increase in the diastolic blood pressure, and characteristic chest X-ray findings. Acute pulmonary edema can also arise from damage to alveolar capillary membranes secondary to an immune reaction or to vasoactive substances in FFP or colloid solutions prepared from human plasma. The use of FFP as a replacement fluid has been associated with complement activation and with allergic reactions that produce urticaria, swelling of oral mucosa, and bronchospasm; these usually respond to antihistamines and corticosteroids. Hypotension and flushing associated with the rapid infusion of albumin in patients taking ACE inhibitors are discussed in Chapter 27. Predominantly ocular (periorbital edema, conjunctival swelling, and tearing) reactions have occurred in donors sensitized to the ethylene oxide gas used to sterilize disposable plastic apheresis kits.[38]

Fatalities During Apheresis. Despite the fact that patients undergoing therapeutic apheresis are often critically ill, fatalities during apheresis are comparatively rare. Estimates of fatality rates range from 3 in 10,000[39] to 1 in 500[40] procedures. Most deaths were due to cardiac arrhythmias or arrest during or shortly after the procedure or to acute pulmonary edema or adult respiratory distress syndrome occurring during a procedure. Rare fatalities resulted from anaphylaxis, vascular perforation, hepatitis, sepsis, thrombosis, and hemorrhage.

Indications for Therapeutic Apheresis

Although therapeutic apheresis has been used in the treatment of many diseases, most published studies are case reports or small uncontrolled series, often providing insufficient evidence of efficacy. Publication bias tends to favor positive results, and physicians should avoid subjecting patients to the risks and high costs of apheresis procedures based on marginal clinical studies. Controlled, randomized, blinded studies of therapeutic apheresis are difficult to conduct, especially because using sham treatments as a control is expensive and carries some risk. However, the complicated apheresis instruments and associated attention from nursing and medical personnel may cre-

ate or amplify a placebo effect and bias the evaluation of clinical improvement.

For many of the diseases being treated, the etiology, pathogenesis, and natural history are incompletely understood, and reductions in such measured variables as complement components, rheumatoid factor, or immune complexes cannot be correlated reliably with changes in disease activity. An example is the use of the erythrocyte sedimentation rate (ESR) as an index of disease activity in rheumatoid arthritis. The ESR invariably decreases during intensive TPE, but this reflects removal of fibrinogen and not necessarily a decrease in disease activity. For the same reasons, the optimal volume and frequency of exchange are often not established. For severe imminently life-threatening disease, when albumin/saline is the replacement fluid, TPE is initially performed daily. After a few days, the fibrinogen or platelet count may be low enough to significantly increase the risk of bleeding. Clinical judgment must then be exercised to decide whether to proceed with TPE using clotting factor/platelet transfusions or to withhold TPE until these parameters normalize. The conditions discussed below are established indications for therapeutic apheresis.[3,20,21,41,42]

Hematologic Conditions

Serum Hyperviscosity Syndrome. Serum hyperviscosity resulting from multiple myeloma or Waldenstrom's macroglobulinemia can cause congestive heart failure; reduced blood flow to the cerebral, cardiac, or pulmonary circulation; or symptoms of headache, vertigo, somnolence, or obtundation. Paraproteins may interfere with hemostasis, leading to hemorrhagic symptoms.

The presence of hyperviscosity correlates only in very general terms with the concentration of paraprotein. Measurement of serum viscosity relative to water is a simple procedure that provides more objective information. For some pathologic proteins, serum viscosity is highly temperature dependent, so serum viscosity should be measured at physiologically relevant temperatures. Normal serum viscosity ranges from 1.4 to 1.8 relative to water. Because most patients are not symptomatic until their relative serum viscosity is more than 4.0 or 5.0, patients with mild elevations may not require treatment. For symptomatic hyperviscosity, a single apheresis procedure is usually highly effective.[23]

Hyperleukocytosis. Leukapheresis is often used to treat the dramatically elevated white cell count that can occur in acute leukemia. Several different thresholds have been used: fractional volume of leukocytes (leukocrit) above 10%; total circulating leukocytes above 100,000/μL; and circulating blasts above 50,000/μL.[43] However, the use of a single laboratory value as an indication for treatment is an oversimplification. Such factors as erythrocyte concentration, leukemic cell type, rate at which the count is rising, potential obstructions to cerebral or pulmonary blood flow, and the patient's coagulation status and general condition must be considered. Most leukemic patients with extreme leukocytosis have significant anemia. Reduced red cell mass reduces blood viscosity, so unless there is an acute need to increase oxygen-carrying capacity, red cells should not be transfused until the hyperviscosity crisis has been resolved.[43]

In some patients with acute blast crisis or in unusual types of leukemia, both the hematocrit and leukocrit are elevated. If there is evidence of cerebral or pulmonary symptoms, rapid reduction of leukocyte concentration should be considered, although the efficacy of such leukocyte reduction is unproved. More commonly, however, the white cell count rises over weeks or longer, and leukocyte reduction can be effected with chemotherapy, with or without leukapheresis. Leukapheresis is sometimes used to reduce the white cell count to <100,000/μL before the start of chemotherapy, to reduce the likelihood of tumor lysis syndrome. However, there have been no controlled clinical trials to substantiate this approach, and it must be recognized that more malignant cells are present outside the circulation than within the bloodstream.

Thrombocythemia. Therapeutic plateletpheresis is usually undertaken for symptomatic patients with platelet counts above 1,000,000/μL. The measured count, by itself, should not determine whether platelet reduction is indicated. In patients with evidence of thrombosis secondary to thrombocythemia, plateletpheresis can be beneficial. The rationale for platelet reduction in bleeding patients with thrombocythemia is less clear. There are no accepted indications for prophylactic plateletpheresis in asymptomatic patients, although the risk of placental infarction and fetal death may justify the procedure in a pregnant woman with severe thrombocythemia.[43]

Thrombotic Thrombocytopenic Purpura/ Hemolytic-Uremic Syndrome (TTP/HUS). The conditions described as TTP/HUS are multisystem disorders, in which platelet/fibrin thrombi occlude the microcirculation. They are characterized by varying degrees of thrombocytopenia, microangiopathic hemolytic anemia, renal dysfunction, neurologic abnormalities, and fever. Patients presenting with fulminant TTP usually have platelet counts below 50,000/μL and lactic dehydrogenase (LDH) levels above 1000 IU/mL, resulting from systemic ischemia and hemolysis.[44] The peripheral blood smear characteristically shows increased numbers of schistocytes. Evidence for disseminated intravascular coagulation is generally absent.

TTP usually develops without obvious cause, although episodes may occur after infections, pregnancy, or use of some common drugs such as ticlopidine, or clopidogrel. Recent reports suggest that it is caused by a transient antibody to a protease (ADAMTS13) that normally cleaves large von Willebrand factor (vWF) multimers. The unusually large vWF multimers avidly aggregate circulating platelets, triggering the syndrome.[45,46] Increasingly, cases of recurrent or relapsing TTP are being recognized.

HUS is a similar condition that occurs more commonly in children than adults. HUS may follow diarrheal infections with verotoxin-secreting strains of *Escherichia coli* (strain 0157:H7) or *Shigella*. Compared with patients who have classic TTP, those with HUS have more renal dysfunction and less prominent neurologic and hematologic findings. Most patients with HUS do not have antibody to the vWF protease and have normal concentrations of vWF protease. TTP/HUS can occur after treatment with certain cytotoxic drugs, including mitomycin C. A microangiopathic hemolysis similar to TTP/HUS can occur in organ or stem cell transplant recipients receiving cyclosporine and tacrolimus.[47,48] Transplant-associated microangiopathic hemolysis appears to be less responsive to therapy and probably represents a different disease process.[48]

TPE with plasma or Plasma Cryoprecipitate Reduced replacement has become the treatment of choice for TTP/HUS.[49,50] Protease levels have been shown to be stable for at least 2 weeks in citrated plasma stored at 37 C.[51] TPE is now thought to remove both antibody to the protease and vWF and to replace deficient protease. Other largely unproved treatments include prednisone, antiplatelet agents, splenectomy, vincristine, rituximab, and intravenous immunoglobulin. Because platelet transfusions have anecdotally been associated with disease exacerbation and death, they are usually contraindicated (except in the presence of life-threatening hemorrhage).

TPE is typically performed daily for 1 to 2 weeks, but the intensity and duration of treatment should be guided by the individual patient's course. Occasionally, prolonged courses of treatment are required. Therapeutic plasma exchange has impressively improved the survival rate in TTP, from being almost universally fatal before 1964 to 80% survival in a recent series.[49] Signs of response to therapy include a rising platelet count and reduction of LDH between procedures. As patients recover to near normal LDH and platelet count (100-150,000/µL), TPE is discontinued. Some programs switch from intensive TPE to intermittent plasma exchange or simple plasma infusion, but the efficacy of this approach has not been established.[52] Despite the success of TPE, TTP/HUS remains a serious condition. Treatment failures continue to occur and to cause major organ damage or death.

Complications of Sickle Cell Disease. Several complications of sickle cell disease are syndromes that can be treated by red cell exchange. These conditions include stroke or impending stroke, acute chest syndrome, and multiorgan failure. Either manual or automated techniques can be used for red cell exchange, but automated techniques are faster and better controlled. The goal is to replace red cells containing hemoglobin S with a sufficient number of red cells containing hemoglobin A so that the overall proportion of hemoglobin A in the blood is 60% to 80%. Some centers provide partially phenotypically matched red cells (eg, C, E, and K1) to avoid alloimmunizing long-term transfusion recipients to these antigens. At the end of the procedure, the patient's hematocrit should be no higher than 30% to 35% to avoid increased blood viscosity. Chronic erythrocytapheresis can be used to manage iron overload in patients requiring long-term transfusion therapy.[53]

Cryoglobulinemia

Significant elevations of cryoglobulins may cause cold-induced vascular occlusion, abnormalities of coagulation, renal insufficiency, or peripheral nerve damage. Removal of cryoglobulins by apheresis can be used to treat acute symptomatic episodes, but definitive therapy depends on identifying and treating the underlying causative condition.

Neurologic Conditions

Myasthenia Gravis. Myasthenia gravis results from autoantibody-mediated blockade of the acetylcholine receptor located on the postsynaptic motor endplate of muscles. Standard treatment includes steroids and acetylcholinesterase inhibitors. TPE is used as adjunctive treatment for patients experiencing exacerbations not controlled by medications and for patients being prepared for thymectomy. A typical treatment protocol is five or six TPE procedures over l to 2 weeks. Concurrent immunosuppression to prevent antibody rebound is recommended. Chronic TPE has been used with some success in a small number of patients.

Acute Guillain-Barré Syndrome. Guillain-Barré syndrome is an acute autoimmune demyelinating polyneuropathy that can produce dramatic paralysis in otherwise healthy individuals. The cause is unknown; many cases appear to follow benign viral infections or *Campylobacter jejuni* infection. Most patients recover spontaneously, but as many as one in six may become unable to walk or may develop respiratory failure requiring ventilatory support. Early treatment is beneficial for patients with rapidly progressive disease. The response to therapy is inferior in pa-

tients who remain untreated for several weeks. Recent controlled studies suggest that intravenous immunoglobulin gives results equivalent to five TPE procedures over a 2-week period.[54] A cost-effectiveness analysis has suggested that TPE is less costly than a course of intravenous immune globulin.[55] Multicenter trials have suggested that TPE, if initiated early, can decrease the period of minimal sensorimotor function.[56] Patients whose illness is not acute in onset, is not characteristic of Guillain-Barré syndrome, or in whom nerve conduction studies show complete axonal block may have a poorer prognosis and less response to apheresis therapy.

Chronic Inflammatory Demyelinating Polyneuropathy. Chronic inflammatory demyelinating polyneuropathy (CIDP), often seen in HIV patients, is a group of disorders with slow onset and progressive or intermittent course, characterized by elevated spinal fluid protein, marked slowing of nerve conduction velocity, and segmental demyelination of peripheral nerves. Various sensorimotor abnormalities result. Polyneuropathy may also occur in the POEMS syndrome, characterized by polyneuropathy, organomegaly, endocrinopathy, MGUS (monoclonal gammopathy of unknown significance), and skin changes. Corticosteroids are the first-line treatment for CIDP. TPE and intravenous immunoglobulin have equivalent efficacy in patients unresponsive to corticosteroids.[57]

Polyneuropathy Associated with Monoclonal Gammopathy of Undetermined Significance. When polyneuropathy is associated with monoclonal paraproteins of uncertain significance, TPE has been shown to be effective for all variants.[58,59]

Renal Diseases

Rapidly progressive glomerulonephritis (RPGN) associated with antibodies to basement membranes of glomeruli and alveoli, which may result in pulmonary hemorrhage (Goodpasture's disease), usually responds to TPE as an adjunct to immunosuppressive drugs.[41] TPE accelerates the disappearance of antibodies to basement membranes and improves renal function. TPE is particularly effective in halting pulmonary hemorrhage in these patients, even if renal function does not completely normalize following treatment. Therapeutic apheresis has been used in treating the vasculitis associated with RPGN and the presence of antineutrophil cytoplasmic antibody (ANCA-positive RPGN).[60,61] TPE is most effective in the more severe cases.[41]

Myeloma light chains may be toxic to renal tubular epithelium and cause renal failure in up to 10% of cases. TPE is useful as adjunctive therapy in some myeloma patients with cast nephropathy but is not associated with improved survival.[41,62]

Other Conditions

TPE has been used as adjunctive treatment for a variety of multisystem diseases. A combination of steroid, cytotoxic agents, and TPE has been used for severely ill patients with polyarteritis nodosa,[63] although most rheumatologic conditions respond poorly to TPE. Clinical trials using standard TPE have not shown benefit in the treatment of systemic lupus erythematosus, polymyositis, dermatomyositis, or scleroderma.[21] Immunoadsorption columns are of benefit in patients with rheumatoid arthritis refractory to medical management.[64]

Homozygous Type II Familial Hypercholesterolemia. Homozygous hypercholesterolemia, a rare disorder of the receptor for low-density lipoproteins, results in severe premature atherosclerosis and early death from coronary artery disease. Prolonged reduction in circulating lipids can be achieved with repeated TPE, often with selective adsorption or filtration techniques.[43] Heterozygous hypercholesterolemia results from several gene defects in the LDL receptor. Some patients with heterozygous hypercholesterolemia also develop high levels of cholesterol and are at increased risk for developing premature atherosclerotic heart disease.

Two apheresis systems for selective LDL removal in patients with homozygous or heterozygous hypercholesterolemia have been cleared by the FDA. The Liposorber LA-150 (Kaneka Pharma America, New York, NY) is based on a dextran sulfate adsorption system. The H.E.L.P. LDL system (B. Braun, Melsugen, Germany) is a heparin-induced LDL cholesterol precipitation system. The LDL apheresis procedure selectively removes apolipoprotein-B-containing cholesterols such as LDL and very LDL, sparing high-density lipoprotein (HDL) cholesterol. This provides an advantage over standard apheresis, which removes all plasma proteins, including the "protective" HDL. The procedure acutely lowers levels of targeted cholesterols by 60% to 70%. Treatment is usually performed every 1 to 2 weeks, and cholesterol-lowering drugs are generally employed simultaneously. Several studies have shown that use of LDL apheresis can achieve significant lowering of lipids in nearly all patients with severe hypercholesterolemia.[65,66] Promising results have also been reported from a system capable of direct adsorption of LDL and Lp(a) (DALI) from whole blood.[67]

Refsum's Disease (Phytanic Acid Disease). Refsum's disease is a rare inborn error of metabolism resulting in toxic levels of phytanic acid, causing neurologic, cardiac, skeletal, and skin abnormalities.[21] TPE is useful in conjunction with a phytanic-acid-deficient diet and should be started as soon as possible, before permanent damage occurs.

Staphylococcal Protein A Immunoadsorption

SPA immunoadsorption is approved by the FDA for treatment of acute and chronic immune thrombocytopenic purpura. The device is also FDA-approved to treat adults with rheumatoid arthritis unresponsive to disease-modifying antirheumatic drugs.[64] Although not FDA-approved, this technique has been used, with limited success, to treat other autoimmune thrombocytopenias.[68] Many of these protocols are still experimental and randomized trials have not been conducted. Anecdotal cases of TTP/HUS refractory to TPE that have responded to SPA immunoadsorption have also been reported.[69]

Photopheresis

Photopheresis is a technique that involves the treatment of patients with psoralens, the separation of lymphocytes by apheresis, and treatment of the cells with ultraviolet radiation. This renders the lymphocytes and other nucleated cells incapable of division. The treated cells are then reinfused. This procedure, also known as extracorporeal photochemotherapy, has been approved by the FDA for the treatment of cutaneous T-cell lymphoma and is considered the first line of treatment for the erythrodermic phase of this disease.[70] Clinical trials are under way to determine the efficacy of photopheresis in the following conditions: cellular-mediated rejection of heart and lung allografts, and acute and chronic graft-vs-host disease following allogeneic marrow transplant. This technology is not available in most apheresis centers.

References

1. Silva MA, ed. Standards for blood banks and transfusion services. 23rd ed. Bethesda, MD: AABB, 2005.

2. Code of federal regulations. Title 21 CFR Part 640. Washington, DC: US Government Printing Office, 2004 (revised annually).

3. McLeod BC. Introduction to the third special issue: Clinical applications of therapeutic apheresis. J Clin Apheresis 2000;15(½):2-3.

4. Burgstaler EA. Current instrumentation for apheresis. In: McLeod BC, Price TH, Weinstein R, eds. Apheresis: Principles and practice. 2nd ed. Bethesda, MD: AABB Press, 2003:95-130.

5. Vamvakas EC, Pineda AA. Selective extraction of plasma constituents. In: McLeod BC, Price TH, Weinstein R, eds. Apheresis: Principles and practice. 2nd ed. Bethesda, MD: AABB Press, 2003:437-76.

6. Berger GM, Firth JC, Jacobs P, et al. Three different schedules of low-density lipoprotein apheresis compared with plasmapheresis in patients with homozygous familial hypercholesterolemia. Am J Med 1990;88:94-100.

7. Silva MA, Brecher ME. Summary of the AABB interorganizational taskforce on bacterial contamination of platelets, fall 2004 impact survey. Transfusion 2005 (in press).

8. Food and Drug Administration. Memorandum: Revised guideline for the collection of Platelets, Pheresis. (October 7, 1988) Rockville, MD: CBER Office of Communication, Training, and Manufacturers Assistance, 1988.

9. Food and Drug Administration. Memorandum: Volume limits for automated collection of source plasma. (November 4, 1992) Rockville, MD: CBER Office of Communication, Training, and Manufacturers Assistance, 1992.

10. Food and Drug Administration. Memorandum: Requirements for infrequent plasmapheresis donors. (March 10, 1995) Rockville, MD: CBER Office of Communication, Training, and Manufacturers Assistance, 1995.

11. Food and Drug Administration. Guidance for industry: Recommendations for collecting red blood cells by automated apheresis methods. (January 30, 2001; technical correction February 13, 2001) Rockville, MD: CBER Office of Communication, Training, and Manufacturers Assistance, 2001.

12. Vamvakas EC, Pineda AA. Determinants of the efficacy of prophylactic granulocyte transfusions: A meta-analysis. J Clin Apheresis 1997; 12:74-81.

13. Stroncek DF, Yau YY, Oblitas J, Leitman SF. Administration of G-CSF plus dexamethasone produces greater granulocyte concen-

trate yields while causing no more donor toxicity than G-CSF alone. Transfusion 2001;41: 1037- 44.

14. Strauss RG. Neutrophil collection and transfusions. In: Simon TL, Dzik WH, Snyder EL, et al, eds. Rossi's principles of transfusion medicine. 3rd ed. Baltimore, MD: Lippincott Williams and Wilkins, 2002:258-67.

15. McCullough J. Granulocyte transfusion. In: Petz LD, Swisher SN, Kleinman S, et al, eds. Clinical practice of transfusion medicine. 2nd ed. New York: Churchill-Livingstone, 1996: 413-32.

16. Barnes A, DeRoos A. Increased granulocyte yields obtained with an oral three-dose prednisone premedication schedule (abstract). Am J Clin Pathol 1982;78:267.

17. Strauss RG, Ghodsi Z. Cataracts in neutrophil donors stimulated with adrenal corticosteroids. Transfusion 2001;41:1464-8.

18. Stroncek DF, Matthews CL, Follman D, Leitman SF. Kinetics of G-CSF induced granulocyte mobilization in healthy subjects: Effects of route of administration and addition of dexamethasone. Transfusion 2002;42: 597-602.

19. Szczepiorkowski ZM, ed. Standards for cellular therapy product services. 1st ed. Bethesda, MD: AABB, 2004.

20. Smith JW, Weinstein R, Hillyer KL for the AABB Hemapheresis Committee. Therapeutic apheresis: A summary of current indications categories endorsed by the AABB and the American Society for Apheresis. Transfusion 2003;43:820-2.

21. Strauss RG, Ciavarella D, Gilcher RO, et al. An overview of current management. J Clin Apheresis 1993;8:189-272.

22. Jones HG, Bandarenko N. Management of the therapeutic apheresis patient. In: McLeod BC, Price TH, Weinstein R, eds. Apheresis: Principles and practice. 2nd ed. Bethesda, MD: AABB Press, 2003:253-82.

23. McLeod BC. Therapeutic plasma exchange. In: Simon TL, Dzik WH, Snyder EL, et al, eds. Rossi's principles of transfusion medicine. 3rd ed. Baltimore, MD: Lippincott Williams and Wilkins, 2002:662-82.

24. Williams WJ, Katz VL, Bowes WA. Plasmapheresis during pregnancy. Obstet Gynecol 1990;76:451-7.

25. Orlin JB, Berkman EM. Partial plasma replacement: Removal and recovery of normal plasma constituents. Blood 1980;56:1055-9.

26. Weinstein R. Basic principles of therapeutic blood exchange. In: McLeod BC, Price TH, Weinstein R, eds. Apheresis: Principles and practice. 2nd ed. Bethesda, MD: AABB Press, 2003:295-320.

27. Brecher ME, Owen HG, Bandarenko N. Alternatives to albumin: Starch replacement for plasma exchange. J Clin Apheresis 1997;12: 146-53.

28. Kiprov DD, Golden P, Rohe R, et al. Adverse reactions associated with mobile therapeutic apheresis; analysis of 17,940 procedures. J Clin Apheresis 2001;16:130-3.

29. Weinstein R. Prevention of citrate reactions during therapeutic plasma exchange by constant infusion of calcium gluconate with the return fluid. J Clin Apheresis 1996;11:204-10.

30. Olbricht CJ, Schaumann D, Fischer D. Anaphylactoid reactions, LDL apheresis with dextran sulphate, and ACE inhibitors. Lancet 1993;341:60-1.

31. Robinson A. Untoward reactions and incidents in machine donor apheresis. Transfus Today 1990;7:7-8.

32. McLeod BC, Sniecinski I, Ciavarella D, et al. Frequency of immediate adverse effects associated with therapeutic apheresis. Transfusion 1999;39:282-8.

33. McLeod BC, Price TH, Owen H, et al. Frequency of immediate adverse effects associated with apheresis donation. Transfusion 1998;38: 938-43.

34. Westphal RG. Complications of hemapheresis. In: Westphal RG, Kasprisin DO, eds. Current status of hemapheresis: Indications, technology and complications. Arlington, VA: AABB, 1987:87-104.

35. Askari S, Nollet K, Debol SM, et al. Transfusion-related acute lung injury during plasma exchange: Suspecting the unsuspected. J Clin Apheresis 2002;17:93-6.

36. Duntley P, Siever J, Korwes ML, et al. Vascular erosion by central venous catheters. Clinical features and outcome. Chest 1992;101:1633-8.

37. Quillen K, Magarace L, Flanagan J, Berkman EM. Vascular erosion caused by a double-lumen central venous catheter during therapeutic plasma exchange. Transfusion 1995; 35:510-2.

38. Leitman SF, Boltansky H, Alter HJ, et al. Allergic reactions in healthy plateletpheresis donors caused by sensitization to ethylene oxide gas. N Engl J Med 1986;315:1192-6.

39. Gilcher RO. Apheresis: Principles and technology of hemapheresis. In: Simon TL, Dzik WH, Snyder EL, et al, eds. Rossi's principles of transfusion medicine. 3rd ed. Baltimore, MD: Lippincott Williams and Wilkins, 2002:648-58.

40. Schmitt E, Kundt G, Klinkmann H. Three years with a national apheresis registry. J Clin Apheresis 1992;7:58-72.

41. Madore F, Lazarus JM, Brady HR. Therapeutic plasma exchange in renal diseases. J Am Soc Nephrol 1996;7:367-86.

42. McLeod BC. Apheresis principles and practice. 2nd ed. Bethesda, MD: AABB Press, 2003.

43. Klein HG. Principles of apheresis. In: Anderson KC, Ness PM, eds. Scientific basis of transfusion medicine. 2nd ed. Philadelphia: WB Saunders, 2000:553-68.

44. Cohen JA, Brecher ME, Bandarenko N. Cellular source of serum lactate dehydrogenase elevation in patients with thrombotic thrombocytopenic purpura. J Clin Apheresis 1998;13:16-9.

45. Furlan M, Robles R, Galbusera M, et al. von Willebrand factor-cleaving protease in thrombotic thrombocytopenic purpura and the hemolytic-uremic syndrome. N Engl J Med 1998;339:1578-84.

46. Tsai H-M, Chun-Yet Lian E. Antibodies to von Willebrand factor-cleaving protease in acute thrombotic thrombocytopenic purpura. N Engl J Med 1998;339:1585-94.

47. McLeod BD. Thrombotic microangiopathies in bone marrow and organ transplant patients. J Clin Apheresis 2002;17:118-23.

48. George JN, Li X, McMinn JR, Terrell DR, et al. Thrombotic thrombocytopenic purpura-hemolytic uremic syndrome following allogeneic HPC transplantation: A diagnostic dilemma. Transfusion 2004;44:294-304.

49. George JN, Rizui MA. Thrombocytopenia. In: Beutler E, Lichtman MA, Coller BS, et al, eds. Williams' hematology. 6th ed. New York: McGraw-Hill, 2001:1495-539.

50. Rock G, Shumak KH, Sutton DM, et al. Cryosupernatant as replacement fluid for plasma exchange in thrombotic thrombocytopenic purpura. Br J Haematol 1996;94:383-6.

51. Gerritsen HE, Robles R, Lammle B, Furlan M. Partial amino acid sequence of purified von Willebrand factor-cleaving protease. Blood 2001;98;1654-61.

52. Bandarenko N, Brecher ME, and members of the US TTP Apheresis Study Group. United States Thrombotic Thrombocytopenic Purpura Apheresis Study Group (US TTP ASG): Multicenter survey and retrospective analysis of current efficacy of therapeutic plasma exchange. J Clin Apheresis 1998;13:133-41.

53. Adans DM, Schultz WH, Ware RE, Kinney TR. Erythrocytapheresis can reduce iron overload and prevent the need for chelation therapy in chronically transfused pediatric patients. J Pediatr Hematol Oncol 1996;18:46-50.

54. Plasma Exchange/Sandoglobulin Guillain-Barré Syndrome Trial Group. Randomized trial of plasma exchange, intravenous immunoglobulin, and combined treatments in Guillain-Barré syndrome. Lancet 1997;349:225-30.

55. Nagpal S, Benstead T, Shumak K, et al. Treatment of Guillain-Barré syndrome: A cost-effectiveness analysis. J Clin Apheresis 1999;14:107-13.

56. Guillain-Barré Syndrome Study Group. Plasmapheresis and acute Guillain-Barré syndrome. Neurology 1985;35:1096-104.

57. vanDoorn PA, Vermeulen M, Brand A. Intravenous immunoglobulin treatment in patients with chronic inflammatory demyelinating polyneuropathy. Arch Neurol 1991;48:217-20.

58. Dyck PJ, Low PA, Windebank AJ, et al. Plasma exchange in polyneuropathy associated with monoclonal gammopathy of undetermined significance. N Engl J Med 1991;325:1482-6.

59. Simovic D, Gorson KC, Popper AH. Comparison of IgM-MGUS and IgG-MGUS polyneuropathy. Acta Neurol Scand 1998;97:194-200.

60. Frasca GM, Zoumparidis NG, Borgnino LC, et al. Plasma exchange treatment in rapidly progressive glomerulonephritis associated with anti-neutrophil cytoplasmic autoantibodies. Int J Artif Organs 1992;3:181-4.

61. Pusey CD, Rees AJ, Evans JJ, et al. A randomized controlled trial of plasma exchange in rapidly progressive glomerulonephritis without anti-GBM antibodies. Kidney Int 1991;40:757-63.

62. Johnson WJ, Kyle RA, Pineda AA, et al. Treatment of renal failure associated with multiple myeloma. Arch Intern Med 1990;150:863-9.

63. Guillevin L, Lhote F, Leon A, et al. Treatment of polyarteritis nodosa related to hepatitis B virus with short-term steroid therapy associated with antiviral agents and plasma exchanges: A prospective trial in 33 patients J Rheumatol 1993;20:289-98.

64. Felson DT, LaValley MP, Baldassare AR, et al. The Prosorba column for treatment of refractory rheumatoid arthritis: A randomized, double-blind, sham-controlled trial. Arthritis Rheum 1999;42:2153-9.

65. Kroon AA, Aengevaeren WRM, van der Werf T, et al. LDL-apheresis atherosclerosis regression study (LAARS): Effect of aggressive versus conventional lipid lowering treatment on coronary atherosclerosis. Circulation 1996;93:1826-35.

66. Thompson GR, Maher VMG, Matthews S, et al. Familial hypercholesterolemia regression study: A Randomized trial of low-density-lipoprotein apheresis. Lancet 1995;345:811-16.

67. Bosch T, Lennertz A, Schenzle D, et al. Direct adsorption of low density lipoprotein and lipoprotein (a) from whole blood: Results of the first clinical long-term multicenter study

using DALI apheresis. J Clin Apheresis 2002; 17:161-9.

68. Handelsman H. Office of health technology assessment report, No. 7. Protein A columns for the treatment of patients with idiopathic thrombocytopenic purpura and other indications. Rockville, MD: DHHS, PHS, Agency for Health Care Policy and Research, 1991:1-8.

69. Gaddis TG, Guthrie TH, Drew MJ, et al. Treatment of refractory thrombotic thrombocytopenic purpura with protein A immunoadsorption. Am J Hematol 1997;55:55-8.

70. Lim HW, Edelson RL. Photopheresis for treatment of cutaneous T-cell lymphoma. Hematol Oncol Clin North Am 1995;9:1117-26.

Blood Component Testing and Labeling

EACH DONOR UNIT must be tested and properly labeled before its release for transfusion. Although the scope and characteristics of donor tests changed with the release of new tests and the advent of new regulatory requirements, the intent of donor testing remains constant: to enhance the safety of the blood supply. This chapter presents the general principles that apply to testing and labeling donor blood, and it provides a description of the specific tests that are required or done voluntarily at most blood banks on each donation. Discussion of the infectious complications of blood transfusion is found in Chapter 28. Other aspects of component preparation are covered in Chapter 8.

Testing

General Requirements

Each laboratory needs to develop standard operating procedures for the performance of blood component testing strictly in compliance with current instructions provided by the test manufacturers. Testing must be performed in a planned, orderly manner under a quality plan and a written set of procedures that instruct the staff how to perform testing, under what circumstances additional testing needs to be done, and what to do if things go wrong. The facilities and equipment must be adequate for the activity being conducted. Access to the area must be limited. The environment must be controlled so that temperature specifications for the tests will be met, and the test will not be adversely affected by the environment. The test materials and equipment in use must be those previously approved and validated by the facility. If a facility uses reagents or equipment from several different manufacturers, the facility is responsible for documentation that validation of the equipment or reagent combination for each test in use has occurred and that staff have been trained on the most current applicable instructions. For tests required by the Food and Drug Administration (FDA)[1] and/or AABB *Standards for Blood Banks and Transfusion Services,* all reagents used must meet or exceed the requirements of the FDA.[2(p9)] If the manufacturer of a licensed test supplies controls, they must be used for that test. However, if these controls are used for calibration, different controls must be used to verify test performance. These controls may need to be purchased separately. The manufacturer defines acceptable sample (specimen) requirements and considerations that usually include the presence and nature of anticoagulant, the age of suitable samples, and permissible storage intervals and conditions. Tests must be performed on a properly identified sample from the current donation. Testing must be completed for each blood donation before release. Each test result must be recorded concurrently with its observation; interpretation is to be recorded only when testing has been completed. Testing results must be recorded and records maintained so that any results can be traced for a specific unit and/or component.

The facility should have a policy for notifying donors of positive infectious disease test results. Test results are confidential and must not be released to anyone (other than the donor) without the donor's written consent. At the time of donation, the donor must be told if the policy is to release positive test results to state or local public health agencies, and the donor must agree to those conditions before phlebotomy. Donors must sign a consent form before they donate blood acknowledging that the facility maintains a registry of donors who gave disqualifying donor histories or have positive infectious disease results. The donor must also be informed if the sample will undergo research testing, including investigational new drug (IND) protocols. The most problematic notifications are those in which the donor has a false-positive test result. For some analytes [eg, antibodies to hepatitis C virus (anti-HCV) or human immunodeficiency virus, types ½ (anti-HIV-1/2)], confirmatory or supplemental testing is routinely performed for donor counseling purposes and possible donor reentry, if applicable. In the case of a minor, state and local laws apply.[3]

Required Tests

ABO group and Rh type must be determined at each donation. A sample from each donation intended for allogeneic use must be tested for the following[1,2(p33)]:

- Syphilis
- Hepatitis B surface antigen (HbsAg)
- HIV nucleic acid (individual or combined HIV/HCV assay)
- HCV nucleic acid (individual or combined HIV/HCV assay)
- Anti-HIV-1
- Anti-HIV-2
- Antibodies to hepatitis B core antigen (anti-HBc)
- Anti-HCV
- Antibodies to human T-cell lymphotropic viruses, types I/II (anti-HTLV-I/II)

A combination test for anti-HIV-1/2 may be used. A test for alanine aminotransferase (ALT) is not required by the FDA or the AABB. Recommendations for labeling units associated with an elevated ALT have been released by the FDA.[4]

Equipment Requirements

All equipment used for testing must be properly calibrated and validated upon installation, after repairs, and periodically. There must be a schedule for planned maintenance. All calibration, maintenance, and repair activities must be documented for each instrument. Software used to control the instrument or to interface with the institution's computer system must also be properly validated.[5]

Records Requirements

Records must show each production step associated with each blood component from its source to its final disposition.[6,7] Records must be kept in a manner that protects the identity and personal information of the donor from discovery by anyone other than the facility doing the donor recruitment, qualification, and blood collection, with the exception of government agencies that require certain test-positive results to be reported by law for public health purposes. Testing records on donor units must be kept in a manner that makes it possible to investigate adverse consequences to a recipient. In addition, donor testing records must be suitable for look-back to previously donated components when a donor's blood gives positive results on a new or improved infectious disease test.

Previous records of a donor's ABO and D typing results must be reviewed and compared with the ABO and D test findings on the current donation. This is a very valuable quality check on both the sample identity correctness and the operation of the laboratory. If a discrepancy is found between any current or historic test required, the unit must not be released until there is unequivocal resolution of the discrepancy.[2(p39)]

ABO and D Testing

Every unit of blood intended for transfusion must be tested for ABO and D.[2(p32),8] The ABO group must be determined by testing donor red cells with reagent anti-A and anti-B, and donor serum or plasma with A_1 and B red cells. The Rh type must be determined by testing donor red cells with anti-D serum. Red cells that are nonreactive with anti-D in direct agglutination tests must be tested by a method designed to detect weak D. Red cells that react with anti-D either by direct agglutination or by the weak D test must be labeled Rh positive. Red cells that are nonreactive with anti-D by direct agglutination and the weak D test must be labeled Rh negative. Some of the automated techniques have sufficient D sensitivity to obviate the need for a weak D test. These instruments add reagents, incubate reagent and sample appropriately, read the reaction, and provide a result ready for interpretation. In addition, the automated devices incorporate positive sample identification with the use of barcode readers and use anticoagulated blood so that only one tube is needed for both red cell and plasma sampling. See Chapter 13 and Chapter 14 for a more complete discussion of the principles of ABO and D testing.

Antibody Screening

Blood from donors with a history of transfusion or pregnancy must be tested for unexpected antibodies. Because it is usually impractical to segregate blood that should be tested from units that need not be tested, most blood centers test all donor units for unexpected red cell antibodies. Donor serum or plasma may be tested against individual or pooled reagent red cells of known phenotypes. Methods must be those that demonstrate clinically significant red cell antibodies. See Methods Section 3 for antibody detection techniques and Chapter 19 for a discussion of antibody detection.

Serologic Test for Syphilis

Serologic testing for syphilis (STS) has been carried out on donor samples for over 50 years. Although experimental studies in the 1980s showed that survival of spirochetes at 4 C is dependent on the concentration, it is not known how long the spirochete (*Treponema pallidum*) survives at refrigerated temperatures in a naturally infected blood component.[9] The last reported transfusion transmitted case of syphilis was reported in fresh blood components in 1969.[10]

The majority of screening tests for syphilis in US blood collection centers are microhemagglutinin or cardiolipin-based tests that are typically automated. Donor units testing positive for syphilis (STS) may not be used for allogeneic transfusion. Results can be confirmed before a donor is notified. Volunteer donors are much more likely to have a false-positive test result than a true-positive one.

Viral Marker Testing

Two screening methods are widely used to detect viral antigens and/or antibodies. The first is the enzyme-linked immunosorbent assay (EIA). The EIA tests for the viral antigen HBsAg employ a solid support (eg, a bead or microplate) coated with an unlabeled antiserum against the antigen. The indicator material is the same or another antibody, labeled with an enzyme whose presence can be detected by a color change in the substrate. If the specimen contains antigen, it will bind to the solid-phase antibody and will, in turn, be bound by the enzyme-labeled indicator antibody. To screen for viral antibodies, ie, anti-HIV-1, anti-HIV-2, anti-HBc, anti-HCV, or anti-HTLV-I/II, the solid phase (a bead or microtiter well) is coated with antigens prepared from the appropriate viral recombinant proteins or synthetic peptides. The second technology for virus detection is based on nucleic acid amplification and detection of viral nuclear material.[11] The RNA viruses being

tested for routinely are HIV and HCV. Two experimental tests for West Nile virus (WNV) are undergoing study nationwide.[12,13] Nucleic acid testing (NAT) for HBsAg is undergoing clinical trials in some centers.

In the capture approach frequently used in assays, serum or plasma is incubated with fixed antigen. If present, antibody binds firmly to the solid phase and remains fixed after excess fluid is washed away. An enzyme-conjugated preparation of antigen or antiglobulin is added; if fixed antibody is present, it binds the labeled antigen or antiglobulin, and the antigen-antibody-antigen (or antiglobulin) complex can be quantified by measuring enzyme activity. One assay for anti-HBc uses an indirect capture method (competitive assay), in which an enzyme-antibody conjugate is added to the solid-phase antigen along with the unknown specimen. Any antibody present in the unknown specimen will compete with the enzyme-conjugated antibody and significantly reduce the level of enzyme fixed, compared with results seen when nonreactive material is present. Antigens used in the viral antibody screening tests may be made synthetically by recombinant technology or extracted from viral particles.

NAT is a powerful but expensive technology that reduces the exposure window for HIV and HCV by detecting very low numbers of viral copies after they appear in the bloodstream. Primers for HCV and HIV viruses are placed in microplate wells, either separately or in combination according to the specific test design. In the use of pooled sera, 16 to 24 donor samples are mixed and tested. If viral RNA matching the fragments already in the well is present in the donor samples, heat-cycling nucleic acid amplification using a heat-cycling technique will cause the viral fragments to multiply and be easily detectable. The microplate with the aliquot of pooled sera is placed in the well with the viral primers and substrate so that if the primers and viral material in the donor samples are the same, the primer and viral particles will increase geometrically with each cycle. Viral presence can then be detected reliably. When a pool is found to be positive, all the individual samples making up the pool are tested separately for the individual viruses HIV and HCV to find the positive donor sample. The second major advantage of this test is the relative lack of false-positive results as long as sample and laboratory cross-contamination are controlled.[12]

For most of the assays, samples giving nonreactive results on the initial screening test, as defined by the manufacturer's package insert, are considered negative and need not be tested further. Samples that are reactive on the initial screening test must be repeated in duplicate. Reactivity in one or both of the repeated tests constitutes a positive result and is considered repeatedly reactive. All components must be discarded in this case. If both the duplicate repeat tests are nonreactive, the test is interpreted as having a negative result.

Before a donor is designated as antigen- or antibody-positive, a status that may have significant clinical and social consequences and cause permanent exclusion from blood donation, it is important to determine whether the screening result is a true- or false-positive result.

Invalidation of Test Results

In the course of viral marker testing, it may be necessary to invalidate test results if the test performance did not meet the requirements of the manufacturer's package insert (eg, faulty equipment, improper procedure, compromised reagents), or if the control results do not meet the acceptance criteria defined in the package insert. All results, both the reactive and the nonreactive, obtained in the run must be declared invalid; all specimens involved must be tested in a new run, which becomes the initial test of record.[13]

However, if the batch controls are acceptable and no error is recognized in test performance, the reactive and nonreactive results from the initial run remain as the initial test of record for the specimens involved. Specimens with reactive results must be retested in duplicate, as required by the manufacturer's instructions.

Before a test run is invalidated, the problems observed should be reviewed by a supervisor or equivalent, causes should be analyzed, and corrective action should be taken, if applicable. A record of departure from normal standard operating procedures should be prepared, with a complete description of the reason for invalidation and the nature of corrective actions.[13]

Use of External Controls

Other considerations may need to be addressed before the invalidation of test results when external controls are used.[13] Internal controls are the validation materials provided with the licensed assay kit; they are used to demonstrate that the test performs as expected. External controls generally consist of at least one positive control and one negative control. If the negative control from the kit is used to calculate the assay cutoff, it cannot be used as an assay control reagent for testing. An external negative control should be used in its place (see Table 7-1). External controls are frequently used to demonstrate the ability of the test to identify weakly reactive specimens. External controls are surrogate specimens, either purchased commercially or developed by the institution, that are not a component of the test kit; they are used for surveillance

Table 7-1. Use of External Controls

Test Kit Reagents	Used to Calculate Assay Cutoff?	External Controls Required?
Negative control only	Yes	Yes–negative control
	No	No
Positive control only	Yes	Yes–positive control
	No	No
Both positive and negative controls	Yes	Yes–positive and negative controls

of test performance. External controls are tested in the same manner as donor samples to augment blood safety efforts and to alert the testing facility to the possibility of an increasing risk of error.

Before being entered into routine use, external controls must be qualified, lot by lot, because each control lot may vary with the test kit. One way to qualify an external control is:

1. Run the external control for 2 days, four replicates per day, using two to three different test kit lots. The performance of the external controls must meet specified requirements before use.

2. If the external controls do meet the specifications, the acceptable sample-to-cutoff ratio for the external control (eg, within three standard deviations of the mean) must be determined.

Additional qualification testing must be performed whenever a new lot of test kits or external controls is introduced.

When a change of test kit lot occurs, replicates (eg, 20 replicates) of the external control should be run with the current kit lot and the new lot. The new sample-to-cutoff ratio and limits should be determined.

Users should verify special requirements for external control handling in pertinent state, federal, and international regulations, as applicable.

A facility may invalidate *nonreactive* test results on the basis of external controls, but if the assay was performed in accordance with manufacturer's specifications and the internal controls performed as expected, external controls cannot be used to invalidate *reactive* test results. The use of external controls may be more stringent than, but must be consistent with, the package insert's criteria for rejection of test results. Observation of donor population data, such as an unexpectedly increased reactive rate within a test run, may cause non-reactive results to be considered invalid. The next assay, performed on a single aliquot from affected specimens, becomes the initial test of record for those samples nonreactive in the invalidated run. However, reactive results obtained in a run with an unexpectedly increased reactive rate may not be invalidated unless the entire run fails to meet the performance criteria specified in the package insert. Such reactive results remain the initial test of record. The samples must be tested in duplicate as the repeat test.

External controls may also be used to invalidate a duplicate repeat test run when an assay run is valid by test kit acceptance criteria and both the repeated duplicate tests are nonreactive. The duplicate samples may be repeated in duplicate; the second duplicate test becomes the test of record. If either of the original duplicate repeat tests is reactive, the donor(s) must be classified as repeatedly reactive and no further repeat screening tests should be performed.

When samples are reactive on the *initial* screening test, allogeneic donor units must be quarantined until the results of duplicate repeat testing are available. Components associated with repeatedly reactive test results must not be used for allogeneic transfusion. Supplemental or confirmatory testing may be performed on samples that are repeatedly reactive to obtain additional information for donor counseling and possible reentry, depending on the viral marker and availability of approved assays.

Supplemental Tests: Neutralization

In confirmatory antigen neutralization tests (eg, HBsAg), the reactive specimen is incubated with human serum known to contain antibody specific for the antigen in question. If incubation causes the positive reaction to disappear or to diminish by at least 50% (or the percentage specified in the package insert) and all controls behave as expected, the presence of antigen is confirmed and the original result is considered a true positive. If incubation with a known antibody does not affect subsequent reactivity, the original reactivity is considered a false-positive result. Known positive and negative control samples must be tested in parallel with donor or patient samples. Parallel incubations must be performed with a preparation known to contain antibody specific for the antigen in question and with a preparation known to be free of both antigen and antibody. If the positive and negative control values do not fall within limits stated in the package insert, the test must be repeated.

Supplemental Test for EIA-Reactive Anti-HIV-1/2, -HTLV I/II, and -HCV Tests

Western blot is the method most frequently used for the confirmation of repeatedly reactive anti-HIV EIA tests. The technique separates antigenic viral material into bands according to molecular weight. The material is transferred to nitrocellulose membranes. Antibody in the test serum reacts with the individual bands, depending on the specificity. Most persons infected with HIV, whether asymptomatic or exhibiting AIDS, show multiple bands, representing antibodies to virtually all of the various gene products. A fully reactive test serum should react with the p17, p24, and p55 *gag* proteins; the p31, p51, and p66 *pol* proteins; and the gp41, gp120, and gp160 *env* glycoproteins. Western blot results in EIA-reactive blood donor samples are classified as positive, negative, or indeterminate. Positive results are those with reactivity to at least two of the following HIV proteins: p24, core protein; gp41, transmembrane protein; and gp120/160, external protein and external precursor protein. Indeterminate results are those with other patterns of reactivity.

An immunofluorescence assay (IFA) is used in some blood centers as an alternative to Western blot testing. Cells infected with virus are fixed on a slide. The sample is incubated with the fixed cells. Antibody in the sample will bind to the antigen sites on the viral particles. The reaction mixture is incubated with fluorescent-labeled antihuman IgG. Following incubation and washing, binding of the labeled antihuman IgG is read using a fluorescence microscope, with subsequent interpretation of the fluorescence pattern.

Although there are FDA-approved Western blot confirmatory tests for anti-HIV, the Western blot test using recombinant DNA and viral lysate antigens for anti-HTLV-I/II has not been approved by the FDA. An appropriate supplemental test to confirm a reactive anti-HTLV test result is to repeat the test using another manufacturer's EIA test. If that test is repeatedly reactive, the result is considered confirmed. If the test is negative, the anti-HTLV test result is considered a false-positive result.

The FDA has approved a recombinant immunoblot assay (RIBA) system to further differentiate anti-HCV EIA repeatedly reactive samples. The RIBA system is based on the fusion of HCV antigens to human superoxide dismutase in the screening test and to a recombinant superoxide dismutase in the confirmatory test to detect nonspecific reactions. A positive result requires reactivity to two HCV antigens and no reactivity to superoxide dismutase. Reactivity to only one HCV antigen or to one HCV antigen and superoxide dismutase is classified as an indeterminate reaction. Results are usually presented as positive, negative, or indeterminate. As with all procedures, it is essential to follow the manufacturer's instructions for classification of test results. The use of nucleic acid amplification testing is discussed in Chapter 28.

Cytomegalovirus Testing

Optional tests may be performed on units intended for recipients with special needs. For example, cytomegalovirus (CMV) testing is a commonly performed optional test. CMV can persist in the tissues and leukocytes of asymptomatic individuals for years after initial infection. Blood from persons lacking antibodies to the virus has reduced risk of transmitting infection compared with untested (nonleukocyte-reduced) units. Only a small minority of donor units with positive test results for anti-CMV will transmit infection. However, there is presently no way to distinguish infective antibody-positive units from noninfective units containing anti-CMV. Routine testing for anti-CMV is not required by AABB *Standards*,[2(p43)] but, if it is performed, the usual quality assurance considerations apply. The most common CMV antibody detection methods in use are EIA and latex agglutination. Other methods, such as indirect hemagglutination, complement fixation, and immunofluorescence, are also available.

Labeling, Records, and Quarantine

Labeling

Labeling is a process that includes a final review of records of donor history, collection, testing, blood component modification, quality control functions, and any additional information obtained after donation. This also includes a review of labels attached to the components and checks to ensure that all labels meet regulatory requirements and are an accurate reflection of the contents of the blood or blood components.[1,8]

All labeling of blood components must be performed in compliance with AABB *Standards*[2(p12)] and FDA regulations. Blood centers and transfusion services must ensure that labeling is specific and controlled. Before the labeling process begins, there should be a mechanism or procedure in place that ensures the use of appropriate labels. This process should include assurance of acceptable label composition, inspection on receipt, secure storage and distribution of labels, archiving of superseded labels, and availability of a master set of labels in use. In addition, procedures should address generation of labels, changes in labels, and modification of labels to reflect label control of altered or new components. Labels should be checked for the proper product code for the component being labeled, which is based on collection method, anticoagulant, and modifications to the component during processing. All aspects of labeling (the bag label as well as the *Circular of Information for the Use of Human Blood and Blood Components*,[14] including the label size, type size, wording, spacing, and the base label adhesive) are strictly controlled.

ISBT 128

The ISBT 128 labeling system is an internationally defined system based on barcode symbology called Code 128. It standardizes the labeling of blood so that bar-coded labels can be read by blood centers and transfusion services around the world. The system allows for each number assigned to a unit of blood (blood identification number) to be unique. The unique number will allow tracking of a unit of blood from donor to recipient, regardless of where the unit was drawn or transfused. As outlined in the *United States Industry Consensus Standard for the Uniform Labeling of Blood and Blood Components Using ISBT 128*,[15] the information appearing on the label, the location of the label, and the exact wording on the label are standardized.

ISBT 128 differs from its predecessor, which used CODABAR symbology, by including more specific information on the label. One advantage of the standardized system is that additional information on the label allows for better definition of product codes. Other changes include an expanded donation identification number to include the collection facility's identification; bar-coded manufacturer's lot number, bag type, etc; bar-coded expiration date; and special testing barcode. A benefit will

be that the use of standardized computer-generated barcode labels (with better differentiation between components, preparation methods, and expiration dates) enhances efficiency, accuracy, and ultimately safety of labeled components. For example, the ISBT 128 label shows conspicuously that an autologous, biohazard unit is not a standard unit by making the blood type a different, smaller size and filling the space usually reserved for blood type with a biohazard symbol. Adherence to the guidelines ensures compliance with AABB standards[2(p12)] and FDA regulations. The United States blood banking community has recently been prompted by a general directive from the Secretary of Health and Human Services and a subsequent proposal from the FDA for uniform acceptance of this more comprehensive labeling system. Until the new international guidelines are implemented, the 1985 FDA Uniform Labeling Guideline remains in effect. More information on ISBT 128 is available from the International Council on Commonality in Blood Banking Automation at www.iccbba.com.

Label Requirements

The following pieces of information are required[2(p12),16,17] in clear readable letters on a label firmly attached to the container of all blood and component units:

- The proper name of the component, in a prominent position.
- A unique numeric or alphanumeric identification that relates the original unit to the donor and each component to the original unit.
- For components, the name, address, and FDA license number or registration number (whichever is appropriate) of the facility that collected the blood and/or the component. The label must include the name and location of all facilities performing any

part of component manufacturing. This includes facilities that wash, irradiate, and reduce leukocytes by filtration. If a process is performed under contract, and the process is performed under processes controlled by the contracting facility, only that facility's name is required in this case. There should not be more than two alphanumeric identifiers on the unit.

■ The expiration dates, including the date and year; if the shelf life is 72 hours or less, the hour of expiration must be stated.

■ The amount of blood collected.

■ The kind and quantity of anticoagulant (not required for frozen, deglycerolized, rejuvenated, or washed red cells).

■ For all blood and blood components, including pooled components, the approximate volume of the component must appear on the container.

■ Recommended storage temperature.

■ ABO group and Rh type.

■ Interpretation of unexpected red cell antibody tests for plasma-containing components when positive (not required for cryoprecipitate or frozen, deglycerolized, rejuvenated, or washed RBCs).

■ Results of unusual tests or procedures performed when necessary for safe and effective use. Routine tests performed to ensure the safety of the unit need not be on the label if they are listed in the *Circular of Information for the Use of Human Blood and Blood Components.*[14]

■ Reference to the *Circular of Information for the Use of Human Blood and Blood Components,*[14] which must be available for distribution, and contains information about actions, indications, contraindications, dosage,

administration, side effects, and hazards.

■ Essential instructions or precautions for use, including the warning that the component may transmit infectious agents, and the statements: "Rx only" and "Properly Identify Intended Recipient."

■ The appropriate donor classification statement—"autologous donor," "paid donor," or "volunteer donor"—in type no less prominent than that used for the proper name of the component.

■ Any additives, sedimenting agents, or cryoprotective agents that might still be present in the component.

Special Labeling

■ Cellular blood components issued as "Leukocytes Reduced" must be labeled as such.

■ The name and final volume of the component and a unique identifier for a pool must appear on all pooled components.

■ The number of units in a pool and their ABO group and Rh type must be on the label or an attached tie tag.

■ Identification numbers of the individual units in a pool should not be on the label but must be in the records of the facility preparing the pool.

■ Cellular blood components issued as "CMV negative" must be labeled as such.

■ Irradiated blood components must carry the appropriate irradiated label.

Records

Current good manufacturing practice regulations, as defined by Title 21 CFR Parts 200 and 600,[6,7,16,18] state that master production and control records must be a part of the labeling process. These records must be described in the facility's procedures. Before labeling, these records must be reviewed for accuracy and completeness. Appropriate signatures and dates (either electronic or manual) must document the review process.

Control Records

Control records include but may not be limited to:

- Donation process: that all questions are answered on the donor card, consent is signed, all prequalifying tests are acceptable (eg, hemoglobin, blood pressure), and a final review is documented by qualified supervisory personnel.
- Infectious disease testing: if performed at the collecting facility, that tests have acceptable quality control and performance; that daily equipment maintenance was performed and was acceptable; and that final results are reviewed to identify the date and person performing the review.
- Donor deferral registry: That the list of deferred donors has been checked to ensure that the donor is eligible.
- Component preparation: that all blood and blood components were processed and/or modified under controlled conditions of temperature and other physical requirements of each component.
- Transfer of records: if testing is performed at an outside facility, that all records of that facility are up to date and that the appropriate licensure is indicated. Records, either electronic or manual, must transfer data appropriately. All electronically transferred test records must be transmitted by a previously validated system.

Transfer of those results must be performed by a system that properly identifies test results to all appropriate blood and blood components.

- Quarantine: that any nonconforming unit is appropriately isolated.

Production Records

Master production records must be traceable back to:

- Dates of all processing or modification.
- Identification of the person and equipment used in the process steps.
- Identification of batches and in-process materials used.
- Weights and measures used in the course of processing.
- In-laboratory control results (temperatures, refrigerator, etc).
- Inspection of labeling area before and after use.
- Results of component yield when applicable.
- Labeling control.
- Secondary bag and containers used in processing.
- Any sampling performed.
- Identification of person performing and checking each step.
- Any investigation made on nonconforming components.
- Results of examinations of all review processes.

Quarantine

Before final labeling, there must be a process to remove nonconforming blood and blood components from the labeling process until further investigation has occurred. This process must be validated to capture and isolate all blood and blood components that do not conform to requirements in any of the critical areas of collecting, testing, and processing. This process must also capture verbal (eg, telephone calls) information submitted to the collection facility after the collection process. All nonconforming units must remain in quarantine until they are investigated and all issues are resolved. The units may then be discarded, labeled as nonconforming units (eg, autologous units), or labeled appropriately for transfusion if the investigation resolved the problems. If the nonconformance cannot be resolved and the units are from an allogeneic donation, they must be discarded.

References

1. Code of federal regulations. Title 21 CFR 610.40. Washington, DC: US Government Printing Office, 2004 (revised annually).
2. Silva MA, ed. Standards for blood banks and transfusion services. 23rd ed. Bethesda, MD: AABB, 2005.
3. Dodd RY, Stramer SL. Indeterminate results in blood donor testing: What you don't know can hurt you. Transfus Med Rev 2000;14:151-9.
4. Food and Drug Administration. Memorandum: Recommendations for labeling and use of units of whole blood, blood components, source plasma, recovered plasma or source leukocytes obtained from donors with elevated levels of alanine aminotransferase (ALT). (August 8, 1995) Rockville, MD: CBER Office of Communication, Training, and Manufacturers Assistance, 1995.
5. Code of federal regulations. Title 21 CFR 606.60. Washington, DC: US Government Printing Office, 2004 (revised annually).
6. Code of federal regulations. Title 21 CFR 606.160. Washington, DC: US Government Printing Office, 2004 (revised annually).
7. Code of federal regulations. Title 21 CFR 606.165. Washington, DC: US Government Printing Office, 2004 (revised annually).
8. Code of federal regulations. Title 21 CFR 640.5. Washington, DC: US Government Printing Office, 2004 (revised annually).
9. van der Sluis JJ, ten Kate FJ, Vuzevski VD, et al. Transfusion syphilis, survival of *Treponema pallidum* in donor blood. II. Dose dependence of experimentally determined survival times. Vox Sang 1985;49:390-9.
10. Chambers RW, Foley HT, Schmidt PJ. Transmission of syphilis by fresh blood components. Transfusion 1969;9:32-4.
11. Busch MP, Stramer SL, Kleinman SH. Evolving applications of nucleic acid amplification assays for prevention of virus transmission by blood components and derivatives. In: Garratty G, ed. Applications of molecular biology to blood transfusion medicine. Bethesda, MD: AABB, 1997:123-76.
12. Vargo K, Smith K, Knott C, et al. Clinical specificity and sensitivity of a blood screening assay for detection of HIV-1 and HCV RNA. Transfusion 2002;42:876-85.
13. Food and Drug Administration. Guidance for industry. Revised recommendations regarding invalidation of test results of licensed and 510(k)-cleared blood-borne pathogen assays used to test donors. (July 11, 2001) Rockville, MD: CBER Office of Communication, Training, and Manufacturers Assistance, 2001.
14. AABB, American Red Cross, and America's Blood Centers. Circular of information for the use of human blood and blood components. Bethesda, MD: AABB, 2002.
15. Food and Drug Administration. Guidance for Industry: United States industry consensus standard for the uniform labeling of blood and blood components using ISBT 128, Version 1.2.0. (November 28, 1999) Rockville, MD: CBER Office of Communication, Training, and Manufacturers Assistance, 1999.
16. Code of federal regulations. Title 21 CFR 606.210, and 606.211. Washington, DC: US Government Printing Office, 2004 (revised annually).
17. Food and Drug Administration. Guidelines for the uniform labeling of blood and blood components. (August 1985) Rockville, MD: CBER Office of Communication, Training and Manufacturers Assistance, 1985.
18. Code of federal regulations. Title 21 CFR Part 210, 211 and 606. Washington, DC: US Government Printing Office, 2004 (revised annually).

Suggested Reading

AABB, American Red Cross, and America's Blood Centers. Circular of information for the use of human blood and blood components. Bethesda, MD: AABB, 2002.

Chapter 8

Collection, Preparation, Storage, and Distribution of Components from Whole Blood Donations

DONOR CENTERS AND transfusion services share a common goal in blood component production: to provide a safe and efficacious component that benefits the intended recipient. To this end and in keeping with Food and Drug Administration (FDA) current good manufacturing practice regulations, all processes involved in the collection, testing, preparation, storage, and transport of blood and components are monitored for quality, including procedures, personnel, reagents, equipment, and the contents of the components themselves. Processes should ensure the potency and purity of the final product, minimize microbial contamination and proliferation, and prevent or delay the detrimental physical and chemical changes that occur when blood is stored.

Blood Component Descriptions

Readers should refer to Chapters 21, 23, and 24 and the current *Circular of Information for the Use of Human Blood and Blood Components*[1] for more detailed indications and contraindications for transfusion.

Whole Blood

Fresh Whole Blood contains all blood elements plus the anticoagulant-preservative in the collecting bag. It is used commonly as a source for component production. After 24-hour storage, it essentially becomes red cells suspended in a protein solution equivalent to liquid plasma, with a minimum hematocrit of approximately 33%.

Red Blood Cells

Red Blood Cells (RBCs) are units of Whole Blood with most of the plasma removed (see Method 6.4). If prepared from whole blood collected into citrate-phosphate-dextrose (CPD), citrate-phosphate-dextrose-dextrose (CP2D), or citrate-phosphate-dextrose-adenine (CPDA-1), the final hematocrit must be ≤80%. Additive red cell preservative systems consist of a primary collection bag containing an anticoagulant-preservative with at least two satellite bags integrally attached; one is empty and one contains an additive solution (AS). AS contains sodium chloride, dextrose, adenine, and other substances that support red cell survival and function up to 42 days[2] (see Table 8-1). The volume of the AS in a 450-mL collection set is 100 mL and the volume in 500-mL sets is 110 mL. AS is added to the red cells remaining in the primary bag after most of the plasma has been removed. This allows blood centers to use or recover a maximum amount of plasma, yet still prepare a red cell component with a final hematocrit between 55% and 65%, a level that facilitates excellent flow rates and allows easy administration.

RBCs can be prepared at any time during their shelf life, but AS must be added within the time frame specified by the manufacturer, generally within the first 72 hours of storage. Shelf life at 1 to 6 C storage depends on the anticoagulant-preservative used and the method of preparation.

Platelets

Platelet concentrates (Platelets) are prepared from units of whole blood that have not been allowed to cool below 20 C. Platelet-rich plasma (PRP) is separated within 4 hours after completion of the phlebotomy or within the time frame specified in the directions for the use of the blood collecting, processing, and storage system—typically 8 hours.[3] The platelets are concentrated by an additional centrifugation step and the removal of most of the supernatant plasma. A procedure for preparation of platelets from single units of whole blood appears in Method 6.13. The final component should contain resuspended platelets in an amount of plasma adequate to maintain an acceptable pH; generally, 40 to 70 mL is used. Although not approved in the United States, platelet concentrates are commonly manufac-

Table 8-1. Content of Additive Solutions (mg/100 mL)

	AS-1 (Adsol)	AS-3 (Nutricel)	AS-5 (Optisol)
Dextrose	2200	1100	900
Adenine	27	30	30
Monobasic sodium phosphate	0	276	0
Mannitol	750	0	525
Sodium chloride	900	410	877
Sodium citrate	0	588	0
Citric acid	0	42	0

tured in Europe using buffy coat as an intermediate product. In this schema, the initial centrifugation is a "hard-spin" in which the platelets are concentrated in the buffy coat. The supernatant platelet-poor plasma and the red cells can be expressed using a top-and-bottom device. The buffy coats can then be centrifuged in a "soft-spin" to remove the white cells or, more commonly, pooled before storage (not currently allowed by the FDA), then soft-spun as a pooled concentrate, with expression of the PRP.[4-6]

Plasma

Plasma in a unit of Whole Blood can be separated at any time during storage, up to 5 days after the expiration date of the Whole Blood. When stored frozen at −18 C or colder, this component is known as Plasma and can be used up to 5 years after the date of collection. If not frozen, it is called Liquid Plasma, which is stored at 1 to 6 C and transfused up to 5 days after the expiration date of the Whole Blood from which it was prepared.

Fresh Frozen Plasma (FFP) is plasma prepared from whole blood, either from the primary centrifugation of whole blood into red cells and plasma or from a secondary centrifugation of PRP. The plasma must be frozen within 8 hours of collection.[3] See Methods 6.10 and 6.13.

Blood centers often convert plasma and liquid plasma to an unlicensed component, "Recovered Plasma (plasma for manufacture)," which is usually shipped to a fractionator and processed into derivatives such as albumin and/or immune globulins. To ship recovered plasma, the collecting facility must have a "short supply agreement" with the manufacturer.[7] Because recovered plasma has no expiration date, records for this component must be retained indefinitely.

See further discussion of additional plasma products later in the chapter.

Cryoprecipitated AHF

Cryoprecipitated antihemophilic factor (AHF) is the cold-insoluble portion of plasma that precipitates when FFP is thawed between 1 to 6 C. It is essentially a concentrate of high-molecular-weight glycoproteins also known as CRYO. This component is prepared from a single Whole Blood unit collected into CPDA-1, CPD, or CP2D and suspended in less than 15 mL of plasma. It contains ≥80 IU Factor VIII (AHF), >150 mg of fibrinogen, and most of the Factor XIII originally present in the fresh plasma. CRYO contains both the procoagulant activity (Factor VIII) and the von Willebrand factor of the Factor VIII von Willebrand complex.

Once separated, CRYO is refrozen within 1 hour of preparation and stored at −18 C or colder for up to 1 year after the date of phlebotomy. See Method 6.11 for a preparation procedure.

Plasma Cryoprecipitate Reduced

If cryoprecipitate has been removed from plasma, this must be stated on the label. When stored at −18 C or colder, this component has a 12-month expiration date from the date of collection.[8(p59)] This component is used primarily in the treatment of thrombotic thrombocytopenic purpura.[9]

Granulocytes

Granulocytes are usually collected by apheresis techniques; however, buffy coats harvested from fresh Whole Blood units can provide a source ($<1 \times 10^9$) of granulocytes in urgent neonatal situations. Their effectiveness is controversial, however.[10] Granulocytes should be transfused as soon as possible after collection but may be stored at 20 to 24 C without agitation for up to 24 hours. Arrangements for pre-collection testing are often useful. This product is becoming obsolete.

Collection

Blood component quality begins with a healthy donor and a clean venipuncture site to minimize bacterial contamination. To prevent activation of the coagulation system during collections, blood should be collected rapidly and with minimal trauma to tissues. Although the target collection time is usually 4 to 10 minutes, one study has shown platelets and fresh frozen plasma to be satisfactory after collection times of up to 15 minutes.[11] The facility's written procedures should be followed regarding these collection times.

There should be frequent, gentle mixing of the blood with the anticoagulant. If prestorage filtration is not intended after collection, the tubing to the donor arm may be stripped into the primary collection bag, allowed to fill, and segmented, so that it will represent the contents of the donor bag for compatibility testing. Blood is then cooled toward 1 to 6 C unless it is to be used for room temperature component production, in which case it should be cooled toward, but not below, 20 C. Chapter 4 discusses blood collection in detail.

Anticoagulants and Preservatives

Whole blood is collected into a bag that contains an FDA-approved anticoagulant-preservative solution designed to prevent clotting and to maintain cell viability and function during storage. Table 8-2 compares some common solutions. Citrate prevents coagulation by chelating calcium, thereby inhibiting the several calcium-dependent steps of the coagulation cascade.[2]

The FDA approves 21-day storage at 1 to 6 C for red cells from whole blood collected in CPD and CP2D and 35-day storage for red cells collected in CPDA-1.[12] Most blood centers now collect up to 500 mL ± 50 mL (450-550 mL) whole blood in bags specifically designed for this larger volume. Blood bags intended for a collection volume of 450 mL ± 45 mL of whole blood (ie, 405-495 mL) contain 63 mL of anticoagulant-pre-

Table 8-2. Anticoagulant-Preservative Solutions (mg in 63 mL) for 450 mL Collections

	CPD	CP2D	CPDA-1
Ratio (mL solution to blood)	1.4:10	1.4:10	1.4:10
FDA-approved shelf life (days)	21	21	35
Content			
Sodium citrate	1660	1660	1660
Citric acid	206	206	206
Dextrose	1610	3220	2010
Monobasic sodium phosphate	140	140	140
Adenine	0	0	17.3

With 500 mL collections, the volume is 70 mL and the content 10% to 11% higher.

servative. The volume of anticoagulant-preservative in 500 mL ±50 mL bags is 70 mL. The allowable range of whole blood collected is dependent upon the collection bag selected and can vary with manufacturer, but the total amount collected including testing samples must not exceed 10.5 mL/kg donor weight per donation.

If only 300 to 404 mL of blood is collected into a blood bag designed for a 450-mL[8(p28)] collection, the red cells may be used for transfusion provided the unit is labeled "Red Blood Cells Low Volume." However, other components should not be prepared from these low-volume units. If a whole blood collection of less than 300 mL is planned, the volume of anticoagulant-preservative solution in that bag should be reduced proportionately (see Chapter 4 for calculations), to ensure that the correct amount of anticoagulant is used (ratio of anticoagulant: whole blood).

Transportation from a Collection Site

Whole blood should be transported from the collection site to the component preparation laboratory as soon as possible. Units should be cooled toward 1 to 6 C unless platelets are to be harvested, in which case, units should be cooled toward, but not below, 20 C. The time between collection and the separation of components must not exceed the time frame specified in the directions for use of the blood collection,[3] processing, and storage system.

Prestorage Processing

Differential Centrifugation

To simplify the separation of whole blood into its component parts, blood is collected into primary bags to which up to three satellite bags are attached.[5] Set design is based on intended use: RBCs, platelets, FFP, Cryoprecipitated AHF, or neonatal aliquots. Refer to Methods Section 6 for specific component preparation procedures. Whole blood must be separated and prepared components placed into their required storage temperatures within the anticoagulant-preservative manufacturer's recommended times of collection.[3] Records of component preparation should identify each individual performing a significant step in processing.

Because red cells, platelets, and plasma have different specific gravities, they are separated using differential centrifugation.[13] Rotor size, speed, and duration of spin are critical variables in centrifugation. Method 7.4 describes how to calibrate a centrifuge for platelet separation, but each centrifuge must be calibrated for optimal speeds and spin times for each combination of components prepared in like fashion and for each different type of collection bag. Times include the time of acceleration and "at speed," not deceleration time. Once the operating variables are identified for component production, timer accuracy, rpm, and temperature (if appropriate), centrifuges should be monitored periodically to verify equipment performance.

Another practical way to assess centrifugation is to monitor quality control data on components prepared in each centrifuge. If component quality does not meet defined standards, eg, if platelet concentrate yields are inconsistent, the entire process should be evaluated. Factors affecting the quality assessment are the calibration of the centrifuge, the initial platelet count on the whole blood donations, storage time, conditions between blood collection and platelet preparation, sampling technique, and counting methods.

Large centrifuges rotate at high speeds, exerting gravitational forces of thousands of pounds on blood bags. Weaknesses in these blood bags or the seals between tubing segments can cause rupture and leakage. The addition of filters for blood sets presents different challenges for cup insertion. Blood bags may be overwrapped with plastic bags to contain any leaks. Bags should be positioned so that a broad surface faces the outside wall of the centrifuge to reduce the centrifugal force on blood bag seams.

Contents in opposing cups of the centrifuge must be equal in weight to improve centrifuge efficiency and prevent damage to the rotor. Dry balancing materials are preferable to liquid material. Weighted rubber discs and large rubber bands are excellent and come in several thicknesses to provide flexibility in balancing. Swinging centrifuge cups provide better separation between cells and plasma than fixed-angle cups.

Testing and Labeling of Donor Units

Chapter 7 contains detailed information on testing and labeling blood components.

Filtration

During inline filtration of whole blood, the anticoagulated whole blood is filtered by gravity through an inline leukocyte reduction filter contained in the collection system. The filtered whole blood may be manufactured into leukocyte-reduced RBCs. Whole blood leukocyte reduction filters retain the platelets to a variable degree, so platelet concentrates cannot be routinely prepared. However, newly designed platelet sparing filters are under investigation. This filtration should occur within the time specified by the filter manufacturer.

A leukocyte reduction filter can be attached to a unit of Whole Blood or RBCs using a sterile connection device. Ideally, such filtration should occur as early as possible after collection but must conform to the manufacturer's recommendations for the specific filter in use. This method may be preferable if special units are to be selected for leukocyte reduction.

During inline filtration of red cells, platelets and/or plasma are first removed from the whole blood donation and the additive solution is transferred to the red cells. The red cells are then filtered through an inline filter into a secondary storage container. This filtration step should occur as early in the shelf life as possible and within the allowed time frame for the specific filter in use.

Leukocyte-reduced platelets may be prepared from PRP using inline leukocyte reduction filtration.[14] FFP manufactured using this intermediate step typically will have a leukocyte content of $<5 \times 10^6$.

Freezing

Acellular Components

When stored at -18 C or colder, FFP contains maximum levels of labile and nonlabile clotting factors (about 1 IU per mL) and has a shelf life of 12 months from the date of collection. FFP frozen and maintained at -65 C may be stored up to 7 years.

See Method 6.10 for preparation details. Plasma can be rapidly frozen by placing the bag 1) in a dry ice-ethanol or dry ice-antifreeze bath, 2) between layers of dry ice, 3) in a blast freezer, or 4) in a mechanical freezer maintained at -65 C or colder. Plasma frozen in a liquid bath should be overwrapped with a plastic bag to protect the container from chemical alteration. When a mechanical freezer is used, care must be taken to avoid slowing the freezing process by introducing too many units at one time.

It is prudent practice to use a method to facilitate detection of inadvertent thawing of plasma during storage, such as:

1. Pressing a tube into the bag during freezing to leave an indentation that

disappears if the unit thaws. Remove tube(s).

2. Freezing the plasma bag in a flat, horizontal position but storing it upright. Air bubbles trapped along the bag's uppermost broad surface during freezing will move to the top if the unit is thawed in a vertical position.

3. Placing a rubber band around the liquid plasma bag and removing it after freezing to create an indentation that disappears with thawing.

Plasma separated and frozen at −18 C between 8 and 24 hours (eg, plasma that does not meet the stricter time requirements of FFP) may be labeled as "Plasma Frozen Within 24 Hours after Phlebotomy." It contains all the stable proteins found in FFP (see Table 21-3). FFP thawing guidelines apply.

Cellular Components

Frozen storage can significantly extend the shelf life of red cell components. Unfortunately, the process can also cause cell damage and add considerable expense.

Effects of Freezing and Thawing. When unprotected cells are frozen, damage may result from cellular dehydration and from mechanical trauma caused by intracellular ice crystals. At rates of freezing slower than 10 C/minute, extracellular water freezes before intracellular water, producing an osmotic gradient that causes water to diffuse from inside the cell to outside the cell. This leads to intracellular dehydration. Controlling the freezing rate, however, is not sufficient by itself to prevent cellular damage, so cryoprotective agents must be used.

Cryoprotective agents are classified as penetrating and nonpenetrating. Penetrating agents such as glycerol are small molecules that freely cross the cell membrane

into the cytoplasm. The intracellular cryoprotectant provides an osmotic force that prevents water from migrating outward as extracellular ice is formed. A high concentration of cryoprotectant prevents formation of ice crystals and consequent membrane damage.[15] Glycerol, a trihydric alcohol, is a colorless, sweet-tasting, syrup-like fluid that is miscible with water. Pharmacologically, glycerol is relatively inert.

Nonpenetrating cryoprotective agents (eg, hydroxyethyl starch) are large molecules that do not enter the cell. The molecules protect the cells by a process called "vitrification" because they form a noncrystalline "glassy" shell around the cell. This prevents loss of water and dehydration injury and alters the temperature at which the solution undergoes transition from liquid to solid.

Freezing of RBCs. Frozen preservation of RBCs with glycerol is primarily used for storing units with rare blood types and autologous units. Frozen cells can be effectively stockpiled for military mobilization or civilian disasters, but the high cost and the 24-hour shelf life after deglycerolization make them less useful for routine inventory management. Recently, an effectively closed system was approved with a 2-week postthaw shelf life when the blood is collected in CPDA-1, frozen within 6 days, and stored at −80 C.

Two concentrations of glycerol have been used to cryopreserve red cells, as shown in Table 8-3. This chapter and Methods 6.7 and 6.8 discuss only the high-concentration glycerol technique used by most blood banks. Modifications have been developed for glycerolizing, freezing, storing, thawing, and deglycerolizing red cells and are discussed elsewhere.[16] Several instruments are available that partially automate glycerolization and deglycerolization of red cells. The manufacturer of each instrument provides detailed instructions for its use.

Table 8-3. Comparison of Two Methods of Red Blood Cell Cryopreservation

Consideration	High-Concentration Glycerol	Low-Concentration Glycerol
Final glycerol concentration (wt/vol)	Approx. 40%	Approx. 20%
Initial freezing temperature	−80 C	−196 C
Freezing rate	Slow	Rapid
Freezing rate controlled	No	Yes
Type of freezer	Mechanical	Liquid nitrogen
Storage temperature (maximum)	−65 C	−120 C
Change in storage temperature	Can be thawed and refrozen	Critical
Type of storage	Polyvinyl chloride; polyolefin	Polyolefin
Shipping	Dry ice	Liquid nitrogen
Special deglycerolizing equipment required	Yes	No
Deglycerolizing time	20-40 minutes	30 minutes
Hematocrit	55-70%	50-70%

Blood intended for freezing can be collected into CPD, CP2D, or CPDA-1 and stored as Whole Blood or RBCs (including AS-RBCs). Ordinarily, red cells are glycerolized and frozen within 6 days of collection or rejuvenated and frozen up to 3 days after they expire, but RBCs preserved in AS have been frozen up to 42 days after collection, with adequate recovery.[17,18]

Some glycerolization procedures require removal of most of the plasma or additive from the RBCs; others do not. The concentration of glycerol used for freezing is hypertonic to blood. Its rapid introduction can cause osmotic damage to red cells, which manifests as hemolysis only after thawing. Therefore, when initiating the cryopreservation process, glycerol should be introduced slowly to allow equilibration within the red cells.

The US Department of Defense has adopted a method for high-concentration glycerolization that uses an 800-mL primary collection container suitable for freezing (see Method 6.8). Because the cytoprotective agent for freezing is transferred directly into the primary collection containers, there is less chance of contamination and/or identification error. In addition, the amount of extracellular glycerol is smaller and it is more efficient to store and ship units prepared by this method.

Storage Bags. Storage bag composition can affect the freezing process; less hemolysis may occur in polyolefin than in some polyvinyl chloride (PVC) bags. Contact between red cells and the PVC bag surface may cause an injury that slightly increases hemolysis upon deglycerolization. In addition, polyolefin bags are less brittle at −80 C and less likely to break during shipment and handling than PVC bags.

Freezing Process. Red cells frozen within 6 days of collection with a final glycerol concentration of 40% (wt/vol) must be stored at –65 C or colder. Red cells are usually placed in canisters to protect the plastic bag during freezing, storage, and thawing.

Although up to 18 hours at room temperature may elapse between glycerolizing and freezing without increased postthaw hemolysis, an interval not exceeding 4 hours is recommended.[16] With current 40% (wt/vol) glycerol methods, controlled rate freezing is unnecessary; freezing is accomplished by placing the RBC container into a –80 C freezer.

Refreezing Deglycerolized RBCs. It may occasionally be desirable to refreeze thawed RBC units that have not been used as expected or have been unintentionally thawed. Units that were deglycerolized, stored 20 hours at refrigerator temperature, and then reglycerolized and refrozen showed no loss of adenosine triphosphate (ATP), 2,3-diphosphoglycerate (2,3-DPG), or in-vivo survival,[19] and RBCs subjected three times to glycerolizing, freezing, and thawing exhibited a 27% loss of total hemoglobin.[20] AABB *Standards for Blood Banks and Transfusion Services* does not address refreezing thawed units because this should not be considered a routine practice. If thawed units are refrozen, the records should document the valuable nature of such units and the reasons for refreezing them.

Freezing of Platelets. Perhaps because of their greater complexity, platelets appear to sustain greater injury during cryopreservation than red cells, although several protocols have successfully used dimethyl sulfoxide as a cryoprotectant.[21,22] Because postthaw platelet recovery and function are significantly reduced when compared with those of liquid-stored platelets, the clinical use of cryopreserved platelets is not widespread. The primary use of this procedure is to freeze autologous platelets for future use. Platelet cryopreservation is essentially a research technique.

Irradiation

Cellular blood components may be irradiated before storage to prevent transfusion-associated graft-vs-host disease (GVHD). This does not shorten the shelf life of platelets or granulocytes, but red cells expire 28 days after irradiation or at the end of the storage period, whichever comes first.

Pooling

Sterile connection devices are used to attach additional bags and compatible tubing to a blood bag without breaking the sterile integrity of the system. The shelf life of components thus prepared is the same as those prepared in a closed system except for Pooled Platelets, which expire 4 hours after pooling. All sterile connection device welds must be inspected for completeness, integrity, leakage, and air bubbles; procedures must address the action to take if the weld is not satisfactory. Record-keeping should include documentation of the products welded, weld quality control, and lot numbers of disposables.[23]

Cryoprecipitated AHF

Units of CRYO may be pooled before labeling, freezing, and storage. If pooled promptly after preparation using aseptic technique and refrozen immediately, the resulting component is labeled "Cryoprecipitated AHF Pooled," with the number of units pooled stated on the label. The volume of saline, if added to facilitate pooling, must also appear on the label. The statement may appear in the *Circular of Information for the Use of Human Blood and Blood Components*[1] instead of on the container label.

The facility preparing the pool must maintain a record of each individual donor traceable to the unique identifier used for the pooled component.[8(p26)]

If an open-system pool or component is to be stored frozen, it should be placed in the freezer within 6 hours after the seal has been broken. The AABB and the FDA require transfusion within 4 hours for pooled thawed components stored at 20 to 24 C.[8(p58)]

Platelets

Prestorage pooling of PRP whole-blood-derived platelets is possible using a sterile connection device and a storage container suitable for storage of a high-yield platelet concentrate. Platelet concentrates can be leukocyte-reduced using inline filtration[14] or they can be pooled into a pooling container, then subsequently leukocyte-reduced by filtration and stored in a storage container. Although current FDA requirements limit the dating of these pools to 4 hours, studies of such prestorage leukocyte-reduced pooled platelet concentrates show good preservation of platelet function without any evidence of a mixed lymphocyte reaction, with up to 7 days of storage.[24] However, the AABB and FDA require transfusion of pooled platelets within 4 hours of pooling.

As indicated earlier, buffy-coat-derived platelets are commonly pooled before storage with filtration of the PRP after centrifugation.[4-6]

Storage

Refrigerated Storage

Blood must be stored only in refrigerators that, by design and capacity, maintain the required blood storage temperatures of 1 to 6 C throughout their interior space. There must be a system to monitor temperatures continuously and record them at least every 4 hours, and an alarm system with an audible signal that activates before blood reaches unacceptable storage temperatures.

Interiors should be clean, adequately lighted, and well organized. Clearly designated and segregated areas are needed for: 1) unprocessed blood; 2) labeled blood suitable for allogeneic transfusion; 3) rejected, outdated, or quarantine blood; 4) autologous blood; and 5) biohazardous autologous blood. Refrigerators used for the storage of blood and blood components may also be used for blood derivatives, tissues, patient and donor specimens, and blood bank reagents.

Refrigerators for blood storage outside the blood bank, as may be found in surgical suites or emergency rooms, must meet these same standards. Temperature records are required at all times when blood is present. It is usually most practical to make blood bank personnel responsible for monitoring these refrigerators.

Frozen Storage

The FDA licenses Red Blood Cells Frozen for storage up to 10 years when prepared with high glycerol (40% wt/vol) methods. Units stored for up to 21 years have been transfused successfully. A facility's medical director may wish to extend the storage period; however, storage beyond 10 years requires exceptional circumstances. The distinctive nature of such units and the reason for retaining them past the 10-year storage period should be documented. As units are put into long-term storage, many consider it prudent to freeze samples of serum or plasma for subsequent testing should new donor screening tests be introduced in the future. The type of any specimen saved, date of collection, date of freezing, and specimen location, if necessary, should be included in records of frozen blood.

Not all such specimens may meet the sample requirements of new tests. If stored samples are not available or inappropriate for testing, blood centers may attempt to call the donor back for subsequent testing. Frozen rare RBCs that have not been tested for all required disease markers should be transfused only after weighing the risks and benefits to the patient. The label should indicate that the unit has not been completely tested and should identify the missing test(s) results.

Blood freezers have the same temperature monitoring and alarm requirements as blood refrigerators and must be kept clean and well organized. Freezers designated for plasma storage must maintain temperatures colder than –18 C (many function at –30 C or colder); RBC freezers must maintain temperatures colder than –65 C (many maintain temperatures colder than –80 C). Self-defrosting freezers must maintain acceptable temperatures throughout their defrost cycle.

Freezer alarm sensors should be accessible and located near the door, although older units may have sensors located between the inner and outer freezer walls where they are neither apparent nor accessible. In such cases, the location of the sensor can be obtained from the manufacturer and a permanent mark placed on the wall at that location. Clinical engineers may be able to relocate the sensor thermocouple for easier use.

Liquid nitrogen tanks used for blood storage also have alarm system requirements. The level of liquid nitrogen should be measured and the sensor placed somewhere above the minimum height needed.

Room Temperature Storage

Platelets require gentle, continuous agitation during storage because stationary platelets display increased lactate pro-duction and a decrease in pH. Elliptical, circular, and flat-bed agitators are available for tabletop or chamber use. Elliptical rotators are not recommended for use with storage bags made of polyolefin without plasticizer (PL-732).[25]

Other components that require 20 to 24 C temperatures, eg, cryoprecipitate, can be stored on a tabletop in any room with an appropriate ambient temperature, provided the temperature is recorded every 4 hours during storage. Because room temperatures fluctuate, "environmental" or "platelet chambers" have been developed to provide consistent, controlled room temperatures. These chambers are equipped with circulating fans, temperature recorders, and alarm systems.

Liquid Storage

Red Blood Cells

Biochemical changes occur when red cells are stored at 1 to 6 C; these changes, some of which are reversible, contribute to the "storage lesion" of red cells and to a reduction in viability and levels of 2,3-DPG affecting oxygen delivery to tissues.[26] The most striking biochemical changes that affect stored red cells are listed in Table 8-4, but some of these changes rarely have clinical significance, even in massively transfused recipients. Hemoglobin becomes fully saturated with oxygen in the lungs but characteristically releases only some of its oxygen at the lower oxygen pressure (pO_2) of normal tissues. The relationship between pO_2 and oxygen saturation of hemoglobin is shown by the oxygen dissociation curve (see Fig 8-1). Release of oxygen from hemoglobin at a given pO_2 is affected by ambient pH, intracellular red cell levels of 2,3-DPG, and other variables. High levels of 2,3-DPG in the red cells cause greater oxygen release at a given pO_2, which occurs as an adap-

Table 8-4. Biochemical Changes in Stored Non-Leukocyte-Reduced Red Blood Cells

Variable	CPD		CPDA-1				AS-1	AS-3	AS-5
	Whole Blood		Whole Blood	Red Blood Cells	Whole Blood	Red Blood Cells	Red Blood Cells	Red Blood Cells	Red Blood Cells
Days of Storage	0	21	0	0	35	35	42	42	42
% Viable cells (24 hours posttransfusion)	100	80	100	100	79	71	76 (64-85)	84	80
pH (measure at 37 C)	7.20	6.84	7.60	7.55	6.98	6.71	6.6	6.5	6.5
ATP (% of initial value)	100	86	100	100	56 (±16)	45 (±12)	60	59	68.5
2,3-DPG (% of initial value)	100	44	100	100	<10	<10	<5	<10	<5
Plasma K+ (mmol/L)	3.9	21	4.20	5.10	27.30	78.50*	50	46	45.6
Plasma hemoglobin	17	191	82	78	461	658.0*	N/A	386	N/A
% Hemolysis	N/A	N/A	N/A	N/A	N/A	N/A	0.5	0.9	0.6

*Values for plasma hemoglobin and potassium concentrations may appear somewhat high in 35-day stored RBC units; the total plasma in these units is only about 70 mL.

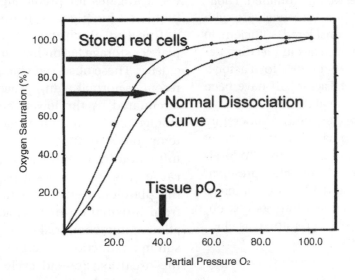

Figure 8-1. Oxygen dissociation of hemoglobin under normal circumstances and in Red Blood Cells (RBCs) stored in excess of 14 days. At tissue pO_2 (40 mm Hg), 25% to 30% of the oxygen is normally released. In stored RBCs, this will decrease to 10% to 15%.

tive change in anemia; lower red cell levels of 2,3-DPG increase the affinity of hemoglobin for oxygen, causing less oxygen release at the same pO_2. In red cells stored in CPDA-1 or in current additive systems, 2,3-DPG levels fall at a linear rate to zero after approximately 2 weeks of storage. This is caused by a decrease in intracellular pH caused by lactic acid, which increases the activity of a diphosphatase.[26] This causes the dissociation curve to shift to the left, resulting in less oxygen release (Fig 8-1).

Upon entering the recipient's circulation, stored red cells regenerate ATP and 2,3-DPG, resuming normal energy metabolism and hemoglobin function as they circulate in the recipient. It takes approximately 12 hours for severely depleted red cells to regenerate half their 2,3-DPG levels, and about 24 hours for complete restoration of 2,3-DPG and normal hemoglobin function.[26,27]

Red cells lose potassium and gain sodium during the first 2 to 3 weeks of storage at 1 to 6 C because sodium/potassium adenosine triphosphatase, which pumps sodium out of red cells and replaces it with potassium, has a very high temperature coefficient and functions poorly in the cold. Supernatant levels of potassium in a unit of CPDA-1 RBCs have been reported to increase from 5.1 mmol/L on the day of collection to 23 mmol/L on day 7 and 75 mmol/L on day 35. Intracellular levels of potassium will be replenished after transfusion.

Supernatant potassium levels in red cell components seem high when compared with levels in units of Whole Blood of equivalent age. However, the smaller supernatant fluid volumes must be considered when determining total potassium load. Blood stored at 1 to 6 C for more than 24 hours has few functional platelets, but levels of coagulation Factors II, VII, IX, X, and fibrinogen are well maintained. Labile factors (Factors V and VIII) decrease with time and are not considered sufficient to correct specific deficiencies in bleeding patients, although levels of 30% for Factor V and 15% to 20% for Factor VIII have been reported in Whole Blood stored for 21 days, and platelets stored at room temperature have been shown to have Factor V levels of 47% (see Chapter 21) and Factor VIII levels of 68% after 72 hours.[13] For better preservation of Factors V and VIII and platelets, whole blood is separated into its component parts and the plasma is stored as FFP.

Platelets

Platelets stored in the liquid state at 20 to 24 C are suspended in either autologous anticoagulated plasma (United States and Europe) or in platelet additive solutions (Europe). Under these conditions, the current shelf life of the platelets in most countries is 5 days (Table 8-5). This time limitation is partly related to concerns about storage-related deterioration in product potency[28] and partly to the potential for bacteria to grow rapidly in this temperature range.[29-30] With regard to potency, liquid-stored platelets undergo in-vitro changes, which are related to the duration of storage and are collectively known as the platelet storage lesion.[31,32] This is characterized by a change in platelet shape from discoid to spherical; the generation of lactic acid from glycolysis, with an associated decrease in pH; the release of cytoplasmic and granule contents; a decrease in various in-vitro measures of platelet function, particularly osmotic challenge; shape changes induced by adenosine diphosphate; and reduction in in-vivo recovery and survival. The in-vitro measures are useful measures of qualitative potency, but controversy still exists regarding their utility as practi-

cal surrogates for predicting in-vivo viability and function.[33] Attempts to date to define the biochemical nature of the platelet storage lesion have not been conclusive. These observed changes may represent a normal aging process, which is attenuated by the lower temperature of storage (20-24 C), rather than the in-vivo temperature of 37 C. However, a role for mitochondrial injury as a contributing cause of these changes is plausible. Resting platelets derive substantial energy from β-oxidation of fatty acids.[34] Alteration in mitochondrial integrity would result in a reduction in carbon flux through the tricarboxylic acid cycle and require energy metabolism through glycolysis, with increased lactate production. Such a reduction would compromise the generation of efficient ATP and result in a decrease in the metabolic pool of ATP and, therefore, the energy charge of the platelet.[35] This decrease in the energy charge would be expected to affect membrane integrity, resulting in a leakage of cytoplasmic contents, a diminished response to physiologic stimuli, and an inability to repair oxidized membrane lipids, with subsequent distortions in platelet morphology.[36]

Shelf Life

The maximum allowable storage time for a blood component held under acceptable temperatures and conditions is called its "shelf life." For red cells, the criteria for determining shelf life for an approved anticoagulant-preservative require that at least 75% of the original red cells (from a normal allogeneic donor) be in the recipient's circulation 24 hours after transfusion. For other components, their shelf life is based on functional considerations. Storage times are listed in Table 8-5.

Table 8-5. Expiration Dates for Selected Blood Components[8(pp53-60)]

Category	Expiration
Whole Blood	ACD/CPD/CP2D – 21 days
	CPDA-1 – 35 days
Whole Blood Irradiated	Original outdate (see outdates above per anticoagulant) or 28 days form date of irradiation, whichever is sooner
Red Blood Cells (RBCs)	ACD/CPD/CP2D – 21 days
	CPDA-1 – 35 days
	Open system – 24 hours
	Additive solutions – 42 days
RBCs Washed	24 hours
RBCs Leukocytes Reduced	ACD/CPD/CP2D – 21 days
	CPDA-1 – 35 days
	Open system – 24 hours
	Additive solutions – 42 days
RBCs Rejuvenated	24 hours
RBCs Rejuvenated Washed	24 hours
RBCs Irradiated	Original outdate above or 28 days from date of irradiation, whichever is sooner
RBCs Frozen 40% Glycerol	10 years
RBCs Frozen 20% Glycerol	10 years
RBCs Deglycerolized	24 hours – or 14 days depending on method
RBCs Open System	24 hours
RBCs Open System – Frozen	10 years, 24 hours after thaw
RBCs Closed System – Frozen	10 years, 2 weeks after thaw as approved by the FDA
RBCs Frozen – Liquid Nitrogen	10 years
Platelets	24 hours to 5 days, depending on collection system*
Platelets Pooled or in Open System	4 hours, unless otherwise specified
Platelets Leukocytes Reduced	Open system – 4 hours
	Closed system – no change from original expiration date*
Platelets Irradiated	Open system – 4 hours
	Closed system – no change from original expiration date
Granulocytes	24 hours
FFP	12 months (–18 C)
	7 years (–65 C), as approved by the FDA

(cont'd)

Table 8-5. Expiration Dates for Selected Blood Components[8(pp53-60)] (cont'd)

Category	Expiration
FFP Thawed	24 hours
FFP Thawed – Open System	24 hours
Plasma Frozen within 24 hours after Phlebotomy	12 months
Plasma Frozen within 24 hours after Phlebotomy Thawed	24 hours
Thawed Plasma	<5 days if whole blood derived 24 hours if apheresis
Plasma Liquid	5 days after expiration of RBCs
Plasma Cryoprecipitate Reduced Frozen	12 months
Plasma Cryoprecipitate Reduced Frozen	24 hours to 5 days
Cryoprecipitated AHF	12 months
Cryoprecipitated AHF Thawed	4 hours if open system or pooled, 6 hours if single unit

*Maximum time without agitation is 24 hours.

Poststorage Processing

Additional discussion of some of the following topics can be found in Chapters 21 and 22.

Filtration for Leukocyte Reduction

Only special leukocyte reduction filters reliably provide the ≥99.9% (log 3) removal needed to meet the 5×10^6 specification.[37] Red cell leukocyte reduction filters contain multiple layers of synthetic nonwoven fibers that retain white cells and platelets, allowing red cells to flow through. Leukocyte reduction filters are commercially available in a number of set configurations to facilitate filtration during the separation process at the bedside or in the laboratory before issue.[38] Intact leukocyte removal efficiency is best when performed soon after collection; therefore, prestorage leukocyte reduction is preferred.[39]

There were concerns that early removal of leukocytes would allow bacteria, present at the time of collection, to proliferate. However, studies suggest that early removal (within 24 hours) in the case of RBCs may reduce the likelihood of significant bacterial contamination.[40] Bedside filtration, particularly of platelets, may not be as effective in preventing reactions in multitransfused patients and is less desirable for this reason than prestorage leukocyte reduction.[41] Bedside filtration has also caused hypotensive reactions.[42] Cytokines and other substances that accumulate during storage (particularly in platelet components) may account for some failures of bedside filtration to prevent febrile reactions[43] (see Chapter 27). Furthermore, quality control is difficult to attain at the bedside.[44]

Thawing

Thawing FFP

FFP is thawed either at temperatures between 30 and 37 C or in an FDA-cleared device.[8(p59)] It is then known as "FFP Thawed" and should be transfused immediately or stored between 1 and 6 C for no more than 24 hours. The expiration date and time must be indicated on the label.

FFP thawed in a waterbath should be protected so that entry ports are not contaminated with water. This can be accomplished by wrapping the container in a plastic overwrap, or by positioning the container upright with entry ports above the water level. Microwave devices should be shown not to exceed temperature limits and not to damage the plasma proteins, and there should be a warning device to indicate if the temperature rises unacceptably. As with any device, there should be a procedure for the quality control of indicated functions.

When whole-blood-derived FFP prepared in a closed system is thawed but not transfused within 24 hours, the label must be modified. This product should be labeled "Thawed Plasma" and can be stored at 1 to 6 C and transfused up to 5 days after thawing. It is similar to FFP except for a reduction in both Factor V and Factor VIII, particularly Factor VIII.

Thawing CRYO

CRYO is thawed at temperatures between 30 to 37 C for no more than 15 minutes [CFR 606.122(n) (4)]. Bags should not remain at 30 to 37 C once thawed, so that degradation of Factor VIII is minimized. As with FFP, entry ports should be protected from water contamination if the unit is thawed in a waterbath. Single-unit thawed CRYO must be transfused immediately or can be stored at room temperature (20 to 24 C) for no more than 6 hours.

All pooled CRYO, whether prepared in an open or a closed system, must be transfused within 6 hours after thawing, or 4 hours after pooling, whichever comes first. CRYO may be pooled into one bag after thawing to simplify transfusion to a patient requiring multiple units. The pooled product is assigned a unique pool number, but records must document the individual units included. See Method 6.12 for guidelines on how to thaw and pool CRYO for transfusion.

Thawing and Deglycerolizing RBCs

The protective canister and enclosed frozen cells may be placed directly in a 37 C dry warmer or can be overwrapped and immersed in a 37 C waterbath. Units frozen in the primary collection bag system should be thawed at 42 C.[16] The thawing process takes at least 20 to 25 minutes and should not exceed 40 minutes. Gentle agitation may be used to speed thawing.

Thawed cells contain a high concentration of glycerol that must be reduced gradually to avoid in-vivo or in-vitro hemolysis. Deglycerolization is achieved by washing the red cells with solutions of decreasing osmolarity. In one procedure (see Method 6.9), glycerolized cells are diluted with 150 mL of 12% saline, then washed with 1 L of 1.6% saline, followed by 1 L of 0.9% saline with 0.2% dextrose. The progressive decrease in osmolarity of the washing solutions causes osmotic swelling of the cells, so each solution must be added slowly, with adequate time allowed for mixing and osmotic equilibration. Any of the commercially available instruments for batch or continuous-flow washing can be used to deglycerolize red cells frozen in a high concentration of glycerol. Because there are many potentially important variations in deglycerolization protocols for each instrument, personnel in each facility should not only follow the manufacturer's instructions, but also validate the local process. The process selected must ensure adequate removal of cryoprotectant agents, minimal free hemoglobin, and recovery of greater than 80% of the original red cell volume after the deglycerolization process.[8(p27)]

When deglycerolization is complete, the integrally connected tubing should be filled with an aliquot of red cells and sealed in such a manner that it can be detached for subsequent compatibility testing. The label must identify both the collecting facility and the facility that prepares the deglycerolized unit if it is different from the collection facility.

When glycerolized frozen red cells from persons with sickle cell trait are suspended in hypertonic wash solutions during deglycerolization and centrifuged, they form a jelly-like mass and hemolyze.[16] Modified wash procedures using only 0.9% saline with 0.2% dextrose after the addition of 12% saline can eliminate this problem.[45] In some cryopreservation programs, donations are screened for the presence of hemoglobin S before being frozen.

When glycerolization or deglycerolization involves entering the blood bag, the system is considered "open" and the resulting suspension of deglycerolized cells can be stored for only 24 hours at 1 to 6 C. A method for glycerolization and deglycerolization in an effectively closed system allows for the resulting suspension of deglycerolized red cells to be stored for 2 weeks at 1 to 6 C. This method allows more effective inventory management of the deglycerolized RBC units.

When deglycerolized RBCs are stored at 1 to 6 C for periods up to 14 days, the major changes observed are increased concentrations of potassium and hemoglobin in the supernatant fluid. Red cells that have undergone gamma irradiation and subsequent storage at 1 to 6 C tolerate freezing with no more detectable damage than unirradiated cells.[46,47]

Irradiation

Blood components that contain viable lymphocytes (including red cell, platelet, and granulocyte components) should be irradiated to prevent proliferation of transfused T lymphocytes in recipients at risk of acquiring, or from donors at risk of causing, GVHD. The AABB and FDA recommend a minimum 25 Gy dose of gamma radiation to the central portion of the container, with no less than 15 Gy delivered to any part of the bag.[8(p26)]

Irradiation is accomplished using cesium-137 or cobalt-60, in self-contained blood irradiators or hospital radiation therapy machines. More recently, an x-ray device has been developed that is capable of adequate dose delivery. Measurement of dose distribution; verification of exposure time, proper mechanical function, and turntable rotation; and adjustment of exposure time as the radioactive source decays should be addressed in the facility's procedures.[48] Records must be maintained, and all steps, supplies, and equipment used in the irradiation process must be documented.

To confirm the irradiation of individual units, radiochromic film labels (available commercially) may be affixed to bags before irradiation. When exposed to an adequate amount of radiation, the film portion of the label darkens, indicating that the component has been exposed to an adequate radiation dosage. Because irradiation damages red cells and reduces the overall viability (24-hour recovery),[49] red cell components that have been irradiated expire on their originally assigned outdate or 28 days from the date of irradiation, whichever comes first. Platelets sustain minimal damage from irradiation, so their expiration date does not change.[50] Irradiated blood is essential for patients at risk from transfusion-associated GVHD, including fetuses receiving intrauterine transfusion, select immunocompetent or immunocompromised recipients, recipients who are undergoing hematopoietic transplantation, recipients of platelets selected for HLA or platelet compatibility, and recipients of donor units from blood relatives.

Washing

Washing a unit of RBCs with 1 to 2 L of sterile normal saline removes about 99% of plasma proteins, electrolytes, and antibodies. Automated and manual washing methods remove some of the leukocytes in the RBCs, but not enough to prevent alloimmunization. Up to 20% of the red cell mass may be lost depending on the protocol used. Washed red cells must be used within 24 hours because preparation is usually accomplished in an open system, and removal of the anticoagulant-preservative solution compromises long-term preservation of cell viability and function.

Platelets can be washed with normal saline or saline-buffered with ACD-A or citrate, using manual or automated methods. The procedures may result in a reduction in radiolabeled recovery (about 33% less), but not in survival of the washed platelets[51]; white cell content is not significantly changed. Washed platelets must be used within 4 hours of preparation.

Pooling

When a patient requires multiple units of Platelets, pooling them into a single bag simplifies issue and transfusion. This product should be labeled "Platelets Pooled." If Platelets contain a significant number of red cells and ABO groups are mixed, plasma antibodies should be compatible with any visible red cells present in the pool. Only one unique number is affixed to the final component, but records must reflect the pooling process and all units included in the pool. This pooled product has an expiration time of 4 hours.

Single CRYO units may be pooled after thawing and labeled appropriately. The AABB and FDA require transfusion of CRYO within 4 hours of pooling and subsequent storage at 20 to 24 C.

Volume Reduction

Platelets may be volume-reduced in order to decrease the total volume of the component transfused or partially remove supernatant substances, such as ABO alloantibodies. The former need may arise in patients with small intravascular volumes or those with fluid overload (eg, resulting from renal or cardiac failure). The latter need may be better addressed by washing (see below). If sterility is broken, the expiration of the product becomes 4 hours. If sterility is not broken (eg, a sterile connection device is used[23]), removal of the supernatant still reduces glucose availability and buffering capacity, and the subsequent storage of the platelets is in a suboptimal environment. Transfusion as soon as possible is generally advocated.

Aliquoting

Blood components may be aliquoted in smaller volumes into other containers in order to meet the needs of very-low-volume transfusion recipients or to provide a component to meet the needs of patients with fluid overload. The composition of red cell and plasma components is not altered by aliquoting, unlike volume reduction. Therefore, the expiration date is not altered if a sterile connection device is used to perform the aliquoting.[23] The shelf life and viability of platelets, however, are dependent on the storage bag, plasma volume, and storage environment. Removing aliquots of platelets from the "mother" bag changes the storage environment of the platelets remaining in the "mother" bag. If the altered storage environment does not meet the storage bag manufacturer's requirements, the expiration period of the remaining component should also be modified.

Rejuvenation

It is possible to restore levels of 2,3-DPG and ATP in red cells stored in CPD or CPDA-1 solutions by adding an FDA-licensed solution containing pyruvate, inosine, phosphate, and adenine (see Method 6.6). RBCs may be rejuvenated after 1 to 6 C storage up to 3 days after expiration; then, they may be glycerolized and frozen in the same manner as fresh red cells. If rejuvenated RBC units are to be transfused within 24 hours, they may be stored at 1 to 6 C; however, they must be washed before use to remove the inosine, which might be toxic to the recipient. The blood label and component records must indicate the use of rejuvenating solutions.

Inspection, Shipping, Disposition, and Issue

Inspection

Stored blood components are inspected immediately before issue for transfusion or shipment to other facilities.[8(pp14,15)] These inspections must be documented; records should include the date, donor number, description of any abnormal units, the action taken, and the identity of personnel involved. Visual inspections cannot always detect contamination or other deleterious conditions; nonetheless, blood components that look abnormal must not be shipped or transfused.

Deleterious conditions should be suspected if[52]: 1) segments appear much lighter in color than what is in the bag (for AS-RBCs), 2) the red cell mass looks purple, 3) a zone of hemolysis is observed just above the cell mass, 4) clots are visible, 5) blood or plasma is observed in the ports or at sealing sites in the tubing, or (6) the plasma or supernatant fluid is murky, purple, brown, or red. A green hue from light-induced changes in bilirubin pigments need not cause the unit to be rejected. Mild lipemia, characterized by a milky appearance, does not render a donation unsuitable provided that all infectious disease testing can be performed. Grossly lipemic specimens are unsuitable.

A component that is questioned for any reason should be quarantined until a responsible person determines its disposition. Evaluation might include inverting the unit gently a few times to mix the cells with the supernatant fluid because considerable undetected hemolysis, clots, or other alterations may be present in the undisturbed red cells. If, after resuspension, resettling, and careful examination, the blood no longer appears abnormal, it may be returned to inventory. Appropriate records should be maintained documenting the actions taken, when, and by whom. Units of FFP and CRYO should be inspected when they are removed from frozen storage for evidence of thawing and refreezing and for evidence of cracks in the tubing or plastic bag. Unusual turbidity in thawed components may be cause for discard.

All platelet components should be inspected before release and issue. Units with macroscopically visible platelet aggregates should not be used for transfusion. Some facilities assess the "swirling" appearance of platelets by holding platelet bags up to a light source and gently tapping them. This swirl phenomenon correlates well with pH values associated with adequate platelet in-vivo viability.[53] Some platelet components have been noted to contain small amounts of particulate matter. These components are suitable for use.

Bacterial contamination of transfusion components is rare because of the use of aseptic technique and screening for bacteria in platelets, the availability of closed systems for collection and preparation, and careful control of storage conditions. Sterility testing of blood components plays a role in validating initial production processes. If a transfusion component has an abnormal appearance, or if an adverse clinical reaction appears to be related to contaminated donor blood, culturing should be performed and a Gram's stain should be evaluated.

Microbiologists can best advise blood center staff on sample requirements and appropriate test methods for detecting potential blood contaminants, including cryophilic microorganisms. Making cultures directly from the contents of the bag and from the recipient can provide useful diagnostic information.

Any facility that collected a reportedly contaminated component should be notified so that donor bacteremia, potentially inadequate donor arm preparation, or improper handling or pooling technique can be investigated. The donor's health should be reviewed, and other components prepared from that collection should be withdrawn.

Shipping

Shipment to areas outside the facility requires additional packaging. Transport containers or coolers and packaging procedures must be validated before use to verify that they are able to maintain blood components at required temperatures for the intended time and conditions. Containers must also be able to withstand leakage, pressure, and other conditions incidental to routine handling. Refer to Chapter 2 for more information on shipping regulations and guidelines.

Simple exposure to temperatures outside the acceptable range does not necessarily render blood unsuitable for transfusion. Exceptions may be made under unusual circumstances such as for autologous units or cells of a rare phenotype, but the records must document the reasons for preserving the unit, the evaluation of its continued suitability for transfusion, and the identity of the person responsible for the decision.

Other factors to consider when assessing component acceptability after transport include the length of time in shipment, mode of transportation, magnitude of variance above or below the acceptable range, presence of residual ice in the shipping box, appearance of the unit(s), age of the unit(s), and likelihood of additional storage before transfusion. The shipping facility should be notified when a receiving facility observes that acceptable transport temperatures have been exceeded.

Whole Blood and RBCs

Liquid Whole Blood and RBCs shipped from the collection facility to another facility must be transported in a manner that ensures a temperature of 1 to 10 C. The upper limit of 10 C can be reached in 30 minutes if a unit of blood taken from 5 C storage is left at an ambient temperature of 25 C. Smaller units, as are commonly used for pediatric patients, can warm even more quickly.

Wet ice, securely bagged to prevent leakage, is the coolant of choice to maintain required temperatures during transport and shipping. An appropriate volume is placed on top of the units within the cardboard box or insulated container. Clinical coolant packs or specially designed containers may also be used to maintain acceptable transport temperatures. Super-cooled ice (eg, large blocks of ice stored at –18 C) in contact with Whole Blood or RBCs may result in temperatures below 1 C, with resultant hemolysis of the red cells.

Platelets and Granulocytes

Every reasonable effort must be made to ensure that platelets and granulocytes are maintained at 20 to 24 C during shipment. A well-insulated container without added ice, or with a commercial coolant designed to keep the temperature at 20 to 24 C, is recommended. Fiber-filled envelopes or newspaper are excellent insulators. For very long distances or travel times in excess of 24 hours, double-insulated containers may be needed.

Frozen Components

Frozen components must be packaged for transport in a manner designed to keep them frozen. This may be achieved by using a suitable quantity of dry ice in well-insulated containers or in standard shipping cartons lined with insulation material, such as plastic air bubble packaging or dry packaging fragments. The dry ice, obtained as sheets, may be layered at the bottom of the container, between each layer of frozen components, and on top.

Shipping facilities should determine optimal conditions for shipping frozen components, which depend on the temperature requirements of the component, the distance to be shipped, the shipping container used, and ambient temperatures to be encountered. Procedures and shipping containers should be validated and periodically monitored. The receiving facility should always observe the shipment temperature and report unacceptable findings to the shipping facility.

Red cells cryopreserved with high-concentration glycerol (40% wt/vol) tolerate fluctuations in temperatures between –85 C and –20 C with no significant change in in-vitro recovery or 24-hour posttransfusion survival, so transport with dry ice is acceptable. Blood shipments containing dry ice as a coolant are considered "dangerous goods," and special packaging and labeling requirements apply (see Chapter 2). Shipping boxes containing dry ice must not be completely sealed so that the carbon dioxide gas released as the dry ice sublimes can escape without risk of explosion.

Disposition

Both blood collection sites and transfusion services must maintain records on all blood components handled so that units can be tracked from collection to final disposition. Units of blood that cannot be released for transfusion should be returned to the provider or discarded as biohazardous material. The nature of the problem disqualifying the unit should be investigated and the results reported to the blood supplier. Findings may indicate a need to improve phlebotomy techniques, donor screening methods, or the handling of units during processing, storage, or transport.

Disposal procedures must conform to the local public health code for biohazardous waste. Autoclaving or incineration is recommended. If disposal is carried out off-site, a contract with the waste disposal firm must be available and should specify that appropriate Environmental Protection Agency, state, and local regulations are followed (see Chapter 2 for the disposal of biohazardous waste).

Issuing from a Transfusion Service

Blood transported short distances within a facility, eg, to the patient care area for transfusion, requires no special packaging other than that dictated by perceived safety concerns and institutional preferences. However, blood should never unnecessarily be allowed to reach temperatures outside its accepted range. Specific transport guidelines may be warranted if transport time is prolonged.

Units that have left the control of the transfusion service or donor center and then have been returned must not be reissued for transfusion unless the following conditions have been met:

1. The container closure has not been penetrated, entered, or modified in any manner.
2. Red cell components have been maintained continuously between 1 and 10 C, preferably 1 to 6 C. Blood centers and transfusion services usually do not reissue RBC units that have remained out of a monitored refrigerator or a validated cooler for longer than 30 minutes because, beyond that time, the temperature of the component may have risen above 10 C.
3. At least one sealed segment of integral donor tubing remains attached to the red cell component, if the blood has left the premises of the issuing facility.
4. Records indicate that the blood has been reissued and has been inspected before reissue.

Blood Component Quality Control

Ensuring safe and efficacious blood components requires applying the principles of quality assurance to all aspects of component collection, preparation, testing, storage, and transport. All procedures and equipment in use must be validated before their implementation and periodically monitored thereafter. Staff must be appropriately trained and their compe-

tency evaluated. The contents of final products should be periodically assessed to make sure that they meet expectations. How much quality control is performed is best determined by the institution, with input from the compliance officer and consideration of AABB and FDA requirements. See Appendix 8-1.

Quality Control of Equipment

Continuous Temperature Monitoring Systems

Most blood refrigerators, freezers, and chambers have built-in temperature monitoring sensors connected to recording charts or digital readout systems for easy surveillance. Digital recording devices measure the differences in potential generated by a thermocouple; this difference is converted to temperature. Because warm air rises, temperature-recording sensors should be placed on a high shelf and immersed in a volume of liquid not greater than the volume of the smallest component stored. Either a glass container or a plastic blood bag may be used. Recording charts and monitoring systems must be inspected daily to ensure proper function.

When recording charts or tapes are changed, they should be dated inclusively (ie, start and stop dates), and labeled to identify the facility, the specific refrigerator or freezer, and the person changing the charts. Any departure from normal temperature should be explained in writing on the chart beside the tracing or on another document and should include how the stored components were managed. A chart with a perfect circle tracing may indicate that the recorder is not functioning properly or is not sensitive enough to record the expected variations in temperature that occur in any actively used refrigerator.

Blood banks with many refrigerators and freezers may find it easier to use a central alarm monitoring system that monitors all equipment continuously and simultaneously and prepares a hard copy tape of temperatures at least once every 4 hours. These systems have an audible alarm that sounds as soon as any connected equipment reaches its predetermined temperature alarm point and indicates the equipment in question. Blood storage equipment so monitored does not require a separate independent recording chart.

Thermometers

Visual thermometers in blood storage equipment provide ongoing verification of temperature accuracy. One should be immersed in the container with the continuous monitoring sensor. The temperature of the thermometer should be compared periodically with the temperature on the recording chart. If the two do not agree within 2 C, both should be checked against a thermometer certified by the National Institute of Standards and Technology (NIST) and suitable corrective action should be taken (see Method 7.2). (A 2 C variation between calibrated thermometers allows for the variation that may occur between thermometers calibrated against the NIST thermometers.)

Thermometers also help verify that the temperature is appropriately maintained throughout the storage space. Large refrigerators or freezers may require several thermometers to assess temperature fluctuations. In addition to the one immersed with the continuous monitoring sensor (usually located on a high shelf), at least one other in a similar container is placed on the lowest shelf on which blood is stored. The temperature in both areas must be within the required range at all times.

Either liquid-in-glass (analog) thermometers or electronic and thermocouple (digital) devices can be used for assessing storage temperatures, as long as their accuracy is calibrated against a NIST-certified thermometer or a thermometer with a NIST-traceable calibration certificate (see Method 7.2). Of equal importance is that they be used as intended, according to the manufacturer's recommendations.

Alarm Systems

To ensure that alarm signals will activate at a temperature that allows personnel to take proper action before blood reaches undesirable temperatures, both temperature of activation and power source are tested periodically. The electrical source for the alarm system must be separate from that of the refrigerator or freezer; either a continuously rechargeable battery or an independent electrical circuit served by an emergency generator is acceptable.

Method 7.3.1 provides a detailed procedure to test the temperatures of activation for refrigerator alarms. Suggestions for freezer alarms are in Method 7.3.2 Thermocouple devices that function at freezer temperatures are especially useful for determining the temperature of activation with accuracy when sensors are accessible. When they are not, approximate activation temperatures can be determined by checking a freezer's thermometer and recording chart when the alarm sounds after it is shut down for periodic cleaning or maintenance. It can also be assessed by placing a water bottle filled with cold tap water against the inner freezer wall where the sensor is located.

When the alarm goes off, usually in a short time, the recording chart can be checked immediately for the temperature of activation. There must be written instructions for personnel to follow when the alarm sounds. These instructions should include steps to determine the immediate cause of the temperature change and ways to handle temporary malfunctions, as well as steps to take in the event of prolonged failure. It is important to list the names of key people to be notified and what steps should be taken to ensure that proper storage temperature is maintained for all blood, components, and reagents.

Quality Control of Red Blood Cells

RBCs prepared without additive solutions must have a hematocrit ≤80%. This should be established during process validation and periodically confirmed by quality control procedures. RBCs Leukocytes Reduced should contain <5 × 10[6]residual leukocytes and retain 85% of the original red cells.[54] Quality control should demonstrate that at least 95% of units sampled meet this specification. Units tested must meet the leukocyte reduction specification.[6,8(p28)] (See Appendix 8-1.)

Quality Control of Platelets

The quality of every method of platelet preparation must be assessed periodically. Data must show that at least 90% of components tested contain an acceptable number of platelets (5.5 × 10[10] for whole-blood-derived platelets) and have a plasma pH of 6.2 or higher at the end of the allowable storage period.[8(p36)]

Prestorage leukocyte-reduced Platelets derived from filtration of platelet-rich plasma must contain less than 8.3 × 10[5] residual leukocytes per unit to be labeled as leukocyte reduced. Validation and quality control should demonstrate that at least 95% of units sampled meet this requirement.[8(p31)]

Quality Control of Cryoprecipitated AHF

AABB *Standards for Blood Banks and Transfusion Services* requires that all tested individual units of CRYO contain a minimum of 80 IU of Factor VIII and 150 mg of fibrinogen.[8(p30)] Each pool must have a Factor VIII content of at least 80 mg times the number of donor units in the pool; for fibrinogen, the content should be 150 mg times the number of donor units.[8(p30)] (See Appendix 8-1.)

References

1. AABB, American National Red Cross, and America's Blood Centers. Circular of information for the use of human blood and blood components. Bethesda, MD: AABB, 2002.

2. Buetler E. Liquid preservation of red blood cells. In: Simon TL, Dzik WH, Snyder EL, et al, eds. Rossi's principles of transfusion medicine. 3rd ed. Philadelphia: Lippincott Williams & Wilkins, 2002:50-61.

3. Code of federal regulations. Title 21 CFR 640.24(b) and 640.34(b). Washington, DC: US Government Printing Office, 2004 (revised annually).

4. Pietersz RN, van der Meer PF, Steneker I, et al. Preparation of leukodepleted platelet concentrates from pooled buffy-coats: Prestorage filtration with Autostop BC. Vox Sang 1999;76: 231-6.

5. Boomgaard MN, Joustra-Dijkhuis AM, Gouwerok CW, et al. In vitro evaluation of platelets, prepared from pooled buffy-coats, stored for 8 days after filtration. Transfusion 1994;34:311-6.

6. van der Meer PF, Pietersz RN, Tiekstra MJ, et al. WBC-reduced platelet concentrates from pooled buffy-coats in additive solution: An evaluation of in vitro and in vivo measures. Transfusion 2001;41:917-22.

7. Code of federal regulations. Title 21 CFR 601.22. Washington, DC: US Government Printing Office, 2004 (revised annually).

8. Silva MA, ed. Standards for blood banks and transfusion services. 23rd ed. Bethesda, MD: AABB, 2005.

9. Owens MR, Sweeney JD, Tahhan RH, et al. Influence of type of exchange fluid on survival in therapeutic apheresis for thrombotic thrombocytopenic purpura. J Clin Apheresis 1995;10:178-82.

10. Rosenthal J, Mitchell SC. Neonatal myelopoiesis and immunomodulation of host defenses. In: Petz LD, Swisher SN, Kleinman S, et al, eds. Clinical practice of transfusion medicine. 3rd ed. New York: Churchill Livingstone, 1996:685-703.

11. Huh YO, Lichtiger B, Giacco GG, et al. Effect of donation time on platelet concentrates and fresh-frozen plasma. Vox Sang 1989;56:21-4.

12. Code of federal regulations. Title 21 CFR 610.53 (c). Washington, DC: US Government Printing Office, 2004 (revised annually).

13. Calhoun L. Blood product preparation and administration. In: Petz LD, Swisher SN, Kleinman S, et al, eds. Clinical practice of transfusion medicine. 3rd ed. New York: Churchill Livingstone, 1996:305-33.

14. Sweeney JD, Holme S, Heaton WAL, Nelson E. White cell-reduced platelet concentrates prepared by in-line filtration of platelet-rich plasma. Transfusion 1995;35:131-6.

15. Valeri CR. Frozen preservation of red blood cells. In: Simon TL, Dzik WH, Snyder EL, et al, eds. Rossi's principles of transfusion medicine. 3rd ed. Philadelphia: Lippincott Williams & Wilkins, 2002:62-8.

16. Meryman HT, Hornblower M. A method for freezing and washing RBCs using a high glycerol concentration. Transfusion 1972;12:145-56.

17. Lovric VA, Klarkowski DB. Donor blood frozen and stored between –20 C and –25 C with 35-day liquid post-thaw shelf-life. Lancet 1989;i:71-3.

18. Rathbun EJ, Nelson EJ, Davey RJ. Post-transfusion survival of red cells frozen for 8 weeks after 42-day liquid storage in AS-3. Transfusion 1989;29:213-7.

19. Kahn RA, Auster MJ, Miller WV. The effect of refreezing previously frozen deglycerolized red blood cells. Transfusion 1978;18:204-5.

20. Myhre BA, Nakasako YUY, Schott R. Studies on 4 C stored frozen reconstituted red blood cells. III. Changes occurring in units which have been repeatedly frozen and thawed. Transfusion 1978;18:199-203.

21. Angelini A, Dragani A, Berardi A, et al. Evaluation of four different methods for platelet freezing: In vitro and in vivo studies. Vox Sang 1992;62:146-51.

22. Borzini P, Assali G, Riva MR, et al. Platelet cryopreservation using dimethylsulfoxide/polyethylene glycol/sugar mixture as cytopreserving solution. Vox Sang 1993;64:248-9.

23. Food and Drug Administration. Memorandum: Use of an FDA cleared or approved sterile connection device (STCD) in blood bank practice. (July 29, 1994) Rockville, MD: CBER Office of Communication, Training, and Manufacturers Assistance, 1994.

24. Sweeney JD, Kouttab NM, Holme SH, et al. Prestorage pooled whole blood derived leukoreduced platelets stored for seven days preserve acceptable quality and do not show evidence of a mixed lymphocyte reaction. Transfusion 2004;44:1212-9.

25. Moroff G, Holme S. Concepts about current conditions for the preparation and storage of platelets. Transfus Med Rev 1991;5:48-59.

26. Högman CF, Meryman HT. Storage parameters affecting red blood cell survival and functions after transfusion. Transfus Med Rev 1999;13:275-6.

27. Heaton A, Keegan T, Holme S. In vivo regeneration of red cell 2,3-diphosphoglycerate following transfusion of DPG-depleted AS-1, AS-3 and CPDA-1 red cells. Br J Haematol 1989;71:131-6.

28. Sweeney JD, Holme S, Heaton WAL. Quality of platelet concentrates. In: Van Oss CJ, ed. Transfusion immunology and medicine. New York: Marcel Dekker, 1995:353-70.

29. Heal JM, Singl S, Sardisco E, et al. Bacterial proliferation in platelet concentrates. Transfusion 1996;26:388-9.

30. Punsalang A, Heal JM, Murphy PJ. Growth of gram-positive and gram-negative bacteria in platelet concentrates. Transfusion 1989;29:596-9.

31. Murphy S. Platelet storage for transfusion. Semin Hematol 1985;22:165-77.

32. Murphy S, Rebulla P, Bertolini F, et al. In vitro assessment of the quality of stored platelet concentrates. The BEST (Biomedical Excellence of Safer Transfusion) Task Force of the International Society of Blood Transfusion. Transfus Med Rev 1994;8:29-36.

33. Rinder HM, Smith BR. In vitro evaluation of stored platelets: Is there hope for predicting post-transfusion platelet survival and function? Transfusion 2003;43:2-6.

34. Murphy S. The oxidation of exogenously added organic anions by platelets facilitates maintenance of pH during their storage for transfusion at 22 C. Blood 1995;85:1929-35.

35. Holme S, Heaton WA, Courtright M. Platelet storage lesion in second-generation containers: correlation with platelet ATP levels. Vox Sang 1987;53:214-20.

36. Holme S, Sawyer S, Heaton A, Sweeney JD. Studies on platelets exposed or stored at temperatures below 20 C or above 24 C. Transfusion 1997;37:5-11.

37. Dzik S. Leukodepletion blood filters: Filter design and mechanisms of leukocyte removal. Transfus Med Rev 1993;7:65-77.

38. Leukocyte reduction. Association Bulletin 99-7. Bethesda, MD: AABB, 1999.

39. Heaton A. Timing of leukodepletion of blood products. Semin Hematol 1991;28:1-2.

40. Buchholz DH, AuBuchon JP, Snyder EL, et al. Effects of white cell reduction on the resis-

tance of blood components to bacterial multiplication. Transfusion 1994;34:852-7.

41. Sweeney JD, Kouttab N, Penn LC, et al. A comparison of prestorage leukoreduced whole blood derived platelets with bedside filtered whole blood derived platelets in autologous stem cell transplant. Transfusion 2000;40:794-800.

42. Cyr M, Hume H, Sweeney JD, et al. Anomaly of the des-Arg9-bradykinin metabolism associated with severe hypotensive reaction during blood transfusions: A preliminary report. Transfusion 1999;39:1084-8.

43. Heddle NM, Klama L, Singer J, et al. The role of the plasma from platelet concentrates in transfusion reactions. N Engl J Med 1994;331:625-8.

44. Sweeney JD. Quality assurance and standards for red cells and platelets. Vox Sang 1998;74:201-5.

45. Meryman HT, Hornblower M. Freezing and deglycerolizing sickle-trait red blood cells. Transfusion 1976;16:627-32.

46. Suda BA, Leitman SF, Davey RJ. Characteristics of red cells irradiated and subsequently frozen for long-term storage. Transfusion 1993;33:389-92.

47. Miraglia CC, Anderson G, Mintz PD. Effect of freezing on the in vivo recovery of irradiated cells. Transfusion 1994;34:775-8.

48. Food and Drug Administration. Guidance for industry: Gamma irradiation of blood and blood components: A pilot program for licensing. (March 15, 2000) Rockville, MD: CBER Office of Communication, Training, and Manufacturers Assistance, 2000.

49. Moroff G, Holme S, AuBuchon JP, et al. Viability and in vitro properties of gamma irradiated AS-1 red blood cells. Transfusion 1999;39:128-34.

50. Sweeney JD, Holme S, Moroff G. Storage of apheresis platelets after gamma radiation. Transfusion 1994;34:779-83.

51. Pineda AA, Zylstra VW, Clare DE, et al. Viability and functional integrity of washed platelets. Transfusion 1989;29:524-7.

52. Kim DM, Brecher ME, Bland LA, et al. Visual identification of bacterially contaminated red cells. Transfusion 1992;32:221-5.

53. Bertoloni F, Murphy S. A multicenter inspection of the swirling phenomenon in platelet concentrates prepared in routine practice. Transfusion 1996;36:128-32.

54. Dumont LJ, Dzik WH, Rebulla P, Brandwein H, and the Members of the BEST Working Party of the ISBT. Practical guidelines for process validation and process control of white cell-reduced blood components: Report of the Biomedical Excellence for Safer Transfusion (BEST) Working Party of the International Society of Blood Transfusion (ISBT). Transfusion 1996;36:11-20.

Appendix 8-1. Component Quality Control

Component	Specifications and Standards*	AABB Standards[†]
Red Blood Cells	Hematocrit ≤80% (in all)	5.7.5.1
Red Blood Cells Leukocytes Reduced	Retain 85% of original red cells, 95% of tested units <5 × 10^6 leukocytes in the final container	5.7.5.6
Cryoprecipitated AHF	Factor VIII: ≥80 IU/bag (100%) Fibrinogen ≥150 mg/bag (100%)	5.7.5.14
Platelets	≥5.5 × 10^{10} platelets per unit and pH ≥6.2 in 90% of units tested	5.7.5.16
Platelets Leukocytes Reduced	≥5.5 × 10^{10} platelets in 75% of units tested, ≥6.2 pH in 90% of units tested, and <8.3 × 10^5 leukocytes in 95% of units tested	5.7.5.17
Platelets Pheresis	≥3.0 × 10^{11} platelets in final container of components tested; and pH ≥6.2 in 90% of units tested	5.7.5.19
Platelets Pheresis Leukocytes Reduced	<5.0 × 10^6 leukocytes in 95% of components tested *and* ≥3.0 × 10^{11} platelets in the final container and pH ≥6.2 in 90% tested units	5.7.5.20
Granulocytes Pheresis	≥1.0 × 10^{10} granulocytes in at least 75% of components tested	5.7.5.21
Irradiated components	25 Gy delivered to the central portion of the container; minimum of 15 Gy at any point in the component	5.7.4.2

*The *specification* is the threshold value; the *standard* is the percentage of tested units meeting or exceeding this threshold. The manufacturing procedures used should be validated as capable of meeting these standards before implementation and routine QC. The number of units tested during routine QC should be such as to have a high level of assurance that conformance with these standards is being achieved.

[†]Silva MA, ed. Standards for blood banks and transfusion services. 23rd ed. Bethesda, MD: AABB, 2005.

Chapter 9

Molecular Biology in Transfusion Medicine

P ROTEINS ARE MACROMOLECULES composed of amino acids, the sequences of which are determined by genes. Lipids and carbohydrates are not encoded directly by genes; genetic determination of their assembly and functional structures results from the action of different protein enzymes. Blood group antigens can be considered gene products, either directly, as polymorphisms of membrane-associated proteins, or indirectly, as carbohydrate configurations catalyzed by glycosyltransferases.

From DNA to mRNA to Protein

Structure of DNA

A gene consists of a specific sequence of nucleotides located at a specific position (locus) along a chromosome. Each chromosome consists of long molecules or strands of deoxyribonucleic acid (DNA). DNA is composed of the sugar deoxyribose, a phosphate group, the purine bases adenine (A) and guanine (G), and the pyrimidine bases thymine (T) and cytosine (C). The combination of a sugar, a phosphate group, and a base is called a nucleotide. A double strand of DNA consists of two complementary (nonidentical) single strands held together by hydrogen bonds between specific base pairings of A-T and G-C. The two strands form a double helix configuration with the sugar-phosphate backbone on the outside and the paired bases on the inside (see Fig 9-1). DNA synthesis is catalyzed by DNA polymerase, which adds a deoxyribonucleotide to the 3′ end of the existing chain. The 3′ and 5′ notation refers to the carbon position of the deoxyribose linkage to the phosphate group. Phosphate groups bridge the sugar groups between the fifth carbon atom of one deoxyribose molecule and the third carbon atom of the adjacent deoxyribose

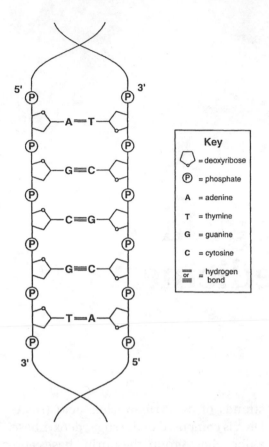

Key

⬠	= deoxyribose
Ⓟ	= phosphate
A	= adenine
T	= thymine
G	= guanine
C	= cytosine
═ or ≡	= hydrogen bond

Figure 9-1. Schematic representation of the base pairing of double-stranded DNA.

molecule and thus create the backbone of the DNA strand. DNA polymerase-dependent synthesis always occurs in the direction of 5′ to 3′.

DNA Transcription

Linear sequences of nucleotides along the DNA strands constitute the genes. Genes occupy a constant location (locus) in the DNA of a specific chromosome; the loci of most known genes have been identified due to the human genome project. For protein synthesis to occur (see Fig 9-2), the information encoded in the DNA sequence must be copied into RNA (transcription) and transported to the cytoplasmic organelles called ribosomes where protein as-

sembly takes place (translation). Transcription is done by copying one strand of the DNA into a primary ribonucleic acid transcript, which is then modified into messenger ribonucleic acid (mRNA). The mRNA represents a single stranded linear sequence of nucleotides that differs from DNA in the sugar present in its backbone (ribose instead of deoxyribose) and the replacement of thymine by uracil (U), which also pairs with adenine. DNA transcription is catalyzed by the enzyme RNA polymerase. RNA polymerase binds tightly to a specific DNA sequence called the promoter, which contains the site at which RNA synthesis begins (see Fig 9-3). Proteins called transcription factors are required for RNA polymerase to bind to DNA and for transcription to occur. Regulation of transcription can lead to increased, decreased, or absent expression of a gene. For instance, a single base-pair mutation in the transcription factor binding site of the Duffy gene promoter impairs the promoter activity and is responsible for the Fy(a–b–) phenotype.[1]

After binding to the promoter, RNA polymerase opens up the double helix of a local region of DNA, exposing the nucleotides on each strand. The nucleotides of one exposed DNA strand act as a template for complementary base pairing; RNA is synthesized by the addition of ribonucleotides to the elongating chain. As RNA polymerase moves along the template strand of DNA, the double helix is opened before it and closes behind it like a zipper. The process continues, usually 0.5 to 2 kb downstream of the poly-A signal, whereupon the enzyme halts synthesis and releases both the DNA template and the new RNA chain.

mRNA Processing

Shortly after the initiation of transcription, the newly formed chain is capped at

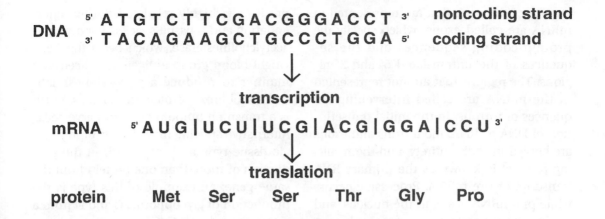

Figure 9-2. Model of a nucleotide sequence. The sequence is fictitious.

its 5′ end by the addition of a methylated G nucleotide. The 5′ cap is important for initiating protein synthesis and possibly for protecting the mRNA molecule from degradation during its transport to the cytoplasm. At the 3′ end of the mRNA, a multiprotein cleavage-polyadenylation complex carries out a two-step process that cleaves the new RNA at a specific sequence and then attaches 100 to 200 copies of adenylic acid, called the poly-A tail. The poly-A tail functions in the export of mature mRNA from the cell nucleus to the cytoplasm, in the stabilization of the mRNA, and as a ribosomal recognition signal required for efficient translation.

In eukaryotic cells, the nucleotide sequence of a gene often contains certain regions that are represented in the mRNA and other regions that are not represented. The

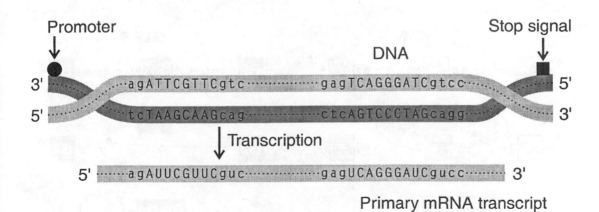

Figure 9-3. The promoter sequence (●) contains the starting site for RNA synthesis. RNA polymerase binds to the promoter and opens up a local region of the DNA sequence. One strand of DNA (the lower one in this figure) acts as a template for complementary base pairing. The RNA polymerase copies the DNA in a 5′ to 3′ direction until it encounters a stop signal (■). Lowercase letters represent nucleotides in introns; uppercase letters represent coding bases in exons. The sequence is fictitious.

regions of the gene that are represented in mRNA are called exons, which specify the protein-coding sequences and the sequences of the untranslated 5′ and 3′ regions. The regions that are not represented in the mRNA are called intervening sequences or introns. In the initial transcription of DNA to RNA, the introns and exons are copied in their entirety, and the resulting product is known as the primary RNA transcript or pre-mRNA. Processing occurs while pre-mRNA is still in the nucleus, and the introns are cut out by a process known as RNA splicing (see Fig 9-4).

RNA splicing depends on the presence of certain highly conserved sequences consisting of GU at the 5′ splice site (donor site) and AG at the 3′ splice site (acceptor site). Additionally, an adenosine residue within a specific sequence in the intron participates in a complex reaction along with a very large ribonucleoprotein complex called the spliceosome. The reaction results in cleavage and joining of the 5′ and 3′ splice sites, with release of the intervening sequence as a lariat. Substitution of any of these highly conserved sequences can result in inaccurate RNA splicing (see Fig 9-4). Splicing of

pre-RNA is highly regulated during differentiation and is tissue-specific. For example, acetylcholinesterase, which bears the Cartwright blood group antigen, is spliced in a manner to produce a glycosylphosphatidylinositol-linked protein in red cells, but it is a transmembrane protein in nerve cells.[2] Alternative splicing may also occur in a single tissue type and may result in the production of more than one protein from the same gene; an example of this type is the production of glycophorins C and D from a single glycophorin C (GPC) gene.[3]

Translation of mRNA

The bases within a linear mRNA sequence are read (or translated) in groups of three, called codons. Each three-base combination codes for one amino acid. There are only 20 amino acids commonly used for protein synthesis, and there are 64 ($4 \times 4 \times 4$) possible codons. Most amino acids can be specified by each of several different codons, a circumstance known as "degeneracy" or "redundancy" in the genetic code. For example, lysine can be specified

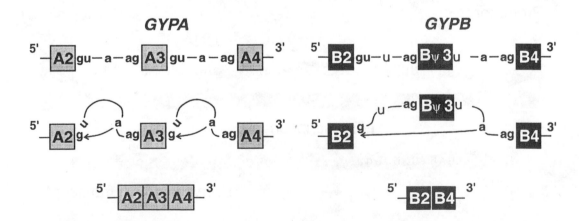

Figure 9-4. Substitution of two nucleotides (boldface) in the intron sequences flanking exon 3 of *GYPB* prevents normal splicing. Instead, all nucleotides between the 5′ donor site of the second intron and the 3′ acceptor site of the third intron are excised. Because exon 3 is not translated, it is called a pseudoexon (Ψ).

by either AAA or AAG. Methionine has only the single codon AUG. Three codons (UAA, UGA, and UAG) function as stop signals; when the translation process encounters one of them, peptide synthesis stops.

For the translation of codons into amino acids, cytoplasmic mRNA requires the assistance of transfer RNA (tRNA) molecules. The tRNA molecules interact with the mRNA through specific base pairings and bring with them the amino acid specified by the mRNA codon. Thus, the amino acids are linked in amino to carboxyl peptide bonds forming a growing polypeptide chain. Proteins are synthesized such that the initial amino acid has an unlinked amine (NH_2) group and ends with a terminal carboxylic acid (COOH) group. Protein synthesis occurs on ribosomes, which are large complexes of RNA and protein molecules; ribosomes bound to the rough endoplasmic reticulum are the site of synthesis of membrane and secretory proteins, whereas free ribosomes are the site of synthesis of cytosolic proteins. The ribosome binds to the tRNA and to the mRNA, starting at its 5′ end (amino terminal). Therefore, protein synthesis occurs from the amino-terminal end toward the carboxyl-terminal end. The protein is produced sequentially until a stop codon is reached, which terminates the translation process and releases the newly synthesized protein.

Many of the steps in the pathway of RNA synthesis to protein production are closely regulated at different levels to control gene expression. Control steps include: initiation of transcription, proofreading of the transcription process, addition of the poly-A tail, transportation of mRNA to the cytosol, initiation of translation, and elongation of the polypeptide chain. Moreover, tissue-specific and differentiation or stage-specific transcription factors, as well as hormone response elements and regulatory elements at the 5′ and 3′ ends of mRNA, can affect gene expression.

Genetic Mechanisms that Create Polymorphism

Despite the redundancy inherent in degeneracy of the genetic code, molecular events such as substitution, insertion, or deletion of a nucleotide may have far-reaching effects on the protein encoded. Some of the blood group polymorphisms observed at the phenotypic level can be traced to small changes at the nucleotide level. The sequence in Fig 9-2, which is not meant to represent a known sequence, can be used to illustrate the effects of minute changes at the nucleotide level, discussed below.

Nucleotide Substitution

Nucleotide substitutions in the genomic DNA can have profound effects on the resultant protein. Many blood group antigens are the result of single nucleotide changes at the DNA level. The nucleotide changes are transcribed into the RNA, which alters the sequence of the codon. In some instances, the codon change results in the incorporation of a different amino acid. For example, a change in the DNA sequence from a T to a C at a given position would result in an mRNA change from U to G. Any one of three possible outcomes can follow the substitution of a single nucleotide:

1. Silent mutation. For example, the substitution of an A with a C in the third position of the DNA coding strand for serine (UCU) in Fig 9-2 also codes for serine (UCG). Thus, there would be no effect on the protein because the codon would still be translated as serine.

2. Missense response. The substitution of a G with an A in the second position of the DNA coding strand for the second serine changes the product of the codon from serine (UCG) to leucine (UUG). Many blood group polymorphisms reflect a single amino acid change in the underlying molecule. For example, the K2 antigen has threonine, but K1 has methionine, as the amino acid at position 193. This results from a single C to T substitution in exon 6 of the Kell (*KEL*) gene.[4]

3. Nonsense response. The substitution of a G with a T in the second position of the DNA coding strand for serine (UCG) results in the creation of the codon (UAG), which is one of the three stop codons. No protein synthesis will occur beyond this point, resulting in a shortened or truncated protein. Depending upon where this nonsense substitution occurs, the synthesized protein may be rapidly degraded or may retain some function in its abbreviated form. The Cromer blood group antigens reside on the decay-accelerating factor (DAF) membrane protein. In the null (Inab) phenotype, a G to A nucleotide substitution of the *DAF* gene creates a stop codon at position 53, and the red cell has no DAF expression.[5]

A nucleotide substitution outside an exon sequence may alter splicing and lead to the production of altered proteins, as seen with the altered expression of glycophorin B (GPB)[6] or in the failure to produce a normal amount of protein, as in the Dr(a–) phenotype of Cromer.[7] In *GYPB*, the gene that encodes GPB, substitutions of two conserved nucleotides required for RNA splicing and present in the glycophorin A gene result in the excision of exon 3 as well as introns 2 and 3 of *GYPB*

(see Fig 9-4). Because exon 3 is a coding exon in *GYPA* but is noncoding in *GYPB*, it is called a pseudoexon in *GYPB*.

Nucleotide Insertion and Deletion

Insertion of an entirely new nucleotide results in a frameshift, described as +1, because a nucleotide is being added. Nucleotide deletion causes a –1 frameshift. A peptide may be drastically altered by the insertion or deletion of a single nucleotide. For example, the insertion of an A after the second nucleotide of the noncoding DNA strand of Fig 9-2 would change the reading frame of the mRNA to UAU CAG AAG CUG CCC UGG and represent the polypeptide isoleucine-valine-phenylalanine-aspartic acid-glycine-threonine.

Genetic Variability

Gene conversion and crossing over may occur between homologous genes located on two copies of the same chromosome that are misaligned during meiosis. Examples of homologous genes encoding blood group antigens are the *RHD* and *RHCE* genes of the Rh blood group system and *GYPA* and *GYPB*, which encode the antigens of the MNS blood group system.

Single Crossover

A single crossover is the mutual exchange of nucleotides between two homologous genes. If crossover occurs in a region where paired homologous chromosomes are misaligned, two hybrid genes are formed in reciprocal arrangement (see Fig 9-5). The novel amino acid sequences encoded by the nucleotides at the junction of the hybrid gene may result in epitopes recognized by antibodies in human serum and are known to occur in at least three blood group systems: Rh, MNS, and Gerbich.

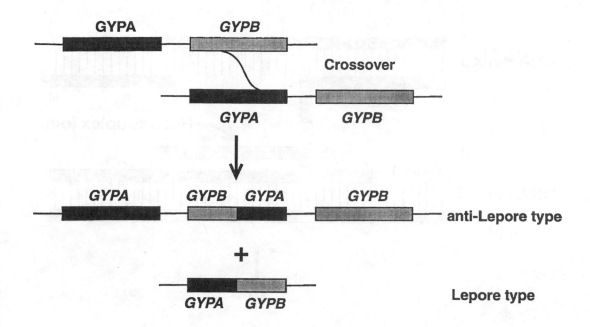

Figure 9-5. Single crossover: exchange of nucleotides between misaligned homologous genes. The products are reciprocal.

Gene Conversion

The process of gene conversion is thought to consist of crossover, a general DNA recombination process, and DNA repair during meiosis. The result is that nucleotides from one homologous gene are inserted into another gene without reciprocal exchange. At the site of chromosome crossover during meiosis, a heteroduplex joint can form; this is a staggered joint between nucleotide sequences on two participating DNA strands (see Fig 9-6). A second type of gene conversion occurs in meiosis when the DNA polymerase switches templates and copies information from a homologous sequence. This event is usually the result of mismatch repair; nucleotides removed from one strand are replaced by repair synthesis using the homologous strand as a template.

Molecular Techniques

The development of modern molecular techniques has greatly expanded our knowledge of all biologic systems. These same techniques are also applicable to the diagnosis of disease, the practice of forensic science, the generation of recombinant proteins, and the production of functional genes for gene therapy. Many of these processes begin with DNA typing and analysis, techniques that are reviewed below.

Isolation of Nucleic Acids

The first step in most molecular biology techniques is the isolation and purification of nucleic acid, either DNA or RNA. For applications of interest to the blood banking community, the desired nucleic

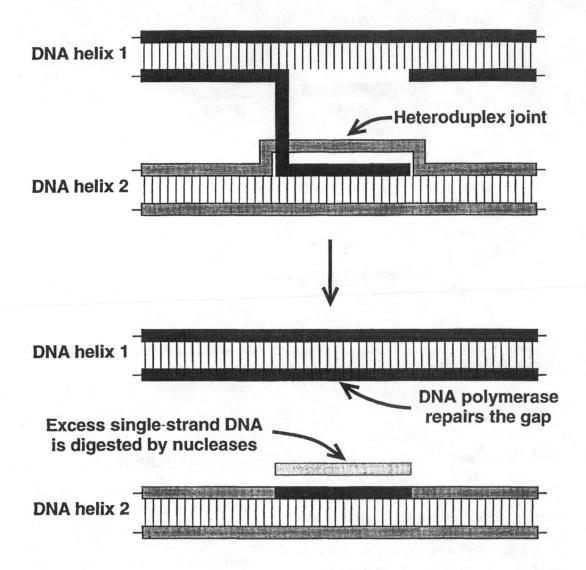

Figure 9-6. Gene conversion: a heteroduplex joint forms between homologous sequences on two genes. DNA polymerase repairs the double strands. Any excess single-stranded DNA is degraded by nucleases, producing a hybrid gene on one chromosome but not on the other.

acid is typically human genomic DNA and mRNA. Genomic DNA is present in all nucleated cells and can be isolated from peripheral blood white cells or from buccal tissue obtained by a simple cheek swab. Both nucleated cells and reticulocytes are cell-specific sources of mRNA.

Manufacturers offer kits for the isolation of human genomic DNA from whole blood,

cells, and tissues. These kits vary in the quantity and quality of the DNA isolated, in rough proportion to the cost and ease of use of the kit. High-quality DNA is of high molecular weight and is relatively free of contamination by protein or RNA. DNA purity is assessed by the ratio of its optical density (OD) at 260 nm to that at 280 nm, with the OD 260/280 ratio for pure DNA being 1.8. Low ratios (<1.6) indicate that the DNA is contaminated with protein or materials used in the isolation procedure, and high ratios (>2.0) indicate that the DNA is contaminated with RNA. If the DNA is pure and of sufficient concentration, it can be quantitated by measurement of the OD at 260 nm. If the DNA is impure or in low concentration, it is best quantitated by electrophoresis in agarose gel along with DNA standards of known concentration, followed by visualization of the DNA with ethidium bromide staining.

For certain molecular biology techniques such as polymerase chain reaction (PCR), the quantity and quality of the genomic DNA used as starting material are not crucial, and good results can be obtained with even nanogram quantities of DNA that has been degraded into small fragments. For other molecular biology techniques, such as cloning, larger quantities of high-molecular-weight DNA are required.

One nucleated cell contains about 6 pg of genomic DNA. Based on an average white cell count of 5000/μL, each milliliter of peripheral blood contains about 30 μg of DNA. Commercial DNA isolation kits typically yield in excess of 15 μg of DNA per milliliter of whole blood processed.

Polymerase Chain Reaction

The introduction of the PCR technique has revolutionized the field of molecular genetics.[8] This technique permits specific DNA sequences to be multiplied rapidly and precisely in vitro. PCR can amplify, to a billionfold, a single copy of the DNA sequence under study, provided a part of the nucleotide sequence is known. The investigator must know at least some of the gene sequence in order to synthesize DNA oligonucleotides for use as primers. Two primers are required: a forward primer (5') and a reverse primer (3'). These are designed so that one is complementary to each strand of DNA, and, together, they flank the region of interest. Primers can be designed that add restriction sites to the PCR product to facilitate its subsequent cloning or labeled to facilitate its detection. Labels may incorporate radioactivity, or, more frequently, a nonradioactive tag, such as biotin or a fluorescent dye. The PCR reaction is catalyzed by one of several heat-stable DNA polymerases isolated from bacterial species that are native to hot springs or to thermal vents on the ocean floor. The thermostability of these enzymes allows them to withstand repeated cycles of heating and cooling.

Reaction Procedure

The amplification technique is simple and requires very little DNA (typically <100 ng of genomic DNA). The DNA under study is mixed together with a reaction buffer, excess nucleotides, the primers, and polymerase (see Fig 9-7). The reaction cocktail is placed in a thermocycler programmed to produce a series of heating and cooling cycles that result in exponential amplification of the DNA. The target DNA is initially denatured by heating the mixture, which separates the double-stranded DNA into single strands. Subsequent cooling in the presence of excess quantities of single-stranded forward and reverse primers allows them to bind or anneal with complementary sequences on the single-stranded template DNA. The specific cooling temperature is calculated to be appropriate for the primers being used. The reaction mixture is then heated to the optimal temperature for the thermo-stable DNA polymerase, which generates a new strand of DNA on the single-strand template, using the nucleotides as build-

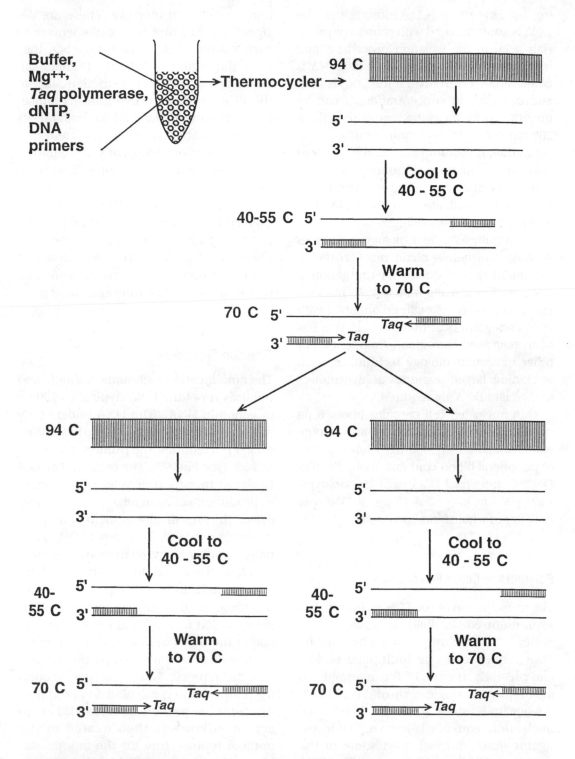

Figure 9-7. The polymerase chain reaction results in the exponential amplification of short DNA sequences such that the target sequence is amplified over a billionfold after 20 cycles. (*Taq* polymerase is used here as an example of a thermostable DNA polymerase.)

ing blocks for elongation. The next cycle denatures newly formed double strands, and the single-stranded DNA copies serve as templates for subsequent synthesis. The number of DNA copies doubles with each cycle, such that after 20 cycles, there is a billionfold amplification of the target DNA.

The amplified DNA may be analyzed by agarose gel electrophoresis in the presence of ethidium bromide, which binds to DNA and is visible under ultraviolet light. The DNA will be present as a single discrete band equivalent in length to the distance between the 5′ ends of the primers. The amplified DNA can also be differentiated by size using capillary electrophoresis. Alternatively, the DNA sample can be blotted onto a membrane and hybridized to a labeled, allele-specific probe. This is known as a dot blot and is particularly useful when multiple samples are being analyzed for the same polymorphism.

Variations of the PCR have been developed to meet specific needs. For instance, "long-distance" PCR, which has a mixture of thermostable polymerases, can amplify much larger targets (up to 40 kilobases in length) than those typically amplified by conventional PCR (up to 2 kilobases in length). It is even possible to perform PCR in situ, in tissue and cells. A related technology, the ligase chain reaction (LCR), uses a thermostable DNA ligase instead of a thermostable DNA polymerase. Rather than amplification of a DNA target segment located between two flanking primers using a DNA polymerase as occurs in PCR, in the LCR direct primer ligation occurs with no amplification of an intervening DNA segment. Other PCR variations include multiplex PCR, in which multiple independent segments of DNA are co-amplified in the same reaction, and kinetic PCR, in which the amplification product is measured in real time in order to quantitate the amount of starting nucleic acid.

Applications of PCR

Amplification of minute quantities of DNA to detectable levels may significantly affect the practice of transfusion medicine. In screening donor blood for infectious agents, PCR has become the procedure of choice and thus eliminate our reliance on seroconversion, which occurs well after exposure to viruses or other pathogens (see Chapter 28). Blood centers have been using nucleic acid amplification testing (NAT) to identify the presence of HIV and HCV RNA in donor samples; detection of West Nile virus RNA has been performed as an investigational test. Detection of viral RNA involves three steps: extraction, amplification, and detection. Extraction may occur following centrifugation steps to concentrate the virus and remove contaminants. Otherwise, RNA extraction can occur first followed by capture of viral RNA onto a molecule that is immobilized on a solid phase or onto magnetic particles in solution (this procedure is referred to as target capture). Once immobilized, the impurities may be removed by a series of wash steps. Before amplification, viral RNA must be converted to DNA; this is accomplished by the enzyme, reverse transcriptase (RT). Amplification of the DNA then can occur through multiple intermediates. In the case of PCR, the amplified product is DNA (and is synthesized using thermostable *Taq* DNA polymerase), whereas, in the case of transcription-mediated amplification, the amplified product is RNA (and is synthesized using T7 RNA polymerase) (see Fig 9-8). Detection of the amplified product can occur by capture of the amplified DNA on nitrocellulose or by enzyme immunoassay or chemiluminescence. Currently, NAT for blood donor screening has been implemented for HIV and hepatitis C; NAT for hepatitis B is under development. NAT for other agents (eg, human T-cell lymphotropic virus, hepatitis A virus, parvovirus B19) is not widely available.

PCR is being used for prenatal determination of many inheritable disorders, such as sickle cell disease, in evaluating hemolytic disease of the fetus and newborn, to type fetal amniocytes,[9] to quantitate residual white cells in filtered blood, and for tracing donor leukocytes in transfusion recipients (chimerism). Long-distance PCR is used for cloning, sequencing, and chromosome mapping, and reverse transcriptase (RT)-PCR is used for studying gene expression and cDNA cloning. LCR has special applicability in transfusion medicine because of its powerful ability to detect genetic variants. In the field of transplantation, PCR using sequence-specific oligonucleotide probes or sequence-specific primers is used to determine HLA types (see Chapter 17).

Restriction Endonucleases

The discovery of bacterial restriction endonucleases provided the key technique for DNA analysis. These enzymes, found in different strains of bacteria, protect a bacteria cell from viral infection by degrading viral DNA after it enters the cytoplasm. Each restriction endonuclease recognizes only a single specific nucleotide sequence, typically consisting of four to six nucleotides. These enzymes cleave the DNA strand wherever the recognized sequence occurs, generating a number of DNA fragments whose length depends upon the number and location of cleavage sites in the original strand. Many endonucleases have been purified from different species of bacteria; the name of each enzyme reflects its host bacterium, eg, Eco RI is isolated from *Escherichia coli*, Hind III is from *Hemophilus influenzae*, and Hpa I is from *Hemophilus parainfluenzae*.

Restriction Fragment Length Polymorphism Analysis

The unique properties of restriction endonucleases make analysis of restriction fragment length polymorphism (RFLP) suitable for the detection of a DNA polymorphism. The changes in nucleotide sequence described above (substitution, insertion, deletion) can alter the relative locations of restriction nuclease cutting sites and thus alter the length of DNA fragments produced. RFLPs are detected using Southern blotting and probe hybridization (see Fig 9-9).

The isolated DNA is cleaved into fragments by digestion with one or more restriction endonucleases. The DNA fragments are separated by electrophoresis through agarose gel and then transferred onto a nylon membrane or nitrocellulose paper. Once fixed to a nylon membrane or nitrocellulose paper, the DNA fragments are examined by application of a probe, which is a small fragment of DNA whose nucleotide sequence is complementary to the DNA sequence under study. A probe may be an artificially manufactured oligonucleotide or may derive from cloned complementary DNA. The probe is labeled with a radioisotope or another indicator that permits visualization of the targeted DNA restriction fragments and is then allowed to hybridize with the Southern blot. Unbound excess probe is washed off, and hybridized DNA is visualized as one or more bands of specific size, dictated by the specific nucleotide sequence. If several individuals are analyzed for polymorphism, several different banding patterns may be observed.

RFLP analysis has been used in gene mapping and analysis, linkage analysis, characterization of HLA genes in transplantation, paternity testing, and forensic science.

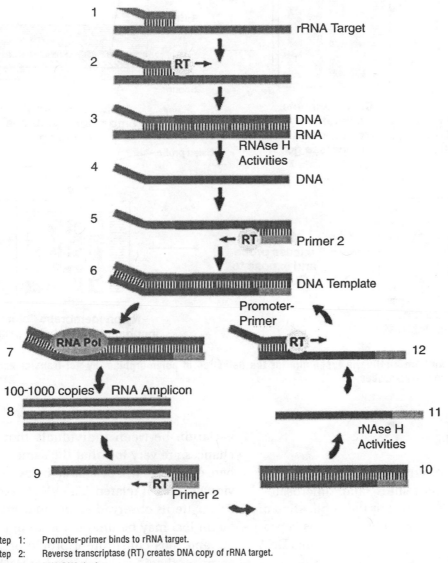

Step 1:   Promoter-primer binds to rRNA target.
Step 2:   Reverse transcriptase (RT) creates DNA copy of rRNA target.
Step 3:   RNA:DNA duplex.
Step 4:   RNAse H activities of RT degrade the rRNA.
Step 5:   Primer 2 binds to the DNA and RT creates a new DNA copy.
Step 6:   Double-stranded DNA template with a promoter sequence.
Step 7:   RNA polymerase (RNA Pol) initiates transcription of RNA from DNA template.
Step 8:   100-1000 copies of RNA amplicon are produced.
Step 9:   Primer 2 binds to each RNA amplicon and RT creates a DNA copy.
Step 10:   RNA:DNA duplex.
Step 11:   RNAse H activities of RT degrade the rRNA.
Step 12:   Promoter-primer binds to the newly synthesized DNA. RT creates a double-stranded DNA and the autocatalytic cycle
           repeats, resulting in a billion-fold amplification.

Figure 9-8. Transcription-mediated amplification cycle.

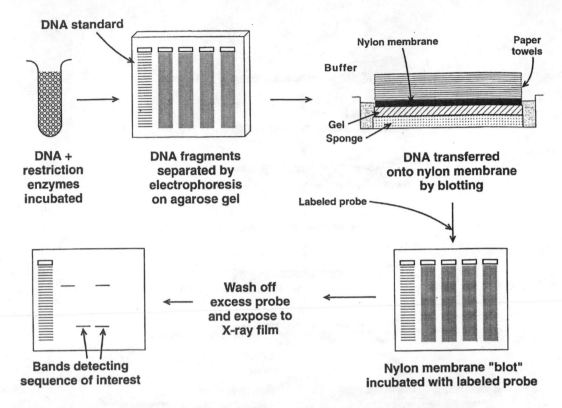

Figure 9-9. Southern blotting: a technique for the detection of polymorphism by gel-transfer and hybridization with known probes.

DNA Profiling

Regions of DNA that show great allelic variability ("minisatellites" and "microsatellites") can be studied by the application of RFLP mapping and/or PCR analysis (a process sometimes called DNA profiling, DNA typing, or DNA fingerprinting). Minisatellites or variable number of tandem repeat (VNTR) loci consist of tandem repeats of a medium-sized (6-100 base-pair) sequence, whereas microsatellites or short tandem repeat (STR) loci consist of tandem repeats of a short (typically four base pair) sequence. These regions are almost always found in the noncoding regions of DNA. Variability stems from differences in the number of repeat units contained within the fragments. There is so much

variation between individuals that the chances are very low that the same numbers of repeats will be shared by two individuals, even if related. The VNTR and/or STR patterns observed at four to eight different loci may be unique for an individual and thus constitute a profile or "fingerprint" that identifies his or her DNA.

When DNA profiling was developed, testing was performed by RFLP analysis. DNA profiling is now increasingly done by amplification of selected, informative VNTR and/or STR loci using locus-specific oligonucleotide primers, followed by measurement of the size of the PCR products produced. PCR products can be separated by size by electrophoresis through polyacrylamide gel and detected by silver staining, or, if the PCR products incorporate a fluorescent tag, by fluorescent detection systems including those designed for automated DNA sequencing. Comparison of the VNTR and STR PCR products with a standard-size ladder distinguishes the alleles present in the sample.

DNA profiling is a technique that is extremely powerful for identifying the source of human DNA; therefore, it has applications in forensic and paternity testing, as well as in the documentation of chimerism, which is of special importance in monitoring allogeneic hematopoietic transplantation.

DNA Cloning

PCR may also be used for analysis of mRNA, which is an especially useful source of genetic material because only the exons of the gene are present. By a modification of PCR called RT-PCR, the single-stranded mRNA is converted to double-stranded DNA. The enzyme RT is used to generate a single strand of DNA, which serves as a template for a second strand generated by DNA polymerase. The product is complementary DNA (cDNA) and it is the DNA molecule of choice for cloning and sequencing.

In gene cloning, the DNA containing the gene of interest is inserted into a vector, which is a self-replicating genetic element such as a virus (eg, the bacteriophage lambda gt11) or a plasmid. Plasmids are small circular molecules of double-stranded DNA that occur naturally in bacteria and typically confer antibiotic resistance. After the gene has been inserted into the DNA of the vector, the recombinant DNA can be introduced into a bacterial host where it undergoes replication. Because many vectors carry genes for antibiotic resistance, this characteristic can be exploited by growing the host bacteria in the presence of the appropriate antibiotic; only bacteria that have

successfully incorporated the recombinant vector will survive to form colonies or clones. Each individual vector potentially contains a different cDNA sequence. The sum of bacterial clones harboring recombinant vectors is called a DNA library. Libraries can be obtained from many commercial sources or can be produced by the individual investigator. The library can be probed through a technique similar to Southern blotting, with an oligonucleotide probe based on part of a known sequence. Positive clones can be selected and a pure culture grown in large quantities. Once purified, the cloned DNA can be recovered for use as a probe or for detailed molecular characterization.

The ability to insert genes into the genomes of virtually any organism, including bacteria, plants, invertebrates (such as insects), and vertebrates (such as mammals), permits not only gene characterization but also genetic engineering, including the production of recombinant proteins (see below) and gene therapy. Although still in the developmental stages, gene therapy promises to have a role in the management of disorders as diverse as inherited genetic diseases, human immunodeficiency virus, and cancer, and in the development of novel vaccines.[10,11]

DNA Sequencing

A major worldwide scientific effort called the Human Genome Project has obtained the complete nucleotide sequence of the human genome as well as the genomes of several other key organisms. The initiative also improved DNA sequencing technology. Realization of both goals has had a positive impact on transfusion practice. The identification of all human genes[12,13] provides a complete blueprint of the proteins that are relevant in transfusion medicine. In turn, this information has helped in the development of recombinant proteins for use as transfusion components and in-vitro test reagents. It also plays a role in clarifying the disorders that afflict transfusion recipients.

Advances in DNA sequencing have taken the field a long way from the cumbersome manual techniques common in research laboratories until recently.[14] Automated DNA sequencers using laser detection of fluorescently labeled sequencing products detect all four nucleotide bases in a single lane on polyacrylamide gel and can be optimized for specialty applications such as heterozygote detection and sizing of PCR fragments. Automated DNA sequencers using capillary electrophoresis are especially useful for the rapid sequencing of short DNA templates. DNA sequence can also be obtained using mass spectrometry. Automated sequencers will become increasingly common in clinical laboratories as this technology evolves. If it can be made cost-effective for routine use, then DNA sequencing could become a routine genotyping method.

DNA Microarrays

The complexity of the human genome requires that the differential expression of multiple genes be analyzed at once to understand normal biologic processes as well as changes in diseases. A powerful technique to accomplish this goal is DNA microarrays or gene chips.[15] In this method, tens of thousands of separate DNA molecules are spotted or synthesized on a small area of a solid support, often a glass slide. The DNA can be generated by PCR or oligonucleotide synthesis. This microarray is then probed, in a process analogous to Southern blotting, using cDNA created from the total mRNA expressed at a given time by a cell or tissue. The result is a picture of the gene expression profile of the tissue for all of the genes on the microarray. Also, microarrays can be used for comparative genomics and genotyping, an application for blood groups.

Recombinant Proteins

The technology to make recombinant proteins includes in-vitro systems in bacteria, yeast, insect cells, and mammalian cells, as well as in-vivo systems involving transgenic plants and animals.[16] First, a source of DNA corresponding in nucleic acid sequence to the desired protein is prepared, typically by cloning the cDNA and ligating it into a suitable expression vector. Then, the expression vector containing the DNA of interest is transfected into the host cell, and the DNA of interest is transcribed under the control of the vector promoter. Next, the resulting mRNA is translated into protein by the host cell.

Posttranslational modifications such as the addition of carbohydrates to the new protein will be carried out by the host cell. If specific posttranslational modifications required for the new protein's function cannot be carried out by the host cell, then it may be necessary to endow the host cell with additional capabilities; for example, by cotransfection with the cDNA for a specific enzyme. In some cases, posttranslational modification may not be crucial for a recombinant protein to be effective; for instance, granulocyte colony-stimulating factor (G-CSF) is produced in a nonglycosylated form in *E. coli* (filgrastim) and in a glycosylated form in yeast (lenograstim).

Recombinant proteins are finding multiple uses in transfusion medicine, as therapeutic agents and vaccine components, in component preparation, in virus diagnosis, and in serologic testing. Recombinant human erythropoietin,[17] G-CSF and GM-CSF,[18] interferon-alpha, interleukin-2, interleukin-11, and Factors VIII,[19] IX,[20] VII, and VIIa[21] are all available and finding clinical acceptance. For instance, recombinant erythropoietin can be used to increase red cell production in anemic patients before surgery, reducing the need for allogeneic blood.[22] It can also be used to increase the amount of autologous red cells that can be withdrawn before surgery from non-anemic patients.[23] Moreover, it has revolutionized the management of renal transplant candidates whose kidneys are too impaired to produce endogenous erythropoietin.

Recombinant human thrombopoietin may be of value in augmenting platelet yields from apheresis donors but is unlikely to significantly reduce the need for platelet transfusions when given to thrombocytopenic patients.[24] In the coagulation arena, recombinant proteins such as protein C, antithrombin, and hirudin are approved by the Food and Drug Administration for use, and tissue factor pathway inhibitor, Factor XIII, and von Willebrand factor appear promising. Recombinant myeloid growth factors such as G-CSF are used to enhance yields of progenitor cells during apheresis and to support patients following chemotherapy and hematopoietic transplantation.[25]

Recombinant proteins can be used as transfusion components.[26] Recombinant human hemoglobin has been produced in a number of in-vitro expression systems and in vivo in transgenic swine and may be useful as a noninfectious blood substitute.[27] Recombinant human serum albumin has been produced in yeast. Alphagalactosidase, an enzyme that is capable of converting group B cells into group O cells, has been produced in a recombinant form that can modify group B units for transfusion to group A and O recipients.[28] These recombinant proteins and other products under development will undoubtedly affect the variety of transfusion components that will become available in the future.

Recombinant proteins corresponding to proteins from clinically relevant viruses, bacteria, and parasites, some of which may be transmitted by blood transfusion, may be used as vaccine components[29] and as antigens in test kits for the detection of antibodies. Cells transfected with appropriate vectors can be induced to express recombinant proteins on the membrane surface and, as such, may become useful as genetically engineered reagent cells for in-vitro testing.

Gene Therapy

Gene therapy refers to the introduction of nonself genetic material into cells to treat or prevent disease. At present, gene therapy is restricted to somatic cells because of ethical concerns about the transfer of genes to germ-line cells. More than 3500 patients have been administered gene therapy in clinical trials,[30] but results overall have been disappointing largely due to problems with delivery (transfection) of the genetic material (transgene) into cells and the limited lifespan of the successfully transfected cells.

There are different types of vectors (gene-delivery vehicles) that deliver genes to cells, including viral vectors (retrovirus, adenovirus, adeno-associated virus, vaccinia, herpes simplex), naked DNA, and modified DNA. Genetic material can also be transferred to cells by physical means such as electroporation (use of an electric field). As methods for gene delivery improve, it is anticipated that the benefits of gene therapy will become more apparent.

Gene therapy can be used to replace a defective gene, leading to increased production of a specific protein as in the replacement of Factor VIII or IX for patients with hemophilia,[31] or it can be used to downregulate (reduce) expression of an undesirable gene. The latter can be accomplished by the introduction of DNA sequences (antisense oligonucleotides) corresponding to the antisense strand of the mRNA, which then interferes with translation of the mRNA into protein.

Protein and RNA Targeted Inactivation

More recently, novel pharmacologic agents have been developed that interfere with specific molecules produced by cancer cells or infectious particles. One such example is imatinib mesylate (Gleevec, Novartis Pharmaceuticals, East Hanover, NJ), which binds specifically to the Bcr-Abl protein and blocks its tyrosine kinase activity in malignant white cells. It specifically blocks the binding site for adenosine triphosphate on the kinase, thus inhibiting its ability to phosphorylate intracellular proteins.[32] The inactivation prevents Bcr-Abl-induced malignant cell proliferation and anti-apoptosis. Normal kinase signaling pathways are largely unaffected.

Another promising therapy is RNA interference, which has its historical roots as a research tool used to characterize the function of known genes. RNA interference is based on an antiviral mechanism in which dsRNA is delivered to a cell and is subsequently processed into small (21-25 bp) interfering RNA (siRNA) molecules. The siRNA molecules silence the expression of a target gene in a sequence-specific manner. More important, RNA interference has potential as a therapeutic strategy to silence cancer-related genes or infectious diseases like viral hepatitis.[33]

References

1. Tournamille C, Colin Y, Cartron JP, Le Van Kim C. Disruption of a GATA motif in the Duffy gene promoter abolishes erythroid gene expression in Duffy-negative individuals. Nat Genet 1995;10:224-8.

2. Li Y, Camp S, Taylor P. Tissue-specific expression and alternative mRNA processing of the mammalian acetylcholinesterase gene. J Biol Chem 1993;268:5790-7.

3. Le Van Kim C, Mitjavila MT, Clerget M, et al. An ubiquitous isoform of glycophorin C is produced by alternative splicing. Nucleic Acids Res 1990;18:3076.

4. Lee S, Wu X, Reid M, et al. Molecular basis of the Kell (K1) phenotype. Blood 1995;85:912-16.

5. Lublin DM, Mallinson G, Poole J, et al. Molecular basis of reduced or absent expression of decay-accelerating factor in Cromer blood group phenotypes. Blood 1994;84:1276-82.

6. Kudo S, Fukuda M. Structural organization of glycophorin A and B genes: Glycophorin B gene evolved by homologous recombination at Alu repeat sequences. Proc Natl Acad Sci U S A 1989;86:4619-23.

7. Lubin DM, Thompson ES, Green AM, et al. Dr(a−) polymorphism of decay accelerating factor. Biochemical, functional, and molecular characterization and production of allele-specific transfection. J Clin Invest 1991;87:1945-52.

8. Erlich HA. Principles and applications of the polymerase chain reaction. Rev Immunogenet 1999;1:127-34.

9. Bennett PR, Le Van Kim C, Colin Y, et al. Prenatal determination of fetal RhD type by DNA amplification. N Engl J Med 1993;329:607-10.

10. Friedmann T. Overcoming the obstacles to gene therapy. Sci Am 1997;276:80-5.

11. Hillyer CD, Klein HG. Immunotherapy and gene transfer in the treatment of the oncology patient: Role of transfusion medicine. Transfus Med Rev 1996;10:1-14.

12. International Human Genome Sequencing Consortium. Initial sequencing and analysis of the human genome. Nature 2001;409:860-921.

13. Venter JC, Adams MD, Myers EW, et al. The sequence of the human genome. Science 2001;291:1304-51.

14. Griffin HG, Griffin AM. DNA sequencing. Recent innovations and future trends. Appl Biochem Biotechnol 1993;38:147-59.

15. Duggan DJ, Bittner M, Chen Y, et al. Expression profiling using cDNA microarrays. Nat Genet 1999;21:S10-14.

16. Lubon H, Paleyanda RK, Velander WH, Drohan WN. Blood proteins from transgenic animal bioreactors. Transfus Med Rev 1996; 10:131-43.

17. Cazzola M, Mercuriali F, Brugnara C. Use of recombinant human erythropoietin outside the setting of uremia. Blood 1997;89:4248-67.

18. Ganser A, Karthaus M. Clinical use of hematopoietic growth factors. Curr Opin Oncol 1996; 8:265-9.

19. VanAken WG. The potential impact of recombinant factor VIII on hemophilia care and the demand for blood and blood products. Transfus Med Rev 1997;11:6-14.

20. White GC II, Beebe A, Nielsen B. Recombinant factor IX. Thromb Haemost 1997;78:261-5.

21. Lusher JM. Recombinant factor VIIa (NovoSeven) in the treatment of internal bleeding in patients with factor VIII and IX inhibitors. Haemostasis 1996;26(Suppl 1):124-30.

22. Braga M, Gianotti L, Gentilini O, et al. Erythropoietic response induced by recombinant human erythropoietin in anemic cancer patients candidate to major abdominal surgery. Hepatogastroenterology 1997;44:685-90.

23. Cazenave JP, Irrmann C, Waller C, et al. Epoetin alfa facilitates presurgical autologous blood donation in non-anaemic patients scheduled for orthopaedic or cardiovascular surgery. Eur J Anaesthesiol 1997;14:432-42.

24. Kuter DJ. What ever happened to thrombopoietin? Transfusion 2002;42:279-83.

25. Ketley NJ, Newland AC. Haemopoietic growth factors. Postgrad Med J 1997;73:215-21.

26. Growe GH. Recombinant blood components: Clinical administration today and tomorrow. World J Surg 1996;20:1194-9.

27. Kumar R. Recombinant hemoglobins as blood substitutes: A biotechnology perspective. Proc Soc Exp Biol Med 1995;208:150-8.

28. Lenny LL, Hurst R, Zhu A, et al. Multiple-unit and second transfusions of red cells enzymatically converted from group B to group O: Report on the end of phase 1 trials. Transfusion 1995;35:899-902.

29. Ellis RW. The new generation of recombinant viral subunit vaccines. Curr Opin Biotechnol 1996;7:646-52.

30. Mountain A. Gene therapy: The first decade. Trends Biotechnol 2000;18:119-28.

31. Kaufman RJ. Advances toward gene therapy for hemophilia at the millennium. Hum Gene Therapy 1999;10:2091-107.

32. Druker BJ, Tamura S, Buchdunger E, et al. Effects of a selective inhibitor of the Abl tyrosine kinase on the growth of Bcr-Abl positive cells. Nat Med 1996;2:561-6.

33. Radhakrishnan SK, Layden TJ, Gartel AL. RNA interference as a new strategy against viral hepatitis. Virology 2004;323:173-81.

34. Farese AM, Schiffer CA, MacVittie TJ. The impact of thrombopoietin and related mpl-ligands on transfusion medicine. Transfus Med Rev 1997;11:243-55.

35. Barbara JA, Garson JA. Polymerase chain reaction and transfusion microbiology. Vox Sang 1993;64:73-81.

36. Power EG. RAPD typing in microbiology—a technical review. J Hosp Infect 1996;34:247-65.

37. Larsen SA, Steiner BM, Rudolph AH, Weiss JB. DNA probes and PCR for diagnosis of parasitic infections. Clin Microbiol Rev 1995;8:1-21.

38. Weiss JB. DNA probes and PCR for diagnosis of parasitic infections. Clin Microbiol Rev 1995;8:113-30.

39. Majolino I, Cavallaro AM, Scime R. Peripheral blood stem cells for allogeneic transplantation. Bone Marrow Transplant 1996;18(Suppl 2):171-4.

40. Gretch DR. Diagnostic tests for hepatitis C. Hepatology 1997;26:43S-7S.

41. Pena SD, Prado VF, Epplen JT. DNA diagnosis of human genetic individuality. J Mol Med 1995;73:555-64.

42. van Belkum A. DNA fingerprinting of medically important microorganisms by use of PCR. Clin Microbiol Rev 1994;7:174-84.

43. Siegel DL. Research and clinical applications of antibody phage display in transfusion medicine. Transfus Med Rev 2001;15:35-52.

44. Hyland CA, Wolter LC, Saul A. Identification and analysis of Rh genes: Application of PCR and RFLP typing tests. Transfus Med Rev 1995;9:289-301.

Suggested Reading

Denomme G, Lomas-Francis C, Storry RJ, Reid ME. Approaches to molecular blood group genotyping and their applications. In: Stowell C, Dzid W, eds. Emerging technologies in transfusion medicine. Bethesda, MD: AABB Press, 2003:95-129.

Garratty G, ed. Applications of molecular biology to blood transfusion medicine. Bethesda, MD: AABB, 1997.

Lewin B. Genes VII. Oxford: Oxford University Press, 2000.

Sheffield WP. Concepts and techniques in molecular biology—an overview. Transfus Med Rev 1997; 11:209-23.

Appendix 9-1. Molecular Techniques in Transfusion Medicine

Technique	Applications	Examples	References
PCR	Infectious disease testing	Viruses, bacteria, parasites	35 36 37, 38
	Polymorphism detection	HLA, blood group antigens	1, 39
	Prenatal detection	Rh	9
Recombinant proteins/ DNA cloning	Therapy	Erythropoietin, thrombopoietin, G-CSF	17, 18, 34
	Apheresis	G-CSF	39
	Infectious disease testing	Viral testing	40
	Recombinant components	Coagulation factors	19
		Hemoglobin	27
	Component processing	Alpha-galactosidase	28
	Vaccine production	Hepatitis, malaria, HIV	27-29
DNA profiling	Human identification	Chimerism, forensic science	41
	Bacterial identification	Bacterial typing	42
DNA sequencing	Polymorphism detection, heterozygote detection	HLA	14
Phage display/ repertoire cloning	Monoclonal antibody production	Anti-D	43
RFLP	Polymorphism detection	HLA, blood group antigens	44

PCR = polymerase chain reaction; G-CSF = granulocyte colony-stimulating factor; HIV = human immunodeficiency virus; RFLP = restriction fragment length polymorphism.

Chapter 10

Blood Group Genetics

LANDSTEINER'S DISCOVERY OF the ABO blood group system demonstrated that human blood expressed inheritable polymorphic structures. Shortly after the discovery of the ABO system, red cells proved to be an easy and accessible means to test for blood group polymorphisms in individuals of any age. As more blood group antigens were described, blood group phenotyping provided a wealth of information about the polymorphic structures expressed on proteins, glycoproteins and glycolipids on red cells, and the genetic basis for their inheritance.

Basic Principles

Inheritance of transmissible characteristics or "traits," including blood group antigens, forms the basis of the science of genetics. The genetic material that determines each trait is found in the nucleus of a cell. This nuclear material is called chromatin and is primarily made up of DNA (see Chapter 9). When a cell divides, the chromatin loses its homogenous appearance and forms a number of rod-shaped organelles called chromosomes. Encoded in the chromatin or chromosomal DNA are units of genetic information called genes. The genes are arranged in a specific order along a chromosome with the precise gene location known as the locus.

Chromosomes

The number of chromosomes and chromosome morphology are specific for each species. Human somatic cells have 46 chromosomes that exist as 23 pairs (one-half of each pair inherited from each parent). Twenty-two of the pairs are alike in both males and females and are called autosomes; the sex chromosomes, XX in females and XY in males, are the remaining pair.

Each chromosome consists of two arms joined at a primary constriction, the centromere. The two arms are usually of different lengths: the short, or petite, arm is termed "p," and the long arm is termed "q." The arms of individual chromosomes are indicated by the chromosome number followed by a p or q (ie, Xp is the short arm of the X chromosome; 12q is the long arm of chromosome 12). When banded and stained, each chromosome displays a unique pattern of bands, which are numbered from the centromere outward (see Fig 10-1). Chromosomes are identified by the location of the centromere and their banding patterns. The locations of individual genes along the chromosome may be physically "mapped" to specific band locations.

Lyonization

In the somatic cells of females, only one X chromosome is active. Inactivation of one of the X chromosomes is a random process that occurs within days of fertilization. Once an X chromosome has become inactivated, all of that cell's clonal descendants have the same inactive X. Hence, inactivation is randomly determined but once the decision is made, the choice is permanent. This process is termed lyonization.

Mitosis and Meiosis

Cells must replicate their chromosomes as they divide so that each daughter cell receives the full complement of genetic information. Cell division is of two kinds: mitosis and meiosis. Mitosis is the process whereby the body grows or replaces dead or injured somatic cells. This process consists of five stages: prophase, prometaphase, metaphase, anaphase, and telophase. The end result after cytokinesis is two complete daughter cells, each with a nucleus containing all the genetic infor-

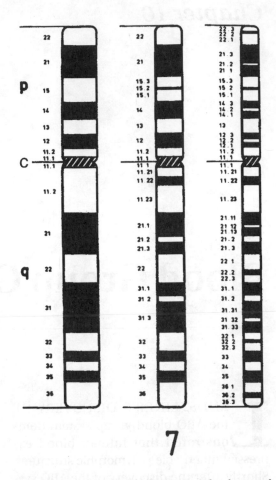

Figure 10-1. Diagram of Giemsa-stained normal human chromosome 7. With increased resolution (left to right), finer degrees of banding are evident. Bands are numbered outward from the centromere (c), which divides the chromosome into p and q arms.[1]

mation of the original parent cell (Fig 10-2).

Meiosis occurs only in primordial cells destined to mature into haploid gametes. Diploid cells that undergo meiosis give rise to haploid gametes (sperm and egg cells with only 23 chromosomes). Hence, somatic cells divide by mitosis, giving rise to diploid cells that have a 2N chromosome complement. Gametes formed following meiosis are haploid, with a 1N chromosome complement. It is during meiosis that genetic diversity occurs. One type of diversity is the

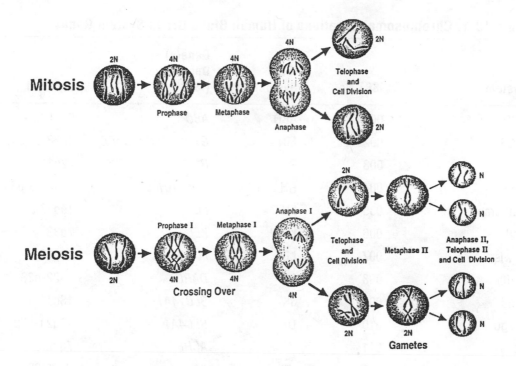

Figure 10-2. The two types of cell division are mitosis and meiosis.

independent assortment of maternal and paternal homologous chromosomes that occurs during division I of meiosis. By the end of meiosis, gametes are formed with an assortment of maternal and paternal chromosomes. The other type of diversity occurs when homologous pairs of chromosomes line up during the first prophase. The homologous chromosomes genetically recombine in a process called chromosomal crossing over (see below). Therefore, not only are the chromosomes shuffled during meiosis, but also portions of chromosomes are recombined to shuffle the genes of an individual chromosome.

Genetics and Heredity

Alleles

Alternative forms of genes, any one of which may occupy a single locus on homologous chromosomes, are called al-

leles. The ISBT terminology distinguishes between the alleles for blood group antigens (ie, the genetic polymorphisms) and the antigens that they encode. For example, the major antigens of the ABO system are A, B, and O, yet the alleles are A^1, B^1, and O^1. In the Kell system, two alleles, K and k, determine the K and k antigens, respectively. Individuals who have identical alleles at a given locus on both chromosomes are *homozygous* for the allele (eg, A^1/A^1 or K/K or k/k). In the *heterozygous* condition, the alleles present at the particular locus on each chromosome are nonidentical (eg, A^1/O^1 or A^1/B^1 or K/k). Table 10-1 summarizes genotypes and chromosomal locations for the 29 blood group antigen systems.

Individuals who are homozygous for an allele in some blood group systems may have more antigen expressed on their red cells than persons who are heterozygous for that allele. For example, red cells from a

Table 10-1. Chromosomal Locations of Human Blood Group System Genes*

System	ISBT No.	ISBT Symbol	Gene(s) Designation (ISGN)	Location
ABO	001	ABO	ABO	9q34.2
MNS	002	MNS	GYPA, GYPB, GYPE	4q28.2-q31.1
P	003	P1	P1	22q11.2-qter
Rh	004	RH	RHD, RHCE	1p36.13-p34.3
Lutheran	005	LU	LU	19q13.2
Kell	006	KEL	KEL	7q33
Lewis	007	LE	FUT3	19p13.3
Duffy	008	FY	DARC	1q22-q23
Kidd	009	JK	SLC14A1	18q11-q12
Diego	010	DI	SLC4A1	17q21-q22
Yt	011	YT	ACHE	7q22.1
Xg	012	XG	XG	Xp22.32
Scianna	013	SC	SC	1p34
Dombrock	014	DO	DO	12p12.3
Colton	015	CO	AQP1	7p14
Landsteiner-Wiener	016	LW	LW	19p13.3
Chido/Rodgers	017	CH/RG	C4A, C4B	6p21.3
H	018	H	FUT1	19q13.3
Kx	019	XK	XK	Xp21.1
Gerbich	020	GE	GYPC	2q14-q21
Cromer	021	CROM	DAF	1q32
Knops	022	KN	CR1	1q32
Indian	023	IN	CD44	11p13
OK	024	OK	CD147	19p13.3
RAPH	025	MER2	MER2	11p15.5
JMH	026	JMH	SEMA7A	15q22.3-q23
I	027	I	CGNT2	6p24
Globoside	028	P	B3GALT3	3q25
GIL	029	GIL	AQP3	9q13

*Modified from Zelinski[1]; Garratty et al[2]; and Denomme et al.[3]

person whose phenotype is Jk(a+b–) have a "double dose" of the *Jk^a* allele and, as a result, express more Jk^a antigen on the red cell surface than an individual whose phenotype is Jk(a+b+) (a single dose of the *Jk^a* allele). The difference in amount of antigen expressed on the red cell membrane between a homozygous and a heterozygous phenotype can often be detected serologically and is termed the dosage effect. For example, some anti-Jk^a sera may give the following pattern of reactivity:

Antibody	Phenotype of RBC Donor	
	Jk(a+b–)	Jk(a+b+)
Anti-Jk^a	3+	2+

Dosage effect is not seen with all blood group antigens or even with all antibodies of a given specificity. Antibodies that typically demonstrate dosage include those in the Rh, MNS, Kidd, and Duffy blood group systems.

Alleles arise by genetic changes at the DNA level and may result in a different expressed phenotype. Some of the changes found among blood group alleles may result from:

- Missense mutations (a single nucleotide substitution leading to the coding of a different amino acid)
- Nonsense mutations (a single nucleotide substitution leading to the coding of a stop codon)
- Mutations in motifs involved in transcription
- Mutations leading to alternate RNA splicing
- Deletion of a gene, exon, or nucleotide(s)
- Insertion of an exon or nucleotide(s)
- Alternate transcription initiation site
- Chromosome translocation
- Gene conversion or recombination
- Crossing over

Mutations may result in the creation of new polymorphisms associated with the altered gene. Figure 10-3 illustrates how mutations in the genes that code for the MNS blood group antigens have resulted in the creation of various low-incidence MNS system antigens.

Allele (Gene) Frequencies

The frequency of an allele (or its gene frequency) is the proportion that it contributes to the total pool of alleles at that locus within a given population at a given time. This frequency can be calculated from phenotype frequencies observed within a population. The sum of allele frequencies at a given locus must equal 1.

The Hardy-Weinberg Law

The Hardy-Weinberg law is based on the assumption that genotypes are distributed in proportion to the frequencies of individual alleles in a population and will remain constant from generation to generation if the processes of mutation, migration, etc do not occur. For example, the Kidd blood group system is basically a two-allele system (*Jk^a* and *Jk^b*; the silent *Jk* allele is extremely rare) that can be used to illustrate the calculation of gene frequencies. This calculation uses the Hardy-Weinberg equation for a two-allele system. If p is the frequency of the *Jk^a* allele and q is the frequency of the *Jk^b* allele, then the frequencies of the three combinations of alleles can be represented by the equation $p^2 + 2pq + q^2 = 1$ where:

p	=	frequency	of	*Jk^a* allele
q	=	frequency	of	*Jk^b* allele
p^2	=	frequency	of	*Jk^a/Jk^a* genotype
2pq	=	frequency	of	*Jk^a/Jk^b* genotype
q^2	=	frequency	of	*Jk^b/Jk^b* genotype

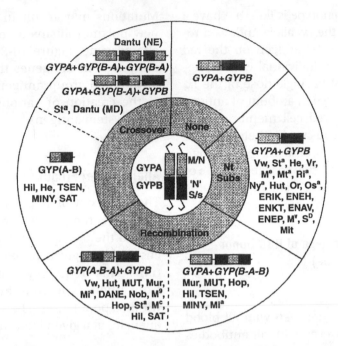

Figure 10-3. How crossover, recombination, and nucleotide substitution (nt subs) result in variations of genes producing glycophorin A and B. The changes are associated with the presence of various low-incidence MNS system antigens. (Modified from Reid.[4])

Using the observation that 77% of individuals within a population express Jk[a] antigen on their red cells, then:

$$p^2 + 2pq \quad = \quad \text{frequency of persons who are Jk(a+) and carry the } Jk^a \text{ allele}$$
$$= \quad 0.77$$

$$q^2 = 1 - (p^2 + 2pq) = \quad \text{frequency of persons who are Jk(a–) (homozygous for the } Jk^b \text{ allele)}$$

$$q^2 = 1 - 0.77 \quad = \quad 0.23$$
$$q \quad = \quad \sqrt{0.23}$$
$$q \quad = \quad 0.48 \text{ (allele frequency of } Jk^b)$$

Because the sum of frequencies of both alleles must equal 1.00,

$$p + q \quad = \quad 1$$
$$p \quad = \quad 1 - q$$
$$p \quad = \quad 1 - 0.48$$
$$p \quad = \quad 0.52 \text{ (allele frequency of } Jk^a)$$

Once the allele frequencies have been calculated, the number of Jk(b+) individuals (both homozygous and heterozygous) can be calculated as:

$$2pq + q^2 \quad = \quad \text{frequency of Jk(b+)}$$
$$= \quad 2 (0.52 \times 0.48) + (0.48)^2$$
$$= \quad 0.73$$

If both anti-Jk[a] and anti-Jk[b] sera are available, allele frequencies can be determined more easily by direct counting. As shown in Table 10-2, the random sample of 100 people tested for Jk[a] and Jk[b] antigens possess a total of 200 alleles at the Jk locus (each person inherits two alleles, one from each parent). There are two Jk^a alleles inherited by

Table 10-2. Gene Frequencies in the Kidd Blood Group System Calculated Using Direct Counting Method*

Phenotype	No. of Individuals	No. of Kidd Genes	Gene Frequencies (%)	
			Jk^a	Jk^b
Jk(a+b−)	28	56	56	0
Jk(a+b+)	49	98	49	49
Jk(a−b+)	23	46	0	46
Totals	100	200	105	95
Gene Frequency			0.525	0.475

*Assumes absence of silent *Jk* allele.

each of the 28 individuals who phenotype as Jk(a+b−), for a total of 56 alleles. There are 49 Jk^a alleles in the individuals who are Jk(a+b+), for a total of 105 alleles or a gene frequency of 0.52 (105 ÷ 200). The frequency of Jk^b is 95 ÷ 200 = 0.48.

The Hardy-Weinberg law is generally used to calculate allele and genotype frequencies in a population when the frequency of one genetic trait (eg, antigen phenotype) is known. However, it relies on certain assumptions: no mutation; no migration (in or out) of the population; lack of selective advantage/disadvantage of a particular trait; and a large enough population so that chance alone cannot alter an allele frequency. If all of these conditions are present, the gene pool is in equilibrium and allele frequencies will not change from one generation to the next. If these assumptions do not apply, changes in allele frequencies may occur over a few generations and can explain many of the differences in allele frequencies between populations.

Segregation

The term segregation refers to the concept that the two members of a single gene pair (alleles) are never found in the same gamete but always segregate and pass to different gametes. In blood group genetics, this can be illustrated by the inheritance of the *ABO* alleles (Fig 10-4). In this example, the members of the parental generation (P₁) are homozygous for an *A* allele and an *O* allele. All members of the first filial generation (F₁) will be heterozygous (*A/O*) but will still express the blood group A antigen (*O* is a silent allele). If an F₁ individual mates with an *A/O* genotypic individual, the resulting progeny [termed the second filial generation: (F₂)] will blood group as A (either heterozygous or homozygous) or group O. If the F₁ individual mated with a heterozygous group B person (*B/O*), the offspring could have the blood group A, B, AB, or O.

Independent Assortment

Mendel's law of independent assortment states that genes determining various traits are inherited independently from each other. For example, if one parent is group A (homozygous for *A*) and K+k+, and the other parent is group B (homozygous for *B*) and K−k+ (homozygous for *k*), all the F₁ children would be group AB; half would be K+k+ and half K−k+ (Fig 10-5). A second filial generation could manifest any of the following phenotypes: group A,

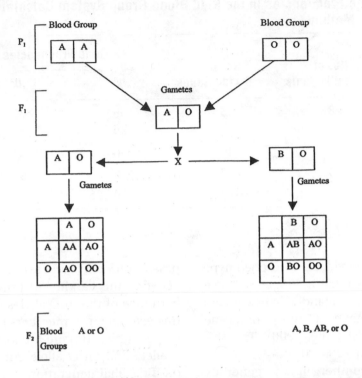

Figure 10-4. Mendel's law of independent segregation demonstrated by the inheritance of ABO genes.

K+k+; group AB, K+k+; group B, K+k+; group A, K–k+; group AB, K–k+; group B, K–k+. The proportions would be 1:2:1:1:2:1.

Independent assortment applies if the genes are on different chromosomes or on distant portions of the same chromosome. One exception to this rule is that closely linked genes on the same chromosome do not sort independently but often remain together from one generation to another. This observation is termed linkage.

Linkage

Genetic linkage is defined as the tendency for alleles close together on the same chromosome to be transmitted together. During mitosis, each pair of homologous chromosomes undergoes a series of recombinations. The resultant reciprocal exchange of segments between the chromatids is termed crossing over (Fig 10-6). Genes close together on a chromosome tend to be transmitted together during these recombinations and their alleles, therefore, do not segregate independently. Sometimes, the linkage is very tight so that recombination rarely occurs. The strength of linkage can be used as a unit of measurement to estimate the distance between different loci. This type of analysis can help in identifying, mapping, and diagnosing the genes responsible for certain inherited diseases.

The demonstration of linkage between the gene controlling ABH secretion (*Se*) and the expression of Lutheran blood group antigens (Lu^a, Lu^b) was the first recognized example of autosomal linkage in humans.[5] Analysis of this relationship also provided the first evidence in humans of recombination due to crossing-over and helped dem-

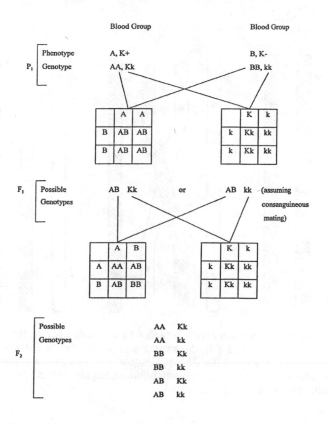

Figure 10-5. Mendel's law of independent assortment demonstrated by the inheritance of ABO and Kell genes.

onstrate that crossing-over occurs more often in females than in males.

Linkage Disequilibrium

When two loci are closely linked, alleles at those loci tend to be inherited together and are said to constitute a haplotype. Again, the close linkage between the loci controlling expression of M and N and of S and s is an example of linkage disequilibrium. The approximate frequencies of each of the four alleles are:

$M = 0.53$ $S = 0.33$
$N = 0.47$ $s = 0.67$

If the alleles of the M, N, S, and s antigens segregated independently, the expected frequency of each haplotype would be the product of the frequencies of the individual alleles. However, the frequencies observed are not those expected:

		Expected Frequency	Observed Frequency
MS	=	$0.53 \times 0.33 = 0.17$	0.24
Ms	=	$0.53 \times 0.67 = 0.36$	0.28
NS	=	$0.47 \times 0.33 = 0.16$	0.08
Ns	=	$0.47 \times 0.67 = \underline{0.31}$	$\underline{0.40}$
Total		1.00	1.00

This is an example of linkage disequilibrium: the tendency of specific combinations of alleles at two or more linked loci to be inherited together more frequently than would be expected by chance.

Another commonly cited example of linkage disequilibrium occurs in the HLA system (see Chapter 17). The combination

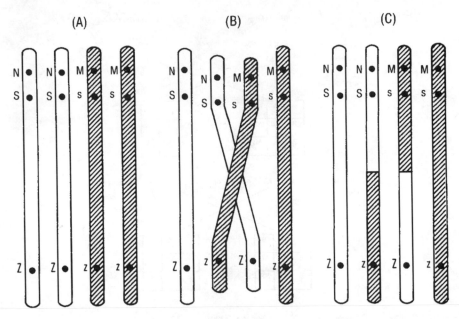

Figure 10-6. Very closely linked loci are rarely affected by crossing over so that alleles of those loci are inherited together (N and S, M and s in the example shown). Loci on the same chromosome that are not closely linked (the *Ss* locus and the *Zz* locus shown) can demonstrate crossing over. Crossing over is one kind of recombination. It occurs between homologous chromatids during meiosis, resulting in segregation of alleles on the same chromosome.

of HLA-A1 with HLA-B8 occurs in some populations approximately five times more frequently than would be expected based on the frequencies of the individual alleles, an example of *positive* linkage disequilibrium. Linkage disequilibrium may be positive or negative, and it may indicate a selective advantage of one haplotype over another. Over many generations, the alleles of even closely linked loci may reach equilibrium and associate according to their individual frequencies in the population.

When there is linkage equilibrium, the alleles at two loci associate with frequencies that reflect their individual frequencies. For example, if alleles in the population have the following frequencies:

Y	0.53	*Z*	0.30
y	0.47	*z*	0.70
Total	1.00		1.00

then the frequencies of the combination should be the product of the frequency of each allele:

YZ	0.53×0.3	=	0.16
Yz	0.53×0.7	=	0.37
yZ	0.47×0.3	=	0.14
yz	0.47×0.7	=	0.33
Total			1.00

In such a case, the alleles are in linkage equilibrium because they are inherited independently.

Patterns of Inheritance
Dominant and Recessive Traits

Traits are the observed expression of genes. A trait that is observable when the determining allele is present is called *domi-*

nant; when different alleles on homologous chromosomes each produce an observable trait, the term *co-dominant* is used. A *recessive* trait is observable only when the allele is not paired with a dominant allele (two recessive alleles are present). Describing traits as dominant and recessive depends on the method used to detect gene products. Observable traits are called *phenotypes*. Thus, blood group antigen typing using antisera identifies a phenotype. In some cases, *genotypes* may be inferred from the phenotype, especially when family studies are performed, but genotypes are not usually determined directly by typing red cells.

Autosomal Dominant Trait

An autosomal dominant trait shows a characteristic pattern of inheritance. The trait appears whenever an individual possesses the allele. Figure 10-7(A) presents a pedigree showing the pattern of autosomal dominant inheritance. Typically, each person with the trait has at least one parent with the trait, continuing backward through generations.

Autosomal Recessive Trait

People who exhibit a recessive trait are homozygous for the encoding allele. Their parents may or may not express the trait. However, parents who lack the trait must be *carriers*, ie, heterozygotes for an allele whose presence is not phenotypically apparent.

If the frequency of the variant allele is low, the recessive trait will be rare and generally will occur only in members of one generation, not in preceding or successive generations unless consanguineous mating occurs. Blood relatives are more likely to carry the same rare allele than unrelated persons from a random population. When offspring are homozygous for a *rare* allele

(frequency: <1:10,000) and display the trait, the parents are often blood relatives [Fig 10-7(B)]. Recessive traits may remain unexpressed for many generations, so that the appearance of a rare recessive trait does not necessarily imply consanguinity, although family ethnicity and geographic origin may be informative. A higher frequency for a recessive allele indicates the less likelihood of consanguinity. Traits inherited in either autosomal dominant or autosomal recessive fashion typically occur with equal frequency in males and females.

Sex-Linked Dominant or Co-dominant Trait

A male always receives his single X chromosome from his mother. The predominant feature of X-linked inheritance, of either dominant or recessive traits, is absence of male-to-male (father-to-son) transmission of the trait. Because a male passes his X chromosome to all his daughters, all daughters of a man expressing a *dominant* X-linked trait also possess the allele and the trait. If a woman expresses a dominant trait, but is heterozygous, each child, male or female, has a 50% chance of inheriting that allele and thus the trait [Fig 10-7(C)]. If the mother possesses the determining allele on both X chromosomes, all her children will express the trait. X-linked dominant traits tend to appear in each generation of a kindred, but without male-to-male transmission. A sex-linked dominant trait of interest in blood group genetics is the Xg blood group system.

Sex-Linked Recessive Trait

Hemophilia A provides a classic example of X-linked recessive inheritance [Fig 10-7(D)]. Males inherit the trait from carrier mothers or, very rarely, from a mother who is homozygous for the allele and

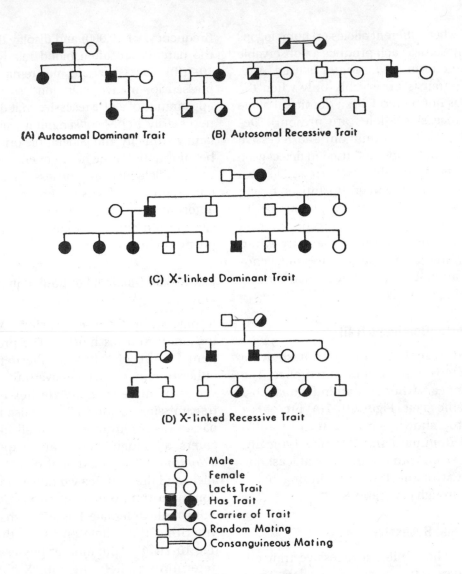

Figure 10-7. Four pedigrees showing different patterns of inheritance.

therefore expresses the trait. In the mating of a normal male and a carrier female, one half of the male offspring are affected and one half of the females are carriers. Among the children of an affected male and a female who lacks the determining allele, all sons are normal and all daughters are carriers.

If the recessive X-linked allele is rare, the trait will be exhibited almost exclusively in males. If the X-linked allele occurs more frequently in the population, affected females will be seen because the likelihood increases that an affected male will mate with a carrier female and produce daughters, half of whom will be homozygous for the abnormal allele.

Blood Group Co-dominant Traits

Blood group antigens, as a rule, are expressed as co-dominant traits: heterozygotes express the products of both alleles. If an individual's red cells type as both K+ and k+, the *K/k* genotype may be inferred.

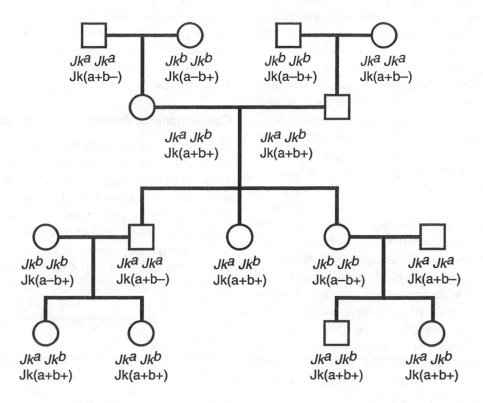

Figure 10-8. Inheritance and co-dominant expression of Kidd blood group antigens.

Figure 10-8 shows the inheritance patterns of the two active alleles of the Kidd blood group system (Jk^a and Jk^b) and the co-dominant phenotypic expression of the two respective antigens Jk^a and Jk^b.

In the ABO system, the situation is more complex. The genes of the ABO system do not code for membrane proteins but control production of enzymes termed glycosyltransferases. These enzymes add specific sugars to a precursor structure on the red cell membrane, resulting in specific antigen expression. In an A^1/A^2 heterozygote, the phenotype is A$_1$; the presence of the A^2 allele cannot be inferred. Although the A^1 allele appears dominant to that of the A^2 allele by simple cell typing, techniques that identify the specific transferases reveal that an A^1/A^2 heterozygote does generate the products of both alleles, ie, both A$_1$ and A$_2$

transferases. Similarly, in an A^2/O person, A^2 is dominant to O. The O allele codes for a specific protein, but this protein (transferase) is nonfunctional. The presence of ABO genes can be demonstrated by molecular techniques (see Chapter 13).

Chromosomal Assignment

The loci of all major blood group genes have been mapped to one or another of the 22 pairs of autosomes, as shown in Table 10-1. The Xg and XK loci are the only blood group genes mapped to the X chromosome.

Interaction among alleles or the products of different genes may modify the expression of a trait. The terms "suppressor" and "modifier" are used to describe genes that affect the expression of other genes;

however, the mechanism of these postulated gene interactions is not always fully understood. Some observations in blood group serology have been explained by gene interaction: weakening of the D antigen expression when the *C* allele is present in *cis* (on the same chromosome) or in *trans* (on the paired chromosome),[6] and the suppression of Lutheran antigen expression by the dominant modifier gene, *In(Lu)*.[7]

When products of two different genes are important in the sequential development of a biochemical end product, the gene interaction is called epistasis. Failure to express A or B antigens if H substance has not first been produced (absence of the *H* gene) is an example of epistasis. A mutation database of gene loci encoding common and rare blood group antigens has been established (Blood Group Antigen Mutation Database) and is available on the Internet (see http://www.bioc.aecom.yu.edu/bgmut/index.htm).

Population Genetics

Some understanding of population genetics is essential for parentage testing and helpful in such clinical situations as predicting the likelihood of finding blood compatible with a serum that contains multiple antibodies. Calculations use published phenotype frequencies.

Phenotype Frequencies

The frequencies of blood group phenotypes are obtained by testing many randomly selected people of the same race or ethnic group and observing the proportion of positive and negative reactions with a specific blood group antibody. In a blood group system, the sum of phenotype frequencies should equal 100%. For example, in a Caucasian population, 77% of randomly selected individuals are Jk(a+).

The frequency of Jk(a–) individuals should be 23%. If blood is needed for a patient with anti-Jk[a], 23% or approximately one in four ABO-compatible units of blood should be compatible.

Calculations for Combined Phenotypes

If a patient has multiple blood group antibodies, it may be useful to estimate the number of units that will have to be tested in order to find units of blood negative for all the antigens. For example, if a patient has anti-c, anti-K, and anti-Jk[a], how many ABO-compatible units of blood would have to be tested to find 4 units of the appropriate phenotype?

	Phenotype Frequency (%)
c–	20
K–	91
Jk(a–)	23

To calculate the frequency of the combined phenotype, the individual frequencies are multiplied because the phenotypes are independent of one another. Thus, the proportion of persons who are c– is 20%. Of the 20% of c– individuals, 91% are K–; hence, 18% ($0.20 \times 0.91 = 0.18$) are c– and K–. Of this 18% of c–K– individuals, 23% will be Jk(a–); therefore, only 4% of individuals will have c–K–Jk(a–) blood ($0.2 \times 0.91 \times 0.23 = 0.04$). Therefore, of 100 units tested, 4 compatible units should be found. Calculations such as this influence decisions about asking for assistance from the local blood supplier or reference laboratory when trying to find compatible blood for an alloimmunized patient.

Parentage Testing

Blood group antigens, many of which are expressed as co-dominant traits with simple Mendelian modes of inheritance, are useful in parentage analyses. If one assumes maternity and that test results are accurate, paternity can be excluded in either of two ways:

1. *Direct* exclusion of paternity is established when a genetic marker is present in the child but is absent from the mother and the alleged father. Example:

Blood Group Phenotype

Child	Mother	Alleged Father
B	O	O

The child has inherited a *B* gene, which could not be inherited from either the mother or the alleged father, assuming that neither the mother nor the alleged father is of the rare O_h phenotype. Based on the phenotypes of mother and child, the *B* gene must have been inherited from the biologic father and is called a paternal *obligatory gene*.

2. Exclusion is *indirect* when the child lacks a genetic marker that the alleged father (given his observed phenotype) must transmit to his offspring. Example:

Blood Group Phenotype

Child	Mother	Alleged Father
Jk(a+b–)	Jk(a+b–)	Jk(a–b+)

In this case, the alleged father is presumably homozygous for Jk^b and should have transmitted Jk^b to the child.

Direct exclusion is more convincing than indirect exclusion when trying to establish parentage. Apparent indirect exclusion can sometimes result from the presence of a silent allele. In the example above, the alleged father could have one silent allele (*Jk*), which was transmitted to the child. The child's genotype could be Jk^aJk instead of the far more common Jk^aJk^a. Interpretation of phenotypic data must take into account all biologic and analytic factors known to influence results.

When the alleged father cannot be excluded from paternity, it is possible to calculate the probability of paternity. The probability that the alleged father transmitted the paternal obligatory genes is compared with the probability that any other randomly selected man from the same ethnic/racial population could have transmitted the genes. The result is expressed as a likelihood ratio (paternity index) or as a percentage (posterior probability of paternity given some prior probability). Methods for parentage analysis often include the study of many genetic systems other than red cell blood groups [ie, HLA and short tandem repeat (STR) systems]. Many parentage testing laboratories employ the STR method of DNA analysis (see Chapter 9) as a means of evaluating cases of disputed parentage. The AABB has developed standards for laboratories that perform parentage studies.[8]

Chimerism

A chimera is one whose cells are derived from more than one distinct zygotic line. Although rare, this may occur when an anastomosis occurs within the vascular tissues of twin embryos, or when two fertilized zygotes fuse to form one individual. This condition, although not hereditary, leads to dual (multiple) phenotypic populations of cells within one individual. Blood types of such rare individuals may demonstrate a mixed-field appearance, with distinct populations of cells of the person's true genetic type, as well as cells of the implanted type. Chimeras also demonstrate immune tolerance: a genetically group O person with implanted A cells does not produce anti-A. More commonly, chimeras are artificial and arise from the transfer of actively dividing cells, eg, through hematopoietic transplantation (see Chapter 25).

Blood Group Nomenclature

The terminology and notations for blood group systems embody many inconsistencies because blood group serologists failed to follow conventions of classic Mendelian genetics. Listed below are a few examples of the confusion engendered by many decades of uncoordinated scientific publications.

1. An allele that determines a dominant trait often is signified by a capital letter; one that determines a recessive trait is denoted by both lowercase letters. The *A* and *B* co-dominant genes of the ABO system are signified by a capital letter. The *O* gene is also given a capital but does not present as a dominant trait. Without prior knowledge, it would be impossible for one to recognize that these notations represent allelic products in a blood group system.

2. Some co-dominant traits have been designated with capital letters and allelic relationships with lowercase letters; for example, *K* and *k* of the Kell blood group system and *C* and *c* of the Rh system.

3. Some co-dominant traits have identical base symbols but different superscript symbols, such as Fy^a and Fy^b (Duffy system) and Lu^a and Lu^b (Lutheran system).

4. In some allelic pairs, the lower frequency antigen is expressed with an "a" superscript (Wr^a has a lower frequency than Wr^b). In other allelic pairs, the "a" superscript denotes the higher incidence antigen (Co^a has a higher frequency than Co^b).

5. Some authors have denoted the absence of a serologic specificity with a base symbol devoid of superscripts, and others use a lowercase version of the base symbol. In the Lutheran system, the assumed amorphic gene is called *Lu*, not *lu*, whereas the amorph in the Lewis system is *le*.

6. Numeric terminology was introduced for some blood group systems, resulting in mixtures of letters and numbers for antigen designations, eg, K, Kp^a, and K11.

Colloquial use of these terminologies, even in some published articles and texts, has compounded their improper use. Early model computers or printers also did not easily accept certain terminologies (eg, superscripts, subscripts, unusual fonts).

In recent years, concerted attempts have been made to establish rational, uniform criteria for the notations used to designate phenotype, genotype, and locus information for blood group systems. Issitt and Crookston[9] and Garratty et al[2] presented guidelines for the nomenclature and terminology of blood groups. The International Society of Blood Transfusion (ISBT) Working Party on Terminology for Red Cell Surface Antigens has provided a standardized system for classifying blood group antigens (see Appendix 6). Similar international committees have established principles for assigning nomenclature of the hemoglobins, immunoglobulin allotypes, histocompatibility antigens, clusters of differentiation, STR sequences, and other serum protein and red cell enzyme systems. Although many of the older terminologies must be retained to avoid even further confusion, common conventions now exist for correct usage.

The ISBT terminology for red cell antigens was devised as a numeric nomenclature suitable for computerization. A six-digit designation indicates each blood group specificity. The first three numbers identify the blood group system and the last three numbers identify the individual specificity. This numeric terminology is designed mainly for computer databases and is not necessarily intended to supplant more common usage.

For ISBT classification, each defined blood group system must be genetically distinct. Assignment of antigens to a specific blood group system is dependent on genetic, serologic, and/or biochemical relationships. Gene cloning has made the task of assignment more definitive and has allowed some designations previously unproved by traditional family studies (ie, the expansion of the Diego system to include a number of low-incidence antigens).

Some antigens, however, have not yet been proven to be part of a recognized system. Collections (termed the 200 series) are apparently related sets of antigens for which definitive genetic information is lacking. Other isolated antigens of high (901 series) or low (700 series) incidence are listed together until genetic information becomes available. In recent years, the number of antigens in these three series has dramatically declined as further genetic and biochemical data allow reassignment.

Correct Terminology

The following are accepted conventions for expressing red cell antigen phenotypes and genotypes.[2]

1. Genes encoding the expression of blood group antigens are written in italics (or underlined if italics are not available). If the antigen name includes a subscript (A_1), generally the encoding gene is expressed with a superscript (A^1).

2. Antigen names designated by a superscript or a number (eg, Fy^a, Fy:1) are written in normal (Roman) script. Numeric designations are written on the same line as the letters. Superscript letters are lowercase. (Some exceptions occur, based on historic usage: hr^s, hr^B.)

3. When antigen phenotypes are expressed using single letter designations, results are usually written as + or –, set on the same line as the letter(s) of the antigen: K+ k–.

4. To express phenotypes of antigens designated with a superscript letter, that letter is placed in parentheses on the same line as the symbol defining the antigen: Fy(a+) and Fy(a–).

5. For antigens designated by numbers, the symbol defining the system is notated in capital letters followed by a colon, followed by the number representing the antigen tested. Plus signs do not appear when test results are positive (K:1), but a minus sign is placed before negative test results: K:1, K:–1. If tests for several antigens in one blood group have been done, the phenotype is designated by the letter(s) of the locus or blood group system followed by a colon, followed by antigen numbers separated by commas: K:–1,2,–3,4. Only antigens tested are listed; if an antibody defining a specific antigen was not tested, the number of the antigen is not listed: K:–1,–3,4.

Although numeric terminology has been devised for various systems and antigens, it should not be assumed that it must replace conventional terminology. The use of conventional antigen names is also acceptable. In some systems, notably Rh, multiple terminologies exist and not all antigens within the system have names in each type.

References

1. Zelinski T. Chromosomal localization of human blood group genes. In: Silberstein LE, ed. Molecular and functional aspects of blood group antigens. Bethesda, MD: AABB, 1995: 41-73.
2. Garratty G, Dzik W, Issitt PD, et al. Terminology for blood group antigens and genes—his-

torical origins and guidelines in the new millennium. Transfusion 2000;40:477-89.

3. Denomme G, Lomas-Francis C, Storry JR, Reid ME. Approaches to blood group molecular genotyping and its applications. In: Stowell C, Dzik W, eds. Emerging diagnostic and therapeutic technologies in transfusion medicine. Bethesda, MD: AABB Press, 2003: 95-129.

4. Reid ME. Molecular basis for blood groups and functions of carrier proteins. In: Silberstein LE, ed. Molecular and functional aspects of blood group antigens. Bethesda, MD: AABB, 1995:75-125.

5. Mohr J. A search for linkage between the Lutheran blood group and other hereditary characters. Acta Path Microbiol Scand 1951; 28:207-10.

6. Araszkiewicz P, Szymanski IO. Quantitative studies on the Rh-antigen D effect of the C gene. Transfusion 1987;27:257-61.

7. Crawford NM, Greenwait TJ, Sasaki T. The phenotype Lu(a–b–) together with unconventional Kidd groups in one family. Transfusion 1961;1:228-32.

8. Gjertson D, ed. Standards for parentage testing laboratories. 6th ed. Bethesda, MD: AABB, 2004.

9. Issitt PD, Crookston MC. Blood group terminology: Current conventions. Transfusion 1984; 24:2-7.

Appendix 10-1. Glossary of Terms in Blood Group Genetics

Allelic:	Pairs of genes located at the same site on chromosome pairs.
Centromere:	A constricted region of a chromosome that connects the chromatids during cell division.
Chromatid:	One of the two potential chromosomes formed by DNA replication of each chromosome before mitosis and meiosis. They are joined together at the centromere.
Chromatin:	The deeply staining genetic material present in the nucleus of a cell that is not dividing.
Chromosome:	A linear thread made of DNA in the nucleus of the cell.
Co-dominant:	A gene that expresses a trait regardless of whether or not an alternative allele at the same locus is also expressed on the other parental chromosome.
Crossing over:	The process of breaking single maternal and paternal DNA double helices in each of two chromatids and rejoining them to each other in a reciprocal fashion, which results in the exchange of parts of homologous chromosomes.
Dominant:	A gene that expresses a trait that does not allow the expression of a trait encoded by an alternative allele at the same locus on the other parental chromosome.
Gene:	The basic unit of heredity, made of DNA. Each gene occupies a specific location on a chromosome.
Locus:	The site of a gene on a chromosome.
Lyonization:	The inactivation of one of the female X chromosomes during embryogenesis. This inactivated chromosome forms the Barr body in the cell nucleus.
Meiosis:	A process of two successive cell divisions producing cells, egg, or sperm that contain half the number of chromosomes found in somatic cells.
Mitosis:	Division of somatic cells resulting in daughter cells containing the same number of chromosomes as the parent cell.
Recessive:	A gene that in the presence of its dominant allele does not express itself. A recessive trait is apparent only if both alleles are recessive.
Sex-linked:	A gene contained within the X or Y chromosome.
Somatic cell:	Nonreproductive cells or tissues.
X-linked:	A gene on the X chromosome for which there is no corresponding gene on the Y chromosome.

Chapter 11

Immunology

THE IMMUNE RESPONSE is a highly evolved innate and adaptive system that is fundamental for survival. It has a sophisticated ability to distinguish self from nonself and provides a memory bank that allows the body to rapidly respond to recurring foreign organisms. A healthy immune response can recognize foreign material or pathogens that invade the body and can initiate a series of events to eliminate these pathogens with minimal or no prolonged morbidity to the host.

The numerous components of the immune system work in delicate balance to ensure a state of health. This may include destruction of abnormal/malignant cells, removal of harmful bacteria or viruses, and/or an inflammatory response to promote healing. If the immune system becomes hyperreactive, the body may attack its own tissue or organs (autoimmune disease), or allergies may develop. If hyporeac-

tive, the host may be susceptible to a wide variety of infectious agents or proliferation of malignant cells. The ultimate goal of immune activity is to maintain this delicate balance.

Immune Response

The immune response can be classified into two categories: the innate response and the adaptive (acquired) response. Innate responses are indiscriminate: the same mechanisms can be deployed against invasive organisms or harmful stimuli. In contrast, the adaptive response recognizes specific features of the harmful stimuli and provides a customized response based on previous experiences (Fig 11-1). The adaptive response is a late evolutionary development, found only in vertebrates. Innate immunity, on the other hand, uses universal properties and processes such as epithelial barriers, proteolytic enzymes,

11

243

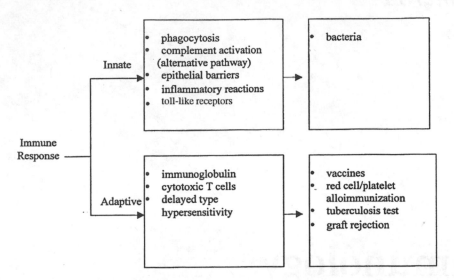

Figure 11-1. Examples of the factors used in innate and adaptive immunity and examples of the two types of immunity.

cellular phagocytosis, and inflammatory reactions. It is important to note that innate and adaptive immunity are complementary—not mutually exclusive—immune responses. Regardless of the classification, the immune response reflects the complex interaction of cells, tissues, organs, and soluble factors. Appendix 11-1 describes some frequently used immunology terms.

Immunoglobulin Superfamily

Molecules that belong to the immunoglobulin superfamily (IgSF) of receptors play a critical role in the recognition of foreign antigens. Antigen recognition is accomplished through receptors that are found in a soluble form and on the surface of lymphoid cells. Figure 11-2 illustrates the similar structure of some of these immunology receptors. The overall structure of these receptors is very similar, and it has been proposed that they arose from a common ancestral gene. The basic structure is similar to the domains of the immunoglobulin molecule; hence,

these receptors have been grouped into a single superfamily of molecules. Examples of these receptors include: immunoglobulins, T-cell receptor (TCR), major histocompatibility complex (MHC) Class I and Class II molecules, and receptors for growth factors and cytokines. There are several hundred members of the IgSF (ie, immunoglobulin receptors, integrins, etc).[2]

Major Histocompatibility Complex

The MHC is a large cluster of genes. In humans, the MHC includes the genes of the HLA system and genes that encode other proteins such as tumor necrosis factor (TNF), some complement components, and some heat shock proteins.[3] The genes that encode MHC molecules are located on the short arm of chromosome 6. There are three classes of these molecules.

MHC Class I Molecules

MHC Class I molecules are found on almost all cells in the body. The molecules are defined by three major Class I genes

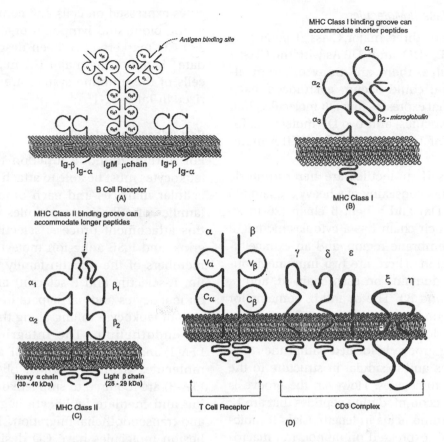

Figure 11-2. Structures of some receptors found on various cells in the immune system.[1]

designated HLA-A, -B, and -C. Hence, each individual will express six distinct Class I HLA molecules: two HLA-A, two HLA-B, and two HLA-C. Each locus has many alleles; more than 50 have been defined for HLA-A; more than 75 for HLA-B; and more than 30 for HLA-C.

The structure of a Class I HLA molecule is illustrated in Fig 11-2. Each molecule contains a heavy chain (45 kDa) and a smaller (12 kDa) peptide chain called β_2-microglobulin. The heavy chain has a cytoplasmic tail, a transmembrane region, and three extracellular immunoglobulin-like domains. β_2-microglobulin is noncovalently associated with the heavy chain and is not a transmembrane protein. This protein is required for Class I MHC expres-

sion and function on the cell surface. The antigen-binding groove of the Class I molecule is formed by the α_1 and α_2 domains of the heavy chain. The structure of the antigen-binding groove consists of a platform made up of eight parallel β strands that is supported by two α helices.[4] The peptides displayed in the antigen-binding groove are 8 to 12 amino acids long and represent hydrolyzed proteins that have been synthesized within the antigen-presenting cell; hence, they are referred to as endogenous antigens. The endogenous source of proteins indicates that the genes encoding the protein also must reside in the cell. These proteins could be the product of host genes including tumorigenic genes or genes from viruses or intracellular bacteria.

MHC Class II Molecules

There are three major Class II gene loci: HLA-DR, -DQ, and -DP. As with the Class I molecules, there are many different alleles that could occupy each locus. Each individual expresses four DR molecules, four DQ molecules, and two DP molecules, for a total of 10 forms of Class II HLA molecules.

Class II molecules are heterodimeric structures consisting of a heavy α chain (30 to 34 kDa) and a light β chain (26 to 29 kDa). Each chain has a cytoplasmic tail, a transmembrane region, and an extracellular portion. There are two immunoglobulin-like domains on each chain (α_1 and α_2 and β_1 and β_2). The α_2 and β_2 domains for each gene have a constant structure; the α_1 and β_1 domains are diverse. The antigen-binding groove is located within the α_1, β_1 domains and is similar in structure to the Class I molecules. However, the groove is larger, accommodating peptides that are 12 to 20 amino acids in length. Class II molecules are expressed on monocytes, macrophages, dendritic cells, and B lymphocytes. The antigenic peptides displayed in the groove of Class II HLA molecules come from proteins that have been phagocytosed or endocytosed by antigen-presenting cells. These proteins are termed exogenous antigens and include most bacteria, parasites, and viral particles released from other cells.[5]

MHC Class III Molecules

There are approximately 20 genes in the Class III region of the MHC. These genes code for proteins of the complement system and proinflammatory molecules such as TNF.

Cluster of Differentiation (CD) Molecules

The CD designation is a nomenclature system used to describe numerous molecules expressed on cells and components of the blood and lymphoid organs. Over 200 CD markers have been described to date.[3] Some of the major CD markers on cells of the immune system are summarized in Table 11-1.

Cell Adhesion Molecules

For normal immune function to occur, leukocytes must be able to attach to extracellular matrices and each other. Three families of adhesion molecules facilitate this attachment process: selectins, integrins, and IgSF adhesion molecules. The members of the selectin family (L-selectin, E-selectin, and P-selectin) are found on leukocytes and participate in the process of leukocyte rolling along the vascular endothelium. The integrins (VAL, LFA-1, and MAC-I) and the IgSF adhesion molecules (ICAMs, VCAMs, LFA-2, and LFA-3) are required to stop leukocyte rolling and mediate leukocyte aggregation and transendothelial migration.[6] Most adhesion molecules have CD designations (eg, LFA-2 is CD2 and LFA-3 is CD58).[7]

Signal Transduction

Signal transduction is the process of sending signals between or within cells that results in the initiation or inhibition of gene transcription. Cell surface activation signals associated with the immune response are initiated by extracellular interaction of various ligands and receptors. Many of these ligands and receptors have CD designations. Any defect or deficiency in the signal transduction process can have significant consequences on the normal functioning of the immune system. For example, severe combined immunodeficiency disease can result from a deficiency of Jak3, which impairs signal transduction of a specific cytokine receptor subunit.[7]

Table 11-1. Some Major CD Antigens on Cells of the Immune System

CD Designation	Cell Population	Other Cells with Antigen	Comments
CD1	Cortical thymocytes	Some APCs, some B cells	Strength of expression is inverse to expression of TCR/CD3
CD2	Pan-T marker, present on early thymocytes	NK cells	This is a sheep-cell rosette receptor; activation and adhesion function (LFA-2)
CD3	T lymphocytes	——	Functions as a signal transduction complex
CD4	Developing and mature thymocytes and on 2/3 of peripheral T cells	T helper cells and some macrophages	Adhesion molecule that mediates MHC restriction; signal transmission; HIV receptor
CD5	Pan-T marker, from late cortical stage	B cells of chronic lymphocytic leukemia; possibly long-lived autoreactive B cells	Function unknown; possibly involved in costimulatory effects of cell-to-cell adhesion
CD8	Developing and mature thymocytes and cytotoxic T lymphocytes	None	Adhesion molecule that mediates MHC restriction; signal transmission
CD14	Monocytes	——	LPS receptor
CD16	Macrophages, neutrophils, NK cells	——	FcγRIII (low-affinity Fc receptor for IgG)
CD19	B lymphocytes	——	Signaling (also called B4)
CD20	B lymphocytes	——	Signaling (also called B1)

(cont'd)

Table 11-1. Some Major CD Antigens on Cells of the Immune System (cont'd)

CD Designation	Cell Population	Other Cells with Antigen	Comments
CD21	Mature B cells	Possibly macrophages	This is a receptor for C3d (CR2); also receptor for EBV
CD25	Activated T and B cells	Macrophages; virally transformed cells	High-affinity IL-2 receptor, earlier called TaC
CD34	Stem cells	Hematopoietic cells; endothelial cells	Called "stem cell antigen"; used in the laboratory to isolate hematopoietic precursor cells; physiologic function unknown
CD35	Mature and activated B cells	Red cells, macrophages, granulocytes, dendritic cells	This is a receptor for C3b (CR4)
CD45	Immature and mature B and T cells	All cells of hematopoietic origin except red cells	Also called leukocyte common antigen (LCA); different leukocytes have different isoforms
CD56	NK cells	NKT cells	NK cell adhesion and lineage marker for NK cells; innate immunity
CD71	Early thymocytes; activated T and B cells	Activated hematopoietic cells; proliferating cells of other somatic lines; reticulocytes	This is the transferrin receptor

CD = clusters of differentiation; APCs = antigen-presenting cells; NK = natural killer; TCR = T-cell receptor; MHC = major histocompatibility complex; HIV = human immunodeficiency virus; IL = interleukin; NKT = natural killer T.

Organs of the Immune System

Numerous organs are involved in the immune system. The central organs include the marrow, liver, and thymus. Peripheral organs are the lymph nodes and spleen. The gastrointestinal tract-associated lymphoid tissue and bronchus-associated lymphoid tissue also play an important role involving both central and peripheral functions.

Cells of the Immune System

The primary cells involved in the adaptive immune system are lymphocytes—B cells, T cells, and antigen-presenting cells. Other cells such as macrophages are involved in the induction of the immune response, and both macrophages and polymorphonuclear leukocytes participate in various inflammation responses associated with the immune response. All of these cells are of hematopoietic origin (ie, marrow-derived) and are formed from a single progenitor called a pluripotent hematopoietic stem cell. As illustrated in Fig 11-3, the pluripotent stem cell can give rise to two lineages: myeloid and lymphoid. Granulocytes (neutrophils, basophils, and eosinophils), platelets, mast cells, red cells, and macrophages arise from myeloid progenitors. T and B lymphocytes are formed from lymphoid progenitors. Dendritic cells and natural killer (NK) cells are also derived from the pluripotent stem cell; however, their precise origin is unknown.

Lymphocytes

The two major lineages of lymphocytes are B cells and T cells. B cells are derived from the marrow and T cells are derived from T-cell precursors produced in the marrow, which migrate to the thymus. B cells are the precursors of the cells that make antibody (plasma cells). T cells consist of subpopulations that either help in antibody formation (helper T cells), kill target cells (cytotoxic T cells), induce inflammation (delayed hypersensitivity T cells), or inhibit the immune response (regulatory T cells).

B Lymphocytes

Each B cell can recognize one (or a limited set) of antigen epitopes through receptors on the cell surface. These receptors are similar to IgM and IgD molecules, which are produced and transported to the membrane surface. When the immunoglobulin receptor binds to a specific antigen, the cell is stimulated to divide and differentiate into a plasma cell. The plasma cell can secrete a soluble form of the immunoglobulin "receptor" known as antibody. The antibody secreted is specific for the same antigen that interacted with the cell-bound immunoglobulin receptor.

The B-cell receptor (BCR) has one additional heavy chain domain (C_H4) compared to secreted immunoglobulin. This domain is required to anchor the receptor to the cell membrane. Several accessory molecules on the surface of B cells are closely associated with the BCR and are important for signal transduction. Some of these accessory molecules include Igα, Igβ, MHC Class II molecules, complement receptors, and some CD markers (see Table 11-2). All of these components are part of the BCR antigen complex (some of these structures are illustrated in Fig 11-2).

The challenge for the body is to have B lymphocytes that can recognize each of the thousands of different foreign antigens encountered over a lifetime. The immune system has a unique approach to ensure this diversity. The human genome is known to contain approximately 40,000 genes. The B

Table 11-2. Receptors/Markers Present on Macrophages, Monocytes, and B Lymphocytes

Marker	Function
Macrophages and Monocytes	
Complement receptors	
CR1 (C3b receptors, CD35)	Binds to cells coated with C3b
CR3 (C3bi receptor, CDIIb)	Adhesion and activation
Cytokine receptors (IL-1, IL-4, IFNγ) and migration-inhibition factor	Receptors that bind cytokines signaling activation and other cell functions
Fc receptors	
FcγRI (CD64)	High affinity for IgG
FcγRII (CD32)	Medium affinity for IgG
FcγRIII (CD16)	Low affinity for IgG
FcγRII (CD23)	Low-affinity receptor for the Fc of IgE
Leukocyte function antigen (LFA1 or CD11a)	Adhesion and activation
Mannose/fucose receptors	Binds sugars on microorganisms
P150,95 (cD11c)	Adhesion and activation
B Lymphocytes	
CD5	Cell marker that identifies a subset of B cells predisposed to autoantibody production
CD19, 20, and 22	Primary cell markers used to distinguish B cells
CD72-78	Other cell markers that identify B cells
Complement receptors C3b (CR1, CD35); C3d (CR2, CD21)	Play a role in cell activation and "homing" of cells
Igα	Transport and assemble IgM monomers in the cell membrane
Igβ	Accessory molecules that interact with the transmembrane segments of IgM
MHC Class II (DP, DQ, DR)	Present on antigen-presenting cells and is critical for initiating T-cell-dependent immune responses

cells in the body probably make more than 100 million different antibody proteins that are expressed as immunoglobulin receptors. Because the human body does not have enough genes to code for the millions of different foreign proteins that the immune system must have the capability to recognize, a process called gene rearrangement is used to create the required diversity.[9]

Several genes code for the heavy chain and light chain that make up the immunoglobulin receptor on B cells. The loci for genes that code for the heavy chain are on chromosome 14 and the loci that code for the light chains are on chromosome 2 (κ light chain) or chromosome 22 (λ light chain). Three gene loci contribute to the diversity of the immunoglobulin receptor: V (variable), D (diversity), and J (joining). The

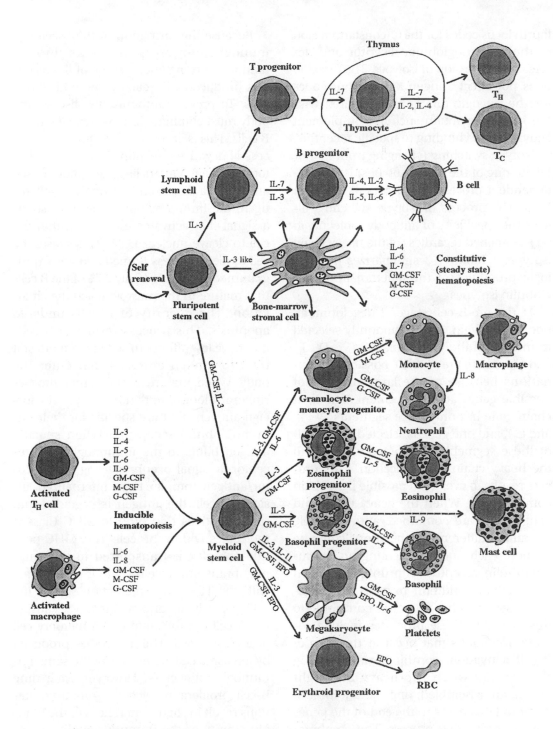

Figure 11-3. The pluripotent stem cell, in the upper middle part of the diagram, gives rise to the lymphoid stem cell and to the myeloid stem cell, from which all other lines of blood cells derive. Cytokines from marrow stromal cells influence the replication and differentiation of stem and later cells. Cytokines from activated members of the highly differentiated T-cell and macrophage lines exert major effects at all stages of myeloid and lymphoid development. (Used with permission from Goldsby et al.[8])

fourth locus codes for the C (constant) region of the immunoglobulin receptor and defines the expression of isotypes. The C region does not affect antigen binding but codes for the biologic functions associated with the immunoglobulin such as complement activation and binding to specific receptors.

Isotype switching (changing from IgM or IgD to one of the other isotypes) is a T-cell-dependent process that occurs at the DNA level. The process of isotype switching allows the specificity of antibody molecule to be maintained regardless of the heavy chain isotype.[9,10] Table 11-3 summarizes the biologic properties of the different immunoglobulin isotypes.

At the pre-B-cell stage of development, one heavy chain gene is randomly selected from each of the four segments (V_H, D_H, J_H, and C_H). There are over 10^4 possible combinations because of the large number of possible genes at each segment. The light chain gene has only three segments (V_L, J_L, and C_L), and one gene is selected from each of these segments in a process similar to the heavy chain gene selection. This process results in over 1000 possible light chain combinations. When the heavy chain and light chains are combined, approximately 10 million different combinations could be formed, each one representing an immunoglobulin receptor with unique antigen specificity. In addition to gene rearrangement, several other processes contribute to this diversity. These processes include somatic mutations that occur at the time of B-cell activation, combinatorial shuffling that occurs when the heavy and light chains are assembled, and the addition of random DNA bases to the end of the genes during the joining process. The combination of all of these processes ensures that B cells have immunoglobulin receptors specific for any foreign antigen that could be encountered (approximately 10^{11} antigen specificities).[9-11]

Because the formation of the B-cell immunoglobulin receptor occurs through random rearrangement, some of the receptors produced will react to the body's own cells. To prevent autoimmune disease, the body must eliminate or downregulate these B cells. This is accomplished through a process of negative selection.[12] When a B cell is formed, it encounters large quantities of self antigen. If a B cell binds strongly to self antigen, the immunoglobulin receptor sends a signal that activates enzymes within the cell to cleave nuclear DNA. This causes the cell to die, a process termed apoptosis (programmed cell death). Only 25% of the B cells that mature in the marrow reach the circulation. The majority of B cells undergo apoptosis. This process results in B cells that have low affinity to self antigen but still bind to foreign antigens that enter the body. When mature B cells enter the peripheral blood circulation, they bind foreign antigens that are specific for their immunoglobulin receptors. When specific antigen binds to the immunoglobulin receptor, a signal occurs causing the receptor/antigen complex to be internalized. Inside the cell, the antigen is degraded into small peptides that bind to MHC Class II molecules within the cell. This MHC-peptide complex is transported to the outer membrane of the cell where it can interact with the TCR. This interaction signals the cell to produce various cytokines, causing the B cell to proliferate into a memory cell or a plasma cell. The antibodies produced by a plasma cell are always of the same immunoglobulin class. However, each time B-cell proliferation occurs, somatic mutations result in slight differences in the binding affinity of the immunoglobulin receptor. Because immunoglobulin receptors with the highest binding affinity will be the ones most likely to encounter antigen, this process preferentially results in proliferation of B cells with the highest affinity for

Table 11-3. Characteristics and Biologic Properties of Human Immunoglobulins

Class	IgG	IgA	IgM	IgD	IgE
Structure					
H-chain isotype	γ	α	μ	δ	ε
Number of subclasses	4	2	1	?	?
L-chain, types	κ,λ	κ,λ	κ,λ	κ,λ	κ,λ
Molecular weight (daltons)	150,000	180,000-500,000	900,000	180,000	200,000
Exists as polymer	No	Yes	Yes	No	No
Electrophoretic mobility	γ	γ	between γ and β	between γ and β	fast γ
Sedimentation constant (in Svedberg units)	6-7S	7-15S	19S	7S	8S
Gm allotypes (H chain)	+	0	0	0	0
Km allotypes (Kappa L chain: formerly Inv)	+	+	+	?	?
Am allotypes	0	+	0	0	0
Serum concentration (mg/dL)	1000-1500	200-350	85-205	3	0.01-0.07
Total immunoglobulin (%)	80	15	5	<0.1	<0.1
Synthetic rate (mg/kg/day)	33	24	6-7	<0.4	<0.02
Serum half-life (days)	23	6	5	2-8	1-5
Distribution (% of total in intravascular space)	45	42	76	75	51
Present in epithelial secretions	No	Yes	No	No	No
Antibody activity	Yes	Yes	Yes	Probably no	Yes
Serologic characteristics	Usually nonagglutinating	Usually nonagglutinating	Usually agglutinating	?	?
Fixes complement	Yes	No	Yes	No	No
Crosses placenta	Yes	No	No	No	No

antigen. This preferential selection is termed a focused immune response.[5,13,14]

T Lymphocytes

There are two major types of T cells: cytotoxic T cells and helper T cells. These two cell types can be differentiated by the pre- sence of specific CD markers on the cell. Cytotoxic T cells are positive for the surface marker CD8 and negative for CD4 and make up approximately one-third of the circulating T cells in the peripheral blood. Helper T cells are CD4 positive and CD8 negative and represent approximately two-thirds of the circulating T cells. Helper T cells recognize antigen presented by Class II HLA molecules, whereas cytotoxic T cells recognize antigen in the context of Class I HLA molecules. Approximately 5% of peripheral blood T cells are negative for both CD4 and CD8.

T cells go through a process of positive and negative selection in the thymus during T-cell ontogeny. If a T cell is able to recognize self MHC antigens, it survives (positive selection) and migrates to the medulla of the thymus. In the medulla, the T cells undergo a process (negative selection) that deletes T cells with high affinity for self MHC antigens. T cells that fail to recognize self MHC antigens undergo apoptosis. The primary goal is to select T cells that recognize self MHC molecules that have foreign peptides in their groove. The process is so exquisite that approximately 10% of T cells have the ability to react with foreign MHC complexes, which forms the major basis of transplantation rejection. In the end, only 5% of the cells in the thymus survive both positive and negative selection and become mature T cells.[5,13,15]

The receptor on the T cell that is responsible for MHC/peptide recognition is the TCR (see Fig 11-2). There are two major types of TCRs: those that express α and β chains or γ and δ chains as part of the TCR complex. Approximately 90% of all T cells bear α, β chains. Each transmembrane chain has two domains (one variable, the other constant). These chains are produced through a process of gene rearrangement in a manner similar to MHC and immunoglobulin receptors. The number of possible TCR α and β specificities is estimated at 10^{15}. The TCRs bearing γ and δ are expressed on 5% to 15% of T cells, predominantly by those T cells in the mucosal endothelium. These T cells appear to play an important role in protecting the mucosal surfaces of the body from foreign bacteria.

The TCR is noncovalently associated with the CD3 complex, which is made up of three pairs of dimers. This CD3 complex is responsible for signal transduction once peptide is recognized by the TCR.[16]

Recognition by Cytotoxic T Cells. Cytotoxic T cells recognize peptides associated with Class I MHC molecules. As discussed previously, these peptides may be derived from self proteins or proteins from intracellular viruses or microbes. The TCR-2 receptor on the cytotoxic T cell recognizes the peptide-MHC Class I molecule in combination with a co-receptor (CD8) on the T cell. These interactions signal the cell to produce proteins (eg, perforin) that disrupt the integrity of the target cell membrane, resulting in cell death. During this process, cytokines [TNF-α and interferon-γ (IFNγ)] are also produced. These cytokines prevent replication of virus that may be shed from the cell during cell death; hence, the infection is stopped through these processes. Although the process is an extremely effective mechanism for killing cells infected with virus, the process can be harmful to the host. The cytokines produced to prevent viral replication can cause adverse effects including the damage or destruction of healthy host tissue. Liver damage associated with hepatitis B infection is an example of morbidity caused by the cytotoxic T-cell response.[5,11]

Stimulation of B Cells. B-cell activation can occur through activation by T cells or by a mechanism independent of T-cell interaction. These two mechanisms are described below.

T-Cell-Dependent Stimulation. Helper T-cell receptors recognize foreign peptides in the antigen-binding groove of Class II MHC molecules in combination with CD4. This TCR-CD4 interaction with MHC Class II upregulates the expression of CD80/86 on the surface of antigen-specific B cells. CD80/86 reacts with the ligand CD28 on the T-cell surface, causing upregulation of the CD40 ligand (CD40L), which engages with CD40 on B cells. This cascade of signals is important for cytokine production, which results in the isotype switch response by the B cell. The production of interleukin (IL)-4 causes B cells to switch from IgM to IgG4 and IgE. The production of transforming growth factor β (TGF-β) and IL-10 causes the B cell to switch to IgA1 and IgA2. If there is an absence or impaired function of the ligand interaction isotype, switching can be affected. For example, if the CD40L-CD40 interaction is impaired, isotype switching will not occur and only IgM antibody is produced. This clinical situation is termed hyper-IgM immune deficiency.[7]

T-Cell-Independent Stimulation. B cells can be activated to produce antibodies by polysaccharides, lipopolysaccharides, and polymeric proteins independent of T-cell interaction. The B cells react directly with these molecules, producing a rapid immune response to pathogens. However, there are disadvantages to this mechanism: the process is ineffective for the production of memory B cells; antibody affinity maturation is poor; and isotype switching is not induced. The T-cell-independent process can also cause antibody production by B cells whose immunoglobulin is specific for antigens other than those found on the pathogen; hence, both protective antibodies and autoantibodies may be produced. When autoantibodies are produced through this mechanism, transient clinical symptoms of autoimmune disease may occur.[7]

NK Cells

NK cells do not express T-cell receptors or B-cell receptors and represent approximately 10% of the lymphocyte population. These cells have the ability to kill some cells infected with viruses and some tumor cells. NK cells do this by a mechanism termed antibody-dependent cellular cytotoxicity or ADCC. ADCC occurs when viral proteins are expressed on the surface of an infected cell, usually as a result of viral budding. The proteins are recognized as foreign by the immune system and antibodies are produced, which later bind to the viral proteins expressed on the infected cell. NK cells recognize the presence of antibody bound on the surface of the cells via their Fcγ receptors. The NK cells produce perforins, which cause lysis of the virus-infected cells by a mechanism that is not entirely understood.[5]

Phagocytic Cells

Phagocytes include cells such as monocytes and polymorphonuclear granulocytes (eosinophils, basophils, and neutrophils). Some monocytes migrate into tissues (liver, lungs, spleen, kidney, lymph nodes, and brain) and become tissue macrophages. The polymorphonuclear granulocytes are rapidly produced and live only for a short time (several days). The neutrophil is the most abundant granulocyte. These cells respond to chemotactic agents such as complement fragments and cytokines, causing them to migrate to the site of inflammation. Eosinophils represent only 2% to 15% of the white cells and play an important role in regulating the inflammatory response by releasing an antihistamine. These cells may also play a role in phagocytosing and killing microorganisms. Basophils make up less than 0.2% of the total leukocyte pool. These cells also respond to chemotactic factors and are involved in the allergic response. Historically, this network of phagocytic cells was called the reticuloendothelial system but is now termed the mononuclear phagocytic system.

The ability of cells to phagocytose is accomplished through the presence of receptors on the cell membrane. There are many types of receptors including: mannose-fucose receptors that bind to sugars on the surface of microorganisms, Fc receptors that bind to IgG, and complement receptors. A summary of some membrane receptors found on macrophages and monocytes is found in Table 11-2. The internalization and processing of particulate matter occur through the production of enzymes (peroxidase and acid hydrolases).[5] Under optimal cytokine conditions, macrophages and monocytes can become formal antigen-presenting cells; therefore, their ability to ingest and process foreign molecules is an essential part of the adaptive immune response.

Soluble Components of the Immune Response

There are three major soluble components of the immune response: immunoglobulins, complement, and cytokines.

Immunoglobulins

Immunoglobulins are the proteins that can be cell bound and serve as antigen receptors on B cells (see section on B lymphocytes) or can be secreted in a soluble form as antibodies. The molecular development of the immunoglobulin molecule is discussed in the section on B lymphocytes. The structures of the different types of immunoglobulin are discussed below.

Each monomeric immunoglobulin molecule consists of two identical heavy chains and two identical light chains. The heavy chains consist of approximately 450 amino acids with a molecular weight of approximately 50 to 77 kDa. There are five heavy chain classes termed isotypes. They include mu (μ), gamma (γ), alpha (α), delta (δ), and epsilon (ε). The light chains are smaller (approximately 210 amino acids; molecular weight 25 kDa) and can be either kappa (κ) or lambda (λ). The heavy and light chains

of the immunoglobulin molecule are held together by disulfide bonds. The polypeptide chains (both heavy and light) are looped, forming globular structures called the immunoglobulin domain. On each chain, there is a variable domain in which the amino acid sequence is diverse, giving the immunoglobulin its specificity. The epitopes expressed in this region are termed idiotypes. The remaining domains on both the heavy and light chains are called constant domains and have similar amino acid sequences, depending on the isotype. The hinge area of the molecule (between C_H1 and C_H2, as shown in Fig 11-4) gives the molecule flexibility, allowing the two antigen-binding components to operate independently. The biologic functions of the molecule are associated with the constant domains on the heavy chain. These functions include: placental transfer, macrophage binding, and complement activation.[4]

Interchain Bonds

Each light chain is joined to one heavy chain by a disulfide bond. One or more disulfide bonds link the two heavy chains at a point between C_H1 and C_H2, in an area of considerable flexibility called the hinge region. It is these interchain disulfide bonds that are the target of reducing agents used to produce "chemically modified" anti-D reagent.

Fab and Fc Fragments

Polypeptides can be cleaved at predictable sites by proteolytic enzymes. Much information about immunoglobulin structure and function is derived from the study of cleavage fragments generated by papain digestion of Ig molecules. Papain cleaves the heavy chain at a point just above the hinge, creating three separate fragments. Two are identical, each consisting of one

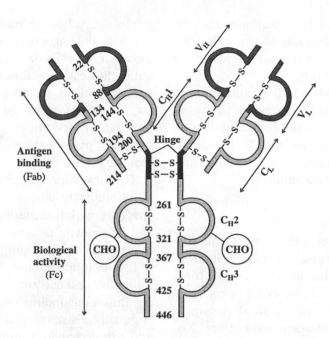

Figure 11-4. The basic four-chain immunoglobulin unit. Idiotypic specificity resides in the variable domains of heavy and light chains (V_H and V_L). Antigen-binding capacity depends on intact linkage between one light chain (V_L and C_L) and the amino-terminal half of one heavy chain (V_H and C_H1), the Fab fragments of the molecule. Disulfide bonds in the hinge region join carboxy-terminal halves of both heavy chains (C_H1 and C_H3, plus C_H4 for μ and ε heavy chains), to form the Fc fragment. (Used with permission from Goldsby et al.[8])

light chain linked to the N-terminal half of one heavy chain; the other fragment consists of the C-terminal halves of the heavy chains, still joined to one another by the hinge-region disulfide bonds. The two identical N-terminal fragments, which retain the specificity of the antibody, are called Fab fragments. The joined C-terminal halves of the heavy chains constitute a nonantibody protein fragment capable of crystallization, called the Fc fragment.

Immunoglobulin Polymers

Disulfide bonds may also join some Ig monomeric units to one another to form larger polymeric molecules; only IgM and IgA can form polymers. IgG, IgE, and IgD exist only in the monomeric form; there are no polymeric forms of these Ig classes. The IgM synthesized by unstimulated B cells and expressed on the membrane as the immunoglobulin receptor is expressed in the monomeric form. As mentioned previously, the μ heavy chain has four constant domains in the membrane form of IgM. The fourth domain allows the IgM monomer to bind to the cell membrane as the immunoglobulin receptor. Following clonal expansion and differentiation to a plasma cell, the activated cell produces μ chains with one less constant domain. While still in the plasma-cell cytoplasm, five IgM monomers are joined by the formation of disulfide bonds between the C_H3 domains and C_H4 domains.[5] The result is a pentamer that is secreted to the exterior of the cell and constitutes the form in which IgM accumulates in body fluids.

Secreted IgA exists in both monomeric and polymeric forms. Monomeric forms predominate in the bloodstream, but dimers and trimers that are secreted by B cells in mucosal surfaces and exocrine tissue are the biologically active form.

Other Chains

Pentameric IgM and the dimers and trimers of IgA contain a 15-kDa polypeptide called the J chain. Before the polymer leaves the plasma-cell cytoplasm, this chain attaches to the terminal constant domain of two adjacent monomers. No matter how many monomers constitute the polymer, there will be only one J chain. Its function is not fully understood.

The polymeric Ig molecules present in epithelial secretions also exhibit a subunit called the secretory component. The secretory component appears to protect the biologically important surface antibodies from proteolysis in the enzyme-rich secretions of respiratory and alimentary tracts.

Individual Immunoglobulin Classes

IgM. IgM is the first Ig class produced by the maturing B cell. It is the first to appear in the serum of maturing infants and the first to become detectable in a primary immune response. Secreted pentameric IgM normally constitutes 5% to 10% of the immunoglobulin in normal serum. Very few of these large molecules diffuse into interstitial fluid.

Although the five monomers comprise 10 antigen-combining sites, only five sites are readily available to combine with most antigens; hence, IgM is described as pentavalent. Because of their large size and multivalency, IgM molecules readily bind to antigens on particulate surfaces, notably those on red cells or microorganisms. IgM antibodies can crosslink cells expressing a specific antigen, forming a clump of cells (agglutination). Although extremely useful as a laboratory endpoint, agglutination probably plays a relatively minor role in biologic events.

The most important biologic effect of IgM is its ability to activate the complement cascade, which enhances inflammatory and phagocytic defense mechanisms and may produce lysis of antigen-bearing cells.

IgG. Immunoglobulin G exists only as a monomer and accounts for 75% to 80% of the immunoglobulins present in serum. It is equally distributed in the intravascular and extravascular compartments. In vivo, cells or particles coated with IgG undergo markedly enhanced interactions with cells that have receptors for the Fc portion of γ chains, especially neutrophils and macrophages.

IgG molecules can be classified into four subclasses: IgG1, IgG2, IgG3, and IgG4. Structurally, these subclasses differ primarily in the characteristics of the hinge region and the number of inter-heavy-chain disulfide bonds. Biologically, they have significantly different properties. IgG3 has the greatest ability to activate complement, followed by IgG1 and, to a much lesser extent, IgG2. IgG4 is incapable of complement activation. IgG1, IgG3, and IgG4 readily cross the placenta. IgG1, IgG2, and IgG4 have a half-life of 23 days, significantly longer than that of other circulating immunoglobulins; however, the half-life of IgG3 is only slightly longer than IgA and IgM. IgG1 and IgG3 readily interact with the Fc receptors on phagocytic cells, but IgG4 and IgG2 have low affinity for these receptors with the exception that IgG2 has an affinity similar to IgG1 and IgG3 for an allotype of Fcγ receptor IIa.

IgA. Although there is a large body content of IgA (10% to 15% of serum immunoglobulin concentration), relatively little is found in the blood. Most of the IgA exists in mucosal secretions. Secretory IgA protects the underlying epithelium from bacterial and viral penetration. Polymeric IgA is thought to combine with environmental antigens, forming complexes that are eliminated as surface secretions are excreted. This process may be important in controlling the development of hypersensitivity. The heavy chain of IgA has no complement-binding site; hence, IgA cannot activate complement through the classical pathway. IgA can activate complement through the alternative pathway (see below).

IgE. The concentration of serum IgE is measured in nanograms, compared with milligram levels for other immunoglobulins. Even when patients with severe allergies have markedly elevated serum concentrations of IgE, the absolute level is minimal compared with other immunoglobulins. Most IgE is present as monomers tightly bound to the membrane of basophilic granulocytes or mast cells. IgE is responsible for immediate hypersensitivity events, such as allergic asthma, hay fever, and systemic anaphylactic reactions. Although IgE appears to be involved in reactions to protozoal parasites, no specific protective mechanisms have been identified.

IgD. Serum contains only trace amounts of IgD. Most IgD exists as membrane immunoglobulin on unstimulated B cells. The function of IgD is unknown, but it may be important for lymphocytic differentiation, which is triggered by antigen binding, and in the induction of immune tolerance.

Complement

Complement is the term applied to a system of 25 to 30 serum and membrane proteins that act in a cascading manner—similar to the coagulation, fibrinolytic, and kinin systems—to produce numerous biologic effects. The participating proteins remain inactive until an event initiates the process, following which the product of one reaction becomes the catalyst for the next step (see Fig 11-5). Each evolving enzyme or complex can act on multiple substrate molecules, creating the potential for tremendous amplification of an initially modest or localized event.

Complement has three major roles: promotion of acute inflammatory events; alteration of surfaces so that phagocytosis is enhanced; and the modification of cell membranes, which leads to cell lysis. These actions cause destruction of bacteria, protect against viral infection, eliminate protein complexes, and enhance development of immune events. However, activation of complement can also initiate inflammatory and immune processes that may harm the host and mediate destruction of host cells, especially those in the blood.

Different mechanisms[17] exist for activating the complement cascade: the classical pathway, which is initiated by interaction between an antibody and its antigen, and the alternative pathway, which is usually not antibody mediated.

The Classical Pathway

For the classical pathway of complement activation to occur, an immunoglobulin must react with target antigen. Combination with antigen alters the configuration of the Fc portion of the immunoglobulin, rendering accessible an area in one of the heavy-chain constant domains that interacts with the C1 component of complement. C1 can combine only with Ig molecules having an appropriate heavy-chain configuration. This configuration exists in

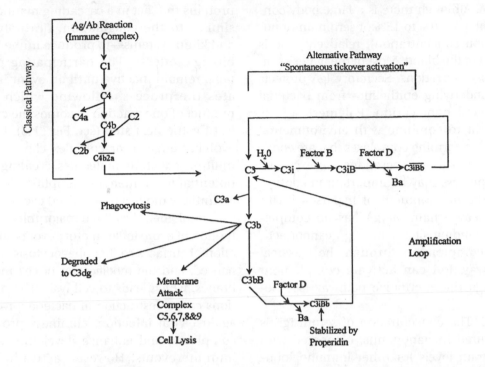

Figure 11-5. Diagram illustrating the activation of complement by the classical and alternative pathways. (Used with permission from Heddle.[1])

the μ heavy chain and in the γ chains in IgG subclasses 1, 2, and 3.

The C1 component of complement attaches to activation sites on the Fc portion of two or more Ig monomers. The pentameric IgM molecule provides an abundance of closely configured Fc monomers; hence, a single IgM molecule can initiate the complement cascade. For IgG antibodies to activate the sequence, two separate molecules must attach to antigen sites close together.[3] Hence, complement activation by IgG antibodies depends not only on the concentration and avidity of the antibody, but also on the topography of the antigen.

Circulating C1 is a macromolecule consisting of three distinct proteins (C1q, C1r, and C1s). When an antigen-antibody reaction occurs, two or more chains of C1q attach to the C_H2 domain of IgG or the C_H3 domain of IgM. This causes a conforma-

tional change, resulting in activation of two C1r molecules that then cleave two C1s molecules into activated $\overline{\text{C1s}}$ (a strong serine esterase). The C1r, C1s, and C1q complex is stabilized by Ca^{2+} ions. In the absence of Ca^{2+}, the complex dissociates. Thus, chelating agents often used in the laboratory, such as citrate and oxalate anticoagulants, prevent the stabilization of the C1 complex and subsequent activation of complement proteins.

Activated $\overline{\text{C1s}}$ works on two substrates. C1s cleaves C4 into two fragments: a large fragment (C4b) and a smaller fragment (C4a) that has modest anaphylatoxic activity. Most of the C4b generated is inactivated; however, some C4b binds to the cell surface and acts as a binding site for C2. C1s also cleaves the bound C2, releasing a fragment called C2b. The C2a fragment that remains bound to C4 forms an activated complex C4b2a, also known as C3 convertase. Each C3 convertase can cleave more than 200 native C3 molecules, splitting the molecule into two fragments. A small fragment (C3a) that has anaphylatoxic activity is released into the plasma; the larger fragment (C3b) attaches to proteins and sugars on the cell surface.

The classical pathway and the alternative pathway are both means of generating a C3 convertase. Once C3 has been cleaved, the same events occur in the two pathways.

The Alternative Pathway

The alternative pathway allows complement activation in the absence of an antigen/antibody interaction. This pathway is a first-line antimicrobial defense for vertebrates and a mechanism whereby prevertebrates can enhance their inflammatory effectiveness. The alternative pathway is a surface-active phenomenon that can be triggered by such initiators as dialysis membranes; the cell wall of many bacteria, yeasts, and viruses; protein complexes, including those containing antibodies that do not bind complement; anionic polymers such as dextran; and some tumor cells. The alternative pathway of complement activation can also occur spontaneously in the plasma at a slow but steady rate (tickover activation) (see Fig 11-5).

Four proteins participate in the alternative pathway: factor B, factor D, properdin (factor P), and C3. Fluid-phase C3 undergoes continuous but low-level spontaneous cleavage, resulting in C3i that is rapidly inactivated by fluid-phase control proteins. If C3i encounters factor B, a complex called C3iB is formed and additional interactions can occur. Factor D acts on bound factor B, generating a C3iBb complex capable of cleaving C3 into C3a and C3b. Most of the C3b generated in the fluid phase is inacti-

vated; however, if C3b binds to a foreign surface such as a bacteria cell wall, the activation of the complement cascade can be accelerated.

When C3b binds to a cell surface, factor B is bound to give C3bB. Factor D can also react with this cell-bound substrate, releasing the small Ba fragment leaving cell-bound C3bBb. This complex will dissociate unless it is stabilized by properdin, resulting in the complex C3bBbP. Like the C4b2a complex of the classical pathway, C3bBbP is capable of converting more C3 into C3b. In summary, both the classical and alternative pathways result in C3b generation. The C3 convertase of the classical pathway is C4b2a, whereas the C3 convertases of the alternative pathway are C3iBb in the fluid phase and C3bBbP when cell bound.

The Membrane Attack Complex

The final phase of activation is called the membrane attack complex and can occur once C3b has been cleaved through either the classical or alternative pathway. C3 convertase cleaves C5 into two fragments: a small peptide (C5a) having potent anaphylatoxin activity and a larger fragment (C5b). The C5b fragment binds C6, C7, C8, and up to 14 monomers of C9, resulting in a lytic hole in the membrane. Small amounts of lysis can occur when C8 is bound; however, the binding of C9 facilitates cell lysis.

The binding of C3b to a cell membrane is the pivotal stage of the pathway. The cell-bound C3b can proceed to activate the membrane attack complex (C5-C9) and cause cell lysis; alternatively, inhibitors may stop the activation sequence, leaving the cell coated with C3b. Factor I is an inhibitor that can cleave cell-bound C3b, leaving iC3b on the membrane. These two subcomponents of C3 (C3b, iC3b) can facilitate phagocytosis by acting as opsonins. However, C3b can be further cleaved, leaving a small fragment called C3dg. It is the C3dg molecule that is detected by the anti- C3d component in anticomplement reagents used for the direct antiglobulin test.

Complement Receptors

Some phagocytic cells have receptors that can bind to C3 on the cell. Four different complement receptors have been identified on phagocytic cells: CR1, CR2, CR3, and CR4.[18]

CR1. CR1 is found on a variety of cells. On red cells and platelets, the CR1 receptor plays an important role in clearing immune complexes. On phagocytic cells and B lymphocytes, it is an opsonic receptor that is involved in lymphocyte activation. CR1 also plays a regulatory role in complement activation by assisting factor I in cleaving C3b into iC3b and C3dg.

CR2. CR2 is found on B cells, some epithelial cells, and follicular dendritic cells. It plays an important role in mediating B-cell activation. It is also the receptor for interferon α and the Epstein-Barr virus.

CR3. CR3 is found on cells of the myeloid lineage. CR3 mediates phagocytosis of particles coated with iC3b and is also an important adhesion molecule capable of binding to certain types of bacteria and yeast.

CR4. CR4 is found on both lymphoid and myeloid cells. Its function is not well characterized, but it appears to have opsonic activity for iC3b, and it plays a role in adhesion.

Regulation of Complement Activation

There is a need to control or regulate the enzyme and activation factors of the complement cascade. The regulatory actions of these control proteins prevent damage to host tissue. These control systems (Table 11-4) act by several different mechanisms: direct inhibition of serine proteases, decay and destruction of convertases, and control of membrane attack complexes.[19]

Physiologic Effects of Complement Activation

Opsonization. Neutrophils and macrophages phagocytose any particle that protrudes from the surface of a cell or microorganism with no regard to the nature of the material. Phagocytosis is more intense if the particle adheres firmly to the membrane of the phagocytic cell. To achieve adherence, phagocytic cells have various receptor molecules such as the Fc receptors for certain immunoglobulins and receptors for C3b. The enhancement of phagocytosis resulting from antibody or complement coating of cells is called opsonization.

Anaphylatoxins Promote Inflammation. Complement fragments C3a and C5a are anaphylatoxins and they play an important role in acute inflammation. These anaphylatoxins bind to receptors on mast cells and basophils, causing them to release histamine and other biologic response modifiers that can be associated with anaphylaxis. More frequently, anaphylatoxins affect vascular permeability, membrane adhesion properties, and smooth-muscle contraction that constitute a large part of the acute inflammatory response. C5a and C3a also cause neutrophils and macrophages to migrate to the site of complement activation.

Cytokines

Throughout this chapter, inference has been made to a number of soluble mediators termed cytokines. Cytokines are a diverse group of intracellular signaling peptides and glycoproteins that have molecular weights ranging from 6,000 to 60,000 daltons. Each cytokine is secreted by particular cell types in response to dif-

Table 11-4. Summary of the Inhibitors of Complement Activation

Complement Control Proteins	Function
Inhibition of Serine Protease	
C1 inhibitor	A serine protease inhibitor that binds and activates C1r and C1s
Decay/Destruction of Convertases	
Factor I plus C4 binding protein (C4-bp)	Catabolizes C4 in the fluid phase
C4-bp	Causes dissociation of C2a from C4b2a
Decay accelerating factor (DAF, CD55)	Inhibits the binding of C2 to C4b
	Causes dissociation of C2 from C4b
Complement receptor 1 (CR1, CD35)	Accelerates the dissociation of C3bBb
Membrane cofactor protein (MCP)	Prompts catabolism of C4b by factor I and is a cofactor with factor I to cleave C3b
Factor H	Causes dissociation of Bb from C3I and C3b and is a cofactor to factor I for catabolism of C3i and C3b
Factor I	Cleaves and degrades C3b using one of three cofactors: factor H (plasma), CR1, or MCP (membrane-bound)
Membrane Attack Complex (MAC)	
S protein (Vitronectin)	Binds to the C5b67 complex preventing insertion into the lipid bilayer
C8-binding protein (CD59)	This cell-bound protein binds to C8 preventing C9 from inserting into the membrane
MAC-inhibiting protein (MIP)	Inhibitor of C9, also known as homologous restriction factor (HRF)

ferent stimuli and has been implicated in a wide variety of important regulatory biologic functions such as inflammation, tissue repair, cell activation, cell growth, fibrosis, and morphogenesis. One cytokine can have several different functions, depending on the type of cell to which it binds. Several hundred different cytokines have been described. Some of the cytokines involved in immune functions are summarized in Table 11-5.[1,5] Cytokines have been implicated in a variety of clinically important factors of transfusion medicine (hemolytic and febrile transfu-sion reactions, immunomodulation, stem cell collection, etc) (see Chapter 27).

Immunology Relating to Transfusion Medicine

Several examples of how the immune system relates to situations encountered in transfusion medicine are described below, including red cell alloimmunization, platelet alloimmunization, immune-mediated red cell destruction, and reagent antibody production.

Table 11-5. Summary of Some Cytokines Involved in the Immune System, Their Site of Production, and Function[1]

Cytokine	Produced by	Primary Functions
Interleukins		
IL-1	Many cells (eg, APCs, endothelial cells, B cells, fibroblasts)	T-cell activation, neutrophil activation, stimulates marrow, pyrogenic, acute-phase protein synthesis
IL-2	Activated T_H cells	T-cell growth, chemotaxis, macrophage activation
IL-4	Activated T_H cells	B-cell activation, B-cell differentiation, T-cell growth, T_H2 differentiation
IL-6	Many cells (eg, T cells, APCs, B cells, fibroblasts, and endothelial cells)	B-cell differentiation, pyrogenic, acute-phase protein synthesis
IL-8	Many cells (eg, macrophages and endothelial cells)	Inflammation, cell migration/ chemotaxis
IL-10	Activated T_H2 cells	Suppression of T_H1 cells, inhibits antigen presentation, inhibits cytokine production (IL-1, IL-6, TNFα, and IFN)
Others		
TNF	Macrophages and lymphocytes	Neutrophil activation, pyrogenic, acute-phase protein synthesis
Interferon γ (IFNγ)	T cells	Phagocyte activation
Transforming growth factor-β (TGF-β)	Various cells	Stimulates connective tissue growth and collagen formation, inhibitory function
Colony-stimulating factors (GM-CSF, M-CSF, G-CSF)	Various cells	Growth and activation of phagocytic cells

APCs = antigen-presenting cells; G-CSF = granulocyte colony-stimulating factor; GM-CSF = granulocyte macrophage–colony-stimulating factor; M-CSF = macrophage colony-stimulating factor; TNF = tumor necrosis factor.

Red Cell Alloimmunization

The mechanism of red cell alloimmunization is not well understood. When allogeneic red cells are transfused, some of the red cells fragment as they age or when they pass through the spleen, thus releasing membrane-bound red cell proteins into the bloodstream as the fragments degrade. Both formal antigen-presenting cells and B lymphocytes can present antigen either as a primary immune response (formal antigen presentation by dendritic cells) or in the secondary immune response by B cells.

HLA Alloimmunization to Platelets

Leukocyte reduction of red cells and platelets to a threshold of 5×10^6 per product has been shown to reduce HLA alloimmunization, possibly by the following mechanism. Donor leukocytes express both Class I and Class II MHC antigens. Some of the donor Class II MHC antigens will contain peptides that originated from the MHC Class I antigens on the donor's cells. Most of the transfusion recipient's T cells recognize self-MHC-carrying foreign peptides. However, as mentioned previously, a small percentage of T cells (<10%) are able to recognize foreign-MHC-carrying foreign peptides. When platelets are transfused, the recipient's T helper cells recognize the foreign MHC Class II complex on the donor leukocytes. If a signal occurs, the T cells activate recipient B cells, which have also bound donor MHC Class I antigen fragments to their Ig receptor, resulting in cell proliferation and MHC Class I (HLA) antibody production (Fig 11-6). In this case, the donor's leukocytes serve as the antigen-presenting cells. This major mechanism is termed "direct allorecognition" because the recipient's T cells are directly stimulated by donor antigen-presenting cells.[20] Alternatively, the process of antigen presentation and immune recognition of foreign HLA peptides can occur by the recipient's own immune system. This alternative form of allorecognition is termed "indirect" and is the classical alloimmune response seen for most foreign antigens. Leukocyte reduction appears to be effective in reducing HLA alloimmunization because antigen presentation by donor leukocytes is reduced and the amount of HLA Class I antigens transfused is greatly reduced.

Immune-Mediated Red Cell Destruction

The activation of complement and/or the presence of IgG on the red cell surface can trigger red cell destruction by predominantly two mechanisms: intravascular hemolysis and extravascular red cell destruction (Fig 11-7). Intravascular hemolysis occurs when complement is activated, resulting in activation of the membrane attack complex. As the integrity of the membrane is disrupted, hemoglobin is released into the plasma. Free hemoglobin binds to haptoglobin and is excreted in the urine. The heme portion of hemoglobin binds to albumin, forming methemalbumin, which can be visually detected in plasma by a brownish green discoloration. At times, the inhibitors of complement stop the cascade, leaving C3b on the red cells. This complement fragment has chemotactic activity for phagocytic cells and these cells have receptors for C3b. C3b-coated red cells adhere to phagocytic cells but are relatively ineffective at triggering phagocytosis. Enzymes can cleave the cell-bound C3b, leaving a small fragment (C3dg) present on the cells. C3dg-sensitized red cells survive normally because phagocytic cells do not have receptors for C3dg. If IgG is present on the red cells, binding to Fcγ receptors will occur, resulting in phagocytosis. If both IgG and

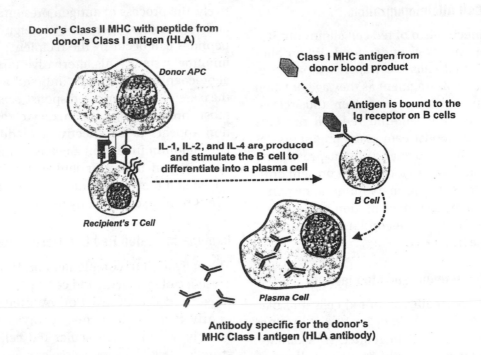

Figure 11-6. Diagram illustrating the major mechanism of HLA alloimmunization due to leukocytes present in platelet transfusion. (Used with permission from Heddle.[1])

C3b are present on the red cells, clearance of the cells may be enhanced, probably because of the chemotactic function of C3b and its adherence capability.

Reagent Antibodies

Heterogeneous antibodies are not optimal as reagents for use in serologic testing because they can vary in concentration, serologic properties, and epitope recognition and can contain other antibodies of unwanted specificity. The ideal serum for serologic testing is a concentrated suspension of highly specific, well-characterized, uniformly reactive, immunoglobulin molecules. Until the 1970s, the only way to obtain reagents was to immunize animals or humans with purified antigens and then perform time-consuming and sometimes unpredictable separation techni-

ques in an attempt to purify the resulting sera. Monoclonal antibody production provided an alternative to human and animal sources of these proteins. Using this approach, a single B-cell clone is propagated in cell culture and the supernatant fluid from the culture contains antibody of a single specificity. However, there are problems with this approach. Normal B cells reproduce themselves only a limited number of times; hence, the cultured cell lines survive only a short time.

In 1976, Köhler and Milstein[21] provided a solution to this problem. Plasma cells of normal antibody-producing capacity were fused to neoplastic plasma cells of infinite reproductive capacity (ie, myeloma cells). Techniques had previously been developed that cause cell membranes to merge, allowing the cytoplasm and the nucleus of two

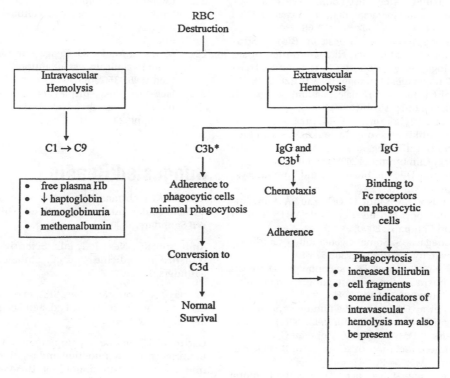

*Ineffective mediator of phagocytosis.

†Due to the chemotactic ability of C3b, extravascular destruction may be enhanced when both IgG and C3b are present on the red cells.

Figure 11-7. Summary of intravascular and extravascular red cell destruction.

different kinds of cells to fuse into a single cell. These plasma cell/myeloma cell hybrids can be maintained in cell culture for prolonged periods, producing large quantities of the selected antibody.

The exquisite specificity of monoclonal antibodies is both an advantage and a disadvantage for reagent use. An antibody that gives strong and specific reactions with one epitope of a multivalent antigen molecule may fail to react with cells whose antigen expression lacks that particular configuration. Thus, reagent preparations typically used in the laboratory are blends of several different monoclonal products, thereby increasing the range of variant phenotypes that the antiserum can identify. Single or blended monoclonal preparations often re-

act more strongly than immune-serum preparations when tested against cells with weakly expressed antigens.

Phage technology is under investigation as an approach for producing genetically engineered antibodies for a variety of therapeutic treatments,[22] as well as for use as typing reagents.[23]

References

1. Heddle NM. Overview of immunology. In: Reid ME, Nance SJ, eds. Red cell transfusion. A practical guide. Totowa, NJ: Humana Press, 1998:13-37.
2. Barclay AN. Membrane proteins with immunoglobulin-like domains—a master superfamily of interaction molecules. Semin Immunol 2003;15:215-3.

3. Marsh SG, Albert ED, Bodmer WF, et al. Nomenclature for factors of the HLA system, 2002. Hum Immunol 2002;63:1213-68.

4. Santos-Aguado J, Barbosa JA, Biro A, Strominger JL. Molecular characterization of serologic recognition sites in the human HLA-A2 molecule. J Immunol 1988;141:2811-18.

5. Roitt I, Brostoff J, Male D. Immunology. 5th ed. St. Louis: Mosby, 1998.

6. Ono SJ, Nakamura T, Miyazaki D, et al. Chemokines: Roles in leukocyte development, trafficking, and effector function. J Allergy Clin Immunol 2003;111:1185-99.

7. Huston DP. The biology of the immune system. JAMA 1997;278:1804-14.

8. Goldsby RA, Kindt TJ, Osborne BA. Kuby immunology. 4th ed. New York: WH Freeman and Company, 2000.

9. Tonegawa S. Somatic generation of antibody diversity. Nature 1983;302:575-81.

10. Alt FW, Backwell TK, Yancopoulos GD. Development of the primary antibody repertoire. Science 1987;238:1079-87.

11. Janeway CA Jr. How the immune system recognizes invaders. Sci Am 1993;269(3):73-9.

12. Russell DM, Dembic Z, Morahan G, et al. Peripheral deletion of self-reactive B cells. Nature 1991;354:308-11.

13. Weissman IL, Cooper MD. How the immune system develops. Sci Am 1993;269(3):64-71.

14. Paul WE. Infectious diseases and the immune system. When bacteria, viruses and other pathogens infect the body, they hide in different places. Sci Am 1993;269(3):90-7.

15. Marrack P, Lo D, Brinster R, et al. The effects of thymus environment on T cell development and tolerance. Cell 1988;53:627-34.

16. Clevers H, Alarcon B, Willeman T, Terhorst C. The T cell receptor/CD3 complex: A dynamic protein ensemble. Annu Rev Immunol 1988; 6:629-62.

17. Sakamoto M, Fujisawa Y, Nishioka K. Physiologic role of the complement system in host defense, disease, and malnutrition. Nutrition 1998;14:391-8.

18. Roitt I. Essential immunology. 8th ed. Oxford: Blackwell Scientific Publications, 1994.

19. Devine DV. The regulation of complement on cell surfaces. Transfus Med Rev 1991;5:123-31.

20. Semple JW, Freedman J. Recipient antigen-processing pathways of allogeneic platelet antigens: Essential mediators of immunity. Transfusion 2002;42:958-61.

21. Köhler G, Milstein C. Derivation of specific antibody-producing tissue culture and tumor lines by cell fusion. Eur J Immunol 1976;6:511-19.

22. Marks C, Marks JD. Phage libraries—a new route to clinically useful antibodies. N Engl J Med 1996;335:730-3.

23. Siegel DL. Phage display tools for automated blood typing (abstract). Transfusion 2004; 44(Suppl):2A.

Suggested Reading

Abbas AK, Lichtman AH, Pober JS, eds. Cellular and molecular immunology. 4th ed. Philadelphia: WB Saunders, 2000.

Anderson KC, Ness PM, eds. Scientific basis of transfusion medicine. 2nd ed. Philadelphia: WB Saunders, 1999.

Barclay AN, Brown MH, Law SKA, et al. The leukocyte antigen factsbook. 2nd ed. San Diego, CA: Academic Press, 1997.

Carroll MC. The role of complement and complement receptors in induction and regulation of immunity. Annu Rev Immunol 1998;16:545-68.

Janeway CA. Immunobiology: The immune system in health and disease. 5th ed. New York: Garland Publishing, 2001.

Marchalonis JJ, Schluter SF, Bernstein RM, et al. Phylogenetic emergence and molecular evolution of the immunoglobulin family. Adv Immunol 1998; 70:417-506.

Muller D. The molecular biology of autoimmunity. Immunol Allerg Clin North Am 1996;16:659-82.

Paul WE. Fundamental immunology. 5th ed. Philadelphia: Lippincott Williams & Wilkins, 2003.

Paul W, Raghavan M, Bjorkman PJ. Fc receptors and their interactions with immunoglobulins. Annu Rev Cell Dev Biol 1996;12:181-220.

Stites DP, Terr AI, Parslow TG, eds. Medical immunology. 10th ed. Stamford, CT: Appleton & Lange, 2001.

Vamvakas EC, Blajchman MA, eds. Immunomodulatory effects of blood transfusion. Bethesda, MD: AABB Press, 1999.

Appendix 11-1. Definitions of Some Essential Terms in Immunology

Adhesion molecule: Any of the many membrane molecules expressed on white cells and endothelial cells that allow cells to come into close apposition with each other.

Allotypic: Variations in the amino acid structure of heavy and light chains unrelated to antibody specificity. Present in some but *not all* members of the species.

Antibody: Immunoglobulin secreted by the plasma-cell progeny of B lymphocytes after stimulation by a specific immunogen. Immunoglobulin molecules on the surface of unstimulated lymphocytes serve as antigen receptors.

Antigen: Any material capable of specific combination with antibody or with cell-surface receptors of T lymphocytes. Often used as a synonym for "immunogen," although some antigens that react with products of the immune response are not capable of eliciting an immune response.

Antigen-presenting cell: A cell capable of incorporating antigenic epitopes into MHC Class II molecules and displaying the epitope-MHC complex on its membrane.

Clone: A population of genetically identical cells derived from successive divisions of a single progenitor cell.

Cytokine: A low-molecular-weight protein, secreted from an activated cell, that affects the function or activity of other cells.

Epitope: The small portion of an immunogen, usually 5 to 15 amino acids or 3 to 5 glycosides, that combines specifically with the antigen receptor of a T or B lymphocyte.

Idiotype: The molecular configuration unique to the variable portion of an antigen-receptor molecule, reflecting the DNA rearrangement occurring in earliest lymphocyte differentiation and conferring upon the cell its specificity of antigen recognition.

Immune system: A collective term for all the cells and tissues involved in immune activity. It includes, in addition to lymphocytes and cells of monocyte/macrophage lineage, the thymus, lymph nodes, spleen, marrow, portions of the liver, and the mucosa-associated lymphoid tissue.

Immunogen: A material capable of provoking an immune response when introduced into an immunocompetent host to whom it is foreign.

Ligand: A molecule, either free in a fluid milieu or present on a membrane, whose three-dimensional configuration allows it to form a tightly fitting complex with a cell-surface molecule (its receptor) of complementary shape.

MHC Class I molecules: Heterodimeric membrane proteins determined by genes in the MHC, consisting of a highly polymorphic α chain linked noncovalently with the nonpolymorphic β_2-microglobulin chain; these molecules present antigen to CD8+ T cells and are the site of HLA antigens of the HLA-A, HLA-B, and HLA-C series.

MHC Class II molecules: Heterodimeric membrane proteins determined by genes in the MHC, consisting of two transmembrane polypeptide chains; these molecules present antigen to CD4+ T cells and exhibit the HLA-DP, HLA-DQ, and HLA-DR series of antigens.

Phagocytosis: The process whereby macrophages and granulocytes ingest particulate material present in the surrounding milieu and subject it to intracellular alteration.

Receptor: A cell-membrane protein molecule whose three-dimensional configuration allows it to form a tightly fitting complex with another molecule (called its ligand) of complementary shape.

Chapter 12

Red Cell Antigen-Antibody Reactions and Their Detection

DEMONSTRATION OF RED cell antigen-antibody reactions is key to immunohematology. The combination of antibody with antigen may produce a variety of observable results. In blood group serology, the most commonly observed reactions are agglutination, hemolysis, and precipitation.

Agglutination is the antibody-mediated clumping of particles that express antigen on their surface. Agglutination of red cells occurs because antibody molecules bind to antigenic determinants on multiple adjacent red cells, linking them together to form a visible aggregate. Agglutination is the endpoint for most tests involving red cells and blood group antibodies and is the primary reaction type discussed in this chapter. In some tests, antibody directly bridges the gap between adjacent cells; in others, antibody molecules attach to, but do not agglutinate, the red cells, and an additional step is needed to induce visible ag-

glutination or to otherwise measure the reaction.

Hemolysis is the rupture of red cells with release of intracellular hemoglobin. In-vitro antibody-mediated hemolysis depends on activity of the membrane attack unit of complement. Hemolysis does not occur if the antigen and antibody interact in serum that lacks complement, or in plasma in which the anticoagulant has chelated the cations (calcium and magnesium) necessary for complement activation. In tests for antibodies to red cell antigens, hemolysis is a positive result because it demonstrates the union of antibody with antigen that activates the complement cascade. (The actions of complement are described in Chapter 11.) Pink or red supernatant fluid in a test system of serum and red cells is an important observation that may indicate that antigen-antibody binding has taken place. Some antibodies that are lytic in vitro (eg, anti-Vel, anti-Le[a], and anti-Jk[a]) may

12

271

cause intravascular hemolysis in a transfusion recipient.

Precipitation is the formation of an insoluble, usually visible, complex when soluble antibody reacts with soluble antigen. Such complexes are seen in test tubes as a sediment or ring and in agar gels as a white line. Precipitation is the endpoint of procedures such as immunodiffusion and immunoelectrophoresis.

Precipitation may not occur, even when soluble antigen and its specific antibody are present. Precipitation of the antigen-antibody complex requires that antigen and antibody be present in optimal proportions. If antibody is present in excess, too few antigen sites exist to crosslink the molecules and a lattice structure is not formed. Antigen-antibody complexes form but do not accumulate sufficiently to form a visible lattice. This phenomenon is called a *prozone*.

The combination of soluble antigen with soluble antibody may also result in a full or partial neutralization of the antibody. Although a visible precipitate is often not produced, such inhibition can be useful in antibody identification procedures by selectively eliminating specific antibodies.

Factors Affecting Red Cell Agglutination

Agglutination is a reversible chemical reaction and is thought to occur in two stages: 1) sensitization, the attachment of antibody to antigen on the red cell membrane; and 2) formation of bridges between the sensitized red cells to form the lattice that constitutes agglutination. Various factors affect these two stages and can be manipulated to enhance (or decrease) agglutination. The effects of enhancement techniques on the two stages cannot always be clearly differentiated.[1]

Stage One: Sensitization

Initially, the antigen and antibody must come together and interact in a suitable spatial relationship. The chance of association between antibody and antigen can be enhanced in a number of ways, such as agitation or centrifugation, or by varying the relative concentration of antibody and antigen. As shown in Fig 12-1, antibody and antigen must complement each other with both a structural (steric) and a chemical fit.

For sensitization to occur, a noncovalent chemical bond must form between antigen and antibody. The forces holding antigens and antibodies together are generally weak (compared with covalent bonds that hold molecules together) and are active only over a very short distance. The antigen-antibody combination is reversible, and random bonds are constantly made and broken until a state of equilibrium is attained.

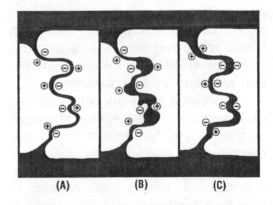

Figure 12-1. Antigen-antibody "goodness of fit." For maximum complementarity, both structural fit and complementary distribution of chemical groups must be achieved. (A) Good structural fit with complementary chemical attraction. (B) Chemical groups are complementary, but structural fit is poor. (C) Good structural fit, but chemical groupings are not attractive and may repel each other. (Reprinted with permission from Moore.[2])

Chemical Bonding

Various types of chemical bonds are responsible for the binding of antibody to antigen, including hydrogen bonds, hydrophobic bonds, electrostatic or ionic bonds, and van der Waals forces. These types of chemical bonds are relevant to immunohematology because different types of bonds have different thermodynamic characteristics; they are either exothermic or endothermic. Thermodynamic characteristics, in turn, may affect the serologic phenomena observed in the test system. For example, carbohydrate antigens tend to form exothermic hydrogen bonds with the antibody-combining site, so the bond is stronger at lower temperatures. In contrast, hydrophilic bonds formed with protein antigens are endothermic, so these bonds are enhanced at higher reaction temperatures.

Equilibrium (Affinity) Constant of the Antibody

The equilibrium constant or affinity constant (K_o) of a reaction is determined by the relative rates of association and dissociation (see Fig 12-2). For each antigen-antibody reaction, the K_o varies. The K_o reflects the degree to which antibody and antigen associate and bind to one another ("goodness of fit") and the speed of the reaction. The higher the K_o value, the better the association or "fit." When the K_o is large, the reaction occurs more readily and is more difficult to dissociate; such antibodies may have a greater clinical importance. When the K_o is small, a higher ratio of antibody to antigen may be required for detection.

   The degree of antigen-antibody "fit" is influenced by the type of bonds predominating. Hydrophobic bonds are usually associated with higher K_o than hydrogen bonds. The K_o is also affected by physical

All chemical reactions are reversible. Antigen (Ag)-antibody (Ab) reactions may be expressed as

$$Ag + Ab \underset{\longleftarrow}{\overset{\longrightarrow}{}} AgAb$$

The reaction proceeds until a state of equilibrium is reached. This is controlled by the rate constants of association (k_a) and dissociation (k_d).

$$Ag + Ab \underset{k_d}{\overset{k_a}{\rightleftarrows}} AgAb$$

By the law of mass action, the speed of the reaction is proportional to the concentrations of the reactants and their product. The equilibrium constant (K_o) is a function of these intrinsic association constants for the antibody being tested.

$$\frac{[AbAg]}{[Ab][Ag]} = \frac{k_a}{k_d} = K_o$$

Figure 12-2. The law of mass action and the equilibrium constant.

conditions such as the temperature at which the reaction occurs, the pH and ionic strength of the suspending medium, and the relative antigen-to-antibody concentrations. In laboratory tests that use agglutination as an endpoint, altering the physical conditions of the system can increase or decrease the test's sensitivity.

Temperature

Most blood group antibodies react within restricted temperature ranges. Typically, these antibodies fall into two broad categories: those optimally reactive at "cold" temperatures (eg, 4 to 25 C) and those optimally reactive at "warm" temperatures (eg, 30 to 37 C). Antibodies that react in vitro only at temperatures below 30 C rarely cause destruction of transfused antigen-positive red cells and are generally considered clinically insignificant. Many of these "cold-reactive" antibodies have been found to be IgM, whereas their "warm-reactive" counterparts have often been found to be IgG. This has led to the mistaken conclusion by many that antibody class determines the temperature of bonding (and clinical significance). Instead, however, the temperature of optimal antigen-antibody reactivity has more to do with the type of reaction and the chemical nature of the antigen than with the antibody class. Carbohydrate antigens are more commonly associated with "cold-reactive" antibodies and protein antigens with "warm-reactive" antibodies.

pH

Changes in pH can affect electrostatic bonds. For most clinically significant blood group antibodies, optimal pH has not been determined but is assumed to approximate the physiologic pH range. Occasional antibodies, notably some examples of anti-M, react best at a lowered pH. For most routine testing, a pH around 7.0 should be used. Stored saline often has a pH of 5.0 to 6.0. Buffered saline is an alternative and may be particularly helpful in solid-phase testing.[3]

Incubation Time

The time needed to reach equilibrium differs for different blood group antibodies. Significant variables include temperature requirements, immunoglobulin class, and specific interactions between antigen configuration and the Fab site of the antibody. The addition of enhancement agents to the system can decrease the incubation time needed to reach equilibrium.

For saline systems in which antiglobulin serum is used to demonstrate antibody at-tachment, 30 to 60 minutes of incubation at 37 C is adequate to detect most clinically significant antibodies. For some weakly reactive antibodies, association may not reach equilibrium at 30 minutes and extending the incubation time may increase sensitivity of the test. Prolonging the incubation time beyond 60 minutes has few disadvantages except for the delay before results are available.

Incubation time at 37 C can usually be reduced to 10 to 15 minutes if a low-ionic-strength saline (LISS) solution is used (including LISS additive solutions). The use of water-soluble polymers such as polyethylene glycol (PEG) can also reduce the necessary incubation time, although for different reasons. (See section on Enhancement of Antibody Detection and Method Section 3.)

Ionic Strength

In normal saline, Na^+ and Cl^- ions cluster around and partially neutralize opposite charges on antigen and antibody molecules. This hinders the association of antibody with antigen. By lowering the ionic strength of the reaction medium, however, this shielding effect can be weakened and electrostatic attractions enhanced. Reducing the salt concentration of the serum-cell system increases the rate at which antibody and antigen come into proximity and may increase the amount of antibody bound. Extending the incubation time in LISS systems may result in a loss of sensitivity.[4] (See section on LISS and LISS Additives.)

Antigen-Antibody Proportions

An excess of antigen to antibody should result in increased antibody uptake. For inhibition or adsorption tests, such an excess of antigen is desirable. For most red cell tests, however, antigen excess reduces the number of antibody molecules bound per red cell, limiting their ability to agglutinate. Antibody excess is, therefore, desirable in most routine test systems. A commonly used ratio in red cell serology is 2 drops of serum to 1 drop of a 2% to 5% red cell suspension. If the antibody is weakly reactive, increasing the quantity of antibody present can increase the test's sensitivity. Very rarely, significant antibody excess may inhibit direct agglutination, producing a prozone phenomenon comparable to what occurs with precipitation reactions. Usually, however, increasing antibody concentration enhances the sensitivity of agglutination tests. Reducing the concentration of red cells from 5% to 2% or 3% doubles the serum-to-cell ratio, as does adding 4 drops of serum to the standard cell suspension. Sometimes, it is useful to increase the volume of serum to 10 or even 20 drops, particularly during an investigation of a hemolytic transfusion reaction in which routine testing reveals no antibody. Alterations in the volume of serum or plasma significantly affect the ionic strength of test systems in which LISS has reduced the dielectric constant, so procedures must be modified so that the appropriate ratio of serum to LISS is maintained. Chapters 18 and 19 give more details about antibody detection and pretransfusion testing.

Stage Two: Agglutination

Once antibody molecules attach to antigens on the red cell surface, the sensitized cells must be linked into a lattice. This allows visualization of the reaction. The size and physical properties of the antibody molecules, the concentration of antigen sites on each cell, and the distance between cells all have an effect on the development of agglutinates.

The bridges formed between antibodies interlinked to antigen sites on adjacent red cells usually result from chance collision of the sensitized cells. Under isotonic conditions, red cells cannot approach each other closer than a distance of 50 to 100 Å.[1] IgG molecules characteristically fail to bridge this distance between red cells and cause sensitization without lattice formation. For larger, multivalent IgM molecules, however, direct agglutination occurs easily. The location and density of antigen sites on the cells may also allow some IgG antibodies to cause direct agglutination; A, B, M, and N antigens, for example, are on the outer edges of red cell glycoproteins and have relatively high densities, allowing IgG antibodies to crosslink.

Red cells suspended in saline have a net negative charge at their surface and therefore repel one another. Negatively charged molecules on the red cell membrane cause mutual repulsion of red cells. This repulsion may be decreased by various laboratory manipulations and by inherent or altered red cell membrane characteristics.

Various strategies are used to overcome this repulsion and to enhance agglutination. Centrifugation physically forces the cells closer together. The indirect antiglobulin test (IAT) uses antiglobulin serum to crosslink the reaction. Other methods include reducing the negative charge of surface molecules (eg, proteolytic enzymes), reducing the hydration layer around the cell (eg, albumin), and introducing positively charged macromolecules (eg, Polybrene®) that aggregate the cells.[1]

Inhibition of Agglutination

In agglutination inhibition tests, the presence of either antigen or antibody is detected by its ability to inhibit agglutination in a system with known reactants (see Chapter 19). For example, the saliva from a secretor contains soluble blood group antigens that combine with anti-A, -B, or -H. The indicator system is a standardized dilution of antibody that agglutinates the corresponding cells to a known degree. If the saliva contains blood group substance, incubating saliva with antibody will wholly or partially abolish agglutination of cells added to the incubated mixture. The absence of expected agglutination indicates the presence of soluble antigen in the material under test. Agglutination of the indicator cells is a negative result.

Enhancement of Antibody Detection

Albumin Additives

Although used routinely for many years as an enhancement medium, albumin itself probably does little to promote antibody uptake (Stage 1). Much of the enhancement effect attributed to albumin may be due to its attributes as a low-ionic-strength buffer. Albumin may influence agglutination by reducing the repulsion between cells, thus predisposing antibody-coated cells to agglutinate. Bovine serum albumin is available as solutions of 22% or 30% concentration.

Enzymes

The proteolytic enzymes used most often in immunohematology laboratories are bromelin, ficin, papain, and trypsin. While enhancing agglutination by some antibodies, the enzymes destroy certain red cell antigens, notably M, N, S, Fy[a], and Fy[b].

Proteolytic enzymes reduce the red cell surface charge by cleaving polypeptides containing negatively charged sialic acid

molecules from polysaccharide chains. Sialic acid is a major contributor to the net negative charge at the red cell surface. Any mechanism that reduces the net charge should enhance red cell agglutination, and red cells pretreated with proteolytic enzymes often show enhanced agglutination by IgG molecules.

Polyethylene Glycol

PEG is a water-soluble linear polymer used as an additive to potentiate antigen-antibody reactions.[5] It has been suggested that PEG promotes antibody uptake through steric exclusion of water molecules in the diluent, such that antigens and antibody molecules come into closer proximity, resulting in increased cell-antibody collisions and subsequent antibody binding. Multiple studies have shown that PEG increases the detection of potentially clinically significant antibodies and decreases the detection of clinically insignificant antibodies.[6]

Anti-IgG is usually the antihuman globulin (AHG) reagent of choice with PEG testing, to avoid false-positive reactions with some polyspecific AHG reagents. Commercially available PEG reagents may be prepared in a LISS solution. PEG can be used in tests with eluates, as well as with serum or plasma. PEG can enhance warm-reactive autoantibodies and thus may be advantageous in detecting weak serum autoantibodies for diagnostic purposes. On the other hand, this enhancement may be disadvantageous when trying to detect alloantibodies in the presence of autoantibodies. In such cases, testing the serum by LISS or a saline IAT may allow for the detection or exclusion of alloantibodies without interference from autoantibodies.

Centrifugation of PEG with test serum and red cells before washing should be avoided because the nonspecific aggregates generated by PEG may not disperse. After incubation with PEG, test cells should be washed immediately in saline for the antiglobulin test.

Precipitation of serum proteins when PEG is added has been reported; this problem appears to be related to elevated serum globulin levels.[6] This problem becomes apparent when the IgG-coated red cells are nonreactive. At least four washes of the red cells at the antiglobulin phase, with agitation, will ensure that the red cells are fully resuspended and will serve to prevent this problem from occurring.

LISS and LISS Additives

LISS (approximately 0.03 M) greatly increases the speed of antibody sensitization of red cells, compared with normal saline (approximately 0.17 M). To prevent lysis of red cells at such a low ionic strength, a nonionic substance such as glycine is incorporated in the LISS.

Most laboratories use a LISS additive reagent, rather than LISS itself. These commercially available LISS additives may contain albumin in addition to ionic salts and buffers. LISS solutions increase the rate of antibody association (Stage 1) when volume proportions are correct. (See Methods 3.2.2 and 3.2.3.) Increasing the volume of serum used in a test will increase the ionic strength of the test; hence, any alteration in prescribed volumes of serum used requires adjustment of the LISS volume or omission of LISS. For this reason, the use of LISS for routine titration studies and for some other tests is problematic. When LISS is used as an additive reagent, the manufacturer's instructions must be followed.

The Antiglobulin Test

In 1945, Coombs, Mourant, and Race[7] described procedures for detecting attachment of antibodies that did not produce agglutination. This test uses antibody to human globulins and is known as the antiglobulin test. It was first used to demonstrate antibody in serum, but later the same principle was used to demonstrate in-vivo coating of red cells with antibody or complement components. As used in immunohematology, antiglobulin testing generates visible agglutination of sensitized red cells. The direct antiglobulin test (DAT) is used to demonstrate in-vivo sensitization of red cells. An IAT is used to demonstrate in-vitro reactions between red cells and antibodies that sensitize, but do not agglutinate, cells that express the corresponding antigen.

Principles of the Antiglobulin Test

All antibody molecules are globulins. Animals injected with human globulins produce antibody to the foreign protein. After the animal serum is adsorbed to remove unwanted agglutinins, it will react specifically with human globulins and can be called AHG serum. AHG sera with varying specificities can be produced, notably, anti-IgG and antibodies to several complement components. Hybridoma techniques are used for the manufacture of most AHG. These techniques are more fully described in Chapter 11.

Anti-IgG combines mainly with the Fc portion of the sensitizing antibody molecules, not with any epitopes native to the red cell (see Fig 12-3). The two Fab sites of the AHG molecule form a bridge between adjacent antibody-coated cells to produce visible agglutination. Cells that have no globulin attached will not be agglutinated. The strength of the observed agglutination is usually proportional to the amount of bound globulin.

AHG will react with human antibodies and complement molecules that are bound

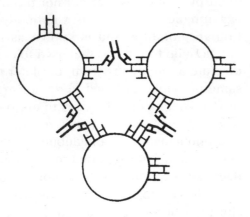

Figure 12-3. The antiglobulin reaction. Anti-human IgG molecules are shown reacting with the Fc portion of human IgG coating adjacent red cells (eg, anti-D coating D-positive red cells).

to red cells or are present, free, in serum. Unbound globulins may react with AHG, causing false-negative antiglobulin tests. Unless the red cells are washed free of unbound proteins before addition of AHG serum, the unbound globulins may neutralize AHG and cause a false-negative result.

Direct Antiglobulin Testing

The DAT is used to demonstrate in-vivo coating of red cells with antibodies or complement, in particular IgG and C3d. Washed red cells from a patient or donor are tested directly with AHG reagents (see Method 3.6). The DAT is used in investigating autoimmune hemolytic anemia (AIHA), drug-induced hemolysis, hemolytic disease of the fetus and newborn, and alloimmune reactions to recently transfused red cells.

Indirect Antiglobulin Testing

In indirect antiglobulin procedures, serum (or plasma) is incubated with red cells, which are then washed to remove unbound globulins. Agglutination that occurs when AHG is added indicates that antibody has bound to a specific antigen present on the red cells. The specificity of the antibody may be known and the antigen unknown, as in blood group phenotyping with an AHG-reactive reagent such as anti-Fy[a]. The presence or specificity of antibody may be unknown, as in antibody detection and identification tests. Or, in other applications, such as the crossmatch, the serum and cells are unknown. This procedure is used to determine whether any sort of antigen-antibody interaction has occurred.

Methods have been developed that obviate the need to wash coated red cells before adding antiglobulin reagent. Column agglutination technology, described later in this chapter, is an example. It uses a microcolumn filled with mixtures of either glass beads or gel, buffer, and sometimes reagents and can be used for direct or indirect antiglobulin procedures. Density barriers allow separation of test serum (or plasma) from red cells, making a saline washing phase unnecessary.

Antiglobulin Reagents

Monospecific antibodies to human globulins can be prepared by injecting animals with purified IgG, IgA, IgM, C3, or C4. Such sera require adsorption to remove unwanted (eg, heterophile) antibodies from the monospecific AHG reagent. These animal-made antisera are polyclonal in nature. Monospecific monoclonal reagents can also effectively be prepared from hybridomas (see Chapter 11). Monospecific animal or hybridoma-derived antibodies can be combined into reagent preparations containing any desired combination of specificities, or different clones all recognizing the same antigen specificity can be combined into a single reagent. Thus, reagents may be polyclonal, monoclonal, blends of monoclonal, or blends of monoclonal and polyclonal antibodies.

The Food and Drug Administration (FDA) has established definitions for a variety of AHG reagents,[8] as shown in Table 12-1. Antisera specific for other immunoglobulins (IgA, IgM) or subclasses (IgG1, IgG3, etc) exist but are rarely standardized for routine test tube methods and must be used with rigorous controls.

Polyspecific AHG

Polyspecific AHG reagents are used for DATs and, in some laboratories, for routine compatibility tests and antibody detection. These reagents contain antibody to human IgG and to the C3d component of human complement. Other complement antibodies may be present, including anti-C3b, -C4b, and -C4d. Currently available, commercially prepared, polyspecific antiglobulin sera contain little, if any, activity against IgA and IgM heavy chains. However, some reagents may react with IgA or IgM molecules because the polyspecific mixture may react with lambda and kappa light chains, which are present in immunoglobulins of all classes.

Because most clinically significant antibodies are IgG, the most important function of polyspecific AHG, in most procedures, is detection of IgG. The anticomplement

Table 12-1. Antihuman Globulin Reagents

Antibody Designation on Container Label		Definition*
(1)	Anti-IgG, -C3d; Polyspecific	Contains anti-IgG and anti-C3d (may contain other anticomplement and anti-immunoglobulin antibodies).
(2)	Anti-IgG	Contains anti-IgG with no anticomplement activity (not necessarily gamma chain specific).
(3)	Anti-IgG; heavy chains	Contains only antibodies reactive against human gamma chains.
(4)	Anti-C3b	Contains only C3b antibodies with no anti-immunoglobulin activity. Note: The antibody produced in response to immunization is usually directed against the antigenic determinant, which is located in the C3c subunit; some persons have called this antibody "anti-C3c." In product labeling, this antibody should be designated anti-C3b.
(5)	Anti-C3d	Contains only C3d antibodies with no anti-immunoglobulin activity.
(6)	Anti-C4b	Contains only C4b antibodies with no anti-immunoglobulin activity.
(7)	Anti-C4d	Contains only C4d antibodies with no anti-immunoglobulin activity.

*As defined by the FDA.[8]

component has limited usefulness in cross-matching and in antibody detection because antibodies detectable only by their ability to bind complement are quite rare. Anti-C3d activity is important, however, for the DAT, especially in the investigation of AIHA. In some patients with AIHA, C3d may be the only globulin detectable on their red cells.[9]

Monospecific AHG Reagents

Licensed monospecific AHG reagents in common use are anti-IgG and anti-C3b, -C3d. The FDA has established labeling requirements for other anticomplement reagents, including anti-C3b, anti-C4b, and anti-C4d, but these products are not generally available. If the DAT with a polyspecific reagent reveals globulins on red cells, monospecific AHG reagents are used to characterize the coating proteins.

Anti-IgG

Reagents labeled "anti-IgG" contain no anticomplement activity. The major component of anti-IgG is antibody to human gamma heavy chains, but unless labeled as "heavy-chain-specific," these reagents may exhibit some reactivity with light chains, which are common to all immunoglobulin classes. An anti-IgG reagent not designated "heavy-chain-specific" must be considered theoretically capable of reacting with light chains of IgA or IgM. A positive DAT with such an anti-IgG does not definitively prove the presence of IgG, although it is quite rare to have an in-vivo coating with IgA or IgM in the absence of IgG. Many workers prefer anti-IgG over polyspecific AHG in antibody detection and compatibility tests because anti-IgG AHG does not react with complement

bound to red cells by cold-reactive antibodies that are not clinically significant.

Anti-C3b, -C3d

Anti-C3b, -C3d reagents prepared by animal immunization contain no activity against human immunoglobulins and are used in situations described for anti-C3d. This type of anti-C3d characteristically reacts with C3b and possibly other epitopes present on C3-coated red cells. Murine monoclonal anti-C3b, -C3d reagent is a blend of hybridoma-derived antibodies.

Role of Complement in Antiglobulin Reactions

Complement components may attach to red cells in vivo or in vitro by one of two mechanisms:
1. Complement-binding antibody specific for a red cell antigen may cause attachment of complement to the cell surface as a consequence of complement activation by the antigen-antibody complex.
2. Immune complexes, not specific for red cell antigens, may be present in plasma and may activate complement components that adsorb onto red cells in a nonspecific manner. Attachment of complement to the membrane of cells not involved in the specific antigen-antibody reaction is often described as "innocent bystander" complement coating.

Red cells coated with elements of the complement cascade may or may not undergo hemolysis. If the cascade does not go to completion, the presence of bound early components of the cascade can be detected by anticomplement reagents. The component most readily detected is C3 because several hundred C3 molecules may be bound to the red cell by the attachment of only a few antibody molecules. C4 coating also can be detected, but C3 coating has more clinical significance.

Complement as the Only Coating Globulin

Complement alone, without detectable immunoglobulin, may be present on washed red cells in certain situations.

1. IgM antibodies reacting in vitro occasionally attach to red cell antigens without agglutinating the cells, as is seen with IgM antibodies to Lewis antigens. IgM coating is difficult to demonstrate in AHG tests, partly because IgM molecules tend to dissociate during the washing process and partly because polyspecific AHG contains little if any anti-IgM activity. IgM antibodies may activate complement, and the IgM reactivity can be demonstrated by identifying the several hundred C3 molecules bound to the cell membrane near the site of antibody attachment.

2. About 10% to 20% of patients with warm AIHA have red cells with a positive DAT due to C3 coating alone.[10] No IgG, IgA, or IgM coating is demonstrable with routine procedures, although some specimens may be coated with IgG at levels below the detection threshold for the DAT.

3. In cold agglutinin syndrome, the cold-reactive autoantibody can react with red cell antigens at temperatures up to 32 C.[11] Red cells passing through vessels in the skin at this temperature become coated with autoantibody, which activates complement. If the cells escape hemolysis, they return to the central circulation, where the temperature is 37 C, and the autoantibody dissociates

from the cells, leaving complement components firmly bound to the red cell membrane. The component usually detected by AHG reagents is C3d.

4. Immune complexes that form in the plasma and bind weakly and nonspecifically to red cells may cause complement coating. The activated complement remains on the red cell surface after the immune complexes dissociate. C3 remains as the only detectable surface globulin.

IgG-Coated Cells

The addition of IgG-coated cells to negative antiglobulin tests (used to detect IgG) is required for antibody detection and crossmatching procedures.[12(p33)] These sensitized red cells should react with the antiglobulin sera, verifying that the AHG reagent was functional. Reactivity with IgG-sensitized cells demonstrates that, indeed, AHG was added and it had not been neutralized. Tests need to be repeated if the IgG-coated cells are not reactive.

Testing with IgG-sensitized cells does not detect all potential failures of the antiglobulin test.[13-15] Partial neutralization of the AHG may not be detected at all, particularly if the control cells are heavily coated with IgG. Errors in the original test, such as omission of test serum, improper centrifuge speed, or inappropriate concentrations of test red cells, may yield negative test results but positive results with control cells. Oversensitized control cells may agglutinate when centrifuged.

Complement-coated cells can also be prepared and are commercially available. They can be used in some cases to control tests with complement-specific reagents.

Some sources of error in antiglobulin tests are listed in Tables 12-2 and 12-3.

Table 12-2. Sources of Error in Antiglobulin Testing—False-Negative Results

Neutralization of Antihuman Globulin (AHG) Reagent

■ Failure to wash cells adequately to remove all serum/plasma. Fill tube at least ¾ full of saline for each wash. Check dispense volume of automated washers.

■ If increased serum volumes are used, routine wash may be inadequate. Wash additional times or remove serum before washing.

■ Contamination of AHG by extraneous protein. Do not use finger or hand to cover tube. Contaminated droppers or wrong reagent dropper can neutralize entire bottle of AHG.

■ High concentration of IgG paraproteins in test serum; protein may remain even after multiple washes.[13]

Interruption in Testing

■ Bound IgG may dissociate from red cells and either leave too little IgG to detect or may neutralize AHG reagent.

■ Agglutination of IgG-coated cells will weaken. Centrifuge and read immediately.

Improper Reagent Storage

■ AHG reagent may lose reactivity if frozen. Reagent may become bacterially contaminated.

■ Excess heat or repeated freezing/thawing may cause loss of reactivity of test serum.

■ Reagent red cells may lose antigen strength on storage. Other subtle cell changes may cause loss of reactivity.

Improper Procedures

■ Overcentrifugation may pack cells so tightly that agitation required to resuspend cells breaks up agglutinates. Undercentrifugation may not be optimal for agglutination.

■ Failure to add test serum, enhancement medium, or AHG may cause negative test.

■ Too heavy a red cell concentration may mask weak agglutination. Too light suspension may be difficult to read.

■ Improper/insufficient serum:cell ratios.

Complement

■ Rare antibodies, notably some anti-Jk^a, -Jk^b, may only be detected when polyspecific AHG is used and active complement is present.

Saline

■ Low pH of saline solution can decrease sensitivity.[3] Optimal saline wash solution for most antibodies is pH 7.0 to 7.2.

■ Some antibodies may require saline to be at specific temperature to retain antibody on the cell. Use 37 C or 4 C saline.

Table 12-3. Sources of Error in Antiglobulin Testing—False-Positive Results

Cells Agglutinated Before Washing

■ If potent agglutinins are present, agglutinates may not disperse during washing. Observe cells before the addition of antihuman globulin (AHG) or use control tube substituting saline for AHG; reactivity before the addition of AHG or in saline control invalidates AHG reading.

Particles or Contaminants

■ Dust or dirt in glassware may cause clumping (not agglutination) of red cells. Fibrin or precipitates in test serum may produce cell clumps that mimic agglutination.

Improper Procedures

■ Overcentrifugation may pack cells so tightly that they do not easily disperse and appear positive.

■ Centrifugation of test with polyethylene glycol or positively charged polymers before washing may create clumps that do not disperse.

Cells That Have Positive Direct Antiglobulin Test (DAT)

■ Cells that are positive by DAT will be positive in any indirect antiglobulin test. Procedures for removing IgG from DAT-positive cells are given in Methods 2.13 and 2.14.

Complement

■ Complement components, primarily C4, may bind to cells from clots or from CPDA-1 donor segments during storage at 4 C and occasionally at higher temperatures. For DATs, use red cells anticoagulated with EDTA, ACD, or CPD.

■ Samples collected in tubes containing silicone gel may have spurious complement attachment.[14]

■ Complement may attach to cells in specimens collected from infusion lines used to administer dextrose-containing solutions. Strongest reactions are seen when large-bore needles are used or when sample volume is less than 0.5 mL.[15]

Other Methods to Detect Antigen-Antibody Reactions

The following methods represent alternatives to traditional tube testing and use of antiglobulin serum. Some methods do not allow detection of both IgM and IgG antibodies and may not provide information on the phase and temperature of reactivity of antibodies that is obtained when traditional tube tests are used.

Solid-Phase Red Cell Adherence Tests

Solid-phase microplate techniques use immobilized antigen or antibody. In a direct test, antibody is fixed to a microplate well and red cells are added. If the cells express the corresponding antigen, they will adhere across the sides of the well; if no antigen-antibody reaction occurs, the red cells pellet to the bottom of the well when centrifuged.[16] An indirect test uses red cells of known antigenic composition bound to a well. The test sample is added to the red-cell-coated wells and allowed to react with the cells, after which the plates are washed free of unbound proteins. The indicator for attached antibody is a suspension of anti-IgG-coated red cells. The reaction is positive if the indicator cells adhere across the sides of the well. If they pellet to the bottom when centrifuged, it demonstrates that no antigen-antibody reaction has occurred (see Fig 12-4).[17] In the indirect test, isolated membrane components (eg, specific proteins), rather than intact cells, can be affixed to the microwell. Solid-phase attachment of antigen or antibody is an integral part of other tests, such as the monoclonal antibody-specific immobilization of erythrocyte antigens (MAIEA) assay, discussed below. Solid-phase systems have also been devised for use in detecting platelet antibodies and in tests for syphilis, cytomegalovirus, and hepatitis B surface antigen.[17-20]

Column Agglutination Technology

Various methods have been devised in which red cells are filtered through a column containing a medium that separates selected red cell populations. As commercially prepared, the systems usually employ a card or strip of microtubes, rather than conventional test tubes. They allow simultaneous performance of several tests. Usually, a space or chamber at the top of each column is used for red cells alone or to incubate red cells and serum or plasma. As the cells pass through the column (usually during centrifugation), the column medium separates agglutinated from unagglutinated red cells, based on aggregate size.[17] Alternatively, in some tests, specific antisera or proteins can be included in the column medium itself; cells bearing a specific antigen are selectively captured as they pass through the medium. When the column contains antiglobulin serum or a protein that specifically binds immunoglobulin, the selected

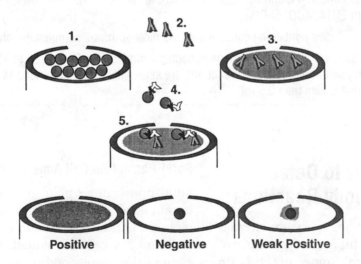

Figure 12-4. An indirect solid-phase test. A monolayer of red cells is affixed to a microwell (1). Test serum is added. If antibody (2) is present, it binds to antigens on the affixed red cells (3). Indicator red cells coated with IgG and anti-IgG (4) are added. The anti-IgG portion binds to any antibody attached to the fixed red cells (5). In a positive test, the indicator red cells are effaced across the microwell. In a negative test, the indicator cells do not bind but pellet to the center of the well when centrifuged. Weak reactions give intermediate results.

cells will be those sensitized with immunoglobulin. By using a centrifuge time and speed that allow red cells to enter the column but leave serum or plasma above, the need for saline washing for antiglobulin tests can be eliminated.[21]

Typically in column tests, negative test cells pellet to the bottom of the column. In positive tests, the cells are captured at the top, or in the body, of the column. An advantage of most such systems is the stability of the final reaction phase, which can be read by several individuals or, in some cases, documented by photocopying. Column tests generally have sensitivity similar to LISS antiglobulin methods, but such tests have reportedly performed less well in detecting weak antibodies, especially those in the ABO system.[22]

In 1986, Lapierre et al developed a process leading to a technology that uses a column of gel particles.[23] As commercially prepared, the gel test uses six microtubes instead of test tubes, contained in what is called a card or strip. The gel particles function as filters that trap red cell agglutinates when the cards are centrifuged. Gels containing antiglobulin serum are used to capture sensitized, but unagglutinated, cells. Gels with various antisera can be used for phenotyping cells (see Fig 12-5).

In another column agglutination technology, a column of glass microbeads in a diluent is used instead of gel. As with the gel test, the beads may either entrap agglutinated cells or antisera, such as anti-IgG, can be added to the diluent.[24]

Automated Testing Platforms

Several automated devices have been developed for the detection of antigen-antibody reactions. All steps in the testing process, from sample aliquotting to reporting results, are performed by the system. These test systems permit the per-

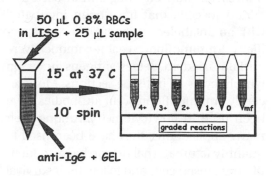

Figure 12-5. Gel test.

formance of multiple tests, using solid-phase, gel-column, and/or microtiter plate technology. The systems are controlled by a computer program and positive sample identity can be ensured by barcode technology. The test system's computer may be integrated into a laboratory's information system for results reporting. Automated test systems may be particularly useful in institutions performing large volumes of patient or donor testing.

Immunofluorescence

Immunofluorescence testing allows identification and localization of antigens inside or on the surface of cells. A fluorochrome such as fluorescein or phycoerythrin can be attached to an antibody molecule, without altering its specificity or its ability to bind antigen. Attachment of fluorescein-labeled antibody to cellular antigen makes the antibody-coated cells appear brightly visible yellow-green or red (depending on the fluorochrome).

Immunofluorescent antibodies can be used in direct or indirect procedures, with the fluorescence analogous to agglutination as an endpoint. In a direct test, the fluorescein-labeled antibody is specific for a single antigen of interest. In an indirect test, fluorescein-labeled antiglobulin serum is added to cells that have been incubated with an unlabeled antibody of known specificity. Immunofluorescent techniques were initially used to detect antigens in or on lymphocytes or in tissue sections. More recently, immunofluorescent antibodies have been used in flow cytometry. Among their many applications, they have been used to quantify fetomaternal hemorrhage, to identify transfused cells and follow their survival in recipients, to measure low levels of cell-bound IgG, and to distinguish homozygous from heterozygous expression of blood group antigens.[25]

Enzyme-Linked Immunosorbent Assay

Enzyme-linked immunosorbent assays (ELISAs) are used to measure either antigen or antibody. Enzymes such as alkaline phosphatase can be bound to antibody molecules without destroying either the antibody specificity or the enzyme activity. ELISAs have been used to detect and measure cell-bound IgG and to demonstrate fetomaternal hemorrhage. When red cells are examined, the test often is called an enzyme-linked antiglobulin test (ELAT).

Monoclonal Antibody-Specific Immobilization of Erythrocyte Antigens Assay

In the MAIEA assay, red cells are incubated with two antibodies. One contains human alloantibody to a blood group antigen and the other is a nonhuman (usually mouse monoclonal) antibody that reacts with a different portion of the same membrane protein. The red cells are lysed and the membrane solubilized, then added to a microwell coated with goat antimouse antibody. This antibody then captures the mouse antibody attached to the membrane protein (with the human

antibody also attached). Conjugated antihuman antibody is added, which reacts with the bound human antibody and gives an ELISA-readable reaction. Thus far, this method has been used primarily to isolate specific membrane structures for blood group antigen studies.[26,27]

References

1. van Oss CJ. Immunological and physiochemical nature of antigen-antibody interactions. In: Garratty G, ed. Immunobiology of transfusion medicine. New York: Marcel Dekker, Inc., 1994:327-64.
2. Moore BPL. Antibody uptake: The first stage of the hemagglutination reaction. In: Bell CA, ed. A seminar on antigen-antibody reactions revisited. Arlington, VA: AABB, 1982:47-66.
3. Rolih S, Thomas R, Fisher E, Talbot J. Antibody detection errors due to acidic or unbuffered saline. Immunohematology 1993; 9:15-18.
4. Jørgensen J, Nielsen M, Nielsen CB, Nørmark J. The influence of ionic strength, albumin and incubation time on the sensitivity of the indirect Coombs' test. Vox Sang 1980;36:186-91.
5. Nance SJ, Garratty G. Polyethylene glycol: A new potentiator of red blood cell antigen-antibody reactions. Am J Clin Pathol 1987;87:633-5.
6. Issitt PD, Anstee DJ. Applied blood group serology. 4th ed. Durham, NC: Montgomery Scientific Publications, 1998:47-8.
7. Coombs RRA, Mourant AE, Race RR. A new test for the detection of weak and "incomplete" Rh agglutinins. Br J Exp Pathol 1945; 26:255-66.
8. Code of federal regulations. Title 21 CFR 660.55. Washington, DC: US Government Printing Office, 2004 (revised annually).
9. Packman CH. Acquired hemolytic anemia due to warm-reacting autoantibodies. In: Beutler E, Lichtman MA, Coller BS, et al, eds. Williams' hematology. 6th ed. New York: McGraw Hill, 2001:639-48.
10. Sokol RJ, Hewitt S, Stamps BK. Autoimmune haemolysis: An 18-year study of 865 cases referred to a regional transfusion centre. Br Med J 1981;282:2023-7.
11. Packman CH. Cryopathic hemolytic syndromes. In: Beutler E, Lichtman MA, Coller

BS, et al, eds. Williams' hematology. 6th ed. New York: McGraw-Hill, 2001:649-55.

12. Silva MA, ed. Standards for blood banks and transfusion services. 23rd ed. Bethesda, MD: AABB, 2005.

13. Ylagen ES, Curtis BR, Wildgen ME, et al. Invalidation of antiglobulin tests by a high thermal amplitude cryoglobulin. Transfusion 1990;30:154-7.

14. Geisland JR, Milam JD. Spuriously positive direct antiglobulin tests caused by silicone gel. Transfusion 1980;20:711-13.

15. Grindon AJ, Wilson MJ. False-positive DAT caused by variables in sample procurement. Transfusion 1981;21:313-14.

16. Rolih SD, Eisinger RW, Moheng JC, et al. Solid phase adherence assays: Alternatives to conventional blood bank tests. Lab Med 1985;16: 766-70.

17. Walker P. New technologies in transfusion medicine. Lab Med 1997;28:258-62.

18. Plapp FV, Sinor LT, Rachel JM, et al. A solid phase antibody screen. Am J Clin Pathol 1984; 82:719-21.

19. Rachel JM, Sinor LT, Beck ML, Plapp FV. A solid-phase antiglobulin test. Transfusion 1985;25:24-6.

20. Sinor L. Advances in solid-phase red cell adherence methods and transfusion serology. Transfus Med Rev 1992;6:26-31.

21. Malyska H, Weiland D. The gel test. Lab Med 1994;25:81-5.

22. Phillips P, Voak D, Knowles S, et al. An explanation and the clinical significance of the failure of microcolumn tests to detect weak ABO and other antibodies. Transfus Med 1997;7:47-53.

23. Lapierre Y, Rigal D, Adam J, et al. The gel test: A new way to detect red cell antigen-antibody reactions. Transfusion 1990;30:109-13.

24. Reis KJ, Chachowski R, Cupido A, et al. Column agglutination technology: The antiglobulin test. Transfusion 1993;33:639-43.

25. Garratty G, Arndt P. Applications of flow cytofluorometry to transfusion science. Transfusion 1994;35:157-78.

26. Petty AC. Monoclonal antibody-specific immobilisation of erythrocyte antigens (MAIEA). A new technique to selectively determine antigenic sites on red cell membranes. J Immunol Methods 1993;161:91-5.

27. Petty AC, Green CA, Daniels GL. The monoclonal antibody-specific antigens assay (MAIEA) in the investigation of human red-cell antigens and their associated membrane proteins. Transfus Med 1997;7:179-88.

Chapter 13

ABO, H, and Lewis Blood Groups and Structurally Related Antigens

THE ABO, AS well as the H, Lewis, I, and P, blood group antigens reside on structurally related carbohydrate molecules. The antigens arise from the action of specific glycosyltransferases that add individual sugars sequentially to sites on short chains of sugars (oligosaccharides) on common precursor substances. Interactions of the *ABO, Hh, Sese,* and *Lele* gene products affect the expression of the ABO, H, and Lewis antigens. Refer to Appendix 6 for ISBT numbers and nomenclature for the blood groups.

The ABO System

The ABO system was discovered when Karl Landsteiner recorded the agglutination of human red cells by the sera of other individuals in 1900[1] and, in the following year, detailed the patterns of reactivity as three types, now called groups A, B, and O.[2,3] He found that serum from group A individuals agglutinated the red cells from group B individuals, and, conversely, the serum from group B individuals agglutinated group A red cells. A and B were thus the first red cell antigens to be discovered. Red cells that were not agglutinated by the serum of either the group A or group B individuals were later called group O; the serum from group O individuals agglutinated the red cells from both group A and group B individuals. Von Decastello and Sturli in 1902 discovered the fourth group, AB.[4] The importance of Landsteiner's discovery is the recognition that antibodies to A and B antigens are present when the corresponding antigen is missing. Routine ABO typing procedures developed from these and later studies.[5]

The ABO antigens and antibodies remain the most significant for transfusion practice. It is the only blood group system in which the reciprocal antibodies (see Table 13-1)

Table 13-1. Routine ABO Typing

Reaction of Cells Tested with		Reaction of Serum Tested Against			Interpre-tation	Incidence (%) in US Population	
Anti-A	Anti-B	A$_1$ Cells	B Cells	O Cells	ABO Group	Whites	Blacks
0	0	+	+	0	O	45	49
+	0	0	+	0	A	40	27
0	+	+	0	0	B	11	20
+	+	0	0	0	AB	4	4

+ = agglutination; 0 = no agglutination.

are consistently and predictably present in the sera of most people who have had no exposure to human red cells. Due to these antibodies, transfusion of ABO-incompatible blood may cause severe intravascular hemolysis as well as the other manifestations of an acute hemolytic transfusion reaction (see Chapter 27). Testing to detect ABO incompatibility between a recipient and the donor is the foundation on which all pretransfusion testing is based.

Genetics and Biochemistry

The genes for all of the carbohydrate antigens discussed in this chapter encode specific glycosyltransferases, enzymes that transfer specific sugars to the appropriate carbohydrate chain acceptor; thus, the antigens are indirect products of the genes. Genes at three separate loci (*H*, *Se*, and *ABO*) control the occurrence and the location of the A and B antigens. The *H* and *Se* (secretor) loci, officially named *FUT1* and *FUT2*, respectively, are on chromosome 19 and are closely linked. Each locus has two recognized alleles, one of which has no demonstrable product and is considered an amorph. The active allele at the *H* locus, *H*, produces a transferase that acts

at the cellular level to form the H antigen on red cells. The amorph, *h*, is very rare. The active allele at the *Se* locus, *Se*, produces a transferase that also acts to form H antigen, but primarily in secretions such as saliva.[6] Eighty percent of individuals are secretors. The amorphic allele is *se*. The enzymes produced by *H* and *Se* alleles are both fucosyltransferases, but they have slightly different activity. H antigen on red cells and in secretions is the substrate for the formation of A and B antigens.

There are three common alleles at the *ABO* locus on chromosome 9, *A*, *B*, and *O*.[7] The *A* and *B* alleles encode glycosyltransferases that produce the A and B antigens respectively; the *O* allele does not encode a functional enzyme.[8] The red cells of group O individuals lack A and B antigens but carry an abundant amount of H antigen, the unconverted precursor substance on which A and B antigens are built.

The carbohydrate chains (oligosaccharides) that carry ABH antigens can be attached to either protein (glycoprotein), sphingolipid (glycosphingolipid), or lipid (glycolipid) carrier molecules. Glycoproteins and glycosphingolipids carrying A or B antigens are integral parts of the membranes of red cells, epithelial cells, and endothelial cells (Fig 13-1) and are also present in soluble form in plasma. Glycoproteins secreted in body fluids such as saliva contain molecules that may, if the person possesses an *Se* allele, carry A, B, and H antigens. A and B antigens that are unattached to carrier protein or lipid molecules are also found in milk and urine as free oligosaccharides.

The transferases encoded by the *A, B, H,* and *Se* alleles add a specific sugar to a precursor carbohydrate chain. The sugar that is added is referred to as immunodominant because when it is removed from the structure, the specific blood group activity is lost. The sugars can be added only in a sequential manner. H structure is made first, then sugars for A and B antigens are added to H. The *H* and *Se* alleles encode a fucosyltransferase that adds fucose (Fuc) to the precursor chain; thus, fucose is the immunodominant sugar for H (see Fig 13-2). The *A* allele encodes *N*-acetyl-galactosaminyltransferase that adds *N*-acetyl-D-

galactosamine (or Gal*N*Ac) to H to make A antigen on red cells. The *B* allele encodes galactosyltransferase that adds D-galactose (or Gal) to H to make B antigen. Group AB individuals have alleles that make transferases to add both Gal*N*Ac and Gal to the precursor H antigen. Attachment of the A or B immunodominant sugars diminishes the serologic detection of H antigen so that the expressions of A or B antigen and of H antigen are inversely proportional. Rare individuals who lack both *H* and *Se* alleles (genotype *hh* and *sese*) have no H and, therefore, no A or B antigens on their red cells or in their secretions (see O$_h$ phenotype below). However, H, A, and B antigens are found in the secretions of some *hh* individuals who appear, through family studies, to possess at least one *Se* allele (see para-Bombay phenotype below).

The oligosaccharides to which the A or B immunodominant sugars are attached may exist as simple repeats of a few sugar molecules linked in linear fashion, or as part of more complex structures, with many sugar residues linked in branching chains. Differ-

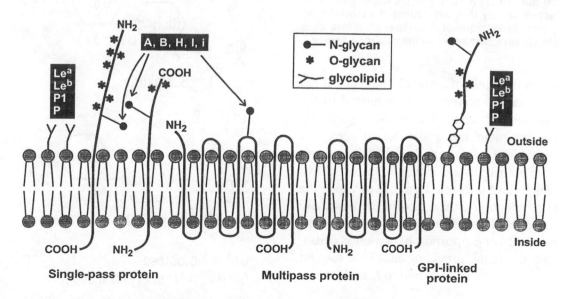

Figure 13-1. Schematic representation of the red cell membrane showing antigen-bearing glycosylation of proteins and lipids. GPI = glycophosphatidylinositol. (Courtesy of ME Reid, New York Blood Center.)

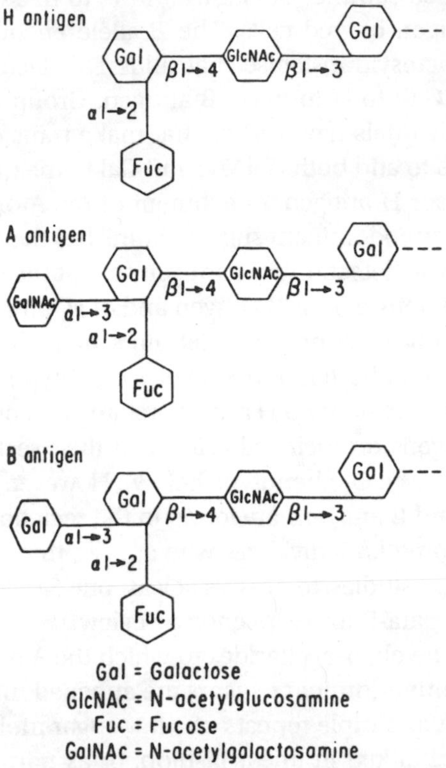

H antigen

A antigen

B antigen

Gal = Galactose
GlcNAc = N-acetylglucosamine
Fuc = Fucose
GalNAc = N-acetylgalactosamine

Figure 13-2. Gal added to the subterminal Gal confers B activity; GalNAc added to the subterminal Gal confers A activity to the sugar. Unless the fucose moiety that determines H activity is attached to the number 2 carbon, galactose does not accept either sugar on the number 3 carbon.

ences between infants and adults in cellular A, B, and H activity may be related to the number of branched structures present on cellular membranes at different ages. The red cells of infants are thought to carry predominantly linear carbohydrate chains, which have only one terminus to which the H (and subsequent A and/or B) sugars can be added. In contrast, the red cells of adults carry a high proportion of branched carbohydrate chains, providing additional sites for conversion to H and then to A and B antigens.

A, B, and H antigens are constructed on carbohydrate chains that are characterized by different linkages and composition of the

terminal disaccharide; there are at least six of these types of disaccharide linkages.[9] Type 1 chains and Type 2 chains differ in the linkage of the terminal Gal to GlcNAc disaccharide (see Fig 13-3). Type 1 A, B, and H structures are present in secretions, plasma, and endodermally derived tissues. They are not synthesized by red cells but are incorporated into the red cell membrane from the plasma. Type 2 chains are the predominant ABH-carrying oligosaccharides on red cells and are also found in secretions. Type 3 chains (repetitive form) are found on red cells from group A individuals.[10] They are synthesized by the addition of Gal to the terminal GalNAc Type 2 A chains, thus forming Type 3 H; Type 3 H chains are subsequently converted to Type 3 A by the addition of GalNAc through the action of A_1-transferase, but not by A_2-transferase (see Fig 13-4).

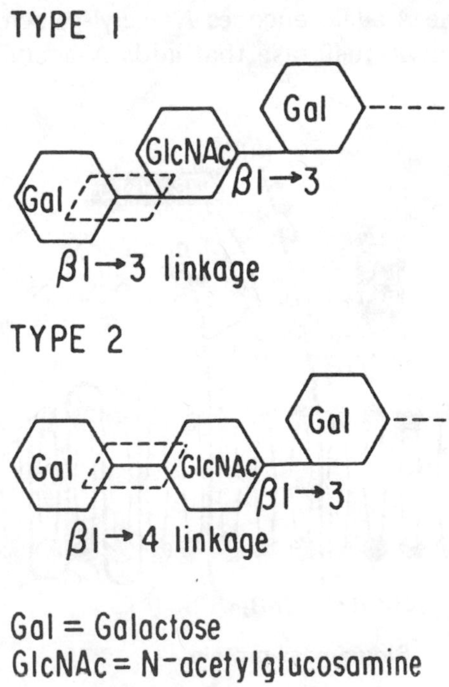

TYPE 1

$\beta 1 \rightarrow 3$ linkage

TYPE 2

$\beta 1 \rightarrow 4$ linkage

Gal = Galactose
GlcNAc = N-acetylglucosamine

Figure 13-3. Type 1 and 2 oligosaccharide chains differ only in the linkage between the GlcNAc and the terminal Gal.

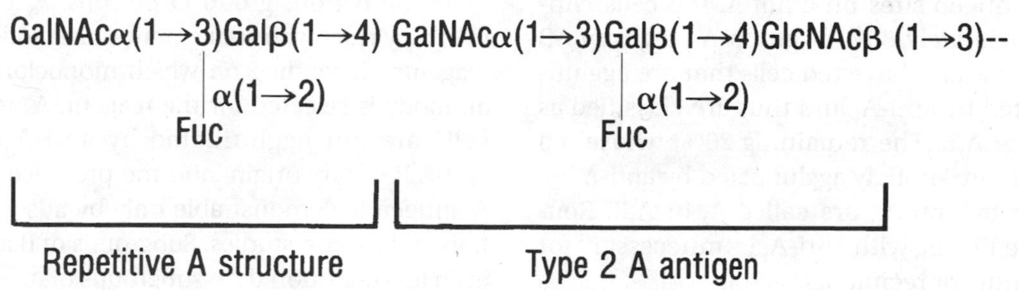

GalNAcα(1→3)Galβ(1→4) GalNAcα(1→3)Galβ(1→4)GlcNAcβ (1→3)--

$\quad$ | α(1→2) $\qquad\qquad\qquad$ | α(1→2)

$\quad$ Fuc $\qquad\qquad\qquad\qquad$ Fuc

$\lfloor$_____$\rfloor$ $\lfloor$_____$\rfloor$

Repetitive A structure $\qquad$ Type 2 A antigen

Figure 13-4. Type 3 A antigen structure.

Active alleles *H* and *Se*, of the *FUT1* and *FUT2* genes, encode fucosyltransferases with a high degree of homology. The enzyme produced by *H* acts primarily on Type 2 chains, which are prevalent on the red cell membranes. The enzyme produced by *Se* prefers, but is not limited to, Type 1 chains and acts primarily in the secretory glands.

ABO Genes at the Molecular Level

Yamamoto et al[11] have shown that *A* and *B* alleles differ from one another by seven nucleotide differences, four of which resulted in amino acid substitutions at positions 176, 235, 266, and 268 in the protein sequence of the A and B transferases. Recent crystallography of A- and B-transferases demonstrated the role of these critical amino acids in substrate recognition.[12]

The initial *O* allele examined had a single nucleotide deletion that resulted in a frame shift and premature stop codon resulting in the predicted translation of a truncated (ie, inactive) protein. Subsequently, other *O* alleles have been identified as well as mutations of *A* and *B* alleles that result in weakened expression of A and B antigens (reviewed elsewhere).[13,14] The *A₂* allele encodes a protein with an additional 21 amino acids.

Antigens

Agglutination tests are used to detect A and B antigens on red cells. Reagent antibodies frequently produce weaker reactions with red cells from newborns than with red cells from adults. Although A and B antigens can be detected on the red cells of 5- to 6-week-old embryos, A and B antigens are not fully developed at birth, presumably because the branching carbohydrate structures develop gradually. By 2 to 4 years of age, A and B antigen expression is fully developed and remains fairly constant throughout life.

Subgroups

ABO subgroups are phenotypes that differ in the amount of antigen carried on red cells and, for secretors, soluble antigen present in the saliva. Subgroups of A are more commonly encountered than subgroups of B. The two principal subgroups of A are A_1 and A_2. Red cells from A_1 and A_2 persons both react strongly with reagent anti-A in direct agglutination tests. The serologic distinction between A_1 and A_2 cells can be determined by testing with anti-A_1 lectin (see anti-A_1 below). There is both a qualitative and quantitative difference between A_1 and A_2.[15] The A_1-transferase is more efficient at converting H substance into A antigen and is capable of making the repetitive Type 3 A structures. There are about 10.5×10^5 A antigen sites on adult A_1 red cells, and about 2.21×10^5

A antigen sites on adult A_2 red cells.[9] Approximately 80% of group A or group AB individuals have red cells that are agglutinated by anti-A_1 and thus are classified as A_1 or A_1B. The remaining 20%, whose red cells are strongly agglutinated by anti-A but not by anti-A_1, are called A_2 or A_2B. Routine testing with anti-A_1 is unnecessary for donors or recipients.

Subgroups weaker than A_2 occur infrequently and, in general, are characterized by decreasing numbers of A antigen sites on the red cells and a reciprocal increase in H antigen activity. Subgroups are most often recognized when there is a discrepancy between the red cell (forward) and serum (reverse) grouping. Generally, classification of weak A subgroups (A_3, A_x, A_m, A_{el}) is based on the:

1. Degree of red cell agglutination by anti-A and anti-A_1.
2. Degree of red cell agglutination by human and some monoclonal anti-A,B.
3. Degree of red cell agglutination by anti-H (*Ulex europaeus*).
4. Presence or absence of anti-A_1 in the serum.
5. Presence of A and H substances in the saliva of secretors.
6. Adsorption/elution studies.
7. Family (pedigree) studies.

Identification of the various A subgroups is not routinely done. The serologic classification of A (and B) subgroups was developed using human polyclonal anti-A, anti-B, and anti-A,B reagents. These reagents have been replaced by murine monoclonal reagents, and the reactivity is dependent upon which clone(s) is selected by the manufacturer. There are, however, some characteristics that should be noted. A_3 red cells give a characteristic mixed-field pattern when tested with anti-A from group B or O donors. A_x red cells are characteristically not agglutinated by human anti-A from group B persons but are agglutinated by anti-A,B from group O persons. A_x red cells may react with some monoclonal anti-A reagents, depending on which monoclonal antibody is selected for the reagent. A_{el} red cells are not agglutinated by anti-A or anti-A,B of any origin, and the presence of A antigen is demonstrable only by adsorption and elution studies. Subgroups of B are even less common than subgroups of A.

Molecular studies have confirmed that A and B subgroups are heterogeneous, and the serologic classification does not consistently correlate with genomic analysis; multiple alleles yield the same weakened phenotype, and, in some instances, more than one phenotype has the same allele.[16]

Antibodies to A and B

Ordinarily, individuals possess antibodies directed toward the A or B antigen absent from their own red cells (see Table 13-1). This predictable complementary relationship permits ABO testing of sera as well as of red cells (see Methods 2.2 and 2.3). One hypothesis for the development of these antibodies is based on the fact that the configurations that confer A and B antigenic determinants also exist in other biologic entities, notably bacteria cell walls. Bacteria are widespread in the environment, and their presence in intestinal flora, dust, food, and other widely distributed agents ensures a constant exposure of all persons to A-like and B-like antigens. Immunocompetent persons react to the environmental antigens by producing antibodies to those that are absent from their own systems. Thus, anti-A is produced by group O and group B persons and anti-B is produced by group O and group A persons. Group AB people, having both antigens, make neither antibody. This "environmental" explanation for the emergence of anti-A and anti-B remains a hypothesis that has not been proven.

Time of Appearance

Anti-A and anti-B produced by an infant can generally be detected in serum after 3 to 6 months of life. Most of the anti-A and anti-B present in cord blood are of maternal origin, acquired by the placental transfer of maternal IgG; occasionally, infants can be found who produce these antibodies at the time of birth.[17(p124)] Thus, anti-A and anti-B detected in the sera of newborns or infants younger than 3 to 6 months cannot be considered valid. Antibody production increases, reaching the adult level at 5 to 10 years of age, and declines later in life. Elderly people usually have lower anti-A and anti-B levels than young adults.

Reactivity of Anti-A and Anti-B

IgM is the predominant immunoglobulin class of anti-A produced by group B individuals and anti-B produced by group A individuals, although small quantities of IgG antibody are also present. IgG is the dominant class of anti-A and anti-B of group O serum.[17(p124)] Because IgG readily crosses the placenta and IgM does not, group A or B infants of group O mothers are at higher risk for ABO hemolytic disease of the fetus and newborn (HDFN) than the infants of group A or B mothers; but severe HDFN can also occur in infants of group A and group B mothers.

Both IgM and IgG anti-A and anti-B preferentially agglutinate red cells at room temperature (20-24 C) or below and efficiently activate complement at 37 C. The complement-mediated lytic capability of these antibodies becomes apparent if serum testing includes an incubation phase at 37 C. Sera from some people will cause hemolysis of ABO-incompatible red cells at temperatures below 37 C. Hemolysis due to ABO antibodies should be suspected when the supernatant fluid of the serum test is pink to red or when the cell button is absent or reduced in size. Hemolysis must be interpreted as a positive result. Because the hemolysis is complement-mediated, it will not occur if plasma is used for testing, or if reagent red cells are suspended in solutions that contain EDTA or other agents that prevent complement activation.

Reactivity of Anti-A,B (Group O Serum)

Serum from a group O individual contains an antibody designated as anti-A,B because it reacts with both A and B red cells, and the anti-A and anti-B cannot be separated by differential adsorption. In other words, after adsorption of group O serum, an eluate prepared from the group A or group B adsorbing cells reacts with both A and B test cells. Saliva from a secretor of either A or B substance inhibits the activity of anti-A,B against A or B red cells, respectively.

Anti-A₁

Anti-A_1 occurs as an alloantibody in the serum of 1% to 2% of A_2 individuals and 25% of A_2B individuals.[15] Sometimes, Anti-A_1 can also be found in the sera of individuals with other weak subgroups of A. Anti-A_1 can cause discrepancies in ABO testing and incompatibility in crossmatches with A_1 or A_1B red cells. Anti-A_1 usually reacts better or only at temperatures well below 37 C and is considered clinically insignificant unless there is reactivity at 37 C. When reactive at 37 C, only A_2 or O red cells should be used for transfusion.

In simple adsorption studies, the anti-A of group B serum appears to contain separable anti-A and anti-A_1. Native group B serum agglutinates A_1 and A_2 red cells; after adsorption with A_2 red cells, group B serum reacts only with A_1 red cells. If further tests are performed, however, the differences in

A antigen expression between A_1 and A_2 red cells appear to be quantitative rather than qualitative.[9]

A reliable anti-A_1 reagent from the lectin of *Dolichos biflorus* is commercially available or may be prepared (see Method 2.10). The raw plant extract will react with both A_1 and A_2 red cells, but an appropriately diluted reagent preparation will not agglutinate A_2 cells and thus constitutes an anti-A_1.

Routine Testing for ABO

Routine testing for determining the ABO group consists of testing the red cells with anti-A and anti-B (cell or forward type) and testing the serum or plasma with A_1 and B red cells (serum or reverse type). Both red cell and serum testing are required for routine ABO tests on donors and patients because each serves as a check on the other.[18(pp32,37)] The two exceptions to performing both cell and serum testing are confirmation testing of the ABO type of donor units that have already been labeled and testing blood of infants less than 4 months of age; in both of these instances, only ABO testing of red cells is required.

Anti-A and anti-B typing reagents agglutinate most antigen-positive red cells on direct contact, even without centrifugation. Anti-A and anti-B in the sera of some patients and donors are too weak to agglutinate red cells without centrifugation or prolonged incubation. Serum tests should be performed by a method that will adequately detect the antibodies—eg, tube, microplate, or column agglutination techniques. Procedures for ABO typing by slide, tube, and microplate tests are described in Methods 2.1, 2.2, and 2.3.

Additional reagents, such as anti-A,B for red cell tests and A_2 and O red cells for serum tests, are not necessary for routine testing but are helpful in resolving typing discrepancies (see below). The use of anti-A,B may not have the same benefit in detecting weak subgroups when testing with monoclonal reagents (depending on the clones used) as when human polyclonal reagents were in use. Many monoclonal ABO typing reagents have been formulated to detect some of the weaker subgroups. Manufacturers' inserts should be consulted for specific reagent characteristics. Special techniques to detect weak subgroups are not routinely necessary because a typing discrepancy (eg, the absence of expected serum antibodies) usually distinguishes these specimens from group O specimens.

The A_2 red cells are intended to facilitate the recognition of anti-A_1. Because most group A specimens do not contain anti-A_1, routine use of this reagent is not necessary.

Discrepancies Between Red Cell and Serum Tests

Table 13-1 shows the results and interpretations of routine red cell and serum tests for ABO. A discrepancy exists when the results of red cell tests do not agree with serum tests. When a discrepancy is encountered, the discrepant results must be recorded, but interpretation of the ABO group must be delayed until the discrepancy has been resolved. If the specimen is from a donor unit, the unit must not be released for transfusion until the discrepancy has been resolved. When the blood is from a potential recipient, it may be necessary to administer group O red cells of the appropriate Rh type before the investigation has been completed. It is important to obtain sufficient pretransfusion blood samples from the patient to complete any additional studies that may be required.

Red cell and serum test results may be discrepant because of intrinsic problems with red cells or serum, or technical errors. Discrepancies may be signaled either because negative results are obtained when positive results are expected, or positive results are found when tests should have been negative (see Table 13-2).

Specimen-Related Problems in Testing Red Cells

ABO testing of red cells may give unexpected results for many reasons.

1. Red cells from individuals with variant *A* or *B* alleles may carry poorly expressed antigens. Antigen expres-

Table 13-2. Possible Causes of ABO Typing Discrepancies

Category	Causes
Red cell weak/ missing reactivity	ABO subgroup Leukemia/malignancy Transfusion Intrauterine fetal transfusion Transplantation Excessive soluble blood group substance
Extra red cell reactivity	Autoagglutinins/excess protein coating red cells Unwashed red cells: plasma proteins Unwashed red cells: antibody in patient's serum to reagent constituent Transplantation Acquired B antigen B(A) phenomenon Out-of-group transfusion
Mixed-field red cell reactivity	Recent transfusion Transplantation Fetomaternal hemorrhage Twin or dispermic (tetragametic) chimerism
Serum weak/missing reactivity	Age related (<4-6 months old, elderly) ABO subgroup Hypogammaglobulinemia Transplantation
Serum extra reactivity	Cold autoantibody Cold alloantibody Serum antibody to reagent constituent Excess serum protein Transfusion of plasma components Transplantation Infusion of intravenous immune globulin

sion may also be weakened on the red cells of some persons with leukemia or other malignancies.

2. A patient who has received red cell transfusions or a marrow transplant may have circulating red cells of more than one ABO group and constitute a transfusion or transplantation chimera (see Mixed-Field Agglutination below).

3. Exceptionally high concentrations of A or B blood group substances in the serum can combine with and neutralize reagent antibodies to produce an unexpected negative reaction against serum- or plasma-suspended red cells.

4. A patient with potent autoagglutinins may have red cells so heavily coated with antibody that the red cells agglutinate spontaneously in the presence of diluent, independent of the specificity of the reagent antibody.

5. Abnormal concentrations of serum proteins or the presence in serum of infused macromolecular solutions may cause the nonspecific aggregation of serum-suspended red cells that simulates agglutination.

6. Serum- or plasma-suspended red cells may give false-positive results with monoclonal reagents if the serum or plasma contains a pH-dependent autoantibody.[19,20] Serum- or plasma-suspended red cells may also give discrepant results due to an antibody to a reagent dye/constituent[21] or to proteins causing rouleaux.

7. Red cells of some group B individuals are agglutinated by a licensed anti-A reagent that contains a particular murine monoclonal antibody, MHO4. These group B individuals had excessively high levels of *B* allele-specified galactosyltransferase, and the designation B(A) was given to this blood group phenotype.[22]

8. Red cells of individuals with the acquired B phenotype typically agglutinate strongly with anti-A and weakly with anti-B, and the serum contains strong anti-B. The acquired B phenotype arises when microbial deacetylating enzymes modify the A antigen by altering the A-determining sugar (*N*-acetylgalactosamine) so that it resembles the B-determining galactose. The acquired B phenomenon is found most often in individuals with the A_1 phenotype.

9. Inherited or acquired abnormalities of the red cell membrane can lead to what is called a polyagglutinable state. The abnormal red cells can be unexpectedly agglutinated by human reagent anti-A, anti-B, or both because human reagents will contain antibodies to the so-called cryptantigens that are exposed in polyagglutinable states. In general, monoclonal anti-A and anti-B reagents will not detect polyagglutination.

Specimen-Related Problems in Testing Serum or Plasma

ABO serum/plasma tests are also subject to false results.

1. Small fibrin clots that may be mistaken for agglutinates may be seen in ABO tests with plasma or incompletely clotted serum.

2. Negative or weak results are seen in serum tests from infants under 4 to 6 months of age. Serum from newborns is not usually tested because antibodies present are generally passively transferred from the mother.

3. Unexpected absence of ABO agglutinins may be due to the presence of an A or B variant.

4. Patients who are immunodeficient due to disease or therapy may have

such depressed immunoglobulin levels that there is little or no ABO agglutinin activity. Samples from elderly patients whose antibody levels have declined with age or from patients whose antibodies have been greatly diluted by plasma exchange procedures may also have unexpectedly weak agglutinins.

5.   If the patient has received a marrow transplant of a dissimilar ABO group, serum antibodies will not agree with red cell antigens. For example, a group A individual who receives group O marrow may have circulating group O red cells and produce only anti-B in the serum. Refer to Chapter 25 for more information on the effects of ABO-mismatched transplants.

6.   Cold allo- or autoantibodies that react at room temperature can react with one or both reverse grouping cells. For example, if the patient has a room-temperature-reactive anti-M, it may cause an unexpected reaction with M-positive A_1 and/or B reagent red cells.

7.   Antibodies to constituents of the diluents used to preserve reagent A_1 and B red cells can agglutinate the cells independent of ABO antigens and antibodies.

8.   Abnormal concentrations of proteins, altered serum protein ratios, or the presence of high-molecular-weight plasma expanders can cause nonspecific red cell aggregation or rouleaux that is difficult to distinguish from true agglutination. Rouleaux formation is easily recognized on microscopic examination if the red cells assume what has been described as a "stack of coins" formation.

9.   Recent transfusion with plasma components containing ABO agglutinins may cause unexpected reactions.

10.   Recent infusion of intravenous immune globulin that may contain ABO isohemagglutinins can cause unexpected reactions.

Mixed-Field Agglutination

Occasional samples are encountered that contain two distinct, separable populations of red cells. Usually, this reflects the recent transfusion of group O red cells to a non-group-O recipient or receipt of a marrow transplant of an ABO group different from the patient's own. Red cell mixtures also occur in a condition called blood group chimerism, resulting either from intrauterine exchange of erythropoietic tissue by fraternal twins or from mosaicism arising through dispermy. In all such circumstances, ABO red cell tests may give a mixed-field pattern of agglutination. Mixed-field reactions due to transfusion last only for the life of the transfused red cells. After hematopoietic transplantation, the mixed-field reaction usually disappears when the patient's own red cells are no longer produced. Persistent mixed-cell populations do occur in some marrow recipients. Mixed-field reactions that arise through blood group chimerism may persist throughout the life of the individual. For more information regarding the transfusion and evaluation of hematopoietic transplant patients, refer to Chapters 21 and 25.

Technical Errors

Technical errors leading to ABO discrepancies include:

1.   Specimen mix-up.
2.   Red cell suspensions are too heavy or too light.
3.   Failure to add reagents.
4.   Missed observation of hemolysis.
5.   Failure to follow manufacturer's instructions.

6. Under- or overcentrifugation of tests.

7. Incorrect interpretation or recording of test results.

Resolving ABO Discrepancies

The first step in resolving an apparent serologic problem should be to repeat the tests on the same sample. If initial tests were performed on red cells suspended in serum or plasma, the testing should be repeated after washing the red cells several times with saline. Washing the red cells can eliminate many problems for red cell typing that are associated with plasma proteins. If the discrepancy persists, the following initial steps can be incorporated into the investigation.

1. Obtain the patient's diagnosis, historical blood group, and history of previous transfusions, transplantation, and medications.

2. Review the results of the antibody detection test against group O red cells and autologous red cells to detect possible interference from allo- or autoantibodies.

3. Obtain a new blood specimen and test the new sample if a discrepancy due to a contaminated specimen is suspected.

In addition to a discrepancy between the red cell and serum tests, an ABO discrepancy may also exist when the observed reactivity is not in agreement with a previous type on record. The first step in resolving this type of discrepancy is to obtain a new blood specimen.

Resolving Discrepancies Due to Absence of Expected Antigens

The cause of a discrepancy can sometimes be inferred from the strength of the reactions obtained in red cell or serum tests. For example, serum that strongly agglutinates group B red cells but not A_1 cells probably comes from a group A person, even though the red cells are not agglutinated by anti-A or anti-B. The following procedures can be used to enhance the detection of weakly expressed antigens.

1. Incubate washed red cells with anti-A, anti-B, and anti-A,B for 15 minutes at room temperature to increase the association of antibody with antigen. Incubating the test system for 15 to 30 minutes at 4 C may further enhance antibody attachment. An inert (eg, 6% albumin) or autologous control for room temperature and 4 C tests is recommended. The manufacturer's directions for any reagent should be consulted for possible comments or limitations.

2. Treat the patient's red cells with a proteolytic enzyme such as ficin, papain, or bromelin. Enzyme treatment increases the antigen-antibody reaction with anti-A or anti-B. In some instances, reactions between reagent antibody and red cells expressing antigens will become detectable at room temperature within 30 minutes if enzyme-treated red cells are employed. Enzyme-treated group O red cells and an autologous control must be tested in parallel as a control for the specificity of the ABO reaction. The manufacturer's directions should be consulted for possible comments or limitations.

3. Incubate an aliquot of red cells at room temperature or at 4 C with anti-A or anti-B (as appropriate) to adsorb antibody to the corresponding red cell antigen for subsequent elution (see Method 2.4). Group A or B (as appropriate) and O red cells should be subjected to parallel adsorption and elution with any reagent to serve as positive and nega-

tive controls. Anti-A$_1$ lectin should not be used for adsorption/elution studies because in a more concentrated form, such as an eluate, it may react nonspecifically with red cells. Test the eluate against group A$_1$, B, and O cells. Unexpected reactivity in control eluates invalidates the results obtained with the patient's red cells. This indicates that the adsorption/elution procedure was not performed correctly, another antibody is present (ie, in a polyclonal reagent), or the specificity of a monoclonal reagent is not distinct enough for the reagent to be used by this method.

4. Test the saliva for the presence of H and A or B substances (see Method 2.5). Saliva tests help resolve ABO discrepancies only if the person is a secretor. This may be surmised from the Lewis phenotype but may not be known until after the saliva testing is complete. See the discussion on Lewis antigens.

Resolving Discrepancies Due to Absence of Expected Antibodies

1. Incubate the serum with A$_1$ and B red cells for 15 to 30 minutes at room temperature. If there is still no reaction, incubate at 4 C for 15 to 30 minutes. It is recommended to include an autocontrol and group O red cells for room temperature and 4 C testing to control for reactivity of common cold autoagglutinins.

2. Treat the A$_1$ and B reagent cells with a proteolytic enzyme such as ficin, papain, or bromelin. Enzyme-treated group O and autologous red cells must be tested in parallel as a control for reactivity. The manufacturer's directions should be consulted for possible comments or limitations.

Resolving Discrepancies Due to Unexpected Red Cell Reactions with Anti-A and Anti-B

Red cell ABO tests sometimes give unexpected positive reactions. For example, reagent anti-A may weakly agglutinate red cells from a sample in which the serum gives reactions expected of a normal group B or O sample. The following paragraphs describe some events that can cause unexpected reactions in ABO typing tests and the steps that can be taken to identify them.

B(A) Phenotype. When cells react weakly with monoclonal anti-A and strongly with anti-B, and the serum reacts with A$_1$ red cells, but not B cells, the B(A) phenotype should be suspected. Verification that the anti-A reagent contains the discriminating MHO4 clone confirms the suspicion. B(A) red cells can show varying reactivity with anti-A; the majority of examples react weakly, and the agglutinates are fragile and easily dispersed, although some examples have reacted as strongly as 2+.[22] Sera from these individuals agglutinate both A$_1$ and A$_2$ cells. Except for newborns and immunocompromised patients, serum testing should distinguish this phenomenon from the AB phenotype in which a subgroup of A is accompanied by anti-A$_1$. Testing with an anti-A without the MHO4 clone should resolve the discrepancy. The recipient can be considered a group B.

Acquired B Phenotype. Red cells agglutinated strongly by anti-A and weakly by anti-B and a serum containing strong anti-B suggest the acquired B state. The acquired B phenomenon is found most often in individuals with the A$_1$ phenotype; a few examples of A$_2$ with acquired B have been found. Most red cells with acquired B antigens react weakly with anti-B, but occasional examples are agglutinated quite strongly. Behavior with monoclonal anti-B reagents varies with the particular clone used. Acquired B antigens had been observed with increased frequency in tests with certain FDA-licensed monoclonal anti-B blood grouping reagents containing the ES-4 clone,[23] but the manufacturers have lowered the pH of the anti-B reagent so the frequency of the detection of acquired B is similar to polyclonal anti-B or have discontinued the use of that clone. To confirm that group A red cells carry the acquired B structure:

1. Check the patient's diagnosis. Acquired B antigens are usually associated with tissue conditions that allow colonic bacteria to enter the circulation, but acquired B antigens have been found on the red cells of apparently normal blood donors.[23]

2. Test the patient's serum against autologous red cells or known acquired B cells. The individual's anti-B will not agglutinate his or her own red cells or red cells known to be acquired B.

3. Test the red cells with monoclonal anti-B reagents for which the manufacturer's instructions give a detailed description. Unlike most human polyclonal antibodies, some monoclonal antibodies do not react with the acquired B phenotype; this information may be included in the manufacturer's directions.

4. Test the red cells with human anti-B serum that has been acidified to pH 6.0. Acidified human anti-B no longer reacts with the acquired B antigen.

Antibody-Coated Red Cells. Red cells from infants with HDFN or from adults suffering from autoimmune or alloimmune conditions may be so heavily coated with IgG antibody molecules that they agglutinate spontaneously in the presence of reagent diluents containing high protein concentrations. Usually, this is at the 18% to 22% range found in some anti-D reagents,

but, sometimes, the sensitized red cells also agglutinate in ABO reagents with protein concentrations of 6% to 12%. Methods 2.12 or 2.14 may be used to remove much of this antibody from the red cells so that the cells can be tested reliably with anti-A and anti-B.

Red cells from a specimen containing cold-reactive IgM autoagglutinins may autoagglutinate in saline tests. Incubating the cell suspension briefly at 37 C and then washing the cells several times with saline warmed to 37 C can usually remove the antibodies. If the IgM-related agglutination is not dispersed by this technique, the red cells can be treated with the sulfhydryl compound dithiothreitol (DTT) (see Method 2.11).

Resolving Discrepancies Due to Unexpected Serum Reactions

The following paragraphs describe some events that can cause unexpected or erroneous serum test results and the steps that can be taken to resolve them.

1. Reactivity of the A_1 reagent cells when anti-A is strongly reactive with the red cells suggests the presence of anti-A_1 in the serum of an A_2 or A_2B individual. To demonstrate this as the cause of the discrepancy:

    a. Test the red cells with anti-A_1 lectin to differentiate group A_1 from A_2 red cells.

    b. Test the serum against several examples of each of the following: A_1, A_2, and O red cells. Only if the antibody agglutinates all A_1 red cells and none of the A_2 or O red cell samples can it be called anti-A_1.

2. Strongly reactive cold autoagglutinins, such as anti-I, anti-IH, anti-IA, and anti-IB, can agglutinate red cells of adults, including autologous cells and reagent red cells, at room temperature (20-24 C). With few excep-

tions, agglutination caused by the cold autoagglutinin is weaker than that caused by anti-A and anti-B. The following steps can be performed when such reactivity interferes to the point that the interpretation of serum tests is difficult.

a. Warm the serum and reagent red cells to 37 C before mixing and testing. Incubate at 37 C for 1 hour and perform a "settled" reading (ie, observe for agglutination without centrifugation). Rare weakly reactive examples of IgM anti-A or anti-B may not be detected by this method.

b. Remove the cold autoagglutinin from the serum using a cold autoadsorption method as described in Method 4.6. The adsorbed serum can then be tested against A_1 and B reagent red cells.

3. Unexpected alloantibodies that react at room temperature, such as anti-P_1 or anti-M, may agglutinate the red cells used in serum tests if the cells carry the corresponding antigen. One or more of the reagent cells used in the antibody detection test may also be agglutinated if the serum and cell mixture was centrifuged for either a room temperature or 37 C reading; a rare serum may react with an antigen of low incidence on the serum testing cells that is not present on cells used for antibody detection. Steps to determine the correct ABO type of sera containing cold-reactive alloantibodies include:

a. Identify the room temperature alloantibody, as described in Chapter 19, and test the reagent A_1 and B cells to determine which, if either, carries the corresponding antigen. Obtain A_1 and B red cells that lack the an-

tigen and use them for serum testing.

b. Raise the temperature to 30 to 37 C before mixing the serum and cells, incubate for 1 hour, and perform a "settled" reading (ie, without centrifugation). If the thermal amplitude of the alloantibody is below the temperature at which anti-A and anti-B react, this may resolve the discrepancy.

c. If the antibody detection test is negative, test the serum against several examples of A_1 and B red cells. The serum may contain an antibody directed against an antigen of low incidence, which will be absent from most randomly selected A_1 and B red cells.

4. Sera from patients with abnormal concentrations of serum proteins, or with altered serum protein ratios, or who have received plasma expanders of high molecular weight can aggregate reagent red cells and mimic agglutination. Some of these samples cause aggregation of the type described as rouleaux. More often, the aggregates appear as irregularly shaped clumps that closely resemble antibody-mediated agglutinates. The results of serum tests can often be corrected by diluting the serum 1:3 in saline to abolish its aggregating properties or by using a saline replacement technique (see Method 3.4).

The H System

On group O red cells, there is no A or B antigen, and the membrane expresses abundant H. Because H is a precursor of A and B antigens, A and B persons have less H substance than O persons. The amount of H antigen detected on red cells with the anti-H lectin *Ulex europaeus* is, in order of diminishing quantity, $O>A_2>B>A_2B>A_1>A_1B$.

Occasionally, group A_1, A_1B, or (less commonly) B individuals have so little unconverted H antigen on their red cells that they produce anti-H. This form of anti-H is generally weak, reacts at room temperature or below, and is not considered clinically significant. Individuals of the rare O_h phenotype (see below), whose red cells lack H, have a potent and clinically significant alloanti-H in their serum (in addition to anti-A and anti-B).

O_h Phenotype

The term O_h or Bombay phenotype has been used for the very rare individuals whose red cells and secretions lack H, A, and B antigens and whose plasma contains potent anti-H, anti-A, and anti-B.[6] This phenotype was first discovered in Bombay, India. The phenotype initially mimics normal group O but becomes apparent when serum from the O_h individual is tested against group O red cells, and strong immediate-spin agglutination and/or hemolysis occurs. The anti-H of an O_h person reacts over a thermal range of 4 to 37 C with all red cells except those of other O_h people. O_h persons must be transfused only with O_h blood because their non-red-cell-stimulated antibodies rapidly destroy cells with A, B, or H antigens. If other examples of O_h red cells are available, further confirmation can be obtained by demonstrating compatibility of the serum with O_h red cells. At the genotypic level, the O_h phenotype arises from the inheritance of *hh* at the *H* locus and *sese* at the *Se* locus. Because the *Se* allele is necessary for the formation of Le^b, O_h red cells will be Le(a+b–) or Le(a–b–).

Para-Bombay Phenotype

The para-Bombay phenotype designation, A_h, B_h, and AB_h, is classically used for individuals who are H-deficient secretors, ie, those who have an inactive H-transferase but have active Se-transferase. The red cells lack serologically detectable H antigen but carry small amounts of A and/or B antigen (sometimes detectable only by adsorption/elution tests), depending on the individual's alleles at the *ABO* locus. Tests with anti-A or anti-B reagents may or may not give weak reactions, but the cells are nonreactive with anti-H lectin or with anti-H serum from O_h persons. Individuals with the para-Bombay phenotype have a functional *Se* allele and thus will express A, B, and H antigens in their plasma and secretions. The sera of A_h and B_h people contain anti-H and/or anti-IH in addition to the expected anti-A or anti-B.

H-deficient secretors may also be group O. These individuals will have traces of H antigen, but no A or B antigen, on their red cells and only have H in their secretions.

In 1994, Kelly et al reported the molecular bases for the Bombay and para-Bombay phenotypes.[24] Many mutations at the *H* locus have subsequently been associated with H-deficiency.

The Lewis System

The Lewis system antigens, Le^a and Le^b, result from the action of a glycosyltransferase encoded by the *Le* allele that, like the A, B, and H glycosyltransferases, adds a sugar to a precursor chain. Le^a is produced when *Le* is inherited with *sese* and Le^b is produced when *Le* is inherited with at least one *Se* allele. When the silent or amorphic allele *le* is inherited, regardless of the secretor allele inherited, no Le^a or Le^b is produced. Thus, Le^a and Le^b are not antithetical antigens produced by alleles; rather, they result from the interaction of independently inherited alleles.

The Lewis antigens are not intrinsic to red cells but are expressed on glycosphingolipid Type 1 chains adsorbed from plasma onto red cell membranes. Plasma lipids exchange freely with red cell lipids.

Gene Interaction and the Antigens

The synthesis of the Lewis antigens is dependent upon the interaction of two different fucosyltransferases: one from the *Se* locus and one from the Lewis locus. Both enzymes act upon the same precursor Type 1 substrate chains. The fucosyltransferase encoded by the *Le* allele attaches fucose in $\alpha(1\rightarrow4)$ linkage to the subterminal GlcNAc; in the absence of the transferase from the *Se* allele, this configuration has Le^a activity. This product cannot be further glycosylated. Le^b occurs when the Type 1 precursor is converted to Type 1 H by the fucosyltransferase from the secretor allele, and subsequently acted upon by the fucosyltransferase from the *Le* allele. This Le^b configuration has two fucose moieties.[9] Thus, Le^b reflects the presence of both the *Le* and *Se* alleles. *Le* without *Se* results in Le^a activity only; *Se* with the amorphic allele *le* will result in

no secretion of Le^a or Le^b and the red cells will have the Le(a–b–) phenotype.

Table 13-3 shows phenotypes of the Lewis system and their frequencies in the population. Red cells that type as Le(a+b+) are rare in people of European and African origin but are relatively common in persons of Asian origin, due to a fucosyltransferase encoded by a variant secretor allele that competes less efficiently with the Le fucosyltransferase.[9]

Lewis Antibodies

Lewis antibodies occur almost exclusively in the sera of Le(a–b–) individuals, usually without known red cell stimulus. Those individuals whose red cell phenotype is Le(a–b+) do not make anti-Le^a because small amounts of unconverted Le^a are present in their saliva and plasma. It is most unusual to find anti-Le^b in the sera of Le(a+b–) individuals, but anti-Le^b may exist along with anti-Le^a in the sera of Le(a–b–) individuals. Lewis antibodies are often found in the sera of pregnant women who transiently demonstrate a Le(a–b–) phenotype. The Lewis antibodies, however, are almost always IgM and do not cross the placenta. Because of this and because Lewis antigens are poorly developed at birth, the antibodies are not associated

Table 13-3. Phenotypes in the Lewis System and Their Incidence

Reactions with Anti-			Adult Phenotype Incidence %	
Le^a	Le^b	Phenotype	Whites	Blacks
+	0	Le(a+b–)	22	23
0	+	Le(a–b+)	72	55
0	0	Le(a–b–)	6	22
+	+	Le(a+b+)	Rare	Rare

+ = agglutination; 0 = no agglutination.

with HDFN. Lewis antibodies may bind complement, and fresh serum that contains anti-Le^a (or infrequently anti-Le^b) may hemolyze incompatible red cells in vitro. Hemolysis is more often seen with enzyme-treated red cells than with untreated red cells.

Most Lewis antibodies agglutinate saline-suspended red cells of the appropriate phenotype. The resulting agglutinates are often fragile and are easily dispersed if red cell buttons are not resuspended gently after centrifugation. Agglutination sometimes is seen after incubation at 37 C, but rarely of the strength seen in tests incubated at room temperature. Some examples of anti-Le^a, and less commonly anti-Le^b, can be detected in the antiglobulin phase of testing. Sometimes this reflects complement bound by the antibody if a polyspecific reagent (ie, containing anticomplement) is used. In other cases, antiglobulin reactivity results from an IgG component of the antibody.

Sera with anti-Le^b activity can be divided into two categories. The more common type reacts best with Le(b+) red cells of group O and A$_2$; these antibodies have been called anti-Le^{bH}. Antibodies that react equally well with the Le^b antigen on red cells of all ABO phenotypes are called anti-Le^{bL}.

Transfusion Practice

Lewis antigens readily adsorb to and elute from red cell membranes. Transfused red cells shed their Lewis antigens and assume the Lewis phenotype of the recipient within a few days of entering the circulation. Lewis antibodies in a recipient's serum are readily neutralized by Lewis blood group substance in donor plasma. For these reasons, it is exceedingly rare for Lewis antibodies to cause hemolysis of transfused Le(a+) or Le(b+) red cells. It is not considered necessary to type donor blood for the presence of Lewis antigens before transfusion or when crossmatching for recipients with Lewis antibodies; red cells that are compatible in tests at 37 C can be expected to survive normally in vivo.[25,26]

Lewis Antigens in Children

Red cells from newborn infants usually do not react with either human anti-Le^a or anti-Le^b and are considered to be Le(a–b–). Some can be shown to carry small amounts of Le^a when tested with potent monoclonal anti-Le^a reagents. Among children, the incidence of Le(a+) red cells is high and that of Le(b+) red cells low, reflecting a greater production of the *Le* allele-specific transferase in infants; the *Se* allele-specific transferase is produced in lower levels. The phenotype Le(a+b+) may be transiently observed in children as the *Se* allele transferase levels increase toward adult levels. Reliable Lewis typing of young children may not be possible because test reactions may not reflect the correct phenotype until approximately 2 to 3 years of age.[25]

The I/i Antigens and Antibodies

Cold agglutinins with I specificity are frequently encountered in sera of normal individuals. The antibody is usually not clinically significant and reacts with all red cells except cord cells and the rare i adult phenotype. I and i antigens, however, are not antithetical but are expressed in a reciprocal relationship. At birth, infant red cells are rich in i; I is almost undetectable. Thus, for practical purposes, cord cells are considered to be I–, i+. During the first 2 years of life, I antigen gradually increases at the expense of i. The red cells of most adults are strongly reactive with anti-I and react weakly or not at all with anti-i. Rare adults have red cells that carry high levels of i and only trace amounts of I; these red cells have the i adult phenotype. There is no true I– or i– phenotype.

The I and i antigens on red cells are internal structures carried on the same glycoproteins and glycosphingolipids that carry H, A, or B antigens and in secretions on the same glycoproteins that carry H, A, B, Le^a, and Le^b antigens. The I and i antigens are located closer to the membrane than the terminal sugars that determine the ABH antigens. The i structure is a linear chain of at least two repeating units of *N*-acetylgalactosamine [Galβ(1→4)GlcNAcβ(1→3)]. On the red cells of adults, many of these linear chains are modified by the addition of branched structures consisting of GlcNAc in a β(1→6) linkage to a galactose residue internal to the repeating sequence. The branching configuration confers I specificity.[27,28] Different examples of anti-I appear to recognize different portions of the branched oligosaccharide chain. As branching occurs and as the sugars for H, A, and B antigens are added, access of anti-i and anti-I may be restricted.[25]

The I antigen, together with the i antigen, used to comprise the Ii Blood Group Collection in the ISBT nomenclature. Recent cloning of the gene that encodes the transferase responsible for converting i active straight chains into I active branched chains and identification of several mutations responsible for the rare i adult phenotype have caused the I antigen to be assigned to the new I Blood Group System; the i antigen remains in the Ii collection.[29]

Antibodies to I/i

Anti-I is a common, benign autoantibody found in the serum of many normal healthy individuals that behaves as a cold agglutinin at 4 C with a titer of <64. Agglutination with adult red cells and weaker or no agglutination with cord cells is the classic reactivity. Some stronger examples agglutinate cells at room temperature; others may react only with the strongest I+ red cells and give inconsistent reactions. Incubating tests in the cold enhances anti-I reactivity and helps to confirm its identity; albumin and testing enzyme-treated red cells also enhance anti-I reactivity.

Autoanti-I assumes pathologic significance in cold agglutinin syndrome (CAS), in which it behaves as a complement-binding antibody with a high titer and high thermal amplitude. The specificity of the autoantibody in CAS may not be apparent when the undiluted sample is tested (I adult and cord cells may react to the same strength even at room temperature); titration studies and/or thermal amplitude studies may be necessary to define the specificity (see Chapter 20). Anti-I is often made by patients with pneumonia due to *Mycoplasma pneumoniae*. These patients may experience transient hemolytic episodes due to the antibody.

Autoanti-i is less often implicated in symptomatic disease than anti-I. On rare occasions, anti-i may be seen as a relatively weak cold autoagglutinin reacting preferentially at 4 C. Anti-i reacts strongest with cord and i adult red cells, and weakest with I adult red cells. Patients with infectious mononucleosis often have transient but potent anti-i.

Table 13-4 illustrates the serologic behavior of anti-I and anti-i at 4 C and 22 C. Reaction strengths should be considered relative; clear-cut differences in reactivity between the two are seen only with weaker examples of the antibodies. Titration studies may be needed to differentiate strong examples of the antibodies.

Serum containing anti-I or anti-i is sometimes reactive at the antiglobulin phase of

Table 13-4. Comparative Serologic Behavior of the I/i Blood Group Antibodies with Saline Red Cell Suspensions

Temperature	Cell Type	Anti-I	Anti-i
4 C	I adult	4+	0-1+
	i cord	0-2+	3+
	i adult	0-1+	4+
22 C	I adult	2+	0
	i cord	0	2-3+
	i adult	0	3+

testing when polyspecific antihuman globulin is used. Such reactions rarely indicate antibody activity at 37 C. Rather, complement components are bound when serum and cells interact at lower temperatures; during the 37 C incubation, the antibody dissociates but the complement remains bound to the red cells. Thus, the antiglobulin phase reactivity is usually due to the anticomplement in a polyspecific antiglobulin reagent. Usually, avoiding room temperature testing and using anti-IgG instead of a polyspecific antihuman globulin help to eliminate detection of cold autoantibodies. Cold autoadsorption to remove the autoantibody from the serum may be necessary for stronger examples; cold autoadsorbed serum or plasma can also be used in ABO typing (see Method 4.6). The prewarming technique can also be used once the reactivity has been confirmed as cold autoantibody (see Method 3.3).

Complex Reactivity

Some antibodies appear to recognize I determinants with attached H, A, or B immunodominant sugars. Anti-IH occurs quite commonly in the serum of A_1 individuals; it reacts stronger with red cells that have high levels of H as well as I (ie, group O and A_2 red cells) and weaker, if at all, with group A_1 cells of adults or cord cells of any group. Anti-IH should be suspected when serum from a group A patient causes direct agglutination of all cells used for antibody detection but is compatible with all or most group A donor blood. Other examples of complex reactivity include anti-IA, $-IP_1$, -IBH, $-ILe^{bH}$, and -iH.

The P Blood Group and Related Antigens

The P blood group has traditionally consisted of the P, P_1, and P^k antigens, and later Luke (LKE). However, the biochemistry and molecular genetics, although not yet completely understood, make it clear that at least two biosynthetic pathways and genes at different loci are involved in the development and expression of these antigens. Thus, in ISBT nomenclature, the P antigen is assigned to the new globoside (GLOB) blood group system, the P_1 antigen is assigned to the P blood group system, and P^k and LKE remain in the globoside collection of antigens.[29] For simplicity, these antigens are often referred to as the P blood group.

The first antigen of the P blood group was discovered by Landsteiner and Levine in 1927, in a series of animal experiments that led also to the discovery of M and N. Originally called P, the name of the antigen was later changed to P_1. The designation P has since been reassigned to an antigen present on almost all human red cells. The P^k antigen is also present on almost all human red cells, but it is not readily detected unless P is absent, eg, in the rare P_1^k or P_2^k phenotypes. The null phenotype, p, is very rare. LKE antigen is present on almost all red cells except those of the rare phenotypes p or P^k and in about 2% of P+ red cells.

Common and Rare Phenotypes

There are two common phenotypes associated with the P blood group, P_1 and P_2, and three rare phenotypes, p, P_1^k, and P_2^k, as shown in Table 13-5. The P_1 phenotype describes those red cells that react with anti-P_1 and anti-P; red cells that do not react with anti-P_1, but do react with anti-P, are of the P_2 phenotype. When red cells are tested only with anti-P_1 and not with anti-P, the phenotype should be written as P_1+ or P_1–.

Biochemistry and Genetics

The P blood group antigens, like the ABH antigens, are sequentially synthesized by the addition of sugars to precursor chains. The different oligosaccharide determinants of the P blood group antigens are shown in Fig 13-5. All the antigens are exclusively expressed on glycolipids on human red cells, not on glycoproteins.[30] The precursor of P_1 can also be glycosylated to Type 2H chains, which carry ABH antigens.

There are two distinct pathways for the synthesis of the P blood group antigens as shown in Fig 13-6. The common precursor is lactosylceramide, also known as ceramide dihexose or CDH. One pathway results in the formation of paragloboside and P_1. Paragloboside is also the Type 2 precursor for ABH antigens. The other pathway results in the formation of the globoside series of antigens: P^k, P, and LKE.

The genes encoding the glycosyltransferases that are responsible for synthesizing P^k from lactosylceramide and for converting P^k to P were cloned in 2000. Several mutations that result in the p and P^k phenotypes have been identified.[31-33] The genetic relationship between P_1, P and P^k is still not understood. Red cells of the p phenotype are

Table 13-5. Phenotypes of the P Blood Group and Related Antigens

Reactions with Anti-					Phenotype Incidence (%)	
P_1	P	P^k	P_1+P+P^k	Phenotype	Whites	Blacks
+	+	0	+	P_1	79	94
0	+	0	+	P_2	21	6
0	0*	0	0	p		
+	0	+	+	P_1^k	All extremely rare	
0	0	+	+	P_2^k		

*Usually negative, occasionally weakly positive.

	Lactosylceramide (CDH)	Galβ(1→4)Glc-Cer
P^k	Globotriosylceramide (CTH)	Galα(1→4)Galβ(1→4)Glc-Cer
P	Globoside	GalNAcβ(1→3)Galα(1→4)Galβ(1→4)Glc-Cer
LKE	Sialosylgalactosylgloboside	NeuAcα(2→3)Galβ(1→3)GalNAcβ(1→3)Galα(1→4)Galβ(1→4)Glc-Cer
	Paragloboside	Galβ(1→4)GlcnAcβ(1→3)Galβ(1→4)Glc-Cer
P_1	Galactosylparagloboside	Galα(1→4)Galβ(1→4)GlcnAcβ(1→3)Galβ(1→4)Glc-Cer

Figure 13-5. Some biochemical structures of P blood group antigens.

P_1– in addition to being P– and P^k–; the P_1– status of p red cells cannot be explained. The P_1 gene is located on chromosome 22 and the P gene is located on chromosome 3.

Anti-P_1

The sera of P_1– individuals commonly contain anti-P_1. If sufficiently sensitive techniques are applied, it is likely that anti-P_1 would be detected in the serum of virtually every person with P_1– red cells.[25] The antibody reacts optimally at 4 C but may occasionally be detected at 37 C. Anti-P_1 is nearly always IgM and has not been reported to cause HDFN. Only rarely has it been reported to cause hemolysis in vivo.[17(p139),34]

The strength of the P_1 antigen varies widely among different red cell samples, and antigen strength has been reported to diminish when red cells are stored. These characteristics sometimes create difficulties in identifying antibody specificity in serum with a positive antibody screen. An antibody that reacts weakly in room temperature testing can often be shown to have anti-P_1 specificity by incubation at lower temperatures or by the use of enzyme-treated red cells. Hydatid cyst fluid or P_1 substance derived from pigeon eggs inhibits the activity of anti-P_1. Inhibition may be a useful aid to

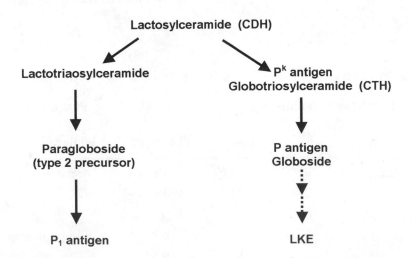

Figure 13-6. Biosynthesis of P blood group antigens.

antibody identification, especially if anti-P_1 is present in a serum with antibodies of other specificities.

Rare Antibodies

Alloanti-P, found as a naturally occurring potent hemolytic antibody in the sera of P_1^k and P_2^k individuals, reacts with all red cells except those of the rare p and P^k phenotypes. Anti-P can be IgM or a mixture of IgM and IgG. Anti-PP_1P^k, formerly called anti-Tj^a, is produced by individuals of the p phenotype without red cell stimulation and reacts with all red cells except those of the rare p phenotype. Anti-PP_1P^k can be separated into its components (anti-P, anti-P_1, and anti-P^k) through adsorptions. These components can be IgM and/or IgG, react over a broad thermal range, and can efficiently bind complement, which make them potent hemolysins. Anti-PP_1P^k has caused hemolytic transfusion reactions and, occasionally, HDFN.[17(p139)] There is an association between both anti-P and anti-PP_1P^k and spontaneous abortions occurring early in pregnancy[35,36]

Autoanti-P associated with paroxysmal cold hemoglobinuria is a cold-reactive IgG autoantibody that is described as a biphasic hemolysin.[17(pp220-1)] The antibody typically does not react in routine test systems, but is demonstrable only by the Donath-Landsteiner test (see Chapter 20).

P Antigens as Receptors for Pathogens

The P blood group antigens are receptors for several pathogens. P, P_1, P^k, and LKE are receptors for uropathogenic *Escherichia coli*; P^k and P_1 are receptors for toxins from enterohemorrhagic *E. coli*[37]; and the meningitis-causing bacterium *Streptococcus suis* binds to P^k antigen.[38] The P antigen (globoside) has also been shown to serve as a receptor for erythrovirus (parvovirus) B19, which causes erythema in-

fectiosum (Fifth disease). Individuals of p phenotype who lack globoside are naturally resistant to infection with this pathogen.[39]

References

1. Landsteiner K. Zur Kenntnis der antifermentativen, lytischen und agglutinierenden Wirkungen des Blutserums und der Lymph. Zbl Balk 1900;27:367.

2. Landsteiner K. Uber Agglutinationserscherschein ungen normalen menschlichen Blutes. Wien Klin Wochenschr 1901;14:1132-4.

3. Garratty G, Dzik W, Issitt PD, et al. Terminology for blood group antigens and genes—historical origins and guidelines in the new millennium. Transfusion 2000;40:477-89.

4. Von Decastello A, Sturli A. Yber due usiaglutinie im Serumgesunder und lronker Menschen. Munchen Med Wochenschr 1902;26:1090-5.

5. Watkins WM. The ABO blood group system: Historical background. Transfus Med 2001; 11:243-65.

6. Oriol R, Candelier JJ, Mollicone R. Molecular genetics of H. Vox Sang 2000;78(Suppl 2):105-8.

7. Yamamoto F. Molecular genetics of ABO. Vox Sang 2000;78(Suppl 2):91-103.

8. Yamamoto F. Molecular genetics of the ABO histo-blood group system. Vox Sang 1995;69:1-7.

9. Daniels G. Human blood groups. 2nd ed. Oxford: Blackwell Science, 2002.

10. Clausen H, Levery SB, Nudelman E, et al. Repetitive A epitope (type 3 chain A) defined by group A_1-specific monoclonal antibody TH-1: Chemical basis of qualitative A_1 and A_2 distinction. Proc Natl Acad Sci U S A 1985;82:1199-203.

11. Yamamoto F, Clausen H, White T, et al. Molecular genetic basis of the histo-blood group ABO system. Nature 1990;345:229-33.

12. Patenaude SI, Seto NOL, Borisova SN, et al. The structural basis for specificity in human ABO(H) blood group biosynthesis (letter). Nat Struct Biol 2002;9:685-90.

13. Lee AH, Reid ME. ABO blood group system: A review of molecular aspects. Immunohematology 2000;16:1-6.

14. Olsson ML, Chester MA. Polymorphism and recombination events at the *ABO* locus: A major challenge for genomic ABO blood grouping strategies. Transfus Med 2001;11:295-313.

15. Reid ME, Lomas-Francis C. The blood group antigen factsbook. 2nd ed. San Diego, CA: Academic Press, 2004.

16. Olsson ML, Irshaid NM, Hosseini-Maaf B, et al. Genomic analysis of clinical samples with serologic ABO blood grouping discrepancies: Identification of 15 novel A and B subgroup alleles. Blood 2001;98:1585-93.

17. Mollison PL, Engelfriet CP, Contreras M. Blood transfusion in clinical medicine. 10th ed. Oxford: Blackwell Scientific Publications, 1997.

18. Silva MA, ed. Standards for blood banks and transfusion services. 23rd ed. Bethesda, MD: AABB, 2005.

19. Spruell P, Chen J, Cullen K. ABO discrepancies in the presence of pH-dependent autoagglutinins (abstract). Transfusion 1994;34(Suppl): 22S.

20. Kennedy MS, Waheed A, Moore J. ABO discrepancy with monoclonal ABO reagents caused by pH-dependent autoantibody. Immunohematology 1995;11:71-3.

21. Garratty G. In vitro reactions with red blood cells that are not due to blood group antibodies: A review. Immunohematology 1998;14:1-11.

22. Beck ML, Yates AD, Hardman J, Kowalski MA. Identification of a subset of group B donors reactive with monoclonal anti-A reagent. Am J Clin Pathol 1989;92:625-9.

23. Beck ML, Kowalski MA, Kirkegaard JR, Korth JL. Unexpected activity with monoclonal anti-B reagents (letter). Immunohematology 1992;8: 22.

24. Kelly RJ, Ernst LK, Larsen RD, et al. Molecular basis for H blood group deficiency in Bombay (O_h) and para-Bombay individuals. Proc Natl Acad Sci U S A 1994;91:5843-7.

25. Issitt PD, Anstee DJ. Applied blood group serology. 4th ed. Durham, NC: Montgomery Scientific Publications, 1998.

26. Waheed A, Kennedy MS, Gerhan S, Senhauser DA. Success in transfusion with cross-match-compatible blood. Am J Clin Pathol 1981;76:294-8.

27. Yu L-C, Twu Y-C, Chang C-Y, Lin M. Molecular basis of the adult I phenotype and the gene responsible for the expression of the human blood group I antigen. Blood 2001;98: 3840-5.

28. Yu L-C, Twu Y-C, Chou M-L, et al. The molecular genetics of the human *I* locus and molecular background explain the partial association of the adult I phenotype with congenital cataracts. Blood 2003;101:2081-8.

29. Daniels GL, Cartron JP, Fletcher A, et al. International Society of Blood Transfusion Committee on terminology for red cell surface antigens: Vancouver report. Vox Sang 2003;84: 244-7.

30. Yang Z, Bergstrom J, Karlsson KA. Glycoproteins with Galα4Gal are absent from human erythrocyte membranes, indicating that glycolipids are the sole carriers of blood group P activities. J Biol Chem 1994;269:14620-4.

31. Hellberg A, Poole J, Olsson ML. Molecular basis of the globoside-deficient P^k blood group phenotype. J Biol Chem 2002;277;29455-9.

32. Furukawa K, Iwamura K, Uchikawa M, et al. Molecular basis for the p phenotype. J Biol Chem 2000;275:37752-6.

33. Koda Y, Soejima M, Sato H, et al. Three-base deletion and one-base insertion of the α(1,4) galactosyltransferase gene responsible for the p phenotype. Transfusion 2002;42:48-51.

34. Arndt PA, Garratty G, Marfoe RA, Zeger GD. An acute hemolytic transfusion reaction caused by an anti-P_1 that reacted at 37 C. Transfusion 1998;38:373-7.

35. Shirey RS, Ness PM, Kickler TS, et al. The association of anti-P and early abortion. Transfusion 1987;27:189-91.

36. Cantin G, Lyonnais J. Anti-PP$_1$P^k and early abortion. Transfusion 1983;23:350-1.

37. Spitalnik PF, Spitalnik SL. The P blood group system: Biochemical, serological, and clinical aspects. Transfus Med Rev 1995;9:110-22.

38. Haataja S, Tikkanen K, Liukkonen J, et al. Characterization of a novel bacterial adhesion specificity of *Streptococcus suis* recognizing blood group P receptor oligosaccharides. J Biol Chem 1993;268:4311-17.

39. Brown KE, Hibbs JR, Gallinella G, et al. Resistance to parvovirus B19 infection due to lack of virus receptor (erythrocyte P antigen). N Engl J Med 1994;330:1192-6.

Suggested Reading

Chester MA, Olsson ML. The ABO blood group gene: A locus of considerable genetic diversity. Transfus Med Rev 2001;15:177-200.

Daniels G. Human blood groups. 2nd ed. Oxford: Blackwell Science Publications, 2002.

Hanfland P, Kordowicz M, Peter-Katalinic J, et al. Immunochemistry of the Lewis blood-group system: Isolation and structure of Lewis-c active and related glycosphingolipids from the plasma of blood-group O Le(a–b–) nonsecretors. Arch Biochem Biophys 1986;246:655-72.

Issitt PD, Anstee DJ. Applied blood group serology. 4th ed. Durham, NC: Montgomery Scientific Publications, 1998.

Judd WJ. Methods in immunohematology. 2nd ed. Durham, NC: Montgomery Scientific Publications, 1994.

Lee AH, Reid ME. ABO blood group system: A review of molecular aspects. Immunohematology 2000;16:1-6.

Morgan WTJ, Watkins WM. Unraveling the biochemical basis of blood group ABO and Lewis antigenic specificity. Glycoconj J 2000;17:501-30.

Olsson ML, Chester MA. Polymorphism and recombination events at the *ABO* locus: A major challenge for genomic ABO blood grouping strategies. Transfus Med 2001;11:295-313.

Palcic MM, Seto NOL, Hindsgual O. Natural and recombinant A and B gene encoded glycosyltransferases. Transfus Med 2001;11:315-23.

Rydberg L. ABO-incompatibility in solid organ transplant. Transfus Med 2001;11:325-42.

Watkins WM. The ABO blood group system: Historical background. Transfus Med 2001;11:243-65.

Yamamoto F. Cloning and regulation of the *ABO* genes. Transfus Med 2001;11:281-94.

Chapter 14

The Rh System

THIS CHAPTER USES the DCE nomenclature—a modification of the
nomenclature originally proposed
by Fisher and Race,[1] which has been able
to accommodate our present understanding of the genetics and biochemistry of this
complex system. The Rh-Hr terminology
of Wiener is presented only in its historical context, as molecular genetic evidence
does not support Wiener's one-locus theory.

The D Antigen and Its Historical Context

Discovery of D

The terms "Rh positive" and "Rh negative"
refer to the presence or absence of the red
cell antigen D. The first human example
of the antibody against the antigen later
called D was reported in 1939 by Levine
and Stetson[2]; the antibody was found in
the serum of a woman whose fetus had
hemolytic disease of the fetus and newborn (HDFN) and who experienced a
hemolytic reaction after transfusion of
her husband's blood. In 1940, Landsteiner
and Wiener[3] described an antibody obtained by immunizing guinea pigs and
rabbits with the red cells of Rhesus mon-
keys; it agglutinated the red cells of approximately 85% of humans tested, and
they called the corresponding determinant the Rh factor. In the same year, Levine and Katzin[4] found similar antibodies
in the sera of several recently delivered
women, and at least one of these sera
gave reactions that paralleled those of the
animal anti-Rhesus sera. Also in 1940,
Wiener and Peters[5] observed antibodies of
the same specificity in the sera of persons
whose red cells lacked the determinant
and who had received ABO-compatible
transfusions in the past. Later evidence
established that the antigen detected by

animal anti-Rhesus and human anti-D were not identical, but, by that time, the Rh blood group system had already received its name. Soon after anti-D was discovered, family studies showed that the D antigen is genetically determined; transmission of the trait follows an autosomal dominant pattern.

Clinical Significance

After the A and B antigens, D is the most important red cell antigen in transfusion practice. In contrast to A and B, however, persons whose red cells lack the D antigen do not regularly have anti-D. Formation of anti-D results from exposure, through transfusion or pregnancy, to red cells possessing the D antigen. The D antigen has greater immunogenicity than other red cell antigens; it is estimated that 30% to 85%[6,7] of D– persons who receive a D+ transfusion will develop anti-D. Therefore, in most countries, the blood of all recipients and all donors is routinely tested for D to ensure that D– recipients are identified and given D– blood.

Other Rh Antigens

By the mid-1940s, four additional antigens—C, E, c, and e—had been recognized as belonging to what is now called the Rh system. Subsequent discoveries have brought the number of Rh-related antigens to 49 (Table 14-1), many of which exhibit both qualitative and quantitative variations. The reader should be aware that these other antigens exist (see the suggested reading list), but, in most transfusion medicine settings, the five principal antigens (D, C, E, c, e) and their corresponding antibodies account for the vast majority of clinical issues involving the Rh system.

Although Rh antigens are fully expressed at birth with antigen detection as early as 8 weeks' gestation,[10] they are present on red cells only and are not detectable on platelets, lymphocytes, monocytes, neutrophils, or other tissues.[11,12]

Genetic and Biochemical Considerations

Attempts to explain the genetic control of Rh antigen expression were fraught with controversy. Wiener[13] proposed a single locus with multiple alleles determining surface molecules that embody numerous antigens. Fisher and Race[14] inferred from the existence of antithetical antigens the existence of reciprocal alleles at three individual but closely linked loci. Tippett's prediction[15] that two closely linked structural loci on chromosome 1 determine the production of Rh antigens has been shown to be correct.

RH Genes

Two highly homologous genes on the short arm of chromosome 1 encode the nonglycosylated polypeptides that express the Rh antigens (Fig 14-1).[16,17] One gene, designated *RHD*, determines the presence of a membrane-spanning protein that confers D activity on the red cell. In Caucasian D– persons, the *RHD* gene is deleted; the D– phenotype in some other populations (persons of African descent, Japanese, and Chinese) is associated with an inactive, mutated, or partial *RHD* gene.[18] The inactive *RHD* gene or pseudogene (*RHD*Ψ) responsible for the D– phenotype in some Africans has been described.[19]

The *RHCE* gene determines the C, c, E, and e antigens; its alleles are *RHCe*, *RHCE*, *RHcE*, and *RHce*.[20] Evidence derived from

Table 14-1. Antigens of the Rh Blood Group System and Their Incidence

Numeric Designation	Antigen Name	Incidence (%)*			Numeric Designation	Antigen Name	Incidence (%)*		
		White	Black	Overall			White	Black	Overall
Rh1	D	85	92		Rh32	Rh32	<0.01	1	
Rh2	C	68	27		Rh33	Har			<0.01
Rh3	E	29	22		Rh34	Bastiaan			>99.9
Rh4	c	80	96		Rh35	Rh35			<0.01
Rh5	e			98	Rh36	Be^a			<0.1
Rh6	f	65	92		Rh37	Evans			<0.01
Rh7	Ce	68	27		Rh39	C-like			>99.9
Rh8	C^w	2	1		Rh40	Tar			<0.01
Rh9	C^x			<0.01	Rh41	Ce-like	70		
Rh10	V	1	30		Rh42	Ce^s	<0.1	2	
Rh11	E^w			<0.01	Rh43	Crawford			<0.01
Rh12	G	84	92		Rh44	Nou			>99.9
Rh17	Hr$_0$			>99.9	Rh45	Riv			<0.01
Rh18	Hr			>99.9	Rh46	Rh46			>99.9
Rh19	hr^s			98	Rh47	Dav			>99.9
Rh20	VS	<0.01	32		Rh48	JAL			<0.01
Rh21	C^G			68	Rh49	STEM	<0.01	6	
Rh22	CE			<1	Rh50	FPTT			<0.01
Rh23	D^w			<0.01	Rh51	MAR			>99.9
Rh26		80	96		Rh52	BARC			<0.01
Rh27	cE	28	22		Rh53	JAHK			<0.01
Rh28				<0.01	Rh54	DAK			<0.01
Rh29	total Rh			>99.9	Rh55	LOCR			<0.01
RH30	Go^a	0	<0.01		Rh56	CENR			<0.01
Rh31	hr^B			98					

*Incidence in White and Black populations where appropriate.[8,9]

transfection studies[21] indicates that both C/c and E/e reside on a single polypeptide product.

Biochemical and Structural Observations

The predicted products of both *RHD* and *RHCE* are proteins of 417 amino acids that, modeling studies suggest, traverse the red cell membrane 12 times and display only short exterior loops of amino acids (Fig 14-1). The polypeptides are fatty acylated and, unlike most blood-group-associated proteins, carry no carbohydrate residues.

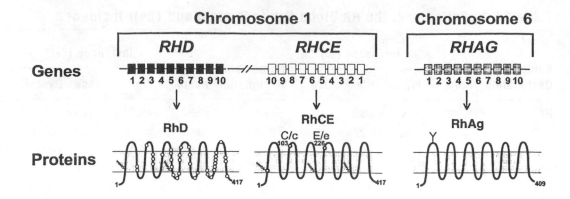

Figure 14-1. Schematic representation of *RHD*, *RHCE*, and *RHAG* genes and RhD, RhCE, and RhAG proteins. ○ on RhD represents amino acid differences between RhD and RhCE. ○ on RhCE indicates the critical amino acids involved in C/c and E/e antigen expression.

Considerable homology exists between the products of *RHD* and *RHCE*; the products of the different alleles of *RHCE* are even more similar.[18] C and c differ from one another in only four amino acids, at positions 16, 60, 68, and 103, of which only the difference between serine and proline at 103 appears to be critical. The presence of proline or alanine at position 226 distinguishes E from e. The D polypeptide, by contrast, possesses 32 to 35 amino acids that will be perceived as foreign by D–individuals.

Within the red cell membrane, the Rh polypeptides form a complex with the Rh-associated glycoprotein (RhAG), which has 37% sequence homology with the Rh polypeptides but is encoded by the *RHAG* gene on chromosome 6 (Fig 14-1).[22]

The study of Rh_{null} red cells, which lack all Rh antigens, reveals that this complex (Rh proteins and RhAG) is essential for expression of other membrane proteins. Rh_{null} cells lack LW antigens, are negative for Fy5 of the Duffy system, and have weakened expression of the antigens carried on glycophorin B (S, s, and U).[23] Although Rh/RhAG proteins play a structural role in the red cell membrane as evidenced by red cell mor-

phology changes in Rh_{null} syndrome (see later in this chapter), their function remains unknown. There is evidence, however, that the RhAG protein plays a role in ammonium transport.[24,25]

Rh Terminology

Three systems of nomenclature were developed to convey genetic and serologic information about the Rh system before the recent advances in our understanding of the genetics.

System Terminology

The Rh-Hr terminology derives from Wiener,[13] who believed the *RH* gene product to be a single entity he called an agglutinogen. An agglutinogen was characterized by numerous individual specificities, called factors, that were identified by specific antibodies. This theory was incorrect, but for the designation of phenotype, particularly in conversation, many serologists use a shorthand system based on Wiener's Rh-Hr notation. The phenotype notations convey haplotypes with the single letters R and r. R is used for haplotypes that produce D, r for haplotypes that do not produce D. Subscripts or, occasionally, superscripts indicate the combinations of other antigens present. For example, R_1 indicates *DCe* haplotype; R_2 indicates *DcE*; r indicates *dce*; R_0 indicates *Dce*; and so on (Table 14-2).

CDE terminology was introduced by Fisher and Race,[1] who postulated three sets of closely linked genes (*C* and *c*, *D* and *d*, and *E* and *e*). Both gene and gene product have the same letter designation, with italics used for the name of the gene. A modified CDE terminology is now commonly used to communicate research and serologic findings. Rosenfield and coworkers[26] proposed a system of nomenclature based on serologic observations. Symbols were not intended to convey genetic information, merely to facilitate communication of phenotypic data. Each antigen is given a number, generally in the order of its discovery or its assignment to the Rh system. Table 14-1 lists the Rh system antigens by number designation, name, and incidence.

Determining Phenotype

In clinical practice, five blood typing reagents are readily available: anti-D, -C, -E, -c, and -e. Routine pretransfusion studies include only tests for D. Other reagents are used principally in the resolution of antibody problems or in family studies. The assortment of antigens detected on a person's red cells constitutes that person's Rh phenotype. Table 14-3 shows reaction patterns of cells tested with antibodies to the five antigens and the probable Rh phenotype in modified Wiener terminology.

Serologic Testing for Rh Antigen Expression

Expression of D

D– persons either lack *RHD*, which encodes for the D antigen, or have a nonfunctional *RHD* gene. Most D– persons are homozygous for *RHce*, the gene encoding c and e; less often they may have *RHCe* or *RHcE*, which encode C and e or c and E, respectively. The *RHCE* gene, which produces both C and E, is quite rare in D– or D+ individuals.

The D genotype of a D+ person cannot be determined serologically; dosage studies are not effective in showing whether an individual is homozygous or heterozygous for *RHD*. Using serologic tests, *RHD* genotype can be assigned only by inference from the antigens associated with the presence of D. Molecular techniques, however, allow the determination of D genotype.[19,27,28]

Interaction between genes results in so-called "position effect." If the interaction is between genes or the product of genes on the same chromosome, it is called a *cis* effect. If a gene or its product interacts with one on the opposite chromosome, it is called a *trans* effect. Examples of both effects were first reported in 1950 by Lawler and Race,[29] who noted as a *cis* effect that the E antigen produced by *DcE* is quantitatively

Table 14-2. The Principal *RH* Gene Complexes and the Antigens Encoded

Haplotype	Genes Present	Antigens Present	Phenotype
R^1	RHD,RHCe	D,C,e	R_1
R^2	RHD,RHcE	D,c,E	R_2
R^0	RHD,RHce	D,c,e	R_0
R^z	RHD,RHCE	D,C,E	R_z
r'	RHCe	C,e	r'
r''	RHcE	c,E	r''
r	RHce	c,e	r
r^y	RHCE	C,E	r^y

Table 14-3. Determination of Likely Rh Phenotypes from the Results of Tests with the Five Principal Rh Blood Typing Reagents

Reagent					Antigens Present	Probable Phenotype
Anti-D	Anti-C	Anti-E	Anti-c	Anti-e		
+	+	0	+	+	D,C,c,e	R_1r
+	+	0	0	+	D,C,e	R_1R_1
+	+	+	+	+	D,C,c,E,e	R_1R_2
+	0	0	+	+	D,c,e	R_0R_0/R_0r
+	0	+	+	+	D,c,E,e	R_2r
+	0	+	+	0	D,c,E	R_2R_2
+	+	+	0	+	D,C,E,e	R_1R_z
+	+	+	+	0	D,C,c,E	R_2R_z
+	+	+	0	0	D,C,E	R_zR_z
0	0	0	+	+	c,e	rr
0	+	0	+	+	C,c,e	r'r
0	0	+	+	+	c,E,e	r''r
0	+	+	+	+	C,c,E,e	r'r''

weaker than E produced by *cE*. They noted as *trans* effects that both C and E are weaker when they result from the genotype *DCe/DcE* than when the genotypes are *DCe/ce* or *DcE/ce*, respectively.

Expression of C, c, E, e

To determine whether a person has genes that encode C, c, E, and e, the red cells are tested with antibody to each of these antigens. If the red cells express both C and c or both E and e, it can be assumed that the corresponding genes are present in the individual. If the red cells carry only C *or* c, or only E *or* e, the person is assumed to be homozygous for the particular allele.

Ethnic Origin

Ethnic origin influences deductions about genotype because the incidence of Rh genes differs from one geographic group to another. For example, a White person with the phenotype Dce would probably be *Dce/ce*, but, in a Black person, the genotype could as likely be either *Dce/Dce* or *Dce/ce*. Table 14-4 shows the incidence of D, C, E, c, and e antigens in White and Black populations.

Gene Frequency

The phenotype DCcEe (line 3 of Table 14-3) can arise from any of several genotypes. In any population, the most probable genotype is *DCe/DcE*. Both these haplotypes encode D; a person with this phenotype will very likely be homozygous for the *RHD* gene, although heterozygous for the *RHCE* gene (*Ce/cE*). Some less likely genotypes could result if the person is heterozygous at the *D* locus (for example, *DCe/cE*, *DcE/Ce*, or *DCE/ce*), but these are uncommon in all populations. Table 14-4 gives the incidence of the more common genotypes in D+ persons. The figures given are for Whites and Blacks. The absence of the *RHD* gene is uncommon in other ethnic groups.

Determining Genotype

Identifying antigens does not always allow confident deduction of genotype. Presumptions regarding the most probable genotype rest on the incidence of antigenic combinations determined from population studies in different ethnic groups. Inferences about genotype are useful in population studies, paternity tests, and in predicting the Rh genes transmitted by the husband/partner of a woman with Rh antibodies (Table 14-4).

Molecular techniques are now available that can determine Rh genotype. Determi-

Table 14-4. Incidence of the More Common Genotypes in D+ Persons*

Antigens Present	Genotype DCE	Genotype Mod. Rh-hr	Incidence (%) Whites	Incidence (%) Blacks	Homo- Whites	Hetero- Whites	Homo- Blacks	Hetero- Blacks
D,C,c,e	*DCe/ce*	R^1r	31.1	8.8				
	DCe/Dce	R^1R^0	3.4	15.0	10	90	59	41
	Dce/Ce	R^0r'	0.2	1.8				
D,C,e	*DCe/DCe*	R^1R^1	17.6	2.9	91	9	81	19
	DCe/Ce	R^1r'	1.7	0.7				
D,c,E,e	*DcE/ce*	R^2r	10.4	5.7	10	90	63	37
	DcE/Dce	R^2R^0	1.1	9.7				
D,c,E	*DcE/DcE*	R^2R^2	2.0	1.3	87	13	99	1
	DcE/cE	R^2r''	0.3	<<0.1				
D,C,c,E,e	*DCe/DcE*	R^1R^2	11.8	3.7				
	DCe/cE	R^1r''	0.8	<0.1	89	11	90	10
	DcE/Ce	R^2r'	0.6	0.4				
D,c,e	*Dce/ce*	R^0r	3.0	22.9	6	94	46	54
	Dce/Dce	R^0R^0	0.2	19.4				

Likelihood of Zygosity for D (%) spans the Homo-/Hetero- columns.

*For the rare phenotypes and genotypes not shown in this table, consult the Suggested Readings listed at the end of this chapter.

nations of genotype with polymerase chain reaction methods can be made using DNA harvested from white cells or amniocytes[19,27,28] or from noncellular fetal DNA in maternal plasma.[30] Rarely, DNA genotype results will disagree with serologic findings.

Weak D

Most D+ red cells show clear-cut macroscopic agglutination after centrifugation with reagent anti-D and can be readily classified as D+. Red cells that are not immediately or directly agglutinated cannot as easily be classified. For some D+ red cells, demonstration of the D antigen requires incubation with the anti-D reagent or addition of antihuman globulin (AHG) serum after incubation with anti-D [indirect antiglobulin test (IAT)]. These cells are considered D+, even if an additional step in testing is required.

In the past, red cells that required additional steps for the demonstration of D were classified as D^u. The term D^u is no longer considered appropriate; red cells that carry weak forms of D are classified as D+ and should be described as "weak D." Improvement of polyclonal reagents and the more widespread use of monoclonal anti-D reagents have resulted in the routine detection of some D+ red cells that would have been considered weak D when tested with less sensitive polyclonal reagents. Additionally, monoclonal anti-D may react by direct agglutination with epitopes of D that had previously required more sensitive test methods or, occasionally, may fail to react with some epitopes of the D antigen. Conversely, some monoclonal anti-D may react by direct testing with rare D epitopes that were not detected with polyclonal reagents (eg, DHAR and Crawford). It is important to realize that anti-D reagents differ among manufacturers and to know the characteristics of the product being used.

Quantitative Weak D

In the majority of cases, this form of the weak D phenotype is due to an *RHD* gene encoding an altered RhD protein associated with reduced D antigen expression on the red cell membrane. The transmembrane or cytoplasmic location of the amino acid changes in the altered D protein does not result in the loss of D epitopes; thus, the production of alloanti-D as in the partial D phenotype (see partial D) would not be expected.[31,32] Weak D expression is fairly common in Blacks, often occurring as part of a *Dce* haplotype. Genes for weak D expression are less common in Whites and may be seen as part of an unusual *DCe* or *DcE* haplotype.

Red cell samples with a quantitative weak D antigen either fail to react or react very weakly in direct agglutination tests with most anti-D reagents. However, the cells will react strongly by an IAT.

Red cells from some persons of the genotype *Dce/Ce* have weakened expression of D, a suppressive effect exerted by *RHC* in the *trans* position to *RHD* on the opposite chromosome. Similar depression of D can be seen with other *RHD* haplotypes accompanied by *RHCe* in *trans* position. Many of the weak D phenotypes due to position effect that were reported in the early literature appear as normal D.

Partial D

The concept that the D antigen consists of multiple constituents arose from observations that some people with D+ red cells produced alloanti-D that was nonreactive with their own cells. Most D+ persons who produce alloanti-D have red cells that react strongly when tested with anti-D. But some, especially those of the DVI phenotype, give weaker reactions than normal D+ red cells or react only in the AHG test. Red cells lacking components of the D antigen have been referred to in the past as "D mosaic" or "D variant." Current terminology more appropriately describes these red cells as "partial D."

Categorization of partial D phenotypes was performed by cross-testing red cells with alloanti-D produced by D+ persons. The four categories initially described by Wiener have been expanded considerably over the years. Tests of many monoclonal anti-D reagents with red cells of various D categories suggest that the D antigen comprises numerous epitopes. Partial D phenotypes can be defined in terms of their D epitopes. Tippett et al[33] established at least 10 epitopes but point out that the D antigen is not large enough to accommodate more than eight distinct epitopes and there must be considerable overlap between them. A current model describes 30 epitopes,[34] thus demonstrating the dynamic nature of the D-epitope model as it is revised due to variation in reagents and techniques. Dogma regarding the existence of many discrete epitopes is giving way to a model that is more topographic in nature, with the fit of antibody to antigen described as a "footprint."[35]

Molecular studies have elucidated the genetic mechanisms behind many of the partial D phenotypes and have shown that the phenotypes arise as the result of exchange between the *RHCE* gene and the *RHD* gene or from single-point mutations.[9,18]

Significance of Weak/Partial D in Blood Donors

AABB *Standards for Blood Banks and Transfusion Services*[36(p32)] requires donor blood specimens to be tested for weak expression of D and to be labeled as D+ if the test is positive. Transfusion of blood with weak expression of the D antigen to D– recipients is not recommended due to the fact that some weak or partial D red cells could elicit an immune response to D.[37] Weak forms of the D antigen, however, seem to be less immunogenic than normal D+ blood; transfusion of a total of 68 units of blood with weak D to 45 D– recipients failed to stimulate production of a single example of anti-D.[38]

Hemolytic transfusion reactions and HDFN due to weak D red cells were reported in the early literature, but it is probable that, with currently available reagents, the responsible cells would have been considered D+.[39]

Significance of Weak/Partial D in Recipients

The transfusion recipient whose red cells test as weak D is sometimes a topic of debate. Most of these patients can almost always receive D+ blood without risk of immunization, but if the weak D expression reflects the absence of one or more D epitopes, the possibility exists that transfusion of D+ blood could elicit the production of alloanti-D. This is especially true in persons of the DVI phenotype. The same possibility exists, however, for persons whose partial D red cells react strongly with anti-D reagents. AABB *Standards for Blood Banks and Transfusion Services*[36(p48)] only requires recipients' specimens to be tested with anti-D by direct agglutination. The test for weak D is not required. Currently available, licensed anti-D reagents are sufficiently potent that most patients with weak D are found to be D+. The few patients classified as D–, whose D+ status is only detectable by an IAT, can receive D– blood without problems. Some serologists consider this practice wasteful of D– blood and prefer to test potential recipients for weak D, then issue D+ blood when indicated.

If D+ blood is given to recipients of the weak D phenotype, it is important to safeguard against careless or incorrect interpretation of tests. D– recipients erroneously classified as D+, possibly due to a positive direct antiglobulin test (DAT) causing a false-positive test for weak D, run the risk of immunization to D if given D+ blood. Individuals whose weakly expressed D antigen is detectable only by an IAT will be classified as D– recipients if an IAT is not performed. However, if they donate blood subsequently, they will be classified as D+ at the time of blood donation. Personnel in blood centers and transfusion services should be prepared to answer questions from puzzled donors or their physicians. This can present special problems in autologous donations, when the D– patient's own blood is labeled as D+. In this case, confirmation of the patient's D status by the IAT resolves the apparent discrepancy between recipient and donor types.

Other Rh Antigens

Numbers up to 56 have been assigned to Rh red cell antigens (see Table 14-1); some of the numbers are now obsolete because antigens have been rescinded or reassigned. Of the currently included 49, most beyond D, C, c, C^w, E, and e and their corresponding antibodies are encountered much less frequently in routine blood transfusion therapy.

Cis Product Antigens

The membrane components that exhibit Rh activity have numerous possible antigenic subdivisions. Each gene or gene complex determines a series of interrelated surface structures, of which some portions are more likely than others to elicit an immune response. The polypeptides determined by the genes in the haplotype *DCe* express determinants ad-

ditional to those defined as D, C, and e. These include Ce (rh_i), a *cis* product that almost always accompanies C and e when they are encoded by the same haplotype. The Ce antigen is absent from red cells on which the C and e were encoded by different haplotypes, for example, in a person of the genotype *DCE/ce*. Similar *cis* product antigens exist for c and e determined by the same haplotype (the antigen called ce or f), for c and E (cE), and for C and E (CE).

Although antibodies directed at *cis* product antigens are encountered infrequently, it would not be correct to consider them rare. Such antibodies may be present but unnoticed in serum containing antibodies of the more obvious Rh specificities; only adsorption with red cells of selected phenotypes would demonstrate their presence. Anti-f (ce) may be present, for example, as a component of some anti-c and anti-e sera, but its presence would have little practical significance. The additional antibody should not confuse the reaction patterns given by anti-c and anti-e because all red cells that react with anti-f will express both c and e. A person with the genotype *DCe/DcE* who makes anti-f may receive c– or e– red cells because cells of either phenotype would also be f–.

Anti-Ce is frequently the true specificity of the apparent anti-C that a *DcE/DcE* person produces after immunization with C+ blood. This knowledge can be helpful in establishing an individual's Rh genotype. If anti-Ce is the predominant specificity in a reagent anti-C, the individual whose weak C antigen resulted from a *DCE* haplotype may be mistyped unless test methods and control red cells are chosen carefully.[40]

The G Antigen and Cross-Reactions

The G antigen results from serine at position 103 of the Rh polypeptides and is encoded by either *RHD* or *RHCE*.[41] As a result, the G antigen is almost invariably present on red cells possessing either C or D. Antibodies against G appear superficially to be anti-C+D, but the anti-G activity cannot be separated into anti-C and anti-D. The fact that G appears to exist as an entity common to C and D explains the fact that D– persons immunized by C–D+ red cells sometimes appear to have made anti-C as well as anti-D, and why D– persons who are exposed to C+D– red cells develop antibodies appearing to contain an anti-D component. Differentiation of anti-D, -C, and -G is not necessary in the pretransfusion setting because virtually all D–C– red cells are G–. In obstetric patients, however, some serologists believe it is essential to distinguish the antibody specificities to determine the need for Rh immune globulin prophylaxis.[42] Differential adsorption and elution studies to distinguish anti-D, -C, and -G are outlined by Issitt and Anstee.[43]

Rare red cells have been described that possess G but lack D and C. The r^G phenotype is found mostly in Blacks; generally, the G antigen is weakly expressed and is associated with the presence of the VS antigen. The r^G phenotype has been described in Whites but is not the same as r^G in Blacks. Red cells also exist that express partial D but lack G entirely, for example, persons of the DIIIb phenotype.[39]

Variant Antigens

Although red cells from most people give straightforward reactions with reagent anti-D, anti-C, anti-E, anti-c, and anti-e sera, some cells give atypical reactions and other seemingly normal red cells stimulate the production of antibodies that do not react with red cells of common Rh phenotypes. It has been convenient to consider C and c, and E and e as antithetical antigens at specific surface sites. Antigens that behave as if they have an antithetical relationship to C/c or E/e have been found, mainly in Whites. The most common is C^w, but the relationship is phenotypic only because C^w and C^x are antithetical to the high-incidence antigen, MAR. Variant forms of the e antigen have been identified, for example, hr^S or hr^B antigens (Rh19 and Rh31, respectively). Persons who are e+ and hr^S– and/or hr^B– are found more frequently in Black populations.[9] The absence of hr^B is associated in most cases with the presence of the VS antigen.[44]

Rh_{null} Syndrome and Other Deletion Types

Rh_{null}

The literature reports at least 43 persons in 14 families whose red cells appear to have no Rh antigens; others are known but have not been reported. The phenotype, described as Rh_{null}, is produced by at least two different genetic mechanisms. In the more common regulator type of Rh_{null}, mutations occur in the *RHAG* gene that result in the complete absence of the core Rh complex (Rh polypeptides and RhAG) that is necessary for the expression of Rh antigens.[18] Such persons transmit normal *RHD* and *RHCE* genes to their offspring.

The other form of Rh_{null}, the amorph type, has a normal *RHAG* gene; however, there is a mutation in each *RHCE* gene together with the common deletion of *RHD* (as in D– individuals).[18] The amorph type of Rh_{null} is considerably rarer than the regulator type. Parents and offspring of this type of Rh_{null} are obligate heterozygotes for the amorph.

majority of c– donor blood will be negative for the E antigen.

Rh Typing

Routine Rh typing for donors and patients involves only the D antigen. Tests for the other Rh antigens are performed when identifying unexpected Rh antibodies, obtaining compatible blood for a patient with an Rh antibody, investigating parentage or other family studies, selecting a panel of phenotyped cells for antibody identification, or evaluating whether a person is likely to be homozygous or heterozygous for *RHD*.

In finding compatible blood for a recipient with a comparatively weak Rh antibody, tests with potent blood typing reagents more reliably confirm the absence of antigen than mere demonstration of a compatible crossmatch. Determination of the patient's Rh phenotype may help confirm the antibody specificity and indicate which other Rh antibodies could also be present.

Routine Testing for D

Until recently, high-protein anti-D reagents of human polyclonal origin that were suitable for slide, tube, or microplate tests were used for most routine testing. More recently, monoclonal anti-D reagents have become widely available. Tests may employ red cells suspended in saline, serum, or plasma, but test conditions should be confirmed by reading the manufacturer's directions before use. Procedures for microplate tests are similar to those for tube tests, but very light suspensions of red cells are used.

Slide tests produce optimal results only when a high concentration of red cells and protein are combined at a temperature of 37 C. A disadvantage of the slide test is evaporation of the reaction mixture, which can cause the red cells to aggregate and be misinterpreted as agglutination. There are also greater biohazardous risks associated with increased potential for spillage of the specimen during manipulation. Representative procedures for tube, slide, and microplate tests are given in Methods 2.6, 2.7, and 2.8.

Techniques to demonstrate weak D are required by AABB *Standards* only for donor blood or for testing blood from neonates born to Rh-negative women to determine Rh immune globulin candidacy.[36(pp32,48)] When there is an indication to test for weak D, an IAT should be performed (Method 2.9). A reliable test for weak D expression cannot be performed on a slide.

High-Protein Reagents

Some anti-D reagents designated for use in slide, rapid tube, or microplate tests contain high concentrations of protein (20-24%) and other macromolecular additives. Such reagents are nearly always prepared from pools of human sera and give rapid reliable results when used in accordance with manufacturers' directions. High-protein levels and macromolecular additives may cause false-positive reactions. A false-positive result could cause a D– patient to receive D+ blood and become immunized. An appropriate control tested according to the manufacturer's directions must be performed.

Control for High-Protein Reagents

Manufacturers offer their individual diluent formulations for use as control reagents. The nature and concentration of additives differ significantly among reagents from different manufacturers and may not produce the same pattern of false-positive reactions. If red cells exhibit aggregation in the control test, the results of the anti-D test cannot be considered valid. In most cases the presence or absence of D can be determined with other reagents, as detailed later in this chapter.

Misleading Results with High-Protein Reagents

False Positives. The following circumstances can produce false-positive red cell typing results.

1. Cellular aggregation resulting from immunoglobulin coating of the patient's red cells or serum factors that induce rouleaux will give positive results in both the test and the control tubes. Serum factors can be eliminated by thoroughly washing the red cells (with warm saline if cold agglutinins are present or suspected) and retesting. If the cells in the control test remain unagglutinated and the anti-D test gives a positive result, the red cells are D+. If agglutination still occurs in the control tube, the most likely explanation is immunoglobulin coating of the red cells, which should then be tested with low-protein reagents.

2. Red cell aggregation, simulating agglutination, may occur if red cells and anti-D are incubated too long and excessive evaporation occurs during the slide test. It is important to follow the manufacturer's recommendations to interpret the test within the recommended period.

False Negatives. The following circumstances can produce false-negative red cell typing results.

1. Too heavy a red cell suspension in the tube test or too weak a suspension in the slide test may weaken agglutination.

2. Saline-suspended red cells must not be used for slide testing.

3. Red cells possessing weakly expressed D antigen may not react well within the 2-minute limit of the slide test or upon immediate centrifugation in the tube test.

Low-Protein Reagents

The low-protein Rh reagents in current use are formulated predominantly with monoclonal antibodies. Immunoglobulin-coated red cells can usually be successfully typed with low-protein Rh reagents that contain saline-agglutinating antibodies.

Monoclonal Source Anti-D

Monoclonal anti-D reagents are made predominantly from human IgM antibodies, which require no potentiators and agglutinate most D+ red cells from adults and infants in a saline system. Monoclonal anti-D reagents usually promote reactions stronger than those with polyclonal IgG reagents, but they may fail to agglutinate red cells of some partial D categories. Adding small amounts of IgG anti-D to the monoclonal IgM antibodies provides a reagent that will react with weak or partial D red cells in antiglobulin tests. Certain rare D+ red cells (DHAR, DVa, DVc, Rh43+) may react at immediate spin with some of these blended reagents, but, with other reagents, these same cells may be nonreactive in an IAT or reactive only in an IAT.

Licensed monoclonal/polyclonal or monoclonal/monoclonal blends can be used by all routine typing methods and are as satisfactory as high-protein reagents in an IAT for weak D. False-negative findings can result, however, if tests using monoclonal reagents are incubated in excess of a manufacturer's product directions. These reagents, prepared in a low-protein medium, can be used to test red cells with a positive

DAT, provided those tests are not subjected to an IAT.

Control for Low-Protein Reagents

Most monoclonal blended reagents have a total protein concentration approximating that of human serum. False-positive reactions due to spontaneous aggregation of immunoglobulin-coated red cells occur no more often with this kind of reagent than with other saline-reactive reagents. False-positive reactions may occur in any saline-reactive test system if the serum contains cold autoagglutinins or a protein imbalance causing rouleaux and the red cells are tested unwashed. It is seldom necessary to perform a separate control test. Absence of spontaneous aggregation can usually be demonstrated by observing absence of agglutination by anti-A and/or anti-B in the cell tests for ABO. For red cell specimens that show agglutination in all tubes (ie, give the reactions of group AB, D+), a control should be performed as described by the reagent manufacturer; this is not required when donors' cells are tested. In most cases, a suitable control is a suspension of the patient's red cells with autologous serum or with 6% to 8% bovine albumin, although exceptions have been noted.[46] If the test is one of several performed concurrently and in a similar manner, any negative result serves as an adequate control. For example, a separate control tube would be required only for a red cell specimen that gives positive reactions with all the Rh reagents (ie, is typed as D+C+E+c+e+).

Testing for D in Hemolytic Disease of the Fetus and Newborn

Because red cells from an infant suffering from HDFN are coated with immunoglobulin, a low protein reagent is usually necessary for Rh testing. Occasionally, the infant's red cells may be so heavily coated with antibody that all antigen sites are occupied, leaving none available to react with a low protein antibody of appropriate specificity. This "blocking" phenomenon should be suspected if the infant's cells have a strongly positive DAT and are not agglutinated by a low protein reagent of the same specificity as the maternal antibody.

Anti-D is the specificity responsible for nearly all cases of blocking by maternal antibody. It is usually possible to obtain correct typing results with a low protein anti-D after 45 C elution of the maternal antibody from the cord blood red cells. (See Method 2.12.) Elution liberates enough antigen sites to permit red cell typing, but it must be performed cautiously because overexposure to heat may denature or destroy Rh antigens.

Tests for Antigens Other than D

Reagents are readily available to test for the other principal Rh antigens: C, E, c, and e. These are formulated as either low-protein (usually monoclonal or monoclonal/polyclonal blends) or high-protein reagents. High-protein reagents of any specificity have the same problems with false-positive results as high-protein anti-D and require a comparable control test performed concurrently and under the same conditions. Observation of a negative result in the control test for anti-D may not properly control the tests for other Rh antigens because results with anti-D are usually obtained after immediate centrifugation; tests for the other Rh antigens are generally incubated at 37 C before centrifugation.

Rh reagents may give weak or negative reactions with red cells possessing variant antigens. This is especially likely to happen if anti-e is used to test the red cells from Blacks, among whom variants of e are relatively common.[9] It is impossible to obtain anti-e reagents that react strongly and consistently with the various qualitative and quantitative variants of e. Variable reactivity with anti-C reagents may occur if the *DCE* or *CE* haplotypes are responsible for the expression of C on red cells. Variant E and c antigens have been reported but are considerably less common.

Whatever reagents are used, the manufacturer's directions must be carefully followed. The IAT must not be used unless the manufacturer's instructions state explicitly that the reagent is suitable for this use. The pools of human source sera (nonmonoclonal) used to prepare reagents for the other Rh antigens may contain antiglobulin-reactive, "contaminating" specificities. Positive and negative controls should be tested; red cells selected for the positive control should have a single dose of the antigen or be known to show weak reactivity with the reagent.

Additional Considerations in Rh Testing

The following limitations are common to all Rh typing procedures, including those performed with high-protein reagents.

False-Positive Reactions

The following circumstances can produce false-positive red cell typing results.
1. The wrong reagent was inadvertently used.
2. An unsuspected antibody of another specificity was present in the human source reagent. Antibodies for antigens having an incidence of less than 1% in the population may occasionally be present and cause false-positive reactions, even when the manufacturer's directions are followed. For crucial determinations, many workers routinely perform replicate tests using reagents from different sources. Replicate testing is not an absolute safeguard, however, because reagents from different manufacturers may not be derived from different sources.
3. Polyagglutinable red cells may be agglutinated by any reagent containing human serum. Although antibodies that agglutinate these surface-altered red cells are present in most adult human sera, polyagglutinins in reagents very rarely cause problems. Aging, dilution, and various steps in the manufacturing process tend to eliminate these predominantly IgM antibodies.
4. Autoagglutinins and abnormal proteins in the patient's serum may cause false-positive reactions when unwashed red cells are tested.
5. Reagent vials may become contaminated with bacteria, with foreign substances, or with reagent from another vial. This can be prevented by the use of careful technique and the periodic inspection of the vials' contents. However, bacterial contamination may not cause recognizable turbidity because the refractive index of bacteria is similar to that of high-protein reagents.

False-Negative Reactions

The following circumstances can produce false-negative red cell typing results.
1. The wrong reagent was inadvertently used.
2. The reagent was not added to the tube. It is good practice to add serum to all the tubes before adding the red cells and any enhancement medium.
3. A specific reagent failed to react with a variant form of the antigen.
4. A reagent that contains antibody directed predominantly at a *cis*-prod-

uct Rh antigen failed to give a reliably detectable reaction with red cells carrying the individual antigens as separate gene products. This occurs most often with anti-C sera.

5. The manufacturer's directions were not followed.

6. The red cell button was shaken so roughly during resuspension that small agglutinates were dispersed.

7. Contamination, improper storage, or outdating cause antibody activity to deteriorate. Chemically modified IgG antibody appears to be particularly susceptible to destruction by proteolytic enzymes produced by certain bacteria.

References

1. Race RR. The Rh genotypes and Fisher's theory. Blood 1948; special issue 2:27-42.

2. Levine P, Stetson RE. An unusual case of intragroup agglutination. JAMA 1939;113: 126-7.

3. Landsteiner K, Wiener AS. An agglutinable factor in human blood recognized by immune sera for rhesus blood. Proc Soc Exp Biol NY 1940;43:223.

4. Levine P, Katzin EM. Isoimmunization in pregnancy and the variety of isoagglutinins observed. Proc Soc Exp Biol NY 1940;43: 343-6.

5. Wiener AS, Peters HR. Hemolytic reactions following transfusions of blood of the homologous group, with three cases in which the same agglutinogen was responsible. Ann Intern Prn Med 1940;13:2306-22.

6. Frohn C, Dümbgen L, Brand J-M, et al. Probability of anti-D development in D– patients receiving D+ RBCs. Transfusion 2003;43: 893-8.

7. Mollison PL, Engelfriet CP, Contreras M. Blood transfusion in clinical medicine. 10th ed. Oxford: Blackwell Scientific Publishers, 1997.

8. Daniels GL, Fletcher A, Garratty G, et al. Blood group terminology 2004: From the International Society of Blood Transfusion committee on terminology for red cell surface antigens. Vox Sang 2004;87:304-16.

9. Reid ME, Lomas-Francis C. The blood group antigen factsbook. 2nd ed. London: Academic Press, 2004.

10. Gemke RJBJ, Kanhai HHH, Overbeeke MAM, et al. ABO and Rhesus phenotyping of fetal erythrocytes in the first trimester of pregnancy. Br J Haematol 1986;64:689-97.

11. Dunstan RA, Simpson MB, Rosse WF. Erythrocyte antigens on human platelets. Absence of Rh, Duffy, Kell, Kidd, and Lutheran antigens. Transfusion 1984;24:243-6.

12. Dunstan RA. Status of major red cell blood group antigens on neutrophils, lymphocytes and monocytes. Br J Haematol 1986;62:301-9.

13. Wiener AS. Genetic theory of the Rh blood types. Proc Soc Exp Biol Med 1943;54:316-19.

14. Fisher RA, Race RR. Rh gene frequencies in Britain. Nature 1946;157:48-9.

15. Tippett P. A speculative model for the Rh blood groups. Ann Hum Genet 1986;50:241-7.

16. Colin Y, Chérif-Zahar B, Le Van Kim C, et al. Genetic basis of RhD-positive and RhD-negative blood group polymorphisms as determined by southern analysis. Blood 1991;78: 2747-52.

17. Arce MA, Thomson ES, Wagner S, et al. Molecular cloning of RhD cDNA derived from a gene present in RhD-positive, but not RhD-negative individuals. Blood 1993;82:651-5.

18. Huang CH, Liu PZ, Cheng JG. Molecular biology and genetics of the Rh blood group system. Semin Hematol 2000;37:150-65.

19. Singleton BK, Green CA, Avent ND, et al. The presence of an *RHD* pseudogene containing a 37 base pair duplication and a nonsense mutation in Africans with the Rh D-negative blood group phenotype. Blood 2000;95:12-8.

20. Mouro I, Colin Y, Chérif-Zahar B, et al. Molecular genetic basis of the human Rhesus blood group system. Nat Genet 1993;5:62-5.

21. Smythe JS, Avent ND, Judson PA, et al. Expression of *RHD* and *RHCE* gene products using retroviral transduction of K562 cells establishes the molecular basis of Rh blood group antigens. Blood 1996;87:2968-73.

22. Ridgwell K, Spurr NK, Laguda B, et al. Isolation of cDNA clones for a 50 kDa glycoprotein of the human erythrocyte membrane associated with Rh (rhesus) blood-group antigen expression. Biochem J 1992;287:223-8.

23. Tippett P. Regulator genes affecting red cell antigens. Transfus Med Rev 1990;4:56-68.

24. Hemker MB, Goedel C, van Zwieten R, et al. The Rh complex exports ammonium from human red blood cells. Br J Haematol 2003; 122:333-40.

25. Westhoff CM, Seigel D, Burd C, Foskett JK. Mechanism of genetic complementation of ammonium transport in yeast by human

erythrocyte Rh-associated glycoprotein. J Biol Chem 2003;279:17443-8.

26. Rosenfield RE, Allen FH Jr, Swisher SN, Kochwa S. A review of Rh serology and presentation of a new terminology. Transfusion 1962;2:287-312.

27. Wagner FF, Flegel WA. *RHD* gene deletion occurred in the Rhesus box. Blood 2000;95:3662-8.

28. Chiu RW, Murphy MF, Fidler C, et al. Determination of RhD zygosity: Comparison of a double amplification refractory mutation system approach and a multiplex real-time quantitative PCR approach. Clin Chem 2003;47:667-72.

29. Lawler SD, Race RR. Quantitative aspects of Rh antigens. Proceedings of the International Society of Hematology 1950:168-70.

30. Lo YMD, Hjelm NM, Fidler C, et al. Prenatal diagnosis of fetal RhD status by molecular analysis of maternal plasma. N Engl J Med 1998;339:1734-8.

31. Wagner F, Gassner C, Müller T, et al. Molecular basis of weak D phenotypes. Blood 1999;93:385-93.

32. Wagner FF, Frohmajer A, Ladewig B, et al. Weak D alleles express distinct phenotypes. Blood 2000;95:2699-708.

33. Tippett P, Lomas-Francis C, Wallace M. The Rh antigen D: Partial D antigens and associated low incidence antigens. Vox Sang 1996;70:123-31.

34. Scott ML. Section 1A: Rh serology. Coordinator's report. 4th International Workshop on Monoclonal Antibodies Against Human Red Cell Surface Antigens, Paris. Transfus Clin Biol 2002;9:23-9.

35. Chang TY, Siegel DL. Genetic and immunological properties of phage-displayed human anti-Rh(D) antibodies: Implications for Rh(D) epitope topology. Blood 1998;91:3066-78.

36. Silva MA, ed. Standards for blood banks and transfusion services. 23rd ed. Bethesda, MD: AABB, 2005.

37. Flegel WA, Khull SR, Wagner FF. Primary anti-D immunization by weak D type 2 RBCs. Transfusion 2000;40:428-33.

38. Schmidt PJ, Morrison EG, Shohl J. The antigenicity of the Rh_o D^u blood factor. Blood 1962;20:196-202.

39. Daniels G. Human blood groups. 2nd ed. Oxford: Blackwell Scientific Publications, 2002.

40. Van Loghem JJ. Production of Rh agglutinins anti-C and anti-E by artificial immunization of volunteer donors. Br Med J 1947;ii:958-9.

41. Faas BHW, Beckers EAM, Simsek S, et al. Involvement of Ser103 of the Rh polypeptides in G epitope formation. Transfusion 1996;36:506-11.

42. Shirey RS, Mirabella DC, Lumadue JA. Differentiation of anti-D, -C, and -G: Clinical relevance in alloimmunized pregnancies. Transfusion 1997;37:493-6.

43. Issitt PD, Anstee DJ. Applied blood group serology. 4th ed. Durham, NC: Montgomery Scientific Press, 1998:350-3.

44. Reid ME, Storry JR, Issitt PD, et al. Rh haplotypes that make e but not hr^B usually make VS. Vox Sang 1997;72:41-4.

45. Shirey RS, Edwards RE, Ness PM. The risk of alloimmunization to c (Rh4) in R_1R_1 patients who present with anti-E. Transfusion 1994;34:756-8.

46. Rodberg K, Tsuneta R, Garratty G. Discrepant Rh phenotyping results when testing IgG-sensitized rbcs with monoclonal Rh reagents (abstract). Transfusion 1995;35(Suppl):67S.

Suggested Reading

Agre P, Cartron JP. Molecular biology of the Rh antigens. Blood 1991;78:551-3.

Avent ND, Reid ME. The Rh blood group system: A review. Blood 2000;95:375-87.

Cartron JP. Defining the Rh blood group antigens. Blood Rev 1994;8:199-212.

Daniels G. Human blood groups. 2nd ed. Oxford: Blackwell Scientific Publications, 2002.

Issitt PD. An invited review: The Rh antigen e, its variants, and some closely related serological observations. Immunohematology 1991;7:29-36.

Issitt PD. The Rh blood group. In: Garratty G, ed. Immunology of transfusion medicine. New York: Marcel Dekker, 1994:111-47.

Issitt PD. The Rh blood group system 1988: Eight new antigens in nine years and some observations on the biochemistry and genetics of the system. Transfus Med Rev 1989;3:1-12.

Issitt PD, Anstee DJ. Applied blood group serology. 4th ed. Durham, NC: Montgomery Scientific Press, 1998.

Lomas-Francis C, Reid ME. The Rh blood group system: The first 60 years of discovery. Immunohematology 2000;16:7-17.

Race RR, Sanger R. Blood groups in man. 6th ed. Oxford: Blackwell Scientific Publications, 1968.

Reid ME, Ellisor SS, Frank BA. Another potential source of error in Rh-Hr typing. Transfusion 1975;15:485-8.

Reid ME, Lomas-Francis C. The blood group antigen factsbook. 2nd ed. London: Academic Press, 2004.

Sonneborn H-H, Voak D, eds. A review of 50 years of the Rh blood group system. Biotest Bulletin 1997; 5(4):389-528.

Vengelen-Tyler V, Pierce S, eds. Blood group systems: Rh. Arlington, VA: American Association of Blood Banks, 1987.

White WD, Issitt CH, McGuire D. Evaluation of the use of albumin controls in Rh typing. Transfusion 1974;14:67-71.

Chapter 15

Other Blood Groups

THERE ARE MANY antigens on red cells in addition to the ones mentioned in previous chapters. These antigens are grouped into blood group systems, collections, and a series of independent antigens, composed mostly of antigens of low or high incidence. A blood group system is a group of one or more antigens governed by a single gene locus or by a complex of two or more closely linked homologous genes that have been shown to be phenotypically and genetically related to each other and genetically distinct from other blood group systems. A collection is a group of antigens shown to have a phenotypic, biochemical, or genetic relationship to each other; however, there is insufficient information or data that shows them to be a distinct blood group system genetically independent from other blood group systems. Table 10-1 lists the blood group systems, as defined by the International Society of Blood Transfusion

(ISBT) working party on blood group terminology, and their gene location.[1-3] Additional information on ISBT terminology for all the antigens mentioned in this chapter can be found in Appendix 6. Table 15-1 shows the serologic behavior and characteristics of the major blood group antibodies derived from human sources. The major systems will be discussed first in the chapter, followed by the other blood group systems, collections, and independent high-incidence and low-incidence antigens. In each grouping, the order will reflect the ISBT number order.

Distribution of Antigens

Antigens present in almost all persons are known as high-incidence antigens, whereas antigens found in very few persons are termed very low-incidence antigens. The frequency of these high- or low-incidence antigens may also differ by ethnic group.

Table 15-1. Serologic Behavior of the Principal Antibodies of Different Blood Group Systems

Antibody	In-Vitro Hemolysis	Saline		Albumin		Papain/Ficin		Associated with	
		4 C	22 C	37 C	AHG	37 C	AHG	HDFN	HTR
Anti-M	0	Most	Some	Few	Few	0	0	Few	Few
Anti-N	0	Most	Few	Occ.	Occ.	0	0	Rare	No
Anti-S	0	Few	Some	Some	Most	See text		Yes	Yes
Anti-s	0	No	Few	Few	Most	See text		Yes	Yes
Anti-U	0	No	Occ.	Some	Most	Most	Most	Yes	Yes
Anti-Lu^a	0	Some	Most	Few	Few	Few	Few	No	No
Anti-Lu^b	0	Few	Few	Few	Most	Few	Few	Mild	Yes
Anti-K	0		Few	Some	Most	Some	Most	Yes	Yes
Anti-k	0		Few	Few	Most	Some	Most	Yes	Yes
Anti-Kp^a	0		Some	Some	Most	Some	Most	Yes	Yes
Anti-Kp^b	0		Few	Few	Most	Some	Most	Yes	Yes
Anti-Js^a	0		Few	Few	Most	Few	Most	Yes	Yes
Anti-Js^b	0		0	0	Most	Few	Most	Yes	Yes
Anti-Le^a	Some	Most	Most	Some	Some	Some	Most	No	Rare
Anti-Le^b	Some	Most	Most	Some	Some	Some	Most	No	No
Anti-Fy^a	0		Rare	Rare	Most	0	0	Yes	Yes
Anti-Fy^b	0		Rare	Rare	Most	0	0	Mild	Yes
Anti-Jk^a	Some		Few	Few	Most	Some	Most	Mild	Yes
Anti-Jk^b	Some		Few	Few	Most	Some	Most	Mild	Yes
Anti-Xg^a	0		Few	Few	Most	0	0	No report	
Anti-Di^a	0		Some	Some	Most	Some	Some	Yes	Yes
Anti-Di^b	0				Most	Some	Some	Yes	Yes
Anti-Yt^a	0		0	0	Most	0	Some	No	Yes
Anti-Yt^b	0				All			No report	
Anti-Do^a	0		0	0	Some	Some	Most	No	Yes
Anti-Do^b	0				All	All	All	No	Yes
Anti-Co^a	0		0	0	Some	Some	Most	Yes	Yes
Anti-Co^b	0		0	0	Some	Some	Most	Mild	Yes
Anti-Sc1	0				All			No	No
Anti-Sc2	0		Some	Some	Most	Most	Most	No	No

AHG = Antihuman globulin; HDFN = Hemolytic disease of the fetus and newborn; HTR = Hemolytic transfusion reaction; Occ. = Occasionally. The reactivity shown in the table is based on the tube methods in common use. If tests are carried out by more sensitive test procedures (such as in capillary tubes, in microtiter plates, or by the albumin layering method), direct agglutination (before the antiglobulin phase) may be observed more often with some antibodies. Blank spaces indicate a lack of sufficient data for generalization about antibody behavior.

Antigens that occur as codominant traits, such as Jk^a and Jk^b, may have a variable incidence and may differ in ethnic groups. For an illustration, the Duffy glycoprotein is known to be a receptor for the parasite *Plasmodium vivax*, one of the causative agents of malaria. In West Africa, where malaria is endemic, the Fy(a–b–) red cell phenotype, very rare in Whites, occurs with an incidence of greater than 80%.

Each of the known antigens described in this chapter was initially identified through the detection of its specific antibody in a serum. Tables listing phenotype frequencies among Whites and Blacks in the US population are given throughout this chapter. Frequencies among other groups in the population are not given because data are scanty and wide differences between groups of diverse Asian, South American, or Native American origins make generalizations about phenotypes inappropriate.

MNS System

M, N, S, s, and U Antigens

The MNS system is a complex system of over 40 antigens carried on two glycophorin molecules or hybrid molecules of the two proteins. The M, N, S, s, and U antigens are the most important antigens of the MNS system with regard to transfusion medicine. They have also been important to our understanding of biochemistry and genetics. The M and N antigens are located on glycophorin A (GPA). The S, s, and U antigens are located on glycophorin B (GPB). Table 15-2 shows the frequencies of the common phenotypes of the MNS system. There is considerable linkage disequilibrium between M,N and S,s due to the gene location on the chromosome. For example, the gene complex producing N with s is much more common than that producing N with S. The MNSs genes *GYPA* and *GYPB* are in very close proximity on chromosome 4.[4] See the section below on Genes Encoding Glycophorins and Chapters 9 and 10 for more information about gene interactions.

Red cells that lack S and s may be negative for a high-incidence antigen called U; persons who lack U may make anti-U when exposed to U+ red cells.

Low-Incidence Antigens of the MNS System

The MNS system includes several low-incidence antigens. Recent biochemical data

Table 15-2. Phenotypes and Frequencies in the MNS System

| Reactions with Anti- | | | | | | Phenotype Frequency (%) | |
M	N	S	s	U	Phenotype	Whites	Blacks
+	0				M+N−	28	26
+	+				M+N+	50	44
0	+				M−N+	22	30
		+	0	+	S+s−U+	11	3
		+	+	+	S+s+U+	44	28
		0	+	+	S−s+U+	45	69
		0	0	0	S−s−U−	0	Less than 1
		0	0	(+)	S−s−U+w	0	Rare*

*May not be detected by some antisera and are listed as U−.

attribute the reactivity of various low-incidence determinants to one or more amino acid substitutions, variation in the extent or type of glycosylation, or the existence of a hybrid sialoglycoprotein (SGP).

Genes Encoding Glycophorins

The genes encoding the MNS system antigens are located on chromosome 4 at 4q28-q31. The gene that encodes GPA is called *GYPA* and the gene that encodes GPB is *GYPB*. The similarities in amino acid sequences of GPA and GPB suggest that both genes derive from a common ancestral gene. *GYPA* and *GYPB* consist of seven and five exons, respectively. The genes share >95% identity. Although the genes are highly homologous, *GYPB* results in a shorter protein because a point mutation at the 5′ splicing site of the third intron prevents transcription of exon 3, called pseudo exon 3. Following the homologous sequences, *GYPA* and *GYPB* differ significantly in the 3′ end sequences.

Hybrid Molecules

Pronounced SGP modifications occur in hybrid molecules that may arise from unequal crossing over or gene conversion between *GYPA* and *GYPB*. Hybrid SGPs may carry the amino-terminal portion of GPA and the carboxy-terminal portion of GPB, or vice versa. Other hybrids appear as a GPB molecule with a GPA insert or a GPA molecule with a GPB insert. The low-incidence antigens Hil (MNS20), St^a (MNS15), Dantu (MNS25), and Mur (MNS10), among others, are associated with hybrid SGPs. Some variants are found in specific ethnic groups. For example, the Dantu antigen occurs predominantly in Blacks, although the antigen is of low incidence.

Many of the MNS low-incidence antigens were categorized into a subsystem called the Miltenberger system, based on reactivity with selected sera. As more antigens have been identified and knowledge of the genetic events that give rise to these novel antigens has increased, it is clear that the Miltenberger subsystem is outdated. These antigens, such as Mi^a, Vw, Hil, etc, should be considered glycophorin variants.

Biochemistry of the MNS System

Antigens of the MNS system are carried on GPA and GPB, which are single-pass transmembrane glycoproteins. The carboxy (C) terminal of each glycophorin extends into the cytoplasm of the red cell, and a hydrophobic segment is embedded within the lipid bilayer. An amino (N) terminal segment extends into the extracellular environment. The molecules are sensitive to cleavage at varying positions by certain proteases (see Fig 15-1).

There are approximately 1,000,000 copies of GPA per red cell. M and N blood group antigen activity resides on the extracellular segment, a sequence of 72 amino acids with carbohydrate side chains attached within the first 50 residues of the amino terminal. When GPA carries M antigen activity (GPA^M), the first amino acid residue is serine and the fifth is glycine. When it carries N antigen activity (GPA^N), leucine and glutamic acid replace serine and glycine at positions one and five, respectively (see Fig 15-1).

Red cells that lack most or all of GPA are described as En(a–). These rare En(a–) individuals may produce antibodies (collectively called anti-En^a) that react with various portions of the extracellular part of the glycoprotein. Some En(a–) persons may produce an antibody against an antigen called Wr^b that is part of the Diego blood group system. Wr^b arises from an interaction between GPA and the anion exchange molecule, AE-1 (also known as band 3).[5]

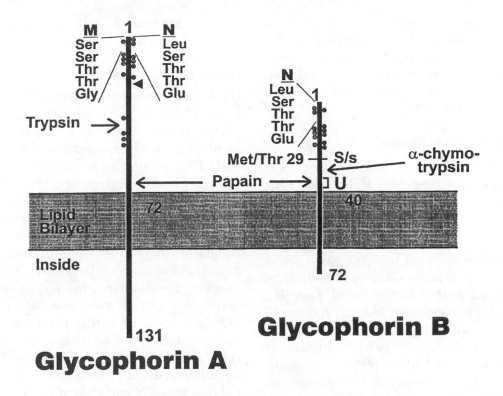

Figure 15-1. Schematic diagram of glycophorin A and glycophorin B. The amino acid sequences that determine M, N, S, and s are given. ● indicates an *O*-linked oligosaccharide side chain, ◀ indicates an *N*-linked polysaccharide side chain. Approximate locations of protease cleavage sites are indicated. (Courtesy New York Blood Center.)

GPB is a smaller protein than GPA, and there are fewer (approximately 200,000) copies per red cell. GPB carries S, s, and U antigens. GPB that expresses S activity has methionine at position 29; GPB with s activity has threonine at that position (see Fig 15-1). The N-terminal 26 amino acids of GPB are identical to the sequence of GPA^N, which accounts for the presence of an N antigen (known as 'N') on all red cells of normal MNS types. Red cells that lack GPB altogether lack not only S, s, and U activity but also 'N'. Immunized individuals of the rare M+N–S–s–U– phenotype can produce a potent anti-N (anti-U/GPB) that reacts with all red cells of normal MNS types, whether N-positive or N-negative, and

should be considered clinically significant. Some S–s– red cells also have a variant GPB.

The Effect of Proteolytic Enzymes on MNS Antigens

Proteolytic enzymes, such as ficin or papain, cleave red cell membrane SGPs at well-defined sites. Reactivity with anti-M and anti-N is abolished by commonly used enzyme techniques. The effect of different enzymes on the expression of MNS system antigens reflects the point at which the particular enzyme cleaves the antigen-bearing SGP and the position of the antigen relative to the cleavage site (see Fig 15-1). Sensitivity of the antigens to proteases may help in the identification of antibodies to M and N antigens, but the effects of proteases on tests for the S and s antigens are more variable. In addition, the S antigen is sensitive to trace amounts of chlorine bleach.[6]

MNS System Antibodies

The antibodies most commonly encountered are directed at the M, N, S, and s antigens.

Anti-M

Anti-M is detected frequently as a saline agglutinin if testing is done at room temperature. Anti-M is often found in the sera of persons who have had no exposure to human red cells. Although M antibodies are generally thought to be predominantly IgM, many examples that are partly or wholly IgG are frequently found. However, these antibodies are rarely clinically significant. Some examples of anti-M cause stronger agglutination if the pH of the test system is reduced to 6.5 and when testing red cell samples possessing a double-dose expression of the M antigen. Examples that react at 37 C or at the antiglobulin phase of testing should be considered potentially significant. Compatibility testing performed by a strictly prewarmed method (see Method 3.3) should eliminate the reactivity of most examples of anti-M. In a few exceptional cases, anti-M detectable at the antiglobulin phase has caused hemolytic disease of the fetus and newborn (HDFN) or hemolysis of transfused cells.

Anti-N

Anti-N is comparatively rare. Examples are usually IgM and typically appear as weakly reactive cold agglutinins. Some powerful and potentially significant IgG examples have been observed in a few persons of the rare phenotypes M+N–S–s–U– and M+N–S–s–U+^{w}

because these people lack or possess an altered form of GPB.

Antibodies to S, s, and U

Unlike anti-M and anti-N, antibodies to S, s, and U usually occur following red cell immunization. All are capable of causing hemolytic transfusion reactions (HTRs) and HDFN. Although a few saline-reactive examples have been reported, antibodies to S, s, and U are usually detected in the antiglobulin phase of testing. Most, but not all, investigators[7] have found that papain or ficin destroys the reactivity of S+ red cells with anti-S. Depending on the enzyme solution used, the reactivity of anti-s with s+ cells can be variable.[8(p477)] Most examples of anti-U react equally with untreated and enzyme-treated red cells, but there have been examples of broadly reactive anti-U, which detect an enzyme-sensitive determinant.

Anti-U is rare but should be considered when serum from a previously transfused or pregnant Black person contains antibody to a high-incidence antigen.

Antibodies to Low-Incidence Antigens

There are many examples of antibodies to low-incidence antigens, such as anti-M^g or anti-V^w, in the MNS blood group system. Many of these antibodies occur as a saline agglutinin in sera from persons who have no known exposure to human red cells. The rarity of these antigens makes it unlikely that the antibodies will be detected if present.

Kell System

Kell System Antigens

Kell system antigens are expressed on the red cell membrane in low density and are weakened or destroyed by treatment with reducing agents and with acid. The antigens are carried on one protein and encoded by a single gene. For an in-depth review, see Lee, Russo, and Redman.[9]

K and k

The K antigen was first identified in 1946 because of an antibody that caused HDFN. The allele responsible for the K antigen is present in 9% of Whites and approximately 2% of Blacks. The existence of the expected allele for k was confirmed when an antithetical relationship was established between K and the antigen detected by anti-k. Anti-k reacts with the red cells of over 99% of all individuals.

Other Kell Blood Group Antigens

Other antithetical antigens of the Kell system include Kp^a, Kp^b, and Kp^c; Js^a and Js^b; K11 and K17; and K14 and K24. Not all theoretically possible genotype combinations have been recognized in the Kell system. For example, Kp^a and Js^a have never been found to be produced by the

same chromosome. Kp^a is an antigen found predominantly in Whites, and Js^a is found predominantly in Blacks. The haplotype producing K and Kp^a has also not been found. Table 15-3 shows some phenotypes of the Kell system. The table also includes K_o, a null phenotype in which the red cells lack all of the antigens of the Kell system. Several high-incidence antigens were assigned to the Kell system because the identifying antibodies were found to be nonreactive with K_o red cells. For simplicity, various Kell antigens of high and low incidence have not been included in the table.

Phenotypes with Depressed Kell Antigens

K_{mod} is an umbrella term used to describe phenotypes characterized by weak expression of Kell system antigens. Adsorption/elution tests are often necessary for their detection. The K_{mod} phenotype is thought to arise through several different point mutations of the *KEL* gene. Red cells of persons with some Gerbich negative

Table 15-3. Some Phenotypes and Frequencies in the Kell System

Reactions with Anti-							Frequency (%)	
K	k	Kp^a	Kp^b	Js^a	Js^b	Phenotype	Whites	Blacks
+	0					K+k−	0.2	Rare
+	+					K+k+	8.8	2
0	+					K−k+	91.0	98
		+	0			Kp(a+b−)	Rare	0
		+	+			Kp(a+b+)	2.3	Rare
		0	+			Kp(a−b+)	97.7	100
				+	0	Js(a+b−)	0.0	1
				+	+	Js(a+b+)	Rare	19
				0	+	Js(a−b+)	100.0	80
0	0	0	0	0	0	K_o	Exceedingly rare	

phenotypes also exhibit depressed Kell phenotypes (see the Gerbich System). Persons of the Ge:–2,–3 and Ge:–2,–3,–4 (Leach) phenotypes have depression of at least some Kell system antigens.

The presence of the Kp^a allele weakens the expression of other Kell antigens when in *cis* position. For example, the k antigen of Kp(a+) red cells reacts more weakly than expected and, when tested with weaker examples of anti-k, may be interpreted as k–.

Biochemistry of the Kell System

The Kell system antigens are carried on a 93-kD single-pass red cell membrane protein. Kell system antigens are easily inactivated by treating red cells with sulfhydryl reagents such as 2-mercaptoethanol (2-ME), dithiothreitol (DTT), or 2-aminoethylisothiouronium bromide (AET). Such treatment is useful in preparing red cells that artificially lack Kell system antigens to aid in the identification of Kell-related antibodies. Treatment with sulfhydryl reagents may impair the reactivity of other antigens (LW^a, Do^a, Do^b, Yt^a, and others). Thus, although treatment with these reagents may be used in antibody problem solving, specificity must be proven by other means. As expected, Kell system antigens are also destroyed by ZZAP, a mixture of DTT and enzyme (see Methods 3.10, 4.6, and 4.9). This susceptibility to sulfhydryl reagents suggests that disulfide bonds are essential to maintain activity of the Kell system antigens. This hypothesis has been supported by the biochemical characterization of Kell proteins deduced from cloned DNA[10]; they exhibit a number of cysteine residues in the extracellular region. Cysteine readily forms disulfide bonds, which contribute to the folding of a protein. Antigens that reflect protein conformation will be susceptible to any agent that interferes with its tertiary structure. Kell antigens are also destroyed by treatment with EDTA-glycine acid.

The function of the Kell protein is unknown, but it has structural similarities to a family of zinc-binding neutral endopeptidases. It has most similarity with the common acute lymphoblastic leukemia antigen (CALLA or CD10), a neutral endopeptidase on leukocytes.[8(pp647-648)]

Kx Antigen, the McLeod Phenotype, and Their Relationship to the Kell System

Although the Kell system locus is on the long arm of chromosome 7 and the Kx locus (*XK*) is on the Xp21 region of the X chromosome, evidence suggests that the Kell and Kx proteins form a covalently linked complex on normal red cells.[8] On red cells that carry normal expressions of Kell antigens, Kx appears to be poorly expressed. It is believed that this finding represents steric interference by the Kell glycoprotein in the approach of anti-Kx to its antigen. Red cells of K$_o$ individuals react strongly with anti-Kx. Similarly, the removal or denaturation of Kell glycoproteins with AET or DTT renders the cells strongly reactive with anti-Kx.

It is believed that the presence of the glycoprotein on which Kx is carried is essential for the antigens of the Kell system to attach to or be expressed normally on red cells. Therefore, a lack of Kx is associated with poor expression of Kell system antigens.

Red cells that lack Kx exhibit not only markedly depressed expression of Kell system antigens but also shortened survival, reduced deformability, decreased permeability to water, and acanthocytic morphology. This combination or group of red cell abnormalities is called the McLeod phenotype, after the first person in whom these observations were made. Persons with McLeod red cells also have a poorly defined abnormality of the neuromuscular system, characterized by persistently elevated serum levels of the enzyme creatine phosphokinase and, in older people, disordered muscular function. The McLeod phenotype arises through deletion and mutations of the *XK* locus of chromosome X.

In a few instances, the McLeod phenotype has been found in patients with chronic granulomatous disease (CGD), in which granulocytes exhibit normal phagocytosis of microorganisms but an inability to kill ingested pathogens. The McLeod phenotype associated with CGD appears to result from deletion of a part of the X chromosome that includes the *XK* locus as well as the gene responsible for X-linked CGD.

Kell System Antibodies

Anti-K and Anti-k

Because the K antigen is strongly immunogenic, anti-K is frequently found in sera from transfused patients. Rare examples of anti-K have appeared as a saline agglutinin in sera from subjects never exposed to human red cells. Most examples are of immune origin and are reactive in antiglobulin testing; some bind complement.

Some workers have observed that examples of anti-K react less well in tests that incorporate low-ionic-strength-saline (LISS) solutions (notably the Polybrene test) than in saline tests or tests that include albumin. Others, however, have not shown differences in antibody reactivity, testing many examples of anti-K in low ionic systems. Anti-K has caused HTRs on numerous occasions, both immediate and delayed. Anti-K can cause severe HDFN and fetal anemia may be caused by the immune destruction of K+ erythroid progenitor cells by macrophages in the fetal liver.[11]

Because over 90% of donors are K–, it is not difficult to find compatible blood for patients with anti-K. Anti-k has clinical and serologic characteristics similar to anti-K but occurs much less frequently. Only about one person in 500 lacks the k antigen and finding compatible blood is correspondingly more difficult.

Other Kell System Antibodies

Anti-Kp[a], anti-Kp[b], anti-Js[a], and anti-Js[b] are all much less common than anti-K but show similar serologic characteristics and are considered clinically significant. Any of them may occur following transfusion or fetomaternal immunization. Antibody frequency is influenced by the immunogenicity of the particular antigen and by the distribution of the relevant negative phenotypes among transfusion recipients and positive phenotypes among donors. In Black patients frequently transfused with phenotypically matched blood, usually from other Black donors, anti-Js[a] is relatively common. This is due to the approximate 20% incidence of the Js[a] antigen in the Black population (see Table 15-3). Ordinarily, however, these antibodies are rare. Assistance from a rare donor file is usually needed to find compatible blood for patients immunized to the high-incidence antigens Kp[b] and Js[b]. Anti-Ku is the antibody characteristically seen in immunized K_o persons. It has been reported to cause a fatal HTR,[12] and it appears to be directed at a single determinant because it has not been separable into other Kell specificities. However, antibodies to other Kell system antigens may be present in serum containing anti-Ku. Some people of the K_{mod} phenotype have made a Ku-like antibody.

Duffy System

Duffy System Antigens

The antigens Fy[a] and Fy[b] are encoded by a pair of codominant alleles at the Duffy

(*FY*) locus on chromosome 1. Anti-Fy^a and anti-Fy^b define the four phenotypes observed in this blood group system, namely: Fy(a+b–), Fy(a+b+), Fy(a–b+), and Fy(a–b–) (see Table 15-4). In Whites, the first three phenotypes are common and Fy(a–b–) individuals are extremely rare. However, the incidence of the Fy(a–b–) phenotype among Blacks is 68%.

The Duffy gene encodes a glycoprotein that is expressed in other tissues, including the brain, kidney, spleen, heart, and lung. The Fy(a–b–) individual can be the result of the *FyFy* genotype or null phenotype. However, in many Black Fy(a–b–) individuals, the transcription in the marrow is prevented and Duffy protein is absent from the red cells. These individuals have an allele that is the same in the structural region as the *Fy^b* gene that prevents the transcription.[8(p439)] However, the Duffy protein is expressed normally in nonerythroid cells of these persons.[13] Other Fy(a–b–) individuals either appear to have a total absence or markedly altered Duffy glycoprotein.[8(pp457-458)] This affects other cell lines and tissues, not only the red cells. Those individuals who have absent or altered glycoprotein can make anti-Fy3, which will react with cells that are Fy(a+) and/or Fy(b+).

A rare inherited form of weak Fy^b called Fy^x has been described and is probably due to a point mutation. The Fy^x antigen may go undetected unless potent anti-Fy^b is used in testing. The Fy5 antigen appears to be defined by an interaction of the Duffy and Rh gene products because it is not expressed on Rh$_{null}$ red cells. The Fy6 antigen has been described only by murine monoclonal antibodies and is not present on red cells that are Fy(a–b–) and Fy:–3,–5.[8(p448)]

Biochemistry of the Duffy System

In red cells, the Duffy gene encodes a multipass membrane glycoprotein. The antigens Fy^a, Fy^b, and Fy6 are located on the N-terminal of the Duffy glycoprotein and are sensitive to denaturation by proteases such as ficin, papain, and α-chymotrypsin, unlike Fy3 or Fy5. Fy3 has been located on the last external loop of the Duffy glycoprotein. It is unaffected by protease treatment (reviewed in Pierce and Macpherson).[14] The glycoprotein is the receptor for the malarial parasite *Plasmodium vivax*, and persons whose red cells lack Fy^a and Fy^b are resistant to that form of the disease. In sub-Saharan Africa, notably West Africa, the resistance to *P. vivax* malaria conferred by the Fy(a–b–) phenotype may have favored its natural selection, and most individuals are Fy(a–b–).

The Duffy gene has been cloned[13] and the Duffy glycoprotein has been identified as an erythrocyte receptor for a number of

Table 15-4. Phenotypes and Frequencies in the Duffy System

Reactions with Anti-		Phenotype	Adult Phenotype Frequency (%)	
Fy^a	Fy^b		Whites	Blacks
+	0	Fy(a+b–)	17	9
+	+	Fy(a+b+)	49	1
0	+	Fy(a–b+)	34	22
0	0	Fy(a–b–)	Very rare	68

chemokines, notably interleukin-8.[15] Because chemokines are biologically active molecules, it has been postulated that Duffy acts as a sponge for excess chemokines, without ill effect on the red cells.

Duffy System Antibodies

Anti-Fy^a is quite common and may cause HDFN and HTRs. Anti-Fy^b is rare and generally is weakly reactive. Anti-Fy^b can cause rare mild HDFN and has been responsible for mostly mild HTRs. Both antibodies are usually IgG and react best by antiglobulin testing. The glycoprotein that expresses the antigens is cleaved by most proteases used in serologic tests, so anti-Fy^a and anti-Fy^b are usually nonreactive in enzyme test procedures.

Weak examples of anti-Fy^a or anti-Fy^b may react only with red cells that have a double dose of the antigen. In Whites, red cells that express only one of the two antigens are assumed to come from persons homozygous for the gene and to carry a double dose of the antigen. In Blacks, such cells may express the antigen only in single dose and may not give the expected strong reaction with antibodies that show dosage. For example, the patient typing Fy(a+b–) may be *Fy^{a}Fy*.

Anti-Fy3 was first described in the serum of a White person of the Fy(a–b–) phenotype and is directed at the high-incidence antigen Fy3. The only cells with which it is nonreactive are Fy(a–b–). Unlike Fy^a and Fy^b, the Fy3 antigen is unaffected by protease treatment, and anti-Fy3 reacts well with enzyme-treated cells positive for either Fy^a or Fy^b. Anti-Fy3 is rare but is sometimes made by Black Fy(a–b–) patients lacking Fy3 who have been immunized by multiple transfusions.

Two other rare antibodies have been described, both reactive with papain-treated red cells. One example of anti-Fy4 has been reported. It reacted with red cells of the Fy(a–b–) phenotype and with some Fy(a+b–) and Fy(a–b+) red cells from Blacks but not with Fy(a+b+) red cells, suggesting reactivity with a putative product of the *Fy* gene. However, different reference laboratories obtained equivocal results and evidence for the existence of the Fy4 antigen is weak.

Anti-Fy5 is similar to anti-Fy3, except that it fails to react with Rh$_{null}$ red cells that express Fy3 and is nonreactive with cells from Fy(a–b–) Blacks. It may react with the red cells from Fy(a–b–) Whites. This provided a previously unrecognized distinction between the Fy(a–b–) phenotype so common in Blacks and the one that occurs, but very rarely, in Whites.[8(p447)]

Anti-Fy6 is a murine monoclonal antibody that describes a high-incidence antigen in the same region as Fy^a and Fy^b. The antibody reacts with all Fy(a+) and/or Fy(b+) red cells, is nonreactive with Fy(a–b–) red cells, but, unlike anti-Fy3, is nonreactive with enzyme-treated red cells.

Kidd System

Jk^a and Jk^b Antigens

The Jk^a and Jk^b antigens are located on the urea transporter, encoded by the *HUT 11* gene on chromosome 18. Jk(a–b–) red cells, which lack the JK protein, are more resistant to lysis by 2M urea.[16] Red cells of normal Jk phenotype swell and lyse rapidly in a solution of 2M urea.

The four phenotypes identified in the Kidd system are shown in Table 15-5. The Jk(a–b–) phenotype is extremely rare, except in some populations of Pacific Island origin. Two mechanisms have been shown to produce the Jk(a–b–) phenotype.[17] One is the homozygous presence of the silent *Jk* allele. The other is the action of a dominant inhibitor gene called *In(Jk)*. The dominant suppression of Kidd antigens is similar to

Table 15-5. Phenotypes and Frequencies in the Kidd System

Reactions with Anti-			Phenotype Frequency (%)	
Jk^a	Jk^b	Phenotype	Whites	Blacks
+	0	Jk(a+b−)	28	57
+	+	Jk(a+b+)	49	34
0	+	Jk(a−b+)	23	9
0	0	Jk(a−b−)	Exceedingly rare	

the *In(Lu)* suppression of the Lutheran system.

Kidd System Antibodies

Anti-Jk^a and Anti-Jk^b

Anti-Jk^a was first recognized in 1951 in the serum of a woman who had given birth to a child with HDFN. Two years later, anti-Jk^b was found in the serum of a patient who had suffered a transfusion reaction. Both antibodies react best in antiglobulin testing, but saline reactivity is sometimes observed in freshly drawn specimens or when antibodies are newly forming. Both anti-Jk^a and anti-Jk^b are often weakly reactive, perhaps because, sometimes, they are detected more readily through the complement they bind to red cells. Some examples may become undetectable on storage. Other examples may react preferentially with red cells from homozygotes.

Some workers report no difficulties in detecting anti-Jk^a and anti-Jk^b in low ionic tests that incorporate anti-IgG. Others find that an antiglobulin reagent containing an anticomplement component may be important for the reliable detection of these inconsistently reactive antibodies. Stronger reactions may be obtained with the use of polyethylene glycol (PEG) or enzyme-treated red cells in antiglobulin testing.

Kidd system antibodies occasionally cause HDFN, but it is usually mild. These antibodies are notorious, however, for their involvement in severe HTRs, especially delayed hemolytic transfusion reactions (DHTRs). DHTRs occur when antibody develops so rapidly in an anamnestic response to antigens on transfused red cells that it destroys the still-circulating red cells. In many cases, retesting the patient's pretransfusion serum confirms that the antibody was undetectable in the original tests.

Anti-Jk3

Sera from some rare Jk(a−b−) persons have been found to contain an antibody that reacts with all Jk(a+) and Jk(b+) red cells but not with Jk(a−b−) red cells. Although a minor anti-Jk^a or anti-Jk^b component is sometimes separable, most of the reactivity has been directed at an antigen called Jk3, which is present on both Jk(a+) and Jk(b+) red cells.

Other Blood Group Systems

So far, this chapter has been devoted to blood group systems of red cell antigens of which the principal antibodies may be seen fairly frequently in the routine blood typing laboratory. The other blood group systems listed in Table 10-1 will be reviewed here briefly; the interested reader should refer to other texts and reviews for greater detail.

Lutheran System

Lu[a] and Lu[b] Antigens

The phenotypes of the Lutheran system, as defined by anti-Lu[a] and anti-Lu[b], are shown in Table 15-6. The Lu(a–b–) phenotype is very rare and may arise from one of three distinct genetic circumstances (reviewed in Pierce and Macpherson[14]). In the first, a presumably amorphic Lutheran gene (*Lu*) is inherited from both parents. In the second and most common, the negative phenotype is inherited as a dominant trait attributed to the independently segregating inhibitor gene, *In(Lu)*, which prevents the normal expression of Lutheran and certain other blood group antigens (notably P_1, I, AnWj, In[a], and In[b]). The third Lu(a–b–) phenotype is due to an X-borne suppressor, recessive in its effect.

Other Lutheran Blood Group Antigens

A series of high-incidence antigens (Lu4, Lu5, Lu6, Lu7, Lu8, Lu11, Lu12, Lu13,

Table 15-6. Phenotypes and Frequencies in the Lutheran System in Whites*

Reactions with Anti-		Phenotype	Phenotype Frequency (%)
Lu[a]	Lu[b]	Phenotype	
+	0	Lu(a+b–)	0.15
+	+	Lu(a+b+)	7.5
0	+	Lu(a–b+)	92.35
0	0	Lu(a–b–)	Very rare

*Insufficient data exist for the reliable calculation of frequencies in Blacks.

Lu16, Lu17, and Lu20) has been assigned to the Lutheran system because the corresponding antibodies do not react with Lu(a–b–) red cells of any of the three genetic backgrounds. Two low-incidence antigens, Lu9 and Lu14, have gained admission to the Lutheran system because of their apparent antithetical relationship to the high-incidence antigens Lu6 and Lu8, respectively.

Au[a] (Lu18), an antigen of relatively high incidence [90% of all populations are Au(a+)] and its antithetical partner, Au[b] (Lu19), present in 50% of Whites and 68% of Blacks, have been shown to belong to the Lutheran system.[18,19]

Biochemistry of the Lutheran System

Lutheran antigens are carried on a glycoprotein bearing both *N*-linked and *O*-linked oligosaccharides. This protein exists in two forms and has been shown to have a role in cell adhesion. The antigens are destroyed by trypsin, α-chymotrypsin, and sulfhydryl-reducing agents.[20] These results and results of immunoblotting experiments suggest the existence of interchain or intrachain disulfide bonds. Tests performed with monoclonal anti-Lu[b] suggest that the number of Lu[b] antigen sites per red cell is low, approximately 600-1600 per Lu(a+b+) red cell and 1400-3800 per Lu(a–b+) red cell.[21]

The *Lu* and *Se* (secretor) loci were shown to be linked in 1951, the first recorded example of autosomal linkage in humans. The two loci have been assigned to chromosome 19. The gene encoding the Lu glycoproteins has been cloned.[22]

Lutheran System Antibodies

The first example of anti-Lu[a] (-Lu1) was found in 1945 in a serum that contained several other antibodies. Anti-Lu[a] and anti-Lu[b] are not often encountered. They are most often produced in response to pregnancy or transfusion but have occurred in the absence of obvious red cell stimulation. Lutheran antigens are poorly developed at birth. It is not surprising that anti-Lu^a has not been reported to cause HDFN; neither has it been associated with HTRs. Anti-Lu^b has been reported to shorten the survival of transfused red cells but causes no, or at most very mild, HDFN. Most examples of anti-Lu^a and some anti-Lu^b will agglutinate saline-suspended red cells possessing the relevant antigen, characteristically producing a mixed-field appearance with small to moderately sized, loosely agglutinated clumps of red cells interspersed among many unagglutinated red cells.

Diego System

Diego System Antigens

The Diego system consists of two independent pairs of antithetical antigens, called Di^a/Di^b and Wr^a/Wr^b. The system also contains a large number of low-incidence antigens as seen in Appendix 6. The antigens are located on AE-1 (band 3), which is encoded by a gene on chromosome 17. The Di^a and Di^b antigens are useful as anthropologic markers because the Di^a antigen is almost entirely confined to populations of Asian origin and Native North and South Americans, in which the incidence of Di^a can be as high as 54%.[8(p583)]

The Wr^a and Wr^b antigens are located on AE-1 in close association with GPA. Wr^b expression is dependent upon the presence of GPA (see MNS Blood Group System).

Diego System Antibodies

Anti-Di^a may cause HDFN or destruction of transfused Di(a+) red cells. Anti-Di^b is rare but clinically significant. Anti-Wr^a is fairly common and can occur without red cell alloimmunization. It is a rare cause of

HTR or HDFN. Anti-Wr^b is a rarely encountered antibody that may be formed by rare Wr(a+b–) and some En(a–) individuals. Anti-Wr^b may recognize an enzyme-resistant or enzyme-sensitive antigen.[23] It should be considered to have potential to destroy Wr(b+) red cells.[8(p589)]

Cartwright System

Cartwright Antigens

The Yt (Cartwright) blood group system consists of two antigens, Yt^a and Yt^b (see Table 15-7). A gene on chromosome 7 encodes the antigens. The Yt antigens are located on red cell acetylcholinesterase (AChE),[24] an enzyme important in neural transmission, but the function of which is unknown on red cells. Enzymes have a variable effect on the Yt^a antigen but 0.2M DTT appears to destroy the Yt^a antigen expression.

Cartwright Antibodies

Some examples of anti-Yt^a are benign. A few cases of anti-Yt^a have shown accelerated destruction of transfused Yt(a+) red cells. Prediction of the clinical outcome by the monocyte monolayer assay has proved successful.[25,26] Anti-Yt^a is not known to cause HDFN. Anti-Yt^b is rare and has not been implicated in HTR or HDFN.

Xg System

Xg^a Antigen

In 1962, an antibody was discovered that identified an antigen more common among women than among men. This would be expected of an X-borne characteristic because females inherit an X chromosome from each parent, whereas males inherit X only from their mother. The antigen was named Xg^a in recognition of its X-borne manner of inheritance. Table 15-8 gives the phenotype frequencies among White

Table 15-7. Phenotype Frequencies in Other Blood Group Systems with Co-Dominant Antithetical Antigens

System	Reactions with Anti-		Phenotype	Phenotype Frequency in Whites (%)*
Yt	Yt^a	Yt^b		
	+	0	Yt(a+b−)	91.9
	+	+	Yt(a+b+)	7.9
	0	+	Yt(a−b+)	0.2
Dombrock	Do^a	Do^b		
	+	0	Do(a+b−)	17.2
	+	+	Do(a+b+)	49.5
	0	+	Do(a−b+)	33.3
Colton	Co^a	Co^b		
	+	0	Co(a+b−)	89.3
	+	+	Co(a+b+)	10.4
	0	+	Co(a−b+)	0.3
	0	0	Co(a−b−)	Very rare
Scianna	Sc1	Sc2		
	+	0	Sc:1,−2	99.7
	+	+	Sc:1,2	0.3
	0	+	Sc:−1,2	Very rare
	0	0	Sc:−1,−2	Very rare
Indian	In^a	In^b		
	+	0	In(a+b−)	Very rare
	+	+	In(a+b+)	<1
	0	+	In(a−b+)	>99
Diego	Di^a	Di^b		
	+	0	Di(a+b−)	Rare
	+	+	Di(a+b+)	Rare
	0	+	Di(a−b+)	>99.9

*There are insufficient data for the reliable calculation of frequencies in Blacks.

males and females. Enzymes, such as papain and ficin, denature the antigen. The gene encoding Xg^a has been cloned.[27,28]

Xg^a Antibody

Anti-Xg^a is an uncommon antibody that usually reacts only in antiglobulin testing. Anti-Xg^a has not been implicated in HDFN or HTRs. Anti-Xg^a may be useful for tracing the transmission of genetic traits associated with the X chromosome, although linkage with the Xg locus has been demonstrated for few traits to date.

Scianna System

Scianna Antigens

Five antigens—Sc1, Sc2, Sc3, Rd, and STAR—are recognized as belonging to the Scianna blood group system. Scianna antigens are expressed by the red cell adhesion protein ERMAP.[3] Sc1 is a high-inci-

Table 15-8. Frequencies of the Xg(a+) and Xg(a−) Phenotypes in White Males and Females

Phenotype	Phenotype Frequency (%)	
	Males	Females
Xg(a+)	65.6	88.7
Xg(a−)	34.4	11.3

Frequencies are based on the combined results of testing nearly 7000 random blood samples from populations of Northern European origin. There are insufficient data for reliable calculation of frequencies in Blacks.

dence antigen, whereas Sc2 occurs very infrequently. Sc1 and Sc2 behave as products of allelic genes (see Table 15-7). Sc3 is thought to be present on the red cells of any individual who inherits a functional *Sc¹* or *Sc²* gene, analogous to Fy3. Rd and STAR are low-incidence antigens recently assigned to the Scianna system. The antigens are resistant to enzymes routinely used in blood group serology. The gene encoding the Scianna antigens is located on chromosome 1.

Scianna Antibodies

The antibodies are rare. Anti-Sc1 has not been reported to cause HTR or HDFN. Anti-Sc2 has caused positive DATs in the neonate but no clinical HDFN.

Dombrock Blood Group System

Dombrock Antigens

Initially, this blood group system consisted of Do^a and Do^b, with the phenotype frequency as shown in Table 15-7. The discovery that red cells negative for the high-incidence antigen Gy^a were Do(a–b–)[29] has led to the recent expansion of the Dombrock blood group system. Three high-incidence antigens are Gy^a, Hy, and Jo^a. The interrelationship of the phenotypes is shown in Table 15-9.[30] Gy(a–) red cells represent the null phenotype. The Gy(a+^{w}), Hy–, and Jo(a–) phenotypes have been found exclusively in Blacks. The Dombrock antigens are located on a glycoprotein of 46 to 58 kD, the function of which is unknown.

Dombrock Antibodies

Anti-Do^a and anti-Do^b are uncommon antibodies and are usually found in sera containing multiple red cell antibodies. This can make the detection and identification of anti-Do^a and anti-Do^b difficult. Anti-Do^a has caused HDFN and HTR.[31] HDFN due to anti-Do^b has not been reported, but examples have caused HTR. Antibodies to Gy^a, Hy, and Jo^a may cause shortened survival of transfused antigen-positive red cells or mild HDFN. Reactivity of Dombrock antibodies may be enhanced by papain or ficin treatment of

Table 15-9. Relationship of the Dombrock Blood Group Antigens

Phenotype	Do^a	Do^b	Gy^a	Hy	Jo^a
Normal Do(a+b−)	+	0	+	+	+
Normal Do(a+b+)	+	+	+	+	+
Normal Do(a−b+)	0	+	+	+	+
Gy(a−)	0	0	0	0	0
Hy−	0	(+)	(+)	0	(+)
Jo(a−)	(+)	(+)	+	(+)	0

(+) = weak antigen expression.

red cells but is weakened or destroyed by sulfhydryl reagents.

Colton System

Colton Antigens

The Colton system consists of Co^a, a high-incidence antigen; Co^b, a low-incidence antigen; and Co3, an antigen (like Fy3) considered to be the product of either the *Co^a* or *Co^b* gene. The antigens are products of a gene on chromosome 7. The phenotype frequencies in Whites are shown in Table 15-7. The Colton antigens have been located on membrane protein CHIP 28 (Aquaporin), which functions as the red cell water transporter.[32]

Colton Antibodies

Anti-Co^a has been implicated in HTRs and HDFN.[8] Anti-Co^b has caused an HTR and mild HDFN. Enzyme treatment of red cells enhances reactions with the Colton antibodies.

LW System

LW Antigens

Table 15-10 shows the LW phenotypes and their frequencies. The antigens are denatured by sulfhydryl reagents, such as DTT, and by pronase but are unaffected by papain or ficin. There are reported cases of both inherited and acquired LW(a–b–) individuals.

Association with Rh

LW^a is more strongly expressed on D+ than D– red cells. However, the gene encoding the LW antigens is independent of the genes encoding the Rh proteins. Genetic independence was originally established through the study of informative families in which LW has been shown to segregate independently of the *RH* genes. The *LW* gene has been assigned to chro-

Table 15-10. Phenotypes and Frequencies in the LW System in Whites

Reactions with Anti-			
LW^a	LW^b	Phenotype	Phenotype Frequency (%)
+	0	LW(a+b–)	>99%
+	+	LW(a+b+)	<1%
0	+	LW(a–b+)	Very rare
0	0	LW(a–b–)	Very rare

mosome 19 and has been cloned. The glycoprotein it encodes has homology with cell adhesion molecules.[33]

Red cells from persons of the Rh$_{null}$ phenotype are LW(a–b–). It appears that the LW glycoprotein requires an interaction with Rh proteins for expression, although the basis of this interaction is not clear. (For a review of the evolution of the LW system, see Storry.[34])

LW Antibodies

Anti-LW^a has not been reported to cause HTRs or HDFN and both D+ and D– LW(a+) red cells have been successfully transfused into patients whose sera contained anti-LW^a. Reduced expression of LW antigens can occur in pregnancy and some hematologic diseases. LW antibodies may occur as an autoantibody or as an apparent alloantibody in the serum of such individuals. Anti-LW^{ab} has been reported in LW(a–b–) individuals as well as in patients with suppressed LW antigens.[19]

Chido/Rodgers System

Chido/Rodgers Antigens

The Chido (Ch) and Rodgers (Rg) antigens are high-incidence antigens present on the complement component C4. The antigens are not intrinsic to the red cell. In antigen-positive individuals, the antigens are adsorbed onto red cells from the plasma through an attachment mechanism that remains unclear.[35] Ch has been subdivided into six antigens and Rg into two antigens. A ninth antigen, WH, requires the interaction of Rg1 and Ch6 for expression. C4 is encoded by two linked genes, *C4A* and *C4B,* on chromosome 6.

Existing sera are poorly classified, but the phenotype frequency may be considered as in Table 15-11. The antigens are destroyed by papain/ficin treatment but unaffected by DTT/AET treatment.

Chido/Rodgers Antibodies

Antibodies to Ch and Rg are generally benign but may be a great nuisance in serologic investigations. Rapid identification is possible using red cells coated with C4 or by inhibition with pooled plasma from antigen-positive individuals. (See Method 3.9.) The antibodies are nonreactive with enzyme-treated red cells.

Gerbich System

Gerbich Antigens

The Gerbich system includes eight antigens, of which three (Ge2, Ge3, and Ge4) are of high incidence and five (Wb, Ls[a], An[a], Dh[a], and GEIS) are of low incidence. Several phenotypes that lack one or more of the high-incidence antigens are shown in Table 15-12; all are rare. Red cells with the Gerbich or Leach phenotype have a weakened expression of some Kell system antigens. Ge2, Ge4, Wb, Ls[a], An[a], Dh[a], and GEIS are destroyed by papain and ficin, but Ge3 resists protease treatment.

Table 15-11. Some Blood Group Antigens with Phenotypic Relationships

| Antigens | Phenotypes | Approximate Frequency (%) | |
		Whites	Blacks
Chido (Ch) and Rodgers (Rg)	Ch+,Rg+	95.0	
	Ch−,Rg+	2.0	
	Ch+,Rg−	3.0	
	Ch−,Rg−	Very rare	
Cost (Cs[a])* and York (Yk[a])	Cs(a+),Yk(a+)	82.5	95.6
	Cs(a+),Yk(a−)	13.5	3.2
	Cs(a−),Yk(a+)	2.1	0.6
	Cs(a−),Yk(a−)	1.9	0.6
Knops-Helgeson (Kn[a]) and McCoy (McC[a])	Kn(a+),McC(a+)	97.0	95.0
	Kn(a+),McC(a−)	2.0	4.0
	Kn(a−),McC(a+)	1.0	1.0
	Kn(a−),McC(a−)	Rare	Rare

*Although Cs[a] is not part of the Knops blood group system, there is a phenotypic association between Yk[a] and Cs[a].

Table 15-12. Ge– Phenotypes

Phenotype	Antibody Produced
Ge: −2,3,4 (Yus type)	Anti-Ge2
Ge:−2,−3,4 (Gerbich type)	Anti-Ge2 or -Ge3
Ge:−2,−3,−4 (Leach type)	Anti-Ge2, -Ge3, or -Ge4

The antigens of the Gerbich blood group system are carried on glycophorin C (GPC) and glycophorin D (GPD). GPC carries Ge3 and Ge4, whereas GPD carries Ge2 and Ge3. An[a] is carried on an altered form of GPD. Dh[a] and Wb are located on altered forms of GPC. Ls[a] is found on an altered form of GPC and GPD.[36] The proteins are the product of a single gene, *GYPC*, on chromosome 2. GPC is approximately four times more abundant than GPD. The mechanism whereby these two proteins are derived from a single gene involves an alternative initiation site in the gene. GPC and GPD interact directly with protein band 4.1 in the membrane skeleton. It is clear that the interaction is important in maintaining cell shape because deficiencies of either band 4.1 or GPC/D cause elliptocytosis.[36]

Gerbich Antibodies

The antibodies that Ge-negative individuals may produce are shown in Table 15-12; they may be immune or occur without red cell stimulation. Anti-Ge is usually IgG but may have an IgM component. The clinical significance of the antibodies is variable. Antibodies to the Gerbich antigens may be a rare cause of HDFN.

Cromer System

Cromer Antigens

A total of 13 antigens have been assigned to the Cromer blood group system: 10 high-incidence antigens and three low-incidence antigens (see Table 15-13). Tc[a] is antithetical to the low-incidence antigen Tc[b] in Blacks and to Tc[c] in Whites. WES[b] is the high-incidence antigen antithetical to WES[a]. Cr[a], Dr[a], Es[a], UMC, GUTI, SERF, and ZENA are not associated with low-incidence antigens. IFC is absent only in the null phenotype (Inab).

The antigens are located on the complement regulatory protein called decay-accelerating factor (DAF). The protein is encoded by *DAF*, one gene of the regulators of complement activation (RCA) complex, on chromosome 1. The antigens are on leukocytes, platelets, and trophoblasts of the placenta as well as in soluble form in the serum/plasma and urine.[37] The antigens are not affected by ficin or papain. DTT or AET may weaken the antigens but do not completely destroy them.[37]

Cromer Antibodies

Antibodies to antigens of the Cromer system are immune-mediated and extremely uncommon. Most examples of anti-Cr[a], -WES[b], and -Tc[a] have been found in the sera of Black individuals. Anti-GUTI was found in a Canadian of Chilean ancestry.[37] The clinical significance of the antibodies is variable, and some examples cause decreased survival of transfused red cells. The antibodies will not cause HDFN because the placenta tissue is a rich source of DAF, which is thought to adsorb the maternal antibodies.[37]

Table 15-13. Antigens of High and Low Incidence in the Cromer Blood Group System

Antigen	Incidence (%)
Cr^a	>99
Tc^a	>99
Tc^b	<1
Tc^c	<1
Dr^a	>99
Es^a	>99
IFC	>99
WES^a	<1
WES^b	>99
UMC	>99
GUTI	>99
SERF	>99
ZENA	>99

Knops System

Knops Antigens

Most of the eight Knops system antigens (Kn^a, Kn^b, McC^a, McC^b, Sl^a, Yk^a, Vil, and Sl3) have been located on the C3b/C4b receptor (CR1), the primary complement receptor on red cells. A gene on chromosome 1 encodes CR1. Kn^a, McC^a, Sl^a, Yk^a, and Sl3 are high-incidence antigens. Kn^b, McC^b, and Vil are low-incidence antigens. Some variation in frequency is observed between the red cells of Whites and Blacks (see Table 15-11).

The Knops system antigens are not destroyed by ficin or papain but may be weakened or destroyed by DTT or AET.

Knops Antibodies

The antibodies commonly show variable weak reactivity in the antiglobulin phase of testing but may continue to react even at high dilutions. Moulds et al[38] have shown that the variable reactivity of anti-CR1-related sera is a direct reflection of the number of CR1 sites that exhibit both size and expression polymorphisms and vary widely among individuals. The antibodies are of no clinical significance.

Indian System

In^a and In^b are located on CD44, a protein of wide tissue distribution with the characteristics of a cell adhesion molecule. In^a is a low-incidence antigen, and In^b is of high incidence (see Table 15-7). In^b shows reduced expression on Lu(a–b–) red cells of the *In(Lu)* type but is normally expressed on Lu(a–b–) red cells from persons homozygous for the *amorph* or possessing the X-borne suppressor gene. The antigens are destroyed by papain and ficin as well as by reducing agents such as 0.2 M DTT. There are few data on the clinical significance of the corresponding antibodies.

Other Blood Group Systems

Ok System

The Ok system consists of a single high-incidence antigen, Ok^a. The few rare Ok(a–) individuals to date have been Japanese. Proteases do not seem to weaken expression of Ok^a in routine agglutination tests. Anti-Ok^a reacts optimally by an indirect antiglobulin test and appears to be clinically significant in transfusion therapy, causing rapid destruction of Ok(a+) red cells.

Raph System

The Raph system consists of a single antigen, MER2. Anti-MER2 has been reported in three Israeli Jews. All three were on renal dialysis, raising the possibility that antibody production may be associated with kidney disease. The MER2 antigen has been detected on the red cells of 92% of those tested. The MER2 antigen is sensitive to DTT but is not affected by treatment with ficin, papain, or chloroquine. The antibodies have been IgG and some have bound complement. To date, there has been no information on whether these antibodies are capable of causing HTR or HDFN.

John Milton Hagen System

The John Milton Hagen (JMH) antigen is carried on a GPI-linked CD108 glycoprotein. JMH antigen decreases over time. The JMH– phenotype can be transient. The JMH– phenotype can be acquired or inherited. The antigen is destroyed or altered by ficin or papain treatment and by AET or DTT treatment.

Antibodies that react with JMH show variation in reactivity and are usually weak. Autoanti-JMH can often be found in older people, along with an acquired absent or weak JMH antigen expression. The antibody is not routinely considered capable of HTR or HDFN.

GIL System

There is one antigen of high frequency, GIL, in this system. GIL is located on aquaporin 3 (AQP3), which is a glycerol transporter. The antibody has not been reported to cause HDFN or HTR.

Blood Group Collections

In addition to the blood group systems, there are collections of antigens that exhibit shared characteristics but do not as yet meet the criteria for blood group system status defined by the ISBT. They include Cost (ISBT 205), Er (ISBT 208), and Vel (ISBT 211).

Cost

Cs^a and Cs^b are all that remain of this collection after the Knops antigens were identified on CR1. Cs^a occurs in a frequency greater that 98% in most populations, whereas Cs^b appears in about 34% of the population.[19] There is, however, an unexplained connection between the Yk^a and Cs^a antigens, such that red cells negative for one antigen are often weak or negative for the other. (See Table 15-11.) The antigens are not destroyed by ficin, papain, or DTT. Anti-Cs^a behaves similarly to antibodies produced to the Knops system antigens and is not considered clinically significant.

Er

The Er collection consists of two antigens, which give rise to four phenotypes: Er(a+b–), Er(a+b+), Er(a–b+), and Er(a–b–). Er^a is a high-incidence antigen present on the red cells of >99% of all individuals, but Er^b has a prevalence of less than 1%. The presence of a silent third allele, *Er*, is thought to account for the Er(a–b–) phenotype, as demonstrated by family studies. The antigens are not destroyed by ficin, papain, or DTT but are destroyed by EDTA-glycine acid.

Vel

The Vel collection was recently created to include two serologically related antigens of high incidence, Vel and ABTI.

Vel is a high-incidence antigen that is unaffected by protease and sulfhydryl treatment. It is well developed at birth, but antigen expression is variable.[8] Despite its occurrence after known immunizing stimuli, anti-Vel is most commonly IgM. It has been reported to range from causing only a positive DAT in the neonate to causing severe HDFN.[19] It has been implicated in HTRs. Anti-Vel binds complement, and in-vitro hemolysis of incompatible red cells is often seen when testing freshly drawn serum containing this antibody. Reactivity of anti-Vel is usually enhanced by enzyme treatment of red cells expressing the antigen.

High-Incidence Red Cell Antigens Not Assigned to a Blood Group System or Collection

Table 15-14 lists the antigens of high incidence that are independent of a blood group system or collection. Persons who make alloantibody to a specific blood group antigen necessarily have red cells lacking that antigen. For this reason, antibodies directed at high-incidence antigens are rarely encountered. The antibodies corresponding to these antigens usually react best by antiglobulin testing.

Lan Antigen

Lan is a high-incidence antigen that is resistant to enzyme-treatment and to 0.2 M DTT treatment. A weak form of the Lan antigen has been reported.[19] Anti-Lan is characteristically IgG, may bind complement, and may cause HTRs. Cases of HDFN due to anti-Lan have been mild even though the Lan antigen is present on cord red cells.[19]

At^a Antigen

At^a is a high-incidence antigen that is resistant to enzyme treatment and to 0.2 M DTT treatment. The At(a–) phenotype has been found only in Black individuals.[19] Anti-At^a is characteristically IgG. The antibody appears to cause only moderate HTRs and no clinical HDFN.[19]

Table 15-14. Some Antigens of High Incidence Not Assigned to a Blood Group System or Collection

Name	Symbol
August	At^a
Langereis	Lan
Sid	Sd^a
Duclos	
	Jr^a
	Emm
	AnWj
	PEL
	MAM

Jr^a Antigen

Jr^a is a high-incidence antigen that is resistant to enzyme treatment and to 0.2 M DTT treatment. The Jr(a–) phenotype is more commonly found in Japanese individuals but has been found in other populations as well.[8(pp805-806)] Anti-Jr^a has been shown to cause reduced red cell survival.[8(pp805-806)] Other examples of anti-Jr^a have shown little or no clinical significance in HDFN or HTR.[8(p806),39]

AnWj Antigen

AnWj is a high-incidence antigen that is resistant to enzyme treatment but weakened by 0.2 M DTT treatment.[19] The antigen is carried on CD44, which also carries the Indian blood group system antigens. The AnWj antigen is weakened on the red cells from individuals with the *In(Lu)* gene (see section on Lutheran System). Some patients with Hodgkin's disease may experience a long-term suppression of the AnWj antigen.[8(pp783-784)] The AnWj antigen is the receptor for *Haemophilus influenzae.*[8(pp784-785)] Anti-AnWj has been implicated in severe HTRs but not in HDFN because the antigen is not present on cord red cells.

Sd^a Antigen

Sd^a is an antigen of fairly high incidence, widely distributed in mammalian tissues and body fluids. The antigen is variably expressed on the red cells of Sd(a+) individuals. Sd^a expression may diminish during pregnancy and the Sd(a–) phenotype is observed in 30% to 75% of pregnant women. The antigen is not present on cord cells. The strongest expression of Sd^a has been observed on polyagglutinable red cells of the Cad phenotype. The frequency of Sd(a–) blood is considered to be around 9%, but weakly positive reactions are often difficult to distinguish from negative ones.

Anti-Sd^a can be reactive by antiglobulin testing. Microscopic examination of positive reactions generally shows mixed-field agglutination, with relatively small, tightly agglutinated clumps of red cells present against a background of free red cells. These agglutinates are refractile and may have a shiny appearance. Because the majority of the examples of anti-Sd^a are IgM, the wide use of anti-IgG means that many examples of anti-Sd^a are no longer detected. Anti-Sd^a is not considered to be clinically significant. However, there have been reported cases of HTRs with red cells with strong Sd^a expression.[8(pp816-817)]

The immunodominant sugar of Sd^a is N-acetylgalactosamine (GalNAc), also the immunodominant sugar of the A blood group antigen and of the Tamm-Horsfall glycoprotein, found in human and guinea pig urine. Anti-Sd^a activity can be inhibited by incubation with urine from guinea pigs or from Sd(a+) humans. See Method 3.11 for the performance of a urine neutralization of anti-Sd^a.

Low-Incidence Red Cell Antigens Not Assigned to a Blood Group System or Collection

Many independent low-incidence red cell antigens have been recognized in addition to a growing number that have been assigned to the MNS, Rh, and Diego systems. Table 15-15 lists those that have been studied and shown to be inherited in a dominant manner. Antibodies specific for these low-incidence antigens react with so few random blood samples that they virtually never cause difficulties in selecting blood for transfusion but may be implicated in some rare cases of HDFN. The antibodies are of interest to the serologist, however, because of the unexpectedly high incidence with which they occur, often without an identifiable antigenic stimulus.

Table 15-15. Antigens of Low Incidence Not Assigned to a Blood Group System or Collection

Batty (By)	Livesay (Li^a)
Biles (Bi)	Milne
Box (Bx^a)	Oldeide (Ol^a)
Christiansen (Chr^a)	Peters (Pt^a)
HJK	Rasmussen (RASM)
HOFM	Reid (Re^a)
JFV	REIT
JONES	SARA
Jensen (Je^a)	Torkildsen (To^a)
Katagiri (Kg)	

The antigens occur with a frequency of 1 in 500 or less.

Antibodies to Low-Incidence Antigens

Antibodies to low-incidence antigens have sometimes been implicated in transfusion reactions and HDFN. These antibodies are usually encountered by chance, when the red cells used for antibody detection or selected for crossmatching happen to carry the corresponding antigen.

Antibodies to low-incidence antigens may also be present as unsuspected contaminants in blood typing reagents prepared from human serum and may cause false-positive test results if the red cells tested carry the antigen. Testing with reagents from different manufacturers may not eliminate this error because it is not uncommon for a single individual with an uncommon antibody to provide the serum used for reagent preparation by different manufacturers.

Some antibodies to low-incidence antigens react as saline agglutinins. They can also occur as IgG antibodies reactive only by antiglobulin testing, even if there has been no exposure to red cell immunization. It is common for several low-incidence antibodies to occur together in a single serum; multiple specificities are especially likely in sera from patients with autoimmune conditions.

Bg (Bennett-Goodspeed) Antigens

Antibodies directed at certain leukocyte antigens sometimes cause confusing reactions in serologic tests with red cells. At least three separate specificities have been given names as Bg antigens: Bg^a corresponds to HLA-B7; Bg^b corresponds to HLA-B17; and Bg^c corresponds to HLA-A28. A fourth antibody in some antileukocyte sera reacts with red cells of persons who express HLA-A10. The so-called Bg antigens are expressed to variable degrees on red cells, with the result that reactions of differing strengths are observed when a single serum containing "anti-Bg" is tested with different Bg+ red cells. Reactivity is most commonly observed in antiglobulin testing, but highly potent anti-Bg sera may directly agglutinate red cells with an unusually strong expression of the Bg antigens.

Confident and precise classification of reactivity is made difficult by the weak expression of these antigens on some red cells and by multiple specificities among different examples of the Bg antibodies. These antibodies may also occur as unsuspected contaminants in human source blood typing sera, where they may cause false-positive reactions with cells having unusually strong expression of the corresponding Bg antigen. Bg-related antigens are denatured by chloroquine diphosphate or a solution of glycine-HCl/EDTA.

References

1. Garratty G, Dzik W, Issitt PD, et al. Terminology for blood group antigens and genes—historical origins and guidelines in the new millennium. Transfusion 2000;40:477-89.
2. Daniels GL, Anstee DJ, Cartron JP, et al. Terminology for red cell surface antigens. ISBT Working Party Oslo Report. International Society of Blood Transfusion. Vox Sang 1999;77:52-7.
3. Daniels GL, Cartron JP, Fletcher A, et al. International Society of Blood Transfusion Committee on terminology for red cell surface antigens: Vancouver Report. Vox Sang 2003;84:244-7.
4. Race RR, Sanger R. Blood groups in man. 6th ed. Oxford: Blackwell Scientific Publications, 1975.
5. Bruce LJ, Ring SM, Anstee DJ, et al. Changes in the blood group Wright antigens are associated with a mutation at amino acid 658 in human erythrocyte band 3: A site of interaction between band 3 and glycophorin A under certain conditions. Blood 1995;85:299-306.
6. Rygiel SA, Issitt CH, Fruitstone MJ. Destruction of the S antigen by Clorox (abstract). Transfusion 1983;23:410.
7. Case J. The behavior of anti-S antibodies with ficin-treated human red cells. In: Abstracts of

volunteer papers. 30th Annual Meeting of the American Association of Blood Banks. Washington, DC: American Association of Blood Banks, 1977:36.

8. Issitt PD, Anstee DJ. Applied blood group serology. 4th ed. Durham, NC: Montgomery Scientific, 1998.

9. Lee S, Russo D, Redman CM. The Kell blood group system: Kell and XK membrane proteins. Semin Hematol 2000;37:113-21.

10. Zelinski T, Coghlan G, Myal Y, et al. Genetic linkage between the Kell blood group system and prolactin-inducible protein loci: Provisional assignment of KEL to chromosome 7. Ann Hum Genet 1991;55:137-40.

11. Daniels G, Hadley A, Green CA. Causes of fetal anemia in hemolytic disease due to anti-K (letter). Transfusion 2003;43:115-16.

12. Lin M, Wang CL, Chen FS, et al. Fatal hemolytic transfusion reaction due to anti-Ku in a K_{null} patient. Immunohematol 2003;19:19-21.

13. Chaudhuri A, Polyakova J, Zbrezezna V, et al. Cloning of glycoprotein D cDNA which encodes the major subunit of the Duffy blood group system and the receptor for the *Plasmodium vivax* malaria parasite. Proc Natl Acad Sci U S A 1993;90:10793-7.

14. Pierce SP, Macpherson CR, eds. Blood group systems: Duffy, Kidd and Lutheran. Arlington, VA: American Association of Blood Banks, 1988.

15. Horuk R, Chitnis C, Darbonne W, et al. A receptor for the malarial parasite *Plasmodium vivax*: The erythrocyte chemokine receptor. Science 1993;261:1182-4.

16. Heaton DC, McLoughlin K. Jk(a–b–) red blood cells resist urea lysis. Transfusion 1982;22:70-1.

17. Mougey R. The Kidd blood group system. In: Pierce SR, Macpherson CR, eds. Blood group systems: Duffy, Kidd and Lutheran. Arlington, VA: American Association of Blood Banks, 1988:53-71.

18. Zelinski K, Kaita H, Coghlan G, Philipps S. Assignment of the Auberger red cell antigen polymorphism to the Lutheran blood group system: Genetic justification. Vox Sang 1991; 61:275-6.

19. Reid ME, Lomas-Francis C. The blood group antigen factsbook. 2nd ed. San Diego, CA: Academic Press, 2004.

20. Daniels G. Effect of enzymes on and chemical modifications of high-frequency red cell antigens. Immunohematology 1992;8:53-7.

21. Merry AH, Gardner B, Parsons SF, Anstee DJ. Estimation of the number of binding sites for a murine monoclonal anti-Lu^b on human erythrocytes. Vox Sang 1987;53:57-60.

22. Crew VK, Green C, Daniels G. Molecular bases of the antigens of the Lutheren blood group system. Transfusion 2003;43:1729-37.

23. Storry JR, Reid ME, Chiofolo JT, et al. A new Wr(a+b–) Proband with anti-Wr^b recognizing a ficin sensitive antigen (abstract). Transfusion 2001;41(Suppl):23S.

24. Spring FA. Characterization of blood-group-active erythrocyte membrane glycoproteins with human antisera. Transfus Med 1993;3: 167-78.

25. Eckrich RJ, Mallory DM. Correlation of monocyte monolayer assays and posttransfusion survival of Yt(a+) red cells in patients with anti-Yt^a (abstract). Transfusion 1993;33 (Suppl):18S.

26. Garratty G, Arndt P, Nance S. The potential clinical significance of blood group alloantibodies to high frequency antigens (abstract). Blood 1997;90(Suppl):473a.

27. Ellis NA, Ye T-Z, Patton S, et al. Cloning of *PBDX*, a *MIC2*-related gene that spans the pseudoautosomal boundary on chromosome Xp. Nat Genet 1994;6:394-9.

28. Ellis NA, Tippett P, Petty A, et al. *PBDX* is the *XG* blood group gene. Nat Genet 1994;8:285-90.

29. Banks JA, Parker N, Poole J. Evidence to show that Dombrock antigens reside on the Gy^a/Hy glycoprotein. Transfus Med 1992;(Suppl) 1:68.

30. Scofield TL, Miller JP, Storry JR, et al. Evidence that Hy– RBCs express weak Jo^a antigen. Transfusion 2004;44:170-2.

31. Judd WJ, Steiner EA. Multiple hemolytic transfusion reactions caused by anti-Do^a. Transfusion 1991;31:477-8.

32. Smith BL, Preston GM, Spring F, et al. Human red cell aquaporin CHIP. J Clin Invest 1994;94: 1043-9.

33. Bailly P, Hermand P, Callebaut I, et al. The LW blood group glycoprotein is homologous to intercellular adhesion molecules. Proc Natl Acad Sci U S A 1994;91:5306-10.

34. Storry JR. Review: The LW blood group system. Immunohematology 1994;8:87-93.

35. Moulds JM, Laird-Fryer B, eds. Blood groups: Chido/Rodgers, Knops/McCoy/York and Cromer. Bethesda, MD: American Association of Blood Banks, 1992.

36. Reid ME, Spring FA. Molecular basis of glycophorin C variants and their associated blood group antigens. Transfus Med 1994;4:139-46.

37. Storry JR, Reid ME, The Cromer blood group system: A review. Immunohematology 2002; 18:95-101.

38. Moulds JM, Moulds JJ, Brown M, Atkinson JP. Antiglobulin testing for CR1-related (Knops/McCoy/Swain-Langley/York) blood group an-

tigens: Negative and weak reactions are caused by variable expression of CR1. Vox Sang 1992;62:230-5.

39. Kwon M, Ammeus M, Blackall D. A Japanese patient with a Jr[a] antibody: Apparent lack of clinical significance despite multiple incompatible transfusions (abstract). Transfusion 2001;41(Suppl):58S.

Suggested Reading

Akane A, Mizukami H, Shiono H. Classification of the standard alleles of the MN blood group system. Vox Sang 2000;79:183-7.

Liu M, Jiang D, Liu S, et al. Frequencies of the major alleles of Diego, Dombrock, Yt, and Ok blood group systems in the Chinese, Han, Hui, and Tibetan nationalities. Immunohematology 2003;19:22-5.

Lögdberg L, Reid M, Miller J. Cloning and genetic characterization of blood group carrier molecules and antigens. Transfus Med Rev 2002;16:1-10.

Pogo AO, Chaudhuri A. The Duffy protein: A malarial and chemokine receptor. Semin Hematol 2000;37:122-9.

Reid ME. The Dombrock blood group system: A review. Transfusion 2003;43:107-14.

Reid ME, Rios M, Yazdanbakhsh K. Applications of molecular biology techniques to transfusion medicine. Semin Hematol 2000;37:166-76.

Reid ME, Storry JR. Low-incidence MNS antigens associated with single amino acid changes and their susceptibility to enzyme treatment. Immunohematology 2001;17:76-81.

Chapter 16

Platelet and Granulocyte Antigens and Antibodies

ANTIBODIES REACTIVE WITH antigens expressed on platelets and leukocytes are assuming increasing importance. Some blood group antigens are shared by red cells, white cells, and platelets; others are specific to certain cell types. This chapter discusses antibodies directed at antigens expressed on platelets and neutrophils, with an emphasis on those specific for these cells. HLA antibodies and antigens are covered more fully in Chapter 17.

Platelet Antigens

Antigens Shared with Other Tissues

Platelets express a variety of antigenic markers on their surface. Some of these antigens are shared with other cell types, as in the case of ABH antigens and HLA antigens, which are shared with virtually all nucleated cells in the body. Others are observed to be essentially platelet specific.

ABH Antigens

The ABH antigens expressed on platelets are a combination of structures intrinsic to the plasma membrane and those adsorbed from the plasma. The amount of ABH antigen present on platelets is quite variable from individual to individual, with from 5% to 10% of non-group-O individuals expressing extremely elevated amounts of A or B substance on their platelets. These people appear to have a "high-expresser" form of glycosyltransferase in their sera. Although platelets are often transfused without regard to ABO compatibility, in some cases, ABO antibodies (particularly IgG antibodies of high titer in group O recipients) may react with platelets carrying large amounts of A or B antigen.[1] High-expresser platelets are particularly vulnerable to this type of immune destruction. ABO antibodies in recipients may also cause reduced survival of ABO-incompatible platelets from normal-expresser phenotype donors, causing occasional patients to exhibit refractoriness to platelet transfusions on this basis.

Other red cell antigens—including Le^a, Le^b, Ii, and P^2 as well as the Cromer antigens associated with decay accelerating factor[3]—are also found on platelets, but there is no evidence that antibodies to these antigens significantly reduce platelet survival in vivo.

HLA Antigens

HLA antigens are found on the surfaces of both platelets and white cells (see Chapter 17). In fact, platelets are the major source of Class I HLA antigens in whole blood.[2] Recent evidence indicates that most Class I HLA molecules on platelets are integral membrane proteins, and smaller amounts may be absorbed from surrounding plasma.[3]

HLA alloantibodies do not occur naturally, arising only after sensitization by pregnancy or blood transfusion. Studies of HLA alloimmunization in patients transfused with platelets document the development of antibodies within 3 to 4 weeks after primary exposure and as early as 4 days after secondary exposure in patients previously transfused or pregnant.[4] The likelihood of HLA alloimmunization by transfusion in patients not previously sensitized is variable,[4,5] and the risk of HLA alloimmunization appears to be related to the underlying disease as well as to the immunosuppressive effects of treatment regimens. Platelets carry Class I HLA antigens but lack Class II antigens, which are necessary for primary sensitization. Therefore, exposure to leukocytes expressing HLA antigens during transfusion is the principal cause of primary HLA alloimmunization.

Platelet Transfusion Refractoriness

A less-than-expected increase in platelet count occurs in about 20% to 70% of multitransfused thrombocytopenic patients,[6] and patients treated for malignant hematopoietic disorders are particularly likely to become refractory to platelet transfusions. A widely accepted definition of refractoriness was used in a randomized controlled clinical trial of platelet transfusion therapy, sponsored by the National Institutes of Health (NIH). In this study, two consecutive 1-hour posttransfusion platelet corrected count increments (CCI) of less than 5000 platelets $\times$ m^2 body surface area/µL indicated refractoriness.[7] Others have used less stringent criteria (eg, three platelet transfusions over a 2-week period that yield inadequate posttransfusion platelet counts).[8,9] Response is often determined by calculating either a CCI or a posttransfusion platelet recovery (PPR) between 10 and 60 minutes after transfusion (see Table 16-1). Responses of 7500 platelets $\times$ m^2 body surface area/µL or 20% can be considered acceptable from the CCI or the PPR calculation, respectively.

Alloimmune platelet refractoriness is most often the result of HLA sensitization and can be diagnosed by demonstration of significant levels of HLA antibodies. Patient serum is tested against a panel of lymphocytes (or synthetic beads bearing Class I antigens) that represent most of the Class I HLA specificities in the population. A panel-reactive antibody (PRA) score of 20% or higher is evidence that HLA sensitization may be contributing to the platelet refractoriness (see Chapter 17).

Although platelet alloimmunization is one cause of refractoriness, there are multi-

Table 16-1. Determination of Response to Transfused Platelets

Calculation of Corrected Count Increment (CCI)

$$CCI = \frac{\text{Body Surface Area } (m^2) \times \text{Platelet Count Increment} \times 10^{11}}{\text{No. of Platelets Transfused}}$$

EXAMPLE: If 4×10^{11} platelets are transfused to a patient whose body surface area is 1.8 m^2 and the increase in posttransfusion platelet count is 25,000/µL, then:

$$CCI = \frac{1.8\ m^2 \times 25,000/\mu L \times 10^{11}}{4 \times 10^{11}} = 11,250 \text{ platelets} \times m^2/\mu L$$

Calculation of Posttransfusion Platelet Recovery (PPR)

$$PPR(\%) = \frac{\text{Estimated Total Blood Volume}^* \times \text{Platelet Count Increment}}{\text{No. of Platelets Transfused}}$$

*Total blood volume can be estimated in adult patients as 75 mL/kg

EXAMPLE: If 4×10^{11} platelets are transfused to a 70-kg patient and the increase in posttransfusion platelet count is 25,000/µL, then:

$$PPR = \frac{70\ kg \times 70\ mL/kg \times 25,000\ \text{plts}/\mu L \times 10^3}{4 \times 10^{11} \text{platelets}} = 30.6\%$$

ple, nonimmune reasons why transfused platelets may not yield the expected increase in platelet count [eg, sepsis, disseminated intravascular coagulation (DIC), or the administration of certain drugs]. Some of the most commonly cited nonimmune causes of platelet refractoriness are listed in Table 16-2. A study of patients undergoing marrow transplant suggested that patient-related variables such as total body irradiation, advanced disease status, and liver dysfunction are important predictors of poor platelet count increments as well.[10,11] Even when possible immune causes of refractoriness are identified, nonimmune factors are often simultaneously present.

Several strategies may be considered when selecting platelets for patients with immune-mediated refractoriness. When antibodies to HLA antigens are demonstrated, a widely used approach is to supply apheresis platelets matched to the patient's HLA type.[12] A disadvantage is that a pool of several thousand HLA-typed potential apheresis donors is necessary to find sufficient HLA-compatible matches.[13] Moreover, donor selection on the basis of HLA type can lead to the exclusion of donors with HLA types different from that of the recipient but potentially effective if the recipient is alloimmunized to other antigenic determinants.[14] For patients who are likely to require multiple platelet transfusions, HLA typing should be performed in advance of a planned course of treatment.

It is important to understand the degree of match that may be provided (see Table 16-3). Platelets received following a request for "HLA-matched" platelets are typically the closest match obtainable within the constraints of time and donor availability. In one study,[15] 43% of platelets provided as

Table 16-2. Some Nonimmune Causes of Platelet Refractoriness

Massive bleeding
Fever
Sepsis
Splenomegaly (splenic sequestration)
Disseminated intravascular coagulation
Allogeneic transplantation
Poor storage of platelets before transfusion
Effects of drugs (may include immune
    mechanisms)
Intravenous amphotericin B
Thrombotic thrombocytopenic purpura

HLA-matched were relatively poor grade B or C matches. The most successful responses occur with the subset of grade A and B1U or B2U HLA matches, but mismatches for some antigens (B44, 45) that are poorly expressed on platelets can be useful. According to AABB *Standards for Blood Banks and Transfusion Services*,[16(p43)] HLA-matched platelets should be irradiated to prevent transfusion-associated graft-vs-host disease.

A second approach to provide effective platelets is to use a pretransfusion platelet crossmatching assay. This approach can be used to predict and, therefore, avoid subsequent platelet transfusion failures.[17] The solid-phase red cell adherence test (SPRCA) is the most widely used method for platelet crossmatching, and test results are reasonably predictive of posttransfusion platelet counts.[18-20] Compared with HLA matching, crossmatching can prove both more convenient and economically advantageous. It avoids exclusion of HLA-mismatched but compatible donors and has the added advantage of selecting platelets when the antibody (-ies) involved is (are) directed at a platelet-specific antigen. Platelet crossmatching, however, will not always be successful, particularly when patients are highly alloimmunized (PRA >50%). In these instances, finding sufficient compatible units may be problematic, and selection of HLA-matched platelets may be more practical. Although the incidence of platelet-specific antibodies causing patients to be refractory to most or all attempted platelet transfusions is very small, this possibility should be investigated when most of the attempted crossmatches are positive. If platelet-specific antibodies are present, donors of known platelet antigen phenotype or

Table 16-3. Degree of Matching for HLA-Matched Platelets

Match Grade	Description	Examples of Donor Phenotypes for a Recipient Who Is A1,3;B8,27
A	4-antigen match	A1,3;B8,27
B1U	1 antigen unknown or blank	A1,-;B8,27
B1X	1 cross-reactive group	A1,3;B8,7
B2UX	1 antigen blank and 1 cross-reactive	A1,-;B8,7
C	1 mismatched antigen present	A1,3;B8,35
D	2 or more mismatched antigens present	A1,32;B8,35
R	Random	A2,28;B7,35

family members, who are more likely to share the patient's phenotype, should be tested.

An alternative approach to supplying HLA-compatible transfusions is to determine the specificity of the patient's HLA antibodies and select donors whose platelets lack the antigens with which the antibodies react. This is termed the antibody specificity prediction (ASP) method.[8] One study compared the effectiveness of transfused platelets selected by the ASP method with those selected on the basis of HLA matching, platelet crossmatching, or on a random basis.[8] Platelets selected by the ASP method were equally effective as those selected by HLA matching or by crossmatching, and superior to randomly selected platelets. In addition, from a file of HLA-typed donors, many more potential donors were identified by the ASP method than were available using traditional HLA matching criteria, making the acquisition of compatible platelets for alloimmunized refractory patients much more feasible.

A further refinement of HLA matching was proposed by Duquesnoy.[21] A computerized algorithm—HLA Matchmaker, available at http://tpis.upmc.edu/tpis/HLAMatchmaker—is employed for evaluation of the molecular similarities and differences between HLA Class I epitopes. First developed to aid in locating compatible organs for alloimmunized prospective renal transplant patients, the strategy is based on the concept that immunogenic epitopes are represented by amino acid triplets on exposed parts of protein sequences of the Class I alloantigens that are accessible to alloantibodies. Using this scheme, many Class I HLA antigens classified as mismatches to a patient's HLA type have no incompatible exposed amino acid triplets and, therefore, would not be expected to elicit an antibody response. The pool of potentially compatible HLA-selected donors is thereby greatly

expanded. Although this strategy may prove useful in selecting platelet donors for refractory patients, it has not yet been evaluated in a clinical trial for this purpose and remains to be validated for this indication.

Prevention of Platelet Alloimmunization

Once refractoriness resulting from platelet alloimmunization is established, it is very difficult, if not impossible, to reverse. Therefore, in addition to developing methods of selecting compatible platelet donors for the refractory patient, several strategies have been evaluated to *prevent* alloimmunization to platelets from occurring in the first place. They include reduction in the number of leukocytes in the platelet products and ultraviolet B (UVB) irradiation. The report of the Trial to Reduce Alloimmunization to Platelets (TRAP) Study Group[7] indicated that use of either leukocyte-filtered or UVB-irradiated blood components reduced the incidence of HLA antibody generation from 45% to between 17% and 21%. The incidence of platelet refractoriness was reduced from 16% to between 7% and 10%. Although a relationship had been reported between alloimmunization and the number of donor exposures in one report,[22] a second study[23] found no relationship between the number of donor exposures and the rate or severity of alloimmunization. The TRAP study found that leukocyte reduction, not the number of donor exposures, was significant in modifying the rate of alloimmunization. Thus, leukocyte-reduced, pooled, whole-blood-derived platelets appear to be clinically equivalent to apheresis platelets, at least in terms of reducing primary alloimmunization.[24]

Antibodies to HLA antigens may be detected by lymphocytotoxicity tests or by many of the platelet antibody tests discussed below. Lymphocytotoxicity tests detect complement-binding antibodies capable of killing lymphocytes. One strategy for managing patients who are receiving multiple platelet transfusions and who have developed clinical refractoriness is to test for the presence of HLA antibodies using a lymphocytotoxicity antibody screen against a panel of lymphocytes representing most of the Class I HLA antigens present in the donor population. Reactivity to greater than 20% of the cells in the panel (PRA >20%) indicates that HLA sensitization may be at least a contributing cause of the platelet refractoriness. Newer, more sensitive HLA antibody detection techniques such as the Flow PRA[25] (One Lambda, Canoga Park, CA) have been adapted to a PRA result format, and some HLA testing laboratories use these methods instead of the traditional lymphocytotoxicity test.

The laboratory detection of lymphocytotoxic antibodies does not necessarily indicate that the patient will experience reduced survival of transfused platelets. Moreover, HLA antibodies may disappear from the patient's plasma despite continued exposure through transfusions.[26] A fuller discussion of HLA antibody and antigen testing can be found in Chapter 17.

Platelet-Specific Alloantigens

To date, 22 platelet-specific alloantigens have been characterized as to their localization to platelet surface glycoprotein structures, quantification of their density on the platelet surface, and determination of DNA polymorphisms in genes encoding for them (see Table 16-4).[27] Several others have been described serologically, but genetic polymorphisms underlying them have not yet been determined.[28] The term "platelet specific," is a misnomer for some of these markers because they may be found on other types of cells as well (especially endothelial cells). However,

their chief clinical importance remains linked to their presence on platelets. Of the dozens of recognized platelet membrane glycoproteins, at least five [GPIa, Ib (alpha and beta), IIb, IIIa, and CD109] are polymorphic and have been demonstrated to be alloimmunogenic.[28] In addition, rare individuals who lack a sixth membrane glycoprotein, GPIV (CD36), may become sensitized to this antigen.[29] Approximately 3% to 5% of individuals of Asian or African ethnicity lack GPIV on their platelets[30] and can become immunized by transfusion or pregnancy.[31] Although antibodies to these various membrane glycoproteins may be associated, in rare instances, with refractoriness to platelet transfusions, alloantibodies to platelet-specific antigens are more often associated with the alloimmune syndromes posttransfusion purpura (PTP) and neonatal alloimmune thrombocytopenia (NAIT).

Several antigen systems on platelets are now recognized[32] (Table 16-4).[27,33] The nomenclature adopted by the International Society of Blood Transfusion classifies the systems numerically according to the date of publication and alphabetically to reflect their frequency in the population.[34] As with red cells, different terminologies for platelet antigens often coexist. The first recognized antigen,[35] Zw[a], is now designated HPA-1a of the HPA-1 system. The HPA-1a antigen is often better known as Pl[A1]. HPA-1a is present on the platelets of about 98% of persons of European ethnicity and anti-HPA-1a (anti-Pl[A1]) is the most frequently encountered clinically significant platelet-specific antibody in this population. Its antithetical antigen, HPA-1b (Pl[A2]), occurs in 27% of this population.

The HPA-1a and HPA-1b alleles reside on the platelet membrane glycoprotein GPIIIa. Patients with Glanzmann's thrombasthenia Type I, a disorder of platelet function, lack

Table 16-4. Alloantigenic Polymorphisms of Platelet Glycoproteins that Have Been Implicated in Alloimmune Syndromes*

HPA System Name	Antigens (Familiar Names)	Phenotypic Frequencies	GP Location	Amino Acid Substitution	Alloimmune Syndromes
POLYMORPHISMS OF GLYCOPROTEIN IIIa					
HPA-1	HPA-1a, (Pl[A1], Zw[a])	98%	IIIa	Leu↔Pro33	NAIT, PTP
	HPA-1b, (Pl[A2], Zw[b])	27%	IIIa		
HPA-4	HPA-4a (Pen[a], Yuk[b])†	99.9%	IIIa	Arg↔Gln143	NAIT, PTP
	HPA-4b (Pen[b], Yuk[a])	<1%	IIIa		
HPA-6	HPA-6bw (Ca[a], Tu[a])	<1%	IIIa	Arg↔Gln489	NAIT
HPA-7	HPA-7bw (Mo)	<1%	IIIa	Pro↔Ala407	NAIT
HPA-8	HPA-8bw (Sr[a])	<1%	IIIa	Arg↔Cys636	NAIT
HPA-10	HPA-10bw (La[a])	<1%	IIIa	Arg↔Gln62	NAIT
HPA-11	HPA-11bw (Gro[a])	<1%	IIIa	Arg↔His633	NAIT
HPA-14	HPA-14bw (Oe[a])	<1%	IIIa	Lys611 Deleted	NAIT
HPA-16	HPA-16bw (Duv[a])	<1%	IIIa	Ile↔Thr140	NAIT
POLYMORPHISMS OF GLYCOPROTEIN IIb					
HPA-3	HPA-3a (Bak[a], Lek[a])	85%	IIb	Ile↔Ser843	NAIT, PTP
	HPA-3b (Bak[b], Lek[b])	63%	IIb		
HPA-9	HPA-9bw (Max[a])	0.6%	IIb	Val↔Met837	NAIT

(cont'd)

Table 16-4. Alloantigenic Polymorphisms of Platelet Glycoproteins that Have Been Implicated in Alloimmune Syndromes* (cont'd)

HPA System Name	Antigens (Familiar Names)	Phenotypic Frequencies	GP Location	Amino Acid Substitution	Alloimmune Syndromes
POLYMORPHISMS OF GLYCOPROTEIN Ia					
HPA-5	HPA-5a (Br^b, Zav^b)	99%	Ia		
	HPA-5b (Br^a, Zav^a)	20%	Ia	glu↔Lys505	NAIT, PTP
HPA-13	HPA-13bw (Sit^a)	<0.2%	Ia	Thr↔Met799	NAIT
POLYMORPHISMS OF GLYCOPROTEIN Ib					
HPA-2	HPA-2a (Ko^b, Sib^b)	99%	Ib alpha		
	HPA-2b (Ko^a, Sib^a)	15%	Ib alpha	Thr↔Met145	NAIT
HPA-12	HPA-12bw (Iy^a)	0.3%	Ib beta	Gly↔Glu15	NAIT
OTHER PROBABLE PLATELET ALLOANTIGEN SPECIFICITIES					
HPA-15	HPA-15a (Gov^b)	80%	CD109		
	HPA-15b (Gov^a)	60%	CD109	Tyr↔Ser703	NAIT, PTP

*Modified from Kroll.[27] GP = glyprotein; NAIT = neonatal alloimmune thrombocytopenia; PTP = posttransfusion purpurpa.

this glycoprotein and, therefore, do not express HPA-1 antigens. The HPA-1 polymorphism arises by the substitution of a single base pair (leucine in HPA-1a and proline in HPA-1b) at amino acid position 33 of the protein's DNA coding sequence. GPIIIa is also the carrier of HPA-4, -6, -7, -8, -10, -11, -14, and -16 antigens. Alleles in each of these systems also arise as a result of single amino acid substitutions at different positions. The HPA-2 antigen system is situated on GPIb alpha; the HPA-3 system on GPIIb; and the HPA-5 system on GPIa.[36,37]

On the platelet membrane, most of the glycoproteins that carry these "platelet-specific" antigens are present as heterodimeric compounds, ie, each consists of two different glycoprotein molecules (see Fig 16-1[38]). Therefore, platelet glycoprotein names are often paired (eg, Ia/IIa, IIb/IIIa, or Ib/IX), referring to the alpha and beta chains in each complex. GPIb/IX is a leucine-rich membrane glycoprotein that serves as a receptor for von Willebrand factor on platelets. The Ia/IIa and IIb/IIIa complexes are members of a broadly distributed family of adhesion molecules called integrins. Integrins are essential for platelet adhesion and aggregation because the molecules serve as receptors for ligands such as fibrinogen (IIb/IIIa), von Willebrand factor (Ib/IX), and collagen (Ia/IIa). When present on other cells, the glycoprotein pairings may differ. For example, on platelets, GPIIIa is normally paired with GPIIb. On endothelial cells, fibroblasts, and smooth muscle, however, GPIIIa is paired with a different glycoprotein. Thus, these cells share the

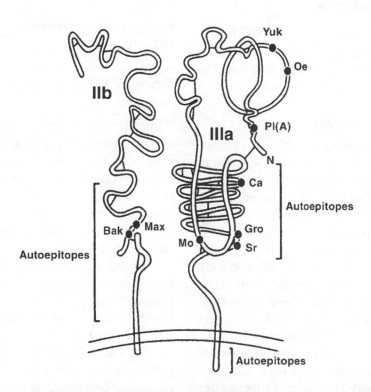

Figure 16-1. Schematic diagram of platelet glycoprotein complex IIb/IIIa. Dots and letters (Yuk, Oe, Pl[a], Ca, Gro, Sr, Mo, Bak, Max) designate positions and names of recognized allotypic epitopes. The molecular regions where autoepitopes have been recognized are indicated by brackets.[38]

HPA alloantigens found on the GPIIIa molecule, but not those found on the GPIIb molecule.

CD109 is an exception to the heterodimeric rule, occurring as a monomeric structure on the platelet membrane. This GPI-linked protein is found on activated T cells, cultured endothelial cells, several tumor cell lines, as well as platelets.[39] Two alloantigens designated HPA-15wb (Gov[a]) and HPA-15wa (Gov[b]) have been localized to platelet CD109.[39] Unlike most platelet-specific alloantigens, both alleles are highly expressed [0.53% (Gov[b]) and 0.47% (Gov[a])] in persons of European ethnicity (Table 16-4). Sensitization to Gov alloantigens has been associated with platelet refractoriness, NAIT, and PTP, albeit usually together with other alloantibodies to platelet antigens.[40]

Clinical Importance of Platelet-Specific Antigens and Antibodies

Neonatal Alloimmune Thrombocytopenia

Neonatal alloimmune thrombocytopenia (variously abbreviated NAIT, NATP, etc) is described in Chapter 23.

Posttransfusion Purpura

Posttransfusion purpura (PTP) is characterized by the development of dramatic, sudden, and self-limiting thrombocytopenia 5 to 10 days after a blood transfusion in a patient with a history of sensitization by pregnancy or transfusion. Coincident with the thrombocytopenia is the development of a potent platelet-specific alloantibody in the patient's serum, usually anti-HPA-1a. Other specificities have been implicated, almost always associated with antigens on GPIIb/IIIa.[37,41] PTP differs from transfusion reactions caused by red cell antibodies because the patient's own antigen-negative (usually HPA-1a-negative) platelets as well as any transfused antigen-positive platelets (which may be accompa-

nied by clinically severe reactions) are destroyed. Transfusion of antigen-negative platelets may be of value during the acute phase of PTP; however, such platelets have a reduced in-vivo survival.[42] Plasmapheresis—once the treatment of choice—has largely been supplanted by the use of intravenous immune globulin (IGIV). The mechanism by which these treatments are efficacious is unknown. Platelet antibody assays usually reveal a serum antibody with HPA-1a specificity. Typing of the patient's platelets after recovery will document a HPA-1a-negative phenotype or analogous typing for other platelet-specific antigen systems. Following recovery, future transfusions should be provided using washed antigen-negative RBC units if possible. Washed RBC units may offer some protection against recurrence, although at least one case of PTP caused by antibody to HPA-5b was precipitated by transfusion of a washed RBC unit.[43]

Testing for Platelet-Specific Antigens and Antibodies

Clinically useful platelet antibody assays emerged later than serologic assays to diagnose immunologic disorders involving red cells. This is mainly because it is difficult to separate platelets from whole blood specimens and to distinguish antibody-dependent endpoints from nonspecific changes that occur in platelets under assay conditions. Three types of platelet antibody detection methods have been developed[44] (Table 16-5). The earliest were Phase I assays that involved mixing patient serum with normal platelets and used platelet function-dependent endpoints such as alpha granule release, aggregation, or agglutination. Phase II tests measured either surface or total platelet-associated immunoglobulin on patient

Table 16-5. Platelet Antibody Assays

Phase I Assays
Platelet aggregation
Inhibition of platelet aggregation
Inhibition of clot retraction
Inhibition of platelet migration
Complement fixation
Platelet factor 3 release
^{51}Chromium release
^{14}C-Serotonin release

Phase II Assays
Detection of platelet surface-associated immunoglobulin
■ Platelet suspension immunofluorescence test (PSIFT)
■ Flow cytometry
■ Radioimmunoassay (^{125}I staphylococcal Protein A,^{125}I antihuman immunoglobulin, polyclonal or monoclonal)
■ Antiglobulin consumption (two-stage assay)
■ Solid-phase red cell adherence
Detection of total platelet-associated immunoglobulin
■ Nephelometry
■ Electroimmunoassay
■ Radial immunodiffusion

Phase III Assays
Monoclonal antibody immobilization of platelet antigens (MAIPA)
Antigen capture ELISA (ACE)
Modified antigen capture ELISA (MACE)
Immunobead assay
Immunoblotting

platelets or on normal platelets after sensitization with patient serum. Phase III solid-phase assays were developed in which the binding of antibodies to isolated platelet surface glycoproteins is detected. The test methods are examples of Phase I, II, and III assays; variations of each test method are also used. Lymphocytotoxicity tests are discussed in Chapter 17.

Mixed Passive Hemagglutination Assay (MPHA). A Phase II assay used for the detection of platelet-specific antibodies as well as for platelet crossmatching is the MPHA. Shibata et al were the first to use this method to detect and identify clinically

significant platelet alloantibodies.[45] A modification of MPHA, the SPRCA, is widely used.[18] In this assay, intact platelets are immobilized in the round-bottom wells of a microtiter tray and are sensitized with antibody to be detected. After washing, detector red cells previously coated with an antibody specific for human immunoglobulin are added. After incubation from several hours to overnight, the tray is subjected to a slow centrifugation and examined visually. If antibody is bound to the immobilized platelets, the indicator red cells fail to form a compact button in the center of the well because they are evenly distributed like a "carpet" over the antibody-coated platelets. In a negative reaction, a red cell button forms in the center of the well. A limitation of the MPHA assay is that it fails to distinguish platelet-specific from non-platelet-specific antibodies. A modification of the MPHA assay, the Capture-P (Imucor Gamma, Norcross, GA), is available as a commercial kit and is most often marketed for platelet cross-matching.[18] SPRCA testing may be modified by treatment of target platelets with chloroquine or acid,[46,47] which disrupts the Class I HLA heavy chain-peptide-β_2-microglobulin trimolecular complex. This modifies antigenic epitopes, reducing the binding of specific antibodies directed against HLA on platelets. However, strong HLA antibodies may still bind, giving the impression that the antibody is directed to non-HLA antigens.

Flow Cytometry. Another example of a Phase II assay is platelet antibody detection using immunofluorescence. Originally a slide-based method,[48] the technique now uses flow cytometry to detect platelet-reactive antibody in patient sera that binds to intact platelets.[49] In the assay, washed platelets are sensitized with patient or control serum for up to 60 minutes, usually at room temperature. The platelets are then washed repeatedly to remove nonspecific immunoglobulins, and platelet-bound antibodies are detected with a fluorescent-labeled (usually fluorescein isothiocyanate, FITC) polyclonal or monoclonal antibody specific for human immunoglobulin. The platelets are analyzed in the flow cytometer and results can be expressed as a ratio of the mean or peak channel fluorescence of normal platelets sensitized with patient serum over that of normal platelets incubated in normal serum. In order to prevent nonspecific binding of the immunoglobulin probe via Fc receptors on the target platelets, the probe antibodies are enzyme treated to remove the Fc end of the molecule. There-

fore, binding of the labeled probe can be assumed to be via its F(ab')$_2$ or antigen-specific end. A second fluorescent label [eg, phycoerythrin (PE)] can be attached to an antihuman IgM probe to detect IgM platelet antibodies. Because FITC and PE fluoresce with peak light intensities at different wavelengths when exposed to the monochromatic argon laser in the flow cytometer (520-nm green light and 580-nm reddish-orange light, respectively), cells labeled with FITC can be distinguished from those labeled with PE. Both anti-IgG and anti-IgM labeled with different fluorochromes can be added to the same tube with washed sensitized platelets for the simultaneous detection of antiplatelet IgG and IgM.

Flow cytometry has proven to be a very sensitive method for detection of alloantibodies. The assay is capable of detecting very small numbers of antibody molecules bound to platelets as is the case with alloantibodies specific for antigens of the HPA-5 (Br) system having only 1000 to 2000 sites per platelet. Moreover, some alloantibodies that are specific for labile epitopes that are unreliably detected in Phase III assays can be detected on intact platelets using flow cytometry.

Because the target platelets used in the assay are intact, flow cytometry does not differentiate between platelet-specific (ie, platelet glycoprotein directed) and non-platelet-specific antibodies. Examples of the latter are HLA and ABO antibodies. This is an advantage when the method is used to detect antibodies that will affect the success of a platelet transfusion, and, for this reason, flow cytometry has been advocated as a platelet crossmatching method. However, when used to investigate cases of suspected NAIT or PTP, the method has a potential drawback—the more relevant platelet-specific antibodies characteristic in these diseases can be obscured by non-platelet-specific reactivity.

Monoclonal Antibody-Specific Immobilization of Platelet Antigen (MAIPA). An example of a Phase III assay is the MAIPA,[50-52] perhaps the most widely used assay to detect platelet-specific antibodies. The assay requires the use of murine monoclonal antibodies (MoAbs) that recognize the target antigens of interest but do not compete with the human antibody being detected. In the assay, target platelets are simultaneously sensitized with patient serum and a murine MoAb recognizing the desired target molecule on the platelet surface. After the initial sensitization step, platelets are washed and solubilized in a nonionic detergent. After centrifugation to remove cytoskeletal fragments, an aliquot of the supernatant lysate is added to wells of a microtiter tray containing immobilized goat antibody specific for mouse IgG. The MoAb is thereby captured and the platelet surface glycoprotein with its bound human antibody is immobilized. After a wash step, the human antibody is detected with an enzyme-labeled goat antihuman immunoglobulin probe.

There are several other versions of Phase III assays in use today, including the antigen capture enzyme-linked immunosorbent assay (ACE), the modified antigen capture ELISA (MACE),[53,54] and the commercially available GTI PAKPLUS[55] (GTI, Waukesha, WI). Each relies on MoAbs to immobilize only the glycoproteins of interest, thereby reducing or eliminating interfering reactions due to non-platelet-specific antibodies, especially anti-HLA, which, if present, is detected only in wells containing pools of immobilized HLA Class I antigens.

Platelet Typing Using Molecular Methods. Molecular typing by polymerase chain reaction (PCR) is available for many platelet antigens. Because immunophenotyping is limited by the shortage of characterized typing antisera and by low platelet counts, several DNA-based HPA typing techniques, such as restriction fragment length polymorphism (RFLP) analysis and sequence-specific oligonucleotide hybridization, have been developed.[56,57] All of these techniques are reliable, but they are also laborious and time-consuming. For this reason, PCR genotyping with sequence-specific primers (SSP) appears to be much more practical to use.[58,59] In a recent workshop, SSP-PCR was the most common and reliable method of determining platelet antigens,[60] making it feasible for genotyping HPAs independent of the patient's platelet count and of rare typing sera.[61]

Autoimmune Platelet Disorders

Idiopathic (Autoimmune) Thrombocytopenic Purpura

Autoantibodies directed against platelet antigens may result in thrombocytopenia. Chronic idiopathic thrombocytopenic purpura (ITP), most often a disease in adults, is characterized by an insidious onset and moderate thrombocytopenia that may exist for months to years before diagnosis. Females are twice as likely to be affected as males. Spontaneous remissions are rare, and treatment is usually required to raise the platelet count. First-line therapy consists of steroids, high-dose IGIV or Rh immunoglobulin (RhIG), followed by splenectomy in nonresponders. Many other therapies have been used in patients who fail to respond to splenectomy. Results have varied. Chronic autoimmune thrombocytopenia may be idiopathic or associated with other diseases (eg, HIV infection, malignancy, other autoimmune conditions). Acute ITP is mainly a childhood disease characterized by abrupt onset of severe thrombocytopenia and bleeding symptomatology, often after a viral infection. The majority of cases resolve spontaneously over a 2- to 6-month period. If treatment is required, IGIV or RhIG infusions are usually effective in raising the platelet count. Steroids are used less often because of serious side effects in children. Splenectomy, if used, is reserved for those children whose disease is severe and lasts longer than 6 months, similar to chronic ITP in adults.

Testing for Platelet Autoantibodies

Numerous Phase I, II, and III platelet antibody assays have been developed to detect relevant autoantibodies in ITP patients. Although many tests have been demonstrated to be quite sensitive, particularly in detecting total or cell surface platelet-associated immunoglobulins (Phase II assays),[62] none has been sufficiently specific to be particularly useful in either the diagnosis or management of ITP. The American Society of Hematology's practice guidelines for ITP state that serologic testing is unnecessary, assuming the clinical findings are compatible with the diagnosis.[63] However, platelet antibody tests may be helpful in the evaluation of patients suspected of having ITP when other, nonimmune causes may be present.

The goal of serologic testing in ITP is to detect autoantibody bound to the patient's own platelets with or without demonstration of similar reactivity in the patient's plasma. Most of the newer assays offered for evaluation of patients suspected of having ITP are Phase III assays, designed to detect immunoglobulin binding to platelet-specific epitopes found on platelet glycoprotein complexes GPIIb/IIIa, GPIa/IIa, and/or GPIb/IX.

These solid-phase GP-specific assays appear to have improved specificity in distinguishing ITP from nonimmune thrombocytopenia when compared to Phase II assays, but this is often balanced by a decrease in sensitivity.[64] Moreover, all of these methods have limited usefulness in patients who have very low platelet counts that prevent adequate numbers of platelets to be collected for use in the tests.

One commercially available Phase III test, the GTI PAKAUTO,[65] uses eluates prepared from washed patient platelets. The eluates are tested against a panel of MoAb-immobilized platelet GP complexes, and antibody binding is detected using an enzyme-linked antihuman immunoglobulin probe. In the indirect phase of the assay, patient plasma is tested against the same glycoprotein panel. In general, plasma antibodies are detected less often than antibodies in the eluates. ITP patients may have antibodies that are reactive with one or several GP targets. To date, there is no correlation between the specificity of autoantibodies in ITP and disease severity.

Drug-Induced Immune Platelet Disorders

Thrombocytopenia associated with specific drugs is not uncommon. Drugs often implicated include quinidine/quinine, sulfa drugs, heparin, and colloidal gold. Both drug-dependent and drug-independent antibodies may be produced. Drug-independent antibodies, although stimulated by drugs, do not require the continued presence of the drug to react with platelets and are serologically indistinguishable from other platelet autoantibodies. (Unlike typical autoimmune thrombocytopenia, these antibodies are transient except when caused by therapy with gold, which is excreted very slowly.) Drug-dependent antibodies result when a drug combines with platelets in such a way as to create neoantigens to which antibodies are formed. The drug must be present for the antibody to react. These antibodies can cause a thrombocytopenia of sudden and rapid onset, usually resolving when the drug is discontinued.

Testing for Drug-Dependent Platelet-Reactive Antibodies

Serology. Virtually any platelet serology test that is used to detect platelet-bound immunoglobulin can be modified for use in the detection of drug-dependent platelet-reactive antibodies. In performing drug-dependent antibody testing, it is essential to establish the proper positive and negative controls for the assay. Each serum or plasma sample suspected of containing drug-dependent antibody must be tested against normal target platelets in the presence and absence of drug. Moreover, at least one normal serum should be tested with and without drug to control for any possible drug-related platelet effect that does not require specific antibody. Finally, a positive control serum known to be reactive with the drug being assayed should be tested with and without drug to complete the evaluation. A positive result must show that the serum is positive against normal target platelets in the presence of drug and not without drug, and that the drug did not nonspecifically cause a positive result in the target platelet. Likewise, the positive control must be positive with the drug and negative without it.

Flow Cytometry. The flow cytometry test can be readily adapted to detect both IgG and IgM drug-dependent platelet antibodies.[53,66] In this modification, fluorescence of normal platelets sensitized with the patient's serum in the presence of drug can be compared with that of the patient's sample without drug or to a normal serum with drug to determine relative intensity of labeling. Flow cytometry has proven to have superior sensitivity to other assays for detection of quinine-quinidine- and sulfonamide-dependent platelet-reactive antibodies.[53] Table 16-6 shows other agents for which drug-dependent platelet-reactive an-

tibodies have been detected and confirmed by flow cytometry in a large platelet immunology reference laboratory.

Flow cytometry has its limitations, as do other antibody detection methods, in detecting drug-dependent antibodies. For many drugs, the optimal concentration to demonstrate in-vitro binding of antibody has not been determined. Probably the most extensively studied drugs in this regard are quinine or quinidine.[67] Another cause of poor sensitivity is the weak binding of drug to platelets, leading to rapidly declining numbers of drug molecules on the platelet surface once drug is removed from the environment of the platelet. It is therefore important to maintain a critical concentration of drug in all washing buffers before addition of probe at the end of an assay.[66] Yet another potential reason for insensitivity is that a patient may not be sensitized to the native drug but, rather, to a metabolite of the drug. Antibodies dependent on metabolites of acetaminophen and sulfamethoxazole have been reported.[68,69]

A number of other assays have been adopted for the detection of drug-dependent platelet antibodies. Among these are the SPRCA.[70,71] Phase I assays have also been modified for detection of heparin-dependent platelet antibodies (see below). In some cases, determination of the specific glycoprotein to which antibody is directed by Phase III assays may provide useful clinical information. For example, drug-dependent antibody to GPIb/IX was associated with a more acute, but reversible, quinine-induced thrombocytopenia, whereas antibody to GPIIb/IIIa was associated with a more prolonged course.[72]

Heparin-Induced Thrombocytopenia

Two types of heparin-induced thrombocytopenia (HIT) have been recognized. Type I, of nonimmune origin, presents with

Table 16-6. Drugs Confirmed to Elicit Drug-Dependent Platelet-Reactive Antibodies In Vitro Using Flow Cytometry Testing

abciximab	heparin	ranitidine
acetaminophen	ibuprofen	rifampin
carbamazepine	levofloxacin	sulfamethoxazole
ceftazidime	loracarbef	sulfisoxazole
ceftizoxime	naproxen	suramin
ceftriaxone	orbofiban	tirofiban
ciprofloxacin	oxaliplatin	trimethoprim
eptifibatide	phenytoin	vancomycin
esomeprazole	propoxyphene	xemilofiban
fentanyl	quinidine	
fexofenadine	quinine	

mild transient thrombocytopenia within minutes to several days after heparin exposure but generally resolves despite ongoing heparin therapy and is not clinically important. In contrast, immune, or Type II, HIT may lead to life- and limb-threatening thrombotic complications and requires careful evaluation and management of afflicted patients.

The exact incidence of immune HIT is unknown, but it may develop in up to 3% of patients treated with unfractionated heparin. Low-molecular-weight heparin is less likely to be associated with either antibody production or thrombocytopenia.[73] Bovine heparin appears somewhat more likely to cause HIT than porcine heparin.[74] A reduction in baseline platelet count by at least 50% occurs generally within 5 to 14 days after primary exposure and sooner after secondary exposure to the drug. The platelet count is often less than 100,000/μL and usually recovers within 5 to 7 days upon discontinuation of heparin.

About 30% of patients with HIT, or approximately 0.9% of patients who receive heparin, develop thrombosis, which can occur in the arterial, venous, or both systems.[75,76] Patients may develop cardiovascular problems, myocardial infarction, limb ischemia, deep venous thrombosis, or ischemia of other organs. The thrombotic complications may force limb amputation or may prove fatal.

Thrombosis or an unexplained decrease in platelet count while on heparin therapy should raise concern about HIT. *Heparin, including heparin flushes and heparin-coated catheters, should be discontinued,* and the patient should be evaluated for laboratory evidence of HIT and signs of thrombosis. In mild-to-moderate thrombocytopenia, monitoring of platelet counts and observation may be sufficient, but because of the high risk of thrombosis, treatment with alternative anticoagulants is generally recommended. Warfarin should be avoided in the early treatment of HIT because it does not prevent thrombosis in this setting and may provoke limb-threatening venous gangrene by reducing levels of naturally occurring anticoagulants faster than it reduces activated coagulation factors. However, warfarin can and should be used after the patient is anticoagulated with alternative drugs. Suitable anticoagulants approved by the Food and Drug Administration (FDA) include hirudin (a natural thrombin inhibitor) and argatroban. Selected patients may also benefit from thrombolectomy or thrombolytic therapy. Platelet transfusion should be avoided, given that bleeding is a rare complication in HIT, and administration of platelets may precipitate thrombosis.[77-79]

Heparin forms a complex with platelet factor 4 (PF4), a tetrameric protein released from platelet alpha granules. Antibodies (IgG, IgM, and some IgA) form against various epitopes on this complex and attach to platelet Fcγ IIa receptors, whereby platelets become activated. The antibody may also bind to the complexes at other sites, notably on endothelial cells. Thus, HIT might involve activation and damage not only of platelets but also of endothelium, causing increased susceptibility to thrombosis. This new understanding of the mechanism of heparin antibodies is exploited by ELISA tests in which microwells are coated with the complexes rather than with the platelets themselves.[80]

Testing for Heparin-Dependent Antibodies

The PF4 ELISA is an example of a Phase III assay for HIT. Target complexes of PF4 and heparin or heparin-like molecules are immobilized on a solid phase. To perform the test, patient serum is added to premade complexes of PF4 and heparin or heparin-like molecules (eg, polyvinyl sulfate, PVS) alone and in the presence of high-dose (100 U/mL) heparin. Heparin-dependent antibody binds to the complexes and is detected via enzyme-conjugated antihuman immunoglobulin. An optical density value above 0.4 in the PF4-PVS well that is inhibited by high-dose heparin confirms the presence of a heparin-dependent antibody in the patient's sample. Although IgG antibodies are the most clinically relevant antibodies causing this syndrome,[81] occasional patients with HIT appear to have only non-IgG (IgM or IgA) antibodies.[82] The PF4 ELISA detects but

does not differentiate IgG, IgM, and IgA antibodies that bind to the PF4-heparin complex.

The ^{14}C-serotonin release assay (SRA) is an example of a Phase I assay for detection of heparin-dependent antibodies.[83] Normal, fresh target platelets are incubated with ^{14}C-serotonin that is taken up into the dense granules of the platelets. Then, target platelets are exposed to patient serum in the presence of low and high concentrations of heparin. Release of at least 20% of the radioactive label at the low dose of heparin and inhibition of this release at the high dose confirms the presence of heparin-dependent antibodies. Other functional tests used to detect heparin-dependent antibodies include the heparin-induced platelet aggregation test and the heparin-induced platelet activation test.

The PF4 ELISA and the SRA are both more sensitive and specific than the platelet aggregation test for the detection of heparin-dependent platelet antibodies in patients for whom there is clinical suspicion of HIT.[83-85] However, in asymptomatic patients receiving heparin or in those who have not yet received the drug, neither test is sufficiently predictive of HIT to warrant its use in screening.

Granulocyte Antigens

Analogous to platelet alloantigens, neutrophil alloantigens are implicated in clinical syndromes including neonatal alloimmune neutropenia (NAN), transfusion-related acute lung injury (TRALI), immune neutropenia after marrow transplantation, refractoriness to granulocyte transfusion, and chronic benign autoimmune neutropenia of infancy. A neutrophil equivalent of PTP has not been described. To date, seven neutrophil alloantigens have been described, including localization to neutrophil surface glycoprotein structures and, in some cases, determination of DNA polymorphisms in genes encoding for them (see Table 16-7).

The first granulocyte-specific antigen, NA1 (HNA-1a), was described in 1966 by Lalezari and Bernard.[86] HNA-1a and its antithetical antigen, HNA-1b, are present on FcγRIIIb. Antibodies to HNA-1a and -1b have been implicated in TRALI, NAN, and autoimmune neutropenia of infancy. About 0.1% of individuals of European ethnicity have neutrophils with no detectable FcγRIIIb (NA$_{null}$). The FcγRIII protein also carries the neutrophil alloantigen SH (HNA-1c).[87] NB1 (HNA-2a) is found on another granulocyte surface glycoprotein, CD177, the function of which is still undetermined. HNA-2a has been reported to have an allele, NB2, but the product of this gene cannot be reliably identified with alloantisera, and no MoAb specific for NB2 has been identified; therefore, the existence of a second allele to HNA-2a (NB1) is unproven.[88] HNA-2a has been associated with TRALI and NAN. The DNA sequence of the NB1(HNA-2a) gene has been determined as have the molecular polymorphisms associated with HNA-1a and HNA-1b and HNA-1c on the gene for FcγRIII. Therefore, genotyping for these specificities can be performed on genomic DNA using PCR-SSP.[89] Reduced expression of granulocyte antigens occurs in paroxysmal nocturnal hemoglobinuria, chronic myelogenous leukemia, and in premature infants.

Additional antigens on granulocytes are shared with other cells and are not granulocyte-specific. These include 5b (HNA-3a), MART^a (HNA-4a), and OND^a (HNA-5a). The HNA-3a is located on a 70- to 95-Kd protein that has not yet been cloned. HNA-3a is also expressed on the surface of lymphocytes. The antibodies directed at this antigen are

Table 16-7. Neutrophil Alloantigens

Antigen System	Allele	HNA Designation	Antigen Frequency (%)		Glycoprotein Location
			White	Black	
Neutrophil-specific					
NA	NA1	HNA-1a	46	46	FcγRIIIb (CD16)
NA	NA2	HNA-1b	88	84	FcγRIIIb (CD16)
SH	SH	HNA-1c	5	22	FcγRIIIb (CD16)
NB	NB1	HNA-2a	97		CD177
Neutrophil-nonspecific					
5	5b	HNA-3a	97		70-95 kD GP
MART	MART^a	HNA-4a	99		CD11b
OND	OND^a	HNA-5a	99		CD11a

usually agglutinins; they occasionally occur in women after pregnancy and may be associated with febrile transfusion reactions. Potent anti-HNA-3a agglutinins in transfused plasma have been responsible for fatal TRALI.[90-92] MART[a] and OND[a], both high-incidence antigens, are also present on monocytes and lymphocytes. MART[a] has been localized to the alpha M chain (CD11b) of the C3bi receptor (CR3) and results from a single nucleic acid substitution. MART[a] has been recently reported to cause NAN.[93] OND[a] is expressed on the alpha L integrin unit, leukocyte function antigen-1 (CD11a) and also results from a single nucleotide substitution. This marker, found in a chronically transfused aplastic anemia patient, has not been reported to be associated with clinical disease.

Clinical Syndromes in Which Granulocyte-Specific Alloantigens Are Implicated

Nonhemolytic, febrile transfusion reactions are often associated with granulocyte antibodies. Although such reactions are more often caused by antibodies to Class I HLA antibodies directed at Class I epitopes present on granulocytes, granulocyte-specific antibodies have been associated with clinical syndromes similar to those seen with antibodies to red cell and platelet antigens.

Neonatal Alloimmune Neutropenia

NAN is caused by maternal antibodies against alloantigens of fetal neutrophils; the most frequent specificities seen are against NA1, NA2, and NB1 antigens (see Table 16-7). NAN most often occurs in women of the neutrophil alloantigen phenotypes NA1/NA1 and NA2/NA2; it may also occur in women of the rare NA_{null} phenotype who lack the FcγRIII protein. The neutropenia in all these cases can oc-

casionally be life-threatening because of increased susceptibility to infection. Management with antibiotics, IGIV, granulocyte colony-stimulating growth factor, and/or plasma exchange may be helpful.

TRALI

TRALI is an acute, often life-threatening reaction characterized by respiratory distress, hypo- or hypertension, and noncardiogenic pulmonary edema that occurs within 6 hours of a transfusion of a plasma-containing blood component. TRALI has been reported to be induced by neutrophil antibodies, although more recent reports are more likely to implicate antibodies to both Class I and II HLA antigens.[94] In TRALI, the causative antibodies are most often found in the plasma of the blood donor (see Chapters 17 and 27). Recent reports have postulated that another etiology for TRALI is possible. This theory suggests that two events must coincide for TRALI to occur: 1) the patient must have a predisposing clinical condition that releases cytokines or other factors that prime neutrophils, causing adherence to endothelium, and 2) the patient must receive a transfusion of biologically active lipids (which also stimulate neutrophils) from stored blood components.[95] In one study, neutrophil antibodies were detected in only three of 10 incidents of TRALI, and none of the donors had HLA antibodies.

Autoimmune neutropenia, usually occurring in adults, may be idiopathic or may occur secondary to such diseases as rheumatoid arthritis, systemic lupus erythematosus, or bacterial infections. In autoimmune neutropenia of infancy, usually occurring in children between the ages of 6 months to 2 years, the autoantibody has a neutrophil antigen specificity (usually HNA-1a and -1b) in about half the cases.

The condition is usually self-limiting (with recovery usually in 7-24 months) and the condition is relatively benign and manageable with antibiotics.[96] Drug-dependent antibodies can also cause neutropenia.

Testing for Granulocyte Autoantibodies

Tests for granulocyte antibodies are not widely performed, although the implication of neutrophil antibodies as a cause of TRALI has increased the demand for this laboratory resource. Agglutination tests performed in tube, capillary, or microplate formats use heat-inactivated serum in the presence of EDTA and require fresh granulocytes. Immunofluorescence tests, read with either a fluorescence microscope or a flow cytometer, are also used and are capable of detecting granulocyte-bound antiglobulin. A combination of agglutination and immunofluorescence tests is beneficial.[97] Other methods include chemiluminescence and a MoAb-specific immobilization of granulocyte antigens (MAIGA) assay, similar to the MAIPA assay. An advantage of the MAIGA assay is its ability to differentiate readily between HLA and granulocyte-specific antibodies.

References

1. Ogasawara K, Ueki J, Takenaka M, Furihata K. Study on the expression of ABO antigens on platelets. Blood 1993;82:993-9.
2. Bialek J, Bodmer W, Bodmer J, Payne R. Distribution and quantity of leukocyte antigens in the formed elements of blood. Transfusion 1966;6:193-204.
3. Feuerstein N, Mono DS, Cooper HL. Phorbolester effect in platelets, lymphocytes, and leukemic cells (HL-60) is associated with enhanced phosphorylation of Class I HLA antigens. Biochem Biophys Res Commun 1985; 126:206-13.
4. Howard JA, Perkins HA. The natural history of alloimmunization to platelets. Transfusion 1978;18:496-503.
5. Godeau B, Fromont P, Seror T, et al. Platelet alloimmunization after multiple transfu-

6. Dzik WH. Leukoreduced blood components: Laboratory and clinical aspects. In: Simon TL, Dzik WH, Snyder EL, et al, eds. Rossi's principles of transfusion medicine. 3rd ed. Philadelphia, PA: Lippincott Williams and Wilkins, 2002:270-87.
7. The Trial to Reduce Alloimmunization to Platelets Study Group. Leukocyte reduction and ultraviolet B irradiation of platelets to prevent alloimmunization and refractoriness to platelet transfusions. N Engl J Med 1997; 337:1861-9.
8. Petz LD, Garratty G, Calhoun L, et al. Selecting donors of platelets for refractory patients on the basis of HLA antibody specificity. Transfusion 2000;40:1446-56.
9. Koerner TAW, Vo TL, Wacker KE, Strauss RG. The predictive value of three definitions of platelet transfusion refractoriness (abstract). Transfusion 1988;28:33S.
10. Ishida A, Handa M, Wakui M, et al. Clinical factors influencing post-transfusion platelet increment in patients undergoing hematopoietic progenitor cell transplantation—a prospective analysis. Transfusion 1998;38: 839-47.
11. Bishop J, McGrath K, Wolf M, et al. Clinical factors influencing the efficacy of pooled platelet transfusions. Blood 1988;71:383-7.
12. Moroff G, Garratty G, Heal JM, et al. Selection of platelets for refractory patients by HLA matching and prospective crossmatching. Transfusion 1992;32:633-40.
13. Bolgiano DC, Larson EB, Slichter SJ. A model to determine required pool size for HLA-typed community donor apheresis programs. Transfusion 1989;29:306-10.
14. Duquesnoy RJ, Filip DJ, Rodey G, et al. Successful transfusion of platelets "mismatched" for HLA antigens to alloimmunized thrombocytopenic patients. Am J Hematol 1997;2: 219-26.
15. Dahlke MB, Weiss KL. Platelet transfusions from donors mismatched from cross-reactive HLA antigens. Transfusion 1984;24:299-302.
16. Silva MA, ed. Standards for blood banks and transfusion services. 23rd ed. Bethesda, MD: AABB, 2005.
17. Rachel JM, Summers TC, Sinor LT, et al. Use of a solid phase red blood cell adherence method for pretransfusion platelet compatibility testing. Am J Clin Pathol 1988;90:63-8.
18. Rachel JM, Sinor LT, Tawfik OW, et al. A solid-phase red cell adherence test for platelet crossmatching. Med Lab Sci 1985;42:194-5.
19. O'Connell BA, Schiffer CA. Donor selection for alloimmunized patients by platelet cross-

sions: A prospective study of 50 patients. Br J Haematol 1992;81:395-400.

matching of random-donor platelet concentrates. Transfusion 1990;20:314-7.

20. Friedberg RC, Donnelly SF, Mintz PD. Independent roles for platelet crossmatching and HLA in the selection of platelets for alloimmunized patients. Transfusion 1994;34: 215-20.

21. Duquesnoy RJ. HLA Matchmaker: A molecularly based algorithm for histocompatibility determination. I. Description of the Algorithm. Hum Immunol 2002;63:339-52.

22. Gmür J, von Felten A, Osterwaider B, et al. Delayed alloimmunization using random single donor platelet transfusions: A prospective study of thrombocytopenic patients with acute leukemia. Blood 1983;62:473-9.

23. Dutcher JP, Schiffer CA, Aisner J, Wiernik PH. Alloimmunization following platelet transfusion: The absence of a dose-response relationship. Blood 1981;57:395-8.

24. Kruskall MS. The perils of platelet transfusions (editorial). N Engl J Med 1997;337:1914-5.

25. Gebel HM, Bray RA. Sensitization and sensitivity: Defining the unsensitized patient. Transplantation 2000;69:1370-4.

26. Murphy MF, Metcalfe P, Ord J, et al. Disappearance of HLA and platelet-specific antibodies in acute leukemia patients alloimmunized by multiple transfusions. Br J Haematol 1987;67:255-60.

27. Kroll H. Human platelet alloantigens (HPA). [Available at http://www.uniklinikum-giessen.de/immunologie/hkroll/HPAs.htm (accessed January 2005).]

28. Newman PJ, Valetin N. Human platelet alloantigens: Recent findings, new perspectives. Thromb Haemost 1995;84:234-9

29. Greenwalt DE, Lipsky RH, Ockenhouse CF, et al. Membrane glycoprotein CD36: A review of its roles in adherence, signal transduction, and transfusion medicine. Blood 1992;80:1105-15.

30. Curtis BR, Aster RH. Incidence of the Nak(a)-negative platelet phenotype in African Americans is similar to that of Asians. Transfusion 1996;36:331-4.

31. Curtis GR, Ali S, Glazier AM, et al. Isoimmunization against CD36 (glycoprotein IV): Description of four cases of neonatal isoimmune thrombocytopenia and brief review of the literature. Transfusion 2002;42:1173-9.

32. Curtis BR, McFarland JG, Gottschall JL. Platelet immunology and alloimmunization. In: Simon TL, Dzik WH, Snyder EL, et al, eds. Rossi's principles of transfusion medicine. 3rd ed. Philadelphia, PA: Lippincott Williams and Wilkins, 2002:203-18.

33. McFarland J. Nomenclature update: HLA, HPA and RBCs. Platelet-specific antigen nomenclature. In: The compendium: A selection of short topic presentations. Bethesda, MD: AABB, 1997.

34. Metcalfe P, Watkins NA, Ouwehand WH, et al. Nomenclature of human platelet antigens. Vox Sang 2003;85:240-5.

35. van Loghem JJ, Dorfmeijer H, van der Hart M. Serological and genetical studies on a platelet antigen (Zw). Vox Sang 1959;4:161-9.

36. Aster RH. Platelet-specific alloantigen systems: History, clinical significance and molecular biology. In: Nance ST, ed. Alloimmunity: 1993 and beyond. Bethesda, MD: AABB, 1993:83-116.

37. von dem Borne AEGKr, Simsek S, van der Schoot S, et al. Platelet and neutrophil alloantigens: Their nature and role in immune-mediated cytopenias. In: Garratty G, ed. Immunobiology of transfusion medicine. New York: Marcel Dekker, 1994:149-71.

38. Müeller-Eckhardt C. Platelet autoimmunity. In: Silberstein LE, ed. Autoimmune disorders of blood. Bethesda, MD: AABB, 1996:115-50.

39. Smith JW, Hayward CP, Horsewood P, et al. Characterization and localization of the Gova/b alloantigens to the glycosylphosphatidylinositol-anchored protein CDw109 on human platelets. Blood 1995;86; 2807-14.

40. Berry JE, Murphy CM, Smith GA, et al. Detection of Gov system antibodies by MAIPA reveals an immunogenicity similar to the HPA-5 alloantigens. Br J Haematol 2000;110: 735-42.

41. McFarland JG. Posttransfusion purpura. In: Popovsky MA, ed. Transfusion reactions. 2nd ed. Bethesda, MD: AABB Press, 2001:187-212.

42. Brecher ME, Moore SB, Letendre L. Posttransfusion purpura: The therapeutic value of Pl^{A1}-negative platelets. Transfusion 1990;30: 433-5.

43. Christie D, Pulkrabek S, Putnam J, et al. Posttransfusion purpura due to an alloantibody reactive with glycoprotein Ia/IIa (anti-HPA-5b). Blood 1991;77:2785-9.

44. Sinha RK, Kelton JG. Current controversies concerning the measurement of platelet associated IgG. Transfus Med Rev 1990;2:121-35.

45. Shibata Y, Juji T, Nishizawa Y, et al. Detection of platelet antibodies by a newly developed mixed passive agglutination with platelets. Vox Sang 1981;41:25-31.

46. Neumuller J, Tohidast-Akrad M, Fisher M, Mayr WR. Influence of chloroquine or acid treatment of human platelets on the antigenicity of HLA and the "thrombocyte-specific" glycoproteins Ia/IIa, IIb, and IIb/IIIa. Vox Sang 1993;65:223-31.

47. Gouttefangeas C, Diehl M, Keilholz W, et al. Thrombocyte HLA molecules retain nonrenewable endogenous peptides of mega-

karyocyte lineage and do not stimulate direct allocytotoxicity in vitro. Blood 2000;95:3168-75.

48. von dem Borne AEGKr, Verheugt FWA, Oosterhof F, et al. A simple immunofluorescence test for the detection of platelet antibodies. Br J Haematol 1978;39:195-207.

49. Garratty G, Arndt P. Applications of flow cytofluorometry to transfusion science. Transfusion 1995;35:157-78.

50. Kiefel V, Santoso S, Weisheit M, Müeller-Eckhardt C. Monoclonal antibody-specific immobilization of platelet antigens (MAIPA): A new tool for the identification of platelet-reactive antibodies. Blood 1987;70:1722-6.

51. Kiefel V. The MAIPA assay and its applications in immunohematology. Transfus Med 1992;2:181-8.

52. Morel-Kopp MC, Daviet L, McGregor J, et al. Drawbacks of the MAIPA technique in characterizing human anti-platelet antibodies. Blood Coag Fibrinol 1996;7:144-6.

53. Visentin GP, Wolfmeyer K, Newman PJ, Aster RH. Detection of drug-dependent, platelet-reactive antibodies by antigen-capture ELISA and flow cytometry. Transfusion 1990;30:694-700.

54. Menitove JE, Pereira J, Hoffman R, et al. Cyclic thrombocytopenia of apparent autoimmune etiology. Blood 1989;73:1561-9.

55. GTI PAKPLUS[TM] platelet antibody screening kit (package insert). Waukesha, WI: GTI, 1996.

56. McFarland JG, Aster RH, Bussel JB, et al. Prenatal diagnosis of neonatal alloimmune thrombocytopenia using allele-specific oligonucleotide probes. Blood 1991;78:2276-82.

57. Simsek S, Faber NM, Bleeker PM, et al. Determination of human platelet antigen frequencies in the Dutch population by immunophenotyping and DNA (allele-specific restriction enzyme) analysis. Blood 1993;82:835-40.

58. Skogen B, Bellissimo D, Hessner M, et al. Rapid determination of platelet alloantigen genotypes by polymerase chain reaction using allele-specific primers. Transfusion 1994;34:955-60.

59. Kluter H, Fehlau K, Panzer S, et al. Rapid typing for human platelet antigen systems-1, -2, -3 and -5 by PCR amplification with sequence-specific primers. Vox Sang 1996;71: 121-5.

60. Panzer S. Report on the Tenth International Platelet Genotyping and Serology Workshop on behalf of the International Society of Blood Transfusion. Vox Sang 2001;80:72-8.

61. Meyer O, Hildebrandt M, Schulz B, et al. Simultaneous genotyping of human platelet antigens (HPA) 1 through 6 using new sequence-specific primers for HPA-5. Transfusion 1999;39:1256-8.

62. George JN. Platelet immunoglobulin G: Its significance for the evaluation of thrombocytopenia and for understanding the origin of α-granule proteins. Blood 1990;76:859-70.

63. George JN, Woolf SH, Raskob GE, et al. Idiopathic thrombocytopenic purpura: A practice guideline developed by explicit methods for the American Society of Hematology. Blood 1996;88:3-40.

64. Warner MN, Moore JC, Warkentin TE, et al. A prospective study of protein-specific assays used to investigate idiopathic thrombocytopenic purpura. Br J Haematol 1999;104:442-7.

65. GTI PAKAUTO[TM] ELISA screening test for autoantibodies to platelet glycoproteins IIb/IIIa, Ib/IX and Ia/IIa (package insert). Waukesha, WI: GTI, 2004.

66. Curtis BR, McFarland JG, Wu GG, et al. Antibodies in sulfonamide-induced immune thrombocytopenia recognize calcium-dependent epitopes on the glycoprotein IIb/IIIa complex. Blood 1994;84:176-83.

67. Christie DJ, Aster RH. Drug-antibody-platelet interaction in quinine- and quinidine-induced thrombocytopenia. J Clin Immunol 1982;70:989-98.

68. Eisner EV, Shahidi NT. Immune thrombocytopenia due to a drug metabolite. N Engl J Med 1972;87:376-81.

69. Kiefel V, Santoso S, Schmidt S, et al. Metabolite-specific IgG and drug-specific antibodies IgG, IgM in two cases of trimethoprim-sulfamethoxazole-induced immune thrombocytopenia. Transfusion 1987;27:262-5.

70. Sinor LT, Stone DL, Plapp FV, et al. Detection of heparin-IgG immune complexes on platelets by solid phase red cell adherence assays. (Immucorrespondence) Norcross, GA: Immucor, 1990.

71. Leach MF, Cooper LK, AuBuchon JP. Detection of drug-dependent, platelet-reactive antibodies by solid-phase red cell adherence assays. Br J Haematol 1997;97:755-61.

72. Nieminen U, Kekomäki R. Quinidine-induced thrombocytopenia purpura: Clinical presentation in relation to drug-dependent and drug-independent platelet antibodies. Br J Haematol 1992;80:77-82.

73. Warkentin TE, Levine M, Hirsh J, et al. Heparin-induced thrombocytopenia in patients treated with low molecular weight heparin or unfractionated heparin. N Engl J Med 1995; 332:1330-5.

74. Warkentin TE. Pork or beef? Ann Thorac Surg 2003;75:15-6.

75. Nand S, Wong W, Yuen B, et al. Heparin-induced thrombocytopenia with thrombosis. Am J Hematol 1997;56:12-6.

76. Warkentin TE, Kelton JG. A 14-year study of heparin-induced thrombocytopenia. Am J Med 1996;101:502-7.

77. Warkentin TE, Chong BA, Greinacher A. Heparin-induced thrombocytopenia: Towards consensus. Thromb Haemost 1998;79:1-7.

78. Cancio LC, Cohen DJ. Heparin-induced thrombocytopenia thrombosis. J Am Coll Surg 1998;186:76-91.

79. Gupta AK, Kovacs MJ, Sauder DN. Heparin-induced thrombocytopenia. Ann Pharmacother 1998;32:55-9.

80. GTI-HAT™ for the detection of heparin-associated antibodies (package insert). Waukesha, WI: GTI, 1997.

81. Suh JS, Malik MI, Aster RH, Visentin GP. Characterization of the humoral immune response in heparin induced thrombocytopenia. Am J Hematol 1997;54:196-201.

82. Amiral J, Wolf M, Fischer A, et al. Pathogenicity of IgA and/or IgM antibodies to heparin-PF4 complexes in patients with heparin induced thrombocytopenia. Br J Haematol 1996;92:954-9.

83. Sheridan D, Carter C, Kelton JG. A diagnostic test for heparin-induced thrombocytopenia. Blood 1986;67:27-30.

84. Pouplard C, Amiral J, Borg JY, et al. Decision analysis for use of platelet aggregation test, carbon 14-serotonin release assay, and heparin platelet factor 4 enzyme-linked immunosorbent assay for diagnosis of heparin-induced thrombocytopenia. Am J Clin Pathol 1999;111:700-6.

85. Lindhoff-Last E, Gerdsen F, Ackermann H, et al. Determination of heparin platelet factor 4 IgG antibodies improves diagnosis of heparin-induced thrombocytopenia. Br J Haematol 2001;113:886-90.

86. Lalezari P, Bernard JE. An isologous antigen-antibody reaction with human neutrophils related to neonatal neutropenia. J Clin Invest 1966;45:1741-50.

87. Steffensen R, Gulen T, Varming K, Jersild C. FcγRIIIb polymorphism: Evidence that NA1/ NA2 and SH are located in two closely linked loci and that the SH allele is linked to the NA1 allele in the Danish population. Transfusion 1999;39:593-8.

88. Stroncek D. Neutrophil alloantigens. Transfus Med Rev 2002;16:67-75.

89. Hessner MJ, Curtis BR, Endean DJ, Aster RH. Determination of neutrophil antigen gene frequencies in five ethnic groups by polymerase chain reaction with sequence-specific primers. Transfusion 1996;36:895-9.

90. Nordhagen R, Conradi M, Promtord SM. Pulmonary reaction associated with transfusion of plasma containing anti-5b. Vox Sang 1986; 51:102-8.

91. Davoren A, Curtis RBR, Shulman IA, et al. TRALI due to granulocyte-agglutinating human neutrophil antigen-3a (5b) alloantibodies in donor plasma: A report of 2 fatalities. Transfusion 2003;43:641-5.

92. Kopko PM, Marshall CS, MacKenzie MR, et al. Transfusion-related acute lung injury: Report of a clinical look-back investigation. JAMA 2002;287:1968-71.

93. Fung UL, Willett JE, Pitcher LA, et al. Confirming an alloimmune neonatal neutropenia due to anti-HLA-4a (MART) by DNA characterization. Presented at the 7th European symposium on platelet, granulocyte and red cell immunobiology, Lago Maggiore, Italy, April 11-14, 2002.

94. Flesch BK, Neppert J. Transfusion-related acute lung injury caused by human leukocyte antigen Class II antibody. Br J Haematol 2002;116:673-6.

95. Silliman R, Paterson AJ, Dickey WO, et al. The association of biologically active lipids with the development of transfusion-related acute lung injury: A retrospective study. Transfusion 1997;37:719-26.

96. Bux J, Behrens G, Jaeger G, et al. Diagnosis and clinical course of autoimmune neutropenia in infancy: Analysis of 240 cases. Blood 1998;91:81-6.

97. Bux J, Chapman J. Report on the second international granulocyte serology workshop. Transfusion 1997;37:977-83.

Chapter 17

The HLA System

THE HLA SYSTEM includes a complex array of genes and their protein products. HLA antigens contribute to the recognition of self and nonself, to the immune responses to antigenic stimuli, and to the coordination of cellular and humoral immunity. The HLA genes, which are located in the major histocompatibility complex (MHC) on the short arm of chromosome 6, code for glycoprotein molecules found on cell surface membranes. Class I molecules are found on the surface of platelets and of all nucleated cells of the body. Mature red cells usually lack HLA antigens demonstrable by conventional methods, but nucleated immature erythroid cells express them. MHC Class II antigens are restricted to a few cell types; the most important are B lymphocytes, macrophages, and dendritic cells. Other terms that have been applied to antigens of the HLA system are: major histocompatibility locus antigens, transplantation antigens, and tissue antigens.

The HLA antigen molecules play a key role in antigen presentation. Immunologic recognition of differences in HLA antigens is probably the first step in the rejection of transplanted tissue. The HLA system is second in importance only to the ABO antigens in influencing the long-term survival of transplanted solid organs and is of paramount significance in hematopoietic progenitor cell (HPC) transplantation. HLA antigens and antibodies are also important in such complications of transfusion therapy as platelet refractoriness, febrile non-hemolytic transfusion reactions (FNHTRs), transfusion-related acute lung injury (TRALI), and posttransplant and posttransfusion graft-vs-host disease (GVHD).

Studies correlating HLA polymorphisms with susceptibility and disease resistance began soon after serologic techniques for HLA Class I typing were developed. Historically, HLA antigen typing has been of value in parentage testing and in forensic investigations. Molecular analysis of the HLA region permits selection of more closely matched donors for HPC transplantation, for investigation of disease associations, and for anthropologic population studies. Because of the polymorphic nature of the HLA genes, a complex nomenclature has been developed to refer to the unique allele sequences based on the relationship of the allele to the serologic specificity of the corresponding antigen.[1]

Genetics of the Major Histocompatibility Complex

Class I and II HLA antigens are cell surface glycoproteins that are products of closely linked genes mapped to the p21.3 band on the short arm of chromosome 6 (Fig 17-1). This genomic region is called the MHC and is usually inherited en bloc as a haplotype. Each of the several loci has multiple alleles with codominant expression of the products from each chromosome. The HLA system is the most polymorphic system of genes described in humans.

The *HLA-A*, *HLA-B*, and *HLA-C* genes encode the corresponding Class I antigens A, B, and C. The *HLA-DR*, *HLA-DQ*, and *HLA-DP* gene cluster codes for the synthesis of correspondingly named Class II antigens. Located between the Class I and Class II genes is a group of non-HLA genes that code for molecules that include the complement proteins C2, Bf, C4A, C4B; a steroid enzyme (21-hydroxylase); and a cytokine (tumor necrosis factor). This region is referred to as MHC Class III.

Organization of HLA Genetic Regions

The HLA Class I region contains, in addition to the classical genes *HLA-A*, *HLA-B*, and *HLA-C*, other gene loci designated *HLA-E*, *HLA-F, HLA-G*, *HFE*, *HLA-J*, *HLA-K*, *HLA-L*, *MICA*, and *MICAB*. These latter genes encode the nonclassical or Class Ib HLA proteins, characterized by limited polymorphism and low levels of expres-

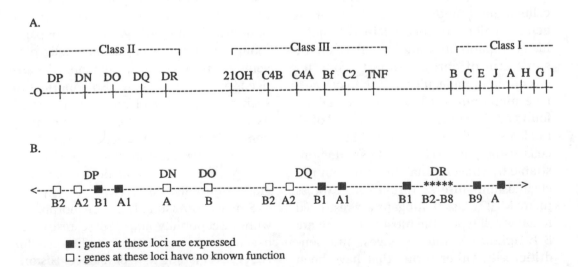

Figure 17-1. (A) The major histocompatibility complex located on the short arm of chromosome 6. The centromere is to the left. The key Class I, II, and III genetic loci are shown. The Class III region contains complement system genes (C2, Bf, C4A, C4B), the 21-hydroxylase gene (21OH), and the gene for tumor necrosis factor (TNF). (B) Greater detail of the Class II region.

sion.[2] Some Class I genes express nonfunctional proteins or are not able to express a protein. Genes unable to express a functional protein product are termed pseudogenes and presumably represent an evolutionary dead end. HLA-E regulates natural killer cells. HLA-G is expressed by the trophoblast and may be involved in the development of maternal immune tolerance of the fetus. Hereditary hemochromatosis (HH), an iron overload disorder with a 10% carrier frequency in Northern Europeans, is associated with two missense mutations in a Class I-like gene.[3] The gene conferring HH was initially named *HLA-H*; however, the *HLA-H* designation had already been assigned to an HLA Class I pseudogene by the World Health Organization (WHO) Nomenclature Committee.[4] The gene conferring HH is now called *HFE*. Class I molecules are also located outside the MHC, such as CD1, which can present nonprotein antigens (such as lipids) to T cells.

The genomic organization of the MHC Class II region (HLA-D region) is more complex. An MHC Class II molecule consists of a noncovalent complex of two structurally similar chains, the α-chain and the β-chain. Both of these chains are encoded within the MHC. The polymorphism of HLA Class II molecules results from differences in both the α-chain and the β-chain; this depends on the Class II isoform. For example, with HLA-DR, the α-chain is monomorphic, but the β-chain is very polymorphic. Multiple loci code for either alpha or beta chains of the Class II MHC proteins. Different haplotypes have different numbers of Class II genes and pseudogenes. The proteins coded by the *DRA* gene and the *DRB1* gene result in HLA-DR1 through HLA-DR18. The products of the *A* gene and the *B3* gene (if present) express HLA-DR52; those of the *A* gene and the *B4* gene (if present) express HLA-DR53; and those of the *A*

gene and *B5* gene (if present) express HLA-DR51. The HLA-DQ1 through DQ9 antigens are expressed on the glycoproteins coded by the *DQA1* and *DQB1* genes in the *DQ* gene cluster. Many of the other genes of the *DQ* cluster are probably pseudogenes. A similar organization is found in the *HLA-DP* gene cluster.

The MHC Class III region contains four complement genes, whose alleles are generally inherited together as a unit, termed a complotype. There are more than 10 different complotypes inherited in humans. Two of the Class III genes, *C4A* and *C4B*, code for variants of the C4 molecule. These variants have distinct protein structure and function; the C4A molecule (if present) carries the Rodgers antigen and the C4B molecule (if present) carries the Chido antigen, both of which are adsorbed onto the red cells of individuals who possess the gene.

Patterns of Inheritance

Although the organization of the MHC is complicated, its inheritance follows the established principles of genetics. Every person has two different copies of chromosome 6 and, thus, possesses two HLA haplotypes, one from each parent. An individual's haplotype is typically determined by typing multiple family members from different generations and observing which alleles are inherited together. The expressed gene products constitute the phenotype, which can be determined for an individual by typing for the HLA antigens. Because the HLA genes are autosomal and codominant, the phenotype represents the combined expression of both haplotypes. Figure 17-2 illustrates inheritance of haplotypes.

Finding HLA-Identical Siblings

Each child inherits one copy of chromosome 6 from each parent; hence, one MHC

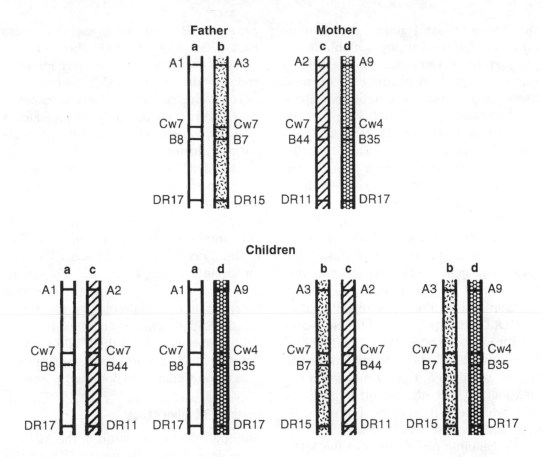

Figure 17-2. The linked genes on each chromosome constitute a haplotype. To identify which haplotypes a person possesses, one must know the antigens present and also the inheritance pattern in the specific kindred. The observed typing results of the father in this family are interpreted into the following phenotype: A1,3;B7,8;Cw7,-;DR15,17. The observed results plus the family study reveal the haplotypes of the father to be: a = A1,Cw7,B8,DR17 and b = A3,Cw7,B7,DR15. Offspring of a single mating pair must have one of only four possible combinations of haplotypes, assuming there has been no crossing-over.

haplotype is inherited from each parent. Because each parent has two different copies of chromosome 6, four different combinations of haplotypes are possible in the offspring (assuming no recombination). This inheritance pattern is important in predicting whether family members will be compatible donors for transplantation. The chance that two siblings will be HLA-identical is 25%. The chance that any one patient with "n" siblings will have at least one HLA-identical sibling is $1-(3/4)^n$.

Having two siblings provides a 44% chance and three siblings a 58% chance that one sibling will be HLA-identical. No matter how many siblings are available for typing (aside from identical twins), the probability will never be 100% for finding an HLA-identical sibling.

Absence of Antigens

Usually, both copies of the genes within the MHC are expressed as antigens; however, in certain individuals, only one antigen can be identified. This may occur if the individual is homozygous for the allele, or if appropriate antisera are not available to type the individual's antigen (referred to as a blank allele). Very rarely, the absence of an antigen can result from a null allele. A null allele is characterized by substitutions within the coding region of the gene that prevent the expression of a functional protein at the cell surface. Such inactivation of a gene may be caused by nucleotide substitutions, deletions, or insertions, which lead to a premature cessation in the antigen's synthesis. When referring to phenotypes, a blank is often written as "x" (for A locus), "y" (for B locus), or "–" (for any locus) (eg, A1,x;B7,40 or A1,–;B7,40). Family studies must be performed to determine the correct genotype.

Crossing-Over

The genes of the HLA region occasionally demonstrate chromosome crossover, in which segments containing linked genetic material are exchanged between the two chromosomes during meiosis or gametogenesis (see Fig 10-6). These recombinants are then transmitted as new haplotypes to the offspring. Crossover frequency is in part related to the physical distance between genes. For example, the *HLA-A*, *HLA-B*, and *HLA-DR* loci are close together, with 0.8% crossover between the *A* and *B* loci and 0.5% between the *B* and *DR* loci. In family studies and in parentage testing, the possibility of recombination must be considered.

Linkage Disequilibrium

The MHC system is so polymorphic that, theoretically, the number of possible unique HLA phenotypes is greater than the global human population. Moreover, new HLA alleles are constantly being discovered and characterized. As of 2004, there were 309 *HLA-A*, 563 *HLA-B*, and 368 *DRB1* alleles. In reality, many HLA haplotypes are overrepresented compared with what would be expected if the distribution of HLA genes were random. The phenomenon of linkage disequilibrium accounts for the discrepancy between expected and observed HLA haplotype frequencies.

Expected frequencies for HLA haplotypes are derived by multiplication of the frequencies of each allele. For example, in individuals of European ancestry, the overall frequency of the gene coding for HLA-A1 is 0.15 and that for HLA-B8 is 0.10; therefore, 1.5% (0.15 × 0.10) of all HLA haplotypes in this population would be expected to contain genes coding for both HLA-A1 and HLA-B8 if they were randomly distributed. The actual frequency of the A1 and B8 combination, however, is 7% to 8% in this population. Certain allelic combinations occur with increased frequency in different racial groups and constitute common haplotypes in those populations. These are called ancestral haplotypes because they appear to be inherited from a single common ancestor. The most common ancestral haplotype in Northern Europeans, the A1, B8, DR3, DQ2 haplotype, includes both Class I and Class II regions. It is unclear whether ancestral haplotypes represent relatively young haplotypes that have not had sufficient time to undergo recombination, or whether they are old haplotypes that are resistant to recombination because of selection. Linkage disequilibrium in the HLA system is important in studies of parentage because haplotype frequencies in the relevant population make the transmission of certain gene combinations more likely than others. Linkage disequilibrium also affects the likelihood of finding suitable unrelated donors for HLA-matched platelet transfusions and for HPC transplantation.

Biochemistry, Tissue Distribution, and Structure

The HLA antigens are cell surface glycoproteins. HLA Class I molecules contain one copy of two polypeptides: a heavy chain, which is attached to the membrane, and a light chain, which is called β_2-microglobulin. The HLA Class II molecules are composed of one copy each of an α-chain and a β-chain, both of which are attached to the cell surface. HLA antigens are divided into Class I and Class II based on their function, tissue distribution, and biochemistry.

Characteristics of Class I and Class II Antigens

Class I antigens (HLA-A, -B, and -C) have a molecular weight around 57,000 daltons and consist of two chains: a glycoprotein heavy chain (45,000 daltons) encoded on the short arm of chromosome 6 and, as a light chain, the β_2-microglobulin molecule (12,000 daltons) encoded by a gene on chromosome 15. The heavy chain penetrates the cell membrane. β_2-microglobulin is not attached to the cell membrane; it associates with the heavy chain via the latter's nonvariable ($\alpha3$) domain but is not covalently bound to it (see Fig 17-3). The external portion of the heavy chain consists of three amino acid domains ($\alpha1$, $\alpha2$, and $\alpha3$), of which the outermost $\alpha1$ and $\alpha2$ domains contain the polymorphic regions conferring the HLA antigen specificity.

Class I molecules are found on platelets and on most nucleated cells in the body, with some exceptions such as neurons, cor-

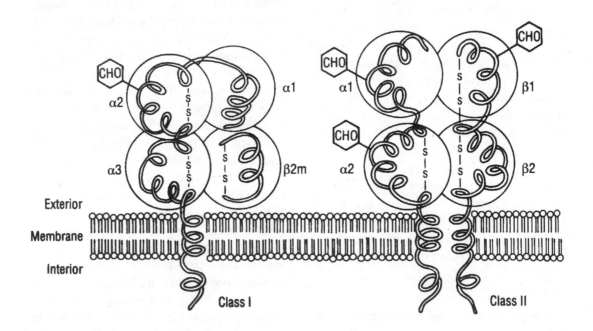

Figure 17-3. Stylized diagram of Class I and Class II MHC molecules showing α and β polypeptide chains, their structural domains, and attached carbohydrate units.

neal epithelium, trophoblast, and germinal cells. Only vestigial amounts remain on mature red cells, with certain allotypes better expressed than others. These Class I polymorphisms were independently recognized as red cell alloantigens by serologists and were designated as Bennett-Goodspeed (Bg) antigens. The specificities called Bg^a, Bg^b, and Bg^c are identified as HLA-B7, HLA-B17, and HLA-A28, respectively. Platelets express primarily HLA-A and HLA-B antigens. HLA-C antigens are present at very low levels and Class II antigens are generally not expressed at all on platelets.

Class II antigens (HLA-DR, -DQ, and -DP) have a molecular weight of approximately 63,000 daltons and consist of two structurally similar glycoprotein chains (α and β), both of which traverse the membrane (see Fig 17-3). The extramembranous portion of each chain has two amino acid domains, of which the outermost domain contains the variable regions of the Class II alleles. The expression of Class II antigens is more restricted than that of Class I. Class II antigens are expressed constitutively on B lymphocytes, monocytes, and cells derived from monocytes such as macrophages and dendritic cells, intestinal epithelium, and early hematopoietic cells. There is also constitutive expression of Class II antigens on some endothelial cells, especially those lining the microvasculature. However, in general, endothelium, particularly that of larger blood vessels, is negative for Class II antigen expression, although its presence can be induced (for instance, by interferon-gamma during immune activation). T lymphocytes are negative for Class II antigen expression but become positive when activated. Class II antigens are expressed abnormally in autoimmune disease and on some tumor cells.

Soluble HLA Class I and Class II antigens shed from cells are found in blood and body fluids and may play a role in modulating immune reactivity.[5] Levels of soluble HLA increase with infection [including human immunodeficiency virus (HIV)], inflammatory disease, and transplant rejection, and decline with progression of malignancy. Levels of soluble HLA in blood components are proportionate to the number of residual donor leukocytes and to the length of storage.[6] Soluble HLA in blood components may be involved in the immunomodulatory effect of blood transfusion.

Configuration

A representative three-dimensional structure of these molecules can be obtained by X-ray crystallographic analysis of purified HLA antigens. The outer domains, which contain the regions of amino acid variability and the antigenic epitopes of the molecules, form a structure known as the "peptide-binding groove." Alleles defined by polymorphisms in the HLA gene sequences have unique amino acid sequences and, therefore, form unique binding grooves, each able to bind different classes of peptides. The peptide-binding groove is critical for the functional aspects of HLA molecules (see section on Biologic Function).

Nomenclature

An international committee sponsored by the World Health Organization establishes the nomenclature of the HLA system. It is updated regularly to incorporate new HLA alleles. HLA antigens are designated by a number following the letter that denotes the HLA series (eg, HLA-A1 or HLA-B8). Previously, antigenic specificities that were not fully confirmed carried the prefix "w" (eg, HLA-Aw33). When identification of the antigen became definitive, the WHO Nomenclature Committee dropped the "w" from the designation. The Committee meets regularly to update nomenclature by recognizing new specificities or genetic loci. The "w" prefix is no longer applied in this manner and is now used only for the following: 1) Bw4 and Bw6, to distinguish these "public" antigens from other B locus alleles; 2) all C locus specificities, to avoid confusion with members of the complement system; and 3) Dw and DP specificities that were defined by mixed lymphocyte reactions and primed lymphocyte typing. The numeric designations for the HLA-A and HLA-B specificities were assigned based on the order of their discovery.

Splits

Refinement of serologic methods permitted antigens previously believed to represent a single specificity to be "split" into specificities that were serologically (and, later, genetically) distinct. The designation for an individual antigen that is a split of an earlier recognized antigen often includes the number of the parent antigen in parentheses, eg, HLA-B44 (12).

Shared Determinants

As the specificity of HLA typing sera improved, it was found that some epitopes, the part of the antigen that binds antibody, were common to several antigens. Antibodies to these epitopes identified antigens that constituted a group, of which the individual members could be identified by antisera with more restricted activity.

Cross-Reactive Groups

In addition to "splits," HLA antigens and antigen groups may have other epitopes in common. Antibodies that react with these shared determinants often cause cross-reactions in serologic testing. The collective term for a group of HLA antigens that exhibit such cross-reactivity is cross-reactive group (CREG).

"Public" Antigens

In addition to splits and CREGs, HLA proteins have reactivity that is common to many different HLA specificities. Called "public" antigens, these common amino acid sequences appear to represent the less variable portion of the HLA molecule. Two well-characterized "public" antigens, HLA-Bw4 and HLA-Bw6, are found in the HLA-B series. The Bw4 antigen is also found on some A locus molecules. "Public" antigens are clinically important because patients exposed to foreign HLA antigens via pregnancy, transfusion, or transplantation can make antibodies to them. A single antibody, when directed against a "public" antigen, can resemble the sum of multiple discrete alloantibodies.

Nomenclature for HLA Alleles

As nucleotide sequencing is used to investigate the HLA system, increasing numbers of HLA alleles are being identified, many of which share a common serologic phenotype. The minimum requirement for designation of a new allele is the sequence of exons two and three for HLA Class I and exon two for HLA Class II (*DRB1*). These exons encode the variable amino acids that confer HLA antigen specificity. A uniform nomenclature has been adopted that takes into account the locus, the major serologic specificity, and the allele determined by molecular typing techniques. For example, isoelectric focusing, amino acid sequencing, and nucleotide sequencing have identified several unique variants of HLA-DR4. The first HLA-DR4 variant is designated *DRB1*0401*, indicating the locus (DR), the protein (β1 chain), an asterisk to represent that an allele name follows, the major serologic specificity (04 for HLA-DR4), and the allele number (variant 01). For Class I alleles, the name of the locus, for example HLA-B, is followed by an asterisk and then a number of digits. The first two digits correspond to the serologic specificity of the antigen. The third and fourth digits are used to list the subtypes, numbers being assigned in the order in which the DNA sequences have been determined. Therefore, *B*2704* represents the HLA-B locus, with a serologic specificity of B27, and was the fourth allele described in this family (see Table 17-1). Finally, the nomenclature can accommodate alleles with silent mutations, ie, those that have different DNA sequences but identical amino acid sequences and null alleles.

Biologic Function

The essential function of the HLA system is self/nonself discrimination. Discrimination of self from nonself is accomplished by the interaction of T lymphocytes with peptide antigens. T lymphocytes interact with peptide antigen only when the T-cell receptor (TCR) for antigen engages both an HLA molecule and the antigenic peptide contained with its peptide-binding groove. This limitation is referred to as "MHC restriction."[7]

In the thymus, T lymphocytes whose TCRs bind to a self HLA molecule are selected (positive selection), with the exception of those whose TCRs also bind to a peptide derived from a self antigen, in which case they are deleted (negative selection). Some self-reactive T cells escape negative selection, however. If not functionally inactivated, for instance, by the mechanism of anergy, these self-reactive T cells may become involved in an autoimmune process. (See Chapter 11.)

Role of Class I

Class I molecules are synthesized, and peptide antigens are inserted into the peptide-binding groove, in the endoplasmic reticulum. Peptide antigens that fit into the Class I peptide-binding groove are typically eight or nine amino acids in length and are derived from proteins that

Table 17-1. HLA Nomenclature

Genetic Locus	Antigenic Specificity	Allele	Number of Identified Alleles	Polypeptide Location
HLA-A	A1 to A80	*A*0101 to *8001*	207	a
HLA-B	B7 to B81	*B*0702 to *8301*	412	a
HLA-C	Cw1 to Cw10	*Bw*0102 to *1802*	100	a
DRA	DR1 to DR18	*DRA*0101 to *0102*	2	a
DRB1		*DRB1*0101 to *1608*	271	β1
DQA1	DQ1 to DQ9	*DQA1*0101 to *0601*	20	a
DQB1		*DQB1*0501 to *0402*	45	β1
DPA1	DPw1 to DPw6	*DPA1*0103 to *0401*	19	a1
DPB1		*DPB1*0101 to *8901*	93	β1

are made by the cell (endogenous proteins). These endogenous proteins, which may be normal self proteins, altered self proteins such as those found in cancer cells, or viral proteins such as those found in virus-infected cells, are degraded in the cytosol by a large multifunctional protease (LMP) and transported to the endoplasmic reticulum by a transporter associated with antigen processing (TAP). The LMP and TAP genes are both localized to the MHC.

Class I molecules are transported to the cell surface where they are available to interact with CD8-positive T lymphocytes. If the TCR of a T lymphocyte can bind the antigenic peptide in the context of the specific Class I molecule displaying it, then this binding activates the cytotoxic properties of the T cell, which will then attack the cell, characteristically eliciting an inflammatory response. The presentation of antigen by Class I molecules is especially important in a host's defense against viral pathogens and against malignant transformation. Tumor cells that do not express Class I escape this immune surveillance.

Role of Class II

Class II molecules, like Class I molecules, are synthesized in the endoplasmic reticulum, but peptide antigens are not inserted into the peptide-binding groove here. Instead, an invariant chain (Ii) is inserted. The Class II-invariant chain molecule is transported to an endosome where the invariant chain is removed by a specialized Class II molecule called DM (whose locus is also localized to the MHC). A Class II antigenic peptide is then inserted into the peptide-binding groove. Peptide antigens that fit into the Class II peptide-binding groove are typically 12 to 25 amino acids in length and are derived from proteins that are taken up by the cell by endocytosis (exogenous proteins). Exogenous proteins, which may be normal self proteins or proteins derived from pathogens such as bacteria, are degraded to peptides by enzymes in the endosomal pathway. Class II molecules are then transported to the cell surface where they are available to interact with CD4-positive T lymphocytes, which secrete immunostimulatory cytokines in response. This mechanism is especially important for the production of antibodies.

Detection of HLA Antigens and Alleles

Methods for the detection of HLA antigens and alleles fall into three groups: molecular (DNA-based), serologic, and cellular assays. Detailed procedures of commonly used assays are provided in the current edition of the American Society for Histocompatibility and Immunogenetics *Laboratory Manual*. Depending on the clinical situation, a particular HLA antigen detection or typing method may be preferable (Table 17-2).

DNA-Based Assays

DNA-based typing has several advantages over serologic and cellular assays: high sensitivity and specificity; small sample volumes; decreased turnaround time, for some methods, as short as a few hours; and absence of the need for cell surface antigen expression or cell viability. Although serologic methods can readily distinguish only about 21 serologic specificities, high-resolution DNA-based methods can detect up to 368 alleles.

Polymerase Chain Reaction Testing

Polymerase chain reaction (PCR) technology allows amplification of large quanti-

Table 17-2. HLA Typing Methods and Appropriate Applications

Method	Clinical Application	Resolution
SSP (PCR)	Solid organ, related and unrelated HPC transplantation	Serologic to allele level, higher resolution with large number of primers
DNA sequencing	Unrelated HPC transplantation, resolution of typing problems with other methods, characterization of new alleles	Allele level
Forward SSOP hybridization	Solid organ and HPC transplantation (can accommodate high-volume testing)	Serologic to allele level
Reverse SSOP hybridization	Solid organ, related and unrelated HPC transplantation	Serologic, higher resolution with larger number of probes
Microlympho-cytotoxicity	Solid organ transplantation, evaluation of platelet refractoriness, HLA typing (Class I only) of platelet recipients and platelet donors	Serologic specificity

ties of a particular target segment of genomic DNA. Low- to intermediate-resolution typing detects the HLA serologic equivalents with great accuracy; eg, it distinguishes DR15 from DR16, whereas high-resolution typing distinguishes individual alleles, eg, DRB1*0101 from DRB1*0102. Several PCR-based methods have been developed, of which two general approaches are described below.

Oligonucleotide Probes. The first technique uses sequence-specific oligonucleotide probes (SSOPs) and is known as PCR-SSO, PCR-SSOP, or allele-specific oligonucleotide (ASO) hybridization.[8] A PCR product amplified from genomic DNA is applied to a membrane or filter to which the labeled SSOPs are hybridized. These short DNA probes will hybridize with the complementary sequences and identify groups of alleles or individual alleles. Advantages are that all Class II loci can be typed and highly specific information obtained. Disadvantages include potential difficulty in interpretation of results and the need to use multiple filters and perform multiple amplifications and subsequent hybridizations. A variation of this technique, the reverse line or dot blot, eliminates the need for multiple filters and hybridizations by incorporation of a label (such as biotin) into the PCR product during its amplification from genomic DNA. The PCR product is then hybridized to a membrane containing all the relevant SSOPs and its pattern of hybridization with the SSOPs revealed by detection of the incorporated label. In the past few years, a new method for establishing HLA genotypes that features arrays of oligonucleotide probes on a solid phase has begun to appear in HLA typing laboratories. The microbead array assay is an SSOP method for HLA-A, -B, and -DR antigen level typing.

This technique also has the ability for low-to-intermediate resolution DNA-based tissue typing, with a reduction in sample processing time.

Sequence-Specific Primers. A second major technique uses sequence-specific primer pairs (SSPs) that target and amplify a particular DNA sequence.[9] This method requires the performance of multiple PCR reactions in which each reaction is specific for a particular allele or group of alleles. Direct visualization of the amplified alleles is seen after agarose gel electrophoresis. Because SSPs have such specific targets, presence of the amplified material indicates presence of the corresponding allele(s). The pattern of positive and negative PCR amplifications is examined to determine the HLA alleles present. Primer pair sets are available that can determine the full HLA-A, -B, -C, -DR, -DQ, and -DP type.

Sequence-Based Typing

High-resolution nucleic acid sequencing of HLA alleles generates allele-level sequences that are used to characterize new allele(s). With the ever-increasing availability and ease of use of automated sequencers, sequence-based typing has become a routine HLA typing method in some HLA laboratories.

Serologic Assays

Lymphocytotoxicity

The microlymphocytotoxicity test can be used to detect HLA-A, -B, -C, -DR, and -DQ antigens. Lymphocytes are used for testing because they are readily obtained from anticoagulated peripheral blood and, unlike granulocytes, give reproducible results. Lymphocytes obtained from lymph nodes or spleen may also be used. HLA typing sera are obtained primarily from multiparous women. Some mouse monoclonal antisera are also available.

HLA sera of known specificities are placed in wells of a microdroplet test plate. A suspension of lymphocytes is added to each well. Rabbit complement is then added and, if sufficient antibody has bound to the lymphocyte membranes, the complement cascade will be activated through the membrane attack complex, leading to lymphocytotoxicity. Damage to the cell membrane can be detected by the addition of dye: cells that have no attached antibody, no activated complement, and no damage to the membrane keep the vital dyes from penetrating; cells with damaged membranes allow the dye to enter. The cells are examined for dye exclusion or uptake under phase contrast microscopy. If a fluorescent microscope is available, fluorescent vital dyes can also be used.

Because HLA-DR and HLA-DQ antigens are expressed on B cells and not on resting T cells, typing for these antigens usually requires that the initial lymphocyte preparation be manipulated before testing to yield an enriched B-cell population. This is typically accomplished by the use of magnetic beads, to which monoclonal antibodies to B cells have been bound.

The interpretation of serologic reactions requires skill and experience. Control wells of known reactivity and careful quality control of reagents are required, especially for the activity of the complement used to induce lymphocytotoxicity. In addition, antigen assignments can be made only on the basis of results obtained with multiple antisera because few reagent antisera have sufficient monospecific reliability to be used alone. The extreme polymorphism of the HLA system, the variation in antigen frequencies among different racial groups, the reliance on biologic antisera and living target cells, and the complexities introduced by splits, CREGs, and "public" antigens all contribute to difficulties in accurate serologic HLA typing.

Antibodies in Patients

Microlymphocytotoxicity testing can be used to test serum specimens against selected target cells. This is routinely done in HLA crossmatching, which consists of testing serum from a potential recipient against unfractionated lymphocytes (or fractionated T and B lymphocytes) from a potential donor. A variation of the microlymphocytotoxicity test, which uses an antiglobulin reagent, is one of the methods used to increase sensitivity. Flow cytometry is also used as an independent method to increase the sensitivity of the crossmatch.

Testing the patient's serum against a panel of 30 to 60 or more different target cells can assess the extent of HLA alloimmunization. The percent of the panel cells to which the recipient has formed cytotoxic antibodies is referred to as the panel reactive antibody (PRA) level. Determination of PRA can be useful in the investigation of FNHTRs, in the workup of platelet refractoriness, and in following patients who are awaiting cadaver solid organ transplants. This "HLA antibody screen" not only detects the presence of HLA antibodies but also may allow their specificity to be determined. The presence of HLA antibodies can also be demonstrated by using an enzyme-linked immunosorbent assay with solid-phase HLA antigens or by flow cytometric analysis using antigen-coated beads.

Cellular Assays

Historically, the mixed lymphocyte culture (MLC) (also called mixed leukocyte culture, mixed lymphocyte reaction, or MLR) was used to detect genetic differences in the Class II region. In the MLR, lymphocytes from different individuals are cultured together and have the opportunity to recognize foreign HLA-D region antigens and to respond by proliferating.

The HLA System and Transfusion

HLA system antigens and antibodies play important roles in a number of transfusion-related events. They include alloimmunization and platelet refractoriness, FNHTR, TRALI, and posttransfusion GVHD. HLA antigens are highly immunogenic. In response to pregnancy, transfusion, or transplantation, immunologically normal individuals are more likely to form antibodies to HLA antigens than to any other antigen system.

Platelet Refractoriness

The incidence of HLA alloimmunization and platelet refractoriness among patients receiving repeated transfusions of cellular components is 20% to 71%.[10] The refractory state exists when transfusion of suitably preserved platelets fails to increase the recipient's platelet count. Platelet refractoriness may be due to clinical factors such as sepsis, high fever, disseminated intravascular coagulopathy, medications, hypersplenism, complement-mediated destruction, or a combination of these, or it may have an immune basis. (See Chapter 16 for more information about platelets.)

Antibody Development

Antibodies against HLA antigens usually cause immune-mediated platelet refractoriness, but antibodies to platelet-specific or ABH antigens may also be involved. HLA alloimmunization can follow pregnancy, transfusion, or organ transplantation because the foreign antigens are the donor MHC antigens themselves. A common example of this is the development of HLA antibodies directed against Class I antigens that occurs with transfusion of platelets, which express only Class

I antigens. The presence, in the transfused component, of leukocytes bearing Class I and II antigens elicits alloimmunization. The likelihood of immunization can be lessened with leukocyte-reduced blood components, or by treatment with ultraviolet light, which alters the co-stimulatory molecules or impairs antigen-presenting cell activity. The threshold level of leukocytes required to provoke a primary HLA alloimmune response is unclear and probably varies among different recipients. Some studies have suggested that 5×10^6 leukocytes per transfusion may represent an immunizing dose. In patients who have been previously sensitized by pregnancy or transfusion, exposure to even lower numbers of allogeneic cells is likely to provoke an anamnestic antibody response.

Finding Compatible Donors

The HLA antibody response of transfused individuals may be directed against individual specificities present on donor cells or against "public" alloantigens. Precise characterization may be difficult. An overall assessment of the degree of HLA alloimmunization can be obtained by measuring the PRA of the recipient's serum. Platelet-refractory patients with a high PRA are broadly alloimmunized and may be difficult to support with platelet transfusions. HLA-matched platelets, obtained by plateletpheresis, benefit some, but not all, of these refractory patients. Because donors with a four-antigen match for an immunized recipient are hard to find, strategies for obtaining HLA-matched platelets vary. Selection of partially mismatched donors, based on serologic cross-reactive groups, has been emphasized, but such donors may fail to provide an adequate transfusion response in vivo. An alternative approach to the selection of donors is based on matching for "public" specificities rather than cross-reactive private antigens. Obtaining an adequate number of readily available HLA-typed donors can prove difficult; it has been estimated that a pool of 1000 to 3000 or more donors would be needed to provide the transfusion requirements of most HLA-alloimmunized patients.[11] Use of single antigen beads to identify HLA antibody specificities precisely can allow a better selection of donors who have acceptable mismatched antigens.[12]

In the past, it was recommended that patients who were at risk of becoming alloimmunized and refractory be serologically Class I HLA-typed early in the course of their illness, when enough lymphocytes were present in the peripheral blood to obtain a reliable HLA type. Intensive chemotherapy makes it very difficult to obtain enough cells for such typing. More recently, with the advent of molecular typing techniques, a patient's HLA alleles can be determined using genomic DNA isolated from very small numbers of white cells or even nonblood tissue (eg, buccal swabs).

HLA-alloimmunized patients often respond to crossmatch-compatible platelets selected using patient serum and samples of apheresis platelets in a platelet antibody assay. Crossmatching techniques may assess compatibility for both HLA and platelet-specific antibodies.[13] These histocompatible platelet components are further discussed in Chapter 21.

Febrile Nonhemolytic Transfusion Reactions

HLA antibodies, as well as granulocyte and platelet-specific antibodies, have been implicated in the pathogenesis of FNHTRs. The recipient's antibodies, reacting with transfused antigens, elicit the release of cytokines (eg, interleukin-1) capable of causing fever. Serologic investigation, if undertaken, may require multiple techniques and target cells from a number of different donors (see Chapter 27).

Transfusion-Related Acute Lung Injury

In TRALI, a transfusion reaction that is being recognized with increasing frequency, acute noncardiogenic pulmonary edema develops in response to transfusion. Pathogenesis appears to reflect the presence of HLA antibodies in donor blood, which react with and fix complement to granulocytes of the recipient, leading to severe capillary leakage and pulmonary edema. Rarely, HLA antibodies of the recipient react with transfused leukocytes from the donor (see Chapter 27). Cases of TRALI have been reported that appear to be caused by donor antibodies against Class II antigens in recipients. Because Class II antigens are not expressed on neutrophils, an alternate explanation for activation of neutrophils in these instances is required. One hypothesis is that Class II antigens on the recipient's pulmonary macrophages are targeted by these complement-activating antibodies. Subsequent release of cytokines and chemokines results in the recruitment and activation of neutrophils in the lungs.[14]

Chimerism and Posttransfusion Graft-vs-Host Disease

Chimerism refers to the presence of donor cells in the recipient. Persistent chimerism after blood transfusion may lead to the development of GVHD in the recipient. The development of posttransfusion GVHD depends on several factors: the degree to which the recipient is immunocompromised; the number and viability of lymphocytes in the transfused component; and the degree of HLA similarity between donor and recipient. The observation of posttransfusion GVHD with the use of fresh blood components from blood relatives has highlighted the role of the HLA system in GVHD.

Figure 17-4 illustrates the conditions for increased risk of GVHD. The parents have one HLA haplotype in common. Each child, therefore, has a one in four chance of inheriting the same haplotype from each parent, and Child #1 is homozygous for the shared parental HLA haplotype. Transfusion of blood from this person to an unrelated recipient who did not have this haplotype would have no untoward consequences. If, however, Child #1 were a directed donor for the relatives heterozygous for that haplotype (both parents and Child #3), the recipient would not recognize any foreign antigens on the transfused lymphocytes and would not eliminate them. The donor cells, however, would recognize the recipient's foreign HLA antigens, would become activated, proliferate, and attack the host. To avoid this situation, it is recommended that all cellular components known to be from blood relatives be irradiated before transfusion. Other specially chosen donor units, such as HLA-matched platelets, may also present an increased risk of posttransfusion GVHD. Rarely, transfusion-associated GVHD has occurred after the transfusion of blood from an unrelated donor.[15]

Chimerism is also proposed to be responsible for the maintenance of tolerance in some organ transplant recipients[16] and for the maintenance of HLA sensitization.[17] It has been postulated that scleroderma is a form of GVHD resulting from chimeric cells derived from fetal cells transferred across the placenta during pregnancy.[18]

Hemolytic Transfusion Reactions

HLA incompatibility has rarely been implicated as a cause of shortened red cell

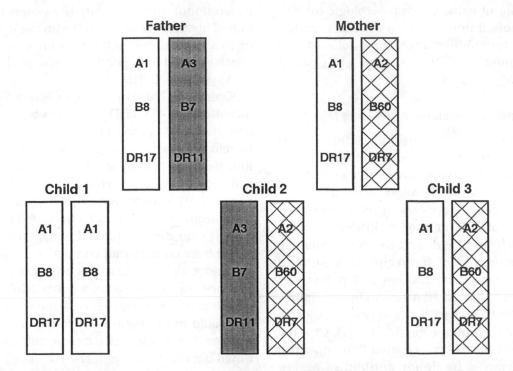

Figure 17-4. HLA haplotypes in a family at risk for transfusion-associated GVHD. In contrast to the family shown in Fig 17-2, each parent shares a common HLA haplotype, HLA-A1,B8,DR17. Child 1 is homozygous for the haplotype shared by the parents and by child 3. The lymphocytes of child 1 are capable of producing posttransfusion GVHD if transfused to either parent or to child 3.

survival in patients with antibodies to HLA antigens such as Bg^a(B7), Bg^b(B17), and Bg^c(A28) that are expressed, although weakly, on red cells (see Chapter 15). Such an incompatibility may not be detected with conventional pretransfusion testing.

HLA Testing and Transplantation

HLA testing is an integral part of organ transplantation. The extent of testing differs for different types of transplants. Organ transplantation is discussed in greater detail in Chapter 26.

Hematopoietic Progenitor Cell Transplants

It has long been recognized that disparity within the HLA system represents an important barrier to successful HPC transplantation.[19] HLA similarity and compatibility between the donor and the recipient are required for engraftment and to prevent GVHD, but some degree of rejection or GVHD remain common problems for recipients of allogeneic HPCs, despite immunosuppressive conditioning.

Candidate donors and recipients are typed for their HLA-A, -B, -C, -DR and -DQ alleles. The goal is to match, as closely as possible, the alleles of the prospective donor and recipient at the *HLA-A, -B*, and *-DRB1* loci, with the optimal match being an allele-level match.[20] Some transplant programs additionally match for *HLA-C* and *-DQ* alleles. Molecular HLA typing is performed on samples from both the donor and recipient for optimal assessment of Class I and II region compatibility. Although HLA-identical sibling donors remain the best choice for HPC transplantation, there is increasing use of unrelated donors identified by searching the file of 5 million HPC donors listed in the National Marrow Donor Program's registry of volunteer donors. The use of umbilical cord blood stem cells and hematopoietic stem cell grafts that have undergone T-cell depletion may allow greater donor-recipient mismatches.[21,22]

Kidney and Pancreas Transplants

ABO compatibility is the most important factor determining the immediate survival of kidney transplants. Because ABH antigens are expressed in varying amounts on all cells of the body, transplanted ABO-incompatible tissue comes into continuous contact with the recipient's ABO antibodies. Of particular importance is the expression of ABH antigens on vascular endothelial cells because the vascular supply in the transplant is a common site for rejection.

Both the recipient and the donor are ordinarily tested for ABO, HLA-A, -B, and -DR antigens. HLA-C and -DQ testing is also usually performed. Before surgery, a major crossmatch of recipient serum against donor lymphocytes is required. ASHI *Standards for Histocompatibility Testing*[23] require that the crossmatch be performed using a method more sensitive than routine microlymphocytotoxicity testing, such as prolonged incubation, washing, augmentation with antihuman globulin reagents, or flow cytometry. Flow cytometry is the most sensitive method and is especially useful because it can best predict early acute re-

jection and delayed graft function, both of which are strong predictors of chronic rejection and long-term allograft survival.[24] In patients undergoing cadaveric kidney retransplantation, the 7-year graft survival rate using the T-cell flow crossmatch to select the donor kidney was comparable to that of patients undergoing primary cadaveric transplantation (68% vs 72%) and was significantly better than that of regraft patients for whom only the antiglobulin lymphocytotoxicity crossmatch was used (45%).[25] Because HLA antibody responses are dynamic, the serum used for the crossmatch is often obtained within 48 hours of surgery and is retained in the frozen state for any required subsequent testing. An incompatible crossmatch with unfractionated or T lymphocytes is a contraindication to kidney transplantation. The significance of a positive B-cell crossmatch is unclear.

Serum from a patient awaiting cadaver-donor kidney transplant surgery is tested at regular intervals for the degree of alloimmunization by determining the PRA. In addition, many laboratories identify the specificities of HLA alloantibodies formed. If an antibody with a defined HLA specificity is identified in a recipient, it is a common practice to avoid the corresponding antigen when allocating a deceased donor allograft. The serum samples used for periodic PRA testing are usually frozen. The samples with the highest PRA are often used, in addition to the preoperative sample, for pretransplant crossmatching. The necessity of a prospective crossmatch for recipients with no evidence of HLA sensitization has been questioned. Prompt transplantation with reduced cold ischemia time for the renal allograft may provide greater benefit to the patient than prospective crossmatching, provided 1) a very sensitive method for antibody detection, such as flow cytometry, has been used[26,27] and 2) it is absolutely certain that the patient has had no additional sensitizing event (ie, immunization or transfusions within 2 weeks before or any time since that serum was screened).

The approach to kidney transplants using living donors is different. In the past, when several prospective living donors were being considered, MLC testing between the recipient and the donors was sometimes performed, but it is rarely performed today. HLA matching of recipients with kidney donors (both living and cadaveric donor) contributes to long-term allograft survival by decreasing the likelihood of chronic rejection. In 1996, the projected 20-year allograft survival rates were 57% for two-haplotype-matched sibling donors, 30% for one-haplotype-matched parental donors, and 18% for cadaver donors.[28] For cadaver donors with no mismatches with the recipient for HLA-A, -B, and -DR, the projected 20-year allograft survival was 40%. Surprisingly, projected survival for allografts from living, unrelated donors is similar to those from parental donors.[29] Recently, the 1-year survival rates for grafts from living and cadaver renal donors were 93.9% and 87.7% respectively, and the half-lives of living-donor and cadaver-donor renal allografts were 21.6 and 13.8 years, respectively.[30]

Other Solid Organ Transplants

For liver, heart, lung, and heart/lung transplants, ABO compatibility remains the primary immunologic system for donor selection, and determining pretransplant ABO compatibility between donor and recipient is mandatory. HLA-A, -B, and -DR testing of potential recipients is required, and the transplant crossmatch must be available before transplantation when the recipient has demonstrated presensitization, except for emergency situations. Levels of HLA compatibility do correlate with graft survival after heart transplantation, but prospective HLA matching has been difficult to implement.[31]

Parentage and Other Forensic Testing

HLA typing (particularly DNA-based HLA typing) has proven useful in forensic testing. In parentage testing, HLA typing alone can exclude about 90% of falsely accused males. With the addition of red cell antigen typing, the exclusion rate rises to 95% and exceeds 99% when typing for red cell enzymes and serum proteins is included. Haplotype frequencies, rather than gene frequencies, are used in these calculations because linkage disequilibrium is so common in the HLA system. It is important, however, to keep in mind the racial differences that exist in HLA haplotype frequencies; recombination events must also be considered.

Other useful DNA-based assays for forensic testing are detection of alleles with variable numbers of tandem repeats and alleles with variation in the number of short tandem repeats, which assess other polymorphic, non-HLA genetic regions. DNA-based assays allow identification of individuals on the basis of extremely small samples of fluid or tissue, such as hairs, epithelial cells, or semen.

HLA and Disease

For some conditions, especially those believed to have an autoimmune etiology, an association exists between HLA phenotype and occurrence of clinical disease (see Table 17-3).[32-34] HLA-associated diseases have several features in common. They are known or suspected to be inherited, display a clinical course with acute

Table 17-3. HLA-Associated Diseases

Disease	HLA	RR [32-37]
Celiac disease	DQ2	>250
Ankylosing spondylitis	B27	>150
Narcolepsy	DQ6	>38
Subacute thyroiditis	B35	14
Type I diabetes	DQ8	14
Multiple sclerosis	DR15, DQ6	12
Rheumatoid arthritis	DR4	9
Juvenile rheumatoid arthritis	DR8	8
Grave's disease	DR17	4

RR = relative risk.

exacerbations and remissions, usually have characteristics of autoimmune disorders, and the exact cause is unknown. Evidence has been accumulating that implicates the HLA molecules themselves in disease susceptibility. For instance, resistance to cerebral malaria results from a strong cytotoxic T-cell response to particular malarial peptides that are restricted by (fit into the peptide-binding grooves of) two specific HLA molecules.[35] Another mechanism that could lead to the association of HLA phenotype and disease is the presence of a Class I or II heterodimer encoded by a specific allele that preferentially presents autoantigens to the T-cell receptor.

The ancestral haplotype A1, B8, DR3, DQ2 discussed previously (under Linkage Disequilibrium) is associated with susceptibility to Type 1 diabetes, lupus, celiac disease, common variable immunodeficiency and IgA deficiency, myasthenia gravis, and also with an accelerated course of HIV infection, likely due to the presence of multiple genes.[36] However, HLA typing has only limited value in assessing risk for most diseases because the association is incom-

plete, often giving false-negative and false-positive results. The association of HLA-B27 and ankylosing spondylitis in those of European ancestry is instructive. The test is highly sensitive; more than 90% of such patients with ankylosing spondylitis possess the HLA-B27 antigen. On the other hand, specificity is low; only 20% of individuals with the B27 antigen will develop ankylosing spondylitis. A second condition, narcolepsy, is strongly associated with the HLA allele *DQB1*0602*.[37] As with the case of HLA-B27 and ankylosing spondylitis, over 90% of individuals with narcolepsy are positive for *HLA-DQB1*0602*, but only a minority of individuals with this marker develop the disease.

The degree of association between a given HLA type and a disease is often described in terms of relative risk (RR), which is a measure of how much more frequently a disease occurs in individuals with a specific HLA type when compared to individuals not having that HLA type. Calculation of RR is usually based on the cross-product ratio of a 2×2 contingency table. However, because the HLA system is so highly polymorphic, there is an increased possibility of finding an association between an HLA antigen and a disease by chance alone. Therefore, calculation of RR for HLA disease associations is more complex and is typically done by Haldane's modification of Woolf's formula.[38-39] The RR values for some diseases associated with HLA are shown in Table 17-3.

References

1. Schreuder GMTh, Hurley CK, Marsh SGE, et al. The HLA dictionary 2001: A summary of HLA-A, -B, -C, -DRB1/3/4/5, -DQB1 alleles and their association with serologically defined HLA-A, -B, -C, -DR, and -DQ antigens. Hum Immunol 2001;62:826-49.

2. Braud VM, Allan DSJ, McMichael AJ. Functions of nonclassical MHC and non-MHC-encoded class I molecules. Curr Opin Immunol 1999;11:100-8.

3. Feder JN, Gnirke A, Thomas W, et al. A novel MHC class I-like gene is mutated in patients with hereditary haemochromatosis. Nat Genet 1996;13:399-408.

4. Bodmer JG, Parham P, Albert ED, Marsh SG. Putting a hold on "HLA-H." Nat Genet 1997; 15:234-5.

5. McDonald JC, Adamashvili I. Soluble HLA: A review of the literature. Hum Immunol 1998; 59:387-403.

6. Ghio M, Contini P, Mazzei C, et al. Soluble HLA class 1, HLA class II, and Fas ligand in blood components: A possible key to explain the immunomodulatory effects of allogeneic blood transfusion. Blood 1999;93:1770-7.

7. Zinkernagel RM, Doherty PC. The discovery of MHC restriction. Immunol Today 1997;18: 14-7.

8. Cao K, Chopek M, Fernandez-Vina MA. High and intermediate resolution DNA typing systems for class I HLA-A, -B, -C genes by hybridization with sequence-specific oligonucleotide probes (SSOP). Rev Immunogenet 1999;1:177-208.

9. Welsh K, Bunce M. Molecular typing for the MHC with PCR-SSP. Rev Immunogenet 1999; 1:157-76.

10. Dzik WH. Leukoreduced blood components: Laboratory and clinical aspects. In: Simon TL, Dzik WH, Snyder EL, et al, eds. Rossi's principles of transfusion medicine. 3rd ed. Baltimore, MD: Lippincott Williams and Wilkins, 2002:270-87.

11. Bolgiano DC, Larson EB, Slichter SJ. A model to determine required pool size for HLA-typed community donor apheresis programs. Transfusion 1989;29:306-10.

12. Pei R, Lee JH, Shih NJ, et al. Single human leukocyte antigen flow cytometry beads for accurate identification of human leukocyte antigen antibody specificities. Transplantation 2003;75:43-9.

13. Friedberg RC. Independent roles for platelet crossmatching and HLA in the selection of platelets for alloimmunized patients. Transfusion 1994;34:215-20.

14. Kopko PM, Popovsky MA, MacKenzie MR, et al. HLA class II antibodies in transfusion-related acute lung injury. Transfusion 2001;41: 1244-8.

15. Gorman TE, Julius CJ, Barth RF, et al. Transfusion-associated graft-vs-host disease. A fatal case caused by blood from an unrelated HLA homozygous donor. Am J Clin Pathol 2000; 113:732-7.

16. Starzl TE, Demetris AJ, Murase N, et al. Chimerism after organ transplantation. Curr Opin Nephrol Hypertens 1997;6:292-8.

17. Sivasai KSR, Jendrisak M, Duffy BF, et al. Chimerism in peripheral blood of sensitized patients waiting for renal transplantation. Transplantation 2000;69:538-44.

18. Artlett CM, Smith JB, Jimenez SA. Identification of fetal DNA and cells in skin lesions from women with system sclerosis. N Engl J Med 1998;338:1186-91.

19. Thomas ED. Bone marrow transplantation: A review. Semin Hematol 1999;36:95-103.

20. Mickelson EM, Petersdorf E, Anasetti PM, et al. HLA matching in hematopoietic cell transplantation. Hum Immunol 2000;61:92-100.

21. Kurtzberg J, Laughlin M, Graham ML, et al. Placental blood as a source of hematopoietic stem cells for transplantation into unrelated recipients. N Engl J Med 1996;335:157.

22. Aversa F, Tabilio A, Velardi A. Treatment of high-risk acute leukemia with T cell depleted stem cells from related donors with one fully mismatched HLA haplotype. N Engl J Med 1998;339:1186-93.

23. Standards for histocompatibility testing. Mt. Laurel, NJ: American Society for Histocompatibility and Immunogenetics, 1998.

24. Utzig MJ, Blumke M, Wolff-Vorbeck G, et al. Flow cytometry cross-match: A method for predicting graft rejection. Transplantation 1997;63:551-4.

25. Bryan CF, Baier KA, Nelson PW, et al. Long-term graft survival is improved in cadaveric renal retransplantation by flow cytometric crossmatching. Transplantation 2000;66: 1827-32.

26. Taylor CJ, Smith SI, Morgan CH, et al. Selective omission of the donor crossmatch before renal transplantation: Efficacy, safety, and effects of cold storage time. Transplantation 2000;69:719-23.

27. Gebel HM, Bray RA. Sensitization and sensitivity: Defining the unsensitized patient. Transplantation 2000;69:1370-4.

28. Terasaki PI, Cho Y, Takemoto S, et al. Twenty-year follow-up on the effect of HLA matching on kidney transplant survival and prediction of future twenty-year survival. Transplant Proc 1996;28:1144-5.

29. Terasaki PI, Cecka JM, Gjertson DW, Takemoto S. High survival rates of kidney transplants from spousal and living unrelated donors. N Engl J Med 1995;333:333-6.

30. Hariharan S, Johnson CP, Bresnahan BA, et al. Improved graft survival after renal transplantation in the United States, 1988 to 1996. N Engl J Med 2000;342:605-12.

31. Ketheesan N, Tay GK, Witt CS, et al. The significance of HLA matching in cardiac transplantation. J Heart Lung Transplant 1999;18:226-30.

32. Thorsby E. Invited anniversary review: HLA associated diseases. Hum Immunol 1997;53:1-11.

33. Pile KS. HLA and disease associations. Pathology 1999;31:202-12.

34. Howell WM, Jones DB. The role of human leukocyte antigen genes in the development of malignant disease. J Clin Pathol Mol Pathol 1995;48:M302-6.

35. Hill AV. The immunogenetics of resistance to malaria. Proc Assoc Am Physicians 1999;111:272-7.

36. Price P, Witt C, Allcock R, et al. The genetic basis for the association of the 8.1 ancestral haplotype (A1, B8, DR3) with multiple immunopathological diseases. Immunol Rev 1999;167:257-74.

37. Pelin Z, Guilleminault C, Risch N, et al. HLA-DQB1*0602 homozygosity increases relative risk for narcolepsy but not for disease severity in two ethnic groups. US Modafinil in Narcolepsy Multicenter Study Group. Tissue Antigens 1998;51:96-100.

38. Haldane JBS. The estimation and significance of the logarithm of a ratio of frequencies. Ann Hum Genet 1955;20:309-11.

39. Woolf B. On estimating the relation between blood groups and disease. Ann Hum Genet 1955;19:251-3.

Suggested Reading

ASHI Clinical Affairs Committee. Guidelines for clinical histocompatibility practice. Mt. Laurel, NJ: American Society for Histocompatibility and Immunogenetics, 1999.

Phelan DL, Mickelson EM, Noreen HS, et al. ASHI laboratory manual. 4th ed. Mt. Laurel, NJ: American Society for Histocompatibility and Immunogenetics, 2001.

Standards for histocompatibility testing. Mt. Laurel, NJ: American Society for Histocompatibility and Immunogenetics, 1998.

Chapter 18

Pretransfusion Testing

THE PURPOSE OF pretransfusion testing is to select blood components that will not cause harm to the recipient and will have acceptable survival when transfused. If performed properly, pretransfusion tests will confirm ABO compatibility between the component and the recipient and detect most clinically significant unexpected antibodies.

The AABB *Standards for Blood Banks and Transfusion Services*[1] requires that the following procedures be performed before blood components are issued for transfusion:

- Positive identification of the recipient and the recipient's blood sample.
- ABO group and Rh typing of the recipient's blood.
- Red cell antibody detection tests for clinically significant antibodies using the recipient's serum or plasma.
- Comparison of current findings on the recipient's sample with records of previous results.

- Confirmation of the ABO group of red cell components.
- Confirmation of the Rh type of Rh-negative red cell components.
- Selection of components of ABO group and Rh type appropriate for the recipient.
- Performance of a serologic or computer crossmatch.
- Labeling of products with the recipient's identifying information.

Transfusion Requests

Requests for transfusion may be submitted electronically or on paper and must contain sufficient information for positive recipient identification. *Standards*[1(p36)] requires two independent identifiers to identify the patient. These identifiers could be the patient's first and last names, an identification number unique to that individual, a birth date, or other identifying system. Other information necessary

18

to process the request includes identification of the component needed, the quantity, any special requests such as irradiation, gender and age of the recipient (42 CFR 493.1241), and the name of the responsible physician. The diagnosis and the recipient's history of transfusion and pregnancy may be helpful in problem-solving. Each facility should have a written policy defining request acceptance criteria. Blood requests that lack the required information, are inaccurate, or are illegible should not be accepted.[1(p36)] Telephoned requests are acceptable in urgent situations but should be documented, for example, in a telephone log; a subsequent request as a written authorization is to be made within 30 days.[2]

Patient Identification

Collection of a properly labeled blood sample from the intended recipient is critical to safe blood transfusion. Most hemolytic transfusion reactions result from errors in sample or patient identification.[3,4] The person drawing the blood sample must identify the intended recipient in a positive manner. Each facility must develop and implement policies and procedures for patient identification and specimen collection.

Most hospitals identify patients with an identification wristband. Ideally, this wristband is placed on the patient before specimen collection and remains on the patient until discharge. The same identifying information on the specimen tube submitted for testing will be used to label blood components and this information will be compared against the patient's wristband at the time of transfusion. Some hospitals use an internally generated or commercially available identification band with a substitute or additional "blood bank number" as the unique patient identifier. Commercial systems vary in design: color-coded numbers on wristbands, tubes, and units; a wristband with an embosser for label printing; and a system for barcoding that provides positive sample and patient identification.

Hospital policies generally require phlebotomists to collect blood specimens only from patients who have an attached patient identification wristband. However, in some circumstances, it may not be possible for the patient to wear an identification wristband, and an alternative means of positive patient identification may be needed. The use of wristbands is difficult when the patient has total body burns, when the patient is an extremely premature infant, or when the wristband is inaccessible during surgery. Some facilities allow identifying information to be placed on a patient's ankle or forehead. Intraoperative patient identification procedures may allow the use of an alternative identification process in lieu of an inaccessible wristband. It is important to remind clinical personnel that transfusions should not be administered to a patient who lacks positive identification.

When the patient's identity is unknown, an emergency identification method may be used. This patient identification must be attached to the patient and affixed or reproduced on blood samples. This identification must be cross-referenced with the patient's name and hospital identification number or code when they become known. When hospitals allow the use of confidential or alias names, the facility must have policies and procedures that govern their use.

Outpatients may be identified with the use of a patient wristband for the purpose of blood sample collection. Alternative methods of positive patient identification include a driver's license or other photographic identification. Whenever possible, the patient should be asked to state his or her name and to provide confirmation of birth date and address. If a discrepancy is noted, the sample must not be collected until the patient's identity has been clarified.

The identification of specimens used for preadmission testing must meet the same requirements as those used for inpatient transfusion—there must be no doubt about the identity of the specimen and the patient. With the advent of patient admission on the same day as surgery, hospitals have devised several mechanisms to identify patients when specimens have been collected several days or weeks before surgery. One option is to require that the patient wear an identification wristband. Other facilities use a unique number on specimens and on a patient identification form that the patient must provide on the day of surgery in order for the preadmission specimen to be valid for transfusion.[5] An alternative procedure is to place on the patient's medical record the wristband used during specimen collection. This wristband would be attached to the patient upon arrival on the day of surgery after proper identification of the patient.[6]

Regardless of the system used, it must be well known to all those who collect blood specimens and be followed routinely. Ideally, patient identification procedures should be used as a matter of course to identify patients for all treatment methods, not solely transfusions.

Sample Labeling

Before leaving the patient, the phlebotomist must label the blood sample tubes with two independent patient identifiers and the date of collection. Either handwritten or imprinted labels may be used as long as the information on the label is identical to that on the wristband and request. There must be a mechanism to identify the phlebotomist[1(p37)]; this certifi-

cation may be placed on the label of the tube, placed on the requisition, or documented in a computer system.

Confirming Sample Identity in the Laboratory

When a sample is received in the laboratory, a trained member of the staff must confirm that the information on the label and on the transfusion request is identical. If there is any doubt about the identity of the patient, a new sample must be obtained.[1(p37)] It is unacceptable for anyone to correct identifying information on an incorrectly labeled sample. Each laboratory should establish policies and procedures that define identifying information and describe how to document receipt of mislabeled specimens.

Blood Sample

Pretransfusion testing may be performed on either serum or plasma. Plasma may be the preferred specimen for some methods such as tests using gel technology. Incompletely clotted blood samples may cause small fibrin clots that trap red cells into aggregates that could resemble agglutinates. Plasma collected from patients with high levels of fibrinogen or patients with dysproteinemia may demonstrate rouleaux. Rouleaux formation can be mistaken for agglutination. Clotting may be incomplete in specimens not intended to be anticoagulated, such as patients who have been treated with heparin. Adding thrombin or protamine sulphate to the sample usually corrects the problem.

It is permissible to collect blood from an infusion line. To avoid interference from residual intravenous fluid, the tubing should be flushed with saline, and 5 mL or a volume of blood approximately twice the fluid volume in the line should be withdrawn and discarded before sample collection.[7]

Appearance of Sample

The appearance of the serum or plasma may create difficulties in detecting antibody-induced hemolysis. Whenever possible, a hemolyzed sample should be replaced with a new specimen. Test results observed with lipemic serum can be difficult to evaluate. On occasion, it may be necessary to use hemoglobin-tinged or lipemic serum or plasma. If hemolyzed samples are used, it should be noted in the patient testing records to differentiate hemolysis as a result of an antigen-antibody reaction. Each institution should have a procedure describing the indications for using hemolyzed and lipemic specimens.

Age of Sample

Blood samples intended for use in cross-matching should be collected no more than 3 days before the intended transfusion unless the patient has not been pregnant or transfused within the preceding 3 months. If the patient's transfusion or pregnancy history is uncertain or unavailable, compatibility tests must be performed on blood samples collected within 3 days of RBC transfusions.[1(p38)] This is to ensure that the sample used for testing reflects the recipient's current immunologic status because recent transfusion or pregnancy may stimulate production of unexpected antibodies. Because it is not possible to predict whether or when such antibodies will appear, a 3-day limit has been selected as an arbitrary interval expected to be both practical and safe. It is short enough to reflect acute changes in immunologic status but long enough to allow the results of preadmission testing completed on Friday (day 0) to be used for surgical cases performed on Monday

(day 3). The 3-day requirement applies only to patients who have been transfused or pregnant within the last 3 months, but many laboratories prefer to standardize their operations by setting a 3-day limit on all specimens used for pretransfusion testing.

Each institution should have a policy that defines the length of time samples may be used. Testing of stored specimens should be based on the specimen storage limitations in the reagent manufacturer's information circulars. Lack of appropriate storage space may also limit the length of time specimens are stored.

Retaining and Storing Blood Samples

The recipient's blood specimen and a sample of the donor's red cells must be stored at refrigerator temperature for at least 7 days after each transfusion.[1(p37)] Donor red cells may be from the remainder of the segment used in the crossmatch or a segment removed before issuing the blood. If the opened crossmatch segment is saved, it should be placed in a tube labeled with the unit number and sealed or stoppered. Keeping the patient's and donor's samples allows repeat or additional testing if the patient experiences adverse effects.

Serologic Testing

The patient's ABO group and Rh type must be determined in order to transfuse ABO- and Rh-compatible components. *Standards*[1(pp37,38)] requires that the red cells of the intended recipient be typed for ABO and Rh and the serum/plasma be tested for expected and unexpected antibodies before components containing red cells are issued for transfusion. There should be written procedures for exceptions during emergencies. When only plasma and platelets or Cryoprecipitated AHF are being infused, historical testing information in the patient's record may be used. Refer to Table 18-1 for selection of the ABO types for red cell and plasma transfusion when ABO-identical products are not available.

ABO Grouping and Rh Typing of the Recipient

To determine the ABO group of the recipient, red cells must be tested with anti-A and anti-B, and the serum or plasma with A_1 and B red cells. The techniques used and interpretation of the results are described in Chapter 13. Any discrepant results should be resolved before blood is given. If transfusion is necessary before resolution, the patient should receive group O red cells.

The patient's red cells must be tested with anti-D, with suitable observations or controls to avoid a false-positive interpretation. Chapter 14 contains a more extensive discussion of Rh typing reagents, appropriate control techniques, and weak D types. If problems in D typing arise, the patient should be given Rh-negative blood until the problem has been resolved. Testing a recipient's red cells for weak D is not necessary because giving Rh-negative cells causes no

harm to recipients with the weak D phenotype. Omitting the test for weak D prevents misinterpretations arising from the presence of a positive direct antiglobulin test (DAT). However, some transfusion services test patient pretransfusion specimens for weak D in order to identify patients who could be given Rh-positive blood components, thus reserving the Rh-negative components for patients who are D–. Routine testing for other Rh antigens is not required.

Detecting Unexpected Antibodies to Red Cell Antigens

Before deciding upon routine procedures for antibody detection, the blood bank director must approve which antibodies are considered potentially clinically significant. In general, an antibody is considered potentially clinically significant if antibodies of that specificity have been associated with hemolytic disease of the fetus and newborn, a hemolytic transfusion reaction, or notably decreased survival of transfused red cells. Antibodies reactive at 37 C and/or in the antiglobulin test are more likely to be clinically significant than cold-reactive antibodies.[8]

Numerous serologic techniques have been developed that are suitable for detec-

Table 18-1. Selection of Components When ABO-Identical Donors Are Not Available

	ABO Requirements
Whole Blood	Must be identical to that of the recipient.
Red Blood Cells	Must be compatible with the recipient's plasma.
Granulocytes Pheresis	Must be compatible with the recipient's plasma.
Fresh Frozen Plasma*	Must be compatible with the recipient's red cells.
Platelets Pheresis	All ABO groups are acceptable; components compatible with the recipient's red cells are preferred.
Cryoprecipitated AHF	All ABO groups are acceptable.

*Also see Table 21-5.

tion of blood group antibodies (see Chapter 12 and Chapter 19). Goals in providing compatible blood for a recipient are to:

■ Detect as many clinically significant antibodies as possible.

■ Detect as few clinically insignificant antibodies as possible.

■ Complete the procedure in a timely manner.

Standards[1(p38)] requires that tests for unexpected antibodies use unpooled reagent red cells in a method that detects clinically significant antibodies and includes an antiglobulin test preceded by incubation at 37 C.

Each negative antiglobulin test must be followed by a control system of IgG-sensitized cells (check cells). If alternative procedures are used, there must be documentation of equivalent sensitivity, and the manufacturer's specified controls must be used.

The method chosen should have sufficient sensitivity to detect very low levels of antibody in a recipient's serum. Transfusion of antigen-incompatible red cells to a recipient with a weakly reactive antibody may result in rapid anamnestic production of antibody, with subsequent red cell destruction. The same antibody detection procedure may be used for all categories of specimens, including pretransfusion and prenatal tests on patients and screening of donor blood. Once a procedure has been adopted, the method must be described in the facility's standard operating procedures manual.

Reading and Interpreting Reactions

In serologic testing, the hemolysis or agglutination that constitutes the visible endpoint of a red cell antigen-antibody interaction must be observed accurately and consistently. The strength of agglutination or degree of hemolysis observed with each cell sample should be recorded immediately after reading. All personnel in a laboratory should use the same interpretations and notations and be consistent in grading (eg, 0-4+) reactions. Some laboratories prefer to use a numeric scoring (eg, 0-12) system to indicate reaction strength. Refer to Method 1.8 for grading and scoring. An optical aid such as a concave mirror enhances visualization in reading tube tests. Microscopic observation is not routinely recommended in manufacturer's inserts for enhancement media. A microscope can be useful in distinguishing rouleaux from true agglutination. Microscopic reading may also allow for the detection of specific patterns of agglutination that are characteristic of some antibodies. For example, anti-Sd[a] typically produces small refractile agglutinates in a sea of free red cells, giving the appearance of a mixed-field appearance. If gel or solid phase is used, the manufacturer's directions must be followed for reading and interpreting positive and negative reactions.

Autologous Control

An autologous control or DAT is not required as a part of pretransfusion testing. It is of limited value, even for patients who have recently been transfused, and should be used only when antibody identification is required.

Practical Considerations

Antibody detection tests may be performed in advance of, or together with, a crossmatch between the patient's serum/plasma and donor red cells. Performing antibody detection tests before crossmatching permits early recognition and identification of clinically significant antibodies. This allows for the selection of the appropriate crossmatch procedure and acquisition of units with special antigen blood types (eg, e– units).

Comparison with Previous Records

Results of ABO and Rh tests on a current specimen must be compared with previous transfusion service records if there has been prior testing during the past 12 months, and the comparison must be documented.[1(p39)] Errors in identification and/or testing may be detected when discrepancies are found between previous and current ABO and Rh results.

Records are also to be reviewed for the presence of clinically significant red cell antibodies, for difficulties in testing, for the occurrence of significant adverse reactions, and for special transfusion requirements.[1(p39)] Clinically significant red cell alloantibodies may become undetectable in a recipient's serum over time. Between 30% and 35% of antibodies become undetectable within 1 year and nearly 50% become undetectable after 10 or more years.[9]

Crossmatching Tests

Unless there is an urgent need for blood, a crossmatch must be performed for red cell transfusion. The crossmatch shall use procedures to demonstrate ABO incompatibility and clinically significant antibodies to red cell antigens. Blood lacking the relevant antigens is to be selected for transfusion when a patient has clinically significant antibody identified currently or historically, even though the antibody is presently nonreactive.[1(pp39,40)] The crossmatch shall include the antiglobulin test. When no clinically significant antibodies are detected in current antibody screening tests and there is no record of previous detection of such antibodies,[1(p40)] then only a method to detect ABO incompatibility, such as an immediate-spin or computer crossmatch, is required. It is very rare for the antiglobulin phase of the crossmatch to detect a clinically significant unexpected antibody if the patient's antibody detection test is negative.[10,11]

The potential benefits of omitting a routine antiglobulin crossmatch include decreased turnaround time, decreased workload, reduced reagent costs, and more effective use of blood inventory. Omitting the antiglobulin phase of the crossmatch for patients who meet the criteria must be in approved written standard operating procedures. The methods used for serologic crossmatching may be the same as those used for red cell antibody detection or identification or they may be different. For example, gel methods may be used for both antibody detection and identification, but the crossmatch may be performed using a tube test.

Repeat Testing of Donor Blood

A serologic test to confirm the ABO group of all RBC units and the Rh type of RBC units labeled as Rh-negative must be performed before transfusion. Confirmatory testing for weak D is not required. This confirmatory testing is to be performed on a sample obtained from an attached segment. Any discrepancies are to be resolved before the unit is issued for transfusion.[1(p37)]

Suggested Procedures for Routine Crossmatching

Red cells used for crossmatching must be obtained from a segment of tubing originally attached to the blood container. For routine tube testing, the cells may be washed and resuspended to 2% to 5% in saline. Washing the donor's red cells removes small fibrin clots and some cold agglutinins that may interfere with interpretation of results. Because the ratio of serum to cells markedly affects the sensitivity of agglutination tests, it is important to stay within the 2% to 5% cell suspension range or as specified by the manufacturer's instructions. For example, if too many red cells are present, weak antibodies may be missed because too few antibody molecules bind to each cell. Many laboratorians find that a 2% to 3% concentration yields the best results. For tests using column (gel) or solid-phase microplate systems, follow the manufacturer's directions.

The simplest serologic crossmatch method is the immediate-spin saline technique, in which serum is mixed with saline-suspended red cells at room temperature and the tube is centrifuged immediately. The immediate-spin crossmatch method is designed to detect ABO incompatibilities between donor red cells and recipient serum. It can be used as the sole crossmatch method only if the patient has no present or previous clinically significant antibodies. Because the testing is performed at room temperature, antibodies such as anti-M, -N, and -P_1 may be detected that were not observed if antibody detection tests omitted room-temperature testing. A sample immediate-spin crossmatch technique is described in Method 3.1. An antiglobulin crossmatch procedure that meets the requirements of *Standards* for all routine situations is described in Method 3.2.

Type and Screen (Antibody Detection Test)

Type and screen is a policy in which the patient's blood sample is tested for ABO, Rh, and unexpected antibodies, then stored in the transfusion service for future crossmatch if a unit is needed for transfusion. Crossmatched blood is not labeled and reserved for patients undergoing surgical procedures that rarely require transfusion. The blood bank must have enough donor blood available to meet unexpected needs of patients undergoing operations under a type and screen policy. If transfusion becomes necessary, ABO- and Rh-

compatible blood can be safely released after an immediate-spin or computer crossmatch, if the antibody screen is negative and there is no history of clinically significant antibodies. However, if the antibody screen is positive, the antibody(ies) must be identified and antigen-negative units for the clinically significant antibodies identified must be available for use if needed.

Routine Surgical Blood Orders

Blood ordering levels for common elective procedures can be developed from previous records of blood use. Because surgical requirements vary among institutions, routine blood orders should be based on local transfusion utilization patterns. The surgeons, anesthesiologists, and the medical director of the blood bank should agree on the number of units required for each procedure. See Chapter 3 for a more detailed discussion of blood ordering protocols. Routine blood order schedules are successful only when there is cooperation and confidence among the professionals involved in setting and using the guidelines.

Once a surgical blood ordering schedule has been established, the transfusion service routinely crossmatches the predetermined number of units for each patient undergoing the designated procedures. Routine orders may need to be modified for patients with anemia, bleeding disorders, or other conditions in which increased blood use is anticipated. As with other circumstances that require rapid availability of blood, the transfusion service staff must be prepared to provide additional blood if the need arises.

Computer Crossmatch

When no clinically significant antibodies have been detected by antibody screening and history review, it is permissible to omit the antiglobulin phase of the crossmatch and perform only a procedure to detect ABO incompatibility. Computerized matching of blood can be used to fulfill the requirement, provided that the following conditions have been met[1(pp40,41)]:

- The computer system has been validated, on site, to ensure that only ABO-compatible whole blood or red cells have been selected for transfusion.
- Two determinations of the recipient's ABO group as specified in *Standards* are made, one on a current specimen and a second one by one of the following methods: by retesting the same sample, by testing a second current sample, or by comparison with previous records.
- The computer system contains the unit number, component name, ABO group, and Rh type of the component; the confirmed donor unit ABO group; two unique recipient identifiers; and the recipient's ABO group, Rh type, and antibody screen results.
- A method exists to verify correct entry of data before the release of blood components.
- The system contains logic to alert the user to discrepancies between the donor ABO group and Rh type on the unit label and the interpretation of the blood group confirmatory test, and to ABO incompatibility between recipient and donor unit.

Butch et al[12,13] and Safwenberg et al[14] have described in detail a model computer crossmatch system. Potential advantages of a computer crossmatch include decreased workload, reduced sample volume required for testing, reduced exposure of personnel to blood specimens, and better use of blood inventory.

Compatibility Testing for Neonates Less than 4 Months of Age

Requirements for compatibility testing for neonates less than 4 months of age are discussed in Chapter 24. An initial pretransfusion specimen must be obtained from the infant to determine ABO and Rh type. For ABO typing, testing the cells with anti-A and anti-B is the only test required. Serum or plasma from either the infant or the mother may be used to detect unexpected red cell antibodies and for crossmatching. The infant's serum need not be tested for ABO antibodies unless a non-group-O infant is to receive non-group-O cells that are incompatible with passively acquired anti-A or anti-B. This antibody most often comes from the mother but can be present from group O RBCs or plasma from incompatible platelets. Test methods in this case are to include an antiglobulin phase using either donor or reagent A_1 or B red cells. If no clinically significant unexpected antibodies are present, it is unnecessary to crossmatch donor red cells for the initial or subsequent transfusions. Repeat testing may be omitted for infants less than 4 months of age during any one hospital admission as long as they are receiving only group O cells.[1(p42)]

Interpretation of Antibody Screening and Crossmatch Results

Most samples tested have a negative antibody screen and are crossmatch-compatible with units selected. A negative antibody screen, however, does not guarantee that the serum does not have clinically significant red cell antibodies, only that it contains no antibodies that react with the screening cells by the techniques employed.

Furthermore, a compatible crossmatch does not guarantee normal red cell survival.

Table 18-2 reviews the possible causes of positive pretransfusion tests. Most of what is known about red cell antigen and antibody reactions comes from work performed in tube testing. This information is not necessarily applicable to antibody detection tests using other technologies such as solid-phase microtiter plates or column technologies. Spurious or unexpected reactions in these other technologies may have the same or other causes than those seen in the tube tests. Depending on the antigen/antibody reaction strength and the testing conditions, not all of the scenarios will result in positive tests.

The cause of the serologic problems should be identified before transfusion. Chapter 19 reviews techniques for problem resolution. If the patient is found to have clinically significant antibodies, units issued for transfusion should be nonreactive for such antigens when tested with licensed reagents (see Selection of Units, Other Blood Groups). When the antibody identified is considered clinically insignificant (eg, anti-A_1, -M, -N, -P_1, -Le^a, and/or -Le^b) and is not reactive at 37 C,[15] random units may be selected for crossmatch.

Labeling and Release of Crossmatched Blood at the Time of Issue

Standards[1(p44)] requires that the following activities take place at the time of issue:

- A tag or label indicating the recipient's two independent identifiers, donor unit number, and compatibility test interpretation, if performed, must be attached securely to the blood container.

- A final check of records maintained in the blood bank for each unit of blood or component must include:
  1. Two independent identifiers, one of which is usually the patient's name.
  2. The recipient's ABO group and Rh type.
  3. The donor unit or pool identification number.
  4. Donor's ABO and, if required, Rh type.
  5. The interpretation of the crossmatch tests (if performed).
  6. The date and time of issue.
  7. Special transfusion requirements (eg, cytomegalovirus-reduced-risk, irradiated, or antigen-negative).

- There must be a process to confirm that the identifying information, the request, the records, and the blood or component are in agreement and that discrepancies have been resolved before issue.

Additional records that may be of use include those that identify the person issuing the blood and the person to whom the blood was issued or the destination of the unit.

After the transfusion, a record of the transfusion shall be made a part of the patient's medical record. This information may be part of a computer record or a paper form. Records must contain the identification of the person(s) performing the test and, if blood is issued before the resolution of compatibility problems, the final status of the serologic findings.

There should be a system to ensure that the proper blood component is issued for the intended patient. Before issuing a unit of blood or component, personnel must ensure that the product is acceptable for use, the unit is checked to make sure it does not have an abnormal color or ap-

Table 18-2. Causes of Positive Pretransfusion Tests*

Negative Antibody Screen, Incompatible Immediate-Spin Crossmatch
- Donor red cells are ABO-incompatible, caused by error in selecting donor unit, patient specimen, or labeling the donor unit.
- Donor red cells are ABO-incompatible, caused by failure to detect weak expressions of antigens.
- Donor red cells are polyagglutinable.
- Anti-A_1 in the serum of an A_2 or A_2B individual.
- Other alloantibodies are reactive at room temperature (eg, anti-M).
- Rouleaux formation.
- Cold autoantibodies (anti-I), especially if immediate spin is not tested on antibody detection screen.

Negative Antibody Screen, Incompatible Antiglobulin Crossmatch
- Donor red cells have a positive direct antiglobulin test.
- Antibody reacts only with red cells having strong expression of a particular antigen either because of dosage effect (eg, Rh, Kidd, Duffy, and MN antigens) or because of intrinsic variation in antigen strength (eg, P_1).
- Antibody reacts with a low-incidence antigen present on the donor red cells.
- Passively transferred antibody is present—significant levels of circulating anti-A or -B may be present after infusion of ABO-incompatible platelets to a recipient.

Positive Antibody Screen, Compatible Crossmatches
- Auto-anti-IH (-H).
- Anti-Le^{bH}.
- Antibodies are dependent on reagent cell diluent.
- Antibodies demonstrating dosage effect and red cells of the unit are from heterozygotes (ie, express a single dose of antigen).

Positive Antibody Screen, Incompatible Crossmatches, Negative Auto Control
- Alloantibody(ies).
- Unexpected interactions with reagent red cells.

Positive Antibody Screen, Incompatible Crossmatches, Positive Auto Control, Negative Direct Antiglobulin Test
- Antibody to ingredient in enhancement media.

Positive Antibody Screen, Incompatible Crossmatches, Positive Auto Control
- Alloantibody is present and patient is experiencing either a delayed serologic or hemolytic transfusion reaction.
- Passively transferred alloantibody from a derivative reactive with the recipient's cells (eg, intravenous immune globulin).
- Cold-reactive autoantibody.
- Warm-reactive autoantibody.
- Rouleaux formation.
- Reagent-related problems.

*Causes are dependent upon serologic methods used.

pearance, the container is not leaking, and the product is not outdated.

Final identification of the recipient and the blood container rests with the transfusionist, who must identify the patient and donor unit and certify that identifying information on forms, tags, and labels is in agreement (see Chapter 22).

Selection of Units

ABO Compatibility

Whenever possible, patients should receive ABO-identical blood; however, it may be necessary to make alternative selections. If the component to be transfused contains 2 mL or more of red cells, the donor's red cells must be ABO-compatible with the recipient's plasma.[1(p40)] Because plasma-containing components can affect the recipient's red cells, the ABO antibodies in transfused plasma should be compatible with the recipient's red cells when feasible. Requirements for components and acceptable alternative choices are summarized in Table 18-1.

Rh Type

Rh-positive blood components should routinely be selected for D+ recipients. Rh-negative units will be compatible but should be reserved for D– recipients. D– patients should receive red-cell-containing components that are Rh-negative to avoid immunization to the D antigen. Occasionally, ABO-compatible Rh-negative components may not be available for D– recipients. In this situation, the blood bank physician and the patient's physician should weigh alternative courses of action. Depending on the childbearing potential of the patient and the volume of red cells transfused, it may be desirable to administer Rh Immune Globulin to a D– patient given Rh-positive blood.[16]

Other Blood Groups

Antigens other than ABO and D are not routinely considered in the selection of units of blood. However, if the recipient has a clinically significant unexpected antibody, antigen-negative blood should be selected for crossmatching. If the antibody is weakly reactive or no longer demonstrable, a licensed reagent should be used to confirm that the donor units are antigen negative. If there is an adequate quantity of the patient's serum, or if another patient's serum with the same antibody specificity is available, and that antibody reacts well with antigen-positive red cells, that serum may be used to screen for antigen-negative units. Those units found to be antigen negative must be confirmed with a licensed reagent, when available. When licensed reagents are not available (eg, anti-Lan or anti-Yt[a]), expired reagents or stored serum specimens from patients or donors can be used, provided that controls tested on the day of use are acceptable (see the Food and Drug Administration Compliance Program Guidance Manual, Chapter 42, Blood and Blood Products). When crossmatch-compatible units cannot be found, the medical director should be involved in the decision to transfuse the patient. (See Chapter 19 and Chapter 20 for additional information on issuing crossmatch-incompatible units.) Antigen-negative units are not usually provided for the patient who has antibodies that are not clinically significant. Sometimes, problems associated with crossmatching units for patients with these antibodies may be avoided by altering the serologic technique used for the crossmatch.

Blood Administered in Urgent Situations

When blood is urgently needed, the patient's physician must weigh the risk of transfusing uncrossmatched or partially crossmatched blood against the risk of delaying transfusion until compatibility testing is complete. Ideally, a transfusion service physician should provide consultation. The risk that the transfused unit might be incompatible may be judged to be less than the risk of depriving the patient of oxygen-carrying capacity of that transfusion. See Chapter 21.

Required Procedures

When blood is released before pretransfusion testing is complete, the records must contain a signed statement of the requesting physician indicating that the clinical situation was sufficiently urgent to require release of blood.[1(p46)] Such a statement does not absolve blood bank personnel from their responsibility to issue properly labeled donor blood that is ABO-compatible with the patient. When urgent release is requested, blood bank personnel should:

1. Issue uncrossmatched blood, which should be:
   a. Group O Red Blood Cells if the patient's ABO group is unknown. It is preferable to give Rh-negative blood if the recipient's Rh type is unknown, especially if the patient is female with the potential to bear children.
   b. ABO and Rh compatible, if there has been time to test a current specimen. Previous records must not be used, nor should information be taken from other records such as cards, identification tags, or driver's license.
2. Indicate in a conspicuous fashion on the attached tag or label that compatibility testing was not complete at the time of issue.
3. Begin compatibility tests and complete them promptly (for massive transfusion, see below). If incompatibility is detected at any stage of testing, the patient's physician and the transfusion service physician should be notified immediately.

Massive Transfusion

Massive transfusion is defined as infusion, within a 24-hour period, of a volume of blood approximating the recipient's total blood volume. Exchange transfusion of an infant is considered a massive transfusion.

Following massive transfusion, the pretransfusion sample no longer represents the blood currently in the patient's circulation and its use for crossmatching has limited benefit. It is only important to confirm ABO compatibility of units administered subsequently. The blood bank director may implement a more limited pretransfusion testing protocol to be used in these situations. This protocol should be in writing to ensure consistent application by all laboratory personnel.

Blood Administered After Non-Group-Specific Transfusion

Transfusion services sometimes release units for transfusion during emergencies before they receive a sample for blood typing. When it arrives, the sample is a pretransfusion specimen. In most cases, the sample is tested and units of that ABO group are issued for transfusion without concern for anti-A and/or anti-B remaining from the initial emergency-release units. Because most donor units are RBCs with comparatively little supernatant plasma, or RBCs (Additive Solution Added) with even less residual plasma, the risks involved in following this practice are minimal. For example, the patient may exhibit a transient positive DAT.

In some cases, when large volumes of red cells are transfused, or when young children or infants receive transfusions, passively acquired ABO antibodies may be detected,[17] and it may be appropriate to demonstrate compatibility of red cells of the patient's original ABO group with a freshly drawn serum specimen. If the crossmatch is incompatible because of ABO antibodies, transfusion with red cells of the alternative group should be continued.

If the change in blood type involves only the Rh system, return to type-specific blood is simple because antibodies are unlikely to be present in the plasma of either the recipient or the donor. If a patient has received blood of an Rh type other than his or her own before a specimen has been collected for testing, it may be difficult to determine the correct Rh type. If there is any question about the recipient's D type, Rh-negative blood should be transfused if possible. The use of Rh Immune Globulin prophylaxis should be considered when Rh-positive components are transfused to Rh-negative patients. See Chapter 21.

References

1. Silva MA, ed. Standards for blood banks and transfusion services. 23rd ed. Bethesda, MD: AABB, 2005.
2. Code of federal regulations. Title 42 CFR 493.1241. Washington, DC: US Government Printing Office, 2004 (revised annually).
3. Sazama K. Reports of 355 transfusion associated deaths: 1976 through 1985. Transfusion 1990;30:583-90.
4. Linden JV, Wagner K, Voytovich AE, Sheehan J. Transfusion errors in New York State: An analysis of 10 years' experience. Transfusion 2000;40:1207-13.
5. Butch SH, Stoe M, Judd WJ. Solving the same-day admission identification problem (abstract). Transfusion 1994;34(Suppl):93S.
6. AuBuchon JP. Blood transfusion options: Improving outcomes and reducing costs. Arch Pathol Lab Med 1997;121:40-7.
7. Procedures for the collection of diagnostic blood specimens by venipuncture. 3rd ed. NCCLS document H3-A2, approved standard. Villanova, PA: National Committee for Clinical Laboratory Standards, 1991.
8. Issitt PD, Anstee DJ. Applied blood group serology. Durham, NC: Montgomery Scientific Publications, 1998:873-905.
9. Ramsey G, Smietana SJ. Long term follow-up testing of red cell alloantibodies. Transfusion 1994;34:122-4.
10. Oberman HA. The present and future crossmatch. Transfusion 1992;32:794-5.
11. Meyer EA, Shulman IA. The sensitivity and specificity of the immediate-spin crossmatch. Transfusion 1989;29:99-102.
12. Butch SH, Judd WJ, Steiner EA, et al. Electronic verification of donor-recipient compatibility: The computer crossmatch. Transfusion 1994;34:105-9.
13. Butch SH, Judd WJ. Requirements for the computer crossmatch (letter). Transfusion 1994;34:187.
14. Safwenberg J, Högman CF, Cassemar B. Computerized delivery control a useful and safe complement to the type and screen compatibility testing. Vox Sang 1997;72:162-8.
15. Shulman IA, Petz LD. Red cell compatibility testing: Clinical significance and laboratory methods. In: Petz LD, Swisher SN, Kleinman S, eds. Clinical practice of transfusion medicine. 3rd ed. New York: Churchill Livingstone, 1996:199-244.
16. Pollack W, Ascari WQ, Crispen JF, et al. Studies on Rh prophylaxis II: Rh immune prophylaxis after transfusion with Rh-positive blood. Transfusion 1971;11:340-4.
17. Garratty G. Problems associated with passively transfused blood group alloantibodies. Am J Clin Pathol 1998;109:169-77.

Suggested Reading

Beck ML, Tilzer LL. Red cell compatibility testing: A perspective for the future. Transfus Med Rev 1996;10:118-30.

Brecher ME. Collected questions and answers. 7th ed. Bethesda, MD: AABB, 2001:49-56.

Butch SH for the Scientific Section Coordinating Committee. Guidelines for implementing an electronic crossmatch. Bethesda, MD: AABB, 2003.

Butch SH, Oberman HA. The computer or electronic crossmatch. Transfus Med Rev 1997;11:256-64.

Frohn C, Dumbgen L, Brand JM, et al. Probability of anti-D development in D– patients receiving D+ RBCs. Transfusion 2003;43:893-8.

Garratty G. How concerned should we be about missing antibodies to low-incidence antigens? (editorial) Transfusion 2003;43:844-7.

Issitt PD. From kill to overkill: 100 years of (perhaps too much) progress. Immunohematology 2000; 16:18-25.

Lumadue JA, Biyd JS, Ness PM. Adherence to a strict specimen-labeling policy decreases the incidence of erroneous blood grouping of blood bank specimens. Transfusion 1997;37:1169-72.

Padget BJ, Hannon JL. Variations in pretransfusion practices. Immunohematology 2003;19:1-6.

Rossmann SN for the Scientific Section Coordinating Committee. Guidelines for the labeling of specimens for compatibility testing. Bethesda, MD: AABB, 2002.

Schonewille H, van Zijl AM, Wijermans PW. Importance of antibodies against low-incidence RBC antigens in complete and abbreviated cross-matching. Transfusion 2003;43:939-44.

Initial Detection and Identification of Alloantibodies to Red Cell Antigens

R ED CELL ALLOANTIBODIES other than naturally occurring anti-A or -B are called unexpected red cell alloantibodies. Depending upon the group of patients or donors studied and the sensitivity of the test methods used, alloantibodies can be found in 0.3% to 38% of the population.[1,2] Alloantibodies react only with allogeneic red cells, whereas red cell autoantibodies react with the red cells of the antibody producer. Immunization to red cell antigens may result from pregnancy, transfusion, transplantation or from injections with immunogenic material. In some instances, no specific immunizing event can be identified. These naturally occurring antibodies are a result of exposure to environmental, bacterial, or viral antigens that are similar to blood group antigens. Also, antibodies detected in serologic tests can be passively acquired. These antibodies may be acquired from injected immunoglobulins, donor plasma, or passenger lymphocytes in transplanted organs or hematopoietic progenitor cells.

Significance of Alloantibodies

Alloantibodies to red cell antigens may be initially detected in any test that uses serum or plasma (eg, ABO test, antibody detection test, crossmatch) or in an eluate prepared from red cells coated with alloantibody. Once an antibody is detected, its specificity should be determined and its clinical significance assessed.

A clinically significant red cell antibody, although difficult to define, could be characterized as an antibody that shortens the survival of transfused red cells or has been associated with hemolytic disease of the fetus and newborn (HDFN). The degree of clinical significance varies with antibodies of the same specificity. Some antibodies cause destruction of incompatible red cells within hours or even minutes, others decrease the survival by only a few days, and some cause no discernible red cell destruction. Antibodies of some specificities are known to cause HDFN, whereas others may cause a positive direct antiglobulin test (DAT) in the fetus without clinical evidence of HDFN.

Reported experience with other examples of antibody with the same specificity can be used in assessing clinical significance. Table 15-1 summarizes the expected reactivity and clinical significance of commonly encountered alloantibodies. Daniels et al[3] have published a review of these and other specificities. For some antibodies, few or no data exist, and decisions must be based on the premise that clinically significant antibodies are usually those active at 37 C and/or by an indirect antiglobulin test (IAT). It is not true, however, that all antibodies active in vitro at 37 C and/or by an IAT are clinically significant.

Antibodies encountered in pretransfusion testing should be identified to assess the need to select antigen-negative red cell components for transfusion. Patients with clinically significant antibodies should, whenever practical, receive red cells that have been tested and found to lack the corresponding antigen. In prenatal testing, the specificity and immunoglobulin class of an antibody influence the likelihood of HDFN. The results of antibody identification tests on donor blood may be used to characterize the units for labeling before transfusion and to procure blood typing reagents or teaching samples.

General Procedures

The techniques employed for antibody detection and antibody identification are similar. Antibody identification methods can be more focused and based on the reactivity patterns seen in the antibody detection test.

Each facility should establish which techniques for antibody detection and identification will be employed routinely. Sometimes, it is valuable to develop flowcharts to clearly guide the technologist through the process of selecting additional techniques to identify antibody specificities. This approach is helpful in expediting the identification process and minimizing unnecessary testing.

Specimen Requirements

Either serum or plasma may be used for antibody detection and identification. Plasma is not suitable for detecting complement-activating antibodies. A 5- to 10-mL aliquot of whole blood usually contains enough serum or plasma for identifying simple antibody specificities; more may be required for complex studies. When autologous red cells are studied, the use of a sample anticoagulated with EDTA avoids problems associated with the in-vitro uptake of complement components by red cells, which may occur in clotted samples.

Medical History

It is useful to know a patient's clinical diagnosis, history of transfusions or pregnancies, and recent drug therapy when performing an antibody identification. For example, in patients who have had recent red cell transfusions, the circulating blood may contain sufficient donor cells to make red cell phenotyping studies difficult to interpret. Special procedures to separate the autologous red cells for typing may be required (see Method 2.15). Other special procedures may be required for patients with autoantibodies.

Reagents

Antibody Detection Red Cells

Group O red cells suitable for antibody screening are commercially available and are offered as sets of either two or three vials of single-donor red cells. Pooled antibody detection cells (usually from two donors) can only be used in testing serum samples from donors.

The decision to use two or three cells in an antibody detection test should be based on circumstances in each individual laboratory. The reagent red cells are selected to express the antigens associated with most commonly encountered antibodies. Reagent cells licensed by the Food and Drug Administration (FDA) for this purpose must express the following antigens: D, C, E, c, e, M, N, S, s, P_1, Le^a, Le^b, K, k, Fy^a, Fy^b, Jk^a, and Jk^b.[4] Some weakly reactive antibodies react only with red cells from donors who are homozygous for the genes controlling the expression of these antigens, a serologic phenomenon called dosage. Antibodies in the Rh, Duffy, MNS, and Kidd systems most commonly demonstrate dosage. Reagent red cells should be refrigerated when not in use and should not be used for antibody detection beyond their expiration date.

Antibody Identification Panels

Identification of an antibody to red cell antigen(s) requires testing the serum against a panel of selected red cell samples with known antigen composition for the major blood groups. Usually, they are obtained from commercial suppliers, but institutions may assemble their own by using red cells from local sources. Panel cells are (except in special circumstances) group O, allowing serum of any ABO group to be tested.

Each cell of the panel is from a different individual. The cells are selected so that, taking all the cells into account, a distinctive pattern of positive and negative reactive reactions exists for each of many antigens. To be functional, a reagent red cell panel must make it possible to identify with confidence those clinically significant alloantibodies that are most frequently encountered, such as anti-D, -E, -K, and -Fy^a. The phenotypes of the reagent red cells should be distributed such that single specificities of the common alloantibodies can be clearly identified and most others excluded. Ideally, the pattern of reactivity for most examples of single alloantibodies will not overlap with any other; eg, all of the K+ samples should not be the only ones that are also E+. It may also be valuable to include red cell samples with a double dose of the antigen in question for antibodies that frequently show dosage. To lessen the possibility that chance alone has caused an apparently definitive pattern, there must be a sufficient number of red cell samples that lack, and sufficient red cell samples that express, most of the antigens listed in Table 19-1.

Commercially prepared panels are generally issued every 2 to 4 weeks. Each panel contains different red cell samples with different antigen patterns, so it is essential to use the phenotype listing sheet that comes with the panel in use. Commercial cells usually come as a 2% to 5% suspension in a preservative medium that can be used directly from the vial. Washing is generally unnecessary unless the media in which the reagent cells are suspended are suspected of interfering with alloantibody identification.

Panel cells should not be used beyond the expiration date; however, this is not always practical. Most serologists use in-date reagent cells for initial antibody identification panels and, if necessary, use expired reagent cells for exclusion or confirmation of specificity. Each laboratory must establish and validate a policy for the use of expired reagent cells.[5]

Table 19-1. A Reagent Red Cell Panel for Alloantibody Identification

Sample #	Rh Phenotype	Rh C	C^w	c	D	E	e	Kell K	Duffy Fy^a	Fy^b	Kidd Jk^a	Jk^b	P P_1	Lewis Le^a	Le^b	MNS M	N	S	s
1	r'r	+	0	+	0	0	+	0	+	0	+	+	+	0	+	+	+	0	+
2	R_1^w	+	+	0	+	0	+	+	+	+	0	+	+	+	0	+	+	+	+
3	R_1	+	0	0	+	0	+	0	0	+	+	+	0	0	+	+	0	+	0
4	R_2	0	0	+	+	+	0	0	+	+	0	+	+	+	0	0	+	0	+
5	r''r	0	0	+	0	+	+	0	0	+	0	0	0	0	+	+	+	+	0
6	r	0	0	+	0	0	+	+	0	+	+	0	+	0	0	+	+	0	+
7	r	0	0	+	0	0	+	0	+	0	+	0	+	0	+	0	0	+	0
8	r	0	0	+	0	0	+	0	0	+	0	+	+	+	0	0	+	0	+
9	r	0	0	+	0	0	+	0	+	0	+	0	0	0	+	+	+	+	0
10	R_0	0	0	+	+	0	+	0	0	0	+	+	+	0	0	+	+	+	+

+ Denotes presence of antigen; 0 denotes absence of antigen.

Antiglobulin Reagents

To detect clinically significant antibodies, most antibody identification tests include an antiglobulin phase. Either polyspecific or IgG-specific antiglobulin reagents may be used. Polyspecific reagents may detect, or detect more readily, antibodies that bind complement. This may be of value in the detection of certain Kidd antibodies.[6] Although this may be advantageous in some instances, many serologists prefer to use IgG-specific reagents to avoid unwanted reactivity resulting from in-vitro complement binding by cold-reactive antibodies.

Enhancement Media

Although the test system may consist solely of serum and red cells (reagent red cells as provided by the manufacturer or saline-suspended red cells), most serologists use some type of enhancement medium. Many different media are available, including low-ionic-strength saline (LISS), polyethylene glycol (PEG), and 22% to 30% albumin. For the initial antibody identification panel, most laboratories use the same enhancement method used in their routine antibody detection tests. Additional enhancement techniques may be employed for more complex studies. Enhancement techniques are discussed later in this chapter.

Autologous Control (Autocontrol)

It may be helpful to know how a serum under investigation reacts with autologous red cells. This helps determine whether alloantibody, autoantibody, or both are present. Serum that reacts only with the reagent red cells usually contains only alloantibody, whereas reactivity with both reagent and autologous red cells suggests the presence of autoantibody or autoantibody plus alloantibody. However, a patient with alloantibodies to antigens ex-pressed on recently transfused red cells may have circulating donor red cells coated with alloantibodies, resulting in a positive autocontrol. Because this result may be misinterpreted as being due to autoantibody, a detailed history of recent transfusions should be obtained for all patients with a positive DAT or positive autocontrol.

The autologous control, in which serum and autologous cells undergo the same test conditions as serum and reagent cells, is not the same as a DAT. Incubation and the presence of enhancement reagents may cause reactivity in the autologous control that is only an in-vitro phenomenon. If the autocontrol is positive in the antiglobulin phase, a DAT should be performed. If the DAT is positive, elution studies should be considered if the patient has been recently transfused, if there is evidence of immune hemolysis, or if the results of serum studies prove inconclusive. A reactive DAT may also indicate the presence of autoantibody. If autoantibody is detected in the serum, adsorption studies may be necessary to detect coexisting alloantibodies.

Basic Antibody Identification Techniques

For initial panels, it is common to use the same methods and test phases used in the antibody detection test or crossmatch. Some serologists may choose to include an immediate centrifugation reading and/or a room temperature incubation and reading without adding an enhancement medium. This may enhance the detection of certain antibodies (anti-M, -N, -P_1, -I, -Le^a, or -Le^b) and may help to explain reactions detected at other phases. Many institutions omit these steps to avoid finding antibodies that react only at lower temperatures and have little or no clinical significance. Test observation after 37 C incubation may detect some antibodies (eg, potent anti-D, -K, or -E) that can cause direct agglutination of red cells. Other antibodies (eg, anti-Le[a], -Jk[a]) may be detected by their lysis of antigen-positive red cells during the 37 C incubation. Some serologists believe that because clinically significant antibodies will be detected with the IAT, the reading after 37 C can be safely omitted. This omission will lessen the detection of unwanted positive reactions resulting from clinically insignificant cold-reactive auto- and alloantibodies.[7,8]

The phenotype of the reactive antibody detection cells will provide clues to the specificity or help exclude specificities. This information is useful for selecting cells that would be most informative in additional testing.

If the patient has previously identified antibodies, this may affect panel selection. For example, if the patient is known to have anti-e, it will not be helpful to test the serum against a panel of 10 red cell samples, nine of which are e+. Testing a panel of selected e– red cell samples will better reveal any newly formed antibodies.

Sometimes, the patient's phenotype influences the selection of reagent cells. For example, if the patient is D– and the serum is reactive with D+ cells in the screening test, an abbreviated panel or select cell panel of D– red cell samples may be tested. This can both confirm the presence of anti-D and demonstrate the presence or absence of additional antibodies, while minimizing the amount of testing required.[9]

Interpreting Results

Antibody screening results are interpreted as positive or negative based on the presence or absence of reactivity (eg, agglutination). Interpretation of panel results can be a more complex process combining technical knowledge and intuitive skills. Panel results generally will include both positive and negative results at different phases of testing, each of which should be explained by the final conclusion. Determination of the patient's red cell phenotype and the probability of antibody specificity can also play roles in the final interpretation.

Positives and Negatives

Both positive and negative reactions are important in antibody identification. Positive reactions indicate the phase and strength of reactivity (see Method 1.8 for grading agglutination), which can suggest certain specificities. Positive reactions also can be compared to the antigen patterns expressed by the panel cells to help assign specificity. Single alloantibodies usually yield definite positive and negative reactions that create a clear-cut pattern with antigen-positive and -negative reagent red cell samples. For example, if a serum reacts only with cells 4 and 5 of the reagent red cell panel shown in Table 19-1, anti-E is very likely present. Both reactive samples express E and all nonreactive samples lack E.

Negative reactions are important in antibody identification because they allow tentative exclusion of antibodies to antigens expressed on the nonreactive cells. Exclusion of antibodies is an important step in the interpretation process and must be performed to ensure proper identification of all the antibodies present.

Exclusion or "Crossing Out"

A widely used first approach to the interpretation of panel results is to exclude specificities based on nonreactivity with the serum tested. Such a system is sometimes referred to as a "cross-out" or "rule-out" method. Once results have been recorded on the worksheet, the antigen profile of the first nonreactive cell is examined. If an antigen is *present* on the cell and the serum *did not react* with the cell, the presence of the corresponding antibody may be, at least tentatively, excluded. Many technologists will cross out that antigen from the listing on the panel sheet to facilitate the process. After all antigens present on that cell have been crossed off, interpretation proceeds with the other nonreactive cells and additional specificities are excluded. In most cases, this process will leave a group of antibodies that still have not been excluded.

Next, the cells reactive with the serum are evaluated. The pattern of reactivity for each nonexcluded specificity is compared to the pattern of reactivity obtained with the test serum. If there is a pattern that matches exactly, that is most likely the specificity of the antibody in the serum. However, if there are remaining specificities that have not been excluded, additional testing may be needed to eliminate remaining possibilities and to confirm the specificity identified. This requires testing the serum against cells selected for specific antigenic characteristics. For example, this approach could be employed if the pattern of positive reactions exactly fits anti-Jk^a, but anti-K and anti-S have not been excluded. Then serum should be tested against selected cells, ideally with the following phenotypes: Jk(a–), K–, S+; Jk(a–), K+, S–; and Jk(a+), K–, S–. The reaction pattern with these cells should both confirm the presence of anti-Jk^a and include or exclude anti-K and anti-S.

Although the exclusion (cross-out) approach often identifies simple antibody specificities, it should be considered only a provisional step, particularly if the cross-out was completed based on the nonreactivity of cells with weaker (eg, heterozygous) expression of an antigen (see Variations in Antigen Expression).

Probability

To ensure that an observed pattern is not the result of chance alone, conclusive antibody identification requires serum to be tested against sufficient reagent red cell samples that lack, and that express, the antigen that corresponds to the apparent specificity of the antibody.

A standard approach (based on Fisher's exact method[10]) has been to require, for each specificity identified, three antigen-positive cells that react and three antigen-negative cells that fail to react. This standard is not always possible, but it works well in practice, especially if cells with strong antigen expression are available. A somewhat more liberal approach is derived from calculations by Harris and Hochman,[11] whereby minimum requirements for a probability (p) value of 0.05 are met by having two positive and three negative cells, or one positive and seven negative cells (or the reciprocal of either combination). Comparative p values are shown in Table 19-2. The use of two positive and two negative cells is also an acceptable approach for antibody confirmation.[12] Additional details on calculating probability may be found in the suggested readings by Race and Sanger, Menitove, and Kanter. The possibility of false-negative results with antigen-positive cells must be considered as well as unexpected positives, ie, false-positive results due either to the presence of an additional antibody specificity or an error in the presumptive antibody identification.

Phenotype of Autologous Red Cells

Once an antibody has been tentatively identified in a serum, it is often helpful to

Table 19-2. Probability Values

No. Tested	No. Positive	No. Negative	p (Fisher[10])	p (Harris and Hochman[11])
5	3	2	0.100	0.035
6	4	2	0.067	0.022
6	3	3	0.050	0.016
7	5	2	0.048	0.015
7	4	3	0.029	0.008
8	7	1	0.125	0.049
8	6	2	0.036	0.011
8	5	3	0.018	0.005
8	4	4	0.014	0.004
9	8	1	0.111	0.043
9	7	2	0.028	0.008
9	6	3	0.012	0.003
10	9	1	0.100	0.039
10	8	2	0.022	0.007
10	7	3	0.008	0.002
10	6	4	0.005	0.001
10	5	5	0.004	0.001

demonstrate the presence or absence of the corresponding antigen on the autologous red cells. For example, if serum from an untransfused individual appears to contain anti-Fy^a but the autologous red cells have a negative DAT and type as Fy(a+), the data are clearly in conflict and further testing is indicated.

Determination of the patient's phenotype can be difficult if the patient has been transfused recently, generally within 3 months. If a pretransfusion specimen is available, these red cells should be used to determine the phenotype. Alternatively, the patient's own red cells can be separated from the transfused red cells and then typed (see Methods 2.15 and 2.16). The use of potent blood typing reagents, appropriate controls, and observation for mixed-field reactions often allow an unseparated specimen to be phenotyped. Phenotyping results on posttransfusion samples can be misleading, however, and should be interpreted with caution.[13] If there is little uncertainty about antibody identification, extensive efforts to separate and type the patient's own red cells are not necessary. Compatible antiglobulin crossmatch,[14(p40)] of antigen-negative donor units provides additional confirmation of antibody specificity. Definitive testing can be performed on the patient's red cells after a sufficient period without red cell transfusion. In a chronically transfused patient, definitive testing can be performed after an interval during which only antigen-negative blood has been given. Any antigen-positive red cells detected after prolonged transfusion of antigen-negative blood would presumably be the patient's own.

Complex Antibody Problems

Not all antibody identifications are simple. The exclusion procedure does not always lead directly to an answer and additional approaches may be required. Figure 19-1 shows some approaches to identifying antibodies in a variety of situations when the autocontrol is negative. Additional approaches may be needed if the autocontrol is positive; they are discussed later in this chapter.

Variations in Antigen Expression

For a variety of reasons, antibodies do not always react with *all* cells positive for the corresponding antigen. Basic interpretation by exclusion, as described previously, may result in a given specificity being excluded because the sample is nonreactive with an antigen-positive red cell sample, despite the presence of the antibody. Technical error, weak antibody reactivity, and variant or weak antigenic expression are all possible causes. Therefore, whenever possible, antibody specificities should be excluded only on the basis of cells known to bear a strong expression of the antigen. Enhancement techniques often help resolve problems associated with variations in antigen expression (see Methods 3.2.2, 3.2.3, 3.2.4, 3.5.5, and 3.5.6).

Zygosity

Reaction strength of some antibodies may vary from one red cell sample to another due to a phenomenon known as dosage, in which antibodies react preferentially with red cells from persons homozygous for the gene that determines the antigen (ie, possessing a "double dose" of the antigen). Red cells from individuals heterozygous for the gene may express less antigen and may react weakly or be nonreactive. Alloantibodies vary in their tendency to recognize dosage. Many antibodies to antigens in the Rh, Duffy, MNS, and Kidd systems have this trait.

Variation in Adults and Infants

Some antigens (eg, I, P_1, Le^a, and Sd^a) are expressed to varying degrees on red cells from different adult donors. This variation is unrelated to zygosity; however, the antigenic differences can be demonstrated serologically. Certain antibodies (eg, anti-I, -Le^a) demonstrate weaker reactivity with cord red cells than with red cells from adults (see Table 19-3).

Changes with Storage

Blood group antibodies may give weaker reactions with stored red cells than with fresh red cells. Some antigens (eg, Fy^a, Fy^b, M, P_1, Kn^a/McC^a, Bg)[17] deteriorate during storage more rapidly than others and the rate varies among red cells from different donors. Because red cells from donors are often fresher than commercial reagent cells, some antibodies give stronger reactions with suspensions of donor cells than with reagent cells. Frozen storage of red cells may result in antigen deterioration that can cause misleading antibody identification results.

The pH or other characteristics of storage media can affect the rate of antigen deterioration.[17,18] For example, Fy^a and Fy^b antigens may be weakened when the cells are stored in a suspending medium of low pH and low ionic strength. Alternatively, certain antibodies may demonstrate stronger or weaker reactions with red cells from different manufacturers using different suspending media. The age and nature of the specimen must also be considered when typing red cells. Antigens on cells from clotted samples tend to deteriorate faster than antigens on cells collected in citrate anticoagulants such as ACD or CPD. Red cells in

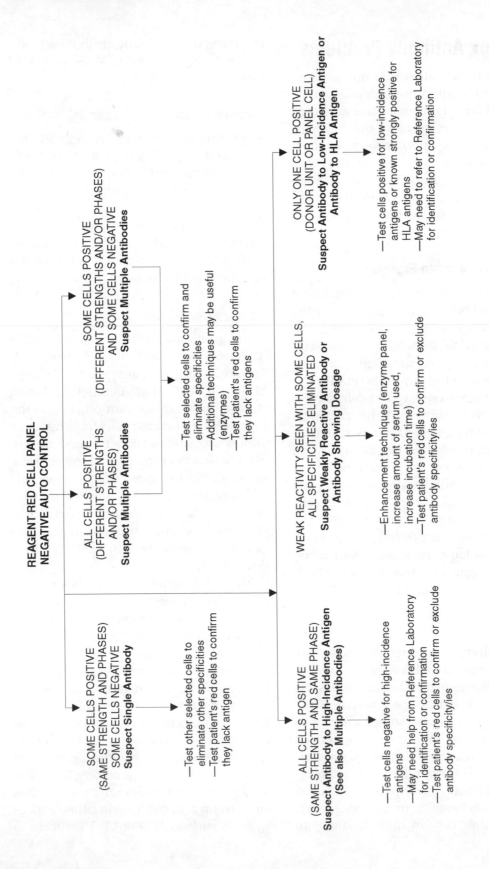

Figure 19-1. Approaches for identifying antibodies (modified from Brendel[15]).

Table 19-3. Antigen Expression on Cord Red Blood Cells*

Expression	Antigens
Negative	Le^a, Le^b, Sd^a, Ch, Rg, AnWj
Weak	I, H, P$_1$, Lu^a, Lu^b, Yt^a, Vel, Bg, McC^a, Yk^a, S1^a, Cs^a, Hy, Gy, Jo^a, Do^a, Do^b, Fy3
Strong	i, LW^a, LW^b

*Modified from Reid.[16]

donor units collected into these anticoagulants generally retain their antigens throughout the standard shelf life of the blood component. EDTA samples up to 14 days old are suitable for antigen typing; however, the manufacturer's instructions should be consulted when using commercial typing reagents.[19]

No Discernible Specificity

Factors other than variation in antigen expression may contribute to difficulty in interpreting results of antibody identification tests. If the reactivity obtained with the serum is very weak and/or if the cross-out process has excluded all likely specificities, alternative approaches to interpretation should be used.

Antigens Present in Common

Instead of excluding antibodies to antigens on nonreactive cells, one can observe what antigens are common to the reactive cells. For example, if the cells reacting at room temperature are all P$_1$+, yet not all the P$_1$+ cells react, the antibody could be an anti-P$_1$ that does not react with cells having a weaker expression of the antigen. (Sometimes, such cells are marked on the panel sheet as "+w.") With this in mind, one could use a method to enhance anti-P$_1$, such as testing at colder temperatures.

If all the reactive cells are Jk(b+), but not all the Jk(b+) cells react, the reactive ones might all be Jk(a–b+), with a double-dose expression of the antigen. Enhancement techniques, such as enzymes, LISS, or PEG, may then help demonstrate reactivity with all the remaining Jk(b+) cells. Typing the patient's cells to confirm they lack the corresponding antigen can also be very helpful.

Inherent Variability

Nebulous reaction patterns that do not appear to fit any particular specificity are characteristic of antibodies, such as anti-Bg^a, that react with HLA antigens on red cells. These antigens vary markedly in their expression on red cells from different individuals. Rarely, a pattern of clear-cut reactive and nonreactive tests that cannot be interpreted is due to the incorrect typing of reagent red cells. If the cell is from a commercial source, the manufacturer should be notified immediately of the discrepancy.

Unlisted Antigens

Sometimes a serum sample reacts with an antigen not routinely listed on the antigen profile supplied by the reagent manufacturer; Yt^b is one example. Even though serum studies yield clear-cut reactive and nonreactive tests, anti-Yt^b may not be suspected. In such circumstances, it is useful to ask the manufacturer for additional phenotype information. If the appropriate blood typing reagent is available, reactive and nonreactive red cell samples, as well as the autologous red cells, can be tested. These problems often have to be referred to an immunohematology reference laboratory.

ABO Type of Red Cells Tested

A serum sample may react with many or all of the group O reagent red cell samples, but not with red cells of the same ABO phenotype as the autologous red cells. This occurs most frequently with anti-H, -IH, or -Le^{bH}. Group O and A$_2$ red cells have large amounts of H antigen; A$_1$ and A$_1$B red cells express very little H (see Chapter 13). Sera containing anti-H or -IH react strongly with group O reagent red cell samples, but autologous A$_1$ or A$_1$B red cells or donor cells used for crossmatching may be weakly reactive or nonreactive. Anti-Le^{bH} reacts strongly with group O, Le(b+) red cells, but reacts weakly or not at all with Le(b+) red cells from A$_1$ or A$_1$B individuals. Such antibodies should be suspected when the antibody screen, which uses group O red cells, is strongly reactive, but serologically compatible A$_1$ or A$_1$B donor samples can be found without difficulty.

Multiple Antibodies

When a serum contains two or more alloantibodies, it may be difficult to interpret the results of testing performed on a single panel of reagent red cells. The presence of multiple antibodies may be suggested by a variety of test results.

1. *The observed pattern of reactive and nonreactive tests does not fit that of a single antibody.* When the exclusion approach fails to indicate a specific pattern, it is helpful to see if the pattern matches any two combined specificities. For example, if the reactive cells (see Table 19-1) are numbers 2, 4, 5, and 7, none of the specificities remaining after crossing-out exactly fits that pattern, but if both K and E are considered together, a pattern is discerned. Cells 2 and 7 react because of anti-K, cells 4 and 5 because of anti-E. If the typing patterns for no two specificities fit the reaction pattern, the possibility of more than two antibodies must be considered. The more antibodies a serum contains, the more complex the identification and exclusion of specificities will be, but the basic process remains the same.

2. *Reactivity is present at different test phases.*
   When reactivity occurs at several phases, each phase should be evaluated separately. The pattern seen at room temperature may indicate a different specificity from the pattern of antiglobulin results. It is also helpful to look at variability in the strength of reactions seen at each phase of testing. Table 15-2 provides information on the characteristic reactivity phase of several antibodies.

3. *Unexpected reactions are obtained when attempts are made to confirm the specificity of a suspected single antibody.*
   If a serum suspected of containing anti-e reacts with additional samples that are e–, another antibody may be present or the suspected antibody may not be anti-e. Testing a panel of selected e– red cell samples may help indicate an additional specificity.

4. *No discernible pattern emerges.*
   When uniform or variable reaction strengths are observed, and dosage or

other variation in antigen strength does not provide an explanation, additional approaches and methods of testing are indicated. Some helpful steps include:

a. If strong positive results were obtained, use the exclusion method with nonreactive cells to eliminate some specificities from initial consideration.

b. If weak or questionable positive results were obtained, test the serum against cells carrying a strong expression of antigens corresponding to any suspected specificities and combine this with methods to enhance reactivity.

c. If the patient has not been recently transfused, type the patient's red cells and eliminate from consideration specificities that correspond to antigens on the autologous cells.

d. Use methods to inactivate certain antigens on the red cells, eg, enzyme treatment to render cells negative for antigens such as Fy^a, Fy^b, and S.

e. Use adsorption/elution methods to separate antibodies.

f. Enhance antibody reactivity by using a more sensitive method (eg, PEG). These and other methods that may be helpful are discussed below.

Antibodies to High-Incidence Antigens

If all reagent red cell samples are reactive, but the autocontrol is nonreactive, an alloantibody to a high-incidence antigen should be considered, especially if the strength and test phase of reactions are uniform for all cells tested. Antibodies to high-incidence antigens can be identified by testing red cells of selected rare phenotypes and by testing the patient's autologous red cells with sera known to contain antibodies to high-incidence antigens. Knowing the race or ethnic origin of the antibody producer can help in selecting additional tests to be performed. Cells that are null for all antigens in a system (eg, Rh_{null} or K_o) or modified red cells (eg, dithiothreitol-treated cells, see Method 3.10) can help limit possible specificities to a particular blood group.

If cells negative for particular high-incidence antigens are not available, cells positive for lower-incidence alleles can sometimes be helpful. Weaker reactivity with Co(a+b+) cells when compared with common Co(a+b-) cells, for instance, might suggest anti-Co^a. Antibodies to high-incidence antigens may be accompanied by other antibodies to common antigens, which can make identification much more difficult. Because the availability of cells negative for high-incidence antigens is limited, it may be necessary to refer specimens suspected of containing antibodies to high-incidence antigens to an immunohematology reference laboratory.

Serologic Clues

Knowledge of the serologic characteristics of particular antibodies to high-incidence antigens can help in identification.

1. Reactivity in tests at room temperature suggests anti-H, -I, -P_1, -P, -PP_1P^k (-Tj^a), -LW (some), -Ge (some), -Sd^a, or -Vel.

2. Lysis of reagent red cells when testing with fresh serum is characteristic of anti-Vel, -P, - PP_1P^k, and -Jk3. It is also seen with some examples of anti-H and -I.

3. Reduced or absent reactivity in enzyme tests occurs with anti-Ch, -Rg, -In^b, -JMH, or -Ge2 and is seen with some examples of anti-Yt^a.

4.   Weak nebulous reactions in the antiglobulin phase are often associated with anti-Kn^a, -McC^a, -Yk^a, and -Cs^a. Complement-binding autoantibodies, such as anti-I or anti-IH, give similar results when polyspecific antiglobulin reagents are used.

5.   Antibodies such as anti-U, -McC^a, -Sl^a, -Js^b, -Hy, -Jo^a, -Tc^a, -Cr^a, and -At^a should be considered if the serum is from a Black individual because the antigen-negative phenotypes occur almost exclusively in Blacks. Individuals with anti-Kp^b are almost always White. Anti-Di^b is usually found among Asian, South American Indians, and Native American populations.[16(pp526,527)]

Interpreting a Positive DAT

When a patient produces antibody directed to a high-incidence antigen after transfusion, the posttransfusion red cells may have a positive DAT, and both serum and eluate may react with all cells tested. Because this pattern of reactivity is identical to that produced by many warm-reactive autoantibodies that may also appear after transfusion, these two scenarios can be very difficult to differentiate. A posttransfusion alloantibody to a high-incidence antigen would be expected to produce a DAT of mixed-field appearance (ie, some cells agglutinated among many unagglutinated cells) because only the transfused red cells would be coated with antibody. In practice, however, weak sensitization and mixed-field sensitization can be difficult to differentiate. If a pretransfusion red cell sample is not available, it may be helpful to use cell separation procedures to isolate autologous cells for testing. Performing a DAT on autologous cells and/or testing the posttransfusion serum with DAT-negative autologous cells may help to distinguish autoantibody from alloantibody. Chapter 15 discusses additional serologic characteristics of antibodies reacting with high-incidence red cell antigens.

Antibodies to Low-Incidence Antigens

Reactions between a serum sample and a single donor or reagent red cell sample may be caused by an antibody to a low-incidence antigen, such as anti-Wr^a. If red cells known to carry low-incidence antigens are available, the serum can be tested against them, or the one reactive red cell sample can be tested with known examples of antibodies to low-incidence antigens. A single serum often contains multiple antibodies to low-incidence antigens; therefore, the expertise and resources of an immunohematology reference laboratory may be required to confirm the suspected specificities.

Serologic Strategies

If an antibody to a low-incidence antigen is suspected, transfusion should not be delayed while identification studies are undertaken. If an antibody in the serum of a pregnant woman is thought to be directed against a low-incidence antigen, testing the father's red cells can predict the possibility of incompatibility with the fetus, and identifying the antibody is unnecessary. If a newborn has a positive DAT, testing of the mother's serum or an eluate from the infant's cells against the father's red cells (assuming they are ABO-compatible) can implicate an antibody to a low-incidence antigen as the probable cause; identifying the antibody is usually of little importance.

Some reference laboratories do not attempt to identify antibodies to low-incidence antigens because they are often only of academic interest. Identification may be made when time permits and suitable reagents are available.

Unexpected Positive Results

When a serum reacts with a panel cell designated as positive for a low-incidence antigen, further testing to exclude the antibody is usually unnecessary. For every antigen of low incidence represented on a panel, there are many more that are not represented and are also not excluded by routine testing. Reactivity against low-incidence antigens is not uncommon; although the antigens are rare, antibodies against some of the low-incidence antigens are much less rare. Presumably, the testing is being performed because the serum contains some other antibody and reactivity with the cell expressing the low-incidence antigen is a coincidental finding. This may complicate interpretation of the panel results but rarely requires confirmation of antibody specificity or typing of donor blood to ensure the absence of the antigen. If typing is desired, a negative crossmatch with the patient's serum is sufficient demonstration that the antigen is absent. Many antibodies to low-incidence antigens are reactive only at temperatures below 37 C and are of doubtful clinical significance.

When the serum reacts only with red cells from a single donor unit or reagent cell, the other possibilities to consider are that the reactive donor red cells are ABO-incompatible, have a positive DAT, or are polyagglutinable.

Antibodies to Reagent Components and Other Anomalous Serologic Reactions

Antibodies to a variety of drugs and additives can cause positive results in antibody detection and identification tests. The mechanisms are probably similar to those discussed in Chapter 20.

Most of these anomalous reactions are in-vitro phenomena and have no clinical significance in transfusion therapy other than causing laboratory problems that delay needed transfusions. They rarely cause erroneous interpretations of ABO typing that could endanger the patient. For a more detailed discussion, see the suggested reading by Garratty.

Ingredients in the Preservative Solution

Antibodies that react with an ingredient in the solution used to preserve reagent red cells (eg, chloramphenicol, neomycin, tetracycline, hydrocortisone, EDTA, sodium caprylate, or various sugars) may agglutinate cells suspended in that solution. Reactivity may occur with cells from several commercial sources or may be limited to cells from a single manufacturer. The autologous control is often nonreactive, unless the suspension of autologous red cells is prepared with the manufacturer's red cell diluent or a similar preservative. Such reactions can often be circumvented by washing the reagent cells with saline before testing. The role of the preservative can often be confirmed by adding the medium to the autologous control and converting a nonreactive test to a positive test. In some cases, however, washing the reagent cells does not circumvent reactivity and the resolution may be more complex.

Ingredients in Enhancement Media

Antibodies reactive with ingredients in other reagents, such as commercially prepared LISS additives or albumin, can cause agglutination in tests using reagent, donor, and/or autologous red cells. Ingredients that have been implicated include parabens (in some LISS additives), sodium caprylate (in some albumins), and thimerosal (in some LISS/saline preparations). Antibody to ingredients in enhancement media may be suspected if the autologous control is positive but the DAT is negative. Omitting the enhancement medium will usually circumvent this reactivity.

In some cases, antibodies dependent upon reagent ingredients will show blood group specificity, eg, paraben-dependent anti-Jk^a, caprylate-dependent anti-c. The autocontrol may be reactive if the patient's own red cells carry the antigen, but the DAT should be negative.

Problems with Red Cells

The age of the red cells can cause anomalous serologic reactions. Antibodies exist that react only with stored red cells; they can cause agglutination of reagent red cells by all techniques and enhanced reactivity in tests with enzyme-treated red cells. Such reactivity is not affected by washing the red cells, and the autocontrol is usually nonreactive. No reactivity will be seen in tests on freshly collected red cells, ie, from freshly drawn donor or autologous blood samples.

The Patient with a Positive Autocontrol

No Recent Transfusions

Reactivity of serum with the patient's own cells may indicate the presence of autoantibody (see Chapter 20). If this reactivity occurs at room temperature or below, the cause is often anti-I or another cold autoagglutinin. Reactivity of the autocontrol in the antiglobulin phase usually signifies a positive DAT and the possibility of autoantibody. If, in addition, the serum reacts with all cells tested, autoadsorption or other special procedures may be necessary to determine whether autoantibody in the serum is masking any significant alloantibodies. If the serum is not reactive or shows only weak reactivity, an eluate may demonstrate more potent autoantibody.

A negative DAT but a positive autocontrol by an IAT is unusual and may indicate antibody to a reagent constituent causing in-vitro reactivity with all cells, including the patient's own. It may also indicate the presence of warm autoantibodies or cold autoagglutinins such as anti-I, -IH, or -Pr reacting by IAT when enhancement media are used.

Cold Autoantibodies. Potent cold autoagglutinins that react with all cells, including the patient's own, can create special problems, especially when reactivity persists at temperatures above room temperature. Cold autoagglutinins may be benign or pathologic. (See Chapter 20 for a more detailed discussion.)

There are different approaches to testing a serum with a potent cold agglutinin. One approach is to determine if the thermal amplitude is high enough (usually 30 C or above) that the antibody has clinical significance. For identification purposes and determination of thermal amplitude, in-vitro autoadsorption of the serum must be avoided by keeping the freshly collected blood warm (37 C) until the serum is separated. For purposes of detecting potentially clinically significant antibodies, methods that circumvent the cold autoantibody are commonly used.

Procedures for the detection of alloantibodies in the presence of cold-reactive autoantibodies are discussed in Chapter 20 and include:

1. Prewarmed techniques, in which red cells and serum to be tested, and saline used for washing, are incubated at 37 C before they are combined (see Method 3.3).
2. The use of anti-IgG rather than polyspecific antiglobulin serum.
3. Cold autoadsorption, to remove autoantibodies but not alloantibodies.

4. Adsorption with rabbit red cells.

Dealing with Warm Autoantibodies. Patients with warm-reactive autoantibody present in their sera create a special problem because the antibody reacts with virtually all cells tested. If such patients are to be transfused, it is important to detect any clinically significant alloantibodies that the autoantibody may mask. Techniques are discussed in Chapter 20 and Methods 4.9, 4.10, 4.11, and 4.12.

Reactivity of most warm-reactive autoantibodies is greatly enhanced by such methods as PEG and enzymes, and to lesser extent by LISS and albumin. It may be advantageous to perform antibody detection tests without the enhancement media usually employed. If tests are nonreactive, the same procedure can be used for compatibility tests, without the need for adsorptions.

Recent Transfusions

If the autocontrol is positive in the antiglobulin phase, there may be antibody-coated cells in the patient's circulation, causing a positive DAT, which may show mixed-field reactivity. Elution may be helpful, especially when tests on serum are inconclusive. For example, a recently transfused patient may have a positive autocontrol and serum that reacts weakly with most but not all Fy(a+) red cells. It may be possible to confirm anti-Fy^a specificity by elution, which concentrates into a small fluid volume the immunoglobulin molecules present in small numbers on the red cells in the whole blood sample. It is rare for transfused cells to make the autocontrol positive at other test phases, but it can occur, especially with a newly developing or cold-reactive alloantibody.

If the positive DAT does not have a mixed-field appearance and, especially, if the serum is reactive with all cells tested, the possibility of autoantibody should be considered. Detection of masked alloantibodies may require allogeneic adsorptions.

Accurate phenotyping of red cells may be difficult if the DAT is reactive in any patient, whether or not there has been recent transfusion. A positive DAT will cause the cells to be reactive in any test requiring the addition of antiglobulin serum and with some reagent antibodies (notably those in the Rh system) in a high protein medium. With rare exception, most monoclonal reagents not tested by an IAT can give valid phenotyping results despite a positive DAT.[20]

Immunohematology Reference Laboratories

When antibody problems cannot be resolved or when rare blood is needed, immunohematology reference laboratories can provide consultation and assistance through their access to the American Rare Donor Program (see Method 3.13).

Selecting Blood for Transfusion

Once an antibody has been identified, it is important to decide its clinical significance. Antibodies reactive at 37 C and/or by IAT are potentially clinically significant and those reactive at room temperature and below are not; however, there are many exceptions. For example, anti-Ch, anti-Rg, and many of the Knops and Cost antibodies have little or no clinical effect despite reactivity by an IAT. Anti-Vel, -P, and -PP$_1$P^k (-Tj^a) may react only at cold temperatures yet may cause red cell destruction in vivo. Comparison with documented cases in the literature and consultation with immunohematology reference laboratories should provide guidance about previous examples of similar specificities.

Phenotyping Donor Units

Whenever possible, red cell units selected for transfusion to a patient with a potentially clinically significant antibody should be tested and found to be negative for the appropriate antigen. Even if the antibody is no longer detectable, the red cells of all subsequent transfusions to that patient should lack the antigen, to prevent a secondary immune response. The transfusion service must maintain records of all patients in whom significant antibodies have been previously identified.[14(pp38,72)] An antiglobulin crossmatch procedure is required if the serum contains, or has previously contained, a significant antibody.

A potent example of the antibody should be used to identify antigen-negative blood. Often, this is a commercial antiserum, but to save expensive or rare reagents, units can first be tested with the patient's serum. The absence of antigen, in nonreactive units, can then be confirmed with the commercial reagent. If the antibody is of unusual specificity or one for which commercial reagents are not available, a stored sample from the sensitized patient can be used to select units for transfusion at a later time, especially if the patient's later specimens lose reactivity. If a patient's serum is to serve as a typing reagent, it should be well characterized and retain its reactivity after storage, and appropriate negative and weak-positive controls should be used at the time of testing. The FDA has established the following criteria for licensing some reagents[21]:

1. Anti-K, anti-k, anti-Jk^a, anti-Fy^a, and anti-C^w: dilution of 1:8 to give at least 1+ reaction.
2. Anti-S, anti-s, anti-P$_1$, anti-M, anti-I, anti-c (saline), anti-e (saline), and anti-A$_1$: dilution of 1:4 to give at least 1+ reaction.
3. Most other specificities: undiluted, must give at least a 2+ reaction.

Reagents prepared in-house from sera that meet these dilution criteria can be used.

Source of Antibodies

When selecting units for patients with clinically significant antibodies, some serologists recommend typing the chosen units with antibodies from two different sources, but others consider it unnecessary, especially when potent reagents are available. Different lots of antibody from the same manufacturer and even reagents from different manufacturers may not have been prepared from different source material because manufacturers often share the same resources.

Labeling Units

If a donor unit from a blood establishment is to be labeled with the results of special antigen typing, use of licensed (commercial) reagents is preferred. If no licensed reagent is available, the unit may be labeled with appropriate wording (eg, "Tested and found to be negative for XX antigen using unlicensed typing reagents").[22] Except for results of ABO and D typing, there is no requirement that results of antigen typing appear on the label of donor units. The establishment may use a tie tag attached to the unit for the additional labeling.

When to Test

For certain antibody specificities, typing of donor units may not be necessary and the patient's serum can be used to select serologically compatible red cells. This is especially true for antibodies that characteristically react below 37 C (eg, anti-M, -N, -P$_1$, -Le^a, -Le^b, -A$_1$) and do not ordinarily exhibit an anamnestic response to the transfusion of antigen-positive red cells.

It is rarely necessary to provide antigen-negative donor units as a prophylactic measure for patients whose cells lack an antigen but who do not have detectable antibody. However, special consideration is sometimes given to certain Rh antibodies. When a patient of the R_1R_1 phenotype has anti-E detected in the serum, some workers suggest that donor blood be negative for both the E and c antigens,[23] based on the assumption that the stimulus to produce the anti-E may also have stimulated an anti-c or anti-cE that remains undetected by routine tests. For an R_2R_2 patient with demonstrated anti-C, the use of C–, e– donor blood may be considered. When an antibody has not been specifically demonstrated, but cannot conclusively be excluded, it may be appropriate to transfuse blood that lacks the antigen.

Tests to Predict Clinical Significance

Certain laboratory procedures have been used to predict the significance of particular antibodies. The monocyte monolayer assay, which quantifies rosetting and/or phagocytosis of antibody-sensitized red cells, can be used to predict the in-vivo clinical significance of some antibodies. The test for antibody-dependent cellular cytotoxicity (ADCC), which measures lysis of antibody-coated cells, and the chemiluminescence assay, which measures the respiratory release of oxygen radicals after phagocytosis of antibody-coated cells, have been helpful in predicting in-vivo antibody reactivity, particularly for severity of HDFN. For cold-reactive antibodies, in-vitro thermal amplitude studies can predict the likelihood of in-vivo problems.

In-vivo tests may also be used to evaluate significance of a given antibody. The most common technique is infusion of radiolabeled, antigen-positive red cells, usually tagged with ^{51}Cr. It is possible to measure survival of 1 mL or less of infused cells. Flow cytometry can also be used to measure the survival of infused cells, but a larger aliquot of red cells (about 10 mL) is generally required. Small aliquots of incompatible cells may have a faster rate of destruction than an entire unit of red cells.

When Blood of Rare Type Is Needed

Blood of a rare type includes not only units negative for high-incidence antigens but also blood negative for a combination of common antigens. When a patient has multiple antibodies, it can be helpful to determine the frequency of compatible donors. To calculate this, the frequency of random donors negative for one antigen must be multiplied by the frequency of donors negative for each of the other antigens. For example, if a serum contains anti-c, -Fy^a, and -S, and, among random donors, 18% are c–, 34% are Fy(a–), and 45% are S–, the frequency of compatible units would be: $0.18 \times 0.34 \times 0.45 = 0.028$. If the patient is group O, then, because 45% of random donors are group O, 1.3% (0.028×0.45) of random donors would be compatible with the patient's serum. If any of these three antibodies occurred singly, finding compatible blood would not be too difficult. Clearly, when all three antibodies are present, a large number of random donors would be necessary to provide even one unit. The preceding calculation uses frequencies in populations of European ethnicity. If the donor population is predominantly of a different origin, frequencies for that group, if available, should be used.

When units of rare (<1 in 5000) or uncommon (<1 in 1000) type are needed, the American Rare Donor Program can be very helpful. This program, which can be accessed only by personnel of an accredited immunohematology reference laboratory, can identify blood suppliers known either to have units available (usually frozen red cells) or to have eligible donors who may be asked to donate (see Method 3.13).

Family members offer another potential source of rare blood donors. Siblings are often the best source of serologically compatible blood for patients with multiple antibodies or antibodies to high-incidence antigens. The absence of high-incidence antigens usually reflects inheritance of the same rare blood group gene from each parent, and offspring of the same parents are far more likely to have the same two rare genes than someone in the general population. In most cases, blood from the patient's parents or children (and some siblings) will carry only a single dose of the relevant antigen; if transfusion is essential, and there is no alternative to giving incompatible blood, these heterozygous donors would be considered preferable to random donors. Occasionally, blood from a parent or child also lacks the high-incidence antigen.

In HDFN or other alloantibody-associated problems in infants, the mother, if ABO compatible, is often the logical donor. If the mother's red cells are transfused, it is helpful to retain the plasma for use as a rare reagent.

If the clinical situation allows, autologous transfusion should be considered for patients for whom compatible blood is difficult to find. For some patients with multiple antibodies for whom autologous transfusion is not an option, it may be necessary to determine whether any of the antibodies is likely to be significantly less destructive than the others and, in a critical situation, give blood incompatible for that particular antigen.

Frequency of Antibody Testing

Once an antibody has been identified in a patient's serum, how frequently should antibody detection and identification tests be performed? A primary antibody response will produce detectable antibody as early as 7 to 10 days but typically over a period of 2 weeks to several months. A secondary immune response produces detectable antibody in a shorter time, as early as 2 to 7 days and usually within 20 days. Shulman[24] found that, in a small number of patients, "new" antibodies could be detected within 1 to 2 days after transfusion. AABB *Standards for Blood Banks and Transfusion Services*[14(p38)] requires that, for a patient who has been pregnant or received red cells within the preceding 3 months, antibody detection and compatibility tests must be performed on a specimen obtained within 3 days of the next scheduled transfusion. The transfusion service may consider testing a fresher specimen if clinical evidence suggests failure of recently transfused red cells to survive as expected.

If a patient has previously identified clinically significant antibodies, antigen-negative red cells must be selected for all future transfusions, even if the antibodies are no longer detectable. In addition, an antiglobulin crossmatch must be performed using antigen-negative red cells.

It is rarely necessary to repeat identification of known antibodies. AABB *Standards* states that in patients with previously identified antibodies, methods of testing shall be those that identify *additional* clinically significant antibodies.[14(p38)] Each laboratory should define and validate methods for the detection of additional antibodies in these patients. Depending on the specificity of the known antibody, repeated testing of the patient's serum against routine antibody detection cells is often not informative. It is more useful to test against cells negative for the antigen(s) to which the patient has antibody and positive for other major antigens. This allows detection of most additional antibodies that might develop. Usually, appropriate cells can be selected from available red cell panels. Selection of test cells may be simplified if the patient's cells are known to express a given antigen. The selected cells need not be positive for that antigen because the corresponding antibody would not be anticipated.

Selected Serologic Procedures

Many techniques and methods may be useful in antibody identification. Some of the methods given here are used routinely by many laboratories; others are alternatives that may apply only in special circumstances. It is important to remember that no single method is optimal for detecting *all* antibodies in all samples. Any laboratory performing antibody detection or identification should have standard procedures for routine testing and have access to at least some alternative approaches. Additional procedures are available in a variety of references (see Suggested Reading).

Enhancement Techniques

When a pattern of weak reactions fails to indicate specificity, or when the presence of an antibody is suspected but cannot be demonstrated, use of the following procedures may be helpful. An autologous control should be included with each test performed.

LISS and PEG

The rationale for these procedures and some technical details are discussed in Chapter 12 and Method 3.2. Each may be used to enhance reactivity and reduce incubation time. LISS methods include the use of low-ionic-strength saline for resus-

pension of test cells and, more commonly, the use of commercially available low-ionic-strength additive media. The use of a LISS additive requires no preparatory stages, but care should be taken to adhere closely to the manufacturer's product insert to ensure that the appropriate proportion of serum to LISS is achieved. Commercially prepared LISS additives may include other enhancement components besides low-ionic-strength saline. Commercially prepared PEG additives are also available and may contain additional enhancing agents. Because LISS and PEG enhance autoantibody activity, their use may create problems with certain samples.[25,26]

Enzyme Techniques

Treatment of red cells with proteolytic enzymes enhances their reactivity with antibodies in the Rh, P, I, Kidd, Lewis, and some other blood group systems and simultaneously destroys or weakens reactivity with other antibodies, most notably those in the Duffy and MNS systems (see Table 19-4). The clinical significance of antibodies that react only with enzyme techniques is questionable. The literature indicates that "enzyme-only" antibodies may have no clinical significance.[28] Procedures for the preparation and use of proteolytic enzyme solutions are given in Methods 3.5 through 3.5.6.

Temperature Reduction

Some alloantibodies (eg, anti-M, -N, -P$_1$, -Le^a, -Le^b, -A$_1$) that react at room temperature react better at lower temperatures; specificity may be apparent only below 22 C. An autocontrol is especially important for tests at cold temperatures because many sera also contain anti-I or other cold-reactive autoantibodies.

Increased Serum-to-Cell Ratio

Increasing the volume of serum incubated with a standard volume of red cells may enhance the reactivity of antibodies present in low concentration. One acceptable procedure is to mix 5 to 10 volumes of serum with one volume of a 2% to 5% saline suspension of red cells and incubate for 60 minutes at 37 C; periodic mixing during incubation promotes contact between red cells and antibody molecules. It is helpful to remove the serum before washing the red cells for the antiglobulin test because the standard three or four washes may be insufficient to remove all the unbound immunoglobulin present in the additional volume. Additional washes are not recommended because bound antibody molecules may dissociate. Increasing the serum-to-red cell ratio is not appropriate for tests using a low-ionic-strength medium or requiring specific proportions of serum and additive.

Increased Incubation Time

For most antibodies, a 15-minute incubation period is insufficient to achieve equilibrium and the observed reactions may be weak, particularly in saline or albumin media. Extending incubation to 30 to 60 minutes may improve reactivity and help clarify the observed pattern of reactions.

Extended incubation may have a negative effect when LISS or PEG are used. If incubation exceeds the recommended times for these methods, antibody reactivity may be lost. Care must be taken to use all reagents according to the manufacturer's directions.

Alteration of pH

Decreasing the pH of the reaction system to 6.5 enhances the reactivity of certain antibodies, notably some examples of anti-M.[29] If anti-M is suspected because the only cells agglutinated are M+N–, modifying the serum to a pH of 6.5 may reveal a definitive pattern of anti-M reactivity. The addition of one volume of 0.1 N HCl to nine volumes of serum brings the pH to approximately 6.5. The acidified serum should be tested against known M– cells as a control for nonspecific agglutination. Similarly, some examples of anti-P may benefit from a lower pH.[30]

Low pH, however, significantly decreases reactivity of some antibodies.[31] If unbuffered saline used for cell suspensions and for washing has a pH much below 6.0, antibodies in the Rh, Duffy, Kidd, and MNS systems may lose reactivity. Use of phosphate-buffered saline (see Method 1.7) can control pH and enhance detection of antibodies poorly reactive at a lower pH.[32]

Techniques to Isolate, Remove, or Depress Antibody Reactivity

It is sometimes useful to decrease or eliminate the reactivity of an antibody. This can be done by inhibiting the antibody with specific substances, by physically removing immunoglobulin molecules, or by removing (or weakening) corresponding antigens from the red cells. Such methods can help confirm suspected specificities and promote identification of additional antibodies.

Inhibition Tests

Soluble forms of some blood group antigens exist in such body fluids as saliva, urine, or plasma, or can be prepared from other sources. These substances can be used to inhibit reactivity of the corresponding antibody. If, for example, a suspected anti-P_1 does not give a definitive agglutination pattern, loss of reactivity after addition of soluble P_1 substance strongly suggests that this is the specificity. A parallel dilution control with saline is essential.

Inhibition can also be used to neutralize antibodies that mask the concomitant presence of nonneutralizable antibodies. The following soluble blood group substances can be used in antibody identification tests:

1. *Lewis substances.* Le^a and/or Le^b substances are present in the saliva of persons who possess the *Le* gene. Le^a substance is present in the saliva of Le(a+b–) individuals, and Le(a–b+) persons have both Le^a and Le^b substances in their saliva (see Method 2.5). Commercially prepared Lewis substance is also available.

2. *P$_1$ substance.* Soluble P$_1$ substance is present in hydatid cyst fluid and can be prepared from pigeon egg whites. P$_1$ substance is available commercially.

3. *Sd^a substance.* Soluble Sd^a blood group substance is present in various body fluids; the most abundant source is urine.[33] To confirm anti-Sd^a specificity in a serum sample, urine from a known Sd(a+) individual (or a pool of urine specimens) can be used to inhibit reactivity. Urine known to lack Sd^a substance, or saline, should be used as a negative control (see Method 3.11).

4. *Chido and Rodgers substances.* Ch and Rg antigens are epitopes of the fourth component of human complement (C4).[34,35] Anti-Ch and -Rg react by an IAT with the trace amounts of C4 present on normal red cells. If red cells are coated in vitro with excess C4,[36] these antibodies may cause direct agglutination. A useful test to identify anti-Ch and -Rg is by the inhibition of the antibodies with plasma from Ch+, Rg+ individuals (see Method 3.9).

5. *Blood group sugars.* Sugars that correspond to the immunodominant configurations of A, B, H, and some other red cell structures can be used to inhibit antibodies. Inhibiting anti-A or -B may allow a serum to be tested against non-group-O cells.

Inactivation of Blood Group Antigens

Certain blood group antigens can be destroyed or weakened by suitable treatment of the cells (see Table 19-4). Modified cells can be useful both in confirming the presence of suspected antibodies and in detecting additional antibodies. This can be

Table 19-4. Alteration of Antigens by Various Agents*

Agent	Antigens Usually Denatured or Altered[†]
Proteolytic enzymes[‡]	M, N, S, Fy^a, Fy^b, Yt^a, Ch, Rg, Pr, Tn, Mg, Mi^a/Vw, Cl^a, Je^a, Ny^a, JMH, some Ge, In^b
DTT	Yt^a, JMH, Kn^a, McC^a, Yk^a, LW^a, LW^b, all Kell, Lutheran, Dombrock, and Cromer blood group antigens
ZZAP (a combination of DTT and proteolytic enzymes)	Alteration of all the antigens listed above

*Modified from Wilkinson.[27]

[†]Some antigens listed may be weakened rather than completely denatured. Appropriate controls should be used with modified cells.

[‡]Different proteolytic enzymes may have different effects on certain antigens.

especially helpful if the antigen is one of high incidence and antigen-negative cells are rare.

Proteolytic enzymes are commonly used to alter red cell antigens. Ficin, papain, trypsin, and bromelin, the enzymes most frequently used, remove antigens such as M, N, Fy^a, Fy^b, Xg^a, JMH, Ch, and Rg (see Table 19-4). Depending on the specific enzyme and method used, other antigens may be altered or destroyed. Antigens inactivated by one proteolytic enzyme will not necessarily be inactivated by other enzymes.

Sulfhydryl reagents such as 2-amino-ethylisothiouronium bromide (AET) or dithiothreitol (DTT) (see Method 3.10) can be used to weaken or destroy antigens in the Kell system and some other anti-gens.[37-39] ZZAP reagent, which contains proteolytic enzyme and DTT,[40] denatures antigens sensitive to DTT (eg, all Kell system antigens) in addition to enzyme-sensitive antigens (see Method 4.9). Glycine-HCl/EDTA treatment of red cells also destroys Bg and Kell system antigens. However, with the exception of Er^a antigen,[41] other antigens outside the Kell system that are often destroyed by sulfhydryl reagents remain intact (see Methods 2.14 and 4.2). Chloroquine diphosphate can be used to weaken the expression of Class I HLA antigens (Bg antigens) on red cells.[42] Chloroquine treatment also weakens some other antigens, including Rh antigens (see Method 2.13).

Adsorption

Antibody can be removed from a serum sample by adsorption to red cells carrying the corresponding antigen. After the antibody attaches to the membrane-bound antigens and the serum and cells are separated, the specific antibody remains attached to the red cells. It may be possible to harvest the bound antibody by elution.

Adsorption techniques are useful in such situations as:

1. Separating multiple antibodies present in a single serum.
2. Removing autoantibody activity to permit detection of coexisting allo-antibodies.
3. Removing unwanted antibody (often anti-A and/or anti-B) from serum that contains an antibody suitable for reagent use.
4. Confirming the presence of specific antigens on red cells through their ability to remove antibody of corresponding specificity from previously characterized serum.
5. Confirming the specificity of an antibody by showing that it can be adsorbed only to red cells of a particular blood group phenotype.

Adsorption serves different purposes in different situations; there is no single procedure that is satisfactory for all purposes. A basic procedure for an antibody adsorption can be found in Method 3.12. The usual serum-to-cell ratio is one volume of serum to an equal volume of washed red cells. To enhance antibody uptake, the proportion of antigen can be increased by using a larger volume of cells. The incubation temperature should be that at which the antibody is optimally reactive. Pretreating red cells with a proteolytic enzyme may enhance antibody uptake and reduce the number of adsorptions required for complete removal of antibody. Because some antigens are destroyed by proteases, antibodies directed against these antigens will not be removed by enzyme-treated red cells.

In separating mixtures of antibodies, the selection of red cells of the appropriate phenotype is extremely important and depends on the object of the separation. If none of the antibodies in the serum has been identified, weakly reactive cells may be used, on the assumption that they are reactive with only a single antibody. The phenotype of the person producing the antibody gives a clue to what specificities might be present, and cells intended to separate those particular antibodies can be chosen. If one or more antibodies have been identified, cells lacking those antigens are usually chosen so that only one antibody is removed. Adsorption requires a substantial volume of red cells. Vials of reagent red cells usually will not suffice, and blood samples from staff members or donor units are the most convenient sources.

Elution

Elution frees antibody molecules from sensitized red cells. Bound antibody may be released by changing the thermodynamics of antigen-antibody reactions, by neutralizing or reversing forces of attraction that hold antigen-antibody complexes together, or by disturbing the structure of the antigen-antibody binding site. The usual objective is to recover bound antibody in a usable form.

Various elution methods have been described. Selected procedures are given in Methods 4.1 through 4.5. No single method is best in all situations. Use of heat or freeze-thaw elution is usually restricted to the investigation of HDFN due to ABO incompatibility because these elution procedures rarely work well for antibodies outside the ABO system. Acid or organic solvent methods are used for elution of warm-reactive auto- and alloantibodies.

Technical factors that influence the success of elution procedures include:

1. *Incorrect technique.* Such factors as incomplete removal of organic solvents or failure to correct the tonicity or pH of an eluate may cause the red cells used in testing the eluate to hemolyze or to appear "sticky." The presence of stromal debris may interfere with the reading of tests. Careful technique and strict adherence to protocols should eliminate such problems.

2. *Incomplete washing.* The sensitized red cells must be thoroughly washed before elution to prevent contamination of the eluate with residual serum antibody. If it is *known* that the serum does not contain antibody, saline washing may not be necessary. Six washes with saline are usually adequate, but more may be needed if the serum contains a high-titer antibody. To determine the efficacy of the washing process, supernatant fluid from the final wash phase should be tested for antibody activity and should be nonreactive.

3. *Binding of proteins to glass surfaces.* If the eluate is prepared in the same test tube that was used during the sensitization phase (eg, in an adsorption/elution process), antibody nonspecifically bound to the test tube surface may dissociate during the elution. Similar binding can also occur from a whole blood sample if the patient has a positive DAT and free antibody in the serum. To avoid such contamination, the washed red cells should be transferred into a clean test tube before the elution procedure is begun.

4. *Dissociation of antibody before elution.* IgM antibodies, such as anti-A or -M, may spontaneously dissociate from the cells during the wash phase. To minimize this loss of bound antibody, cold (4 C) saline can be used for washing. Although this is not a concern with most IgG antibodies, some low-affinity IgG antibodies can also be lost during the wash phase. If such antibodies are suspected, wash-

ing with cold LISS instead of normal saline may help maintain antibody association.

5.   *Instability of eluates.* Dilute protein solutions, such as those obtained by elution into saline, are unstable. Eluates should be tested as soon after preparation as possible. Alternatively, bovine albumin may be added to a final concentration of 6% w/v and the preparation stored frozen. Eluates can also be prepared directly into antibody-free plasma, 6% albumin, or a similar protein medium instead of into saline.

Elution techniques are useful for:

1.   Investigation of a positive DAT (see Chapter 20).

2.   Concentration and purification of antibodies, detection of weakly expressed antigens, and identification of multiple antibody specificities. Such studies are used in conjunction with an appropriate adsorption technique, as described above and in Method 2.4.

3.   Preparation of antibody-free red cells for use in phenotyping or autologous adsorption studies. Procedures used to remove cold- and warm-reactive autoantibodies from red cells are discussed in Method 4.6 and Method 4.9, and a discussion of autologous adsorption of warm-reactive autoantibodies appears in Chapter 20.

Combined Adsorption-Elution

Combined adsorption-elution tests can be used to separate mixed antibodies from a single serum, to detect weakly expressed antigens on red cells, or to help identify weakly reactive antibodies. The process consists of first incubating serum with selected cells, then eluting antibody from the adsorbing red cells. Both the eluate

and treated serum can be used for further testing. Unmodified red cells are generally used for adsorption and subsequent elution; elution from enzyme- or ZZAP-treated cells may create technical problems.

Use of Sulfhydryl Reagents

Sulfhydryl reagents, such as DTT and 2-mercaptoethanol (2-ME), cleave the disulfide bonds that join the monomeric subunits of the IgM pentamer. Intact 19S IgM molecules are cleaved into 7S subunits, which have altered serologic reactivity.[43] The interchain bonds of 7S Ig monomers are relatively resistant to such cleavage (see Chapter 11 for the structure of immunoglobulin molecules). Sulfhydryl reagents are used to diminish or destroy IgM antibody reactivity. DTT also destroys certain red cell antigens. The applications of DTT and 2-ME in immunohematology include:

1.   Determining the immunoglobulin class of an antibody (see Method 3.8).

2.   Identifying specificities in a mixture of IgM and IgG antibodies, particularly when an agglutinating IgM antibody masks the presence of IgG antibodies.

3.   Determining the relative amounts of IgG and IgM components of a given specificity (eg, anti-A or -B).

4.   Dissociating red cell agglutinates caused by IgM antibodies (eg, the spontaneous agglutination of red cells caused by potent autoantibodies) (see Method 2.11).

5.   Dissociating IgG antibodies from red cells using a mixture of DTT and a proteolytic enzyme (ZZAP reagent) (see Method 4.9).

6.   Converting nonagglutinating IgG antibodies into direct agglutinins.[44] Commercially prepared, chemically

modified, blood typing reagents for use in rapid saline tube, slide, or microplate tests have been manufactured in this manner (see Chapter 12).

7. Destroying selected red cell antigens (eg, those of the Kell, Dombrock, Cartwright, and LW systems) for use in antibody investigations (see Method 3.10).

Titration

The titer of an antibody is usually determined by testing serial twofold dilutions of the serum against selected red cell samples. Results are expressed as the reciprocal of the highest serum dilution that shows macroscopic agglutination. Titration values can provide information about the relative amount of antibody present in a serum, or the relative strength of antigen expression on red cells.

Titration studies are useful in the following situations:

1. *Prenatal studies.* When the antibody is of a specificity known to cause HDFN or its clinical significance is unknown, the results of titration studies may contribute to the decision about performing invasive procedures, eg, amniocentesis (see Chapter 23 and Method 5.3).

2. *Antibody identification.* Some antibodies that agglutinate virtually all reagent red cell samples may produce an indication of specificity by demonstrating reactivity of different strength with different samples in titration studies. For example, potent autoanti-I may react in the undiluted state with both adult and cord red cells, but titration may reveal reactivity at a higher dilution with adult I+ red cells than with cord red cells.

Most weakly reactive antibodies lose reactivity when diluted even modestly, but some antibodies that give weak reactions when undiluted continue to react at dilutions as high as 1 in 2048. Such antibodies include anti-Ch, -Rg, -Cs^a, -Yk^a, -Kn^a, -McC^a, -JMH, and other specificities. When weak reactions are observed in indirect antiglobulin tests, titration may be used to indicate specificity within this group. Not all antibodies of the specificities mentioned demonstrate such "high titer, low avidity" characteristics. Thus, although demonstration of these serologic characteristics may help point to certain specificities, failure to do so does not eliminate those possibilities. Antibodies of other specificities may sometimes react at high titers. Details of titration are given in Method 3.7 and Method 3.9.

3. *Separating multiple antibodies.* Titration results may suggest that one antibody reacts at higher dilutions than another. This information can allow the serum to be diluted before testing against a cell panel, effectively removing one antibody and allowing identification of the other.

Other Methods

Methods other than traditional tube techniques may be used for antibody identification. Some are especially useful for identifying individual antibody specificities, for dealing with small volumes of test reagents, for batch testing, or for use with automated systems. Such methods include testing in capillary tubes, microplates, or by solid phase; enzyme-linked immunosorbent assays; and column agglutination (eg, gel techniques). Other methods useful in laboratories with specialized equipment include radioimmuno-assay, immunofluorescence (including flow cytometric procedures), immunoblotting, and immunoelectrode biosensing. Some of these methods are discussed in Chapter 12.

References

1. Giblett ER. Blood group alloantibodies: An assessment of some laboratory practices. Transfusion 1977;17:299-308.

2. Walker RH, Lin DT, Hatrick MB. Alloimmunization following blood transfusion. Arch Pathol Lab Med 1989;113:254-61.

3. Daniels G, Poole J, deSilva M, et al. The clinical significance of blood group antibodies. Tranfus Med 2002;12:287-95.

4. Code of federal regulations. Title 21 CFR Part 660.33. Washington, DC: US Government Printing Office, 2004 (revised annually).

5. Standards Source – 4.3.2.1. (January 2004) Bethesda, MD: AABB, 2004.

6. Howard JE, Winn LC, Gottlieb CE, et al. Clinical significance of anti-complement component of antiglobulin antisera. Transfusion 1982;22:269-72.

7. Judd WJ, Fullen DR, Steiner EA, et al. Revisiting the issue: Can the reading for serologic reactivity following 37 C incubation be omitted? Transfusion 1999;39:295-9.

8. Issitt PD. Antibody screening: Elimination of another piece of the test (editorial). Transfusion 1999;39:229-30.

9. Shulman IA, Calderon C, Nelson JM, Nakayama R. The routine use of Rh-negative reagent red cells for the identification of anti-D and the detection of non-D red cell antibodies. Transfusion 1994;34:666-70.

10. Fisher RA. Statistical methods and scientific inference. 2nd ed. Edinburgh, Scotland: Oliver and Boyd, 1959.

11. Harris RE, Hochman HG. Revised p values in testing blood group antibodies. Transfusion 1986;26:494-9.

12. Kanter MH, Poole G, Garratty G. Misinterpretation and misapplication of p values in antibody identification: The lack of value of a p value. Transfusion 1997;37:816-22.

13. Reid ME, Oyen R, Storry J, et al. Interpretation of RBC typing in multi-transfused patients can be unreliable (abstract). Transfusion 2000;40 (Suppl):123.

14. Silva MA, ed. Standards for blood banks and transfusion services. 23rd ed. Bethesda, MD: AABB, 2005.

15. Brendel WL. Resolving antibody problems. In: Pierce SR, Wilson JK, eds. Approaches to serological problems in the hospital transfusion service. Arlington, VA: AABB, 1985:51-72.

16. Reid ME, Lomas-Francis C. The blood group antigen factsbook. 2nd ed. New York: Academic Press, 2004.

17. Issitt PD, Anstee DJ. Applied blood group serology. 4th ed. Durham, NC: Montgomery Scientific Publications, 1998.

18. Malyska H, Kleeman JE, Masouredis SP, et al. Effects on blood group antigens from storage at low ionic strength in the presence of neomycin. Vox Sang 1983;44:375-84.

19. Westhoff CM, Sipherd BD, Toalson LD. Red cell antigen stability in K_3EDTA. Immunohematology 1993;9:109-11.

20. Rodberg K, Tsuneta R, Garratty G. Discrepant Rh phenotyping results when testing IgG-sensitized rbcs with monoclonal Rh reagents (abstract). Transfusion 1995;35(Suppl):67.

21. Code of federal regulations. Title 21 CFR Part 660.25. Washington, DC: US Government Printing Office, 2004 (revised annually).

22. Food and Drug Administration. Compliance program guidance manual. Chapter 42; inspection of licensed and unlicensed blood banks, brokers, reference laboratories, and contractors—program 7342.001. Attachment C—Product testing system, blood grouping and typing (ABO and Rh), and compatibility testing. Rockville, MD: CBER Office of Communication, Training, and Manufacturers Assistance, 2003. [Available at http://www.fda.gov/cber/cpg.htm.]

23. Shirey RS, Edwards RE, Ness PM. The risk of alloimmunization to c (Rh4) in R_1R_1 patients who present with anti-E. Transfusion 1994;34:756-8.

24. Shulman IA. Controversies in red blood cell compatibility testing. In: Nance SJ, ed. Immune destruction of red blood cells. Arlington, VA: AABB, 1989:171-99.

25. Reisner R, Butler G, Bundy K, Moore SB. Comparison of the polyethylene glycol antiglobulin test and the use of enzymes in antibody detection. Transfusion 1996;36:487-9.

26. Issitt PD, Combs MR, Bumgarner DJ, et al. Studies of antibodies in the sera of patients who have made red cell autoantibodies. Transfusion 1996;36:481-6.

27. Wilkinson SL. Serological approaches to transfusion of patients with allo- or auto-antibodies. In: Nance SJ, ed. Immune destruction of red blood cells. Arlington, VA: AABB, 1989:227-61.

28. Issitt PD, Combs MR, Bredehoeft SJ, et al. Lack of clinical significance of "enzyme-only"

red cell alloantibodies. Transfusion 1993;33: 284-93.

29. Beattie KM, Zuelzer WW. The frequency and properties of pH-dependent anti-M. Transfusion 1965;5:322-6.

30. Judd WJ. A pH dependent autoagglutinin with anti-P specificity. Transfusion 1975;15:373-6.

31. Bruce C, Watt AH, Hare V, et al. A serious source of error in antiglobulin testing. Transfusion 1986;26:177-81.

32. Rolih S, Thomas R, Fisher F, Talbot J. Antibody detection errors due to acidic or unbuffered saline. Immunohematology 1993;9:15-8.

33. Morton J, Pickles MM, Terry AM. The Sd^a blood group antigen in tissues and body fluids. Vox Sang 1970;19:472-82.

34. O'Neil GJ, Yang SY, Tegoli J, et al. Chido and Rodgers blood groups are distinct antigenic components of human complement, C4. Nature 1978;273:668-70.

35. Tilley CA, Romans DG, Crookston MC. Localization of Chido and Rodgers to the C4d fragment of human C4 (abstract). Transfusion 1978;18:622.

36. Judd WJ, Kreamer K, Moulds JJ. The rapid identification of Chido and Rodgers antibodies using C4d-coated red blood cells. Transfusion 1981;21:189-92.

37. Advani H, Zamor J, Judd WJ, et al. Inactivation of Kell blood group antigens by 2-aminoethylisothiouronium bromide. Br J Haematol 1982;51:107-15.

38. Branch DR, Muensch HA, Sy Siok Hian AL, Petz LD. Disulfide bonds are a requirement for Kell and Cartwright (Yt^a) blood group antigen integrity. Br J Haematol 1983;54:573-8.

39. Moulds J, Moulds MM. Inactivation of Kell blood group antigens by 2-amino-ethylisothiouronium bromide. Transfusion 1983;23:274-5.

40. Branch DR, Petz LD. A new reagent (ZZAP) having multiple applications in immunohematology. Am J Clin Pathol 1982;78:161-7.

41. Liew YW, Uchikawa M. Loss of Er^a antigen in very low pH buffers. Transfusion 1987;27:442-3.

42. Swanson JL, Sastamoinen R. Chloroquine stripping of HLA A,B antigens from red cells (letter). Transfusion 1985;25:439-40.

43. Freedman J, Masters CA, Newlands M, et al. Optimal conditions for use of sulphydryl compounds in dissociating RBC antibodies. Vox Sang 1976;30:231-9.

44. Romans DG, Tilley CA, Crookston MC, et al. Conversion of incomplete antibodies to direct agglutinins by mild reduction. Evidence for segmental flexibility within the Fc fragment of immunoglobulin G. Proc Natl Acad Sci U S A 1977;74:2531-5.

Suggested Reading

Boorman KE, Dodd BE, Lincoln PJ. Blood group serology. 6th ed. Edinburgh, Scotland: Churchill Livingstone, 1988.

Crookston MC. Soluble antigens and leukocyte related antibodies. Part A. Blood group antigens in plasma: An aid in the identification of antibodies. In: Dawson RD, ed. Transfusion with "crossmatch incompatible" blood. Washington, DC: AABB, 1975: 20-5.

Daniels G. Human blood groups. 2nd ed. Oxford, England: Blackwell Scientific Publications, 2002.

Engelfriet CP, Overbeeke MAM, Dooren MC, et al. Bioassays to determine the clinical significance of red cell antibodies based on Fc receptor-induced destruction of red cells sensitized by IgG. Transfusion 1994;14:617-26.

Garratty G. In-vitro reactions with red blood cells that are not due to blood group antibodies: A review. Immunohematology 1998;14(1):1-11.

Issitt PD, Anstee DJ. Applied blood group serology. 4th ed. Durham, NC: Montgomery Scientific Publications, 1998.

Johnson ST, Rudmann SV, Wilson SM, eds. Serologic problem-solving strategies: A systematic approach. Bethesda, MD: AABB, 1996.

Judd WJ. Elution of antibody from red cells. In: Bell CA, ed. A seminar on antigen-antibody reactions revisited. Washington, DC: AABB, 1982:175-221.

Judd WJ. Methods in immunohematology. 2nd ed. Durham, NC: Montgomery Scientific Publications, 1994.

Kanter MH. Statistical analysis. In: Busch MP, Brecher ME, eds. Research design and analysis. Bethesda, MD: AABB, 1998:63-104.

Mallory D, ed. Immunohematology methods and procedures. Rockville, MD: American Red Cross, 1993.

Marsh WL, Reid ME, Kuriyan M, et al. A handbook of clinical and laboratory practices in the transfusion of red blood cells. Moneta, VA: Moneta Medical Press, 1993.

Menitove JE. The Hardy-Weinberg principle: Selection of compatible blood based on mathematic principles. In: Fridey JL, Kasprisin CA, Chambers LA, Rudmann SV, eds. Numbers for blood bankers. Bethesda, MD: AABB, 1995:1-11.

Mollison PL, Engelfriet CP, Contreras M. Blood transfusion in clinical medicine. 10th ed. London: Blackwell Scientific Publications, 1997.

Race RR, Sanger R. Blood groups in man. 6th ed. Oxford, England: Blackwell Scientific Publications, 1975.

Reid ME, Lomas-Francis C. The blood group antigen factsbook. 2nd ed. New York: Academic Press, 2004.

Rolih S. A review: Antibodies with high-titer, low-avidity characteristics. Immunohematology 1990; 6:59-67.

Telen MJ. New and evolving techniques for antibody and antigen identification. In: Nance ST, ed. Alloimmunity: 1993 and beyond. Bethesda, MD: AABB, 1993:117-39.

Chapter 20

The Positive Direct Antiglobulin Test and Immune-Mediated Red Cell Destruction

THE DIRECT ANTIGLOBULIN test (DAT) is generally used to determine if red cells have been coated in vivo with immunoglobulin, complement, or both. A positive DAT, with or without shortened red cell survival, may result from:

1. Autoantibodies to intrinsic red cell antigens.
2. Alloantibodies in a recipient's circulation, reacting with antigens on recently transfused donor red cells.
3. Alloantibodies in donor plasma, plasma derivatives, or blood fractions that react with antigens on the red cells of a transfusion recipient.
4. Alloantibodies in maternal circulation that cross the placenta and coat fetal red cells.
5. Antibodies directed against certain drugs that bind to red cell membranes (eg, penicillin).
6. Nonspecifically adsorbed proteins, including immunoglobulins, associated with hypergammaglobulinemia

or recipients of high-dose intravenous gammaglobulin,[1,2] or modification of the red cell membrane by certain drugs, eg, some cephalosporins.

7. Red-cell-bound complement. This may be due to complement activation by alloantibodies, autoantibodies, drugs, or bacterial infection.
8. Antibodies produced by passenger lymphocytes in transplanted organs or hematopoietic components.[3]

A positive DAT does not necessarily mean that a person's red cells have shortened survival. Small amounts of both IgG and complement appear to be present on all red cells. A range of 5 to 90 IgG molecules/red cell[4] and 5 to 40 C3d molecules/red cell[5] appears to be normal on the red cells of healthy individuals.

The DAT can detect a level of 100 to 500 molecules of IgG/red cell and 400 to 1100 molecules of C3d/red cell, depending on the reagent and technique used. Positive DATs without clinical manifestations of immune-mediated red cell destruction are reported in 1 in 1000 up to 1 in 14,000 blood donors and 1% to 15% of hospital patients.[4]

Most blood donors with positive DATs appear to be perfectly healthy, and most patients with positive DATs have no obvious signs of hemolytic anemia, although some may show slight evidence of increased red cell destruction.[4,6(p222)] Elevated levels of IgG or complement have been noted on the red cells of patients with sickle cell disease, β-thalassemia, renal disease, multiple myeloma, autoimmune disorders, AIDS, and other diseases with elevated serum globulin or blood urea nitrogen (BUN) levels with no clear correlation between a positive DAT and anemia.[1,2,7] Interpretation of positive DATs should include the patient's history, clinical data, and the results of other laboratory tests.

The Direct Antiglobulin Test

The principles of the DAT are discussed in Chapter 12. Although any red cells may be tested, EDTA-anticoagulated blood samples are preferred to prevent in-vitro fixation of complement. If red cells from a clotted blood sample have a positive DAT due to complement, the results should be confirmed on cells from a freshly collected or EDTA-anticoagulated specimen if those results are to be used for diagnostic purposes.

Most DATs are initially performed with a polyspecific antihuman globulin (AHG) reagent capable of detecting both IgG and C3d (see Method 3.6). If positive, tests with specific anti-IgG and anticomplement reagents may be appropriate. Occasionally, polyspecific AHG reagents react with cell-bound proteins other than IgG or C3d (eg, IgM, IgA, or other complement components); specific reagents to distinguish these proteins are not readily available in most laboratories. If cord blood samples are to be tested, it is appropriate to use anti-IgG only because hemolytic disease of the fetus and newborn (HDFN) results from the fetal red cells becoming sensitized with maternally derived IgG antibody and complement activation rarely occurs.[3]

The Pretransfusion DAT and the Autologous Control

Neither the AABB, in the *Standards for Blood Banks and Transfusion Services*,[8] nor any other accrediting agency requires a DAT or an autologous control (autocontrol) as part of pretransfusion testing. Studies have shown that eliminating the DAT/autocontrol portion of routine pretransfusion testing carries minimal risk.[9]

Evaluation of a Positive DAT

Extent of Testing

Clinical considerations should dictate the extent to which a positive DAT is evaluated. Dialogue with the attending physician is important. Interpretation of the significance of serologic findings requires knowledge of the patient's diagnosis; recent drug, pregnancy, and transfusion history; and information on the presence of acquired or unexplained hemolytic anemia. The results of serologic tests alone are not diagnostic; their significance must be assessed in conjunction with clinical information and such laboratory data as hematocrit, bilirubin, haptoglobin, and reticulocyte count. When investigating a transfusion reaction, performance of the DAT on postreaction specimens is part of the initial transfusion reaction investigation. The DAT may be positive if sensitized red cells have not been destroyed or negative if hemolysis and rapid clearance have occurred. Positive DAT results should be further evaluated. The patient's history is important in interpreting a posttransfusion reaction positive DAT (see Chapter 27).

Answers to the following questions may help decide what investigations are appropriate:

1. *Is there any evidence of in-vivo red cell destruction?* Reticulocytosis, spherocytes observed on the peripheral blood film, hemoglobinemia, hemoglobinuria, decreased serum haptoglobin, and elevated levels of serum unconjugated bilirubin or lactate dehydrogenase (LDH), especially LDH1, may be associated with increased red cell destruction. If an anemic patient with a positive DAT does show evidence of hemolysis, testing to evaluate a possible immune etiology is appropriate. IF THERE IS NO EVIDENCE OF INCREASED RED CELL DESTRUCTION, NO FURTHER STUDIES ARE NECESSARY, unless the patient needs transfusion and the serum contains incompletely identified unexpected antibodies to red cell antigens.

2. *Has the patient been recently transfused?* Many workers routinely attempt to determine the cause of a positive DAT when the patient has received transfusions within the previous 3 months because the first indication of a developing immune response may be the attachment of antibody to recently transfused red cells. Antibody may appear as early as 7 to 10 days (but typically 2 weeks to several months) after transfusion in primary immunization and as early as 2 to 7 days (but usually within 20 days) in a secondary response; these alloantibodies could shorten the survival of red cells already transfused or given subsequently.

Studies have shown that the positive DAT and reactive eluates can persist for more than 300 days following a transfusion reaction, which is far longer than the transfused cells would be expected to survive, suggesting that autologous as well as transfused red cells are sensitized following a transfusion reaction.[10,11] A mixed-field appearance in the posttransfusion DAT may or may not be observed.

3. *Is the patient receiving any drugs, such as cephalosporins, procainamide, intravenous penicillin, or α-methyldopa?* Cephalosporins are associated with positive DATs; the second- and third-generation cephalosporins can be associated with immune red cell destruction.[12] In one study, 21% of patients receiving procainamide developed a positive DAT (three of whom had evidence of hemolytic anemia).[13] A high incidence (39%) of positive DATs has been reported in patients taking Unasyn.[14] Although not commonly seen in recent years, approximately 3% of patients receiving intravenous penicillin, at very high doses, and 15% to 20% of patients receiving α-methyldopa will develop a positive DAT. However, fewer than 1% of those patients who develop a positive DAT have hemolytic anemia. Positive DATs associated with other drugs are rare. If a positive DAT is found in a patient receiving such drugs, the attending physician should be alerted so that appropriate surveillance for red cell destruction can be maintained. If red cell survival is not shortened, no further studies are necessary.

4. *Has the patient received marrow, peripheral blood stem cells, or an organ transplant?* Passenger lymphocytes of donor origin produce antibodies directed against ABO or other antigens on the recipient's cells, causing a positive DAT.[3]

5. *Is the patient receiving IGIV or intravenous RhIG?* Immune Globulin, Intravenous (IGIV) may contain ABO antibodies, anti-D, or, sometimes, other antibodies. Intravenous Rh Immune Globulin (RhIG) causes Rh-positive patients to develop a positive DAT.[15]

6. *Is the patient septic?* Complement activation can occur in septic patients, leading to intravascular hemolysis. This is most often seen in cases of polyagglutination resulting from organisms that produce neuraminidase.

Serologic Studies

Three investigative approaches are helpful in the evaluation of a positive DAT.

1. Test the DAT-positive red cells with anti-IgG and anti-C3d reagents to characterize the types of proteins coating the red cells.

2. Test the serum/plasma to detect and identify clinically significant antibodies to red cell antigens.

3. Test an eluate (see Methods 4.1 through 4.5) prepared from the coated red cells with a panel of reagent red cells to define whether the coating protein has red cell antibody activity. When the only coating protein is complement, eluates are frequently nonreactive. However, an eluate from the patient's red cells coated only with complement should be tested if there is clinical evidence of antibody-mediated hemolysis. The eluate preparation can concentrate small amounts of IgG that may not be detectable on direct testing using routine methods. Results of these tests combined with the patient's history and clinical data should assist in classification of the problems involved.

See Appendix 20-1 for an example of an algorithm for investigating a positive DAT (excluding investigation of HDFN).

Elution

Elution frees antibody from sensitized red cells and recovers antibody in a usable form. Details of eluate preparation are given in Chapter 19 and in Methods 4.1 through 4.5. Commercial elution kits are also available. Table 20-1 lists the advantages and disadvantages of several common elution methods; no single elution method is ideal in all situations. Although many elution methods damage or destroy the red cells, certain techniques (see Methods 2.11, 2.12, 2.13, and 2.14) remove antibody but leave the cells sufficiently intact to allow testing for various antigens or for use in adsorption procedures. Some antigens may be altered by elution, however, and appropriate controls are essential.

In cases of HDFN or hemolytic transfusion reactions, specific antibody (or antibodies) is usually detected in the eluate, which may or may not be detectable in the serum. In the case of transfusion reactions, newly developed antibodies initially detectable only in the eluate are usually detectable in the serum after about 14 to 21 days. Eluate preparation from the patient's red cells often concentrates antibody activity and may facilitate identification of weakly reactive serum antibodies.

When the eluate reacts with all the cells tested, autoantibody is the most likely explanation, especially if the patient has not been recently transfused. WHEN NO UNEXPECTED ANTIBODIES ARE PRESENT IN THE SERUM, AND IF THE PATIENT HAS NOT BEEN RECENTLY TRANSFUSED, NO FURTHER SEROLOGIC TESTING OF AN AUTOANTIBODY IS NECESSARY.

A nonreactive eluate prepared from IgG-coated red cells may have several causes.

Table 20-1. Antibody Elution Techniques

Method	Advantages	Disadvantages
Heat (56 C)	Good for ABO-HDFN; quick and easy	Poor recovery of other blood group allo- and autoantibodies
Freeze-thaw	Good for ABO-HDFN; quick method; requires small volume of red cells	Poor recovery of other blood group allo- and autoantibodies
Cold acid	Quick and easy; adequate for most warm auto- and alloantibodies; commercial kits available	Possible false-positive elution (see Leger et al[16])
Digitonin acid	Nonhazardous; good recovery of most antibodies	Time-consuming washing of stroma
Dichloromethane/ Methylene chloride	Noncarcinogenic, nonflammable; good for IgG auto- and alloantibodies	Vapors harmful

Compiled from Judd[17] and South et al.[18]

One cause may be that the eluate was not tested against cells positive for the corresponding antigen, notably group A or group B cells, or antigens of low incidence, which are absent from most reagent cell panels. If a non-group-O patient has received plasma containing anti-A or anti-B (as in transfusion of group O platelets), and the recipient appears to have immune hemolysis, the eluate can be tested against A and/or B cells. If the expected ABO antibodies are not detected, other causes of the positive DAT should be sought. It may be appropriate to test the eluate against red cells from recently transfused donor units, which could have caused immunization to a rare antigen, or, in HDFN, against cells from the father, from whom the infant may have inherited a rare gene. Pursuing the cause of a nonreactive eluate for patients with no evidence of hemolysis is usually not indicated. Toy et al[1] showed that 79% of hospital patients with a positive DAT have a nonreactive eluate. It is suggested that at least one contributing factor to these positive DAT results is nonspecific uptake of proteins on the red cells, which occurs in patients with elevated gamma globulin levels.[1,2]

Reactivity of eluates can be enhanced by testing them against enzyme-treated cells or by the use of enhancement techniques such as polyethylene glycol (PEG). Antibody reactivity can be increased by the use of a concentrated eluate, either by alteration of the fluid-to-cell ratio or by use of commercial concentration devices. Washing the red cells with low-ionic-strength saline (LISS) or cold wash solutions may prevent the loss of antibody while the cells are being prepared for elution.

Certain elution methods give poor results with certain antibodies. When eluates are nonreactive yet clinical signs of red cell destruction are present, elution by a different method may be helpful. If both serum and eluate are nonreactive at all test phases and if the patient has received high-dose intravenous penicillin or other drug therapy, testing to demonstrate drug-related antibodies should be considered.

Immune-Mediated Hemolysis

Immune-mediated hemolysis (immune hemolysis) is the shortening of red cell survival by the product(s) of an immune response. If marrow compensation is adequate, the reduced red cell survival may not result in anemia. Immune hemolysis is only one cause of hemolytic anemia, and many causes of hemolysis are unrelated to immune reactions. The serologic investigations carried out in the blood bank do not determine whether a patient has a "hemolytic" anemia. The diagnosis of hemolytic anemia rests on clinical findings and such laboratory data as hemoglobin or hematocrit values; reticulocyte count; red cell morphology; bilirubin, haptoglobin, and LDH levels; and, sometimes, red cell survival studies. The serologic findings help determine whether the hemolysis has an immune basis and, if so, what type of immune hemolytic anemia is present. This is important because the treatment for each type is different.

The terms hemolysis and hemolytic are frequently used to indicate both intravascular and extravascular red cell destruction; however, this may be misleading. In-vivo lysis of cells and release of free hemoglobin within the intravascular compartment (ie, resulting in hemoglobinemia and hemoglobinuria) is uncommon and, often, dramatic. Extravascular hemolysis, which is more common, is characterized by an increase in serum bilirubin, but not by hemoglobinemia and hemoglobinuria. As a description of in-vitro antibody reactivity, hemolysis or lysis of the red cells with release of free hemoglobin to the surrounding media is both obvious and rare.

Immune hemolytic anemias can be classified in various ways. One classification system is shown in Table 20-2. Autoimmune hemolytic anemias (AIHAs) are subdivided into five major types: warm antibody AIHA (WAIHA), cold agglutinin syndrome (CAS), mixed-type AIHA, paroxysmal cold hemoglobinuria (PCH), and DAT-negative AIHA. Not all cases fit neatly into these categories. Drugs (discussed in a later section of this chapter) may also induce immune hemolysis. The prevalence of each type can vary depending on the patient population studied. Table 20-3 shows the serologic characteristics of the autoimmune and drug-induced hemolytic anemias.

DATs performed with IgG- and C3-specific AHG reagents as well as the serum and eluate studies described earlier can be used to help classify AIHAs. Three additional procedures may be useful: a cold agglutinin titer and thermal amplitude studies (Methods 4.7 and 4.8) and the Donath-Landsteiner test for PCH (Method 4.13).

The binding of antibody to red cells does not, in itself, damage the cells. It is the phenomena that the bound antibody-antigen complex promotes that may eventually damage cells. These include complement binding, adherence to Fc receptors on macrophages leading to phagocytosis, and cytotoxic lysis. The IgG subclass of bound antibody may be significant. IgG1 is the subclass most commonly found, sometimes alone but often in combination with other subclasses. The other IgG subclasses occur more often in combination with other subclasses than alone. In general, IgG3 antibodies have the most destructive

Table 20-2. Classification of Immune Hemolytic Anemias

Autoimmune Hemolytic Anemia (AIHA)

1. Warm autoimmune hemolytic anemia
   a. primary (idiopathic)
   b. secondary [to such conditions as lymphoma, systemic lupus erythematosus (SLE), carcinoma, or to drug therapy]
2. Cold agglutinin syndrome
   a. primary (idiopathic)
   b. secondary (to such conditions as lymphoma, mycoplasma pneumonia, infectious mononucleosis)
3. Mixed-type AIHA
   a. primary (idiopathic)
   b. secondary (to such conditions as SLE, lymphoma)
4. Paroxysmal cold hemoglobinuria
   a. primary (idiopathic)
   b. secondary (to such conditions as syphilis, viral infections)
5. DAT-negative AIHA
   a. primary (idiopathic)
   b. secondary (to such conditions as lymphoma, SLE)

Drug-Induced Hemolytic Anemia

Alloimmune Hemolytic Anemia

1. Hemolytic disease of the fetus and newborn
2. Hemolytic transfusion reaction

---

effects, followed by IgG1. IgG2 antibodies are associated with less destruction and IgG4 with little to no destruction.

The number of antibody molecules per red cell also plays a role. The number of antibody molecules on the red cells of apparently healthy blood donors with positive DATs (<200 molecules/red cell) is far less than that usually seen in patients with AIHA.[4,5] Some patients with apparent immune hemolysis may have negative DATs.

Warm Antibody Autoimmune Hemolytic Anemia

The most common type of AIHA is associated with warm-reactive (37 C) antibodies. Typical serologic findings are described below.

DAT

When IgG-specific and complement-specific AHG reagents are used, three pat-

Table 20-3. Serologic Findings in Immune Hemolytic Anemias

	WAIHA	CAS	Mixed-Type AIHA	PCH	Drug-Induced
Percent of cases	48%[19] to 70%[3]	16%[3] to 32%[19]	7%[19] to 8%[20]	Rare in adults; 32% in children[21]	12%[3] to 18%[19]
DAT	IgG: 20%[3] to 66%[19] IgG + C3: 24%[19] to 63%[3] C3: 7%[19] to 14%[3]	C3 only: 91%[19] to 98%[3]	IgG + C3: 71%[19] to 100%[3] C3: 13%[3]	C3 only: 94%[19] to 100%[3]	IgG: 94%[19] IgG + C3: 6%[19]
Immunoglobulin type	IgG (sometimes IgA or IgM, rarely alone)	IgM	IgG, IgM	IgG	IgG
Eluate	IgG antibody	Nonreactive	IgG antibody	Nonreactive	IgG antibody
Serum	57% react by saline-IAT; 13% hemolyze enzyme-treated RBCs at 37 C; 90% agglutinate enzyme-treated RBCs at 37 C; 30% agglutinate untreated RBCs at 20 C; rarely agglutinate untreated RBCs at 37 C[3]	IgM agglutinating antibody; titer usually >1000 at 4 C; usually react at 30 C in albumin; monoclonal antibody in chronic disease[3]	IgG IAT-reactive antibody plus IgM agglutinating antibody, usually react at 30-37 C in saline; high titer at 4 C (classic CAS) or low titer (<64) at 4 C[3,19,20,22]	IgG biphasic hemolysin (Donath-Landsteiner antibody)[3]	IgG antibody similar to WAIHA[3]
Specificity	Rh specificity; other specificities have been reported*	Usually anti-I but can be anti-i; rarely anti-Pr[23]	Usually specificity is unclear[19,20,22] Can be anti-I, -i, or other cold agglutinin specificities	Anti-P (nonreactive with p and P^k RBCs)	Specificity often Rh related[23]

*See text.

terns of reactivity may be found: coating with IgG alone, with complement alone, or with both. In approximately 1% of cases, the DAT will be positive with a poly-specific AHG reagent but negative with IgG- and complement-specific AHG reagents. Some of these may be due to attachment of IgM or IgA alone if reactivity with these immunoglobulins has not been excluded by the manufacturer.[3,19]

Serum

Autoantibody in the serum typically is IgG and reacts by indirect antiglobulin testing against all cells tested.[3] If the autoantibody has been adsorbed by the patient's red cells in vivo, the serum may contain very little free antibody. The serum will contain antibody after all the specific antigen sites on the red cells have been occupied and no more antibody can be bound in vivo. In such cases, the DAT is usually strongly positive. Approximately 50% of patients with WAIHA have serum antibodies that react with untreated saline-suspended red cells. When testing with PEG, enzyme-treated red cells, or solid-phase methods, over 90% of these sera can be shown to contain autoantibody. Approximately one-third of patients with WAIHA have cold-reactive autoagglutinins demonstrable in tests at 20 C, but cold agglutinin titers at 4 C are normal. The presence of this cold agglutinin does not mean the patient has CAS in addition to WAIHA.[3]

Eluate

The presence of the IgG autoantibody on the red cells may be confirmed by elution at least upon initial diagnosis and/or at pretransfusion testing. (See Methods 4.1, 4.2, and 4.5.) Typically, the eluate reacts with virtually all cells tested, with reactivity enhanced in tests against enzyme-treated cells or when PEG is used. The eluate will usually have no serologic activity if the only protein coating the red cells is complement components. Occasionally, antibody not detected by the DAT will be detected in the eluate, possibly due to the concentrating effect of eluate preparation.

Specificity of Autoantibody

The specificity of autoantibodies associated with WAIHA is complex. In routine tests, all cells tested are usually reactive. Some autoantibodies that have weaker or negative reactivity with cells of rare Rh phenotypes, such as D– – or Rh_{null}, appear to have broad specificity in the Rh system. Apparent specificity for simple Rh antigens (D, C, E, c, e) is occasionally seen, either as the sole autoantibody or as a predominant portion, based on stronger reactivity with cells of certain phenotypes. Such reactivity is often termed a "relative" specificity. Such relative specificity in a serum may be mistaken for alloantibody, but cells negative for the apparent target antigen can adsorb and remove the "mimicking" specificity.[23,24]

Unusual Specificities. Apart from Rh specificity, warm autoantibodies with many other specificities have been reported, eg, specificities in the LW, Kell, Kidd, Duffy, and Diego systems.[24] Dilution and selective adsorption of eluates may uncover specificity or relative specificity of autoantibodies. Patients with autoantibodies of Kell, Rh, LW, Ge, Sc, Lu, and Lan specificities may have depressed expression of the respective antigen and the DAT may be negative or very weakly positive.[24]

Practical Significance. Tests against red cells of rare phenotype and by special techniques have limited clinical application. In rare instances of WAIHA involving IgM agglutinins, determining autoantibody specificity may help differentiate such cases from typical CAS.[25] It is rarely, if ever, necessary to ascertain autoantibody specificity in order to select antigen-negative blood for transfusion. If apparent specificity is directed to a high-incidence antigen (eg, anti-U), or when the autoantibody reacts with all red cells except those of a rare Rh phenotype (eg, D– –, Rh_{null}), compatible donor blood is unlikely to be available and there is little point in determining specificity. Such blood, if available, should be reserved for alloimmunized patients of that uncommon phenotype.

Transfusion-Stimulated Autoantibodies. Transfusion itself may lead to the production of autoantibodies that may persist and cause positive DATs for some time after transfusion yet not cause obvious red cell destruction. Such cell-bound autoantibodies sometimes display blood group specificity (eg, E, K, Jk^a). The positive DAT may persist long after transfused red cells should have disappeared from the circulation, apparently adsorbed to the patient's own antigen-negative red cells.[11]

Transfusion of Patients with Warm-Reactive Autoantibodies

Inherent Risks. Patients with warm-reactive autoantibodies range from those with no apparent decreased red cell survival to those with life-threatening anemia. Patients with little or no evidence of significant in-vivo red cell destruction tolerate transfusion quite well.

When autoantibody is active in serum, it may be difficult to exclude the presence of alloantibodies, which increases the risk of an adverse reaction. Transfusion may stimulate alloantibody production, complicating subsequent transfusions. Transfusion may intensify the autoantibody, inducing or increasing hemolysis and making serologic testing more difficult. Transfusion

may depress compensatory erythropoiesis. Destruction of transfused cells may increase hemoglobinemia and hemoglobinuria. In patients with active hemolysis, transfused red cells may be destroyed more rapidly than the patient's own red cells. In rare cases, this may promote hypercoagulability and disseminated intravascular coagulation (DIC). Transfusion reactions, if they occur, may be difficult to investigate.

Transfusion in WAIHA. Transfusion is especially problematic for patients with rapid in-vivo hemolysis, who may present with a very low hemoglobin level and hypotension. Reticulocytopenia may accompany a rapidly falling hematocrit, and the patient may exhibit coronary insufficiency, congestive heart failure, cardiac decompensation, or neurologic impairment. Under these circumstances, transfusion is usually required as a lifesaving measure. The transfused cells may support oxygen-carrying capacity until the acute hemolysis diminishes or other therapies can effect a more lasting benefit. These patients represent a significant challenge because serologic testing may be complex while clinical needs are acute.

Transfusion should not be withheld solely because of serologic incompatibility. The volume transfused should usually be the smallest amount required to maintain adequate oxygen delivery, not necessarily to reach an arbitrary hemoglobin level. Volumes of about 100 mL may be appropriate.[3] The patient should be carefully monitored throughout the transfusion.

Transfusion in Chronic WAIHA. Most patients with WAIHA have a chronic stable anemia, often at relatively low hemoglobin levels. Those with hemoglobin levels above 8 g/dL rarely require transfusion, and many patients with levels of 5 g/dL (or even lower) can be managed with bed rest and no transfusions. Transfusion will be required if the anemia progresses or is accompanied by such symptoms as severe angina, cardiac decompensation, respiratory distress, and cerebral ischemia.

Most patients with chronic anemia due to WAIHA tolerate transfusion without overt reactions, even though the transfused cells may not survive any better than their own. Because transfusion may lead to circulatory overload or to increased red cell destruction, the decision to transfuse should be carefully considered. A few patients without acute hemolysis have had severe hemolytic reactions after transfusion. This may be due to the sudden availability of large volumes of donor cells and the exponential curve of decay, by which the number of cells hemolyzed is proportional to the number of cells present.[3,6(pp230,369)]

Selecting Blood. If the decision is made to transfuse, selection of appropriate donor blood is essential. It is important to determine the patient's ABO and Rh type and, if time permits, to detect potentially clinically significant alloantibodies. Adsorption and other special techniques described later in this chapter can greatly reduce the risk of undetected alloantibodies but may be time-consuming. If clinically significant alloantibodies are present, the transfused cells should lack the corresponding antigen(s).

If the autoantibody has apparent and relatively clear-cut specificity for a single antigen (eg, anti-e) and there is active ongoing hemolysis, blood lacking that antigen may be selected. There is evidence that, in some patients, such red cells survive better than the patient's own red cells.[6(p230),20] In the absence of hemolysis, autoantibody specificity is not important, although donor units negative for the antigen may be chosen because this is a simple way to circumvent the autoantibody and detect potential alloantibodies. If the autoantibody shows broader reactivity, reacting with all cells but showing some relative specificity (eg, it reacts preferentially with e+ red cells), the use of blood lacking the corresponding antigen is debatable. It may be undesirable to expose the patient to Rh antigens absent from autologous cells, especially D and especially in females who may bear children later, merely to improve serologic compatibility testing with the autoantibody (eg, when a D– patient has autoanti-e).

In many cases of WAIHA, no autoantibody specificity is apparent. The patient's serum reacts with all red cell samples to the same degree or reacts with red cells from different donors to varying degrees for reasons seemingly unrelated to Rh phenotypes. Even if specificity is identified, the exotic cells used for such identification are not available for transfusion. The most important consideration in such cases is to exclude the presence of clinically important alloantibodies *before* selecting either phenotypically similar or dissimilar, crossmatch-incompatible red cells for transfusion. In extremely rare cases in which there is severe and progressive anemia, it may be essential to transfuse blood that does not react with the patient's autoantibody.

Frequency of Testing. Although AABB *Standards*[8(p38)] requires that a sample be tested every 3 days, some serologists contend that, in these difficult cases, the continued collection and testing (to include antibody investigation) of patient samples are unnecessary.[26] Others disagree with that opinion. In studies of patients with WAIHA, there was 12% to 40% alloimmunization, with many alloantibodies developing after recent transfusions.[27,28] These two papers offer methods to assist in the detection of alloantibodies in the presence of autoantibodies. For patients with previously identified clinically significant antibodies, *Standards*[8(p38)] requires that methods of testing shall be those that identify additional clinically significant antibodies. It is the exclusion of newly formed alloantibodies that is of concern. Autoantibodies that react with all reagent red cells, even weakly, are capable of masking alloantibody reactivity; the serologic reactivity is not necessarily additive.[29] Due to the presence of autoantibodies, all crossmatches will be incompatible. This is unlike the case of clinically significant alloantibodies, where a compatible crossmatch with antigen-negative red cells can be obtained. Monitoring for evidence of red cell destruction due to *alloantibodies* is difficult in patients who already have AIHA; the patient's own red cells and transfused red cells will have shortened survival. In patients who have autoantibodies without hemolytic anemia, transfused red cells should have normal survival.

An alternative transfusion management protocol proposed by one group uses prophylactic antigen-matched units for patients with warm autoantibodies where feasible, in combination with streamlined adsorption procedures.[30] Such a protocol depends on the ability to maintain an adequate inventory of antigen-negative units.[31]

IgM Warm AIHA

AIHA associated with IgM agglutinins that react at 37 C is unusual but is characterized by severe hemolysis.[25,32-34] The prognosis for these patients is poor.

DAT

The patient's red cells are typically spontaneously agglutinated, requiring disruption of the IgM agglutinin by dithiothreitol in order to obtain accurate DAT (and ABO/Rh) results. Complement is usually detected on the red cells. In one series, IgG was detected in 17% of cases and IgM in 28%. By a more sensitive flow cytometric method, red cell-bound IgM was detected on 82% of patients' red cells not reacting with anti-IgM by tube DAT.[33]

Serum

Warm IgM autoagglutinins are typically weak and sometimes are enhanced in the presence of albumin or when the serum is acidified.[33] Occasionally, optimal reactivity is between 20 C and 30 C, rather than 37 C. These antibodies have low or negligible antibody titers; a 4 C titer of <64 easily differentiates this IgM warm antibody from those seen in CAS.

Eluate

IgM agglutinins are often detected in an eluate when inspected at the agglutinin phase before proceeding to the antiglobulin test.

Cold Agglutinin Syndrome

Cold agglutinin syndrome (also called cold hemagglutinin disease, CHD) is the hemolytic anemia most commonly associated with cold-reactive autoantibodies and accounts for approximately 16% to 32% of all cases of immune hemolysis.[3,19] (See Table 20-3.) It occurs as an acute or chronic condition. The acute form is often secondary to lymphoproliferative disorders (eg, lymphoma) or *Mycoplasma pneumoniae* infection. The chronic form is often seen in elderly patients, sometimes associated with lymphoma, chronic lymphocytic leukemia, or Waldenstrom's macroglobulinemia. Acrocyanosis and hemoglobinuria may occur in cold weather. CAS is often characterized by rapid agglutination, at room temperature, of red cells in an EDTA specimen. Clumping of red cells may be obvious in such a sample, sometimes so strong that the cells appear to be clotted. Problems with ABO and Rh typing and other tests are not uncommon. Maintaining the EDTA specimen at 37 C and washing the red cells with 37 C saline is usually necessary to disperse the cold autoagglutinin before performing ABO and Rh typing and the DAT.

DAT

Complement is the only protein detected on the red cells in almost all cases. If other proteins are detected, a negative control for the DAT, eg, 6% to 10% albumin, should be tested to ensure that the cold autoagglutinin is not causing a false-positive test.

The cold-reactive autoagglutinin is usually IgM, which binds to red cells in the comparatively low temperature of the peripheral circulation and causes complement components (C3 and C4 in particular) to attach to the red cells. As the red cells circulate to warmer areas, the IgM dissociates, but the complement remains. Red-cell-bound C3b can react with the CR1 or CR3 receptors of macrophages in the reticuloendothelial system. More of the red cell destruction occurs in the liver. Regulatory proteins convert the bound C3 and C4 to C3dg and C4d, and it is the anti-C3d component of polyspecific AHG reagents that accounts for the positive DAT. The presence of C3dg alone does not shorten red cell survival because macrophages have no C3dg or C3d receptors.

Serum

IgM cold-reactive autoagglutinins associated with immune hemolysis usually react ≥30 C and have a titer ≥1000 when tested at 4 C; they rarely react with saline-suspended red cells above 32 C. If 30% bovine albumin is included in the reaction medium, 100% and 70% of clinically significant examples will react at 30 C or 37 C, respectively.[35] Occasionally, pathologic cold agglutinins will have a lower titer (ie, <1000), but they will have a high thermal amplitude (ie, reactive at 30 C with or without the addition of albu-

min). Hemolytic activity against untreated red cells can be demonstrated sometimes at 20 to 25 C, and, except in rare cases with Pr specificity, enzyme-treated red cells are hemolyzed in the presence of adequate complement.

Determination of the true thermal amplitude or titer of the cold autoagglutinin requires that the specimen be collected and maintained strictly at 37 C until the serum and cells are separated, to avoid in-vitro autoadsorption. Alternatively, plasma can be used from an EDTA-anticoagulated specimen that has been warmed for 10 to 15 minutes at 37 C (with repeated mixing) and then separated from the cells, ideally at 37 C. This should release autoadsorbed antibody back into the plasma.

In chronic CAS, the IgM autoagglutinin is usually a monoclonal protein with kappa light chains. In the acute form induced by *Mycoplasma* or viral infections, the antibody is polyclonal IgM with normal kappa and lambda light-chain distribution. Rare examples of IgA and IgG cold-reactive autoagglutinins have also been described.

Eluate

Elution is seldom necessary in obvious cases of CAS. If the red cells have been collected properly and washed at 37 C, there will be no immunoglobulin on the cells and no reactivity will be found in the eluate.

Specificity of Autoantibody

The autoantibody specificity in CAS is usually of academic interest only. CAS is most often associated with antibodies with I specificity.[3,23] Less commonly, i specificity is found, usually associated with infectious mononucleosis.[3] On rare occasions, cold-reactive autoagglutinins with Pr or other specificities are seen[3,23] (see Method 4.7). Dilution of the serum may be necessary to demonstrate specificity of very high-titer antibodies.

Autoantibody specificity is not diagnostic for CAS. Autoanti-I may be seen in healthy subjects as well as patients with CAS. The nonpathologic forms of autoanti-I, however, rarely react to titers above 64 at 4 C, and are usually nonreactive with I– (i cord and i adult) red cells at room temperature. In contrast, the autoanti-I of CAS may react quite strongly with I– red cells in tests at room temperature, and equal or even stronger reactions are observed with I+ red cells. Autoanti-i reacts in the opposite manner, demonstrating stronger reactions with I– red cells than with red cells that are I+. Procedures to determine the titers and specificities of cold-reactive autoantibodies are given in Method 4.6 and Method 4.7.

Pretransfusion Testing. Antibody detection tests should be performed in ways that minimize cold-reactive autoantibody activity yet still permit detection of clinically significant alloantibodies. The use of albumin and other potentiators may increase the reactivity of the autoantibodies. To avoid the detection of bound complement, most serologists use an IgG-specific reagent, rather than a polyspecific AHG serum. Additionally, a prewarming technique may be used (see Method 3.3).

Adsorption Procedures. When cold-reactive autoantibody reactivity continues to interfere with antibody detection tests (eg, when performed strictly at 37 C), cold autoadsorption studies (see Method 4.6) can be helpful. One or two cold autoadsorptions should remove enough autoantibody to make it possible to detect alloantibodies at 37 C that were otherwise masked by the cold-reactive autoantibody; many cold autoadsorptions would be required to remove enough of the cold-reactive autoantibody for room temperature testing. If the patient has been recently transfused, rabbit red cells may be used to remove autoanti-I and -IH from sera[36]; clinically significant alloantibodies, notably anti-B, -D, -E, Vel, and others, have been removed by this method.[37,38] A preparation of rabbit red cell stroma is commercially available. Alternatively, allogeneic adsorption studies at 4 C can be performed as for WAIHA (see below).

Mixed-Type AIHA

Although about one-third of patients with WAIHA have nonpathologic IgM antibodies that react to high titer at low temperature, another group of patients with WAIHA have cold agglutinins that react at or above 30 C. This latter group is referred to as "mixed-type" AIHA and can be subdivided: patients with high titer, high thermal amplitude IgM cold antibodies (the rare WAIHA plus classic CAS) and patients with normal titer (<64 at 4 C), high thermal amplitude cold antibodies.[19,20,22,39] Patients with mixed-type AIHA often present with hemolysis and complex serum reactivity present in all phases of testing. Typical serologic findings are described below.

DAT

When the patient has WAIHA plus classic CAS, both IgG and C3 are usually detectable on the patient's red cells. When the cold agglutinin has a normal titer, but high thermal amplitude (greater than or equal to 30 C), IgG and/or C3 may be detectable on the red cells.[3]

Serum

Both warm-reactive IgG autoantibodies and cold-reactive, agglutinating IgM autoantibodies are present in the serum. These usually result in reactivity at all phases of testing, with virtually all cells tested. The IgM agglutinating autoantibody(ies) reacts at 30 C or above. If adsorption studies are done to detect alloantibodies, it may be necessary to perform adsorptions at both warm and cold temperatures.

Eluate

A suitably prepared eluate will contain a warm-reactive IgG autoantibody.

Specificity of Autoantibodies

The unusual cold-reactive IgM agglutinating autoantibody can have specificities typical of CAS (ie, I or i) but often has no apparent specificity.[19,20,22] The warm-reactive IgG autoantibody often appears serologically indistinguishable from specificities encountered in typical WAIHA.

Transfusion in Mixed-Type AIHA

If blood transfusions are necessary, the considerations in the selection of blood for transfusion are identical to those described for patients with acute hemolysis due to WAIHA (see above).

Paroxysmal Cold Hemoglobinuria

The rarest form of DAT-positive AIHA is PCH. In the past, it was characteristically associated with syphilis, but this association is now unusual. More commonly, PCH presents as an acute transient condition secondary to viral infections, particularly in young children. In such cases, the biphasic hemolysin (see below) may only be transiently detectable. PCH can also occur as an idiopathic chronic disease in older people. One large study found that none of 531 adults having well-defined immune hemolytic anemias had Donath-Landsteiner hemolysins, whereas 22 of 68 (32%) children were shown to have Donath-Landsteiner hemolysins.[21]

DAT

PCH is caused by an IgG complement-fixing antibody, but, as with IgM cold-reactive autoagglutinins, it reacts with red cells in colder areas of the body (usually the extremities), causes C3 to bind irreversibly to red cells, and then the antibody dissociates from the red cells as the blood circulates to warmer parts of the body. Red cells washed in a routine manner for the DAT are usually coated only with complement components, but IgG may be detectable on cells that have been washed with cold saline and tested with cold anti-IgG reagent.[3] Keeping the system nearer its optimal binding temperature allows the cold-reactive IgG autoantibody to remain attached to its antigen.

Serum

The IgG autoantibody in PCH is classically described as a biphasic hemolysin because binding to red cells occurs at low temperatures but hemolysis does not occur until the coated red cells are warmed to 37 C. This is the basis of the diagnostic test for the disease, the Donath-Landsteiner test (see Method 4.13). The autoantibody may agglutinate normal red cells at 4 C but rarely to titers greater than 64. Because the antibody rarely reacts above 4 C, the serum is usually compatible with random donor cells by routine crossmatch procedures and pretransfusion antibody detection tests are usually nonreactive.

Eluate

Because complement components are usually the only globulins present on circulating red cells, eluates prepared from red cells of patients with PCH are almost always nonreactive.

Specificity of Autoantibody

The autoantibody of PCH has most frequently been shown to have P specificity, reacting with all red cells by the Donath-Landsteiner test (including the patient's own red cells) except those of the very rare p or P^k phenotypes. Exceptional examples with other specificities have been described.[6(p221),23]

Transfusion in PCH

Transfusion is rarely necessary for adult patients with PCH, unless their hemolysis is severe. In children, especially under age 6, the thermal amplitude of the antibody tends to be much wider than in adults and hemolysis more brisk, so transfusion may be required as a lifesaving measure. Although there is some evidence that p red cells survive better than P+ (P_1+ or P_1−) red cells,[6(p221)] the prevalence of p blood is approximately 1 in 200,000 and the urgent need for transfusion usually precludes attempts to obtain this rare blood. Transfusion of random donor blood should not be withheld from PCH patients whose need is urgent. Red cells negative for the P antigen should be considered only for those patients who do not respond adequately to random donor blood.[3]

DAT-Negative AIHA

Clinical evidence of hemolytic anemia is present in some patients whose DAT is nonreactive. Frequently, autoantibody cannot be detected in either eluate or serum. There may be several reasons the DAT is negative. The autoantibody may be IgA or IgM.[3,40] Antibodies with low binding affinity may dissociate from the red cells during saline washing of the cells for the DAT. Washing with ice cold (eg, 4 C) LISS or saline may help retain antibody on the cells; a control (eg, 6-10% albumin) is necessary to confirm that cold autoagglutinins are not causing the positive results.[3,40] There may be too few antibody molecules on the cell for detection by routine methods but enough to be demonstrable by methods such as flow cytometry, enzyme-linked antiglobulin tests, solid phase, PEG, direct Polybrene, column agglutination, or concentrated eluate.

Nonroutine Reagents

The causative antibody may be IgM or IgA not detected by routine AHG reagents. Anti-IgG, anti-C3d, and the combined anti-C3b, -C3d reagents are the only licensed products available in the United States for use with human red cells. AHG reagents that react with IgA, IgM, or C4 are available commercially but have been prepared for use with endpoints other than agglutination. These must be used cautiously and their hemagglutinating reactivity carefully standardized by the user.[3] Quality control must be rigorous because agglutination with AHG reagents is more sensitive than precipitation; a serum that appears to be monospecific by precipitation tests may react with several different proteins when used in agglutination tests.

Antigen Depression

Patients with autoantibodies of Kell, Rh, LW, Ge, Sc, Lu, and Lan specificities may have depressed red cell expression of the respective antigens. When this occurs, antibody may be detected in the serum and eluate, but the DAT may be negative or very weakly positive. This may provide in-vivo protection of autologous cells. Donor cells of common specific antigen type may be destroyed, but cells lacking the corresponding antigen (usually high-incidence) may survive well. When the autoantibody subsides, autologous cells again express normal amounts of antigen.[6(p228),24]

Serologic Problems with Autoantibodies

In pretransfusion tests on patients with auto-antibodies, the following problems may arise:

1. Cold-reactive autoantibodies can cause autoagglutination, resulting in erroneous determinations of ABO and Rh type.
2. Red cells strongly coated with globulins may undergo spontaneous agglutination with high-protein, anti-Rh, blood-typing reagents, and occasionally even with low-protein reagents.[41]
3. The presence of free autoantibody in the serum may make antibody detection and crossmatching tests difficult to interpret. If time permits, the presence or absence of unexpected, clinically important alloantibody(ies) should be determined (see Methods 4.9 through 4.12) before blood is transfused.

Although resolving these serologic problems is important, delaying transfusion in the hope of finding serologically compatible blood may cause greater danger to the patient in some cases. Only clinical judgment can resolve this dilemma; therefore, dialogue with the patient's physician is important.

Resolution of ABO Problems

There are several approaches to the resolution of ABO typing problems associated with cold-reactive autoagglutinins. Often, it is only necessary to maintain the blood sample at 37 C immediately after collection and to wash the red cells with warm (37 C) saline before testing. It is helpful to perform a parallel control test, using 6% to 10% bovine albumin in saline, to determine if autoagglutination persists. If the control test is nonreactive, the results obtained with anti-A and anti-B are usually valid. If autoagglutination still occurs, it may be necessary to treat the red cells with sulfhydryl reagents.

Because cold-reactive autoagglutinins are almost always IgM and sulfhydryl reagents denature IgM molecules, reagents such as 2-mercaptoethanol (2-ME) or dithiothreitol (DTT) can be used to abolish autoagglutination (see Method 2.11). Treating the red cells with ZZAP reagent as in the preparation for adsorptions can also be used (see Method 4.10). Appropriate controls are essential for all tests.

When the serum agglutinates group O reagent red cells, the results of serum tests may be unreliable. Repeating the tests using prewarmed serum and group A, B, and O red cells at 37 C will often resolve any discrepancy, but weak anti-A and/or -B in some patients' sera may not react at 37 C. Alternatively, adsorbed serum (either auto-adsorbed or adsorbed with allogeneic group O red cells) can be used. Because rabbit red cells express a B-like antigen, sera adsorbed with rabbit red cells or stroma may not contain anti-B, and sera adsorbed in this manner should not be used for ABO serum tests.

Resolution of Rh Problems

Autoagglutination of red cells by cold- or spontaneous agglutination of red cells by warm-reactive autoantibodies may also cause discrepant Rh typing. The same procedures described for the resolution of ABO problems, with the exception of using ZZAP-treated red cells, may be useful. Also, IgG antibody can be dissociated from the cells by treatment with chloroquine diphosphate (Method 2.13), or by glycine-HCl/EDTA (Method 2.14), methods that leave red cells intact for subsequent typing. IgM-coated cells can be treated with sulfhydryl reagents (such as 2-ME or DTT, Method 2.11) to circumvent autoagglutination and spontaneous agglutination.

Detection of Alloantibodies in the Presence of Warm-Reactive Autoantibodies

If the patient who has warm-reactive autoantibodies in the serum needs transfusion, it is important to evaluate the possible simultaneous presence of alloantibodies to red cell antigens. Some alloantibodies may make their presence known by reacting more strongly or at different phases than the autoantibody, but quite often studies may not suggest the existence of masked alloantibodies.[29] It is helpful to know which of the common red cell antigens are lacking on the patient's red cells, to predict which clinically significant alloantibodies the patient may have produced or may produce. Antigens absent from autologous cells could well be the target of present or future alloantibodies. When the red cells are coated with IgG, antiglobulin-reactive reagents cannot be used to test IgG-coated cells unless the IgG is first removed (see Methods 2.13 and 2.14). Low-protein antisera (eg, monoclonal reagents) that do not require an antiglobulin test may be helpful in typing the DAT-positive red cells. Cell separation procedures (see Methods 2.15 and 2.16) may be necessary if the patient has been transfused recently.

Methods to detect alloantibodies in the presence of warm-reactive autoantibodies attempt to remove, reduce, or circumvent the autoantibody. Antibody detection methods that use PEG, enzymes, column agglutination, or solid-phase red cell adherence generally enhance autoantibodies. Testing LISS- or saline-suspended red cells may avoid autoantibodies but allow detection of most significant alloantibodies. Other procedures involve adsorption, the principles of which are discussed in Chapter 19. Two widely used approaches are discussed below.

Autologous Adsorption

In a patient who has not been recently transfused, autologous adsorption (see Method 4.9) is the best way to detect alloantibodies in the presence of warm-reactive autoantibodies. The adsorbed serum can be used in the routine antibody detection procedure.

Autoadsorption generally requires some initial preparation of the patient's red cells. At 37 C, in-vivo adsorption will have occurred and all antigen sites on the patient's own red cells may be blocked. It may be necessary, therefore, to remove autoantibody from the red cells to make sites available for adsorption. A gentle heat elution at 56 C for 5 minutes can dissociate some of the bound IgG. This can be followed by treatment of the autologous red cells with proteolytic enzymes to increase their capacity to adsorb autoantibody. Treatment of the red cells with ZZAP, a mixture of papain or ficin and DTT (see Method 4.9) accomplishes both of these actions in one step; the sulfhydryl component makes the IgG molecules more susceptible to the protease and dissociates the antibody molecules from the cell. Multiple sequential autoadsorptions with new aliquots of red cells may be necessary if the serum contains high levels of autoantibody. Once the autoantibody has been removed, the adsorbed serum is examined for alloantibody activity.

If the patient is to be transfused, it can be advantageous to collect and save additional aliquots of pretransfusion cells, to be used for later adsorptions.

Autologous adsorption is not recommended for patients who have been recently transfused, because they may have an admixture of transfused red cells that might adsorb alloantibody. Red cells normally live for about 110 to 120 days. In patients with AIHA, autologous and transfused red cells can be expected to have shortened survival. However, determining how long transfused red cells remain in circulation in patients who need repeated transfusions is not feasible. It has been demonstrated that very small amounts (<10%) of antigen-positive red cells are capable of removing alloantibody reactivity in in-vitro studies[42]; therefore, it is recommended to wait for 3 months after transfusion before autologous adsorptions are performed.

Allogeneic Adsorption

The use of allogeneic red cells for adsorption may be helpful when the patient has been recently transfused or when insufficient autologous red cells are available. The goal is to remove autoantibody and leave the alloantibody in the adsorbed serum. The adsorbing cells must not have the antigens against which the alloantibodies react. Because alloantibody specificity is unknown, red cells of different phenotypes will usually be used to adsorb several aliquots of the patient's serum.

Given the number of potential alloantibodies, the task of selecting cells may appear formidable. However, the selected cells need only demonstrate those few alloantibodies of clinical significance likely to be present. These include the common Rh antigens (D, C, E, c, and e), K, Fy^a and Fy^b, Jk^a and Jk^b, and S and s. Cell selection is made easier by the fact that some antigens can be destroyed by appropriate treatment (eg, with enzymes) before use in adsorption procedures. Antibodies to high-incidence antigens cannot be excluded by allogeneic

adsorptions because the adsorbing cells will almost invariably express the antigen and adsorb the alloantibody along with autoantibody.

Patient's Phenotype Unknown. When the patient's phenotype is not known, group O red cell samples of three different Rh phenotypes (R_1R_1, R_2R_2, and rr) should be selected (see Method 4.10). One should lack Jk^a and another Jk^b. If treated with ZZAP, these cells would also lack all antigens of the Kell system and enzyme-sensitive antigens (see Table 19-3). If ZZAP is not available, cells treated only with proteolytic enzyme can be used, but at least one of the adsorbing cells must be K– because Kell system antigens will not be destroyed. Untreated cells may be used, but antibody may be more difficult to remove and the adsorbing cells must, at a minimum, include at least one negative for the S, s, Fy^a, Fy^b, and K antigens in addition to the Rh and Kidd requirements above.

Each aliquot may need to be adsorbed two or three times. The fully adsorbed aliquots are tested against reagent red cells known either to lack or to carry common antigens of the Rh, MNS, Kidd, Kell, and Duffy blood group systems. If an adsorbed aliquot is reactive, that aliquot (or an additional specimen similarly adsorbed) should be tested to identify the antibody. Adsorbing several aliquots with different red cell samples provides a battery of potentially informative specimens. For example, if the aliquot adsorbed with Jk(a–) red cells subsequently reacts only with Jk(a+) red cells, the presence of alloanti-Jk^a can confidently be inferred.

Patient's Phenotype Known. If the patient's Rh and Kidd phenotypes are known or can be determined, adsorption can be performed with a single sample of allogeneic ZZAP-treated red cells of the same Rh and Kidd phenotypes as the patient (see Method 4.11).

Problems Encountered. Occasionally autoantibody will not be removed by three sequential adsorptions. Further adsorptions can be done, but multiple adsorptions have the potential to dilute the serum. If the adsorbing cells do not appear to remove the antibody, the autoantibody may have an unusual specificity that does not react with the cells used for adsorption. For example, autoantibodies with Kell, LW, or En^{a}FS specificity would not be removed by ZZAP-treated cells (see Table 19-3 for a list of antigens altered by various agents).

Autoantibodies Mimicking Alloantibodies

Sometimes, autoantibodies have patterns of reactivity that are easily mistaken for alloantibody. For example, the serum of a D– patient may have apparent anti-C and -e reactivity. The anti-C reactivity may reflect warm-reactive autoantibody even if the patient's cells lack C. The autoantibody nature of the reactivity can be demonstrated by autologous and allogeneic adsorption studies. In this case, the apparent alloanti-C would be adsorbed by C– red cells, both autologous and allogeneic. This is quite unlike the behavior of a true alloanti-C, which would be adsorbed only by C+ red cells. In one study,[43] the serum prepared from an initial autoadsorption would often retain autoantibodies that mimicked alloantibodies in addition to the true alloantibody(ies) present. Serum prepared from an initial alloadsorption most often contains only alloantibodies. The differences in the auto- or alloantibody nature of specificities detected in the autoadsorbed serum as compared to the alloadsorbed serum reflect an inefficiency of autologous adsorption. This is primarily due to limited volumes of autologous cells available for removing all autoantibody reactivity from the serum.[43]

Detection of Alloantibodies in the Presence of Cold-Reactive Autoantibodies

Cold-reactive autoagglutinins rarely mask clinically significant alloantibodies if serum tests are conducted at 37 C and if IgG-specific reagents are used for the antiglobulin phase. In rare instances, it may be necessary to perform autoadsorption at 4 C (see Method 4.6). Achieving the complete removal of potent cold-reactive autoagglutinins is very time-consuming and is usually unnecessary. Removal of sufficient cold autoagglutinins may be facilitated by treating the patient's cells with enzymes or ZZAP before adsorption.

Drug-Induced Immune Hemolytic Anemia

Drugs sometimes induce the formation of antibodies, either against the drug itself or against intrinsic red cell antigens, that may result in a positive DAT, immune red cell destruction, or both. Some of the antibodies produced appear to be dependent on the presence of the drug (ie, drug dependent) for their detection or destructive capability, whereas others do not (ie, drug independent). In some instances, a reactive DAT may result from nonimmunologic effects of the drugs. Drugs that have been reported to cause hemolytic anemia and/or a positive DAT are listed in Appendix 20-2.

Theories of the Immune Response and Drug-Dependent Antibodies

Numerous theories have been suggested to explain how drugs induce immune responses and what relation such responses may have to the positive DAT and immune-mediated cell destruction observed in some patients. For many years, drug-associated positive DATs were classified into four mechanisms: drug adsorption (penicillin-type), immune complex formation, autoantibody production, and nonspecific adsorption. Such classification has been useful, but many aspects lacked definitive proof. In addition, some drugs created immune problems involving aspects of more than one mechanism. More recent theories, still unproven, tend toward a more comprehensive approach.[44-48]

Most drugs are probably capable of binding loosely, or firmly, to circulating cells, which can lead to an immune response. Figure 20-1 illustrates this concept. Antibodies can be formed to the drug itself or to the drug plus membrane components. When an antibody is formed to the drug plus membrane components, the antibody may recognize primarily the drug or primarily the membrane. One or all three of these antibody populations may be present.

Serologic and Clinical Classification

Drug-induced antibodies can be classified into three groups according to their clinical and serologic characteristics.[3] In one group, the drug binds firmly to the cell membrane and antibody is apparently largely directed against the drug itself. This was called the drug adsorption mechanism. Antibodies to penicillin are the best described of this group.

The second group of drug-dependent antibodies reacts with drugs that do not bind well to the cell membrane (eg, quinidine, ceftriaxone). The reactive mechanism of these antibodies was previously thought to be due to drug/antidrug immune complex formation, but the theory has never been proven.[48] Antibodies in this group may cause acute intravascular hemolysis and may be difficult to demonstrate serologically. Testing for this type of drug antibody

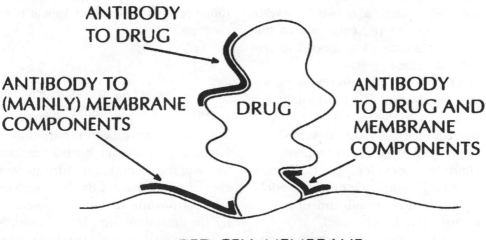

ANTIBODY TO DRUG

ANTIBODY TO (MAINLY) MEMBRANE COMPONENTS

DRUG

ANTIBODY TO DRUG AND MEMBRANE COMPONENTS

RED CELL MEMBRANE

Figure 20-1. Proposed unifying theory of drug-induced antibody reactions (based on a cartoon by Habibi as cited by Garratty[23]). The thicker darker lines represent antigen-binding sites on the F(ab) region of the drug-induced antibody. Drugs (haptens) bind loosely, or firmly, to cell membranes and antibodies may be made to: a) the drug [producing in-vitro reactions typical of a drug adsorption (penicillin-type) reaction]; b) membrane components, or mainly membrane components (producing in-vitro reactions typical of autoantibody); or c) part-drug, part-membrane components (producing an in-vitro reaction typical of the so-called immune complex mechanism).[23(p55)]

is still referred to as the "immune complex" method.

Antibodies of the third group (eg, methyldopa, procainamide, and fludarabine) have serologic reactivity independent of the drug, despite the fact that it was the drug that originally induced the immune response. Serologically, they behave as autoantibodies.

Drug-Dependent Antibodies Reactive with Drug-Treated Red Cells: Penicillin-Type Antibodies

The clinical and laboratory features of drug-induced immune hemolytic anemia operating through this mechanism are:

1. The DAT is strongly positive due to IgG coating. Complement coating may also be present.
2. Antibody eluted from the patient's red cells reacts with drug-treated red cells but not with untreated red cells.
3. The serum contains a high-titer IgG antibody (especially when the target is penicillin or cefotetan) reactive with the drug-treated red cells but not with the untreated red cells, unless the patient also has alloantibodies to red cell antigens.
4. For penicillin, the hemolysis-inducing dose is millions of units daily for a week or more; for other drugs, eg, cefotetan, a single 1 to 2 g dose has been implicated in immune hemolysis.
5. Hemolysis develops gradually but may be life-threatening if the etiology is unrecognized and drug administration is continued.
6. Discontinuation of the drug is usually followed by increased cell survival, although hemolysis of decreasing severity may persist for several weeks.

Approximately 3% of patients receiving large doses of penicillin intravenously (ie, millions of units per day) will develop a positive DAT; only occasionally will these patients develop hemolytic anemia.[6(p231)] A possible mechanism for the positive DAT is given in Fig 20-2. The penicillin becomes covalently linked to the red cells in vivo. If the patient has antibodies to penicillin, they bind to the penicillin bound to the red cells. The result is that the penicillin-coated red cells become coated with IgG. If cell destruction occurs, it takes place extravascularly, probably in the same way that red cells coated with IgG alloantibodies are destroyed. Intravascular hemolysis is rare.

Many cephalosporins, which are related to penicillins, behave in a similar manner. The cephalosporins are generally classified by "generations," based on their effectiveness against gram-negative organisms (see Table 20-4). Approximately 4% of patients receiving first- or second-generation cephalosporins develop a positive DAT.[48] Dramatically reduced red cell survival has been associated with second- and third-generation cephalosporins.[12,47,49-53] The prevalence and severity of cephalosporin-induced immune red cell destruction appear to be increasing.[3]

Drug-Dependent Antibodies Reacting by the "Immune Complex" Mechanism

Many drugs have been reported as causing hemolytic anemia by this mechanism. Some of the second- and third-generation cephalosporins react by this mechanism; anti-ceftriaxone has been detected only by the immune complex method.[49] The following observations are characteristic:

1. Complement may be the only globulin easily detected on the red cells, but IgG may be present.
2. The serum antibody can be either IgM or IgG, or IgM with IgG.
3. A drug (or metabolite) must be present in vitro for demonstration of the

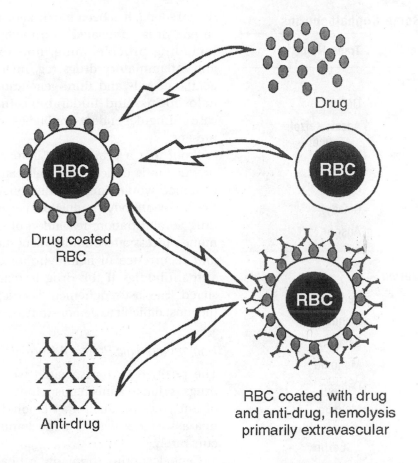

Drug

RBC

Drug coated
RBC

RBC

Anti-drug

RBC coated with drug
and anti-drug, hemolysis
primarily extravascular

Figure 20-2. The drug-adsorption mechanism. The drug binds tightly to the red cell membrane proteins. If a patient develops a potent drug antibody, it will react with the cell-bound drug. Such red cells will yield a positive result in the DAT using anti-IgG reagents. Complement is usually not activated and lysis is primarily extravascular in nature. Penicillin-G is the prototype drug.

antibody in the patient's serum. Antibodies may cause hemolysis, agglutination, and/or sensitization of red cells in the presence of the drug.

4. The patient need only take a small amount of the drug.

5. Acute intravascular hemolysis with hemoglobinemia and hemoglobinuria is the usual presentation. Renal failure is quite common.

6. Once antibody has been formed, severe hemolytic episodes may recur after exposure to very small quantities of the drug.

Drug-Independent Antibodies: Autoantibody Production

Some drugs induce autoantibodies that appear serologically indistinguishable from those of WAIHA. Red cells are coated with IgG, and the eluate as well as the serum react with virtually all cells tested in the absence of the drug. Blood group specificity has been demonstrated at times, similar to that seen in AIHA. The antibody has no in-vitro activity with the drug, directly or indirectly.

The best studied of such cases are those induced by α-methyldopa. A closely related

Table 20-4. Some Cephalosporins

Generic Name	Trade Name*
First Generation	
cefadroxil	Duricef
cefazolin	Ancef, Kefzol, Zolicef
cephalexin	Keflex
cephalothin	Keflin
cephapirin	Cefadyl
cephradine	Anspor
Second Generation	
cefaclor	Ceclor
cefamandole	Mandol
cefmetazole	Zefazone
cefonicid	Monocid
cefotetan	Cefotan
cefoxitin	Mefoxin
cefuroxime	Zinacef, Kefurox, Ceftin
cefuroxime axetil	Ceftin
Third Generation	
cefixime	Suprax
cefoperazone	Cefobid
cefotaxime	Claforan
ceftazidime	Fortaz, Ceptaz, Pentacef, Tazicef, Tazidime
ceftizoxime	Ceftizox
ceftriaxone	Rocephin
Fourth Generation	
cefepime	Maxipime

*Several forms are marketed under other trade names. This list is intended to be informative, not inclusive.

drug, L-dopa, has been implicated, as have several drugs unrelated to α-methyldopa, including procainamide, nonsteroidal anti-inflammatory drugs (eg, mefenamic acid), second- and third-generation cephalosporins, and fludarabine. In some cases, drug-dependent antibodies are also present.

Proof that a drug causes autoantibody production is difficult to obtain. Sufficient evidence would include: demonstration that autoantibody production began after drug administration; resolution of the immune process after withdrawal of the drug; *and* recurrence of hemolytic anemia or autoantibodies if the drug is readministered. The last requirement is crucial and the most difficult to demonstrate.

Nonimmunologic Protein Adsorption

The positive DAT associated with some drugs is due to a mechanism independent of antibody production. Hemolytic anemia associated with this mechanism occurs rarely.

Cephalosporins (primarily cephalothin) are the drugs with which this was originally associated. Red cells coated with cephalothin (Keflin) and incubated with normal plasma will adsorb albumin, IgA, IgG, IgM, and C3 in a nonimmunologic manner. If this occurs, a positive indirect antiglobulin test will be seen with AHG reagents.

Other drugs that may cause nonimmunologic adsorption of proteins and a positive DAT include diglycoaldehyde, suramin, cisplatin, clavulanate (in Timentin and Augmentin), sulbactam in Unasyn,[54] and tazobactam (in Tazocin and Zosyn).[55,56]

Laboratory Investigation of Drug-Induced Antibodies

The drug-related problems most commonly encountered in the blood bank are those associated with a positive DAT. Typical DAT results are shown in Table 20-3. Recent red cell transfusions and/or dramatic hemolysis may result in a weak DAT by the time hemolysis is suspected.

The patient's serum should be tested for unexpected antibodies by routine procedures. If the serum does not react with untreated red cells, the tests should be repeated against ABO-compatible red cells in the presence of the drug(s) suspected of causing the problem. Techniques are given in Method 4.14 and Method 4.15.

If the drug has already been reported as causing hemolytic anemia, testing methods may be available in the case reports. If such information is not available, an initial screening test can be performed with a solution of the drug at a concentration of approximately 1 mg/mL in phosphate-buffered saline at a pH optimal for solubility of the drug.

If these tests are not informative, attempts can be made to coat normal red cells with the drug, and the patient's serum and an eluate from the patient's red cells can be tested against the drug-coated red cells. This is the method of choice when penicillin or cephalosporins are thought to be implicated. Results definitive for a penicillin-induced positive DAT are reactivity of the eluate against penicillin-coated red cells and absence of reactivity between the eluate and uncoated red cells.

The immune response may be due to a metabolite of a drug rather than the drug itself. If the clinical picture is consistent with immune-mediated hemolysis and the above tests are noninformative, it may be helpful to test drug metabolites (see Method 4.16).

Normal sera commonly agglutinate and/or sensitize cephalosporin-treated red cells due to the nonspecific uptake of protein discussed above. This problem can be overcome by testing a 1 in 20 dilution of the patient's serum and a normal serum control against the cephalosporin-treated red cells.

During the testing of cefotetan-treated red cells, a 1 in 100 dilution of the patient's serum should be tested because it has been shown that some normal sera appear to contain "naturally occurring" antibodies to cefotetan, some of which still react weakly at a 1 in 20 dilution.[57,58] Cefotetan antibodies associated with drug-induced immune hemolytic anemia have very high antiglobulin titers (4000 to 256,000).[49]

Two other observations have been made regarding the testing of cefotetan antibodies: 1) the last wash from the eluate preparation may react with cefotetan-treated red cells (possibly due to the high-titer antibodies and/or the antibody affinity), and 2) drug-independent antibodies may be detected in the serum and eluate and hemolysis may be inadvertently attributed to idiopathic WAIHA.[49]

References

1. Toy PT, Chin CA, Reid ME, Burns MA. Factors associated with positive direct antiglobulin tests in pretransfusion patients: A case control study. Vox Sang 1985;49:215-20.
2. Heddle NM, Kelton JG, Turchyn KL, Ali MAM. Hypergammaglobulinemia can be associated with a positive direct antiglobulin test, a nonreactive eluate, and no evidence of hemolysis. Transfusion 1988;28:29-33.
3. Petz LD, Garratty G. Immune hemolytic anemias. 2nd ed. Philadelphia: Churchill Livingstone, 2004.
4. Garratty G. The significance of IgG on the red cell surface. Transfus Med Rev 1987;1:47-57.
5. Freedman J. The significance of complement on the red cell surface. Transfus Med Rev 1987;1:58-70.
6. Mollison PL, Engelfriet CP, Contreras M. Blood transfusion in clinical medicine. 10th ed. Oxford, England: Blackwell Scientific Publications, 1997.
7. Clark JA, Tanley PC, Wallas CH. Evaluation of patients with positive direct antiglobulin tests and nonreactive eluates discovered during pretransfusion testing. Immunohematology 1992;8:9-12.
8. Silva MA, ed. Standards for blood banks and transfusion services. 23rd ed. Bethesda, MD: AABB, 2005.

9.   Judd WJ, Barnes BA, Steiner EA, et al. The evaluation of a positive direct antiglobulin test (autocontrol) in pretransfusion testing revisited. Transfusion 1986;26:220-4.

10. Salama A, Mueller-Eckhardt C. Delayed hemolytic transfusion reactions. Evidence for complement activation involving allogeneic and autologous red cells. Transfusion 1984; 24:188-93.

11. Ness PM, Shirey RS, Thoman SK, Buck SA. The differentiation of delayed serologic and delayed hemolytic transfusion reactions: Incidence, long-term serologic findings, and clinical significance. Transfusion 1990;30: 688-93.

12. Garratty G. Immune cytopenia associated with antibiotics. Transfus Med Rev 1993;7:255-67.

13. Kleinman S, Nelson R, Smith L, Goldfinger D. Positive direct antiglobulin tests and immune hemolytic anemia in patients receiving procainamide. N Engl J Med 1984;311:809-12.

14. Lutz P, Dzik W. Very high incidence of a positive direct antiglobulin test (+DAT) in patients receiving Unasyn® (abstract). Transfusion 1992;32(Suppl):23S.

15. Garratty G. Problems associated with passively transfused blood group alloantibodies. Am J Clin Pathol 1998;109:769-77.

16. Leger RM, Arndt PA, Ciesielski DJ, Garratty G. False-positive eluate reactivity due to the low-ionic wash solution used with commercial acid-elution kits. Transfusion 1998;38: 565-72.

17. Judd WJ. Elution—dissociation of antibody from red blood cells: Theoretical and practical considerations. Transfus Med Rev 1999; 13:297-310.

18. South SF, Rea AE, Tregellas WM. An evaluation of 11 red cell elution procedures. Transfusion 1986;26:167-70.

19. Sokol RJ, Hewitt S, Stamps BK. Autoimmune haemolysis: An 18 year study of 865 cases referred to a regional transfusion centre. Br Med J 1981;282:2023-7.

20. Shulman IA, Branch DR, Nelson JM, et al. Autoimmune hemolytic anemia with both cold and warm autoantibodies. JAMA 1985;253: 1746-8.

21. Göttsche B, Salama A, Mueller-Eckhardt C. Donath-Landsteiner autoimmune hemolytic anemia in children. A study of 22 cases. Vox Sang 1990;58:281-6.

22. Sokol RJ, Hewitt S, Stamps BK. Autoimmune haemolysis. Mixed warm and cold antibody type. Acta Haematol 1983;69:266-74.

23. Garratty G. Target antigens for red-cell-bound autoantibodies. In: Nance SJ, ed. Clinical and basic science aspects of immunohematology. Arlington, VA: AABB, 1991:33-72.

24. Garratty G. Specificity of autoantibodies reacting optimally at 37 C. Immunohematology 1999;15:24-40.

25. Freedman J, Wright J, Lim FC, Garvey MB. Hemolytic warm IgM autoagglutinins in autoimmune hemolytic anemia. Transfusion 1987;27:464-7.

26. Judd WJ. Investigation and management of immune hemolysis: Autoantibodies and drugs. In: Wallace ME, Levitt JS, eds. Current applications and interpretations of the direct antiglobulin test. Arlington, VA: AABB, 1988:47-103.

27. Leger RM, Garratty G. Evaluation of methods for detecting alloantibodies underlying warm autoantibodies. Transfusion 1999;39:11-16.

28. Branch DR, Petz LD. Detecting alloantibodies in patients with autoantibodies (editorial). Transfusion 1999;39:6-10.

29. Church AT, Nance SJ, Kavitsky DM. Predicting the presence of a new alloantibody underlying a warm autoantibody (abstract). Transfusion 2000;40(Suppl):121S.

30. Shirey RS, Boyd JS, Parwani AV, et al. Prophylactic antigen-matched donor blood for patients with warm autoantibodies: An algorithm for transfusion management. Transfusion 2002;42:1436-41.

31. Garratty G, Petz LD. Approaches to selecting blood for transfusion to patients with autoimmune hemolytic anemia (editorial). Transfusion 2002;42:1390-2.

32. Garratty G, Arndt P, Domen R, et al. Severe autoimmune hemolytic anemia associated with IgM warm autoantibodies directed against determinants on or associated with glycophorin A. Vox Sang 1997;72:124-30.

33. Garratty G, Arndt P, Leger R. Serological findings in autoimmune hemolytic anemia associated with IgM warm autoantibodies (abstract). Blood 2001;98(Suppl 1):61a.

34. Nowak-Wegrzyn A, King KE, Shirey RS, et al. Fatal warm autoimmune hemolytic anemia resulting from IgM autoagglutinins in an infant with severe combined immunodeficiency. J Pediatr Hematol Oncol 2001;23:250-2.

35. Garratty G, Petz LD, Hoops JK. The correlation of cold agglutinin titrations in saline and albumin with haemolytic anemia. Br J Haematol 1975;35:587-95.

36. Marks MR, Reid ME, Ellisor SS. Adsorption of unwanted cold autoagglutinins by formaldehyde-treated rabbit erythrocytes (abstract). Transfusion 1980;20:629.

37. Dzik W, Yang R, Blank J. Rabbit erythrocyte stroma treatment of serum interferes with recognition of delayed hemolytic transfusion reactions (letter). Transfusion 1986;26:303-4.

38. Mechanic SA, Maurer JL, Igoe MJ, et al. Anti-Vel reactivity diminished by adsorption with rabbit RBC stroma. Transfusion 2002;42:1180-3.

39. Garratty G, Arndt PA, Leger RM. Serological findings in autoimmune hemolytic anemia (AIHA) associated with both warm and cold autoantibodies (abstract). Blood 2003;102 (Suppl 1):563a.

40. Garratty G. Autoimmune hemolytic anemia. In: Garratty G, ed. Immunobiology of transfusion medicine. New York: Marcel Dekker, 1994:493-521.

41. Garratty G, Postoway N, Nance SJ, Brunt DJ. Spontaneous agglutination of red cells with a positive direct antiglobulin test in various media. Transfusion 1984;24:214-7.

42. Laine EP, Leger RM, Arndt PA, et al. In vitro studies of the impact of transfusion on the detection of alloantibodies after autoadsorption. Transfusion 2000;40:1384-7.

43. Issitt PD, Combs MR, Bumgarner DJ, et al. Studies of antibodies in the sera of patients who have made red cell autoantibodies. Transfusion 1996;36:481-6.

44. Salama A, Mueller-Eckhardt C. Immune-mediated blood cell dyscrasias related to drugs. Semin Hematol 1992;29:54-63.

45. Petz LD, Mueller-Eckhardt C. Drug-induced immune hemolytic anemia. Transfusion 1992;32:202-4.

46. Shulman NR, Reid DM. Mechanisms of drug-induced immunologically mediated cytopenias. Transfus Med Rev 1993;7:215-29.

47. Christie DJ. Specificity of drug-induced immune cytopenias. Transfus Med Rev 1993;7:230-41.

48. Garratty G. Drug-induced immune hemolytic anemia. In: Garratty G, ed. Immunobiology of transfusion medicine. New York: Marcel Dekker, 1994:523-51.

49. Arndt PA, Leger RM, Garratty G. Serology of antibodies to second- and third-generation cephalosporins associated with immune hemolytic anemia and/or positive direct antiglobulin tests. Transfusion 1999;39:1239-46.

50. Gallagher NI, Schergen AK, Sokol-Anderson ML, et al. Severe immune-mediated hemolytic anemia secondary to treatment with cefotetan. Transfusion 1992;32:266-8.

51. Garratty G, Nance S, Lloyd M, Domen R. Fatal immune hemolytic anemia due to cefotetan. Transfusion 1992;32:269-71.

52. Stroncek D, Procter JL, Johnson J. Drug-induced hemolysis: Cefotetan-dependent hemolytic anemia mimicking an acute intravascular immune transfusion reaction. Am J Hematol 2000;64:67-70.

53. Viraraghavan R, Chakravarty AG, Soreth J. Cefotetan-induced haemolytic anaemia. A review of 85 cases. Adv Drug React Toxicol Rev 2002;21:101-7.

54. Garratty G, Arndt PA. Positive direct antiglobulin tests and haemolytic anemia following therapy with beta-lactamase inhibitor containing drugs may be associated with non-immunologic adsorption of protein onto red blood cells. Br J Haematol 1998;100:777-83.

55. Broadberry RE, Farren TW, Kohler JA, et al. Haemolytic anaemia associated with Tazobactam (abstract). Vox Sang 2002;83(Suppl 2):227.

56. Arndt PA, Leger RM, Garratty G. Positive direct antiglobulin tests and haemolytic anaemia following therapy with the beta-lactamase inhibitor, tazobactam, may also be associated with non-immunologic adsorption of protein onto red blood cells (letter). Vox Sang 2003;85: 53.

57. Arndt P, Garratty G. Is severe immune hemolytic anemia, following a single dose of cefotetan, associated with the presence of "naturally-occurring" anti-cefotetan? (abstract) Transfusion 2001;41(Suppl):24S.

58. Arndt PA. Practical aspects of investigating drug-induced immune hemolytic anemia due to cefotetan or ceftriaxone—a case study approach. Immunohematology 2002;18:27-32.

Suggested Reading

Dacie J. Historical review. The immune haemolytic anaemias: A century of exciting progress in understanding. Br J Haematol 2001;114:770-85.

Engelfriet CP, Overbeeke MAM, von dem Borne AEGKr. Autoimmune hemolytic anemia. Semin Hematol 1992;29:3-12.

Garratty G. Novel mechanisms for immune destruction of circulating autologous cells. In: Silberstein LE, ed. Autoimmune disorders of blood. Bethesda, MD: AABB, 1996:79-114.

Garratty G. Autoantibodies induced by blood transfusion (editorial). Transfusion 2004:445-9.

Mack P, Freedman J. Autoimmune hemolytic anemia: A history. Transfus Med Rev 2000;14:223-33.

Petz LD, Garratty G. Immune hemolytic anemias. 2nd ed. Philadelphia: Churchill Livingstone, 2004.

Petz LD. A physician's guide to transfusion in autoimmune haemolytic anaemia. Br J Haematol 2004; 124:712-16.

Appendix 20-1. An Example of an Algorithm for Investigating a Positive DAT (Excluding Investigation of HDFN)

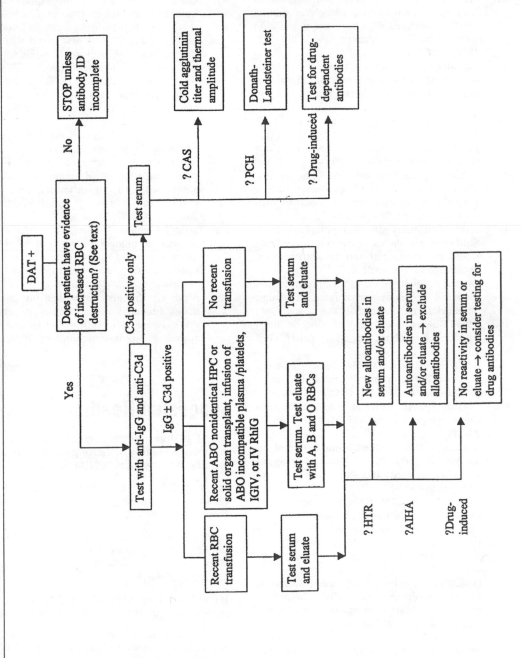

Appendix 20-2. Some Drugs Associated with Immune Hemolysis and/or Positive DATs Due to Drug-Induced Antibodies

Drug	Therapeutic Category	Possible Mechanism
Acetaminophen	Analgesic, antipyretic	DD-IC
Aminopyrine	Analgesic, antipyretic	DD-IC
Amphotericin B	Antifungal, antibiotic	DD-IC
Ampicillin	Antibacterial	DD-IC
Antazoline	Antihistamine	DD-IC
Apazone (azapropazone)	Anti-inflammatory, analgesic	DI, DD-DA
Buthiazide (butizide)	Diuretic, antihypertensive	DD-IC
Carbenicillin	Antibacterial	DD-DA
Carbimazole	Thyroid inhibitor	DD-IC
Carboplatin	Antineoplastic	DD-DA, DD-IC
Carbromal	Sedative; hypnotic	DD-DA
Catergen	Diarrheal astringent, treatment of hepatic disease	DI
Cephalosporins	Antibacterials	
First generation		NIA, DD-DA
Second generation		DD-IC, DD-DA, DI
Third generation		DD-IC, DD-DA, DI
Chaparral		DI
Chlorpropamide	Antidiabetic	DD-IC
Chlorpromazine	Antipsychotic	DI, DD-IC
Cisplatin	Antineoplastic	NIA
Cladribine (chlorodeoxyadenosine)	Antineoplastic	DI
Clavulanate potassium	β-lactamase inhibitor/antibacterial	NIA
Cyanidanol		DI, DD-DA, DD-IC
Cyclofenil	Gonad-stimulating principle	DI
Cyclosporine	Immunosuppressive	DI
Diclofenac	Anti-inflammatory	DI, DD-IC
Diethylstilbestrol	Estrogen	DD-IC
Diglycoaldehyde	Antineoplastic	NIA
Dipyrone	Analgesic, antipyretic	DD-IC, DD-DA
Elliptinium acetate	Antineoplastic	DD-IC
Erythromycin	Antibacterial	DD-DA
Etodolac	Anti-inflammatory, analgesic	IC
Fenfluramine	Anorexic	?
Fenoprofen	Anti-inflammatory, analgesic	DI, DD-IC
Fludarabine	Antineoplastic	DI
Fluorescein	Injectable dye	DD-DA, DD-IC
Fluorouracil	Antineoplastic	DD-IC
Glafenine	Analgesic	DI, DD-IC
Hydralazine	Antihypertensive	DD-IC
Hydrochlorothiazide	Diuretic	DD-IC
Ibuprofen	Anti-inflammatory	DI
Insulin	Antidiabetic	DD-DA?, DD-IC
Interferon	Antineoplastic, antiviral	DI
Isoniazid	Antibacterial, tuberculostatic	DD-DA?, DD-IC
Levodopa	Antiparkinsonian, anticholinergic	DI
Mefenamic acid	Anti-inflammatory	DI
Mefloquine	Antimalarial	DD-IC

(cont'd)

Appendix 20-2. Some Drugs Associated with Immune Hemolysis and/or Positive DATs Due to Drug-Induced Antibodies (cont'd)

Drug	Therapeutic Category	Possible Mechanism
Melphalan	Antineoplastic	DD-IC
6-Mercaptopurine	Antineoplastic	DD-DA
Methadone	Narcotic analgesic	?
Methicillin	Antibacterial	DD-DA
Methotrexate	Antineoplastic, antimetabolite	DD-IC
Methyldopa	Antihypertensive	DI
Moxalactam (latamoxef)	Antibacterial	DD-IC, DI
Nafcillin	Antibacterial	DD-DA
Nomifensine	Antidepressant	DI, DD-IC
p-Aminosalicylic acid	Antitubercular	DD-IC
Penicillin G	Antibacterial	DD-DA
Phenacetin	Analgesic, antipyretic	DI, DD-IC
Piperacillin	Antibacterial	DD-DA, DD-IC
Podophyllotoxin	Antineoplastic, cathartic	?
Probenecid	Uricosuric	DD-IC
Procainamide	Cardiac depressant, antiarrhythmic	DI
Propyphenazone	Analgesic, antipyretic, anti-inflammatory	DD-IC
Pyramidon	Analgesic, antipyretic	DD-IC
Quinidine	Cardiac depressant, antiarrhythmic	DD-DA, DD-IC
Quinine	Antimalarial	DD-IC
Ranitidine	Antagonist (to histamine H_2 receptors)	?
Rifampin (rifampicin)	Antibacterial, antitubercular	DD-IC
Sodium pentothal	Anesthetic	DD-IC
Stibophen	Antischistosomal	DD-IC
Streptomycin	Antibacterial, tuberculostatic	DI, DD-DA, DD-IC
Sulbactam sodium	β-lactamase inhibitor/antibacterial	NIA
Sulfonamides	Antibiotics	DD-IC
Sulfonylurea derivatives	Antidiabetic	DD-IC
Sulindac	Anti-inflammatory	DD-DA, DI
Suprofen	Anti-inflammatory, analgesic	DD-IC, DI
Suramin	Antitrypanosomal, antifilarial	NIA
Temafloxacin	Antibacterial	DD-IC
Teniposide	Antineoplastic	DI, DD-IC
Tetracycline	Antibacterial, antirickettsial, antiamebic	DD-DA?, DD-IC
Thiopental	Anesthetic	DD-IC
Tolbutamide	Antidiabetic	DD-DA
Tolmetin	Anti-inflammatory	DI, DD-IC
Triamterene	Diuretic	DD-IC
Trimellitic anhydride	Used in preparation of dyes, resins, etc	?
Zomepirac	Analgesic, anti-inflammatory	DD-DA, DD-IC, DI

Mechanisms listed are based on descriptions in the literature.[3,44-48]
DAT = Direct antiglobulin test.
DD-DA = Drug-dependent. Drug adsorbed onto red cells; antibody reacts with drug on cells.
DD-IC = Drug-dependent. "Immune complex mechanism." Requires drug, serum, and red cells for serologic demonstration. For most of these drugs, there are only single or very few case reports.
DI = Drug-independent. Associated with autoantibodies similar to those in AIHA. Drug not required for in-vitro demonstration. Mechanisms of autoantibody production may vary.
NIA = Nonimmunologic adsorption of proteins.
? = Mechanism unclear or unknown.

Chapter 21

Blood Transfusion Practice

T HE DECISION TO transfuse, like any other therapeutic decision, should be based on the risks, benefits, and alternatives of treatment. Unfortunately, data regarding the indications for transfusion are frequently not available and recipients run the risk of both overtransfusion and undertransfusion. Transfusions based solely on laboratory test "triggers," in particular, are problematic. Consensus statements on the use of blood components such as those produced by the National Institutes of Health (NIH) help guide therapy but cannot substitute for clinical judgment.

Red Blood Cell Transfusion
Physiologic Principles

The primary indication for transfusion of Red Blood Cells (RBCs) is to restore or maintain oxygen-carrying capacity to meet tis-sue demands; transfusion to replace red cells destined for destruction in hemolytic disease of the newborn is discussed in Chapter 24. Because demand for oxygen varies greatly among different individuals in different clinical circumstances, measurement of only the hematocrit or the hemoglobin concentration ("the hemoglobin") cannot accurately assess the need for transfusion.[1-3]

Normal Oxygen Supply and Demand

Tissues at rest have a baseline demand for oxygen, particularly the heart, kidneys, brain, liver, and gastrointestinal tract; consumption by muscle is very low at rest. The oxygen content of blood (mL O_2/mL blood) is determined by the hemoglobin, the binding coefficient of hemoglobin for oxygen, the oxygen saturation of hemoglobin, and a small quantity of oxygen dissolved in the plasma. This is described as:

$$O_2 \text{ content} = (Hb \times 1.39 \times \%sat) + (pO_2 \times 0.003)$$

Tissue oxygen consumption is calculated as the difference between oxygen delivery in the arterial blood and oxygen return by the venous blood:

$$O_2 \text{ consumption} = \text{Cardiac output} \times Hb \times 1.39 \times (\%sat_{arterial} - \%sat_{venous})/100$$

which is expressed as

$$(\text{mL } O_2/\text{minute}) = L/\text{minute} \times g/L \times \text{mL } O_2/g$$

The oxygen saturation of arterial and venous hemoglobin varies with the partial pressure of oxygen. Under normal circumstances the pO_2 falls from 100 mm Hg in the arteries to 40 mm Hg in the veins as the tissues extract oxygen, and hemoglobin saturation falls from near 100% in the arteries to approximately 75% in the veins; thus, the oxygen extraction ratio is 0.25. That is, the hemoglobin "gives up" only 25% of its oxygen. When tissue demand for oxygen increases or the supply of oxygen decreases, the tissues extract a greater fraction of oxygen from the plasma and from hemoglobin; this results in a lower venous pO_2 and decreased oxygen saturation of the venous blood. Studies in primates suggest that a critical point of limited oxygen delivery is reached when the oxygen extraction ratio approaches twice normal or 0.50.[2]

Under normal resting conditions, the body has a large reserve of oxygen supply relative to demand. In the average adult, approximately 1000 mL/minute is available to the tissues and only 250 mL/minute is consumed as follows:

O_2 supply (Calculation assumes a hemoglobin of 140 g/L and a pO_2 of 100)

$$
\begin{aligned}
&= \text{Cardiac output} \times O_2 \text{ content}_{arterial}\\
&= 5 \text{ L/minute} \times [(140 \times 1.39 \times 100\%)\\
&\quad + (100 \times 0.003)]\\
&= 5 \text{ L/minute} \times 200 \text{ mL } O_2/L\\
&= 1000 \text{ mL } O_2/\text{minute}
\end{aligned}
$$

O_2 consumption = Cardiac output $\times$ (O_2 content$_{arterial}$ – O_2 content$_{venous}$)

$$
\begin{aligned}
&= 5 \text{ L/minute} \times (200 \text{ mL } O_2/L -\\
&\quad 150 \text{ mL } O_2/L)\\
&= 5 \text{ L/minute} \times 50 \text{ mL } O_2/L =\\
&\quad 250 \text{ mL } O_2/\text{minute}
\end{aligned}
$$

Compensation for Anemia

The above equations demonstrate that any decrease in oxygen content due to anemia can be compensated for by an increase in cardiac output.[1,2] This occurs because of increased cardiac work and also because anemia decreases blood viscosity, and thus peripheral vascular resistance. The increase in oxygen supply provided by increased cardiac output is augmented by increased oxygen extraction. Oxygen extraction is augmented acutely by a decrease in tissue oxygen tension, acting at the steep portion of the hemoglobin-oxygen dissociation curve[1] (see Fig 8-1), and by acidosis, which promotes oxygen dissociation from hemoglobin. Over time, an increase in red cell 2,3-diphosphoglycerate (2,3-DPG) concentration also has a significant positive effect on oxygen unloading.

Measuring the Adequacy of Oxygen Supply

As shown above, multiple factors determine oxygen delivery to the tissues, except at the lower extremes. Therefore, measurements in addition to the hemoglobin must be used to guide most transfusion decisions. The adequacy of the oxygen supply depends on the partial pressure of inspired oxygen, gas exchange in the lungs, the patient's cardiac performance, hemoglobin, oxygen-hemoglobin affinity, and current oxygen demand; all but the oxygen-hemoglobin affinity are subject to substantial variation. For patients in an intensive care unit or in the operating room, direct measurement of the cardiac output and mixed venous oxygen tension, in association with hemoglobin level, may serve as more physiologic guides for transfusion decisions than hemoglobin alone. Nonetheless, most such decisions will continue to be made based on hemoglobin and standard clinical assessment.

Determinants of cardiac performance include the patient's intravascular volume, the anemia-related reduction in peripheral vascular resistance, the presence of coronary artery disease or other forms of heart disease, and the patient's age. Tissue oxygen debt results when oxygen demand exceeds supply; tissues convert to anaerobic metabolism and produce increased quantities of lactic acid. Metabolic acidosis, in turn, impairs cardiac performance, further decreasing perfusion and tissue oxygen delivery, leading to greater tissue hypoxia in a vicious cycle.

Treating Inadequate Oxygen Supply

RBC transfusion is the most direct means of raising the hemoglobin concentration. Other ways to improve oxygen supply relative to demand include increasing tissue perfusion (maximizing cardiac performance), increasing oxygen saturation with supplemental oxygen or mechanical ventilation, and decreasing tissue oxygen demands with bed rest, antipyretics, and avoidance of hypertension.

For example, a patient with a hemoglobin of 6 g/dL and a cardiac index of 5 L/minute/m^2 has decreased oxygen delivery.

Assuming that oxygen extraction remains constant, oxygen delivery could be normalized by an increase in the hemoglobin concentration to 9 g/dL, or by an increase in the cardiac index to 7 L/minute/m^2. A smaller increase in hemoglobin would blunt the required increase in cardiac index.

Red-Cell-Containing Components

Whole Blood

Whole Blood provides oxygen-carrying capacity, stable coagulation factors (the concentrations of Factors V and VIII decrease during storage), and blood volume expansion. Thus, it is useful for patients with concomitant red cell and volume deficits, such as actively bleeding patients, and will help support coagulation in appropriate clinical settings such as liver transplantation.[4] In fact, Whole Blood is rarely available for allogeneic transfusion; RBCs and asanguinous solutions have become the standard for most cases of active bleeding in trauma and surgery, with supplementation of hemostatic elements as needed. The major use of Whole Blood in the United States today is for autologous transfusion (see Chapter 5).

Red Blood Cells

Red cell components are indicated for the treatment of patients who require an increase in oxygen-carrying capacity and red cell mass.[5] The transfusion of red cells increases oxygen-carrying capacity with less expansion of blood volume per unit than Whole Blood. This is important for patients who are at risk for circulatory overload (eg, neonates or patients with congestive heart failure). In a typical adult in the absence of bleeding, hemolysis, or major fluid shifts, one RBC unit is expected to raise the hemoglobin concentration by approximately 1 g/dL, or the hematocrit by 3%.

Selection of Whole Blood and Red Cell Components

Whole Blood must be ABO identical. RBC units need not be ABO identical but must be compatible with ABO antibodies in the recipient's plasma. Rh-negative recipients should receive Rh-negative Whole Blood or red cell components. In cases of trauma or massive transfusion, it may be necessary to use Rh-positive components, as discussed below. See Table 21-1 for blood group selection in red cell transfusion. Selection of RBC units for patients with blood group alloantibodies is discussed in Chapter 19.

Indications for Transfusion

Several organizations have published guidelines for RBC transfusion.[3,6,7] Reviews of indications for transfusion are also available.[1,8,9]

Blood Loss and Perioperative Transfusion

For actively bleeding patients, the goal of initial treatment should be to prevent the development of hypovolemic shock by stopping the bleeding and restoring intravascular volume. Efforts to restore volume by the infusion of crystalloid or colloid so-lutions take precedence over restoration of oxygen-carrying capacity and should be started immediately. In situations of acute bleeding, guidelines suggest transfusing patients who have lost 30% to 40% of their blood volume in conjunction with other measures to correct and maintain total blood volume.[3,6] Patients with cardiac or other disease may require replacement sooner. Healthy resting adults have been demonstrated to tolerate acute isovolemic hemodilution to hemoglobin concentrations as low as 5 g/dL without demonstrating evidence of inadequate oxygenation.[10] In patients who refuse transfusion on religious grounds and undergo surgery, mortality increases progressively below postoperative hemoglobin levels of 5 or 6 g/dL, particularly for those with cardiovascular disease.[11]

Perioperative transfusion accounts for 55% to 65% of red cell component use.[12] Randomized trials have demonstrated the safety of a "transfusion trigger" of 8 g/dL of hemoglobin in patients undergoing cardiovascular surgery,[13,14] orthopedic surgery,[15] and acute gastrointestinal bleeding.[16] Even before most of this evidence was available, an NIH consensus conference on perioperative red cell transfusion[7] emphasized that a hemoglobin of 10 g/dL was inappropriate as a guideline or transfusion trigger in the perioperative setting and suggested a he-

Table 21-1. Suggested ABO Group Selection Order for Transfusion of RBCs

Recipient ABO Group	Component ABO Group			
	1st Choice	2nd Choice	3rd Choice	4th Choice
AB	AB	A	B	O
A	A	O		
B	B	O		
O	O			

moglobin of 7 g/dL as a level at which transfusion was frequently required in otherwise healthy individuals with acute anemia. Factors to be considered in making an individual transfusion decision included "the duration of the anemia, the intravascular volume, the extent of the operation, the probability of massive blood loss, and the presence of coexisting conditions such as impaired pulmonary function, inadequate cardiac output, myocardial ischemia, or cerebrovascular or peripheral circulatory disease."[7] The guidelines also emphasized that transfusion does not improve wound healing, which depends on pO_2 rather than total oxygen content of the blood.

A guideline by an American Society of Anesthesiologists task force[3] cited a hemoglobin below 6 g/dL as "almost always" indicating transfusion, a hemoglobin above 10 g/dL as rarely indicating transfusion, and the range in between as the realm of clinical judgment. A task force of the College of American Pathologists reached a similar conclusion and proposed several objective measures that might indicate red cell transfusion for hemoglobin levels in the range of 6 to 10 g/dL, including tachycardia or hypotension in the face of normovolemia, a mixed venous pO_2 of <25 torr, an oxygen extraction ratio >50%, or a total oxygen consumption of <50% of baseline.[6]

In the past, there was some concern that transfusions of a single RBC unit were likely to represent unnecessary intervention. However, if transfusion of a single unit will achieve the desired clinical outcome, then only one unit should be transfused. Transfusing additional units in this setting will increase the risk of transfusion without any additional benefit.

Anemia

Among medical patients, those with cardiovascular and malignant diseases ac-count for a large proportion of those receiving RBC units.[13] In a prospective randomized trial of red cell transfusion, anemic but euvolemic patients in the intensive care unit (ICU) were assigned to either "restrictive" or "liberal" transfusion regimens that maintained the hemoglobin between 7 and 9 g/dL or between 10 and 12 g/dL, respectively.[17] The mortality rate during hospitalization (but not at 30 days) was significantly lower in the restrictive-strategy group (22.3% vs 28.1%, p = 0.05). No difference in mortality rate was seen among all patients with clinically significant cardiac disease. One third of the restrictive group avoided transfusion, and total red cell use was half that of the liberal group. These authors concluded that a restrictive strategy of red cell transfusion is at least as effective as, and possibly superior to, a liberal transfusion strategy in critically ill patients, with the possible exception of the subset of patients with acute myocardial infarction (MI) and unstable angina. Reanalysis of the patients in this study with cardiovascular disease showed a trend, albeit not statistically significant, toward increased mortality in the restrictive group among patients with MI and unstable angina.[18]

A retrospective study of a large number of elderly (>65 years old) patients hospitalized with acute MI divided into groups according to admission hematocrit compared 30-day mortality rates in patients who received transfusion and those who did not.[19] Transfusion appeared beneficial in patients with a hematocrit <30%. This result persisted when data were adjusted for multiple clinical and institutional factors.

Patients with chronic anemia tolerate a low hemoglobin better than those with acute anemia because of cardiovascular compensation and increased oxygen extraction. Moreover, patients at bed rest who are not febrile, who do not have congestive heart failure, and who are not hypermetabolic have low oxygen requirements and may tolerate anemia remarkably well. However, the high oxygen needs of cardiac muscle may precipitate angina in patients with cardiac disease and anemia. A hemoglobin concentration of 8 g/dL adequately meets the oxygen needs of most patients with stable cardiovascular disease.

Although it is desirable to prevent unnecessary transfusions, anemic patients who are symptomatic should receive appropriate treatment. Anemia may cause symptoms of generalized weakness, headache, dizziness, disorientation, breathlessness, palpitations, or chest pain, and signs include pallor (not cyanosis) and tachycardia. Elwood and coworkers[20] could not correlate symptoms with the hemoglobin level in patients with chronic iron deficiency anemia and a hemoglobin as low as 8 g/dL. A study of the use of erythropoietin demonstrated improvement in symptoms as hemoglobin is raised to 10 g/dL, but no change above that level.[21] Patients with chronic hypoproliferative anemia who are known to be transfusion dependent should be maintained at a level that prevents symptoms by establishing a transfusion schedule and then adjusting it as needed.

Platelet Transfusion

Physiologic Principles

Hemostasis occurs in four phases: the vascular phase, the formation of a platelet plug, the development of fibrin clot on the platelet plug, and the ultimate lysis of the clot. Platelets are essential to the formation of the primary hemostatic plug and provide the surface upon which fibrin forms. Deficiencies in platelet number and/or function can have unpredictable effects that range from clinically insignifi-

cant prolongation of the bleeding time to major life-threatening hemorrhage. Platelet plug formation results from the combined processes of adhesion, activation and release, aggregation, and procoagulant activity.[22] Platelet adhesion to damaged endothelium is mediated largely by the von Willebrand factor (vWF), which binds to the surface glycoprotein (GP) receptor GPIb-IX-V complex. The process of activation and release causes a dramatic change in platelet shape, with extension of pseudopod-like structures, a change in the binding properties of membrane activation proteins, secretion of internal granule contents, and activation of several metabolic pathways. These changes have many effects, including the recruitment of additional platelets, which aggregate with the help of fibrinogen or vWF binding to platelet surface glycoproteins. Finally, the platelet membrane procoagulant activity localizes and directs formation of fibrin.

Assessing Platelet Function

Decreased platelet numbers may result from decreased production, increased destruction, or splenic sequestration. Platelet function may be adversely affected by such factors as drugs, liver or kidney disease, sepsis, fibrin(ogen) degradation products, cardiopulmonary bypass, and primary marrow disorders. Platelet hemostasis is assessed by the medical history, physical examination, and laboratory tests including platelet count and bleeding time or in-vitro platelet function assays (eg, PFA100). Patients with inadequate platelet number or function may demonstrate petechiae, easy bruising, mucous membrane bleeding, nose and gum bleeding, and hematuria. Preprocedure platelet counts have predicted bleeding in some studies[23,24] but not in others.[25-27]

Bleeding time measures both the vascular phase and the platelet phase of hemostasis. Although the bleeding time may be a useful diagnostic test in the evaluation of patients with known or suspected abnormalities of platelet function, it is a poor predictor of surgical bleeding[28] and is not a reliable indicator of the need for platelet transfusion therapy.[29] The in-vitro measurement of platelet function is useful but, like the bleeding time, is a poor predictor of bleeding.[30]

Platelet Life Span and Kinetics

Platelets normally circulate with a life span of 10.5 days,[31] and platelets that have been properly collected and stored have a near normal residual mean life span of 4 to 5 days when reinfused into the original donor. Conditions that shorten platelet life span include splenomegaly, sepsis, drugs, disseminated intravascular coagulation (DIC), auto- and alloantibodies, endothelial cell activation, and platelet activation (eg, cardiopulmonary bypass or intra-aortic balloon pumps). Because a relatively constant number of platelets (7,000-10,000/μL/day) are consumed by routine plugging of minor endothelial defects, the fraction of the circulating platelet pool required for maintenance functions increases as the total number of platelets declines. Therefore, the life span of native and transfused platelets decreases with progressive thrombocytopenia.[31] The response to platelet transfusion is best assessed by observing whether bleeding stops and by measuring the posttransfusion platelet increment. The posttransfusion increment is generally measured between 10 minutes and 1 hour after completion of the transfusion and is expressed as a corrected count increment (CCI) or percent recovery, as outlined in Chapter 16. Two consecutive poor responses suggest platelet refractoriness.

Platelet Components

Platelets

A single unit of Platelets prepared from an individual unit of Whole Blood may be adequate for transfusion to neonates or infants, but, for adults, 4 to 6 units are ordinarily pooled for transfusion to achieve a dose greater than 3.0×10^{11} platelets. This should increase the platelet count by 30,000 to 60,000/μL.

Platelets Pheresis

Units of platelets prepared by apheresis technology ("single-donor platelets") have a platelet content similar to that of pooled platelets from four to six donors and, depending on the equipment used, may have a reduced leukocyte content. The fact that a single such unit can provide an entire transfusion facilitates provision of compatible platelets to recipients who are refractory because of alloimmunization. Transfusion of recipients who are refractory to platelet transfusions is discussed in Chapter 16.

Selection of Platelets

ABO Matching

Because ABO antigens are present on the platelet surface, recovery of group A platelets transfused into group O patients is somewhat decreased,[32] but this effect is not usually clinically significant (see Chapter 16). Transfusion of ABO-incompatible plasma present in platelet components may also result in a blunted posttransfusion platelet count increment.[33] Hemolysis occurs rarely in this setting but it frequently causes a positive direct antiglobulin test (DAT), which may increase costs and charges to the patient for serologic investigation. Moreover, a retrospective analysis suggested that survival after marrow transplantation was significantly reduced in patients who received substantial amounts of ABO-incompatible plasma from platelet transfusion,[34] and it has been suggested that infusion of soluble A and B antigen in platelet or plasma components may have a similar adverse effect mediated by immune complex function.[35] Therefore, it may be prudent to use ABO-matched platelets, particularly for patients requiring repeated transfusions. However, urgently needed transfusions should not be delayed in order to obtain them.

For infants, it is desirable to avoid administration of plasma that is incompatible with the infant's red cells; if platelets containing compatible plasma are not available, the plasma can be reduced (see Method 6.15). This is rarely necessary in adults or older children, although significant hemolysis has been reported after transfusion of group O Platelets Pheresis with high-titer anti-A or B.[36] If transfused ABO antibodies are detectable in the recipient, it may become necessary to use group O RBC units.

Matching for Rh

The D antigen is not detectable on platelets, and posttransfusion survival of platelets from Rh-positive donors is normal in recipients with anti-D. However, platelet components contain small numbers of red cells so Rh-negative individuals may become alloimmunized by platelet components from Rh-positive donors. For immunocompetent normal Rh-negative females of childbearing potential, it is especially desirable to avoid administration of platelets from Rh-positive donors; however, if this is unavoidable, Rh Immune Globulin (RhIG) should be admin-

istered. If hematoma formation is an issue, an intravenous form of RhIG is available. A full dose of RhIG, which is considered immunoprophylactic for up to 15 mL of Rh-positive red cells, should protect against the red cells in a minimum of 30 units of Rh-positive Platelets or 7 units of Rh-positive Platelets Pheresis.

Therapeutic Platelet Transfusion

Significant bleeding due to thrombocytopenia or abnormal platelet function is an indication for "therapeutic" platelet transfusion.[37] The decision to transfuse platelets depends on the cause of bleeding, the patient's clinical condition, and the number and function of the circulating platelets.[3,38-40] Platelet transfusions are most likely to be of benefit when thrombocytopenia is the primary hemostatic defect. The goal is to maintain counts >50,000/µL. Other blood components may also be required in patients with multiple defects. Bleeding due to the defects in platelet function that follow cardiopulmonary bypass surgery or to the ingestion of aspirin-containing compounds, glycoprotein IIb/IIIa antagonists (eg, abciximab), and P2 inhibitors (eg, clopidigrel and ticlopidine) often responds to platelet transfusion. Other defects such as those found in uremia or von Willebrand disease respond less well because the transfused platelets tend to acquire the same defect.

Prophylactic Platelet Transfusion

Indications for prophylactic platelet transfusion are more controversial than for therapeutic rationales. A threshold of 20,000/µL or less for patients with chemotherapy-induced thrombocytopenia has been used by many physicians, but prospective randomized trials have shown that a threshold of 10,000/µL in stable patients is equally safe and results in significant decreases in platelet usage.[41-43] A higher transfusion trigger is often used for patients with fever, evidence of rapid consumption, high white cell counts, coagulation defects, and intracranial lesions.[38] In contrast, many stable thrombocytopenic patients can tolerate platelet counts as low as 5000/μL.[41]

Despite the widespread use of prophylactic platelet transfusions, few studies have documented their clinical benefit. One study comparing patients given prophylactic transfusions with patients transfused only for clinically significant bleeding demonstrated a significant decrease in bleeding, but the number of patients in the study was too small to show a difference between the groups in overall survival or in deaths due to bleeding.[44] Of interest, the prophylactic group received twice as many platelet transfusions, and there was a suggestion that refractoriness developed more often in this group. This observation raises the caveat that prophylactic platelet transfusion may be most relevant to patients in whom thrombocytopenia is expected to be a temporary condition.[38] If thrombocytopenia or platelet dysfunction will be prolonged, the development of refractoriness may limit the response to platelets, particularly if immune function is normal as it is in patients with aplastic anemia or congenital thrombocytopathies.

Patients with severe preoperative thrombocytopenia are generally assumed to benefit from prophylactic platelet transfusion, but this has not been demonstrated in experimental studies. The threshold for such prophylaxis is typically set at platelet counts between 50,000 and 100,000/μL.[3] Prophylactic transfusion of platelets has been investigated in circumstances in which thrombocytopenia is expected to develop intraoperatively, either because of dilution[45] or cardiopulmonary bypass[46]; in both cases,

prophylaxis was ineffective. Although it endorsed the logic of prophylactic platelet transfusion for thrombocytopenic patients undergoing surgery, the NIH consensus panel[38] suggested that such transfusions were most appropriate for patients in whom hemorrhage could not be observed or in whom it occurred at a site where it could be critical in small amounts (eg, in the central nervous system). Published guidelines[3,39] suggest a platelet transfusion trigger of 50,000/μL for most major surgery, with counts "near" 100,000/μL possibly required for patients undergoing neurosurgery or ophthalmic procedures.[39] Prophylactic platelet transfusion may also be useful for patients who are having surgery and who have a platelet function defect,[39] including that due to treatment with abciximab.[47]

Refractoriness to Platelet Transfusion

Platelet refractoriness, defined as a poor increment following a dose of platelets, can result from either immune or nonimmune mechanisms and is discussed in detail in Chapter 16 and other reviews.[48,49] The antibodies that cause immune refractoriness may have either allo- or autoreactivity, with alloantibodies most commonly directed against Class I HLA antigens. Autoantibodies occur in immune thrombocytopenic purpura (ITP) (see Chapter 16). Nonimmune causes of the refractory state include infection, splenomegaly, drugs (particularly amphotericin B), and accelerated platelet consumption (see Table 16-3).

Contraindications to Platelet Transfusion

There are several conditions for which platelet transfusions may be requested but are contraindicated. Relative contraindications include conditions in which the likelihood of benefit is remote; transfusion in this setting merely wastes a valuable component. Examples include prophylactic platelet transfusions in stable patients with ITP[50] or platelet refractoriness. For ITP patients undergoing splenectomy, transfusion of platelets should be delayed until the vascular pedicle is clamped. Platelet transfusion should be avoided for patients with thrombotic thrombocytopenic purpura (TTP) or active heparin-induced thrombocytopenia except in life- or organ-threatening hemorrhage. These conditions are associated with platelet thrombi, and major thrombotic complications may follow platelet transfusions.[51]

Granulocyte Transfusion

The use of granulocyte transfusions for adult recipients is rare. New antibiotics, adverse effects attributable to granulocyte transfusions, the advent of recombinant growth factors, and difficulty demonstrating efficacy have contributed to this decline. Nevertheless, in selected patients, transfused granulocytes may produce clinical benefits,[52] particularly with the larger granulocyte doses available from donors treated with granulocyte colony-stimulating factor.[53] Attention to HLA compatibility is also required for alloimmunized recipients.[54] The preparation, storage, and pretransfusion testing of granulocytes are discussed in Chapter 6, and their use in neonates is discussed in Chapter 24.

Indications and Contraindications

The goals of granulocyte transfusion should be clearly defined before a course of therapy is initiated. In general, the patient should meet the following minimum conditions:
1.   Neutropenia (granulocyte count less than 500/µL).

2.   Fever for 24 to 48 hours, positive bacterial or fungal blood cultures, or progressive parenchymal infection unresponsive to appropriate antibiotic therapy.
3.   Myeloid hypoplasia.
4.   A reasonable chance for recovery of marrow function.

Patients with documented granulocyte dysfunction, such as those with chronic granulomatous disease, may also be candidates to receive granulocyte transfusions during life-threatening episodes of infection or while awaiting hematopoietic progenitor cell transplantation.

Other Considerations

Granulocyte components contain significant amounts of red cells, which must be crossmatch compatible and Rh specific, particularly for females with childbearing potential. Granulocytes should be irradiated to avoid the risk of graft-vs-host disease (GVHD). If cytomegalovirus (CMV) transmission is an issue, its risk can be reduced by the use of a CMV-seronegative donor (leukocyte reduction filters are contraindicated). For alloimmunized recipients, donors should be matched by HLA typing or leukocyte crossmatching.[52,54]

Special Cellular Blood Components

Leukocyte Reduction

The approximate leukocyte content of common blood components is summarized in Table 21-2.[55-59] Leukocyte reduction has been used for some time for select groups of patients. Current federal guidelines[57,58] and AABB *Standards for Blood Banks and Transfusion Services*[59(pp25,28,29,31,32)] define a leukocyte-reduced component as one with $<5 \times 10^6$ residual donor leukocytes

Table 21-2. Approximate Leukocyte Content of Blood Components (per Unit)[55-59]

Whole Blood	10^9
RBCs	10^8
RBCs Washed	10^7
RBCs Deglycerolized	10^6-10^7
RBCs Leukocytes Reduced (by filtration)*	$<5 \times 10^6$
Platelets Pheresis	10^6-10^8
Platelets	10^7
Platelets Pheresis Leukocytes Reduced*	$<5 \times 10^6$
Platelets Leukocytes Reduced	$<8.3 \times 10^5$
Platelets Pooled Leukocytes Reduced	$<5 \times 10^6$
FFP Thawed	$<0.6 \times 10^6$ - 1.5×10^7

*Leukocyte reduction with third-generation leukocyte adsorption filter.

per final product (this includes RBCs; Platelets Pheresis; and pooled Platelets). AABB *Standards*[59(p31)] requires $<8.3 \times 10^5$ leukocytes in Platelets Leukocytes Reduced, which are prepared from a single unit of Whole Blood, to achieve the requirement for a pool of 6 platelet units. Draft guidance from the Food and Drug Administration (FDA) recommends quality control to indicate with 95% confidence that more than 95% of blood units meet these criteria. By comparison, European guidelines define leukocyte-reduced components as those with $<1 \times 10^6$ residual leukocytes per unit and require that there should be no more than a 10% failure rate in the process.

Published data demonstrate that leukocyte reduction reduces the risk of:
1. Febrile nonhemolytic reactions (see Chapter 27).
2. CMV transmission.[60]
3. HLA alloimmunization that may lead to patients becoming refractory to platelet transfusions.[61]

Controversial and unproven indications for leukocyte reduction include:
1. Reduction of immunomodulation that may lead to an increased risk of cancer recurrence or bacterial infections.[62]
2. Reduction in the risk of prion disease.
3. Reduction in the risk of *Yersinia enterocolitica* contamination of RBC units.[63]

Many studies have investigated the possibility that leukocyte reduction can reduce the incidence of clinical outcomes due to transfusion-related immunomodulation, but the results are contradictory.[62] One such proposal was that savings related to reduced immunomodulation could offset the costs of leukocyte reduction, but this was not demonstrable in a large prospective randomized trial.[64] Nonetheless, several countries have converted to a leukocyte-reduced blood supply, and this subject remains controversial.[65]

Irradiation

Irradiation of a cellular blood component is the only accepted method to prevent GVHD. GVHD has been reported after transfusion of leukocyte-reduced components.[66] For more details on GVHD and indications for irradiation, see Chapter 27.

Replacement of Coagulation Factors

Physiologic Principles

Coagulation results from a complex but ordered enzyme cascade occurring on the surface of platelets and cells that express tissue factor (see Fig 21-1). The coagulation cascade is typically divided into the intrinsic and the extrinsic pathways, the

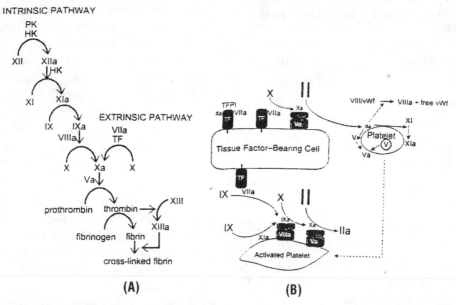

(A)   **(B)**

Roberts HR, Monroe DM III, Hoffman M. Molecular biology and biochemistry of the coagulation factors and pathways of hemostasis. In: Beutler E, Lichtman MA, Coller BS, et al. Williams' hematology. 6th ed. New York: McGraw-Hill, 2001:1409-34.

Figure 21-1. (A) The classic cascade model of coagulation reactions was based on in-vitro experimental data in cell-free systems. The term extrinsic reflects the fact that tissue factor does not circulate in plasma. (B) More recent evidence emphasizes that the coagulation reactions occur on the surfaces of tissue factor-bearing cells at the site of injury and on the surface of platelets that are subsequently recruited. HK = high-molecular-weight kininogen, PK = prekallikrein, TF = tissue factor, TFPI = tissue factor pathway inhibitor. (Adapted with permission from Roberts et al.[67])

in-vitro activity of which can be measured by the activated partial thromboplastin time (aPTT) and prothrombin time (PT), respectively, but, *in vivo*, the cascades are interdependent.[67] The central procoagulant enzyme is thrombin, which is activated by both pathways.

Minimal levels of coagulation factors (see Table 21-3) are required for normal formation of fibrin and hemostasis, so normal plasma contains coagulation factors in excess, a reserve that usually allows patients to tolerate replacement of one or more blood volumes of red cells and crystalloid without needing Fresh Frozen Plasma (FFP). Patients with liver disease have less physiologic reserve and are more susceptible to dilutional coagulopathy.

Monitoring Hemostasis

The PT, aPTT, and measurement of fibrinogen level are commonly used to monitor coagulation. Results should be interpreted with four considerations in mind: 1) mild prolongations of the PT or aPTT occur before the residual factor concentration falls below the level normally needed for hemostasis; 2) conversely, the PT and aPTT are relatively insensitive to low fibrinogen levels; 3) significant deficiencies of coagulation factors (or the presence of coagulation factor inhibitors) cause clearly prolonged values for the PT or aPTT; and 4) an infusion of FFP that increases the concentration of factors by 20% will have a far greater impact on a greatly

Table 21-3. Coagulation Factors

Factor	Name	In-vivo Half-life	In-vitro, 4 C Half-life	% of Normal Needed for Hemostasis	% In-vivo Recovery	Initial Therapeutic Dose
I	Fibrinogen	3-6 days	Years	12-50	50-70	1 bag cryoprecipitate/7 kg body weight
II	Prothrombin	2-5 days	>21 days	10-25	50	10-20 units/kg body weight
V	Labile factor, Proaccelerin	4.5-36 hours	10-14 days	10-30	~80	10-20 mL plasma/kg body weight
VII	Stable factor, Proconvertin	2-5 hours	>21 days	>10	100	10-20 units/kg body weight
VIII	Antihemophilic factor	8-12 hours	7 days	30-40	60-70	See Table 21-6
IX	Plasma thromboplastin component, Christmas factor	18-24 hours	>21 days	15-40	20	See Table 21-6
X	Stuart-Prower factor	20-42 hours	>21 days	10-40	50-95	10-20 units/kg body weight
XI	Plasma thromboplastin antecedent (PTA)	40-80 hours	>28 days	20-30	90	10-20 mL/kg body weight
XIII	Fibrin stabilizing factor	12 days	>21 days	<5	50-100	500 mL plasma every 3 weeks
AT	Antithrombin	60-90 hours	>42 days	80-120	50-100	40-50 IU/kg body weight

Notes:
1. All dosings are provided as a general guideline for initial therapy; the exact loading dose and maintenance intervals should be individualized for each patient.
2. One unit of coagulation factor is present in each mL of Fresh Frozen Plasma.
3. DDAVP is the treatment of choice for patients with hemophilia A who are responders.
4. Composite data from the following references:

a. Beutler E, Lichtman MA, Coller BS, Kipps TL, eds. Williams' hematology. 5th ed. New York: McGraw-Hill, 1995:1413-58, 1657.
b. Mollison PL, Engelfriet CP, Contreras M. Blood transfusion in clinical medicine. 10th ed. Oxford: Blackwell Scientific Publications, 1997:459-88.
c. Huestis DW, Bove JR, Case J, eds. Practical blood transfusion. 4th ed. Boston, MA: Little Brown and Co, 1988:319.
d. Counts RB, Haisch C, Simon TL, et al. Hemostasis in massively transfused trauma patients. Ann Surg 1979;190:91-9.
e. Package inserts.

prolonged PT or aPTT than on a mildly prolonged PT or aPTT. For example, the infusion of two units of FFP in a patient with a PT of 14.5 seconds (normal: 11 to 13 seconds) is unlikely to provide any clinical benefit and is also unlikely to correct the PT to the normal range.

Guidelines typically cite a PT 1.5 times the upper limit of normal[3] or the midpoint of the normal range[39] and an aPTT 1.5 times the upper limit of normal[3,39] as thresholds at which therapeutic or prophylactic replacement may be indicated in an appropriate clinical setting. Of note, however, studies have consistently shown that the PT and aPTT, even when elevated to this degree, have little predictive value for bleeding complications of invasive procedures including paracentesis or thoracentesis,[25] liver biopsy,[26,27] angiography,[23] or central venous catheter placement.[24]

Components and Products Available for Coagulation Factor Replacement

The plasma components that are available differ according to the timing of freezing and/or thawing and variations in preparation (see Chapter 8). FFP contains all the clotting factors, including labile Factors V and VIII. Other forms of plasma have lower levels of labile factors but could substitute for FFP for most of the indications for which the latter is transfused. Plasma Cryoprecipitate Reduced has a decreased content of vWF and is used specifically for treatment of TTP (see Chapter 6). Pooled Plasma, Solvent/Detergent-Treated is no longer available in the United States.

Cryoprecipitated AHF (CRYO) is a concentrate of high-molecular-weight plasma proteins that precipitate in the cold, including vWF, Factor VIII, fibrinogen, Factor XIII, and fibronectin (see Chapter 8).

Plasma derivatives are concentrates of specific plasma proteins from large pools of plasma or cryoprecipitate. Cohn fractionation, which relies on the precipitation of various plasma proteins in cold ethanol-water mixtures, was developed during World War II and is still used with some modifications.[68] After fractionation, derivatives undergo further processing to purify and concentrate the proteins and inactivate contaminating viruses. Virus-inactivation procedures include heat treatment, microfiltration, the use of chemical solvents and detergents, and affinity column purification. Factors VIII, IX, VIIa, and antithrombin are also produced by recombinant DNA technology. These products appear to be efficacious and are not known to carry any infectious risk.

The specific activity (factor units/mg protein) of presently available concentrates has been dramatically increased in concentrates prepared with affinity columns or by recombinant technology. Moreover, HIV, HBV, and HCV transmission appear to be absent in patients with hemophilia treated exclusively with new preparations.[69] Unfortunately, their cost has also increased due to the increased complexity of manufacturing and the protein losses resulting from extensive manipulation. Coagulation factor concentrates are supplied in lyophilized form and the factor activity is stated on the label.[69] Currently available products for replacement of Factors VIII and IX are listed in Table 21-4.

Selection of ABO-Compatible Plasma

Because of its long shelf life, group-specific or compatible plasma (see Table 21-5) is typically available. (Note that platelet transfusions usually contain a volume of plasma equivalent to one unit of FFP, and limitations in availability may

Table 21-4. Available Coagulation Factor Concentrates

Product Type	Product	Approved Indications	Comment
Factor VIII, fractionated	Humate-P	Factor VIII and vWF repl.	Contains vWF
	Koate-HP	Factor VIII replacement	Contains vWF
	Koate-DVI	Factor VIII replacement	Contains vWF
Factor VIII, affinity purified	Alphanate	Factor VIII replacement	Contains vWF
Factor VIII, immunaffinity purified	Hemofil-M	Factor VIII replacement	
	Monarc M	Factor VIII replacement	
	Monoclate-P	Factor VIII replacement	
Factor VIII, recombinant	Kogenate FS Helixate FS	Factor VIII replacement	Contains trace amounts of human albumin
	Recombinate (Bioclate)	Factor VIII replacement	
	ReFacto	Factor VIII replacement	Does not contain human albumin
Factor VIII, porcine	Hyate C	Factor VIII inhibitor tx.	
Factor IX, affinity purified	AlphaNine-SD	Factor IX replacement	
Factor IX, immunaffinity purified	Mononine	Factor IX replacement	
Factor IX, recombinant	BeneFIX	Factor IX replacement	Does not contain human albumin
Factor IX complex	Bebulin VH	Factor IX replacement	Contains Factor II, Factor X, trace Factor VII
	Konyne 80	Factor IX replacement Factor VIII inhibitor tx. Warfarin reversal	Contains Factor II, Factor X, some Factor VII
	Profilnine SD	Factor IX replacement	Contains Factor II, Factor X, some Factor VII
	Proplex T	Factor IX and Factor VII replacement Factor VIII inhibitor tx.	Contains Factor II, Factor VII, and Factor X
Factor IX complex, activated	Autoplex-T	Factor VIII inhibitor tx.	Contains Factor IIa, Factor VIIa, and Factor Xa
	FEIBA VH	Factor VIII inhibitor tx.	Contains Factor IIa, Factor VIIa, and Factor Xa
Factor VIIa, recombinant	NovoSeven	Factor VIII inhibitor tx.	Does not contain human albumin

Table 21-5. Suggested ABO Group Selection Order for Transfusion of Plasma

Recipient ABO Group	Component ABO Group			
	1st Choice	2nd Choice	3rd Choice	4th Choice
AB	AB	(A)	(B)	(O)
A	A	AB	(B)	(O)
B	B	AB	(A)	(O)
O	O	A	B	AB

(Blood groups in parentheses represent choices with incompatible plasma, listed in "least incompatible" order.)

require infusion of incompatible plasma in this context.)

Indications for FFP

Guidelines exist for the appropriate use of FFP.[3,39,70] FFP is the only approved component for clinically significant deficiency of Factors II, V, X, and XI. Plasma is most often used in patients with multiple factor deficiencies, including those with liver disease, dilutional and consumption coagulopathy, or a need for rapid reversal of warfarin treatment. It is of limited clinical benefit in patients with inhibitors to any coagulation factor. Plasma Cryoprecipitate Reduced may be more effective than FFP for some patients receiving plasma exchange treatment for TTP or hemolytic-uremic syndrome[71] (see Chapter 6).

Vitamin K Deficiency and Warfarin Reversal

The most common cause of multiple coagulation factor abnormalities among hospitalized patients is deficiency of the vitamin-K-dependent factors due to treatment with the vitamin K antagonist warfarin (Coumadin) or nutritional deficiency.[67] Vitamin K is a fat-soluble vitamin required for hepatocellular synthesis of coagulation Factors II, VII, IX, and X, as well as the anticoagulant proteins C and S. Body stores of vitamin K last only 2 weeks, so deficiency may occur in hospitalized patients unable to tolerate normal food intake. Absorption of vitamin K requires precursor metabolism by bacteria in the intestine and the action of bile salts; therefore, deficiencies can occur with antibiotic use, obstructive jaundice, and fat malabsorption syndromes.

Vitamin K depletion or warfarin usually cause a prolongation of the PT that is out of proportion to the aPTT because Factor VII, which has the shortest half-life of the vitamin-K-dependent factors, has little effect on the aPTT. Deficiency of vitamin K is best managed by treatment of the underlying condition and by administration of vitamin K.[67] If liver function is adequate, coagulation factors will return to effective levels in about 12 hours.

Although most patients with vitamin K deficiency do not require plasma, plasma transfusion is occasionally needed to treat active bleeding or to prepare for emergency invasive procedures.[67] Transfusion of 10 to 15 mL of plasma per kg of body weight will generally achieve hemostatic coagulation factor levels in patients with warfarin-induced coagulopathy. One form of Factor IX complex concentrate is licensed for warfarin reversal (see Table 21-4) but carries a significant risk of thrombotic complications and is rarely used for this indication. Concurrent vitamin K supplementation should also be given unless only transient correction is desired. Although the International Normalized Ratio can provide useful information about response to therapy, the need for additional treatment should be guided by the clinical response and not by the results of laboratory tests. As discussed above, it is rarely necessary to correct the PT or aPTT to normal to achieve adequate hemostasis.

Liver Disease

Patients with liver disease have multiple derangements that contribute to an increased bleeding tendency. These abnormalities include portal hypertension and engorgement of systemic collateral venous shunts; splenomegaly with secondary thrombocytopenia; decreased synthesis of all coagulation factors except Factor VIII; dysfibrinogenemia; decreased clearance of fibrin, fibrinogen degradation products, and fibrinolytic activators; and decreased synthesis of inhibitors of the fibrinolytic system. As in vitamin K deficiency, the short half-life of Factor VII causes the PT to be prolonged more than the aPTT, and, for the same reason, FFP infusion corrects the PT for only about 4 hours.[72] Because the defect in hepatocellular disease is in primary protein synthesis, supplemental vitamin K will not usually correct the abnormality. However, because it is one of the few treatable causes of coagulopathy in liver disease, a trial of replacement vitamin K may be indicated.

FFP corrects coagulation factor deficiencies found in severe liver disease, but is often used inappropriately. The most common error is to attribute all bleeding to coagulopathy and to give systemic treatment when the cause is localized bleeding. For example, bleeding at the operative site after cardiac surgery usually responds better to local hemostatic measures than to intravenous infusion of FFP. A second common error in treating liver-associated

coagulopathy is overdependence on the PT. Again, a normal PT is rarely, if ever, required for the cessation of serious bleeding, and the goal of FFP therapy in severe liver disease should be to correct or prevent bleeding complications. If FFP is to be used prophylactically before an invasive procedure, it should be given immediately before the procedure.

Patients with liver disease may also have abnormalities of platelet plug formation and fibrinolysis. In addition, severe splenomegaly may impair the response to platelet transfusions. Platelet function in some patients with liver disease can be enhanced by administration of 1-deamino-8-D-arginine vasopressin (desmopressin, DDAVP).[73] Cryoprecipitated AHF should be given if there is severe hypofibrinogenemia or bleeding related to dysfibrinogenemia. The increase in systemic fibrinolysis associated with severe liver disease may not respond to FFP alone, and antifibrinolytic agents in combination with plasma therapy can be useful in these patients (see below).

Dilutional Coagulopathy

Massive blood loss and replacement with crystalloid and/or colloid solutions may produce a dilutional coagulopathy,[74] but most patients can tolerate loss and replacement of at least one blood volume without developing impaired hemostasis.[75] Shock accompanying traumatic hemorrhage also contributes to the coagulopathy (see Chapter 27). In the setting of trauma, thrombocytopenia generally develops before plasma clotting factors are diluted to the point of causing impaired hemostasis, and adequate platelet replacement generally has priority.[75] However, in elective surgical patients, coagulation factor deficits may predominate.[74] FFP may be beneficial if the PT and/or aPTT are greater than 1.5 times normal.[3,39] If surgical hemostasis has not been achieved and significant continued bleeding is expected, FFP may be indicated.[39]

Patients undergoing plasmapheresis without plasma replacement develop a variety of coagulation factor deficits, particularly hypofibrinogenemia, depending on the volume and frequency of the exchanges.[76] Although these changes can be striking, most authors have concluded that routine supplements with FFP in patients with normal liver function are unnecessary, particularly for alternate-day regimens.

Other Conditions

Plasma exchange is lifesaving in TTP (see Chapter 6). FFP may be an adjunct to treatment of DIC. Hereditary angioneurotic edema results from a congenital deficiency of C1-esterase inhibitor, an inhibitory protein that regulates complement activation. Patients with this condition develop localized edema and may experience lifethreatening obstruction of the upper respiratory tract following complement activation. FFP or Liquid Plasma contain normal levels of C1-esterase inhibitor and FFP transfusion appeared to prevent attacks at the time of oral surgery in one study.[77] There are rare anecdotal reports of exacerbation of angioneurotic edema with FFP administration. The need for treatment of isolated deficiency of Factors II, V, VII, X, or XI is uncommon; guidelines for initial therapy are given in Table 21-3 (however, for a more complete treatment, refer to one of the standard hematology or coagulation texts).

Plasma can also be used to replace proteins C and S, and antithrombin; these are discussed separately below.

Misuse of Fresh Frozen Plasma

Plasma should not be used as a volume expander, as a nutritional source, or to enhance wound healing.[38,70,75] Transfusing plasma for volume expansion carries a risk of infectious disease transmission and other transfusion reactions (eg, allergic) that can be avoided by using crystalloid or colloid solutions. Plasma is also not a suitable source of immunoglobulins for patients with severe hypogammaglobulinemia because more effective preparations exist (immunoglobulin for intravenous or intramuscular use).

FFP is often given prophylactically to patients with mild to moderate prolongation of the PT or aPTT before invasive procedures, but there is little or no evidence that this prevents bleeding complications. Because these tests do not accurately predict the risk of bleeding when mildly prolonged, there is little logic for a transfusion intended to "improve" the results.

Cryoprecipitated AHF Transfusion

CRYO is the only concentrated fibrinogen product currently available for systemic use, and intravenous supplementation of fibrinogen is its primary clinical use, particularly in DIC. A second major use has been in patients with severe von Willebrand disease, but there are Factor VIII concentrates that contain vWF and are more appropriate if available (see Table 21-4). CRYO can be used in isolated Factor XIII deficiency and to ameliorate the platelet dysfunction associated with uremia. It is also used topically as a fibrin sealant, although a commercial preparation is available. CRYO is seldom used for patients with hemophilia because Factor VIII concentrates are available commercially and have been processed to reduce or eliminate the risk of blood-borne viral infection; CRYO is used as a last resort for this indication. Because CRYO contains

ABO antibodies, consideration should be given to ABO compatibility when the infused volume will be large relative to the recipient's red cell mass.

Calculating the CRYO Dose for Fibrinogen Replacement

On average, one unit of CRYO contains approximately 250 mg of fibrinogen; the minimum required by AABB *Standards* is 150 mg.[59(p30)] The amount of transfused CRYO required to correct the fibrinogen level depends upon the nature of the bleeding episode and the severity of the initial deficiency and can be calculated as follows:

1. Weight (kg) × 70 mL/kg = blood volume (mL).
2. Blood volume (mL) × (1.0 – hematocrit) = plasma volume (mL).
3. Mg of fibrinogen required = (Desired fibrinogen level in mg/dL – initial fibrinogen level in mg/dL) × plasma volume (mL) ÷ 100 mL/dL.
4. Bags of CRYO required = mg of fibrinogen required ÷ 250 mg fibrinogen/ bag of CRYO

This calculation assumes that 100% of administered fibrinogen is recovered as measurable intravascular fibrinogen, but, because the content of CRYO is variable, further refinements are unproductive.

von Willebrand Syndromes

von Willebrand syndromes are the most common major inherited coagulation abnormalities.[78] These conditions are usually autosomal dominant and represent a collection of quantitative and qualitative abnormalities of vWF, the most important protein mediating platelet adhesion to damaged endothelial surfaces. The protein also transports Factor VIII. As a result, patients with von Willebrand syndromes have varying degrees of abnormal platelet plug formation and partial deficiency of Factor VIII. The former may manifest as a prolonged bleeding time and the latter as a prolonged aPTT, but these abnormalities vary between syndromes. vWF exists in the plasma as a family of multimeric molecules with a wide range of molecular weights. The high-molecular-weight species of vWF are the most hemostatically effective. Laboratory evaluation demonstrates a specific deficiency in the level of vWF, often measured as ristocetin cofactor activity because vWF is required for the platelet-agglutinating effect of ristocetin in vitro.

Mild cases of von Willebrand syndrome can often be treated with DDAVP, which causes a release of endogenous stores of Factor VIII and vWF. Many Factor VIII concentrates do not contain therapeutic levels of vWF, but several with satisfactory levels are commercially available and one is licensed for this indication (see Table 21-4). In the absence of a suitably therapeutic virus-inactivated concentrate, severe von Willebrand syndrome can be treated with CRYO. The quantity of CRYO required to treat bleeding episodes or to prepare for major surgery varies greatly among patients with von Willebrand syndromes. In addition to the clinical response of the patient, the template bleeding time, the level of Factor VIII, or the ristocetin cofactor activity may help to guide therapy.

Fibrinogen Abnormalities

Hypofibrinogenemia may occur as a rare isolated congenital deficiency, may be acquired as part of the DIC syndrome, or may be due to obstetric complications such as abruptio placentae. Dysfibrinogenemias may be congenital or acquired and represent conditions in which fibrinogen is present as measured by immunoassays but functionally defective as measured by the thrombin time. Patients with severe liver disease frequently exhibit a dysfibrinogenemia.

Disseminated Intravascular Coagulation

DIC occurs when circulating thrombin induces widespread fibrin formation in the microcirculation and consumption of platelets and coagulation factors, particularly fibrinogen, prothrombin, Factor V, and Factor VIII. Fibrin strands in the microcirculation may cause mechanical damage to red cells, a condition called microangiopathic hemolysis, manifest as schistocytes (fragmented red cells) in the circulation. Widespread microvascular thrombi promote tissue ischemia and release of tissue factor, which further activates thrombin. Lysis of microvascular fibrin causes increased quantities of fibrin degradation products to enter the bloodstream.

Several clinical conditions can initiate DIC, including shock, tissue ischemia, sepsis, hemolytic transfusion reactions, disseminated cancer (particularly adenocarcinoma), acute promyelocytic leukemia, tumor lysis syndrome, and obstetric complications such as amniotic fluid embolism. The common precipitating event is a procoagulant signal for thrombin production that exceeds the normal physiologic defenses against disseminated thrombin activity. Treatment of DIC depends on correcting the underlying problem and preventing further hypotension and tissue ischemia. Replacement therapy focuses on the building blocks of the thrombus (platelets and fibrinogen), and secondarily on other coagulation factors, including Factors VIII, XIII, V, and II. Thus, in bleeding patients, platelet transfusion is indicated when the platelet count falls below 50,000/µL, and cryoprecipitate is supplemented if the fibrinogen level is below 100 mg/dL. FFP is indicated in the setting of hemorrhage that results from DIC once the fibrinogen is above 100 mg/dL.

Topical Use

The fibrinogen in CRYO has been used during surgery as a topical hemostatic preparation, so-called fibrin sealant or fibrin glue, made from one or two units of CRYO, which may be of autologous origin. The fibrinogen is converted to fibrin by the action of bovine thrombin at the site that is bleeding or to be "glued." Commercial preparations of fibrin sealant are available that have a higher fibrinogen concentration than that of CRYO and include human thrombin and bovine aprotinin (see below) to decrease the lysis of the resulting fibrin. These pooled, virus-inactivated products have been licensed for the reduction of bleeding in cardiovascular surgery,[79] for repairing splenic trauma, and for colostomy closure. Fibrin sealants have also been used for a variety of indications in which it is desired to bind two tissue surfaces together, including repair of the dura mater or eardrum.

Use of bovine thrombin can stimulate the formation of antibodies against thrombin and other contaminant proteins including Factor V.[80] These antibodies can cross-react with human thrombin and Factor V, causing abnormal clotting times and, in some cases, bleeding. For this reason, it has been suggested that use of "homemade" fibrin sealants be replaced by use of the commercial product.[80]

Hemophilia A

Each unit of CRYO prepared from a single blood donation should contain a minimum of 80 international units (IU) of Factor VIII.[59(p30)] Although no longer the component of choice, CRYO can serve as replacement therapy for patients with hemophilia A if virus-inactivated Factor VIII concentrates are unavailable.[39] If CRYO is used, the amount required to provide a therapeutic dose of Factor VIII is based on calculations similar to those used for AHF.

Hemophilia A is a sex-linked recessive trait (ie, affected males, carrier females) causing deficiency of Factor VIII (antihemophilic factor, AHF).[81] The responsible genes usually produce a protein with reduced activity, so immunologic measurement of Factor VIII antigen gives normal results despite deficient Factor VIII coagulant activity. In contrast, antigen is typically depressed in von Willebrand disease. Characteristic laboratory findings include a prolonged aPTT, normal PT and template bleeding time, and decreased Factor VIII activity.

The severity of hemophilia A depends on the patient's level of Factor VIII activity, and this varies; patients with severe hemophilia have Factor VIII levels below 1%, whereas those with moderate disease typically have 1% to 5% activity, and severity is mild with levels of 6% to 30%.[81] One unit of Factor VIII activity is defined as the Factor VIII content of 1 mL of fresh, citrated, pooled normal plasma. The measured level of Factor VIII can be expressed as a concentration, as percent activity, or as a decimal fraction. For example, a patient with mild hemophilia with one-tenth the normal activity of Factor VIII can be said to have a Factor VIII level of 10 units/dL or 0.1 unit/mL or 10% activity.

Patients with mild-to-moderate hemophilia can often be managed without replacement therapy.[81] Careful attention to local hemostasis and the use of topical antifibrinolytics may prevent the need for further replacement. Systemic levels of Factor VIII can be raised in mild hemophilia with the use of DDAVP, which stimulates the release of endogenous Factor VIII from storage sites. However, DDAVP is ineffective in patients with severe hemophilia A; in such cases, Factor VIII replacement is required. The amount of Factor VIII infused depends upon whether therapy is intended to prevent bleeding or, if bleeding has occurred, the nature of the bleeding episode and the severity of the initial deficiency (see Table 21-6). For example, treatment for hemarthrosis ordinarily requires more Factor VIII than epistaxis.

Calculating the Dose of Factor VIII

When the desired result is determined (see Table 21-6), the amount of Factor VIII required for transfusion can be calculated by one of the following formulas:

$$\text{Factor VIII dose (IU/kg)} =$$
$$\text{Desired factor increase (\%)} \times 0.5 \text{ (1 IU/kg typically raises the Factor VIII level by 2\%)}$$

$$\text{Total dose} =$$
$$(\text{Patient mass} \times 70\text{mL/kg}) \times (1 - \text{Hct}) \times (\text{Desired activity} - \text{current activity})$$

Example: A 70-kg patient with severe hemophilia has an initial Factor VIII level of 2% (0.02 unit/mL) and a hematocrit of 40%. How many units of Factor VIII concentrate should be given to raise his Factor VIII level to 50% (0.5 unit/mL)?

$$(70 \times 70) \times (1 - 0.4) \times (0.5 - 0.02) = 1411 \text{ units}$$

The therapy of choice for severe hemophilia A is a Factor VIII concentrate (see Table 21-4). CRYO could be used to supply 1411 units of Factor VIII, but, at 80 IU per bag, this would require at least 18 bags (and 18 allogeneic donor exposures). The half-life of Factor VIII is about 12 hours, so infusions are repeated at 8- to 12-hour intervals

Table 21-6. General Factor Replacement Guidelines for the Treatment of Bleeding in Hemophilia

Indication	Initial Minimum Desired Factor Level (%)	Factor VIII Dose* (IU/kg)	Factor IX Dose* (IU/kg)	Duration (days)
Severe epistaxis, oral mucosal bleeding[†]	20-30	10-15	20-30	1-2
Hemarthrosis, hematoma, persistent hematuria,[‡] gastrointestinal tract bleeding, retroperitoneal bleeding	30-50	15-25	30-50	1-3
Trauma without signs of bleeding, tongue/ retropharyngeal bleeding[†]	40-50	20-25	40-50	2-4
Trauma with bleeding, surgery,[§] intracranial bleeding[§]	100	50	100	10-14

Data from USP.[69]

*Dosing intervals are based on a half-life for Factor VIII of 8 to 12 hours (2 to 3 doses/day) and a half-life for Factor IX of 18 to 24 hours (1 to 2 doses/day). Maintenance doses of one half the initial dose may be given at these intervals. The frequency depends on the severity of bleeding, with more frequent dosing for serious bleeding.

[†]In addition to antifibrinolytics.

[‡]Painless spontaneous hematuria usually requires no treatment. Increased oral or intravenous fluids are necessary to maintain renal output.

[§]Continuous factor infusion may be administered. Following the initial loading dose, a continuous infusion at a dose of 3 IU/kg per hour is given. Subsequent doses are adjusted according to the plasma factor levels.

to maintain hemostatic levels. The duration of treatment with Factor VIII infusions depends upon the type and location of the hemorrhage or the reason for prophylaxis, and the clinical response of the patient (see Table 21-6). After major surgery, the Factor VIII level should be maintained above 40% to 50% for at least 10 days. When elective surgery is planned, Factor VIII assays should be made available to serve as a guide to therapy.

Treatment of Inhibitors of Factor VIII

About 10% to 35% of patients with hemophilia A, typically, those with severe dis-ease or genetic defects involving large portions of the molecule, develop a detectable inhibitor to human Factor VIII.[68,81] These antibodies are directed against the active site of Factor VIII, rendering the patient relatively unresponsive to infusion. Patients having an elective invasive procedure should be screened for such inhibitors. Management is difficult; approaches have included attempts to overwhelm the inhibitor with very large doses of human Factor VIII; use of porcine Factor VIII, which has low cross-reactivity with human Factor VIII antibody[81]; use of Factor VIII bypassing agents including Factor IX complex, activated Factor IX complex, and activated Factor VII (see Table 21-4); and desensitization therapy. The latter includes large daily doses of AHF in conjunction with corticosteroids or Immunoglobulin Intravenous (IGIV) and cyclophosphamide. Success rates of 50% to 80% are reported. If hemorrhage is life-threatening, intensive plasmapheresis to remove the inhibiting antibody, coupled with immunosuppression, as well as infusions of Factor VIII and possibly antifibrinolytic therapy (see below), can be employed.

Hemophilia B

Factor IX deficiency (hemophilia B, Christmas disease) is clinically indistinguishable from Factor VIII deficiency in that both are sex-linked disorders that cause a prolonged aPTT in the presence of a normal PT and bleeding time.[81] The disorder is confirmed by specific measurement of Factor IX activity. Factor IX complex concentrate has been used for treatment of hemophilia B for the past 2 decades, but the new, more pure forms of Factor IX concentrate (see Table 21-4) are preferred because they carry much less risk of inducing thrombosis.[82]

The formula for calculating of Factor IX dosage is similar to that for Factor VIII, but the units to be given should be doubled because only half of the infused Factor IX dose is recovered in the vascular space. The biologic half-life is 18 to 24 hours, so doses are given 1 or 2 times/day. As with hemophilia A, recommended dose and treatment schedules vary with the severity and type of bleeding (see Table 21-6).

Immunoglobulin, Intravenous

IGIV is prepared from modified Cohn fraction II and subjected to virus inactivation. Preparations intended for intramuscular administration contain aggregates that may activate the complement and kinin systems and produce hypotensive and/or anaphylactoid reactions if administered intravenously, but the intravenous product contains almost exclusively monomeric IgG molecules.[83]

The indications for the use of IGIV are evolving.[83,84] Some conditions in which IGIV is used are listed in Table 21-7. Infusion of IGIV can induce such reactions as headache, vomiting, volume overload, allergic reactions, renal failure, and pulmonary reactions, but they can usually be prevented by infusing slowly and pretreating with diphenhydramine and/or hydrocortisone. Passively transferred blood group allo- and autoantibodies and/or therapy-induced hypergammaglobulinemia may cause a positive DAT result in recipients, but significant hemolysis is rarely noted.

Antiprotease Concentrates

Antithrombin, also known as heparin cofactor, is a serine protease inhibitor synthesized in the liver.[85] It circulates in normal plasma at a concentration of 15 mg/dL but is typically measured as % activity, with a normal range of 84% to 116%. Antithrombin inactivates serine proteases including thrombin, and Factors IXa, Xa, XIa, and XIIa by covalently bonding at the serine site, followed by a conformation change.[86] This activity is greatly accelerated by heparin, which induces a conformation change in antithrombin and helps approximate thrombin and antithrombin as well.

Patients who are deficient in antithrombin are prone to thromboembolic complications.[87] Such deficiency can be congenital or acquired. Acquired deficiency occurs in a wide variety of disease states, including decreased synthesis due to liver

Table 21-7. Potential Indications and Clinical Uses for Intravenous Immunoglobulin Preparations

Congenital immune deficiencies
  Hypogammaglobulinemia and agammaglobulinemia
  Selective antibody deficiency
  IgG subclass deficiency and recurrent infection
  Premature newborns
  Acquired antibody deficiency
  Malignancies with antibody deficiency and recurrent infection: multiple myeloma,
    chronic lymphocytic leukemia
  Protein-losing enteropathy
  Drug- or radiation-induced humoral immunodeficiency

Prophylaxis or treatment of bacterial and viral diseases
  Pediatric HIV infection for prevention of bacterial and secondary viral infections
  Cytomegalovirus infection in transplant recipients
  Neonatal sepsis

Other
  HIV-related immune thrombocytopenic purpura
  Immune cytopenias (ITP, NAIT, PTP, WAIHA)
  Kawasaki syndrome
  Guillain-Barré syndrome and chronic inflammatory demyelinating neuropathy
  Acquired Factor VIII inhibitors
  Myasthenia gravis
  Multiple sclerosis

---

disease or malnutrition; losses due to nephrotic syndrome and gastrointestinal states; accelerated consumption as in DIC, surgery or trauma, and preeclampsia; and associated with pharmacotherapy including heparin, L-asparaginase, and oral contraceptives.

Antithrombin is stable in plasma so deficiency can be treated with FFP or with Liquid or Thawed Plasma. A heat-treated concentrate of antithrombin is also available; recombinant and transgenic sources are under investigation.

Clinical uses of antithrombin have recently been reviewed.[87] Antithrombin is approved for use in hereditary antithrombin deficiency as part of the treatment for thromboembolic episodes and for prophylactic use in perioperative, postoperative, and peripartum settings. Several off-label uses of antithrombin exist, eg, patients with low antithrombin levels and DIC, neonates born to mothers with antithrombin deficiency, and liver transplant recipients.

The half-life of purified antithrombin is long, approximately 60 to 90 hours,[88] but is abbreviated when replacement is for consumptive states. The dose is calculated on the basis of an expected increment of 1.4% per U per kg, with an initial target of 120%. Other available concentrates of antiproteases include alpha-1-proteinase inhibitor (alpha-1-antitrypsin). C1-esterase inhibitor is not available in the United States.

Protein C and Protein S

Protein C and protein S are vitamin-K-dependent proteins with anticoagulant effects.[86] Protein S is a cofactor for activated protein C, which, in turn, inactivates Factor Va and Factor VIIIa. Patients with deficiencies of protein C or protein S have a predisposition to thrombotic complications and are often treated with anticoagulants.[85] Warfarin treatment, however, can cause these vitamin-K-dependent proteins to decrease to dangerously low levels, leading to skin necrosis and exacerbating thrombosis. Transfusion of FFP can serve as an immediate source of supplemental protein C or protein S for patients with severe deficiencies, and a human protein C concentrate is under development.

Patients with heterozygous protein C deficiency have plasma levels 40% to 60% of normal and characteristically have minimal symptoms, rarely requiring treatment with protein C supplementation.[85] If treatment is needed for a thrombotic episode, anticoagulants suffice. Homozygous protein C deficiency causes neonatal purpura fulminans, which requires immediate administration of protein C, along with complex regulation of the rest of the coagulation cascade. The half-life of infused protein C is 6 to 16 hours.

Colloid Solutions

Human albumin (5% and 25%) and plasma protein fraction (PPF) provide volume expansion and colloid replacement without risk of transfusion-transmitted viruses.[89]

PPF has a greater concentration of nonalbumin plasma proteins than 5% albumin. Pharmacologic agents such as hydroxyethyl starch or dextran are also commonly used for volume expansion.

Physiology of Albumin

The total body albumin mass is about 300 g, of which 40% (120 g) is in the plasma. Daily albumin synthesis in a normal adult approximates 16 g. Albumin has complex roles in normal physiology and disease in addition to its obvious one of maintenance of intravascular volume.[90] Hypoalbuminemia resulting from decreased synthesis, increased catabolism or losses, and shifts between different fluid compartments is common in acute and chronic illness.

Replacement

Albumin solutions are effective volume expanders, with the promise of better intravascular fluid retention than simpler and less expensive crystalloids (eg, normal saline or lactated Ringer's solution). Because hypoalbuminemia is involved in the pathogenesis of many disease states and may correlate with their prognosis, it has been tempting to try to alter their course by exogenous supplementation, particularly in view of the perceived low risk status of albumin solutions. However, this low-risk is in question.

Indications for albumin approved by a consensus panel[91] include:

1. Volume replacement in nonhemorrhagic shock unresponsive to crystalloid or in the presence of capillary leak syndromes.
2. Volume replacement after the first day in patients with extensive burns (>50%) unresponsive to crystalloid.
3. Replacement after removal of large volumes (>4 L) of ascitic fluid in patients unresponsive to crystalloid.
4. Replacement of ascitic fluid or postoperative treatment of ascites and peripheral edema in hypoalbuminemic liver transplant recipients.
5. Replacement during large-volume plasma exchange.
6. Volume replacement in patients with severe necrotizing pancreatitis.

7. Diarrhea (>2 L/day) in hypoalbuminemic (<2.0 g/dL) patients on enteral feedings, unresponsive to short chain peptide supplementation.

Nonalbumin colloid solutions were considered less expensive first alternatives in several of these situations.

In spite of the conceptual attractiveness, the long history of albumin replacement, and the consensus on its use, a number of prospective randomized trials have suggested that albumin use was ineffective or increased mortality. A meta-analysis of 30 randomized trials including 1419 patients grouped according to indication (namely, hypovolemia, burns, and hypoproteinemia) demonstrated higher mortality with albumin treatment for each of the groups.[92] In response to this outcome, the authors of the meta-analysis called for an immediate review of albumin use in critically ill patients.

Special Transfusion Situations

Thalassemia

Thalassemia and sickle cell disease are inherited syndromes characterized by deficient or abnormal hemoglobin structures and anemia. Thalassemia is caused by a deficiency in alpha or beta chain production that ranges from mild to severe. Total absence of synthesis of one of the alpha chains is lethal in utero; absence of beta chain synthesis (thalassemia major) results in a progressive anemia in the newborn period. In an attempt to compensate for significant degrees of anemia, hematopoietic tissue expands, causing characteristic bone abnormalities and enlargement of the liver and spleen. Tissue iron accumulates as a result of increased adsorption and transfusion (see Chapter 27). The only current cure for thalassemia is hemato-

poietic transplantation, but because the anemia can be controlled with red cell transfusions and concurrent iron chelation therapy, the use of this expensive and potentially hazardous therapy is controversial. Transfusion of thalassemia patients is discussed in Chapter 24.

Sickle Cell Disease

Sickle cell disease (SCD) results from a single base substitution in the gene for the beta chain of hemoglobin. The hemoglobin of individuals homozygous for this abnormality can irreversibly polymerize and cause red cells to deform or "sickle." Such cells may initiate blockage of the microvasculature directly or in association with endothelial damage and thrombosis. They also have a decreased life span, so SCD patients have a variably compensated hemolytic anemia. Sickling, which can be triggered by fever, infection, or hypoxia, can lead to a variety of complications or "crises," including pain crisis due to musculoskeletal or other tissue ischemia, splenic or pulmonary sequestration crisis (chest syndrome), aplastic crisis due to transient marrow suppression by viruses (particularly parvoviruses), leg ulcers, priapism, tissue infarction, and stroke.

Most patients with sickle cell disease are asymptomatic most of the time and do not require routine transfusion. Although sickling can be prevented or reversed by maintaining the level of normal hemoglobin above 50% to 70%, the risks from alloimmunization, iron overload, and disease transmission outweigh the benefits of prophylactic transfusion in most patients. Moreover, uncomplicated pain crises do not respond well to simple transfusion. Simple transfusion is indicated for symptomatic anemia, aplastic crises, and blood loss. Sometimes, patients with a history of stroke or pulmonary or cardiac disease are sometimes treated with a hypertransfusion protocol or chronic red cell exchange program to maintain their hematocrit at 25% to 30% and the proportion of hemoglobin S below about 30%. Care should be taken to avoid raising the hematocrit above 35% because of the risks of hyperviscosity. Red cell exchange is used to manage and/or prevent life- or organ-threatening complications, particularly stroke and pulmonary crisis. Red cell exchange has also been used to prepare patients for surgery, but a randomized controlled trial did not support this measure over simple transfusion to a hemoglobin of 10 g/dL.[93]

The clinical management of sickle cell disease is complex and the reader is referred to recent reviews for more details.[94,95] Patients with thalassemia and sickle cell disease can receive standard red cell components. However, leukocyte reduction is generally offered to avoid febrile, nonhemolytic transfusion reactions. Phenotyping the patient's red cells and providing antigen-matched units for transfusion helps reduce alloimmunization to red cell antigens and delayed hemolytic transfusion reactions, although the cost and logistics of such a program may be impractical for many institutions. A frequent compromise is to match for Rh system and K antigens. Patients with SCD should be given hemoglobin-S-negative RBC units. For more details, see Chapter 24.

Transfusing Known Incompatible Blood

Clinicians must occasionally transfuse a patient for whom no serologically compatible RBC units are available. This most often occurs in patients with autoantibodies, which typically react with all red cells; however, once alloantibodies are ruled out, the transfused cells are expected to survive as long as autologous cells. Other situations in which all units appear incompatible include the presence of alloantibodies to high-incidence antigens and multiple antibody specificities.

If serologic testing fails to resolve the problem, or if the problem is identified but time is not sufficient for acquisition of compatible units, the physician must weigh the risks and benefits of transfusion and consider what alternative therapies are suitable. If the need is sufficiently urgent, incompatible red cells of the patient's ABO and Rh type may have to be given. Depending on the alloantibody, incompatible transfusion does not always result in immediate hemolysis, and the incompatible cells may remain in the circulation long enough to provide therapeutic benefit.[96]

If time permits and if equipment is available, the survival of a radiolabeled aliquot of the incompatible cells can be determined. Alternatively, an "in-vivo crossmatch" can be performed by cautiously transfusing 25 to 50 mL of the incompatible cells, watching the patient's clinical response, and checking a 30-minute posttransfusion specimen for hemoglobin-tinged serum. Such assessment does not guarantee normal survival, but it can indicate whether an acute reaction will occur. If no adverse symptoms or hemolysis are observed, the remainder of the unit can be transfused slowly with careful clinical monitoring. If the transfusion need is life-threatening, RBC units may sometimes be given without special testing, but clinical staff should be prepared to treat any reaction that may result.

Transfusing Patients with Autoimmune Hemolytic Anemia

Because of the serologic difficulties that accompany autoimmune hemolytic anemia and the expected short red cell survival, a conservative approach to transfusion is recommended. The presence of underlying alloantibodies should be investigated before beginning transfusions, time permitting. It is very helpful to establish the patient's phenotype before transfusion in order to simplify subsequent investigation for the presence of possible alloantibodies. Chapter 20 contains a more complete discussion.

Massive Transfusion

Massive transfusion is defined as replacement approximating or exceeding the patient's blood volume within a 24-hour interval. The most important factor in supporting tissue oxygenation is maintenance of adequate blood flow and blood pressure by infusing a sufficient volume of crystalloid or blood components to correct or prevent hypovolemic shock.

Emergency Issue

The transfusion service should establish a standard operating procedure for emergency provision of blood. Immunohematologic testing is relatively time-consuming, so it may have to be abbreviated in trauma cases or other hemorrhagic emergencies. Because ABO-compatible components are entirely compatible in the vast majority of cases, particularly if the patient has never been transfused before, group O RBCs are often used for emergency transfusion before completion of any compatibility tests. In this situation, Rh-negative RBCs should be used for females of childbearing potential because of the concern for immunizing such individuals and possibly causing hemolytic disease of the newborn in the future. For women beyond their childbearing years or men, only the current presence of anti-D is a concern. Because this antibody is no more common than certain other blood group alloantibodies, Rh-positive RBCs can be used with similar safety.

The use of so-called "universal donor" RBCs, as discussed above, has several drawbacks. Group O RBCs are typically in short supply because of demographic differences between the donor and recipient populations in the United States, and such universal donor practices accentuate this problem. ABO typing can be performed very quickly, and, in most emergencies, there is time for ABO typing of the recipient and provision of ABO-specific components. Second, transfusion of large quantities of group O RBCs before a recipient blood sample is obtained may obscure subsequent immunohematologic testing. Therefore, even if universal donor RBCs are to be used, a blood sample should be obtained before transfusion; this is possible in all but the most dire cases of exsanguinating hemorrhage. Finally, unexpected blood group antibodies can cause fatal transfusion reactions, particularly in multitransfused patients such as those with SCD or liver disease who present to an emergency room with severe anemia or bleeding. In such situations, a call to another hospital transfusion service at which the patient was previously transfused can be life-saving. Individuals caring for such patients must understand the above principle concerning the priority of volume deficits over anemia.

Emergency situations should not be construed as justification for exceptions to strict identification of recipient blood samples. On the contrary, increased attention to patient identification is warranted, and one indication for use of universal donor RBCs is in situations when multiple trauma victims arrive concurrently, when there is a high risk of recipient misidentification.

AABB *Standards* requires physicians who order transfusion before completion of standard compatibility tests to document the need by signing some type of "emergency release form."[59(p46)] This documentation should be required only after the emergency is over, typically within 24 hours, and signatures on such forms should not be construed as a release of the transfusion service's responsibility. The transfusion service must insist on strict identification of samples, documentation of unit disposition, and documentation of the emergency status of the transfusion. However, it also has the responsibility to perform testing on a STAT basis, provide consultation, and avoid unnecessarily restrictive practices.

Changing Blood Types

The transfusion service should establish guidelines for switching blood types during massive transfusion. An alternative to ABO-identical RBCs is the use of ABO-compatible units (see Table 21-1). The age and sex of the patient are important considerations. For example, when transfusing a young group B, Rh-negative woman, it is preferable to switch to group O, Rh-negative RBCs before switching to group B, Rh-positive cells. The clinical situation should be evaluated by the transfusion service's physician. If the continuing transfusion requirement is expected to exceed the available supply of Rh-negative blood, evaluation of the change to Rh-positive blood should be made early, to conserve blood for other recipients. Once the patient receives one or more Rh-positive units, there may be little advantage in returning to Rh-negative blood.

Coagulation Support During Massive Transfusion

Massive transfusion is often associated with coagulation abnormalities that may manifest as microvascular bleeding (MVB) in the form of oozing from multiple IV sites, failure of blood shed into body cavities to clot, and bleeding from tissue surfaces on which hemostasis was previously obtained. These situations have been attributed to the dilution of platelets or coagulation factors, but consumptive coagulopathy also plays a role (see Chapter 27). Inadequate volume resuscitation and poor tissue perfusion not only promote the release of tissue procoagulant material leading to DIC but also result in lactic acidosis, acidemia, and poor myocardial performance. If MVB occurs, the results of platelet counts, fibrinogen level, PT, and aPTT ideally should guide the need for hemostatic components. Empiric therapy with platelets and/or plasma may be initiated immediately after specimens are obtained. Additional tests may be indicated to evaluate the possibility of DIC. In this situation, a platelet count less than 50,000/µL and a fibrinogen level less than 100 mg/dL are better predictors of hemorrhage than the PT and aPTT.[97] PT results below 1.5 times normal are usually associated with adequate hemostasis during surgery.[3] In most adult patients, these levels are encountered only after transfusion of 15 to 20 RBC units (1.5 to 2 red cell volumes). FFP or platelets should not be administered in a fixed ratio to the number of RBC units given.

Hypothermia, Tissue Oxygenation, and 2,3-DPG

Hypothermia as a complication of transfusion is discussed in Chapter 27. In hypovolemic shock, the underlying pathophysiologic defect is inadequate tissue oxygenation. Oxygen supply to the tissues is determined by many factors, the most important of which are blood flow (perfusion) and hemoglobin concentration. The level of 2,3-DPG decreases in stored RBCs, and this decrease has been suggested as a potential cause of poor tissue oxygenation after massive transfusion. Low 2,3-DPG levels have not been shown to be detrimental to massively transfused patients, although for infants undergoing exchange transfusion, blood with near-normal 2,3-DPG levels is frequently requested. Within 3 to 8 hours after transfusion, previously stored red cells regenerate 50% of normal 2,3-DPG levels.[98]

Pharmacologic Alternatives to Transfusion

Concern over the risks and limitations of transfusion has led to examination of pharmacologic alternatives. Such alternatives might: 1) stimulate increased production or release of blood elements that otherwise would require replacement (eg, erythropoietin); 2) substitute for a blood component (eg, colloid solutions or oxygen-carrying solutions including chemically modified hemoglobins); or 3) alter physiologic mechanisms to reduce the need for replacement (eg, fibrinolytic inhibitors).[99]

Recombinant Growth Factors

Growth factors are low-molecular-weight protein hormones that regulate hematopoiesis by specific interaction with receptors found on progenitor cells. The use of growth factors to stimulate endogenous blood cell production is an important alternative to the use of blood.[100]

Erythropoietin

Recombinant erythropoietin (EPO) is a growth factor that stimulates RBC production.[100] It has been approved for presurgical administration to increase preoperative hemoglobin and hematocrit levels; typical dose regimens range from 300 to 600 U/kg by subcutaneous injection weekly. The use of EPO has markedly reduced the need for transfusion in patients with end-stage renal disease and is indicated for the treatment of anemia in patients infected with human immunodeficiency virus. Intensive EPO treatment (40,000 units weekly) reduced the transfusion requirement of ICU patients.[101] It may also have a role in treating anemia due to chronic disease or to receipt of other medications that suppress the marrow.

Other Blood Cell Growth Factors

Granulocyte-macrophage colony-stimulating factor (GM-CSF) and G-CSF stimulate marrow production of granulocytes.[100] G-CSF is approved for the treatment of chemotherapy-induced neutropenia, for patients undergoing peripheral blood progenitor cell collection and therapy, and for patients with chronic neutropenia. The use of these stimulants decreases the duration of neutropenia, increases tolerance to cytotoxic drugs, and decreases the need for granulocyte transfusions. GM-CSF is approved for use in patients undergoing autologous marrow transplantation. Another potential use for GM-CSF and G-CSF is support of patients undergoing allogeneic marrow transplantation or patients receiving antiviral agents that suppress the marrow. Recombinant interleukin-11 is licensed for cancer patients with thrombocytopenia, but other activators for thrombopoietin receptors have been disappointing and none are available at this time.

Oxygen Therapeutics (Carriers)

Stroma-free hemoglobin solution, in which free hemoglobin has been separated from cell membranes, has several characteristics that render it unsuitable as a blood substitute, including a low p50, short circulation time, high oncotic pressure, and vasopressor/nephrotoxic properties.[102,103]

However, chemical modifications of hemoglobin solutions may successfully overcome these disadvantages and such products are in Phase III clinical trials at the time of this writing. Patients in these trials have survived very severe anemia (residual cellular hemoglobin as low as 1 g/dL) without significant toxicity when supported by these agents.[104] Bovine hemoglobin is approved for veterinary use. Hemoglobin produced by recombinant DNA techniques has also been investigated. Finally, fluorocarbon products that bind oxygen have been extensively investigated.[103] One of the latter, Fluosol, was approved by the FDA for use during percutaneous transluminal angioplasty, but it is no longer available in the United States.

DDAVP

DDAVP is a synthetic analogue of the hormone vasopressin that lacks significant pressor activity.[99,105] First used in the treatment of diabetes insipidus, DDAVP is also useful in promoting hemostasis because of its ability to cause the release of endogenous stores of high-molecular-weight vWF from the vascular subendothelium and the concomitant increase in Factor VIII. Because of its effect on Factor VIII and vWF, DDAVP is used as a hemostatic agent in patients with mild-to-moderate hemophilia A and in patients with some von Willebrand syndromes. Because platelet adhesion and the subsequent formation of a platelet plug depend upon vWF, DDAVP may also be beneficial in a wide variety of platelet function disorders, including uremia, cirrhosis, drug-induced platelet dysfunction (including aspirin), primary platelet disorders, and myelodysplastic syndromes.[99,105,106]

DDAVP can be administered intravenously, subcutaneously, or intranasally. It is usually given as a single injection (0.3 to 0.4 µg/kg) to treat bleeding or for prophylaxis before a procedure. Doses are not usually repeated within a 24- to 48-hour period because of tachyphylaxis (the loss of biologic effect with repeated administration of an agent) and the induction of water retention and hyponatremia. Some patients experience facial flushing or mild hypotension, but side effects are rare. Its effect on vWF occurs within 30 minutes and lasts 4 to 6 hours.[105]

Fibrinolytic Inhibitors

Epsilon aminocaproic acid (EACA) and tranexamic acid—synthetic analogues of lysine—competitively inhibit fibrinolysis by saturating the lysine binding sites at which plasminogen and plasmin bind to fibrinogen and fibrin. The drugs can be used locally or systemically and can be given orally. Aprotinin is a polypeptide prepared from bovine lung that inhibits proteinases including plasmin, kallikrein, trypsin, and, to some extent, urokinase. Thus, it has an antifibrinolytic action but may also inhibit coagulation because kallikrein activates Factor XII. Aprotinin is used intravenously. Because it is a polypeptide, hypersensitivity reactions can occur.[99,107]

Antifibrinolytic agents have been used successfully in cardiac surgery, prostatectomy, and liver transplantation. EACA and tranexamic acid can also be used locally at sites where fibrinolysis contributes to bleeding, as from mucosal lesions of the mouth and gastrointestinal tract, and are of benefit in the control of hemorrhage following dental extractions in patients with hemophilia and in the control of gastrointestinal bleeding. EACA and tranexamic acid may be helpful in controlling bleeding due to severe thrombocytopenia. Systemic administration of fibrinolytic inhibitors has been associated with serious thrombotic complications, including ureteral obstruction due to clot formation and thrombosis of large arteries and veins. When used in excessive doses, fibrinolytic inhibitors can prolong the bleeding time. These drugs should be employed by physicians with experience in their use.

All three of these antifibrinolytic agents, as well as DDAVP, have been used in an attempt to decrease blood use in cardiac surgery, and meta-analyses have shown a decrease in the proportion of patients receiving allogeneic RBCs, the number of units transfused,[108,109] estimated blood losses,[108] and the number of patients requiring reoperation for bleeding.[108,109] Of the three agents, a much larger data base exists for aprotinin, which is the most frequently used. DDAVP was not effective overall but may be useful in patients taking aspirin.[108] Of concern has been a trend toward increased thrombotic complications (myocardial infarction and graft thrombosis) with aprotinin, but they do not appear to be statistically significant.[107,108] Unfortunately, very large studies would be required to demonstrate whether the risk profile of these agents is superior to that of blood, particularly in view of the decreasing risks of transfusion.

Oversight of Transfusion Practice

Of the various institutions that regulate or accredit aspects of transfusion, the Joint Commission for Accreditation of Healthcare Organizations (JCAHO) has historically emphasized oversight of transfusion practice as a requirement for accreditation. As part of its performance improvement standards, the JCAHO requires collection of data regarding the use of blood and scores the institution on the appropriateness of the selected performance measures and the size of the data sample.[110] Moreover, the JCAHO standards require that the medical staff take the leadership role in measurement, assessment, and improvement of clinical processes related to the use of blood and blood components. This assessment process must include peer review, and its findings must be communicated to involved staff members as well as being a part of the renewal of their clinical privileges.

Typically, this function has been delegated to a medical staff committee, often a dedicated "Transfusion Committee." The medical director of the transfusion service should be a member of the committee. This committee should review blood bank activities and statistics, blood ordering, and transfusion practices and should have a process to review records of patients transfused with blood or components. The committee should monitor significant developments in transfusion medicine that would affect patients in the health-care institution and take appropriate action regarding these developments.

The College of American Pathologists (CAP) laboratory accreditation program also requires transfusion oversight. This is mandated by its general standard on quality control and improvement, which states that the blood bank director must evaluate the appropriateness of any laboratory's output in a multidisciplinary fashion.[111] Moreover, the CAP accreditation checklist for blood banks seeks documentation that ". . . the transfusion service medical director actively participates in establishing criteria and in reviewing cases not meeting transfusion audit criteria."[112]

Finally, the AABB *Standards* requires that there be a peer-review program that monitors appropriateness of use of blood components.[59(p86)]

References

1. Welch HG, Meehan KR, Goodnough LT. Prudent strategies for elective red blood cell transfusion. Ann Intern Med 1992;116:393-402.

2. Wilkerson DK, Rosen AL, Gould SA, et al. Oxygen extraction ratio: A valid indicator of myocardial metabolism in anemia. J Surg Res 1987; 42:629-34.

3. Practice guidelines for blood component therapy: Report by the American Society of Anesthesiologists Task Force on Blood Component Therapy. Anesthesiology 1996;84:732-47.

4. Laine E, Steadman R, Calhoun L, et al. Comparison of RBCs and FFP with whole blood during liver transplant surgery. Transfusion 2003;43:322-7.

5. American Association of Blood Banks, America's Blood Centers, American Red Cross. Circular of information for the use of human blood and blood components. Bethesda, MD: AABB, 2002.

6. Practice parameter for the use of red blood cell transfusions: Developed by the Red Blood Cell Administration Practice Guidelines Development Task Force of the College of American Pathologists. Arch Pathol Lab Med 1998; 122:130-8.

7. National Institutes of Health Consensus Development Conference. Perioperative red blood cell transfusion. JAMA 1988;260:2700-3.

8. Hébert PC, Schweitzer I, Calder L. Review of the clinical practice literature on allogeneic red blood cell transfusion. Can Med Assoc J 1997;156(Suppl):S9-26.

9. Goodnough LT, Brecher ME, Kanter MH, AuBuchon JP. Transfusion medicine: First of two parts. N Engl J Med 1999;340:438-47.

10. Weiskopf RB, Viele MK, Feiner J, et al. Human cardiovascular and metabolic response to acute, severe isovolemic anemia. JAMA 1998;279:217-21.

11. Carson JL, Noveck H, Berlin JA, Gould SA. Mortality and morbidity in patients with very low postoperative Hb levels who decline blood transfusion. Transfusion 2002;42:812-8.

12. Vamvakas EC. Epidemiology of red blood cell transfusion. Transfus Med Rev 1996;10:44-61.

13. Bracey AW, Radovancevic R, Riggs SA, et al. Lowering the hemoglobin threshold for transfusion in coronary artery bypass procedures: Effect on patient outcome. Transfusion 1999; 39:1070-7.

14. Johnson RG, Thurer RL, Kruskall MS, et al. Comparison of two transfusion strategies after elective operations for myocardial revascularization. J Thorac Cardiovasc Surg 1992;104:307-14.

15. Carson JL, Terrin ML, Barton FB, et al. A pilot randomized trial comparing symptomatic vs. hemoglobin-level-driven red blood cell transfusions following hip fracture. Transfusion 1998;38:522-9.

16. Blair SD, Janvrin SB, McMollum CN, et al. Effect of early blood transfusion on gastrointestinal hemorrhage. Br J Surg 1986;73:783-5.

17. Hébert PC, Wells G, Blajchman MA, et al. A multicenter, randomized, controlled clinical trial of transfusion requirements in critical care. N Engl J Med 1999;340:409-17.

18. Hébert PC, Yetisir E, Martin C. Is a low transfusion threshold safe in critically ill patients with cardiovascular diseases? Critical Care Med 2001;29:227-34.

19. Wu WC, Rathore SS, Wang Y, et al. Blood transfusion in elderly patients with acute myocardial infarction. N Engl J Med 2001; 345:1230-6.

20. Elwood PC, Waters WR, Green WJW, et al. Symptoms and circulating hemoglobin level. J Chronic Dis 1969;21:615-28.

21. Canadian Erythropoietin Study Group. Association between recombinant human erythropoietin and quality of life and exercise capacity of patients receiving hemodialysis. Br Med J 1990;300:573-8.

22. Parise LV, Smyth SS, Collor BS. Platelet morphology, biochemistry, and function. In: Beutler E, Lichtman MA, Coller BS, et al. Williams' hematology. 6th ed. New York: McGraw-Hill, 2001:1357-408.

23. Darcy MD, Kanterman RY, Kleinhoffer MA, et al. Evaluation of coagulation tests as predictors of angiographic bleeding complications. Radiology 1996;198:741-4.

24. Doerfler ME, Kaufman B, Goldenberg AS. Central venous catheter placement in patients with disorders of hemostasis. Chest 1996;110:185-8.

25. McVay PA, Toy P. Lack of increased bleeding after paracentesis and thoracentesis in patients with mild coagulopathy. Transfusion 1991;31:164-71.

26. Ewe K. Bleeding after liver biopsy does not correlate with indices of peripheral coagulation. Dig Dis Sci 1981;26:388-93.

27. McVay PA, Toy P. Lack of increased bleeding after liver biopsy in patients with mild hemostatic abnormalities. Am J Clin Pathol 1990;94: 747-53.

28. Lind SE. Review: The bleeding time does not predict surgical bleeding. Blood 1991;77: 2547-52.

29. Rodgers RP, Levin J. A critical appraisal of the bleeding time. Semin Thromb Hemost 1990; 16:1-20.

30. Despotis GJ, Goodnough LT. Management approaches to platelet-related microvascular bleeding in cardiothoracic surgery. Ann Thorac Surg 2000;70:S20-32.

31. Hanson SR, Slichter SJ. Platelet kinetics in patients with bone marrow hypoplasia: Evidence for a fixed platelet requirement. Blood 1985;66:1105-9.

32. Aster RH. Effect of anticoagulant and ABO incompatibility on recovery of transfused human platelets. Blood 1965;26:732-43.

33. Heal JM, Masel D, Rowe JM, Blumberg N. Circulating immune complexes involving the ABO system after platelet transfusion. Br J Haematol 1993;85:566-72.

34. Benjamin RB, Antin JH. ABO-incompatible bone marrow transplantation: The transfusion of incompatible plasma may exacerbate regimen-related toxicity. Transfusion 1999; 39:1273-4.

35. Heal JM, Blumberg N. The second century of ABO: And now for something completely different. Transfusion 1999;39:1155-9.

36. McManigal S, Sims KL. Intravascular hemolysis secondary to ABO incompatible platelet products; an underrecognized transfusion reaction. Am J Clin Pathol 1999;111:202-6.

37. Norfolk DR, Ancliffe PJ, Contreras M, et al. Synopsis of background papers (Consensus Conference on Platelet Transfusion). Br J Haematol 1998;101:609-14.

38. National Institutes of Health Consensus Development Conference. Platelet transfusion therapy. Transfus Med Rev 1987;1:195-200.

39. Development Task Force of the College of American Pathologists. Practice parameter for the use of fresh frozen plasma, cryoprecipitate, and platelets. JAMA 1994;271:777-81.

40. Schiffer CA, Anderson KC, Bennett CL, et al. Platelet transfusion for patients with cancer: Clinical practice guidelines of the American Society of Clinical Oncology. J Clin Oncol 2001;19:1519-38.

41. Gmur J, Burger J, Schanz U, et al. Safety of stringent prophylactic platelet transfusion policy for patients with acute leukemia. Lancet 1991;338:1224-6.

42. Wandt H, Frank M, Ehninger G, et al. Safety and cost effectiveness of a 10×10^9/L trigger for prophylactic platelet transfusions compared with the traditional 20×10^9/L trigger; a prospective comparative trial in 105 patients with acute myeloid leukemia. Blood 1991;10:3601-6.

43. Rebulla P, Finazzi G, Morangoni F, et al. The threshold of prophylactic platelet transfu-sions in adults with acute myeloid leukemia. N Engl J Med 1997;337:1870-5.

44. Murphy S, Litwin S, Herring LM, et al. Indications for platelet transfusion in children with acute leukemia. Am J Hematol 1982;12:347-56.

45. Reed RL, Ciavarella D, Heimbach DM, et al. Prophylactic platelet administration during massive transfusion; a prospective, randomized, double-blind clinical study. Ann Surg 1986;203:40-8.

46. Simon TL, Akl BF, Murphy W. Controlled trial of routine administration of platelet concentrates in cardiopulmonary bypass surgery. Ann Thorac Surg 1984;37:359-64.

47. Nguyen CM, Harrington RA. Glycoprotein IIb/IIIa receptor antagonists; a comparative review of their use in percutaneous coronary intervention. Am J Cardiovasc Drugs 2003;3: 423-36.

48. McFarland JG. Matched apheresis platelets. In: McLeod BC, Price TH, Weinstein R, eds. Apheresis: Principles and practice. 2nd ed. Bethesda, MD: AABB Press, 2003:199-220.

49. Kickler TS, Herman JH, eds. Current issues in platelet transfusion therapy and platelet allo-immunity. Bethesda, MD: AABB Press, 1999.

50. Warkentin TE. Management of immune thrombocytopenia. In: Simon TL, Dzik WH, Snyder EL, et al, eds. Rossi's principles of transfusion medicine. 3rd ed. Baltimore, MD: Lippincott Williams and Wilkins, 2002:367-95.

51. Gordon LI, Kwaan HC, Rossi EC. Deleterious effects of platelet transfusions and recovery thrombocytosis in patients with thrombotic microangiopathy. Semin Hematol 1987;24: 194-201.

52. Strauss RG. Granulocyte transfusion. In: McLeod BC, Price TH, Weinstein R, eds. Apheresis: Principles and practice. 2nd ed. Bethesda, MD: AABB Press, 2003:237-52.

53. Price TH. The current prospects for neutrophil transfusions for the treatment of granulo-cytopenic infected patients. Transfus Med Rev 2000;14:2-11.

54. Vamvakas EC, Pineda A. Determinants of the efficacy of prophylactic granulocyte transfusions: A meta-analysis. J Clin Apheresis 1997; 12:74-81.

55. Gresens CJ, Paglieroni TG, Moss CB, et al. WBC populations in thawed fresh frozen plasma (abstract). Transfusion 1999;39(Suppl): 99S.

56. Stringham JC, Bull DA, Fuller TC, et al. Avoidance of cellular blood product transfusions in LVAD recipients does not prevent HLA allosensitization. J Heart Lung Transplant 1999;18(2):160-5.

57. Food and Drug Administration. Memorandum: Recommendations and license requirements for leukocyte-reduced blood products. (May 29, 1996) Rockville, MD: CBER Office of Communication, Training, and Manufacturers Assistance, 1996.

58. Food and Drug Administration. Draft guidance for industry: Prestorage leukocyte reduction with whole blood and blood components intended for transfusion. (January 23, 2001) Rockville, MD: CBER Office of Communication, Training, and Manufacturers Assistance, 2001.

59. Silva MA, ed. Standards for blood banks and transfusion services. 23rd ed. Bethesda, MD: AABB, 2005.

60. Preiksaitis J. The cytomegalovirus-"safe" blood product: Is leukoreduction equivalent to antibody screening? Transfus Med Rev 2000;14:112-36.

61. The trial to reduce alloimmunization to platelets study group. Leukocyte reduction and ultraviolet B irradiation of platelets to prevent alloimmunization and refractoriness to platelet transfusions. N Engl J Med 1997;337:1861-9.

62. Vamvakas EC, Dzik WH, Blajchman MA. Deleterious effects of transfusion associated immunomodulation: Appraisal of the evidence and recommendations for prevention. In: Vamvakas EC, Blajchman MA, eds. Immunomodulatory effects of blood transfusion. Bethesda, MD: AABB Press, 1999:253-85.

63. Krishnan LA, Brecher ME. Transfusion transmitted bacterial infection. Hematol Oncol Clin North Am 1995;9:167-85.

64. Dzik WH, Anderson JK, O'Neill EM, et al. A prospective, randomized clinical trial of universal WBC reduction. Transfusion 2002;42:1114-22.

65. Vamvakas EC, Blajchman MA. Universal WBC reduction: The case for and against. Transfusion 2001;41:691-712.

66. Akahoshi M, Takanashi M, Masuda H, et al. Case reports: A case of transfusion-associated graft-versus-host disease not prevented by white cell-reduction filters. Transfusion 1992; 32:169-72.

67. Roberts HR, Monroe DM III, Hoffman M. Molecular biology and biochemistry of the coagulation factors and pathways of hemostasis. In: Beutler E, Lichtman MA, Coller BS, et al. Williams' hematology. 6th ed. New York: McGraw-Hill, 2001:1409-34.

68. van Aken WG. Preparation of plasma derivatives. In: Simon TL, Dzik WH, Snyder EL, et al, eds. Rossi's principles of transfusion medicine. 3rd ed. Baltimore, MD: Lippincott Williams and Wilkins, 2002:304-15.

69. The United States Pharmacopoeial Convention, Inc. Hemophilia management. Transfus Med Rev 1998;12:128-40.

70. British Committee for Standards in Haematology, Working Party of the Blood Transfusion Task Force. Guidelines for the use of fresh frozen plasma. Transfus Med 1992;2:557-63.

71. Rock G, Shumak KH, Sutton DM, et al. Cryosupernatant as replacement fluid for plasma exchange in thrombotic thrombocytopenic purpura. Members of the Canadian Apheresis Group. Br J Haematol 1996;94: 383-6.

72. Spector I, Corn M, Ticktin HE. Effect of plasma transfusions on the prothrombin time and clotting factors in liver disease. N Engl J Med 1966;275:1032-7.

73. Mannucci PM, Vicente V, Vianello L, et al. Controlled trial of desmopressin in liver cirrhosis and other conditions associated with a prolonged bleeding time. Blood 1986;67:1148-53.

74. Murray DJ, Pennell BJ, Weinstein SL, Olson JD. Packed red cells in acute blood loss: Dilutional coagulopathy as a cause of surgical bleeding. Anesth Analg 1995;80:336-42.

75. National Institutes of Health Consensus Development Conference. Fresh frozen plasma; indications and risks. JAMA 1985;253:551-3.

76. Weinstein R. Basic principles of therapeutic blood exchange. In: McLeod BC, Price TH, Weinstein R, eds. Apheresis: Principles and practice. 2nd ed. Bethesda, MD: AABB Press, 2003:295-320.

77. Jaffee CJ, Atkinson JP, Gelfand JA, Frank MM. Hereditary angioedema: The use of fresh frozen plasma for prophylaxis in patients undergoing oral surgery. J Allergy Clin Immunol 1975;545:386-93.

78. Ginsburg D. von Willebrand disease. In: Beutler E, Lichtman MA, Coller BS, et al, eds. Williams' hematology. 6th ed. New York: McGraw-Hill, 2001:1813-28.

79. Rousou J, Levitsky S, Gonzalez-Levin J, et al. Randomized clinical trial of fibrin sealant in patients undergoing resternotomy or reoperation after cardiac operations. J Thorac Cardiovasc Surg 1989;97:194-203.

80. Streiff MB, Ness PM. Acquired FV inhibitors: A needless iatrogenic complication of bovine thrombin exposure. Transfusion 2002;42:18-26.

81. Roberts HR, Hoffman M. Hemophilia A and hemophilia B. In: Beutler E, Lichtman MA, Coller BS, et al, eds. Williams' hematology. 6th ed. New York: McGraw-Hill, 2001:1639-71.

82. Smith KJ. Factor IX concentrates: The new products and their properties. Transfus Med Rev 1992;6:124-36.

83. Nydegger UE, Mohacsi PJ. Immunoglobulins in clinical medicine. In: Simon TL, Dzik WH, Snyder EL, et al, eds. Rossi's principles of transfusion medicine. 3rd ed. Baltimore, MD: Lippincott Williams and Wilkins, 2002:316-32.

84. Kobayashi RH, Stiehm ER. Immunoglobulin therapy. In: Petz LD, Swisher SN, Kleinman S, et al, eds. Clinical practice of transfusion medicine. 3rd ed. New York: Churchill Livingstone, 1995:985-1010.

85. Goodnight SW, Griffin JH. Hereditary thrombophilia. In: Beutler E, Lichtman MA, Coller BS, et al, eds. Williams' hematology. 6th ed. New York: McGraw-Hill, 2001:1697-714.

86. Griffin JH. Control of coagulation reactions. In: Beutler E, Lichtman MA, Coller BS, et al, eds. Williams' hematology. 6th ed. New York: McGraw-Hill, 2001:1435-49.

87. Bucar SJ, Levy JH, Despotis GJ, et al. Uses of antithrombin III concentrate in congenital and acquired deficiency states. Transfusion 1998;38:481-98.

88. Friedman KE, Menitove JE. Preparation and clinical use of plasma and plasma fractions. In: Beutler E, Lichtman MA, Coller BS, et al, eds. Williams' hematology. 6th ed. New York: McGraw-Hill, 2001:1917-34.

89. McClelland DBL. Safety of human albumin as a constituent of biologic therapeutic products. Transfusion 1998;38:690-4.

90. Doweiko JP, Nompleggi DJ. The role of albumin in human physiology and pathophysiology. Part III: Albumin and disease states. J Parenter Enteral Nutr 1991;15:476-83.

91. Vermeulen LC Jr., Ratko TA, Erstad BL, et al. A paradigm for consensus. The University Hospital consortium guidelines for the use of albumin, nonprotein colloid, and crystalloid solutions. Arch Intern Med 1995;155:373-9.

92. Cochrane Injuries Group Albumin Reviewers. Human albumin administration in critically ill patients: Systemic review of randomized controlled trials. Br Med J 1998;317:235-46.

93. Vichinsky EP, Haberkern CM, Newmayer L, et al. A comparison of conservative and aggressive transfusion regimens in the perioperative management of sickle cell disease. N Engl J Med 1995;333:206-13.

94. Rosse W, Telen M, Ware R. Transfusion support for patients with sickle cell disease. Bethesda, MD: AABB Press, 1998.

95. The National Institutes of Health, National Heart, Lung and Blood Institute, Division of Blood Diseases and Resources. The management of sickle cell disease. 4th ed. Bethesda, MD: NHLBI, 2002. (Available at http://www.nhlbi.nih.gov/health/prof/blood/sickle/sc_mngt.pdf.)

96. Mollison PL, Engelfriet CP, Contreras M. Blood transfusion in clinical medicine. 10th ed. Oxford, England: Blackwell Scientific Publications, 1998.

97. Ciavarella D, Reed RL, Counts RB, et al. Clotting factors and the risk of diffuse microvascular bleeding in the massively transfused patient. Br J Haematol 1987;67:365-8.

98. Heaton A, Keegan T, Holme S, et al. In vivo regeneration of red cell 2,3-diphosphoglycerate following transfusion of DPG-depleted AS-1, AS-3 and CPDA-1 red cells. Br J Haematol 1989;71:131-6.

99. Mannucci PM. Drug therapy: Hemostatic drugs. N Engl J Med 1998;339:245-53.

100. Kruskall MS. Biologic response modifiers—hematopoietic growth factors. In: Petz LD, Swisher SN, Kleinman S, et al, eds. Clinical practice of transfusion medicine. 3rd ed. New York: Churchill Livingstone, 1996:1023-39.

101. Corwin HL, Gettinger A, Pearl RG, et al. Efficacy of recombinant human erythropoietin in critically ill patients: A randomized, controlled trial. JAMA 2002;288:2827-35.

102. Spence RK. Blood substitutes. In: Petz LD, Swisher SN, Kleinman S, et al, eds. Clinical practice of transfusion medicine. 3rd ed. New York: Churchill Livingstone, 1996:967-84.

103. Stowell CP, Levin J, Spiess BD, Winslow RM. Progress in the development of RBC substitutes. Transfusion 2001;41:287-99.

104. Gould S, Moore ED, Hoyt DB, et al. The life-sustaining capacity of human polymerized hemoglobin when red cells might be unavailable. J Am Cell Surg 2002;195:445-52.

105. Schulman S. DDAVP, the multipotent drug in patients with coagulopathies. Transfus Med Rev 1991;5:132-44.

106. Shattil SJ, Abrams CS, Bennett JS. Acquired qualitative platelet disorders due to diseases, drugs, and foods. In: Beutler E, Lichtman MA, Coller BS, et al, eds. Williams' hematology. 6th ed. New York: McGraw-Hill, 2001:1583-602.

107. Bachman F. Disorders of fibrinolysis and use of antifibrinolytic agents. In: Beutler E, Lichtman MA, Coller BS, et al, eds. Williams' hematology. 6th ed. New York: McGraw-Hill, 2001:1829-40.

108. Laupacis A, Fergusson D. Drugs to minimize perioperative blood loss in cardiac surgery: Meta-analysis using perioperative blood transfusion as the outcome. Anesth Analg 1997;85:1258-67.

109. Munoz JJ, Birkmeyer NJ, Birkmeyer JD, et al. Is epsilon-aminocaproic acid as effective as aprotinin in reducing bleeding with cardiac surgery? A meta-analysis. Circulation 1999; 99:81-9.

110. Joint Commission for Accreditation of Healthcare Organizations. 2004 Comprehensive accreditation manual for hospitals, standard PI.3.1.1 and MS.8.1.3 and MS.8.3.

Oakbrook, IL: Joint Commission Resources, 2004.

111. Hamlin WB. Requirements for accreditation by the College of American Pathologists Laboratory Accreditation Program. Arch Pathol Lab Med 1999;123:465-7.

112. CAP Transfusion Medicine Checklist. Revision date 12/31/2003. Northfield, IL: College of American Pathologists, 2003.

Chapter 22

Administration of Blood and Components

G OOD TRANSFUSION PRACTICE requires that comprehensive policies and procedures for blood administration be designed to prevent errors. The development of these policies should be a collaborative effort between the medical director of the transfusion service, the directors of the clinical services, both nursing and medical, and all personnel involved in blood administration. Policies and procedures must be accessible, periodically reviewed for appropriateness, and monitored for compliance. In addition to blood administration policies and procedures, this chapter discusses pretransfusion preparation, issuing of blood components, the equipment used in blood administration, and compatible intravenous solutions.

Pre-Issue Events

Patient Education and Consent

Patients who are aware of the steps involved in a transfusion will experience less anxiety. This is important not only for an adult but also for any child who has the ability to understand the process. In the latter situation, it is appropriate to educate the parents, so that they are better prepared to support their child throughout the transfusion. The transfusionist should explain how the transfusion will be given, how long it will take, what the expected outcome is, what symptoms to report, and that vital signs will be taken. The physician has a responsibility to explain the benefits and risks of transfusion therapy as well as the alternatives in a fashion that the patient can comprehend. Other than in emergency situations, the patient should be given an opportunity to ask questions, and his or her informed choice should be documented. State and local laws govern the process of obtaining and documenting the consent of the patient. Some states have specific requirements for blood transfusion consent. Institutions should be careful to ensure that their individual processes and procedures comply with applicable laws.

Individual institutions have different requirements for obtaining and documenting this interaction, as well as different policies about how often it is necessary. Some facilities require the use of a formal consent form, which provides information in understandable language, signed by the patient. Others expect the physicians to make a note in the medical record stating that the risks of, and alternatives to, blood transfusions were explained and that the patient consented. If a patient is unable to give consent, a responsible family member should be asked. If no family member is available or if the emergency need for transfusion leaves no time for consent, it is prudent to note this in the medical record.[1-3]

Prescription and Special Instructions

There must be documentation of the order by the physician for the blood component(s).[4] Although a telephone order may be acceptable during urgent situations, this must be followed by a written request. Special instructions should be indicated regarding the transfusion relating to the:

- *Component*—eg, washed, irradiated, leukocyte-reduced, cytomegalovirus negative
- *Patient*—eg, premedication, timing
- *Process*—flow rates, rate of infusion, use of a blood warmer or electromechanical pump
- Need for *emergency release*

Component Considerations

Some components require special preparation before release for transfusion. Because these steps are time-consuming and may significantly shorten the shelf life of the component, preparation should be carefully coordinated with the anticipated time of transfusion. The transfusion service must strive to make every effort to ensure that the component is ready when needed, but not so early that it expires before administration.

Medical and nursing staffs need to be aware of special requirements for preparation and to understand that these times cannot be significantly shortened, even in urgent situations. Close communication is required. Some examples of pretransfusion processing procedures are given in Table 22-1.

Patient Considerations

Patients with a history of recurrent allergic transfusion reactions may benefit from premedication with antihistamines or by slowing the rate of transfusion. Routine premedication with antipyretics should be discouraged because delaying a rise in temperature may mask one sign of a hemolytic reaction and partly because they may be ineffective.[5-7]

Antipyretics typically do not mask other clinical features of hemolysis, such as changes in blood pressure, pulse, or respiration. Premedication orders should be carefully timed with the anticipated administration of the unit. Medication ordered intravenously may be given immediately before the start of the transfusion, but orally administered drugs need to be given 30 to 60 minutes before the start of the transfusion.

Process Considerations

Blood warmers and electromechanical pumps need to be available if required for the transfusion.

Emergency Release

Blood may be released without completing pretransfusion testing if it is urgently needed for a patient's survival, provided that: 1) the records properly document

Table 22-1. Component Preparation Times

Component	Minimum Time*	Shelf Life
RBCs: saline-washed	45 minutes	24 hours
RBCs: thawed-deglycerolized	75 minutes	24 hours or 2 weeks[†]
Fresh Frozen Plasma: thawed	30 minutes	24 hours
Thawed Plasma	—	5 days
Platelets: pooled	15 minutes	4 hours
CRYO: thawed (single unit)	15 minutes	6 hours
CRYO: pooled	15 minutes	4 hours

*Will vary with institutional procedures.
[†]Depends on the method used.
RBCs = Red Blood Cells; CRYO = Cryoprecipitated AHF.

the emergency request and 2) the issued units are of an ABO group unlikely to cause immediate harm to the recipient.

Venous Access

To avoid any delay in transfusion and potential wastage of blood components, venous access should be established before the component is issued. If a pre-existing line is to be used, it should be checked for patency; signs of infiltration, inflammation, or infection; and the compatibility of any intravenous solutions (see below). Many venous access devices can be used for blood component transfusion. Selection depends on the location, size, and integrity of the patient's veins; the type of medication or solution to be infused; the type of component to be transfused; the volume and timing of the administration; the possibility of interactions among parenteral solutions; and expected duration of intravenous therapy.

The lumen of needles or catheters used for blood transfusion should be large enough to allow appropriate flow rates without damaging the vein. There are no strict guidelines limiting the size of the catheter or needles used for transfusion. An 18-gauge catheter provides good flow rates for cellular components without excessive discomfort to the patient, but patients with small veins require much smaller catheters. High-pressure flow through needles or catheters with a small lumen may damage red cells[8-10] unless the transfusion component is sufficiently diluted.[10] Undiluted preparations of red cells flow very slowly through a 23-gauge needle, but dilution with saline to increase the flow rate may cause unwanted volume expansion. Even in patients with cardiac disease or volume expansion, transfusions should be able to be given safely within 4 hours. For rare patients unable to tolerate a transfusion within 4 hours, local policy should be developed regarding whether to split units or to discard the unused portion. Specific models of infusion pumps have been approved for use in blood transfusion. These pumps maintain a constant delivery of blood, and studies have indicated no significant evidence of hemolysis as the needle size varies.[11]

Central venous catheters are used for medium- and long-term therapy or for the administration of solutions potentially toxic to a peripheral vein to allow the dilution achieved with high-volume blood flow. Some catheters are placed via special introducing needles and guide-wires; others are surgically implanted. Catheters with a multilumen design have separate infusion ports for each lumen, permitting the simultaneous infusion of fluids without intermixture in the infusion line, thereby avoiding the potential for hemolysis from incompatible fluids.

Need for Compatibility Testing

The transfusion service personnel determine what pretransfusion testing is required. Compatibility testing must be performed for transfusion of Whole Blood, components with a clinically significant red cell content, and all red cell components. For test and specimen requirements, refer to Chapter 18. Compatibility testing other than ABO and Rh typing is not required for platelet and plasma components, but most facilities require that the recipient's ABO and D types be known (on file) before such components are selected for issue. Whenever possible, plasma-containing components should be compatible with the patient's red cells (see Chapter 21).

Blood Issue and Transportation

Delivering Blood to the Patient Area

Institutions should define blood pick-up and delivery policies and appropriate training programs for the staff assigned to these functions. Blood is not routinely dispensed from the controlled environment of the blood bank until all testing is completed, the patient is properly prepared, and the transfusionist is ready to begin the procedure. There must be a mechanism to identify the intended recipient and the requested component at the time of issue. It is optimal to identify the transporter.

Transfusion service personnel will review identifying information, inspect the appearance of the component before release, and ensure there is a system to maintain proper storage temperature during transport. The safest practice is to issue one unit to one patient at a time. For patients who are rapidly bleeding or who have multiple venous access sites, multiple units may be issued to a single patient. It is not recommended that blood for two or more patients be issued simultaneously to one transporter because this could increase the chance of transfusion error. However, logistical considerations may make this impractical. The transporter should transport the blood to the intended site of transfusion without delay—preferably to the transfusionist. It is preferable to place the unit of blood in a protective container that would contain any spillage in the event of inadvertent breakage during transport.

The responsibility for accurately identifying a transfusion component rests with both the transfusion service personnel who issue the blood and the transfusionist who receives it. Before a unit of blood is issued, transfusion service personnel complete the following steps:

1. The records that identify the intended recipient and the requested component are reviewed.

2. The identifiers (*Standards* requires at least two) of the intended recipient, the ABO and D type of the recipient, the component unit number, the ABO and D type of the donor unit, and the interpretation of compatibility tests (if performed) are re-

corded on a transfusion form for each unit. This form, or a copy, becomes a part of the patient's permanent medical record after completion of the transfusion. In some institutions, the transfusion form is attached to the unit and, therefore, serves as the tie tag that is required and described below. This form typically will have fields to identify the transfusionist and co-identifier (if required) and other information, such as pre- and posttransfusion vital signs, amount of blood given, whether a reaction occurred, etc.

3. A tie tag or label with the name and identification number of the intended recipient, the component unit number, and the interpretation of compatibility tests (if performed) must be securely attached to the blood container.

4. The appearance of the unit is checked before issue and a record is made of this inspection.

5. The expiration date (and time if applicable) is checked to ensure that the unit is suitable for transfusion.

6. The name of the person issuing the blood and the date and time of issue are recorded. Recording the name of the transporter to whom the blood is issued is optimal.

Delay in Starting the Transfusion

Ideally, blood should be requested from the blood bank only at the time when it is intended to be administered. If the transfusion cannot be initiated promptly, the blood should be returned to the blood bank for storage, unless the transfusion to the originally intended recipient can be completed within 4 hours. It should not be left at room temperature or stored in an unmonitored refrigerator. Units re-turned to the blood bank after a period outside monitored refrigeration will be unsuitable for reissue if the sterility of the container is compromised or if the temperature has risen to 10 C or above, which is generally considered to happen in less than 30 minutes. If the units have been kept in suitable conditions, such as iced coolers that have been validated for several hours of storage, longer periods are acceptable. Requirements for blood collected intraoperatively differ. See Table 5-8. Units that have been entered (punctured) after release from the blood bank cannot be accepted into general inventory for later reissue.

Pre-Administration Events
Identifying the Recipient and Donor Unit

Accurate identification of the transfusion component and the intended recipient may be the single most important step in ensuring transfusion safety.[12-15] Most hemolytic transfusion reactions and deaths occur because of inadvertent administration of ABO-incompatible red cells.[14-15] Plasma and platelets are also capable of causing serious transfusion reactions.[16] Identification and labeling of donor blood are discussed in Chapter 7; procedures to identify the patient's specimen used for compatibility testing are discussed in Chapter 18. The most important steps in safe transfusion administration are clerical and occur when the transfusion service issues blood for a specific patient and when the blood is administered.

The transfusionist who administers the blood represents the last point at which identification errors can be detected before transfusion of the component is initiated. The transfusionist must check all identifying information immediately before beginning the transfusion and record that this information has been checked and found to be correct, typically, on the transfusion form. Any discrepancy must be resolved before the transfusion is started. It is common practice in many institutions that a second person (co-identifier) confirms the identity of the blood unit and of the patient. Some institutions may require that the transfusionist check for documentation of patient consent before blood is given. It is also common practice to check the ABO and D type as written in the transfusion form with a record of ABO and D type in the patients' chart. The following information, however, *must* be reviewed and found to be correct:

1. *Physician's order.* The nature of the blood or component should be checked against the physician's written order to verify that the correct component and dose (number of units) are being given. All identification attached to the container must remain attached until the transfusion has been completed.

2. *Recipient identification.* The patient's identifiers on the patient's identification band must be identical with the identifiers attached to the unit. It is desirable to ask the patient to state his or her name, if capable of so doing, because the information on the identification band may be in error.[17]

3. *Unit identification.* The unit identification number on the blood container, the transfusion form, and the tie tag attached to the unit (if not the same as the latter) must agree.

4. *ABO and D.* The ABO and D type on the primary label of the donor unit must agree with those recorded on the transfusion form. The recipient's ABO and D type must be recorded on the transfusion form. The patient's type and the type of the com-

ponent may not be identical (see Chapter 21), but the information on the transfusion form and that on the container label must be the same.

5. *Expiration.* The expiration date and time of the component should be verified as acceptable.

6. *Compatibility.* The interpretation of compatibility testing (if performed) must be recorded on the transfusion form and on the tag attached to the unit (if not the same). If blood was issued before compatibility tests were completed, this must be conspicuously indicated.

In certain clinical situations, such as the operating room (OR), emergency room, or in the outpatient setting, an identifying band may not be attached to all patients at the time of transfusion. Wristbands are frequently removed in the OR for arterial line insertions and identity confirmation may not be possible in this manner. Furthermore, a co-identifier confirming identity, although always desirable, may not function for all circumstances in this setting. Institutions should address such clinical situations, and site-specific transfusion protocols should be developed.[18]

Starting the Transfusion

After checking all the identifying information, the transfusionist (and co-identifier) must indicate in the medical record that the identification was correct (such as by signing the transfusion form) to document who started the transfusion and to record the date and time. Vital signs should be taken and recorded, if not done previously. A record of the date and time of transfusion, the name and volume of the component, and vital signs may be required on other parts of the medical record, such as intake/output records, anesthesia records, or intensive care flow sheets, depending on the institution's policy. This may suffice for documentation purposes.

Several reports have documented the occurrence of errors at the point of blood administration.[19-22] In particular, Baele and colleagues[19] studied the charts and records of 808 patients who received 3485 units of blood over a period of 15 months, to determine if there had been errors in blood administration. They detected 165 errors occurring after blood units had left the blood bank, 15 of which were considered to be major. Seven of the major errors involved patient misidentification that resulted in blood being given to patients for whom it was not intended, constituting 0.74% of patients and 0.2% of units. One error resulted in an ABO-incompatible hemolytic reaction that was not reported to the blood bank. Eight other major errors occurred in four patients (0.5%), including the administration of five allogeneic units to a patient for whom autologous blood was available, and the transfusion of one anemic patient whose doctor had ordered only a crossmatch. The remaining 150 errors included misrecording (n = 61), mislabeling (n = 6), and failure to adequately document the transfusion (n = 83).

Both mechanical barrier systems[23] and electronic means of patient and product identifications are marketed to supplement (but not substitute for) the paper identification process. In electronic systems, a bar code or radio frequency identifiers are attached to the blood component (and transfusion form) that, when scanned/read, will match the patient's information on the identification band.[24] It is likely that these electronic means will find more widespread use in the future. Empiric experience with medication administration, however, suggests that unanticipated side effects of such procedures may need consideration.[25]

Compliance with institutional blood administration policies requires a Quality Assurance/Continuous Improvement program in which continued monitoring and re-education of staff occur when variance with procedures is observed. Such an approach has been initiated in some institutions, resulting in improvement in transfusion practice.[26] Direct observation of administration[27] or educational videos[28] may also be useful.

Administration

Infusion Sets

Any blood component must be administered through a filter designed to retain blood clots and particles potentially harmful to the recipient.[4,29(p48)] All filters and infusion devices must be used according to the manufacturer's directions.

Standard Sets

Standard blood infusion sets have inline filters (pore size: 170 to 260 microns), drip chambers, and tubing in a variety of configurations. Sets should be primed according to the manufacturer's directions, using either the component itself or a solution compatible with blood (see the section on Compatible IV Solutions). For optimal flow rates and performance, filters should be fully wetted. Drip chambers should be half-filled to allow observation of blood flow.

Many institutions have a policy of changing sets after every transfusion or of limiting their use to several units or several hours in order to reduce the risks of bacterial contamination. A reasonable time limit is 4 hours; this is consistent with the 4-hour outdate that the Food and Drug Administration (FDA) places on blood in an open system held at room temperature. Most standard filters are designed to filter 2 to 4 units of blood, but if the first unit required 4 hours for infusion, the filter should not be reused. The filter traps cell aggregates, cellular debris, and coagulated proteins, resulting in a high protein concentration at the filter surface. The high protein milieu and room temperature conditions promote growth of any bacteria that might be present. Accumulated material also slows the rate of flow.[30]

Special Sets

High flow sets for rapid transfusion have large filter surface areas, large-bore tubing, and may have an inline hand pump. Sets designed for rapid infusion devices also may have "prefilters" to retain particles over 300 microns in diameter and to extend the life of standard blood filters "downstream." Gravity-drip sets for the administration of platelets and cryoprecipitate have small drip chamber/filter areas, shorter tubing, and smaller priming volumes. Syringe-push sets for component administration have the smallest priming volumes and an inline blood filter that may be inconspicuous.

Microaggregate Filters

Microaggregate filters are designed for the transfusion of red cells. Microaggregates (smaller than 170 microns in size) pass through standard blood filters. Screen- or depth-type filters have an effective pore size of 20 to 40 microns and trap the microaggregates composed of degenerating platelets, leukocytes, and fibrin strands that form in blood after 5 or more days of refrigerated storage.

Microaggregate filters may be used for other components if this use is mentioned in the manufacturer's instructions; how-ever, the large volume required for priming causes a significant portion of these components to be lost if the set is not flushed with saline afterward. Depth-type micro-aggregate filters, or any filters capable of removing leukocytes, must not be used for the transfusion of granulocyte concentrates.[29(p48)] Hemolysis of red cells has been reported with microaggregate filters.[30]

Leukocyte Reduction Filters

Special "third-generation" blood filters can reduce the number of leukocytes in red cell or platelet components to less than 5×10^6, a level that reduces the risk of HLA alloimmunization and the transmission of cytomegalovirus as well as the incidence of febrile nonhemolytic transfusion reactions[31-35] (see Chapters 8, 21, and 27). These filters contain multiple layers of synthetic nonwoven fibers that selectively retain leukocytes but allow red cells or platelets to pass, depending on the filter type. Selectivity is based on cell size, surface tension characteristics, the differences in surface charge, density of the blood cells, and, possibly, cell-to-cell interactions and cell activation/adhesion properties.[36] Because filters for red cells and filters for platelets do not use the same technology for leukocyte removal and may have strict priming and flow rate requirements, they must be used only with their intended component and only according to the manufacturer's directions.[37]

The use of these filters at the bedside is more complex than the use of standard infusion sets. The filters are expensive and can be ineffective or may clog, if improperly used.[38-40] Those designed only for gravity infusion should not be used with infusion pumps or applied pressure. A quality control program that measures the effectiveness of leukocyte reduction is important, but impractical, at the bedside; therefore, adherence to proper protocol is very important.

Blood Warmers

It is desirable for the medical staff of the transfusion service to participate in the assessment and selection of transfusion equipment and ensure that such items are included in the facility's quality assurance program. The performance of devices such as blood warmers or infusion pumps must be validated before the equipment is used and must be monitored regularly throughout the facility to identify malfunctions and ensure appropriate use. This characteristically requires cooperation among personnel of several hospital departments, including transfusion medicine, nursing, anesthesiology, quality assurance, and clinical engineering.

Patients who receive blood or plasma at rates faster than 100 mL/minute for 30 minutes are at increased risk for cardiac arrest unless the blood is warmed.[41] Rapid infusion of large volumes of cold blood can lower the temperature of the sinoatrial node to below 30 C, at which point an arrhythmia can occur.

Transfusions at such rapid rates generally occur only in the OR or trauma settings. There is no evidence that patients receiving 1 to 3 units of blood over several hours have a comparable risk for arrhythmias; therefore, routine warming of blood is not recommended.[42] Several types of blood warmers are available: thermostatically controlled waterbaths; dry heat devices with electric warming plates; and high-volume countercurrent heat exchange with water jackets.[43] Blood warming devices must not raise the temperature of blood to a level that causes hemolysis.[29(p6)]

Devices should have a visible thermometer and, ideally, an audible alarm that sounds before the manufacturer's designated temperature limit is exceeded. The standard operating procedure for warming blood should include guidelines on performing temperature and alarm checks, and instructions on what action to take when warmers are out of range or the alarm activates.[44] Conventional microwave ovens and microwave devices for thawing plasma are not designed for warming other blood components and can damage red cells.

Electromechanical Infusion Devices

Mechanical pumps that deliver infusions at a controlled rate are useful, especially for very slow rates of transfusion used for pediatric, neonatal, and selected adult patients. Some pumps use a mechanical screw drive to advance the plunger of a syringe filled with blood; others use roller pumps or other forms of pressure applied to the infusion tubing. Although some can be used with standard blood administration sets, many require special plastic disposables or tubing supplied by the manufacturer. Blood filters can be added to the required setups upstream of the pumps.

The manufacturer should be consulted before blood is administered with an infusion pump designed for crystalloid or colloid solutions. Many induce hemolysis, but of a magnitude that does not adversely affect the patient.[43] Red cells in components with high hematocrit and high viscosity are more likely to be hemolyzed when infused under pressure than red cells in Whole Blood or red cell components prepared in a manner that reduces viscosity, such as additive solutions.[45] Platelets and granulocytes appear to sustain no adverse effects when infused with a pumping device.[46,47] Proper training of personnel and appropriate policies for maintenance and quality control should reduce the chances of damage to transfused components.

Pressure Devices

Urgent transfusion situations may require flow rates faster than gravity can provide. The simplest method to speed infusion is to use an administration set with an inline pump that the transfusionist squeezes by hand. Pressure bags specially designed as compression devices are also available. These devices operate much like blood pressure cuffs except that they completely encase the blood bag and apply pressure more evenly to the bag's surface. Such devices should be carefully monitored during use because pressures greater than 300 mm Hg may cause the seams of the blood bag to rupture or leak and air embolism is a concern. Large-bore needles are traditionally recommended for venous access when the use of external pressure is anticipated, but recent data question this practice.[11] Manually forcing red cells through a small-gauge line has been shown to cause hemolysis.[45]

Devices for intraoperative and postoperative blood collection are discussed in Chapter 5.

Compatible IV Solutions

AABB *Standards for Blood Banks and Transfusion Services*[29(p48)] and the *Circular of Information for the Use of Human Blood and Blood Components*[48] are explicit in stating that medications must not be added to blood or components. If red cells require dilution to reduce their viscosity or if a component needs to be rinsed from the blood bag or tubing, normal saline (0.9% sodium chloride injection, USP) can be used. Red cells prepared with an additive solution (AS) ordinarily do not require dilution. These red cell components have a hematocrit of approximately 60%. Other solutions intended for intravenous use may be added to blood or components or may come into contact with blood in an administration set only if they have been approved for this use by the FDA or if there is documentation to show that their addition to blood is safe and efficacious.[29(p6),48] Calcium-free, isotonic electrolyte solutions that meet the above requirements also may be used, but they usually are more expensive than saline and offer little benefit in routine transfusion. Lactated Ringer's solution, 5% dextrose, and hypotonic sodium chloride solutions should not be added to blood. Dextrose solution may cause red cells to clump in the tubing and, more important, to swell and hemolyze as dextrose and associated water diffuse from the medium into the cells. Lactated Ringer's solution contains enough ionized calcium (3 mEq/L) to overcome the chelating agents in anticoagulant-preservative or additive solutions, which results in clot development.[49-51]

Patient Care During Transfusion

The transfusionist should either remain with, or be in a position to closely observe, the patient for at least the first 15 minutes of the infusion. The transfusion should be started slowly at a rate of approximately 2 mL/minute except during urgent restoration of blood volume. Catastrophic reactions from acute hemolysis, anaphylaxis, transfusion-related acute lung injury, or bacterial contamination can become apparent after a very small volume enters the patient's circulation (see Chapter 27).

After the first 15 minutes, some institutions record vital signs, but this is unnecessary if the patient's condition is satisfactory. The rate of infusion can be increased to that specified in the order or to be consistent with institutional practice (approximately 4 mL/minute). The desirable rate of infusion depends upon the patient's blood volume, cardiac status, and hemodynamic condition. No experimental or clinical data exist to support a specific time restriction; however, the *Circular of Information*[48] gives 4 hours as the maximum duration for an infusion. Maximum time should not be confused with recommended time. Most RBC units are transfused within 1 to 2 hours, whereas platelet or plasma transfusions are commonly administered over a shorter period (30 to 60 minutes). However, there is no physiologic reason to administer compatible red cells more slowly than plasma or platelets and rapid infusion of these products may increase the risk of adverse events. If rapid transfusion is needed, blood can be infused as rapidly as the patient's circulatory system will tolerate and the type of vascular access will allow.

If it is anticipated that an infusion time of longer than 4 hours may be required, the physician covering the transfusion service should be notified to assess the specific clinical situation. Administration rates are calculated by counting the drops per minute in the drip chamber and dividing this number by the "drop/mL" rating of the infusion system. Blood may flow more slowly than desired as a result of obstruction of the filter or when there is excessive viscosity of the component. Steps to investigate and correct the problem include the following:

■ Elevate the blood container to increase hydrostatic pressure.
■ Check the patency of the needle.
■ Examine the filter of the administration set for excessive debris.
■ Consider the addition of 50 to 100 mL of saline to a preparation of red cells, if there is an order permitting such addition.

Clinical personnel should continue to observe the patient periodically throughout the transfusion (eg, every 30 minutes) and up to an hour after completion.

Action for Suspected Reactions

Most transfusions proceed without complication, but when adverse reactions do occur, medical and nursing staff must be prepared to deal with them immediately. Different types of reactions, their etiology, symptoms, treatment, and prevention are discussed in Chapter 27. Because severity can vary significantly and symptoms are not specific, all transfusions must be carefully monitored and stopped as soon as a reaction is suspected. It may be helpful to summarize common symptoms and the immediate steps to take on the transfusion form that accompanies the unit. This eliminates the need to search for instructions and helps standardize patient care in an urgent situation.

Post-Administration Events

After each unit of blood has been infused, personnel should measure vital signs; record the time, the volume, and the component given; record the patient's condition; and record the identity of the person who stopped the transfusion (if not the transfusionist), made the observations, and measured and recorded vital signs. Many transfusion services require that a copy of the completed transfusion form be returned to the laboratory to document the unit's disposition for laboratory records. The empty blood bag need not be returned after uncomplicated transfusions, but bags, tubing, and attached solutions should be returned to the transfusion service if a complication occurs.

Some transfusion services choose to have all bags returned following all transfusions in order to investigate reactions that may not be evident at the time of transfusion. Proper biohazard precautions should be used in the handling of entered containers and used administration sets. The patient should remain under observation after the transfusion has been completed, if this is practical. Because not all severe reactions are immediately apparent, all patients who receive transfusions in outpatient or home care settings, or their caretakers, must be given clearly written instructions outlining posttransfusion care, a description of the signs and symptoms of acute and delayed reactions, and the appropriate action to take if such are noted.

Quality Assurance

The process of blood administration should begin and end with patient safety in mind, starting with the generation of an appropriate order; continuing through collection of the patient's pretransfusion specimen, preparation and delivery of the unit, identification of the unit with the recipient, and selection and proper use of equipment; and concluding with patient care during the transfusion and maintenance of appropriate records. Policies, procedures, training, and assessment are all critical to this process and must be monitored as parts of blood usage review.

Periodic auditing of the blood administration process and forms should be performed in order to identify patterns of nonconformance. Errors, regardless of clinical outcome, should be subjected to root-cause analysis because such errors are often indicative of systematic problems.

References

1. Sazama K. Practical issues in informed consent for transfusion. Am J Clin Pathol 1997; 107:572-4.
2. Holland PV. Consent for transfusion: Is it informed? Transfus Med Rev 1997;11:274-85.
3. Williams FG. Consent for transfusion: A duty of care. Br Med J 1997;315:380-1.
4. Code of Federal Regulations. 42 CFR 482.23(c)(2). Washington, DC: US Government Printing Office, 2004 (revised annually).
5. Wang SE, Lara PN, Lee-Ow A, et al. Acetaminophen and diphenhydramine as premedication for platelet transfusions: A prospective randomized double-blind placebo-controlled trial. Am J Hematol 2002;70: 191-4.
6. Agostini JV, Leo-Summers LS, Inouye SK. Cognitive and other adverse effects of diphenhydramine use in hospitalized older patients. Arch Intern Med 2001;161:2091-7.
7. Patterson BJ, Freedman J, Blanchette V, et al. Effect of pre-medication guidelines and leukoreduction on the rate of febrile nonhemolytic platelet transfusions. Transfus Med 2000;10:199-206.
8. Wilcox GJ, Barnes A, Modanlou H. Does transfusion using a syringe infusion pump and small gauge needle cause hemolysis? Transfusion 1981;21:750-1.
9. Herrera AJ, Corless J. Blood transfusions: Effect of speed of infusion and of needle gauge on hemolysis. J Pediatr 1981;99:757-8.
10. de la Roche MR, Gauthier L. Rapid transfusion of packed red blood cells: Effects of dilution, pressure, and catheter size. Ann Emerg Med 1993;22:1551-5.
11. Frelich R, Ellis MH. The effect of external pressure, catheter gauge, and storage time on hemolysis in RBC transfusion. Transfusion 2001;41:799-802.
12. AuBuchon JP, Kruskall MS. Transfusion safety: Realizing efforts with risks. Transfusion 1997;37:1211-15.
13. McClelland DBL, Phillips P. Errors in blood transfusion in Britain: Survey of hospital haematology departments. Br Med J 1994; 308:1205-6.
14. Linden JV, Wagner K, Voytovich AE, Sheehan J. Transfusion errors in New York State: An analysis of 10 years' experience. Transfusion 2000;40:1207-13.
15. Sazama K. Reports of 355 transfusion-associated deaths: 1976-1985. Transfusion 1990;30: 583-90.
16. McManigal S, Simms KL. Intravascular hemolysis secondary to ABO incompatible

platelet products. Am J Clin Pathol 1999;11: 202-6.

17. Renner SW, Howanitz PJ, Bachner P. Wrist band identification error reporting in 712 hospitals. Arch Pathol Lab Med 1993;117: 573-7.

18. Vicki C, Bower J. Blood administration in perioperative settings. AORN J 1997;66:133-43.

19. Baele PL, De Bruyere M, Deneys V, et al. Bedside transfusion errors. Vox Sang 1994;66:117-21.

20. Murphy MF, Atterbury CLJ, Chapman JF, et al. The administration of blood and blood components and the management of transfused patients. Transfus Med 1999;9:227-38.

21. Ibojie J, Urbaniak SJ. Comparing near misses with actual mistransfusion events: A more accurate reflection of transfusion error. Br J Haematol 2000;108:458-60.

22. Galloway M, Woods R, Whitehead S, et al. An audit of error rates in a UK district hospital transfusion laboratory. Transfus Med 1999;9: 199-203.

23. Wenz B, Burns ER. Improvement in transfusion safety using a new blood unit and and patient identification system as part of safe transfusion practice. Transfusion 1991;31: 401-3.

24. Jensen NJ, Crosson JT. An automated system for bedside verification of the match between patient identification and blood unit identification. Transfusion 1996;36:216-21.

25. Patterson ES, Cook RI, Render ML. Improving patient safety by identifying side effects from introducing bar coding in medication administration. J Am Med Inform Assoc 2002;9: 540-3.

26. Shulman IA, Lohr K, Derdiarian A, Picukaric JM. Monitoring transfusionist practices: A strategy for improving transfusion safety. Transfusion 1994;34:11-15.

27. Whitsett CF, Robichaux MG. Assessment of blood administration procedures: Problems identified by direct observation and administrative incident reporting. Transfusion 2001; 41:581-6.

28. Broods JP, Combest TG. In-service training with videotape is useful in teaching transfusion medicine principles. Transfusion 1996; 36:739-42.

29. Silva MA, ed. Standards for blood banks and transfusion services. 23rd ed. Bethesda, MD: AABB, 2005.

30. Schmidt WF, Kim HC, Tomassini N, Schwartz E. Red blood cell destruction caused by a micro-pore blood filter. JAMA 1982;248:1629-32.

31. Stack G, Pomper GJ. Febrile allergic and nonimmune transfusion reactions. In: Simon TL,

Dzik WH, Stowell CP, et al, eds. Principles of transfusion medicine. 3rd ed. Baltimore, MD: Williams and Wilkins, 2002:831-51.

32. Novotny VM, van Doorn R, Witvliet MD, et al. Occurrence of allogeneic HLA and non-HLA antibodies after transfusion of prestorage filtered platelets and red blood cells: A prospective study. Blood 1995;85:1736-41.

33. Brand A, Claas FH, Voogt PJ, et al. Alloimmunization after leukocyte-depleted multiple random donor platelet transfusions. Vox Sang 1998;54:160-6.

34. Bowden RA, Slichter SJ, Sayers M, et al. A comparison of leukocyte-reduced and cytomegalovirus (CMV) seronegative blood products for the prevention of transfusion-associated CMV infection after marrow transplant. Blood 1995;86:3598-603.

35. Narvios AB, Przepiorka K, Tarrand J, et al. Transfusion support using filtered unscreened blood products for cytomegalovirus negative allogeneic marrow transplant recipients. Bone Marrow Transplant 1998;22:575-7.

36. Buril A, Beugeling T, Feijen J, van Aken WG. The mechanisms of leukocyte removal by filtration. Transfus Med Rev 1995;9:145-66.

37. Dzik WH. Leukoreduced blood components: Laboratory and clinical aspects. In: Simon TL, Dzik WH, Stowell CP, et al, eds. Principles of transfusion medicine. 3rd ed. Baltimore, MD: Williams and Wilkins, 2002:270-87.

38. Sprogre-Jakobsen U, Saetre AM, Georgsen J. Preparation of white cell-reduced red cells by filtration: Comparison of a bedside filter and two blood bank filter systems. Transfusion 1995;35:421-6.

39. Ledent E, Berlin G. Inadequate white cell reduction by bedside filtration of red cell concentrates. Transfusion 1994;34:765-8.

40. Kao KJ, Hudson S, Orsini LA, et al. Effect of in vitro storage time of platelet concentrates on clogging of white cell reduction filters. Transfusion 1994;34:740-1.

41. Boyan CP, Howland WS. Cardiac arrest and temperature of bank blood. JAMA 1963;183: 58-60.

42. Calhoun L. Blood product preparation and administration. In: Petz LD, Swisher SN, Kleinman S, eds. Clinical practice of transfusion medicine. 3rd ed. New York: Churchill Livingstone, 1996:305-33.

43. Iserson KV, Huestis DW. Blood warming: Current applications and techniques. Transfusion 1991;31:558-71.

44. Uhl L, Pacini D, Kruskall MS. A comparative study of blood warmer performance. Anesthesiology 1992;77:1022-8.

45. Burch KJ, Phelps SJ, Constance TD. Effect of an infusion device on the integrity of whole

blood and packed red cells. Am J Hosp Pharm 1991;48:92-7.

46. Snyder EL, Ferri PM, Smith EO, Ezekowitz MD. Use of electromechanical infusion pump for transfusion of platelet concentrates. Transfusion 1984;24:524-7.

47. Snyder EL, Malech HL, Ferri PM, et al. In vitro function of granulocyte concentrates following passage through an electromechanical infusion pump. Transfusion 1986;26:141-4.

48. American Association of Blood Banks, America's Blood Centers, American Red Cross. Circular of information for the use of human blood and blood components. Bethesda, MD: AABB, 2002.

49. Ryden SE, Oberman HA. Compatibility of common intravenous solutions with CPD blood. Transfusion 1975;15:250-5.

50. Dickson DN, Gregory MA. Compatibility of blood with solutions containing calcium. S Afr Med J 1980;57:785-7.

51. Strautz RL, Nelson JM, Meyer EA, Shulman IA. Compatibility of ADSOL-stored red cells with intravenous solutions. Am J Emerg Med 1989;7:162-4.

Chapter 23

Perinatal Issues in Transfusion Practice

PREGNANCY PRESENTS SPECIAL immunohematologic problems for the transfusion service. The mother may exhibit alloimmunization to antigens on fetal cells, and the fetus may be affected by maternal antibodies provoked by previous pregnancies, by previous or present transfusions, or by the ongoing pregnancy. This chapter discusses hemolytic disease of the fetus and newborn (HDFN) and neonatal alloimmune thrombocytopenia (NAIT)—the two primary immunohematologic concerns during the perinatal period. Also included is a brief discussion of neonatal thrombocytopenia secondary to maternal idiopathic thrombocytopenic purpura.

Hemolytic Disease of the Fetus and Newborn

In HDFN, fetal red cells become coated with IgG alloantibody of maternal origin, directed against a paternally inherited antigen present on the fetal cells that is absent from maternal cells. The IgG-coated cells may undergo accelerated destruction both before and after birth, but the severity of the disease can vary from serologic abnormalities detected in an asymptomatic infant to intrauterine death.

Pathophysiology

Accelerated red cell destruction stimulates increased production of red cells, many of which enter the circulation prematurely as nucleated cells, hence the term "erythroblastosis fetalis." Severely affected fetuses may develop generalized edema, called "hydrops fetalis." In HDFN resulting from anti-D, erythropoiesis in the fetal liver may be so extensive that portal circulation is disrupted and albumin synthesis impaired, thereby reducing plasma colloid osmotic pressure. The severe anemia may cause cardiovascular failure, tissue hypo-

23

xia, and death in utero. Intrauterine transfusion may be lifesaving in these circumstances. If live-born, the severely affected infant exhibits profound anemia and heart failure.[1] Less severely affected infants continue to experience accelerated red cell destruction, which generates large quantities of bilirubin. Unlike HDFN due to anti-D, HDFN due to anti-K1 results from suppression of fetal erythropoiesis in addition to causing peripheral red cell destruction.[2]

Before birth severs the communication between maternal and fetal circulation, fetal bilirubin is processed by the mother's liver. At birth, the infant's immature liver is incapable of conjugating the amount of bilirubin that results from destruction of antibody-coated red cells. Unconjugated bilirubin is toxic to the developing central nervous system (CNS), causing brain damage referred to as "kernicterus." For the live-born infant with HDFN and rising levels of unconjugated bilirubin, kernicterus may pose a greater clinical danger than the consequences of anemia.[3] Prematurity, acidosis, hypoxia, and hypoalbuminemia increase the risk of CNS damage. Decisions about undertaking exchange transfusion are based primarily on the bilirubin level, the rate of bilirubin accumulation, and, to a lesser degree, on the severity of the anemia. Recently, the American Academy of Pediatrics has published guidelines aimed toward preventing and managing hyperbilirubinemia in infants ≥35 weeks of gestation.[4]

Mechanisms of Maternal Immunization

HDFN is often classified into three categories, on the basis of the specificity of the causative IgG antibody. In descending order of potential severity, they are:

1. D hemolytic disease caused by anti-D alone or, less often, in combination with anti-C or anti-E. (The Rh blood group is discussed in greater detail in Chapter 14.)
2. "Other" hemolytic disease caused by antibodies against other antigens in the Rh system or against antigens in other systems; anti-c and anti-K1 are most often implicated.[5]
3. ABO HDFN caused by anti-A,B in a group O woman or by isolated anti-A or anti-B.

In all but ABO HDFN, maternal antibodies reflect alloimmunization by pregnancy or transfusion. Rising titers of antibody can be documented, at least in the first affected pregnancy, and the infant may be symptomatic at birth as a result of effects on the fetus in utero. In contrast, ABO fetomaternal incompatibility cannot be diagnosed during pregnancy and the infant is rarely symptomatic at birth.

Pregnancy as the Immunizing Stimulus

Pregnancy causes immunization when fetal red cells, possessing a paternal antigen foreign to the mother, enter the maternal circulation as a result of fetomaternal hemorrhage (FMH). FMH occurs in the vast majority of pregnancies, usually during the third trimester and during delivery.[6] Delivery is the most common immunizing event, but fetal red cells can also enter the mother's circulation after amniocentesis, spontaneous or induced abortion, chorionic villus sampling, cordocentesis, rupture of an ectopic pregnancy, and blunt trauma to the abdomen.

Immunogenic Specificities. The antigen that most frequently induces immunization is D, but, in theory, any red cell antigen present on fetal cells and absent from the mother can stimulate antibody production. One retrospective study determined that there was a 0.24% prevalence of production of clinically significant antibodies other than anti-D during pregnancy. Because other red cell antigens are less immuno-genic than D, sensitization is more likely to result from exposure to a large volume of red cells, such as during blood transfusion. Immunization to D, on the other hand, can occur with volumes of fetal blood less than 0.1 mL.[7]

Frequency of Immunization. The probability of immunization to D correlates with the volume of D-positive red cells entering the D-negative mother's circulation.[6] The overall incidence of D sensitization in untreated D-negative mothers of D-positive infants is about 16%; 1.5% to 2% become sensitized at the time of their first delivery, an additional 7% become sensitized within 6 months of the delivery, and the final 7% become sensitized during the second affected pregnancy.[8] The sensitization during the second affected pregnancy probably reflects primary immunization during the first D-positive pregnancy and delivery that happened without production of detectable levels of antibody. The small numbers of D-positive fetal red cells entering the maternal circulation early during the second affected pregnancy constitute a secondary stimulus sufficient to elicit overt production of IgG anti-D. In susceptible women not immunized after two D-positive pregnancies, later pregnancies may be affected but with diminished frequency. The incidence of the more common genotypes in D-positive individuals can be found in Table 14-4. This can be used to get a general idea of the likelihood of how often an infant with a D-positive father and D-negative mother will express the D antigen.

Once immunization has occurred, successive D-positive pregnancies often manifest HDFN of increasing severity, particularly between the first and second affected pregnancies. After the second affected pregnancy, the history is predictive of outcome, although, in rare instances, some women have a stable or diminishing pattern of clinical disease in subsequent pregnancies.

Effect of ABO Incompatibility. Rh immunization of untreated D-negative women occurs less frequently after delivery of an ABO-incompatible D-positive infant than when the fetal cells are ABO-compatible with the mother. ABO incompatibility between mother and fetus has a substantial but not absolute protective effect against maternal immunization by virtue of the increased rate of red cell destruction by anti-A or anti-B. The rate of immunization is decreased from 16% to between 1.5% and 2%.[7]

Transfusion as the Immunizing Stimulus

It is extremely important to avoid transfusing D-positive whole blood or red cells to D-negative females of childbearing potential because anti-D stimulated by transfusion characteristically causes severe HDFN in subsequent pregnancies with a D-positive fetus. Red cells present in platelet or granulocyte concentrates can constitute an immunizing stimulus; if components from D-positive donors are necessary for young D-negative female recipients, Rh immunoprophylaxis should be considered. This is discussed further in Chapter 21.

The risk of immunization to a red cell antigen other than D after an allogeneic red cell transfusion has been estimated to be 1% to 2.5% in the general hospital population.[7] This will endanger the fetus only if the antibody is IgG and directed against an antigen that is also present on the fetal red cells. For a couple planning to have children, the woman should not be transfused with red cells from her sexual partner or his blood relatives. This form of directed donation increases the risk that the mother will be immunized to paternal red cell, leukocyte, and/or platelet antigens, which could cause alloimmune cytopenias in future children who share the same paternal antigens. Programs using parents as directed donors for their sick newborns deserve special consideration because of these unique issues in the face of strong parental desires.[9,10]

ABO Antibodies

The IgG antibodies that cause ABO HDFN nearly always occur in the mother's circulation without a history of prior exposure to human red cells. ABO HDFN can occur in any pregnancy, including the first. It is restricted almost entirely to group A or B infants born to group O mothers because group O individuals make the IgG antibody, anti-A,B. Group A or B mothers with an A- or B-incompatible fetus predominantly produce IgM antibody, with only small amounts of IgG antibody capable of crossing the placenta.

Prenatal Evaluation

Maternal History

Information about previous pregnancies or blood transfusions is essential in evaluating fetal risk. Invasive tests, which carry risk to the fetus, should be performed only for pregnancies in which the fetus is at risk for HDFN, by history and/or serologic testing. For a woman with a history of an infant with hydrops fetalis due to anti-D, there is a 90% or more chance of a subsequent fetus being similarly affected.[5] In contrast, during the first sensitized pregnancy, the risk of a hydropic fetus is 8% to 10%. Experience with other alloantibodies has not been as extensive as with anti-D; in some series, anti-c and anti-K1 were by far the most common causes of severe HDFN, other than anti-D.[5,11]

Serologic Studies

Alloantibodies capable of causing HDFN can be detected during pregnancy. Initial studies should be performed on all pregnant women as early in pregnancy as possible; they should include tests for ABO and D, and a screen for unexpected red cell antibodies.[12] If a woman's red cells are not directly agglutinated by anti-D, testing for weak D is not required. When testing for weak D is not performed, women with weak D will be labeled as D negative, although they are in fact D positive; the only potential negative outcome is that these women will receive unnecessary Rh Immune Globulin (RhIG). Women with some partial D phenotypes, such as D^{VI}, will also most likely type as D negative in direct tests, and, in the absence of weak D testing, these women are also candidates for RhIG antenatal prophylaxis.

With the application of molecular techniques, knowledge of the *RHD* gene is evolving. Not all weak D red cells are the result of a decreased expression of the D antigen, but, rather, some have altered RhD proteins. Consequently, these patients are at risk for immunization when exposed to the D antigen, explaining formation of anti-D in some patients classified as weak D. As more is learned about the D antigen, the distinction between partial D and weak D is blurring.[13,14]

Whether or not prophylaxis would be successful in the setting of partial D remains unknown. The appropriate dose is also subject to speculation. As a result, some practitioners administer RhIG to these women, whereas others consider it unnecessary. Very rarely, a mother with partial D antigen produces anti-D as a result of pregnancy.

If weak D testing is performed and the test is clearly positive, the woman should be regarded as D positive. If testing for weak D is not performed, women whose red cells do not react in direct tests with anti-D can be considered candidates for RhIG prophylaxis. Some laboratories continue to do weak D testing to avoid confusion in the interpretation of the FMH screen during postpartum testing.[12] Chapter 14 contains a more complete discussion of the Rh blood group.

A woman should be classified as D positive if the test for either D or weak D is positive. If a D-negative woman has a negative initial antibody screen, the test can be repeated at 28 weeks' gestation before administration of RhIG to detect immunization that might have occurred before 28 weeks, in accordance with AABB recommendations. Because the incidence of immunization during this period of pregnancy is extremely low, the American College of Obstetricians and Gynecologists (ACOG) points out that no data exist that support the cost-effectiveness of this practice.[15] Repeat antibody screening of D-positive women may be recommended if there is a history of clinically significant red cell antibodies associated with HDFN, previous blood transfusion, or trauma to the abdomen.

Antibody Specificity. All positive screens for red cell antibodies require identification of the antibody.[12] The mere presence of an antibody, however, does not indicate that HDFN will occur. Non-red-cell-stimulated IgM antibodies, notably anti-Le[a] and anti-I, are relatively common during pregnancy but do not cross the placenta. In addition, the fetal red cells may lack the antigen corresponding to the mother's antibody; the likelihood of fetal involvement can often be predicted by typing the father's red cell antigens.[16] The laboratory report on prenatal antibody studies should include sufficient information to aid the clinician in determining the clinical significance of the identified antibody.

Typing the Fetus. The fetal D type can be established by using the polymerase chain reaction (PCR) to amplify DNA obtained from amniotic fluid, chorionic villus samples, or by serologic typing of fetal blood obtained by cordocentesis.[17] Chorionic villus

sampling is discouraged because it causes FMH and has been associated with more severe HDFN. Amniotic fluid samples are recommended over cordocentesis because cordocentesis has a fourfold or higher rate of perinatal loss over amniocentesis.[18] The use of molecular techniques can help detect variations in the *RHD* gene that might go undetected using serology alone. It is preferable that both paternal and maternal blood samples accompany the fetal samples.[19] Fetal DNA typing is also available for Jk[a]/Jk[b],[20] K1/K2,[21] c,[22] and E/e[23] antigens. A more recent development in fetal RhD typing involves the isolation of free fetal DNA in the maternal serum. Although not routinely available in the United States at this time, this will likely replace amniocentesis for fetal genotyping in the near future.[24]

Maternal Antibody Titer

Antibody titrations can help in decisions about the performance and the timing of invasive procedures, especially if the antibody is anti-D. The antibody titer should be established in the first trimester to serve as a baseline, and the specimen should be frozen for future comparisons (see Method 5.3).[7] Because invasive tests will not be undertaken before 16 to 18 weeks' gestation, no further titration is indicated until this time. The true significance of an antibody titer in maternal serum is controversial because some studies have shown poor correlation between the level of the titer and effects on the fetus. For antibodies other than anti-D, critical titers have not been identified, although a critical titer similar to that used in cases of anti-D alloimmunization is often utilized.[25] These techniques continue to be performed because they represent a noninvasive way to try to assess the presence and severity of alloimmunization. When performed, it is important that successive titrations use the same methods and test cells of the same red cell phenotype. Testing previously frozen serum samples in parallel with a current specimen minimizes the possibility that changes in the titer result from differences in technique. The critical titer for anti-D (the level below which HDFN and hydrops fetalis are considered so unlikely that no further invasive procedures will be undertaken) should be selected at each facility and is usually 16 or 32 in the antihuman globulin phase.[26,27] Follow-up testing is recommended for any titer greater than 8.[26] The critical titer for anti-K1 may be lower than anti-D, typically a value of 8.[25,28] Currently, it is not recommended that gel technology be used for prenatal antibody titration because of the lack of data showing a correlation between gel and tube agglutination titers.[12]

Other Measures of HDFN Severity

Numerous laboratory procedures have been investigated to improve the accuracy of predicting the severity of hemolysis.[29] The antibody titer discussed above is not always reliable, nor is the serial change in titer. Functional assays, including measures of adherence, phagocytosis, antibody-dependent cytotoxicity, and chemiluminescence have been investigated, but their use has been limited and remains controversial. These procedures are usually performed in referral centers and may be useful when additional information is required to manage difficult and complex cases.

Amniotic Fluid Analysis

A good index of intrauterine hemolysis and fetal well-being is the level of bilirubin pigment found in amniotic fluid obtained by amniocentesis. Amniocentesis is usually performed in alloimmunized women who have a history of previously affected pregnancies or have an antibody titer at or above the critical titer.[28] Because fetal anemia secondary to K1 alloimmunization is not always associated with elevated levels of bilirubin in amniotic fluid, it has been recommended that fetal blood sampling be used instead of serial amniocentesis when anti-K1 is detected in a pregnant woman.[2]

Amniotic fluid is obtained by inserting a long needle through the mother's abdominal wall and uterus into the uterine cavity under continuous ultrasound guidance. The aspirated fluid is scanned spectrophotometrically at wavelengths of 350 to 700 nm. Peak absorbance of bilirubin is at 450 nm. An increase in optical density from the projected baseline at 450 nm (ΔOD_{450}) is a measure of the concentration of bile pigments.[30,31] The ΔOD_{450} value is plotted on a graph against the estimated length of gestation, because bile pigment concentration has different clinical significance at different gestational ages. Liley's system[31] (Fig 23-1) of predicting the severity of fetal disease based on the ΔOD_{450} has been used for decades. It delineates three zones to estimate severity of disease: a top zone (zone 3) indicates severe disease, the bottom zone (zone 1) indicates mild or no disease, and mid-zone (zone 2) values require repeat determination to establish a trend. This method is applicable to pregnancies from 27 weeks through term. Queenan et al[32] have proposed a system for managing D-immunized pregnancies based on the ΔOD_{450} from as early as 14 weeks' gestation. They identified four zones (Fig 23-2), with early invasive intervention recommended if ΔOD_{450} values fall in the highest zone. With both systems, the severity of HDFN is more accurately predicted with serial ΔOD_{450} measurements than with a single observation, to evaluate whether readings are falling, rising, or stable. In general, the higher the pigment concentration, the more se-

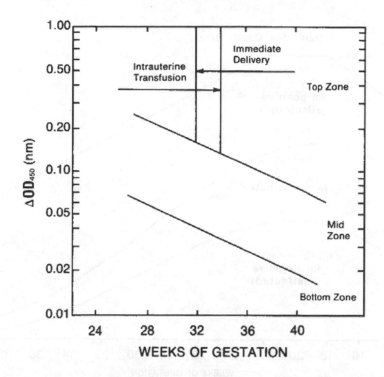

Figure 23-1. Liley graph for collecting data from amniotic fluid studies. Intrauterine transfusion should be done if the ΔOD_{450} value is in the top zone before 32 weeks' gestation. After 34 weeks, top zone values indicate immediate delivery. Either intrauterine transfusion or immediate delivery may be indicated for top zone ΔOD_{450} between 32 and 34 weeks, depending on studies of fetal maturity. Modified from Liley.[31]

vere the intrauterine hemolysis. It is important to perform an ultrasound to establish the correct gestational age so that the test can be interpreted and the course of therapy for a particular ΔOD_{450} will be appropriate.[18] Alternatively, a ΔOD_{450} value in the upper mid-zone of the Liley curve indicates the need for fetal blood sampling.

Amniocentesis, particularly if the needle goes through the placenta, or cordocentesis may cause FMH, which can boost the titer of existing red cell alloantibody, thereby increasing the severity of HDFN, or inducing immunization to additional antigens.[18] Therefore, when amniocentesis or cordocentesis is performed for any reason on a D-negative woman who does not have anti-D, Rh immunoprophylaxis should be given.

Percutaneous Umbilical Blood Sampling

In the early 1980s, the use of sophisticated ultrasound equipment made it feasible to direct a needle into an umbilical blood vessel, preferably the vein at its insertion into the placenta, and obtain a fetal blood sample. Percutaneous umbilical blood sampling (PUBS, or cordocentesis) allows direct measurement of hematologic and biochemical variables. Determination of the fetal hematocrit provides an accurate assessment of the severity of fetal hemolytic disease.[18] It is important to verify that the sample has been obtained from the fetus. Fetal and maternal red cells can be distinguished because of differences in red cell size and red cell phenotyping, as well as by the presence of fetal hemoglobin.[33]

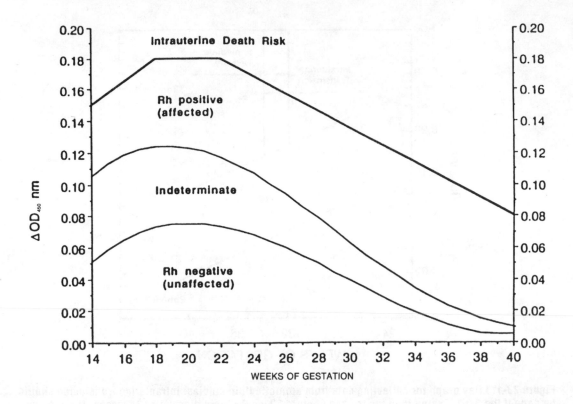

Figure 23-2. Amniotic fluid ΔOD_{450} management zones. (Reproduced with permission from Queenan et al.[32])

The fetal mortality of intrauterine fetal blood sampling has been reported to be 1% to 2%,[34] and the procedure carries a high risk of FMH. Its use is recommended only for certain circumstances, such as when serial amniotic fluid determinations indicate severe HDFN, when hydrops is present, when the D titer is high or rising, or when HDFN occurred in previous pregnancies. In addition to diagnosis, PUBS allows treatment of the affected fetus.

Doppler Flow Studies

Because fetal anemia results in increased cardiac output, several investigators have measured various blood velocities in fetal vessels using Doppler ultrasonography to determine the clinical status of the fetus in a noninvasive manner.[18,35] Recent stud-

ies have found good correlation between middle cerebral artery (MCA) peak velocity, fetal hemoglobin, and ΔOD_{450} readings.[36] Many centers routinely use an MCA peak systolic velocity value of greater than 1.5 multiples of the median to proceed with cordocentesis to determine if the fetus is anemic. In such centers, amniocentesis is performed only after 35 weeks' gestation when MCA Doppler is associated with a high false-positive rate for the diagnosis of fetal anemia (Moise K, personal communication).

Suppression of Maternal Alloimmunization

Several approaches to suppress maternal alloimmunization have been attempted, two of which have limited clinical benefit in reducing maternal antibody levels: intensive plasma exchange and the administration of immunoglobulin (intravenous) (IGIV).[5,18] Plasma exchange can reduce antibody levels by as much as 75%. Unfortunately, rebound usually follows because the IgG antibody is mostly extravascular and antigen exposure may be ongoing. Plasma exchange has been proposed as a way to delay the need for fetal intervention, particularly when there is a previous pregnancy complicated by early hydrops.[37] In this setting, plasma exchange can delay the need for more invasive procedures until the second trimester. The AABB and the American Society for Apheresis (ASFA) categorize plasma exchange as treatment Category III because its efficacy and safety have not been proven for this indication (see Chapter 6). With the increasing safety of intrauterine transfusion through ultrasound guidance and the decreasing incidence of HDFN due to anti-D, the use of plasma exchange as a treatment modality has declined.

IGIV infusion has also been shown to stabilize anti-D titers, with best results obtained when started before 28 weeks' gestation and when the fetus is not hydropic.[38] In a small study assessing the efficacy of IGIV, it was found to be well tolerated and there was a decrease in hemolysis.[39] The mechanism of IGIV effect is not clear, although it may work by saturating placental Fc receptors and inhibiting the transplacental transfer of maternal antibody or by suppressing ingestion of IgG-coated red cells by the fetal reticuloendothelial system. An alternative explanation is that the introduction of anti-idiotype antibodies modifies maternal antibody production. IGIV has also been used with plasma exchange to reduce the antibody rebound that has been seen following plasma exchange.[18] Until larger studies assessing safety and efficacy can be per-

formed, intrauterine transfusion remains the mainstay of standard therapy.

Intrauterine Transfusion

Intrauterine transfusion can be performed by the intraperitoneal route (IPT) or the direct intravascular approach (IVT) by the umbilical vein. In many instances, IVT is the procedure of choice, but there may be problems of access that make IPT preferable; a combination may also be used to minimize peaks and troughs of fetal hematocrit between procedures. Intrauterine transfusion is seldom feasible before the 20th week of gestation; once initiated, transfusions are usually administered periodically until delivery. It is important that blood is available and ready at the time of the first diagnostic, and subsequent, cordocenteses. If fetal anemia is detected, an intrauterine transfusion can be performed at once, minimizing fetal risks. The interval between transfusions depends on the presence or absence of hydrops, the gestational age, and the amount of blood infused. Good outcomes are achieved over 80% of the time and 94% of nonhydropic fetuses survive.[40] Because intrauterine transfusion carries a 1% to 2% risk of perinatal loss, it should be performed only after careful clinical evaluation.[18,34,41,42] Other perinatal conditions that have been treated with intrauterine transfusion include parvovirus infection, large FMH, and alpha thalassemia.[43]

Techniques

IPT is performed through a needle passed, with ultrasonographic monitoring, through the mother's abdominal wall into the abdominal cavity of the fetus. Transfused red cells enter the fetal circulation through lymphatic channels that drain the peritoneal cavity. In IVT, the umbilical vein is penetrated under ultrasound guidance, and a blood sample is taken to verify positioning in the fetal vasculature. Injection of saline can also confirm correct placement because it can be visualized by ultrasound. Blood is infused directly, as either a simple transfusion or as a partial exchange transfusion. IVT can be particularly valuable for very severe cases of HDFN associated with hydrops fetalis. In hydropic infants, red cells administered by IPT are not efficiently absorbed.

Selection of Red Cells

The red cells used should be group O, D-negative, or negative for the antigen corresponding to the mother's antibody if the specificity is not anti-D. Blood for intrauterine transfusion should be irradiated (see Chapter 27), and should be cytomegalovirus (CMV)-reduced-risk. It may also be desirable to transfuse blood that is known to lack hemoglobin S in order to transfuse red cells with maximal oxygen-transporting capacity, in the setting of low oxygen tension. For optimal survival of the transfused cells, blood used for intrauterine transfusion should be drawn as recently as possible, generally less than 7 days old.

The hematocrit of the RBCs prepared for exchange transfusion is usually high to minimize the chance of volume overload in the fetus. Washed, irradiated maternal blood has also been used for intrauterine transfusion.[44] To remove the offending antibody, the red cells are washed and resuspended in saline to a final hematocrit between 75% and 85%. Washed or deglycerolized preparations have been used as a means to remove plasma, anticoagulant/preservative solutions, and excess electrolytes that might accumulate during prolonged storage. Blood for intrauterine transfusions and all blood and cellular components subsequently transfused in the neonatal period should be irradiated to prevent transfusion-associated graft-vs-host disease because the fetus is considered immunologically naïve and tolerant.[45,46]

Volume Administered

The volume transfused varies with the technique used as well as the fetal size, initial hematocrit, and gestational age. For IPT, a volume calculated by the formula $V = (\text{gestation in weeks} - 20) \times 10 \text{ mL}$ appears to be well tolerated by the fetus. The volume of red cells transfused by IVT can be calculated by the following formula.[47]

$$\text{Fetoplacental volume (mL)} = \text{ultrasound estimated fetal weight} \text{ (g)} \times 0.14$$

$$\text{Volume to transfuse (mL)} = \frac{\text{Fetoplacental volume} \times (\text{Hct after IVT} - \text{Hct before IVT})}{\text{Hct of donor cells}}$$

where Hct = hematocrit

Transfusion is repeated on the basis of an estimated decline in fetal hematocrit of approximately 1% per day in an effort to maintain the fetal hematocrit in the range of 27% to 30%.[48]

Postpartum Evaluation

It may be desirable to collect a sample of cord blood, preferably by cannulation of an umbilical vessel at delivery, from newborns where there is a risk of HDFN (eg, Rh-positive infants born to Rh-negative mothers, type A and B infants born to type O mothers). This sample should be identified as cord blood and labeled in the delivery suite with the mother's name, the date, and two unique forms of identification for the infant (eg, name and medical record number).

In cases of suspected HDFN, samples of both cord and maternal blood should be tested. When the mother is known to have antibodies capable of causing HDFN, the hemoglobin or hematocrit and the bilirubin level of cord blood should also be determined. If the mother is D negative and the infant D positive, the mother's blood should be tested to determine the volume of FMH, as discussed later. Testing cord blood may present some special problems, which are described below.

ABO Testing

ABO testing on newborns relies entirely on red cell typing because ABO antibodies in cord serum are nearly always of maternal origin and are IgG. However, in the investigation of possible HDFN due to ABO incompatibility, cord serum should be tested for antiglobulin-reactive ABO antibodies. Also, if the infant will receive non-group-O red cells, testing must be taken to the antiglobulin phase.[49(p42)]

D Testing

Newborns who have had successful intrauterine transfusions often type at birth as D negative or very weakly positive because over 90% of their circulating red cells may be those of the donors. The ABO and direct antiglobulin tests may also give misleading results. If the infant's red cells are heavily coated with IgG antibodies, tests with anti-D may give either false-positive or false-negative results (see Chapter 14).

Antiglobulin Testing

The direct antiglobulin test (DAT) is usually strongly positive in HDFN resulting from anti-D or antibodies to other blood groups; reactions are much weaker or even negative in HDFN resulting from ABO antibodies. However, the strength of the DAT does not correlate with the severity of hemolysis, especially in ABO HDFN. Infants who have received an intrauterine transfusion may have a weakly positive DAT with a mixed-field pattern of agglutination. If the DAT on cord cells is positive, the antibody can be eluted from the red cells and tested for specificity. It is not necessary to make and test an eluate if the maternal serum has been shown to contain a single red cell antibody. All clinically significant red cell antibodies in the maternal serum must be respected. (See the section on Selection of Blood, later in this chapter.) If the DAT is positive and the maternal antibody screen is negative, investigation should turn toward ABO antibodies or HDFN caused by an antibody directed against a low-incidence antigen not present on reagent red cells.

Evaluation of ABO Antibodies. ABO HDFN may be suspected on clinical grounds even though the DAT is negative. Testing the eluate from the cord cells against A_1 and B red cells should establish the diagnosis of ABO HDFN. Cord blood or peripheral blood serum should be tested by an indirect antiglobulin technique against A_1, B, and O red cells. The presence of anti-A, anti-B, or anti-A,B confirms the potential for ABO HDFN. It is often possible to elute anti-A and/or anti-B from the infant's red cells despite a negative DAT, but this step is not necessary for the presumptive diagnosis. In the rare cases of ABO HDFN that require transfusion, D-compatible group O blood should be transfused, whether or not the diagnosis has been serologically confirmed. Nonimmune causes of hyperbilirubinemia and hemolysis should still be considered in an infant with a negative DAT before concluding that it is due to ABO HDFN because other hematologic disorders might be present.[50]

Antibodies to Low-Incidence Antigens.
If ABO HDFN is ruled out, antibody against a low-incidence red cell antigen should be suspected. Testing an eluate or maternal serum against the father's red cells with an antiglobulin technique may provide an answer. Maternal serum must be ABO compatible, if it is used. If either or both of these tests are positive, it indicates that the infant has an antigen of paternal origin that the mother lacks, causing her to make an IgG antibody directed against this antigen. Unless the mother has been exposed to red cells from the father or his blood relations, transfusion would be an unlikely immunizing event for a low-incidence antigen. Because there should be no difficulty in obtaining compatible blood, diagnostic studies can be performed after initial clinical concerns have been resolved. If the DAT is positive and all attempts to characterize a coating red cell antibody are consistently negative, causes of a false-positive DAT should be considered (see Chapter 20).

Exchange Transfusion

Exchange transfusion for HDFN achieves several desired effects, including:
1. Removal of antibody-coated fetal red cells.
2. Removal of maternal antibody.
3. Removal of bilirubin.
4. Replacement of red cells, thereby treating anemia.

The red cells used for replacement must be compatible with the causative antibody. Fresh Frozen Plasma is frequently used to reconstitute whole blood because it provides coagulation factors. Platelet values should also be monitored and transfusion used as necessary. Plasma frozen within 24 hours and thawed plasma can be used too, with the understanding that there might be decreases in the activity of the labile clotting Factors V and VIII.

Selection of Blood

In most cases, the mother's serum is used for crossmatching and the red cells selected for transfusion are compatible with her ABO antibodies as well as any additional antibody(ies) responsible for the hemolytic process. Group O red cells resuspended in AB plasma are commonly used. In ABO HDFN, the red cells used for exchange must be group O. If the antibody is anti-D, the red cells must be D negative, but not every exchange transfusion requires group O RBCs. If mother and infant are ABO-identical, group-specific red cells or whole blood can be used. If the implicated antibody is not anti-D, D-positive red cells may be given to a D-positive infant.

Maternal serum or plasma is the specimen of choice for crossmatching in exchange transfusion; it is available in large quantities, decreases the volume of blood taken from the infant, has the red cell antibody present in high concentration, and can be analyzed accurately and completely before delivery. On the other hand, use of maternal serum may be problematic if it contains antibodies directed against antigens not present on the infant's red cells because of other sources of sensitization, or if it contains IgM antibodies that have not crossed the placenta. These additional antibodies could complicate the serologic picture.

If maternal blood is not available or is unsuitable for crossmatching, the infant's serum and/or, preferably, an eluate from the infant's red cells can be used for crossmatching. The concentration of antibody in the infant's serum may be low, especially if most of the molecules are bound to the red cells. Use of the eluate or serum, or of both together, may be indicated if attempts to obtain a maternal specimen would delay therapy. Blood used for exchange transfusion should be irradiated. Typically, a volume of twice the infant's blood volume is used for exchange.[51]

Subsequent Transfusion

Bilirubin may reaccumulate rapidly after a successful exchange transfusion despite appropriate phototherapy. This occurs because most bilirubin in extravascular fluid will reequilibrate by entering the intravascular space and also because residual antibody-coated cells continue to hemolyze. If rising bilirubin levels make a second or third exchange transfusion necessary, the same considerations of red cell selection and crossmatching apply.

Infants who have undergone intrauterine transfusion need to be followed closely after birth because intrauterine transfusion suppresses fetal erythropoiesis. Weekly hematocrit and reticulocyte counts should be performed on the neonate for a 1- to 3-month period.[18] Many of these infants will subsequently develop anemia and need to be supported with red cell transfusion until their own production begins, as evidenced by reticulocytosis and age-appropriate hemoglobin levels.[18,52]

Antibody Against a High-Incidence Antigen

Rarely, the mother's antibody reacts with a high-incidence antigen and no compatible blood is available. If this problem is recognized and identified before delivery, the mother's siblings can be evaluated for compatibility and suitability, or compatible donors can be sought through a rare donor file. Maternal red cells can also be collected and frozen. Any products collected from blood relatives must be irradiated. If this very rare event is not recognized until after delivery, three choices are available:

1. Collect blood from the mother, if the obstetrician agrees. Remove as much plasma as possible, preferably by saline washing, and resuspend the red cells in compatible plasma to the desired hematocrit.
2. If time permits, test the mother's siblings or other close relatives for compatibility and eligibility.
3. Use incompatible donor blood for the exchange transfusion if the clinical situation is sufficiently urgent. The exchange will reduce the bilirubin load, the most heavily antibody-coated cells, and the number of unbound antibody molecules. However, residual antibody will attach to the transfused cells, and one or more additional exchanges will probably be needed as bilirubin accumulates.

Rh Immune Globulin

RhIG is a concentrate of predominantly IgG anti-D derived from pools of human plasma. A full dose of anti-D (300 µg, 1500 IU, or the actual content of a "dose" as indicated by the individual manufacturer[53]) is sufficient to counteract the immunizing effects of 15 mL of D-positive red cells; this corresponds to approximately 30 mL of fetal whole blood. RhIG is available in a reduced dose, approximately 50 µg, which is protective for up to 2.5 mL of D-positive fetal red cells. This dose can be used for first-trimester abortion or miscarriage, when the total blood volume of the fetus is less than 2.5 mL. However, because of fears of miscalculating the length of pregnancy and concerns of inadvertently mixing up inventory resulting in undertreatment, a full dose is usually administered and these low doses are frequently not stocked. The protective effect of RhIG on D-negative individuals exposed to D-positive cells probably results from interference with antigen recognition in the induction phase of primary immunization.[54]

RhIG is available in two formulations: 1) for intramuscular (IM) injection only and 2) for either IM or intravenous (IV) administration. The dose of the intravenous preparation is expressed in international units (5 IU is equivalent to 1 µg), with 1500 IU (300 µg) neutralizing 17 mL of D-positive red cells, according to the package insert.

Antepartum Administration

Widespread postpartum use of Rh immunoprophylaxis has reduced pregnancy-associated immunization to the D antigen to 1% to 2%.[8] This risk is further decreased to 0.1% if RhIG is also given antepartum at 28 weeks of gestation.[7] The ACOG recommends antepartum RhIG prophylaxis at 28 weeks of gestation, based on the observation that, of women who develop anti-D during pregnancy, 92% do so at or after 28 weeks.[7,15]

Blood obtained before injection of RhIG should be tested for ABO and D. A D-negative woman who has antibodies other than anti-D (eg, anti-G) is still a candidate for anti-D immunoprophylaxis. When the mother receives RhIG during pregnancy, the infant may be born with a positive DAT, but without hemolysis. The mother's serum will often exhibit anti-D reactivity. There must be good communication between the patient's physician and the blood bank staff at the institution where delivery takes place, to ensure correct interpretation of laboratory tests made at the time of delivery. The half-life of an injected dose of RhIG, in the absence of significant FMH, is approximately 21 days. Therefore, of 300 µg of anti-D given at 28 weeks, 20-30 µg could remain at the time of delivery 12 weeks later. Some practitioners will administer another dose of RhIG if delivery is delayed beyond 40 weeks.[18] Anti-D can be detected in the maternal circulation for as long as 6 months.

Postpartum Administration

Cord blood from infants born to D-negative mothers should be tested for the D antigen. A D-negative woman with a D-positive infant should receive one full dose of RhIG within 72 hours of delivery, unless she is known to be alloimmunized to D previously. The presence of residual anti-D from antepartum RhIG does not indicate ongoing protection.

Active vs Passive Antibody. In-vitro clues can help distinguish passively administered RhIG from the anti-D formed as a result of active alloimmunization. Passively acquired anti-D is entirely IgG; if a woman's anti-D is saline-reactive or can be completely or partially inactivated by treating the serum with 2-mercaptoethanol or dithiothreitol, it has an IgM component and probably represents active immunization. Passively acquired anti-D rarely achieves an antiglobulin titer above 4, so a high-titered antibody or rising antibody titer is likely to indicate active immunization. It is desirable to obtain confirmation from the physician's records, but RhIG should always be given when doubt cannot easily be resolved. It should also be given if there is any problem determining the Rh type.

Postpartum Evaluation. A sample of the mother's blood should be drawn, preferably within 1 hour after delivery, and evaluated for FMH of a quantity greater than that for which 300 µg RhIG is immunosuppressive. If the screening test demonstrates the presence of fetal cells, the extent of FMH must be determined so that an appropriate dose of RhIG can be administered.[49(pp48,49),55]

Postpartum RhIG should be given within 72 hours of delivery. If prophylaxis is delayed, the likelihood that alloimmunization will be prevented decreases. Despite the decrease seen, the ACOG recommends that treatment still be administered because some studies have found partial protection has occurred as late as 13 days after exposure and, possibly, as late as 28 days.[15]

The following women are *not* candidates for RhIG:

1. The D-negative woman whose infant is D-negative.
2. Any D-positive woman. Very rare cases of HDFN have been reported in infants whose mothers had a weak/partial D phenotype, but routine RhIG prophylaxis is not routinely recommended for women of the weak/partial D phenotype.[12]
3. A D-negative woman known to be immunized to D.

Other Indications for RhIG

RhIG should be given to a D-negative woman after any obstetric event that might allow fetal cells to enter the mother's circulation: spontaneous or therapeutic abortion, ectopic pregnancy, amniocentesis, chorionic villus sampling, molar pregnancy, cordocentesis, antepartum hemorrhage, blunt abdominal trauma, or fetal death.[55] As mentioned earlier, at 12 weeks of gestation or earlier, a 50 µg dose of RhIG would be adequate to protect against the small fetal blood volume during the first trimester. From 13 weeks' gestation until term, a full dose of RhIG should be given. At <20 weeks, the fetal blood volume is rarely more than 30mL,[56] small enough that a single dose of 300 µg Rh immune globulin will be sufficient for prophylaxis for any FMH. Therefore, it is not necessary to quantitate fetal red cells in the maternal circulation before 20 weeks of gestation.[57]

Amniocentesis

Amniocentesis can cause FMH and consequent Rh immunization. The D-negative woman who has amniocentesis at 16 to 18 weeks' gestation for genetic analysis should receive a full dose of RhIG at that time, a second full dose at 28 weeks of gestation, and the usual postpartum dose if the infant is D positive. If a nonimmunized D-negative woman undergoes amniocentesis for any reason in the second or third trimester, a full dose of RhIG is indicated. If the procedure is repeated more than 21 days later, an additional full dose should be given.[18] If amniocentesis is performed to assess fetal maturity, and if delivery is expected within 48 hours of the procedure, RhIG can be withheld until the infant is born and confirmed to be D positive. If more than 48 hours will elapse, RhIG should be given following amniocentesis. If delivery occurs within 21 days thereafter and there is no evidence of a massive FMH,[15] additional RhIG may not be essential, but prudent management suggests repeat RhIG administration at delivery.

Screening for Large-Volume FMH

Postpartum administration of RhIG may not prevent immunization if the quantity of D-positive fetal red cells entering the mother's circulation exceeds the immunosuppressive capacity of RhIG. One 300-µg dose protects against 15 mL of D-positive red cells or 30 mL of fetal blood. Only 0.3% of pregnancies are estimated to sustain FMH greater than 30 mL, but large FMH is an important and preventable cause of failed immunoprophylaxis.[7] The ACOG recommends postpartum testing for large FMH only for high-risk pregnancies,[15] but Ness and colleagues[58] showed that testing based only on the ACOG criteria would miss 50% of mothers exposed to large-volume FMH. AABB *Standards for Blood Banks and Transfusion Services* requires examination of a postpartum specimen from all D-negative women at risk of immunization, to detect the presence of FMH that requires more than one dose of RhIG.[49(p49)] In rare cases, a massive FMH can cause fetal death and infuse enough Rh-positive cells into the maternal circulation to simulate a weak D phenotype in an Rh-negative patient.[15,59] Unless recognized and treated with an adequate dose of RhIG, this will likely lead to alloimmunization.

"Microscopic Weak D." In the past, some workers looked for D-positive red cells in the mother's D-negative blood by examining the antiglobulin phase of the test for D microscopically ("microscopic weak D test"); mixed-field reactivity indicated a substantial admixture with D-positive cells. This procedure should not be used to identify large FMH, however, because of its lack of reliability.[60]

The Rosette Test. The rosette test demonstrates small numbers of D-positive cells in a D-negative suspension. The suspension is incubated with an anti-D reagent of human origin, and antibody molecules attach to sites on D-positive cells in the suspension. Indicator D-positive cells are added, which react with antibody molecules bound to the surface of the already-present D-positive cells and form visible agglutinates (rosettes) around them (see Method 5.1). This method will detect FMHs of approximately 10 mL,[60] a sensitivity that provides a desirable margin of safety for a screening test. Weak D-positive cells do not react as strongly in the rosette procedure as normal D-positive cells. If the newborn has a weak D phenotype, FMH can be evaluated by the Kleihauer-Betke acid-elution test (see below), which identifies fetal hemoglobin, not a surface antigen. In all cases, the rosette test gives only qualitative results and a positive result must be followed by a quantitative test, such as an acid-elution procedure. Other tests that can be used to detect and/or quantify FMH are flow cytometry, gel agglutination, and the enzyme-linked antiglobulin test (ELAT, which is in limited use). Each of these methods has various advantages and disadvantages that must be evaluated by each institution. The use of nucleic acid amplification techniques, designed to detect very small amounts of fetal cells, remains a research endeavor.[61-63]

Quantifying FMH

Historically, quantification of FMH has been achieved by the Kleihauer-Betke acid-elution test, which relies on the differences between fetal and adult hemoglobin in resistance to acid elution (see Method 5.2). Results are reported as a percentage of fetal cells, but the precision and accuracy of the procedure may be poor. Because 300 µg of RhIG will protect against FMH of 30 mL of D-positive fetal blood, the number of doses of RhIG required is determined by dividing the estimated volume of fetal blood present by 30.

For example:

1. Kleihauer-Betke test results reported as 1.3%
2. $(1.3/100) \times 5000$ mL* = 65 mL of fetal blood
3. $65/(30$ mL per dose) = 2.2 doses of RhIG required

* = mother's arbitrarily assigned blood volume

Because quantification by this procedure is inherently inaccurate and because the consequences of undertreatment can be serious, it is desirable to provide a safety margin in calculating RhIG dosage. One approach is as follows:

1. When the number to the right of the decimal point is less than 5, round down and add one dose of RhIG (example: If the calculation comes to 2.2 doses, give 3 doses).

2. When the number to the right of the decimal point is 5 or greater, round up to the next number and add one dose of RhIG (example: If the calculation comes to 2.8 doses, give 4 doses). (See Table 23-1).

Not more than five doses of RhIG should be injected intramuscularly at one time. For larger quantities, injections can be spaced over a 72-hour period for the patient's comfort; an optimal time sequence has not been established. The intravenous preparation of RhIG can be used when higher doses are required. According to the package insert, a maximum dose of 300 IU should be given at each injection, every 8 hours, until the total calculated dose has been administered.

Neonatal Immune Thrombocytopenia

Maternal IgG antibodies to platelets can cross the placenta and cause severe antenatal and neonatal thrombocytopenia. Two categories of immune thrombocytopenia are recognized, and the distinction between them is therapeutically important.

Neonatal Alloimmune Thrombocytopenia

The mechanism of NAIT is similar to that of HDFN. Fetal platelets, expressing a paternal antigen absent from the mother's cells, may enter the mother's circulation during gestation or delivery. If she becomes immunized, the maternal IgG antibody crosses the placenta and causes fetal and neonatal thrombocytopenia. The maternal platelet count remains normal. The incidence of NAIT is approximately 1 in 1500 to 2000 live births.[64,65] NAIT is the cause of the majority of cases of intracranial hemorrhage due to thrombocytopenia, greater than all other etiologies of thrombocytopenia combined.[66]

Unlike HDFN, NAIT often affects firstborn children, with about 50% to 60% of cases occurring in a woman's first child. The thrombocytopenia is self-limiting, normally resolving in 2 to 3 weeks. NAIT varies in severity from mild thrombocytopenia with no clinical signs to overt clinical bleeding. The incidence of intracranial hemorrhage has been reported as 10% to 30%, with approximately half occurring in utero.[65,67] Recurrence in subsequent pregnancies is frequent, with equal or increasing severity, so

Table 23-1. RhIG Dosage for Massive Fetomaternal Hemorrhage, Based on the Acid Elution Test

% Fetal Cells	Vials of RhIG to Inject	Dose	
		In µg	In IU
0.3 - 0.8	2	600	3000
0.9 - 1.4	3	900	4500
1.5 - 2.0	4	1200	6000
2.1 - 2.5	5	1500	7500

Notes:
1. Based on a maternal blood volume of 5000 mL.
2. 1 vial of 300 µg (1500 IU) is needed for each 15 mL fetal red cells or 30 mL fetal whole blood.

a woman known to be alloimmunized must receive skilled antenatal attention.

Serologic Testing

Serologic diagnosis should be sought in a woman whose infant has had NAIT if further pregnancies are planned. Several platelet-specific antigen systems have been associated with NAIT, with HPA-1a antigen (Pl^{A1}) accounting for the vast majority of cases in Caucasians.[64] Pregnancy, rather than transfusion, is the usual immunizing event. Approximately 2% of the population is HPA-1a negative; approximately 10% of HPA-1a-negative women with HPA-1a-positive infants become immunized.[68] Some studies have shown an association between developing anti-HPA-1a and possessing the HLA phenotype DRw52a.[66,68] Chapter 16 contains more information about platelet antigens. Although antibodies to HLA Class I antigens are frequently encountered in pregnancy, and platelets express Class I antigens, this is a rare cause of NAIT, and the true role of HLA antibodies in this setting remains controversial.[69,70]

Any family with a history of an infant born with a platelet count of <50,000/μL should be evaluated. Ideally, serologic testing uses maternal serum and maternal and paternal whole blood from which platelets are isolated. Maternal serum is screened for both platelet-nonspecific and platelet-specific antibodies against paternal cells, as well as panels of phenotyped platelets. Maternal and paternal platelet typing can be performed using serologic and/or molecular typing methods. Some clinicians have proposed screening pregnant women for HPA-1a antigen because it is the most commonly implicated antigen causing incompatibility in Caucasians. Because only 10% of HPA-1a-negative women are truly at risk for forming antibody, and, of those, only

about 33% will have neonates with clinically important thrombocytopenia, this has not been widely adopted. In addition, the cost and logistics of performing platelet antigen typing are impediments to broad implementation.[65,71]

Prenatal Considerations

With knowledge of antibody specificity and gene frequencies, the likelihood of subsequent offspring being affected can be predicted (see Table 16-1). The recognized platelet-specific antigens occur in diallelic systems, so typing the father's platelets indicates zygosity. If the father is homozygous for the expression of the antigen, there is no need to determine the fetal antigen status because all offspring will be affected. If the father is heterozygous for the expression of the antigen, then there is a 50% chance that subsequent offspring will have the offending antigen. In an at-risk pregnancy, the genotype of the fetus (and by inference the platelet phenotype) can be determined by DNA typing on fetal cells obtained by amniocentesis.

When the risk of NAIT is high, a fetal blood sample for platelet count determination can be obtained by cordocentesis as early as 20 weeks' gestation. Because cordocentesis carries a risk of serious bleeding in a thrombocytopenic fetus, compatible platelets must be available at the time of the procedure and are often infused if the platelet count is low. Some institutions will infuse platelets during the procedure, before knowing the platelet count, because of the risk of bleeding during the cannulation itself. When the fetus is found to be thrombocytopenic, the mother is often given infusions of IGIV in weekly doses of 1 g/kg, with or without steroids, until delivery.[64-67,72] Alternatively, some would recommend empiric treatment with

IGIV in cases of a homozygous paternal genotype for the specific platelet antigen or in situations when PCR performed on amniotic fluid reveals that the fetus carries that platelet antigen. Many centers will proceed with elective cesarean section instead of cordocentesis near term to determine the fetal platelet count.

Sources of Platelets. Maternal platelets are often prepared for use at cordocentesis or delivery. The mother will undergo required testing for infectious disease markers. Prior administration of high-dose IGIV may cause false-positive immunoassays; therefore, it is desirable to test the mother before initiating IGIV therapy. Those with confirmed positive results (eg, hepatitis C virus, which is transmitted more efficiently by transfusion than perinatally) should not be used as a source of platelets because these results are more likely to represent maternal infection. Of note, pregnancy itself can also cause false-positive results on serologic infectious disease tests.

Platelets can be collected either from the mother or from another donor whose platelets lack the corresponding antigen and whose plasma is compatible with the fetal red cells. If maternal platelets are used, the antibody-containing plasma should be removed or reduced and the platelets resuspended in compatible plasma or saline with reduced volume (see Method 6.15). All components for intrauterine transfusion must be irradiated (see Chapter 27) and should be CMV-reduced risk.[73]

Scheduling Therapy. Various strategies have been used in the management of fetal thrombocytopenia. Although weekly platelet transfusions have been used in the past, the inherent risk of repeated cordocentesis makes the administration of IGIV to the mother the preferred treatment in the United States. Practice is different in Europe, where weekly platelet transfusions are still performed. Platelet transfusion and re-

peated cordocentesis are reserved for patients when noninvasive forms of therapy are not effective. Another approach is administration of a single platelet transfusion just before delivery if cordocentesis reveals severe thrombocytopenia. This approach is usually reserved for pregnancies at extreme risk for intracranial hemorrhage.

Management After Delivery

Platelet counts can continue to decrease after birth and should be monitored. For patients at increased risk of bleeding due to severe thrombocytopenia, compatible platelets should be given prophylactically. If compatible platelets are not available, the use of high-dose IGIV should be considered, but response to this treatment is variable. In patients who do respond, platelet counts usually start increasing within 24 to 48 hours, although it may take longer in some patients.[64] Because response is slow, the neonate with an urgent need for transfusion and no available compatible platelets can receive platelets from random donors, frequently resulting in an adequate response. For patients requiring platelet transfusion, giving concurrent IGIV can accelerate the recovery of the patient's own platelets and shorten the period of transfusion dependency. If the patient has mild thrombocytopenia without bleeding, it can be managed without specific therapeutic intervention.

Thrombocytopenia Secondary to Maternal ITP

Infants born to mothers with active idiopathic (immune) thrombocytopenic purpura (ITP) are often not profoundly thrombocytopenic and have a smaller risk of hemorrhage than infants with NAIT.[69,74] The antibody in ITP is usually IgG, which readily crosses the placenta. Occasionally, delivery of a severely thrombocytopenic infant has led to the diagnosis of previously unsuspected ITP in a moderately affected mother (postpartum platelet count 75,000-100,000/µL). Such cases of mild ITP should be distinguished from gestational thrombocytopenia, in which a mother with no history of autoimmune thrombocytopenia has a platelet count less than 150,000/µL. In cases of maternal ITP, the risk of severe fetal thrombocytopenia (usually defined as a platelet count less than 50,000/µL) is 7% to 10%.[74,75] The risk of intracranial hemorrhage in infants born to mothers with ITP is low (≤1%), with only a few cases reported in the literature. This is lower than the rate in NAIT because, infants born to mothers with ITP are generally born with higher platelet counts and their platelet function is not impaired, as it seems to be in NAIT. Routine fetal platelet assessment is not recommended and cesarean section is reserved for obstetric indications only.[74,76]

The antibody in ITP has broad reactivity against platelets. If the infant has a high concentration of antibody, there will be uniformly short survival of platelets from random donors, from the mother, or from other family members. Responses do sometimes occur, and, in the presence of hemorrhage, platelet transfusions will be used as emergency therapy.[69] IGIV therapy may also be effective for severe autoimmune thrombocytopenia.[66,72,74,76]

References

1. Goodstein M. Neonatal red cell transfusion. In: Herman JH, Manno CS, eds. Pediatric transfusion therapy. Bethesda, MD: AABB Press, 2002:39-91.
2. Vaughn JI, Manning M, Warwick RM, et al. Inhibition of erythroid progenitor cells by anti-Kell antibodies in fetal alloimmune anemia. N Engl J Med 1998;338:798-803.
3. Dennery PA, Seidman DS, Stevenson DK. Neonatal hyperbilirubinemia. N Engl J Med 2001;344:581-90.
4. American Academy of Pediatrics Subcommittee on Hyperbilirubinemia. Management of hyperbilirubinemia in the newborn infant 35 or more weeks of gestation. Clinical practice guideline. Pediatrics 2004;114:297-316.
5. Bowman JM. Intrauterine and neonatal transfusion. In: Anderson KC, Ness PM, eds. Scientific basis of transfusion medicine: Implications for clinical practice. Philadelphia: WB Saunders, 2000:307-20.
6. Bowman JM. Treatment options for the fetus with alloimmune hemolytic disease. Transfus Med Rev 1990;4:191-207.
7. Bowman JM. The prevention of Rh immunization. Transfus Med Rev 1988;2:129-50.
8. Bowman JM. Controversies in Rh prophylaxis. Who needs Rh immune globulin and when should it be given? Am J Obstet Gynecol 1985;151:289-94.
9. Strauss RG, Burmeister LE, Johnson K, et al. Randomized trial assessing the feasibility and safety of biologic parents as RBC donors for their preterm infants. Transfusion 2000;40:450-6.
10. Elbert C, Strauss RG, Barrett F, et al. Biological mothers may be dangerous blood donors for their neonates. Acta Hematol 1991;85:189-91.
11. Geifman-Holtzman O, Wojtowycz M, Kosmas K, Artal R. Female alloimmunization with antibodies known to cause hemolytic disease. Obstet Gynecol 1997;89:272-5.
12. Judd WJ. Practice guidelines for prenatal and perinatal immunohematology, revisited. Transfusion 2001;41:1445-52.
13. Legler TJ, Maas JH, Köhler M, et al. RHD sequencing: A new tool for decision making on transfusion therapy and provision of Rh prophylaxis. Transfus Med 2001;11:383-8.
14. Wagner FF, Frohmajer A, Ladewig B, et al. Weak D alleles express distinct phenotypes. Blood 2000;95:2699-708.
15. Prevention of Rh D alloimmunization. ACOG Practice Bulletin Number 4. Washington, DC: American College of Obstetricians and Gynecologists, May 1999.
16. Kanter MH. Derivation of new mathematic formulas for determining whether a D-positive father is heterozygous or homozygous for the D antigen. Am J Obstet Gynecol 1992;166:61-3.
17. Bennett PR, Le Van Kim C, Colon Y, et al. Prenatal determination of fetal RhD type by DNA amplification. N Engl J Med 1993;329:607-10.
18. Moise KJ. Management of Rhesus alloimmunization in pregnancy. Obstet Gynecol 2002;100:600-11.

19. Singleton BK, Green CA, Avent ND, et al. The presence of an RHD pseudogene containing a 37 base pair duplication and a nonsense mutation in Africans with the Rh D-negative blood group phenotype. Blood 2000;95:12-8.

20. Hessner MJ, Pircon RA, Luhm RA. Development of an allele specific polymerase chain reaction assay of prenatal genotyping of Jk[a] and Jk[b] of the Kidd blood group system (abstract). Am J Obstet Gynecol 1998;178(Suppl): 52S.

21. Lee S, Bennett PR, Overton T, et al. Prenatal diagnosis of Kell blood group genotypes: KEL1 and KEL2. Am J Obstet Gynecol 1996; 175:445-9.

22. Le Van Kim C, Mouro I, Brossard Y, et al. PCR-based determination of the Rhc and RhE status of the fetus at risk for Rhc and RhE hemolytic disease. Br J Haematol 1994;88: 193-5.

23. Spence WC, Potter P, Maddalena A, et al. DNA-based prenatal determination of the RhEe genotype. Obstet Gynecol 1995;86:670-2.

24. Randen I, Hauge R, Kjeldsen-Kragh J, Fagerhol MK. Prenatal genotyping of RHD and SRY using maternal blood. Vox Sang 2003;85:300-6.

25. Issitt PD, Anstee DJ. Applied blood group serology. 4th ed. Durham, NC: Montgomery Scientific Publications, 1998:1067-9.

26. Management of isoimmunization in pregnancy. ACOG Educational Bulletin Number 227. Washington, DC: American College of Obstetricians and Gynecologists, 1996.

27. Gottvall T, Hilden JO. Concentration of anti-D antibodies in Rh(D) alloimmunized pregnant women as a predictor of anemia and/or hyperbilirubinemia in their newborn infants. Acta Obstet Gynecol Scand 1997;76:733-8.

28. Bowman JM, Pollock JM, Manning FA, et al. Maternal Kell blood group alloimmunization. Obstet Gynecol 1992;79:239-44.

29. Hadley AG. Laboratory assays for predicting the severity of haemolytic disease of the fetus and newborn. Transpl Immunol 2002;10:191-8.

30. Hume HA. Fetal and neonatal transfusion therapy. In: Pomphilon DH, ed. Modern transfusion medicine. Boca Raton, FL: CRC Press, 1995:193-215.

31. Liley AW. Liquor amnii analysis in the management of the pregnancy complicated by rhesus sensitization. Am J Obstet Gynecol 1961;82:1359-70.

32. Queenan JT, Tomai TP, Ural SH, King JC. Deviation in amniotic fluid optical density at a wavelength of 450 nm in Rh-immunized pregnancies from 14 to 40 weeks' gestation: A proposal for clinical management. Am J Obstet Gynecol 1993;168:1370-6.

33. Steiner EA, Judd WJ, Oberman HA, et al. Percutaneous umbilical blood sampling and umbilical vein transfusions: Rapid serologic differentiation of fetal blood from maternal blood. Transfusion 1990;30:104-8.

34. Ludomirsky A. Intrauterine fetal blood sampling—a multicenter registry evaluation of 7462 procedures between 1987-1991 (abstract). Am J Obstet Gynecol 1993;168:318.

35. Mari G, Deter RL, Carpenter FL, et al. Noninvasive diagnosis by Doppler ultrasonography of fetal anemia due to maternal red-cell alloimmunization. N Engl J Med 2000;342:9-14.

36. Nishie EN, Brizot ML, Liao AW, et al. A comparison between middle cerebral artery peak systolic velocity and amniotic fluid optical density at 450 nm in the prediction of fetal anemia. Am J Obstet Gynecol 2003;188:214-9.

37. Quillen K, Berkman EM. Introduction to therapeutic apheresis. In: McLeod BC, Price TH, Weinstein R, eds. Apheresis: Principles and practice. 2nd ed. Bethesda, MD: AABB Press, 2003:49-69.

38. Margulies M, Voto LS, Mathet E, Margulies M. High dose intravenous IgG for the treatment of severe Rhesus alloimmunization. Vox Sang 1991;61:181-9.

39. Ulm B, Kirchner G, Svolba G, et al. Immunoglobulin administration to fetuses with anemia due to alloimmunization to D. Transfusion 1999;39:1235-8.

40. Ghidini A, Sepulveda W, Lockwood CJ, Romero R. Complications of fetal blood sampling. Am J Obstet Gynecol 1993;168:1339-44.

41. Weiner CP, Okamura K. Diagnostic fetal blood sampling-technique related losses. Fetal Diagn Ther 1996;11:169-75.

42. Schumacher B, Moise KJ Jr. Fetal transfusion for red blood alloimunization in pregnancy (review). Obstet Gynecol 1996;88:137-50.

43. Skupski DW, Wolf CF, Bussel JB. Fetal transfusion therapy. Obstet Gynecol Surg 1996;51:181-92.

44. Gonsoulin WJ, Moise KJ, Milam JD, et al. Serial maternal blood donations for intrauterine transfusion. Obstet Gynecol 1990;75: 158-62.

45. Sanders MR, Graeber JE. Posttransfusion graft-versus-host disease in infancy. J Pediatr 1990;117:159-63.

46. Linden JV, Pisciotto PT. Transfusion-associated graft-versus-host disease and blood irradiation. Transfus Med Rev 1992;6:116-23.

47. Mandelbrot L, Daffos F, Forestier F, et al. Assessment of fetal blood volume for computer-

assisted management of in utero transfusion. Fetal Ther 1988;3:60-6.

48. Moise KJ, Carpenter RJ, Kirshon B, et al. Comparison of four types of intrauterine transfusion: Effect on fetal hematocrit. Fetal Ther 1989;4:126-37.

49. Silva MA, ed. Standards for blood banks and transfusion services. 23rd ed. Bethesda, MD: AABB, 2005.

50. Herschel M, Karrison T, Wen M, et al. Isoimmunization is unlikely to be the cause of hemolysis in ABO-incompatible but direct antiglobulin test-negative neonates. Pediatrics 2002;110:127-30.

51. Koenig JM. Evaluation and treatment of erythroblastosis fetalis in the neonate. In: Christensen RD, ed. Hematologic problems of the neonate. Philadelphia: WB Saunders Company, 2000:185-207.

52. Saade GR, Moise KJ, Belfort MA, et al. Fetal and neonatal hematologic parameters in red cell alloimmunization: Predicting the need for late neonatal transfusions. Fetal Diagn Ther 1993;8:161-4.

53. Moise KJ, Brecher ME. Package insert for Rhesus immune globulin (letter). Obstet Gynecol 2004;103:998-9.

54. Mollison PL, Engelfriet CP, Contreras M. Blood transfusion in clinical medicine. 10th ed. Oxford, England: Blackwell Scientific Publications, 1997.

55. Hartwell EA. Use of Rh immune globulin. ASCP Practice Parameter. Am J Clin Pathol 1998;110:281-92.

56. Nicolaides KH, Clewell WH, Rodeck CH. Measurement of human fetoplacental blood volume in erythroblastosis fetalis. Am J Obstet Gynecol 1987;157:50-3.

57. Vengelen-Tyler V, Telen MJ. Collected questions and answers. 5th ed. Bethesda, MD: AABB, 1997:52-3.

58. Ness PM, Baldwin ML, Niebyl JR. Clinical high risk designation does not predict excess fetal maternal hemorrhage. Am J Obstet Gynecol 1987;156:154-8.

59. Owen J, Stedman CH, Tucker TL. Comparison of predelivery versus postdelivery Kleihauer-Betke stains in cases of fetal death. Am J Obstet Gynecol 1989;161:663-6.

60. Sebring ES. Fetomaternal hemorrhage—incidence and methods of detection and quantitation. In: Garratty G, ed. Hemolytic disease of the newborn. Arlington, VA: AABB, 1984:87-117.

61. Duguid JKM, Bromilow IM. Laboratory measurement of fetomaternal hemorrhage and its clinical relevance. Transfus Med Rev 1999; 13:43-8.

62. Riley JZ, Ness PM, Taddie SJ, et al. The detection and quantitation of fetal-maternal hemorrhage using an enzyme-linked antiglobulin test (ELAT). Transfusion 1982;22:472-4.

63. Bayliss KM, Kueck BD, Johnson ST, et al. Detecting fetomaternal hemorrhage: A comparison of five methods. Transfusion 1991;31:303-7.

64. Uhrynowska M, Maslanka K, Zupanska B. Neonatal thrombocytopenia: Incidence, serological and clinical observations. Am J Perinatol 1997;14:415-18.

65. Williamson LM, Hackett G, Rennie J, et al. The natural history of fetomaternal alloimmunization to the platelet-specific antigen HPA-1a (Pl^{A1}, Zw^a) as determined by antenatal screening. Blood 1998;92:2280-7.

66. Bussel JB. Alloimmune thrombocytopenia in the fetus and newborn. Semin Thromb Hemost 2001;27:245-52.

67. Johnson JA, Ryan G, al-Musa A, et al. Prenatal diagnosis and management of neonatal alloimmune thrombocytopenia. Semin Perinatol 1997;21:45-52.

68. Waters AW, Murphy M, Hambley H, Nicolaides K. Management of alloimmune thrombocytopenia in the fetus and neonate. In: Nance SJ, ed. Clinical and basic science aspects of immunohematology. Arlington, VA: AABB, 1991:155-77.

69. Blanchette VS, Kuhne T, Hume H, Hellman J. Platelet transfusion therapy in newborn infants. Transfus Med Rev 1995;9:215-30.

70. Maes LY, Gautreaux M, Southgate WM, Lazarchick J. Evidence of neonatal alloimmune thrombocytopenia mediated by anti-HLA antibodies (abstract). Transfusion 2001;41 (Suppl):20S.

71. Murphy MF, Williamson LM, Urbaniak SJ. Antenatal screening for fetomaternal alloimmune thrombocytopenia; should we be doing it? Vox Sang 2002;83(Suppl 1):409-16.

72. Gaddipati S, Berkowitz RL, Lembet AA, et al. Initial fetal platelet counts predict the response to intravenous gammaglobulin therapy in fetuses that are affected by PL^{A1} incompatibility. Obstet Gynecol 2001;185:976-80.

73. Leukocyte reduction. Association Bulletin 99-7. Bethesda, MD: AABB, 1999.

74. Bussel JB. Immune thrombocytopenia in pregnancy: Autoimmune and alloimmune. J Reprod Immunol 1997;37:35-61.

75. Payne SD, Resnik R, Moore TR, et al. Maternal characteristics and risk of severe neonatal thrombocytopenia and intracranial hemorrhage in pregnancies complicated by autoimmune thrombocytopenia. Am J Obstet Gynecol 1997;177:149-55.

76. Blanchette VS, Kirby MA, Turner C. Role of intravenous immunoglobulin G in autoimmune hematologic disorders. Semin Hematol 1992;29:72-82.

Chapter 24

Neonatal and Pediatric Transfusion Practice

MANY PHYSIOLOGIC CHANGES accompany the transitions from fetus to neonate, neonate to infant, and throughout childhood. Hematologic values, blood volume, and physiologic responses to stresses such as hypovolemia and hypoxia vary widely. The most rapid changes occur during early infancy. Consequently, discussions of pediatric transfusion are usually divided into two periods: neonates from birth through 4 months, and older infants (>4 months) and children. Some concerns in neonatal transfusion practice overlap with those of the perinatal period and are discussed in Chapter 23.

Advances in medical care now permit the survival of extremely premature neonates. Blood providers must be capable of furnishing blood components that are tailored to satisfy the specific needs of very low birthweight (VLBW <1500 g) and extremely low birthweight (ELBW <1000 g) patients, whose small blood volumes and impaired or immature organ functions provide little margin for safety. Ill neonates are more likely than hospitalized patients of any other age group to receive red cell transfusions.[1] Advances in critical-care neonatology, such as surfactant therapy, nitric oxide therapy, use of high-frequency ventilators, and adherence to transfusion practice guidelines, have diminished the number of blood transfusions given; most are now given to infants with birthweights less than 1000 g.[1] The doses of various components used for simple, small-volume transfusions are given in Table 24-1.[2]

Fetal and Neonatal Erythropoiesis

The predominant sites of hematopoiesis in the developing embryo shift from the wall of the yolk sac to the liver to the mar-

Table 24-1. Volumes for Simple, Small-Volume Transfusions of Neonates

Component	Volume	Estimated Change
RBC	10-15 mL/kg	Hemoglobin ↑ 2-3 g/dL
Platelet	5-10 mL/kg	Platelet ↑ 50,000-100,000/μL
Granulocyte	≥1 × 10^9 neutrophils/kg in volume of 10-15 mL/kg	Repeat until clinical response
FFP	10-15 mL/kg	Factor activity ↑ 15-20%
Cryoprecipitate	1-2 units/10 kg	↑ 60-100 mg/dL fibrinogen (infant) ↑ 5-10 mg/dL fibrinogen (larger child)

Adapted with permission from Roseff.[2]

row in the first 24 weeks.[3] Hematopoiesis is regulated by gradually increasing erythropoietin (EPO) levels stimulated by low oxygen tensions during intrauterine life. Fetal red cells, rich in hemoglobin F, are well adapted to low intrauterine oxygen tensions. The high oxygen affinity of fetal hemoglobin enhances transfer of oxygen from maternal erythrocytes to fetal erythrocytes throughout pregnancy.

The "switch" from fetal to adult hemoglobin begins at about 32 weeks' gestation; at birth, 60% to 80% of the total hemoglobin is hemoglobin F. Preterm neonates, therefore, are born with higher levels of fetal hemoglobin than those born at term. The mean cord hemoglobin of healthy term neonates is 16.9 ± 1.6 g/dL, and that of preterm neonates is 15.9 ± 2.4 g/dL.[4] Hemoglobin concentration gradually falls in the first few weeks of life. This has been called "physiologic anemia of infancy" in term newborns and "physiologic anemia of prematurity" in preterm newborns. The anemia is considered physiologic because it is self-limited, is usually well tolerated, and is not associated with any deleterious effects to the infant. Erythropoietic activity diminishes secondary to an increase in pulmonary blood flow and a rise in arterial pO$_2$, as well as the increase in red cell con-

tent of 2,3-diphosphoglycerate (2,3-DPG) and hemoglobin A, which enhance the release of oxygen to the tissues. As tissue oxygenation improves, levels of EPO decline and erythropoiesis diminishes. This, along with decreased survival of fetal red cells and expansion of the blood volume due to rapid growth, causes the hemoglobin concentration to decline. The rate of decline is dependent on gestational age at birth; hemoglobin may drop to as low as 8.0 g/dL at 4 to 8 weeks of age in preterm infants with birthweights of 1000 to 1500 g, and 7.0 g/dL in neonates with birthweights less than 1000 g.[3]

Despite hemoglobin levels that would indicate anemia in older children and adults, the normally developing infant usually maintains adequate tissue oxygenation. Physiologic anemia requires treatment only if the degree or timing of the anemia causes symptoms in the patient.

Unique Aspects of Neonatal Physiology

Infant Size and Blood Volume

Full-term newborns have a blood volume of approximately 85 mL/kg; preterm low birthweight newborns have an average blood volume of 100 mL/kg. As survival rates continue to improve for infants weighing 1000 g or less at birth, blood banks are being asked to provide blood components for patients whose total blood volume is less than 100 mL on a more frequent basis. The need for frequent laboratory tests has made replacement of iatrogenic blood loss the most common indication for transfusion of low birthweight preterm neonates. However, the previous practice of replacing blood mL for mL is giving way to replacement as needed in order to maintain a target hematocrit in certain clinical situations.[1]

Newborns do not compensate for hypovolemia as well as adults. After 10% volume depletion in a newborn, left ventricular stroke volume is diminished without increasing heart rate. To maintain systemic blood pressure, peripheral vascular resistance increases, and this, combined with a decreased cardiac output, results in poor tissue perfusion, low tissue oxygenation, and metabolic acidosis.[5]

Erythropoietin Response

Erythropoietin response in newborns differs from that in adults and older children. In older children and adults, oxygen sensors in the kidney recognize diminished oxygen delivery and release EPO into the circulation. In the fetus, the oxygen sensor that stimulates EPO production is believed to be the liver, which appears to be programmed for the hypoxic intrauterine environment.

This hyporesponsiveness to hypoxia protects the fetus from becoming polycythemic in utero. Eventually, EPO production shifts from the liver to the kidneys, a developmental change thought to be regulated based on the time of conception, not birth, and possibly not beginning until term. The most premature infants produce the least amount of EPO for any degree of anemia; this may reflect the absence of the developmental shift of erythropoietin production from the liver to the kidneys.[6] Sick preterm neonates who receive many transfusions shortly after birth have reduced circulating levels of fetal hemoglobin. Circulating EPO levels are lower, for a given hematocrit, in preterm neonates with higher proportions of hemoglobin A relative to hemoglobin F, which favors release of oxygen to the tissues.[6] Erythroid progenitor cells in the hypoproliferative marrow of these preterm infants show normal intrinsic sensitivity to EPO. Clinical trials of recombinant human erythropoietin (rHuEPO) in premature neonates show that the number of transfusions and severity of anemia can be lessened.[7] Adverse effects of rHuEPO in this age group are also different from those seen in older children and adults and include transient, reversible neutropenia. Since the adherence to strict transfusion guidelines and the decrease in phlebotomy in VLBW infants, the ultimate role of rHuEPO in the management of "anemia of prematurity" has remained unclear. A recent multicenter study in Europe showed decreased need for transfusion when administering EPO to ELBW infants within 3 to 5 days of life (early EPO administration) and continuing for 9 weeks.[8] The mean number of transfusions dropped from 2.66 to 1.86, with a reduction in donor exposures from 2 to 1. Questions regarding optimal dosing, route of administration, and use of supplemental iron remain to be answered.[1,7-10] In any event, with the tremendous strides made in decreasing donor exposure in transfused newborns by using restrictive transfusion practices alone, the role of EPO for this purpose may no longer be relevant.

Cold Stress

Hypothermia in the newborn causes exaggerated effects, including increased metabolic rate, hypoglycemia, metabolic acidosis, and a tendency toward apneic episodes that may lead to hypoxia, hypotension, and cardiac arrest. Blood used for exchange transfusion should be warmed because blood at room temperature may decrease a newborn's core temperature by 0.7 to 2.5 C. The usual method is to use an inline warmer. Blood, either large or small volumes, should not be warmed under a radiant heater because of the risk of hemolysis in an unmonitored apparatus. When transfusions are given to infants undergoing phototherapy, the tubing should be positioned to minimize exposure to the phototherapy light in order to prevent hemolysis.[11]

Immunologic Status

Infants have an immature and inexperienced cellular and humoral immune system. Antibodies present derive almost entirely from the maternal circulation. Transplacental transfer of immunoglobulin and other proteins is independent of molecular size; IgG (150 kD) is transferred much more readily than albumin (64 kD). In humans, maternal IgM does not reach the fetus and IgA is not readily transferred, although low levels have been found in the newborn.

All four subclasses of IgG are transported across the placenta, but the rate varies between individual mother-fetus pairs. Early in pregnancy (approximately 12 weeks), IgG probably passes from mother to fetus by diffusion, and concentration in fetal serum is low for all subgroups.[12] Between 20 and 33 weeks of gestation, fetal IgG levels rise markedly, apparently because of maturation of a selective transport system that involves, in part, specific protein receptors on the membrane of placental cells. IgG1, the predominant subclass in maternal blood, crosses the placenta first and is transported in greatest quantity. Cord blood has higher antibody concentrations than maternal blood. Catabolism of IgG occurs more slowly in the fetus than in the mother, so that transplacental maternal antibody is conserved during the neonatal period.

A fetus exposed to an infectious process in utero or an infant exposed shortly after birth may produce small amounts of IgM detectable by sensitive techniques, but unexpected red cell alloantibodies of either IgG or IgM class are rarely formed during the neonatal period. The mechanisms responsible for the lack of alloantibody production in the neonate are not clearly understood and are most likely multifactorial, including deficient T helper function, enhanced T suppressor activity, and poor antigen-presenting cell function.[13]

The cellular immune response is critical to the occurrence of transfusion-associated graft-vs-host disease (TA-GVHD). In the newborn, TA-GVHD has been reported most often in the clinical setting of confirmed or suspected congenital immunodeficiency. It is recommended that infants with suspected and/or documented T-cell immunodeficiency receive irradiated blood components. The majority of TA-GVHD cases reported in nonimmunocompromised hosts have occurred in infants who received intrauterine transfusion followed by postnatal exchange transfusion.[14] A proposed explanation is that lymphocytes given during intrauterine transfusion could induce host tolerance, impairing rejection of lymphocytes given in the subsequent exchange transfusions. There have also been rare cases of TA-GVHD reported in association with extreme prematurity, neonatal alloimmune thrombocytopenia, and the use of extracorporeal membrane oxygenation (ECMO).[14,15] Neonates present with TA-GVHD after a longer latent period than adults, with fever occurring at an average of 28 days after exposure, rather than 10 days for immunocompetent adults. There may be several risk factors other than the immune status of the recipient that predispose to TA-GVHD, such as the number and viability of lymphocytes in the transfused component and donor-recipient HLA compatibility. The true incidence of TA-GVHD in the neonatal setting is not known. However, on the basis of data from Japan, it appears that the incidence of reported TA-GVHD is far lower than would be expected.[15] The postulated mechanism for this apparent decreased susceptibility of newborns to TA-GVHD is thought to be extrathymic and/or thymic semitolerance of allogeneic donor T lymphocytes. As for all patients, directed-donor units from biologic relatives must be irradiated.[15,16] There are no data to support the practice of universal irradiation of blood transfused to all infants or children.

Metabolic Problems

Acidosis or hypocalcemia may occur after large-volume whole blood or plasma transfusion because the immature liver of the newborn metabolizes citrate inefficiently. Immature kidneys have reduced glomerular filtration rate and concentrating ability, and newborns may have difficulty excreting excess potassium, acid, and/or calcium.

Potassium

Although potassium levels increase rapidly in the plasma of stored red cells, small-volume, simple transfusions administered slowly have little effect on serum potassium concentration in newborns. It has been calculated that transfusion of 10 mL/kg of red cells (hematocrit 80%) obtained from a unit of blood stored for 42 days in extended storage medium would deliver 2 mL of plasma containing only 0.1 mmol/L of potassium. This is much less than the daily potassium requirement of 2 to 3 mmol/L for a 1-kg patient.[17] However, serum potassium may, rise rapidly after infusion of large volumes of red cells in such circumstances as surgery, exchange transfusion, or extracorporeal circulation, depending upon the plasma potassium levels in the blood and manipulation of the blood component.[18,19] Of interest, a unit of Red Blood Cells (RBCs) preserved in AS-1 will deliver less extracellular potassium compared to the amount in RBCs stored in CPDA-1.[16,20] In stored irradiated blood, the problem of potassium leak is potentiated; for selected patients, it may be desirable to wash irradiated cells, if they have subsequently been stored >24 hours.[19] There are increasing anecdotal reports of infants who receive either older RBC units or units irradiated more than 1 day before transfusion having severe adverse effects (eg, cardiac arrest, death) after transfusion of these products into central lines or intracardiac lines.[21,22]

The untoward consequences of washing blood, such as reducing its shelf life and the possible introduction of bacteria, must be considered. It is preferable to perform irradiation as close to the time of administration as possible, obviating the concern for high levels of potassium in the transfused product.

2,3-Diphosphoglycerate

Neonates with respiratory distress syndrome or septic shock have decreased levels of intracellular red cell 2,3-DPG. Alkalosis and hypothermia may further increase the oxygen affinity of hemoglobin, shifting the dissociation curve to the left and making oxygen even less available to the tissues. Arterial oxygenation may be further compromised by respiratory distress syndrome or other pulmonary disease. Mechanisms that compensate for hypoxia in adults, such as increased heart rate, are limited in newborns. If a large proportion of an infant's blood volume has come from transfusion of 2,3-DPG-depleted blood, this may cause problems that would not affect older children or adults. Because 2,3-DPG levels decline rapidly after the first week of storage, the freshest blood conveniently available (up to 14 days) should be used for exchange transfusion in newborns. For small-volume transfusions, the medical necessity for fresh blood has never been demonstrated and arguments have been raised to suggest it is unnecessary.[1,16,19]

Cytomegalovirus Infection

Perinatal infection with cytomegalovirus (CMV) may occur, acquired either in utero or during the birth process. Neonates can be infected during breast-feeding or by close contact with mothers or nursery personnel. CMV can also be transmitted by transfusion, although the risk from the current blood supply is small.[23,24]

CMV infection in newborns has extremely variable manifestations, ranging from asymptomatic seroconversion to death. Studies of CMV in neonatal transfusion recipients reveal the following observations:

1. The overall risk of symptomatic post-transfusion CMV infection seems to be inversely related to the seropositivity rate in the community. Although many adults are positive for CMV antibodies, the rate of symptomatic CMV infection in newborns is low.

2. Symptomatic CMV infection during the neonatal period is uncommon in children born to seropositive mothers.[25]

3. The risk of symptomatic posttransfusion infection is high in multitransfused preterm infants weighing less than 1200 g who are born to seronegative mothers.[17,26]

4. The risk of acquiring CMV infection is directly proportional to the cumulative number of donor exposures incurred via transfusion.

5. Cytomegalovirus in blood is associated with leukocytes. The risk of virus transmission can be reduced by transfusing CMV-reduced-risk blood from seronegative donors or by using leukocyte-reduced components. Although deglycerolized and washed red cells also have a reduced risk of CMV infection, leukocyte reduction by filtration is the technique of choice.[16,27-30]

Red Cell Transfusions in Infants Less than 4 Months of Age

RBCs are the component most often transfused during the neonatal period. Many of the physiologic considerations mentioned above directly affect decisions regarding indications for transfusion, selection, and administration of red cell components, as well as the requirements for compatibility testing.

Compatibility Testing

Because the neonate and young infant are immunologically immature, alloimmunization to red cell antigens is rare during the neonatal period. A study of 90 neonates who received 1269 transfusions from different donors found no instances of antibody production even with use of very sensitive detection techniques.[31] Other investigators confirm the relative infrequency of alloantibodies directed against red cell, as well as HLA, antigens.[13,28]

Because alloimmunization is extremely rare and repeated testing increases iatrogenic blood loss, AABB *Standards for Blood Banks and Transfusion Services*[32(p42)] requires only limited pretransfusion serologic testing for infants under 4 months old. Initial testing must include ABO and D typing of red cells and a screen for red cell antibodies, using either serum or plasma, from the mother or the infant.

During any one hospitalization, compatibility testing and repeat ABO and D typing may be omitted, provided that the screen for red cell antibodies is negative; that all red cells transfused are group O or ABO-identical or ABO-compatible; and that red cells are either D negative or the same D type as the patient. It is unnecessary to test the infant's serum for anti-A and/or anti-B as a component of blood typing. Before giving non-group-O red cells, the neonate's serum must be checked for passively acquired maternal anti-A or anti-B and must include the antiglobulin phase. If the antibody is present, ABO-compatible red cells lacking the corresponding A or B antigen must be used until the antibody is no longer detected. In this setting, it is not necessary to perform crossmatches. If an unexpected non-ABO red cell antibody is detected in the infant's specimen or the mother's serum contains a clinically significant red cell antibody, the infant should be given either RBC units tested and found to lack the corresponding antigen(s) or units compatible by antiglobulin crossmatch. This practice should continue for as long as maternal antibody persists in the infant's blood. The institution's policy will determine how frequently to recheck the screen for red cell antibodies; once a negative result is obtained, subsequent crossmatches

and/or provision of blood lacking the target antigen are unnecessary. It is important to avoid transfusion of any component that may transfer unexpected antibody or ABO-incompatible antibodies to the infant.

Indications for Red Cell Transfusion

Certain events in the perinatal period cause anemia, for which the benefits of red cell transfusion are unquestioned. These include spontaneous fetomaternal or fetoplacental hemorrhage, twin-twin transfusion, obstetric accidents, and internal hemorrhage. A venous hemoglobin of less than 13 g/dL in the first 24 hours of life indicates significant anemia.[33] For severely anemic neonates with congestive heart failure, it may be necessary to remove aliquots of their dilute blood and transfuse concentrated red cells. This "partial exchange" transfusion will prevent intravascular volume overload. Most red cell transfusions in the neonatal period, however, are given either to replace iatrogenic blood loss or to treat the physiologic decline in hemoglobin (anemia of prematurity) when it complicates clinical problems.

Because tissue demand for oxygen cannot be measured directly and because so many variables determine oxygen availability, no universally accepted criteria exist for transfusion of preterm or term neonates. Despite the widespread use of micromethods for laboratory tests and growing use of bedside or noninvasive monitoring devices, infants still sustain significant cumulative blood loss from laboratory sampling. In a sick neonate, red cell replacement is usually considered when approximately 10% of the blood volume has been removed. The decision to transfuse a newborn for anemia should include evaluation of the hemoglobin levels expected for the patient's age and clinical status, as well as the amount of blood loss over time. Transfusion may be more aggressive in the infant in respiratory distress who is hypoxic and more vulnerable to cerebral hemorrhage.

Considerable controversy surrounds the correlation of the "signs of anemia" in the preterm infant (tachycardia, tachypnea, bradycardia, recurrent apnea, and poor weight gain) with response to red cell transfusions.[1] When red cells are transfused, they are usually given in small volumes of 10 to 15 mL/kg (or less if the infant cannot tolerate this volume). The hematocrit of the red cell component transfused will depend on the anticoagulant/preservative used and how the original unit is processed to provide small component transfusions for neonates. A transfusion of 10 mL/kg of red cells adjusted to a hematocrit greater than 80% just before release for transfusion should raise the hemoglobin concentration by approximately 3 g/dL. A transfusion of 10 mL/kg of red cells in additive solution, which have a hematocrit of approximately 65%, will result in a posttransfusion hemoglobin increment less than 3 g/dL.

Red Cell Components Used for Neonatal Transfusion

The small-volume requirements of transfusion to neonatal recipients make it possible to prepare several aliquots from a single donor unit, thus limiting donor exposure and decreasing donor-related risks. Several technical approaches are available to realize this advantage and to minimize wastage.[34]

Aliquoting for Small-Volume Transfusion

A multiple-pack system is a common technique for providing small-volume red cell transfusions.[34,35] Quad packs, where a single unit of Whole Blood is collected into a bag with four integrally attached containers, can be used to increase the number of transfusions an infant can receive from one donor. Because the original seal remains intact, each container has the expiration date of the original unit. With use of a sterile connecting device, multiple bags called pedi-packs or specially designed syringe systems can be integrally attached to a unit of RBCs after component preparation. This maintains a closed system and further increases the number of small-volume transfusions obtained from a single donor. Sterile connecting devices can be used to prepare small aliquots for transfusion in the blood bank. If aliquots are prepared by entering the bag through a port, the unit and the aliquot are assigned a 24-hour shelf life, if refrigerated.

Each aliquot must be fully labeled as it is prepared, including the time it outdates. The origin and disposition of each aliquot must be recorded. Using these techniques, a recipient can receive multiple small-volume transfusions from a single donation until the expiration of the original unit, thereby reducing donor exposure.[34,36] The disadvantage of any method that creates aliquots from a single donation is that any undetected, transmissible pathogen that might be present in the primary unit can be disseminated to multiple recipients.

In order to prevent waste, many transfusion services assign a unit of RBCs to one or more infants based on their weight. As an example, 1 or 2 lower birthweight infants may be assigned to one unit because they will most likely require the greatest number of transfusions. On the other hand, four larger infants may be assigned to one unit because their transfusion needs will not be as great.[37,38]

Red Cells with Additive Solution

RBCs used for pediatric transfusions were traditionally stored in CPDA-1.[35] Additive solutions (AS) used as anticoagulants/ preservatives contain additional adenine and dextrose and some contain mannitol. There has been concern about the potential side effects of these additives because large amounts of adenine and mannitol have been associated with renal toxicity. Mannitol is also a potent diuretic and, because of its effect on the fluid dynamics in preterm infants, may cause unacceptable fluctuations in cerebral blood flow. The different constituents of these solutions are found in Chapter 8. However, when the dose of transfused red cells is small (5 to 15 mL/kg), the recipient is exposed to relatively small amounts of the preservative solutions. Clinical studies comparing red cells stored in AS-1 and AS-3 solutions have shown no apparent detrimental effects in neonates receiving simple transfusions, and, after adjustment for the lower hematocrit of the component, they are as effective as CPDA-1 cells in increasing hemoglobin. Furthermore, the additional sugars present have been shown to benefit glucose homeostasis in comparison with CPDA-1.[39] Studies on the safety of AS-3-preserved red cells in neonates have been published.[38,40] Because the components of AS-5 are the same as those found in the other additive solutions, it is considered acceptable for use in neonates.

Using theoretical calculations in a variety of clinical situations, Luban et al[41] demonstrated that red cells preserved in extended-storage media present no substantive risks when used for small-volume transfusions. For preterm infants with severe hepatic or renal insufficiency, however, removing the additive-containing plasma may be beneficial. This is particularly important if there will be multiple transfusions that could have a cumulative effect. The safety of red cells stored in additive solutions and used for massive transfusions, such as cardiac surgery or exchange trans-

fusion, has not been studied. Concern still remains regarding the use of blood stored in additive solutions being used outside the setting of simple, small-volume transfusion.[40,41] However, with extensive anecdotal use in large transfusion services, there have not been reports of deleterious effects from the infusion of additive solutions.[42,43]

Whether or not placental/umbilical cord blood will become an acceptable form of neonatal transfusion remains to be seen. Although use of this type of "autologous" blood would eliminate some infectious disease risks, questions regarding quantity, quality, and sterility raise concerns about its safety and efficacy.[18]

Transfusion Administration

Vascular access is often difficult in the tiny newborn and in any infant requiring long-term or repeated intravenous infusions. Within a short time after birth, the umbilical artery may be cannulated. Transfusion through a needle as small as 25-gauge or a vascular catheter as small as 24-gauge has been shown to cause little hemolysis and to be safe when constant flow rates are used. Transfusion through smaller gauge catheters has not been thoroughly evaluated.

It is not usually necessary to warm small-volume transfusions that are given slowly, but it is important to be able to control the volume and rate of infusion. Constant-rate electromechanical syringe delivery pumps provide this control and cause minimal hemolysis, even when used with inline leukocyte reduction filters.[44,45]

The length of the plastic tubing used can add significantly to the volume required for transfusion. Infusion sets identified as suitable for platelets or components have less dead space than standard sets because they have short tubing and a small 170-micron filter. Pediatric microaggregate filters (20-

or 40-micron) are often used for their small priming volume, not for the removal of microaggregates. Hemolysis may occur when stored blood is given by negative pressure filtration through these filters.[46]

Administration rates for RBCs have not been extensively studied, nor are there standard practices; rates of transfusion as well as devices used vary with institutions. The rate of administration of blood and blood components in neonates and infants should be individualized on the basis of the patient's clinical needs. Theoretical concerns regarding rapid changes in intravascular volume and electrolyte changes in these small, labile patients have focused on an increased risk for intracranial hemorrhage. This has not been clearly demonstrated. For simple RBC transfusions, transfusing products over 2 to 4 hours is usually adequate. When there is an urgent need because of shock or severe bleeding, infusion should be as rapid as possible. Products can be transfused safely using a variety of devices. It is important that mechanical systems be tested and validated for use with blood and blood components.

Exchange Transfusion for Hyperbilirubinemia

The fetal liver has limited capacity to conjugate bilirubin. In utero, unconjugated bilirubin crosses the placenta for excretion through the mother's hepatobiliary system. After birth, transient mild hyperbilirubinemia normally occurs during the first week of life and is referred to as "physiologic jaundice." Liver function is less mature, and jaundice worsens in premature neonates. When the level of unconjugated bilirubin is excessive, bilirubin may cross the blood-brain barrier and concentrate in the basal ganglia and cerebellum; the resulting damage to the central nervous system (CNS) is called kernicterus. Photo-

therapy with fluorescent blue lights is the most common treatment for hyperbilirubinemia; exchange transfusion is reserved for phototherapy failures. The most common reason, however, for an exchange to be performed in a neonate is to correct hyperbilirubinemia.

Pathologic processes that may result in excessively high unconjugated bilirubin levels in neonates include immune-mediated hemolysis, nonimmune hemolysis, bile excretion defects and impaired albumin binding. Exchange transfusion removes unconjugated bilirubin and provides additional albumin to bind residual bilirubin. If hyperbilirubinemia is due to antibody-mediated hemolysis, exchange transfusion is of additional benefit by removing free antibody and antibody-coated red cells while providing antigen-negative red cells that will survive normally.

Exchange transfusion should be performed before bilirubin rises to levels at which CNS damage occurs. Several factors affect the threshold for toxicity. CNS damage occurs at lower levels if there is prematurity, decreased albumin binding capacity, or the presence of such complicating conditions as sepsis, hypoxia, acidosis, hypothermia, or hypoglycemia. In full-term infants, kernicterus rarely develops at indirect bilirubin levels less than 25 mg/dL, but, in sick VLBW infants, kernicterus has occurred at levels as low as 8 to 12 mg/dL.[47]

The rate at which bilirubin rises is more predictive of imminent need for exchange transfusion than the absolute level attained. Neonates with severe anemia and a rapid rise in bilibrubin, despite phototherapy, require exchange transfusion. A two-volume exchange transfusion removes approximately 70% to 90% of circulating erythrocytes and about 25% of the total bilirubin. Because of reequilibration between the extravascular tissue and plasma bilirubin, levels may again rise, resulting in the need for a second exchange transfusion.[48] Indications for repeat exchange are similar to those for the initial exchange.

The American Academy of Pediatrics recently released new guidelines for the management of newborn infants born ≥35 weeks of gestation with hyperbilirubinemia. It is hoped that raising awareness about the potential for hyperbilirubinemia in this patient group will reduce its frequency and provide a framework for optimal treatment, to include the use of phototherapy, exchange transfusion, and Immune Globulin, Intravenous (IGIV).[49]

Exchange Transfusion for Other Causes

The safety and efficacy of exchange transfusion in the neonatal period for other indications should be evaluated on a case-by-case basis, using guidelines in published literature. Treatment categories for disorders based on proven vs theoretical benefits have been recommended (see Table 6-1). The treatment of disseminated intravascular coagulation (DIC) using exchange transfusion has yielded variable results, perhaps because only the sickest infants have been selected to receive this therapy. The most important aspect of therapy for neonatal DIC is to treat the underlying disease.

Exchange transfusion is occasionally used to remove other toxins, such as drugs or chemicals given to the mother near the time of delivery, drugs given in toxic doses to the neonate/infant, or substances such as ammonia that accumulate in the newborn because of prematurity or inherited metabolic diseases.[50,51]

Technique of Exchange Transfusion

Choice of Components

Red cells are resuspended in compatible thawed Fresh Frozen Plasma (FFP) for exchange transfusion. If AS-RBC units are used, depending on the clinical situation, some institutions would choose to remove the additive-containing plasma, to reduce the volume transfused. As discussed earlier, washing components may not be necessary or desirable. Many transfusion services use red cells that have been screened and found to lack hemoglobin S for exchange transfusion, to avoid the possibility of intravascular sickling.

The glucose load administered during exchange transfusion can be extremely high. This stimulates the infant to secrete insulin, which may lead to rebound hypoglycemia. It is important to monitor blood glucose levels for the first few hours after the procedure.

Because unconjugated bilirubin binds to albumin, albumin is frequently used to increase intravascular binding. With additional albumin in the circulation, bilirubin from the extravascular space diffuses out to the intravascular space. This, in turn, increases the total quantity of bilirubin removed during the exchange. There have been conflicting results, however, about the efficacy of administering albumin either before or during exchange to enhance bilirubin removal. A study that compared 15 hyperbilirubinemic neonates given albumin with 27 who received none found similar efficiency of bilirubin removal in both groups.[52] Infusing albumin raises the colloid osmotic pressure and increases intravascular volume. Therefore, it should be given cautiously, if at all, to neonates or infants who are severely anemic, have increased central venous pressure, or are in renal or congestive heart failure.

Exchange transfusion may cause dilutional thrombocytopenia and/or coagulopathy that require transfusion of platelets and/or other components containing coagulation factors. Platelet counts and coagulation parameters should be monitored after exchange transfusion.

Volume and Hematocrit

An exchange transfusion equal to twice the patient's blood volume is typically recommended for newborns; rarely is more than one full unit of donor blood required. In practice, the volume calculated for exchange is an estimate. The final hematocrit of transfused blood should be approximately 40% to 50%, with sufficient plasma to provide clotting factors, if needed. In the unusual event that the infant's condition demands a high postexchange hematocrit, a small-volume transfusion of red cells can be given after the exchange, or units with a higher hematocrit used for exchange. It is important to keep the blood mixed during the exchange; if it settles in the container, the final aliquots will not have the intended hematocrit. The infant's hematocrit and bilirubin level should be measured using the last aliquot removed in the exchange.

Vascular Access

Exchange transfusions in the newborn period are usually accomplished via catheters in the umbilical vessels. Catheterization is easiest within hours of birth, but it may be possible to achieve vascular access at this site for several days. The catheters should be radio-opaque to facilitate radiographic monitoring during and after placement. If umbilical catheters are not available for exchange transfusion, small central venous or saphenous catheters may be used.

Methods Used

Two methods of exchange transfusion are in common use. In the isovolumetric method, there is vascular access through two catheters of identical size. Withdrawal and infusion occur simultaneously, regulated by a single peristaltic pump. The umbilical artery is usually used for withdrawal and the umbilical vein for infusion.

The manual push-pull technique can be accomplished through a single vascular access. A three-way stopcock joins the unit of blood, the patient, and an extension tube that leads to the graduated discard container. An inline blood warmer and a standard blood filter should be incorporated in the administration set. The maximum volume of each withdrawal and infusion will depend on the infant's size and hemodynamic status. The rate at which exchange transfusion occurs may alter the infant's hemodynamic status. It is important to maintain careful records during an exchange transfusion. The procedure should take place over 1 to 1.5 hours.

Transfusion of Other Components

Although the percentage of VLBW and ELBW infants being transfused has decreased significantly since the 1980s, between 61% and 94% of these neonatal patients can be expected to receive multiple red cell transfusions. The smallest patients will receive the greatest number of transfusions. It is estimated that a much lower percentage of infants receive other components.[1,9,53,54]

Platelet Transfusion

The normal platelet count of newborns is similar to that of adults. A platelet count less than $150,000/\mu L$ in a full-term or premature infant is abnormal. Approximately 20% of infants in neonatal intensive care units have mild-to-moderate thrombocytopenia, which is the most common hemostatic abnormality in the sick infant.[55] Neonatal thrombocytopenia may result from impaired production or increased destruction of platelets, abnormal distribution, or a dilutional effect secondary to massive transfusion such as exchange transfusion. Increased destruction is the most common cause; it may be associated with a multitude of conditions and is usually transient. Neonatal alloimmune thrombocytopenia is discussed in Chapter 23.

Indications

Platelet transfusion is indicated in neonates and young infants with platelet counts below 50,000/μL who are experiencing bleeding.[55] The use of prophylactic platelet transfusions in the newborn remains controversial. In thrombocytopenic adults, the risk of severe bleeding is rare unless the platelet count is less than 10,000/μL.[56] Conversely, preterm neonates and infants with other complicating illnesses may bleed at higher platelet counts. Factors contributing to this increased risk of bleeding include a quantitatively lower concentration of plasma coagulation factors; circulation of an anticoagulant that enhances inhibition of thrombin; intrinsic or extrinsic platelet dysfunction; and increased vascular fragility.[57] Of major concern is intraventricular hemorrhage, which occurs in up to 40% of preterm neonates in the first 72 hours. Although prophylactic platelet transfusions increase platelet counts and shorten the bleeding time in these infants, the incidence or extent of intraventricular hemorrhage is not reduced.[57] Because of the apparent lack of clinical benefit, controversy exists about the use of platelet transfusion in this setting, as well as the selection of an optimal dose. After a platelet transfusion, a post-transfusion platelet count soon after transfusion can be used to evaluate survival in the circulation but may not pre-dict hemostatic efficacy. Repeated platelet transfusions, without an appropriate rise, may not be beneficial.

Platelet Components

A platelet dose of 5 to 10 mL/kg body weight should raise the platelet count of an average full-term newborn by 50,000 to 100,000/μL, depending on the platelet concentration in the component used.[17,57] The platelet component should be group specific, if possible, and should not contain clinically significant unexpected red cell antibodies. Transfusion of ABO-incompatible plasma is more dangerous in infants than in adults because of their very small blood volumes. If it is necessary to give a platelet unit that contains incompatible plasma (due to antibodies in the ABO or other blood groups), plasma can be removed (see Method 6.15) and the platelets resuspended in saline. FFP can be substituted as the resuspending medium if the patient also requires clotting factors, but it carries the risk of infectious disease transmission. Routine centrifugation of platelets to reduce the volume of transfusion is not necessary.[53,55] If platelets have been volume reduced and placed in a syringe, the pH declines rapidly, a potential problem for an already ill, acidotic patient.[58] Therefore, if there is a need to reduce the volume of platelets, it should be done just before transfusion and the component must be infused within 4 hours, if done in an open system.

Granulocyte Transfusion

Neonates are more susceptible to severe bacterial infection than older children because of both the quantitative and qualitative defects of neutrophil (polymorphonuclear cell or PMN) function and, in the absence of pathogen-specific maternal antibody, to deficiency of humoral immunity. Group B streptococcus is the most frequent cause of early-onset neonatal sepsis, and, despite improvement in antimicrobial therapy and intensive care, it is still associated with a high mortality rate. Controversy surrounds several issues in granulocyte transfusions for neonates, including dose, neutrophil level at which to transfuse, and efficacy as compared to other forms of therapy.[59] Because it appears that efficacy is related to dose, the smaller blood volume of infants and young children may result in these patients having a better response to this form of therapy. A meta-analysis published in 1996 concluded that granulocyte doses greater than 1×10^9 PMN/kg resulted in a better clinical response.[60] Granulocyte concentrates prepared by apheresis are more desirable than those prepared from buffy coats because they produce a higher yield.[17,60] Products collected from donors on a regimen of granulocyte colony-stimulating factor (G-CSF) and steroid mobilization can yield higher numbers of granulocytes than those collected from an unstimulated donor. There have been some encouraging observations on the use of IGIV in the treatment of early neonatal sepsis, although conflicting data result in a lack of consensus on its use.[59,61-64] Preliminary studies of hematopoietic growth factors (eg, G-CSF) show promise in the treatment of overwhelming bacterial infection in the newborn.[59,61,65,66] For adults and larger children, a minimum dose of 1×10^{10} PMN/kg is recommended.[60,67,68]

Indications

Although the precise role of granulocyte transfusion for neonatal sepsis is unclear, certain clinical situations exist in which granulocyte transfusion may be considered as an adjunct to antibiotic therapy. Candidates for possible granulocyte transfusion are infants with strong evidence of bacterial septicemia, an absolute neutrophil count below 3000/µL, and a diminished marrow storage pool, such that less than 7% of their nucleated cells in the marrow are granulocytes at the stage of metamyelocytes or more mature forms.[18,69]

Granulocyte Components

Granulocytes are harvested by standard apheresis techniques. For infants, a dose of 10 to 15 mL/kg is recommended, which is about 1×10^9 to 2×10^9 PMN/kg.[17,60] Because neonatal neutrophil function is often abnormal, the use of granulocyte transfusions in this age group may be beneficial.[17,60,67,70-72] Administration should be continued daily until an adequate white cell mass is achieved or the patient has clinically improved. Based on the fact that granulocyte concentrates contain large numbers of lymphocytes, there is general consensus that all granulocyte transfusions should be irradiated to prevent graft-vs-host disease. For granulocyte transfusions to neonates, donors are usually selected to be CMV seronegative and must be ABO compatible with the infant, in accordance with *Standards*, because there is a significant volume of red cells in these products.[32(p40)] Many institutions also provide products that are D-compatible (see Chapter 21).

Transfusion to Enhance Hemostasis

The elements of the hemostatic system of the newborn are similar to those of older children and adults, but the concentration of many plasma proteins is decreased. Coagulation factors do not cross the placenta, but are independently synthesized by the fetus. Plasma levels of coagulation proteins increase progressively with gestational age. At birth, the infant's prothrombin time and partial thromboplastin time are prolonged, compared to older children and adults, primarily the result of physiologically low levels of the vitamin-K-dependent factors (II, VII, IX, and X) and contact factors (XI, XII, prekallikrein, and high-molecular-weight kininogen).[73] Proteins C and S and antithrombin inhibitors of coagulation are also at low levels. These two systems usually balance each other, so that spontaneous bleeding and thrombosis in the healthy newborn are rare, but very little reserve capacity exists for response to pathologic insults. Therefore, serious bleeding may occur in the first week of life in the sick premature infant as a result of hemostatic immaturity coupled with an acquired disorder of hemostasis.

In addition to having physiologically low levels of the vitamin-K-dependent factors, neonates may also become vitamin-K-deficient during the first 2 to 5 days of life, placing them at risk of bleeding. This "hemorrhagic disease of the newborn" is rare in developed countries because intramuscular vitamin K is routinely given at birth. If vitamin K therapy is omitted, especially if the neonate is breast fed, life-threatening hemorrhage may occur. This should be treated with FFP.[2,74]

Although hereditary deficiencies of coagulation factors may be apparent in the newborn, significant bleeding is rare. Coagulopathy more often results from an acquired defect such as liver disease or DIC.[74] Although component therapy replacement may temporarily correct the hemostatic problem, treatment of the underlying disease will ultimately reduce the need to treat the acquired defect.

Newborns who are heterozygous for deficiencies of inhibitory proteins rarely experience complications in the absence of another pathologic insult. However, the homozygous form of protein C deficiency has caused life-threatening thrombotic complications in the newborn period. In countries where it is available, protein C concentrates prepared from human plasma should be used as the initial treatment for neonates with homozygous protein C deficiency presenting with purpura fulminans. Protein C concentrates may be available on a compassionate use basis in the United States. Otherwise, plasma infusion is used as the initial treatment during the acute event, with subsequent anticoagulant therapy for long-term management.[74,75]

Fresh Frozen Plasma

Fresh frozen plasma may be used to replace coagulation factors in newborns, particularly if multiple factors are involved, such as in vitamin K deficiency. The usual dose is 10 to 15 mL/kg, which should increase factor activity by 15% to 20% unless there is marked consumptive coagulopathy.[74] As with red cell transfusions, there are several methods to provide small-volume FFP infusions while limiting donor exposure and wastage of components. Blood can be collected into a system with multiple integrally attached bags, creating aliquots that can be prepared for freezing.[34] Once thawed, these aliquots can be further divided and used for several patients within a 24-hour period. If not used within 24 hours as aliquots, the thawed plasma (stored at 1 to 6 C) can still be used as a means to decrease donor exposure. As with all patients, newborns must receive FFP that is ABO compatible and free of clinically significant unexpected antibodies. Group AB FFP is often used because a single unit provides compatible small aliquots for several neonates requiring FFP simultaneously.

Cryoprecipitate

Cryoprecipitate is rich in fibrinogen, coagulation Factors VIII and XIII, and von Willebrand factor. This component is often used in conjunction with platelet transfusions to treat DIC in the newborn. In DIC, fibrinogen and platelets are the elements most often severely depleted. The plasma in which the platelets are suspended is a source of stable coagulation factors. Cryoprecipitate provides concentrated levels of additional fibrinogen and storage-labile Factor VIII. For an infant, one bag is sufficient to achieve hemostatic levels. As with FFP and platelets, the cryoprecipitate should be ABO compatible with the neonatal recipient. Directed donor cryoprecipitate is not recommended as first-line therapy in the newborn with hemophilia A because safer alternatives are available. Recombinant Factor VIII products or virus-inactivated, monoclonal-antibody-purified, plasma-derived products are the standard treatment.[76] Cryoprecipitate should be used to treat von Willebrand disease only as a last resort, when safer products are not readily available. More information on the use of cryoprecipitate can be found in Chapter 21.

Neonatal Polycythemia

A venous hematocrit greater than 65% or hemoglobin in excess of 22 g/dL any time in the first week of life defines polycythemia, a condition that occurs in approximately 5% of all newborns. Small-for-gestational-age infants and infants of diabetic mothers are at increased risk for developing polycythemia. As the hematocrit rises above 65%, the viscosity of blood increases exponentially and oxygen transport decreases. For neonates, the exponential rise may occur at a hematocrit closer to 40%.[77] Infants have a limited ability to increase cardiac output to compensate for hyperviscosity and may develop congestive heart failure. Impairment of blood flow can cause CNS abnormalities, pulmonary and renal failure, and necrotizing enterocolitis. Phlebotomy can be used to normalize the hematocrit to 55% to 60% and improve tissue perfusion, while maintaining the blood volume.

To treat polycythemia, whole blood is removed and the volume replaced with crystalloid (such as normal saline), the choice being based on the quantity needed and on the infant's clinical condition. Plasma is not recommended because the volume administered will be insufficient to correct any coagulopathy and because necrotizing enterocolitis has been reported when it is used in this procedure.[78] A formula to approximate the volume of colloid replacement required (and the volume of blood to be drawn) for the exchange is[47]:

$$\text{Volume of replacement fluid} = \text{blood volume} \times \frac{(\text{observed hematocrit} - \text{desired hematocrit})}{\text{observed hematocrit}}$$

Extracorporeal Membrane Oxygenation

ECMO is a modified cardiopulmonary bypass technique that has been used for short-term support for cardiac or respiratory failure. It is performed in specialized centers and only for patients in whom conventional medical therapy has failed and anticipated survival with such therapy is limited (see Table 24-2). The use of ECMO in patients other than neonates is not widespread. The therapy is more successful in infants, whose small blood volume allows for total cardiorespiratory support and whose primary respiratory problem often resolves after 1 to 2 weeks

Table 24-2. Disorders Treated by ECMO

■ Meconium aspiration
■ Diaphragmatic hernia
■ Persistent pulmonary hypertension of the newborn
■ Severe group B streptococcal sepsis

of support. ECMO provides gas exchange independent of the patient's lungs, allowing them time to improve or heal without exposure to aggressive ventilator support and the secondary lung damage this may cause.[79]

Individual ECMO centers establish their own specific criteria for transfusion and blood component selection, and standard transfusion practices are lacking. Because of the combination of factors present (including systemic heparinization, platelet dysfunction, thrombocytopenia, and other coagulation defects) as well as the ECMO circuitry itself, bleeding complications are frequent. The ECMO team should be in close communication with the blood bank or transfusion service staff, and there should be mutual agreement on protocols to ensure consistency of care. Many infants requiring ECMO have been transferred from other hospitals, where they may already have received numerous transfusions. The amount of red cell, platelet, and FFP support required to maintain hematologic and hemodynamic equilibrium will vary depending on the clinical situation and in accordance with the institutions' practices.[68] When platelet transfusion is required, some practitioners think it is important to transfuse through peripheral access to avoid platelet damage, whereas others will transfuse directly into the ECMO circuitry because all blood will eventually flow through the equipment. It is also important to monitor ionized calcium levels

and supplement them as needed.[47,79] (See Tables 24-3 and 24-4.)

Leukocyte Reduction

The benefit of leukocyte reduction of components transfused to infants remains controversial. Difficulty in identifying transfusion reactions in this patient population makes this question hard to study. In addition, infants are rarely alloimmunized because of the immaturity of their immune system during this period of development. The reduction of risk of CMV transmission to infants is the only benefit of leukocyte reduction that has been well documented, as discussed earlier.[16,30,80]

Of interest, a recent study in Canada compared the clinical outcomes of premature infants weighing <1250 g before and after implementation of universal leukocyte reduction. Although neither mortality nor bacteremia were reduced in the setting of universal leukocyte reduction, other secondary clinical outcomes, such as retinopathy of prematurity and bronchopulmonary dysplasia, were improved. Length

Table 24-3. Risks of ECMO

■ Bleeding
■ Thrombosis
■ Thrombocytopenia
■ Neutropenia
■ Platelet dysfunction
■ Stroke
■ Seizure
■ Air embolism
■ Hemolysis
■ Systemic hypertension
■ Cannulization of carotid artery
■ Infectious complications of blood transfusion

Table 24-4. Contraindications for ECMO

- High risk for intraventricular hemorrhage
- Irreversible lung disease
- Systemic bleeding
- Severe asphyxia
- Presence of lethal malformations

of stay was decreased with universal leukocyte reduction.[81]

Transfusion Practices in Older Infants and Children

The indications for transfusion of red cells and other components in older infants (>4 months) and children are similar to those for adults but must take into account differences in blood volume, ability to tolerate blood loss, and age-appropriate hemoglobin and hematocrit levels. The most common indication for red cell transfusion in children is to reverse or prevent tissue hypoxia resulting from decreased red cell mass associated with surgical procedures or in response to anemia of chronic diseases or hematologic malignancies. It is important to remember that normal hemoglobin and hematocrit levels are lower in children than adults. Pediatric patients may remain asymptomatic despite extremely low levels of hemoglobin, particularly if the anemia has developed slowly.

The decision to transfuse should be based not only on the hemoglobin level but also on the presence or absence of symptoms, the functional capacity of the child, the etiology of the anemia, the possibility of using alternative therapies, and the presence or absence of additional clinical conditions that increase the risk for developing hypoxia. If small-volume transfusions are required, many of the methods described to provide small-volume transfusions to neonates could be applied. All pediatric patients over 4 months of age, however, must be tested for ABO and D type as well as for the presence of clinically significant antibodies before red cell transfusions. Compatibility testing must be done in accordance with *Standards*.[32(pp37-41)] Of note, a published abstract reported that leukocyte reduction does decrease the occurrence of febrile nonhemolytic transfusion reactions in pediatric hematology/oncology patients.[82]

Red Cell Support for Children with Hemoglobinopathies

In certain childhood conditions, chronic red cell transfusions are given not only to treat tissue hypoxia but also to suppress endogenous hemoglobin production. Approximately 6% to 10% of children with sickle cell disease suffer a stroke, with two-thirds experiencing a recurrence.[83] The goal of transfusion for these patients is to reduce the risk of stroke by decreasing the percentage of circulating red cells capable of sickling, while simultaneously avoiding an increase in blood viscosity. It is important to remember that raising the hematocrit, without significantly reducing the percent of sickle cells, could increase viscosity and negate any beneficial effects of the transfusion.[83,84] The rate of recurrent stroke can be reduced to less than 10% by maintaining a hemoglobin level of 8 to 9 g/dL, with a hemoglobin S level less than 30%, in children who have had a cerebrovascular accident. This can usually be achieved with a simple or partial exchange transfusion every 3 to 4 weeks. Therapy is continued indefinitely, as cessation can lead to subsequent stroke.[83,84] Because of concern about iron overload, some workers follow several uneventful years of transfusions to keep hemoglobin

S below 30% with a less aggressive protocol that maintains hemoglobin S between 40% and 50%.[84] Erythrocytapheresis has been shown to improve iron balance in a small cohort of patients.[85] Adams et al showed that transfusion to maintain a hemoglobin S level less than 30% in children who have abnormal results on transcranial Doppler ultrasound reduced the risk of a first stroke.[86] The benefits of this transfusion therapy, however, must be weighed against the complications of transfusion, such as iron overload and alloimmunization, as well as the risks of increased donor exposure during erythrocytapheresis. Although simple transfusion increases blood viscosity, exchange transfusion does not. Blood for transfusion to a patient with sickle cell disease should ideally be screened for hemoglobin S. In addition, most centers now provide leukocyte-reduced blood for patients with sickle cell disease to prevent alloimmunization to platelets, which could complicate transplantation.[87]

Red cell transfusions are also used to treat acute complications associated with sickle cell disease, such as splenic sequestration and aplastic crisis.[88] Acute chest syndrome, a new pulmonary infiltrate in a patient with sickle cell disease, other than atelectasis, with additional respiratory symptoms and fever, carries a poor prognosis if untreated. Simple transfusion can be used as a first-line therapy to improve oxygenation. For those patients who continue to deteriorate or who do not improve, red cell exchange transfusion should be performed. There are no randomized controlled trials comparing exchange and simple transfusion in this setting.[89] A study evaluating preoperative transfusion protocols found that a conservative protocol, in which the hemoglobin was raised to 10 g/dL, was as effective in preventing perioperative complications as an aggressive approach to decrease hemoglobin S levels to below 30%.[90]

Patients with sickle cell disease might also be at risk for severe delayed hemolytic transfusion reactions that could be life-threatening because of the coincident suppression of erythropoiesis. When a patient's hemoglobin level decreases after transfusion, this "hyperhemolytic" syndrome—wherein it appears that autologous red cells are destroyed through an innocent bystander mechanism—should be suspected. In these circumstances, transfusion should be stopped and corticosteroid therapy, or a combination of corticosteroid therapy and IGIV, considered, based on reports of efficacy in case studies.[91,92] Autoantibody formation also occurs in these patients after transfusion.[93] In the hope of decreasing the need for transfusion, medical interventions are being explored. One therapy uses hydroxyurea to increase the percentage of hemoglobin F. By having a higher percentage of cells that are hemoglobin F, the formation of hemoglobin S polymers is reduced. In addition, the concomitant decrease in neutrophil counts that accompanies hydroxyurea administration was found to be independently associated with a reduction in the rate of crisis.[94] Marrow transplantation has also been used in some patients and may have a role in the future treatment of patients with sickle cell disease.[95,96]

For children with thalassemia and severe anemia, transfusion not only improves tissue oxygenation but also suppresses erythropoiesis. By suppressing ineffective erythropoiesis, many of the complications associated with the disease are ameliorated. So-called hypertransfusion, in which the pretransfusion hemoglobin is kept between 8 and 9 g/dL, allows normal growth and development, as well as normal levels of activity for the child's age. Supertransfusion programs aim to maintain a pretransfusion hemoglobin concentration between 11 and 12 g/dL, in order to decrease iron absorption from the gastrointestinal tract. The results of maintaining near-normal hemoglobin levels are still controversial. Iron overload is a complication of treatment, requiring chelation therapy beginning early in childhood.[97]

Antibody Production in Sickle Cell and Thalassemia Patients

The frequency of red cell alloimmunization in chronically transfused children varies with the disease, the age of first transfusion, the number of transfusions given, and the ethnic background of donors and recipients, although patients with sickle cell disease have the highest rates of alloimmunization of any patient group.[98-100] Antibodies to the common antigens of the Rh, Kell, Duffy, and Kidd systems are often identified. It may be prudent, therefore, to phenotype the patient's red cell antigens as completely as possible before beginning transfusion therapy and to maintain a permanent record of the results. This can be helpful in selecting compatible blood if alloimmunization occurs. There is evidence that transfusing K, C, and E antigen-negative red cells can significantly reduce the rate of alloimmunization.[101] However, the practice of transfusing only phenotypically matched units is controversial, especially in patients who have not yet developed the corresponding antibody, because many of these units are difficult to obtain.[83,102] A recent survey of 50 academic medical centers in the United States and Canada found that the most common practice is to perform pretransfusion phenotypic matching for C, E, and K.[103] In patients who have already become immunized and who are at high risk of developing additional antibodies, use of pheno-typically matched units may be a reasonable approach to prevent further alloimmunization.[102] Method 2.16 can be used to perform red cell phenotyping on autologous red cells of recently transfused patients.

African Americans with sickle cell disease frequently become immunized because the majority of red cell transfusions are obtained from Caucasian donors, with major differences in antigen exposure. In some areas, blood collectors have developed programs to specifically recruit African American donors to supply blood for patients with sickle cell disease, in order to reduce rates of alloimmunization.[101] Leukocyte-reduced blood components may be of particular value for these chronically transfused patients. One benefit would be to diminish the development of alloimmunization to HLA antigens, in light of the prospect of future marrow transplantation.[87] There are conflicting data whether leukocyte reduction can prevent alloimmunization to red cell transfusion.[104,105] Preventing febrile transfusion reactions is also important for patients who may be receiving a unit of phenotypically matched blood. Discarding such a unit would be both wasteful and may have an impact on the ability to adequately transfuse the patient.[106]

Platelets and Plasma

The indications for FFP and platelet transfusions in older infants and children parallel those for adults. Platelet transfusions are most often given as prophylaxis to children receiving chemotherapy. Prophylactic platelet transfusions are seldom given when platelet counts are above 10,000 to 20,000/μL, but, as with red cell transfusion and hemoglobin, the indication for platelet transfusion should not be based solely on the platelet count. When additive risk factors such as fever, sepsis,

DIC, or clotting abnormalities are present, the platelet count may need to be higher to prevent spontaneous hemorrhage. In the absence of such factors, a much lower level may be safe.[56] In recent studies, the use of ABO-compatible platelets has been associated with better clinical outcomes.[107-109]

References

1. Hume H, Bard H. Small volume red blood cell transfusions for neonatal patients. Transfus Med Rev 1995;9:187-99.

2. Roseff SD, ed. Pediatric transfusion: A physician's handbook. 1st ed. Bethesda, MD: AABB, 2003.

3. Brugnara C, Platt OS. The neonatal erythrocyte and its disorders. In: Nathan DG, Orkin SH, eds. Nathan and Oski's hematology of infancy and childhood. 5th ed. Philadelphia: WB Saunders, 1998:19-52.

4. Blanchette V, Doyle J, Schmidt B, Zipursky A. Hematology. In: Avery GB, Fletcher MA, MacDonald MG, eds. Neonatology: Pathophysiology and management of the newborn. 4th ed. Philadelphia: JB Lippincott, 1994: 952-99.

5. Wallgren G, Hanson JS, Lind J. Quantitative studies of the human neonatal circulation. Acta Paediatr Scand 1967;179(Suppl):43-54.

6. Ohls RK. Evaluation and treatment of anemia in the neonate. In: Christensen RD, ed. Hematologic problems of the neonate. Philadelphia: WB Saunders, 2000:137-69.

7. Ohls RK. Erythropoietin to prevent and treat the anemia of prematurity. Curr Opin Pediatr 1999;11:108-14.

8. Maier RE, Obladen M, Müller-Hansen I, et al. Early treatment with erythropoietin β ameliorates anemia and reduces transfusion requirements in infants with birth weights below 1000 g. J Pediatr 2002;141:8-15.

9. Widness JA, Seward VJ, Kromer IJ, et al. Changing patterns of red cell transfusion in very low birth weight infants. J Pediatr 1996; 129:680-7.

10. Vamvakas EC, Strauss RG. Meta-analysis of controlled clinical trials studying the efficacy of rHuEPO in reducing blood transfusions in the anemia of prematurity. Transfusion 2001;41:406-15.

11. Luban NLC, Mikesell G, Sacher RA. Techniques for warming red blood cells packaged in different containers for neonatal use. Clin Pediatr 1985;24:642-5.

12. Simister NE. Placental transport of immunoglobulin G. Vaccine 2003;21:3365-9.

13. DePalma L. Red cell alloantibody formation in the neonate and infant: Considerations for current immunohematologic practice. Immunohematology 1992;8:33-7.

14. Sanders MR, Graeber JE. Posttransfusion graft-versus-host disease in infancy. J Pediatr 1990; 117:159-63.

15. Ohto H, Anderson KC. Posttransfusion graft-versus-host disease in Japanese newborns. Transfusion 1996;36:117-23.

16. Stauss RG. Data-driven blood banking practices for neonatal RBC transfusions. Transfusion 2000;40:1528-40.

17. Strauss RG. Transfusion therapy in neonates. Am J Dis Child 1991;145:904-11.

18. Strauss RG. Neonatal transfusion. In: Anderson KC, Ness PM, eds. Scientific basis of transfusion medicine. Implications for clinical practice. 2nd ed. Philadelphia: WB Saunders, 2000:321-6.

19. Strauss RG. Routinely washing irradiated red cells before transfusion seems unwarranted. Transfusion 1990;30:675-7.

20. McDonald TB, Berkowitz RA. Massive transfusion in children. In: Jeffries LC, Brecher ME, eds. Massive transfusion. Bethesda, MD: AABB, 1994:97-119.

21. Harris B, Lumadue J, Luban NLC, Pollack M. Transfusion-related hyperkalemic arrest from irradiated packed red blood cells (abstract). Transfusion 1998;38(Suppl):69S.

22. Hall TL, Barnes A, Miller JR, et al. Neonatal mortality following transfusion of red cells with high plasma potassium levels. Transfusion 1993;33:606-9.

23. Pisciotto PT. Cytomegalovirus safety issues in neonatal transfusion. In Hermann JH, Manno CS, eds. Pediatric transfusion therapy. Bethesda, MD: AABB Press, 2002:171-92.

24. Delage G. Transfusion-transmitted infections in the newborn. Transfus Med Rev 1995;9:271-6.

25. Hamprecht K, Maschmann J, Vochem M, et al. Epidemiology of transmission of cytomegalovirus from mother to preterm infant by breastfeeding. Lancet 2001;357:513-8.

26. Adler SP, Chandrika T, Lawrence L, Baggett J. Cytomegalovirus infections in neonates acquired by blood transfusions. Pediatr Inf Dis 1983;2:114-8.

27. Brady MT, Milam JD, Anderson DC. Use of deglycerolized red blood cells to prevent posttransfusion infection with cytomegalovirus in neonates. J Infect Dis 1984;150:334-9.

28. Strauss RG. Selection of white cell-reduced blood components for transfusions during infancy. Transfusion 1993;33:352-7.

29. Bowden RA, Slichter SJ, Sayers M, et al. A comparison of filtered leukocyte-reduced and cytomegalovirus (CMV) seronegative blood products for the prevention of transfusion-associated CMV infection after marrow transplant. Blood 1995;86:3598-603.

30. Gilbert GL, Hayes K, Hudson H, et al. Prevention of transfusion-associated cytomegalovirus infection in infants by blood filtration to remove leukocytes. Lancet 1989;i:1228-31.

31. Ludvigsen C, Swanson JL, Thompson TR, McCullough J. The failure of neonates to form red cell alloantibodies in response to multiple transfusions. Am J Clin Pathol 1987;87:250-1.

32. Silva MA, ed. Standards for blood banks and transfusion services. 23rd ed. Bethesda, MD: AABB, 2005.

33. Pridjian G. Fetomaternal interactions: Placental physiology and its role as a go-between. In: Avery GB, Fletcher MA, MacDonald MG, eds. Neonatology: Pathophysiology and management of the newborn. 5th ed. Philadelphia: JB Lippincott, 1999:125-41.

34. Roseff SD. Pediatric blood collection and transfusion technology. In: Herman JK, Manno CS, eds. Pediatric transfusion therapy. Bethesda, MD: AABB Press, 2002:217-47.

35. Levy GJ, Strauss RG, Hume H, et al. National survey of neonatal transfusion practices, I: Red blood cell therapy. Pediatrics 1993;91:523-9.

36. Cook S, Gunter J, Wissel M. Effective use of a strategy using assigned red cell units to limit donor exposure for neonatal patients. Transfusion 1993;33:379-83.

37. Wang-Rodriguez J, Mannino FL, Liu D, Lane TA. A novel strategy to limit blood donor exposure and blood waste in multiply transfused premature infants. Transfusion 1996;36:64-70.

38. Strauss RG, Burmeister LF, Johnson K, et al. Feasibility and safety of AS-3 red blood cells for neonatal transfusions. J Pediatr 2000;136:215-9.

39. Goodstein MH, Herman JH, Smith JF, et al. Metabolic consequences in very low birth weight infants transfused with older AS-1 preserved erythrocytes. Pediatr Pathol Lab Med 1999;18:173-85.

40. Rock G, Poon A, Haddad R, et al. Nutricel as an additive solution for neonatal transfusion. Transfus Sci 1999;20:29-36.

41. Luban NLC, Strauss RG, Hume HA. Commentary on the safety of red cells preserved in extended-storage media for neonatal transfusions. Transfusion 1991;31:229-35.

42. Tuchschmid P, Mieth D, Burger R, et al. Potential hazard of hypoalbuminemia in new-born babies after exchange transfusions with Adsol red blood cell concentrates (letter). Pediatrics 1990;85:234-5.

43. Brecher ME, ed. Collected questions and answers. 6th ed. Bethesda, MD: AABB, 2000:73-5.

44. Burch KJ, Phelps SJ, Constance TD. Effect of an infusion device on the integrity of whole blood and packed red blood cells. Am J Hosp Pharm 1991;48:92-7.

45. Criss VR, DePalma L, Luban NLC. Analysis of a linear peristaltic infusion device for the transfusion of red cells to pediatric patients. Transfusion 1993;33:842-4.

46. Longhurst DM, Gooch W, Castillo RA. In vitro evaluation of a pediatric microaggregate blood filter. Transfusion 1983;23:170-2.

47. Behrman RE, Kleigman RM, Jenson HB, eds. Nelson's textbook of pediatrics. 16th ed. Philadelphia: WB Saunders, 2000.

48. Koenig JM. Evaluation and treatment of erythroblastosis fetalis in the neonate. In: Christensen RD, ed. Hematologic problems of the neonate. Philadelphia: WB Saunders, 2000:185-207.

49. American Academy of Pediatrics Subcommittee on Hyperbilirubinemia. Management of hyperbilirubinemia in the newborn infant 35 or more weeks of gestation. Clinical Practice Guideline. Pediatrics 2004;114:297-316.

50. Ballard RA, Vincour B, Reynolds JW, et al. Transient hyperammonemia of the preterm infant. N Engl J Med 1978;299:920-5.

51. Leonard JV. The early detection and management of inborn errors presenting acutely in the neonatal period. Eur J Pediatr 1985;143:253-7.

52. Chan G, Schoff D. Variance in albumin loading in exchange transfusions. J Pediatr 1976;88:609-13.

53. Strauss RG, Levy GJ, Sotelo-Avila C, et al. National survey of neonatal transfusion practices: II. Blood component therapy. Pediatrics 1993;91:530-6.

54. Maier RF, Sonntag J, Walka MW, et al. Changing practices of red blood cell transfusions in infants with birth weights less than 1000 g. J Pediatr 2000;136:220-4.

55. Blanchette VS, Kuhne T, Hume H, Hellman J. Platelet transfusion therapy in newborn infants. Transfus Med Rev 1995;9:215-30.

56. Beutler E. Platelet transfusions: The 20,000/μL trigger. Blood 1993;81:1411-13.

57. Andrew M, Vegh P, Caco C, et al. A randomized, controlled trial of platelet transfusions in thrombocytopenic premature infants. J Pediatr 1993;123:285-91.

58. Pisciotto P, Snyder EL, Snyder JA, et al. In vitro characteristics of leukocyte-reduced sin-

gle unit platelet concentrates stored in syringes. Transfusion 1994;34:407-11.

59. Sweetman RW, Cairo MS. Blood component and immunotherapy in neonatal sepsis. Transfus Med Rev 1995;9:251-8.

60. Vamvakas EC, Pineda AA. Meta-analysis of clinical studies of the efficacy of granulocyte transfusions in the treatment of bacterial sepsis. J Clin Apheresis 1996;11:1-9.

61. Rosenthal J, Cairo MS. Neonatal myelopoiesis and immunomodulation of host defenses. In: Petz LD, Swisher SN, Kleinman S, et al, eds. Clinical practice of transfusion medicine. 3rd ed. New York: Churchill Livingstone, 1996:685-703.

62. Jenson HB, Pollock BH. The role of intravenous immunoglobulins for the prevention and treatment of neonatal sepsis. Semin Perinatol 1998;22:50-63.

63. Sandberg K, Fasth A, Berger A, et al. Preterm infants with low immunoglobulin G levels have increased risk of neonatal sepsis but do not benefit from prophylactic immunoglobulin G. J Pediatr 2000;137:623-8.

64. Hill HR. Additional confirmation of the lack of effect of intravenous immunoglobulin in the prevention of neonatal infection (editorial). J Pediatr 2000;137:595-7.

65. Schibler KR, Osborne KA, Leung LY, et al. A randomized, placebo-controlled trial of granulocyte colony-stimulating factor administration to newborn infants with neutropenia and clinical signs of early-onset sepsis. Pediatrics 1998;102:6-13.

66. Calhoun DA, Lunoe M, Du Y, et al. Granulocyte colony-stimulating factor serum and urine concentrations in neutropenic neonates before and after intravenous administration of recombinant granulocyte colony-stimulating factor. Pediatrics 2000;105:392-7.

67. Price TH. The current prospects for neutrophil transfusion for the treatment of granulocytopenic infected patients. Transfus Med Rev 2000;14:2-11.

68. Roseff SD, Luban NLC, Manno CS. Guidelines for assessing appropriateness of pediatric transfusion. Transfusion 2002;42:1398-413.

69. Christensen RD, Bradley PP, Rothstein G. The leukocyte left shift in clinical and experimental neonatal sepsis. J Pediatr 1981;98:101-5.

70. Cairo MS, Rucker R, Bennetts GA, et al. Improved survival of newborns receiving leukocyte transfusions for sepsis. Pediatrics 1984;74:887-92.

71. Cairo MS, Worcester CC, Rucker RW, et al. Randomized trial of granulocyte transfusions versus intravenous immune globulin therapy for neutropenia and sepsis. J Pediatr 1992;120:281-5.

72. Hübel K, Dale DC, Liles WC. Granulocyte transfusion therapy: Update on potential clinical applications. Curr Opin Hematol 2001;8:161-4.

73. Andrew M, Paes B, Johnston M. Development of the hemostatic system in the neonate and young infant. Am J Pediatr Hematol Oncol 1990;12:95-104.

74. Andrew M. Transfusion in the newborn: Plasma products. In: Kennedy M, Wilson S, Kelton J, eds. Perinatal transfusion medicine. Arlington, VA: AABB, 1990:145-77.

75. Monagle P, Michelson AD, Bovill E, Andrew M. Antithrombotic therapy in children. Chest 2001;119(Suppl):344-70S.

76. Pressey JG, Manno CS. Therapy for hemophilia and von Willebrand disease. In: Herman JK, Manno CS, eds. Pediatric transfusion therapy. Bethesda, MD: AABB Press, 2002:355-82.

77. Lindemann R, Haga P. Evaluation and treatment of polycythemia in the neonate. In: Christensen RD, ed. Hematologic problems of the neonate. Philadephia: WB Saunders, 2000:171-83.

78. Black VD, Rumack CM, Lubchenco LD, Koops BL. Gastrointestinal injury in polycythemic term infants. Pediatrics 1985;76:225-31.

79. Kevy SV. Extracorporeal therapy for infants and children. In: Petz LD, Swisher SN, Kleinman S, et al, eds. Clinical practice of transfusion medicine. 3rd ed. New York: Churchill Livingstone, 1996:733-55.

80. Strauss RG. Selection of white cell-reduced blood components for transfusions during early infancy. Transfusion 1993;33:352-7.

81. Fergusson D, Hébert PC, Lee SK, et al. Clinical outcomes following institution of universal leukoreduction of blood transfusions in premature infants. JAMA 2003;289:1950-6.

82. Young G, Jubran RF, Luban NLC. Febrile transfusion reactions in pediatric hematology/oncology patients: The effect of leukodepletion (abstract). Blood 1999;94(Suppl 1):3371a.

83. Sharon BI, Honig GR. Management of congenital hemolytic anemias. In: Simon TL, Dzik WH, Snyder ES, et al, eds. Rossi's principles of transfusion medicine. 3rd ed. Philadelphia: Lippincott Williams and Wilkins, 2002:463-82.

84. Cohen AR, Norris CF, Smith-Whitley K. Transfusion therapy for sickle cell disease. In: Capon SM, Chambers LA, eds. New directions in pediatric hematology. Bethesda, MD: AABB, 1996:39-88.

85. Adams DM, Schultz WH, Ware RF, Kinney TR. Erythrocytapheresis can reduce iron overload and prevent the need for chelation therapy in chronically transfused pediatric patients. J Pediatr Hematol Oncol 1996;18:3-7.

86. Adams RJ, McKie VC, Hsu L, et al. Prevention of a first stroke by transfusions in children with sickle cell anemia and abnormal results on transcranial Doppler ultrasonography. N Engl J Med 1998;339:5-11.

87. Friedman DF, Lukas MB, Jawad A, et al. Alloimmunization to platelets in heavily transfused patients with sickle cell disease. Blood 1996;88:3216-22.

88. National Heart Lung and Blood Institute. The management of sickle cell disease. 4th ed. No. 02-2117. Bethesda, MD: National Institutes of Health, 2002.

89. Platt OS. The acute chest syndrome of sickle cell disease. N Engl J Med 2000;342:1904-7.

90. Vichinsky EP, Heberkern CM, Neumayr L, et al. A comparison of conservative and aggressive transfusion regimens in the perioperative management of sickle cell disease. N Engl J Med 1995;333:206-13.

91. Petz LD, Calhoun L, Shulman IA, et al. The sickle cell hemolytic transfusion reaction syndrome. Transfusion 1997;37:382-92.

92. Win N, Doughty H, Telfer P, et al. Hyperhemolytic transfusion reaction in sickle cell disease. Transfusion 2001;41:323-8.

93. Garratty G. Autoantibodies induced by blood transfusion (editorial). Transfusion 2004;44:5-9.

94. Charash S, Barton FB, Moore RD, et al. Hydroxyurea and sickle cell anemia. Clinical utility of a myelosuppressive "switching" agent. The Multicenter Study of Hydroxyurea in Sickle Cell Anemia. Medicine (Baltimore) 1996;75:300-26.

95. Steinberg MH. Management of sickle cell disease. N Engl J Med 1999;340:1021-30.

96. Woodard P, Jeng M, Handgretinger R, et al. Summary of symposium: The future of stem cell transplantation for sickle cell disease. J Pediatr Hematol Oncol 2002;24:512-4.

97. Hoffbrand AV, Al-Refaie F, Davis B, et al. Long-term trial of deferiprone in 51 transfusion-dependent iron overload patients. Blood 1998;91:295-300.

98. Rosse WF, Gallagher D, Kinney TR, et al. Transfusion and alloimmunization in sickle cell disease. Blood 1990;76:1431-7.

99. Spanos T, Karageorge M, Ladis V, et al. Red cell alloantibodies in patients with thalassemia. Vox Sang 1990;58:50-5.

100. Rosse WF, Telen M, Ware RE. Transfusion support for patients with sickle cell disease. Bethesda, MD: AABB Press, 1998.

101. Smith-Whitley K. Alloimmunization in patients with sickle cell disease. In: Herman JK, Manno CS, eds. Pediatric transfusion therapy. Bethesda, MD: AABB Press, 2002:249-82.

102. Tahhan HR, Holbrook CT, Braddy LR, et al. Antigen-matched donor blood in the transfusion management of patients with sickle cell disease. Transfusion 1994;34:562-9.

103. Afenyi-Annan A, Brecher ME. Pre-transfusion phenotype matching for sickle cell disease patients (letter). Transfusion 2004;44:619-20.

104. Blumberg N, Heal JM, Gettings KF. Leukoreduction of red cell transfusions is associated with a decreased incidence of red cell alloimmunization. Transfusion 2003;43:945-52.

105. Van de Watering L, Jermans J, Witvliet M, et al. HLA and RBC immunization after filtered and buffy coat-depleted blood transfusion in cardiac surgery: A randomized controlled trial. Transfusion 2003;43:765-71.

106. Lane TA, Anderson KC, Goodnough LT, et al. Leukocyte reduction in blood component therapy. Ann Intern Med 1992;117:151-62.

107. Larsson LG, Welsh VJ, Ladd DJ. Acute intravascular hemolysis to out-of-group platelet transfusion. Transfusion 2000;40:902-6.

108. Heal JM, Blumberg N. The second century of ABO: And now for something completely different. Transfusion 1999;39:1155-9.

109. Blumberg N, Heal JM, Hicks GL, Risher WH. Association of ABO-mismatched platelet transfusions with morbidity and mortality in cardiac surgery. Transfusion 2001;41:790-3.

Cell Therapy and Cellular Product Transplantation

T HERAPEUTIC CELLS INCLUDE cell populations collected and processed to provide a special therapeutic effect. The classic example of cell therapy is the use of pluripotent stem cells, which are capable of self-renewal and differentiation into all blood-cell lineages. These stem cells—transplanted in preparations of marrow, stimulated peripheral blood mononuclear preparations, or cord blood—also give rise to other regenerative tissues such as hepatocytes, endothelial cells, and other tissue under the proper microenvironmental circumstances.[1] Other cell populations may serve therapeutic purposes such as immune modulation in posttransplant donor lymphocyte infusion (DLI). The hematopoietic progenitor cells (HPCs), which are committed to a blood-cell lineage, were first studied in the laboratory for their power to give rise to complete, sustained hematopoietic engraftment when given in

sufficient numbers. This chapter primarily discusses the hematopoietic repopulation cells. Cell preparations for HPC transplantation are thought to contain both hematopoietic stem cells (HSCs) capable of self-renewal and HPCs committed to a blood-cell lineage. However, committed progenitor cells lack capacity for sustained self-renewal or the ability to differentiate into other blood-cell lineages. The committed cells are important for the speed of engraftment.[2] Current measurement methods cannot easily separate the earlier and more committed cell populations. Both cell populations are referred to as HPCs in this chapter. HPCs collected from peripheral blood via apheresis are referred to as HPC-A. Those collected by harvesting marrow are termed HPC-M and those from cord blood are called HPC-C.

HPC transplantation has advanced from a research procedure performed in a few centers to a common medical procedure performed in many tertiary care centers. HPC transplantation can be classified according to the source of the HPCs used for engraftment as autologous, allogeneic, syngeneic, and xenogeneic.

Autologous HPC transplantation is technically not a transplant but, rather, the "rescue" of a patient with the patient's own HPCs, which are removed and stored frozen or in nonfrozen conditions for later infusion as protection from the lethal effects of therapeutic or ablative irradiation or chemotherapy. The autologous graft may be manipulated to retain HPCs and leave behind or exclude tumor cells or damaging immune cells. Autologous HPCs are reinfused to repopulate the patient's marrow after an otherwise lethal or near-lethal dose of radiation or chemotherapy given to treat malignancies of the marrow and metastatic or recurrent solid tumors. In the special case of an identical twin donor and recipient, such transplants are referred to as syngeneic.

Allogeneic HPC transplantation involves the infusion of HPCs from another human (an HLA-matched related or unrelated donor) in order to establish donor cell chimerism to rescue the patient from dose-intense therapy and/or as an active immunotherapy against a disease after a potentially lethal dose of radiation or chemotherapy. Such transplants are preferred in patients who have acute myelogenous leukemia (AML), acute lymphocytic leukemia (ALL), severe immunodeficiency, aplastic anemia, marrow involvement with their malignancy, or those who are incapable of supplying their own autologous "normal" HPCs, as with hemoglobinopathies (thalassemias or sickle cell disease). As new indications for transplantation are developed, some others are drastically changed by new discoveries. For instance, patients with chronic myelogenous leukemia (CML) used to receive the largest number of adult hematopoietic transplants; however, imatinib mesylate has been such a successful treatment for this disease that the number of CML transplants has dropped sharply since licensure of this drug.[3]

Another advance in marrow transplantation has been the recognition and exploitation of the effects of transplanted allogeneic immune cells on the malignancy of the patient. Because the transplanted cells are the treatment modality for the patient, the preparation for transplantation needs only to modify the patient's immune system to allow the new cells to engraft. This nonmyeloablative transplantation expands the number of patients eligible for transplant by accepting patients of more advanced age and with more health problems. These patients would not be candidates to enter more toxic myeloablative regimens because the risk of the treatment would be so great. In this setting, chemotherapy and/or low-dose total body irradiation targets the recipient's T lymphocytes to allow tolerance for the healthy, allogeneic graft.

In successful marrow transplants, the cells gradually produce full chimerism in the patient's marrow and attack and eliminate the tumor cells immunologically.[4-6] In patients where healthy cell replacement is the intended result of treatment, such as in children with immune deficiencies, this method allows replacement cells to engraft without putting the child through the danger of full myeloablation. The patient does not have to undergo extensive periods of cytopenia with exposure to infection and bleeding risk. The engrafted cells become the treatment agent, allowing the chemotherapy and/or radiation to be low-dose and relatively low toxicity. This approach uses the immune reconstitution as the tool to control disease, but it is not without risk because the immune cells can also attack the healthy tissues of the patient, causing graft-vs-host disease (GVHD).[7] The number of nonmyeloablative transplants has increased from 20 in 1997 to 870 in 2001, according to the Center for International Blood and Marrow Transplant Research (CIBMTR) reporting system.[3]

Xenogeneic HPC transplantation would involve HPC transplants derived from a nonhuman species. However, because of currently insurmountable immunologic barriers and disease concerns, these transplants are not now clinically feasible.

Sources of progenitor cells include marrow, peripheral blood, umbilical cord blood, and fetal liver (although this source is experimental and not in routine clinical use).[1] Once collected, the HPCs may be subjected to ex-vivo processing, eg, removal of incompatible red cells or plasma and/or cell selection (purging) before the transplantation procedure. In some cases, certain cell populations are "positively" selected (selectively isolated) for their special therapeutic effects. T lymphocytes may be isolated and later infused in measured doses for antitumor effects, thus minimizing GVHD. Separation of cell populations can be accomplished using a cell separation device approved by the Food and Drug Administration (FDA), such as the Isolex system (Baxter Healthcare, Deerfield, IL). Alternatively, some cell populations may be "negatively selected" (culled out or destroyed), as by antibody-mediated lysis of malignant cells or by flow cytometry separation of cell populations in clinical trial situations.

Diseases Treated with Hematopoietic Cell Transplantation

Many diseases have been treated with HPC transplantation.[8] Malignant diseases are the most frequent indications for HPC transplantation. Although many nonma-

lignant diseases have also been treated with life-saving transplantation, as a group, they represent less than 15% of all transplants.[3,9] The success rate of HPC transplantation depends on the condition and age of the patient, type and stage of the disease being treated, the cell dose, and degree of HLA matching between the donor and the patient. Overall, long-term survival rates are generally 30% to 60% for otherwise fatal diseases. Table 25-1 describes general outcomes.[10]

Sources of Hematopoietic Progenitor Cells

Historically, marrow was the primary source of hematopoietic cells for transplantation. However, HPC-A transplants constituted approximately 90% of adult autologous and about half of allogeneic transplantation procedures in the 1998-2000 International Bone Marrow Transplant Registry report.[3] Data on umbilical cord blood transplants have shown promising results in pediatric patients for whom a matched unrelated allogeneic HPC-M or HPC-A donor is unavailable. Clinical studies are in progress to determine 1) the safety and efficacy of cord blood transplantation, 2) whether adults can be successfully transplanted, and 3) the extent of HLA mismatch that can safely and effectively provide durable engraftment.

HPCs from Marrow (Autologous)

Currently, only about 5% of autologous transplants are performed with HPC-M. This source has been largely replaced by mobilized autologous HPC-A.

HPCs from Marrow (Allogeneic)

Allogeneic transplants address the problem of the inability to obtain a tumor-free

Table 25-1. Examples of Diseases Responsive to Hematopoietic Stem Cell Transplantation[10]

Disease	Type of Transplant	Timing	Clinical Results
AML	Allogeneic	First CR	OS 40%-50%
ALL (children)	Allogeneic	Second CR	OS 40%-65%
ALL (high risk)	Allogeneic	First CR	OS 50%
Chronic phase CML	Allogeneic	Chronic phase (CP)	OS 50%-80%
Accelerated phase CML	Allogeneic	Individualized	OS 30%-40%
Blast phase CML	Allogeneic	Second CP	OS 15%-25%
Myelodysplastic syndrome	Allogeneic	Age <60	OS 40%
Aplastic anemia	Allogeneic	Individualized	OS 70%-90%
CLL	Allogeneic or autologous	Participation in clinical trial	Small series of patients with durable CR; nonablative transplants under investigation
Intermediate-grade NHL	Autologous	Chemosensitive relapse	OS 40%-50%
High-risk NHL	Autologous	First CR	OS 50%-60%
Low-grade NHL	Allogeneic or autologous	Chemosensitive relapse	DFS 25%-50% at 5 years
Mantle cell lymphoma	Allogeneic or autologous clinical trial	First CR	Small series with durable CR rates of 25%-50%
Lymphoblastic lymphoma	Allogeneic or autologous clinical trial	Chemosensitive relapse or first CR	Small series with durable CR
NHL or Hodgkin's disease	Allogeneic clinical trial	Advanced refractory disease	DFS 15%-25%
Multiple myeloma	Autologous	Chemosensitive relapse or first CR	OS 50% at 5 years; DFS 20%
High-risk breast, testicular, or ovarian cancer	Autologous clinical trial	Chemosensitive disease	Improved survival over historical controls not confirmed in randomized trials
Renal cell carcinoma	Nonablative allogeneic	Clinical trial	Small series with durable CR
Thalassemia	Allogeneic	Clinical trial	OS 75% for patients without cirrhosis
Sickle cell anemia	Allogeneic	Clinical trial	OS 75%
Autoimmune disorders	Allogeneic	Clinical trial	Small series of remissions

CR = complete response; DFS = disease-free survival; OS = overall survival; AML = acute myelogenous leukemia; CML = chronic myelogenous leukemia; ALL = acute lymphocytic leukemia; CP = chronic phase; NHL = non-Hodgkin's lymphoma. Netter examples used with permission from Icon Learning Systems, a division of MediMedia USA, Inc. All rights reserved.

graft with an autologous transplant for a patient with malignant disease and provide possible immune help after transplantation from graft-vs-tumor response. For other patients, such as those with marrow failure, immunodeficiency, inborn errors of metabolism, or hemoglobinopathy, an allogeneic transplant is the only appropriate type of graft. Sources of allogeneic HPC-M may be from matched or partially matched related or unrelated donors.

Matched, Unrelated Donor Transplantation

Matched, unrelated donor searches can be initiated for the 60% to 70% of candidates without an HLA-identical related (usually sibling) donor. Several marrow donor databases are available worldwide. The largest is the National Marrow Donor Program (NMDP) database. Since its founding in 1986, the NMDP has facilitated approximately 12,000 transplant procedures with a total of over 2000 transplants per year. A directory of transplant centers, outcome results, and charges is available from the NMDP. (See Appendix 11 at the end of the book).

Upon initial search, 80% of transplantation candidates usually find an HLA phenotypic match. However, patients from racial or ethnic minorities have a lower chance of success in such a donor search (Caucasian, 81%; Hispanic, 64%; Asian/Pacific Islander, 55%; African American, 47%; and American Indian/Alaska Native, 50%; according to the NMDP). The median time from initiating a search to receiving a transplant has been 120 days, but a new expedited search and donor preparation program is being implemented to shorten this time.

The NMDP is conducting a clinical trial of HPC-A collections from unrelated, HLA-matched volunteers stimulated with granulocyte colony-stimulating factor (G-CSF or filgrastim).[11] The donors' physical symptoms as well as their attitudes and feelings about the process are being monitored for the trial. The use of HPC-A offers the potential advantage of improved engraftment kinetics and enhanced graft-vs-leukemia (GVL) effect. In allogeneic, related transplant settings clinical trials comparing HPC-M to HPC-A, the latter showed improved survival. Although chronic GVHD was a problem in the HPC-A study arm, it was manageable in a sufficient number of cases to give those patients a survival advantage.[12]

Initially, the most common diagnosis in patients undergoing matched, unrelated donor transplantation was CML. The discovery of imatinib mesylate has revolutionized the treatment of CML such that the most common indication for allogeneic transplantation is acute leukemia followed by non-Hodgkin's lymphomas, multiple myeloma, and other diseases of marrow failure such as aplastic anemia.[13]

Traditionally, HLA typing for Class I (HLA-A and HLA-B) has been dependent on serologic techniques. However, it is likely that the posttransplant complications of GVHD and failure to engraft result from use of phenotypically matched, unrelated donors with significant disparities in alloantigens that were not identified through serologic matching techniques.[14] HLA-A and HLA-B molecular Class I typing, intermediate resolution, and high-resolution typing of Class II alleles are the current standard of care, particularly in unrelated transplants.

The risk of GVHD is greater with HLA Class II disparity than with Class I disparity.[15] HLA typing for HLA-DR and HLA-DQ is routinely performed by DNA-based techniques. Molecular technology provides greater resolution, including subtypes of alleles identified as cross-reactive groups using conventional serologic techniques. Mismatching for a single Class I or Class II antigen has no effect on survival, but mortality increases with more than one Class I mismatch or simultaneous mismatches in Class I and Class II antigens.[15] Recent studies demonstrated the importance of recipient *HLA-DRB1* and *HLA-DQB1* allele disparity in the development of GVHD.[16,17] With further experience in molecular typing and transplant outcomes, the extent to which successfully transplanted cells can tolerate disparities in specific alleles will be elucidated. Although the importance of HLA-A, -B, and -DR disparities is well known, the significance of HLA-C disparity is being investigated. HLA-C typing has been hampered by poor serologic identification, and its significance has been thought, until recently, to play a minor role in the T-cell immune response because of its reduced polymorphism and low level of cell surface expression. Early studies showed that HLA-C antigens can be recognized by alloreactive cytotoxic T lymphocytes and natural killer cells, which may be associated with an increased risk of graft failure.[18]

Graft-vs-Host Disease

The negative outcomes of HLA mismatching are graft rejection, host-vs-graft reactions, and graft-vs-host reactions. In acute GVHD, the transplanted cells may attack the tissues of the recipient early in the engraftment—within 100 days after the initial engraftment-associated events. The skin, the gastrointestinal tract, and the liver are most commonly involved, although usually not concurrently. The site and severity determine the clinical grade of acute GVHD. The risk of GVHD is greater with HLA-mismatched, unrelated and related transplants than with HLA-identical transplants.[19]

Chronic GVHD characteristically occurs spontaneously months after transplanta-tion or after acute GVHD (generally after posttransplant day 50) and may severely affect the patient's quality of life. In addition to the symptoms found in the acute form, chronic autoimmune-type disorders such as biliary cirrhosis, Sjogren's syndrome, and systemic sclerosis may develop as the transplanted immune cells attack the secretory epithelial cells in the saliva glands, the biliary tree, or the patient's connective tissue. Chronic GVHD was reported in 55% to 65% of allogeneic transplant patients who survived beyond day 100 in a large study.[2] Both forms of GVHD impair the patient's immune response and predispose the patient to infections. To decrease or eliminate GVHD in these transplants, HPCs can undergo procedures for T-cell reduction (depletion) and the patient can be treated prophylactically with a variety of immuno-suppressive drug therapies.

GVHD has been associated with both a decreased disease relapse and an improved overall survival in leukemia patients if the GVHD is relatively mild. Such a GVL effect is believed to be secondary to the graft attacking residual malignant cells. A major clinical challenge is to maximize the GVL effect while minimizing the adverse sequelae of GVHD. The mechanism of the GVL effect is incompletely understood, but donor-derived cytotoxic T lymphocytes specific for the patient's minor histocompatibility antigens may contribute to the effect. Donor lymphocyte infusion of therapeutic T cells in patients with leukemic relapse after allogeneic transplantation has been attempted to induce a GVL effect.[20] Conflicting data exist about whether a GVL effect can occur independently of GVHD. A strategy to maximize the GVL effect and minimize GVHD has been to titrate the number of donor lymphocytes until GVHD Grade II-III occurs in order to create a GVL effect without severe GVHD. However, the optimal number of donor lymphocytes capable of inducing a GVL effect without significant GVHD is not known. Immunosuppression, number of T cells transfused, T-cell phenotype, myelosuppression, and the timing of the DLI of therapeutic T cells all play a role in the balance between the GVL effect and GVHD. The GVL effect is best documented in CML and less well shown in AML, ALL, and other lymphoid malignancies.

However, because it is difficult to identify a good HLA match, allogeneic transplantation is associated with a major risk that immunocompetent donor T cells reacting against recipient tissues will cause GVHD. Even in HLA-identical (six-antigen match) donor/recipient pairs, up to 6% of the grafts will fail and GVHD will occur in 20% to 60% of cases as a result of nucleated cells exhibiting minor histocompatibility antigens that are not linked to the major histocompatibility complex antigens.[21] Improved HLA typing techniques now employ molecular techniques that give a fuller picture of the antigen mapping and match/mismatch picture, but serologic terms of estimation of number of matches are still frequently used in clinical descriptions for reference. This occurs despite immunosuppressive therapy administered for several months after the procedure.[22] New and emerging immune cell manipulations are being explored to exploit the cancer-controlling effects of these cells while seeking to avoid the unwanted consequences of GVHD. Extracorporeal photopheresis is being used to treat patients with GVHD and to reduce the dose of immunosuppressive medications required.[23]

HPCs by Apheresis (Autologous)

Autologous HPC-A collection involves mobilizing the hematopoietic cells from the patient's marrow compartment into the peripheral blood with hematopoietic growth factors, most commonly filgrastim, with or without treatment with chemotherapy before collection. Once in the circulation, the HPCs are collected by leukapheresis. HPC-A collection carries no anesthesia risk, is less invasive, and contains fewer tumor cells than marrow harvests.

HPCs by Apheresis (Allogeneic)

Related Transplantation

For adult allogeneic transplantation, the best clinical results are obtained with a completely HLA-matched, related donor. The best chance of finding a six-antigen HLA match is among the patient's genetic sisters and brothers. Parents and children will be at least a haplotype match.

Genetically, there is a 25% chance of a sibling being a complete match, a 50% chance of a haplotype match, and a 25% chance of a complete mismatch. Pediatric patients are more tolerant of partially mismatched grafts and, therefore, have a larger available donor pool.[24] In the rare instance a recipient has an identical twin, a syngeneic transplant may be optimal because the donor and recipient cells are genotypically identical and the risk of GVHD is reduced. However, syngeneic grafts do not provide the graft-vs-tumor effect found in allogeneic transplants.

HPC-A has largely replaced HPC-M for related transplantation.[25] The use of G-CSF in healthy donors has been shown to mobilize sufficient HSCs for allogeneic transplantation,[26] thus avoiding the need for anesthesia and a marrow harvest. Clinical data comparing allogeneic HPC-A vs allogeneic HPC-M from HLA-identical siblings have shown that HPC-A recipients have faster engraftment, improved immune reconstitution, lower transplant-related morbidity, and a similar incidence of acute GVHD.[2,27] Retrospective analyses reported a higher incidence of chronic GVHD in related allogeneic HPC-A recipients.[28] However, a recent prospective randomized study found no difference in the risk of chronic GVHD.[12]

HPCs from Cord Blood

Despite the fact that over 3 million individuals are registered with the NMDP, patients in need of an allogeneic HPC transplant have ≤85% chance of finding a matched donor. Finding and qualifying a willing donor for HPC-A or HPC-M collection typically takes weeks. Because of the time and availability constraints, attention has turned to the third available source—HPC-C. Umbilical cord blood, which in clinical practice is routinely discarded, is being banked as an alternative source of HPCs, especially for children, for whom smaller collection numbers of HPCs are adequate for successful engraftment. The advantages of cord blood as a source of HPCs for transplantation include: no risk to the donor, potential availability of cord blood from donor populations underrepresented in the NMDP, more rapid availability, and possibly lower risk of viral infection and GVHD. Areas of concern regarding HPC-C include ethical and informed consent issues, speed of engraftment, higher mortality in the posttransplant period, and ability to achieve engraftment in adults as a result of the limited number of nucleated cells in cord blood.

Cord blood obtained from a delivered placenta is known to be rich in early and committed progenitor cells.[29] Since the first cord blood transplant was reported in 1989 for Fanconi anemia,[30] more than 2500 patients have received cord blood for a variety of hematologic malignant and nonmalignant conditions.[31]

Cord blood is collected from the placenta at the time of delivery using a variety of techniques, but the preferred system uses a small collection bag (150 to 250 mL) with appropriate anticoagulant. In-vitro data have suggested that placental blood has an increased capacity for proliferation.[32] The volume of units retained for processing is typically 80 to 100 mL (range, 40-240 mL), with a median nucleated cell count of 1.2×10^9 in the units chosen for transplantation and a median CD34+ cell count of 2.7×10^5/kg.[33] Clinical studies have reported successful engraftment in children.[34,35] The median time to neutrophil engraftment (500/ μL) is 30 days; median time to platelet engraftment (50,000/μL) is 56 days.[36] Compared with engraftment observed after allogeneic marrow transplantation, neutrophil and platelet engraftment appear to be delayed. Clinical studies have also suggested that unrelated HPC-C transplants are associated with a lower risk of GVHD compared with unrelated HPC-M transplants in children, even considering the lower risk susceptibility of pediatric patients to GVHD.[31,34,36,37]

Two studies have compared engraftment and outcomes of transplantation of adults with one- or two-antigen mismatched HPC-C, matched HPC-M, and one-antigen mismatched HPC-M. The findings in the two studies were very similar: HPC-M transplant recipients recovered neutrophils on day 18 to 19, and HPC-C recipients recovered neutrophils on day 26 to 27.[38,39] Platelet engraftment in these studies repeated the finding that HPC-M transplantation provided more rapid recovery at 29 days compared with 60 days for HPC-C. Both of these studies found that the HPC-C transplantation compares favorably with one-antigen mismatched HPC-M transplantation, with equal advantage for survival for each group. A matched HPC-M transplant was superior to HPC-C or mismatched HPC-M, but the advantage was small. This is encouraging news for adults who need an HPC-M transplant but have difficulty finding a suitably matched donor. Current clinical trials are testing whether multiple HPC-C units received by adults will facilitate faster engraftment. A study of 23 such recipients with advanced-stage disease showed a mean neutrophil engraftment of 23 days and a 57% chance of disease-free survival after 1 year. In these two-unit transplants, the cells of one of the units prevailed and provided the lasting engraftment population.[40]

Related Cord Blood Donors

Sibling-derived cord blood has been used as a source of hematopoietic engraftment in more than 250 allogeneic transplants in Europe and North America, representing 15% of the allogeneic cord blood transplants.[31,35] The kinetics of hematopoietic recovery are similar to those observed with unrelated cord blood recipients.[31] Times to both platelet and neutrophil engraftment are slower than those observed in HLA-matched sibling marrow transplants. However, recipients of cord blood from HLA-identical siblings have a lower incidence of acute and chronic GVHD compared with marrow from HLA-identical siblings.[31]

Autologous Cord Blood

Companies are marketing the freezing and long-term storage of an infant's cord blood cells to parents, in case the child may need them.[41,42] The chance of an individual needing a cord blood transplant by age 18 is estimated to be 1 in 200,000.[42] The first successful autologous cord blood transplantation procedure was reported in a 14-month-old patient with neuroblastoma.[43]

Cord Blood Banks

The first large-scale community cord blood program was the Placental Blood Program at the New York Blood Center, which began collecting placental prod-

ucts in 1992. The program has stored in excess of 14,000 cord blood units and has provided cells for more than 1500 transplant procedures. The outcomes of the first 562 procedures have been reported in detail.[34] The NMDP has developed a registry of participating cord blood banks. The National Cord Blood Bank of the New York Blood Center, NetCord, Bone Marrow Donors Worldwide, and the Caitlin Raymond Registry are additional search sites available today.

Donor Eligibility

Donor Evaluation: Autologous Setting

In the autologous setting, the major concern regarding eligibility for transplantation arises from the condition of the patient. For HPC-M, the patient's marrow first should be assessed for residual malignancy and marrow cellularity. Patients scheduled for an autologous transplant should undergo an extensive history and physical examination to identify any risks from the marrow harvest and/or apheresis procedures. For HPC-A, the patient/donor is evaluated for the likelihood that he or she can undergo successful mobilization and collection.

Donor Evaluation: Allogeneic Setting

Allogeneic donors must be selected according to their degree of HLA match; qualifications according to the FDA regulations; standards of the AABB, NMDP, and Foundation for the Accreditation of Cellular Therapy (FACT); and physical ability and willingness of the donor to undergo the collection procedure. Ideally, a full six-antigen match should be found; however, transplant procedures have been performed successfully using one-antigen mismatched and haploidentical donors.

Cytomegalovirus (CMV) status of the donor is also a deciding factor in the selection process in the case of CMV-negative recipients. The use of parous females or gender-mismatched individuals as donors is associated with an increased risk of GVHD, as is a history of transfusion in the donor.[44-46] Therefore, the preferred HLA-identical donor would be CMV negative (in the case of CMV-negative recipients); of the same gender as the recipient; if female, nonparous; and untransfused.

Infectious Disease Testing

Autologous and tested allogeneic donors must be screened and tested for certain infectious diseases.[47] In the *Code of Federal Regulations* (CFR) Title 21, sections of the regulations relevant to cell therapy donors are Donor Screening (1271.75), Donor Testing: General (1271.80), and Donor Testing: Specific Requirements (1271.85). The rules are described by the FDA as "comprehensive, but flexible." The donor screening rules are consistent with the 1994 Centers for Disease Control and Prevention (CDC) guidelines to prevent transmission of human immunodeficiency virus (HIV), and 1993 FDA guidelines for prevention of transmission of hepatitis B virus (HBV) and hepatitis C virus (HCV). Testing for syphilis is required, and tissue rich in leukocytes must be tested for human T-cell lymphotropic virus (HTLV) and CMV. They also include requirements for questioning donors about risk factors for variant Creutzfeldt-Jakob disease and new or emerging pathogens such as West Nile virus and severe acute respiratory syndrome, and requirements for tests for carriers of these illnesses as soon as they are practically available. The regulations and guidance are extensive and fit the FDA's stated "layered approach" that intensifies the amount of screening and testing of the donor to the level of risk to which the recipient may be subjected. Thus, unrelated allogeneic donors represent the highest level of risk, whereas family members or regular sexual partners are considered a lower risk source of new exposure to patients.

The donor must be screened in order to minimize the risk of disease transmission to an already immunocompromised recipient. FDA regulations specify that the HPC donor sample should normally be tested up to 7 days before collection, or at the time of collection but before release of the product. HPC-A donor samples may be obtained up to 30 days before collection in order to have infectious disease testing completed before the patient begins myeloablative chemotherapy [21 CFR 1271.80(b)]. For purposes of optimal donor selection, it may be advisable to test the donor earlier in the transplantation workup period as well.[48,49]

The use of approved nucleic acid tests for HIV and HCV has considerably shortened the possible "window period" in donors who may have contracted either of these infections but who do not yet test positive on antibody tests. Donors being stimulated with filgrastim develop higher sample-to-cutoff ratios. This makes false-positive reactions more likely in the immunoassays currently used for infectious disease. False-positive test results for hepatitis B surface antigen and HCV antibody have been associated with G-CSF administration in normal donors.[50,51]

Donors who are confirmed positive for HIV should not be used as a source for the transplant. Other positive disease markers do not necessarily prohibit use of collections from a particular donor (eg, anti-HBc positive), and special evaluation of donors with this marker is under way by the NMDP at this time. The allograft material from such donors may be used when the patient's transplantation physician informs him or her of the status of the donor and documents consent of the patient. Segregated methods of storage must be used for the biohazardous material collected until it is infused so that cross-contamination of other stored products is prevented.[48(p78),49,52]

In cases of allogeneic HPC-C transplants, a sample for infectious disease studies should be obtained from the donor's mother within 48 hours of collection of the cord blood and tested. Any positive results should be reported to the mother and the mother's physician. The HPC-C donation involving a mother or a child who has a positive infectious disease history or results should either be discarded or the patient must go through a special notification and consent process.[52] In cases of allogeneic transplantation, CMV status of the donor and the recipient should be carefully considered.

A recipient may develop primary CMV infection if he or she is CMV negative and receives a CMV-positive graft but may have some protection from the immunity in the graft. CMV-positive individuals receiving a CMV-negative graft may have a severe primary infection of the graft from virus resident in the recipient's tissue.[46]

Collection of Products
HPC-M Collection

A marrow harvest is the same for an allogeneic donor as for an autologous patient. The procedure is performed under sterile conditions in the operating room. The posterior iliac crest provides the richest site of marrow. In the autologous patient, prior radiation therapy to an aspiration site may result in hypocellular yields. In general, these sites are unsuitable for harvest and should be avoided. Once aspirated, the marrow should be mixed and

diluted with an anticoagulant (usually preservative-free heparin and/or ACD). The marrow aliquots are pooled into a sterile vessel or a harvest collection bag equipped with filters of graduated pore size. The marrow is then transferred to a sterile blood bag and transported to the processing laboratory, where samples are removed for graft evaluation, quality assurance testing, possible manipulation of the product, final labeling, and/or cryopreservation.

Collection Targets

The recipient's body weight and type of manipulation of the collection, if any, will determine the volume of marrow to be collected. A frequently used minimum target (after processing), for both autologous and allogeneic transplants, is 2.0×10^8 nucleated cells per kilogram of recipient body weight. Marrow harvests in autologous patients who have received alkylating agents as therapy may yield fewer progenitor cells relative to the total nucleated cells collected. In these cases, extra marrow should be obtained if possible.[53] If the harvested product is to be processed (ie, T-cell depletion, ex-vivo tumor purging), additional marrow (up to double the reinfusion target) should be collected. The NMDP limits the volume harvested from its donors to a maximum of 1500 mL. Many centers use the cell number requested for transplant and the cell count on the product during collection to determine the final collection volume.

Clinical Considerations

The age of the donor and, in the autologous setting, the underlying disease and previous treatment regimen influence the HPC yield (Table 25-2).[54] Autologous or allogeneic donors may require RBC transfusions to replace blood taken with marrow collection. Frequently, allogeneic marrow donors will have an autologous RBC unit collected 2 to 3 weeks before the harvest. Most RBC transfusions occur after the harvest to avoid marrow dilution. Allogeneic blood components must be irradiated if given before or during the procedure, to incapacitate donor lymphocytes from replication and attack of the transplant recipient, possibly causing GVHD. In transplants that require marrow manipulation, such as red cell depletion, the recovered red cells may be returned to the donor.

HPC-A Collection

HPCs can be mobilized into the peripheral blood with the use of recombinant colony-stimulating factors and collected in sufficient numbers to achieve long-term hematopoietic engraftment in a transplant recipient.

CD34

CD34 is the cluster designation given to a transmembrane glycoprotein present on immature hematopoietic cells, some mature endothelial cells, and stromal cells.[55] The antigen has an approximate molecular weight of 110 kD and carries a negative charge. Cells expressing the CD34 antigen encompass the lineage-committed cells as well as the pluripotent stem cells. CD34+ cells purified from marrow are capable of trilineage reconstitution in humans.[55] One to three percent of normal marrow cells express this antigen. In normal peripheral blood, CD34+ cells circulate in low numbers (0.01-0.1%).[56] Monoclonal antibodies (MoAbs) to CD34 have been developed and are used in flow cytometric assays to measure the stem/progenitor content of HPC collections and CD34+ cell concentration in donor peripheral blood.[57]

HPC-A Collection (Autologous)

In the autologous setting, HPC-A donors are routinely mobilized with hematopoietic growth factors (with or without chemotherapy), which include G-CSF and granulocyte-macrophage colony-stimulating factor (GM-CSF) or a combination of the two. Mobilization with chemotherapy or growth factors alone results in a 10- to 30-fold increase in the concentration of HPCs over the steady state.[8] Combined mobilization with growth factors and chemotherapy enriches HPC concentrations 50- to 200-fold.[58] Transplantation of autologous HPC-A results in a reduced time to hematopoietic recovery compared with autologous HPC-M.[59] Platelet reconstitution is most striking and patient hos-

Table 25-2. Factors Reported to Affect the Mobilization of Hematopoietic Cells

1. Mobilization technique
   a. Chemotherapy—degree of transient myelosuppression
   b. Growth factors—type, schedule, dose
   c. Use of combined chemotherapy and growth factors
2. Extent of prior chemotherapy/radiation
3. Type of underlying disease
4. Age of patient
5. Presence of marrow metastases

Adapted with permission from Lane.[54]

pital stays are reduced by 7 to 10 days. Schwella and colleagues[60] demonstrated that the median time to an unsupported platelet count of ≥20,000/µL was 10 days in the group receiving chemotherapy plus G-CSF-mobilized HPCs vs 17 days in the group receiving autologous HPC-M. Effective mobilization in the autologous patient is influenced by previous chemotherapy or radiation.

There is a linear relation between the precollection peripheral blood CD34 count and the volume of blood that needs to be processed to achieve a target dose. Graphs and predictive models would be expected to vary based on the efficiency of CD34+ collection related to the specific equipment and software employed. It would also be expected to be least predictive at low peripheral blood CD34+ concentrations, where the enumeration is least accurate. White cell counts, the number of mononuclear cells, and the number of circulating CD34+ cells have all been used as surrogate markers for the timing of the HPC-A collection.[59,61-63] It has been suggested that the optimal time to begin HPC collection in patients who have been primed with chemotherapy is when the white cell count first exceeds 5×10^9/L.[59] However, the white cell concentration does not correlate with the number of HPCs in the peripheral blood. Phenotypic analysis of CD34+ cells by flow cytometry provides a more real-time measurement of CD34+ cell content in an HPC collection or hematopoietic graft. The technique can be used to indicate the timing of the first collection and the total number of CD34+ cells/kg finally collected (as a function of the volume of blood processed).[56,57,64-66] The length of time for engraftment correlates with the number of CD34+ cells in the collection.[65,67-69] In general, a peripheral blood CD34+ cell concentration of 10/µL can be expected to result in a yield of at least 1.0×10^6 CD34+ cells/kg.[60,61,64]

In most autologous patients, venous access is obtained through a dual- or triple-lumen central venous apheresis catheter. Operators of blood cell separators generally process two to three blood volumes per procedure. In the pediatric setting, it may be necessary to prime the cell separator with compatible, irradiated red cells. The donor will undergo daily procedures of approximately 2 to 5 hours each. Large-volume leukapheresis procedures (processing at least three blood volumes or 15-20 liters) are performed at many centers to reduce the overall number of collections. Investigational studies have suggested that there is equilibration of noncirculating HPCs into the peripheral circulation with large-volume collections.[70-72] Hillyer[73] reported a 2.5-fold increase in colony-forming units–granulocyte-macrophage (CFU-GM) per mL processed in collection when the collection volume was 15 liters compared to the yield in the first blood volume of the collection.

Collection Targets. The adequacy of autologous HPC collection is gauged by the CD34+ dose (the number of CD34+ cells per kilogram of recipient body weight). The reported minimum threshold of CD34+ cells necessary for neutrophil and platelet engraftment in the autologous patient has ranged from 0.75 to 1.0×10^6/kg.[8,64] This minimum target is a broad guideline and higher doses have been associated with accelerated platelet engraftment,[74] reduced febrile complications, and use of antibiotic therapy after transplantation.[75] Recent data support an economic benefit associated with greater CD34+ cell collections (greater or equal to 5.0×10^6/kg) compared to the minimum acceptable collections required for engraftment (1.0×10^6/kg).[76] The type of processing will also influence the volume necessary for collection.

Poor Autologous HPC Mobilization. Patients who have been heavily pretreated with chemotherapy and/or radiation therapy may fail to mobilize enough HPCs after stimulation with growth factors/chemotherapy. The best way to obtain an adequate collection from poorly mobilized patients is unknown. Collection of HPC-M in combination with, or in place of, HPC-A is frequently ineffective in improving engraftment.[77] Second attempts at mobilization with G-CSF alone have been successful in obtaining adequate CD34+ cell counts and can be as effective as G-CSF and chemotherapy.[78] Increasing the dose of G-CSF or combining with GM-CSF has also successfully mobilized some autologous donors after prior failed attempts.[79]

Mobilization can be very difficult in some patients, particularly if they have been heavily pretreated or are older. Another approach to increase production of stem/progenitor cells by growth factors is manipulation of the chemokines that attach the cells to their microenvironment. The interaction of stromal-derived growth factor-1 (SDF-1) and CXCR4, its ligand, controls mobilization. The molecule AMD 3100 was developed originally as a potent and selective inhibitor of CXCR4 in order to control replication of HIV-containing cells. An observed side effect of the drug was a rapid increase in white cells. Broxmeyer and colleagues measured a 40-fold increase in HPCs after injection of AMD 3100 into human volunteers.[80] Phase I and II clinical trials are under way in conjunction with G-CSF to enhance mobilization and HPC-A yields in difficult-to-mobilize patients.[81]

Clinical Considerations for Autologous HPC-A Collection. The frequency and length of HPC-A collections may result in donor discomfort and side effects. Complete blood counts are performed before and after each apheresis procedure to monitor the hematocrit and platelet values. Red cell and/or platelet transfusions may be required. Red cell loss should be minimal in HPC-A collection, but platelet counts typically decrease from 25% to 40% because the HPCs lie close to the platelet layer in the buffy coat. Collection can be performed via peripheral or central venous access. Patients who have received prior chemotherapy are more likely to need a central venous catheter because of poor peripheral access. Catheter-associated thrombosis (either in the catheter or in the vein surrounding it) is the most common complication associated with HPC-A collection.[82]

HPC-A Collection (Allogeneic)

Collection of allogeneic HPCs from HLA-matched relatives is primarily performed using G-CSF mobilization. Typically, donors are given 10 to 16 µg/kg as a subcutaneous injection once or twice daily. The concentration of CD34+ cells in the peripheral blood begins to rise after 3 days of G-CSF administration and peaks after 5 to 6 days. Standard volume leukapheresis (processing 8-9 L) results in a component with the following median values: white cells, 32.4×10^9; mononuclear cell count, 31.4×10^9; CD34+ cells, 330×10^6; platelets, 470×10^9; and RBCs, 7.6 mL.[83] Clinical trials have suggested a minimum dose of 2.0×10^6/kg of CD34+ cells to be adequate for allogeneic HPC-A transplants.[84]

Allogeneic donors with poor venous access may require central venous catheters. In the NMDP report on normal donor collections of HPCs, 5% of men and 20% of women require central venous access for collection.[85] There is a 1% risk of complications associated with these catheters including infection, hemorrhage, and pneumothorax. Thrombocytopenia has been reported as a complication of G-CSF administration and HPC-A collection in healthy donors.[86,87]

There is also a risk in exposing normal donors to G-CSF. Ninety percent of donors experience side effects.[88] The most common complaint is bone pain followed by headaches, body aches, fatigue, nausea, and/or vomiting. Bone pain, headaches, and body aches can be successfully managed with nonsteroidal analgesics such as acetaminophen. As mentioned earlier, false-positive infectious disease serologies have been reported.[51] Serious adverse effects are rare but include reports of splenic rupture,[89,90] neutrophilic infiltration of the skin (Sweet's syndrome),[91] arterial thrombosis,[92] and an anaphylactoid reaction.[93] Donors with complex hemoglobinopathies (eg, sickle trait and β+ thalassemia) have been observed to have complications with G-CSF stimulation for the purpose of becoming an HPC donor.[94,95]

HPC-C Collection

Umbilical cord blood can be collected from either a delivered or an undelivered placenta.[96] Cord blood collection should not interfere with obstetric care of the mother or the infant. If the birth provider intends to collect the cord blood, plans should be made in advance to abandon the collection if care of the mother or the infant requires the care provider's attention instead. Cord blood collected after delivery of the placenta is preferably initiated within 15 minutes of parturition, if adequate volumes are to be obtained.[97] To minimize the risk of bacterial contamination, the surface of the cord should be cleaned with alcohol, then disinfected, in a similar manner to the preparation of skin for a blood donation. A large-bore needle connected to a blood collection bag containing CPDA, CPD, or ACD anticoagulant is inserted into the umbilical vein so that the placental blood drains by gravity into the bag. Alternatively, a delivered placenta can be suspended above the collection bag. CPDA or CPD are the preferred anticoagulants because they are isotonic

and have a neutral pH. However, other closed system arrangements using ACD or heparin are in use in some centers. Informed consent from the biologic mother or legal representative of the child must be obtained, preferably before delivery.

A personal and family medical history of the biologic mother (and, if available, of the infant donor) must be obtained and documented before, or within 48 hours of, the collection. If available, his medical history should be obtained from the biologic father. HPC-C collections are not acceptable for allogeneic use if there is a family history (biologic mother, father, or sibling) of genetic disorders that may affect the graft's effectiveness in the recipient or otherwise expose the recipient to a genetic disorder through the transplant.

Red cells from the HPC-C collection or from the infant donor must be typed for ABO/Rh and a screen for unexpected red cell antibodies must be performed using either the mother's serum or plasma or a sample from either the infant donor or the cord blood collection.[52,56] White cells from the cord blood must be typed for HLA (HLA-A and -B antigen testing, and DNA-based Class II typing) by a laboratory accredited by the American Society of Histocompatibility and Immunogenetics (ASHI) or an equivalent accrediting organization.[49,52] In order for HPC-C to be a feasible alternative to allogeneic HPC-M or HPC-A transplants, it is essential to have a frozen inventory of ready-to-use HLA-typed products.

Samples, preferably from an attached segment, should be frozen for pretransplant confirmation of HLA type by the transplant facility. Many centers freeze a sample of the mother's serum to allow new infectious disease tests to be done if they become available after the HPC-C has been collected and are thought to be important at the time the transplant is planned. The emergence of West Nile virus as a threat to mothers, infants, and transplant recipients is an example. A sample of the mother's blood containing cells or DNA (a dried filter paper sample is adequate) may be useful if questions concerning the child's HLA type arise. These samples from the mother were more useful when HLA typing was done by serologic methods to investigate ambiguous types in the infant. CD34+ cell enumeration at the time of thawing may also be performed to estimate the stem cell content of the HPC-C graft but is useful only if a viability marker is employed so that only viable cells are counted.

The desire to increase the dose of stem cells in HPC-C has fueled interest in ex-vivo expansion of the cells in a laboratory setting.[98] Early clinical trials with expanded cord blood progenitors are promising, having shown successful engraftment; however, no improvement in patient survival has been reported.[99,100] Ex-vivo expansion of cord blood is an area of active experimental investigation.

Processing of Hematopoietic Progenitor Cells

Techniques for Cell Selection and/or Purging of Hematopoietic Progenitor Cells

Selection of the CD34+ Cells

As an HPC undergoes differentiation and maturation, CD34 antigen levels decrease. This property, coupled with the use of MoAbs specific for the different epitopes of the CD34 molecule, permits physical separation procedures. There are several methods of immunoselection available, such as fluorescence-activated cell sorting (FACS) and immunomagnetic beads.[101] Selection of CD34+ HPCs may be associated with a reduction of tumor cells (autologous grafts) or T cells (allogeneic grafts). The clinical utility of CD34 and AC133 selection for tu-

mor or T-cell reduction is under investigation.[102]

Immunomagnetic Separation. Various immunomagnetic separation techniques, direct or indirect, are available. Typically, a CD34 antibody is coupled to a magnetic bead. This complex is incubated with mononuclear cells, and the cells expressing the CD34 antigen bind to the antibody-coated beads, forming rosettes. A magnet is applied to separate the rosetting CD34+ cells from the nonrosetting cells. Bead detachment, which varies among methods, may be accomplished through anti-Fab fragments or enzymatic treatment (eg, chymopapain).[103] The Isolex 300 system (Baxter Healthcare Immunotherapy Division, Irvine, CA), a magnetic cell separator, is a semiautomated instrument for clinical-scale CD34+ selection applications. This method uses antibody-coated Dynal paramagnetic beads to rosette the CD34+ cells. A fully automated device (Isolex 300i, Baxter) and a peptide release agent are available for clinical use.[104] Other techniques of magnetic cell separation employ superparamagnetic microbeads that remain attached to the HPC surface.[105] One such method, magnetic cell sorting (MACS, Miltenyi Biotec, Bergisch Gladbach, Germany), was first introduced on a small scale by Miltenyi.[106] The CliniMACS (Miltenyi Biotec) is a clinical-scale version of the MACS system and is available in the United States for investigational use only. This system employs antibody-conjugated iron-dextran microbeads. The magnetically stained cells are separated over a high gradient magnetic column and a microprocessor controls the elution of the CD34+ cells.

Counterflow Centrifugal Elutriation. Counterflow centrifugal elutriation (CCE) is a method of separating cells based on their size and density. A continuous-flow centrifuge (Beckman Instruments, Palo Alto, CA, and Gambro, Golden, CO) and unique chamber design allow for the basic separation principle: two opposing forces (centrifugal force and counter media flow) acting upon cells at the same time. As cells are pumped into the chamber (centripetal direction), they align according to their sedimentation properties. With adjustment of the counterflow rate, the centrifugal and counterflow forces are balanced, and a gradient of flow rates exists across the chamber. By gradually increasing the flow rate of the medium or decreasing the speed of the rotor, cells can be eluted out of the chamber and collected. Smaller, slower sedimenting cells elute first. Although this technique is used primarily for T-cell depletion, CCE has been applied to CD34+ cell selection. CD34+ cells are heterogeneous and will elute in subset fractions that are useful for repopulation experiments and ex-vivo expansion trials.[107]

Autologous Tumor Purging

Purging or negative selection refers to the removal of tumor cells that may contaminate the autologous graft. In patients with hematopoietic disease or malignancies that frequently involve the marrow (eg, lymphomas), minimal residual disease contributes to relapse.[108] Although autologous HPC-A collections have a lower probability than HPC-M of tumor contamination and fewer tumor cells/mL, they still may contain large numbers of viable tumor cells. Studies have demonstrated that tumor cells may be mobilized from the marrow into the peripheral circulation.[109,110] Whether tumor purging decreases the likelihood of relapse is controversial. Because some purging methods may damage HPCs, the probability of residual disease or relapse should be carefully balanced against the higher graft failure rate or increased mortality from prolonged aplasia that may be associated with tumor purging.[111] Numerous techniques for autologous purging are available. The goal of all purging methods— whether physical, immunologic, or pharmacologic—is the destruction or removal of the malignant clone while maintaining the efficacy of the HPCs necessary for engraftment.[112]

Pharmacologic Techniques. In-vivo antineoplastic therapy produces greater tumor cell kill because of the differential sensitivity of malignant cells over normal cells. In-vitro pharmacologic purging is an effort to expand this therapeutic ratio. In-vitro purging allows for dose and exposure intensification without concern for organ toxicity because higher drug concentrations can be used on isolated hematopoietic grafts ex vivo, which then can be administered in vivo. However, the drug concentration must be at nontoxic levels before reinfusion. Activated oxazaphosphorines (4-hydroperoxycyclophosphamide, mafosfamide) were the most frequently used compounds but are generally no longer in use in the United States. Other chemotherapeutic agents have been investigated in preclinical models but are not in clinical use. Results from purged autologous transplants for AML with either of these drugs showed prolonged aplasia with less than 1% CFU-GM survival.[112]

Physical Techniques. Separation methods based on cell size and density through gradient-generating reagents or CCE do not achieve adequate tumor cell depletion.[111] However, the combined use of physical and immunologic techniques requires further study.

Immunologic Techniques. The development of MoAbs coupled with the discovery of tumor-associated antigens opened the field for immunologic purging.[113] MoAbs may be directed at tumor-specific antigens or cell-differentiation antigens.[111] The immunologic techniques differ primarily by the method of target cell removal. MoAbs are used in conjunction with complement, bound to toxins, or coupled to magnetic beads. The choice of MoAb and the heterogeneity of antigen expression on the target cell affect the success of the purge or the level of depletion. Many investigators employ a cocktail of MoAbs in an effort to enhance the purging efficiency.[114,115] Complement-mediated cytotoxicity is frequently used if the antibody is of IgM isotype or if the expected level of antigen density is high.[111]

Immunomagnetic cell separation, either by direct or indirect method, employs an antibody-coated magnetic bead to target the antigen or antigens of interest. A recent study described a 5-log tumor cell depletion with two cycles using the indirect method for B-cell lymphoma. Colony assays showed only a 20% reduction in CFU-GM and multipotential CFU (CFU-GEMM).[114]

T-Cell Depletion

GVHD is a significant complication in allogeneic HPC transplantation. Because the disease process is mediated by donor T cells that are reactive against the host, depletion strategies are used to target and remove these cells in an effort to decrease the incidence or at least lessen the severity of GVHD. Many of the techniques outlined for positive selection and tumor purging are applicable to T-cell depletion (Table 25-3).[17]

In T-cell-depleted grafts, two major areas of concern are graft failure and recurrent leukemia. Most instances of graft failure (initial or late) are caused by immunologic rejection. Early transplants involving depleted grafts in patients with CML showed a 50% or greater relapse rate. In contrast, patients who developed GVHD had a lower relapse rate. Subsequent clinical and investigational data provided evidence of an immune-mediated GVL effect.[116]

Table 25-3. Methods of T-Cell Depletion

Nonimmunologic
  Counterflow centrifugal elutriation
  Pharmacologic/cytotoxic drugs
Immunologic
  Monoclonal antibodies with or without
      complement
  Immunotoxins
  Immunomagnetic beads

Research and developmental efforts have focused on determining the optimal level of T-cell depletion. Dreger et al[115] reported a comparison of T-cell depletion methods (CAMPATH-1 plus complement, immunomagnetic CD34+ selection, and biotin-avidin-mediated CD34+ selection). The immunomagnetic method provided a 4-log reduction in T cells vs a 3.1-log reduction with the biotin-avidin method. MoAb treatment with autologous complement yielded a 2.1-log reduction. The challenge of minimizing the severity of GVHD and maintaining the GVL effect is ongoing. Additional studies are examining the role of subpopulations of T cells and/or cytokines in potentiating the GVL effect.[117]

ABO Incompatibility

Although HLA compatibility is crucial in the successful engraftment of myelosuppressed or ablated patients, ABO compatibility is not. Pluripotent and very early committed HPCs do not possess ABH antigens, allowing engraftment to occur successfully regardless of the ABO compatibility between the recipient and donor. ABO incompatibility does not affect neutrophil or platelet engraftment, graft failure, or rejection. However, delayed red cell engraftment may occur after a major ABO-incompatible transplant and delayed hemolysis may occur after a minor ABO-incompatible transplant where the donor has antibodies to the recipient's blood cells (Table 25-4).[118]

Major ABO Incompatibility

Major incompatibility occurs when the recipient has ABO antibodies or other red cell antibodies, such as anti-D or anti-Kell, against the donor red cell antigens. The HPC preparation can be processed to remove mature red cells. The group O recipient who receives a group A graft may continue to produce anti-A and anti-B for 3 to 4 months or longer in rare instances, and the presence of anti-A will delay erythropoiesis by the group A graft; group A red cells appear in the circulation when the recipient's anti-A disappears. Granulo-

cyte and platelet production are not affected.[119] Red cell engraftment may be delayed to ≥40 days after the transplantation.[120] Red cells used for transfusion of the recipient must be compatible with both the donor and the recipient. In some centers, group O red cells are given to all major ABO-incompatible transplant recipients in order to avoid confusion. Recommendations for optimal blood component selection are shown in Table 25-5.

Minor ABO Incompatibility

Minor ABO incompatibility occurs when the donor has antibodies against the recipient red cell antigens (such as a group O donor to a non-group O recipient). Be-

Table 25-4. Potential Problems with ABO- and Rh-Incompatible HPC Transplantation

| | Example | | |
Incompatibility	Donor	Patient	Potential Problems
ABO (major)	Group A	Group O	Hemolysis of infused donor RBCs, delay of RBC engraftment, hemolysis at the time of donor RBC engraftment
ABO (minor)	Group O	Group A	Hemolysis of patient RBCs from infused donor plasma; in pediatric cases, hemolysis of patient RBCs 7-10 days after transplant caused by passenger lymphocyte-derived isohemagglutinins
Rh	Negative	Positive	Hemolysis of patient RBCs by donor anti-D produced after engraftment
	Positive	Negative (with anti-D)	Hemolysis of donor RBCs from newly engrafted HPCs (rare), or delayed RBC recovery
Other RBC antigens	Negative	Positive	Hemolysis of patient RBCs by donor antibodies in plasma produced after engraftment
	Positive	Negative (with antibody)	Hemolysis of donor RBCs from newly engrafted HPCs (rare), or delayed RBC recovery

Table 25-5. Transfusion Support for Patients Undergoing ABO-Mismatched Allogeneic HPC Transplantation

Recipient	Donor	Mismatch Type	Phase I — All Components	Phase II — RBCs	Phase II — First Choice Platelets	Phase II — Next Choice Platelets*	Phase II — FFP	Phase III — All Components
A	O	Minor	Recipient	0	A, AB	AB; B; 0	A, AB	Donor
B	O	Minor	Recipient	0	B, AB	AB; A; 0	B, AB	Donor
AB	O	Minor	Recipient	0	AB	A; B; 0	AB	Donor
AB	A	Minor	Recipient	A, 0	AB	A; B; 0	AB	Donor
AB	B	Minor	Recipient	B, 0	AB	B; A; 0	AB	Donor
O	A	Major	Recipient	0	A	AB; B; 0	A, AB	Donor
O	B	Major	Recipient	0	B	AB; A; 0	B, AB	Donor
O	AB	Major	Recipient	0	AB	A; B; 0	AB	Donor
A	AB	Major	Recipient	A, 0	AB	A; B; 0	AB	Donor
B	AB	Major	Recipient	B, 0	AB	B; A; 0	AB	Donor
A	B	Minor & major	Recipient	0	AB	A; B; 0	AB	Donor
B	A	Minor & major	Recipient	0	AB	B; A; 0	AB	Donor

*Platelet concentrates should be selected in the order presented. Modified from Friedberg et al.[121]

Phase I = the time when the patient/recipient is prepared for HPC transplantation.

Phase II = from the initiation of myeloablative therapy until:

For RBC—DAT is negative and antidonor isohemagglutinins are no longer detectable (ie, the reverse typing is donor type).

For FFPs—recipient's erythrocytes are no longer detectable (ie, the forward typing is consistent with donor's ABO group).

Phase III = after the forward and reverse type of the patient are consistent with donor's ABO group.

Beginning from Phase I, all cellular components should be irradiated and leukocyte reduced.

fore infusion of a graft from a plasma-incompatible donor, the plasma may be removed to avoid infusion of preformed anti-A and/or anti-B. Minor ABO-incompatible transplants can be characterized by rather abrupt onset of immune hemolysis, which begins about 7 to 10 days after transplantation and may last for 2 weeks. The direct antiglobulin test (DAT) is positive; anti-A and/or anti-B can be recovered in the eluate and hemoglobinemia and/or hemoglobinuria may occur. An additional 30% of such transplant recipients develop a positive DAT without experiencing gross hemolysis. This phenomenon is the result of red cell antibodies produced by passenger B lymphocytes in the stem cell graft.[121] Non-ABO antibodies from passenger lymphocytes in HPC transplants have also been reported.[122] Although transient, the hemolysis may persist for up to 2 weeks and may require transfusion with group O red cells. Minor ABO-mismatched HPC transplants may be associated with a higher risk of hemolysis, possibly caused by greater B-cell content.[123] In all cases, plasma used for transfusion should be compatible with both the donor and the recipient. In some centers, group AB plasma products are given to all minor ABO-incompatible transplant recipients in order to avoid confusion. RBC transfusions, beginning with the conditioning regimen, should be of donor type. Recommendations for optimal blood component selection are shown in Table 25-5.

Chimerism

In spite of intensive pretransplant chemotherapy and irradiation, some of the host's hematopoietic cells may survive and subsequently coexist with cells produced by the transplanted HPCs. This dual cell population, called partial hematopoietic chimerism, may have an effect on immu-

nologic tolerance.[124] This tolerance develops in successful transplants and allows normal immune reconstitution. Full chimerism (replacement of host marrow cells entirely by donor cells) usually occurs in successful HPC-M transplantation.

Processing in the Presence of ABO Incompatibilities

Major ABO Incompatibility. Two approaches have been employed with major ABO incompatibilities: 1) removal of or decrease in the isoagglutinin level in the recipient or 2) removal of the red cells in the HPC-M collection. Processing is not generally required with HPC-A because such a small volume of red cells is usually included.

Attempts to remove or decrease the isoagglutinin titer in recipients involve the use of one or more large-volume plasma exchanges with or without the subsequent infusion of donor-type red cells as a secondary effort to absorb any additional isoagglutinins.[125,126]

Other approaches to ABO-incompatible products include red cell depletion. The most prevalent method in use is red cell sedimentation.

Some institutions accomplish red cell depletion using density gradient separation and cell washers (Gambro BCT, Lakewood, CO); others use continuous-flow apheresis machines such as the Spectra (Gambro) and the Fenwal CS-3000 (Baxter Healthcare), with mononuclear cell recoveries of 94% and 87% and red cell depletion of 99% and 98%, respectively.

Minor ABO Incompatibility. Theoretically, the level of hemolysis is dependent on the volume of HPC-M infused relative to the recipient's plasma volume and the IgM titer of the donor. Incompatible plasma can be easily removed by centrifugation. Plasma removal using this method removes approximately 75% of the plasma volume while recovering >70% of the initial nucleated cell count. Plasma removal is not generally required in HPC-A because the volume of incompatible plasma is usually small.

Umbilical Cord Blood Processing

Advances in the processing of umbilical cord blood cells have solved the early problems of unacceptably high progenitor cell losses with manipulation.[127] Unlike cryopreservation laboratories that store relatively few autologous or allogeneic HPC-M or HPC-A products (typically, less than a few hundred products at any one time), a successful cord bank would be expected to store thousands of products for prolonged periods. Therefore, attempts to reduce umbilical cord blood bulk (and, therefore, storage space, liquid nitrogen requirements, and cost) have been actively pursued. Currently, many centers are following the approach used by the New York Blood Center, which involves sedimentation and volume reduction before cryopreservation.[128]

Cultures for Microbial Contamination

Sterility is essential in blood products for infusion to immunosuppressed patients. This is particularly important with HPC-M, which is frequently collected in an open system, and with products that require multiple manipulations (Table 25-6).[129-134] Culture growth can result from contamination during collection or product processing, or as a result of an infected catheter or the patient's sepsis. Skin commensals are the predominant isolates from these cultures. In all cases it is important to identify the source, the degree of contamination, and the causative organism, given the fact that this product is intended for transplantation in an immunocompromised recipient. Each product must be tested for microbial contamination at least once during the course of processing, usually just before freezing or infusion with allogeneic transplants.[48] A positive culture does not necessitate immediate discard of the product because these are frequently irreplaceable cells.[135] Thus, positive results need to be reviewed by the appropriate physician on a case-by-case basis and sensitivity tests ordered to better define the organism and to allow for appropriate clinical management at the time of transplant. This should also serve as the impetus to review all procedures and techniques to ensure that they

Table 25-6. Percent Microbial Contamination of Cell Therapy Products

Source of HPCs	No. of Products Tested	% Contaminated	Reference
Marrow	291	0	129
	227	1.3	130
	317	6.0	131
	194	<0.1	132
Peripheral blood	1380	0.65	129
	560	0.7	130
	576	0.5	131
	1040	0.2	133
Cord blood	1000	<1.0*	134

*Initial rates were as high as 28%; however, with improved donor selection and technique, the rate fell to <1%.

provide safeguards to prevent contamination.

Stem Cell Enumeration: CD34 Analysis, Aldehyde Dehydrogenase Activity, and Others

As stem cells differentiate into hematopoietic cells, CD34 surface markers appear. As the cells continue to differentiate and acquire other surface markers, CD34 expression diminishes. Stages of differentiation may be studied by the expression or co-expression of other antigens or properties. There are currently two assays for CD34 that are FDA-cleared for in-vitro diagnostic use. These CD34+ measurement methods are the most widely used for the evaluation of grafts, have the longest history of use, and show the most clinical correlations in the marrow transplantation literature.

The principle of gain and later loss of CD34 expression has been applied to evaluate the quality of HPC grafts. The current approach is to use a method based on multiparameter flow cytometry to determine the number of CD34+ cells and to calculate a subsequent CD34+ dose based on the recipient's weight. Numerous flow cytometric analysis methods for CD34 enumeration exist.[56,136,137] Because these methods differ, correlation of CD34 dose values from site to site is often unreliable. Multiple studies have documented the variability of CD34 analysis methods and results and have examined possible causes of the variability.[56,57,138,139] Because of the "rare event" nature of CD34 enumeration, several procedural components play a critical role in the assay. Selection of the CD34 antibody clone, fluorescent conjugate, lysing solution, lyse-wash format, gating strategy, and the number of events analyzed are some of the factors that influence the end result.[140]

Growing awareness of, and concern about, the need for a standardized approach to CD34 analysis have prompted several collaborative groups such as the International Society for Cellular Therapy (ISCT) to propose guidelines for CD34+ cell determination by flow cytometry.[56,141] Alternate approaches are available and will continue to be developed and investigated as more is discovered about the CD34 antigen and other markers for the pluripotent stem cell.[142]

A second method for enumeration of early cells has gained FDA clearance. The cytosolic expression of aldehyde dehydrogenase (ALDH) in stem cells was found to be the protective property of HSCs in cyclophosphamide treatment of patients and in preservation of stem cells in graft purging with 4HC. Flow cytometric analysis of ALDH-positive cells with the enzymatic excitation and trapping inside the stem cells of a fluorescent substrate (because the fluorophore becomes charged and does not diffuse freely) allows measurement of a viable population enriched in colony-forming progenitor cells. Both long-term repopulating and committed progenitor cells are enriched and the ALDH^{br} contains the population responsible for hematopoietic engraftment of NOD-SCID mice.[143,144] This method to enumerate ALDH^{br} SSc^{lo} cells identifies only cells with intact membranes and is well correlated with engraftment in post-thaw HPC-A grafts.[145] Another measurement technique involving the use of Flk-2 and Thy 1.1^{lo} showed that Flk-2–, Thy 1.1^{lo} cells represented long-term repopulating cells, whereas Flk-2+, Thy 1.1^{lo} cells were short-term engraftment-enhancing cells. These tools may be developed for use in future graft engineering approaches to finely separate early cell populations.[146]

Colony-Forming Cell Assays

Culture systems are available that can demonstrate in-vitro proliferative capacity of a hematopoietic sample. It is thought that short-term (generally within 2 weeks) repopulating potential is produced from the committed HPCs. Long-term repopulating ability is thought to be a result of the pluripotential HPCs that are principally necessary for a complete and sustained engraftment. Cultures may be useful to assess engraftment potential; however, because media, culture techniques, and colony identification are quite variable, interinstitutional comparisons are difficult. Reported CFU-GM doses below which engraftment may be delayed range from 1.5×10^5 to 5.0×10^5/kg.[147]

Long-term cultures are not routinely used clinically because of the 5- to 8-week incubation requirements. However, they may be useful in evaluating developmental procedures involving product manipulation.

Freezing and Storage

Although easily performed by many transplant centers, HPC cryopreservation and reinfusion are not without risk of loss of HPCs. The infusion of cryopreserved cells also results in risks to the recipient, many of which are life-threatening, and some of which are not well understood. The loss of HPCs from cryopreservation and the effect of this loss on engraftment speed have not been quantified. There are multiple aspects to successful cryopreservation of HPCs. Each of these variables affects the recovery of HPCs during the cryopreservation steps and, as with any manufacturing process, must be rigidly controlled for reproducible results. The question that still faces cryopreservation facilities is whether other solutions or processing techniques will provide better cryosurvival of cells, at less cost, with greater simplicity, or with less toxicity to either the recipient or to the cell type being frozen.

HPC-A, HPC-M, and HPC-C are frozen and stored using the same techniques. The general parameters include cryopreservation in dimethylsulfoxide (DMSO) and a source of plasma protein with or without hydroxyethyl starch (HES), cooling at 1 to 3 C/minute, and storage at –80 C or colder. Variations on this technique include the concentration at which the cells are frozen, the amount and source of the plasma protein, and the cooling techniques used.[148] Most of these variations probably have little effect on the survival of the HPCs as shown by the consistent engraftment of cryopreserved components. However, cryopreservation results in the loss of an undefined but potentially substantial proportion of HPCs, and delay in engraftment can occur if the component being frozen has borderline quantities of HPCs. There is also considerable but generally minor toxicity associated with the infusion of cryopreserved cells that must be considered when developing cryopreservation techniques.

Allogeneic Products

The collection of allogeneic marrow is generally timed to coincide with the completion of the recipient's preparative regimen. Because of the brief storage period required, the product is maintained in the liquid state. Unseparated HPC-M can be stored in the liquid state for up to 3 days at either 4 C or 22 C without any significant loss in viability of either uncommitted or committed progenitors. The ability to store unmanipulated marrow under these conditions is vital in the context of the NMDP or other transplant registries where unrelated HPC-M units are collected and then transported great distances for transplantation. Similarly, HPC-A units may be stored in the liquid state under the same conditions as HPC-M for up to 3 days at 4 C.[149,150] The cell concentration is important in determining the storage time and temperature that the cells will tolerate without damage. High concentrations of white cells in liquid storage at room temperature quickly expend the supplies of oxygen and glucose and cause a decrease in pH in the storage medium that is toxic to the cells. A lower concentration of cells (higher volume of suspending medium, often autologous plasma) and refrigerated storage are protective.

Autologous Products

Because of the length of time required for treatment and/or HPC product collection, autologous products are usually cryopreserved and stored until the time of infusion. Cryopreservation also allows HPCs to be collected while the patient is in remission and stored for use in case a relapse occurs (prophylactic storage). At present, no expiration date has been defined for these products; however, HPC-M stored for 11 years has been used for transplantation, with sustained engraftment.[151]

Computer-Controlled Cryopreservation

The purpose of cryopreservation is to freeze cells in such a way as to allow for their long-term storage with a minimal loss of cell viability or reconstitutive ability upon thaw. The main obstacle to maintaining viability during cryopreservation and storage is the formation of intracellular ice crystals along with an increase in external osmolarity, causing exit of water from the cell, both resulting in cell lysis. Thermal shock, the time required for phase change (liquid state to solid state), and the posttransition freezing rate also present specific conditions to be managed for cryopreservation.[152]

The adverse effects caused by the formation of intracellular ice crystals or by cell dehydration can be minimized by a slow cooling rate and the addition of a cryoprotective agent such as DMSO. Cryoprotectants such as DMSO prevent the formation of large ice crystals within the cells by penetrating the cell and providing some balance of the external hyperosmolar solute conditions in the freezing medium surrounding the cell.[153] A commonly used cryoprotectant consists of 20% DMSO and 20% plasma or albumin prepared in a buffered electrolyte solution or tissue culture media. The plasma or albumin provides a protein source, which aids in preventing cell damage during freezing and thawing. The cryoprotectant is combined with an equal volume of product immediately before freezing, resulting in a final cell suspension containing 10% DMSO and 10% plasma.

Phase transition time is a physical phenomenon of freezing water where forming ice crystals release heat energy into the cell solution that needs to be offset by continued cooling to prevent crystallization of ice, thawing, and recrystallization during this energy exchange, with damage to the cell membrane.[152] This method of freezing requires physical conditions that support this process. This may be accomplished by a computerized programmable freezing chamber that adds liquid nitrogen in sufficient amounts to push the freezing process through the phase change smoothly. The freezer is programmed to cool cells at an optimal rate of 1 to 3 C/minute until a temperature of –90 to –100 C is reached.[154-156] With the combination of a cryoprotectant and a programmed rate of freezing, cryopreservation and long-term storage of HPCs are possible, with minimal damage to the cells.

Passive Controlled-Rate Freezing

Mechanical, methanol bath immersion, or "passive controlled-rate" freezing is advocated by some investigators as a simple, reliable, cost-effective, and validated method of managing the physical conditions of cooling as an alternative to a controlled-rate device.[157-159] The principle is that products can be cooled without the aid of a programmable freezer or liquid nitrogen if the conditions of freezing are predetermined, measured, and performed according to standard operating procedures. The products are stored in a –80 C mechanical freezer or colder after the initial freeze. HPCs stored in this fashion have successfully engrafted after as long as 2 years of storage.[159] In some cases, the combination of the metal canisters the bags are placed in, the bag itself, and the volume of product frozen produces a freezing rate of approximately 3 C/minute, which falls within the optimal range previously discussed.[160] The major deterrent to use of mechanical freezers is fear of mechanical failure and the lack of data on long-term storage and engraftment.

Frozen Storage

Although products frozen in a mechanical freezer are stored at –80 to –150 C, products cryopreserved using a programmable freezer generally are stored in a liquid nitrogen freezer. The storage temperature achieved with vapor phase, although not as cold as liquid phase, averages –140 C, a temperature that has been shown to allow for viable long-term marrow storage.[151] The major drawbacks to vapor phase storage include the potential for large fluctuation in temperature when the freezer is entered as well as the variation in storage temperature throughout the freezer itself, dependent on the design of the storage chamber and the procedure for entering and retrieving units. The time to rising temperatures of the stored products in cases of electrical or liquid nitrogen supply emergencies is significantly shorter

than with liquid phase. The advantage of vapor phase storage is the possibly decreased risk of cross-contamination that has become an issue with liquid phase storage.[161]

Storage of Untested or Infectious Products

Regulations [21 CFR 1271.60(a) and 1271.65(a)] and standards[48(p35),49] require alternative storage for products that are untested or have a positive disease marker test result. Some institutions comply by storing all products in vapor phase and physical separation by category of product. Other institutions use an overwrap, placing the component in an outer plastic bag that is sealed before storage. A third alternative is a separate storage compartment for units that are untested or positive for infectious disease markers.

Final Suitability Criteria

Before each autologous or allogeneic unit is released, it must undergo review and meet the predetermined release criteria described in the facility's quality plan. The pertinent facts describing donor selection, product collection, processing, and storage must be reviewed. The container label and associated information must accurately reflect the product classification, storage/preservative medium in the final container, the product content (usually cell content), and results of release testing including infectious disease tests. If exceptions to standard practice were made, they must be explained either on the label or in the accompanying release material.

Transportation and Shipping

In some cases, a hematopoietic component must be transported from one center to another. The product must be positively identified upon its removal from inventory in preparation for shipping. In all cases, precautions should be taken to protect the component from rough handling, out-of-range temperatures, X-ray examination, breakage, and spillage. The shipping container must undergo quality control to ensure that it is capable of holding the expected temperature during shipping. In the case of cryopreserved components, the use of a liquid nitrogen "dry shipper" is desirable. Such "dry shippers" have liquid nitrogen absorbent material between the walls of the container that allows the inside of the container to maintain temperatures in the range of −180 C for up to 10 to 14 days if they are properly filled with liquid nitrogen and shipped in the upright position. Tipping or inversion of the container during shipping permits the liquid nitrogen to drain out, allowing the container to warm toward ambient temperature.

Thawing and Infusion

For all components, final identification is done by the nurse or physician performing the infusion. Flow through the central venous catheter is confirmed and the cells are infused by gravity drip, calibrated pump, or manual push with or without an in-line filter (a standard 170-micron red cell infusion filter is acceptable). Although DMSO was thought to be toxic to HPCs, it is now known to be nontoxic after short-term exposure (up to 1 hour) at the concentration used for cryopreservation of HPCs.[162] However, prolonged exposure to DMSO ex vivo at 22 to 37 C may be harmful to HPCs. To minimize the exposure of thawed cells to DMSO, many centers rapidly thaw one bag at a time near the bedside. Some centers place product bags in secondary containment bags before thaw-

ing; others immerse the bag (all but the access ports) directly into sterile water or saline at 37 to 40 C.[152] The bag is kneaded gently until all solid clumps have thawed. The cells are then infused (usually 10-15 mL per minute). Products may also be washed and resuspended in the laboratory before infusion to prevent cell aggregation.[152]

Side effects associated with infusions include nausea, diarrhea, flushing, bradycardia, hypertension, and abdominal pain. In general, such side effects may justify slowing, but not halting, the infusion until the symptoms pass. A limit of 1 gram of DMSO per kilogram of body weight of the patient at one infusion is recommended to allow the patient to tolerate both the DMSO and the volume infusion effects of the administration. Sudden and severe hypotension can occur in the absence of adequate antihistamine premedication. The patient should receive fluids and treatment to ensure that the urine is "alkalinized." This facilitates the clearance of hemoglobin caused by red cell lysis, which occurs during freezing and reduces the risk of renal complications. If the total infusion volume exceeds 10 mL/kg of recipient body weight, many centers divide the volume over a morning and an afternoon infusion or over 2 consecutive days.

It is best to collect postthaw laboratory samples directly from the patient's infusion bags instead of freezing separate individual specimens because these samples are identical to the infused product.[163]

Evaluation and Quality Control of Hematopoietic Products

Cell Counts

Each hematopoietic product is analyzed to determine the total cell concentration and the mononuclear cell concentration, which are used to calculate the number of cells per kilogram (of the recipient) or cell dose for each product.[48(p55),49] These doses, in combination with other assays, determine the number of collections necessary to achieve engraftment.[135] In addition, they are used to calculate the percent recovery, providing a quality control measure for processing procedures and equipment.[164]

In general, automated cell counts provide the most rapid and accurate value. However, platelet/cellular aggregates in HPC-A or fat globules in HPC-M specimens can falsely decrease or increase cell counts.[135,165] In such cases, manual cell counts may be preferable. It is important that cell counts are not overestimated because this may result in inaccurate estimation of time to engraftment or graft failure.

Engraftment Data

Ultimately, engraftment of neutrophils, platelets, and red cells is the primary determinant of graft quality. Monitoring and documenting days to engraftment for neutrophil and platelet lineage are required by FACT[49] and AABB[48(p41)] for accreditation.

Tumor Cell Detection

Tumor cell detection techniques have been developed to screen products suspected of tumor cell contamination and to evaluate purged products. The majority of these assays use MoAbs that specifically bind tumor antigens. Detection and quantitation can be done by flow cytometry, immunofluorescence, or immunohistochemical staining. Sensitivity varies with technique from 0.1% to 0.0004% of cells examined.[166] Preliminary studies indicate that the presence of tumor cells may be associated with a reduced disease-free survival.[167]

Regulations

In 1997, the FDA announced a new comprehensive approach to the regulation of cellular and tissue-based products.[168] HPCs from placental/umbilical cord blood and peripheral blood were covered by this proposal. Many of the policies, proposed regulations, and guidance documents needed to implement this approach have been published.[47,169-173]

These regulations require establishment registration and listing of facilities collecting, processing, or distributing tissue or cell therapy products. Although the regulations are similar to those for blood donor qualification, there are differences appropriate to the specific tissue source under consideration. The cGTP regulations (found in Title 21 CFR 1271.145 to 320) are specific instructions intended to ensure that facilities establish and maintain a quality program that documents that personnel, procedures, facilities, equipment, supplies, and reagents are set up and maintained in an acceptable and a standard manner. Process control is required: there must be written procedures and documented validation. Products are required to be collected, tested, labeled, and stored in ways that preserve their identity and prevent contamination and cross-contamination. It may be necessary to demonstrate regulatory compliance during FDA inspection visits. Reporting of adverse events (when applicable) is also required within 15 days of receipt of the information if the event is serious as defined in 21 CFR 1271.350. This body of regulations represents a major effort on the part of the FDA to ensure that tissue and cell therapy products are safe for the recipient.

Standards

The AABB and FACT have published separate, but substantially similar, standards for HPCs.[48,49] The AABB *Standards for Cellular Therapy Product Services* addresses the collection, processing, storage, and distribution of HPCs. Other organizations such as the NMDP also publish voluntary standards. FACT standards address clinical issues provided by HPC clinical transplant programs as well as laboratory services performing the collection, processing, storage, and distribution of HPCs. Both AABB and FACT provide an inspection and certification program for requesting members. These program reviews are an important, external, and impartial look at program organization and how the program's organization affects patient outcome. As an outgrowth of the standards writing process, representatives from the constituent organizations of AABB and FACT cooperated to produce a uniformly endorsed *Circular of Information for the Use of Cellular Therapy Products.*[174] In this circular, the organizations agreed upon a number of principles, including a common set of names for cell therapy products. This agreement on product names allowed the International Committee on Commonality of Blood Bank Automation's (ICCBBA) North American Task Force to approve progenitor cell label designs, including ICCBBA's quality design requirements.

References

1. Korbling M, Estrov Z. Adult stem cells for tissue repair—a new therapeutic concept? N Engl J Med 2003;349:570-82.
2. Champlin RE, Schmitz N, Horowitz MM, et al. Blood stem cells compared with bone marrow as a source of hematopoietic cells for allogeneic transplantation. IBMTR Histocompatibility and Stem Cell Sources Working Committee and the European Group for Blood and Marrow Transplantation (EBMT). Blood 2000;95:3702-9.
3. Report on state of the art in blood and marrow transplantation—the IBMTR/ABMTR summary slides with guide (2002). IBMTR/ABMTR Newsletter 2002;9(1):4-11. [Available at http://www.ibmtr.org/newsletter/pdf/2002Feb.pdf.]
4. Champlin R, Khouri I, Anderlini P, et al. Nonmyeloablative preparative regimens for allogeneic hematopoietic transplantation. Biology and current indications. Oncology (Hunting), 2003;17:94-100.
5. Sandmaier BM, McSweeney P, Yu C, Storb R. Nonmyeloablative transplants: Preclinical and clinical results. Semin Oncol 2000;27:78-81.
6. Storb RF, Champlin R, Riddell SR, et al. Nonmyeloablative transplants for malignant disease. Hematology (Am Soc Hematol Educ Program) 2001;375-91.
7. Giralt S, Anagnostopoulos A, Shahjahan M, et al. Nonablative stem cell transplantation for older patients with acute leukemias and myelodysplastic syndromes. Semin Hematol 2002;39:57-62.
8. To LB, Haylock DN, Simmons PJ, Juttner CA. The biology and clinical uses of blood stem cells. Blood 1997;89:2233-58.
9. National Marrow Donor Program Overview (2001 slide presentation). [Available at http://www.nmdp.org/nmdp/slide_presentation.html.]
10. Powderly J, Shea T. Hematopoietic cell transplantation. In: Runge MS, Greganti MA, eds. Netter's internal medicine. Teterboro, NJ: Icon Learning Systems, 2003:401-05.
11. Stroncek DF, Confer DL, Leitman SF. Peripheral blood progenitor cells for HPC transplants involving unrelated donors. Transfusion 2000;40:731-41.
12. Bensinger WI, Martin PJ, Storer B, et al. Transplantation of bone marrow as compared with peripheral-blood stem cells from HLA-identical relatives in patients with hematologic malignancy. N Engl J Med 2001;344:175-81.
13. Beatty PG, Kollman C, Howe CW. Unrelated-donor marrow transplants: The experience of the National Marrow Donor Program. Clin Transpl 1995:271-7.
14. Scott I, O'Shea J, Bruce M, et al. Molecular typing shows a high level of HLA class I incompatibility in serologically well matched donor/patient pairs: Implications for unrelated bone marrow donor selection. Blood 1998;92:4864-71.

15. Petersdorf EW, Gooley TA, Anasetti C, et al. Optimizing outcome after unrelated marrow transplantation by comprehensive matching of HLA class I and II alleles in the donor and recipient. Blood 1998;92:3515-20.

16. Petersdorf EW, Longton GM, Anasetti C, et al. Definition of HLA-DQ as a transplantation antigen. Proc Natl Acad Sci U S A 1996;93: 15358-63.

17. Gajewski J, Gjertson D, Cecka M, et al. The impact of T-cell depletion on the effects of HLA DR beta 1 and DQ beta allele matching in HLA serologically identical unrelated bone marrow transplantation. Biol Blood Marrow Transplant 1997;3:76-82.

18. Petersdorf EW, Longton GM, Anasetti C, et al. Association of HLA-C disparity with graft failure after marrow transplantation from unrelated donors. Blood 1997;89:1818-23.

19. Kanfer E. Graft-versus-host disease. In: Treleaven J, Wiernik P, eds. Color atlas and text of bone marrow transplantation. London: Mosby-Wolfe, 1995:185-8.

20. Kolb HJ, Schattenberg A, Goldman JM, et al. Graft-versus-leukemia effect of donor lymphocyte transfusion in marrow grafted patients. Blood 1995;86:2041-50.

21. Champlin R. Bone marrow transplantation from HLA-matched unrelated donors as treatment for leukemia. J Hematother 1993;2: 323-7.

22. Champlin R, Kyoung L. T-cell depletion to prevent graft-versus-host disease following allogeneic bone marrow transplantation. In: Areman EM, Deeg HJ, Sacher RA, eds. Bone marrow and stem cell processing: A manual of current techniques. Philadelphia: FA Davis, 1992:163-217.

23. Apisarnthanarax N, Donato M, Korbling M, et al. Extracorporeal photopheresis therapy in the management of steroid-refractory or steroid-dependent cutaneous chronic graft-versus-host disease after allogeneic stem cell transplantation: Feasibility and results. Bone Marrow Transplant 2003;31:459-65.

24. Chan KW, Wadsworth LD. Pediatric bone marrow transplantation and processing. In: Areman EM, Deeg HJ, Sacher RA, eds. Bone marrow and stem cell processing: A manual of current techniques. Philadelphia: FA Davis, 1992:363-85.

25. Stroncek D, Anderlini P. Mobilized PBPC concentrates: A maturing blood component (editorial). Transfusion 2001;41:168-71.

26. Bensinger WI, Clift R, Martin P, et al. Allogeneic peripheral blood stem cell transplantation in patients with advanced hematologic malignancies: A retrospective comparison with marrow transplantation. Blood 1996;88: 2794-800.

27. Ottinger HD, Beelen DW, Scheulen B, et al. Improved immune reconstitution after allotransplantation of peripheral blood stem cells instead of bone marrow. Blood 1996;88: 2775-9.

28. Storek J, Gooley T, Siadak M, et al. Allogeneic peripheral blood stem cell transplantation may be associated with a high risk of chronic graft-versus-host disease. Blood 1997;90: 4705-9.

29. Broxmeyer HE, Gluckman E, Auerbach AD, et al. Human umbilical cord blood: A clinically useful source of transplantable hematopoietic stem/progenitor cells. Int J Cell Cloning 1990;8:76.

30. Gluckman E, Broxmeyer HE, Auerbach AD, et al. Hematopoietic reconstitution in a patient with Fanconi anemia by means of umbilical-cord blood from an HLA-identical sibling. N Engl J Med 1989;321:1174-8.

31. Rocha V, Wagner JE, Sobocinski KA, et al. Graft-versus-host disease in children who have received a cord-blood or bone marrow transplant from an HLA-identical sibling. N Engl J Med 2000;342:1846-54.

32. Laughlin MJ, Barker J, Bambach B, et al. Hematopoietic engraftment and survival in adult recipients of umbilical-cord blood from unrelated donors. N Engl J Med 2001; 344:1815-22.

33. Wagner J, Barker J, DeFor T, et al. Transplantation of unrelated donor umbilical cord blood in 102 patients with malignant and non-malignant diseases: Influence of CD34 cell dose and HLA disparity on treatment-related mortality and survival. Blood 2002; 100:1611-18.

34. Rubinstein R, Carrier C, Scaradavou A, et al. Outcomes among 562 recipients of placental-blood transplants from unrelated donors. N Engl J Med 1998;339:1565-77.

35. Wagner JE, Kernan NA, Steinbuch M, et al. Allogeneic sibling umbilical-cord-blood transplantation in children with malignant and non-malignant disease. Lancet 1995; 346:214-9.

36. Locatelli F, Rocha V, Chastang C, et al. Factors associated with outcome after cord blood transplantation in children with acute leukemia. Eurocord-Cord Blood Transplant Group. Blood 1999;93:3662-71.

37. Rocha V, Cornish J, Sievers EL, et al. Comparison of outcomes of unrelated bone marrow and umbilical cord blood transplants in children with acute leukemia. Blood 2001;97: 2962-71.

38. Laughlin MJ, Eapen M, Rubinstein P, et al. Outcomes after transplantation of cord blood or bone marrow from unrelated donors in adults with leukemia. N Engl J Med 2004;351: 2265-75.

39. Rocha V, Labopin M, Sanz G, et al. Transplants of umbilical-cord blood or bone marrow from unrelated donors in adults with acute leukemia. N Engl J Med 2004;351:2276-85.

40. Barker JN, Weisdorf DJ, DeFor TE, et al. Transplantation of two partially HLA-matched umbilical cord blood units to enhance engraftment in adults with hematologic malignancy. Blood 2005;105:1343-7.

41. Mehta SN. Umbilical-blood storage: Uncertain benefits, high price. The Wall Street Journal 1995 Nov 14;Sect B:1-2.

42. Rubin R. A hard sell to bank your baby's blood. US News & World Report 1996 July 29:60-1.

43. Ferreira E, Pasternak J, Bacal N, et al. Autologous cord blood transplantation (letter). Bone Marrow Transplant 1999;24:1041.

44. Flowers MED, Pepe MS, Longton G, et al. Previous donor pregnancy as a risk factor for acute graft-versus-host disease in patients with aplastic anemia treated by allogeneic marrow transplantation. Br J Haematol 1990; 74:492-6.

45. Gale RP, Bortin MM, Van Bekkum DW, et al. Risk factors for acute graft-versus-host disease. Br J Haematol 1987;67:397-406.

46. Bensinger WI, Deeg JH. Transfusion support and donor considerations in marrow transplantation. In: Sacher RA, AuBuchon JP, eds. Marrow transplantation: Practical and technical aspects of stem cell reconstitution. Bethesda, MD: AABB, 1992:157-84.

47. Food and Drug Administration. Eligibility determination for donors of human cells, tissues, and cellular and tissue-based products; final rule (May 25, 2004). Fed Regist 2004;69: 29786-834.

48. Szczepiorkowski ZM, ed. Standards for cellular therapy product services. Bethesda, MD: AABB, 2004.

49. Warkentin PI, ed. Standards for hematopoietic progenitor cell collection, processing and transplantation. 2nd ed. Omaha, NE: Foundation for the Accreditation of Cellular Therapy, 2002.

50. Mair DC, Brecher ME, Hom E, et al. False-positive hepatitis B surface antigen screening test results in patients receiving granulocyte-colony-stimulating factor. Transfusion 1996;36:948-51.

51. Kaufman RM, Goodnough LT, Lublin DM, et al. False-positive hepatitis C screening tests results in healthy allogeneic peripheral blood stem cell donors (abstract). Transfusion 2000; 40(Suppl):S34.

52. International standards for cord blood collection, processing, testing, banking, selection and release. 2nd ed. Omaha, NE: Foundation for the Accreditation of Cellular Therapy, 2001.

53. Treleaven JG. Bone marrow harvesting and reinfusion. In: Gee AP, ed. Bone marrow processing and purging. Boca Raton, FL: CRC Press, 1991:32-4.

54. Lane TA. Mobilization of hematopoietic progenitor cells. In: Brecher ME, Lasky LC, Sacher RA, Issitt LA, eds. Hematopoietic progenitor cells: Processing, standards and practice. Bethesda, MD: AABB, 1995:59-108.

55. Krause DS, Fackler MJ, Civin CI, et al. CD34: Structure, biology, and clinical utility. Blood 1996;87:1-13.

56. Sutherland DR, Anderson L, Keeney M, et al. The ISHAGE guidelines for CD34+ cell determination by flow cytometry. J Hematother 1996;5:213-26.

57. Brecher ME, Sims L, Schmitz J, et al. North American multicenter study on flow cytometric enumeration of CD34+ hematopoietic stem cells. J Hematother 1996;5:227-36.

58. Lie AK, Rawlings TP, Bayly JL, To LB. Progenitor cell yield in sequential blood stem cell mobilization in the same patients: Insights into chemotherapy dose escalation and combination of haemopoietic growth factor and chemotherapy. Br J Haematol 1996;95: 39-44.

59. Leitman SF, Read SJ. Hematopoietic progenitor cells. Semin Hematol 1996;33:341-58.

60. Schwella N, Beyer J, Schwaner I, et al. Impact of preleukapheresis cell counts on collection results and correlation of progenitor-cell dose with engraftment after high-dose chemotherapy in patients with germ cell cancer. Blood 1994;83:3787-94.

61. Elliot C, Samson DM, Armitage S, et al. When to harvest peripheral blood stem cells after mobilization therapy: Prediction of CD34 positive cell yield by preceding day CD34 positive concentration cell in peripheral blood. J Clin Oncol 1996;14:970-3.

62. Owen HG, Brecher ME. Paired randomized comparative study of PBSC collection (abstract). J Clin Apheresis 1997;12:29.

63. Bandarenko N, Sims LC, Brecher ME. Circulating CD34+ counts are predictive of PBSC CD34+ yields (letter). Transfusion 1997;37: 1218.

64. Perez-Simon JA, Caballero MD, Corral M, et al. Minimum number of circulating CD34+ cells to ensure successful leukapheresis and

engraftment in autologous peripheral blood progenitor cell transplantation. Transfusion 1998;38:385-91.

65. Green RHA, Morrison AE, Watson D, et al. The use of peripheral blood CD34 measurements in determining the optimal timing of peripheral blood progenitor cell (PBPC) collections (abstract). J Clin Apheresis 1997;12:47.

66. Yu J, Leisenring W, Bensinger WI, et al. The predictive value of white cell or CD34+ cell count in the peripheral blood for timing apheresis and maximizing yield. Transfusion 1999;39:442-50.

67. Shpall EJ, Champlin R, Glaspy JA. Effect of CD34+ peripheral blood progenitor cell dose on hematopoietic recovery. Biol Blood Marrow Transplant 1998;4:84-92.

68. Schulman KA, Birch R, Zhen B, et al. Effect of CD34+ cell dose on resource utilization in patients after high-dose chemotherapy with peripheral-blood stem-cell support. J Clin Oncol 1999;17:1227.

69. Bensinger W, Appelbaum F, Rowley S, et al. Factors that influence collection and engraftment of autologous peripheral-blood stem cells. J Clin Oncol 1995;13:2547-55.

70. Malachawski ME, Comenzo RL, Hillyer CD, et al. Large-volume leukapheresis for peripheral blood stem cell collection in patients with hematologic malignancies. Transfusion 1992;32:732-5.

71. Passos-Coelho JL, Braine HG, Davis JM, et al. Predictive factors for peripheral-blood progenitor-cell collections using a single large-volume leukapheresis after cyclophosphamide and granulocyte-macrophage colony-stimulating factor mobilization. J Clin Oncol 1995;13:705-14.

72. Hillyer CD, Lackey DA, Hart KK, et al. CD34+ progenitors and colony-forming units-granulocyte macrophage are recruited during large-volume leukapheresis and concentrated by counterflow centrifugal elutriation. Transfusion 1993;33:316-21.

73. Hillyer CD. Large volume leukapheresis to maximize peripheral blood stem cell collection. J Hematother 1993;2:529-32.

74. Glaspy JA, Shpall EJ, LeMaistre CF, et al. Peripheral blood progenitor cell mobilization using stem cell factor in combination with filgrastim in breast cancer patients. Blood 1997;90:2939-51.

75. Scheid C, Draube A, Reiser M, et al. Using at least 5×10^6/kg CD34+ cells for autologous stem cell transplantation significantly reduces febrile complications and use of antibiotics after transplantation. Bone Marrow Transplant 1999;23:1177-81.

76. Glaspy JA. Economic considerations in the use of peripheral blood progenitor cells to support high-dose chemotherapy. Bone Marrow Transplant 1999;23(Suppl 2):S21-7.

77. Watts MJ, Sullivan AM, Leverett D, et al. Back-up bone marrow is frequently ineffective in patients with poor peripheral stem cell mobilization. J Clin Oncol 1998;16:1554-60.

78. Gazitt Y, Shaughnessy P, Liu Q. Differential mobilization of CD34+ cells and lymphoma cells in non-Hodgkin's lymphoma patients mobilized with different growth factors. J Hematother Stem Cell Res 2001;10:167-76.

79. Jennis A, Pecora A, Preti R, et al. High dose G-CSF stem cell mobilization after initial stem cell mobilization failure (abstract). Blood 1998;92(Suppl 1):271a.

80. Broxmeyer HE, Hangoc G, Cooper S, Bridger G. Interference of the SDF-1/CXCR4 axis in mice with AMD 3100 induces rapid high level mobilization of hematopoietic progenitor cells and AMD 3100 acts synergistically with G-CSF and MIP-1 alpha to mobilize progenitors (abstract). Blood 2001;96(Suppl 1):3371a.

81. Devine S, Flomenberg N, Vesole D, et al. Safety and effect on WBC count and CD34 cell mobilization following administration of AMD 3100 to patients with multiple myeloma or non-Hodgkin's lymphoma. Presented at the Eighth Congress of the European Hematology Association, Rotterdam, The Netherlands, July 5-9, 2003.

82. Goldberg SL, Mangan KF, Klumpp TR, et al. Complications of peripheral blood stem cell harvesting: Review of 554 PBSC leukaphereses. J Hematother 1995;4:85-90.

83. Stroncek DF, Clay ME, Smith J, et al. Composition of peripheral blood progenitor cell components collected from healthy donors. Transfusion 1997;37:411-7.

84. Ilhan O, Arslan O, Arat M, et al. The impact of the CD34+ cell dose on engraftment in allogeneic peripheral stem cell transplantation. Transfus Sci 1999;20:69-71.

85. Anderlini P, Rizzo JD, Nugent ML, et al. Peripheral blood stem cell donation: An analysis from the International Bone Marrow Transplant Registry (IBMTR) and European Group for Blood and Marrow Transplant (EBMT) databases. Bone Marrow Transplant 2001;27:689-92.

86. Stroncek DF, Clay ME, Smith J, et al. Changes in blood counts after the administration of granulocyte-colony-stimulating factor and the collection of peripheral blood stem cells from healthy donors. Transfusion 1996;36:596-600.

87. Bandarenko N, Brecher ME, Owen H, et al. Thrombocytopenia in allogeneic peripheral

blood stem cell collections (letter). Transfusion 1996;36:668.

88. Stroncek DF, Clay ME, Petzoldt ML, et al. Treatment of normal individuals with granulocyte colony-stimulating factor: Donor experiences and the effects on peripheral blood CD34+ cell counts and on the collection of peripheral blood stem cells. Transfusion 1996;36:601-10.

89. Becker PS, Wagle M, Matous S, et al. Spontaneous splenic rupture following administration of granulocyte colony-stimulating factor (G-CSF): Occurrence in an allogeneic donor of peripheral blood stem cells. Biol Blood Marrow Transplant 1997;3:45-9.

90. Falzetti F, Aversa F, Minelli O, Tabilil A. Spontaneous rupture of spleen during peripheral blood stem cell mobilization in a healthy donor (letter). Lancet 1999;353:555.

91. Arbetter KR, Hubbard KW, Markovic SN, et al. Case of granulocyte colony-stimulating factor-induced Sweet's syndrome. Am J Hematol 1999;61:126-9.

92. Kawachi Y, Watanabe A, Uchida T, et al. Acute arterial thrombosis due to platelet aggregation in a patient receiving granulocyte colony-stimulating factor. Br J Haematol 1996;94:413-6.

93. Adkins DR. Anaphylactoid reaction in a normal donor given granulocyte colony-stimulating factor (letter). J Clin Oncol 1998;16:812-3.

94. Blau CA. Adverse effects of G-CSF in sickle cell syndromes (letter). Blood 2001;97:3682.

95. Wei A, Grigg A. Granulocyte colony-stimulating factor-induced sickle cell crisis and multiorgan dysfunction in a patient with compound heterozygous sickle cell/β+ thalassemia. Blood 2001;97:3998-9.

96. Rubinstein P, Carrier C, Taylor P, Stevens CE. Placental and umbilical cord blood banking for unrelated marrow reconstitution. In: Brecher ME, Lasky LC, Sacher RA, Issitt LA, eds. Hematopoietic progenitor cells: Processing, standards and practice. Bethesda, MD: AABB, 1995:1-17.

97. Yao AC, Minian M, Lind J. Distribution of blood between infant and placenta after birth. Lancet 1969;ii:871-3.

98. Di Gusto DL, Lee R, Moon J, et al. Hematopoietic potential of cryopreserved and ex vivo manipulated umbilical cord blood progenitor cells evaluated in vitro and in vivo. Blood 1996;87:1261-71.

99. Pecora AL, Stiff P, Jennis A, et al. Prompt and durable engraftment in two older adult patients with high risk chronic myelogenous leukemia (CML) using ex vivo expanded and unmanipulated unrelated umbilical cord blood. Bone Marrow Transplant 2000;25:797-9.

100. Kogler G, Nurnberger W, Fuscher J, et al. Simultaneous cord blood transplantation of ex vivo expanded together with non-expanded cells for high risk leukemia. Bone Marrow Transplant 1999;24:397-403.

101. Silvestri F. CD34+ cell purification by immunomagnetic beads/chymopapain system from normal and myeloid leukemias bone marrow and peripheral blood for research use. In: Wunder E, Sovalat H, Henon P, Serke S, eds. Hematopoietic stem cells: The Mulhouse manual. Dayton, OH: AlphaMed Press, 1995:161-9.

102. Gallacher L, Murdoch B, Wu DM, et al. Isolation and characterization of human CD34⁻Lin⁻ and CD34⁺Lin⁻ hematopoietic stem cells using cell surface markers AC133 and CD7. Blood 2000;95:2813-20.

103. Wunder E, deWynter E. Purification of CD34+ cells. In: Wunder E, Sovalat H, Henon P, Serke S, eds. Hematopoietic stem cells: The Mulhouse manual. Dayton, OH: AlphaMed Press, 1995:125-82.

104. Marolleau JP, Brice P, Cortivo LD, et al. CD34+ selection by immunomagnetic selection (Isolex 300) for patients with malignancies (abstract). Blood 1996;88(Suppl 1):110a.

105. Devernardi N, Camilla C, Traore Y, et al. Antibody-coated magnetic particles for CD34+ cell separation. In: Wunder E, Sovalat H, Henon P, Serke S, eds. Hematopoietic stem cells: The Mulhouse manual. Dayton, OH: AlphaMed Press, 1995:183-200.

106. Miltenyi S, Guth S, Radbruch A, et al. Isolation of CD34+ hematopoietic progenitor cells by high-gradient magnetic cell sorting (MACS). In: Wunder E, Sovalat H, Henon P, Serke S, eds. Hematopoietic stem cells: The Mulhouse manual. Dayton, OH: AlphaMed Press, 1995:201-13.

107. Wunder E, Herbein G, Sovalat H, et al. Separation of hematopoietic cells of different maturity in mononuclear cell subsets generated by elutriation. In: Wunder E, Sovalat H, Henon P, Serke S, eds. Hematopoietic stem cells: The Mulhouse manual. Dayton, OH: AlphaMed Press, 1995:271-9.

108. Brenner MK, Rill DR, Moen RC, et al. Gene-marking to trace origin of relapse after autologous bone-marrow transplantation. Lancet 1993;341:85-6.

109. Ross AA, Cooper BW, Lazarus HM, et al. Detection and viability of tumor cells in peripheral blood stem cell collections from breast cancer patients using immunocytochemical and clonogenic assay techniques. Blood 1993;82:2605-10.

110. Brugger W, Bross KJ, Glatt M, et al. Mobilization of tumor cells and hematopoietic progenitor cells into peripheral blood of patients with solid tumors. Blood 1994;83:636-40.

111. Rowley SD, Davis JM. Purging techniques in autologous transplantation. In: Areman EM, Deeg HJ, Sacher RA, eds. Bone marrow and stem cell processing: A manual of current techniques. Philadelphia: FA Davis, 1992:218-35.

112. Rowley SD, Davis JM. The use of 4-HC in autologous purging. In: Gee AP, ed. Bone marrow processing and purging. Boca Raton, FL: CRC Press, 1991:248-62.

113. Ball ED. Monoclonal antibodies and complement for autologous marrow purging. In: Gee AP, ed. Bone marrow processing and purging. Boca Raton, FL: CRC Press, 1991:281-8.

114. Kvalheim G, Wang MY, Pharo A, et al. Purging of tumor cells from leukapheresis products: Experimental and clinical aspects. J Hematother 1996;5:427-36.

115. Dreger P, Viehmann K, Steinmann J, et al. G-CSF mobilized peripheral blood progenitor cells for allogeneic transplantation: Comparison of T cell depletion strategies using different CD34+ selection systems or CAMPATH-1. Exp Hematol 1995;23:147-54.

116. van der Straaten HM, Fijnheer R, Dekker AW, et al. Relationship between graft-versus-host disease and graft-versus-leukaemia in partial T cell-depleted bone marrow transplantation. Br J Haematol 2001;114:31-5.

117. Krenger W, Ferrara J. Dysregulation of cytokines during graft-versus-host disease. J Hematother 1996;5:3-14.

118. Lopez-Plaza I, Triulzi DJ. Transfusion support in HSCT. In: Ball ED, Lister J, Law P, eds. Hematopoietic stem cell therapy. Philadelphia: Churchill Livingstone, 2000:589-97.

119. Long GD, Blume KG. Allogeneic and autologous bone marrow transplantation. In: Beutler E, Lichtman MA, Coller BS, Kipps TL, eds. Williams' hematology. 5th ed. New York: McGraw-Hill, 1995:172-94.

120. Worel N, Greinix HT, Schneider B, et al. Regeneration of erythropoiesis after related and unrelated donor BMT or peripheral blood HPC transplantation: A major ABO mismatch means problems. Transfusion 2000;40:543-60.

121. Friedberg RC, Andrzejewski C. Transfusion therapy in hematopoietic stem cell transplantation. In: Mintz PD, ed. Transfusion therapy: Clinical principles and practice. 2nd ed. Bethesda, MD: AABB Press, 2005:279-96.

122. Leo A, Mytilineos J, Voso MT, et al. Passenger lymphocyte syndrome with severe hemolytic anemia due to an anti-Jk[a] after allogeneic PBPC transplantation. Transfusion 2000;40:632-6.

123. Salmon JP, Michaux S, Hermanne JP, et al. Delayed massive immune hemolysis mediated by minor ABO incompatibility after allogeneic peripheral blood progenitor cell transplantation. Transfusion 1999;39:824-7.

124. Good R. Mixed chimerism and immunological tolerance. N Engl J Med 1993;328:801-2.

125. Buckner CD, Clift RA, Sanders JE, et al. ABO incompatible marrow transplants. Transplantation 1978;26:233-8.

126. Hershko C, Gale RP, Ho W, Fitchen J. ABH antigens and bone marrow transplantation. Br J Haematol 1980;44:65-73.

127. Broxmeyer HE, Douglas GW, Hangoc G, et al. Human umbilical cord blood as a potential source of transplantable hematopoietic stem/progenitor cells. Proc Natl Acad Sci U S A 1989;86:3828-32.

128. Rubinstein P, Dobrila L, Rosenfield RE, et al. Processing and cryopreservation of placental/umbilical cord blood for unrelated bone marrow reconstitution. Proc Natl Acad Sci U S A 1995;92:10119-22.

129. Webb IJ, Coral FS, Andersen JW, et al. Sources and sequelae of bacterial contamination of hematopoietic stem cell components: Implications for the safety of hematotherapy and graft engineering. Transfusion 1996;36:782-8.

130. Cohen A, Tepperberg M, Waters-Pick B, et al. The significance of microbial cultures of the hematopoietic support for patients receiving high-dose chemotherapy. J Hematother 1996;5:289-94.

131. Padley D, Koontz F, Trigg ME, et al. Bacterial contamination rates following processing of bone marrow and peripheral blood progenitor cell preparations. Transfusion 1996;36:53-6.

132. Lazarus HM, Mogalhaes-Silverman M, Fox RM, et al. Contamination during in vitro processing of bone marrow for transplantation: Clinical significance. Bone Marrow Transplant 1991;7:241-6.

133. Espinosa MT, Fox R, Creger RJ, Lazarus HM. Microbiologic contamination of peripheral blood progenitor cells collected for hematopoietic cell transplantation. Transfusion 1996;36:789-93.

134. Armitage D, Warwick R, Fehily D, et al. Cord blood banking in London: The first 1000 collections. Bone Marrow Transplant 1999;24:130-45.

135. Davis JM, Schepers KG. Quality control of hematopoietic progenitor cell products. In: Brecher ME, Lasky LC, Sacher RA, Issltt LA, eds. Hematopoietic progenitor cells: Process-

ing, standards and practice. Bethesda, MD: AABB, 1995:159-81.

136. Siena S, Bregni M, Brando B, et al. Flow cytometry for clinical estimation of circulating hematopoietic progenitors for autologous transplantation in cancer patients. Blood 1991;77:400-9.

137. Roscoe RA, Rybka WB, Winkelstein A, et al. Enumeration of CD34+ hematopoietic stem cells for reconstitution following myeloablative therapy. Cytometry 1994;16:74-9.

138. Johnsen HE. Report from a Nordic Workshop on CD34+ cell analysis: Technical recommendations for progenitor cell enumeration in leukapheresis from multiple myeloma patients. J Hematother 1995;4:21-8.

139. Chang A, Ma DDF. The influence of flow cytometric gating strategy on the standardization of CD34+ cell quantitation: An Australian multicenter study. J Hematother 1996; 5:605-16.

140. Säberlich S, Kirsch A, Serke S. Determination of CD34+ hematopoietic cells by multiparameter flow cytometry: Technical remarks. In: Wunder E, Sovalat H, Hénon P, Serke S, eds. Hematopoietic stem cells: The Mulhouse manual. Dayton, OH: AlphaMed Press, 1994:45-60.

141. Johnsen HE. Toward a worldwide standard for CD34+ enumeration? (letter) J Hematother 1997;6:83-4.

142. Sims LC, Brecher ME, Gertis K, et al. Enumeration of CD34 positive stem cells: Evaluation and comparison of three methods. J Hematother 1997;6:213-26.

143. Storms RW, Trujillo AP, Springer JB, et al. Isolation of primitive human hematopoietic progenitors on the basis of aldehyde dehydrogenase activity. Proc Natl Acad Sci U S A 1999;96:9118-23.

144. Hess DA, Meyerrose TE, Wirthlin L, et al. Functional characterization of highly purified human hematopoietic repopulating cells isolated according to aldehyde dehydrogenase activity. Blood 2004;104:1648-55.

145. Fallon P, Gentry T, Balber AE, et al. Mobilized peripheral blood SSC^lo ALDH^br cells have the phenotypic and functional properties of primitive hematopoietic progenitor cells and their number correlates with engraftment following autologous transplantation. Br J Haematol 2003;122:99-108.

146. Christensen JL, Weissman IL. Flk-2 is a marker in hematopoietic stem cell differentiation: A simple method to isolate long-term stem cells. Proc Natl Acad Sci U S A 2001;98: 14541-6.

147. Wunder E, Sovalat H, Henon P, Serke S, eds. Hematopoietic stem cells: The Mulhouse

Manual; Dayton, OH: AlphaMed Press, 1995: 126-82.

148. Moroff G, Seetharaman S, Kurtz JW, et al. Retention of cellular properties of PBPCs following liquid storage and cryopreservation. Transfusion 2004;44:245-52.

149. Hechler G, Weide R, Heymanns J, et al. Storage of noncryopreserved peripheral blood stem cells for transplantation. Ann Hematol 1996;72:303-6.

150. Sugrue SR, Hubel AH, McCullough J, et al. The effect of overnight storage of leukapheresis stem cell products on cell viability, recovery and cost. J Hematother 1998;7:431-6.

151. Aird W, Laborpin M, Gorin NC, Anten JH. Long term cryopreservation of human stem cells. Bone Marrow Transplant 1992;9:487-90.

152. Gorin NC. Cryopreservation and storage of stem cells. In: Areman EM, Deeg JH, Sacher RA, eds. Bone marrow and stem cell processing: A manual of current techniques. Philadelphia: FA Davis, 1992:138-41.

153. Meryman HT. Cryoprotective agents. Cryobiology 1971;8:173-83.

154. Leibo SP, Farrant J, Mazur P, et al. Effects of freezing on marrow stem cell suspensions: Interactions of cooling and warming rates in the presence of PVP, sucrose or glycerol. Cryobiology 1970;6:15-32.

155. Mazur P. Theoretical and experimental effects of cooling and warming velocity in the survival of frozen and thawed cells. Cryobiology 1966;2:181-92.

156. Lewis JP, Passovoy M, Trobaugh FE. The effect of cooling regimens on the transplantation potential of marrow. Transfusion 1967;7:17-32.

157. Hernandez-Navarro F, Ojeda E, Arrieta R, et al. Hematopoietic cell transplantation using plasma and DMSO without HES, with nonprogrammed freezing by immersion in a methanol bath: Results in 213 cases. Bone Marrow Transplant 1998;21:511-7.

158. Galmes A, Besalduch J, Bargay J, et al. Cryopreservation of hematopoietic progenitor cells with 5-percent dimethyl sulfoxide at −80 degrees C without rate-controlled freezing. Transfusion 1996;36:794-7.

159. Stiff PJ, Murgo AJ, Zaroules CG, et al. A simplified bone marrow cryopreservation method. Blood 1988;71:1102-3.

160. Stiff PJ, Murgo AJ, Zaroules CG, et al. Unfractionated marrow cell cryopreservation using dimethylsulfoxide and hydroxyethyl starch. Cryobiology 1983;21:17-21.

161. Tedder RS, Zuckerman MA, Goldstone AH, et al. Hepatitis B transmission from contami-

nated cryopreservation tank. Lancet 1995; 346:137-40.

162. Rowley SD, Anderson GL. Effect of DMSO exposure without cryopreservation on hematopoietic progenitor cells. Bone Marrow Transplant 1993;11:389-93.

163. Gee AP. Quality control in bone marrow processing. In: Gee AP, ed. Bone marrow processing and purging: A practical guide. Boca Raton, FL: CRC Press, 1991:19-27.

164. Lasky LC, Johnson NL. Quality assurance in marrow processing. In: Areman EM, Deeg HJ, Sacher RA, eds. Bone marrow and stem cell processing: A manual of current techniques. Philadelphia: FA Davis, 1992:386-443.

165. Bentley SA, Taylor MA, Killian DE, et al. Correction of bone marrow nucleated cell counts for the presence of fat particles. Am J Clin Pathol 1995;140:60-4.

166. Moss TJ. Detection of metastatic tumor cells in bone marrow. In: Gee AP, ed. Bone marrow processing and purging: A practical guide. Boca Raton, FL: CRC Press, 1991:121-35.

167. Pecora AL, Lazarus EM, Cooper B, et al. Breast cancer contamination in peripheral blood cell (PBPC) collections association with bone marrow disease and type of mobilization (abstract). Blood 1997;89(Suppl):99a.

168. Food and Drug Administration. A proposed approach to the regulation of cellular and tissue-based products (March 4, 1997). Fed Regist 1997;62:9721-2.

169. Food and Drug Administration. Human tissue intended for transplantation; final rule, 21 CFR 16 and 1270 (July 29, 1997). Fed Regist 1997;62:40429-47.

170. Food and Drug Administration. Guidance for industry: Screening and testing of donors of human tissue intended for transplantation. (July 29, 1997) Rockville, MD: CBER Office of Communication, Training, and Manufacturers Assistance, 1997.

171. Food and Drug Administration. Draft guidance for industry: Preventive measures to reduce possible risk of transmission of Creutzfeldt-Jakob disease (CJD) and variant Creutzfeldt-Jakob disease (vCJD) by human cells, tissues, and cellular and tissue-based products (HCT/Ps) (June 25, 2002). Fed Regist 2002;67:42789-90.

172. Food and Drug Administration. Request for proposed standards for unrelated allogeneic peripheral and placental/umbilical cord blood hematopoietic stem/progenitor cell products; request for comments (January 20, 1998). Fed Regist 1998;63:2985-8.

173. Food and Drug Administration. Current good tissue practice for human cell, tissue, and cellular and tissue-based product establishments; inspection and enforcement (November 24, 2004). Fed Regist 2004;69:68612-88.

174. AABB, American Red Cross, America's Blood Centers, American Society for Blood and Marrow Transplantation, Foundation for the Accreditation of Cellular Therapy, International Society for Cellular Therapy, National Marrow Donor Program. Circular of information for the use of cellular therapy products. Bethesda, MD: AABB, 2003.

Chapter 26

Tissue and Organ Transplantation

IN RECENT YEARS, the numbers of cornea, bone, skin, heart valve, and other tissue donations and transplants[1-3] have exceeded those of solid organs,[4] such as kidneys, livers, hearts, and lungs. The hospital blood bank, transfusion service, community blood center, and regional blood center are uniquely qualified to provide essential support for organ and tissue transplantation and to serve as tissue banks (Table 26-1).[5] It is common for hospital blood banks to provide transfusion support for organ and tissue recipients and, in some cases, to store, keep records of, and dispense tissue for allografts. AABB *Standards for Blood Banks and Transfusion Services*[6(pp8,14,15,60,79)] addresses the receipt, storage, transportation, and records of tissue allografts. Additional guidance for the collection and preparation of tissue and organ allografts is available from federal and state regulations, Public Health Service Guidelines, and the standards, guidelines, and technical manuals of other national or local organizations.[7-14]

Transplant-Transmitted Diseases and Preventive Measures

The widened availability of tissue and organ grafts has encouraged new clinical uses and highlighted not only their effectiveness and advantages but also their drawbacks, side effects, and complications. Organs and tissues can transmit bacterial, fungal, viral, and prion diseases from the donor to the recipient[3,15-26] (Table 26-2), but careful donor screening and testing, along with disinfection and sterilization steps for specific tissues, can markedly reduce the risk.

Table 26-1. Skills and Experience Appropriate for Institutions Undertaking Tissue Banking

- Community support
- Public accountability
- Public education with a broad-based public information system
- Donor recruitment
- Counseling
- Medical overview
- Donor selection
- Donor testing including automated virology testing to avoid transcription errors
- Cellular cryopreservation
- Temperature-controlled and monitored storage
- Regulatory compliance
- Transportation infrastructure
- Financial relations with hospitals
- Computerized inventory control
- Record-keeping
- Logistics management
- Investigation of adverse reactions
- Peer review of medical, scientific, and operational practice
- Recipient matching
- Concern over the balance of the adequacy and safety of supply
- Reputation for dependable service
- Commitment to research and development
- 24-hours-per-day, 7-days-per-week operation

Reproduced with permission from Warwick et al.[5]

Risk Reduction for Tissues

Crucial to the safety of transplanted tissue is an evaluation of the potential donor's eligibility. Listed below are the questions, examinations, and tests undertaken to ensure that material from the potential donor poses a low threat of disease transmission. Additional measures apply to reproductive tissue donors.[10,11]

1. Review of health history, through interviews with next of kin and/or significant other, and possibly health-care provider, and review of medical records. Review includes an evaluation (although not necessarily rejection for asterisked items*) of the potential donor for:

   a. History of infection,* malignant disease,* or neurodegenerative disease

   b. History of autoimmune processes*

   c. History of exposure to hormone derived from human pituitary gland or dura mater transplant

Table 26-2. Infectious Diseases Reported to Have Been Transmitted by Organ and Tissue Allografts[15-26]

Allograft	Infectious Disease/Disease Agent
Bone	HIV-1 Hepatitis C Hepatitis, unspecified type Bacteria Tuberculosis
Cornea	Hepatitis B Creutzfeldt-Jakob disease Rabies Cytomegalovirus (?) Bacteria Fungus
Dura mater	Creutzfeldt-Jakob disease
Heart valve	Hepatitis B Tuberculosis
Skin	Bacteria Cytomegalovirus (?) HIV-1 (?)
Pericardium	Creutzfeldt-Jakob disease Bacteria
Solid organ (eg, kidney, liver, heart)	HIV-1 Hepatitis B Hepatitis C Cytomegalovirus Epstein-Barr virus Parvovirus Toxoplasmosis Chagas' disease Malaria Bacteria Tuberculosis HHV-8 Strongyloidiasis Sarcoidosis West Nile virus Rabies Lymphocytic choriomeningitis

(cont'd)

Table 26-2. Infectious Diseases Reported to Have Been Transmitted by Organ and Tissue Allografts[15-26] (cont'd)

Allograft	Infectious Disease/Disease Agent
Pancreatic islet	Bacteria
Semen	Hepatitis B
	Hepatitis C (?)
	Gonorrhea
	Syphilis (?)
	HIV-1
	HTLV-I (?)
	Human papilloma virus (?)
	Trichomonas vaginalis
	Chlamydia trachomatis
	Cytomegalovirus (?)
	Ureaplasma urealyticum
	HSV-2
	Mycoplasma hominis
	Group B streptococcus

2. Review for evidence of high-risk behavior (exclusion for any of the donor-deferral criteria included in items 9c, 9e, and 10 of Standard 5.4.1A of *Standards for Blood Banks and Transfusion Services*.[6(pp62-65)]

3. Serologic testing on suitable blood specimens[10] (see below for more detail).
   a. Hepatitis B surface antigen (HBsAg)
   b. Antibodies to human immunodeficiency viruses 1 and 2 (anti-HIV-1 and -2)
   c. Antibody to hepatitis C virus (anti-HCV)
   d. Antibody to human T-cell lymphotropic virus types I and II (anti-HTLV-I and -II)
   e. Serologic test for syphilis

4. Physical examination to detect:
   a. Evidence of intravenous drug use
   b. Jaundice
   c. External signs of infection
   d. Signs of AIDS

5. Review of results of autopsy examination, if performed.

Consent and Donor Eligibility

Written consent for clinical use of any tissue or organ must be obtained from a living donor or from the next of kin of a deceased donor (formerly referred to as a cadaveric donor), except when corneas are procured under statutory consent. State and federal referral statutes and regulations exist, mandating that hospitals 1) maintain policies for notifying organ procurement organizations and appropriate tissue banks, including eye banks, when death of a patient has occurred or is imminent and 2) designate requestors to approach families about organ and tissue donation. All applicable federal, state, and local laws concerning the consent of next of kin must be obeyed. When the next of kin signs consent for tissue donation, he or she should specify which tissues may be donated and whether the permission includes tissue to be used for research or other specific uses.

Living donors and the families of deceased donors are not responsible for expenses involved in recovering and processing donated tissues and organs. Donors do not receive compensation for the donation, although donors of reproductive tissue are often compensated for their time, risk, and inconvenience, and donor families may receive incentives, such as a contribution toward funeral expenses, for donation from deceased donors. Tissues can be recovered up to 24 hours after death if the body is refrigerated within 12 hours of death. Tissues can be recovered up to 15 hours after death if not refrigerated. Organs must be recovered from a donor whose neurologic death has been declared and whose circulation has been maintained (see Table 26-3). Eyes as a source of corneal allografts should be removed as soon as possible after death to ensure viability of endothelial cells.

Each prospective deceased donor must be evaluated against eligibility criteria for the specific tissue(s) and organ(s) to be collected; eg, deceased newborns are not suitable for bone donation because of their cartilaginous skeletal structure but may be candidates for heart valve donation. Although exceptions may be made in specific cases, the medical eligibility of a donor is determined on the basis of absence of infection and malignancy as revealed by the medical history, physical examination, laboratory tests, and autopsy, if performed.

Donation of organs and tissues does not ordinarily cause delays in funerals or prevent family viewing of the body.

Serologic Testing

Federal regulations require that donors of tissues be tested for HBsAg, anti-HIV-1/2, and anti-HCV, and given a syphilis screening test, with tests licensed by the Food and Drug Administration (FDA). Testing must be performed by a laboratory that is certified under the provisions of the Clinical Laboratory Improvement Amendments of 1988[7,8] or that has met equivalent requirements as determined by the Centers for Medicare and Medicaid Services. A screening test approved for cadaveric specimens must be used when available.[27] National standard-setting organizations, such as the American Association of Tissue Banks (AATB),[10] Eye Bank Association of America (EBAA),[12] and the United Network for Organ Sharing (UNOS),[13] may require additional tests for infectious disease markers. The American Society for Reproductive Medicine also has issued recommendations for gamete and embryo donation.[11] For anonymous semen donors, tests for anti-HIV-1/2 and anti-HCV must be repeated on a sample obtained 6 months after donation and the results found negative before semen can be released for use.[9,10] Testing for anti-HBc must also be performed on this sample to rule out hepatitis B infection at the time of collection. ABO typing is required for organ grafts. HLA typing is essential for organ grafts and hematopoietic progenitor cells[13] but not for tissues.[28] Other tests, such as antibody to cytomegalovirus (anti-CMV), are also generally performed on organ donors. For deceased donors, tests are optimally performed on a blood sample obtained before administration of transfusions or fluids; these patients may have re-

Table 26-3. Kinds of Donors Providing Organs and Tissue for Transplantation

Living Donor	Deceased Donor (Neurologic Death)	Deceased Donor (Cardiorespiratory and Neurologic Death)
Amniotic membrane	Heart	Bone
Bone	Kidney	Cartilage
Fetal tissues (mother is the donor)	Liver	Cornea
Foreskin	Lung	Dura mater
Kidney	Pancreas (with or without small intestine)	Fascia lata
Liver		Heart valve
Lung		Marrow
Marrow		Pericardium
Milk		Skin
Pancreas		Tendon
Parathyroid (frequently autologous)		Vascular tissue
Peripheral blood progenitor cells		
Reproductive tissue		
Umbilical cord blood		
Umbilical vein		

ceived large volumes of replacement fluids shortly before death, and the consequent plasma dilution may cause false-negative results.[19,20]

If donor serum collected before blood transfusion or intravenous fluid administration is not available from other sources, a pretransfusion sample is often available from the blood bank because blood banks hold specimens collected for compatibility for at least 7 days. For samples obtained after transfusion or infusion of intravenous fluids, algorithms for determining the suitability of a donor sample are available.[7,8] For example, the sample is not suitable for infectious disease marker testing if either one of the following situations exists:

1. The total volume of colloid (plasma, dextran, platelets, or hetastarch) transfused in 48 hours plus the total volume of crystalloid infused in the hour before the sample is obtained exceed the patient's plasma volume.

2. The sum of the volume of blood transfused (RBCs, whole blood) and colloid transfused in 48 hours plus the total volume of crystalloid infused in the hour before the sample is obtained exceed the patient's blood volume.

Testing of cadaveric blood specimens can be complicated by postmortem hemolysis, which can cause misleading test results (eg, false-positive HBsAg).[15,29] Many tests licensed for use on blood donor specimens are not licensed for use with postmortem specimens, but licensed assays for postmortem specimens are available for anti-HIV-1/2, HBsAg, and HIV-1/HCV nucleic acid.[27]

Bone Banking

Except for blood cells, bone is the most commonly transplanted tissue[1] or organ. When bone grafting is needed, fresh autologous bone, usually removed from the iliac crest during surgery, is generally considered the most effective graft material. As with blood, the use of autologous bone for graft material is not risk free and there may be morbidity and infectious complications. The quantity of bone graft needed for some surgical procedures may make the use of autologous bone impractical. Allografts are used for these patients and for patients in whom the prolongation of surgery, extra bleeding, and potential complications of autograft collection are considered undesirable. Bone allografts have achieved widespread clinical application for acetabular and proximal femur support in revisions of failed hip prostheses; packing of benign bone cysts; spinal fusion to treat disc disease or scoliosis; reconstruction of maxillo-facial defects; and correction of healed fractures. Demineralized bone powder is commonly used by periodontal surgeons to restore alveolar bone in periodontal pockets.

The surgeon today has access to a wide choice of processed bone allografts: freeze-dried or frozen, cancellous or cortical, with or without treatment with sterilants. Common preparations include frozen or freeze-dried cancellous cubes or chips, cortical struts, and cortical-cancellous blocks and dowels. Bone can be stored frozen or, if freeze-dried to a low residual moisture content (6% or less by gravimetric analysis or 8% by nuclear magnetic resonance spectrometry), at room temperature for 5 years (Table 26-4). Frozen bone is processed aseptically, some without a microbial inactivation step. Such tissue carries a greater risk of bacterial contamination. A series of infection cases, including one death, linked to aseptically processed musculoskeletal allografts underscores the importance of recovery cultures of donated tissue.[24] Freeze-dried tissue has undergone extensive processing to remove blood and marrow and may have been exposed to alcohol. Thus, the risk of disease transmission is reduced. Most bone allografts used in the United States are freeze-dried to simplify storage. Some grafts, whether frozen or freeze-dried, may be treated with gamma irradiation or ethylene oxide to reduce the risk of infectious disease transmission. Demineralization of bone is believed to make its proteins and growth factors more readily available, thereby enhancing its capacity to promote healing and bone formation.

The implantation of frozen bone allografts has stimulated blood group antibodies that have been implicated in hemolytic disease of the newborn. Frozen, unprocessed bone allografts contain sufficient red cells to stimulate production of Rh and other red cell antibodies. When indicated, the risk of blood group sensitization can be avoided by using processed frozen or freeze-dried bone allograft, both of which are devoid of blood cells and marrow. With these grafts, matching blood groups of donors and recipients is not necessary. When using unprocessed frozen bone in Rh-negative females with childbearing potential, it is advisable to use bone from Rh-negative donors to prevent alloimmunization or administer Rh immune globulin prophylactically. There is no evidence to date that ABO or Rh incompatibility between the bone

Table 26-4. Recommended Preservation Conditions and Dating Periods for Human Tissue and Organs

	Storage Condition	Dating Period
Tissue		
Bone	−40 C	5 years*
	−20 C	6 months
	1-10 C	5 days
	Liquid nitrogen	Not defined
	Lyophilized, room temperature	5 years*
Tendon	−40 C	5 years*
Fascia lata	Lyophilized, room temperature	5 years*
	−40 C	5 years*
Articular cartilage	−40 C	5 years*
	1-10 C	5 days
	Liquid nitrogen, immersed	Not defined
Skin	1-10 C	14 days
	−40 C	Not defined
	Lyophilized, room temperature	Not defined
Cornea	2-6 C	14 days
Hematopoietic progenitor cells	Liquid nitrogen, immersed	Not defined
	Liquid nitrogen, vapor phase	Not defined
Semen	Liquid nitrogen, immersed	Not defined
	Liquid nitrogen, vapor phase	Not defined
Heart valve, vein, artery	−100 C	Not defined
Dura mater	Lyophilized, room temperature	Not defined
Organ		
Kidney	Refrigerated	48-72 hours
Liver	Refrigerated	8-24 hours
Heart	Refrigerated	3-5 hours
Heart-lung	Refrigerated	3-5 hours
Pancreas	Refrigerated	12-24 hours

*Unless a longer dating period has been validated by the processor.

donor and recipient has an adverse effect on the success of the bone graft.[30]

Skin Banking

A human skin allograft is the dressing of choice for deep burn wounds if sufficient amounts of skin for autografting are unavailable. A skin allograft provides temporary coverage; speeds reepithelialization; acts as a metabolic barrier against loss of water, electrolytes, protein, and heat; and provides a physical barrier to bacterial infection. Skin allografts are replaced periodically until sufficient autograft skin can be obtained. A skin allograft may also be used for donor sites for pedicle flaps and skin autografts, and for traumatically denuded areas or unhealed areas of chronic injury, such as decubitus ulcers.

Following preparation, skin donation involves removing a layer of skin approximately 0.015 inch thick. After collection, refrigerated skin can be stored at 1 to 10 C for up to 14 days. For refrigerated storage, standard tissue-culture nutrient media are used, with added antibiotics. Skin can be frozen soon after collection, usually with 10% to 15% glycerol, although dimethyl sulfoxide (DMSO) is an acceptable alternative.[31] Skin is often cryopreserved on fine-mesh gauze in flat cryopreservation bags. Cryogenic damage is minimized by controlled-rate freezing at about 1 C per minute, or by freezing, using a validated heat sinking method, followed by storage in liquid nitrogen or in a mechanical freezer at a temperature colder than –40 C. Alternatively, skin placed in aluminum plates inside insulated boxes can be placed directly into a –40 C mechanical freezer. This simple process also provides a slow, predictable freezing rate and maintains cellular viability. The optimal freezing procedure and the maximal storage period that maintain viability and structural integrity in the frozen state have not been determined. Skin should be transported to the operating room on wet ice if stored at 4 C, or on dry ice if cryopreserved. A variety of bioengineered skin substitutes, such as cultured keratinocyte allografts and autografts, are available for treatment of acute and chronic wounds. Keratinocytes extracted from foreskin can be seeded onto biodegradable platforms to create bioengineered tissue products used in wound healing or as cadaveric skin substitutes for burns.[32]

Heart Valves

Human heart valve allografts provide long-term function for valve replacement—superior to that of mechanical or porcine valves. Recipients of human heart valve allografts do not require anticoagulation and the incidence of thromboembolism is low. These allografts may rarely transmit bacterial or fungal infection. They are the graft of choice for children, to avoid long-term anticoagulation; for pregnant women, to avoid teratogenic risks of anticoagulants; and for patients with infection at the aortic root. Despite their advantages, widespread use of human valve allografts has been slow because implantation is technically difficult and appropriate size valve allografts are not always readily available.

To obtain allograft valves, hearts are aseptically collected in an operating room, autopsy room, or morgue. Subsequently, in the tissue bank, the pulmonic and aortic valves are dissected out, cryopreserved with DMSO, and stored in liquid nitrogen. Compared with valves stored at 5 C in antibiotics and culture medium, cryopreserved heart valves are associated with increased cell viability; reduced incidence of valve degeneration, rupture, and leaflet perforation; and reduced occurrence of valve-related death.[33]

Records of Stored Tissue Allografts

In two cases in which HIV and HCV were transmitted (through unprocessed frozen bone or organs and tendon allografts, respectively) from two deceased donors to multiple recipients,[22,23] investigations revealed that several hospitals had insufficient records to identify recipients of other tissue from the same infected donors. Voluntary standards of national professional associations and government regulations require tissue banks to have a record-keeping system that identifies the donor and allows tracking of any tissue from the donor (or supplier source) to the consignee.[6(pp12,47,79),10,14,34] Records must show the source facility, the identification number of the donor or lot, storage temperatures, and final disposition of each tissue. These records must be retained at least 10 years beyond the distribution date, transplantation date, disposition date, or expiration date, whichever is latest. Donor eligibility records for dura mater must be retained indefinitely. Hospitals should also have records that identify recipients who received tissue from a specific donor or tissue lot. Hospitals should have procedures in place to recognize adverse outcomes of tissue use and to report them to the tissue bank supplying the tissue.

FDA Regulation of Tissue

The FDA regulates human tissue collected for transplantation.[7,8] There are requirements for infectious disease testing, donor screening, and record-keeping. A tissue establishment must have and follow written, validated procedures to prevent contamination and cross-contamination during processing.[7,35] The FDA has published rules for determining eligibility for donation of human cells, tissues, and cellular and tissue-based products (HCT/Ps)[36] that became effective May 25, 2005. Federal rules also require all facilities that recover, process, store, or distribute HCT/Ps or screen or test the donor to register with the agency and list their products by mailing or faxing Form FDA 3356.[37] Information may be submitted electronically at the FDA website www.fda.gov/cber/tissue/tisreg.htm. Products not covered by these regulations include xenogeneic tissue, vascularized organs, transfusable blood products, products used in the propagation of cells or tissues, and products that are secreted or extracted from cells or tissues. Minimally manipulated marrow, such as marrow that undergoes cell separation, the relevant characteristics of which are not altered by the processing, is not covered.

Under the federal regulations, infectious disease testing is required for allogeneic tissues, except reproductive tissue from sexually intimate partners. Current good tissue practice rules to address concerns about proper handling, storage and processing of tissue have been finalized.[34] Until such time that the comprehensive regulatory framework for human cells, tissues, and cellular and tissue-based products is effective, including donor eligibility requirements, good tissue practice regulations, and appropriate enforcement provisions, human dura mater and human heart valves will remain subject to the medical devices requirements under the Federal Food, Drug, and Cosmetic Act.[38] Federal regulation of tissue banks, formerly under the purview of the FDA's Center for Biologics Research and Review, Office of Blood Research and Review, is now the responsibility of the Center for Biologics Evaluation and Research, Office of Cellular, Tissue, and Gene Therapies' Division of Human Tissues.

The Importance of ABO Compatibility

The ABO antigens are important in transplantation practice because they constitute very strong histocompatibility antigens that are expressed on vascular endothelium. Major ABO mismatching can cause rapid graft rejection due to endothelial damage by ABO antibodies and subsequent widespread thrombosis within the graft. ABO matching is important to the success of vascularized grafts (ie, kidney,[39] heart, liver, and pancreas), but ABO matching is not important in tissue grafts (ie, fascia, bone, heart valves, skin, and cornea).[40]

The definition of an ABO-compatible graft is the same as that for a red cell transfusion. A group O donor of tissue or organ is a universal donor whose graft can be transplanted into recipients of all blood groups. Case reports document rare successful organ transplants with major ABO incompatibility, but these are few in number.[41] In some cases, A_2 donor kidneys can be successfully transplanted into group O recipients with survival comparable to that of group O donor kidneys.[42] ABO-incompatible transplants have occurred, often with fatal results, due to errors of record-keeping or labeling. It has been estimated that inadvertent ABO-incompatible heart or kidney transplants occur with a frequency of 1 per 1000.[43] This underscores the importance of a final ABO check of donor and recipient blood at the transplant facility to reduce this risk.

The Role of Transfusion in Kidney Transplants

In 1973, Opelz et al[44] noted decreasing kidney allograft survival when hemodialysis staff attempted to avoid priming the dialysis equipment with blood and to limit pretransplant blood transfusions. The association between fewer transfusions and declining renal allograft survival led transplant centers to initiate deliberate pretransplant transfusion protocols in the mid-1970s. Subsequent studies have supported the theory that pretransplant blood transfusions enhance renal allograft survival through mechanisms of inducing tolerance that remain imperfectly understood.[45,46] However, with the availability of cyclosporine and other immunosuppressive agents, interest in this approach has waned.[47] If the controversial practice of transfusion to induce tolerance in patients before transplantation is begun, nonleukocyte-reduced Red Blood Cells (RBCs) should be used.[48,49] The introduction of erythropoietin has reduced the need for red cell transfusions in patients awaiting a renal transplant.

Liver Transplants

A liver transplant program presents one of the greatest challenges to the donor center and hospital transfusion service, demanding maximal support in terms of preparedness, supply, and responsiveness. Massive blood loss and hypocoagulability due to preexisting liver disease and/or the anhepatic interval during the procedure create complex problems for the transfusion service. The liver is the major site for synthesis of clotting factors and other essential proteins and is a prime regulator of acid-base, electrolyte, and glucose homeostasis. The three surgical phases of the procedure—recipient hepatectomy, anhepatic interval, and biliary reconstruction—seriously derange these functions.

Support Required

To achieve a successful liver transplant program, a major commitment to this support is required. A successful program requires cooperation and communication among the hospital administration; operating room and intensive care unit; respiratory therapy, radiology, gastroenterology, and anesthesiology services; the coagulation and transfusion laboratories; and the regional donor center. The institutional commitment must extend 24 hours a day, 365 days a year, because there may be no more than a few hours' advance notice of a liver transplant. Consistent availability of blood bank staff on short notice is essential to meet the transfusion requirements. The surgical procedure frequently takes place at night or on weekends because of the availability of the donor organ and in order to avoid disrupting the operating room schedule. The surgical procedure takes an average of 6 to 8 hours but may take up to 24 hours and involve massive blood use and several surgical teams.

The blood bank should be notified as soon as the donor organ becomes available and the decision for transplantation is made. The blood bank obtains a generous blood sample from the recipient for crossmatching, but there may be more than one patient waiting for a liver and the surgeons may be undecided about the specific recipient. Therefore, the blood bank may have to perform numerous crossmatches for patients who may have different ABO groups and/or Rh types. Liver transplant programs initially used hundreds of units of blood and components per patient. Although blood use has steadily declined over the years, liver transplant procedures frequently use a volume of blood components equal to one whole-body blood volume and sometimes several blood volumes. Intraoperative blood recovery frequently plays a major role in the conservation of red cells in such cases.

Considerations of ABO and Rh

Except in emergencies, donor livers should be ABO-compatible with the recipient. ABO-identical RBCs and Fresh Frozen Plasma (FFP) are generally used for transfusion support of group O and group A recipients. Group B recipients who need large quantities of red cells can be switched to group O RBCs. Group AB recipients needing massive transfusion are often switched to group A RBCs to conserve group O RBCs for other patients. If the supply of AB FFP is insufficient, early use of group A RBCs followed by a switch to group A FFP is appropriate. A general rule for massive transfusions is to switch red cells first, then switch plasma, and reverse the order when returning to the patient's original blood group.[46]

Special considerations apply to the recipient of an out-of-group but ABO-compatible liver transplant. In a group A patient receiving a group O liver, lymphocytes of donor origin may produce ABO antibodies that cause hemolysis that begins several days after the procedure and may continue for 2 weeks or longer.[50] Although passenger lymphocytes may produce antibodies in any out-of-group but compatible combination, significant hemolysis is seen most often in the recipient of a group O liver.

Transfusion support of Rh-negative patients not immunized to the D antigen is not standardized.[46] Because successful pregnancy has occurred after liver transplantation, most programs consider it preferable to provide D-negative units to D-negative females with childbearing potential, if needs are expected to be moderate. Should massive blood loss occur, the patient could be switched intraoperatively to D-positive blood, if necessary. For premenopausal females without anti-D, some programs reserve 10 units of D-negative RBCs; if more than 10 units are required, they switch to D-positive blood.[46] Production of anti-D occurs less frequently in D-negative liver transplant patients exposed to the D antigen than in other D-negative patients.[51] In some programs, patients without anti-D who are D-negative postmenopausal females or D-negative males are transfused exclusively with D-positive blood.

Red Cell Alloantibodies

Liver transplant patients with clinically significant red cell alloantibodies represent a special challenge to blood banks. Sometimes, a sufficient quantity of antigen-negative blood can be secured before surgery. Some programs reserve a limited number of antigen-negative units for use at the beginning of surgery, when alloantibody is present, and at the end of massive blood loss, when transfused cells are expected to remain in circulation. Antibody screening during the interval of massive blood loss can help guide use of antigen-positive units during surgery.

Coagulation Considerations

During surgery, hemodilution, platelet consumption, disordered thrombin regulation, and fibrinolysis derange the hemostatic process. The coagulopathy is especially severe during the anhepatic and early reperfusion stage. The following tests are useful: the hematocrit guides the use of red cells, colloids, and crystalloids; the platelet count guides transfusion of platelets; the prothrombin time and activated partial thromboplastin time guide FFP use; and fibrinogen determinations guide use of Cryoprecipitated AHF and antifibrinolytic agents.[46,52,53]

Other Organ Transplants

Blood bank support for cardiac transplantation is very similar to that routinely used for other surgical procedures in which cardiopulmonary bypass is employed. The blood bank may also provide ABO testing and assist in the release of ABO-compatible organs to prevent ABO-mismatched organ transplantation. Pancreatic transplants have comparatively low transfusion requirements, but a specimen from the recipient should routinely be examined for clinically significant unexpected red cell antibodies; in some institutions, the protocol calls for crossmatching several units.

Transfusion Service Support for Organ Transplantation

The blood bank provides vital support for a clinical transplantation program. Close communication with the surgeons and other professionals involved in the program is essential. Transfusion practices in the peritransplant period have a major effect on morbidity, mortality, and graft survival rates.

Potential recipients of solid organ transplants are generally available well before the procedure, so there is ample time to obtain a history and perform laboratory tests. It is important for the transfusion service to know if there have been previous pregnancies, transplants, or transfusions.

Laboratory tests routinely performed include: ABO group and Rh type, the direct antiglobulin test (DAT), a screen for unexpected red cell antibodies, and determination of CMV serostatus. HLA typing and HLA antibody studies are routine for organ recipients.

Passenger lymphocyte hemolysis (typically "ABO"-incompatible hemolysis), as discussed previously in regard to liver transplantation, can occur with other solid organ transplants, such as lung, heart, and kidney. In the case of a recipient receiving an ABO-compatible but non-group-identical organ, prophylactic use of mutually ABO-compatible erythrocytes (compatible for the donor and the recipient) has been suggested for intraoperative and postoperative infusions, during the first postoperative month, or at the appearance of an antibody. At present, there is no consensus on this issue. It is important to remember that if immediate-spin or computer cross-matching is routinely performed after an ABO-unmatched transplant, ABO incompatibility due to these IgG antibodies may be missed. In such cases, the routine use of a crossmatch with an antihuman globulin phase or the use of a DAT (which may detect such cases earlier than a crossmatch) is recommended. If ABO hemolysis is present, the patient should be transfused with group O RBCs.

CMV infection, a serious and often fatal complication in transplant recipients, is related to the presence of CMV in the donor and recipient and the degree to which the recipient is immunosuppressed. The primary test used to determine CMV status is the demonstration of circulating antibody. CMV-seronegative recipients of CMV-seronegative transplants characteristically receive transfusion components processed to reduce risk of CMV transmission, either by preparation from seronegative donors or by leukocyte reduction to 5×10^6 cells/component or below.

References

1. Strong M, Eastlund T, Mowe J. Tissue bank activity in the United States: 1992 survey of AATB-inspected tissue banks. Tissue Cell Rep 1996;3:15-18.
2. 2002 EBAA statistical report. Washington, DC: Eye Bank Association of America, 2002.
3. Yap PL. Viral transmission by blood, organs and tissues. J Hosp Infect 1999;43(Suppl):S137-44.
4. The Organ Procurement and Transplantation Network data reports, 2003. Richmond, VA: United Network for Organ Sharing, 2003.
5. Warwick RM, Eastlund T, Fehily D. Role of the blood transfusion service in tissue banking. Vox Sang 1996;71:71-7.
6. Silva MA, ed. Standards for blood banks and transfusion services. 23rd ed. Bethesda, MD: AABB, 2005.
7. Food and Drug Administration. Human tissue intended for transplantation. Fed Regist 1997; 62:40429-47.
8. Food and Drug Administration. Guidance for industry: Screening and testing of donors of human tissue intended for transplantation. (July 1997) Rockville, MD: CBER Office of Communication, Training, and Manufacturers Assistance, 1997.
9. Centers for Disease Control and Prevention. Guidelines for preventing HIV transmission through organ and tissue transplantation. MMWR 1994;43(RR-8):1-17.
10. Woll J, Kasprisin D, eds. Standards for tissue banking. McLean, VA: American Association of Tissue Banks, 2002.
11. American Society for Reproductive Medicine. Guidelines for gamete and embryo donation. Fertil Steril 2002;77:Suppl 5.
12. Medical standards of EBAA. Washington, DC: Eye Bank Association of America, 2002.
13. Articles of incorporation, by-laws, and policies of UNOS. Richmond, VA: United Network of Organ Sharing, 2004 (revised at least annually).
14. New York State Department of Health. Tissue banks and nontransplant anatomic banks, Part 52. New York State Codes, Rules, and Regulations, Title 10. Albany, NY: New York State Department of Health, 2004. (Available at http://www.wadsworth.org/labert/blood_tissue.)
15. Eastlund T. Infectious disease transmission through cell, tissue and organ transplantation. Reducing the risk through donor selection. Cell Transplant 1995;4:455-77.
16. Eastlund T, Strong DM. Infectious disease transmission through tissue transplantation. In: Phillips GO, ed. Advances in tissue banking. Vol. 7. Singapore: World Scientific, 2004:51-132.
17. CJD and the eye. Monograph 7. London: Royal College of Ophthalmologists, 1998.
18. Hogan RN, Brown P, Heck E, Cavanagh HD. Risk of prion disease transmission from ocular tissue transplantation. Cornea 1999;18:2-11.

19. Human immunodeficiency virus transmitted from an organ donor screened for HIV antibody—North Carolina. MMWR Morb Mortal Wkly Rep 1987;36:306-8.

20. Eastlund T. Hemodilution due to blood loss and transfusion and reliability of cadaver tissue donor infectious disease testing. Cell and Tissue Banking 2000;1:121-7.

21. Linden JV, Critser JK. Therapeutic insemination by donor II: A review of the known risks. Reprod Med Rev 1995;4:19-29.

22. Simonds RJ, Holmberg SD, Hurwitz RL, et al. Transmission of human immunodeficiency virus type 1 from a seronegative organ and tissue donor. N Engl J Med 1992;326:726-32.

23. Conrad EU, Gretch D, Obermeyer K, et al. The transmission of hepatitis C virus by tissue transplantation. J Bone Joint Surg 1995;77A: 214-23.

24. Kainer MA, Linden JV, Whaley DN, et al. Clostridium infections associated with musculoskeletal-tissue allografts. N Engl J Med 2004;350:2564-71.

25. Centers for Disease Control and Prevention. Investigation of rabies infections in organ donor and transplant recipients—Alabama, Arkansas, Oklahoma, and Texas, 2004. MMWR Morb Mortal Wkly Rep 2004;53:586-9.

26. Centers for Disease Control and Prevention. Lymphocytic choriomeningitis virus infection in organ transplant recipients—Massachusetts, Rhode Island, 2005. MMWR Morb Mortal Wkly Rep 2005;54:537-9.

27. Food and Drug Administration. Guidance for industry: Availability of licensed donor screening tests for use with cadaveric blood specimens. (June 23, 2000) Rockville, MD: CBER Office of Communication, Training, and Manufacturers Assistance, 2000.

28. Choo SY, Eastlund T. Tissue transplantation and HLA typing. Tissue Cell Rep 1995;2:3-4.

29. LeFor WM, McGonigle AF, Wright CE, Shires DL. The frequency of false positive HBsAg screening test results with cadaver tissue donors is dependent upon the assay procedure used. Tissue Cell Rep 1996;3:6-170.

30. Eastlund T. Bone transplantation and bone banking. In: Lonstein JE, Bradford DS, Winter RB, Ogilvie JW, eds. Moe's textbook of scoliosis and other spinal deformities. 3rd ed. Philadelphia: WB Saunders, 1995:581-95.

31. Bravo D, Rigley TH, Gibran N, et al. Effect of storage and preservation methods on viability of transplantable human skin allografts. Burns 2000;26:367-78.

32. Phillips TJ. New skin for old: Developments in biological skin substitutes. Arch Dermatol 1998;134:344-9.

33. O'Brien MF, Stafford EG, Gardner MAH, et al. Cryopreserved viable allograft aortic valves. In: Yankoh AC, Hetzer R, Miller DC, et al, eds. Cardiac valve allografts 1972-1987. New York: Springer-Verlag, 1988:311-21.

34. Food and Drug Administration. Current good tissue practice for human cell, tissue, and cellular and tissue-based product establishments; inspection and enforcement; final rule. (November 4, 2004) Fed Regist 2004;69:68611-88.

35. Food and Drug Administration. Guidance for Industry. Validation of procedures for processing human tissues intended for transplantation. (March 2002) Rockville, MD: CBER Office of Communications, Training, and Manufacturers Assistance, 2002.

36. Food and Drug Administration. Eligibility determination for donors of human cells, tissues, and cellular and tissue-based products; final rule. Fed Regist 2004;69:29786-834.

37. Food and Drug Administration. Human cells, tissues, and cellular and tissue-based products; establishment registration and listing; final rule. Fed Regist 2001;66:5447-69.

38. Food and Drug Administration. Human cells, tissues, and cellular and tissue-based products; establishment registration and listing; interim final rule; opportunity for public comment. Fed Regist 2004;69:3823-6.

39. Alkhunaizi AM, de Mattos AM, Barry JM, et al. Renal transplantation across the ABO barrier using A_2 kidneys. Transplantation 1999;67: 1319-24.

40. Eastlund T. The histo-blood group ABO system and tissue transplantation. Transfusion 1998;38:975-88.

41. Alexandre GPJ, Squifflet JP, DeBruyere M, et al. ABO-incompatible related and unrelated living donor renal allografts. Transplant Proc 1986;18:1090-2.

42. Breimer ME, Brynger H, Rydberg L, et al. Transplantation of blood group A_2 kidneys to O recipients. Biochemical and immunological studies of group A antigens in human kidneys. Transplant Proc 1985;17:2640-3.

43. Terasaki PI. Red-cell crossmatching for heart transplants (letter). N Engl J Med 1991;325: 1748-9.

44. Opelz G, Sengar DPS, Mickey MR, Terasaki P. Effect of blood transfusion on subsequent kidney transplants. Transplant Proc 1973;5: 253-9.

45. Blumberg N, Heal JM. Transfusion immunomodulation. In: Anderson KC, Ness PM, eds. Scientific basis of transfusion medicine. 2nd ed. Philadelphia:WB Saunders, 2000:427-43.

46. Dzik WH. Solid organ transplantation. In: Petz LD, Swisher SN, Kleinman S, et al, eds. Clinical practice of transfusion medicine. 3rd

ed. New York: Churchill Livingstone, 1996: 783-806.

47. Lundgren G, Groth CG, Albrechtsen D, et al. HLA matching and pretransplant blood transfusions in cadaveric renal transplantation—a changing picture with cyclosporin. Lancet 1986;ii:66-9.

48. Iwaki Y, Cecka JM, Terasaki PI. The transfusion effect in cadaver kidney transplants, yes or no. Transplantation 1990;49:56-9.

49. Opelz G, Vanrenterghem Y, Kirste G, et al. Prospective evaluation of pretransplant blood transfusions in cadaver kidney recipients. Transplantation 1997;63:964-7.

50. Triulzi DJ, Shirey RS, Ness PM, Klein AS. Immunohematologic complications of ABO-unmatched liver transplants. Transfusion 1992;32:829-33.

51. Casanueva M, Valdes MD, Ribera MC. Lack of alloimmunization to D antigen in D-negative immunosuppressed liver transplant recipients. Transfusion 1994;34:570-2.

52. Triulzi DJ, Bontempo FA, Kiss JE, Winkelstein A. Transfusion support in liver transplantation. Transfus Sci 1993;14:345-52.

53. Motschman TL, Taswell HF, Brecher ME, et al. Blood bank support of a liver transplantation program. Mayo Clin Proc 1989;64:103-11.

Chapter 27

Noninfectious Complications of Blood Transfusion

THIS CHAPTER ADDRESSES four broad categories of transfusion reactions: 1) acute immunologic, 2) acute nonimmunologic, 3) delayed immunologic, and 4) delayed nonimmunologic complications, as shown in Table 27-1.[1,2] For each individual type of reaction, the pathophysiology, treatment, and prevention are discussed. More detailed coverage is available elsewhere.[1] Infectious risks of transfusion are discussed in Chapter 28.

Manifestations

All personnel involved in ordering and administering transfusions must be able to recognize a transfusion reaction so that appropriate actions can be taken promptly. Listed below are signs and symptoms that are typically associated with acute transfusion reactions and can aid in their recognition. In general, one should consider any adverse manifestation occurring at the time of the transfusion to be a transfusion reaction until proven otherwise.

- Fever with or without chills [generally defined for surveillance purposes as a 1 C (2 F) increase in body temperature] associated with transfusion. Fever is the most common symptom of a hemolytic transfusion reaction (HTR),[3] but more frequently it has other causes.

- Shaking chills (rigors) with or without fever.

- Pain at the infusion site or in the chest, abdomen, or flanks.

- Blood pressure changes, usually acute, either hypertension or hypotension. Circulatory shock in combination with fever, severe chills, and high-output cardiac failure suggests acute

Table 27-1. Categories and Management of Adverse Transfusion Reactions*

Acute (<24 hours) Transfusion Reactions–Immunologic

Type	Incidence	Etiology	Presentation	Diagnostic Testing	Therapeutic/Prophylactic Approach
Hemolytic	1:38,000-1:70,000	Red cell incompatibility	Chills, fever, hemoglobinuria, hypotension, renal failure with oliguria, DIC (oozing from IV sites), back pain, pain along infusion vein, anxiety	■ Clerical check ■ DAT ■ Visual inspection (free Hb) ■ Repeat patient ABO, pre- and posttransfusion sample ■ Further tests as indicated to define possible incompatibility ■ Further tests as indicated to detect hemolysis (LDH, bilirubin, etc)	■ Keep urine output >100 mL/hr with fluids and IV diuretic (furosemide) ■ Analgesics (may need morphine) ■ Pressors for hypotension (low-dose dopamine) ■ Hemostatic components (platelets, cryo, FFP) for bleeding
Fever/chill, nonhemolytic	RBCs: 1:200-1:17 (0.5-6%) Plts: 1:100-1:3 (1-38%)	■ Antibody to donor WBCs ■ Accumulated cytokines in platelet unit	Fever, chills/rigors, headache, vomiting	■ Rule out hemolysis (DAT, inspect for hemoglobinemia, repeat patient ABO) ■ Rule out bacterial contamination ■ WBC antibody screen	■ Antipyretic premedication (acetaminophen, no aspirin) ■ Leukocyte-reduced blood
Urticarial	1:100-1:33 (1-3%)	Antibody to donor plasma proteins	Urticaria, pruritis, flushing	■ Rule out hemolysis (DAT, inspect for hemoglobinemia, repeat patient ABO)	■ Antihistamine, treatment or premedication (PO or IV) ■ May restart unit slowly after antihistamine if symptoms resolve

Reaction	Incidence	Cause	Signs/Symptoms	Laboratory Evaluation	Management
Anaphylactic	1:20,000-1:50,000	Antibody to donor plasma proteins (includes IgA, haptoglobin, C4)	Hypotension, urticaria, bronchospasm (respiratory distress, wheezing), local edema, anxiety	■ Rule out hemolysis (DAT, inspect for hemoglobinemia, repeat patient ABO) ■ Anti-IgA ■ IgA, quantitative	■ Trendelenberg (feet up) position ■ Fluids ■ Epinephrine (adult dose: 0.3-0.5 mL of 1:1000 solution SC or IM; in severe cases, 1:10,000 IV) ■ Antihistamines, corticosteroids, beta-2 agonists ■ IgA-deficient blood components
Transfusion-related acute lung injury	1:5,000-1:190,000	WBC antibodies in donor (occasionally in recipient), other WBC-activating agents in components	Hypoxemia, respiratory failure, hypotension, fever, bilateral pulmonary edema	■ Rule out hemolysis (DAT, inspect for hemoglobinemia, repeat patient ABO) ■ WBC antibody screen in donor and recipient. If positive, antigen typing may be indicated ■ WBC crossmatch ■ Chest X-ray	■ Supportive care until recovery ■ Defer implicated donors

Acute (<24 hours) Transfusion Reactions—Nonimmunologic

Reaction	Incidence	Cause	Signs/Symptoms	Laboratory Evaluation	Management
Transfusion-associated sepsis	Varies by component (see Chapter 28)	Bacterial contamination	Fever, chills, hypotension	■ Gram's stain ■ Culture of component ■ Patient culture ■ Rule out hemolysis (DAT, inspect for hemoglobinemia, repeat patient ABO)	■ Broad spectrum antibiotics (until sensitivities completed) ■ Treat complications (eg, shock)

(cont'd)

Table 27-1. Categories and Management of Adverse Transfusion Reactions* (cont'd)

Type	Incidence	Etiology	Presentation	Diagnostic Testing	Therapeutic/Prophylactic Approach
Hypotension associated with ACE inhibition	Dependent on clinical setting	Inhibited metabolism of bradykinin with infusion of bradykinin (negatively charged filters) or activators of prekallikrein	Flushing, hypotension	■ Rule out hemolysis (DAT, inspect for hemoglobinemia, repeat patient ABO)	■ Withdraw ACE inhibition ■ Avoid albumin volume replacement for plasmapheresis ■ Avoid bedside leukocyte filtration
Circulatory overload	<1%	Volume overload	Dyspnea, orthopnea, cough, tachycardia, hypertension, headache	■ Chest X-ray	■ Upright posture ■ Oxygen ■ IV diuretic (furosemide) ■ Phlebotomy (250-mL increments)
Nonimmune hemolysis	Rare	Physical or chemical destruction of blood (heating, freezing, hemolytic drug or solution added to blood)	Hemoglobinuria, hemoglobinemia	■ Rule out patient hemolysis (DAT, inspect for hemoglobinemia, repeat patient ABO) ■ Test unit for hemolysis	■ Identify and eliminate cause
Air embolus	Rare	Air infusion via line	Sudden shortness of breath, acute cyanosis, pain, cough, hypotension, cardiac arrythmia	■ X-ray for intravascular air	■ Place patient on left side with legs elevated above chest and head
Hypocalcemia (ionized calcium)	Dependent on clinical setting	Rapid citrate infusion (massive transfusion of citrated blood, delayed metabolism of citrate, apheresis procedures)	Paresthesia, tetany, arrhythmia	■ Ionized calcium ■ Prolonged Q-T interval on electrocardiogram	■ Slow calcium infusion while monitoring ionized calcium levels in severe cases ■ PO calcium supplement for mild symptoms during apheresis procedures

| | Dependent on clinical setting | Rapid infusion of cold blood | Cardiac arrhythmia | Central body temperature | ■ Employ blood warmer |

Delayed (>24 hours) Transfusion Reactions—Immunologic

Alloimmuni-zation, RBC antigens	1:100 (1%)	Immune response to foreign antigens on RBCs, or WBCs and platelets (HLA)	Positive blood group antibody screening test	■ Antibody screen ■ DAT	■ Avoid unnecessary transfusions ■ Leukocyte-reduced blood
Alloimmuni-zation, HLA antigens	1:10 (10%)		Platelet refractoriness, delayed hemolytic reaction, hemolytic disease of the newborn	■ Platelet antibody screen ■ Lymphocytotoxicity test	■ Avoid unnecessary transfusions ■ Leukocyte-reduced blood
Hemolytic	1:11,000-1:5000	Anamnestic immune response to red cell antigens	Fever, decreasing hemoglobin, new positive antibody screening test, mild jaundice	■ Antibody screen ■ DAT ■ Tests for hemolysis (visual inspection for hemoglobinemia, LDH, bilirubin, urinary hemosiderin as clinically indicated)	■ Identify antibody ■ Transfuse compatible red cells as needed
Graft-vs-host disease	Rare	Donor lymphocytes engraft in recipient and mount attack on host tissues	Erythroderma, maculopapular rash, anorexia, nausea, vomiting, diarrhea, hepatitis, pancytopenia, fever	■ Skin biopsy ■ HLA typing	■ Corticosteroids, cytotoxic agents ■ Irradiation of blood components for patients at risk (including related donors and HLA-selected components)

(cont'd)

Table 27-1. Categories and Management of Adverse Transfusion Reactions* (cont'd)

Type	Incidence	Etiology	Presentation	Diagnostic Testing	Therapeutic/Prophylactic Approach
Posttransfusion purpura	Rare	■ Recipient platelet antibodies (apparent alloantibody, usually anti-HPA-1) destroy autologous platelets	Thrombocytopenic purpura, bleeding, 8-10 days after transfusion	■ Platelet antibody screen and identification	■ IGIV ■ HPA-1-negative platelets ■ Plasmapheresis
Immunomodulation	Unknown	Incompletely understood interaction of donor WBC or plasma factors with recipient immune system	Increased renal graft survival, infection rate, postresection tumor recurrence rate (controversial)	■ None specific	■ Avoid unnecessary transfusions ■ Autologous transfusion ■ Leukocyte-reduced red cells and platelets

Delayed (>24 hours) Transfusion Reactions–Nonimmunologic

Type	Incidence	Etiology	Presentation	Diagnostic Testing	Therapeutic/Prophylactic Approach
Iron overload	Typically after >100 RBC units	Multiple transfusions with obligate iron load in transfusion-dependent patient	Diabetes, cirrhosis, cardiomyopathy	■ Serum ferritin ■ Liver enzymes ■ Endocrine function tests	■ Desferioxamine (iron chelator)

*For platelet refractoriness, see Chapter 16; for septic transfusion reactions, see Table 28-1; for a recent summary of transfusion reactions, see Popovsky.[1]
ACE = angiotensin-converting enzyme; antibody screen = blood group antibody screening test; DAT = direct antiglobulin test; DIC = disseminated intravascular coagulation; FFP = Fresh Frozen Plasma; Hb = hemoglobin; IV = intravenous; IGIV = intravenous immunoglobulin; IM = intramuscular; LDH = lactate dehydrogenase; PO = by mouth; RBC = Red Blood Cell; SC = subcutaneous; WBC = White Blood Cell.

sepsis but may also accompany an acute HTR. Circulatory collapse without fever and chills may be the most prominent finding in anaphylaxis.

- Respiratory distress, including dyspnea, tachypnea, wheezing, or hypoxemia.
- Skin changes, including urticaria, pruritis (itching), flushing, or localized edema (angioedema).
- Nausea with or without vomiting.
- Darkened urine or jaundice. Dark urine may be the earliest indication of an acute hemolytic reaction in anesthetized patients.
- Bleeding or other manifestations of a consumptive coagulopathy.

Acute Transfusion Reactions

Immune-Mediated Hemolysis

Pathophysiology and Manifestations

The most severe hemolytic reactions occur when transfused red cells interact with preformed antibodies in the recipient. In contrast, the interaction of transfused antibodies with the recipient's red cells rarely causes symptoms. However, there may be accelerated red cell destruction, and plasma-containing products with high-titer ABO antibodies can cause acute hemolysis. The interaction of antibody with antigen on the red cell membrane can initiate a sequence of complement activation (see Chapter 11), cytokine and coagulation effects, and other elements of a systemic inflammatory response[4] that result in the clinical manifestations of a severe acute HTR. Severe symptoms can occur after the infusion of as little as 10 to 15 mL of ABO-incompatible red cells. In anesthetized patients who cannot report symptoms, the initial manifestations of an acute HTR may be hemoglobinuria, hypotension, or diffuse bleeding at the surgical site.

Such severe acute HTRs today are usually caused by ABO incompatibility[5] but occasionally may be caused by antibodies with other specificities.[6] In contrast, hemolysis of an entire unit of blood can occur in the virtual absence of symptoms[7] and may be a relatively slow process. In such cases, hemolysis is typically extravascular, without generation of significant systemic levels of inflammatory mediators.

Complement Activation. The binding of antibody to blood group antigens may activate complement, depending on the characteristics of both the antibody and the antigen, including antibody specificity, class, subclass, titer, and antigen density (see Chapter 11). C3 activation releases the anaphylatoxin C3a (see Chapter 11), and red cells coated with C3b are removed by phagocytes with complement receptors, more rapidly than if antibody is present alone. If the enzymatic cascade proceeds to completion and a membrane attack complex is assembled, intravascular hemolysis results, with the production of C5a, which is 100 times as potent an anaphylatoxin as C3a.[3] This sequence is characteristic of ABO incompatibility and causes the cardinal manifestations of hemoglobinemia and, if the renal threshold for hemoglobin is exceeded, hemoglobinuria.[8(p182)] Anaphylatoxins interact with a wide variety of cells, including monocytes/macrophages, granulocytes, platelets, vascular endothelial cells, and smooth muscle cells, the latter leading to hypotension and bronchospasm. Anaphylatoxins also cause the release or production of multiple local and systemic mediators, including granule enzymes, histamine and other vasoactive amines, kinins, oxygen radicals, leukotrienes, nitric oxide, and cytokines.[3] These mechanisms may cause manifestations that mimic allergy, such as flushing and rarely urticaria, wheezing and chest pain or tightness, and abdominal pain, nausea, and vomiting.

With most non-ABO blood group antibodies, complement activation is usually incomplete; hemoglobinemia is absent or mild, but the consequences of complement activation, most notably the release of anaphylatoxins and opsonization of red cells, may still have adverse effects.

Cytokines. The role of cytokines in inflammatory responses (see Chapter 11), including acute HTRs, is increasingly recognized.[9,10] The known activities of inflammatory cytokines, such as tumor necrosis factor α (TNFα), interleukin-1β and -6 (IL-1β, IL-6), and chemokines such as IL-8 and monocyte chemoattractant protein (MCP), suggest that they mediate some of the effects of alloimmune hemolysis. IL-1 and TNF cause fever and hypotension (particularly in synergy), stimulation of endothelial cells to increase expression of adhesion molecules and procoagulant activity, and recruitment and activation of neutrophils and platelets, perhaps through the induction of IL-8 and MCP. Incubation of whole blood with washed, ABO-incompatible red cells in vitro has been shown to cause dramatic increases in TNF, IL-8, and MCP. This cytokine response is complement dependent. A similar model of hemolysis resulting from anti-D (IgG) showed a different pattern of cytokine production with "high-level" responses of IL-8 and MCP and "low-level" responses of IL-1β, IL-6, and TNFα.[9,10]

The relevance of these in-vitro models to HTRs in vivo is suggested by a case in which TNFα and neutrophil elastase levels were found to be elevated when a group O patient received 100 mL of group A red cells; elevation of neutrophil elastase is consistent with IL-8 activity.[11] These findings may lead to new therapeutic options for patients. However, the complete role of cytokines in the consequences of immune hemolysis remains to be defined.

Coagulation Activation. Several mechanisms, including those listed above, may be responsible for abnormalities of coagulation in HTRs.[4] The antigen-antibody interaction may activate the "intrinsic" clotting cascade through Hageman factor. In addition, activated Hageman factor (Factor XIIa) acts on the kinin system to generate bradykinin; bradykinin increases capillary permeability and dilates arterioles, causing a decrease in systemic arterial pressure. Several factors cited above may increase the expression of tissue factor by leukocytes and endothelial cells, including activated complement components, TNFα, and IL-1β. Tissue factor activates the "extrinsic" coagulation pathway, and its release is associated with disseminated intravascular coagulation (DIC), which may, in turn, cause: 1) formation of thrombi within the microvasculature and ischemic damage to tissues and organs; 2) consumption of fibrinogen, platelets, and other coagulation factors; 3) activation of the fibrinolytic system and generation of fibrin degradation products. The outcome can be a hemorrhagic diathesis characterized by generalized oozing or uncontrolled bleeding.

Shock and Renal Failure. Considering the absolute mass of antigen and antibody—and the list of mediators that may be involved in HTRs, including anaphylatoxins, vasoactive amines, kinins, and cytokines—it may not be surprising that shock can occur. Hypotension provokes a compensatory sympathetic nervous system response that produces vasoconstriction in organs and tissues with a vascular bed rich in alpha-adrenergic receptors, notably, the renal, splanchnic, pulmonary, and cutaneous capillaries, aggravating ischemia in these sites.

Renal failure is another sequel of an acute HTR. Although free hemoglobin, historically considered the cause of renal failure, does impair renal function,[12] current thought attributes renal failure largely to hypotension, renal vasoconstriction, antigen-antibody complex deposition, and formation of thrombi in the renal vasculature, all of which compromise renal cortical blood supply.

Frequency

Clerical and other human errors leading to mistaken identity are the most common causes of ABO-incompatible transfusion, occurring either at pretransfusion sample collection, within the transfusion service, or at the time of blood administration. A study of reported transfusion errors in New York State over a 10-year period (the 1990s) estimated the incidence of ABO-incompatible red cell transfusions at 1:38,000. Correction for the expected rate of fortuitously compatible transfusions led to an estimate of the rate of mistransfusion of 1:14,000.[7] A survey of 3601 institutions by the College of American Pathologists found 843 acute HTRs reported over a 5-year period, of which 50 (6%) were fatal.[13] The Serious Hazards of Transfusion (SHOT) initiative in the United Kingdom and Republic of Ireland reported 161 cases of ABO-incompatible transfusion, with nine fatal cases (five definitely related deaths, one probably related death, and three possibly related deaths) in 5 years.[14] Although no precise denominator is available for these confidential reports, it is believed that over 90% of the total transfusions were reviewed and approximately 2.5 million RBC units were issued each year, for a rate of no less than 1 in 78,000. These values probably underestimate the true frequency, because even acute HTRs go unrecognized or unreported. Estimates of mortality rates from acute HTRs are generally in the range of 1 in 1,000,000 transfusions.[5,7,14]

Treatment

The treatment of an acute HTR depends on its severity.[4] Vigorous treatment of hypotension and promotion of adequate renal blood flow are the primary concerns. If shock can be prevented or adequately treated, progression to renal failure may be avoided. Adequacy of renal perfusion can be monitored by measurement of urine output, with a goal of maintaining urine flow rates above 100 mL/hour in adults for at least 18 to 24 hours. The usual first support is intravenous normal saline, but underlying cardiac and/or renal disease may complicate therapy, and it is important to avoid overhydration. Invasive monitoring of pulmonary capillary wedge pressure is recommended in guiding fluid therapy in the face of hemodynamic instability. Diuretics help to improve blood flow to the kidneys and increase urine output. Intravenous furosemide at a dose of 40 to 80 mg for an adult or 1 to 2 mg/kg for a child not only has a diuretic effect but also improves blood flow to the renal cortex. This dose may be repeated once, and the patient should be adequately hydrated. Mannitol, an osmotic diuretic, has been used in the past, but furosemide is better for maintaining renal cortical blood flow. If no diuretic response occurs within a few hours of instituting fluid and diuretic therapy, there is a strong likelihood that acute tubular necrosis has occurred, and further fluid administration may be harmful.

Treatment of hypotension with pressor agents that decrease renal blood flow, such as dopamine in higher doses, should be avoided if possible. The use of low-dose dopamine (2-5 μg/kg/minute), as an agent to protect renal function, has been recommended in the management of acute HTRs.[4] However, evidence suggests that it is not effective in this role, and it has many toxicities.[15]

Consumptive coagulopathy, with resultant bleeding or generalized oozing, may be a prominent clinical finding in some HTRs and may be the initial presentation in an anesthetized patient. Heparin has been recommended by some, both to forestall DIC when an ABO incompatibility is first discovered and to treat the established coagulopathy. Others believe the dangers of heparin outweigh its potential benefits, especially because the immune event that provoked the DIC is self-limited. Administration of Platelets, Fresh Frozen Plasma (FFP), and Cryoprecipitated AHF, a source of fibrinogen and Factor VIII, may be necessary. Red cell exchange may be considered in patients with a significant load of circulating incompatible red cells.

Acute hemolytic reactions are rare and few clinicians have first-hand experience with their treatment. Because medical management of an acute HTR is often complicated and may require aggressive interventions such as hemodialysis, consultation with physicians experienced in the organ systems most damaged or specialists in critical care medicine may be prudent when treating a patient with a severe acute HTR.

Prevention

Because clerical errors cause the majority of acute, immune-mediated HTRs, the best hope for prevention lies in preventing or detecting errors in every phase of the transfusion process. In each institution, there should be systems designed to prevent and detect errors in patient and unit identification at the time of phlebotomy (sample acquisition), at all steps in laboratory testing, at the time of issue, and when the transfusions are given. The SHOT reports document multiple errors in a majority of mistransfusion incidents and particularly emphasize the importance of the bedside check at the time of transfusion.[14] Ensuring that all clinical staff recognize the signs of acute reactions and stop the transfusion before a critical volume of blood has been administered is essential to preventing harm to the patient. Crucial in the prevention of transfusion mishaps are training and assessment of personnel performing transfusions. Active participation by physicians and management, as well as by nursing, technical, and clinical personnel, is essential.

Nonimmune-Mediated Hemolysis

Causes

Red cells may undergo in-vitro hemolysis if the unit is exposed to improper temperatures during shipping or storage or is mishandled at the time of administration. Malfunctioning blood warmers, use of microwave ovens or hot waterbaths, or inadvertent freezing may cause temperature-related damage. Mechanical hemolysis may be caused by the use of roller pumps (such as those used in cardiac bypass surgery), pressure infusion pumps, pressure cuffs, or small-bore needles.[16] Osmotic hemolysis in the blood bag or infusion set may result from the addition of drugs or hypotonic solutions. Inadequate deglycerolization of frozen red cells may cause the cells to hemolyze after infusion. Finally, hemolysis may be a sign of bacterial growth in blood units. In a patient with transfusion-associated hemolysis for which both immune and nonimmune causes have been eliminated, the possibility might be considered that the patient or donor has an intrinsic red cell defect, such as glucose-6-phosphatase dehydrogenase deficiency, causing coincidental hemolysis.

Treatment

Treatment depends on the severity of the reaction. If the patient develops a severe reaction with hypotension, shock, and renal dysfunction, intensive clinical management is required even before the cause of the mishap is investigated. If the patient exhibits only hemoglobinemia and hemoglobinuria, supportive therapy may be sufficient.

Prevention

There should be written procedures for all aspects of procuring, processing, and issuing blood, and administering transfusions. All staff should be trained in the proper use of equipment, intravenous solutions, and drugs used during the administration of blood and blood components. Equipment must be properly maintained and records kept of how and when items are used. Intravenous medications shall not be injected into blood bags, unless approved by the Food and Drug Administration (FDA) or documented to be safe for that purpose,[17(p48)] and care must be exercised in the selection and use of intravenous access devices. Chapter 22 discusses the details of administering transfusions.

Transfusion-Associated Sepsis

Bacterial contamination of transfused blood should be considered if the patient experiences severe rigors, especially if they are accompanied by cardiovascular collapse and/or fever over 40 C.[18] For a more detailed discussion of this potentially life-threatening transfusion complication, see Chapter 28.

Febrile Nonhemolytic Reactions

Pathophysiology and Manifestations

A febrile nonhemolytic transfusion reaction (FNHTR) is often defined as a temperature increase of >1 C associated with transfusion and without any other explanation. Such reactions are often associated with chills or rigors. The 1 C definition is arbitrary; the same events might cause smaller temperature increments. Indeed, some authors discuss reactions characterized by rigors or other symptoms, in the absence of fever, as FNHTRs because of a presumed common mechanism.[2] In one study of 108 reactions characterized by chills, cold, or rigors, only 18 involved a rise in temperature.[19] Febrile reactions complicate 0.5% to 6% of nonleukocyte-reduced red cell transfusions. Previous opportunities for alloimmunization, especially pregnancies and multiple transfusions, increase the frequency of FNHTRs to red cells. The rate of such reactions is much higher after platelet transfusion (1-38%). Most FNHTRs are benign, although some may cause significant discomfort and hemodynamic or respiratory changes. The temperature increase may begin early in the transfusion or be delayed in onset for hours after completion of the transfusion.

Many febrile reactions are thought to result from an interaction between antibodies in the recipient's plasma and antigens present on transfused lymphocytes, granulocytes, or platelets, most frequently HLA antigens. There is also evidence that febrile reactions, particularly those due to platelets, may be caused by the infusion of biologic response modifiers, including cytokines, that accumulate in the blood bag during storage. Cytokine release in the recipient undoubtedly contributes to those reactions that begin with recipient antibody against donor leukocytes.[2,20-22] Because fever may be an initial manifestation of an acute HTR or a reaction to transfusion of blood contaminated with bacteria, any observation of an increase in temperature associated with transfusion warrants prompt attention. The diagnosis of an FNHTR is made after excluding other possible explanations for the fever, particularly a hemolytic or septic reaction. Guidelines for evaluating a suspected acute transfusion reaction are presented later in this chapter.

Treatment

Traditionally, transfusion was discontinued when an FNHTR occurred.[23] However, some clinicians believe that fever should not routinely cause discontinuation of a transfusion,[2,24] depending on whether the patient has symptoms, signs, or laboratory data that suggest hemolysis, transfusion-related acute lung injury (TRALI), or bacterial contamination. The fever of an FNHTR usually responds to antipyretics. Acetaminophen is preferred to the use of salicylates because the former drug does not affect platelet function. Meperidine injection may be useful in patients with severe shaking chills. Antihistamines are not indicated because most FNHTRs do not involve histamine release.

Prevention

Febrile reactions in an alloimmunized individual can often be prevented by transfusion of leukocyte-reduced blood components. Prevention of reactions caused by cytokine accumulation during storage requires that the leukocyte reduction be performed before storage,[2,19] but some patients will still react. With non-leukocyte-reduced platelets, cytokine-mediated reactions may be less frequent when the component(s) are less than or equal to 3 days old. Plasma removal may also decrease febrile reactions. Acetaminophen is commonly given before transfusion, but there is no evidence that the premedication lessens the incidence of FNHTR symptoms due to prestorage leukocyte-reduced platelets.[25]

Allergy; Urticaria (Hives) to Anaphylaxis

Pathophysiology and Manifestations

Allergic reactions to transfusion form a continuum, with the vast majority clustered at the mild end, in the form of urticaria or "hives"—erythematous, sharply circumscribed raised lesions, most often present over the upper trunk and neck, which may itch and which are not usually accompanied by fever or other adverse findings. At the other end of the spectrum are anaphylactic reactions, in which there are systemic symptoms including hypotension, loss of consciousness, shock, and, in rare cases, death. The latter may begin after infusion of only a few milliliters, but less severe reactions tend to take longer to develop. The term "anaphylactoid" is used in transfusion medicine to denote reactions in between these extremes, but it is also used to denote reactions that have clinical similarities to anaphylaxis but different mechanisms. Manifestations of these reactions may involve one or several systems, notably, the skin (urticaria, generalized flushing or rash, localized swelling or "angioedema"), respiratory tract (upper or lower respiratory tract obstruction with cough, hoarseness, stridor, wheezing, chest tightness or pain, dyspnea), the gastrointestinal tract (cramps, nausea, vomiting, diarrhea), or the circulatory system (tachycardia and other arrhythmias including cardiac arrest).[26] Fever is characteristically absent, a feature that aids in differentiating these reactions from hypotension due to a hemolytic reaction or bacterial contamination, and from respiratory compromise caused by TRALI (see below). The severity of allergic transfusion reactions may increase with successive transfusions.

Allergic reactions are attributed to exposure to a soluble substance in donor plasma that binds to preformed IgE antibodies on mast cells, resulting in the activation and release of histamine. This presumption is based on the facts that reactions tend to recur in an affected recipient and that they can be prevented by removal of the plasma from cellular components or, in the case of urticaria, by antihistamines. Anaphylactic and anaphylactoid reactions are sometimes associated with class, subclass, and allotype-specific antibodies against IgA, particularly in IgA-deficient patients.[27] IgE anti-IgA has been demonstrated in two patients with common variable immunodeficiency having reactions to immunoglobulin preparations.[28] However, most of the IgA antibodies to which anaphylactic reactions are attributed are of the IgG or IgM class,[27] and these antibodies are demonstrable in only a minority of the anaphylaxis cases referred for study (17.5% in the series of Sandler et al[27]). Moreover, IgA antibodies are common but anaphylactic reactions are not. Therefore, demonstration of anti-IgA in an individual who has not been transfused does not predict anaphylaxis. Other allergens or other mechanisms are likely.

Severe allergic reactions have been reported in patients with antibodies directed against C4 determinants,[29,30] haptoglobin,[31] and elements of nonbiologic origin such as ethylene oxide used for sterilizing tubing sets.[32] However, the causative antigens have not been identified in the vast majority of cases. Reactions caused by passively transferred donor antibody have rarely been documented.[33,34]

Hypotensive reactions mimicking anaphylaxis have been observed in patients taking angiotensin-converting enzyme (ACE) inhibitors who receive albumin during plasma exchange.[35] They were thought to be due to inhibition of bradykinin catabolism by the ACE inhibitors combined with bradykinin activation by low levels of prekallikrein activator (a Hageman factor fragment) in the albumin used for replacement.

Similarly, bradykinin activation by prekallikrein activity in plasma protein fraction has also been implicated in hypotensive reactions,[36] and a similar mechanism is probably responsible for the many patients taking ACE inhibitors reported to have hypotensive reactions when receiving blood components via bedside leukocyte reduction filters.[37-39] Similar reactions have been observed in association with the contact of plasma with charged dialysis membranes, low-density lipoprotein adsorption columns, and staphylococcal protein A immunoadsorption columns. Other mechanisms that have been proposed include the infusion of complement-derived anaphylatoxins and histamine.[26] The differentiation and appropriate classification of these different reactions will require additional research and refined diagnostic tools.

Frequency

Urticaria may complicate as many as 1% to 3% of transfusions, the observed frequency depending on how vigorously it is sought. The incidence of anaphylactic reactions fortunately is low, estimated to be 1 in 20,000 to 50,000 units. The SHOT data suggest that anaphylaxis is much more common as a complication of plasma and platelet transfusions, than of red cells[14]; although these reactions may have contributed to the death of a few severely ill patients, they were not a primary cause of death. The mortality rate reported to the FDA is about 1 per year.[26]

Treatment

If urticaria is the only adverse event noted, the transfusion may be temporarily interrupted while an antihistamine (eg, diphenhydramine, 25-50 mg) is administered orally or parenterally. If symptoms are mild and promptly relieved, the transfusion may be resumed, provided the interrupted infusion can be completed within the acceptable time (see Chapter 22). If the patient develops severe urticaria, a significant local swelling, respiratory or gastrointestinal symptoms, or hypotension, the transfusion should be discontinued.[26]

The immediate treatment of an anaphylactic transfusion reaction should be to stop the transfusion and treat hypotension by placing the patient in the Trendelenberg (feet up) position and administering a fluid challenge. If the blood pressure does not improve immediately, epinephrine should be given. In mild to moderate cases, epinephrine (1:1000) should be delivered subcutaneously or intramuscularly in a starting dose of 0.3 to 0.5 mL in adults, or 0.01 mL/kg in children. This dose may be repeated a second and third time at 5- to 15-minute intervals. In severe reactions (eg, systolic blood pressure below 80 mm Hg, laryngeal edema with upper airway compromise, or respiratory failure), the drug should be given intravenously (1:10,000) for the most rapid effect because drug absorption is unreliable in hypotensive patients. Aerosolized or intravenous beta-2 agonists and theophylline may be required in selected patients in whom bronchospasm is unresponsive to epinephrine treatment, or in whom epinephrine is ineffective because of pre-existing beta-blocker therapy. Oxygen therapy should be administered as required, with endotracheal intubation if there is significant upper airway obstruction. Continued hemodynamic instability may require invasive hemodynamic monitoring. Under no circumstances should the transfusion be restarted. Coincidental occurrence of myocardial infarction, pulmonary embolism, or other medical catastrophes could present with hypotension and respiratory compromise and should be considered.[26]

Prevention

Recipients who have frequent transfusion-associated urticarial reactions may respond well to administration of antihistamine (eg, 25-50 mg of diphenhydramine) one-half hour before transfusion. However, diphenhydramine should not be given routinely without a history of previous allergic reactions, particularly to elderly patients.[40] If antihistamine administration is insufficient, 100 mg of hydrocortisone given 1 hour before transfusion may be useful. If reactions are recurrent and severe or associated with other allergic manifestations in spite of adequate premedication, transfusion of washed red cell or platelet components, or red cells that have been frozen, thawed, and deglycerolized will usually be tolerated.

Patients who have had a prior life-threatening anaphylactic reaction and who are IgA-deficient or have a demonstrated IgA antibody should receive blood components that lack IgA, either by washing or preparation of components from IgA-deficient blood donors. Severe reactions that are not caused by anti-IgA can be prevented only by maximal antiallergy immunosuppression or washing. A need for red cells may be met by the use of washed or frozen, thawed, and deglycerolized units.[26] Washed platelets are generally not readily available and may result in decreased platelet recovery, function, and survival[41]; therefore, after the first reaction, if there is no evidence that the reaction is mediated by IgA, some centers elect to rechallenge the patient under closely controlled circumstances. Prevention of anaphylactoid reactions in patients such as those with thrombotic thrombocytopenic purpura who absolutely require plasma components may be a tremendous challenge if IgA-deficient donors will not suffice. Pretreatment with antihistamines, corticosteroids (starting with 100 mg of hydrocortisone), and ephedrine may help. Finally, it may be possible to collect and store autologous blood components from patients known to have experienced anaphylactic reactions.

Transfusion-Related Acute Lung Injury

Pathophysiology and Manifestations

TRALI should be considered whenever a transfusion recipient experiences acute respiratory insufficiency and/or X-ray findings are consistent with bilateral pulmonary edema but has no other evidence of cardiac failure or a cause for respiratory failure. The severity of the respiratory distress is usually disproportionate to the volume of blood infused. The reaction typically includes fever, chills, and hypotension, usually occurring during or within 1 to 2 after transfusion, often with an immediate and dramatic onset. Implicated components always have contained plasma, but the volume may be as small as that of a unit of cryoprecipitate or RBCs in an additive solution.[42,43]

Because the manifestations of TRALI are variable and may overlap with those of the patient's underlying medical problems, it is useful to define the syndrome, particularly for the purpose of conducting studies of its epidemiology and pathogenesis. A consensus conference of the blood services in Canada developed such a definition.[44] The panel defined acute lung injury (ALI) as a syndrome of: 1) acute onset; 2) hypoxemia (PaO_2/FIO_2 <300 mm Hg, or O_2 saturation <90% on room air, or other clinical evidence); 3) bilateral lung infiltrates on a chest x-ray; and 4) no evidence of circulatory overload. TRALI is then defined as: 1) new ALI occurring during transfusion or within 6 hours of completion; and 2) no other temporally associated ALI risk factors. If the latter are present, the case is considered "Possible TRALI." Risk factors for ALI include aspiration, pneumonia, toxic inhalation, lung contusion, near drowning, severe sepsis, shock, multiple trauma, burn injury, acute pancreatitis, cardiopulmonary bypass, and drug overdose. It was noted that such a definition will not include cases of mild respiratory embarrassment having a similar pathogenesis, cases of ALI in patients with circulatory overload, and cases in which a transfusion-related process causes worsening of pre-existing ALI.[44]

TRALI may result from multiple mechanisms. Donor antibodies directed against recipient HLA class I or II antigens, or neutrophil antigens of the recipient, have been demonstrated[45-47] and are thought to cause a sequence of events that increase the permeability of the pulmonary microcirculation so that high-protein fluid enters the interstitium and alveolar air spaces. Infrequently, antibodies in the recipient's circulation against HLA or granulocyte antigens initiate the same events.[45,46,48] Although one would expect causative antibodies to be far more common in recipients than donors, the rarity of TRALI due to recipient antibody might be due to the fact that the pool of target leukocytes is much smaller in a cellular blood component than in a recipient's circulation. Monocyte activation, with expression of cytokines including IL-1β, TNFα, and tissue factor, has been demonstrated, and these reactions were highly specific for cells bearing the target antigens.[48] Perfusion of neutrophils, complement, and neutrophil-specific antibody into an ex-vivo rabbit lung preparation causes severe edema,[49] and autopsy studies demonstrate neutrophil aggregation in the lungs of patients who have died of TRALI.[50] These and other observations suggest that pulmonary edema in TRALI is caused by neutrophil-mediated endothelial damage, initiated by antibodies activating neutrophils directly or via activation of monocytes, pulmonary macrophages, and/or endothelial cells.

As the spectrum of antibodies implicated in cases of TRALI broadens, more cases will appear to be antibody-mediated. However, other mechanisms have been proposed as causes for transfusion-related respiratory failure. Severe pulmonary reactions are reported after granulocyte transfusions, particularly in patients with known or unapparent lung infections or with conditions likely to promote prompt complement activation.[51] Other factors may include anaphylatoxins C3a and C5a, aggregation of granulocytes into leukoemboli that lodge in the pulmonary microvasculature, or transfusion of cytokines that have accumulated in stored blood components. Recently, reactive lipid products from donor blood cell membranes have been implicated as potential granulocyte activators in the pathogenesis of TRALI.[52] These substances accumulate during blood bank storage and prime neutrophils to produce vasoactive mediators in response to a second stimulus such as infection. One nested case-control study found that component age and levels of bioactive lipids, but not leukocyte antibodies, were associated with TRALI.[53]

The incidence rate of TRALI is not known, but data from one institution in the 1980s suggest that this complication may occur as frequently as 1 in 5000 transfusions.[45] The passive surveillance data of 5 years of SHOT reports[14] include 70 TRALI cases (approximately 1 per 250,000 total components), of which 18 cases were fatal (includes six definite, two probable, and 10 possible TRALI-related fatalities). In this series, TRALI was the most common cause of morbidity and mortality, ahead of transfusion-associated graft-vs-host disease (TA-GVHD), ABO incompatibility, and bacterial contamination. The SHOT data suggest that the rate of TRALI is higher after plasma and platelet transfusion. Conclusions regarding incidence and fatality rates will, of course, depend on the definition of TRALI used.

Treatment

If any kind of acute pulmonary reaction is suspected, the transfusion should be stopped immediately and the same unit should not be restarted even if symptoms abate. Clinical management focuses on reversing progressive hypoxemia with oxygen therapy and ventilatory assistance, if necessary. The role of intravenous steroids is unproved. Unlike other forms of acute respiratory distress syndrome, most patients recover adequate pulmonary function within 2 to 4 days,[42,45] and the observed mortality is less than 6% to 23% (Holness L, personal communication).

Prevention

If antibody in donor plasma can be shown to have caused an acute pulmonary reaction, blood from that donor should not be used for plasma-containing components. No special precautions are needed for the patient if the problem was donor-specific and components from other donors are available. Current policy in the United Kingdom is not to prepare plasma from female donors.

Circulatory Overload

Pathophysiology and Manifestations

Transfusion therapy may cause acute pulmonary edema due to volume overload, and this can have severe consequences, including death. Few data are available on the incidence rate of transfusion-induced circulatory overload in the general population, but young children and the elderly are considered most at risk, and incidence rates of up to 1% have been observed in a study of elderly orthopedic patients.[54] Rapid increases in blood volume are especially poorly tolerated by patients with compromised cardiac or pulmonary status and/or chronic anemia with expanded plasma volume. The infusion of 25% albumin, which shifts large volumes of extravascular fluid into the vascular space, may also cause circulatory overload. Hypervolemia must be considered if dyspnea, cyanosis, orthopnea, severe headache, hypertension, or congestive heart failure occur during or soon after transfusion. Elevated levels of brain natriuretic peptide may be seen in cases of circulatory overload,[55] and this test may be useful in separating such cases from cases of TRALI.

Treatment

Symptoms usually improve when the infusion is stopped, and it should not be restarted until volume overload has been addressed. Placing the patient in a sitting position may help. Diuretics and oxygen are often indicated and, if symptoms are not relieved, multiple medical interventions may be required, including phlebotomy.

Prevention

Except in conditions of ongoing, rapid blood loss, anemic patients should receive blood transfusions slowly, with attention to total fluid input and output. The administration of diuretics before and during the transfusion may be helpful.

Complications of Massive Transfusion

Among the numerous complications that may accompany massive transfusion, metabolic and hemostatic abnormalities are matters of particular concern. Some or all of the following metabolic derangements can depress left ventricular function: hypothermia from refrigerated blood, citrate toxicity, and lactic acidosis from systemic underperfusion and tissue ischemia, often complicated by hyperkalemia. Metabolic alkalosis due to metabolism of citrate can occur after massive transfusion but is probably not clinically significant. Patients who are losing blood rapidly may have pre-existing or coexisting hemostatic abnormalities or develop them during resuscitation. Hemostatic abnormalities may include dilutional coagulopathy, DIC, and liver and platelet dysfunction.

Citrate Toxicity

Pathophysiology and Manifestations. When large volumes of FFP, Whole Blood, or Platelets are transfused rapidly, particularly in the presence of liver disease, plasma citrate levels may rise, binding ionized calcium and causing symptoms. Citrate is rapidly metabolized, however, so these manifestations are transient.[56] Hypocalcemia is more likely to cause clinical manifestations in patients who are in shock or are hypothermic. Prolonged apheresis procedures put patients, and occasionally blood donors, at some risk. Exchange transfusion, especially in tiny infants who are already ill, requires careful attention to all electrolytes.

A decrease in ionized calcium increases neuronal excitability, leading, in the awake patient or apheresis donor, to symptoms of perioral and peripheral tingling, shivering, and lightheadedness, followed by a diffuse sense of vibration, tetanic symptoms such as muscle cramps, fasciculations and spasm, and nausea. In the central nervous system, hypocalcemia is thought to increase the respiratory center's sensitivity to CO_2, causing hyperventilation. Because myocardial contraction is dependent on the intracellular movement of ionized calcium, hypocalcemia also depresses cardiac function.[57]

Treatment and Prevention. Massively transfused patients, particularly those with severe liver disease or those undergoing rapid apheresis procedures such as peripheral blood progenitor cell collections, may benefit from calcium replacement. It should be noted, however, that empiric replacement therapy in the era before accurate monitoring of ionized calcium was available was associated with iatrogenic mortality.[58] Usually, however, unless a patient or donor has a predisposing condition that hinders citrate metabolism, hypocalcemia due to citrate overload requires no treatment other than slowing the infusion. Calcium must never be added directly to the blood container because the blood will clot.

Hypothermia

Pathophysiology and Manifestations. Ventricular arrhythmias may occur in patients who receive rapid infusions of large volumes of cold blood, and they can be prevented by blood warming.[59] The effect of cold blood is presumed to be more likely if the blood is administered via central catheters positioned close to the cardiac conduction system.[60] Hypothermia increases the cardiac toxicity of hypocalcemia or hyperkalemia and can result in poor left ventricular performance. Other complications of hypothermia include impaired hemostasis[61] and increased susceptibility to wound infections.[62] Blood warming is a must during massive transfusion of cold blood.

Treatment and Prevention. Hypothermia-induced arrhythmias are reduced by avoiding rapid infusion of cold blood into the cardiac atrium. Generalized effects of hypothermia can be prevented by using blood warmers. AABB *Standards for Blood Banks and Transfusion Services* mandates that warmers have a temperature monitor and a warning system to detect malfunction and prevent hemolysis.[17(p6)] Attention to proper protocol is critical during the use of blood warming devices because overheating destroys red cells and has caused fatalities.[5]

Hyperkalemia and Hypokalemia

Pathophysiology. When red cells are stored at 1 to 6 C, the potassium level in the supernatant plasma or additive solution increases. Although the concentration in the plasma/anticoagulant portion of an RBC unit may be high (see Chapter 8), because of the small volume, the total extracellular potassium load is less than 0.5 mEq for fresh units and only 5 to 7 mEq for units at their outdate. This rarely causes hyperkalemic problems in the recipient because rapid dilution, redistribution into cells, and excretion blunt the effect. Hypokalemia is probably more often observed[63] because potassium-depleted red cells reaccumulate this intracellular ion, and citrate metabolism causes movement of potassium into the cells in response to the consumption of protons. Hyperkalemia may be a problem in patients with renal failure and in premature infants and newborns receiving relatively large transfusions, such as in cardiac surgery or exchange transfusion; otherwise, it can be demonstrated only as a transient effect in very rapid transfusion.

Treatment and Prevention. No treatment or preventive strategy is usually necessary, provided the patient is adequately resuscitated from whatever condition required the massive transfusion.[63] For large-volume transfusion to sick infants or adults at risk, many professionals prefer red cells that are no more than 5 to 14 days old or washed units. However, for infants receiving small-volume transfusions infused slowly, units may be used safely until their expiration date.[64] There is no evidence that routine red cell transfusions require manipulation to lower potassium levels, even in patients with no renal function.

Coagulopathy in Massive Transfusion

Pathophysiology. Of greater concern is the occurrence of coagulopathy during massive transfusion. Classically, this coagulopathy is ascribed to dilution of platelets and clotting factors, which occurs as patients lose hemostatically active blood. The lost blood is initially replaced with red cells and asanguinous fluids. Classic studies of military[65] and civilian[66] trauma patients receiving stored Whole Blood demonstrated a progressive increase in the incidence of "microvascular bleeding" (MVB) characteristic of a coagulopathy with increasing transfusion, typically occurring after replacement of two to three blood volumes (20 to 30 Whole Blood units). Although platelet counts, coagulation times, and levels of selected clotting factors all correlated with volume transfused, contrary to expectations from a simple dilutional model, the relationship was marked by tremendous variability. Inspection of laboratory parameters in the patients developing a bleeding diathesis, as well as the response to various hemostatic components, suggested that platelet deficits were more important in causing the bleeding than were coagulation factor deficiencies. MVB typically occurred when the platelet count fell below 50,000 to 60,000/μL. On the other hand, no simple relationship could be determined between a patient's coagulation tests and the onset of bleeding.

Subsequent studies have refined these observations. Significant platelet dysfunction has been demonstrated in massively transfused trauma patients.[67,68] In the studies of Counts and coworkers,[66,69] low fibrinogen and platelet levels were better predictors of hemostatic failure than elevations of prothrombin time (PT) and partial thromboplastin time (PTT), suggesting that consumption coagulopathy was an important factor in addition to dilution. A similar conclusion was reached by Harke and Rahman,[70] who showed that the degree of platelet and clotting abnormalities correlated with the length of time the patient was hypotensive, in groups of patients receiving similar transfusion volumes, also suggesting that the most important cause was DIC due to shock. Taking these data together, Collins[71] concluded that "...coagulopathy in heavily transfused patients was due to hypoperfusion, not transfusion."

These data may not be generalizable to patients undergoing massive transfusion in the "clean" setting of the operating room, where hypotension due to volume loss is prevented. In this setting, coagulation factor levels may indeed have priority over platelet problems.[72]

Treatment and Prevention. The dilutional model of coagulopathy in massive transfusion would suggest that prophylactic replacement of hemostatic components based on the volume of red cells or whole blood transfused would prevent development of a bleeding diathesis. However, prospective studies have consistently shown that such regimens do not work,[73] perhaps due to patient variability. Instead, replacement of platelets and coagulation factors in the massively transfused trauma or surgical patient should be based on characterization of the specific abnormality by use of platelet counts, the PT (international normalized rate), aPTT, and fibrinogen levels. Thromboelastography may also be useful. It is imperative that the laboratory rapidly complete testing. Empiric therapy with platelets and/or plasma may be initiated immediately after specimens are obtained.

Air Embolism

Air embolism can occur if blood in an open system is infused under pressure or if air enters a central catheter while containers or blood administration sets are being changed. It has been reported in association with intraoperative and perioperative blood recovery systems that allow air into the infusion bag.[7] The minimum volume of air embolism that is potentially fatal for an adult is approximately 100 mL.[74] Symptoms include cough, dyspnea, chest pain, and shock.

If air embolism is suspected, the patient should be placed on the left side with the head down, to displace the air bubble from the pulmonic valve. Aspiration of the air is sometimes attempted. However, proper use of infusion pumps, equipment for blood recovery or apheresis, and tubing couplers is still essential to prevent this complication.

Evaluation of a Suspected Acute Transfusion Reaction

The Role of Clinical Personnel Attending the Patient

Medical personnel attending the patient are generally the first to suspect that a transfusion reaction has occurred and the first to take action. The appropriate actions should be specified in the institution's patient care procedures manual, and transfusion service personnel should be prepared to act as consultants.

1. If a transfusion reaction is suspected, the transfusion should be stopped to limit the volume of blood infused.
2. All labels, forms, and patient identification should be checked to determine whether the transfused component was intended for the recipient.
3. An intravenous line should be maintained with normal saline (0.9% sodium chloride), at least until a medical evaluation of the patient has been completed.
4. The transfusion service and the patient's physician should be notified

immediately. A responsible physician should evaluate the patient to determine whether a transfusion reaction is a possibility, what kind it might be, and what immediate actions should be undertaken. The possibilities of acute hemolytic reaction, anaphylaxis, transfusion-induced sepsis, and TRALI should be kept in mind because these conditions require aggressive medical management and must be reported promptly to the laboratory.

5. If the observed events are limited to urticaria or circulatory overload, the transfusion service need not evaluate postreaction blood samples. If there are signs and symptoms other than urticaria or circulatory overload, particularly if there is any possibility of acute HTR, anaphylaxis, TRALI, transfusion-induced sepsis, or other serious problem, a postreaction blood sample(s) should be sent to the laboratory for evaluation. The specimen(s) must be carefully drawn to avoid mechanical hemolysis and must be properly labeled. In addition, the transfusion container with whatever contents remain, the administration set (without the needle), and the attached intravenous solutions should be sent to the laboratory, following standard precautions. In some cases, a postreaction urine sample will be useful.

The Role of the Laboratory

Whenever hemolysis is a possibility, the laboratory should perform three steps as soon as possible after receiving notification and the clinical material: check for clerical errors; perform a visual check for hemolysis; and check for evidence of blood group incompatibility by performing a direct antiglobulin test (DAT) and a reconfirmation of the recipient's ABO type. Some laboratories do not follow this sequence when the only manifestations are urticarial or febrile reactions to ABO-compatible platelets.

Check for Identification Errors

The identification of each patient's sample and the blood component(s) must be checked for errors. If an error is discovered, the patient's physician or other responsible health-care professional must be notified immediately, and a search of appropriate records should be initiated to determine whether misidentification or incorrect issue of other specimens or components has put other patients at risk. Once the acute crisis has passed, each step of the transfusion process should be reviewed to find the source of error.

Visual Check for Hemolysis

The serum or plasma in a postreaction blood specimen must be inspected for evidence of hemolysis and compared with a prereaction sample, if available. Pink or red discoloration after, but not before, the reaction suggests destruction of red cells and release of free hemoglobin. Intravascular hemolysis of as little as 2.5 mL of red cells may produce visible hemoglobinemia.[75] Hemolysis resulting from poor collection technique or other medical interventions can cause hemoglobinemia; if faulty sampling is suspected, examination of a second specimen should resolve the question. Myoglobin, released from injured muscle, may also cause pink or red plasma and might be suspected if a patient has suffered severe trauma or muscle injury.[76(p369)] If the sample is not drawn until 5 to 7 hours after an episode of acute hemolysis, hemoglobin degradation products, especially bilirubin, may be in the bloodstream and cause yellow or brown discol-

oration. An increase in bilirubin may begin as early as 1 hour after the reaction, peak at 5 to 7 hours, and disappear within 24 hours if liver function is normal.

In examining a postreaction urine specimen, it is important to differentiate among hematuria (intact red cells in the urine), hemoglobinuria (free hemoglobin in the urine), and myoglobinuria (free myoglobin in the urine). In acute HTRs, free hemoglobin released from damaged cells can cross the renal glomeruli and enter the urine, but hematuria and myoglobinuria would not be expected. Urine examination should be done on the supernatant fluid after centrifugation of a freshly collected specimen; misinterpretation can occur if free hemoglobin is released when previously intact red cells in a specimen undergo in-vitro hemolysis during transportation or storage.

Serologic Check for Incompatibility

A DAT must be performed on a postreaction specimen, preferably one anticoagulated with a chelating agent (such as EDTA) to avoid in-vitro coating of red cells by complement proteins. If the postreaction DAT is positive, a DAT should be performed on red cells from the pretransfusion specimen (unless this was already done as part of pretransfusion testing) and compared. If transfused incompatible cells have been coated with antibody but not immediately destroyed, the postreaction specimen DAT is likely to be positive, often with a mixed-field agglutination pattern. If the transfused cells have been rapidly destroyed, the postreaction DAT may be negative, particularly if the specimen is drawn several hours later. If both the pre- and postreaction DATs are positive, further workup is required to rule out incompatibility. Comparison of the graded strength of these two tests is not a reliable method to rule this out. Nonimmune hemolysis (eg, from thermal damage or mechanical trauma) causes hemoglobinemia but not a positive DAT. The recipient's ABO type must also be confirmed on the postreaction specimen.

Additional Laboratory Evaluation

If any of the three initial checks and tests (error check, visual inspection for hemoglobinemia, DAT and ABO confirmation) gives positive or suspicious results, the diagnosis of an acute HTR should be vigorously pursued. Even if no error or apparent incompatibility is found, the possibility of an acute HTR should still be considered if the patient's clinical presentation is consistent with such a reaction. The tests listed below help characterize the cause of the HTR, if one has occurred, or help clarify the immunologic and serologic status of patients in whom the diagnosis is unclear. Some or all may be performed following a written institutional protocol or at the discretion of the physician in charge of the transfusion service.

1.   If ABO and Rh typing on the prereaction and postreaction samples do not agree, there has been an error in patient or sample identification, or in testing. If sample mix-up or mislabeling has occurred, another patient's specimen may also have been incorrectly labeled; it is important to check the records of all specimens received at approximately the same time.

2.   Perform ABO and Rh testing on blood from the unit or an attached segment. If blood in the bag is not of the ABO type noted on the bag label, there has been an error in unit labeling.

3.   Perform antibody detection tests on the prereaction and postreaction samples and on the donor blood. If a previously undetected antibody is discovered, it should be identified. Once the antibody has been identified, retained samples from transfused donor units should be tested for the corresponding antigen. If a previously undiscovered antibody is present in a postreaction specimen but not in a prereaction sample, the reason may be 1) a sample identification error, 2) anamnestic antibody production after a recent transfusion, or, less likely, 3) passive transfer of antibody from a recently transfused component. It may be desirable to use enhancement techniques, such as an increased serum-to-cell ratio, low-ionic-strength saline, Polybrene, polyethylene glycol, or enzyme techniques, when retesting the prereaction specimen.

4.   Repeat crossmatch tests, with prereaction and postreaction samples in parallel using the antiglobulin technique. A positive crossmatch in the face of a negative antibody screening test may indicate the presence of an antibody directed against a low-incidence blood group antigen.

5.   Perform DAT and antibody detection tests on additional specimens obtained at intervals after the transfusion reaction. A first postreaction sample may have serologically undetectable levels of a significant alloantibody, especially if all the antibody molecules have attached to the incompatible transfused cells. In this event, antibody levels would rise rapidly, and antibody detection and identification would become possible within a few days.

6.   Perform frequent checks of the patient's hemoglobin values, to see whether the transfused cells produce the expected therapeutic rise, or

whether a decline occurs after an initial increase. In patients with sickle cell anemia, the survival of transfused red cells can be followed by evaluation of the levels of hemoglobin A. In complex cases, phenotypic differences between autologous and transfused cells quantitated by flow cytometry have been used to follow survival.[77]

7. In-vivo red cell survival studies have been used to demonstrate the rare occurrence of an acute HTR in the absence of detectable alloantibody.[78] When the patient is phenotyped in preparation for such studies, it is important that the sample be one that contains only the patient's red cells. This may be difficult if the patient has received transfusions within the previous several weeks. Method 2.15 gives a technique for obtaining autologous red cells from a patient who has been transfused. If an antigen is present on the donor's red cells and absent from those of the patient, its presence or absence in postreaction samples indicates whether the transfused cells have survived and remained in the circulation.

8. Markers of hemolysis, including lactate dehydrogenase, unconjugated bilirubin, and haptoglobin levels, may be useful, particularly if pre- and multiple postreaction measurements are available.

9. Examine the blood remaining in the unit and the administration tubing for evidence of hemolysis, especially if no immune explanation for hemolysis can be demonstrated. Depending on how the blood was handled and administered, hemolysis may be present in the container and the administration tubing, or only in the administration tubing. For example,

if the unit had been inappropriately heated in the container, both the blood in the container and in the administration tubing would be hemolyzed. If a faulty infusion device had been used during blood administration, hemolysis might be present in the administration tubing, but not in the container.

Additional testing may also be useful for significant nonhemolytic reactions.

1. If the presentation suggests an anaphylactic reaction, test the patient's serum for the presence of anti-IgA. Preliminary information can be obtained by quantitation of IgA because most patients with IgA-related anaphylaxis have been IgA deficient.[27] Note, however, that subclass- or allotype-specific antibodies may develop in patients with normal IgA levels.[26] If additional transfusions are required, cellular components can be washed; if plasma (or platelets; see above) is required, IgA-deficient plasma can be used.

2. Examine the returned unit for any abnormal appearance, including clots or any brownish, opaque, muddy, or purple discoloration. If the clinical presentation suggests bacterial sepsis, a Gram stain and bacterial cultures of the contents should be performed, even if the unit looks normal. Blood cultures should also be performed on the patient's blood.[79] Treatment for suspected bacterial contamination should be based on clinical considerations because a delay in therapy may result in severe morbidity or death. Treatment includes prompt intravenous administration of broad-spectrum antibiotics after blood and other appropriate cultures have been obtained, combined with therapy for shock, if present.

3. If the clinical presentation suggests TRALI, test the patient's pretransfusion sample and a sample of the donor's plasma for antibodies to HLA and neutrophil antigens. Crossmatching recipient lymphocytes or granulocytes with implicated donor sera can provide supportive evidence for TRALI.

Delayed Consequences of Transfusion

Alloimmunization to Red Cell Antigens

Pathophysiology

Primary alloimmunization, evidenced by the appearance of newly formed antibodies to red cell antigens, becomes apparent weeks or months after transfusion. It has been estimated that alloimmunization occurs in unselected immunocompetent recipients with a risk of 1% to 1.6% per RBC unit, provided that D-negative recipients receive D-negative cellular components.[80] Hemolysis has been reported in cases of primary immunization, but these reports are controversial,[81] and, even if it occurs, the phenomenon must be very rare and usually subclinical.

Serologic Observations. Once alloimmunization has occurred, blood group antibodies can become undetectable, especially those of the Kidd system. One investigator reported that this occurred to 29% of antibodies after a median of 10 months[82] and to 41% of antibodies after 5 or more years.[83] If red cells that express the antigen are subsequently transfused, however, an anamnestic response may cause the appearance, within hours or days, of IgG antibodies that react with the transfused red cells. In a prospective study, previously undetected alloantibodies were found in 58 of 2082 (2.8%) recipients (37% known previously transfused, 36% previously pregnant)

within 7 days of transfusion.[84] In two of the 58, only the DAT was positive, but, in all others, repeat antibody screening would have detected the new antibody. Regardless, characterization of an eluate is necessary because alloantibodies may be present on the red cells that are not in the serum. If the clinical laboratory discovers an anamnestic response, both the transfusion service director and the patient's clinician should be notified and the possibility of a delayed HTR (DHTR) should be investigated.

Delayed Reactions. In most cases, anamnestic antibody production does not cause detectable hemolysis, leading to the designation "delayed serologic transfusion reaction" (DSTR).[85] However, in some patients, clinically apparent hemolysis will result from the combination of significant levels of antibody with hemolytic potential and large numbers of transfused red cells in the circulation; in the study cited above, only one of the 58 recipients with a new antibody within 7 days of transfusion had clinically evident hemolysis.[84] This translated into a DHTR rate of one per 2082 recipients, or one for every 11,328 units transfused. As would be expected, retrospective studies, which would be similar to the routine experience of a transfusion service, yield a lower rate of DSTRs, but the rate of clinically detectable hemolysis may be roughly equivalent.[85-87] The most common presentation of a DHTR is a declining hemoglobin and a newly positive antibody screen, but fever, leukocytosis, and mild jaundice may be present. Some DHTRs present as the absence of the anticipated increase in hemoglobin after transfusion. Other clinical problems are infrequent; hemoglobinuria is occasionally noted, but acute renal failure is uncommon. However, DHTRs may be particularly problematic in patients with sickle cell disease. In these patients, hemolysis may include autologous red cells, a phenomenon termed sickle cell hemolytic transfusion reaction syndrome (see Chapter 24).[88]

If a DHTR is suspected, a freshly obtained blood sample may be tested for unexpected alloantibodies, both in the serum and, by DAT, on the red cells. Discovery of a new red cell alloantibody in a recently transfused patient with hemolysis strongly suggests a DHTR, and the diagnosis is supported by demonstration of the corresponding antigen on the red cells from a retained segment from one or more transfused units. Antigen typing of the red cells circulating in the patient may also suggest whether the newly incompatible cells have been eliminated, or whether some are still circulating. Repeat antibody screening on the patient's previous specimen will rule out technical errors.

Treatment

Specific treatment is rarely necessary, although it may be prudent to monitor the patient's urine output and renal function and observe for changes in coagulation function. If transfusion is still necessary, donor red cells should lack the antigen corresponding to the newly discovered antibody. Passenger lymphocyte hemolysis, seen after solid organ transplantation, is a variant of DHTR and is covered in Chapter 26.

Prevention

Future transfusions for the patient should lack the antigen(s) responsible for the anamnestic response, even if the antibody again becomes undetectable. Some facilities issue a medical alert card with this information for the patient to carry and present at the time of hospitalization or transfusion in a different facility. It is to prevent these problems that *Standards for Blood Banks and Transfusion Services*

mandates permanent preservation of records of clinically significant antibodies, and review of previous records before red cells are issued for transfusion.[17(pp39,72)] Prospective antigen matching may prevent DHTRs in selected patients, particularly those with sickle cell disease (see Chapters 21 and 24).[89]

Posttransfusion Autoantibody

Occasionally, transfusion of allogeneic red cells and platelets stimulates production of autoantibodies; in some of these patients, hemolytic anemia or thrombocytopenia may occur.[90] See Chapter 20 for more details.

Alloimmunization to Leukocyte Antigens and Refractoriness to Platelet Transfusions

See Chapter 16 and Chapter 17.

Transfusion-Associated Graft-vs-Host Disease

Transfusion-associated graft-vs-host disease is a usually fatal immunologic transfusion complication caused by engraftment and proliferation of donor lymphocytes in a susceptible host.[91] The engrafted lymphocytes mount an immunologic attack against the recipient tissues, including hematopoietic cells, leading to refractory pancytopenia with bleeding and infectious complications, which are primarily responsible for the 90% to 100% mortality rate in afflicted patients. TA-GVHD is rare in US transfusion recipients and has been observed almost exclusively in immunocompromised patients. In contrast, over 200 cases of TA-GVHD have been described in Japan,[92] with incidence rates reaching 1:660 in patients undergoing cardiovascular surgery.[93] Greater genetic homogeneity of the Japanese population and frequent use of fresh Whole

Blood from related donors are thought to be the primary reasons for the surprisingly frequent occurrence of TA-GVHD in that country. The SHOT data[14] demonstrate a significant decline in the incidence of TA-GVHD since the introduction of universal leukocyte reduction, but two cases occurred despite leukocyte reduction. In the first 3 years of this study, the rate of TA-GVHD was approximately 1 per 600,000 cellular components transfused and, in the first 5 years, accounted for a greater number of deaths than acute HTRs and only slightly fewer than did TRALI.

Pathophysiology and Manifestations

The pathophysiology of TA-GVHD is complex and incompletely understood. The overall mechanism includes the escape of donor T lymphocytes present in cellular blood components from immune clearance in the recipient and subsequent proliferation of these cells, which then mount an immune attack on host tissues. Manifestations include fever, enterocolitis, rash, hepatitis, and pancytopenia. The rash typically begins as a blanching, maculopapular erythema of the upper trunk, neck, palms, soles, and earlobes, which becomes confluent with additional findings ranging from edema to widespread blistering. Skin biopsy reveals infiltration of the upper dermis by mononuclear cells and damage to the basal layer of epithelial cells. Hepatitis manifests as elevations in alanine and aspartate aminotransferases, alkaline phosphatase, and bilirubin. Enterocolitis causes anorexia, nausea, and up to 3 to 4 liters per day of secretory diarrhea. Pancytopenia is associated with a hypocellular marrow. Symptoms typically appear within 8 to 10 days of the transfusion but may occur as early as 3 days and as late as 30 days. The diagnosis is proven by demonstration of donor-derived lymphocytes in the recipient's peripheral blood or tissues by HLA typing.[91]

Factors that determine an individual patient's risk for TA-GVHD include whether and to what degree the recipient is immunodeficient, the degree of HLA similarity between donor and recipient, and the number and type of T lymphocytes transfused that are capable of multiplication.[91] TA-GVHD may occur in an immunologically normal recipient if the donor is homozygous for an HLA haplotype for which the recipient is heterozygous, a so-called "one-way" HLA match, and if the component contains viable T cells (the fresher the unit, the higher the risk). Cytokine dysfunction, recruitment of host cells into the immune reaction, and release of biologic mediators, in particular nitric oxide, all play a role in the pathogenesis.[94] Of interest is the fact that TA-GVHD has not been reported in an AIDS patient.

Treatment and Prevention

Treatment of TA-GVHD with immunosuppressive agents has been attempted but rarely succeeds, so prevention is necessary. Irradiation of cellular blood components is the accepted standard method to prevent TA-GVHD. The dose mandated by the FDA is a minimum of 25 Gy targeted to the midline of the container and a minimum dose of 15 Gy delivered to all other parts of the component.[95] This renders T lymphocytes incapable of replication without substantially affecting the function of red cells, platelets, and granulocytes.

AABB *Standards for Blood Banks and Transfusion Services* requires routine irradiation of cellular components from units collected from the recipient's blood relatives, and donors selected for HLA compatibility by typing or crossmatching.[17(p43)] Policies should be in place to define the other groups of patients who should receive irradiated cellular components, and there must be a process for ensuring that once a patient has been determined to be at risk for TA-GVHD, all cellular components will be irradiated as long as clinically indicated.

Published guidelines[96] additionally recommend component irradiation for: 1) hematopoietic progenitor cell (HPC) transplant recipients (this includes allogeneic and autologous HPC transplants), 2) patients with hematologic disorders who will be undergoing allogeneic HPC transplantation imminently, 3) intrauterine transfusions, 4) neonates undergoing exchange transfusion or use of extracorporeal membrane oxygenation, 5) patients with Hodgkin's disease, and 6) patients with congenital cellular immunodeficiencies. TA-GVHD has also been reported in patients with acute lymphoid and myeloid leukemias, chronic lymphocytic leukemia particularly in patients receiving fludarabine phosphate,[91] patients with B-cell malignancies including non-Hodgkin's lymphoma, myeloma, and Waldenstrom's macroglobulinemia,[14] premature or low-birthweight infants without specific immunodeficiency disorders, and children being treated for neuroblastoma and rhabdomyosarcomas.[91]

Posttransfusion Purpura

Pathophysiology and Manifestations

Posttransfusion purpura (PTP) is an uncommon event, although over 200 cases have been published. It is characterized by the abrupt onset of severe thrombocytopenia (platelet count usually <10,000/μL) an average of 9 days after transfusion (range, 1-24 days).[97] Components provoking the reaction have usually been RBCs or Whole Blood, but PTP has also been reported after platelet and plasma transfusion, and after transfusion of frozen deglycerolized RBCs. Most patients have previously been pregnant or transfused. "Wet purpura" is common, and fatal intra-

cranial hemorrhage can occur. The ratio of affected patients is five women to one man, and the median age is 51 years (range, 16-83). Most cases (68%) involve patients whose platelets lack the HPA-1a (Pl^{A1}) antigen (<2% of the population) and who form the corresponding antibody. However, immunization to HPA-1b is reported in 10%, and other platelet antibodies, including HLA antibodies, have been associated with the syndrome as well. PTP is usually self-limited, with full recovery within 21 days. Historically, 10% to 15% of patients have been reported to die from PTP, typically from intracranial bleeding, so treatment is desirable.

The reason for destruction of the patient's own platelets by what appears to be a platelet alloantibody is controversial. Three mechanisms have been proposed, including: 1) formation of immune complexes of patient antibody and soluble donor antigen that bind to Fc receptors on the patient's platelets and mediate their destruction, 2) conversion of antigen-negative autologous platelets to antibody targets by soluble antigen in the transfused component, and 3) cross-reactivity of the patient's antibodies with autologous platelets (ie, the presence of an autoantibody component). The last of these theories has received the most support.

Treatment

Because PTP remits spontaneously, treatment may appear falsely efficacious. Steroids are frequently given but their role is controversial. Plasma exchange can achieve platelet counts of 20,000/μL in 1 to 2 days,[98] but the use of high-dose Immune Globulin Intravenous (IGIV) is now supplanting this therapy.[98,99] With the use of IGIV, recovery to platelet counts of 100,000/μL is typically achieved within 3 to 5 days. As it does in other disorders such as immune thrombocytopenic purpura, IGIV appears to block antibody-mediated clearance of the target cells, although the mechanism of action has not been established. If randomly selected platelets are transfused, patients may experience a febrile transfusion reaction, and, in the vast majority of cases, such transfusions have not been efficacious. Antigen-negative platelets can be of benefit in PTP, and, in conjunction with IGIV, reversal of this disorder in 1 day is now possible.[100,101] Unfortunately, the time necessary to procure such platelets often limits their usefulness. After recovery, some authors have suggested that future transfusions should be from donors lacking the offending antigen, or, if they are not available, washed platelet units.[97]

Immunomodulatory Effects of Transfusion

Transfusion has been known to modulate immune responses since the 1973 observation by Opelz and coworkers[102] of improved renal allograft survival in transfused patients. This beneficial tolerance-inducing effect of transfusion raised concerns that transfusion may have other adverse effects in different clinical settings, including increased rates of postoperative solid tumor recurrence and bacterial infection.[103] Despite numerous retrospective and several large prospective studies, the clinical significance of transfusion-associated immunomodulation and the usefulness of preventive strategies, such as leukocyte reduction of transfused components, remain controversial.[104,105]

Iron Overload

Every RBC unit contains approximately 200 mg of iron. Chronically transfused patients, especially those with hemoglobinopathies, have progressive and continuous accumulation of iron and no physiologic means of excreting it. Storage oc-curs initially in reticuloendothelial sites, but when they are saturated, there is deposition in parenchymal cells. The threshold for clinical damage is lifetime exposure to greater than 50 to 100 RBC units in a nonbleeding person.[106] Iron deposition interferes with function of the heart, liver, and endocrine glands (eg, pancreatic islets, pituitary); hepatic failure and cancer, diabetes mellitus, and cardiac toxicity cause most of the morbidity and mortality. Elevated ferritin levels demonstrate increased iron stores, and tissue damage can be shown with organ-specific assays such as liver enzyme levels or endocrine function tests (eg, glucose, thyroid-stimulating hormone).

Treatment is directed at removing iron without reducing the patient's circulating hemoglobin. Metered subcutaneous infusion of desferoxamine, an iron-chelating agent, can reduce body iron stores in such patients, but the regimen of nightly subcutaneous infusion by pump is arduous and expensive, and compliance is often poor. In transfusion-dependent patients with hemoglobinopathies, red cell exchange can minimize additional iron loads and can reduce the total iron burden.[107] An oral iron chelator has been studied but is not yet available in the United States.

Records of Transfusion Complications

Each transfusion service must maintain indefinitely the records of patients who have had transfusion complications or evidence of alloimmunization. Possible cases of contaminated blood must be reported to the institution where the blood was drawn.

Records must be kept, and consulted, to prevent patients who have had a transfusion reaction from having a recurrence with subsequent transfusions. For example, patients with a history of IgA-related anaphylactic reactions should be transfused with plasma products that lack IgA. A history of repeated or severe FNHTRs might prompt the use of leukocyte-reduced cellular blood components. Red cell alloantibodies may become undetectable over time as discussed above,[82,83] so records should be checked and compatible blood issued in order to prevent a DHTR. Routine checking of previous results of ABO and Rh testing may disclose an error in testing or in the identification of a current sample.

Records of Patients with Special Needs

In addition to records of transfusion reactions, transfusion services should maintain records of patients who need specially prepared or manipulated components. This is especially important in institutions where physicians rotate frequently, and the need for irradiated, leukocyte-reduced, or IgA-deficient components may not be known to a particular physician writing an individual order.

Reporting Transfusion Fatalities

When a complication of blood transfusion has been confirmed to be fatal, it must be reported to the Director, Office of Compliance, Center for Biologics Evaluation and Research, FDA, as soon as possible, with a written report within 7 days (see Chapter 28 for reporting information). Patients who are critically ill and near death often receive transfusions in close temporal proximity to death, and clinical suspicion of cause and effect may occasionally be raised. The overwhelming majority of such deaths are unrelated to transfusion, but if there is a suggestion that a transfusion might have contributed to death, it may be prudent to pursue an investigation.

In the absence of such errors as administration of ABO-incompatible blood or of physiologic events clearly attributable to acute hemolysis, anaphylaxis, TRALI, or sepsis, transfusion is highly unlikely to be acutely responsible for death. The review should include all available medical and laboratory records and the results of an autopsy, if performed. On the other hand, if an investigation does reveal evidence or the possibility of hemolysis, anaphylactic or pulmonary events, unexplained sepsis, or ambiguous identification records, the case may warrant more extensive inquiry.

References

1. Popovsky MA, ed. Transfusion reactions. 2nd ed. Bethesda, MD: AABB Press, 2001.
2. Heddle NM, Kelton JG. Febrile nonhemolytic transfusion reactions. In: Popovsky MA, ed. Transfusion reactions. 2nd ed. Bethesda, MD: AABB Press, 2001:45-82.
3. Davenport RD. Hemolytic transfusion reactions. In: Popovsky MA, ed. Transfusion reactions. 2nd ed. Bethesda, MD: AABB Press, 2001: 1-44.
4. Capon SM, Goldfinger D. Acute hemolytic transfusion reaction, a paradigm of the systemic inflammatory response: New insights into pathophysiology and treatment. Transfusion 1995;35:513-20 [Erratum in Transfusion 1995;35:794].
5. Sazama K. Report of 355 transfusion-associated deaths: 1976-1985. Transfusion 1990;30: 583-90.
6. Del Greco F, Kurtides ES. Kell incompatibility with acute renal failure. Arch Intern Med 1963; 112:727-30.
7. Linden JV, Wagner K, Voytovich AE, Sheehan J. Transfusion errors in New York State: An analysis of 10 years' experience. Transfusion 2000;40:1207-13.
8. Jandl JH. Blood: Textbook of hematology. 2nd ed. Boston: Little, Brown & Co, 1996.
9. Davenport RD, Kunkel SL. Cytokine roles in hemolytic and non-hemolytic transfusion reactions. Transfus Med Rev 1994;8:157-68.
10. Davenport RD. Inflammatory cytokines in hemolytic transfusion reactions. In: Davenport RD, Snyder EL, eds. Cytokines in transfusion medicine: A primer. Bethesda, MD: AABB Press, 1996:85-97.

11. Butler J, Parker D, Pillai R, et al. Systemic release of neutrophil elastase and tumour necrosis factor alpha following ABO incompatible blood transfusion. Br J Haematol 1991;79: 525-6.

12. Savitsky JP, Doczi J, Black J, Arnold JD. A clinical safety trial of stroma-free hemoglobin. Clin Pharmacol Ther 1978;23:73-80.

13. Simon T. Proficiency testing program. CAP Survey 1991 J-C. Northfield, IL: College of American Pathologists, 1991.

14. Asher D, Atterbury CLJ, Chapman C, et al. Serious Hazards of Transfusion (SHOT). Annual Report, 2000-2001. Manchester, UK: Serious Hazards of Transfusion Steering Group, 2002.

15. Marik PE. Low-dose dopamine: A systematic review. Intensive Care Med 2002;28:877-83.

16. Beauregard P, Blajchman MA. Hemolytic and pseudo-hemolytic transfusion reactions: An overview of the hemolytic transfusion reactions and the clinical conditions that mimic them. Transfus Med Rev 1994;8:184-99.

17. Silva MA, ed. Standards for blood banks and transfusion services. 23rd ed. Bethesda, MD: AABB, 2005.

18. Blajchman MA. Transfusion-associated bacterial sepsis: The phoenix rises yet again. Transfusion 1994;34:940-2.

19. Heddle NM, Blajchman MA, Meyer RM, et al. A randomized controlled trial comparing the frequency of acute reactions to plasma-reduced platelets and prestorage WBC-reduced platelets. Transfusion 2002;42:556-66.

20. Ferrara JLM. The febrile platelet transfusion reaction: A cytokine shower. Transfusion 1995; 35:89-90.

21. Davenport RD, Burdick M, Moore SA, Kunkel SL. Cytokine production in IgG-mediated red cell incompatibility. Transfusion 1993;33:19-24.

22. Brand A. Passenger leukocytes, cytokines, and transfusion reactions. N Engl J Med 1994;331: 670-1.

23. Widmann FK. Controversies in transfusion medicine: Should a febrile transfusion response occasion the return of the blood component to the blood bank? Pro. Transfusion 1994;34:356-8.

24. Oberman HA. Controversies in transfusion medicine: Should a febrile transfusion response occasion the return of the blood component to the blood bank? Con. Transfusion 1994;34:353-5.

25. Wang SE, Lara PN, Lee-Ow A, et al. Acetaminophen and diphenhydramine as premedication for platelet transfusions: A prospective randomized double-blind placebo-controlled trial. Am J Hematol 2001;70:191-4.

26. Vamvakas EC, Pineda AA. Allergic and anaphylactic reactions. In: Popovsky MA, ed. Transfusion reactions. 2nd ed. Bethesda, MD: AABB Press, 2001:83-128.

27. Sandler SG, Mallory D, Malamut D, Eckrich R. IgA anaphylactic transfusion reactions. Transfus Med Rev 1995;9:1-8.

28. Burks AW, Sampson HA, Buckley RH. Anaphylactic reactions after gamma globulin administration in patients with hypogammaglobulinemia. N Engl J Med 1986;314:560-4.

29. Lambin P, LePennec PY, Hauptmann G, et al. Adverse transfusion reactions associated with a precipitating anti-C4 antibody of anti-Rodgers specificity. Vox Sang 1984;47:242-9.

30. Westhoff CM, Sipherd BD, Wylie DE, Toalson LD. Severe anaphylactic reactions following transfusions of platelets to a patient with anti-Ch. Transfusion 1992;32:576-9.

31. Shimada E, Tadokoro K, Watamabe Y, et al. Anaphylactic transfusion reactions in haptoglobin-deficient patients with IgE and IgG haptoglobin antibodies. Transfusion 2002;42: 766-73.

32. Leitman SF, Boltansky H, Alter HJ, et al. Allergic reactions in healthy plateletpheresis donors caused by sensitization to ethylene oxide gas. N Engl J Med 1986;315:1192-6.

33. Ramirez MA. Horse asthma following blood transfusion; report of case. JAMA 1919;73:985.

34. Routledge RC, De Kretser DMH, Wadsworth LD. Severe anaphylaxis due to passive sensitization to donor's blood. Br Med J 1976;1:434.

35. Owen HG, Brecher ME. Atypical reactions associated with use of angiotensin-converting enzyme inhibitors and apheresis. Transfusion 1994;34:891-4.

36. Alving BM, Hojima Y, Pisano JJ, et al. Hypotension associated with pre-kallikrein activator (Hageman factor fragments) in plasma protein fraction. N Engl J Med 1978;299:66-70.

37. Shiba M, Tadokoro K, Sawanobori M, et al. Activation of the contact system by filtration of platelet concentrates with a negatively charged white cell-removal filter and measurement of venous blood bradykinin level in patients who received filtered platelets. Transfusion 1997;37:457-62.

38. Hume HA, Popovsky MA, Benson K, et al. Hypotensive reactions: A previously uncharacterized complication of platelet transfusion? Transfusion 1996;36:904-9.

39. Mair B, Leparc GF. Hypotensive reactions associated with platelet transfusions and angiotensin-converting enzyme inhibitors. Vox Sang 1998;74:21-30.

40. Agostini JV, Leo-Summers LS, Inonye SK. Cognitive and other adverse effects of

diphenhydramine use in hospitalized older patients. Arch Intern Med 2001;161:2091-7.

41. Pineda AA, Zylstra VW, Clare DE, et al. Viability and functional integrity of washed platelets. Transfusion 1989;29:524-7.

42. Popovsky MA. Transfusion-related acute lung injury (TRALI). In: Popovsky MA, ed. Transfusion reactions. 2nd ed. Bethesda, MD: AABB Press, 2001:155-70.

43. Zoon KC. Transfusion related acute lung injury ("Dear Colleague" letter). (October 19, 2001) Rockville, MD: CBER Office of Communication, Training, and Manufacturers Assistance, 2001.

44. Kleinman S, Caulfield T, Chan P, et al. Toward an understanding of transfusion-related acute lung injury: Statement of a consensus panel. Transfusion 2004;44:1774-89.

45. Popovsky MA, Moore SB. Diagnostic and pathogenetic considerations in transfusion-related acute lung injury. Transfusion 1985;25: 573-7.

46. Popovsky MA, Haley NR. Further characterization of transfusion-related acute lung injury: Demographics, clinical and laboratory features, and morbidity. Immunohematology 2000;16:157-9.

47. Kao GS, Wood IG, Dorfman DM, et al. Investigations into the role of anti-HLA class II antibodies in TRALI. Transfusion 2003;43: 185-91.

48. Kopko PM, Paglieroni TG, Popovsky MA, et al. TRALI: Correlation of antigen-antibody and monocytes activation in donor-recipient pairs. Transfusion 2003;43:177-84.

49. Seeger W, Schneider U, Kreusler B, et al. Reproduction of transfusion-related acute lung injury in an ex vivo lung model. Blood 1990; 76:1438-44.

50. Dry SM, Bechard KM, Milford EL, et al. The pathology of transfusion-related acute lung injury. Am J Clin Pathol 1999;112:216-21.

51. McCullough J. Granulocyte transfusion. In: Petz LD, Swisher SN, Kleinman S, et al, eds. Clinical practice of transfusion medicine. 3rd ed. New York: Churchill Livingstone, 1996:413-32.

52. Silliman CC, Paterson AJ, Dickey WO, et al. The association of biologically active lipids with the development of transfusion-related acute lung injury: A retrospective study. Transfusion 1997;37:719-26.

53. Silliman CC, Boshkov LK, Mehdizadehkashi Z, et al. Transfusion-related acute lung injury: Epidemiology and a prospective analysis of etiologic factors. Blood 2003;101:454-62.

54. Audet AM, Popovsky MA, Andrzejewski C. Transfusion-associated circulatory overload in orthopedic surgery patients: A multi-insti-

tutional study. Immunohematology 1996;12: 87-9.

55. Bowman RJ, Laudi N, Aslan D, Burgher A. Use of BNP to evaluate TRALI (abstract). Transfusion 2004;44(Suppl):24A.

56. Dzik WH, Kirkley SA. Citrate toxicity during massive blood transfusion. Transfus Med Rev 1988;2:76-94.

57. Olinger GN, Hottenrott C, Mulder DG, et al. Acute clinical hypocalcemic myocardial depression during rapid blood transfusion and postoperative hemodialysis: A preventable complication. J Thorac Cardiovasc Surg 1976; 72:503-11.

58. Howland WS, Jacobs RG, Goulet AH. An evaluation of calcium administration during rapid blood replacement. Anesth Analg 1960;39: 557-63.

59. Boyan CP, Howland WS. Cardiac arrest and temperature of bank blood. JAMA 1963;183: 58-60.

60. Iserson KV, Huestis DW. Blood warming: Current applications and techniques. Transfusion 1991;31:558-71.

61. Valeri CR, Feingold H, Cassidy G, et al. Hypothermia-induced reversible platelet dysfunction. Ann Surg 1987;205:175-81.

62. Sessler DI. Current concepts: Mild perioperative hypothermia. N Engl J Med 1997;336: 1730-7.

63. Collins JA. Problems associated with the massive transfusion of stored blood. Surgery 1974;174:274-95.

64. Liu EA, Manino FL, Lane TA. Prospective, randomized trial of the safety and efficacy of a limited donor exposure transfusion program for premature neonates. J Pediatr 1994; 125:92-6.

65. Miller RD, Robbins TO, Tong MJ, Barton SL. Coagulation defects associated with massive blood transfusion. Ann Surg 1971;174:794-801.

66. Counts RB, Haisch C, Simon TL, et al. Hemostasis in massively transfused trauma patients. Ann Surg 1979;190:91-9.

67. Lim RC, Olcott C, Robinson AJ, Blaisdell FW. Platelet response and coagulation changes following massive blood replacement. J Trauma 1973;13:577-82.

68. Harrigan C, Lucas CE, Ledgerwood KAM, et al. Serial changes in primary hemostasis after massive transfusion. Surgery 1985;98: 836-43.

69. Ciavarella D, Reed RL, Counts RB, et al. Clotting factor levels and the risk of microvascular bleeding in the massively transfused patient. Br J Haematol 1987;67:365-8.

70. Harke H, Rahman S. Haemostatic disorders in massive transfusion. Bibl Haematol 1980; 46:179-88.

71. Collins JA. Recent developments in the area of massive transfusion. World J Surg 1987;11: 75-81.

72. Murray DJ, Pennell BJ, Weinstein SL, Olson JD. Packed red cells in acute blood loss: Dilutional coagulopathy as a cause of surgical bleeding. Anesth Analg 1995;80:336-42.

73. Reed RL, Ciavarella D, Heimbach DM, et al. Prophylactic platelet administration during massive transfusion: A prospective, randomized, double-blind clinical study. Ann Surg 1986; 203:40-8.

74. O'Quin RJ, Lakshminarayan S. Venous air embolism. Arch Intern Med 1982;142:2173-6.

75. Elliott K, Sanders J, Brecher, ME. Transfusion medicine illustrated. Visualizing the hemolytic transfusion reaction. Transfusion 2003;43: 297.

76. Henry JB. Clinical diagnosis and management by laboratory methods. 20th ed. Philadelphia: WB Saunders, 2001.

77. Nance ST. Flow cytometry in transfusion medicine. In: Anderson KC, Ness PM, eds. Scientific basis of transfusion medicine. Philadelphia: WB Saunders, 1994:707-25.

78. Baldwin ML, Barrasso C, Ness PM, Garratty G. A clinically significant erythrocyte antibody detectable only by ^{51}Cr survival studies. Transfusion 1983;23:40-4.

79. Sazama K. Bacteria in blood for transfusion: A review. Arch Pathol Lab Med 1994;118:350-65.

80. Lostumbo MM, Holland PV, Schmidt PJ. Isoimmunization after multiple transfusions. N Engl J Med 1966;275:141-4.

81. Issitt PD, Anstee DJ. Applied blood group serology. 4th ed. Durham, NC: Montgomery Scientific Publications, 1998.

82. Ramsey G, Larson P. Loss of red cell antibodies over time. Transfusion 1988;28:162-5.

83. Ramsey G, Smietana SJ. Long-term follow-up testing of red cell alloantibodies. Transfusion 1994;34:122-4.

84. Heddle NM, Soutar RL, O'Hoski PL, et al. A prospective study to determine the frequency and clinical significance of alloimmunization post-transfusion. Br J Haematol 1995;91: 1000-5.

85. Ness PM, Shirey RS, Thoman SK, Buck SA. The differentiation of delayed serologic and delayed hemolytic transfusion reactions: Incidence, long-term serologic findings, and clinical significance. Transfusion 1990;30: 688-93.

86. Pinkerton PH, Coovadia AS, Goldstein J. Frequency of delayed haemolytic transfusion reactions following antibody screening and immediate-spin crossmatching. Transfusion 1992; 32:814-7.

87. Vamvakas EC, Pineda AA, Reisner R, et al. The differentiation of delayed hemolytic and serologic transfusion reactions: Incidence and predictors of hemolysis. Transfusion 1995;35: 26-32.

88. Garratty G. Severe reactions associated with transfusions of patients with sickle cell disease. Transfusion 1997;37:357-61.

89. Vichinsky EP, Luban NL, Wright E, et al. Prospective RBC phenotype matching in a stroke-prevention trial in sickle cell anemia: A multicenter transfusion trial. Transfusion 2001; 41:1086-92.

90. Petz LD, Garratty G. Immune hemolytic anemias. 2nd ed. Philadelphia: Churchill Livingstone, 2004:335-40.

91. Webb IJ, Anderson KC. Transfusion-associated graft-vs-host disease. In: Popovsky MA, ed. Transfusion reactions. 2nd ed. Bethesda, MD: AABB Press, 2001:171-86.

92. Ohto H, Anderson KC. Survey of transfusion-associated graft-versus-host disease in immunocompetent recipients. Transfus Med Rev 1996;10:31-43.

93. Juji T, Takahashi K, Shibata Y. Post-transfusion graft versus host disease as a result of directed donations from relatives (letter). N Engl J Med 1989;321:56.

94. Ferrara JL, Krenger W. Graft-vs-host disease: The influence of type 1 and type 2 cell cytokines. Transfus Med Rev 1998;12:1-17.

95. Food and Drug Administration. Memorandum. Recommendations regarding license amendments and procedures for gamma irradiation of blood products. (July 22, 1993) Rockville, MD: CBER Office of Communication, Training, and Manufacturers Assistance, 1993.

96. Przepiorka D, LeParc GF, Stovall MA, et al. Use of irradiated blood components. Practice parameter. Am J Clin Pathol 1996;106:6-11.

97. McFarland JG. Postransfusion purpura. In: Popovsky MA, ed. Transfusion reactions. 2nd ed. Bethesda, MD: AABB Press, 2001:187-212.

98. McLeod BC, Strauss RG, Ciavarella D, et al. Management of hematological disorders and cancers. J Clin Apheresis 1996;11:211-30.

99. Mueller-Eckhardt C, Kiefel V. High-dose IgG for post-transfusion purpura revisited. Blut 1988; 57:163-7.

100. Brecher ME, Moore SB, Letendre L. Post-transfusion purpura: The therapeutic value of Pl^{A1}-negative platelets. Transfusion 1990;30: 433-5.

101. Win N, Matthey F, Slater NGP. Blood components—Transfusion support in post-transfusion purpura due to HPA-1a immunization. Vox Sang 1996;71:191-3.

102. Opelz G, Senger DP, Mickey MR, Terasaki PI. Effect of blood transfusions on subsequent

kidney transplants. Transplant Proc 1973;5: 253-9.

103. Blumberg N, Heal JM. Effects of transfusion on immune function: Cancer recurrence and infection. Arch Pathol Lab Med 1994;118: 371-9.

104. Blajchman MA. Allogeneic blood transfusions, immunomodulation, and postoperative bacterial infection: Do we have the answers yet? Transfusion 1997;37:121-5.

105. Vamvakas EC, Blajchman MA, eds. Immunomodulatory effects of blood transfusion. Bethesda, MD: AABB Press, 1999.

106. Sharon BI, Honig GR. Management of congenital hemolytic anemias. In: Simon TL, Dzik WH, Snyder EL, et al, eds. Rossi's principles of transfusion medicine. 3rd ed. Baltimore, MD: Lipincott Williams and Wilkins, 2002:463-82.

107. Adams DM, Schultz WH, Ware RE, Kinney TR. Erythrocytapheresis can reduce iron overload and prevent the need for chelation therapy in chronically transfused pediatric patients. J Pediatr Hematol Oncol 1996;18: 46-50.

Chapter 28

Transfusion-Transmitted Diseases

MANY ADVANCES HAVE been made in the testing of blood donations for infectious diseases. However, the risk of transmitting viral, bacterial, and parasitic diseases via transfusion still exists, and new agents may appear at any time. Thus, infectious complications of transfusion remain an important area of concern in transfusion medicine.

Hepatitis

Hepatitis is inflammation of the liver that can be caused by many different toxins, immunologic processes, or infectious agents. Hepatitis linked to transfusion is almost exclusively caused by viruses. These viruses include hepatitis viruses A-E (HAV, HBV, HCV, HDV, HEV), cytomegalovirus (CMV), Epstein-Barr virus (EBV), and possibly

newly described putative hepatitis viruses (such as TTV and SEN-V). Infectious agents pose a serious threat to transfusion recipients if they persist in the circulation of asymptomatic blood donors and can cause clinically significant acute or chronic disease manifestations in recipients.

The vast majority of posttransfusion hepatitis in the past was attributable to HBV and HCV, both of which can establish prolonged carrier states in donors characterized by high-titer viremia in the absence of symptoms. HBV and HCV also cause significant long-term liver-related morbidity and mortality.[1,2] These viruses are considered in detail below.

HAV and HEV, which are enterically transmitted viruses, circulate only transiently during the acute phase of infection. Because the viremic individual is usually clinically ill and not a candidate for donation, HAV and HEV are not serious threats to transfusion recipients. However, HAV viremia may be present for up to 28 days before symptoms develop, and isolated cases have been reported associated with transfusion of cellular components[3] and outbreaks with Factor VIII concentrate.[4] Because HAV lacks a lipid envelope, it is not inactivated by solvent/detergent treatment; additional inactivation methods are under development to prevent recurrence of such outbreaks. HEV is rare in the United States, and there have been no documented cases of transfusion transmission in this country.

HDV, formerly called the delta agent, can cause infection and serious hepatitis after transfusion or other parenteral exposure. However, because HDV is a defective virus found only in HBV carriers, screening donors for HBV infection simultaneously eliminates the risk of HDV.[5] HGV, also called GBV-C, is distantly related to HCV and has a high prevalence rate (>1%) among asymptomatic donors. Although HGV is unequivocally transfusion-transmissible,[6] a causal relationship has not been established between HGV infection and hepatitis or any other disease manifestation, despite intensive study.

TTV appears similar to HGV with respect to prevalence, transmissibility, and the lack of clinical disease significance. Thus, screening blood donors for HGV or TTV is not currently recommended. Hepatitis associated with CMV or EBV is generally mild in the absence of severe immunosuppression. The frequency and severity of such hepatitis cases do not justify routine screening measures.[7] SEN-V has been associated with transfusion-associated non-A through non-E hepatitis in one study,[8] but a causal association has not been established, nor has SEN-V been significantly associated with chronic non-A through non-E hepatitis. SEN-V appears to be distantly related to TTV and to be a member of a family of small, circular DNA viruses called *Circoviridae*. Screening for these agents is not currently recommended because disease associations have not been established.

Clinical Manifestations of Hepatitis

Most individuals who acquire HBV or HCV infection have a subclinical primary infection without obvious symptoms or physical evidence of disease. Some develop overt hepatitis with jaundice, nausea, vomiting, abdominal discomfort, fatigue, dark urine, and elevation of liver enzymes. Signs and symptoms usually resolve spontaneously. Acute hepatitis C tends to be milder than hepatitis B. Uncommonly, the clinical course of HBV and, rarely, HCV infections may be complicated by fulminant hepatitis. Of greater concern is a propensity of hepatitis C to evolve to chronic hepatitis (75% to 85% of affected individuals), with a significant number demonstrating long-term progression to cirrhosis, liver failure, or hepatocellular carcinoma. Hepatitis A tends to be clinically mild in otherwise healthy hosts and is not known to progress to chronic hepatitis or a chronic carrier state.[9] HEV infection may lead to severe disease in pregnant women.[10] Vaccination is available for hepatitis A and for hepatitis B, and hepatitis B immune globulin (HBIG) has proven useful for post-exposure prophylaxis for hepatitis B and immune serum globulin (ISG) for hepatitis A.

Chronic Carriers of HBV

After initial HBV infection, a proportion of patients fail to clear infectious virus from the bloodstream and become chronic carriers for years or life. HBV carriers produce, in addition to the infectious viral particle, large amounts of noninfectious envelope protein detected by the assay for hepatitis B surface antigen (HBsAg). The risk of becoming an HBsAg carrier is strongly age-dependent; ≤5% of those infected with HBV as adults become chronic HBsAg carriers, whereas ≥95% recover completely and develop protective antibody against HBsAg (anti-HBs). In contrast, before routine prophylactic immune globulin infusion and immunization, 90% or more of infants infected perinatally became carriers and became at risk for progressing to cirrhosis and hepatocellular carcinoma. According to World Health Organization estimates, the number of HBsAg carriers is approximately 400 million worldwide,[11] with a prevalence of up to 10% in some Asian countries, 0.1% to 0.5% in the general US population, and 0.02% to 0.04% in US blood donors. Small proportions (<10%) of HBsAg carriers develop clinical manifestations, such as hepatic insufficiency, cirrhosis, or hepatocellular carcinoma.

Chronic Carriers of HCV

Most people who are initially infected with HCV become chronic HCV carriers, with 75% to 85% having persistent HCV RNA in the serum and liver for years to decades. At least 50% of such HCV carriers have biochemical and histologic evidence of chronic liver inflammation.[12] Despite this chronic inflammatory process, most HCV-infected individuals remain asymptomatic. During the first 20 years after infection, HCV is usually indolent and associated with low mortality and morbidity. Those with clinical liver disease represented about 10% of the entire infected cohort in one study.[13] The risk that and the rate at which chronic hepatitis by itself will progress to cirrhosis is unknown. It is thought that alcohol may play a synergistic role in exacerbating chronic hepatitis C. Posttransfusion HCV in children infected after cardiac surgery appears to resolve more frequently than that in adults

and to be a mild infection at almost 20 years of follow-up.[14]

Recommendations for clinical management of persons with chronic HCV infection were developed by a National Institutes of Health consensus development conference[15] and have been updated and expanded by others.[16]

Markers of Viral Infection

Laboratory tests can identify markers of previous exposure and probable current infectivity for HBV and HCV, which are useful for screening and diagnostic applications. Table 28-1 lists the molecular and serologic markers commonly used in the diagnosis of hepatitis. Figure 28-1 illustrates the sequence of test results typical of individuals with acute HBV infection that completely resolves.

The period between exposure to HBV and emergence of circulating markers of infection (HBV DNA or HBsAg) is usually about 6 weeks.[3,9] HBV DNA, detectable by pooled nucleic acid amplification testing (NAT) techniques, is the first marker to appear, followed by detectable HBsAg. Individual donor NAT (ID-NAT) is able to detect HBV DNA approximately 19 days before minipooled NAT (MP-NAT).[17] Antibody to the HBV core protein (anti-HBc) usually appears several weeks later, first as IgM and then as IgG. The clearance of HBsAg and appearance of anti-HBs signal resolution of infection. However, there has been a report of a fatality, after reactivation of HBV in a patient treated with rituximab, who was previously anti-HBs-reactive.[18] The specific virus showed multiple mutations in major antigenic sites and was thought to escape the patient's endogenous immunity.

Two additional HBV markers, HBeAg or its antibody (anti-HBe), are useful diagnostic and prognostic markers but are not employed in donor screening. An asymptom-

Table 28-1. Molecular and Serologic Tests in the Diagnosis of Viral Hepatitis

HBV

DNA	HBsAg	Anti-HBc Total	IgM	Anti-HBs	HBeAg	Anti-HBe	Interpretation
+	−	−	−	−	−	−	Window period
+	+	+/−	+/−	−	+/−	−	Early acute HBV infection/chronic carrier
+	+	+	+	−	+	−	Acute infection
+/−	−	+	+	−	+/−	+/−	Early convalescent infection/possible early chronic carrier
+/−	+	+	−	−	+/−	+/−	Chronic carrier*
−	−	+	−	+	−	+/−	Recovered infection
−	−	−	−	+	−	−	Vaccinated or recovered infection
−	−	+	−	−	−	−	Recovered infection? False positive?

HDV

RNA	HBsAg	Anti-HBc	IgM	Anti-HBs	Anti-Delta		Interpretation
+	+	+		−	+		Acute or chronic HDV infection
−	−	+		+	+		Recovered infection

HCV

RNA	Anti-HCV (Screening EIA)	Recombinant Antigens (RIBA) 5-1-1	c100-3	c33c	c22-3	Interpretation
+/−	+	Not available				Probable acute or chronic HCV infection (if RNA is positive)
−	+	−	−	−	−	False positive

	RNA			Interpretation
	+/−	+		Probable false positive (if RNA is negative); possible acute infection (if RNA is positive)†
	+/−	+		Early acute or chronic infection (if RNA is positive); false positive or late recovery (if RNA is negative)†
	+	−	+/−	Acute or chronic infection
	−	+	+/−	Recovered HCV†

	RNA	Anti-HAV Total	IgM	Interpretation
HAV	+	+	+	Acute HAV
	−	+	−	Recovered HAV/vaccinated

	RNA	Anti-HEV Total	IgM	Interpretation
HEV	+	+	+	Acute HEV
	−	+	−	Recovered HEV

*Those with HBeAg are more infectious and likely to transmit vertically.

†Anti-5-1-1 and anti-c100-3 generally appear later than anti-c22-3 and anti-c33c during seroconversion and may disappear spontaneously, during immunosuppression or after successful antiviral therapy.

HBsAg = hepatitis B surface antigen; anti-HBc = antibody to hepatitis B core antigen; anti-HBs = antibody to hepatitis B surface antigen; HBeAg = hepatitis B e antigen; anti-HBe = antibody to hepatitis B e antigen; anti-delta = antibody to delta antigen; anti-HAV = antibody to hepatitis A virus; anti-HCV = antibody to hepatitis C virus; anti-HEV = antibody to hepatitis E virus.

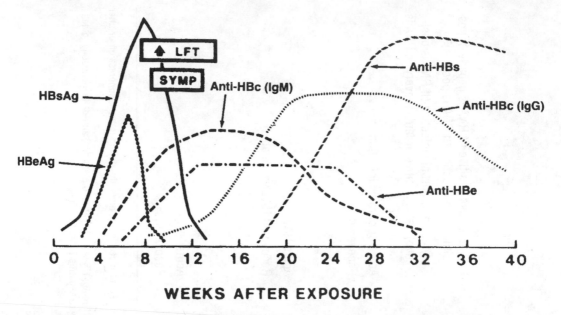

WEEKS AFTER EXPOSURE

Figure 28-1. Serologic markers in hepatitis B virus infection that resolved without complications. In the acute phase, markers often appear before onset of liver function test (LFT) abnormalities and symptoms (SYMP). Anti-HBs and anti-HBc persist after recovery and indicate immunity. In chronic carriers (not shown), HBsAg persists and anti-HBc is usually present, but anti-HBs is absent (HBeAg and anti-HBe may be present, see Table 28-1). HBV DNA (not shown) may be detected approximately 1 to 2 weeks before HBsAg.

atic HBsAg-positive individual may either be in the early phase of acute HBV infection (without anti-HBc or with IgM anti-HBc) or a chronic HBV carrier (with IgG anti-HBc). HBsAg particles are produced in excess during acute and chronic infection; blood from individuals with circulating HBsAg can infect others. Current screening immunoassays detect approximately 0.2 to 0.7 ng/mL HBsAg or $\geq 3 \times 10^7$ particles.[3] The number of HBsAg particles in most acute and chronic infections exceeds this level, but transmission of HBV from HBsAg seronegative donors has been described. NAT testing allows the detection of as few as 10 genomic copies of HBV DNA.[3] The value of NAT for the detection of seronegative donors infected with HBV is under study but may be reduced by high sensitivity of current assays for HBsAg and the relatively slow rise in HBV DNA levels contrasted with HIV and HCV. It is possible that

effective detection of seronegative HBV infected donors by NAT will require testing at the single donation level.[19] HBV vaccines contain noninfectious HBsAg protein, which may result in false-positive HBsAg screening test results for a few days after the inoculation. Resulting protective antibodies are directed against HBsAg; vaccination does not produce anti-HBc.

Tests for antibodies to HCV are enzyme immunoassays (EIAs) using recombinant antigens of HCV coated on a solid phase as the capture reagent. Current assays detect antibodies to c200 (including c33c and c100-3), c22-3, and NS-5. Anti-HCV is detectable by third-generation EIAs approximately 10 weeks after infection. HCV RNA is present at high concentrations in plasma during most of the period from exposure to antibody seroconversion. Anti-HCV is detected in 40% to 50% of samples from patients at initial diagnosis of acute hepatitis, either transfusion-transmitted or community-acquired.[20]

The clinical significance of a positive screening test for anti-HCV in healthy blood donors is unclear without supplemental testing. Approximately 0.21% of US blood donors have repeatedly reactive EIA results.[21] Several generations of recombinant immunoblot assays (RIBA) have been licensed by the Food and Drug Administration (FDA) for further elucidation of repeatedly reactive EIA results. An individual who is positive by RIBA is considered to have true HCV antibody; in 70% to 90% of these cases, HCV nucleic acid is detectable by NAT methods. The infectivity of units that are positive for HCV RNA approaches 100%.[22] In contrast, EIA repeatedly reactive donors with negative or indeterminate RIBA 3.0 results, representing 37% of EIA repeatedly reactive donors, are rarely infected or infectious. Regardless of RIBA results, a donation with a repeatedly reactive EIA result cannot be used for transfusion. Donors with negative RIBA results may be considered for reentry (Table 28-2).

In 1999, NAT for HCV RNA was implemented as a donor screening assay under FDA-sanctioned investigational new drug (IND) protocols. The testing was performed in minipools of samples from 16 to 24 whole blood donations. The rapid increase in viremia and high viral load of seronegative, acutely infected donors allows sensitive detection of HCV RNA even in these diluted pools. The window period for HCV detection with pooled NAT is reduced to 10 to 30 days.[17] After testing over 39 million donors, approximately 1:270,000 donors had been identified as being in the seronegative window with a positive NAT result.[23]

NAT results can be used in lieu of supplemental testing in specific circumstances. An FDA variance is required.[24] It is anticipated that NAT HCV testing will be used in the future for reentry.

Surrogate Markers

Before HCV was identified and anti-HCV testing became feasible, two nonspecific or "surrogate" tests on donor blood were introduced to reduce the risk of non-A, non-B (NANB) hepatitis after transfusion. In 1986 and 1987, the AABB called for testing of whole blood donations for alanine aminotransferase (ALT) and anti-HBc as surrogates for the direct detection of the NANB agent. Current very sensitive tests for anti-HCV have essentially eliminated the value of surrogate tests in preventing hepatitis,[25] but anti-HBc testing continues as recommended by FDA to prevent HBV transmission. HBV from liver transplant donors with reactive anti-HBc and negative HBsAg test results has been transmitted to their recipients, and reports in the literature show that transfusions of blood reactive for anti-HBc and negative for HBsAg have been associated with development of hepatitis B in some recipients. There may also be a small number of potential donors infected with HBsAg mutants of HBV that may not be optimally detected by currently licensed HBsAg tests.[26] Donors who test repeatedly reactive for anti-HBc on two occasions or who test repeatedly reactive on tests from two different manufacturers should be deferred.

Current Risk of Posttransfusion Hepatitis

The risk of posttransfusion HBV or HCV infection decreased dramatically, to an estimated 1 in 60,000 to 1 in 100,000 risk before implementation of HCV NAT.[27] Not a single new case of transfusion-associated HCV has been detected by the CDC Sentinel Counties Viral Hepatitis Surveillance System since 1994 (M. Alter, personal communication, 3/04).[1] The development of progressively improved HCV antibody tests and stringent selection measures for donors have contributed to this remark-

Table 28-2. Reentry of Donors with Repeatedly Reactive Screening Tests

Repeatedly Reactive for					Reentry Status
Anti-HIV-1 or -1/2	Anti-HIV-2	HIV-1-Ag	HBsAg	Anti-HCV	
Initial sample					
Licensed Western blot positive or indeterminate or IFA reactive	Different HIV-2 EIA RR	Confirmed by neutralization	Confirmed by neutralization or anti-HBc RR	RIBA indeterminate or positive	Not eligible for reentry
Licensed Western blot or IFA NR	Different HIV-2 EIA NR and licensed Western blot or IFA NR	Not confirmed by neutralization	HBsAg specificity not confirmed by neutralization and anti-HBc NR	RIBA negative	Evaluate for reentry
Follow-up sample					
(Drawn 6 months later)	(Drawn 6 months later)	(Drawn 8 weeks later)	(Drawn 8 weeks later)	(Drawn 6 months later)	
EIA RR or Western blot positive or indeterminate or IFA reactive	RR HIV-1 or different HIV-2 EIA RR or a licensed Western blot or IFA reactive or indeterminate	HIV-1-Ag RR, neutralization confirmed or not confirmed	HBsAg RR or anti-HBc RR	EIA RR or RIBA indeterminate or positive	Not eligible for reentry
Original EIA method NR and whole virus lysate anti-HIV-1 EIA NR and licensed Western blot or IFA NR	Screening test and a different HIV-2 EIA NR and licensed Western blot or IFA NR	HIV-1-Ag and anti-HIV-1 EIA NR or HIV-1-Ag RR, not confirmed (temporary deferral for additional 8 weeks)	HBsAg NR and anti-HBc NR	Licensed multiantigen EIA method NR and RIBA negative	Eligible for reentry

NR = nonreactive; RR = repeatedly reactive; RIBA = recombinant immunoblot assay; IFA = immunofluorescence assay; EIA = enzyme immunoassay; anti-HIV-1 = antibody to human immunodeficiency virus, type 1; anti-HIV-2 = antibody to human immunodeficiency virus, type 2; HIV-1-Ag = HIV-1 antigen; HBsAg = hepatitis B surface antigen; anti-HCV = antibody to hepatitis C virus; anti-HBc = antibody to hepatitis B core antigen.

able decline, and transfusion is no longer considered a major risk factor for HCV transmission.[28] Nucleic acid screening assays for HCV were implemented by blood centers in 1999. In 3 years of NAT testing, 170 HCV NAT-positive, seronegative donations were identified in the United States among 39.7 million screened donations.[23] NAT has probably reduced the residual risk for HCV transmission to ≤1 in 2,000,000 components transfused.[29,30]

Quarantine and Recipient Tracing

Donations with repeatedly reactive screening test results (HBsAg, anti-HBc, and/or anti-HCV) cannot be used for transfusion. In addition, in-date components from collections preceding the current unsuitable donation may need to be quarantined as follows, and consignee notification for the purpose of recipient tracing (ie, look-back) may be required[31,32]:

For HCV:

- Extending back indefinitely, to the extent that computerized electronic records exist for anti-HCV repeatedly reactive and confirmed donations or repeatedly reactive donations for which supplemental tests were not performed.

- Extending back to January 1, 1988 if computerized electronic records are not available.

For HBsAg and anti-HBc:

- In-date components, extending back 5 years, or 12 months from the most recent negative test result for units that were repeatedly reactive or confirmed, or for which confirmatory testing was not performed.

Depending on the results of licensed supplemental tests and prior screening tests, the quarantined units may be released for transfusion or further manufacture, or may have to be destroyed. Recipients notified as a result of the HCV look-back should be counseled regarding the nature of the subsequent donor test results and offered appropriate testing. If they test positive, life style changes (eg, abstinence from alcohol consumption) and evaluation for chronic liver disease justifying antiviral therapy to reduce the likelihood of disease progression may be warranted. Earlier experiences from Canada and several European countries indicate that the number of transfusion recipients who ultimately benefit from look-back efforts is small.[33] A survey of US blood collection facilities and hospital transfusion services after implementation of targeted HCV look-back resulted in an estimate that notification of the recipients of 98,484 components would result in the identification of 1520 infected persons who were previously unaware of their infection.[34] This would represent less than 1% of the 300,000 still-living recipients who may have acquired infection by blood transfusion. More recently, 0.9% to 5.0% of patients tested for hepatitis C were found to be positive in a review of look-back studies in Canada that notified recipients of any previous transfusions of the risk of HCV and then provided testing; 42% to 58% of the cases were newly identified.[35]

Human Immunodeficiency Viruses

The human immunodeficiency viruses type 1 (HIV-1) and type 2 (HIV-2) are the etiologic agents of AIDS. The AIDS syndrome was recognized in 1981, well before the discovery of the causative virus in 1984. Wider implications of the immune disorder were noted when, in 1982, AIDS was reported in three patients with hemophilia,[36] and in a 17-month-old infant whose multiple transfusions at birth included a unit of platelets from a donor who subsequently developed AIDS.[37] Within a few years, studies established that well over 50% of patients with hemophilia who received clotting factor concentrates in the early 1980s developed HIV-1 infection.[38] In some regions of the United States, up to 1% of single-donor unit transfusions were infected with HIV in the early 1980s.[39]

Clinical Manifestations of HIV Infection

HIV is a cytopathic retrovirus that preferentially infects CD4-positive T lymphocytes (helper T cells) in lymph nodes and other lymphoid tissue.[40] After primary infection, HIV replicates and disseminates initially as cell-free virions, and 10 days to 3 weeks after infection, viremia is first detectable in the plasma. During this time, about 60% of acutely infected persons develop an acute retroviral syndrome, characterized by a flu-like illness with fever, enlarged lymph nodes, sore throat, rash, joint and muscle pain—with or without headache, diarrhea, and vomiting. As HIV-1 antibodies appear, the disease enters a clinically latent stage; however, viral replication and dissemination continue. During this phase, the virus can be transmitted by blood or genital secretions (Fig 28-2).

Persistent infection with an asymptomatic clinical status has been estimated to last a median of 10 to 12 years in the absence of treatment.[41] After years of asymptomatic infection, both plasma viremia and the percentage of infected T lymphocytes

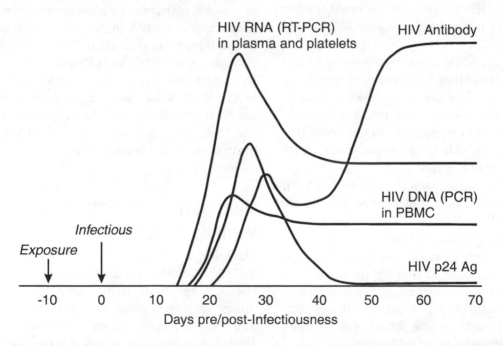

Figure 28-2. Virologic events during primary HIV infection. After initial infection and propagation of HIV in lymph nodes, a blood donor becomes infectious (defined as day 0), with HIV RNA being detectable in plasma on days 14-15, HIV DNA detectable in leukocytes at days 17-20, and HIV antibodies detectable between days 20 and 25. Anti-HIV persists indefinitely but may be lost in the preterminal stage of the disease, in parallel with a surge in viral burden, indicating collapse of the immune system. HIV = human immunodeficiency virus; RT-PCR = reverse transcriptase polymerase chain reaction; PBMC = peripheral blood mononuclear cells.

increase. Loss of the immune functions served by helper T cells impairs immune reactivity, and there may be inappropriate immune activation and cytokine secretion. Eventually, there is a sharp decline in the number of CD4+ T lymphocytes, and the vast majority of infected individuals succumb to opportunistic illnesses fostered by profound immunosuppression.

Enumeration of viral load and CD4+ cells is used to guide clinical and therapeutic management of HIV-infected persons. The AIDS classification system devised by the Centers for Disease Control and Prevention (CDC) is based on the number of CD4+ T cells (<200/μL defines AIDS), the presence or absence of systemic symptoms, and existence of any of the 26 clinical conditions considered to be AIDS-defining illnesses.[42] Among these conditions are otherwise unusual malignancies, such as Kaposi's sarcoma, central nervous system lymphoma, and a wide array of devastating, potentially lethal opportunistic infections with fungi and parasites, the most common being *Pneumocystis carinii* pneumonia.

Advances in treatment of HIV and opportunistic infections have dramatically enhanced the survival of infected persons. Unfortunately, worldwide, the disease is still spreading rapidly and, for the majority of HIV-infected individuals in developing countries, effective therapy is either not available or not affordable.

Risk Factors for HIV Infection

HIV can be transmitted through sexual contact, childbirth, breast-feeding, and parenteral exposure to blood. Those identified early as being at highest risk were men who had sex with other men; commercial sex workers and their contacts; needle-sharing drug users; patients with hemophilia who received human-derived clotting factor concentrates; and, to a les-

ser extent, recipients of blood transfusions. By 1989, the rate of infection in each group was no longer increasing exponentially and appeared to have reached a plateau in the populations most at risk.[43] HIV seroprevalence had stabilized in most US cities. Heterosexual transmission of HIV represented a progressively larger proportion of US HIV infections and AIDS cases reported in the 1990s.[44] This is of importance in transfusion medicine because screening for heterosexual high-risk behavior is more problematic than screening for male-to-male sex and parenteral drug use.[45]

HIV-2 and HIV-1, Group O

First discovered in 1985, HIV-2 causes endemic infection in many countries in West Africa. Although HIV-2 was initially restricted to West Africa, recent studies in European countries such as Great Britain and France (which have significant immigration from West Africa) have observed increasing rates of HIV-2 and other HIV subtypes.[46,47]

The first case of HIV-2 infection in the United States was reported in March 1988 in a young West African who had recently immigrated to the United States.[48] The spectrum of disease attributable to HIV-2 is similar to that caused by HIV-1; however, there appears to be a longer incubation period and lower incidence of progression to AIDS. HIV-2 is spread both sexually and from mother to child, but transmission is less efficient than for HIV-1.

Tests in the United States on parenteral drug users, persons with sexually transmitted diseases, newborn infants, and homosexual men confirm the very limited prevalence and transmission of the agent. HIV-1/HIV-2 combination tests were implemented in the United States in 1992. Since then, three HIV-2-infected donors have been identified; none appeared to have been infected in the United States.[49]

To date, three groups of HIV-1 viruses have been identified: group M (major group); group O (outlier group); and, most recently, group N. Further, there are 10 subtypes (A-J) of group M. None of 97 donors retrospectively identified as being HIV-1 infected in 1985 and three (1%) of 383 donors prospectively identified between 1993 and 1996 were found to have non-B subtypes (two subtype As and one subtype C).[50] Of note, this study did find an increase in *env* gene diversity among HIV-1 group B strains over time and called for continued surveillance for emergence of non-B subtypes and development of test systems for their detection. A follow-up study from these same investigators documented characterized HIV subtypes in 291 infected US donors identified from 1997 through 2000 and identified that six (2%) were non-B subtypes of HIV-1 and one was HIV-2.[51] In Cameroon and surrounding West African countries, an estimated 1% to 2% of HIV infections are caused by group O viral strains.[52] As with HIV-2, group O isolates have rarely been seen outside this geographic area. Concern arose when studies demonstrated that some group O viral isolates were not reliably detected by several EIA tests used for blood donor screening. Of the two FDA-licensed tests for NAT, both were evaluated by the manufacturer for the detection of non-B subtypes including group O and N, using a limited number of specimens. (although neither test detects HIV-2). However, until reliable detection of group O infections is established, the FDA recommends indefinite deferral of blood and plasma donors who were born, resided, or traveled in West Africa since 1977, or had sexual contact with someone identified by these criteria.[53] The risk of group O infection in the United States is very low. In a survey of HIV subtypes in US blood donors over a period spanning two decades, only three non-B subtypes were identified. Two of these three donors were born in Africa.[50]

Transfusion Considerations

Transfusion-Transmitted HIV-1

All blood components can transmit HIV-1. Although approximately 1% of all AIDS exposures have resulted from transfusion or organ or tissue transplantation, the introduction of MP-NAT in 1999 virtually eliminated the risk of transfusion-transmitted HIV.[54] The few cases of HIV infection that have been documented since 1999 were attributed to low-level viremic units that likely would have been detected by ID-NAT.[55-57]

Most but not all recipients of HIV-infected blood transfusions become infected. In one large study, HIV infection developed in 89.5% of recipients who received blood from anti-HIV-positive donors.[58] Transmission rates correlated with component type and viral load in the donation. With the exception of coagulation factor concentrates, plasma derivatives (such as albumin and immune globulins) have not been reported to transmit HIV infection. No transmission of HIV attributable to coagulation factors has been documented in the United States since implementation of full donor screening and virus inactivation techniques in 1987.[59]

Transfusion-Transmitted HIV-2 and HIV-1, Group O

There have been two reports of possible HIV-2 transmission through blood component use, both in Europe. Two women were infected by Whole Blood obtained from a donor who developed AIDS at least 16 years after becoming infected with HIV-2; both women were asymptomatic 14 years after transfusion.[60] Two hemophilia patients who received clotting factors were also infected. Because of their extremely low prevalence, no HIV-2 or HIV-1 group O transmissions have been reported in the United States by blood transfusion or any other transmission route.

Current Risk of Posttransfusion HIV

With screening tests available before 1992, the seronegative interval ("window period") averaged 45 days. More sensitive screening tests for HIV antibody closed the antibody-negative window to approximately 22 days.[17] Introduced in 1996, p24 antigen screening further reduced the potentially infectious window by an estimated 6 days,[61] although it appears that fewer HIV-infected units were intercepted by the introduction of this test than had been expected based on the calculated reduction of the infectious window period. Risk from seronegative donations will vary in proportion to the incidence of HIV infection in the donor community. Overall estimates of posttransfusion HIV risk in the United States since the implementation of HIV NAT are approximately 1 in 2 million screened donations.[23,30]

HIV Testing of Blood Donors

AABB *Standards for Blood Banks and Transfusion Services*[62(pp33,34)] and FDA regulations[63] require that all units of blood and components be nonreactive for anti-HIV-1 and anti-HIV-2 before they are issued for transfusion. HIV-1-antigen (HIV-1-Ag) testing is no more required by the FDA or AABB as long as licensed HIV-1 NAT is in place. Figure 28-3 shows the sequence of screening and confirmatory testing for anti-HIV-1/2.

Because the consequence of missing even one true positive is great, screening tests are designed to have high sensitivity both to immunovariant viruses and to low-titer antibody during seroconversion. EIA-detectable antibody develops 2 to 4 weeks after exposure,[58] days to a week after the onset of symptoms in those who have any recognized acute illness,[64] and about 12 days after detectable viremia by ID-NAT or 9 to 10 days by MP-NAT.[17,65]

A few days later, HIV-1 antibodies become detectable by the HIV-1 Western immunoblot. With very rare exceptions, all persons infected with HIV develop anti-HIV reactivity detectable by EIA and Western blot that persists for life.

More sensitive tests using NAT technologies have been shown to detect additional potentially infectious donors. In February 2002, the FDA approved the first NAT system for screening whole blood donors and issued draft guidance for blood establishments; the final guidance was issued in October 2004.[66,67] It has been estimated that HIV NAT has reduced the window period for HIV from 16 days to 10 days.[17] The use of NAT for donor testing has not only increased sensitivity, but has also decreased the number of false-positive tests, increasing specificity. During the 3 years of investigational HIV NAT, 12 confirmed HIV-1 RNA-positive antibody-negative donors were detected in 37 million donations screened, or 1 in 3.1 million, of which only two were detected by HIV-1 p24 antigen.[23]

Confirmatory Testing for Antibodies to HIV-1/2

If a disease has low prevalence in the tested population, the likelihood is high that most positive screening test results will be false positive. More specific supplemental tests are then required to confirm the screening test results. The most commonly used of these tests for antibodies to HIV-1/2 is the Western blot (see Chapter 7).

According to current FDA and CDC criteria, a sample is defined as anti-HIV-positive if at least two of the following bands are

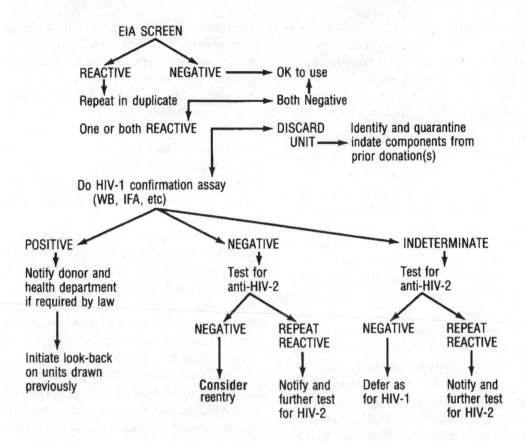

Figure 28-3. Decision tree for anti-HIV-1/HIV-2 testing of blood donors. IFA = immunofluorescence assay; WB = Western blot. If EIA testing is nonreactive, NAT testing must also be nonreactive before release of a donation.

present: p24, gp41, and/or gp120/160.[68] Negative Western blot results have no bands present. Western blot results classified as indeterminate have some bands present but do not have the pattern defining HIV positivity. Individuals infected with HIV may have indeterminate patterns when initially tested but develop additional bands within 6 weeks. Healthy individuals with initial indeterminate patterns continue to have negative or indeterminate results on repeat samples and are negative on clinical examination and additional tests, including viral cultures and NAT. Healthy donors who continue to show the same indeterminate pattern for more than 3 months can be reassured that they are unlikely to have HIV infection, but they are not currently eligible to donate blood. Several groups have identified Western blot patterns in blood donors that were identified as false-positive results; for these, testing (using NAT) is recommended to resolve the infectious status of the donor.[69]

Approximately 50% of all HIV screening EIA repeatedly reactive donors test indeterminate by licensed HIV-1 Western blot assays. However, when these donations were tested by ID-NAT, less than 0.1% were shown to contain HIV-1 RNA (1:1450 RNA-positive, indeterminate donors). When combined with those donations that tested Western blot negative, the frequency of a donor testing HIV repeatedly reactive and then Western blot indeterminate or negative and demonstrating RNA was 1:4.27 million (S. Stramer, personal communication, 3/17/04).

The FDA has approved reentry protocols to qualify donors with negative confirmatory test results as eligible for subsequent donations (see Table 28-2).[70] Reentry currently requires retesting at least 6 months later, to detect delayed seroconversion; the use of EIA tests based on whole-virus lysate; and use of either a licensed Western blot to ensure appropriate sensitivity of the methods or an FDA-licensed immunofluorescence assay.[71] The later sample must also be nonreactive in an EIA test for anti-HIV-2, if standard testing does not include HIV-2. The FDA recently published draft reentry guidelines that will allow reinstatement of donors with indeterminate Western blot results, eliminate the need for viral lysate EIA testing, and include testing by HIV-1 NAT.

NAT results can be used in lieu of supplemental testing in specific circumstances. An FDA variance is required.[24] It is anticipated that NAT HIV-1 testing will be used in the future for reentry.

Positive Tests in Autologous Donors

Whether HIV EIA repeatedly reactive or NAT-positive autologous donations should be withheld from transfusion is controversial.[72] These units may be supplied for autologous use if the following conditions are met: 1) there is a written, signed, and dated request from the patient's physician authorizing this shipment, 2) there is a written statement from the transfusion service indicating willingness to receive this product, and 3) the transfusion service takes responsibility for ensuring that there is documented verification of the accurate identity of the transfusion recipient. These units must be labeled "BIOHAZARD" and "FOR AUTOLOGOUS USE ONLY."

Whether a facility elects to offer autologous services is an internal decision. Institutions should consider, however, that where feasible for a patient, it is generally accepted that the patient should have the option to use his or her blood. In addition, a US Supreme Court decision in the *Bragdon v Abbott* case ruled that HIV-positive individuals are protected under the Americans with Disabilities Act.[73] Whether this would apply to HIV-positive donations that could represent a risk to hospitalized transfused patients remains controversial.

Recipient Tracing (Look-Back)

Identification of persons who have received seronegative or untested blood from a donor later found to be infected by HIV is referred to as "look-back." Because the interval between receipt of an infected transfusion and onset of AIDS can be very long, recipients are usually unaware of their infection and may be infectious to others. To identify these individuals, blood centers must have procedures to notify recipients of previous donations from any donor later found to have a confirmed positive test for anti-HIV or a confirmed positive test for HIV using licensed NAT. If a patient with AIDS is known to have donated previously, recipients of blood or blood components from these donations should be traced and notified. Recipient tracing and testing are usually accomplished through the patient's physician, not through direct contact with the patient. In companion rules, the FDA and the Centers for Medicare and Medicaid Services established timelines and standards defining look-back.[74-77] If recipients of units that were donated at least 12 months before the last known negative test are tested and found negative, earlier recipients are probably not at risk because infectivity earlier than 12 months before a negative screening test is extremely unlikely.

Human T-Cell Lymphotropic Viruses

HTLV, Type I

Human T-cell lymphotropic virus, type I (HTLV-I) was the first human retrovirus isolated and the first to be causally associated with a malignant disease of humans, adult T-cell lymphoma-leukemia (ATL).[58] HTLV-I is also associated with the neurologic condition HTLV-associated myelopathy (HAM), often called tropical spastic paraparesis (TSP). ATL was described before HAM. Both these conditions occur in a small minority (no more than 2-4%) of persons harboring the virus. Infection during childhood is an important aspect of, and possibly a requirement for, developing ATL many years later, whereas childhood or adult infection can cause HAM, with a variable latent period.

Prevalence of HTLV-I infection shows striking geographic clustering, with pockets of high endemicity in parts of southern Japan and certain Pacific Islands; sub-Saharan Africa; and the Caribbean basin, Central America, and South America. Transmission is by mother to child through breast milk, by sexual contact (predominantly male-to-female), and by exposure to blood.

HTLV, Type II

Human T-cell lymphotropic virus, type II (HTLV-II) was described several years after HTLV-I. There is at least 60% similarity of genetic sequences to those of HTLV-I; antibodies to either show strong cross-reactivity in tests with viral lysates. HTLV-II also shows clustering, but in different populations. High prevalence has been noted among some Native American populations and in intravenous drug users in the United States, in whom seroprevalence is 1% to 20%. Rare disease associations with HTLV-II include HAM; its occurrence seems to be somewhat less frequent than with HTLV-I.[58]

Epidemiologic data suggest that there is an excess of infectious syndromes (eg, bronchitis, urinary infections, and pneumonia) among blood donors infected with HTLV-I or -II.[78-81]

Clinical Observations

For both HTLV-I and -II, infection persists lifelong, as does the presence of antibody. Studies of prevalence and transmission use seroconversion as the endpoint for diagnosis. Infection does not cause any recognizable acute events, and with the exception of those developing ATL or HAM, infected individuals experience few, if any, health consequences. Most carriers are asymptomatic and completely unaware of the infection.

Transmission

Both viruses are very strongly cell-associated. Contact with infected viable lymphocytes can cause infection, but plasma appears to be not, or much less, infective. Cellular components from infected donors cause seroconversion in at least 50% of recipients in Japan, but apparently in a much smaller proportion of US recipients.[58] After refrigerated storage for 10 days or more, red cells transfused from an infected donor are far less likely to result in seroconversion, presumably due to degradation of lymphocytes that transmit the virus.[82,83] Transfusion-transmitted HTLV-I infection has been associated with HAM of rather rapid onset and at least one case of ATL.

Donor Tests

Donor screening for anti-HTLV-I began in the United States in late 1988; at that time, the rate of confirmed positive tests was approximately 0.02%, or 1 in 5000 units collected, a figure that has since declined at least 10-fold as seropositive persons have been removed from the donor pool.[84] The combined risk of transfusion-transmitted HTLV-I/II infection has been estimated as about 1 in 641,000 units.[84] Further risk reduction can be expected from the implementation of combination HTLV-I/II EIA tests in blood donor screening. The first such test was licensed in 1998 in the United States. By using viral lysates from both HTLV-I and HTLV-II viruses, the test offers sensitive detection of both anti-HTLV-I and anti-HTLV-II. The originally licensed anti-HTLV-I EIA screening tests might have missed up to 50% of HTLV-II infections.[85]

A donation that is repeatedly reactive on EIA may not be used for transfusion. If a donor tests repeatedly reactive by the EIA screening assay on two or more occasions, he or she should be notified and indefinitely deferred.[85] Another recommended approach is to test donor serum with a second manufacturer's EIA test kit.[86] If that test is also repeatedly reactive, then the donor is indefinitely deferred on the basis of that single donation. Further testing of serum that is repeatedly reactive for anti-HTLV-I/II against antigen preparations specific for the two agents (HTLV-I or HTLV-II), or by NAT on material from peripheral blood mononuclear cells, can characterize the infecting agent. Half or more of US blood donors confirmed infected after EIA screening prove to have HTLV-II infections. Although there is no FDA requirement to perform additional testing (no confirmatory test for HTLV is licensed), most centers do so using an investigational supplemental test or se-

ries of tests in an algorithm if the donation tests repeatedly reactive by both the test-of-record and second HTLV-I/II EIAs; if supplemental tests are positive, the donor is indefinitely deferred (see Table 28-3). Regardless of the results of these investigational supplemental tests, a donor meeting the EIA criteria for indefinite deferral described above must still be indefinitely deferred.

Quarantine and Look-Back

In-date prior collections of blood or components from donors who subsequently are found repeatedly reactive for anti-HTLV-I/II need to be quarantined. Because recipients of units from seropositive donors do not consistently seroconvert and because many seropositive donors have lifelong infection, the time frame for look-back is not self-evident. No requirement for recipient tracing and notification has been established.[85] Screening, in place since 1988, has probably removed from the active donor pool most donors with lifelong infection.

West Nile Virus

West Nile virus (WNV) is a flavivirus primarily transmitted in birds through mosquito bites; humans are incidental hosts. In humans, symptoms range from a mild febrile illness to encephalitis, coma, and death, although about 80% of infected individuals remain asymptomatic. WNV outbreaks have been reported in Europe, the Middle East, and Russia over the past decade and have been associated with human encephalitis and meningitis (in <1%), although no transfusion-associated cases were reported. WNV was observed in the United States, in the metropolitan

Table 28-3. Recommended Actions for HTLV-I/II Testing

| First Donation to Be Tested for HTLV-I/II Antibodies | | | | Subsequent Donation(s) | | | | |
EIA	WB/RIPA	Donation	Donor	EIA	Second Manufacturer	WB/RIPA	Donation	Donor
Repeatedly reactive	Positive	Destroy all components*	Defer and counsel	Not applicable/Donor deferred				
Repeatedly reactive	Negative or indeterm.	Destroy all components*	No action	Repeatedly reactive	Pos	Any result	Destroy all components*	Defer and counsel
				Nonreactive†	Neg	Not done	All components acceptable	No action

*Destroyed unless appropriately labeled as positive for HTLV-I/II antibodies, and labeled for laboratory research use or further manufacture into in-vitro diagnostic reagents.
†Assuming that separate prior donations have been repeatedly reactive for HTLV-I/II antibody no more than once. If separate prior donations had been repeatedly reactive for HTLV-I/II antibodies on two or more occasions, the donor should have been indefinitely deferred.
HTLV-I = human T-cell lymphotropic virus, type I; HTLV-II = human T-cell lymphotropic virus, type II; EIA = enzyme immunoassay; WB = Western blot; RIPA = recombinant immunoprecipitation assay.

New York City area, in 1999. Subsequently, it dispersed rapidly westward throughout the country, spread by infected birds. In 2001, 66 human cases occurred in 10 states. In 2002, 4161 cases of WNV illness were reported in 39 states, including 284 deaths. In 2002, 23 cases were associated with transfusion (with an infected donor identified); Red Blood Cells (RBCs), Fresh Frozen Plasma, and Platelets were implicated.[87] The implicated donations occurred between July 22 and October 6, 2002. Statistical resampling of data available regarding case onset dates during the 2002 epidemic was used to generate estimates of the mean risk of transfusion-associated WNV transmission (per 10,000 donations) for six states and six selected metropolitan areas, with results ranging from a mean of 2.12 to 4.76 and 1.46 to 12.33, respectively.[88]

An FDA guidance document in May 2003 recommended deferral of donors with a diagnosis of WNV infection for 28 days after onset of symptoms or 14 days after resolution, whichever is later, and recommended inquiring whether donors had experienced a fever with headache in the week before donation.[89] However, because most infected persons are asymptomatic, the yield of such measures would be expected to be modest, and testing was sought as the best method to identify infected donors. During the summer and fall of 2003, almost 5 million donations constituting over 95% of collections in the United States were tested for WNV by NAT in minipools of six or 16 samples under one of two IND protocols—one using a polymerase chain reaction method and one using a transcription-mediated amplification method. During 2003, approximately 1000 donors were confirmed as viremic for WNV and approximately 1500 likely infected components were interdicted.[90] However, six probable or confirmed transfusion-as-

sociated WNV cases were reported in 2003; four recipients had WNV encephalitis, one had West Nile fever, and one critically ill patient did not have discernible WNV-compatible illness despite confirmed WNV infection.[91] Some of the donors were identified through retrospective testing of individual samples, and it appears that all were related to specimens with very low viral titers. The number of transfusion-associated cases undoubtedly would have been much higher had widespread testing under IND protocols not been initiated. There were 9862 WNV cases and 264 deaths in the United States overall during this time.

The persistent low-level transmission of WNV by transfusion in 2003 led to the implementation of targeted ID-NAT in high epidemic regions in 2004. This effort successfully interdicted low-level viremic units that would have been missed by MP-NAT.[92,93]

In 2004, the virus appeared predominantly in western states, with California accounting for 31% of cases.[94] Only three states (Hawaii, Alaska, and Washington) remained free of reports of infection in either humans or animals (mammalian and avian). A total of 2470 cases of human WNV infection were reported in 40 states plus the District of Columbia, including 88 fatal cases—far fewer than the previous year. A total of 192 WNV-positive donors were identified, almost all from states west of the Mississippi River.[94] Of these donors, three subsequently reported neuroinvasive WNV illness and 55 subsequently developed WNV fever.[94] One probable transfusion-associated case was reported.[95]

The experience to date indicates that blood screening for WNV has improved blood safety. However, a small risk of WNV transfusion-associated transmission remains. If the number of WNV cases continues to dramatically decline, the need for WNV testing will be reassessed. The FDA has agreed that asking the question concerning fever with headache in the week before donation may be discontinued (K Gregory, personal communication, 3/30/05).

Herpesviruses and Parvovirus

Cytomegalovirus

CMV, a member of the human herpesvirus family, is a ubiquitous DNA virus that causes widespread infection; transmission can occur through infectious body secretions, including urine, oropharyngeal secretions, breast milk, blood, semen, and cervical secretions. About 1% of newborns are infected, transplacentally or through exposure to infected cervical secretions at delivery or by breast milk. In early childhood, CMV is often acquired through close contact, especially in daycare settings; in adulthood, through sexual intercourse. The prevalence of CMV antibodies ranges from 50% to 80% in the general population.[96] The rate increases with age and is generally higher in lower socioeconomic groups, in urban areas, and in developing countries.

Clinical Observations

In persons with an intact immune system, CMV infection may be asymptomatic and remain latent in tissues and leukocytes for many years. Infection, either primary or reactivation of latent infection, can be associated with a mononucleosis-like syndrome of sore throat, enlarged lymph nodes, lymphocytosis, fever, viremia, viruria, and hepatitis. Intrauterine infection may cause jaundice, thrombocytopenia, cerebral calcifications, and motor disabilities; the syndrome of congenital infection causes mental retardation and deafness and may be fatal.

CMV infection can progress to CMV disease and cause serious morbidity and mortality in premature infants, recipients of organ, marrow, or peripheral blood progenitor cell transplants, and in AIDS patients.[96] Pneumonitis, hepatitis, retinitis, and multisystem organ failure are manifestations of CMV disease. CMV infection can result from blood transfusions. Other sources of infection, however, such as organ transplants from CMV-positive donors or reactivation of latent virus, may be as much or more of a risk than transfusion.

Transfusion-Transmitted CMV

Infection with CMV varies greatly according to socioeconomic status and geographic region. Although approximately 50% of blood donors can be expected to be CMV seropositive, it has been estimated that, currently, less than 1% of seropositive cellular blood components are able to transmit the virus.[96,97] Rarely, posttransfusion hepatitis may be due to CMV. The postperfusion mononucleosis syndrome that first focused attention on CMV in transfused components in the early 1960s is now rarely seen. Posttransfusion CMV infection is generally of no clinical consequence in immunocompetent recipients, and intentional selection of CMV-reduced-risk blood (see below) is not warranted.

In light of the potential for severe CMV disease in immunocompromised patients, several categories of recipients have been identified who should be protected from transfusion-transmitted CMV.[7] These include low-birthweight premature infants born to seronegative mothers; seronegative recipients of hematopoietic progenitor cells from CMV-negative donors; seronegative pregnant women, because the fetus is at risk of transplacental infection; and recipients of intrauterine transfusions. In some cases, seronegative recipients of organ transplants from a seronegative donor; seronegative individuals who are candidates for autologous or allogeneic hematopoietic progenitor cell transplants; and those few patients with AIDS who are free of CMV infection are also included.

Preventive Measures

Blood from donors who test negative for CMV antibody has very little risk of transmitting CMV, but the supply of seronegative blood is limited.[96,97] Another approach to reduce risk is to remove leukocytes from donated blood (because leukocytes are the principal reservoir for CMV).[98-100] Although the precise leukocyte population that harbors the virus has not been defined, leukocyte removal with high-efficiency filters, to 5×10^6 leukocytes per component or fewer, can significantly reduce, if not prevent, posttransfusion CMV in high-risk neonates and transplant recipients. Effectively leukocyte-reduced cellular components are considered equivalent to serologically screened components by many experts, although this is controversial.[98-100] The incremental benefit of serologic testing when added to leukocyte reduction has not been established. Prophylactic therapy with CMV immune globulin and prophylactic use of antiviral agents are being investigated as options for high-risk immunosuppressed organ transplant recipients.[96,97]

Epstein-Barr Virus

EBV causes most cases of infectious mononucleosis and is closely associated with the endemic form of Burkitt's lymphoma in Africa and with nasopharyngeal carcinoma. Most persons have been infected by the time they reach adulthood; although usually asymptomatic, infection persists. Infection is spread by contact with infected saliva. Primary infection in children is either asymptomatic or is characterized by a sore throat and enlarged lymph nodes. Primary infection in older, immunologically mature persons usually causes a systemic syndrome, infectious mononucleosis, with fever; tonsillar infection, sometimes with necrotic ulcers; enlarged lymph nodes; hematologic and immunologic abnormalities; and sometimes hepatitis or other organ involvement. EBV infection targets B lymphocytes, which undergo polyclonal proliferation and then induce a T-lymphocyte response, observed as "atypical lymphocytes."

Transfusion-transmitted EBV infection is usually asymptomatic, but it has been a rare cause of the postperfusion syndrome that follows massive transfusion of freshly drawn blood during cardiac surgery and is a rare cause of posttransfusion hepatitis.[101] EBV plays a role in the development of nasopharyngeal carcinoma and at least one form of Burkitt's lymphoma and has the in-vitro capacity to immortalize B lymphocytes. EBV contributes to the development of lymphoproliferative disorders in immunosuppressed recipients of hematopoietic and organ transplants. Given a 90% seropositivity rate for EBV among blood donors and essentially no risk for clinical disease from transfusion-transmitted EBV in immunocompetent recipients, serologic screening for this virus has not been considered helpful. As is the case for CMV, leukocyte reduction of cellular blood components would be expected to reduce the risk of EBV infection in severely immunosuppressed seronegative patients who may be at risk for clinical disease. However, there have been no studies to verify such a reduced risk.

Human Herpesviruses 6 and 8

As with CMV and EBV, human herpesvirus 6 (HHV-6) is a cell-associated virus that integrates with the genome of lymphocytes. The seroprevalence in some adult populations approaches 100%. Primary infection in immunocompetent children is recognized as exanthem subitum, a febrile illness characterized by a rash; it is rarely complicated by involvement of other organ systems. Immunocompromised patients (eg, those with transplants or AIDS) may experience manifestations of reactivation of HHV-6 infection in multiple organ systems. Studies have sought an association between multiple sclerosis and HHV-6 infection, but this remains controversial. With the ubiquity of antibodies to HHV-6 and absence of disease associations after transfusion transmission, no recommendations have been made for protection of seronegative blood recipients from transmission by blood components.[102]

HHV-8 (also known as Kaposi's sarcoma-associated herpesvirus or KSHV) is causally associated with both Kaposi's sarcoma and body cavity-based lymphomas. It has been found in apparently healthy blood donors, but spread appears to be primarily by the venereal route. Low titers of HHV-8 antibodies were found in 11% of 91 healthy US blood donors.[103] Among HHV-8-seropositive women, injection drug use and indices of sexual activity were independent risk factors for HHV-8 infection.[104] In this study, the association with injection drug use suggests that transmission by infected blood is possible. Transmission by organ donation has been documented.[105-107] Epidemiologic studies suggest that blood transfusion is associated with a small risk of HHV-8 transmission.[108]

Parvovirus

Parvovirus B19 is the cause of erythema infectiosum or "fifth disease," a contagious febrile illness of early childhood. Infections in adults may be associated with arthritis but are generally benign. More ominously, parvovirus B19 can infect and lyse red cell precursors in the marrow.[109] This may result in sudden and severe anemia in patients with underlying chronic hemolytic disorders who depend on active erythropoiesis to compensate for shortened red cell survival. Patients with cellular immunodeficiency, including those infected with HIV, are at risk for chronic viremia and associated hypoplastic anemia. Infection during pregnancy predisposes to spontaneous abortion, fetal malformation, and hydrops from severe anemia and circulatory failure.[110]

The red cell P antigen is the cellular receptor for parvovirus B19, and people who do not have the P antigen are naturally resistant to infection.[111] About 30% to 60% of normal blood donors have antibodies to parvovirus B19, which indicates immunity rather than chronic persistent infection.[109] Viremia occurs only in the early phases of infection and there is no evidence for a carrier state; the incidence of viremia in blood donors has been estimated to range from 1 in 3300 to 1 in 40,000.[110] Parvovirus B19 lacks a lipid envelope and is therefore not inactivated by solvent/detergent treatment or heat inactivation using temperatures below 100 C.[109] The virus has been found regularly in clotting factor concentrates and has been transmitted to persons with hemophilia. Rare transmission through cellular blood components and plasma, but not intravenous immunoglobulin and albumin, has been reported.[110]

After the description of parvovirus B19 seroconversion (without clinical illness) in volunteers during Phase IV clinical evaluation of solvent/detergent-treated plasma, derivative manufacturers (with the concurrence of FDA) began development and implementation of NAT screening for high-titer parvovirus B19 viremic donations in minipools. The rationale, supported by observations from the Phase IV evaluation, is that high-titer donations overwhelm neutralizing antibody in plasma pools, allowing transmission of this highly resistant virus by some derivatives. The FDA has classified this MP-NAT as an in-process manufacturing control rather than a donor screening test. Screening of whole blood donations has not been a high priority because of the benign and/or transient nature of most parvovirus disease, the availability of effective treatment (intravenous immunoglobulin) for chronic hematologic sequelae, and the extreme rarity of reports of parvovirus B19 transmission by individual components.[112]

Transmissible Spongiform Encephalopathies

The transmissible spongiform encephalopathies (TSEs) are degenerative brain disorders caused by agents often called prions, postulated to be infectious proteins. They are characterized by long incubation periods, measured in years to decades, and by the extreme resistance of the pathogens to inactivation by physical and chemical methods sufficient for classic pathogens. Two TSEs, Creutzfeldt-Jakob disease (CJD) and variant Creutzfeldt-Jakob disease (vCJD), are of particular interest in transfusion medicine.

Classic CJD

CJD is a degenerative brain disorder that is rapidly fatal once symptoms of progressive dementia and motor disturbances develop. Approximately 85% of cases are sporadic. Symptoms do not develop until many years to several decades after the initial infection. Ten to fifteen percent of cases are familial, associated with inheritance of one of at least 20 described mutations in the prion gene that, in its non-mutated form, encodes for a normal cellular protein. Worldwide, there is about one case of CJD per million people per year, nearly all in older individuals. In sporadic CJD, the vast majority of cases, the mode of acquisition is unknown. The agent causing CJD is resistant to commonly used disinfectants and sterilants. Iatrogenic CJD has been transmitted by administration of growth hormone and gonadotropic hormone derived from pooled human pituitary tissue, through allografts of dura mater, and through reuse of intracerebral electroencephalographic electrodes from infected patients.[113]

Early experimental studies in animals raised the possibility that CJD could be transmitted by blood transfusion. Additionally, iatrogenic transmission from peripheral injection of human pituitary-derived hormones has been observed. Nevertheless, several population-based, case-controlled studies have shown no evidence that blood transfusion is a risk factor for the development of CJD.[114-116]

Individuals at increased risk for CJD are excluded from donating blood; this group includes persons who have received tissue or tissue derivatives known to be a source of the CJD agent (eg, dura mater allografts, pituitary growth hormone of human origin) and persons with a family history of CJD.[117-119] For the purposes of donor exclusion, unit quarantine, and unit destruction, family history has been defined as having one blood relative who has had this diagnosis. However, a donor with CJD in a family member may be accepted if gene sequences have been tested and found to be normal.

Variant CJD

In 1996, the first cases of an unusual CJD outbreak or cluster were described in the

United Kingdom (UK). These cases were later termed variant CJD (vCJD) and appeared to be caused by the same prion responsible for bovine spongiform encephalopathy (BSE). This prion is distinct from the prion found in classical CJD. A donor infected by dietary exposure to BSE during the incubation period of vCJD might theoretically infect a transfusion recipient. Consequently, UK health authorities prohibited the use of UK plasma for further manufacture, restricted the use of UK plasma for children (born on or after 1 January 1996), and implemented universal leukocyte reduction of cellular components (to reduce the prions known to be present in white cells).

Experimental transfusion transmission of BSE to two sheep (and four cases of transmission of natural scrapie—a sheep prion illness) have been reported.[120] Positive transmissions occurred with blood taken at preclinical and clinical stages of infection. Two cases of transfusion-transmitted BSE in humans have been observed[121,122] as a result of surveillance in the UK of 48 individuals identified as having received a labile blood component from a total of 15 donors who later developed vCJD. In the first possible case, the recipient developed symptoms of vCJD 6.5 years after receiving a transfusion of red cells donated by an individual 3.5 years before the donor developed symptoms of vCJD. Although the source of the infection could have been caused by past dietary exposure to the BSE agent, the age of the patient was well beyond that of most vCJD cases, and the chance of observing a case of vCJD in a recipient in the absence of transfusion-transmitted infection was estimated to be about 1 in 15,000 to 1 in 30,000, making dietary transmission unlikely in this case.[121] In the second possible case, the person received a blood transfusion in 1999 from a donor who later developed vCJD. This patient died of causes unrelated to vCJD, but a postmortem examination revealed the presence of the abnormal prion protein in the patient's spleen and in a lymph node.[122] Notably, unlike previous cases of vCJD (by any method of transmission), in which all involved people were homozygous for methionine (MM) at codon 129 of the prion protein gene (*PRNP*), this individual was heterozygous (methionine valine— MV). In the UK, the population distribution of this gene is MM, MV, or VV in 42%, 47%, and 11%, respectively.[123]

In the United States, blood donors who were in the UK or Europe during the years of potential exposure to the BSE agent are deferred based on the duration of residence there. Balancing the theoretical risk against considerations of the adequacy of the blood supply, the recommended deferral is for 3 months of cumulative residence in the UK between 1980 and 1996 (and current and former US military personnel, civilian military employees, and their dependents who were stationed at European bases for 6 months or more during this period) or 5 years of cumulative residence in Europe. Potential donors who may have injected bovine insulin from the UK or received transfusions in the UK during the BSE epidemic are also excluded.[119]

Bacterial Contamination

Bacterial contamination remains an important cause of transfusion morbidity and mortality. Bacterial contamination of blood components accounted for 29 (16%) of the transfusion fatalities reported to the FDA between 1986 and 1991. However, in 2002 alone, there were 17 deaths reported to the FDA from bacterial contamination of blood components, most commonly caused by contaminated apheresis platelets and whole-blood-derived platelets.[124,125] Although the hepatitis viruses, HIV, and WNV have been more prominently featured in the media and remain a primary concern of the public, bacterial contamination is believed to be the most common infectious source of morbidity and mortality related to transfusion. To place the risk of bacterial contamination into some perspective, in 2002, there were 23 transfusion-transmitted cases of WNV identified in the United States.[87] Of these 23 recipients, seven died, but only five of these deaths were associated with WNV meningoencephalitis. Thus, the deaths from bacterial contamination were more than three times more common than those from WNV.

No matter how carefully blood is drawn, processed, and stored, complete elimination of microbial agents is impossible. Bacteria are most often believed to originate with the donor, either from the venipuncture site or from unsuspected bacteremia.[126] Bacterial multiplication is more likely in blood components stored at room temperature than in refrigerated components.[126] Organisms that multiply in refrigerated blood components are often psychrophilic gram-negative organisms (such as *Yersinia enterocolitica, Serratia liquifaciens,* and *Pseudomonas fluorescens*). Gram-positive organisms are more often seen in platelets stored at 20 to 24 C.

For RBCs, the CDC estimates a symptomatic contamination rate of approximately 1 case per million units, primarily with *Y. enterocolitica,* followed by *S. liquifaciens.*[127] In New Zealand, the incidence of symptomatic *Yersinia* contamination of RBC units has been reported to be as high as one in 65,000 units, with a fatality rate of one in 104,000.[128] Transfusion of an RBC unit heavily contaminated with a gram-negative organism is often a rapid and catastrophic event, with a quick onset of sepsis and a greater than 60% mortality rate.[129,130]

Because platelets are stored at 20 to 24 C to retain their viability and function, they serve as an excellent growth medium for bacteria. Sepsis resulting from transfusion of contaminated platelets is believed to be both underrecognized and underreported. Sepsis occurring after transfusion of contaminated platelets is usually not a catastrophic event, but it can occur several hours or longer after transfusion, making it more difficult to connect the transfusion to the sepsis. Because many of the patients infected by bacteria from a platelet transfusion are immunocompromised by their underlying condition and treatment (eg, chemotherapy), the event is frequently attributed to other causes, such as an infected catheter, which often involves the same organisms.

In the United States, 4 million platelet units are transfused annually (1 million apheresis platelets and 3 million whole-blood-derived platelet concentrates).[130] Given that approximately 1:1000 to 1:2000 platelet units are contaminated with bacteria (as measured by aerobic cultures done in multiple studies before 2002), it would be expected that 2000 to 4000 bacterially contaminated units would be transfused.[131] Estimates of the fraction of such units that would result in signs or symptoms have been as low as 1 in 10 cases. However, in the only study that has prospectively cultured platelets that were transfused, symptoms occurred in 3 of 8 (35.8%) patients who received culture-positive but Gram's-stain-negative platelet pools.[132] Notably, six Gram's-stain-positive pools were interdicted and never transfused. Thus, of contaminated products, perhaps 1/10 to 2/5 would be expected to result in clinical sepsis (200 to 1600 cases) if transfused. Data from national passive reporting studies in the United States, Great Britain, and France (Table 28-4) suggest that perhaps 1/5 to 1/3 would result in death (40 to 533 deaths per

Table 28-4. Summary of Organisms Identified in the BaCon, SHOT, and BACTHEM Studies*

Organism	United States[127]	United Kingdom[133]	France[134]	Total
Gram positive				
Bacillus cereus	1	4 (1)	2	7 (1)
Coagulase-negative Staphylococci	9	6 (1)	5	20 (1)
Streptococcus sp.	3 (1)	2		5 (1)
Staphylococcus aureus	4	2 (1)		6 (1)
Propionibacterium acnes			3	3
Subtotal	17 (1 = 6%)[†]	14 (3 = 21%)	10 (0 = 0%)	41 (4 = 10%)
Gram negative				
Klebsiella sp.			2 (1)	2 (1)
Serratia sp.	2 (2)		1 (1)	3 (3)
Escherichia coli	5 (1)	2 (1)	1	8 (2)
Acinetobacter			1	1
Enterobacter sp.	2 (1)	1 (1)	1	4 (2)
Providencia rettgeri	1 (1)			1 (1)
Yersinia enterocolitica	1			1
Subtotal	11 (5 = 45%)	3 (2 = 67%)	6 (2 = 33%)	20 (9 = 45%)
Total	28 (6 = 21%)	17 (5 = 29%)	16 (2 = 13%)	58 (13 = 14%)

*Number of cases (fatalities) and the percent of the subtotal and total cases are listed. This table illustrates that although gram-positive organisms are associated with the majority of reported cases (41/58 = 71/%), gram-negative organisms account for the majority of deaths (9/11 = 82%). Modified with permission from Brecher and Hay.[131]

†There were 17 cases of gram-positive organisms identified in the US study; however, only one case (1/17 = 6%) resulted in a fatality.

year).[127,133,134] This translates to a risk of death from a transfusion of a platelet unit contaminated with bacteria of between 1:7500 to 1:100,000. Clinical observations from university hospitals with heightened awareness of platelet-related sepsis confirm such estimates. A fatality rate of 1:17,000 has been reported by Ness et al, from Johns Hopkins, with pooled whole-blood-derived platelets and 1:61,000 with apheresis platelets.[135] University Hospitals of Cleveland

similarly observed a fatality rate of approximately 1:48,000 per whole-blood-derived platelet concentrate.[136] With the implementation of bacteria detection of platelets (see below), it is anticipated that this rate will be greatly reduced.

Clinical Considerations

Severe reactions are characterized by fever, shock, and disseminated intravascular coagulation (DIC). If bacterial contamination is suspected, the transfusion should be stopped immediately and a Gram's stain and blood culture should be obtained from the unit (not an attached segment of tubing because the bag may be contaminated but an isolated segment of tubing may be sterile) and recipient as promptly as possible after the reaction is observed. Bacterial multiplication may cause the oxygen in an RBC unit to be consumed, resulting in hemoglobin desaturation and erythrocyte lysis, both of which contribute to a darkening of the unit compared to the color of the blood in the attached sealed segments. Color change (to dark purple or black), clots in the bag, or hemolysis suggest contamination, but the appearance of the blood in the bag is often unremarkable. The presence of bacteria on a Gram's stain of the component is confirmatory, but absence of visible organisms does not exclude the possibility. Gram's stain has a sensitivity of only 10^6 to 10^7 CFU/mL. The patient's blood, the suspect component, and intravenous solutions in all the administration tubing used should be cultured.

Treatment should not await the results of these investigations and should include immediate intravenous administration of antibiotics combined with therapy for shock, renal failure, and DIC, if present.

Preventive Measures

Prevention of septic reactions depends upon reducing or preventing contamination of components with bacteria. Careful selection of healthy blood donors is the first and most important step.

The donor's present appearance and recent medical history should indicate good health; additional questioning may be needed if there is a present or recent history of antibiotic use, of medical or surgical interventions, or of any constitutional symptoms. Questions to elicit the possibility of bacteremia are especially important for autologous donors, who may have undergone recent hospitalization, antibiotic therapy, or invasive diagnostic or therapeutic procedures; there have been several reports of *Yersinia* sepsis complications after the infusion of stored autologous blood.

Scrupulous attention must be paid to selecting and cleansing the donor's phlebotomy site. Skin preparation reduces but does not completely abrogate the contamination of components by bacteria. Scarred or dimpled areas associated with previous dermatitis or repeated phlebotomy can harbor bacteria and should be avoided. Green soap must not be used to prepare the phlebotomy site.

Discarding the first aliquot of donor blood removed ("diversion") has been proposed as a measure to reduce bacterial contamination of blood components. This measure would remove the skin core that may enter the collection from the hollow bore needle used in the phlebotomy. Systems have been developed to facilitate the application of this approach and would be expected to reduce skin contaminants (mostly gram-positive organisms).

Phagocytosis of contaminating bacteria by donor white cells in blood components may be important for the minimization of clinical bacterial contamination. Leukocyte removal, with coincident removal of adherent or engulfed bacteria, has been advocated as an approach to reducing *Yersinia* contamination of RBCs.[137,138]

Care in the preparation of components and handling of materials used in blood administration is essential. If a waterbath is used, components should be protected by overwrapping, outlet ports should be inspected for absence of trapped fluid, and the waterbath should be frequently emptied and disinfected.

Worldwide, screening of platelets for bacteria is being implemented. Screening is mandatory in several countries [eg, Belgium (Flemish Red Cross), the Netherlands, Hong Kong (Red Cross), and Wales].[139]

In the United States, the College of American Pathologists (CAP) Commission on Laboratory Accreditation has added a question to the Transfusion Medicine Checklist to assess the presence of a laboratory system to detect bacteria in platelet components (TRM.44955).[140] Similarly, the AABB requires bacteria detection.[62(p11)] Currently, two culture techniques are approved by the FDA for quality control of leukocyte-reduced platelets and are available in the United States. Because of expense and

logistics, whole-blood-derived platelets are often tested in the United States with less sensitive but more rapid detection strategies, such as staining or the use of surrogate markers of bacterial metabolism (eg, pH and glucose). Several other more rapid and sensitive detection strategies are under development or are not readily available. One possible investigative strategy after detecting a confirmed culture-positive platelet unit is outlined in Fig 28-4.

Prospect for Extended Storage

The extent of bacterial growth in platelet components correlates with the duration of storage. In 1983, in recognition of tech-

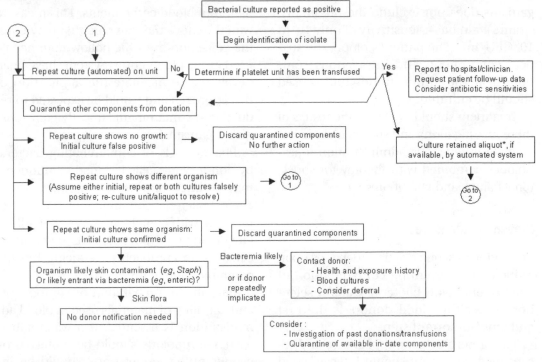

Protocol for Evaluation of Report of Bacterial Growth in Platelet Unit

f pool was cultured, re-culture individual units or their aliquots, if possible.

Figure 28-4. Possible investigative strategy for a positive culture in a platelet unit. Modified with permission.[141]

nically improved storage conditions, the FDA increased storage limits of platelets at room temperature from 3 to 7 days. However, it reduced the limits to a maximum of 5 days in 1986, responding to reports of bacterial contamination after more than 5 days of storage.[142] The use of bacteria detection systems has been given as the rationale for an extension of platelet storage to 7 days in several European countries and is being implemented in the United States.[139]

Syphilis

Syphilis is caused by the spirochete *Treponema pallidum* and is characteristically spread by sexual contact. The phase of spirochetemia is brief and the organisms survive only a few days at 4 C. Although transmission by transfusion is possible, its occurrence is exceedingly rare (the last case reported in the United States occurred in 1965). Syphilis transmission by transfusion may not be effectively prevented by subjecting the donor blood to standard serologic tests for syphilis (STS) because seroconversion often occurs after the phase of spirochetemia. Most positive STS results reflect immunologic abnormalities unrelated to syphilis (biologic false-positives), inadequately treated non-infectious syphilis that is more of a threat to the individual being tested than to a transfusion recipient, or the serologic residual of an effectively treated infection.

A recent series described *T. pallidum* DNA and RNA testing of 169 aliquots from platelet concentrates that were reactive by STS and confirmed positive by fluorescent treponemal antibody absorption.[143] This series included 48 donors who were positive by rapid plasma reagin tests (compatible with recent or active disease). No sample contained *T. pallidum* DNA or RNA, sug-

gesting a low probability that the blood of donors who have a confirmed positive syphilis test result is infectious for syphilis. Nevertheless, a study from the CDC showed that from 1995-2000, 22 primary, 81 secondary, and 413 early latent syphilis cases were identified through blood or plasma donor screening in the United States.[144] Thus, screening of blood donors for syphilis may have broader public health implications. Currently, performance of a STS is still required.[62(pp33,34)]

Tick-Borne Infections

Because many tick-borne infectious agents circulate in the blood, it is theoretically possible that they will be transmitted by transfusion of blood components.

Babesia

Clinical Events

In the United States, the most frequently recognized transfusion-associated tick-borne infection is babesiosis.[145] Babesiosis is usually transmitted by the bite of an infected deer (black-legged) tick and is reported most frequently in the coastal lands and islands of northeastern United States, including Martha's Vineyard, Cape Cod, and Long Island. Geographic areas of the hosts and the vectors appear to be expanding.[146] Transfusion-associated babesiosis has been documented in more than 50 cases, caused mostly by *Babesia microti* from the Northeast, but also by the recently recognized WA1-type *Babesia* parasite, from asymptomatic infected blood donors.[145-147] As humans continue to encroach on the habitat of vectors and natural reservoirs of infection [eg, deer (and other *Cervidae*) and mice populations in the northeastern United States], the incidence of transfusion-transmitted babesiosis may increase.

The vector and reservoir of the *Babesia* more recently found in the northwestern and western United States remain to be defined. *Babesia* species survive blood bank storage for up to at least 35 days and can be transmitted by both RBCs and platelet concentrates. Babesiosis classically causes a febrile illness with hemolytic anemia, but infection can also cause chronic asymptomatic or mildly symptomatic parasitemia. Studies suggest that untreated persons can harbor *B. microti* DNA for long periods, despite mild or absent symptoms, and may transmit infection for months or possibly longer.[148] Symptoms are often so mild that the infection is not recognized, which likely explains the low rate of reported transfusion-transmitted babesiosis. Symptomatic patients develop fever 2 to 8 weeks after transfusion, sometimes associated with chills, headache, hemolysis, or hemoglobinuria. Rarely, life-threatening hemolytic anemia, renal failure, and coagulopathy develop, particularly in asplenic or severely immunocompromised patients.[149]

Preventive Measures

The *Babesia* carrier state may be asymptomatic and may exceed a year in duration. Persons with a history of babesiosis are indefinitely deferred, because lifelong parasitemia can follow recovery from symptomatic illness. Restrictive policies, such as not collecting blood in areas where the disease vectors are endemic during spring and summer months when tick bites are more common, are in practice in some locations but probably are of limited value. No test is available for mass screening to detect asymptomatic carriers of *Babesia* species.

Other Agents

One case of transfusion transmission of Rocky Mountain spotted fever (*Rickettsia rickettsii*) and no cases of human monocytic ehrlichiosis (caused by *Erlichia chaffeensis*) have been documented.[150] A single possible transfusion transmission of the unnamed agent of human granulocytic erlichiosis has been reported.[151] In 1997, Rocky Mountain spotted fever and/or human monocytic erlichiosis developed in National Guard trainees at Fort Chaffee, AR. Ten components donated by infected trainees had been transfused before a recall; however, none of the persons who received blood from infected donors became clinically ill.[152]

Lyme disease is the most common tick-borne infection in the United States. *Borrelia burgdorferi*, the causative spirochete, is transmitted through bites of the deer (black-legged) tick. No transfusion-related cases have been reported, but chronic subclinical infections do occur and experimentally inoculated organisms can survive conditions of frozen, refrigerated, and room temperature storage.[153] On the other hand, the phase of spirochetemia seems to be associated with symptoms that would render a potential donor ineligible, and in two reported cases where the donor became ill shortly after donation, the recipient did not develop infection.[149] Potential donors who give a history of Lyme disease should be completely asymptomatic and should have completed a full course of antibiotic therapy before they are permitted to donate. Transfusion transmission of tick-borne agents is biologically plausible and, for some agents, has been demonstrated. Nevertheless, modifications to current donor screening are not likely to be useful because of their low predictive value and the potential for nonspecific questions to defer large numbers of donors for a small increment in transfusion safety.[153]

Other Nonviral Infectious Complications of Blood Transfusion

Malaria

Malaria is caused by several species of the intraerythrocytic protozoan genus *Plasmodium*. Transmission usually results from the bite of an anopheles mosquito, but infection can follow transfusion of parasitemic blood. Although very rare in the United States, malaria is probably the most commonly recognized parasitic complication of transfusion; the risk in the United States is estimated to be <0.3 case per million transfusions.[154,155] From 1963 to 1999, 93 cases of transfusion-transmitted malaria (10 fatal) in the United States were reported to CDC.[155]

The species involved in transfusion-transmitted malaria in the United States are *P. falciparum* (35%), *P. malariae* (27%), *P. vivax* (27%), and *P. ovale* (5%).[155] Three percent were mixed infections, and 2% were caused by unidentified species. Fever, chills, headache, and hemolysis occur a week to several months after the infected transfusion; morbidity varies but can be severe, and deaths have occurred, especially from *P. falciparum*. Adding to the risk of a fatal outcome may be a lack of immunity in the recipient, the patient's underlying condition(s), and delay in the diagnosis because of lack of suspicion and unfamiliarity with the disease in areas where the parasite is not endemic.

Malaria parasites survive for at least a week in components stored at room temperature or at 4 C. The parasites can also survive cryopreservation with glycerol and subsequent thawing. Any component that contains red cells can transmit infection, via the asexual form of the intraerythrocytic parasite.

Asymptomatic carriers are generally the source of transfusion-transmitted malaria, although their parasite density is very low. Asymptomatic infections rarely persist more than 3 years, but asymptomatic *P. falciparum* and *P. vivax* infections may persist for 5 years, *P. ovale* for 7 years, and *P. malariae* can remain transmissible for the lifetime of the asymptomatic individual. In extreme cases, transmission of *P. vivax*, *P. ovale*, *P. falciparum*, and *P. malariae* have been reported at 27, 7, 13, and 53 years, respectively.[156] There are no practical serologic tests to detect transmissible malaria in asymptomatic donors. Malaria transmission is prevented by deferral of prospective donors with increased risk of infectivity, based on their medical and travel history. The AABB requires that prospective donors who have had a diagnosis of malaria, or who have traveled or lived in a malaria-endemic area and have had unexplained symptoms suggestive of malaria, be deferred for 3 years after becoming asymptomatic.[62(p65)] Individuals who have lived for at least 5 consecutive years in areas in which malaria is considered endemic by the CDC Malarial Branch shall be deferred for 3 years after departure from that area. Individuals who have traveled to an area where malaria is endemic shall be deferred for 12 months after departing that area. These deferral periods apply irrespective of the receipt of antimalarial prophylaxis. Updated information on malaria risks worldwide is available from the CDC, including an on-line resource (http://www.cdc.gov/travel/yb/outline.htm#2).

Chagas' Disease

American trypanosomiasis, or Chagas' disease, is endemic in South and Central

America and is caused by the protozoan parasite *Trypanosoma cruzi*. The human host sustains infection after the bite of reduviid bugs (called cone-nosed or "kissing" bugs), which usually exist in hollow trees, palm trees, and in thatched-roofed mud or wooden dwellings. Naturally acquired Chagas' disease in the United States is exceedingly rare. Five such cases have been recognized in the United States since 1955, the most recent in 1998 in Tennessee.[157]

Clinical Events

T. cruzi infects humans whose skin or mucosa comes in contact with feces of infected reduviid bugs, usually as the result of a bite. Recent infections are usually either asymptomatic or the very mild signs, and symptoms go undetected. Rarely, the site of entry evolves into an erythematous nodule called a chagoma, which may be accompanied by lymphadenopathy. Fever and enlargement of the spleen and liver may follow. Recently infected young children may experience acute myocarditis or meningoencephalitis. Acute infection usually resolves without treatment, but persisting low-level parasitemia is usual and up to one-third of infected individuals develop a chronic form associated with cardiac or gastrointestinal symptoms years or decades later.[158]

Transfusion Considerations

Blood transfusion has been a major source of infection with *T. cruzi* in South American urban centers that receive large numbers of immigrants from rural areas where the parasite is endemic. However, in many countries, serologic screening has been effective in reducing the risk of transfusion-transmitted Chagas' disease. Four cases of transfusion-transmitted Chagas' disease have been reported in the United

States[158]: in New York, Los Angeles, Texas, and Florida. All occurred in immunocompromised patients. Additionally, two cases were reported in Manitoba, Canada. In one interesting study, postoperative blood specimens from 11,430 cardiac surgery patients were tested by EIA and, if repeatedly reactive, were confirmed by radioimmunoprecipitation. Six postoperative specimens (0.05%) were confirmed positive. All six seropositive patients apparently were infected with *T. cruzi* before surgery; however, a diagnosis of Chagas' disease was not known or even considered in any of these patients. No evidence for transfusion-transmitted *T. cruzi* was found.[159]

Reasonably sensitive and specific EIA screening tests for antibodies to *T. cruzi*, as well as confirmatory Western blot and radioimmunoprecipitation assays, have been developed.[158] Testing in several US blood centers located in geographic areas with a large immigrant population from Central or South America found a seroprevalence of 0.1% to 0.2% among at-risk donors, who were identified by questionnaire.[160,161] However, look-back studies identified no infected recipients; it is also likely that not all at-risk donors can be identified by questionnaire.[160] As a consequence, if blood donor screening were to be implemented, testing of all donors might be necessary.

Other Parasites

Toxoplasmosis is caused by the ubiquitous parasite *Toxoplasma gondii,* and infection has been reported as an unusual transfusion complication in immunocompromised patients.[162] The disease has not been considered a problem in routine transfusion practice.

There have been occasional reports of parasitic worm infections transmitted by transfusion in countries other than the

United States.[162] Microfilariasis is a potential transfusion risk in tropical zones, acquired by donors through bites by insects carrying *Wuchereria bancrofti*. Transfusion transmission of *Leishmania* species is a rare risk in countries where such organisms are endemic. Currently, the AABB defers potential donors who have been to Iraq in the previous 12 months as a result of possible *Leishmania* exposure.[163]

Reducing the Risk of Infectious Disease Transmission

Overall, the risk per unit of transfusion-transmitted disease is remarkably low (Table 28-5). This low incidence is due to both donor screening and specific disease testing. Nevertheless, in pooled components, which may contain elements from thousands of donors, the risk of disease transmission is increased. Therefore, several strategies have been developed and implemented to further reduce the risk of disease transmission in pooled acellular components and, in some cases, cellular components.

Inactivation/Destruction of Agents in Derivatives or Plasma Products

The first intervention specifically added to reduce the risk of hepatitis transmission was heating (to 60 C for 10 hours), which has been used for albumin products since at least 1948.[167] In those rare instances when infections occurred with plasma protein fractions prepared with this step, the processing had been compromised.

Immunoglobulins

The plasma fractionation process used for most immunoglobulin products employs cold ethanol precipitation after removal of cryoprecipitate. Historically, when antibodies to HCV were present in the plasma, this process concentrated HCV in the Factor VIII-rich cryoprecipitate and other fractions and left little in the immunoglobulin fraction. The immunoglobulin fraction also has a high concentration of virus-neutralizing antibodies and the resulting product for intramuscular application has a remarkably low risk of virus transmission.[168]

Preparations of immunoglobulin intended for intravenous administration (IGIV) were expected to be similarly free of disease transmission. However, NANB hepatitis transmission did occur in the 1980s during early clinical trials of IGIV products in the United States and with routinely manufactured IGIV products in Europe.[169] In late 1993 and early 1994, a worldwide outbreak with more than 200 reported HCV infections was traced to a single IGIV preparation licensed in the United States.[170,171] In this case, transmission apparently occurred because of lack of virus inactivation steps in the specific manufacturing process for this product[172] and absence of complexing and neutralizing anti-HCV subsequent to anti-HCV screening of plasma donors, with resultant accumulation of virus particles in the immunoglobulin fraction.[170] Anti-HCV-positive source plasma has been excluded from the manufacture of IGIV since 1992.

The importance of the manufacturing method is underscored by outbreaks of HCV infection from intravenous anti-D immunoglobulin in Germany in the late 1970s and in Ireland from the late 1970s to the early 1990s.[173,174] Both products were prepared by anion exchange chromatography rather than cold-ethanol (Cohn) fractionation.[175] To prevent further HCV outbreaks, the FDA has required, since 1994, virus clearance steps in the manufacturing process of immunoglobulin or proof of ab-

Table 28-5. Infectious Risks of Blood Transfusion in the United States

Infectious Agent or Outcome	Estimated Risk per Unit Transfused	Estimated % of Infected Units that Transmit or Cause Clinical Sequelae*	Reference
Viruses			
HIV-1 and -2	1:1,400,000-1:2,400,000	90	23, 29, 30
HTLV-I and -II	1:256,000-1:2,000,000	30	84
HAV	1:1,000,000	90	164
HBV	1:58,000-1:147,000	70	29
HCV	1:872,000-1:1,700,000	90	23, 29, 30
B19 parvovirus	1:3,300-1:40,000	Low	110
Bacteria			
RBCs	1:1000	1:10,000,000 fatal	165
Platelets (screened with Gram's stain, pH, or glucose concentration)	1:2000-1:4000	>40% result in clinical sequelae	30, 132, 166
(screened with early aerobic culture)	<1:10,000	Unknown	
Parasites			
Babesia and malaria	<1:1,000,000†	Unknown	145, 156, 164
Trypanosoma cruzi	Unknown	<20	158

*Units that were confirmed test positive for the infectious agent.
Note: West Nile virus is not included in this table because of regional, temporal, and testing (eg, minipool vs individual donation testing) variation; decreasing rates of infection; and the fact that all testing in the United States is being conducted under an investigational new drug protocol.
†Risk is higher in areas where *Babesia* is endemic.

sence of HCV from the final product by NAT. In addition, NAT technology is now applied to screening of source plasma as an additional layer of safety.

Coagulation Factors

Until the early 1980s, clotting factor concentrates frequently transmitted viral infections. As the significance of HIV transmission was recognized, virus inactivation steps were applied more rigorously to Factor VIII and other clotting factor concentrates, even though these steps were initially introduced in the hope of reducing hepatitis transmission. Unfortunately, a large proportion (over 50%) of the hemophilic population receiving concentrates before processing was improved became infected with HIV. Chronic hepatitis was an additional complication in almost all patients with hemophilia receiving older clotting factor products.[176]

The thermal instability of Factor VIII made it difficult to develop an effective heat treatment, until a practical approach was widely adopted in 1985. Since then, many virus inactivation steps have been introduced, and factor concentrates are now, in general, very safe products. Each process has its own set of advantages and disadvantages. Application of organic solvents and detergents inactivates viruses with a lipid-containing envelope (eg, HIV, HBV, HCV, HTLV, EBV, CMV, HHV-6, HHV-8) but is ineffective against nonenveloped agents such as HAV and parvovirus B19. Virus inactivation steps have the potential drawback of reducing the potency and biologic effectiveness of the product. Another concern is whether virus inactivation steps affect immunogenicity, especially the induction of Factor VIII inhibitors in patients with hemophilia.

Current Risks of Human Plasma Derivatives. Many methods are highly effective against enveloped viruses, but sporadic re-

ports of viral transmission continue to occur, possibly resulting from accident or error during the manufacturing process. The combination of heat treatment, solvent/detergent treatment, and purification steps with monoclonal antibodies provides clotting factor concentrates with a risk of transmitting hepatitis and HIV that is lower than the risk associated with use of Cryoprecipitated Antihemophilic Factor derived from individual voluntary whole blood donations. Documented transmission of HBV, HCV, or HIV by US-licensed plasma derivatives is rare since the introduction of effective virus inactivation procedures and improved viral screening. Although absolute safety of products derived from human plasma cannot be guaranteed, starting with the safest possible donated plasma reduces the viral load and has contributed to the excellent safety record of the products subjected to virus inactivation/removal.[177]

Avoiding Human Plasma. Factor VIII concentrates produced by recombinant DNA technology are licensed for use and have become the preparation of choice for previously untreated patients with hemophilia.[178] Batches are produced by culture of mammalian cells engineered to secrete Factor VIII into the supernatant medium, which is purified by ion-exchange chromatography and immunoaffinity chromatography using a mouse monoclonal antibody. Except for the fact that excipient human albumin is sometimes added to stabilize Factor VIII, the product is free of human proteins, HIV, hepatitis viruses, and other unwanted agents, thus avoiding many of the risks associated with using human plasma. On the other hand, recombinant products have a relatively short history of use and there is no guarantee that they are risk-free.

Plasma

Virus reduction steps, originally developed for purified plasma protein fractions, have also been applied to plasma intended for transfusion. Alternative approaches being studied include organic solvents and detergents and use of photochemicals. Solvent/detergent treatment, which is effective against lipid-enveloped viruses, involves addition of 1% Triton X-100 and 1% tri-n-butyl phosphate (TNBP) to pooled plasma, followed by oil extraction of the TNBP and chromatographic adsorption of the Triton X-100. After several years of experience with this method in Europe, solvent/detergent-treated plasma was transiently available in the United States. However, concern with the use of a pooled product, expense, poor market penetration, and possible thrombotic (or excessive bleeding) events led to the discontinuation of this product. A psoralen (S59) activated by ultraviolet A light is undergoing US clinical trials for pathogen inactivation in platelets and plasma and is available in some countries in Europe.

Processing Cellular Components

Photochemical and chemical pathogen inactivation methods are theoretically applicable to cellular blood components; another organic chemical (S-303) and a nucleic acid targeting compound (PEN 110) have undergone initial clinical evaluation for pathogen inactivation in red cells. These methods have the potential for reliable inactivation of bacteria, viruses, and parasites, including intracellular forms.[179,180] However, both products have been shown to result in the formation of antibodies in recipients. Pathogen reduction trials in platelets (eg, with S-59) have been associated with decreased cell recovery and survival and the need for increased platelet transfusions. Such unintended consequences of pathogen reduction have resulted in some trials being halted and may ulti-mately eliminate such molecules from widespread clinical application.

Reporting Transfusion-Associated Infections

Unexplained infectious disease reported in a transfusion recipient must be investigated for the possibility of transfusion-transmitted illness.[62(pp83,85)] Hepatitis is expected to become apparent within 2 weeks to 6 months if it resulted from transfusion, but, even within this interval, the cause need not necessarily have been blood-borne infection. Blood centers and transfusion services must have a mechanism to encourage recognition and reporting of possible transfusion-associated infections. HIV infection thought to be a result of transfusion should also be reported to the blood supplier, although the interval between transfusion and the recognition of infection or symptoms may be years.

Infection in a recipient should be reported to the collecting agency so that donors shown or suspected of being infectious can be evaluated and recipients of other components from the implicated or other donations can be contacted and, if necessary, tested. A donor who proves to have positive results on tests during the investigation must be placed on an appropriate deferral list.

Reporting Fatalities

The *Code of Federal Regulations* [21 CFR 606.170(b)] requires that fatalities attributed to transfusion complications (eg, hepatitis, AIDS, and hemolytic reactions) be reported to the Director, Center for Biologics Evaluation and Research (CBER), Office of Compliance and Biologics Quality, Attn: Fatality Program Manager (HFM-650), 1401 Rockville Pike, Suite 200N, HFM-650, Rockville, MD

20852-1448. A report should be made as soon as possible by telephone (301-827-6220), fax (301-827-6748), or email to fatalities2@cber.fda.gov and a written report should be submitted within 7 days. Current information can be found on the Internet at http://www.fda.gov/cber/gdlns/bldfatal.pdf.

Management of Posttransfusion Infections

Implicated Donors

If documented transfusion-associated hepatitis, HIV, or HTLV-I/II occurs in a patient who received only a single unit, that donor must be permanently excluded from future donations, and the name placed in a file of permanently deferred individuals. If posttransfusion viral infection occurs after exposure to blood from several donors, it is not necessary to exclude all of the potentially implicated donors. If only a few donors are involved, it may be desirable to recall them to obtain an interim medical history and to perform additional tests. Donors found to have been implicated in more than one case of transfusion-associated viral infection should be appropriately investigated and possibly deferred permanently according to procedures established by the collecting agency.

Notification

A donor who will be permanently excluded as a future blood donor because of a positive test implication in posttransfusion viral infection must be notified of this fact. Follow-up testing should, ideally, be done by the donor's own physician, and the collecting agency should obtain the donor's consent to release available information to a designated health-care provider. If the donor does not have a physician, a blood bank physician or other trained staff member should provide initial counseling and appropriate medical referral. The notification process and counseling must be done with tact and understanding, and the concerns of the donor should be addressed. The donor should be told clearly why he or she is deferred and, when appropriate, about the possibility of being infectious to others. Notification should occur promptly because a delay in notification can delay initiation of treatment or institution of measures to prevent the spread of infection to others.

Use of Immunoglobulins

It is not recommended practice to give intramuscular or intravenous immune serum globulin or HBIG prophylactically to prevent posttransfusion hepatitis[181]; these agents have not been shown to prevent posttransfusion hepatitis B, and the available evidence is conflicting about their effect on posttransfusion hepatitis C.[182,183] If there has been inadvertent transfusion of known marker-positive blood or needle-stick exposure to infectious material, HBIG may prevent or attenuate HBV infection.[184] Prophylaxis with immunoglobulin is ineffective in preventing HCV transmission following occupational exposures and is not recommended for this indication.[185]

References

1. Alter MJ. Epidemiology and prevention of hepatitis B. Semin Liver Dis 2003;23:39-46.
2. Centers for Disease Control and Prevention. Recommendations for prevention and control of hepatitis C virus (HCV) infection and HCV-related chronic disease. MMWR Morb Mortal Wkly Rep 1998;47(No. RR019):1-39.
3. Conry-Cantilena C, Menitove J. Hepatitis. In: Anderson K, Ness P, eds. Scientific basis of transfusion medicine. Implications for clini-

cal practice. Philadelphia: WB Saunders, 2000:472-87.

4. Dodd R. Hepatitis. In: Petz LD, Swisher SN, Kleinman S, et al, eds. Clinical practice of transfusion medicine. 3rd ed. New York: Churchill Livingstone, 1996:847-73.

5. Dienstag JL. Transfusion-transmitted hepatitis B, A, and D. In: Simon TL, Dzik WH, Snyder EL, et al, eds. Rossi's principles of transfusion medicine. 3rd ed. Philadelphia: Lippincott Williams and Wilkins, 2002:733-41.

6. Alter HJ, Nakatsuji Y, Melpolder J, et al. The incidence of transfusion-associated hepatitis G virus infection and its relation to liver disease. N Engl J Med 1997;336:747-54.

7. Sayers M. Cytomegalovirus and other herpesviruses. In: Petz LD, Swisher SN, Kleinman S, et al, eds. Clinical practice of transfusion medicine. 3rd ed. New York: Churchill Livingstone, 1996:875-89.

8. Unemura T, Yeo AET, Sottini A, et al. SEN virus infection and its relationship to transfusion-associated hepatitis. Hepatology 2001;33:1303-11.

9. Alter HJ. Transfusion-transmitted hepatitis C and non-A, non-B, non-C virus infections. In: Simon TL, Dzik WH, Snyder EL, et al, eds. Rossi's principles of transfusion medicine. 3rd ed. Philadelphia: Lippincott Williams and Wilkins, 2002:718-32.

10. Kumar A, Beniwal B, Kar P, et al. Hepatitis E in pregnancy. Obstet Gynecol Surv 2005;60: 7-8.

11. Lee WM. Hepatitis B virus infection. N Engl J Med 1997;337:1733-45.

12. Alter HJ. To C or not to C: These are the questions. Blood 1995;85:1681-95.

13. Seeff LB, Buskell-Bales Z, Wright EC, et al. Long-term mortality after transfusion-associated non-A, non-B hepatitis. The National Heart, Lung, and Blood Institute Study Group. N Engl J Med 1992;327:1906-11.

14. Vogt M, Lang T, Frosner G, et al. Prevalence and clinical outcome of hepatitis C infection in children who underwent cardiac surgery before the implementation of blood-donor screening. N Engl J Med 1999;341:866-70.

15. National Institutes of Health. National Institutes of Health consensus development conference panel statement: Management of hepatitis C. Hepatol 1997;26:2S-10S.

16. Sherman M, Bain V, Villeneuve JP, et al. The management of chronic viral hepatitis: A Canadian consensus conference 2004. Can J Gastroenterol 2004;18:715-28.

17. Busch MP. Closing the windows on viral transmission by blood transfusion. In: Stramer S, ed. Blood safety in the new millennium. Bethesda MD: AABB, 2000:33-54.

18. Westhoff TH, Jochimsen F, Schmittel A, et al. Fatal hepatitis B virus reactivation by an escape mutant following rituximab therapy (letter). Blood 2003;102:1930.

19. Busch MP, Kleinman SH, Jackson B, et al. Nucleic acid amplification testing of blood donors for transfusion-transmitted diseases: Report of the Interorganizational Task Force on Nucleic Acid Amplification Testing of Blood Donors. Transfusion 2000;40:143-59.

20. Alter HJ, Purcell RH, Shih JW, et al. Detection of antibody to hepatitis C virus in prospectively followed transfusion recipients with acute and chronic non-A, non-B hepatitis. N Engl J Med 1989;321:1494-500.

21. Brecher ME, ed. Collected questions and answers. 6th ed. Bethesda, MD: AABB, 2000:21.

22. Van der Poel CL, Cuypers HT, Reesink HW, et al. Confirmation of hepatitis C virus infection by new four-antigen recombinant immunoblot assay. Lancet 1991;337:317-9.

23. Stramer SL, Glynn SA, Kleinman SH, et al for the National Heart, Lung, and Blood Institute Nucleic Acid Test Study Group. Detection of HIV-1 and HCV infections among antibody-negative blood donors by nucleic acid-amplification testing. N Engl J Med 2004;351:760-8.

24. Variance request to use NAT results and be exempted from HIV and HCV supplemental testing in specific circumstances (Association Bulletin #05-03). Bethesda, MD: AABB, 2005.

25. Busch MP, Korelitz JJ, Kleinman SH, et al. Declining value of alanine aminotransferase in screening of blood donors to prevent post-transfusion hepatitis B and C virus infection. The Retrovirus Epidemiology Donor Study. Transfusion 1995;35:903-10.

26. Jongerius JM, Webster M, Cuypers HT, et al. New hepatitis B virus mutant form in a blood donor that is undetectable in several hepatitis B surface antigen screening assays. Transfusion 1998;38:56-9.

27. Alter H. Transfusion-transmitted non-A, non-B and hepatitis C infections. In: Rossi EC, Simon TL, Moss GL, Gould S, eds. Principles of transfusion medicine. 2nd ed. Baltimore, MD: Williams and Wilkins, 1996:687-98.

28. Armstrong GL, Alter MJ, McQuillan GM, Margolis HS. The past incidence of hepatitis C virus infection: Implications for the future burden of chronic liver disease in the United States. Hepatology 2000;31:777-82.

29. Goodnough LT, Shander A, Brecher ME. Transfusion medicine: Looking to the future. Lancet 2003;361:161-9.

30. Busch MP, Glynn SA, Stramer S, et al. A new strategy for estimating risks of transfusion-transmitted viral infections based on rates of

detection of recently infected donors. Transfusion 2005;45:254-64.

31. 65th Blood Product Advisory Committee Meeting (transcripts). March 16, 2000. [Available at http://www.fda.gov/ohrms/dockets/ac/00/transcripts/3603t1.rtp.]

32. Food and Drug Administration. Draft guidance for industry: Current good manufacturing practice for blood and blood components: (1) quarantine and disposition of units from prior collections from donors with repeatedly reactive screening tests for antibody to hepatitis C virus (anti-HCV); (2) supplemental testing and the notification of consignees and blood recipients of donor test results for anti-HCV. (June 17, 1999) Rockville, MD: CBER Office of Communication, Training, and Manufacturers Assistance, 1999.

33. Goldman M, Juodvalkis S, Gill P, Spurli G. Hepatitis C lookback. Transfus Med Rev 1998; 12:84-93.

34. Culver DH, Alter MJ, Mullan RJ, Margolis HS. Evaluation of the effectiveness of targeted lookback for HCV infection in the United States—interim results. Transfusion 2000;40:1176-81.

35. Bowker SL, Smith LJ, Rosychuk RJ, Preiksaitis JK. A review of general hepatitis C virus lookbacks in Canada. Vox Sang 2004;86:21-7.

36. Centers for Disease Control. *Pneumocystis carinii* pneumonia among persons with hemophilia A. MMWR Morb Mortal Wkly Rep 1982;31:365-7.

37. Centers for Disease Control. Possible transfusion-associated acquired immune deficiency syndrome (AIDS)—California. MMWR Morb Mortal Wkly Rep1982;31:652-4.

38. Ragni MV, Winkelstein A, Kingsley L, et al. 1986 update of HIV seroprevalence, seroconversion, AIDS incidence, and immunologic correlates of HIV infection in patients with hemophilia A and B. Blood 1987;70: 786-90.

39. Busch MP, Young MJ, Samson SM, et al. Risk of human immunodeficiency virus (HIV) transmission by blood transfusions before the implementation of HIV-1 antibody screening. The Transfusion Safety Study Group. Transfusion 1991;31:4-11.

40. Levine A, Liebman H. The acquired immunodeficiency syndrome (AIDS). In: Beutler E, Lichtman M, Coller B, Kipps T, eds. Williams' hematology. New York: McGraw-Hill, 1995: 975-97.

41. Mayer A, Busch M. Transfusion-transmitted HIV infection. In: Anderson K, Ness P, eds. Scientific basis of transfusion medicine. Implications for clinical practice. Philadelphia: WB Saunders, 1994:659-68.

42. Centers for Disease Control. 1993 revised classification system for HIV infection and expanded surveillance case definition for AIDS among adolescents and adults. MMWR Morb Mortal Wkly Rep 1992;41:1-19.

43. Brookmeyer R. Reconstruction and future trends of the AIDS epidemic in the United States. Science 1991;253:37-42.

44. Centers for Disease Control and Prevention. US HIV and AIDS cases reported through December 2000. HIV/AIDS Surveillance Report 2000;12(2):1-44. [Available at http://www.cdc.gov/hiv/stats/hasr1202.pdf.]

45. Petersen LR, Doll LS, White CR, et al. Heterosexually acquired HIV infection and the US blood supply: Consideration for screening of potential donors. Transfusion 1993;33:552-7.

46. Simon F, Loussert-Ajaka I, Damond F, et al. HIV type 1 diversity in northern Paris, France. AIDS Res Hum Retroviruses 1996;12:1427-33.

47. Parry JV, Murphy G, Barlow KL, et al. National surveillance of HIV-1 subtypes for England and Wales: Design, methods, and initial findings. J Acquir Immune Defic Syndr 2001;26:381-8.

48. Leads from the MMWR. AIDS due to HIV-2 infection—New Jersey. JAMA 1988;259:969, 972.

49. Sullivan MT, Guido EA, Metler RP, et al. Identification and characterization of an HIV-2 antibody-positive blood donor in the United States. Transfusion 1998;38:189-93.

50. de Oliveira CF, Diaz RS, Machado DM, et al. Surveillance of HIV-1 genetic subtypes and diversity in the US blood supply. Transfusion 2000;40:1399-406.

51. Delwart EL, Orton S, Parekh B, et al. Two percent of HIV-positive US blood donors are infected with non-subtype-B strains. AIDS Res Hum Retroviruses 2003;19:1065-70.

52. Peeters M, Gueye A, Mboup S, et al. Geographical distribution of HIV-1 group O viruses in Africa. AIDS 1997;11:493-8.

53. Food and Drug Administration. Memorandum: Interim recommendations for deferral of donors at increased risk for HIV-1 group O infection. (December 11, 1996) Rockville, MD: CBER Office of Communication, Training, and Manufacturers Assistance, 1996.

54. Kaiser Family Foundation. Cumulative adult/adolescent HIV infection cases reported through 2003 among states with confidential name-based reporting. [Available at http://www.statehealthfacts.kff.org.]

55. Delwart EL, Kalmin ND, Jones TS, et al. First case of HIV transmission by an RNA-

screened blood donation. Vox Sang 2004;86: 771-7.

56. Phelps R, Robbins K, Liberti T, et al. Window-period human immunodeficiency virus transmission to two recipients by an adolescent blood donor. Transfusion 2004;44:929-33.

57. Ling AE, Robbins KE, Brown TM, et al. Failure of routine HIV-1 tests in a case involving transmission with preseroconversion blood components during the infectious window period. JAMA 2000;284:210-4 [comment in JAMA 2000;284:238-40].

58. Fiebig E, Busch MP. Retroviral infections. In: Simon TL, Dzik WH, Snyder EL, et al, eds. Rossi's principles of transfusion medicine. 3rd ed. Philadelphia: Lippincott Williams and Wilkins, 2002:742-56.

59. Tabor E. The epidemiology of virus transmission by plasma derivatives: Clinical studies verifying the lack of transmission of hepatitis B and C viruses and HIV type 1. Transfusion 1999;39:1160-8.

60. Dufoort G, Courouce AM, Ancelle-Park R, Bletry O. No clinical signs 14 years after HIV-2 transmission via blood transfusion (letter). Lancet 1988;ii:510.

61. Kleinman S, Busch MP, Korelitz JJ, Schreiber GB. The incidence/window period model and its use to assess the risk of transfusion-transmitted human immunodeficiency virus and hepatitis C virus infection. Transfus Med Rev 1997;11:155-72.

62. Silva MA, ed. Standards for blood banks and transfusion services. 23rd ed. Bethesda, MD: AABB, 2005.

63. Code of federal regulations. Title 21 CFR 610.40. Washington, DC: US Government Printing Office, 2004 (revised annually).

64. Busch MP. HIV and blood transfusions: Focus on seroconversion. Vox Sang 1994;67 (Suppl 3):13-8.

65. Fiebig EW, Wright DJ, Rawal BD, et al. Dynamics of HIV viremia and antibody seroconversion in plasma donors: Implications for diagnosis and staging of primary HIV infection. AIDS 2003;17:1871-9.

66. Food and Drug Administration. Talk paper: FDA approves first nucleic acid test (NAT) system to screen whole blood donors for infections with human immunodeficiency virus (HIV) and hepatitis C virus (HCV). (February 28, 2002) [Available at http://fda. gov/cber/products/hivhcvgen022702.htm.]

67. Food and Drug Administration. Guidance for industry: Use of nucleic acid tests on pooled and individual samples from donations of whole blood and blood components (including Source Plasma and Source Leukocytes) to adequately and appropriately reduce the risk of transmission of HIV-1 and HCV. (October 21, 2004) Rockville, MD: CBER Office of Communication, Training, and Manufacturers Assistance, 2004. [Available at http://www.fda. gov/cber/gdlns/hivhcvnatbld.htm.]

68. Centers for Disease Control. Interpretive criteria used to report Western blot results for HIV-1-antibody testing: United States. MMWR Morb Mortal Wkly Rep 1991;40:692-5.

69. Kleinman S, Busch MP, Hall L, et al. False-positive HIV-1 test results in a low-risk screening setting of voluntary blood donation. Retrovirus Epidemiology Donor Study. JAMA 1998;280:1080-5.

70. Food and Drug Administration. Memorandum: Revised recommendations for the prevention of human immunodeficiency (HIV) transmission by blood and blood products. (April 23, 1992) Rockville, MD: CBER Office of Communication, Training, and Manufacturers Assistance, 1992.

71. Food and Drug Administration. Memorandum: Use of fluorognost HIV-1 immunofluorescent assay (IFA). (April 23, 1992) Rockville, MD: CBER Office of Communication, Training, and Manufacturers Assistance, 1992.

72. Mintz P. Participation of HIV-infected patients in autologous blood programs. JAMA 1993;269:2892-4.

73. Pub. Law. 101-336, 104 Stat. 327 (1990). Codified at 42 U.S.C. §12101-12213.

74. Food and Drug Administration. Current good manufacturing practice for blood and blood components: Notification of consignees receiving blood and blood components at increased risk for transmitting HIV infection. (September 9, 1996) Fed Regist 1996;61: 47413-23.

75. Health Care Financing Administration. Medicare and Medicaid programs; hospital standard for potentially HIV infectious blood and blood products. (September 9, 1996) Fed Regist 1996;61:47423-34.

76. Code of federal regulations. 42 CFR 610.46-47. Washington, DC: US Government Printing Office, 2004 (revised annually).

77. Code of federal regulations. 21 CFR 482.27(c). Washington, DC: US Government Printing Office, 2004 (revised annually).

78. Murphy EL, Glynn SA, Fridey J, et al. Increased incidence of infectious diseases during prospective follow-up of human T-lymphotropic virus type II- and I-infected blood donors. Retrovirus Epidemiology Donor Study. Arch Intern Med 1999;159:1485-91.

79. Orland JR, Engstrom J, Fridey J, et al. Prevalence and clinical features of HTLV neuro-

logic disease in the HTLV Outcomes Study. Neurology 2003;61:1588-94.

80. Murphy EL, Wang B, Sacher RA, et al. Respiratory and urinary tract infections, arthritis, and asthma associated with HTLV-II and HTLV-I infection. Emerg Infect Dis 2004;10: 109-16.

81. Orland JR, Wang B, Wright DJ, et al. Increased mortality associated with HTLV-II infection in blood donors: A prospective cohort study. Retrovirology 2004;1:4.

82. Levine PH, Manns A. Transfusion transmission of human T-lymphotropic virus types I and II: Lessons to be learned from look-back investigations and implications for patient counseling (editorial). Transfusion 1993;33: 4-6.

83. Kleinman S, Swanson P, Allain JP, Lee H. Transfusion transmission of human T-lymphotropic virus types I and II: Serologic and polymerase chain reaction results in recipients identified through look-back investigations. Transfusion 1993;33:14-8.

84. Schreiber GB, Busch MP, Kleinman SH, Korelitz JJ. The risk of transfusion-transmitted viral infections. The Retrovirus Epidemiology Donor Study. N Engl J Med 1996;334: 1685-90.

85. Food and Drug Administration. Guidance for industry: Donor screening for antibodies to HTLV-II. (August 15, 1997) Rockville, MD: CBER Office of Communication, Training, and Manufacturers Assistance, 1997.

86. Dual enzyme immunoassay (EIA) approach for deferral and notification of anti-HTLV-I/II EIA reactive donors. Association Bulletin 99-9. Bethesda, MD: AABB, 1999.

87. Pealer LN, Marfin AA, Petersen LR, et al for the West Nile Virus Transmission Investigation Team. Transmission of West Nile virus through blood transfusion in the United States in 2002. N Engl J Med 2003;349:1236-45.

88. Biggerstaff BJ, Petersen LR. Estimated risk of transmission of the West Nile virus through blood transfusion in the US, 2002. Transfusion 2003;43:1007-17.

89. Food and Drug Administration. Guidance for industry: Revised recommendations for the assessment of donor suitability and blood and blood product safety in cases of known or suspected West Nile virus infection. (May 1, 2003) Rockville, MD: CBER Office of Communication, Training, and Manufacturers Assistance, 2003.

90. Kleinman S, Glynn SA, Busch M, et al for the NHLBI Retrovirus Epidemiology Study (REDS). The 2003 West Nile virus United States epidemic: The America's Blood Centers experience. Transfusion 2005;45:469-79.

91. Centers for Disease Control and Prevention. Update: West Nile virus screening of blood donations and transfusion-associated transmission—United States, 2003. MMWR Morb Mortal Wkly Rep 2004;53:281-4.

92. Busch MP, Caglioti S, Robertson GF, et al. Screening the blood supply for West Nile virus RNA by nucleic acid amplification testing. N Engl J Med 2005 (in press).

93. Update on WNV-related activities and considerations, 2004; a summary of the WNV Task Force meeting. Association Bulletin #04-03. Bethesda, MD: AABB, 2004.

94. Centers for Disease Control and Prevention. 2004 West Nile virus activity in the United States (reported as of January 11, 2005). [Available at http://www.cdc.gov/ncidod/dvbid/westnile/surv&controlCaseCount04_detailed.htm.]

95. Centers for Disease Control and Prevention. Transfusion-associated transmission of West Nile virus—Arizona, 2004. MMWR Morb Mortal Wkly Rep 2004;53:842-4.

96. Roback JD. Human herpes infections. In: Hillyer CD, Silberstein LE, Ness PM, Anderson KC, eds. Blood banking and transfusion medicine. New York: Churchill Livingstone, 2003:465-85.

97. Roback JD. CMV and blood transfusions. Rev Med Virol 2002;12:211-19.

98. Leukocyte reduction for the prevention of transfusion-transmitted cytomegalovirus. Association Bulletin #97-2. Bethesda, MD: AABB, 1997.

99. Bowden RA, Slichter SJ, Sayers M, et al. A comparison of filtered leukocyte-reduced and cytomegalovirus (CMV) seronegative blood products for the prevention of transfusion-associated CMV infection after marrow transplant. Blood 1995;86:3598-603.

100. Preiksaitis JK. The cytomegalovirus-"safe" blood product: Is leukoreduction equivalent to antibody screening? Transfus Med Rev 2000;14:112-36.

101. McMonigal K, Horwitz CA, Henle W. Postperfusion syndrome due to Epstein-Barr virus. Report of two cases and review of the literature. Transfusion 1983;23:331-5.

102. Campadelli-Fiume G, Mirandola P, Menotti L. Human herpesvirus 6: An emerging pathogen. Emerg Infect Dis 1999;5:353-66.

103. Chatlynne LG, Lapps W, Handy M, et al. Detection and titration of human herpesvirus-8-specific antibodies in sera from blood donors, acquired immunodeficiency syndrome patients, and Kaposi's sarcoma patients us-

ing a whole virus enzyme-linked immunosorbent assay. Blood 1998;92:53-8.

104. Cannon MJ, Dollard SC, Smith DK, et al. Blood-borne and sexual transmission of human herpesvirus 8 in women with or at risk for human immunodeficiency virus infection. N Engl J Med 2001;344:637-43.

105. Luppi M, Barozzi P, Santagostino G, et al. Molecular evidence of organ-related transmission of Kaposi sarcoma-associated herpesvirus or human herpesvirus-8 in transplant patients. Blood 2000;96:3279-81.

106. Regamey N, Tamm M, Wernli M, et al. Transmission of human herpesvirus 8 infection from renal-transplant donors to recipients. N Engl J Med 1998;339:1358-63.

107. Parravicini C, Olsen SJ, Capra M, et al. Risk of Kaposi's sarcoma-associated herpes virus transmission from donor allografts among Italian posttransplant Kaposi's sarcoma patients. Blood 1997;90:2826-9.

108. Mbulaiteye SM, Biggar RJ, Bakaki PM, et al. Human herpesvirus 8 infection and transfusion history in children with sickle-cell disease in Uganda. J Natl Cancer Inst 2003;95:1330-5.

109. Luban NL. Human parvoviruses: Implications for transfusion medicine. Transfusion 1994;34:821-7.

110. Prowse C, Ludlam CA, Yap PL. Human parvovirus B19 and blood products. Vox Sang 1997;72:1-10.

111. Brown KE, Hibbs JR, Gallinella G, et al. Resistance to parvovirus B19 infection due to lack of virus receptor (erythrocyte P antigen). N Engl J Med 1994;330:1192-6.

112. Nucleic acid testing of blood donors for human parvovirus B19 (presentations, public hearing, discussion, and recommendations). 64th meeting of the Blood Products Advisory Committee, Bethesda, MD, September 16, 1999. [Available at http://www.fda.gov/cber/advisory/bp/bpmain.htm.]

113. Manuelidis L. The dimensions of Creutzfeldt-Jakob disease. Transfusion 1994;34:915-28.

114. Ricketts MN, Cashman NR, Stratton EE, El Saadany S. Is Creutzfeldt-Jakob disease transmitted in blood? Emerg Infect Dis 1997;3:155-63.

115. Evatt B, Austin H, Barnhart E, et al. Surveillance for Creutzfeldt-Jakob disease among persons with hemophilia. Transfusion 1998;38:817-20.

116. van Duijn CM, Delasnerie-Laupretre N, Masullo C, et al. Case-control study of risk factors of Creutzfeldt-Jakob disease in Europe during 1993-95. European Union (EU) Collaborative Study Group of Creutzfeldt-Jakob Disease (CJD). Lancet 1998;351:1081-5.

117. Food and Drug Administration. Memorandum: Revised precautionary measures to reduce the possible risk of transmission of Creutzfeldt-Jakob disease (CJD) by blood and blood products. (August 5, 1995) Rockville, MD: CBER Office of Communication, Training, and Manufacturers Assistance, 1995.

118. Food and Drug Administration. Memorandum: Revised precautionary measures to reduce the possible risk of transmission of Creutzfeldt-Jakob disease (CJD) by blood and blood products. (December 11, 1996) Rockville, MD: CBER Office of Communication, Training, and Manufacturers Assistance, 1996.

119. Food and Drug Administration. Draft guidance for industry: Preventive measures to reduce the possible risk of transmission of Creutzfeldt-Jakob disease (CJD) and variant Creutzfeldt-Jakob disease (vCJD) by human cells, tissues, and cellular and tissue-based products (HCT/Ps). (June 25, 2002) Fed Regist 2002;67:42789-90.

120. Hunter N, Foster J, Chong A, et al. Transmission of prion diseases by blood transfusion. J Gen Virol 2002;83:2897-905.

121. Llewelyn CA, Hewitt PE, Knight RS, et al. Possible transmission of variant Creutzfeldt-Jakob disease by blood transfusion. Lancet 2004;363:417-21.

122. Peden AH, Head MW, Ritchie DL, et al. Preclinical vCJD after blood transfusion in a PRNP codon 129 heterozygous patient. Lancet 2004;364:521-9.

123. Nurmi MH, Bishop M, Strain L, et al. The normal population distribution of PRNP codon 129 polymorphism. Acta Neurol Scand 2003;108:374-8.

124. Sazama K. Bacteria in blood for transfusion. A review. Arch Pathol Lab Med 1994;118:350-65.

125. Food and Drug Administration. CBER annual report FY 2002 (October 1, 2001 through September 30, 2002). Rockville, MD: CBER Office of Communication, Training, and Manufacturers Assistance, 2002. [Available at http://www.fda.gov/cber/inside/annrptpart3.htm.]

126. Morrow JF, Braine HG, Kickler TS, et al. Septic reactions to platelet transfusions. A persistent problem. JAMA 1991;266:555-8.

127. Kuehnert MJ, Roth VR, Haley NR, et al. Transfusion-transmitted bacterial infection in the United States, 1998 through 2000. Transfusion 2001;41:1493-9.

128. Theakston EP, Morris AJ, Streat SJ, et al. Transfusion transmitted *Yersinia enterocolitica* infection in New Zealand. Aust N Z J Med 1997;27:62-7.

129. Cookson ST, Arduino MJ, Agucro SM, Jarvis WR, and the Yersinia Study Group. *Yersinia enterocolitica*-contaminated Red Blood Cells

(RBCs)—an emerging threat to blood safety (abstract). In: Program and abstracts of the 36th Interscience Conference on Antimicrobial Agents and Chemotherapy, New Orleans, September 15-18, 1996. Washington, DC: American Society for Microbiology, 1996:237.

130. National Blood Data Resource Center. Comprehensive report on blood collection and transfusion in the United States in 2001. Bethesda, MD: AABB, 2003.

131. Brecher ME, Hay SN. Improving platelet safety: Bacterial contamination of platelets. Curr Hematol Rep 2004;3:121-7.

132. Dykstra A, Hoeltge G, Jacobs M, et al. Platelet bacterial contamination (PBC) rate is surveillance method (SM) dependent (abstract). Transfusion 1998;38(Suppl):104S.

133. Serious Hazards of Transfusion (SHOT). Annual report 2000-2001. Manchester, UK: SHOT Office, 2002. [Available at http://www.shot.demon.co.uk/toc.htm.]

134. Perez P, Salmi LR, Follea G, et al. Determinants of transfusion-associated bacterial contamination: Results of the French BACTHEM case-control study. Transfusion 2001;41:862-71.

135. Ness PM, Braine HG, King K, et al. Single donor platelets reduce the risk of septic transfusion reactions. Transfusion 2001;41:857-61.

136. Engelfriet CP, Reesink HW, Blajchman MA, et al. Bacterial contamination of blood components. Vox Sang 2000;78:59-67.

137. Kim DM, Brecher ME, Bland LA, et al. Prestorage removal of Yersinia enterocolitica from red cells with white cell-reduction filters. Transfusion 1992;32:658-62.

138. Buchholz DH, AuBuchon JP, Snyder EL, et al. Removal of Yersinia enterocolitica from AS-1 red cells. Transfusion 1992;32:667-72.

139. Pietersz RNI, Engelfriet CP, Reesink HW, et al. Detection of bacterial contamination of platelet concentrates. International Forum. Vox Sang 2003;85:224-39.

140. Commission on Laboratory Accreditation. Transfusion medicine checklist. TRM.44955 Phase I. Northfield, IL: College of American Pathologists, January 2003. [Available at http://www.cap.org/html/checklist_html/transfusionmedicine_1202.html.]

141. Brumit MC, Hay SN, Brecher ME. Bacteria detection. In: Brecher ME, ed. Bacterial and parasitic contamination of blood components. Bethesda, MD: AABB Press, 2003:57-82.

142. Anderson KC, Lew MA, Gorgone BC, et al. Transfusion-related sepsis after prolonged platelet storage. Am J Med 1986;81:405-11.

143. Orton SL, Liu H, Dodd RY, Williams AE. Prevalence of circulating Treponema pallidum DNA and RNA in blood donors with confirmed positive syphilis tests. Transfusion 2002;42:94-9.

144. Gardella C, Marfin AA, Kahn RH, et al. Persons with early syphilis identified through blood or plasma donation screening in the United States. J Infect Dis 2000;185:545-9.

145. Leiby DA. Babesia and other parasites. In: Brecher ME, ed. Bacterial and parasitic contamination of blood components. Bethesda, MD: AABB Press, 2003:179-200.

146. Herwaldt BL, Springs FE, Roberts PP, et al. Babesiosis in Wisconsin: A potentially fatal disease. Am J Trop Med Hyg 1995;53:146-51.

147. Herwaldt BL, Kjemtrup AM, Conrad PA, et al. Transfusion-transmitted babesiosis in Washington State: First reported case caused by a WA1-type parasite. J Infect Dis 1997;175:1259-62.

148. Krause PJ, Spielman A, Telford SR 3rd, et al. Persistent parasitemia after acute babesiosis. N Engl J Med 1998;339:160-5.

149. Cable R, Trouern-Trend J. Tick-borne infections. In: Linden JV, Bianco C, eds. Blood safety and surveillance. New York: Marcel Dekker, 2001:399-422.

150. Wells GM, Woodward TE, Fiset P, Hornick RB. Rocky Mountain spotted fever caused by blood transfusion. JAMA 1978;239:2763-5.

151. Eastlund T, Persing D, Mathiesen D, et al. Human granulocytic ehrlichiosis after red cell transfusion (abstract). Transfusion 1999;39(Suppl):117S.

152. Arguin PM, Singleton J, Rotz LD, et al. An investigation into the possibility of transmission of tick-borne pathogens via blood transfusion. Transfusion-Associated Tick-Borne Illness Task Force. Transfusion 1999;39:828-33.

153. McQuiston JH, Childs JE, Chamberland ME, Tabor E for the Working Group on Transfusion Transmission of Tick-Borne Diseases. Transmission of tick-borne agents of disease by blood transfusion: A review of known and potential risks in the United States. Transfusion 2000;40:274-84.

154. Mungai M, Tegtmeier G, Chamberland M, Parise M. Transfusion-transmitted malaria in the United States from 1963 through 1999. N Engl J Med 2001;344:1973-8.

155. Centers for Disease Control and Prevention. Probable transfusion-transmitted malaria—Houston, Texas, 2003. MMWR Morb Mortal Wkly Rep 2003;52:1075-6.

156. Katz LM. Transfusion-induced malaria. In: Brecher ME, ed. Bacterial and parasitic con-

tamination of blood components. Bethesda, MD: AABB Press, 2003:127-55.

157. Herwaldt BL, Grijalva MJ, Newsome AL, et al. Use of polymerase chain reaction to diagnose the fifth reported US case of autochthonous transmission of *Trypanosoma cruzi*, in Tennessee, 1998. J Infect Dis 2000; 181:395-9.

158. Shulman IA. Transfusion of *T. cruzi* infection by blood transfusion. In: Brecher ME, ed. Bacterial and parasitic contamination of blood components. Bethesda, MD: AABB Press, 2003:157-78.

159. Leiby DA, Rentas FJ, Nelson KE, et al. Evidence of *Trypanosoma cruzi* infection (Chagas' disease) among patients undergoing cardiac surgery. Circulation 2000;102:2978-82.

160. Leiby DA, Read EJ, Lenes BA, et al. Seroepidemiology of *Trypanosoma cruzi*, etiologic agent of Chagas' disease, in US blood donors. J Infect Dis 1997;176:1047-52.

161. Shulman IA, Appleman MD, Saxena S, et al. Specific antibodies to *Trypanosoma cruzi* among blood donors in Los Angeles, California. Transfusion 1997;37:727-31.

162. Shulman I, Haimowitz MD. Transmission of parasitic infections by blood transfusion. In: Simon TL, Dzik WH, Snyder EL, et al, eds. Rossi's principles of transfusion medicine. 3rd ed. Philadelphia: Lippincott Williams and Wilkins, 2002:774-83.

163. Deferral for risk of Leishmaniasis exposure. Association Bulletin #03-14. Bethesda, MD: AABB, 2003.

164. US General Accounting Office. Blood supply: Transfusion-associated risks. GAO/PEMD-97-1. Washington, DC: US Government Printing Office, 1997.

165. Brecher ME. Bacterial contamination of blood products. In: Simon TL, Dzik WH, Snyder EL, et al, eds. Rossi's principles of transfusion medicine. 3rd ed. Philadelphia: Lippincott Williams and Wilkins, 2002: 789-801.

166. Rock G, Neurath D, Toye B, et al. The use of a bacteria detection system to evaluate bacterial contamination in PLT concentrates. Transfusion 2004;44:337-42.

167. Suomela H. Inactivation of viruses in blood and plasma products. Transfus Med Rev 1993; 7:42-57.

168. Centers for Disease Control. Safety of therapeutic immune globulin preparations with respect to transmission of human T-lymphotropic virus type III/lymphadenopathy-associated virus infection. MMWR Morb Mortal Wkly Rep 1986;35:231-3. [Erratum in MMWR Morb Mortal Wkly Rep 1986;35:607.]

169. Williams PE, Yap PL, Gillon J, et al. Non-A, non-B hepatitis transmission by intravenous immunoglobulin (letter). Lancet 1988;ii:501. [Erratum in Lancet 1988;ii:584.]

170. Yu MW, Mason BL, Guo ZP, et al. Hepatitis C transmission associated with intravenous immunoglobulins (letter). Lancet 1995;345: 1173-4.

171. Centers for Disease Control. Outbreak of hepatitis C associated with intravenous immunoglobulin administration: United States, October 1993-June 1994. MMWR Morb Mortal Wkly Rep 1994;43:505-9.

172. Farrugia A, Walker E. Hepatitis C virus transmission by intravenous immunoglobulin (letter). Lancet 1995;346:373-5.

173. Meisel H, Reip A, Faltus B, et al. Transmission of hepatitis C virus to children and husbands by women infected with contaminated anti-D immunoglobulin. Lancet 1995;345:1209-11.

174. Power JP, Lawlor E, Davidson F, et al. Hepatitis C viraemia in recipients of Irish intravenous anti-D immunoglobulin (letter). Lancet 1994;344:1166-7.

175. Foster PR, McIntosh RV, Welch AG. Hepatitis C infection from anti-D immunoglobulin (letter). Lancet 1995;346:372.

176. Makris M, Preston FE. Chronic hepatitis in haemophilia. Blood Rev 1993;7:243-50.

177. Prowse C. Kill and cure. The hope and reality of virus inactivation. Vox Sang 1994;67(Suppl 3):191-6.

178. Lusher JM, Arkin S, Abildgaard CF, Schwartz RS. Recombinant factor VIII for the treatment of previously untreated patients with hemophilia A. Safety, efficacy, and development of inhibitors. Kogenate Previously Untreated Patient Study Group. N Engl J Med 1993;328: 453-9.

179. Ben-Hur E, Moor AC, Margolis-Nunno H, et al. The photodecontamination of cellular blood components: Mechanisms and use of photosensitization in transfusion medicine. Transfus Med Rev 1996;10:15-22.

180. Zhang Q-X, Edson C, Budowsky E, Purmal A. Inactine™—a method for viral inactivation in red blood cell concentrates (abstract). Transfusion 1998;38(Suppl):75S.

181. Seeff L. The efficacy of and place for HBIG in the prevention of type B hepatitis. In: Szmuness W, Alter H, Maynard J, eds. Viral hepatitis: 1981 International Symposium. Philadelphia: The Franklin Institute Press, 1982:585-95.

182. Sanchez-Quijano A, Pineda JA, Lissen E, et al. Prevention of post-transfusion non-A, non-B hepatitis by non-specific immunoglobulin in heart surgery patients. Lancet 1988;i:1245-9.

183. Conrad ME. Prevention of post-transfusion hepatitis (letter). Lancet 1988;ii:217.

184. Kobayashi R, Stiehm E. Immunoglobulin therapy. In: Petz LD, Swisher SN, Kleinman S, et al, eds. Clinical practice of transfusion medicine. 3rd ed. New York: Churchill Livingstone, 1996:985-1010.

185. Centers for Disease Control. Recommendations for follow-up of health-care workers after occupational exposure to hepatitis C virus. MMWR Morb Mortal Wkly Rep 1997;46: 603-6.

Suggested Reading

Actions following an initial positive test for possible bacterial contamination of a platelet unit (Association Bulletin #04-07). Bethesda, MD: AABB, 2004.

Criteria for donor deferral in known or suspected common source outbreaks of hepatitis A virus infection (Association Bulletin #04-08). Bethesda, MD: AABB, 2004.

Guidance on management of blood and platelet donors with positive or abnormal results on bacterial contamination tests (Association Bulletin #05-02). Bethesda, MD: AABB, 2005.

Methods

The inclusion of methods in this edition of the *Technical Manual* is a subjective decision of the Technical Manual Program Unit. Readers are encouraged to refer to previous editions of the manual for methods not appearing in this edition because exclusion from the current edition does not necessarily indicate that their use is prohibited. However, some procedures, such as xylene and chloroform elution techniques, were removed because the chemicals used in the procedures could present a safety risk. Thus, readers are cautioned when referring to procedures in previous editions because they have not been reviewed for content and safety.

There are often many different ways to perform the same test procedure. Although some workers may prefer other methods, those given here are reliable, straightforward, and of proven value. Although the investigation of unusual serologic problems often requires flexibility in thought and methodology, the adoption of uniform methods for routine procedures in the laboratory is imperative. In order for laboratory personnel to have reproducible and comparable results in a test procedure, it is essential that everyone in the laboratory perform the same procedure in the same manner.

Methods

General Laboratory Methods

Introduction

The methods outlined in the following sections are *examples* of acceptable procedures. Other acceptable procedures may be used by facilities if desired. To the greatest extent possible, the written procedures conform to the *Guidelines for Clinical Laboratory Technical Procedure Manuals* developed by the National Committee for Clinical Laboratory Standards. As indicated in Title 21 of the Code of Federal Regulations (CFR) Part 606.65(e), the manufacturer's instructions (eg, product insert) for reagents and supplies licensed by the Food and Drug Administration (FDA) should be followed. Any deviation should be validated using appropriate controls and incorporated into a standard operating procedure before approval by the medical director. (Note: Deviations may also require concurrence from the FDA.) It is important to use Standard Precautions when appropriate (see Chapter 2).

Reagent Preparation

Many procedures include formulas for reagent preparation. Labels for reagents prepared in-house must contain the following:

- Name of solution.
- Date of preparation.
- Expiration date (if known).
- Storage temperature and/or conditions.
- Mechanism to identify the person preparing the solution.
- Universal hazardous substance label.

Temperatures

Whenever specific incubation or storage temperatures are given, the following ranges are considered satisfactory:

Stated Temperature	Acceptable Range
4 C	2-8 C
Room temperature	20-24 C
37 C	36-38 C
56 C	54-58 C

Section 1

Centrifugation Variables

Centrifugation speeds (relative centrifugal force) and times should be standardized for each piece of equipment. (See Methods Section 8.)

Reference

Guidelines for clinical laboratory technical procedure manuals. 3rd ed. (NCCLS Document GP2-A3, Vol. 12, No. 10.) Wayne, PA: National Committee for Clinical Laboratory Standards, 1996.

Method 1.1. Transportation and Shipment of Dangerous Goods

Several agencies specify packaging and shipping requirements for dangerous or hazardous materials, depending on how the material is shipped (mail, ground, or air). For transport by mail of infectious materials, clinical specimens, or biologic products, the United States Postal Service (USPS) Dangerous Goods Regulations must be followed.[1,2] For interstate transport of infectious materials by ground or air, the United States Department of Transportation (DOT) regulations apply.[3] Most air carriers apply the International Air Transport Association (IATA)[4] regulations and the technical instructions of the International Civil Aviation Organization (ICAO).[5] These agencies adopt the recommendations of the United Nations (UN) Committee of Experts on the Transport of Dangerous Goods for the international transport of infectious substances and clinical specimens.

The Centers for Disease Control and Prevention (CDC)[6] and the IATA[7] provide packing and labeling requirements for shipments of infectious materials in order to protect the public health by minimizing the potential for direct contact with such materials, contamination of the environment,

and the spread of disease. The CDC also serves as a Center for Applied Biosafety and Training for the World Health Organization (WHO)[8] and for the UN. The Occupational Safety and Health Administration (OSHA)[9] regulates worker safety related to handling, packing, and transport. Both the DOT and the IATA require active training for anyone who packages infectious or toxic materials for shipment.[3,4] DOT and IATA documents offer general shipping advice for all hazardous materials because the regulations are similar and most carriers follow the shipping guidelines set forth in the IATA Dangerous Goods Regulations[4] and the Infectious Substances Shipping Guidelines.[7] Facilities should also consult their local carriers for additional requirements. In general, all dangerous goods regulations are based on public risk from the materials and therefore have specific packaging, labeling, and documentation requirements. It is the responsibility of the shipper of biologic or infectious material to properly classify, package, label, and document the substance being shipped.

Dangerous Goods Classifications

IATA classifies hazards into nine categories:

1. Explosives.
2. Compressed gases.
3. Flammable liquids.
4. Other flammable hazards.
5. Oxygen-rich material, oxidizers, and organic peroxides.
6. Material affecting health, poisons, and infectious substances.
7. Radioactive materials.
8. Corrosive material.
9. Miscellaneous hazards.[4]

The infectious category includes:

■ Infectious substances: microbiologic agents or their toxins that cause, or may cause, disease; also called etiologic agents.

- Biologic products: products that are prepared and shipped in compliance with the provisions of 9 CFR part 102 (Licensed Veterinary Biological Products), 9 CFR part 103 (Biological Products for Experimental Treatment of Animals), 9 CFR part 104 (Imported Biological Products), 21 CFR part 312 (Investigational New Drug Application), 21 CFR parts 600-680 (Biologics), 29 CFR Part 1910.1030 (Occupational Exposure to Bloodborne Pathogens), 42 CFR Part 72 (Interstate Shipment of Etiological Agents), or 49 CFR Parts 171-178 (Hazardous Materials Regulations).
- Clinical or diagnostic specimens: human or animal material (including excreta, secreta, blood and its components, body fluids, tissue) being shipped for the purpose of diagnosis.
- Genetically modified organisms.
- Clinical and medical waste.

Blood Bank Applications

Although the USPS regulates some biologic products, such as live poliovirus vaccine, the DOT and IATA take the position that biologic products and diagnostic specimens may be shipped with less stringent packaging and labeling requirements, unless they contain, or are reasonably believed to contain, an infectious substance. The CDC has proposed regulations to harmonize these requirements with other federal and international requirements.[10] Units of blood that meet disease testing requirements and unscreened blood from healthy donors meeting all FDA donor eligibility criteria including specimens for screening may be shipped without hazard restrictions. Specimens being shipped for initial diagnosis purposes and with a low probability that infectious agents are present are packaged as diagnostic samples (IATA packing instruction 650); specimens from individuals known, or thought likely, to have an infectious disease are shipped as infectious substances (IATA packing instruction 602). The IATA Dangerous Goods Regulations should be consulted for the most recent amendments to ship biologic specimens.

Method 1.1.1. Shipping Diagnostic Specimens and Infectious Substances

Principle

The safe transport of hazardous materials requires that they be packaged in a way to protect the materials and those who handle them. Prevention from leakage and from being crushed in unexpected accidents are required. Primary containers should be leakproof and securely closed. The primary container should be placed in a watertight secondary container. Absorbent material capable of absorbing the entire liquid contents in the package is placed between the primary and secondary containers. The outer packaging should have adequate strength for its intended use and capacity and be labeled in accordance with applicable regulations. Packaging requirements for clinical specimens are similar to those for infectious substances except that performance standards of the packaging materials are less rigorous.

Materials

1. Leakproof, watertight primary container (eg, test tube), heat sealed, crimped, or otherwise reinforced to prevent cap slippage.

2. Leakproof, watertight secondary package (eg, sealable plastic bag or container with screw cap).
3. Nonparticulate absorbent material (eg, paper towels, gauze, disposable diaper).
4. For infectious substances and for total shipment volumes greater than 50 mL (but less than 4000 mL or 4 kg), shock-absorbent material equal in volume to the nonparticulate-absorbent material.
5. Outer packaging.
    a. For infectious substances with a shipping volume greater than 50 mL (but less than 4000 mL or 4 kg), an outer package of corrugated cardboard, fiberboard, wood, metal, or rigid plastic meeting UN strength requirements.
    b. For biologic and diagnostic specimens with a shipping volume less than 50 mL, a noncertified outer container.
6. Coolant material (if necessary).
    a. Wet ice, enclosed in sealed bags to prevent leakage.
    b. Dry ice, not to exceed 5 lb (for air shipments).
7. Itemized listing of package contents.
8. Address label that includes the names, addresses, and contact names and telephone numbers of both the sender and intended recipient.
9. Special labels, as applicable to circumstances (see Table 1.1.1-1).
    a. Diagnostic specimens.
    b. Infectious substances.
    c. Dry ice.
    d. Liquid nitrogen.
    e. Cargo aircraft only.
10. Carrier-specific documents, such as airbills or dangerous goods declarations.

Procedure

1. Place the sealed primary container into the secondary container.
2. Add sufficient absorbent material around the primary container (between the primary and secondary containers) to cover all sides of the primary container and to absorb the entire contents of the primary container should breakage occur.
3. Seal the secondary container securely.
4. Place the secondary container into the applicable outer package.
5. For infectious substances with a shipping volume greater than 50 mL, place shock-absorbent materials at the top, bottom, and sides between the secondary container and the outer packaging. See Fig 1.1.1-1.
6. Place any necessary coolant material (eg, wet ice or dry ice) between the secondary container and the applicable outer packaging. Provide interior support to secure the secondary packaging in the original position because the ice or dry ice melts or dissipates.

PACKAGING FOR A CLINICAL SPECIMEN (VOLUME >50 mL AND <4000 mL)

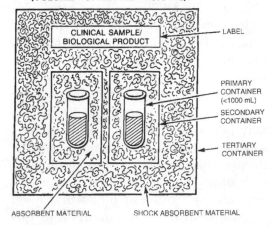

Figure 1.1.1-1. Appropriate packaging of clinical specimen material.

Table 1.1.1-1. Special Labels for Shipping

Clinical (Diagnostic) Specimens

Specimens collected for diagnosis, research, or other purposes must be labeled as biohazardous. Both the primary container and the outer packaging must contain a biohazard label. The outer packaging label must appear as follows:

1. The color of the material on which the label is printed must be *bright orange*, with the biohazard symbol and printing in black.
2. The label must be a *rectangle* measuring 2 inches high by 4 inches long.
3. The biohazard symbol, measuring 1.56 inches in diameter, must be centered on a square measuring 2 inches on each side.
4. The size of the letters, printed in Helvetica, must be:

Biohazard	16 pt.
Clinical specimens	14 pt.
Packaged in compliance with 42 CFR part 72	6 pt.
In case of damage or leakage, notify	10 pt.
Shipper and receiver	10 pt.

Infectious Substances (Etiologic Agents)

For substances known to contain infectious agents or reasonably anticipated to contain such agents, biohazardous labels must be placed on the primary container and outer packaging. The outer packaging label must appear as follows:

1. The color of the material on which the label is printed must be *white*, with the biohazard symbol and printing in black.
2. The label must be a *diamond-on-point* measuring, at a minimum, 4 inches on each side.
3. The biohazard symbol, measuring 0.81 inches in diameter, must be centered on a square measuring 2 inches on each side.
4. The Class 6 symbol for infectious substances must be centered at the bottom of the label.
5. The size of the letters, printed in Helvetica, must be:

Infectious substance	16 pt.
Packaged in compliance with 42 CFR part 72	5 pt.
In case of damage or leakage, notify	7 pt.
Immediately notify	7 pt.
Public Health Authority	7 pt.
In the United States	5 pt.
Centers for Disease Control and Prevention	5 pt.
Atlanta, GA	5 pt.
1-800-232-0124	5 pt.
6	24 pt.

Dry Ice

Packages with dry ice must be labeled with the following information:

1. The diamond-shaped Class 9 symbol for miscellaneous hazardous materials.
2. The words "Dry Ice" or "Carbon Dioxide, Solid."
3. "UN 1845," the United Nations hazardous material category for dry ice (if shipped out of the country).
4. The name of the contents being cooled.
5. The weight of the dry ice in kg (not to exceed 5 lb if transported by air).

Liquid Nitrogen

Packages with liquid nitrogen must be labeled with a green IATA label stating "Contains Cryogenic Liquid."

Cargo Aircraft Only

If the mode of transport is air and more than 50 mL of infectious substance is enclosed, the package must have a warning label "Cargo Aircraft Only" to preclude the carrier from transporting the package on a passenger plane.

7. Enclose the itemized listing of container contents between the secondary and outer packaging.

8. Seal the outer packaging and label with address label and applicable special labels.

9. Complete applicable shipping forms and send them with the package.

Notes

1. Package specimens within a container such that they will remain in an upright position to help prevent leakage.

2. Closures on primary containers can be reinforced with adhesive tape or paraffin. It is not necessary to reinforce unopened evacuated specimen collecting tubes.

3. For infectious substances, the name, address, and telephone number of the shipper must appear on both the secondary and outer shipping containers.

4. Shipments of infectious substances may contain multiple secondary containers, but the total volume of the shipment may not exceed 4 L or 4 kg, excluding the packaging and coolant weights.

5. Primary containers or secondary packaging must be capable of withstanding an internal pressure differential of 95 kPA (0.95 bar, 13.8 lb/in^2) between the temperatures of –40 C and 55 C.

6. Styrofoam, plastic bags, and paper envelopes are unacceptable for outer packaging.

7. UN-certified containers must be able to withstand a 30-foot "drop test," as specified in 49 CFR 178.609, without breaking enclosed tubes. The UN certification number must appear on the container. Noncertified containers must be able to withstand at least a 1.2-meter drop on a hard unyielding surface without release of the container's contents.

8. Ensure that all state and local regulations are followed.

9. Some exceptions may apply for ground transportation.

10. If unsure about how to package and ship materials, contact the CDC.

11. If breakage occurs during shipment, the package should be handled with extreme caution (wear personal protective equipment) and the entire package (including containers, contents, and packaging materials) should be autoclaved before discard. Supervisory personnel should be notified if the contents are lost in transit or if the damage appears related to inadequate packaging by the sender.

12. The carrier, the receiver, or anyone handling damaged or leaking packages must isolate the package and notify the shipper and intended recipient immediately. In addition, for infectious substances, notify the CDC as soon as possible (1-800-232-0124). When notifying the CDC, the caller should provide a description of the condition of the package, the name, address, and telephone number of the shipper, and any other pertinent information, so that decontamination and disposal procedures can be provided.

Additional Considerations with the Use of Dry Ice

1. Solid carbon dioxide or "dry ice" is classified as a hazardous material because it can cause burns on contact and gives off carbon dioxide gas as it volatilizes.

2. Insulated gloves must be worn when handling dry ice; eye protection must be worn when breaking up chunks of solid ice or when breaking apart ice pellets.

3. Dry ice should be handled in a well-ventilated area; its gas can cause light-headedness and, in extreme cases, asphyxiation.

4. When kept in a tightly sealed shipping container, dry ice could rupture the packaging. If dry ice is used, it must be placed outside the secondary packaging or in an overpack with one or more complete packages. The outer packaging must be leakproof. Procedures for packing with dry ice must include instructions for sealing the outer container in a manner that allows the gas to escape and prevents loosening of secondary containers as the dry ice dissipates. Consult the Domestic Mail Manual (section C023),[2] 49 CFR 173.217 and 175.10 (a)(13),[3] IATA Dangerous Goods Regulations,[4] and IATA packing instruction 904.

5. HAZMAT training requirements for dry ice are found in 49 CFR 172.704.[3] Training for staff who come in contact with dry ice should include information on:
   - Potential hazards.
   - Personal protective equipment to use when handling or chipping.
   - Procedures for packing, sealing, labeling, and handling boxes containing dry ice.
   - Special considerations in operating a vehicle used to transport boxes containing dry ice.
   - Procedures for storing or disposing of dry ice (eg, allowing the gas to dissipate by natural means in a well-ventilated area) after a shipment is received.

Additional Considerations with the Use of Liquid Nitrogen

1. Liquid nitrogen is classified as a cryogenic liquid.

2. Insulated gloves, eye protection, and a protective laboratory coat must be worn when working with liquid nitrogen.

3. A watertight material capable of withstanding cryogenic temperatures must be used for the primary container. This container must maintain its containment integrity at the temperature of the refrigerant as well as at the temperature and pressure of air transport if refrigeration is lost.

4. The secondary packaging must be designed to withstand cryogenic temperatures.

5. The design of the outer packaging must allow for relief of pressure when the liquid nitrogen evaporates. A loose-fitting, but secured, container cover or pressure relief valve may be used.

References

1. Code of Federal Regulations. Title 39 CFR. Washington, DC: US Government Printing Office, 2004 (revised annually).

2. Etiologic agent preparations, clinical specimens, and biological products. Domestic Mail Manual (section C023), issue 57, July 10, 2003.

3. Code of Federal Regulations. Title 49 CFR Part 171-180. Washington, DC: US Government Printing Office, 2004 (revised annually).

4. Dangerous goods regulations. 45th ed. Montreal, Canada: International Air Transport Association, 2004 (revised annually).

5. Technical instructions for the safe transport of dangerous goods by air. 2002-2004 ed. Montreal, Canada: International Civil Aviation Organization, Documents 9284 and 9284SU, 2002.

6. Code of Federal Regulations. Title 42 CFR Part 72. Washington, DC: US Government Printing Office, 2004 (revised annually).

7. Infectious substances and diagnostic specimens shipping guidelines. 4th ed. Montreal, Canada: International Air Transport Association, 2003.

8. World Health Organization. Guidelines for the safe transport of infectious substances and diagnostic specimens. Geneva, Switzerland: World Health Organization, 1997.

9. Code of Federal Regulations. Title 29 CFR 1910.1030. Washington, DC: US Government Printing Office, 2004 (revised annually).

10. Centers for Disease Control and Prevention. Packaging and handling of infectious substances and select agents, notice of proposed rulemaking. Fed Regist 1999;64(208):58022-31.

Method 1.1.2. Monitoring Temperature During Shipment of Blood

Principle

Some form of temperature indication or monitoring is desirable when shipping blood. The temperature of the contents of a shipping container used for whole blood or liquid-stored red cell components can be ascertained when the shipment is received, as follows:

Procedure

1. Open the shipping container and promptly place the sensing end of a calibrated liquid-in-glass or electronic thermometer between two bags of blood or components (labels facing out) and secure the "sandwich" with two rubber bands.

2. Close the shipping container.

3. After approximately 3 to 5 minutes, read the temperature.

4. If the temperature of red-cell-containing components exceeds 10 C, quarantine the units until their appropriate disposition can be determined.

Notes

Other suitable methods for monitoring shipments are:

1. Use time/temperature indicators, one such indicator per shipping carton. These indicators will change color or show another visible indication if the temperature has exceeded 10 C.

2. Place a "high-low" thermometer in the shipping container. This simple, reusable thermometer measures and records the highest and lowest temperatures during any period.

Method 1.2. Treatment of Incompletely Clotted Specimens

Principle

Fibrin generation may continue in serum separated from incompletely clotted blood, especially during incubation at 37 C. This produces strands of protein that entrap red cells and make it difficult to evaluate agglutination. Blood from patients who have recently received heparin may not clot at all, and blood from patients with excessive fibrinolytic activity may reliquefy or may contain protein fragments that interfere with examination for agglutination.

Materials

1. Thrombin: dry human/bovine thrombin or thrombin solution (50 units/mL in saline).

2. Glass beads.

3. Protamine sulfate: 10 mg/mL in saline.

4. Epsilon aminocaproic acid (EACA): 0.25 g/mL in saline.

Procedure

1. *To accelerate clotting*: Either of the following techniques may be used:
    a. Add to the specimen the amount of dry thrombin that adheres to the tip of an applicator stick or 1 drop of thrombin solution per mL of whole blood or serum. Allow 10 to 15 minutes for the clot to form. Use standard centrifugation to separate the clot and serum.
    b. Gently agitate the separated serum with small glass beads, at 37 C, for several minutes. Then, use low speed centrifugation to pellet the glass beads. Transfer the serum to another tube.
2. *To neutralize heparin:* Protamine sulfate can be added to the specimen to neutralize heparin; however, excess protamine promotes rouleaux formation and, in great excess, will inhibit clotting. Add 1 drop of protamine sulfate solution to 4 mL of whole blood and wait 30 minutes to evaluate the effect on clotting. If clotting does not occur, add additional protamine sparingly. Note: protamine sulfate may work more rapidly when briefly incubated (5-10 minutes) at 37 C.
3. *To inhibit fibrinolytic activity:* Add 0.1 mL of EACA to 4 mL of whole blood.

Notes

1. The use of anticoagulated (eg, ACD or EDTA) collection tubes may help to avoid the problem of incompletely clotted specimens. The use of anticoagulated specimens must be validated in accordance with each standard operating procedure.
2. Because preparations of human thrombin may contain red cell anti-

bodies, test results must be carefully observed for false-positive reactions. Quality control should be performed on thrombin reagents before or concurrent with their use to identify those with contaminating antibodies.

Method 1.3. Solution Preparation—Instructions

Principle

The basic definitions, calculations, and instructions given below serve as a review of simple principles necessary for solution preparation.

1. Mole, gram-molecular weight: Weight, expressed in grams equal to the atomic or molecular weight of the substance.
2. Molar solution: A one molar (1 M) solution contains one mole of solute in a liter of solvent. The solvent is assumed to be distilled or deionized water unless otherwise indicated.
3. Gram-equivalent weight: Weight, in grams, of a substance that will produce or react with 1 mole of hydrogen ion.
4. Normal solution: A one normal (1 N) solution contains one gram-equivalent weight of solute in a liter of solution.
5. Percentage solutions: The percent designation of a solution gives the weight or volume of solute present in 100 units of total solution. Percent can be expressed as:
    a. Weight/weight (w/w), indicating grams of solute in 100 g of solution.
    b. Volume/volume (v/v), indicating milliliters of solute present in 100 mL of solution.

c. Weight/volume (w/v), indicating grams of solute in 100 mL of solution. Unless otherwise specified, a solution expressed in percentage can be assumed to be w/v.

6. Water of crystallization, water of hydration: Molecules of water that form an integral part of the crystalline structure of a substance. A given substance may have several crystalline forms, with different numbers of water molecules intrinsic to the entire molecule. The weight of this water must be included in calculating molecular weight of the hydrated substance.

7. Anhydrous: The salt form of a substance with no water of crystallization.

8. Atomic weights (rounded to whole numbers): H, 1; O, 16; Na, 23; P, 31; S, 32; Cl, 35; K, 39.

9. Molecular weights:
    HCl: $1 + 35 = 36$; NaCl: $23 + 35 = 58$
    KCl: $39 + 35 = 74$
    H_2O: $(2 \times 1) + 16 = 18$
    NaH_2PO_4: $23 + (2 \times 1) + 31 + (4 \times 16) = 120$
    $NaH_2PO_4 \bullet H_2O$: $23 + (2 \times 1) + 31 + (4 \times 16) + (2 \times 1) + 16 = 138$
    KH_2PO_4: $39 + (2 \times 1) + 31 + (4 \times 16) = 136$
    H_2SO_4: $(2 \times 1) + 32 + (4 \times 16) = 98$

Examples

1. Molar solutions:
    $1 M$ $KH_2PO_4 = 136$ g of solute made up to 1 L.
    $0.15 M$ $KH_2PO_4 = (136 \times 0.15) = 20.4$ g of solute made up to 1 L.
    $0.5 M$ $NaH_2PO_4 = (120 \times 0.5) = 60$ g of solute made up to 1 L.

2. Molar solution with hydrated salt:
    $0.5 M$ $NaH_2PO_4 \bullet H_2O = (138 \times 0.5) =$ 69 g of the monohydrate crystals made up to 1 L.

3. Normal solutions:
    1 N HCl = 36 g of solute made up to 1 L. One mole HCl dissociates into one mole H^+, so gram-equivalent weight and gram-molecular weight are the same.
    12 N HCl = $(36 \times 12) = 432$ g of solute made up to 1 L.
    1 N $H_2SO_4 = (98 \div 2) = 49$ g of solute made up to 1 L. One mole H_2SO_4 dissociates to give two moles of H^+, so the gram-equivalent weight is half the gram-molecular weight.

4. Percent solution:
    0.9% NaCl (w/v) = 0.9 g of solute made up to 100 mL of solution.

Notes

Accurate results require accurate preparation of reagents. It is important to carefully read and follow all instructions and labels.

1. Weigh only quantities appropriate for the accuracy of the equipment. The operator's manual should give these specifications.

2. Prepare the largest volume that is practical. There is greater accuracy in measuring larger volumes than smaller volumes. If a reagent balance is accurate to ±0.01 g, the potential error in weighing 0.05 g (50 mg) will be 20%, whereas the potential error in weighing 0.25 g (250 mg) will be only 4%. If the solution retains its activity when stored appropriately, it is usually preferable to prepare a large volume. If the solution deteriorates rapidly, smaller volumes may be preferred to reduce waste.

3. Note whether a substance is in the hydrated or anhydrous form. If the

instructions give solute weight for one form, and the available reagent is in another form, be sure to adjust the measurements appropriately. For example, if instructions for 0.5 M NaH_2PO_4 call for 60 g, and the reagent is $NaH_2PO_4 \bullet H_2O$, find the ratio between the weights of the two forms. The molecular weight of $NaH_2PO_4 \bullet H_2O$ is 138 and the molecular weight of NaH_2PO_4 is 120. Therefore, the ratio is $138 \div 120 = 1.15$. Multiply the designated weight by the ratio $(60 \text{ g} \times 1.15 = 69 \text{ g})$ to obtain the final weight needed.

4. Dissolve the solute completely before making the solution to the final volume. This is especially important for substances, such as phosphates, that dissolve slowly. For example, to make 500 mL of 0.15 M KH_2PO_4:

   a. Weigh 10.2 g of solute in a weighing boat or glass $[(0.15 \times 136) \div 2]$ because only 500 mL will be made.

   b. Place 350 mL of water in a 500-mL volumetric flask on a magnetic stirrer. Add the stirring bar and adjust it to a slow, steady stirring speed.

   c. Add 10.2 g of salt, then rinse the boat with several aliquots of water until no salt remains. Numerous small-volume rinses remove adherent material more effectively than a few larger volumes. Add the rinse water to the material in the flask and stir until the salt has completely dissolved.

   d. If pH measurement is unnecessary, add water to the 500-mL mark, adjusting the volume for the stirring bar, and mix thoroughly. For solutions needing pH adjustment, see the next step.

5. Adjust the pH of the solution before bringing it to its final volume so that the addition of water (or other solvent) does not markedly change the molarity. For example, to bring 500 mL of 0.1 M glycine to a pH of 3:

   a. Add 3.75 g of glycine (H_2NCH_2COOH: molecular weight, 75) to 400-475 mL of water in a beaker. Dissolve completely, using a magnetic stirrer.

   b. Add a few drops of concentrated (12 N) HCl and measure pH after acid is thoroughly mixed. Continue adding HCl until pH is 3.0.

   c. Transfer the solution to a 500-mL volumetric flask. Rinse beaker and stirring bar with aliquots of water, adding the rinse water to the flask. Use the rinses to contribute to the total 500-mL volume.

   d. Measure the pH of the solution at final volume.

References

1. Remson ST, Ackerman PG. Calculations for the medical laboratory. Boston, MA: Little, Brown & Co., 1977.
2. Henry JB, ed. Clinical diagnosis and management by laboratory methods. 18th ed. Philadelphia: WB Saunders, 1991.

Method 1.4. Serum Dilution

Principle

Serum is sometimes diluted in saline or other diluents to determine its relative antibody concentration. It is customary to express the dilution as 1 part of serum *contained* in the total number of parts of the dilution. For example, to test the serum at one-tenth its original concentration, a dilution of 1 part in 10 may be made by mixing 1 mL of serum with 9 mL of saline. The *final volume is 10*, and the dilution is expressed as a 1 in 10 dilution. The diluted material contains one-tenth (1/10 or 0.1) of the unmodified serum. It is often customary to report the titer of an antibody as the reciprocal of the highest dilution that retains a 1+ agglutination. Therefore, serum that reacts at a dilution of 1/32 is considered to have a titer of 32. Note: A 1 in 10 dilution is 1 part in 9 parts, whereas a 1 to 10 or 1:10 is 1 part in 10 parts.

Procedure

1. Diluting an existing dilution:
    a. A new higher dilution can be prepared from diluted material by adding more diluent. The formula for calculating either the new higher final dilution or the amount of diluent to add to obtain a higher final dilution is:

$$\frac{\text{reciprocal of present serum dilution}}{\text{volume of serum dilution used}}$$

$$= \frac{\text{reciprocal of new final dilution}}{\text{total final volume}}$$

    b. *Example*: Serum dilution is one in two and volume of serum dilution is 1.0 mL. If 4.0 mL of saline is added, what will be the new final dilution?

$$\frac{2}{1} = \frac{X}{5}$$

X = 10 or 1 in 10 dilution

2. Diluting a dilution to a specified volume:
    a. The formula for calculating the volume of diluent to add to a dilution to achieve a certain quantity of a new higher final dilution is:

$$\frac{\text{reciprocal of present dilution}}{\text{volume of present dilution needed}}$$

$$= \frac{\text{reciprocal of final dilution}}{\text{total final volume required}}$$

    b. *Example*: Present serum dilution is one in two, total final volume is 100 mL, and new final serum dilution is 1 in 10. How much serum (diluted one in two) will have to be added to make up a final volume of 100 mL of a 1 in 10 dilution?

$$\frac{2}{X} = \frac{10}{100}$$

X = 20 or 20 mL of serum (dilution of one in two) must be added to 80 mL of diluent to obtain 100 mL of a 1 in 10 dilution.

Method 1.5. Dilution of % Solutions

Procedure

1. Dilutions can be prepared from more concentrated solutions by use of the following formula:

$$(\text{Volume}_1 \times \text{Concentration}_1) = (\text{Volume}_2 \times \text{Concentration}_2)$$
$$V_1 \times C_1 = V_2 \times C_2$$

where V_1 and C_1 represent original volume and concentration, and V_2 and C_2 represent final desired volume and concentration.

2. *Example:* 30% albumin is available, but 2 mL of 6% albumin is needed. How should the albumin be diluted?

$$V_1 \times 30 = 2 \times 6$$
$$30V_1 = 12$$
$$V_1 = 12 \div 30 = 0.4$$

Therefore, mix 0.4 mL of 30% albumin with 1.6 mL saline to obtain 2.0 mL of 6% albumin, or for small-volume use, mix 4 drops 30% albumin with 16 drops saline to obtain 20 drops of 6% albumin.

Method 1.6. Preparation of a 3% Red Cell Suspension

Principle

A 3% red cell suspension is a common reagent in many serologic procedures. The suspension need not be exactly 3%; an approximation achieves the appropriate serum-to-cell ratio for most test procedures and an adequate number of red cells to read and grade the reactions. The following steps are intended to help an individual gain confidence in approximating a 3% red cell suspension visually, both as a suspension of cells and in the appropriate size of the cell pellet achieved after centrifugation.

Materials

1. Whole blood sample.
2. Test tubes.
3. Disposable pipettes (1 mL and 10 mL serologic).
4. Saline.
5. Centrifuge (3000 rpm or equivalent).
6. Commercially prepared 3% reagent red cell suspension.

Procedure

To prepare 10 mL of a 3% red cell suspension:

1. Transfer at least 1 mL of whole blood to a 10-mL tube.
2. Wash the red cells in saline or phosphate-buffered saline (PBS), centrifuging for 5 minutes to pellet the cells. Repeat two or three times. The final supernate should be clear and should be completely removed by aspiration.
3. Transfer 0.3 mL of the washed red cells to a tube with 9.7 mL of saline, PBS, or Alsever's solution.
4. Cap or cover the tube with parafilm. Thoroughly mix the red cells and saline by gently inverting the tube several times.
5. To compare the color and density of the suspension by eye, transfer a volume of the prepared suspension to a 10×75 mm tube. Also transfer a similar volume of a known 3% red cell suspension (eg, commercial reagent red cell suspension) to another 10×75 mm tube. Hold the two tubes in front of a light source to compare them.
6. To compare the size of the cell pellet expected from a 3% red cell suspension, transfer one drop of the prepared suspension to a 10×75 mm tube. Similarly, transfer one drop of a known 3% commercial reagent red cell suspension to another 10×75 mm tube. Centrifuge the tubes in a serologic centrifuge, using the spin time designated for "saline." The size of the two cell pellets should be similar.

Note

For best results use red cell suspensions on the day of preparation only, unless stability for a longer time has been validated.

Method 1.7. Preparation and Use of Phosphate Buffer

Principle

Mixtures of acids and bases can be prepared at specific pH values and used to buffer (render) other solutions to that pH. The following procedure includes a method for preparing phosphate-buffered saline (PBS), which can be used as a diluent in serologic tests.

Reagents

1. Prepare acidic stock solution (solution A) by dissolving 22.16 g of $NaH_2PO_4 \cdot H_2O$ in 1 L of distilled water. This 0.16 M solution of the monobasic phosphate salt (monohydrate) has a pH of 5.0.
2. Prepare alkaline stock solution (solution B) by dissolving 22.7 g of Na_2HPO_4 in 1 L of distilled water. This 0.16 M solution of the dibasic phosphate salt (anhydrous) has a pH of 9.0.

Procedure

1. Prepare working buffer solutions of the desired pH by mixing appropriate volumes of the two solutions. A few examples are:

pH	Solution A	Solution B
5.5	94 mL	6 mL
7.3	16 mL	84 mL
7.7	7 mL	93 mL

2. Check the pH of the working solution before using it. If necessary, add small volumes of acid solution A or alkaline solution B to achieve the desired pH.
3. To prepare PBS of a desired pH, add one volume of phosphate buffer at that pH to nine volumes of normal saline.

References

1. Hendry EB. Osmolarity of human serum and of chemical solutions of biologic importance. Clin Chem 1961;7:156-64.
2. Dacie JV, Lewis SM. Practical haematology. 4th ed. London, England: J and A Churchill, 1968: 540-1.

Method 1.8. Reading and Grading Tube Agglutination

Principle

The purpose of grading reactions is to allow comparison of reaction strengths. This is beneficial in detecting multiple antibody specificities or antibodies exhibiting dosage. The grading of agglutination reactions should be standardized among all members of the laboratory staff, in the interest of uniformity and reproducibility of test results. Most laboratories define their own version of a grading system, which is described in a written procedure available to all staff. Some systems use assigned numeric values (scores) for the observed reactions.

Materials

1. Centrifuged serologic tests for agglutination.
2. Agglutination viewer.

Procedure

1. Gently shake or tilt the tube and resuspend the red cell button in the tube. The tilt technique uses the meniscus to gently dislodge the red cell button from the wall of the tube.
2. Observe the way that cells are dispersed from the red cell button.
3. Record reactivity by comparing the agglutinates to the descriptions in Table 1.8-1. The reactivity should be assessed when the red cells have been

Table 1.8-1. Interpretation of Agglutination Reactions

Macroscopically Observed Findings	Designation	Score
One solid agglutinate	4+	12
Several large agglutinates	3+	10
Medium-size agglutinates, clear background	2+	8
Small agglutinates, turbid background	1+	5
Very small agglutinates, turbid background	1^w	4
Barely visible agglutination, turbid background	w+ or +/−	2
No agglutination	0	0
Mixtures of agglutinated and unagglutinated red cells (mixed field)	mf	
Complete hemolysis	H	
Partial hemolysis, some red cells remain	PH	

completely resuspended from the button.

Interpretation

Refer to Table 1.8-1.

Notes

1. An agglutination viewer may facilitate the reading of tube tests. However, the manufacturer's test recommendation must be followed for interpreting the test results.

2. Serum overlying the centrifuged cell button must be inspected for hemolysis, which is a positive sign of an antigen-antibody reaction, provided the pretest serum was *not* hemolyzed and no hemolytic agent was added to the test.

3. The character of the agglutination should be noted and recorded. This information provides valuable clues in the investigation such as the characteristic refractile agglutination of anti-Sd[a].

4. Mixed-field agglutination is expected when using pooled cells for donor antibody detection and adding check cells to negative antiglobulin tests.

Reference

Race RR, Sanger R. Blood groups in man. 6th ed. Oxford: Blackwell Scientific Publications, 1975.

Red Cell Typing

Method 2.1. Slide Test for Determination of ABO Type of Red Cells

Principle

See Chapter 13 for a discussion of the principles of testing for ABO groups.

Specimen

The reagent manufacturer's instructions must be consulted before slide tests are performed; some manufacturers recommend performing slide tests with whole blood, whereas others specify the use of red cell suspensions of lighter concentrations prepared in saline, serum, or plasma.

Reagents

1. Anti-A.
2. Anti-B.
3. Anti-A,B (optional).

All reagents must be used in accordance with the manufacturer's instructions.

Procedure

1. Place 1 drop of anti-A on a clean, labeled glass slide.
2. Place 1 drop of anti-B on a separate clean, labeled glass slide.
3. Place 1 drop of anti-A,B on a third slide, if parallel tests are to be performed with this reagent, or on a single clean, labeled slide if this is the only test performed.
4. Add to each drop of reagent on the slides 1 drop of well-mixed suspension (in saline, serum, or plasma) of the red cells to be tested. (Consult the reagent manufacturer's instructions to determine the correct cell concentration to be used.)
5. Mix the reagents and red cells thoroughly, using a clean applicator stick for each reagent. Spread the mixture

over an area approximately 20 mm × 40 mm.

6. Gently tilt the slide continuously for up to 2 minutes. Do not place the slide over a heated surface, such as an Rh viewbox, during this period.
7. Read, interpret, and record the results of the reactions on all slides.

Interpretation

1. Strong agglutination of red cells in the presence of any ABO typing reagent constitutes a positive result.
2. A smooth suspension of red cells at the end of 2 minutes is a negative result.
3. Samples that give weak or doubtful reactions should be retested using Method 2.2.

Notes

1. Slide testing imposes a greater risk of exposure to infectious samples. Personnel should follow safety measures detailed in the facility's procedures manual.
2. Slide testing is not suitable for detection of ABO antibodies in serum/plasma.

Method 2.2. Tube Tests for Determination of ABO Group of Red Cells and Serum

Principle

See Chapter 13 for a discussion of the principles of testing for ABO groups. The following procedure is an acceptable representative method, but the manufacturer's instructions for the specific reagents must be consulted.

Specimen

The reagent manufacturer's package insert must be consulted to determine specific specimen requirements. Generally, clotted or anticoagulated blood samples may be used for ABO testing. The red cells may be suspended in autologous serum, plasma, or saline, or may be washed and resuspended in saline.

Reagents

1. Anti-A.
2. Anti-B.
3. Anti-A,B. Note: Use of this reagent is optional.
4. A_1, A_2, and B red cells. They can be obtained commercially or the testing laboratory can prepare a 2% to 5% suspension on each day of use. (Note: The use of A_2 cells is optional.)

All reagents must be used in accordance with the manufacturer's instructions.

Procedures

Testing Red Cells

1. Place 1 drop of anti-A in a clean, labeled test tube.
2. Place 1 drop of anti-B in a clean, labeled tube.
3. Place 1 drop of anti-A,B in a clean, labeled tube, if tests are to be performed with this reagent.
4. Add to each tube 1 drop of a 2% to 5% suspension (in saline, serum, or plasma) of the red cells to be tested. Alternatively, the equivalent amount of red cells can be transferred to each tube with clean applicator sticks.
5. Mix the contents of the tubes gently and centrifuge them for the calibrated spin time.
6. Gently resuspend the cell buttons and examine them for agglutination.

7. Read, interpret, and record the test results. Compare the red cell test results with those obtained in the serum/plasma tests (see below).

Testing Serum/Plasma

1. Label two clean test tubes as A_1 and B. (Note: Label an additional tube if an optional test with A_2 red cells is to be performed.)
2. Add 2 or 3 drops of serum/plasma to each tube.
3. Add 1 drop of A_1 reagent cells to the tube labeled A_1.
4. Add 1 drop of B reagent cells to the tube labeled B.
5. Add A_2 cells to the appropriate tube, if this optional test is being performed.
6. Mix the contents of the tubes gently and centrifuge them for the calibrated spin time.
7. Examine the serum overlying the cell buttons for evidence of hemolysis. Gently resuspend the cell buttons and examine them for agglutination.
8. Read, interpret, and record test results. Compare serum test results with those obtained in testing red cells (see above).

Interpretation

1. Agglutination of tested red cells and either hemolysis or agglutination in tests with serum constitute positive test results.
2. A smooth cell suspension after resuspension of the cell button is a negative test result.
3. Interpretation of serum/plasma and cell tests for ABO is given in Table 13-1.
4. Any discrepancy between the results of the tests with serum/plasma and cells should be resolved before an

interpretation is recorded for the patient's or donor's ABO group (see Chapter 13).

Note

Positive reactions characteristically show 3+ to 4+ agglutination by reagent ABO antibodies; reactions between test serum and reagent red cells are often weaker. The serum tests may be incubated at room temperature for 5 to 15 minutes to enhance weak reactions. See Chapter 13 for a discussion of weakly reactive samples.

Method 2.3. Microplate Test for Determination of ABO Group of Red Cells and Serum

Principle

See Chapter 13 for a discussion of the principles of testing for ABO blood group. Microplate techniques can be used to test for antigens on red cells and for antibodies in serum.

A microplate can be considered as a matrix of 96 "short" test tubes; the principles that apply to hemagglutination in tube tests also apply to tests in microplates.

Microplates may be rigid or flexible, with either U-shaped or V-shaped bottoms. U-shaped bottom plates are more widely used because results can be read either after centrifuging the plate and observing the characteristics of resuspended red cells or by observing the streaming pattern of the cells when the plate is placed at an angle. Either reading technique permits estimation of the strength of agglutination.

Specimen

Refer to Method 2.2.

Equipment

1. Dispensers (optional): Semiautomated devices are available for dispensing equal volumes to a row of wells. Special plate carriers can be purchased to fit common table-top centrifuges.
2. Microplate readers (optional): Automated photometric devices are available that read microplate results by the light absorbance in U-shaped bottom wells to differentiate between positive and negative tests. The microprocessor component of the reader interprets the reactions and prints the blood testing results. The manufacturer's instructions for the collection and preparation of serum/plasma and cell specimens must be followed.
3. Centrifuges: Appropriate conditions must be established for each centrifuge. The following times and relative centrifugal forces, expressed as *g*, are suggested. Consult the manufacturer's directions for specific information.
    For a flexible U-shaped bottom microplate: $700 \times g$ for 5 seconds for red cell testing and serum/plasma testing.
    For a rigid U-shaped bottom microplate: $400 \times g$ for 30 seconds for red cell testing and serum/plasma testing.

Reagents

Many manufacturers supply ABO or Rh typing reagents that are licensed by the Food and Drug Administration (FDA) for use as undiluted reagents in microplate tests.

1. Anti-A.
2. Anti-B.
3. Anti-A,B. Note: Use of this reagent is optional.

4. Group A_1, A_2, and B red cells. They can be obtained commercially or the testing laboratory can prepare a 2% to 5% suspension on each day of use. (Note: The use of A_2 cells is optional.)

Procedure

Testing Red Cells

1. Place 1 drop of anti-A and anti-B in separate clean wells of a U-bottom microplate. If tests with anti-A,B are to be performed, add this reagent to a third well.
2. Add 1 drop of a 2% to 5% saline suspension of red cells to each well containing blood typing reagent.
3. Mix the contents of the wells by gently tapping the sides of the plate.
4. Centrifuge the plate at the appropriate conditions established for the centrifuge.
5. Resuspend the cell buttons by manually tapping the plate or with the aid of a mechanical shaker, or place the plate at an angle for the tilt and stream method.
6. Read, interpret, and record results. Compare red cell test results with those obtained in testing serum/plasma.

Testing Serum/Plasma

1. Add 1 drop of a 2% to 5% suspension of reagent A_1 and B red cells to separate clean wells of a U-bottom microplate. (Note: If an optional test on A_2 cells will be performed, add A_2 cells to a third well.)
2. Add 1 drop of serum or plasma under test to each well.
3. Mix the contents of the wells by gently tapping the sides of the plate.
4. Centrifuge the plate at the appropriate conditions established for the centrifuge.

5. Resuspend the cell buttons by manually tapping the plate or with aid of a mechanical shaker, or place the plate at an angle for the tilt and stream method.

6. Read, interpret, and record results. Compare test results on serum/plasma with those obtained in testing red cells.

Note

To enhance weak serum/plasma reactions, the plates may be incubated at room temperature for 5 to 10 minutes, then the centrifugation, reading, and recording steps may be repeated.

Interpretation

1. Agglutination in any well of red cell tests and hemolysis or agglutination in any well of a serum test constitute positive results.

2. A smooth suspension of red cells after resuspension of the cell button is a negative test.

3. The interpretation of ABO tests is given in Table 13-1.

4. Any discrepancy between results on cell and serum/plasma tests should be resolved before an interpretation is recorded for the patient's or donor's ABO group (see Chapter 13).

Method 2.4. Confirmation of Weak A or B Subgroup by Adsorption and Elution

Principle

See Chapter 13 for a discussion of the principles of testing for ABO groups.

Specimen

Refer to Method 2.2.

Reagents

1. Human anti-A and/or anti-B. Because some monoclonal ABO typing reagents are sensitive to changes in pH and osmolarity, they may not be suitable for use in adsorption/elution tests.

2. Eluting agent: See Methods Section 4.

Procedure

1. Wash 1 mL of the red cells to be tested at least three times with saline. Remove and discard the supernatant saline after the last wash.

2. Add 1 mL of reagent anti-A (if a weak variant of A is suspected) or 1 mL of anti-B (if a weak variant of B is suspected) to the washed cells.

3. Mix the red cells with the reagent antibody and incubate them at 4 C for 1 hour, mixing occasionally.

4. Centrifuge the mixture to pack the red cells. Remove all supernatant reagent.

5. Transfer the red cells to a clean test tube.

6. Wash the cells at least eight times with large volumes (10 mL or more) of cold (4 C) saline. Save an aliquot of the final wash supernatant fluid and test it in parallel with the eluate.

7. Use an elution method suitable for recovery of ABO antibodies, eg, heat or Lui freeze-thaw elution techniques can be used to remove antibody from the cells (see Methods Section 4).

8. Centrifuge to pack the cells and transfer the supernatant eluate to a clean test tube.

9. Test the eluate and the final wash solution (from step 6), in parallel, against two examples of group O cells and two examples of cells expressing the relevant antigen (A_1 cells for suspected anti-A, B cells for anti-B). Add 2 drops of eluate or wash to 1 drop of cells and examine them for agglutination after immediate centrifugation; if negative, incubate 15 to 30 minutes at room temperature. If these phases are both negative, a 15-minute incubation at 37 C and the indirect antiglobulin test may also be performed.

Interpretation

1. The presence of anti-A or anti-B in the eluate, hence the presence of A or B antigen on the test cells, is confirmed if: a) the eluate reacts with both antigen-positive cells, at any phase; b) the eluate is nonreactive at all phases with all group O cells; and c) the final wash solution is nonreactive with all four cells.

    If the eluate does not react with the A or B cells, it may indicate that the test cells do not express the antigen and cannot adsorb the relevant antibody; alternatively, it could reflect failure to prepare the eluate correctly.

    If the eluate reacts with one or both of the A or B cells and also with one or both or all of the O cells, it indicates recovery of some other or additional antibody in the adsorption/elution process.

2. If the final wash solution reacts with the A or B cells, tests on the eluate cannot be considered valid. This can occur if unbound reagent antibody was not adequately removed before beginning the elution, if the cells were not adequately washed, or if there was dissociation of bound antibody during the wash process.

3. A and B cells can be used in the adsorption/elution procedure as positive/negative controls and tested in parallel. Group O cells can also be used as a negative control.

Note

The eluate may be stained by hemoglobin and be difficult to read except at the indirect antiglobulin phase.

Reference

Beattie KM. Identifying the causes of weak or "missing" antigens in ABO grouping tests. In: The investigation of typing and compatibility problems caused by red blood cells. Washington, DC: AABB, 1975:15-37.

Method 2.5. Saliva Testing for A, B, H, Le^a, and Le^b

Principle

Approximately 78% of all individuals possess the *Se* gene that governs the secretion of water-soluble ABH antigens into all body fluids with the exception of cerebrospinal fluid. These secreted antigens can be demonstrated in saliva by inhibition tests with ABH and Lewis antisera (see Chapter 13).

Specimen

1. Collect 5 to 10 mL of saliva in a small beaker or wide-mouthed test tube. Most people can accumulate this amount in several minutes. To encourage salivation, the subject may be asked to chew wax, paraffin, or a clean rubber band, but not gum or

anything else that contains sugar or protein.

2. Centrifuge saliva at 900 to 1000 × g for 8 to 10 minutes.

3. Transfer supernatant to a clean test tube and place it in a boiling water-bath for 8 to 10 minutes to inactivate salivary enzymes.

4. Recentrifuge at 900 to 1000 × g for 8 to 10 minutes, remove clear or slightly opalescent supernatant fluid, and discard the opaque or semisolid material. Dilute the supernatant fluid with an equal volume of saline.

5. Refrigerate, if testing is to be done within several hours. If testing will not be done on the day of collection, freeze the sample and store it at –20 C. Frozen samples retain activity for several years.

Reagents

1. Human (polyclonal) anti-A and anti-B. Note: Some monoclonal reagents may not be appropriate for use; therefore, appropriate controls are essential.

2. Anti-H lectin from *Ulex europaeus* obtained commercially or prepared by saline extraction of *Ulex europaeus* seeds.

3. Polyclonal (rabbit/goat/human) anti-Le^a. There are no published data on the suitability of monoclonal Lewis antibodies.

4. A$_1$ and B red cells, as used in Method 2.2.

5. Group O, Le(a+b–) red cells, as used for antibody detection or identification (see Chapter 19).

6. Specimens, frozen or fresh saliva, from persons known to be secretors

or nonsecretors, to use as positive and negative controls.

Procedures

Selection of Blood Grouping Reagent Dilution

1. Prepare doubling dilutions of the appropriate blood typing reagent.

2. To 1 drop of each reagent dilution, add 1 drop of 2% to 5% saline suspension of red cells. Use A, B, or O cells to determine, respectively, A, B, or H secretor status. Use Le(a+b–) red cells to determine Lewis secretor status.

3. Centrifuge each tube and examine macroscopically for agglutination.

4. Select the highest reagent dilution that gives 2+ agglutination.

Inhibition Test for Secretor Status

1. Add 1 drop of appropriately diluted blood grouping reagent to each of four tubes. For ABH studies, the tubes should be labeled "Secretor," "Nonsecretor," "Saline," and "Unknown." For Lewis studies, they will be "Lewis-positive," "Lewis-negative," "Saline," and "Unknown."

2. Add 1 drop of the appropriate saliva to the "Secretor," "Nonsecretor," and "Unknown" tubes, and 1 drop of saline to the tube marked "Saline."

3. Mix the contents of the tubes. Incubate the tubes for 8 to 10 minutes at room temperature.

4. Add 1 drop of 2% to 5% saline suspension of washed indicator cells to each tube, group A, B, or O for ABH secretor status, as appropriate, or Le(a+) for Lewis testing.

5. Mix the contents of the tubes. Incubate the tubes for 30 to 60 minutes at room temperature.

6. Centrifuge each tube and inspect each cell button macroscopically for agglutination.

Interpretation

1. Agglutination of indicator cells by antibody in tubes containing saliva indicates that the saliva does not contain the corresponding antigen.

2. The failure of known antibody to agglutinate indicator cells after incubation with saliva indicates that the saliva contains the corresponding antigen.

3. The failure of antibody in the saline control tube to agglutinate indicator cells invalidates the results of saliva tests; this usually reflects use of reagents that are too dilute. Redetermine the appropriate reagent dilution, as described above, and repeat the testing.

4. For further interpretation, see Table 2.5-1.

Notes

1. Include, as controls, saliva from a known secretor and nonsecretor. For ABH status, use saliva from previously tested *Se* and *sese* persons. For Lewis testing, use saliva from a person whose red cells are Le(a+b–) or Le(a–b+) as the positive control; use saliva from a Le(a–b–) person as the negative control. Aliquots of saliva from persons of known secretor status may be frozen for later use.

2. This screening procedure can be adapted for the semiquantitation of blood group activity by testing serial saline dilutions of saliva. The higher the dilution needed to remove inhibitory activity, the more blood group substance is present in the saliva.

Table 2.5-1. Interpretation of Saliva Testing

| | Testing with Anti-H | | | |
Unknown Saliva	*Se* Saliva (H Substance Present)	Non-*Se* Saliva (H Substance Not Present)	Saline (Dilution Control)	Interpretation
2+	0	2+	2+	Nonsecretor of H
0	0	2+	2+	Secretor of H

| | Testing With Anti-Le^a | | | |
Unknown Saliva	Le-positive Saliva	Le-negative Saliva	Saline (Dilution Control)	Interpretation
2+	0	2+	2+	Lewis-negative
0	0	2+	2+	Lewis-positive[*]

*A Lewis-positive person shown to be a secretor of ABH can be assumed to have Le^b as well as Le^a in saliva. A Le(a+) person who is *sese* and does not secrete ABH substance will have only Le^a in saliva.

Saliva should be diluted before it is incubated with antibody. To detect or to measure salivary A or B substance in addition to H substance, the same procedure can be used with diluted anti-A and anti-B reagents. The appropriate dilution of anti-A or anti-B is obtained by titrating the reagent against A_1 or B red cells, respectively.

3. A Lewis-positive person shown to be a secretor of A, B, and H can be assumed to have Le^b as well as Le^a in the saliva. A Le(a+) person who does not secrete A, B, or H substances lacks the *Se* gene and will have only Le^a in the saliva.

4. Specimens with a high concentration of soluble antigen may give a false-negative result and require dilution before testing.

Method 2.6. Slide Test for Determination of Rh Type

Principle

See Chapter 14 for a discussion of the principles of Rh typing.

Specimen

Refer to Method 2.2.

Equipment

View box.

Reagents

1. Reagent anti-D: Suitable reagents include polyclonal high-protein or low-protein (eg, monoclonal) reagents. Follow the instructions from the manufacturer of the anti-D in use before performing slide tests; the method presented here is a representative procedure.

2. Rh control reagent: The manufacturer's instructions will indicate the type of reagent to use, if needed.

Procedure

1. Place 1 drop of anti-D onto a clean, labeled slide.

2. Place 1 drop of the appropriate control reagent, if needed, onto a second labeled slide.

3. To each slide, add 2 drops of a well-mixed 40% to 50% suspension (in autologous or group-compatible serum or plasma) of the red cells to be tested.

4. Thoroughly mix the cell suspension and reagent. Using a clean applicator stick for each test, spread (mix) the reaction mixture over an area approximately 20 mm × 40 mm.

5. Place both slides on the viewbox and tilt the slides gently and continuously to observe them for agglutination (see note 1). Most manufacturers stipulate that the test must be read within 2 minutes because drying of the reaction mixture may cause the formation of rouleaux, which may be mistaken for agglutination.

6. Interpret and record the results of the reactions on both slides.

Interpretation

1. Agglutination with anti-D and a smooth suspension on the control slide constitute a positive test result and indicate that the cells being tested are D+.

2. No agglutination with either anti-D or the Rh control suggests that the cells are D–. Testing by the antiglobulin procedure (see Method 2.9) will show weak expression of D on cells that are not agglutinated on slide testing.

3. If there is agglutination on the control slide, results of the anti-D test must not be interpreted as positive without further testing.

4. Drying around the edges of the reaction mixture must not be confused with agglutination.

Notes

1. Slide testing imposes a much greater risk of biohazardous exposure. Personnel should follow safety measures detailed in the facility's procedures manual.

2. For slide tests using low-protein anti-D, a negative result on slide testing with either anti-A or anti-B serves as the control reaction.

Method 2.7. Tube Test for Determination of Rh Type

Principle

See Chapter 14 for a discussion of the principles of Rh typing.

Specimen

Refer to Method 2.2.

Reagents

1. Reagent anti-D: Suitable reagents include polyclonal high-protein or low-protein (eg, monoclonal) reagents. Follow the instructions from the manufacturer of the anti-D in use before performing tube tests. The method presented here is a representative procedure.

2. Rh control reagent: The manufacturer's instructions will indicate the type of control to use, if needed.

Procedure

1. Place 1 drop of anti-D in a clean, labeled test tube.

2. Place 1 drop of the appropriate control reagent, if needed, in a second labeled tube.

3. Add to each tube 1 drop of a 2% to 5% suspension (in saline, serum or plasma) of the red cells to be tested; alternatively, the equivalent amount of red cells can be transferred to each tube with clean applicator sticks.

4. Mix gently and centrifuge for the time and at the speed specified by the manufacturer.

5. Gently resuspend the cell button and examine it for agglutination. If a stick was used to transfer the red cells, adding 1 drop of saline to each tube will make it easier to resuspend the cell button.

6. Grade reactions and record test and control results.

Interpretation

1. Agglutination in the anti-D tube, combined with a smooth suspension in the control tube, indicates that the red cells under investigation are D+.

2. A smooth suspension of red cells in both the anti-D and the control tubes is a negative test result. Specimens from patients may be designated as D− at this point. Donor blood must be further tested for the presence of weak D antigen. The serum-and-cell mixture used in steps 1 through 5, above, may be used to test for weak D, providing the manufacturer's directions state that the reagent is suitable for the test for weak D.

Notes

1. Most commercially prepared antisera provide a 2+ or greater agglutination with D+ cells. A facility may choose to do additional testing on results with an agglutination of less than 2+. Required testing must be defined in the facility's procedures manual.
2. A negative tube test with anti-A and/ or anti-B serves as a valid control when a low-protein anti-D reagent has been used.

Method 2.8. Microplate Test for Determination of Rh Type

Principle

See Chapter 14 for a discussion of the principles of Rh typing

Specimen

Refer to Method 2.2. Clotted or anticoagulated samples may be used for Rh testing. Follow the manufacturer's instructions for specimen preparation when using semiautomated microplate readers.

Reagents

Use only anti-D approved for use in microplate tests (see the discussion in Method 2.3).

Procedure

The following is a representative method; the manufacturer's instructions should be followed for specific reagents and equipment.

1. Place 1 drop of the Rh reagent in a clean well of the microplate. If the reagent requires the use of an Rh control, add 1 drop of the control to a second well.
2. Add 1 drop of a 2% to 5% saline suspension of red cells to each well.
3. Mix the contents of the wells by gently tapping the sides of the plate.
4. Centrifuge the plate at the appropriate conditions established for the centrifuge.
5. Resuspend the cell buttons by manually tapping the plate or with the aid of a mechanical shaker, or place the plate at an angle for the tilt and stream method.
6. Read, interpret, and record the results.
7. Incubate negative tests at 37 C for 15 minutes.
8. Centrifuge the plate at the appropriate conditions established for the centrifuge.
9. Resuspend the cell buttons by manually tapping the plate or with the aid of a mechanical shaker, or place the plate at an angle for the tilt and stream method.
10. Read, interpret, and record the results.

Interpretation

Agglutination with anti-D reagent after the immediate-spin or 37 C incubation phase indicates a positive test provided there is no agglutination with the control reagent. See Table 14-3 for determining Rh phenotypes from reactions obtained with Rh blood typing reagents.

Note

Refer to the manufacturer's instructions for the necessity for weak D testing.

Method 2.9. Test for Weak D

Principle

Some red cells express the D antigen so weakly that most anti-D reagents do not directly agglutinate the cells. Weak D expression can be recognized most reliably by an indirect antiglobulin procedure after incubation of the test red cells with anti-D.

Specimen

Refer to Method 2.2.

Reagents

1. Reagent anti-D: Suitable reagents include polyclonal high-protein or low-protein (eg, monoclonal blend) reagents, but the manufacturer's package insert should be consulted before any anti-D reagent is used for this purpose.
2. Antihuman globulin reagent, either anti-IgG or polyspecific.
3. IgG-coated red cells.

Procedure

If the original, direct test with anti-D was performed by tube testing, the same tube may be used for the weak D test, providing the manufacturer's directions so state. In this case, proceed directly to step 4, after recording the original anti-D tube test as negative.

1. Place 1 drop of anti-D in a clean, labeled test tube.
2. Place 1 drop of the appropriate control reagent in a second labeled test tube.
3. To each tube, add 1 drop of a 2% to 5% suspension in saline of the red cells to be tested. It is permissible to use a direct antiglobulin test (DAT) on the test cells as a control, but an indirect antiglobulin procedure with an Rh control reagent is preferable because this ensures that all reagent components that might cause a false-positive result are represented.
4. Mix and incubate both tubes according to the reagent manufacturer's directions. Typically, this is 15 to 30 minutes at 37 C.
5. If a reading is desired after the 37 C incubation phase, centrifuge the tubes according to the reagent manufacturer's directions.
6. Gently resuspend the cell buttons and examine the tubes for agglutination. If the test red cells are strongly agglutinated in the anti-D tube but not in the control tube, record the test sample as D+ and do not proceed with the antiglobulin phase of the test.
7. If the test cells are not agglutinated or the results are doubtful, wash the cells three or four times with large volumes of saline.
8. Add antiglobulin reagent, according to the manufacturer's directions.
9. Mix gently and centrifuge according to the calibrated spin times.
10. Gently resuspend each cell button, examine the tubes for agglutination, and grade and record the test result.
11. If the test result is negative, add IgG-coated red cells.

Interpretation

1. Either a diluent control or a direct antiglobulin test (DAT) must accompany the test for weak D. Agglutination in the anti-D tube and none in the control tube constitutes a positive test result. If the facility chooses to perform the test for weak D, and the result is clearly positive, the blood should be classified as D+. It is incorrect to report such red cells as being "D–, weak D" or "D–, D^u."
2. Absence of agglutination in the tube with anti-D is a negative result, indicating that the cells do not express D and should be classified as D–.

3.   If there is agglutination at any phase in the control tube, no valid interpretation of the weak D test can be made. If the specimen is from a potential transfusion recipient, Rh-negative blood should be given until the D type can be resolved. If the specimen is from a donor, the unit should not be used for transfusion.

Note

Some facilities may elect to do an additional reading after the 37 C incubation and before completing the antiglobulin phase of testing. Refer to the manufacturer's instructions. If this optional reading is performed, the facility's procedures manual should indicate its policy on the interpretation of this result and on the additional testing requirements.

Method 2.10. Preparation and Use of Lectins

Principle

Saline extracts of seeds react with specific carbohydrates on red cell membranes and make useful typing reagents that are highly specific at appropriate dilutions. Diluted extract of *Dolichos biflorus* agglutinates A_1 red cells but not A_2. *Ulex europaeus* extract reacts with the H determinant; it agglutinates in a manner proportional to the amount of H present ($O>A_2>B>A_1>A_1B$ red cells). Other lectins useful for special purposes include *Arachis hypogaea* (anti-T), *Glycine max* (anti-T, -Tn), *Vicia graminea* (anti-N), and the *Salvia* lectins (*S. horminum*, anti-Tn/Cad; *S. sclarea*, anti-Tn). To investigate red cell polyagglutination, prepare and test the cells with *Arachis*, *Glycine*, *Salvia*, and *Dolichos* lectins. The anticipated reactions with various types of polyagglutinable red cells are shown in Table 2.10-1. If commercially made lectins are used, follow the manufacturer's instructions.

Reagents

Seeds may be obtained from health-food stores, pharmacies, or commercial seed companies. The seeds should be raw.

Procedure

1.   Grind the seeds in a food processor or blender until the particles look like coarse sand. A mortar and pestle may be used, or seeds can be used whole.
2.   In a large test tube or small beaker, place ground seeds and three to four times their volume of saline. (Seeds vary in the quantity of saline they absorb.)
3.   Incubate at room temperature for 4 to 12 hours, stirring or inverting occasionally.
4.   Transfer supernatant fluid to a centrifuge tube and centrifuge it for 5 minutes, to obtain clear superna-

Table 2.10-1. Reactions Between Lectins and Polyagglutinable Red Cells

	T	Th	Tk	Tn	Cad
*Arachis hypogaea**	+	+	+	0	0
Dolichos biflorus†	0	0	0	+	+
Glycine max (soja)	+	0	0	+	+
Salvia sclarea	0	0	0	+	0
Salvia horminum	0	0	0	+	+

*T and Th cells give weaker reactions with *Arachis* after protease treatment; Tk reactivity is enhanced after protease treatment.
†A and AB cells may react due to anti-A reactivity of *Dolichos* lectin.

tant. Collect and filter the supernatant fluid and discard seed residue.

5. Test dilutions of the extract to find dilution for the desired activity. Determine the activity of the extract with the appropriate red cells, as below.

For *Dolichos biflorus*:

a. Add 1 drop of 2% to 5% saline suspension of known A_1, A_2, A_1B, A_2B, B, and O red cells to appropriately labeled tubes.

b. Add 1 drop of the extract to each tube.

c. Centrifuge for calibrated time.

d. Inspect for agglutination and record results.

e. The lectin should agglutinate A_1 and A_1B cells but not A_2, A_2B, B, or O cells. The native extract often agglutinates all the cells tested. To make the product useful for reagent purposes, add enough saline to the extract so that there is 3+ or 4+ agglutination of A_1 and A_1B cells, but not of A_2, A_2B, B, or O cells.

For *Ulex europaeus*:

a. Add 1 drop of 2% to 5% saline suspension of known A_1, A_2, A_1B, B, and O cells to appropriately labeled tubes.

b. Add 1 drop of extract to each tube.

c. Centrifuge for the calibrated time.

d. Inspect for agglutination and record results.

e. The strength of the agglutination should be in the order of $O>A_2>B>A_1>A_1B$.

f. Dilute extract with saline, if necessary, to a point that O cells show 3+ or 4+ agglutination, A_2 and B cells show 1+ to 2+ agglutination, and A_1 or A_1B cells are not agglutinated.

Notes

1. To facilitate grinding hard seeds, the seeds can be covered with saline and soaked for several hours before grinding. The container used for soaking should not be tightly closed because some beans release gas during the soaking process, which could cause the container to explode.

2. The saline extracts may be stored in the refrigerator for several days; they may be stored indefinitely if frozen.

3. Tests should include a positive and negative control.

Method 2.11. Use of Sulfhydryl Reagents to Disperse Autoagglutination

Principle

See Chapter 20 for a discussion of autoagglutination dispersion.

Specimen

Immunoglobulin-coated red cells to be evaluated.

Reagents

1. 0.01 M dithiothreitol (DTT): 0.154 g of DTT dissolved in 100 mL of phosphate-buffered saline (PBS) at pH 7.3, or 0.1 M 2-mercaptoethanol (2-ME), 0.7 mL of stock solution of 14 M 2-ME diluted in 100 mL of PBS at pH 7.3.

2. PBS at pH 7.3.

Procedure

1. Dilute red cells to a 50% concentration in PBS.

2. Add an equal quantity of 0.01 M DTT in PBS, or 0.1 M 2-ME in PBS, to the cells.

3. Incubate at 37 C for 10 minutes (2-ME) or 15 minutes (DTT).
4. Wash cells three times in saline and resuspend them.
5. Dilute the treated red cells to a 2% to 5% concentration in saline for use in blood grouping tests. Verify that red cells do not spontaneously agglutinate before typing or use.

Note

This procedure is normally used only for ABO forward cell typing, Rh testing, and the direct antiglobulin test. At this concentration of DTT, some antigens, in particular Js^a and Js^b, may be weakened or destroyed by 0.01M DTT.

Reference

Reid ME. Autoagglutination dispersal utilizing sulfhydryl compounds. Transfusion 1978;18:353-5.

Method 2.12. Gentle Heat Elution for Testing Red Cells with a Positive DAT

Principle

Red cells heavily coated with IgG may spontaneously agglutinate in high-protein reagents and will cause false-positive AHG test results. To perform red cell antigen typing, it may be necessary to dissociate antibody from the cells by elution without damaging membrane integrity or altering antigen expression. The gentle heat elution procedure employed to prepare immunoglobulin-free red cells differs from procedures intended to recover active antibody.

Reagent

Antihuman globulin.

Specimen

Test cells with a positive direct antiglobulin test (DAT) result.

Procedure

1. Place one volume of washed antibody-coated red cells and three volumes of normal saline in a test tube of appropriate size. In another tube, place the same volumes of saline and washed red cells positive for the antigen under test. This will provide a check that the elution technique does not destroy the antigen reactivity.
2. Incubate the contents of both tubes at approximately 45 C for 10 to 15 minutes. The tubes should be agitated frequently. The time of incubation should be roughly proportional to the degree of antibody coating, as indicated by strength of antiglobulin reactivity.
3. Centrifuge the tubes and discard the supernatant saline.
4. Test the person's cells for degree of antibody removal by comparing a DAT on the treated cells with the antiglobulin results on untreated red cells. If the antibody coating is reduced but still present, steps 1 through 3 can be repeated; the control cells should be subjected to a similar second treatment.
5. Test the treated cells for the desired antigen.

Notes

1. This procedure may be unnecessary if IgM monoclonal reagents are available; these reagents cause direct agglutination and are not usually affected by bound immunoglobulin.

2. As with untreated patient cells, results of antigen testing in recently transfused patients should be interpreted with caution because of the potential presence of donor cells.

Method 2.13. Dissociation of IgG by Chloroquine for Red Cell Antigen Testing of Red Cells with a Positive DAT

Principle

Red cells with a positive direct antiglobulin test (DAT) cannot be tested accurately with blood typing reagents that require an indirect antiglobulin technique. Under controlled conditions, chloroquine diphosphate dissociates IgG from the red cell membrane with little or no damage to its integrity. Use of this procedure permits complete phenotyping of red cells coated with warm-reactive autoantibody, including tests with reagents solely reactive by indirect antiglobulin techniques.

Specimen

Red cells with a positive DAT due to IgG coating.

Reagents

1. Chloroquine diphosphate solution prepared by dissolving 20 g of chloroquine diphosphate in 100 mL of saline. Adjust to pH 5.1 with 1 N NaOH, and store at 2 to 6 C.
2. Control red cells carrying a single-dose expression of antigens for which the test samples are to be phenotyped.
3. Anti-IgG antiglobulin reagent.

Procedure

1. To 0.2 mL of washed IgG-coated cells, add 0.8 mL of chloroquine diphosphate solution. Similarly treat the control sample.
2. Mix and incubate at room temperature for 30 minutes.
3. Remove a small aliquot (eg, 1 drop) of the treated test cells and wash them four times with saline.
4. Test the washed cells with anti-IgG.
5. If this treatment has rendered the cells nonreactive with anti-IgG, wash the total volumes of treated test cells and control cells three times in saline and make a 2% to 5% suspension in saline to use in subsequent blood typing tests.
6. If the treated red cells react with anti-IgG after 30 minutes of incubation with chloroquine diphosphate, steps 3 and 4 should be repeated at 30-minute intervals (for a maximum incubation period of 2 hours), until the sample tested is nonreactive with anti-IgG. Then proceed as described in step 5.

Notes

1. Chloroquine diphosphate does not dissociate complement proteins from the cell membrane. If red cells are coated with both IgG and C3, only anti-IgG should be used in tests performed after chloroquine treatment.
2. Incubation with chloroquine diphosphate should not be extended beyond 2 hours. Prolonged incubation at room temperature or incubation at 37 C may cause hemolysis and loss of red cell antigens.
3. Some denaturation of Rh antigens may occur.
4. Many serologists run chloroquine-treated control cells for each antigen tested. Select control cells that are positive for the antigen correspond-

ing to the antisera that will be used to type the patient's cells.

5. Chloroquine diphosphate may not completely remove antibody from sensitized red cells. DAT results on red cells from some persons, particularly those with a strongly positive initial test, may only be diminished in strength.

6. In addition to its use for removal of autoantibodies, this method can be used for removal of Bg (HLA)-related antigens from red cells. Appropriate Bg controls should be used.

7. If a commercial kit is used, manufacturer's instructions should be followed for testing and controls.

References

1. Edwards JM, Moulds JJ, Judd WJ. Chloroquine diphosphate dissociation of antigen-antibody complexes: A new technique for phenotyping rbcs with a positive direct antiglobulin test. Transfusion 1982;22:59-61.
2. Swanson JL, Sastamoinen R. Chloroquine stripping of the HLA-A,B antigens from red cells (letter). Transfusion 1985;25:439-40.

Method 2.14. Acid Glycine/EDTA Method to Remove Antibodies from Red Cells

Principle

Acid glycine/EDTA can be used to dissociate antibody molecules from red cell membranes. This procedure is routinely used for blood typing tests or adsorption procedures. All common red cell antigens can be detected after treatment with acid glycine/EDTA except antigens of the Kell system, Bg antigens, and Er antigens. Thus, cells treated in this manner cannot be used to determine these phenotypes.

Specimen

Red cells with a positive direct antiglobulin test (DAT).

Reagents

1. 10% EDTA prepared by dissolving 2 g of disodium ethylenediamine tetra-acetic acid (Na_2EDTA) in 20 mL of distilled or deionized water.
2. 0.1 M glycine-HCl buffer (pH 1.5) prepared by diluting 0.75 g of glycine to 100 mL with isotonic (unbuffered) saline. Adjust the pH to 1.5 using concentrated HCl.
3. 1.0 M TRIS-NaCl prepared by dissolving 12.1 g of tris (hydroxymethyl) aminomethane (TRIS) and 5.25 g of sodium chloride (NaCl) to 100 mL with distilled or deionized water.

Procedure

1. Wash the red cells to be treated six times with isotonic saline.
2. In a test tube, mix together 20 volumes of 0.1 M acid glycine-HCl (pH 1.5) with five volumes of 10% EDTA. This is the acid glycine/EDTA reagent.
3. Place 10 volumes of washed red cells in a clean tube.
4. Add 20 volumes of acid glycine/EDTA.
5. Mix the contents of the tube thoroughly.
6. Incubate the mixture at room temperature for no more than 2 to 3 minutes.
7. Add one volume of 1.0 M TRIS-NaCl and mix the contents of the tube.
8. Centrifuge at 900 to 1000 × g for 1 to 2 minutes, then aspirate, and discard the supernatant fluid.
9. Wash the red cells four times with saline.
10. Test the washed cells with anti-IgG; if nonreactive with anti-IgG, the cells

are ready for use in blood typing or adsorption procedures. If the DAT is still positive, one additional treatment can be performed.

Notes

1. Overincubation of red cells with acid glycine/EDTA causes irreversible damage to cell membranes.
2. Include a parallel control reagent, such as 6% bovine albumin or inert plasma, when typing treated red cells.
3. Use anti-IgG, not a polyspecific antiglobulin reagent, in step 10.
4. Many serologists run acid glycine/EDTA treated control cells for each antigen tested. Select control cells that are positive for the antigen corresponding to the antisera that will be used to type the patient's cells.
5. If a commercial kit is used, manufacturer's instructions should be followed for testing and controls.

References

1. Louie JE, Jiang AF, Zaroulis CG. Preparation of intact antibody-free red cells in autoimmune hemolytic anemia (abstract). Transfusion 1986;26:550.
2. Champagne K, Spruell P, Chen J, et al. EDTA/glycine-acid vs. chloroquine diphosphate treatment for stripping Bg antigens from red blood cells (abstract). Transfusion 1996;36(Suppl):21S.
3. Reid ME, Lomas-Francis C. The blood group antigen factsbook. New York: Academic Press, 2004.

Method 2.15. Separation of Transfused from Autologous Red Cells by Simple Centrifugation

Principle

Newly formed autologous red cells generally have a lower specific gravity than transfused red cells and may be separated from the transfused population by simple centrifugation. Newly formed autologous cells concentrate at the top of the column of red cells when blood is centrifuged in a microhematocrit tube, providing a simple method for recovering autologous cells in a blood sample from recently transfused patients. Note: Red cells from patients with hemoglobin S or spherocytic disorders are not effectively separated by this method (see Method 2.16 for an alternative procedure).

Specimen

Red cells from whole blood collected into EDTA.

Materials

1. Microhematocrit centrifuge.
2. Plain (not heparinized) glass or plastic hematocrit tubes.
3. Sealant.

Procedure

1. Wash the red cells three times in saline. For the last wash, centrifuge them at 900 to 1000 g for 5 to 15 minutes. Remove as much of the supernatant fluid as possible without disturbing the buffy coat. Mix thoroughly.
2. Fill 10 microhematocrit tubes to the 60-mm mark with well-mixed washed red cells.
3. Seal the ends of the tubes by heat or with sealant.
4. Centrifuge all tubes in a microhematocrit centrifuge for 15 minutes.
5. Cut the microhematocrit tubes 5 mm below the top of the column of red cells. This 5-mm segment con-

tains the least dense, hence youngest, circulating red cells.

6. Place the cut microhematocrit tubes into larger test tubes (10 or 12 × 75 mm), add saline, and mix well to flush the red cells from the microhematocrit tubes. Then, either a) centrifuge them at 1000 × g for 1 minute and remove the empty hematocrit tubes or b) transfer the saline-suspended red cells to a clean test tube.

7. Wash the separated red cells three times in saline before resuspending them to 2% to 5% in saline for testing.

Notes

1. Separation is better if 3 or more days have elapsed since transfusion than if the sample has been obtained shortly after transfusion.

2. The red cells should be mixed continuously while the microhematocrit tubes are being filled.

3. Separation techniques are only effective if the patient is producing normal or above-normal numbers of reticulocytes. This method will be ineffective in patients with inadequate reticulocyte production.

4. Some red cell antigens may not be as strongly expressed on reticulocytes as on older cells. Particular attention should be given to determinations of the E, e, c, Fy^a, Jk^a, and Ge antigens.

References

1. Reid ME, Toy P. Simplified method for recovery of autologous red blood cells from transfused patients. Am J Clin Pathol 1983;79:364-6.

2. Vengelen-Tyler V, Gonzales B. Reticulocyte rich RBCs will give weak reactions with many blood typing antisera (abstract). Transfusion 1985;25:476.

Method 2.16. Separation of Transfused Red Cells from Autologous Red Cells in Patients with Hemoglobin S Disease

Principle

Red cells from patients with sickle cell disease, either hemoglobin SS or SC, are resistant to lysis by hypotonic saline, in contrast to red cells from normal persons and those with hemoglobin S trait. This procedure permits isolation of autologous red cells from patients with hemoglobin SS or SC disease who have recently been transfused.

Specimen

Red cells to be evaluated.

Reagents

1. Hypotonic saline (0.3% w/v NaCl): NaCl, 3 g; distilled water to 1 L.

2. Normal saline (0.9% w/v NaCl): NaCl, 9 g; distilled water to 1 L.

Procedure

1. Place 4 or 5 drops of red cells into a 10 or 12 × 75-mm test tube.

2. Wash the cells six times with 0.3% NaCl, or until the supernatant fluid no longer contains grossly visible hemoglobin. For each wash, centrifuge at 1000 × g for 1 minute.

3. Wash the cells twice with 0.9% NaCl to restore tonicity. For each wash, centrifuge at 200 × g for 2 minutes to facilitate removal of residual stroma.

4. Resuspend the remaining intact red cells to a 2% to 5% concentration for phenotyping.

Note

Larger volumes, for use in adsorption studies, can be processed in a 16 × 100-mm test tube.

Reference

Brown D. A rapid method for harvesting autologous red cells from patients with hemoglobin S disease. Transfusion 1988;28:21-3.

Antibody Detection, Antibody Identification, and Serologic Compatibility Testing

Method 3.1. Immediate-Spin Compatibility Testing to Demonstrate ABO Incompatibility

Principle

See Chapter 18 for a discussion of the principles of compatibility testing.

Specimen

Patient's serum or plasma may be used. The age of the specimen must comply with the pretransfusion specimen requirements in AABB *Standards for Blood Banks and Transfusion Services.*[1(p38)]

Reagents

1. Normal saline.
2. Donor red cells, 2% to 5% suspension in normal saline or EDTA saline. Some serologists prefer to suspend the donor red cells in EDTA saline because high-titered anti-A or -B can initiate complement coating, which can cause steric hindrance of agglutination.[2] The use of a patient's sample collected in EDTA is an alternative approach to prevent this phenomenon.

Procedure

1. Label a tube for each donor red cell suspension being tested with the patient's serum.
2. Add 2 drops of the patient's serum or plasma to each tube.
3. Add 1 drop of the suspension of donor red cells to the appropriate test tube.
4. Mix the contents of the tube(s) and centrifuge according to the calibration of the centrifuge.

5. Examine the tube(s) for hemolysis, gently resuspend the red cell button(s), and examine for agglutination.

6. Read, interpret, and record test results.

Interpretation

1. Agglutination or hemolysis constitutes a positive (incompatible) test result.

2. A smooth suspension of red cells after resuspension of the red cell button constitutes a negative result and indicates a compatible immediate-spin crossmatch.

References

1. Silva MA, ed. Standards for blood banks and transfusion services. 23rd ed. Bethesda, MD: AABB, 2005.

2. Judd WJ, Steiner EA, O'Donnell DB, Oberman HA. Discrepancies in ABO typing due to prozone; how safe is the immediate-spin crossmatch? Transfusion 1988;28:334-8.

Method 3.2. Indirect Antiglobulin Test (IAT) for the Detection of Antibodies to Red Cell Antigens

Principle

For a discussion of the principles of saline, albumin, low-ionic-strength saline (LISS), and polyethylene glycol (PEG) indirect antiglobulin testing, see Chapters 12, 18, and 19.

Specimen

Serum or plasma may be used. The age of the specimen must comply with pretransfusion specimen requirements in AABB *Standards for Blood Banks and Transfusion Services.*

Reagents

1. Normal saline.

2. Bovine albumin (22% or 30%).

3. LISS made as follows:
   a. Add 1.75 g of NaCl and 18 g of glycine to a 1-liter volumetric flask.
   b. Add 20 mL of phosphate buffer prepared by combining 11.3 mL of 0.15 M KH_2PO_4 and 8.7 mL of 0.15 M Na_2HPO_4.
   c. Add distilled water to the 1-liter mark.
   d. Adjust the pH to 6.7 $\pm$ 0.1 with NaOH.
   e. Add 0.5 g of sodium azide as a preservative.

   Note: LISS may be used as an additive (Method 3.2.2) or for the suspension of test red cells (Method 3.2.3). LISS preparations are also available commercially.

4. PEG, 20% w/v: To 20 g of 3350 MW PEG, add phosphate-buffered saline (PBS) pH 7.3 (see Method 1.7) to 100 mL. PEG is also available commercially.

5. Antihuman globulin (AHG) reagent. Polyspecific or anti-IgG may be used unless otherwise indicated.

6. Commercially available group O antibody detection cells. Pooled group O antibody detection cells may be used only for donor testing. Testing of patients' samples must be performed with unpooled cells.

7. IgG-coated red cells.

Method 3.2.1. Saline Indirect Antiglobulin Test

Procedure

1. Add 2 drops of serum or plasma to properly labeled tubes.

2. Add 1 drop of 2% to 5% saline-suspended reagent group O cells or donor red cells to each tube and mix.

3. Centrifuge and observe for hemolysis and agglutination. Grade and record the results.

4. Incubate at 37 C for 30 to 60 minutes.
5. Centrifuge and observe for hemolysis and agglutination. Grade and record the results.
6. Wash the cells three or four times with saline and completely decant the final wash.
7. Add AHG to the dry cell button according to the manufacturer's directions. Mix well.
8. Centrifuge and observe for agglutination. Grade and record the results.
9. Confirm the validity of negative tests by adding IgG-coated red cells.

Method 3.2.2. Albumin or LISS-Additive Indirect Antiglobulin Test

Procedure

1. Add 2 drops of serum or plasma to properly labeled tubes.
2. Add an equivalent volume of 22% or 30% bovine albumin or LISS additive (unless the manufacturer's directions state otherwise.)
3. Add 1 drop of a 2% to 5% saline-suspended reagent or donor red cells to each tube and mix.
4. For albumin, incubate at 37 C for 15 to 30 minutes. For LISS, incubate for 10 to 15 minutes or follow the manufacturer's directions.
5. Centrifuge and observe for hemolysis and agglutination. Grade and record the results.
6. Perform the test described in Method 3.2.1, steps 6 through 9.

Method 3.2.3. LISS Indirect Antiglobulin Test

Procedure

1. Wash reagent or donor red cells three times in normal saline and completely decant saline.
2. Resuspend the cells to a 2% to 3% suspension in LISS.

3. Add 2 drops of serum to a properly labeled tube.
4. Add 2 drops of LISS-suspended red cells, mix, and incubate at 37 C 10 to 15 minutes or follow the manufacturer's directions.
5. Centrifuge and observe for hemolysis and agglutination by gently resuspending the cell button. Grade and record results.
6. Perform the test described in Method 3.2.1, steps 6 through 9.

Method 3.2.4. PEG Indirect Antiglobulin Test

Procedure

1. For each cell sample to be tested, mix 2 drops of test serum, 4 drops of 20% PEG in PBS, and 1 drop of a 2% to 5% suspension of red cells.
2. Incubate at 37 C for 15 minutes.
3. DO NOT CENTRIFUGE.
4. Wash the cells four times with saline and completely decant the final wash.
5. Perform the AHG test, using anti-IgG, described in Method 3.2.1, steps 7 through 9.
Note: The manufacturer's instructions should be followed for the proper use of commercial PEG solutions.

Interpretation (for Antiglobulin Tests, Methods 3.2.1 through 3.2.4)

1. The presence of agglutination/hemolysis after incubation at 37 C constitutes a positive test.
2. The presence of agglutination after addition of AHG constitutes a positive test.
3. Antiglobulin tests are negative when no agglutination is observed after initial centrifugation and the IgG-coated red cells added afterward are agglutinated. If the IgG-coated red cells are not agglutinated, the nega-

tive result is invalid and the test must be repeated.

Controls

The procedure used for the detection of unexpected antibodies in pretransfusion testing should be checked daily with weak examples of antibody. Control sera can be prepared from reagent grade typing sera diluted with 6% bovine albumin to give 2+ reactions by an IAT. Human sources of IgG antibodies are also acceptable.

Notes

1. The incubation times and the volume and concentration of red cells indicated are those given in the literature. Individual laboratories may choose to standardize techniques with somewhat different values. See Chapter 12 for other limitations when modifying procedures. In all cases, the manufacturer's package insert should be consulted before modifying a procedure.
2. For the saline procedure, step 3 may be omitted to avoid the detection of antibodies reactive at room temperature.
3. For the PEG procedure:
    a. Omit centrifugation after 37 C incubation because red cells will not resuspend readily.
    b. Use anti-IgG rather than poly-specific AHG to avoid unwanted positive reactions due to C3-binding autoantibodies.
4. Steps 6 through 9 of the IAT (Method 3.2.1) must be performed without interruption.

Reference

Silva MA, ed. Standards for blood banks and transfusion services. 23rd ed. Bethesda, MD: AABB, 2005: 38.

Method 3.3. Prewarming Technique

Principle

Prewarming may be useful in the detection and identification of red cell antibodies that bind to antigen only at 37 C. This test is particularly useful for testing sera of patients with cold-reactive autoantibody activity that may mask the presence of clinically significant antibodies. However, use of the prewarming technique for this application has become controversial.[1-2] It has been shown to result in decreased reactivity of some potentially significant antibodies and weak antibodies can be missed.[3] The technique should be used with caution and not used to eliminate unidentified reactivity.

Strong cold-reactive autoantibodies may react in prewarmed tests; other techniques such as cold allo- or autoadsorption or dithiothreitol treatment of plasma may be required to detect underlying clinically significant antibodies.

Specimen

Serum or plasma may be used. The age of the specimen must comply with pretransfusion specimen requirements in AABB *Standards for Blood Banks and Transfusion Services.*[4(p38)]

Reagents

1. Normal saline.
2. Anti-IgG.
3. Commercially available group O antibody detection cells. Pooled group O antibody detection cells may be used only for donor testing. Testing of patients' samples must be done with unpooled cells.
4. IgG-coated red cells.

Procedure

1. Prewarm a bottle of saline to 37 C.
2. Label one tube for each reagent or donor sample to be tested.
3. Add 1 drop of 2% to 5% saline-suspended red cells to each tube.
4. Place the tubes containing red cells and a tube containing a small volume of the patient's serum and a pipette at 37 C; incubate for 5 to 10 minutes.
5. Using the prewarmed pipette, transfer 2 drops of prewarmed serum to each tube containing prewarmed red cells. Mix without removing tubes from the incubator.
6. Incubate at 37 C for 30 to 60 minutes.
7. Without removing the tubes from the incubator, fill each tube with prewarmed (37 C) saline. Centrifuge and wash three or four times with 37 C saline.
8. Add anti-IgG, according to the manufacturer's directions.
9. Centrifuge and observe for reaction. Grade and record the results.
10. Confirm the validity of negative tests by adding IgG-coated red cells.

Notes

1. The prewarming procedure described above will not detect alloantibodies that agglutinate at 37 C or lower and are not reactive in the antiglobulin phase. If detection of these antibodies is desired, testing and centrifugation at 37 C are required. If time permits, a tube containing a prewarmed mixture of serum and cells can be incubated at 37 C for 60 to 120 minutes, and the settled red cells examined for agglutination by resuspending the button without centrifugation.
2. Cold-reactive antibodies may not be detectable when room-temperature saline instead of 37 C saline is used in the wash step.[2] The use of room-temperature saline may avoid the elution of clinically significant antibody(ies) from reagent red cells that can occur with the use of 37 C saline. Some strong cold-reactive autoantibodies, however, may still react and therefore require the use of 37 C saline to avoid their detection.

References

1. Judd WJ. Controversies in transfusion medicine. Prewarmed tests: Con. Transfusion 1995; 35:271-7.
2. Mallory D. Controversies in transfusion medicine. Prewarmed tests: Pro—why, when, and how—not if. Transfusion 1995;35:268-70.
3. Leger RM, Garratty G. Weakening or loss of antibody reactivity after prewarm technique. Transfusion 2003;43:1611-14.
4. Silva MA, ed. Standards for blood banks and transfusion services. 23rd ed. Bethesda, MD: AABB, 2005.

Method 3.4. Saline Replacement to Demonstrate Alloantibody in the Presence of Rouleaux

Principle

Rouleaux are aggregates of red cells that, characteristically, adhere to one another on their flat surface, giving a "stack of coins" appearance when viewed microscopically. Rouleaux formation is an in-vitro phenomenon resulting from abnormalities of serum protein concentrations. The patient is often found to have liver disease, multiple myeloma, or another condition associated with abnormal globulin levels. It may be difficult to detect antibody-associated agglutination in a test system containing rouleaux-promoting serum. In the saline replacement technique, serum and cells are incubated to allow antibody attachment, but the serum is removed and saline is added as the resuspending medium.

Reagents

Saline.

Procedure

After routine incubation and resuspension, proceed with the following steps if the appearance of the resuspended cells suggests rouleaux formation:

1. Recentrifuge the serum/cell mixture.
2. Remove the serum, leaving the cell button undisturbed.
3. Replace the serum with an equal volume of saline (2 drops).
4. Resuspend the cell button gently and observe for agglutination. Rouleaux will disperse when suspended in saline, whereas true agglutination will remain.

Reference

Issitt PD, Anstee DJ. Applied blood group serology. 4th ed. Durham, NC: Montgomery Scientific Publications, 1998:1135.

Method 3.5. Enzyme Techniques

For a discussion of the principles of enzyme testing, see Chapter 19.

Method 3.5.1. Preparation of Ficin Enzyme Stock, 1% w/v

Principle

The enzyme preparations used in blood banking differ from lot to lot; each time a stock enzyme solution is prepared, its reactivity should be tested and incubation periods standardized for optimal effectiveness. See Method 3.5.3.

Reagents

1. Dry enzyme powder, 1 g.
2. Phosphate-buffered saline (PBS), pH 7.3: see Method 1.7.
3. Phosphate buffer, pH 5.4.

Procedure

1. Place 1 g of powdered ficin in a 100-mL volumetric flask. Handle the ficin carefully; it is harmful if it gets in the eyes or is inhaled. It is desirable to wear gloves, mask, and apron, or to work under a hood.
2. Add PBS, pH 7.3 to 100 mL, to dissolve the ficin. Agitate vigorously by inversion, rotate for 15 minutes, or mix with a magnetic stirrer until mostly dissolved. The powder will not dissolve completely.
3. Collect clear fluid, either by filtration or centrifugation, and prepare small aliquots. Store the aliquots at –20 C or colder. Do not refreeze a thawed solution.

Method 3.5.2. Preparation of Papain Enzyme Stock, 1% w/v

Principle

The enzyme preparations used in blood banking differ from lot to lot; each time a stock enzyme solution is prepared, its reactivity should be tested and incubation periods standardized for optimal effectiveness. See Method 3.5.3.

Reagents

1. L-cysteine hydrochloride 0.5 M, 0.88 g in 10 mL distilled water.
2. Dry enzyme powder, 2 g.
3. Phosphate buffer 0.067 M at pH 5.4, prepared by combining 3.5 mL of Na_2HPO_4 and 96.5 mL of KH_2PO_4.

Procedure

1. Add 2 g of powdered papain to 100 mL of phosphate buffer (pH 5.4). Handle papain carefully; it is harmful to mucous membranes. Use appropriate protective equipment.
2. Agitate enzyme solution for 15 minutes at room temperature.
3. Collect clear fluid by filtration or centrifugation.
4. Add L-cysteine hydrochloride and incubate solution at 37 C for 1 hour.
5. Add phosphate buffer (pH 5.4) to final volume of 200 mL. Store aliquots at –20 C or colder. Do not refreeze aliquots.

Method 3.5.3. Standardization of Enzyme Procedures

Principle

For a two-stage enzyme procedure, the optimal treatment time must be determined for each new lot of stock solution. The technique given below for ficin can be modified for use with other enzymes.

Reagents

1. 1% stock solution of ficin in PBS, pH 7.3.
2. Several sera known to lack unexpected antibodies.
3. Anti-D that agglutinates only enzyme-treated D+ red cells and does not agglutinate untreated D+ cells.
4. Anti-Fy^a of moderate or strong reactivity.
5. D+ and Fy(a+b–) red cell samples.
6. Antihuman globulin (AHG) reagent. Polyspecific or anti-IgG may be used unless otherwise indicated.
7. IgG-coated red cells.

Procedure

1. Prepare 0.1% ficin by diluting one volume of stock ficin solution with nine volumes of PBS, pH 7.3.
2. Label three tubes: 5 minutes, 10 minutes, and 15 minutes.
3. Add equal volumes of washed red cells and 0.1% ficin to each tube.
4. Mix and incubate at 37 C for the time designated. Incubation times are easily controlled if the 15-minute tube is prepared first, followed by the 10- and 5-minute tubes at 5-minute intervals. Incubation will be complete for all three tubes at the same time.
5. Immediately wash the red cells three times with large volumes of saline.
6. Resuspend treated cells to 2% to 5% in saline.
7. Label four tubes for each serum to be tested: untreated, 5 minutes, 10 minutes, 15 minutes.
8. Add 2 drops of the appropriate serum to each of the four tubes.
9. Add 1 drop of the appropriate red cell suspension to each of the labeled tubes.
10. Mix and incubate at 37 C for 15 minutes.
11. Centrifuge and examine for agglutination by gently resuspending the red cell button.
12. Proceed with the AHG test described in Method 3.2.1, steps 6 through 9.

Interpretation

Table 3.5.3-1 shows possible results with D+, Fy(a+b–) cells and the sera indicated. In this case, the optimal incubation time would be 10 minutes. Incubation for only 5 minutes does not completely abolish Fy^a activity or maximally enhance anti-D reactivity. Incubation for 15 minutes causes

Table 3.5.3-1. Hypothetical Results with D+, Fy(a+b−) Red Cells

Cells and Enzyme		Inert Serum	Anti-D	Anti-Fy^a
Untreated	37 C incubation	0	0	0
	antihuman globulin test	0	1+	3+
5 minutes	37 C incubation	0	1+	0
	antihuman globulin test	0	2+	1+
10 minutes	37 C incubation	0	2+	0
	antihuman globulin test	0	2+	0
15 minutes	37 C incubation	0	2+	0
	antihuman globulin test	w+	2+	w+

false-positive antiglobulin reactivity with inert serum.

If incubation for 5 minutes overtreats the cells, it is preferable to use a more dilute working solution of enzyme than to reduce incubation time because it is difficult to accurately monitor very short incubation times. Additional tests can evaluate a single dilution at different incubation times, or a single incubation time can be used for different enzyme dilutions.

Method 3.5.4. Evaluating Enzyme-Treated Red Cells

Principle

After optimal incubation conditions have been determined for a lot of enzyme solution, treated red cells should be evaluated before use to demonstrate that they are adequately, but not excessively, modified. Satisfactory treatment produces cells that are agglutinated by an antibody that causes only indirect antiglobulin test reactivity of unmodified cells but are not agglutinated or aggregated by inert serum.

Specimen

Enzyme-treated red cells.

Reagents

1. Sera known to contain antibody that will agglutinate enzyme-treated cells.
2. Sera free of any unexpected antibodies.
3. Antihuman globulin (AHG) reagent. Polyspecific or anti-IgG may be used unless otherwise indicated.
4. IgG-coated red cells.

Procedure

1. Select an antibody that agglutinates enzyme-treated red cells positive for the antigen but gives only AHG reactions with unmodified cells. Many examples of human source anti-D behave in this way.
2. Add 2 drops of the selected antibody-containing serum to a tube labeled "positive."
3. Add 2 drops of a serum free of unexpected antibodies to a tube labeled "negative."
4. Add 1 drop of 2% to 5% suspension of enzyme-treated red cells to each tube.
5. Mix and incubate 15 minutes at 37 C.
6. Centrifuge and resuspend the cells by gentle shaking.

7. Examine macroscopically for the presence of agglutination.
8. Perform the AHG test described in Method 3.2.1, steps 6 through 9, on the tube labeled "negative."

Interpretation

There should be agglutination in the "positive" tube and no agglutination in the "negative" tube. If agglutination occurs in the "negative" tube, the cells have been overtreated; if agglutination does not occur in the "positive" tube, treatment has been inadequate.

Method 3.5.5. One-Stage Enzyme Technique

Specimen

Serum or plasma to be tested.

Reagent

1. Reagent red cells.
2. Antihuman globulin (AHG) reagent. Polyspecific or anti-IgG may be used unless otherwise indicated.
3. IgG-coated red cells.

Procedure

1. Add 2 drops of serum to an appropriately labeled tube.
2. Add 2 drops of a 2% to 5% saline suspension of reagent red cells.
3. Add 2 drops of 0.1% papain solution and mix well.
4. Incubate at 37 C for 15 minutes.
5. Centrifuge; gently resuspend the cells and observe for agglutination. Grade and record the results.
6. Proceed with the AHG test described in Method 3.2.1, steps 6 through 9.

Method 3.5.6. Two-Stage Enzyme Technique

Specimen

Serum or plasma to be tested.

Reagent

1. Reagent red cells.
2. Antihuman globulin (AHG) reagent. Polyspecific or anti-IgG may be used unless otherwise indicated.
3. IgG-coated red cells.

Procedure

1. Prepare a diluted enzyme solution (papain or ficin) by adding 9 mL of PBS, pH 7.3, to 1 mL of stock enzyme.
2. Add one volume of diluted enzyme to one volume of packed, washed reagent red cells.
3. Incubate at 37 C for the time determined to be optimal for that enzyme solution.
4. Wash treated cells at least three times with large volumes of saline and resuspend the cells to a 2% to 5% concentration in saline.
5. Add 2 drops of serum or plasma to be tested to an appropriately labeled tube.
6. Add 1 drop of 2% to 5% suspension of enzyme-treated cells.
7. Mix and incubate for 15 minutes at 37 C.
8. Centrifuge; gently resuspend the cells and observe for agglutination. Grade and record the results.
9. Proceed with the AHG test described in Method 3.2.1, steps 6 through 9.

Notes

1. An alternative method for steps 4 and 5 (Method 3.5.5) or steps 7 and 8 (Method 3.5.6) is to incubate the serum and enzyme-treated cells at 37

C for 60 minutes and examine the settled cells for agglutination without centrifugation. This can be useful for serum with strong cold-reactive agglutinins and can sometimes prevent the occurrence of false-positive results.

2. Microscopic examination is not recommended for routine use and is particularly inappropriate with enzyme enhanced tests; false-positive reactions will often be detected.

3. Either papain or ficin may be used in a two-stage procedure.

4. Enzyme preparations are available commercially. The manufacturer's directions should be followed for appropriate use and quality control.

References

1. Issitt PD, Anstee DJ. Applied blood group serology, 4th ed. Durham, NC: Montgomery Scientific, 1998.
2. Judd WJ. Methods in immunohematology. 2nd ed. Durham, NC: Montgomery Scientific, 1994.

Method 3.6. Direct Antiglobulin Test (DAT)

Principle

See Chapter 20 for a discussion of the principles of direct antiglobulin testing.

Specimen

Red cells from an anticoagulated blood sample.

Reagents

1. Antihuman globulin (AHG) reagent: polyspecific antiglobulin reagent, anti-IgG, anti-complement antisera.

2. A control reagent (eg, PBS) is required when all antisera tested give a positive result.

3. IgG-coated red cells.

Procedure

1. Dispense 1 drop of a 2% to 5% suspension of red cells into each tube.

2. Wash each tube three or four times with saline. Completely decant the final wash.

3. Immediately add antisera and mix. For the amount of antisera required, refer to the manufacturer's directions.

4. Centrifuge according to the manufacturer's directions.

5. Examine the cells for agglutination. Grade and record the reaction.

6. If using polyspecific AHG or anti-C3d, incubate nonreactive tests at room temperature for 5 minutes, then centrifuge, and read again.

7. Confirm the validity of negative tests by adding IgG-coated red cells to tests containing anti-IgG.

8. Centrifuge according to the manufacturer's directions.

9. Examine the cells for agglutination and record the reaction.

Interpretation

1. The DAT is positive when agglutination is observed either after immediate centrifugation or after the centrifugation that followed room-temperature incubation. IgG-coated red cells usually give immediate reactions, whereas complement coating may be more easily demonstrable after incubation.[1,2] Monospecific AHG reagents are needed to confirm which globulins are present.

2. The DAT is negative when no agglutination is observed at either test phase and the IgG-coated cells added in step 7 are agglutinated. If the IgG-coated cells are not agglutinated, the negative DAT result is considered invalid and the test must be repeated. A negative DAT does not necessarily

mean that the red cells have no attached globulin molecules. Polyspecific and anti-IgG reagents detect as few as 200 to 500 molecules of IgG per cell,[1] but patients may experience autoimmune hemolytic anemia when IgG coating is below this level.[2]

3. No interpretation can be made if the results with all antisera used to perform a DAT and the control are reactive. This indicates spontaneous agglutination, which must be resolved before further testing is performed.

Notes

1. Steps 2 through 7 must be performed without interruption.

2. Initial testing may be performed with polyspecific reagent only. If the DAT is negative with polyspecific reagent, no further testing is necessary. If the DAT is positive with polyspecific reagent, perform the DAT test with monospecific reagents, anti-IgG, and anticomplement, to determine which globulins are present.

3. Verification of negative results with anti-C3d is recommended. Refer to the manufacturer's instructions to determine appropriate controls.

References

1. Mollison PL, Engelfriet CP, Contreras M, eds. Blood transfusion in clinical medicine. 10th ed. Oxford, England: Blackwell Scientific Publications, 1997.
2. Petz LD, Garratty G. Immune hemolytic anemia. Philadelphia: Churchill-Livingstone, 2004.

Method 3.7. Antibody Titration

Principle

Titration is a semiquantitative method used to determine the concentration of antibody in a serum sample or to compare the strength of antigen expression on different red cell samples. The usual applications of titration studies are: 1) estimating antibody activity in alloimmunized pregnant women to determine whether and when to perform more complex invasive investigation of the fetal condition (see Chapter 23); 2) elucidating autoantibody specificity (see Chapter 20); 3) characterizing antibodies as high-titer, low-avidity, traits common in antibodies to antigens of the Knops and Chido/ Rodgers systems, Cs[a], and JMH (see Chapter 15); and 4) observing the effect of sulfhydryl reagents on antibody behavior, to determine immunoglobulin class (IgG or IgM). See Method 5.3 for titration studies specifically to assist in monitoring clinically significant antibodies in the pregnant woman.

Specimen

Serum or plasma antibody to be titrated.

Reagents

1. Red cells that express the antigen(s) corresponding to the antibody specificity (ies), in a 2% to 5% saline suspension. Uniformity of cell suspensions is very important to ensure comparability of results.

2. Saline. (Note: Dilutions may be made with albumin if desired.)

Procedure

The master dilution technique for titration studies is as follows:

1. Label 10 test tubes according to the serum dilution (eg, 1 in 1, 1 in 2, etc). A 1 in 1 dilution means one volume of serum undiluted; a 1 in 2 dilution means one volume of serum in a fi-

nal volume of two, or a 50% solution of serum in the diluent. See Methods 1.4 and 1.5.

2. Deliver one volume of saline to all test tubes except the first (undiluted 1 in 1) tube.

3. Add an equal volume of serum to each of the first two tubes (undiluted and 1 in 2).

4. Using a clean pipette, mix the contents of the 1 in 2 dilution several times and transfer one volume into the next tube (the 1 in 4 dilution).

5. Continue the same process for all dilutions, using a clean pipette to mix and transfer each dilution. Remove one volume of diluted serum from the final tube and save it for use if further dilutions are required.

6. Label 10 tubes for the appropriate dilutions.

7. Using separate pipettes for each dilution, transfer 2 drops of each diluted serum into the appropriately labeled tubes and add 2 drops of a 2% red cell suspension. Alternatively, for convenience, add 1 drop of a 3%-4% suspension of red cells as supplied by the reagent manufacturer, although this method is less precise.

8. Mix well and test by a serologic technique appropriate to the antibody (see Chapter 19).

9. Examine test results macroscopically; grade and record the reactions. The prozone phenomenon (see Chapter 12) may cause reactions to be weaker in the more concentrated serum preparations than in higher dilutions. To avoid misinterpretation of results, it may be preferable to examine first the tube containing the most dilute serum and proceed through the more concentrated samples to the undiluted specimen.

Interpretation

1. Observe the highest dilution that produces 1+ macroscopic agglutination. The titer is reported as the reciprocal of the dilution level, eg, 32—*not* 1 in 32 or 1:32 (see Table 3.7-1). If there is agglutination in the tube containing the most dilute serum, the endpoint has not been reached, and additional dilutions should be prepared and tested.

2. In comparative studies, a significant difference in titer is three or more dilutions. Variations in technique and inherent biologic variability can cause duplicate tests to give results that differ by one dilution in either direction. Serum containing antibody at a true titer of 32 may show, on replicate tests, the endpoint in the 1:32 tube, the 1:64 tube, or the 1:16 tube.

3. Titer values alone can be misleading without also evaluating the strength of agglutination. The observed strength of agglutination can be assigned a number and the sum of these numbers for all tubes in a titration study represents the score, another semiquantitative measurement of antibody reactivity. The arbitrarily assigned threshold for significance in comparing scores is a difference of 10 or more between different test samples. See Table 3.7-1.

4. Antibodies with high-titer, low-avidity characteristics generally have a titer greater than 64, with most tubes showing consistently weak reactivity.

Table 3.7-1 shows the results obtained with three sera, each of which shows no more agglutination after 1:256. The differences in score, however, indicate considerable variation in strength of reactivity.

Table 3.7-1. Examples of Antibody Titers, Endpoints, and Scores

| | | \multicolumn{10}{c}{Reciprocal of Serum Dilution} | | |
		1	2	4	8	16	32	64	128	256	512	Titer*	Score
Sample 1	Strength:	3+	3+	3+	2+	2+	2+	1+	±	±	0	64(256)	
	Score:	10	10	10	8	8	8	5	3	2	0		64
Sample 2	Strength:	4+	4+	4+	3+	3+	2+	2+	1+	±	0	128(256)	
	Score:	12	12	12	10	10	8	8	5	3	0		80
Sample 3	Strength:	1+	1+	1+	1+	±	±	±	±	±	0	8(256)	
	Score:	5	5	5	5	3	3	3	2	2	0		33

*The titer is often determined from the highest dilution of serum that gives a reaction ≥1+ (score 5). This may differ significantly from the titration endpoint (shown in parentheses), as with the reactions of an antibody with high-titer, low-avidity characteristics, manifested by Sample 3.

Notes

Titration is a semiquantitative technique. Technical variables greatly affect the results and care should be taken to achieve the most uniform possible practices.

1. Careful pipetting is essential. Pipettes with disposable tips that can be changed after each dilution are recommended.
2. Optimal time and temperature of incubation and time and force of centrifugation must be used consistently.
3. The age, phenotype, and concentration of the test red cells will influence the results. When the titers of several antibody-containing sera are to be compared, all of them should be tested against red cells (preferably freshly collected) from the same donor. If this is not possible, the tests should use a pool of reagent red cells from donors of the same phenotype. When a single serum is to be tested against different red cell samples, all samples should be collected and preserved in the same manner and diluted to the same concentration before use.
4. Completely reproducible results are virtually impossible to achieve. Comparisons are valid only when specimens are tested concurrently. In tests with a single serum against different red cell samples, material from the master dilution must be used for all the tests.
5. Measurements are more accurate with large volumes than with small volumes; a master dilution technique (see above) gives more reliable results than individual dilutions for a single set of tests. The volume needed for all planned tests should be calcu-

lated and an adequate quantity of each dilution prepared.

6. When performing a titration for anti-D for HDFN, see Method 5.3.

Method 3.8. Use of Sulfhydryl Reagents to Distinguish IgM from IgG Antibodies

Principle

Treating IgM antibodies with sulfhydryl reagents abolishes both agglutinating and complement-binding activities. Observations of antibody activity before and after sulfhydryl treatment are useful in determining immunoglobulin class. Sulfhydryl treatment can also be used to abolish IgM antibody activity to permit detection of coexisting IgG antibodies. For a discussion of IgM and IgG structures, see Chapter 11.

Specimen

2 mL of serum or plasma to be treated.

Reagents

1. Phosphate-buffered saline (PBS) at pH 7.3.

2. 0.01 M dithiothreitol (DTT), prepared by dissolving 0.154 g of DTT in 100 mL of pH 7.3 PBS. Store at –18 C or lower.

Procedure

1. Dispense 1 mL of serum or plasma into each of two test tubes.

2. To one tube, labeled dilution control, add 1 mL of pH 7.3 PBS.

3. To the other tube, labeled test, add 1 mL of 0.01 M DTT.

4. Mix and incubate at 37 C for 30 to 60 minutes.

5. Use the DTT-treated and dilution control samples in standard procedures.

Interpretation

1. Reactivity in the dilution control serum and no reactivity in the DTT-treated serum indicates an IgM antibody.

2. Reactivity in the dilution control serum and the DTT-treated serum indicates an IgG antibody or an IgG and IgM mixture. Titration studies may be necessary to distinguish between them. See Table 3.8-1.

Table 3.8-1. Effect of Dithiothreitol on Blood Group Antibodies

Test Sample	Dilution					Interpretation
	1/2	1/4	1/8	1/16	1/32	
Serum + DTT	3+	2+	2+	1+	0	IgG
Serum + PBS	3+	2+	2+	1+	0	
Serum + DTT	0	0	0	0	0	IgM
Serum + PBS	3+	2+	2+	1+	0	
Serum + DTT	2+	1+	0	0	0	IgG + IgM*
Serum + PBS	3+	2+	2+	1+	0	

*May also indicate only partial inactivation of IgM.

3. No reactivity in the dilution control serum indicates dilution of weak antibody reactivity and an invalid test.

Control

A serum or plasma sample known to contain an IgM antibody should be treated and tested in parallel.

Notes

1. 2-mercaptoethanol can also be used for this purpose. See Method 2.11 for preparation.
2. Sulfhydryl reagents used at low concentration may weaken antigens of the Kell system. For investigation of antibodies in the Kell system, it may be necessary to use other methods.
3. Gelling of a serum or plasma sample may be observed during treatment with DTT. This can occur if the DTT has been prepared incorrectly and has a concentration above 0.01 M. Gelling may also occur if serum and DTT are incubated too long. An aliquot of the sample undergoing treatment can be tested after 30 minutes of incubation; if the activity thought to be due to IgM has disappeared, there is no need to incubate further. Gelled samples cannot be tested for antibody activity because overtreatment with DTT causes the denaturation of all serum proteins.

Reference

Mollison PL, Engelfriet CP, Contreras M, eds. Blood transfusion in clinical medicine. 10th ed. Oxford, England: Blackwell Scientific Publications, 1997.

Method 3.9. Plasma Inhibition to Distinguish Anti-Ch and -Rg from Other Antibodies with HTLA Characteristics

Principle

For a discussion of the principles of plasma inhibition of anti-Ch and -Rg, see Chapter 19.

Specimen

Serum or plasma to be tested.

Reagents

1. Reactive red cell samples.
2. A pool of six or more normal plasma samples.
3. 6% bovine albumin, see Method 1.5.
4. Anti-IgG.
5. IgG-coated red cells.

Procedure

1. Prepare serial twofold dilutions of test serum in saline. The dilution range should be from 1 in 2 to 1 in 512, or to one tube beyond the known titer as determined above (Method 3.7). The volume prepared should be not less than 0.3 mL for each red cell sample to be tested.
2. For each red cell sample to be tested, place 2 drops of each serum dilution into each of two sets of appropriately labeled 10 or 12 × 75-mm test tubes.
3. To one set, add 2 drops of pooled plasma to each tube.
4. To the other set, add 2 drops of 6% albumin to each tube.
5. Gently agitate the contents of each tube and incubate the tubes at room temperature for at least 30 minutes.
6. Add 1 drop of a 2% to 5% suspension of red cells to each tube.

7. Gently agitate the contents of each tube and incubate the tubes at 37 C for 1 hour.

8. Wash the cells four times in saline, add anti-IgG, and centrifuge according to the manufacturer's directions.

9. Resuspend the cell buttons and examine for agglutination; confirm all nonreactive tests microscopically. Grade and record the results.

10. Confirm the validity of negative tests by adding IgG-coated red cells.

Interpretation

1. Inhibition of antibody activity in the tubes to which plasma has been added suggests anti-Ch or anti-Rg specificity; this inhibition is often complete.

2. The presence of partial inhibition suggests the possibility of additional alloantibodies. This can be tested by preparing a large volume of inhibited serum and testing it against a reagent red cell panel to see if the non-neutralizable activity displays antigenic specificity.

3. Lack of reactivity in the control (6% albumin) indicates dilution of weakly reactive antibody and an invalid test.

Notes

1. Antibodies to other plasma antigens may also be partially inhibited by plasma.[1]

2. Adsorption with C4-coated red cells is an alternative procedure that may be used for identifying anti-Ch or anti-Rg and for detecting underlying alloantibodies.[2]

References

1. Reid ME, Lomas-Francis C. The blood group antigen factsbook. 2nd ed. New York: Academic Press, 2004.

2. Ellisor SS, Shoemaker MM, Reid ME. Adsorption of anti-Chido from serum using autologous red blood cells coated with homologous C4. Transfusion 1982;22:243-5.

Method 3.10. Dithiothreitol (DTT) Treatment of Red Cells

Principle

DTT is an efficient reducing agent that can disrupt the tertiary structure of proteins by irreversibly reducing disulfide bonds to free sulfhydryl groups. Without tertiary structure, protein-containing antigens can no longer bind antibodies that are specific for them. Red cells treated with DTT will not react with antibodies in the Kell blood group system, most antibodies in the Knops system, or most examples of anti-LW^a, -Yt^a, -Yt^b, -Do^a, -Do^b, -Gy^a, -Hy, and -Jo^a. This inhibition technique may be helpful in identifying some of these antibodies or in determining if a serum contains additional underlying alloantibodies.

Specimen

Red cells to be tested.

Reagents

1. Prepare 0.2 M DTT by dissolving 1 g of DTT powder in 32 mL of phosphate-buffered saline (PBS), pH 8.0. Divide it into 1-mL volumes and freeze aliquots at −18 C or colder.

2. PBS at pH 7.3, see Method 1.7.

3. Red cells known to be positive for the antigen in question and, as a control, red cells known to be positive for K, which is consistently disrupted by DTT.

4. Anti-K, either in reagent form or strongly reactive in a serum specimen.

Procedure

1. Wash one volume of the test cells and the control cells with PBS. After decanting, add four volumes of 0.2 M DTT, pH 8.0.
2. Incubate at 37 C for 30 to 45 minutes.
3. Wash four times with PBS. Slight hemolysis may occur; if hemolysis is excessive, repeat the procedure using fresh red cells and a smaller volume of DTT, eg, two or three volumes.
4. Resuspend the cells to a 2% to 5% suspension in PBS.
5. Test DTT-treated cells with serum containing the antibody in question. Test K+ red cells with anti-K.

Interpretation

1. The control K+ red cells should give negative reactions when tested with anti-K; if not, the DTT treatment has been inadequate. Other antigens in the Kell system can also serve as the control.
2. If reactivity of the test serum is eliminated, the suspected antibody specificity may be confirmed. Enough red cell samples should be tested to exclude most other clinically significant alloantibodies.

Note

Treatment of red cells with 0.2 M DTT, pH 8.0, is optimal for denaturation of all antigens of the Kell, Cartwright, LW, and Dombrock systems, and most antigens of the Knops system. Lower concentrations of DTT may selectively denature particular blood group antigens (ie, 0.002 M DTT will denature only Js^a and Js^b antigens). This property may aid in certain antibody investigations.

Reference

Branch DR, Muensch HA, Sy Siok Hian S, Petz LD. Disulfide bonds are a requirement for Kell and Cartwright (Yt^a) blood group antigen integrity. Br J Haematol 1983;54:573-8.

Method 3.11. Urine Neutralization of Anti-Sd^a

Principle

For a discussion of anti-Sd^a neutralization by urine, see Chapter 15.

Specimen

Serum or plasma suspected of containing anti-Sd^a.

Reagents

1. Urine from a known Sd(a+) individual, or from a pool of at least six individuals of unknown Sd^a type, prepared as follows: Collect urine and immediately boil it for 10 minutes. Dialyze it against phosphate-buffered saline (PBS), pH 7.3, at 4 C for 48 hours. Change PBS several times. Centrifuge. Dispense supernatant into aliquots, which can be stored at −20 C until thawed for use.
2. PBS, pH 7.3. See Method 1.7.

Procedure

1. Mix equal volumes of thawed urine and test serum.
2. Prepare a dilution control tube containing equal volumes of serum and PBS.
3. Prepare a urine control tube by mixing equal volumes of thawed urine and PBS.
4. Incubate all tubes at room temperature for 30 minutes.
5. Mix 1 drop of each test red cell sample with 4 drops from each of the

tubes: neutralized serum, serum with PBS, and urine with PBS. Test each one using standard procedures.

Interpretation

1. Persistent agglutination in the serum sample incubated with urine means either that partial or no neutralization was achieved or that underlying antibodies are present. Microscopic examination may be helpful; agglutination due to anti-Sd^a has a refractile, mixed-field appearance on microscopic examination.

2. No agglutination in the neutralized tube with persistent agglutination in the dilution control tube and absence of hemolysis and agglutination in the urine control tube indicate that the antibody has been neutralized and is quite probably anti-Sd^a.

3. The absence of agglutination in the dilution control tube means that the dilution in the neutralization step was too great for the antibody present and the results of the test are invalid. The urine control tube provides assurance that no substances in the urine are agglutinating or damaging the red cells.

Note

Urine may also contain ABO and Lewis blood group substances, depending upon the ABO, Lewis, and secretor status of the donor.

Reference

Judd WJ. Methods in immunohematology. 2nd ed. Durham, NC: Montgomery Scientific Publications, 1994.

Method 3.12. Adsorption Procedure

Principle

See Chapter 19.

Specimen

Serum or plasma containing antibody to be adsorbed.

Reagents

Red cells (eg, autologous or allogeneic) that carry the antigen corresponding to the antibody specificity to be adsorbed.

Procedure

1. Wash the selected red cells at least three times with saline.

2. After the last wash, centrifuge the red cells at 800 to 1000 $\times$ g for at least 5 minutes and remove as much of the supernatant saline as possible. Additional saline may be removed by touching the red cell mass with a narrow piece of filter paper.

3. Mix appropriate volumes of the packed red cells and serum and incubate at the desired temperature for 30 to 60 minutes.

4. Mix the serum/cell mixture periodically throughout the incubation phase.

5. Centrifuge the red cells at 800 to 1000 $\times$ g for 5 minutes to pack cells tightly. Centrifuge at the incubation temperature, if possible, to avoid dissociation of antibody from the red cell membranes.

6. Transfer the supernatant fluid, which is the adsorbed serum, to a clean test tube. If an eluate is to be prepared, save the red cells.

7. Test an aliquot of the adsorbed serum, preferably against an addi-

tional aliquot of the cells used for adsorption, to see if all antibody has been removed.

Interpretation

If reactivity remains, the antibody has not been completely removed. No reactivity signifies that antibody has been completely adsorbed.

Notes

1. Adsorption is more effective if the area of contact between the red cells and serum is large; use of a large-bore test tube (13 mm or larger) is recommended.
2. Multiple adsorptions may be necessary to completely remove an antibody, but each successive adsorption increases the likelihood that the serum will be diluted and unadsorbed antibodies weakened.
3. Repeat adsorptions should use a fresh aliquot of cells and not the cells from the prior adsorption.
4. Enzyme pretreatment of adsorbing cells can be performed to increase antibody uptake for enzyme-resistant antigens.

Reference

Judd WJ. Methods in immunohematology. 2nd ed. Durham, NC: Montgomery Scientific Publications, 1994.

Method 3.13. Using the American Rare Donor Program

Principle

The American Rare Donor Program (ARDP) helps to locate blood products for patients requiring rare or unusual blood.

The ARDP maintains a database of rare donors submitted by immunohematology reference laboratories that are accredited by the AABB or the American Red Cross (ARC). Donors are considered rare due to the absence of a high-incidence antigen, absence of multiple common antigens, or IgA deficiency.

All requests to the ARDP must originate from an AABB- or ARC-accredited immunohematology reference laboratory to ensure that the patient in question has been accurately evaluated and reported. All shipping and rare unit fees are established by the shipping institution.

Procedure

1. A hospital blood bank, transfusion service, or blood center identifies a patient who needs rare blood.
2. The institution contacts the nearest AABB- or ARC-accredited immunohematology reference laboratory to supply the needed blood.
3. If the laboratory cannot supply the blood, it contacts the ARDP. *All* requests to the ARDP *must* come from an AABB- or ARC-accredited laboratory (or another rare donor program). Requests received directly from a non-accredited facility will be referred to the nearest accredited institution.
4. The institution contacting the ARDP (requesting institution) *must* confirm the identity of the antibody(ies) by serologic investigation or by examining the serologic work performed by another institution.
5. ARDP staff search their database for centers that have identified donors with the needed phenotype and contact the centers for availability of units. ARDP staff give the name(s) of the shipping center(s) to the requesting institution.

6. The requesting and shipping institutions should discuss and agree on charges and testing requirements before units are shipped.
7. If an initial search does not result in a sufficient number of units, the following mechanisms can be used by ARDP staff to obtain needed units: 1) communication to all ARDP participating centers alerting them to search their inventories and/or recruit donors matching the needed phenotype, 2) contacting other rare donor files such as those administered by the World Health Organization, Japanese Red Cross, etc.

Investigation of a Positive Direct Antiglobulin Test

Elution Techniques

The objective of all elution techniques is to interfere with the noncovalent binding forces that hold antibody-antigen complexes together on the red cell surface. The cell membrane can be physically disrupted by heat, ultrasound, freezing and thawing, detergents, or organic solvents. The binding forces of antigen-antibody complexes can be interrupted by alterations in pH or salt concentration. For a comparison of the advantages and disadvantages of various elution methods, see Chapter 20. Selected elution methods follow, including one example of an organic solvent method. The cold-acid elution method (Method 4.1) is the basis of the commercially available acid elution kits commonly used in the United States. Because no single elution method will result in the identification of all antibodies, use of an alternative elution method (eg, organic solvent) may be indicated when a nonreactive eluate is not in agreement with clinical data. The reader should refer to Chapter 2 for the proper handling of hazardous chemicals that are sometimes used in these techniques. Access to a chemical fume hood is desirable when organic solvents are in use.

Very thorough washing of the red cells before elution is essential to ensure that antibody in the eluate is only red cell-bound and does not represent free antibody, eg, from plasma. A control to show that all free antibody has been removed by washing can be obtained by saving the saline from the last wash and testing it in parallel with the eluate. Additionally, transferring the red cells into a clean test tube just before the elution step eliminates the possibility of dissociating antibody that may have nonspecifically bound to the glass test tube during an adsorption or the initial eluate preparation steps.

Method 4.1. Cold-Acid Elution

Principle

Dissociation of antibodies from red cells enables the identification of auto- or allo-antibodies. Elution methods used in conjunction with adsorption techniques are also useful in detecting weak antigen expression on the adsorbing cells and in separating mixtures of antibodies against red cell antigens.

Specimen

Red cells positive by the direct antiglobulin test (DAT) washed six times with large volumes of saline (save the last wash).

Reagents

1. Glycine-HCl (0.1 M, pH 3.0), prepared by dissolving 3.75 g of glycine and 2.922 g of sodium chloride in 500 mL of deionized or distilled water. Adjust the pH to 3.0 with 12 N HCl. Store at 4 C.
2. Phosphate buffer (0.8 M, pH 8.2), prepared by dissolving 109.6 g of Na_2HPO_4 and 3.8 g of KH_2PO_4 in approximately 600 mL of deionized or distilled water and adjusting the final volume to 1 L. Adjust the pH, if necessary, with either 1 N NaOH or 1 N HCl. Store at 4 C (see note 2).
3. NaCl, 0.9%, at 4 C.
4. Supernatant saline from the final wash of red cells to be tested.

Procedure

1. Place 1 mL of red cells in a 13 × 100-mm test tube and chill in an ice water bath for 5 minutes before adding the glycine-HCl.
2. Add 1 mL of chilled saline and 2 mL of chilled glycine-HCl to the red cells.
3. Mix and incubate the tube in an ice water bath (0 C) for 1 minute.
4. Quickly centrifuge the tube at 900 to 1000 × g for 2 to 3 minutes.
5. Transfer the supernatant eluate into a clean test tube and add 0.1 mL of pH 8.2 phosphate buffer for each 1 mL of eluate (see note 3).
6. Mix and centrifuge at 900 to 1000 × g for 2 to 3 minutes.
7. Transfer the supernatant eluate into a clean test tube and test it in parallel with the supernatant saline from the final wash.

Notes

1. Keep glycine-HCl in an ice bath during use, to maintain the correct pH.
2. Phosphate buffer will crystallize during storage at 4 C. Redissolve it at 37 C before use.
3. The addition of phosphate buffer restores neutrality to the acidic eluate. Acidity may cause hemolysis of the reagent red cells used in testing the eluate. The addition of 22% bovine albumin (one part to four parts of eluate) may reduce such hemolysis.

References

1. Judd WJ. Methods in immunohematology. 2nd ed. Durham, NC: Montgomery Scientific Publications, 1994.
2. Rekvig OP, Hannestad K. Acid elution of blood group antibodies from intact erythrocytes. Vox Sang 1977;33:280-5.

Method 4.2. Glycine-HCl/EDTA Elution

Principle

See Method 4.1.

Specimen

Red cells positive by the direct antiglobulin test (DAT) washed six times with large volumes of saline (save the last wash).

Reagents

1.   Disodium EDTA (10% w/v): Na_2EDTA, 10 g; distilled water to 100 mL.
2.   Glycine-HCl (0.1 M at pH 1.5): 0.75 g glycine diluted to 100 mL with 0.9% NaCl; adjust to pH 1.5 with 12 N HCl.
3.   TRIS-NaCl (1 M): Tris(hydroxymethyl) aminomethane [TRIS] or TRIZMA BASE, 12.1 g; 5.25 g NaCl; distilled water to 100 mL.
4.   Supernatant saline from the final wash of the red cells to be tested.

Procedure

1.   In a test tube, mix together 20 volumes (eg, drops) of 0.1 M glycine-HCl buffer and 5 volumes of 10% EDTA. This is the eluting solution.
2.   In a 12 × 75-mm tube, place 10 volumes of packed red cells.
3.   Add 20 volumes of the eluting solution to the red cells, mix well, and incubate at room temperature for 2 minutes. Do not overincubate.
4.   Add 1 volume of TRIS-NaCl, mix, and immediately centrifuge the tube at 900 to 1000 × g for 60 seconds.
5.   Transfer the supernatant eluate into a clean test tube and adjust it carefully dropwise to pH 7.0 to 7.4 with 1 M TRIS-NaCl. The pH can be checked with pH paper.
6.   Centrifuge at 900 to 1000 × g for 2 to 3 minutes to remove the precipitate.
7.   Transfer the supernatant eluate into a clean test tube and test it in parallel with the supernatant saline from the final wash.

Notes

1.   Once the red cells have been rendered DAT negative, they may be tested for the presence of blood group antigens, except those in the Kell system. Treatment with glycine-HCl/EDTA denatures Kell system antigens and Er^a. Wash the red cells at least three times in saline before use.
2.   Red cells modified with glycine-HCl/EDTA may be treated with a protease and used in autologous adsorption studies.
3.   Overincubation with the eluting solution (step 3) will irreversibly damage the red cells.
4.   TRIS-NaCl is very alkaline and only a few drops should be required to attain the desired pH (step 5).
5.   Aliquots of the reagents can be stored frozen and one tube of each can be thawed just before use. The 10% EDTA may precipitate when stored at 2 to 8 C.
6.   Stored eluate (4 C or frozen) may be more stable if albumin is added (1 volume of 30% bovine albumin for every 10 volumes of eluate). If albumin is added to the eluate, it should be added to the last wash.

Reference

Byrne PC. Use of a modified acid/EDTA elution technique. Immunohematology 1991;7:46-7. [Correction note: Immunohematology 1991;7:106.]

Method 4.3. Heat Elution

Principle

Heat elution uses an increase in temperature to dissociate antibodies from red cells. This method is best suited for the investigation of ABO hemolytic disease of the fetus and newborn and for the elution of IgM antibodies from red cells. It should not routinely be used for the investigation of abnormalities caused by IgG auto- or alloantibodies.

Specimen

Red cells positive by the direct antiglobulin test (DAT) washed six times with large volumes of saline; save the last wash (see note).

Reagents

1. 6% bovine albumin (see Method 1.5).
2. Supernatant saline from the final wash of the red cells to be tested.

Procedure

1. Mix equal volumes of washed packed cells and 6% bovine albumin in a 13×100-mm test tube.
2. Place the tube at 56 C for 10 minutes. Agitate the tube periodically during this time.
3. Centrifuge the tube at 900 to 1000 × g for 2 to 3 minutes, preferably in a heated centrifuge.
4. Immediately transfer the supernatant eluate into a clean test tube and test in parallel with the supernatant saline from the final wash.

Note

For optimal recovery of cold-reactive antibodies, the red cells should be washed in ice-cold saline to prevent dissociation of bound antibody before elution.

References

1. Judd WJ. Methods in immunohematology. 2nd ed. Durham, NC: Montgomery Scientific Publications, 1994.
2. Landsteiner K, Miller CP Jr. Serological studies on the blood of primates. II. The blood groups in anthropoid apes. J Exp Med 1925; 42:853-62.

Method 4.4. Lui Freeze-Thaw Elution

Principle

As red cells freeze, extracellular ice crystals form that attract water from their surroundings. This increases the osmolarity of the remaining extracellular fluid, which then extracts water from the red cells. The red cells shrink, resulting in lysis. As the membranes are disrupted, antibody is dissociated. This method is used primarily for the investigation of ABO hemolytic disease of the fetus and newborn.

Specimen

1. Red cells washed six times with large volumes of saline.
2. Supernatant saline from the final wash of the red cells to be tested.

Procedure

1. Mix 0.5 mL of the red cells to be tested with 3 drops of saline in a test tube.
2. Cap the tube, then rotate the tube to coat the tube wall with cells.
3. Place the tube in a horizontal position in a freezer at –6 C to –70 C for 10 minutes.
4. Remove the tube from the freezer and thaw it quickly with warm, running tap water.
5. Centrifuge for 2 minutes at 900 to 1000 × g.
6. Transfer the supernatant to a clean test tube and test it in parallel with the supernatant saline from the final wash.

References

1. Judd WJ. Methods in immunohematology. 2nd ed. Durham, NC: Montgomery Scientific Publications, 1994.
2. Feng CS, Kirkley KC, Eicher CA, et al. The Lui elution technique: A simple and efficient method for eluting ABO antibodies. Transfusion 1985;25:433-4.

Method 4.5. Methylene Chloride Elution

Principle

Organic solvents can influence antigen-antibody dissociation by several mechanisms, including alteration of the tertiary structure of antibody molecules and disruption of the red cell membrane. This method is suitable for elution of IgG auto- and alloantibodies.

Specimen

DAT-positive red cells washed six times with large volumes of saline (save last wash).

Reagents

1. Methylene chloride (dichloromethane).
2. Supernatant saline from final wash of the red cells to be tested.

Procedure

1. Mix 1 mL of red cells, 1 mL of saline, and 2 mL of methylene chloride in a test tube, eg, 13×100 mm.
2. Stopper the tube and mix by gentle agitation for 1 minute.
3. Remove the stopper and centrifuge the tube at $1000 \times g$ for 10 minutes.
4. Remove the *lower* layer of methylene chloride with a transfer pipette and discard it.
5. Place the tube at 56 C for 10 minutes. Stir the eluate constantly with wooden applicator sticks in the first several minutes to avoid it boiling over; thereafter, stir it periodically.
6. Centrifuge at $1000 \times g$ for 10 minutes.
7. Transfer the supernatant eluate into a clean test tube and test it in parallel with the supernatant saline from the final wash.

Reference

Judd WJ. Methods in immunohematology. 2nd ed. Durham, NC: Montgomery Scientific Publications, 1994.

Immune Hemolytic Anemia Serum/Plasma Methods

Included in this section are methods used to remove warm or cold autoantibody reactivity (eg, adsorptions) so that alloantibody detection tests and diagnostic tests for differentiating the immune hemolytic anemias can be performed. See Chapter 20 for a discussion of the immune hemolytic anemias.

Method 4.6. Cold Autoadsorption

Principle

Although most cold autoantibodies do not cause a problem in serologic tests, some potent cold-reactive autoantibodies may mask the concomitant presence of clinically significant alloantibodies. In these cases, adsorbing the serum in the cold with autologous red cells can remove the autoantibody, permitting detection of underlying alloantibodies. In the case of most nonpathologic cold autoantibodies, a simple quick adsorption of the patient's serum with enzyme-treated autologous red cells will remove most cold antibody. See Method 3.5.6. A more efficient method of removing immunoglobulins is the use of ZZAP reagent, a combination of proteolytic enzyme and a powerful reducing agent. ZZAP treatment removes IgM and complement from autologous red cells and uncovers antigen sites that can be used to bind free autoantibody in the serum.

Specimen

1. 1 mL of serum or plasma to be adsorbed.
2. Two 1-mL aliquots of autologous red cells.

Reagents

1. 1% cysteine-activated papain or 1% ficin (see Methods 3.5.1 and 3.5.2).
2. Phosphate-buffered saline (PBS), pH 7.3 (see Method 1.7).
3. 0.2 M dithiothreitol (DTT) prepared by dissolving 1 g of DTT in 32.4 mL of pH 7.3 PBS. Dispense into 3-mL aliquots and store at –18 C or colder.

Procedure

1. Prepare ZZAP reagent by mixing 0.5 mL of 1% cysteine-activated papain with 2.5 mL of 0.2 M DTT and 2 mL of pH 7.3 PBS. Alternatively, use 1 mL of 1% ficin, 2.5 mL of 0.2 M DTT, and 1.5 mL of pH 7.3 PBS. The pH should be between 6.0 and 6.5.
2. Add 2 mL of ZZAP reagent to 1 mL of autologous red cells. Mix and incubate at 37 C for 30 minutes.
3. Wash the cells three times in saline. Centrifuge the last wash for at least 5 minutes at 900 to 1000 × *g* and remove as much of the supernatant saline as possible (see note 1).
4. To the tube of ZZAP-treated red cells, add 1 mL of the autologous serum. Mix and incubate at 4 C for 30 minutes.
5. Centrifuge at 900 to 1000 × *g* for 4 to 5 minutes and transfer the serum into a clean tube.
6. Steps 2 through 5 may be repeated if the first autoadsorption does not satisfactorily remove the autoantibody activity.

7. After the final adsorption, test the serum with reagent red cells for alloantibody activity.

Notes

1. To avoid dilution of the serum and possible loss of weak alloantibody activity, it is important in step 3 to remove as much of the residual saline as possible.
2. If the reactivity of the autoantibody is not diminished, the target autoantigen may have been destroyed by either the enzyme or the DTT. The adsorption should be repeated against untreated autologous red cells washed several times in warm saline.

References

1. Branch DR. Blood transfusion in autoimmune hemolytic anemias. Lab Med 1984;15:402-8.
2. Branch DR, Petz LD. A new reagent (ZZAP) having multiple applications in immunohematology. Am J Clin Pathol 1982;78:161-7.

Method 4.7. Determining the Specificity of Cold-Reactive Autoagglutinins

Principle

For a discussion of specificity of cold-reacting autoantibodies, see Chapter 20.

Specimen

1. Serum, separated at 37 C from a blood sample allowed to clot at 37 C, or plasma, separated from an anti-coagulated sample after periodic inversion at 37 C for approximately 15 minutes.
2. Autologous red cells.

Reagents

Test red cells of the following phenotypes:

1. A pool of two examples of adult group O I adult red cells; they can be the reagent cells routinely used for alloantibody detection.
2. Group O i cord red cells.
3. The patient's own (autologous) red cells, washed at least three times with 37 C saline.
4. Red cells of the same ABO group as the patient, if the patient is not group O. If the patient is group A or AB, use both A$_1$ and A$_2$ cells.
5. Saline or phosphate-buffered saline (PBS), pH 7.3 (see Method 1.7).

Procedure

1. Prepare serial twofold dilutions of the serum or plasma in saline or PBS. The dilution range should be from 1 in 2 to 1 in 4096 (12 tubes), and the volumes prepared should be more than the total volume needed to test all of the desired red cells. See Method 3.7.
2. Label a set of 12 tubes with the dilution (eg, 2, 4, 8, etc) for each of the red cells to be tested (eg, adult, cord, autologous).
3. Dispense 2 drops of each dilution into the appropriate tubes.
4. Add 1 drop of a 3% to 5% saline suspension of each red cell sample to the appropriate set of tubes.
5. Mix and incubate at room temperature for 30 to 60 minutes.
6. Centrifuge for 15 to 20 seconds at 900 to 1000 × g. Examine the tubes one by one macroscopically for agglutination, starting with the set of tubes at the highest dilution for each cell tested (ie, read all the tubes for each dilution as a set). Grade and record the results.
7. Transfer the tubes to 4 C and incubate them at this temperature for 1 to 2 hours.
8. Centrifuge for 15 to 20 seconds at 900 to 1000 × g. Immediately place the tubes in a rack in an ice water bath. Examine the tubes as in step 6. Grade and record the results.

Interpretation

Table 4.7-1 summarizes the reactions of the commonly encountered cold-reactive autoantibodies. In cold agglutinin syn-

Table 4.7-1. Typical Relative Reactivity Patterns of Cold Autoantibodies

Red Cells	Antibody Specificity				
	Anti-I	Anti-i	Anti-I^T	Anti-IH	Anti-Pr
O I adult	+	0/↓	0/↓	+	+
O i cord	0/↓	+	+	↓	+
O i adult	0/↓	+	0/↓	↓	+
A$_1$ I adult	+	0/↓	0/↓	↓	+
Autologous	+	0/↓	0/↓	↓	+
O I enzyme-treated	↑	↑	↑	↑	0

+ = reactive; 0 = nonreactive; ↓ = weaker reaction; ↑ = stronger reaction.

drome, anti-I is seen most frequently, but anti-i may also be encountered. When cord cells react stronger than adult cells, the specificity may be anti-i, but adult i red cells need to be tested to confirm that these reactions are due to anti-i and not anti-I^T. Some examples of anti-I react more strongly with red cells that have a strong expression of H antigen (eg, O and A_2 cells); such antibodies are called anti-IH. Rarely, the specificity may be anti-Pr, which should be suspected if all the cells tested react equally. Anti-Pr can be confirmed by testing enzyme-treated cells; anti-Pr does not react with enzyme-treated cells, whereas anti-I and anti-i react better with enzyme-treated cells. Anti-Pr reacts equally with untreated red cells of I or i phenotypes.

Notes

1. It is important to use separate pipettes or pipette tips for each tube when preparing serum dilutions because the serum carried from one tube to the next when a single pipette is used throughout may cause falsely high titration endpoints. The difference can convert a true titer of 4000 to an apparent titer of 100,000, when the use of separate pipettes is compared with the use of a single pipette.
2. Serum dilutions can be prepared more accurately with large volumes (eg, 0.5 mL) than with small volumes.
3. Potent examples of cold-reactive autoantibodies generally do not show apparent specificity until titration studies are performed; this specificity may not even be apparent with dilutions at room temperature or 4 C. In such circumstances, tests can be incubated at 30 to 37 C. Dif-

ferential reactivity may be more apparent if incubation times are prolonged and agglutination is evaluated after settling, without centrifugation. Settled readings are more accurate after a 2-hour incubation.

4. This procedure can be used to determine both the titer and the specificity. If incubations are started at 37 C (set up prewarmed, and readings are taken sequentially after incubation at each temperature—eg, 37 C, 30 C, room temperature, 4 C), the specificity, titer, and thermal amplitude of the autoantibody can be determined with a single set of serum dilutions.
5. If testing will also be performed at 30 C and 37 C, include a test of the neat (undiluted) serum.

Reference

Petz LD, Garratty G. Immune hemolytic anemias. 2nd ed. Philadelphia: Churchill Livingstone, 2004.

Method 4.8. Cold Agglutinin Titer

Principle

Cold-reactive autoantibodies, if present at very high titers, may suggest a pathologic cold agglutinin disease. This may result in overt hemolysis and systemic symptoms and may indicate underlying B-cell hematologic neoplasia.

Specimen

Serum, separated at 37 C from a sample allowed to clot at 37 C, or plasma, separated from an anticoagulated sample after periodic inversion at 37 C for approximately 15 minutes.

Reagents

1. A pool of 2 examples of washed group O I adult red cells, eg, antibody detection cells.
2. Phosphate-buffered saline (PBS), pH 7.3 (see Method 1.7).

Procedure

1. Prepare serial twofold dilutions of the patient's serum or plasma in PBS. The dilution range should be from 1 in 2 to 1 in 4096 (12 tubes). See Method 3.7.
2. Mix 2 drops of each dilution with 1 drop of a 3% to 5% cell suspension of red cells.
3. Mix and incubate at 4 C for 1 to 2 hours.
4. Centrifuge the tubes for 15 to 20 seconds at 900 to 1000 × g, then place the tubes in a rack in an ice water bath. Examine the tubes one by one macroscopically for agglutination, starting with the tube at the highest dilution. Grade and record the results.

Interpretation

The titer is the reciprocal of the highest serum dilution at which macroscopic agglutination is observed. Titers above 64 are considered elevated, but hemolytic anemia resulting from cold-reactive auto-agglutinins rarely occurs unless the titer is >1000. Titers below 1000 may be obtained when the autoantibody has a different specificity (eg, anti-i), or if the cold agglutinin is of the less common low-titer, high-thermal-amplitude type. If the patient has a positive direct antiglobulin test (DAT) because of complement only and has clinical signs of hemolytic anemia, specificity and thermal amplitude studies should be performed (see Method 4.7).

Notes

1. It is important to use separate pipettes for each tube when preparing serum dilutions because the serum carried from one tube to the next when a single pipette is used throughout may cause falsely high titration endpoints.
2. Serum dilutions can be prepared more accurately with large volumes (eg, 0.5 mL) than with small volumes.

Reference

Petz LD, Garratty G. Immune hemolytic anemias. 2nd ed. Philadelphia: Churchill Livingstone, 2004.

Method 4.9. Autologous Adsorption of Warm-Reactive Autoantibodies

Principle

Warm-reactive autoantibodies in serum may mask the concomitant presence of clinically significant alloantibodies. Adsorption of the serum with autologous red cells can remove autoantibody from the serum, permitting detection of underlying alloantibodies. However, autologous red cells in the circulation are coated with autoantibody. Autologous adsorption of warm-reactive autoantibodies can be facilitated by dissociating autoantibody from the red cell membrane, thereby uncovering antigen sites that can bind free autoantibody to remove it from the serum. Some autoantibody can be dissociated by a gentle heat elution for 3 to 5 minutes at 56 C. Subsequent treatment of the cells with enzymes enhances the adsorption process by removing membrane structures that otherwise hinder the association between antigen and antibody. The most effective procedure involves the use of ZZAP reagent, a mixture of a proteolytic enzyme and a sulfhydryl reagent. ZZAP removes immunoglobulins and complement from the red cells and enhances the adsorption process. Red cells from patients transfused within the last 3 months should not be used for autoadsorption because transfused red cells present in the circulation are likely to adsorb the alloantibodies that are being sought (see Chapter 20).

Specimen

1. 1 mL of serum or plasma (or eluate) to be adsorbed.
2. 2 mL of autologous red cells.

Reagents

1. 1% cysteine-activated papain or 1% ficin (see Methods 3.5.1 and 3.5.2).
2. Phosphate-buffered saline (PBS), pH 7.3 (see Method 1.7).
3. 0.2 M DTT prepared by dissolving 1 g of DTT in 32.4 mL of pH 7.3 PBS. Dispense into 3-mL aliquots and store at –18 C or colder.

Procedure

1. Prepare ZZAP reagent by mixing 0.5 mL of 1% cysteine-activated papain with 2.5 mL of 0.2 M DTT and 2 mL of pH 7.3 PBS. Alternatively, use 1 mL of 1% ficin, 2.5 mL of 0.2 M DTT, and 1.5 mL of pH 7.3 PBS. The pH should be between 6.0 and 6.5.
2. To each of two tubes containing 1 mL of red cells, add 2 mL of ZZAP reagent. Mix and incubate at 37 C for 30 minutes with periodic mixing.
3. Wash the red cells three times in saline. Centrifuge the last wash for at least 5 minutes at 900 to 1000 $\times$ g

and remove as much supernatant saline as possible.
4. Add serum to an equal volume of ZZAP-treated red cells, mix, and incubate at 37 C for approximately 30 to 45 minutes.
5. Centrifuge and carefully remove serum.
6. If the original serum reactivity was only 1+, proceed to step 7; otherwise, repeat steps 4 and 5 once more using the once-adsorbed patient's serum and the second aliquot of ZZAP-treated cells.
7. Test the serum against a specimen of group O reagent cells. If reactivity persists, repeat steps 4 and 5.

Interpretation

One or two adsorptions ordinarily remove sufficient autoantibody so that alloantibody reactivity, if present, is readily apparent. If the twice-autoadsorbed serum reacts with defined specificity, as shown by testing against a small antibody identification panel, then the defined specificity of the antibody is probably an alloantibody. If the serum reacts with all cells on the panel, either additional autoadsorptions are necessary, the serum contains antibody to a high-incidence antigen, or the serum contains an autoantibody (eg, anti-Kp^b) that does not react with ZZAP-treated cells and thus will not be adsorbed by this procedure. To check this latter possibility, test the reactive autoadsorbed serum against reagent cells that have been pretreated with the ZZAP reagent.

Notes

1. ZZAP treatment destroys all Kell system antigens and all other antigens that are destroyed by proteases, eg, M, N, Fy^a, and Fy^b. ZZAP reagent also denatures the antigens of the LW, Cartwright, Dombrock, and Knops

systems. If the autoantibody is suspected to have specificity in any of these latter blood groups, an alternative procedure is to perform auto-adsorption with untreated autologous cells or autologous cells treated only with 1% ficin or 1% cysteine-activated papain.

2. There is no need to wash packed red cells before treatment with ZZAP.

3. Cold autoantibodies reactive at room temperature can also be present in the serum of about 30% of patients with warm-reactive autoantibodies. Removal of these cold antibodies can be facilitated by placing the serum and cell mixture at 4 C for about 15 minutes after incubation at 37 C.

4. As a guide, when the original serum reactivity is 1+ in the low-ionic-strength saline indirect antiglobulin test (LISS-IAT), usually only one adsorption would be required. Antibodies with 2+ to 3+ reactivity will generally be removed in two to three adsorptions. Performing greater than four adsorptions increases the risk of diluting alloantibody reactivity.

Reference

Branch DR, Petz LD. A new reagent (ZZAP) having multiple applications in immunohematology. Am J Clin Pathol 1982;78:161-7.

Method 4.10. Differential Warm Adsorption Using Enzyme- or ZZAP-Treated Allogeneic Red Cells

Principle

Adsorption of serum with selected red cells of known phenotypes will remove auto-antibody and leave antibodies to most blood group systems. The specificity of the antibodies that remain after adsorption can be confirmed by testing against a panel of reagent red cells. This procedure can be used to detect underlying alloantibodies if the patient has been recently transfused, or if insufficient autologous red cells are available and the patient's phenotype is unknown.

Treating the adsorbing cells with enzyme or ZZAP typically enhances the adsorption process. In addition, the treated red cells will lack the antigens destroyed by dithiothreitol (DTT) and/or enzymes (see Chapter 19).

Specimen

Serum/plasma containing warm-reactive autoantibodies or eluate from direct antiglobulin test (DAT)-positive cells.

Reagents

1. 1% cysteine-activated papain or 1% ficin (see Methods 3.5.1 and 3.5.2).

2. ZZAP reagent (papain or ficin plus 0.2 M DTT). See Method 4.9.

3. Phosphate-buffered saline (PBS), pH 7.3 (see Method 1.7).

4. Group O red cells of the phenotypes R_1R_1, R_2R_2, and rr; one of these cells should be Jk(a–b+) and one should be Jk(a+b–). Additionally, if the red cells are to be only enzyme-treated, at least one of the cells should also be K–. They can be reagent cells or from any blood specimen that will yield a sufficient volume of red cells.

Procedure

1. Wash 1 mL of each red cell specimen once in a large volume of saline, centrifuge to pack the cells, and remove the supernatant saline.

2. To each volume of washed packed cells, add one volume of 1% enzyme solution or two volumes of working

ZZAP reagent. Invert several times to mix them.

3. Incubate at 37 C: 15 minutes for enzyme or 30 minutes for ZZAP. Mix periodically throughout incubation.

4. Wash the red cells three times with large volumes of saline. Centrifuge at 900 to 1000 × g for at least 5 minutes and remove the last wash as completely as possible to prevent dilution of the serum.

5. For each of the three red cell specimens, mix one volume of treated cells with an equal volume of the patient's serum and incubate at 37 C for 30 minutes, mixing occasionally.

6. Centrifuge at 900 to 1000 × g for approximately 5 minutes and harvest the supernatant serum.

7. Test the three samples of adsorbed serum against the cells (untreated) used for adsorption, respectively. If reactivity is present, repeat steps 5 through 7 with a fresh aliquot of treated red cells until no reactivity remains. The three samples of adsorbed serum can then be tested against antibody detection/panel cells and the results compared for demonstration of persisting and removed alloantibody activity. See section on allogeneic adsorption in Chapter 20.

Notes

1. If the autoantibody is very strong, three or more aliquots of adsorbing cells should be prepared. If the first adsorption is unsuccessful, the use of a higher proportion of cells to serum/eluate may enhance effectiveness.

2. The adsorbing red cells should be tightly packed to remove residual saline that might dilute the antibodies remaining in the serum/eluate.

3. Agitate the serum/cell mixture during incubation to provide maximum surface contact.

4. A visible clue to the effectiveness of adsorption is clumping of the enzyme- or ZZAP-treated cells when they are mixed with the serum, especially when strong antibodies are present.

5. As a guide, when the original serum reactivity is 1+ in the low-ionic-strength saline indirect antiglobulin test (LISS-IAT), usually only one adsorption would be required. Antibodies with 2+ to 3+ reactivity will generally be removed in two to three adsorptions. Performing greater than four adsorptions increases the risk of diluting alloantibody reactivity.

6. If adsorption with enzyme- or ZZAP-treated cells has no effect on the autoantibody, adsorption with untreated red cells may be tried.

References

1. Branch DR, Petz LD. A new reagent (ZZAP) having multiple applications in immunohematology. Am J Clin Pathol 1982;78:161-7.

2. Judd WJ. Methods in immunohematology. 2nd ed. Durham, NC: Montgomery Scientific Publications, 1994.

Method 4.11. One-Cell Sample Enzyme or ZZAP Allogeneic Adsorption

Principle

If the Rh and Kidd phenotypes of a recently transfused patient are known or can be determined, autoantibody activity can be adsorbed from the serum onto a single allogeneic red cell sample, leaving serum that can be evaluated for the presence of alloantibodies. The red cells used should have the same Rh and Kidd phenotypes as the patient; they can be treated with enzyme or ZZAP to denature antigens (see Chapter 19). This method is a simplified version of the previous adsorption procedure, but it should be used only if the patient's Rh and Kidd phenotypes are known (see the note).

Specimen

Serum, plasma, or eluate to be tested.

Reagents

1. 1% cysteine-activated papain or 1% ficin (see Methods 3.5.1 and 3.5.2).
2. ZZAP reagent (papain or ficin plus 0.2 M DTT). See Method 4.9.
3. ABO-compatible red cells of the patient's Rh and Kidd phenotypes; they can be reagent cells or cells from any blood specimen that will yield sufficient cells.

Procedure

1. Wash the selected allogeneic red cells once in a large volume of saline and centrifuge to pack them.
2. Add one volume of 1% enzyme solution or two volumes of ZZAP reagent to one volume of these packed cells. Invert several times to mix them.
3. Incubate at 37 C: 15 minutes for enzyme or 30 minutes for ZZAP. Mix periodically throughout incubation.
4. Wash the cells three times with saline. Centrifuge at 900 to $1000 \times g$ for at least 5 minutes and remove the last wash as completely as possible to prevent dilution of the serum.
5. To one volume of treated cells, add an equal volume of the patient's serum, mix, and incubate at 37 C for 30 minutes, mixing occasionally.
6. Centrifuge at 900 to $1000 \times g$ for approximately 5 minutes and harvest the supernatant serum.

7. Test the adsorbed serum against the cells (untreated) used for adsorption. If reactivity persists, repeat steps 5 through 7 with a fresh aliquot of treated cells until the serum is no longer reactive.

Note

The s antigen may not be denatured by a particular enzyme or ZZAP solution. The s antigen status of the adsorbing red cells may need to be considered.

Method 4.12. Polyethylene Glycol Adsorption

Principle

Polyethylene glycol (PEG) enhances the adsorption of antibody by untreated red cells. Testing the adsorbed aliquot against a panel of red cells can identify the specificity of antibodies that remain after adsorption. This method can be used for both autologous and allogeneic adsorption.

Specimen

Serum or plasma to be tested.

Reagents

1. PEG, 20% (20 g PEG, 3350 MW, in 100 mL of PBS, pH 7.3) or commercial PEG enhancement reagent.
2. Autologous red cells or ABO-compatible allogeneic red cells of known phenotype.

Procedure

1. Wash aliquots of red cells in large volumes of saline three times and centrifuge for 5 to 10 minutes at $1000 \times g$. Remove all residual saline.
2. To 1 volume (eg, 1 mL) of red cells, add 1 volume of serum and 1 vol-

ume of PEG. Mix well and incubate at 37 C for 15 minutes.

3. Centrifuge the serum/PEG/cell mixture for 5 minutes and harvest the adsorbed serum/PEG mixture.

4. To test the adsorbed serum, add 4 drops of serum to 1 drop of test red cells, incubate for 15 minutes at 37 C, and proceed to the antiglobulin test with anti-IgG. The larger volume of serum tested (4 drops) is required to account for the dilution of the serum by the PEG. See the notes.

5. To check for completeness of adsorption, test the adsorbed serum against the red cells used for the adsorption. If positive, repeat the adsorption by adding the adsorbed serum to a fresh aliquot of red cells but do not add additional PEG. If the test was negative, test the adsorbed serum with a panel of cells.

Notes

1. Red cells for adsorption may be chemically modified (eg, with enzymes or ZZAP) before adsorption if denaturation of antigens is desired.

2. The adsorbing cells should be thoroughly packed to remove any residual saline that could result in dilution of the antibodies remaining in the serum.

3. Test the adsorbed serum on the day it was adsorbed. Weak antibody reactivity may be lost upon storage of PEG-adsorbed sera, possibly due to precipitation of the protein noticeable after 4 C storage.

4. Although many laboratories successfully use the PEG adsorption method, some serologists have reported a weakening or loss of antibody reactivity in some samples when compared with results ob-

tained using a different technique. To accommodate this potential weakening of antibody reactivity, some serologists test 6 drops of the PEG-adsorbed serum.

5. Agglutination of the adsorbing red cells does not occur when PEG is used; therefore, there is no visible clue to the efficiency of the adsorption process. As a guide, when the original serum reactivity is 1+ in low-ionic-strength saline indirect antiglobulin test (LISS-IAT), usually only one adsorption would be required. Antibodies with 2 to 3+ reactivity will generally be removed in two adsorptions.

References

1. Leger RM, Garratty G. Evaluation of methods for detecting alloantibodies underlying warm autoantibodies. Transfusion 1999;39:11-6.
2. Leger RM, Ciesielski D, Garratty G. Effect of storage on antibody reactivity after adsorption in the presence of polyethylene glycol. Transfusion 1999;39:1272-3.

Method 4.13. The Donath-Landsteiner Test
Principle

IgG autoantibodies that cause paroxysmal cold hemoglobinuria (PCH) act as biphasic hemolysins in vitro. The IgG autoantibodies bind to the red cells at cold temperatures, and, as the test is warmed to 37 C, complement is activated and lysis of the red cells occurs. The patient for whom this procedure should be considered is one with a positive direct antiglobulin test (DAT) resulting from C3; demonstrable hemoglobinemia, hemoglobinuria, or both; and no evidence of autoantibody activity in the serum or the eluate made from the DAT-positive cells. For a discussion of PCH, see Chapter 20.

Specimen

Serum separated from a freshly collected blood sample maintained at 37 C.

Reagents

1. Freshly collected pooled normal sera known to lack unexpected antibodies, to use as a source of complement.
2. 50% suspension of washed group O red cells that express the P antigen, eg, antibody detection cells.

Procedure

1. Label three sets of three 10×75-mm test tubes as follows: A1-A2-A3; B1-B2-B3; C1-C2-C3.
2. To tubes 1 and 2 of each set, add 10 volumes (eg, drops) of the patient's serum.
3. To tubes 2 and 3 of each set, add 10 volumes of fresh normal serum.
4. To all tubes, add one volume of the 50% suspension of washed P-positive red cells and mix well.
5. Place the three "A" tubes in a bath of melting ice for 30 minutes and then at 37 C for 1 hour.
6. Place the three "B" tubes in a bath of melting ice and keep them in melting ice for 90 minutes.
7. Place the three "C" tubes at 37 C and keep them at 37 C for 90 minutes.
8. Centrifuge all tubes and examine the supernatant fluid for hemolysis.

Interpretation

The Donath-Landsteiner test is considered positive when the patient's serum, with or without added complement, causes hemolysis in the tubes that were incubated first in melting ice and then at 37 C (ie, tubes A1 and A2), and there is no hemolysis in any of the tubes maintained throughout at 37 C (ie, tubes C1, C2) or in melting ice (ie, tubes B1, B2). The A3, B3, and C3 tubes serve as a control of the normal sera complement source and should not manifest hemolysis.

Notes

1. The biphasic nature of the hemolysin associated with PCH requires that serum be incubated with cells at a cold temperature first (eg, melting ice bath) and then at 37 C.
2. Active complement is essential for demonstration of the antibody. Because patients with PCH may have low levels of serum complement, fresh normal serum should be included in the reaction medium as a source of complement.
3. To avoid loss of antibody by cold autoadsorption before testing, the patient's blood should be allowed to clot at 37 C, and the serum separated from the clot at this temperature.
4. If a limited amount of blood is available (eg, from young children), set up tubes A-1, A-2, A-3 and C-1, C-2; if there is only enough serum for two tests (ie, 20 drops), set up tubes A-2, A-3, and C-2.
5. To demonstrate the P specificity of the Donath-Landsteiner antibody, ABO-compatible p red cells should be tested in a second set of tubes A-1, A-2, and A-3. No lysis should develop in these tubes, confirming the P specificity of the antibody.

References

1. Judd WJ. Methods in immunohematology. 2nd ed. Durham, NC: Montgomery Scientific Publications, 1994.
2. Dacie JV, Lewis SM. Practical hematology. 7th ed. New York: Churchill Livingstone, 1991: 500-1.

Method 4.14. Detection of Antibodies to Penicillin or Cephalosporins by Testing Drug-Treated Red Cells

Principle

See Chapter 20 for a discussion of the mechanisms by which drugs cause a positive direct antiglobulin test (DAT). The preparations of drugs used should, to the extent possible, be the same as those given to the patient. For drugs other than penicillin and the cephalosporins, refer to published reports for the method used to treat the red cells.

Specimen

Serum or plasma and eluate (and last wash) to be studied.

Reagents

1. 0.1 M sodium barbital-buffer (BB) at pH 9.6 to 9.8, prepared by dissolving 2.06 g of sodium barbital in 80 mL of distilled or deionized H_2O. Adjust the pH to between 9.6 and 9.8 with 0.1 N HCl. Bring total volume to 100 mL. Store at 2 to 8 C.
2. Phosphate-buffered saline (PBS), pH 7.3 (see Method 1.7).
3. Drug, eg, penicillin, cephalosporin.
4. Washed, packed, group O red cells.
5. Normal sera/plasma.
6. IgG-coated red cells.

Procedure

1. For penicillin-treated cells, dissolve 600 mg of penicillin in 15 mL of BB. This high pH is optimal, but if the buffer is unavailable, PBS, pH 7.3, can be used. Add 1 mL of red cells. In a separate tube, prepare control cells by adding 1 mL of untreated red cells (without the drug) to 15 mL of the same buffer. Incubate both tubes for 1 hour at room temperature with occasional mixing. Wash three times in saline and store in PBS at 2 to 8 C for up to 1 week. See note 1.
2. For cephalosporin-treated cells, dissolve 400 mg of the drug in 10 mL of PBS, pH 7.3. Add 1 mL of red cells. In a separate tube, prepare control cells by adding 1 mL of untreated red cells (without the drug) to 10 mL of PBS. Incubate both tubes for 1 hour at 37 C with occasional mixing. Wash three times in saline and store in PBS for up to 1 week at 2 to 8 C. See notes 1 and 2.
3. Mix 2 or 3 drops of each specimen (serum, eluate, and last wash) and controls with 1 drop of 5% saline suspension of drug-treated red cells.
4. In parallel, test each specimen and control with the untreated red cells. See notes 3 and 4.
5. Incubate the tests at 37 C for 60 minutes. Centrifuge and examine for hemolysis and agglutination. Record the results.
6. Wash the cells four times in saline and test by an indirect antiglobulin technique using polyspecific anti-human globulin or anti-IgG reagent. Centrifuge and examine for agglutination. Record the results.
7. Confirm the validity of negative tests by adding IgG-coated red cells.

Interpretation

Reactivity (hemolysis, agglutination, and/or positive indirect antiglobulin test) with drug-treated cells, but not with untreated cells, indicates that drug antibodies are present (see notes 3 and 4). No hemolysis will be seen in tests with plasma or the eluate. Antibodies to either penicillin or cephalothin may cross-react with cells treated with the other drug (ie, penicillin antibodies may attach to cephalothin-treated cells and vice versa). Antibodies to other cephalosporins may react with cephalothin-treated cells. It is best to treat cells with the drug that is suspect.

Negative results without a positive control can only be interpreted to mean that drug antibodies were not detected. The drug may or may not be bound to the test red cells.

Notes

1. The volume of drug-treated red cells can be scaled down as long as the ratio of the 40 mg/mL drug solution to red cells is constant; eg, 120 mg penicillin in 3 mL BB plus 0.2 mL red cells or 100 mg cephalosporin in 2.5 mL PBS plus 0.25 mL red cells.[1]
2. Cephalosporins do not require a high pH for optimal coating of red cells. In fact, a lower pH, ie, pH 6 to 7, decreases nonspecific protein adsorption seen when a high pH buffer is used. The least amount of nonspecific protein adsorption by drug-treated red cells will occur if a pH 6.0 buffer is used, but this leads to a slight decrease in coating by the drug.
3. Test normal pooled serum and PBS as negative controls and, when available, a specimen known to contain an antibody to the drug being investigated as a positive control.
4. To control for nonspecific protein adsorption and nonspecific agglutination of normal sera observed with some cephalosporins (eg, cephalothin), test the normal serum and the

test serum at a 1 in 20 dilution in PBS. Normal sera diluted 1 in 20 generally do not react nonspecifically. Thus, reactivity of the diluted serum with the drug-treated cells but not with the untreated cells indicates that drug antibody is present.

5. When testing cefotetan-treated red cells, test the serum at a 1 in 100 dilution in PBS to prevent a false-positive test result. In addition to the nonspecific uptake of protein onto cefotetan-treated red cells, some normal sera appear to have a "naturally occurring" anticefotetan,[2] a few of which react weakly at a 1 in 20 dilution. Cases of cefotetan-induced immune hemolytic anemia are associated with very high antibody titers (eg, mean antiglobulin test titer = 16,000).[3]
6. About 30% of patients with anticefotetan also have a drug-independent antibody[3]; in these cases, the serum and/or eluate, when tested undilute, may react with both the cefotetan-treated and untreated red cells.
7. The last wash control can sometimes react with cefotetan-treated red cells when antibodies to cefotetan are present, regardless of the wash solution used (commercial acid eluate kit wash solution, 4 C LISS, or 4 C PBS) or the number of washes performed.[3]
8. Prepare drug solutions just before use.
9. Drug-treated red cells may be kept in PBS at 4 C for up to 1 week; however, there may be some weakening of drug coating upon storage. Drug-treated and untreated red cells may also be stored frozen.
10. When antibodies are not detected with drug-treated red cells, test by

the immune complex method (Method 4.15). Antibodies to some third-generation cephalosporins (eg, ceftriaxone) do not react with drug-treated red cells.

References

1. Petz LD, Garratty G. Immune hemolytic anemias. 2nd ed. Philadelphia: Churchill Livingstone, 2004.
2. Arndt P, Garratty G. Is severe immune hemolytic anemia, following a single dose of cefotetan, associated with the presence of "naturally occurring" anti-cefotetan? (abstract) Transfusion 2001;41(Suppl):24S.
3. Arndt PA, Leger RM, Garratty G. Serology of antibodies to second- and third-generation cephalosporins associated with immune hemolytic anemia and/or positive direct antiglobulin tests. Transfusion 1999;39:1239-46.

Method 4.15. Demonstration of Immune-Complex Formation Involving Drugs

Principle

For a discussion of the mechanism of drug-induced immune-complex formation, see Chapter 20.

Specimen

The patient's serum.

Reagents

1. The drug under investigation, in the same form (powder, tablet, capsules) that the patient is receiving.
2. Phosphate-buffered saline (PBS) at pH 7.3 (see Method 1.7).
3. Fresh, normal serum known to lack unexpected antibodies, as a source of complement.
4. Pooled group O reagent red cells, 5% suspension, one aliquot treated with a proteolytic enzyme (see Method 3.5.6) and one untreated.
5. Polyspecific antihuman globulin reagent.
6. IgG-coated red cells.

Procedure

1. Prepare a 1 mg/mL solution of the drug in PBS. Centrifuge to remove any particulate matter and adjust the pH of the supernatant fluid to approximately 7 with either 1 N NaOH or 1 N HCl, as required, if the pH is below 5 or above 8.
2. Label two sets of tubes for the following test mixtures:
   a. Patient's serum + drug.
   b. Patient's serum + PBS.
   c. Patient's serum + complement (normal serum) + drug.
   d. Patient's serum + complement (normal serum) + PBS.
   e. Normal serum + drug.
   f. Normal serum + PBS.
3. Add 2 volumes (eg, 2 drops) of each component in the appropriate tubes (eg, 2 drops of serum + 2 drops of drug).
4. Add 1 drop of a 5% saline suspension of untreated group O reagent red cells to one set of tubes. Add 1 drop of a 5% saline suspension of enzyme-treated group O reagent red cells to the second set of tubes.
5. Mix and incubate at 37 C for 1 to 2 hours, with periodic gentle mixing.
6. Centrifuge, examine for hemolysis and agglutination, and record the results.
7. Wash the cells four times in saline and test with a polyspecific antiglobulin reagent.
8. Centrifuge, examine for agglutination, and record the results.
9. Confirm the validity of negative tests by adding IgG-coated red cells.

Interpretation

Hemolysis, direct agglutination, or positive indirect antiglobulin tests can occur together or separately. Reactivity in any of the tests containing the patient's serum to which the drug was added, and absence of reactivity in the corresponding control tests containing PBS instead of the drug, indicate that antibody to the drug is present. See note 4.

Notes

1. The drug may be more easily dissolved by incubation at 37 C and vigorous shaking of the solution. If the drug is in tablet form, crush it with a mortar and pestle and remove any visible outer tablet coating material before adding PBS.
2. Not all drugs will dissolve completely in PBS. Consult the manufacturer or a reference such as the Merck Index for the solubility of the drug in question. A previous report of drug-induced immune hemolytic anemia resulting from the drug in question may provide information on the drug solution preparation.
3. When available, a serum/plasma known to contain antibody with the drug specificity being evaluated should be included as a positive control.
4. Tests without the drug added may be positive if autoantibodies or circulating drug-antibody immune complexes are present in the patient's sample. Autoantibody reactivity would be persistent over time, whereas circulating immune complexes are transient.
5. Testing with enzyme-treated red cells and the addition of fresh normal serum as a source of comple-

ment may increase the sensitivity of the test.

6. If tests for drug antibodies by the immune-complex method and drug adsorption method are noninformative, consider testing with ex-vivo antigen (see Method 4.16).

Reference

Petz LD, Garratty G. Immune hemolytic anemias. 2nd ed. Philadelphia: Churchill Livingstone, 2004.

Method 4.16. Ex-Vivo Demonstration of Drug/Anti-Drug Complexes

Principle

Immune drug/anti-drug complexes can activate complement and cause hemolysis in vivo. These immune complexes may be demonstrable by serologic testing in the presence of the drug, but with some drugs (notably nomifensine), antibodies are directed against metabolites of the drug, rather than the native drug. Serum and/or urine from volunteers who have ingested therapeutic levels of the drug can be used as a source of these metabolites. See note 1.

This procedure is used to investigate drug-associated immune hemolysis, particularly when use of the preceding methods has been noninformative.

Specimen

Patient's serum.

Reagents

1. Polyspecific antihuman globulin (AHG) reagent.
2. Drug metabolites from volunteer drug recipients. See note 2.

a. Volunteer serum (VS) obtained immediately before (VS$_0$), at 1 hour (VS$_1$), and 6 hours (VS$_6$) after drug administration. Divide serum into 1-mL aliquots and store them at 2 to 8 C for a few hours or at –20 C or colder until use.

b. Volunteer urine (VU) obtained immediately before (VU$_0$), at 1 hour (VU$_1$), 3.5 hours (VU$_{3.5}$), 7 hours (VU$_7$), and 16 hours (VU$_{16}$) after drug administration. Divide into 1-mL aliquots and store them at 2 to 8 C for a few hours or at –20 C or colder until use.

3. Fresh normal serum, known to lack unexpected antibodies, as a source of complement.

4. Phosphate-buffered saline (PBS), pH 7.3 (see Method 1.7).

5. Pooled group O reagent red cells washed three times with saline and resuspended to a 5% concentration with PBS.

6. Pooled, enzyme-treated, group O red cells, 5% suspension in PBS.

7. IgG-coated red cells.

Procedure

1. For each volunteer serum and/or volunteer urine sample collected, label two sets of the following test mixtures:
   a. Patient's serum + VS (or VU).
   b. Patient's serum + PBS.
   c. Patient's serum + complement + VS (or VU).
   d. Patient's serum + complement + PBS.
   e. Complement + VS (or VU).
   f. Complement + PBS.

2. Add 0.1 mL of each component to the appropriate tubes.

3. Add 1 drop of a 5% saline suspension of the untreated group O reagent red cells to one set of tubes. Add 1 drop of a 5% saline suspension of enzyme-treated reagent red cells to the second set of tubes.

4. Mix the contents of each tube and incubate at 37 C for 1 to 2 hours, with periodic mixing.

5. Centrifuge, examine for agglutination and/or hemolysis, and record the results.

6. Wash the cells four times with saline and test with a polyspecific antiglobulin reagent.

7. Centrifuge, examine for agglutination, and record the results.

8. Confirm the validity of negative tests by adding IgG-coated red cells.

Interpretation

Hemolysis, direct agglutination, or reactivity with AHG in any of the tubes containing test serum and VS or VU, and absence of reactivity in all the control tubes, indicate antibody against a metabolite of the drug in question.

Notes

1. Approval of the institutional ethics committee should be obtained for the use of volunteers for obtaining drug metabolites.

2. The urine sample collection times given are those optimal for antibodies to nomifensine metabolites; different collection times may be required for other drugs.

3. Complement may be omitted from step 1 if the VS samples have been kept on ice and are used for testing within 8 hours of collection.

4. Testing with enzyme-treated red cells and the addition of fresh normal serum as a source of complement may increase the sensitivity of the test.

References

1. Judd WJ. Methods in immunohematology. 2nd ed. Durham, NC: Montgomery Scientific Publications, 1994.

2. Salama A, Mueller-Eckhardt C. The role of metabolite-specific antibodies in nomifensine-dependent immune hemolytic anemia. N Engl J Med 1985;313:469-74.

Hemolytic Disease of the Fetus and Newborn

Method 5.1. Indicator Cell Rosette Test for Fetomaternal Hemorrhage

Principle

This test detects D+ red cells in the blood of a D– woman whose fetus or recently delivered infant is D+. When reagent anti-D is added to maternal blood containing D+ fetal cells, fetal red cells become coated with anti-D. When D+ reagent cells are subsequently added, easily visible rosettes are formed, with several red cells clustered around each antibody-coated D+ red cell.

Although the number of rosettes is roughly proportional to the number of D+ red cells present in the original mixture, this test provides only qualitative information about fetal-maternal admixture. Specimens giving a positive result should be subjected to further testing to quantify the number of fetal cells. The acid-elution procedure given below and flow cytometry are acceptable choices. If a commercial test is available, the directions in the package insert should be followed.

Specimen

A 2% to 5% saline suspension of washed red cells from a maternal blood sample.

Reagents

Prepared reagents are commercially available. The steps below can be used for in-house preparation.

1. Negative control: a 2% to 5% saline suspension of washed red cells known to be D–.

2. Positive control: a 2% to 5% saline suspension of a mixture containing approximately 0.6% D+ red cells and 99.4% D– red cells. The positive control can be prepared by adding 1 drop

of a 2% to 5% suspension of D+ control cells to 15 drops of a 2% to 5% suspension of washed D– control cells. Mix well, then add 1 drop of this cell suspension to 9 drops of the 2% to 5% suspension of D– red cells. Mix well.

3. Indicator red cells: a 2% to 5% saline suspension of group O, R_2R_2 red cells. Either enzyme-treated or untreated cells in an enhancing medium can be used.

4. Chemically modified or high-protein reagent anti-D serum. Some monoclonal/polyclonal blended reagents are unsuitable for use in this method. The antisera selected for use should be evaluated for suitability before incorporation into the test procedure.

Procedure

1. To each of three test tubes, add 1 drop (or volume specified in the manufacturer's instructions) of reagent anti-D.
2. Add 1 drop of maternal cells, negative control cells, and positive control cells to the appropriately labeled tubes.
3. Incubate at 37 C for 15 to 30 minutes, or as specified by the manufacturer's instructions.
4. Wash cell suspensions at least four times with large volumes of saline, to remove all unbound reagent anti-D. Decant saline completely after last wash.
5. To the dry cell button, add 1 drop of indicator cells and mix thoroughly to resuspend them.
6. Centrifuge the tubes for 15 seconds at 900 to $1000 \times g$.
7. Resuspend cell button and examine the red cell suspension microscopically at 100 to $150 \times$ magnification.
8. Examine at least 10 fields and count the number of red cell rosettes in each field.

Interpretation

The absence of rosettes is a negative result. With enzyme-treated indicator cells, up to one rosette per three fields may occur in a negative specimen. With untreated indicator cells and an enhancing medium, there may be up to six rosettes per five fields in a negative test. The presence of more rosettes than these allowable maxima constitutes a positive result, and the specimen should be examined using a test that quantifies the amount of fetal blood present.

The presence of rosettes or agglutination in the negative control tube indicates inadequate washing after incubation, allowing residual anti-D to agglutinate the D+ indicator cells. A strongly positive result is seen with red cells from a woman whose Rh phenotype is weak D rather than D–; massive fetomaternal hemorrhage may produce an appearance difficult to distinguish from that caused by a weak D phenotype, and a quantitative test for fetal cells should be performed. If the infant's cells are shown to be weak D, a negative result on the mother's specimen should be interpreted with caution. In this situation, a quantitative test that does not rely on D antigen expression should be performed.

Reference

Sebring ES, Polesky HF. Detection of fetal maternal hemorrhage in Rh immune globulin candidates. Transfusion 1982;22:468-71.

Method 5.2. Acid-Elution Stain (Modified Kleihauer-Betke)

Principle

Fetal hemoglobin resists elution from red cells under acid conditions, whereas adult hemoglobin is eluted. When a thin blood smear is exposed to an acid buffer, hemoglobin from adult red cells is leached into the buffer so that only the stroma remains; fetal cells retain their hemoglobin and can be identified by a positive staining pattern. The approximate volume of feto-maternal hemorrhage can be calculated from the percentage of fetal red cells in the maternal blood film.

Specimen

Maternal anticoagulated whole blood sample.

Reagents

Prepared reagents are commercially available in kits. The steps below can be used for in-house preparations.

1. Stock solution A (0.1 M of citric acid). $C_6H_8O_7 \bullet H_2O$, 21.0 g, diluted to 1 liter with distilled water. Keep it in the refrigerator.
2. Stock solution B (0.2 M of sodium phosphate). $Na_2HPO_4 \bullet 7H_2O$, 53.6 g, diluted to 1 liter with distilled water. Keep it in the refrigerator.
3. McIlvaine's buffer, pH 3.2. Add 75 mL of stock solution A to 21 mL of stock solution B. Prepare fresh mixture for each test. This buffer mixture should be brought to room temperature or used at 37 C.
4. Erythrosin B, 0.5% in water.
5. Harris hematoxylin (filtered).
6. 80% ethyl alcohol.
7. Positive control specimen. Ten parts of anticoagulated adult blood, mixed with one part of anticoagulated ABO-compatible cord blood.
8. Negative control specimen. Anticoagulated adult blood.

Procedure

1. Prepare very thin blood smears, diluting blood with an equal volume of saline. Air dry.

2. Fix the smears in 80% ethyl alcohol for 5 minutes.
3. Wash the smears with distilled water.
4. Immerse the smears in McIlvaine's buffer, pH 3.2, for 11 minutes at room temperature or 5 minutes at 37 C. This reaction is temperature-sensitive.
5. Wash the smears in distilled water.
6. Immerse the smears in erythrosin B for 5 minutes.
7. Wash the smears completely in distilled water.
8. Immerse the smears in Harris hematoxylin for 5 minutes.
9. Wash the smears in running tap water for 1 minute.
10. Examine dry using 40× magnification, count a total of 2000 red cells, and record the number of fetal cells observed.
11. Calculate the percent of fetal red cells in the total counted.

Interpretation

1. Fetal cells are bright pink and refractile; normal adult red cells appear as very pale ghosts.
2. The conversion factor used to indicate the volume (as mL of whole blood) of fetomaternal hemorrhage is the percent of fetal red cells observed times 50.

Note

The accuracy and precision of this procedure are poor, and decisions regarding Rh Immune Globulin (RhIG) dosage in massive fetomaternal hemorrhage should be made accordingly. If there is a question regarding the need for additional RhIG, it is preferable to administer another dose to prevent the risks of undertreatment. (See Table 23-1 for dosage.)

Reference

Sebring ES. Fetomaternal hemorrhage—incidence and methods of detection and quantitation. In: Garratty G, ed. Hemolytic disease of the newborn. Arlington, VA: AABB, 1984:87-118.

Method 5.3. Antibody Titration Studies to Assist in Early Detection of Hemolytic Disease of the Fetus and Newborn

Principle

Antibody titration is a semiquantitative method of determining antibody concentration. Serial twofold dilutions of serum are prepared and tested for antibody activity. The reciprocal of the highest dilution of plasma or serum that gives a 1+ reaction is referred to as the titer (ie, 1 in 128 dilution; titer = 128).

In pregnancy, antibody titration is performed to identify women with significant levels of antibodies that may lead to hemolytic disease of the fetus and newborn (HDFN) and, for low-titer antibodies, to establish a baseline for comparison with titers found later in pregnancy. Titration of non-Rh antibodies should be undertaken only after discussion with the obstetrician about how the data will be used in the clinical management of the pregnancy. The significance of titers has been sufficiently established only for anti-D (using a saline technique).

Specimen

Serum for titration (containing potentially significant unexpected antibodies to red cell antigens, 1 mL). If possible, test the current sample in parallel with the most recent previously submitted (preceding) sample from the current pregnancy.

Materials

1. Antihuman IgG: need not be heavy-chain-specific.
2. Isotonic saline.
3. Volumetric pipettes, or equivalent: 0.1- to 0.5-mL delivery, with disposable tips.
4. Red cells: group O reagent red cells, 2% suspension. (See note 1 regarding the selection of red cells for testing.) Avoid using Bg+ red cells because they may result in falsely high values, especially with sera from multiparous women.
5. IgG-coated red cells.

Quality Control

1. Test the preceding sample in parallel with the most recent sample.
2. Prepare the dilutions using a separate pipette for each tube. Failure to do so will result in falsely high titers because of carryover.
3. Confirm all negative reactions with IgG-coated red cells (see step 9 below).

Procedure

1. Using 0.5-mL volumes, prepare serial twofold dilutions of serum in saline. The initial tube should contain undiluted serum and the doubling dilution range should be from 1 in 2 to 1 in 2048 (total of 12 tubes). (See Method 3.7.)
2. Place 0.1 mL of each dilution into appropriately labeled test tubes.
3. Add 0.1 mL of the 2% suspension of red cells to each dilution. Alternatively, for convenience, add 1 drop of a solution of a 3% to 4% suspension of red cells as supplied by the reagent manufacturer, although this method is less precise.

4. Gently agitate the contents of each tube; incubate at 37 C for 1 hour.

5. Wash the red cells four times with saline; completely decant the final wash supernatant.

6. To the dry red cell buttons thus obtained, add anti-IgG according to the manufacturer's directions.

7. Centrifuge as for hemagglutination tests.

8. Examine the red cells macroscopically; grade and record the reactions.

9. Add IgG-coated red cells to all negative tests; recentrifuge and examine the tests for macroscopic agglutination; repeat the testing if the tests with IgG-coated red cells are nonreactive.

Interpretation

The titer is reported as the reciprocal of the highest dilution of serum at which 1+ agglutination is observed. A titer ≥16 (this value may vary according to the laboratory) is considered significant and may warrant further monitoring for HDFN.

Notes

1. The selection of the most suitable phenotype of red cells to use when performing titration studies for HDFN is controversial. Some workers select red cells that have the strongest expression of antigen, such as R_2R_2 for anti-D. Others select red cells with the phenotype that would be expected in fetal circulation—ie, red cells that express a single dose of the antigen, such as R_1r for testing for anti-D. Whichever viewpoint is followed, it is important that the laboratory be consistent and use red cells of the same phenotype for future titrations to test the same patient's serum.

2. Titration studies should be performed upon initial detection of the anti-body; save an appropriately labeled aliquot of the serum (frozen at –20 C or colder) for comparative studies with the next submitted sample.

3. When the titer (eg, >16) and the antibody specificity have been associated with HDFN, it is recommended that repeat titration studies be performed every 2 to 4 weeks, beginning at 18 weeks' gestation; save an aliquot of the serum (frozen at –20 C or colder) for comparative studies with the next submitted sample.

4. When invasive procedures (eg, amniocentesis) have demonstrated fetal compromise and are being used to monitor the pregnancy, use the optimal method for follow-up of fetal well-being. However, if initial studies do not show fetal compromise or the Liley curve result is borderline, additional titrations may be helpful as a means of following the pregnancy in a less invasive manner.

5. Each institution should develop a policy to ensure a degree of uniformity in reporting and interpreting antibody titers.

6. For antibodies to low-incidence antigens, consider using putative paternal red cells, having established that they express the antigen in question.

7. Do not use enhancement techniques [albumin, polyethylene glycol, low-ionic-strength saline (LISS)] or enzyme-treated red cells because falsely elevated titers may be obtained. Gel testing is not recommended.

8. LISS should not be used as a diluent in titration studies; nonspecific uptake of globulins may occur in serum-LISS dilutions.

9. Failure to obtain the correct results may be caused by 1) incorrect technique, notably, failure to use sepa-

rate pipette tips for each dilution or 2) failure to adequately mix thawed frozen serum.

References

1. Issitt PD, Anstee DJ. Applied blood group serology. 4th ed. Durham, NC: Montgomery Scientific Publications, 1998:1067-9.
2. Judd WJ, Luban NLC, Ness PM, et al. Prenatal and perinatal immunohematology: Recommendations for serologic management of the fetus, newborn infant, and obstetric patient. Transfusion 1990;30:175-83.
3. Judd WJ. Methods in immunohematology. 2nd ed. Durham, NC: Montgomery Scientific Publications, 1994.
4. Judd WJ. Practice guidelines for prenatal and perinatal immunhematology, revisited. Transfusion 2001;41:1445-52.

Methods Section 6

Blood Collection, Storage, and Component Preparation

Method 6.1. Copper Sulfate Method for Screening Donors for Anemia

Principle

This method estimates the hemoglobin content of blood from its specific gravity. A drop of blood in contact with copper sulfate solution of specific gravity 1.053 becomes encased in a sac of copper proteinate, which prevents dispersion of the fluid or any change in specific gravity for about 15 seconds. If the specific gravity of the blood is higher than that of the solution, the drop will sink within 15 seconds; if not, the drop will hesitate and remain suspended or rise to the top of the solution. A specific gravity of 1.053 corresponds to a hemoglobin concentration of 12.5 g/dL.

This is not a quantitative test; it shows only whether the prospective donor's hemoglobin is below or above the acceptable level of 12.5 g/dL. False-positive reactions

are rare; donors whose drop of blood sinks nearly always have an acceptable hemoglobin level. False-negative reactions occur fairly commonly and can cause inappropriate deferral.[1,2] Measuring hemoglobin by another method or determining hematocrit sometimes reveals that the prospective donor is acceptable.

Reagents and Materials

1.   Copper sulfate solution at specific gravity 1.053, available commercially. Store it in tightly capped containers to prevent evaporation. The solution should be kept at room temperature or brought to room temperature before it is used.
2.   Sterile gauze, antiseptic wipes, and sterile lancets.
3.   Containers for the disposal of sharps and other biohazardous materials.
4.   Capillary tubes and dropper bulbs or a device to collect capillary blood without contact.

Procedure

1. Into a labeled, clean, dry tube or bottle, dispense a sufficient amount (at least 30 mL) of copper sulfate solution to allow the drop to fall approximately 3 inches. Change the solution daily or after 25 tests. Be sure that the solution is adequately mixed before beginning each day's determinations.

2. Clean the site of the skin puncture thoroughly with antiseptic solution and wipe it dry with sterile gauze.

3. Puncture the finger firmly, near the end but slightly to the side, with a sterile, disposable lancet or spring-loaded, disposable needle system. A good free flow of blood is important. Do not squeeze the puncture site repeatedly because this may dilute the drop of blood with tissue fluid and lower the specific gravity.

4. Collect the blood in a capillary tube without allowing air to enter the tube.

5. Let one drop of blood fall gently from the tube at a height about 1 cm above the surface of the copper sulfate solution.

6. Observe for 15 seconds.

7. Dispose of lancets and capillary tubes in appropriate biohazard containers. Dispose of gauze appropriately; gauze contaminated with droplets of blood that subsequently dry such that the item is stained but not soaked or caked may be considered nonhazardous.

Interpretation

1. If the drop of blood sinks, the donor's hemoglobin is at an acceptable level for blood donation.

2. If the drop of blood does not sink, the donor's hemoglobin may not be at an acceptable level for blood donation. If time and equipment permit, it is desirable to perform a quantitative measurement of hemoglobin or hematocrit.

Notes

1. A certificate of analysis from the manufacturer should be obtained with each new lot of copper sulfate solution.

2. Used solution should be disposed of as biohazardous or chemical material because of the blood in the container. Refer to local and state laws regarding disposal.

3. Use care to prevent blood from contaminating work surfaces, the donor's clothing, or other persons or equipment.

4. Cover the container between uses to prevent evaporation.

References

1. Lloyd H, Collins A, Walker W, et al. Volunteer blood donors who fail the copper sulfate screening test: What does failure mean, and what should be done? Transfusion 1988;28: 467-9.

2. Morris MW, Davey FR. Basic examination of blood. In: Henry JB, ed. Clinical diagnosis and management by laboratory methods. 20th ed. Philadelphia: WB Saunders, 2001: 479-519.

Method 6.2. Arm Preparation for Blood Collection

Detailed instructions are specific to each manufacturer and should be followed as indicated. The following procedure is written in general terms as an example.

Principle

Iodophor compounds, or other sterilizing compounds, are used to sterilize the venipuncture site before blood collection.

Materials

1. Scrub solution: Disposable povidone-iodine scrub 0.75% or disposable povidone-iodine swabstick 10%; available in prepackaged single-use form.
2. Preparation solution: 10% povidone-iodine; available in prepackaged single-use form.
3. Sterile gauze.

Procedure

1. Apply tourniquet or blood pressure cuff; identify venipuncture site, then release tourniquet or cuff.
2. Scrub area at least 4 cm (1.5 inches) in all directions from the intended site of venipuncture (ie, 8 cm or 3 inches in diameter) for a minimum of 30 seconds with 0.7% aqueous solution of iodophor compound. Excess foam may be removed, but the arm need not be dry before the next step.
3. Starting at the intended site of venipuncture and moving outward in a concentric spiral, apply "prep" solution; let stand for 30 seconds or as indicated by manufacturer.
4. Cover the area with dry, sterile gauze until the time of venipuncture. After the skin has been prepared, it must not be touched again. Do not repalpate the vein at the intended venipuncture site.

Notes

1. For donors sensitive to iodine (tincture or povidone preparations), another method (eg, ChloraPrep 2%

chlorhexidine and 70% isopropyl alcohol) should be designated by the blood bank physician. Green soap should not be used.
2. For donors sensitive to both iodine and chlorhexidine, a method using only isopropyl alcohol could be considered. The preferred procedure is the use of a 30-second up-and-down scrub, followed by enough time for the skin to dry. A second scrub is then applied. This method may require a variance from the Food and Drug Administration.
3. Arm preparation methods approved by the Food and Drug Administration are available at http://www.fda.gov/cber/infosheets/armprep.htm.

Reference

Goldman M, Roy G, Frechette N, et al. Evaluation of donor skin disinfection methods. Transfusion 1997;37:309-12.

Method 6.3. Phlebotomy and Collection of Samples for Processing and Compatibility Tests

Principle

Blood for transfusion and accompanying samples is obtained from prominent veins on the donor's arm, usually in the area of the antecubital fossa.

Materials

1. Sterile collection bag containing anticoagulant, with integrally attached tubing and needle.
2. Metal clips and hand sealers.
3. Balance system to monitor volume of blood drawn.
4. Sterile gauze and clean instruments (scissors, hemostats, forceps).

5. Test tubes for sample collection.
6. Device for stripping blood in the tubing.
7. Dielectric sealer (optional).

Procedure

1. Ask donor to confirm his or her identification.
2. Ensure that all labeling on blood container, processing tubes, retention segment, and donor records is correct.
3. Prepare donor's arm as described in Method 6.2.
4. Inspect bag for any defects and discoloration. The anticoagulant and additive solutions should be inspected for particulate contaminants.
5. Position bag below the level of the donor's arm.
    a. If a balance system is used, be sure the counterbalance is level and adjusted for the amount of blood to be drawn. Unless metal clips and a hand sealer are used, make a very loose overhand knot in the tubing. Hang the bag and route the tubing through the pinch clamp. A hemostat should be applied to the tubing before the needle is uncapped to prevent air from entering the line.
    b. If a balance system is not used, be sure to monitor the volume of blood drawn.
6. Reapply tourniquet or inflate blood pressure cuff. Ask the donor to open and close hand until previously selected vein is again prominent.
7. Uncover sterile needle and perform the venipuncture immediately. A clean, skillful venipuncture is essential for collection of a full, clot-free unit. Once the bevel has penetrated the skin, palpation of the skin above the needle stem may be performed with a gloved finger, provided the needle is not touched. When the needle position is acceptable, tape the tubing to the donor's arm to hold the needle in place and cover the site with sterile gauze.
8. Release the hemostat. Open the temporary closure between the interior of the bag and the tubing.
9. Ask the donor to open and close hand slowly every 10 to 12 seconds during collection.
10. Keep the donor under observation throughout the donation process. The donor should never be left unattended during or immediately after donation.
11. Mix blood and anticoagulant gently and periodically (approximately every 45 seconds) during collection. Mixing may be done by hand or by continuous mechanical mixing.
12. Be sure blood flow remains fairly brisk, so that coagulation activity is not triggered. If there is continuous, adequate blood flow and constant agitation, rigid time limits are not necessary. However, units requiring more than 15 minutes to draw may not be suitable for preparation of Platelets, Fresh Frozen Plasma, or Cryoprecipitated AHF. The time required for collection can be monitored by indicating the time of phlebotomy or the maximal allowable time (start time plus 15 minutes) on the donor record.
13. Monitor volume of blood being drawn. If a balance is used, the device will interrupt blood flow after the proper amount has been collected. One mL of blood weighs at least 1.053 g, indicated by the minimum allowable specific gravity for donors. A conve-

nient figure to use is 1.06 g/mL; a unit containing 405 to 550 mL should weigh 429 to 583 g plus the weight of the container and anticoagulant. For a 500-mL bag, this is 565 to 671 g.

14. Clamp the tubing near the venipuncture using a hemostat, metal clip, or other temporary clamp. Release the blood pressure cuff/tourniquet to 20 mm Hg or less and fill the tube(s) for blood processing sample(s) by a method that prevents contamination of the contents of the bag. This can be done in several ways.

   a. If the blood collection bag contains an inline needle, make an additional seal with a hemostat, metal clip, hand sealer, or a tight knot made from previously prepared loose knot just distal to the inline needle. Open the connector by separating the needles. Insert the proximal needle into a processing test tube, remove the hemostat, allow the tube to fill, and reclamp the tubing. The donor needle is now ready for removal.

   b. If the blood collection bag contains an inline processing tube, be certain that the processing tube, or pouch, is full when the collection is complete and the original clamp is placed near the donor needle. The entire assembly may now be removed from the donor.

   c. If a straight-tubing assembly set is used, the following procedure should be followed. Place a hemostat on the tubing, allowing about four segments between the hemostat and the needle. Pull tight the loose overhand knot made in step 3. Release the hemostat and strip

a segment of the tubing free of blood between the knot and the needle (about 1 inch in length). Reapply the hemostat and cut the tubing in the stripped area between the knot and the hemostat. Fill the required tube(s) by releasing the hemostat and then reclamp the tubing with the hemostat. Because this system is open, Biosafety Level 2 precautions should be followed.

15. Deflate the cuff and remove the tourniquet. Remove the needle from the donor's arm, if not already removed. Apply pressure over the gauze and ask the donor to raise his or her arm (elbow straight) and hold the gauze firmly over the phlebotomy site with the other hand.

16. Discard the needle assembly into a biohazard container designed to prevent accidental injury to, and contamination of, personnel.

17. Strip donor tubing as completely as possible into the bag, starting at the seal. Work quickly, to prevent the blood from clotting in the tubing. Invert the bag several times to mix the contents thoroughly; then allow the tubing to refill with anticoagulated blood from the bag. Repeat this procedure a second time.

18. Seal the tubing attached to the collection bag into segments, leaving a segment number clearly and completely readable. Attach a unit identification number to one segment to be stored as a retention segment. Knots, metal clips, or a dielectric sealer may be used to make segments suitable for compatibility testing. It must be possible to separate segments from the unit without breaking sterility of the bag. If a di-

electric sealer is used, the knot or clip should be removed from the distal end of the tubing after creating a hermetic seal.

19. Reinspect the container for defects.

20. Recheck numbers on the container, processing tubes, donation record, and retention segment.

21. Place blood at appropriate temperature. Unless platelets are to be removed, whole blood should be placed at 1 to 6 C immediately after collection. If platelets are to be prepared, blood should not be chilled but should be stored in a manner intended to reach a temperature of 20 to 24 C until platelets are separated. Platelets must be separated within 8 hours after collection of the unit of Whole Blood.

Notes

1. If the needle is withdrawn and venipuncture is attempted again, preparation of the site must be repeated as in Method 6.2.

2. In addition to routine blood donor phlebotomy, this procedure may be adapted for use in therapeutic phlebotomy.

References

1. Silva MA, ed. Standards for blood banks and transfusion services. 23rd ed. Bethesda, MD: AABB, 2005.

2. Smith LG. Blood collection. In: Green TS, Steckler D, eds. Donor room policies and procedures. Arlington, VA: AABB, 1985:25-45.

3. Huh YO, Lightiger B, Giacco GG, et al. Effect of donation time on platelet concentrates and fresh frozen plasma. Vox Sang 1989;56: 21-4.

4. Sataro P. Blood collection. In: Kasprisin CA, Laird-Fryer B, eds. Blood donor collection practices. Bethesda, MD: AABB, 1993:89-103.

Method 6.4. Preparation of Red Blood Cells

Principle

Red Blood Cells (RBCs) are obtained by removal of supernatant plasma from centrifuged Whole Blood. The volume of plasma removed determines the hematocrit of the component. When RBCs are preserved in CPDA-1, maximal viability during storage requires an appropriate ratio of cells to preservative. A hematocrit of 80% or lower ensures the presence of adequate glucose for red cell metabolism for up to 35 days of storage.

Materials

1. Freshly collected Whole Blood, obtained by phlebotomy as described in Method 6.3. Collect blood in a collection unit with integrally attached transfer container(s).

2. Plasma extractor.

3. Metal clips and hand sealer.

4. Clean instruments (scissors, hemostats).

5. Dielectric sealer (optional).

6. Refrigerated centrifuge.

7. Scale.

Procedure

1. Centrifuge whole blood using a "heavy" spin (see Method 7.4), with a temperature setting of 4 C.

2. Place the primary bag containing centrifuged blood on a plasma expressor, and release the spring, allowing the plate of the expressor to contact the bag.

3. Temporarily clamp the tubing between the primary and satellite bags with a hemostat or, if a mechanical

sealer will not be used, make a loose overhand knot in the tubing.

4. If two or more satellite bags are attached, apply the hemostat to allow plasma to flow into only one of the satellite bags. Penetrate the closure of the primary bag. A scale, such as a dietary scale, may be used to measure the expressed plasma. Remove the appropriate amount of plasma to obtain the desired hematocrit.

5. Reapply the hemostat when the desired amount of supernatant plasma has entered the satellite bag. Seal the tubing between the primary bag and the satellite bag in two places.

6. Check that the satellite bag has the same donor number as that on the primary bag and cut the tubing between the two seals.

Notes

1. If blood was collected in a single bag, modify the above directions as follows: after placing the bag on the expressor, apply a hemostat to the tubing of a sterile transfer bag, aseptically insert the cannula of the transfer bag into the outlet port of the bag of blood, release the hemostat, and continue as outlined above. The expiration date will change, however.

2. Collection of blood in an additive solution allows removal of a greater volume of plasma in step 4. After the plasma has been removed, the additive solution is allowed to flow from the attached satellite bag into the red cells. This will result in a hematocrit of 55% to 65%. Be sure that an appropriate label and dating period are used.

3. The removal of 230 to 256 g (225 to 250 mL) of plasma and preservation

Table 6.4-1. Removing Plasma from Units of Whole Blood (To Prepare RBCs in Anticoagulant-Preservative with a Known Hematocrit)

Hematocrit of Segment from Whole Blood Unit	Volume of Plasma to Be Removed	Final Hematocrit of Red Blood Cell Unit
40%	150 mL	56%
39%	150 mL	55%
38%	160 mL	55%
37%	165 mL	54%
36%	170 mL	54%
35%	180 mL	54%
34%	195 mL	55%
33%	200 mL	55%

of the red cells in the anticoagulant-preservative solution will generally result in a red cell component with a hematocrit between 70% and 80%.

4. See Table 6.4-1 to prepare Red Blood Cells with a specific (desired) hematocrit.

Method 6.5. Preparation of Prestorage Red Blood Cells Leukocytes Reduced

Principle

The general principle and materials of Method 6.4 apply, except that the red cells are filtered using a special leukocyte reduction filter. All red cell leukocyte reduction filters licensed in the United States remove platelets to some degree. Anticoagulated whole blood may be filtered, from which only platelet-poor plasma (leukocyte reduced) and red cells may be made. Alternatively, the red cells may be filtered in additive solution, potentially allowing the preparation of platelets, plasma, and red cells. Nonleukocyte-reduced red cells may also undergo leukocyte reduction after preparation by attaching a leukocyte reduction filter connected to a storage container using a sterile connection device.

Procedure

1. Before centrifugation, the anticoagulated Whole Blood may be filtered by hanging the container upside down and allowing the blood to flow through an in-line filter by gravity into a secondary container. The steps in Method 6.4 are then followed (see note 2, for addition of additive solution).

2. The anticoagulated Whole Blood may be centrifuged with the in-line filter attached. After centrifugation, the plasma is expressed. The additive solution is added, and the red cells in the additive solution are filtered by gravity, as in step 1 above.

3. A red cell component prepared using Method 6.4 either in residual anticoagulated plasma or in additive solution (AS-1, AS-3, AS-5) may have a secondary container with an in-line filter attached using a sterile connection device. Filtration can proceed according to the manufacturer's directions using gravity, as in step 1. The timing of this filtration is often within 24 hours of collection but can be up to 5 days.

4. Red cells that are leukocyte reduced are labeled "Red Blood Cells Leukocytes Reduced." There is no specific label for prestorage leukocyte reduction.

Notes

1. If the collection system does not include an in-line filter, a sterile connection device can be used to attach a leukocyte reduction filter to the collection system. The filter should be used according to the manufacturer's directions.

2. Whole-blood-derived platelets can be manufactured only before leukocyte reduction (see Method 6.14).

Method 6.6. Rejuvenation of Red Blood Cells

Principle

Rejuvenation is a process to restore depleted metabolites and improve the function and posttransfusion survival of stored red cells. The rejuvenating solution is not intended for intravenous administration; after warm incubation with the solution, the red cells are washed and either glycerolized for frozen storage or kept at 1 to 6 C for transfusion within 24 hours.

The rejuvenating solution approved by the Food and Drug Administration contains pyruvate, inosine, phosphate, and adenine. Its use is permitted only with RBCs prepared from Whole Blood collected into CPD, CP2D, or CPDA-1, and it may be added at any time between 3 days after collection of the blood and 3 days after the expiration of the unit. However, the use of the rejuvenation solution with RBC units before 14 days of storage is not routinely accepted because the treated cells may develop supranormal levels of 2,3-diphosphoglycerate, which impairs oxygen uptake.

Reagents and Materials

1. RBCs stored at 1 to 6 C and prepared from Whole Blood collected in CPD or CPDA-1. After collection, RBCs

suspended in CPD from day 3 to day 24 (or in CPDA-1 from day 3 to day 38) may be used. The solution is not approved for use with cells stored in additive solutions.

2. Red Blood Cell rejuvenation solution, in 50-mL sterile vial (Rejuvesol, Cytosol Laboratories, Braintree, MA); also called rejuvenating solution.

3. Waterproof plastic bag.

4. Metal clips and hand sealer.

5. Sterile airway.

Procedure

1. Connect the container of rejuvenating solution to the RBCs, using a transfer set and aseptic technique.

2. Allow 50 mL of rejuvenating solution to flow by gravity into the container of red cells. Gently agitate the cell/ solution mixture during this addition. Note: A sterile airway is required if the solution is in a bottle.

3. Seal the tubing near the blood bag and incubate the mixture for 1 hour at 37 C. Either a dry incubator or circulating waterbath can be used. If placed in a waterbath, the container should be completely immersed; use of a waterproof overwrap is essential to prevent contamination.

4. For use within 24 hours, wash the rejuvenated cells with saline (2 L unbuffered 0.9% NaCl) by the use of an approved protocol. Storage of the washed cells from the start of the wash procedure should be at 1 to 6 C for no longer than 24 hours.

5. If the rejuvenated cells are to be cryopreserved, the standard glycerolization protocol adequately removes the rejuvenation solution from the processed cells. Expiration date remains 10 years from the date of collection.

6. Be sure that units are appropriately labeled and that all applicable records are complete.

Reference

Valeri CR, Zaroules CG. Rejuvenation and freezing of outdated stored human red cells. N Engl J Med 1972;287:1307-13.

Method 6.7. Red Cell Cryopreservation Using High-Concentration Glycerol—Meryman Method

Principle

Cryoprotective agents make possible the long-term (10 or more years) preservation of red cells in the frozen state. High-concentration glycerol is particularly suitable for this purpose. A practical method for RBCs collected in a 450-mL bag is described below.

Materials

(See Chapter 8 for additional information on frozen cellular components.)

1. Donor blood, collected into CPD, CD2D, CPDA-1, or AS.
   a. Complete all blood processing on units intended for freezing.
   b. RBCs preserved in CPD or CPDA-1 may be stored at 1 to 6 C for up to 6 days before freezing.
   c. RBCs preserved in AS-1 and AS-3 may be stored at 1 to 6 C for up to 42 days before freezing.
   d. RBCs that have undergone rejuvenation (see Method 6.6) may be processed for freezing up to 3 days after their original expiration.
   e. RBCs in any preservative solution that have been entered for

processing must be frozen within 24 hours of puncturing the seal.

2. Storage containers, either polyvinyl chloride or polyolefin bags.

3. 6.2 M of glycerol lactate solution (400 mL).

4. Cardboard or metal canisters for freezing.

5. Hypertonic (12%) sodium chloride solution.

6. 1.6% NaCl, 1 liter for batch wash.

7. Isotonic (0.9%) NaCl with 0.2% dextrose solution.

8. 37 C waterbath or 37 C dry warmer.

9. Equipment for batch or continuous-flow washing, to deglycerolize cells frozen in high-concentration glycerol.

10. Freezer tape.

11. Freezer (–65 C or colder).

Procedure

Preparing RBCs for Glycerolization

1. Prepare RBCs from Whole Blood units by removal of supernatant anticoagulant-preservative or additive solution. Weigh the RBC unit to be frozen and obtain the net weight of the RBCs. The *combined weight* of the cells and the collection bag should be between 260 g and 400 g.

2. Underweight units can be adjusted to approximately 300 g either by the addition of 0.9% NaCl or by the removal of less plasma than usual. Record the weight and, if applicable, document the amount of NaCl added.

3. Record the Whole Blood number, ABO group and Rh type, anticoagulant, date of collection, date frozen, expiration time, and the identification of the person performing the

procedure. If applicable, document the lot number of the transfer bag.

4. Warm the red cells and the glycerol to at least 25 C by placing them in a dry warming chamber for 10 to 15 minutes or by allowing them to remain at room temperature for 1 to 2 hours. The temperature must not exceed 42 C.

5. Apply a "Red Blood Cells Frozen" label to the freezing bag in which the unit will be frozen. The label must also include: name of the facility freezing the unit; Whole Blood number; ABO group and Rh type; date collected; date frozen; the cryoprotective agent used; and the expiration date.

Glycerolization

1. Document the lot numbers of the glycerol, the freezing bags, and, if used, the 0.9% NaCl.

2. Place the container of red cells on a shaker and add approximately 100 mL of glycerol as the red cells are gently agitated.

3. Turn off the shaker and allow the cells to equilibrate, without agitation, for 5 to 30 minutes.

4. Allow the partially glycerolized cells to flow by gravity into the freezing bag.

5. Add the remaining 300 mL of glycerol slowly in a stepwise fashion, with gentle mixing. Add smaller volumes of glycerol for smaller volumes of red cells. The final glycerol concentration is 40% w/v. Remove any air from the bag.

6. Allow some glycerolized cells to flow back into the tubing so that segments can be prepared.

7. Maintain the glycerolized cells at temperatures between 25 and 32 C until freezing. The recommended in-

terval between removing the RBC unit from refrigeration and placing the glycerolized cells in the freezer should not exceed *4 hours.*

Freezing and Storage

1. Place the glycerolized unit in a cardboard or metal canister and place it in a freezer at –65 C or colder.
2. Label the top edge of the canister with freezer tape marked with the Whole Blood number, ABO group and Rh type, the date frozen, and the expiration date.
3. Do not bump or handle the frozen cells roughly.
4. The freezing rate should be less than 10 mL/minute.
5. Store the frozen RBCs at –65 C or colder for up to 10 years. For blood of rare phenotypes, a facility's medical director may wish to extend the storage period. The unusual nature of such units and the reason for retaining them past the routine 10-year storage period must be documented.

Thawing and Deglycerolizing

1. Put an overwrap on the protective canister containing the frozen cells and place it in either a 37 C waterbath or 37 C dry warmer.
2. Agitate it gently to speed thawing. The thawing process takes at least 10 minutes. Thawed cells should be at 37 C.
3. After the cells have thawed, use a commercial instrument for batch or continuous-flow washing to deglycerolize cells. Follow the manufacturer's instructions.
4. Record the lot numbers and manufacturer of all the solutions and software used. Apply a "Red Blood Cells Deglycerolized" label to the transfer pack and be sure that the label includes identification of the collecting facility, the facility preparing the deglycerolized cells, the ABO group and Rh type of the cells, the Whole Blood number, and the expiration date and time.
5. Dilute the unit with a quantity of hypertonic (12%) NaCl solution appropriate for the size of the unit. Allow it to equilibrate for approximately 5 minutes.
6. Wash the cells with 1.6% NaCl until deglycerolization is complete. Approximately 2 liters of wash solution are required. To check for residual glycerol, see Method 6.8.
7. Suspend the deglycerolized cells in isotonic (0.9%) saline with 0.2% dextrose.
8. Fill the integrally attached tubing with an aliquot of cells sealed in such a manner that it will be available for subsequent compatibility testing.
9. Deglycerolized RBCs must be stored at 1 to 6 C for no longer than 24 hours. (A closed system has been licensed that allows storage of deglycerolized RBCs at 1 to 6 C for 2 weeks.)

Notes

1. An aliquot of the donor's serum or plasma should be frozen and stored at –65 C or colder for possible future use if new diagnostic tests are implemented.
2. When new diagnostic tests have been implemented and stored units do not have aliquots available for testing, the units may have to be issued with a label stating that the test has not been performed. The reason for distributing an untested compo-

nent should be documented. If a specimen from the donor is obtained and tested after the unit was stored, the date of testing should be noted on the unit when it is issued.

Reference

Meryman HT, Hornblower M. A method for freezing and washing RBCs using a high glycerol concentration. Transfusion 1972;12:145-56.

Method 6.8. Red Cell Cryopreservation Using High-Concentration Glycerol—Valeri Method

Principle

RBCs collected in an 800-mL primary collection bag in CPDA-1 and stored at 1 to 6 C for 3 to 38 days can be biochemically rejuvenated and frozen with 40% w/v glycerol in the 800-mL primary container. See Method 6.6 for additional information.

Materials

1. Quadruple plastic bag collection system with 800-mL primary bag.
2. Hand sealer clips.
3. Empty 600-mL polyethylene cryogenic vials (eg, Corning 25702 or Fisher 033746).
4. Sterile connection device with wafers.
5. Freezer tape.
6. 600-mL transfer bag.
7. 50 mL of Red Blood Cell Processing Solution (Rejuvesol, Cytosol Laboratories, Braintree, MA).
8. Heat-sealable 8" × 12" plastic bags.
9. Rejuvenation harness (Fenwal 4C1921 or Cutter 98052).

10. Sterile filtered airway needle (BD 5200), for Fenwal rejuvenation harness only.
11. 500 mL of glycerolyte 57 solution (Fenwal 4A7833) or 500 mL of 6.2 M glycerolization solution (Cytosol PN5500).
12. Labels—Red Blood Cells Frozen Rejuvenated.
13. Corrugated cardboard storage box (7" × 5.5" × 2" outside dimensions).
14. Heat sealing device.
15. Plastic bag for overwrapping.

Procedure

Preparing RBCs for Glycerolization

1. Collect 450 mL of Whole Blood in the primary bag. Invert the bag, fold it about 2 inches from the base, secure the fold with tape, and place the bag upright in a centrifuge. Centrifuge and remove all visible supernatant plasma. The hematocrit of the RBC unit must be 75% ± 5%.
2. Store RBCs at 1 to 6 C in the 800-mL primary bag, along with the adapter port on the tubing that connects the primary bag and transfer pack.
3. Centrifuge the stored cells to remove all visible plasma before undertaking rejuvenation. The gross and net weights of the RBCs should not exceed 352 g and 280 g, respectively.
4. Transfer the plasma to the integrally connected transfer pack, fold the integral tubing, and replace the hand sealer clip (not crimped).
5. Attach an empty 600-mL transfer pack to the integral tubing of the primary collection bag, using a sterile connection device.
6. Transfer 1 mL of plasma to each of three cryogenic vials to be used for future testing.

Biochemical Modification of the Cells

1. Using the Fenwal Rejuvenation Harness: Aseptically insert the needle of the Y-type Fenwal Harness into the rubber stopper of a 50-mL Red Blood Cell Processing Solution bottle and the coupler of the set into the adapter port of the primary collection bag. Insert the filtered airway needle into the rubber stopper of the Red Blood Cell Processing Solution bottle.

2. Using the Cutter Rejuvenation Harness: Aseptically insert the *vented white spike with the drip chamber* into the rubber stopper of the Red Blood Cell Processing Solution bottle and the *nonvented spike* into the special adapter port on the primary collection bag.

3. With gentle manual agitation, allow 50 mL of Red Blood Cell Processing Solution to flow directly into the red cells.

4. Heat-seal the tubing of the harness set that connects the Red Blood Cell Processing Solution to the adapter port. The second tubing of the harness Y-set is used to add glycerol (see below).

5. Completely overwrap the 800-mL primary bag, the integrally connected empty transfer pack, and the coupler of the Y-type harness and incubate them in a 37 C waterbath for 1 hour.

Glycerolization

1. Remove the numbered crossmatch segments, leaving the initial segment and number attached to the collection bag. Weigh the unit.

2. Determine the amount of glycerol to be added, based on the gross or net weight of the unit, from the values shown in Table 6.8-1.

3. Aseptically insert the coupler of the rejuvenation harness into the outlet port of the rubber stopper on the glycerol solution bottle. For the Fenwal harness only, insert a filtered airway needle into the vent portion of the glycerol bottle stopper.

4. Place the bag on a shaker. Add the amount of glycerol shown in Table 6.8-1 for the first volume while the bag is shaking at low speed (180 oscillations/minute).

5. Equilibrate the mixture for 5 minutes without shaking and add the second volume. Equilibrate it for 2 minutes. Add the third volume of glycerol, using vigorous manual shaking.

Table 6.8-1. Amount of Glycerol Needed for Different Weights of Red Cell Units

Gross Weight of Unit (grams)*	Net Weight of Unit (grams)	Initial Addition of Glycerol (mL)	Second Addition of Glycerol (mL)	Third Addition of Glycerol (mL)	Total Glycerol Added (mL)
222-272	150-200	50	50	250	350
273-312	201-240	50	50	350	450
313-402	241-330	50	50	400	500

*Weight of the empty 800-mL primary bag with the integrally attached transfer pack and the adapter port is 72 grams (average).

6. Heat-seal the tubing between the empty bottle of glycerol and the tubing proximal to the adapter port. Ensure that the transfer pack remains integrally attached to the primary collection bag.

7. Centrifuge the mixture of red cells and glycerol *and transfer all visible supernatant glycerol to the transfer pack, resuspend, and mix. Note: This step differs from Method 6.7.*

8. Seal the tubing 4" from the primary collection bag, detach the transfer pack containing the supernatant fluid, and discard it.

9. Affix an overlay blood component label, the facility label, and an ABO/Rh label. Record the expiration date on the label.

10. Weigh the unit just before freezing and record the weight.

11. Fold over the top portion of the primary bag (approximately 2"). Place the primary bag into a plastic bag overwrap and heat-seal the outer bag across the top so that there is as little air as possible between the bags.

12. Place one vial of plasma and the plastic bag containing the glycerolized red cells in the cardboard box. Store the other two vials, suitably identified, at –65 C or colder for future testing, if needed.

13. Affix a "Red Blood Cells Frozen Rejuvenated" label, an ABO/Rh label, a facility label, and the original unit number on the outside of the box. Record separately or affix on the cardboard box the collection, freezing, and expiration dates.

14. Freeze the unit in a –80 C freezer. No more than 4 hours should be allowed to elapse between the time the unit was removed from the 4 C refrigerator and the time the cells are placed in the –80 C freezer.

Thawing and Deglycerolization

See Method 6.7. Note, however, that the supernatant glycerol is removed before freezing. Therefore, only two salt solutions (the hypertonic 12% saline and the 0.9% saline-0.2% dextrose solution) are used in the deglycerolization process.

References

1. Rejuvesol Package insert. Braîntree, MA: Cytosol Laboratories, 2002.
2. Valeri CR, Ragno G, Pivacek LE, et al. A multicenter study of in vitro and in vivo values in human RBCs frozen with 40% (wt/vol) glycerol and stored after deglycerolization for 15 days at 4 C in AS-3: Assessment of RBC processing in the ACP 215. Transfusion 2001; 41:933-9.

Method 6.9. Checking the Adequacy of Deglycerolization of Red Blood Cells

Principle

Glycerolization of red cells for frozen storage creates a hyperosmolar intracellular fluid, which must be restored to physiologically compatible levels before the cells are transfused. Inadequately deglycerolized red cells will be hemolyzed by contact with normal saline, or with serum or plasma if subjected to crossmatching. During deglycerolization, the last solution in contact with the cells is normal saline. The easiest way to determine adequacy of glycerol removal is to determine the level of free hemoglobin (mg/dL) in the final wash. An adequate estimate of hemolysis can be achieved by comparing the color of the final wash fluid with the blocks in a commercially available color comparator. Alternatively, normal saline can be added to an aliquot of deglycerolized cells and the color of the supernatant fluid evaluated against the color comparator.

Materials and Equipment

1. Semiautomated instrument for deglycerolizing cryopreserved RBCs.
2. Transparent tubing, as part of disposable material used to deglycerolize individual unit.
3. Color comparator, available commercially.

Procedure

1. Interrupt the last wash cycle at a point when wash fluid is visible in the tubing leading to the disposal bag.
2. Hold the comparator block next to an accessible segment of tubing, against a well-lighted white background.
3. Note coloration of the wash fluid, which should be no stronger than the block, indicating 3% hemolysis (3% of the red cells are hemolyzed).
4. If the level of hemolysis is excessive, continue the wash process until the color is within acceptable limits.
5. Record observation for the individual unit and for the quality assurance program.
6. If unacceptable hemolysis occurs repeatedly, document corrective action.

Method 6.10. Preparation of Fresh Frozen Plasma from Whole Blood

Principle

Plasma is separated from cellular blood elements and frozen to preserve the activity of labile coagulation factors. Plasma must be placed in the freezer within the time frame required for the anticoagulant or collection process.

Materials

1. Freshly collected Whole Blood, obtained by phlebotomy as described in Method 6.3, in a collection unit with integrally attached transfer container(s).
2. Metal clips and hand sealer.
3. Clean instruments (scissors, hemostats).
4. Dielectric sealer (optional).
5. Plasma extractor.
6. Freezing apparatus.
7. Refrigerated centrifuge.
8. Scale.

Procedure

1. Centrifuge blood soon after collection, using a "heavy" spin (see Method 7.4). Use a refrigerated centrifuge at 1 to 6 C unless also preparing platelets (see Method 6.13).
2. Place the primary bag containing centrifuged blood on a plasma extractor and place the attached satellite bag on a scale adjusted to zero. Express the plasma into the satellite bag and weigh the plasma.
3. Seal the transfer tubing with a dielectric sealer or metal clips but do not obliterate the segment numbers of the tubing. Place another seal nearer the transfer bag.
4. Label the transfer bag with the unit number before it is separated from the original container. Record the volume of plasma on the label.
5. Cut the tubing between the two seals. The tubing may be coiled and taped against the plasma container, leaving the segments available for any testing desired.

6. Place the plasma at –18 C or colder within the time frame required for the anticoagulant or collection process.

Method 6.11. Preparation of Cryoprecipitated AHF from Whole Blood

Principle

Coagulation Factor VIII (antihemophilic factor, AHF) can be concentrated from freshly collected plasma by cryoprecipitation. Cryoprecipitation is accomplished by slow thawing, at 1 to 6 C, plasma that has been prepared for freezing within the time frame required for the anticoagulant or collection process.

Materials

1. Freshly collected Whole Blood, obtained by phlebotomy as described in Method 6.3, in a collection unit with at least two integrally attached transfer containers.
2. Metal clips and hand sealer.
3. Clean instruments (scissors, hemostats).
4. Dielectric sealer (optional).
5. Plasma extractor.
6. Refrigerated centrifuge.
7. Freezing apparatus: suitable freezing devices include blast freezers or mechanical freezers capable of maintaining temperatures of –18 C or colder; dry ice; or an ethanol dry ice bath. In a bath of 95% ethanol and chipped dry ice, freezing will be complete in about 15 minutes.
8. 1 to 6 C circulating waterbath or refrigerator.
9. Scale.

Procedure

1. Collect blood in a collection unit with two integrally attached transfer containers.
2. Centrifuge blood shortly after collection at 1 to 6 C, using a "heavy" spin (see Method 7.4). Collect at least 200 mL (205 g) of cell-free plasma for processing into cryoprecipitate.
3. Promptly place plasma in a freezing device so that freezing is started within the time frame required for the anticoagulant or collection process. Plasma containers immersed in liquid must be protected with a plastic overwrap.
4. Allow the frozen plasma to thaw at 1 to 6 C by placing the bag in a 1 to 6 C circulating waterbath or in a refrigerator. If thawed in a waterbath, use a plastic overwrap (or other means) to keep container ports dry.
5. When the plasma has a slushy consistency, separate liquid plasma from the cryoprecipitate by one of the procedures below:
   a. Centrifuge the plasma at 1 to 6 C using a "heavy" spin. Hang the bag in an inverted position and allow the separated plasma to flow rapidly into the transfer bag, leaving the cryoprecipitate adhering to the sides of the primary bag. Separate the cryoprecipitate from the plasma promptly, to prevent the cryoprecipitate from dissolving and flowing out of the bag. Ten to 15 mL of supernatant plasma may be left in the bag for resuspension of the cryoprecipitate after thawing. Refreeze the cryoprecipitate immediately.
   b. Place the thawing plasma in a plasma expressor when appro-

ximately one-tenth of the contents is still frozen. With the bag in an upright position, allow the supernatant plasma to flow slowly into the transfer bag, using the ice crystals at the top as a filter. The cryoprecipitate paste will adhere to the sides of the bag or to the ice. Seal the bag when about 90% of the cryoprecipitate-reduced plasma has been removed and refreeze the cryoprecipitate immediately.

6. The cryoprecipitate should be refrozen within 1 hour of thawing. Store at –18 C or colder, preferably –30 C or colder, for up to 12 months from the date of blood collection.

Note

Cryoprecipitated AHF may be prepared from Fresh Frozen Plasma at any time within 12 months of collection. The expiration date of Cryoprecipitated AHF is 12 months from the date of phlebotomy, not from the date it was prepared.

Method 6.12. Thawing and Pooling Cryoprecipitated AHF

Principle

Cryoprecipitated AHF should be rapidly thawed at 30 to 37 C but should not remain at this temperature once thawing is complete. The following method permits rapid thawing and pooling of this product.

Materials

1. Circulating waterbath at 37 C (waterbaths designed for thawing plasma

are available commercially, as are specially designed dry heat devices).

2. Medication injection ports.
3. Sterile 0.9% sodium chloride for injection.
4. Syringes and needles.

Procedure

1. Cover the container with a plastic overwrap to prevent contamination of the ports with unsterile water, or use a device to keep the containers upright with the ports above water.
2. Resuspend the thawed precipitate carefully and completely, either by kneading it into the residual 10 to 15 mL of plasma or by adding approximately 10 mL of 0.9% sodium chloride and gently resuspending.
3. Pool by inserting a medication injection site into a port of each bag. Aspirate contents of one bag into a syringe and inject into the next bag. Use the ever-increasing volume to flush each subsequent bag of as much dissolved cryoprecipitate as possible, until all contents are in the final bag.
4. Thawed Cryoprecipitated AHF must be stored at room temperature. If pooled, it must be administered within 4 hours. Thawed single units, if not entered, must be administered within 6 hours of thawing if intended for replacement of Factor VIII. Pools of thawed individual units may not be refrozen.

Method 6.13. Preparation of Platelets from Whole Blood

Principle

Platelet-rich plasma is separated from Whole Blood by "light-spin" centrifugation and the platelets are concentrated by "heavy-spin" centrifugation, with subsequent removal of supernatant plasma (see Method 7.4).

Materials

1. Freshly collected Whole Blood, obtained by phlebotomy as described in Method 6.3, in a collection unit with two integrally attached transfer containers. The final container must be a plastic approved for platelet storage. Keep blood at room temperature (20 to 24 C) before separating platelet-rich plasma from the red cells. This separation must take place within 8 hours of phlebotomy.
2. Metal clips and hand sealer.
3. Scissors, hemostats.
4. Plasma extractor.
5. Dielectric sealer (optional).
6. Centrifuge, calibrated as in Method 7.4.
7. Scale.
8. Rotator.

Procedure

1. Do not chill the blood at any time before or during platelet separation. If the temperature of the centrifuge is 1 to 6 C, set the temperature control of the refrigerated centrifuge at 20 C and allow the temperature to rise to approximately 20 C. Centrifuge the blood using a "light" spin (see Method 7.4).
2. Express the platelet-rich plasma into the transfer bag intended for platelet storage. Seal the tubing twice between the primary bag and Y connector of the two satellite bags and cut between the two seals. Place the red cells at 1 to 6 C.
3. Centrifuge the platelet-rich plasma at 20 C using a "heavy" spin (see Method 7.4).

4. Express the platelet-poor plasma into the second transfer bag and seal the tubing. Some plasma should remain on the platelet button for storage, but no exact volume can be designated. AABB *Standards for Blood Banks and Transfusion Services* requires that sufficient plasma remain with the platelet concentrate to maintain the pH at 6.2 or higher for the entire storage period. This usually requires a minimum of 35 mL of plasma when storage is at 20 to 24 C, but 50 to 70 mL is preferable.
5. The platelet concentrate container should be left stationary, with the label side down, at room temperature for approximately 1 hour.
6. Resuspend the platelets in either of the following ways:
    a. Manipulate the platelet container gently by hand to achieve uniform resuspension.
    b. Place the container on a rotator at room temperature. The slow, gentle agitation should achieve uniform resuspension within 2 hours.
7. Maintain the platelet suspensions at 20 to 24 C with continuous gentle agitation.
8. Platelets should be inspected before issue to ensure that no platelet aggregates are visible.

Notes

The platelet-reduced plasma may be frozen promptly and stored as Fresh Frozen Plasma (FFP), if the separation and freezing are completed within the time frame required for the anticoagulant or collection process. The volume of FFP prepared after platelet preparation will be substantially less than that prepared directly from Whole Blood.

Reference

Silva MA, ed. Standards for blood banks and transfusion services. 23rd ed. Bethesda, MD: AABB, 2005:30.

Method 6.14. Preparation of Prestorage Platelets Leukocytes Reduced from Whole Blood

Principle

Prestorage leukocyte-reduced platelets may be prepared from whole blood using in-line filtration of the platelet-rich plasma (PRP). The resulting intermediate product is a filtered PRP, from which a leukocyte-reduced platelet concentrate and leukocyte-reduced plasma may be manufactured. Materials and procedures are the same as for Method 6.13, except that the PRP is expressed through an in-line filter.

References

1. Sweeney JD, Holme S, Heaton WAL, Nelson E. Leukodepleted platelet concentrates prepared by in-line filtration of platelet rich plasma. Transfusion 1995;35:131-6.
2. Sweeney JD, Kouttab N, Penn LC, et al. A comparison of prestorage leukoreduced whole blood derived platelets with bedside filtered whole blood derived platelets in autologous stem cell transplant. Transfusion 2000;40:794-800.

Method 6.15. Removing Plasma from Platelet Concentrates (Volume Reduction)

Principle

Although optimal storage of platelets requires an adequate volume of plasma, a few patients may not tolerate large-volume infusion. Stored platelets may be centrifuged and much of the plasma removed shortly before transfusion, but appropriate resuspension is essential. The platelets must remain at room temperature, without agitation, for 20 to 60 minutes before resuspension into the remaining plasma. Transfusion must take place within 4 hours of the time the platelet bag was entered. Volume reduction can be performed on individual or pooled units.

No consensus exists regarding the optimal centrifugation rate. One study[1] found 35% to 55% platelet loss in several units centrifuged at 500 × g for 6 minutes, compared with 5% to 20% loss in units centrifuged at 5000 × g for 6 minutes or 2000 × g for 10 minutes. The authors recommend 2000 × g for 10 minutes, to avoid any risk that a higher centrifugal force might inflict on the plastic container. A study by Moroff et al[2] found mean platelet loss to be less than 15% in 42 units centrifuged at 580 × g for 20 minutes. High g forces are of theoretical concern because they may damage the platelets when they are forced against the wall of the container and also increase the possibility of container breakage.

Materials

1. Platelet concentrate(s), prepared as described in Method 6.13.
2. Metal clips and hand sealer.
3. Scissors, hemostats.
4. Dielectric sealer (optional).
5. Centrifuge, calibrated as in Method 7.4.
6. Plasma extractor.

Procedure

1. Pool platelets, if desired, into a transfer pack, using standard technique. Single platelet concentrates may need volume reduction for pediatric

recipients. Apheresis components may be processed directly.

2. Centrifuge at 20 to 24 C, using one of the following protocols:
   a. $580 \times g$ for 20 minutes.
   b. $2000 \times g$ for 10 minutes.
   c. $5000 \times g$ for 6 minutes.

3. Without disturbing the contents, transfer the bag to a plasma extractor. Remove all but 10 to 15 mL plasma from single units, or somewhat more volume, proportionately, from a pool or from a component prepared by apheresis.

4. Mark expiration time on bag as 4 hours after the time the unit was entered.

5. Leave bag at 20 to 24 C without agitation for 20 minutes if centrifuged at $580 \times g$, or for 1 hour if centrifuged at 2000 or $5000 \times g$.

6. Resuspend platelets as described in Method 6.13.

Notes

1. If a sterile connection device is used for removing plasma from a hema-

pheresis component or individual platelet concentrate, the unit can be considered sterile and it is not necessary to impose the 4-hour expiration interval required for entered Platelets. However, no data exist to support storage of reduced volume platelet concentrates; therefore, it is preferable to transfuse them as soon as possible.

2. Reduced-volume platelet concentrates may not be distributed as a licensed product.

3. Platelets that have been pooled must be used within 4 hours of entering the units, whether or not they have been volume-reduced. Pooled platelets may not be distributed as a licensed product.

References

1. Simon TL, Sierra ER. Concentration of platelet units into small volumes. Transfusion 1984;24:173-5.

2. Moroff G, Friedman A, Robkin-Kline L, et al. Reduction of the volume of stored platelet concentrates for use in neonatal patients. Transfusion 1984;24:144-6.

Quality Control

Method 7.1. Quality Control for Copper Sulfate Solution

Either of the two methods presented below is acceptable for quality control of copper sulfate solution.

Method 7.1.1. Functional Validation of Copper Sulfate Solution

Principle

Copper sulfate solution can be checked for suitability in donor screening by observing the behavior (sinking or floating) of drops of blood of known hemoglobin concentration.

Materials

1. Copper sulfate—specific gravity 1.053.
2. Capillary tubes.
3. Worksheet for recording results.

Procedure

1. Obtain several (three to six, if possible) blood samples with known hemoglobin levels. Samples should include hemoglobin levels slightly above and below 12.5 g/dL.
2. Gently place a drop of each blood sample into a vial of copper sulfate solution of stated specific gravity of 1.053.
3. Drops of all blood samples with hemoglobin at or above 12.5 g/dL must sink and those with hemoglobin levels below 12.5 g/dL must float.
4. Record the date of testing; the manufacturer, lot number, and expiration date of the copper sulfate; sample identity; the results; and the identity of the person performing the test.
5. Document the corrective action taken if the results are outside acceptable limits.

Method 7.1.2. Use of Measurement Instruments for Specific Gravity, Density, or Refractive Index of Copper Sulfate Solution

Principle

The specific gravity, density, or refractive index of the copper sulfate solution can be measured directly and the result compared with the value stated by the manufacturer. An error in the specific gravity reading of ±0.0001 corresponds to ±0.06 g/dL hemoglobin in whole blood.[1] Therefore, a copper sulfate solution with a specific gravity of 1.053 ± 0.0003 would result in a corresponding hemoglobin range of 12.5 ± 0.18 g/dL.

Materials

1. Copper sulfate—specific gravity 1.053.
2. Measurement instruments
   • For specific gravity—high-precision hydrometer, with gradations of 0.0005 or smaller.
   • For refractive index—refracto-meter.
3. Pipette.
4. For specific gravity method—graduated cylinder or other container suitable for use with a hydrometer.
5. Alcohol for cleaning hydrometer.
6. Worksheet for recording results.

Procedure

Hydrometer method:
1. Wipe the hydrometer clean with alcohol and dry it.
2. Gently lower the hydrometer into the solution until it floats on its own. Drops of solution on the stem will cause inaccurate readings.
3. To read, observe a point just below the plane of the liquid surface and then raise the line of vision until the surface is seen as a straight line in-

stead of an ellipse. Read at the point where the line intersects the scale on the instrument.

Refractometer method:
1. Follow manufacturer's instructions for operation and maintenance of the instrument.
2. Add a drop of copper sulfate to the refractometer.
3. Observe refractive index.
   Note: Some refractometers designed for urine analysis provide both a refractive index scale and a specific gravity scale. Do not read specific gravity directly from this type of refractometer.
4. A copper sulfate solution with a specific gravity of 1.053 will have a refractive index of about 1.3425 at room temperature.[2]

Both methods:
1. Record the results; the date of testing; the manufacturer, lot number, and expiration date of the copper sulfate solution; the identity of the person performing the test; and the identification of the instrument used for measurement.
2. Document the corrective action taken if the results are outside the acceptable limits.

Note

A liquid densitometer may be used to measure density directly. At 4 C, the density of the solution will be exactly the same as the specific gravity (specific gravity = density of solution/density of water; density of water at 4 C = 1 g/mL). When density is measured at room temperature, a conversion factor of 0.9970 (the density of water at 25 C) is used to calculate specific gravity.[2] Specific gravity of copper sulfate solution at 25 C = the observed density in g/mL divided by 0.9970 g/mL.

References

1. Phillips RA, Van Slyke DD, Hamilton PB, et al. Measurement of specific gravities of whole blood and plasma by standard copper sulfate solutions. J Biol Chem 1950;183:305-30.
2. Blood hemoglobin screening (specific gravity method). Technical Reference Document 12. Arlington, TX: Ricca Chemical Company, 2002.

Method 7.2. Standardization and Calibration of Thermometers

Principle

Thermometers used during laboratory testing and in the collection (donor suitability), processing, and storage of blood components and reagents should be calibrated and standardized to ensure accurate indication of temperatures. Calibration should be performed at temperatures close to the temperature at which the thermometers will be used. Over time, liquid-in-glass thermometers may give a different reading at a given temperature because of permanent changes in the volume of the bulb related to relaxation of the glass.[1] Each thermometer should be calibrated before initial use and periodically thereafter, as well as any time there is reason to suspect change or damage. Calibration must be verified for all electronic thermometers, even those described as "self-calibrating."

Materials

1. National Institute of Standards and Technology (NIST)-certified thermometer or thermometer with NIST-traceable calibration certificate.
2. Thermometer to be calibrated.
3. Suitable container, eg, 250-500 mL beaker.
4. Water.
5. Crushed ice.
6. 37 C waterbath.
7. Worksheet for recording results.

Method 7.2.1. Liquid-in-Glass Laboratory Thermometers

Procedure

1. Before choosing a thermometer for a particular application, consider all the governing factors; be sure that the thermometer will be used at its proper immersion; and follow the manufacturer's instructions for its proper use. When using a certified thermometer, read and follow the applicable notes. Be sure to include any correction factors noted on the certificate for the NIST-traceable thermometer and apply them in calculations.
2. Categorize the thermometers by key factors, such as immersion, increments, and temperature of intended use. Test them in groups, comparing similar thermometers. Do not attempt to compare dissimilar thermometers in a single procedure.
3. Number each thermometer being tested (eg, place a numbered piece of tape around the top of each thermometer or use the manufacturer's serial number).
4. Perform calibration with water at a temperature close to that which the thermometer will monitor.
   a. To calibrate at 37 C, place the thermometers to be tested and the NIST thermometer at a uniform depth in a standard 37 C waterbath, making sure that the tips of all devices are at the same level in the liquid.

b.   To calibrate at 1 to 6 C, fill a suitable container with water. Add crushed ice until the approximate desired temperature is reached. Place the thermometers to be tested and the NIST thermometer at a uniform depth in the water/ice mixture, making sure that the tips of all devices are at the same level and are in the liquid, not the upper ice.

5.   Stir constantly in a random motion until the temperature equilibrates, approximately 3 to 5 minutes.

6.   Observe temperatures. Record each thermometer's identification and results. Acceptance criteria depend on the level of precision required, but, for most blood banking applications, agreement within 1 C between the two thermometers may be considered acceptable. If the reading varies by more than one degree from the standard, the thermometer may be returned to the distributor (if newly purchased), labeled with the correction factor (degrees different from the NIST thermometer) that must be applied to each reading, or discarded.

7.   Complete the calibration record with the date of testing and identity of the person who performed the test.

Notes

1.   If a thermometer is to be used for temperatures over a range greater than a few degrees (eg, 10 degrees), a three-point calibration should be performed. Use water of appropriate temperature. Test at temperatures just below, just above, and at the midway point of intended use. All results should be within 1 C of the NIST thermometer to be considered acceptable.

2.   Thermometers should be observed routinely for any split in the column because this will cause inaccurate readings. The methods for reuniting the separation can be found in NCCLS Standard I2-A2.[2] When this occurs, document corrective action and recalibrate the thermometer.

References

1.   Wise JA. A procedure for the effective recalibration of liquid-in-glass thermometers. NIST Special Publication 819. Gaithersburg, MD: National Institute of Standards and Technology, 1991.

2.   Temperature calibration of water baths, instruments, and temperature sensors. 2nd ed; approved standard I2-A2 Vol. 10 No. 3. Wayne, PA: National Committee for Clinical Laboratory Standards, 1990.

Method 7.2.2. Electronic Oral Thermometers

Procedure

1.   Use any of the following methods to verify calibration:
   a.   Follow manufacturer's instructions for verifying calibration.
   b.   Use a commercially available calibration device by following the instructions provided by the device's manufacturer.
   c.   Calibrate the thermometer by inserting the probe in a 37 C waterbath with a NIST-certified thermometer.

2.   A result is acceptable if the reading on the thermometer agrees with the NIST thermometer within 0.1 C. If expected results are not achieved, unsatisfactory thermometers should be returned to the distributor. Document corrective actions.

3. Record the date of testing, thermometer identification numbers, temperature readings, and the identity of the person performing the test.

Method 7.3. Testing Blood Storage Equipment Alarms

Blood storage refrigerators and freezers must be equipped with a system for continuous temperature monitoring and an audible alarm. If a storage unit goes into alarm, it is essential that personnel know the appropriate actions to take. Directions for such events should be available in a conspicuous location, and personnel should be trained to initiate these actions if the temperature cannot be corrected rapidly. The alarm on each storage unit should be checked periodically for proper functioning. Monthly checks are appropriate until consistent behavior of a particular storage unit has been demonstrated. Thereafter, alarms should be tested regularly and frequently enough to achieve and maintain personnel competency as well as to detect malfunctions. For equipment in good condition, quarterly checks are usually sufficient. Because alarms may be disconnected or silenced during repairs, it is also prudent to verify alarm functioning after repairs.

The high and low temperatures of activation must be checked and the results recorded. AABB *Standards for Blood Banks and Transfusion Services*[1(p5)] requires that the alarm be set to activate at a temperature that will allow appropriate intervention before blood or components reach an undesirable temperature. Because of the diversity of equipment available, it is not possible to give specific instructions for all applicable alarm systems. If the equipment user's manual does not provide suitable directions for testing the alarm, consult the manufacturer or other equipment storage expert. The facility procedures manual must include a detailed description of the method(s) in local use. (See Appendix 10 for quality control testing intervals.)

Method 7.3.1. Testing Refrigerator Alarms

Principle

Refrigerator temperatures may increase beyond acceptable limits for several reasons, including:

1. Improperly closed door.
2. Insufficient refrigerant.
3. Compressor failure.
4. Dirty or blocked heat exchanger.
5. Loss of electrical power.

Materials

1. Calibrated thermometer.
2. Pan large enough to hold the thermocouple container.
3. Water.
4. Crushed ice.
5. Table salt.
6. Worksheet for recording results.

Procedure

1. Verify that the alarm circuits are operating, the alarm is switched on, and the starting temperature is 1 to 6 C. Immerse an easy-to-read calibrated thermometer in the container with the alarm thermocouple.

   For low activation:

2. Place the container with the thermocouple and thermometer in a pan containing an ice and water slush at a temperature of –4 C or colder. To achieve this temperature, add several spoonfuls of table salt to the slush.

3. Close the refrigerator door to avoid changing the temperature of the storage compartment. Keep the container in the pan of cold slush, and

gently agitate it periodically until the alarm sounds.

4. Record this temperature as the low-activation temperature.

For high activation:

5. Place the container with thermocouple and thermometer in a pan containing cool water (eg, 12 to 15 C).

6. Close the refrigerator door. Allow the fluid in the container to warm slowly, with occasional agitation.

7. Record the temperature at which the alarm sounds as the high-activation temperature.

8. Record the date of testing, the refrigerator identification, the thermometer identification, and the identity of the person performing the test.

9. If temperatures of activation are too low or too high, take appropriate corrective actions such as those suggested by the manufacturer, record the nature of the corrections, and repeat the alarm check to document that the corrections were effective.

Notes

1. The thermocouple for the alarm should be easily accessible and equipped with a cord long enough so that it can be manipulated easily.

2. The thermocouple for the continuous temperature monitor need not be in the same container as that of the alarm. If it is in the same container, a notation should be made in the records that explains any out-of-range temperature registered as a result of the alarm check.

3. When the temperatures of alarm activation are checked, the temperature change should occur slowly enough so that the measurements and recording are accurate. Too rapid a change in temperature may give the false impression that the alarm does not sound until an inappropriate temperature is registered.

4. The low temperature of activation should be greater than 1 C (eg, 1.5 C); the high temperature of activation should be less than 6 C (eg, 5.5 C).

5. Alarms should sound simultaneously at the site of the refrigerator and at the location of remote alarms, when employed. If remote alarms are used, the alarm check should include a verification that the alarm sounded at the remote location.

6. The amount of fluid in which the thermocouple is immersed must be no larger than the volume of the smallest component stored in that refrigerator. The thermocouple may be immersed in a smaller volume, but this means that the alarm will go off with smaller temperature changes than those registered in a larger volume of fluid. Excessive sensitivity may create a nuisance.

7. With the one-time assistance of a qualified electrician, the required refrigerator alarm checks of units with virtually inaccessible temperature probes can be performed with an electrical modification cited by Wenz and Owens.[2]

References

1. Silva MA, ed. Standards for blood banks and transfusion services. 23rd ed. Bethesda, MD: AABB, 2005.

2. Wenz B, Owens RT. A simplified method for monitoring and calibrating refrigerator alarm systems. Transfusion 1980;20:75-8.

Method 7.3.2. Testing Freezer Alarms

Principle

Freezer temperatures may rise to unacceptable levels for a variety of reasons.

Common causes of rising temperatures include:

1. Improperly closed freezer door or lid.
2. Low level of refrigerant.
3. Compressor failure.
4. Dirty or blocked heat exchanger.
5. Loss of electrical power.

Materials

1. Protection for the freezer contents, eg, a blanket.
2. Calibrated thermometer or thermocouple independent from that built into the system.
3. Warm water or an oven mitt.
4. Worksheet for recording results.

Procedure

1. Protect frozen components from exposure to elevated temperatures during the test.
2. Use a thermometer or thermocouple, independent from that built into the system, that will accurately indicate the temperature of alarm activation. Compare these readings with the temperatures registered on the recorder.
3. Warm the alarm probe and thermometer slowly (eg, in warm water, by an oven-mitt-covered hand, exposure to air). The specific temperature of activation cannot be determined accurately during rapid warming, and the apparent temperature of activation will be too high.
4. Record the temperature at which the alarm sounds, the date of testing, the identity of the person performing the test, the identity of the freezer and calibrating instrument, and any observations that might suggest impaired activity.

5. Return the freezer and the alarm system to their normal conditions.
6. If the alarm sounds at too high a temperature, take appropriate corrective actions such as those suggested by the manufacturer, record the nature of the correction, and repeat the alarm check to document that the corrections were effective.

Notes

1. Alarms should sound simultaneously at the site of the freezer and at the location of the remote alarms, when employed. If remote alarms are used, the alarm check should include a verification that the alarm sounded at the remote location.
2. Test battery function, electrical circuits, and power-off alarms more frequently than the activation temperature. Record function, freezer identification, date, and identity of person performing the testing.
3. For units with the sensor installed in the wall or in air, apply local warmth to the site or allow the temperature of the entire compartment to rise to the point at which the alarm sounds. Remove the frozen contents or protect them with insulation while the temperature rises.
4. For units with the thermocouple located in antifreeze solution, pull the container and the cables outside the freezer chest for testing, leaving the door shut and the contents protected.
5. For units with a tracking alarm that sounds whenever the temperature reaches a constant interval above the setting on the temperature controller, set the controller to a warmer setting and note the temperature interval at which the alarm sounds.

6. Liquid nitrogen freezers must have alarm systems that activate at an unsafe level of contained liquid nitrogen.

Method 7.4. Functional Calibration of Centrifuges for Platelet Separation

Principle

Successful preparation of platelet concentrates requires adequate but not excessive centrifugation; the equipment used must perform in a consistent and dependable manner. Each centrifuge used to prepare platelets should be calibrated upon receipt and after adjustment or repair. Functional calibration of the centrifuge for both the preparation of platelet-rich plasma (PRP) from whole blood and subsequent preparation of platelet concentrate from PRP can be performed during the same procedure.

Materials

1. Freshly collected whole blood, obtained by phlebotomy into a bag with two integrally attached transfer containers.
2. A specimen of blood from the donor, anticoagulated with EDTA and collected in addition to the specimens drawn for routine processing.
3. Metal clips and hand sealer or dielectric sealer.
4. Clean instruments (scissors, hemostats, tubing stripper).
5. Plasma extractor.
6. Centrifuge suitable for preparation of platelet concentrates.
7. Worksheet for recording results.

Procedure

Preparation of Platelet-Rich Plasma

1. Perform a platelet count on the anticoagulated specimen. If the platelet count is below 133,000/µL, do not use this donor's blood for calibration.
2. Calculate and record the number of platelets in the Whole Blood unit: platelets/µL × 1000 × mL of whole blood = number of platelets in whole blood.
3. Prepare PRP at a selected speed and time. (See "light spin" in Table 7.4-1 or guidance provided by the centrifuge manufacturer.)
4. Place a temporary clamp on the tubing so that one satellite bag is closed off. Express the PRP into the other satellite bag. Seal the tubing close to the primary bag, leaving a long section of tubing, the "tail." Disconnect the two satellite bags from the primary bag. Do not remove the temporary clamp between the satellite bags until the platelets are prepared (see next section).
5. Strip the tubing and "tail" several times so that they contain a representative sample of PRP.
6. Seal off a segment of the "tail" and disconnect it, so that the bag of PRP remains sterile.
7. Perform a platelet count on the sample of PRP in the sealed segment. Calculate and record the number of platelets in the bag of PRP: platelets/µL × 1000 × mL of PRP = number of platelets in PRP.
8. Calculate and record percent yield: (number of platelets in PRP × 100) divided by (number of platelets in whole blood) = % yield.
9. Repeat the above process three or four times with different donors, using different speeds and times of centrifugation, and compare the yields

achieved under each set of test conditions.

10. Select the shortest time/lowest speed combination that results in the highest percent of platelet yield without unacceptable levels of red cell content in the PRP.

11. Record the centrifuge identification, the calibration settings selected, the date, and the identity of the person performing the calibration.

Preparation of Platelets

1. Centrifuge the PRP (as prepared above) at a selected time and speed to prepare platelets. (See "heavy spin" in Table 7.4-1 or guidance provided by the centrifuge manufacturer.)

2. Remove the temporary clamp between the two satellite bags and express the platelet-reduced plasma into the second attached satellite bag, leaving approximately 55 to 60 mL volume in the platelet bag. Seal the tubing, leaving a long section of tubing attached to the platelet bag.

3. Allow the platelets to rest for approximately 1 hour.

4. Place the platelets on an agitator for at least 1 hour to ensure that they are evenly resuspended. Platelet counts performed immediately after centrifugation will not be accurate.

5. Strip the tubing several times, mixing tubing contents well with the contents of the platelet bag. Seal off a segment of the tubing and disconnect it, so that the platelet bag remains sterile.

6. Perform a platelet count on the contents of the segment.

7. Calculate and record the number of platelets in the concentrate: platelets/$\mu L \times 1000 \times mL$ of platelets = number of platelets in platelet concentrate.

8. Calculate and record percent yield.

9. Repeat the above process with PRP from different donors, using different speeds and times of centrifugation, and compare the yields achieved under each set of test conditions.

Table 7.4-1. Centrifugation for Component Preparation

Heavy Spin

Red cells Platelets from whole blood }	$5000 \times g$, 5 minutes*
Cell-free plasma Cryoprecipitate }	$5000 \times g$, 7 minutes*

Light Spin

Platelet-rich plasma	$2000 \times g$, 3 minutes*

To calculate relative centrifugal force in *g*:

$$rcf \text{ (in } g) = 28.38 \times R^\dagger \times (rpm/1000)^2$$

---

*Times include acceleration but not deceleration times. Times given are approximations only. Each individual centrifuge must be evaluated for the preparation of the various components.
†R = radius of centrifuge rotor in inches.

10. Select the shortest time/lowest speed combination that results in the highest percent of platelet yield in the platelet concentrate.

11. Record the centrifuge identification, the calibration settings selected, the date, and the identity of the person performing the calibration.

Notes

1. It is not necessary to perform functional recalibration of a centrifuge unless the instrument has undergone adjustments or repairs, or component quality control indicates that platelet counts have fallen below acceptable levels. However, timer, speed, and temperature calibrations of the centrifuge should occur on a regularly scheduled basis (see Appendix 10).

2. Each centrifuge used for preparing platelets must be calibrated individually. Use the conditions determined to be optimal for each instrument.

3. When counting platelet samples on an instrument intended for whole blood, it may be necessary to use a correction factor to obtain accurate results.

4. When determining the appropriate time and speed of centrifugation, consideration should also be given to other products that will be prepared from the whole blood. Final size and hematocrit of red cell and plasma volume made available for further processing are important factors to consider.

References

1. Kahn R, Cossette I, Friedman L. Optimum centrifugation conditions for the preparation of platelet and plasma products. Transfusion 1976;16:162-5.

2. McShine R, Das P, Smit Sibinga C, Brozovic B. Effect of EDTA on platelet parameters in blood and blood components collected with CPDA-1. Vox Sang 1991;61:84-9.

Method 7.5. Functional Calibration of a Serologic Centrifuge

Principle

Each centrifuge should be calibrated upon receipt, after adjustments or repairs, and periodically. Calibration evaluates the behavior of red cells in solutions of different viscosities, not the reactivity of different antibodies.

For Immediate Agglutination

Materials

1. Test tubes, 10 × 75 mm or 12 × 75 mm (whichever size is routinely used in the laboratory)

2. Worksheet for recording results.

3. For saline-active antibodies:
   - Serum from a group A person (anti-B) diluted with 6% albumin to give 1+ macroscopic agglutination (3 mL of 22% bovine albumin + 8 mL of normal saline = 6% bovine albumin). See Method 1.5.
   - *Positive control:* Group B red cells in a 2% to 5% saline suspension.
   - *Negative control:* Group A red cells in a 2% to 5% saline suspension.

4. For high-protein antibodies:
   - Anti-D diluted with 22% or 30% albumin to give 1+ macroscopic agglutination.
   - *Positive control:* D+ red cells in a 2% to 5% saline suspension.
   - *Negative control:* D– red cells in a 2% to 5% saline suspension.

Procedure

1. For each set of tests (saline and high-protein antibodies), label five test tubes for positive reactions and five for negative reactions.
2. In quantities that correspond to routine use, add diluted anti-B to each of 10 tubes for the saline test and add diluted anti-D to each of 10 tubes for the high-protein test. Add serum and reagents in quantities that correspond to routine use.
3. Add the appropriate control cell suspension to one set of tubes (one positive and one negative tube for the saline test, and one positive and one negative tube for the high-protein antibody test). Centrifuge immediately for the desired time interval (eg, 10 seconds).
4. Observe each tube for agglutination and record observations. (See example in Table 7.5-1.)
5. Repeat steps 2 and 3 for each time interval (eg, 15, 20, 30, and 45 seconds). Do not allow cells and sera to incubate before centrifugation.
6. Select the optimal time of centrifugation, which is the shortest time required to fulfill the following criteria:
   a. Agglutination in the positive tubes is as strong as determined in preparing reagents.
   b. There is no agglutination or ambiguity in the negative tubes.
   c. The cell button is clearly delineated and the periphery is sharply defined, not fuzzy.
   d. The supernatant fluid is clear.
   e. The cell button is easily resuspended.
      In the example shown in Table 7.5-1, these criteria are met by the 30-second and the 45-second spins; the optimal time for these tests in this centrifuge is 30 seconds.
7. Record centrifuge identification, the times selected, the date, and the identity of the person performing the calibration.

For Washing and Antiglobulin Testing

Tests in which antihuman globulin (AHG) serum is added to red cells may require

Table 7.5-1. Example of Serologic Centrifuge Test Results*

Criteria	Time in Seconds				
	10	15	20	30	45
Supernatant fluid is clear	No	No	Yes	Yes	Yes
Cell button is clearly delineated	No	No	No	Yes	Yes
Cells are easily resuspended	Yes	Yes	Yes	Yes	Yes
Agglutination is observed	±	±	1+	1+	1+
Negative tube is negative	Yes	Yes	Yes	Yes	Resuspends roughly

*The optimal time for centrifugation in this example is 30 seconds.

centrifugation conditions different from those for immediate agglutination. Centrifugation conditions appropriate for both washing and AHG reactions can be determined in one procedure. Note that this procedure does not monitor the completeness of washing; use of IgG-coated cells to control negative AHG reactions provides this check. The following procedure addresses only the mechanics of centrifugation.

Materials

1. AHG reagent, unmodified.
2. Saline, large volumes.
3. Test tubes, 10 × 75 mm or 12 × 75 mm (whichever size is routinely used in the laboratory).
4. Worksheet for recording results.
5. *Positive control:* a 2% to 5% saline suspension of D+ red cells incubated for 15 minutes at 37 C with anti-D diluted to give 1+ macroscopic agglutination after addition of AHG.
6. *Negative control:* a 2% to 5% suspension of D+ red cells incubated for 15 minutes at 37 C with 6% albumin. [Note: D– red cells incubated with diluted anti-D may also be used as a negative control.]

Procedure

1. Prepare five test tubes containing 1 drop of positive cells and five tubes containing 1 drop of negative control cells.
2. Fill tubes with saline and centrifuge them in pairs, one positive and one negative, for different times (eg, 30, 45, 60, 90, and 120 seconds). The red cells should form a clearly delineated button, with minimal cells trailing up the side of the tube. After the saline has been decanted, the cell button should be easily resus-

pended in the residual fluid. The optimal time for washing is the shortest time that accomplishes these goals.

3. Repeat washing process on all pairs three more times, using time determined to be optimal.
4. Decant supernatant saline thoroughly.
5. Add AHG to one positive control test tube and one negative control test tube. Centrifuge immediately for the desired interval (eg, 10 seconds).
6. Observe each tube for agglutination and record observations.
7. Repeat steps 5 and 6 for each interval (eg, 15, 20, 30, and 45 seconds). Do not allow cells and AHG to incubate before centrifugation.
8. Select optimal time as in immediate agglutination procedure.
9. Record centrifuge identification, the times selected, the date, and the identity of the person performing the calibration.

Notes

Periodic recalibration is performed to verify that the timing in use continues to be the optimal timing. This may be accomplished by using a shortened version of the procedures outlined above. For example, use the current timing for a particular centrifuge and each medium and those times just above and just below the current timing.

Method 7.6. Performance Testing of Automatic Cell Washers
Principle

Antihuman globulin (AHG) is inactivated readily by unbound immunoglobulin. The red cells to which AHG will be added must be washed free of all proteins and suspended in a protein-free medium. A properly functioning cell washer must add large volumes of saline to each tube, resuspend the cells, centrifuge them adequately to avoid excessive red cell loss, and decant the saline to leave a dry cell button.

Materials

1. Test tubes routinely used in the laboratory, 10 × 75 mm or 12 × 75 mm.
2. Additive routinely used to potentiate antigen-antibody reactions.
3. Human serum, from patient or donor.
4. IgG-coated red cells, known to give a 1 to 2+ reaction in antiglobulin testing.
5. Normal saline.
6. AHG reagent, anti-IgG or polyspecific.
7. Worksheet for recording results.

Procedure

1. To each of 12 tubes, add potentiator and human serum in quantities that correspond to routine use and 1 drop of IgG-coated red cells.
2. Place the tubes in a centrifuge carrier, seat the carrier in the cell washer, and start the wash cycle.
3. After addition of saline in the second cycle, stop the cell washer. Inspect the contents of all tubes. There should be an approximately equal volume of saline in all tubes; some variation is acceptable. Tubes should be approximately 80% full, to avoid splashing and cross-contamination. (Refer to manufacturer's instructions for specific requirements.) Record observations.
4. Observe all tubes to see that the red cells have been completely resuspended. Record observations.

5. Continue the washing cycle.
6. After addition of saline in the third cycle, stop the cell washer and inspect tubes as above. Record observations.
7. Complete the wash cycle.
8. At the end of the wash cycle, inspect all tubes to see that saline has been completely decanted and that each tube contains a dry cell button. Record observations.
9. Add AHG according to the manufacturer's directions, centrifuge, and examine all tubes for agglutination. If the cell washer is functioning properly, the size of the cell button should be the same in all tubes. All tubes should show the same degree of agglutination. Record observations.
10. Record identity of centrifuge, the date of testing, and the identity of the person performing the testing.

Notes

1. Further investigation is needed if:
   a. The amount of saline varies significantly from tube to tube or cycle to cycle.
   b. The cell button is not resuspended completely after being filled with saline.
   c. Any tube has weak or absent agglutination in the antiglobulin phase.
   d. Any tube has a significant decrease in the size of the cell button.
2. Cell washers that automatically add AHG should also be checked for uniform addition of AHG. In step 9 above, AHG would be added automatically, and failure of addition would be apparent by absence of agglutination. The volume of AHG

should be inspected and found to be equal in all tubes. The volume of AHG delivered automatically by cell washers should be checked monthly to ensure that it is as specified in the manufacturer's directions and that delivery is uniform in all tubes.

3. Some manufacturers market AHG colored with green dye for use in automated cell washers so that it will be immediately obvious if no reagent has been added.

Method 7.7. Monitoring Cell Counts of Apheresis Components

Principle

When cellular components are prepared by apheresis, it is essential to determine cell yields without compromising the sterility of the component.

Materials

1. Component collected by apheresis.
2. Metal clips and hand sealer or dielectric sealer.
3. Tubing stripper.
4. Clean instruments (scissors, hemostats).
5. Test tubes.
6. Cell-counting equipment.
7. Worksheet for recording results.

Procedure

1. Ensure that the contents of the apheresis component bag are well mixed.
2. Strip the attached tubing at least four times, mixing the contents of the tubing with the contents of the bag, to ensure that the contents of the tubing accurately represent the entire contents of the bag.

3. Seal a 5- to 8-cm (2- to 3-inch) segment distal to the collection bag. There should be approximately 2 mL of fluid in the segment. Double-seal the end of the tubing next to the component bag and detach the segment.
4. Empty the contents of the segment into a suitably labeled tube.
5. Determine and record cell counts in cells/mL.
   a. For results reported as cells/μL, change values to cells/mL by multiplying by 1000 (or 10^3).
   b. For results reported as cells/L, change values to cells/mL by dividing by 1000 (or 10^3).
6. Multiply cells/mL by the volume of the component, in mL, to obtain total cell count in the component.
7. Record component's identity, the date, and the identity of the person performing the testing.

Note

Refer to manufacturer's directions for any additional requirements.

Method 7.8. Manual Method for Counting Residual White Cells in Leukocyte-Reduced Blood and Components

Principle

The residual white cell content of leukocyte-reduced whole blood and components can be determined using a large-volume hemocytometer. For red-cell-containing components, the red cells in the aliquot to be counted are first lysed. Crystal violet is used to stain the leukocyte nuclei. The Nageotte counting chamber has a volume 56 times that of the standard hemocytometer. Accuracy of counting is improved by examining a larger volume of minimally diluted specimen, compared with standard counting techniques.

Materials

1. Hemocytometer chamber with 50 µL counting volume (eg, Nageotte Brite Line Chamber).
2. Crystal violet stain: 0.01% w/v crystal violet in 1% v/v acetic acid (eg, Turks solution).
3. Red cell lysing agent (eg, Zapoglobin, Coulter Electronics, Hialeah, FL), for red-cell-containing components only.
4. Pipettor (40 µL and 100 µL) with disposable tips.
5. Talc-free gloves, clean plastic test tubes, plastic petri dish, filter paper.
6. Light microscope with 10× ocular lens and 20× objective.
7. Worksheet for recording results.

Procedure

1. Dilute and stain leukocyte-reduced blood and component samples as follows:
   a. *For Red-Cell-Containing Components*
      1) Pipette 40 µL of lysing agent into a clean test tube.
      2) Place a representative sample of the component to be tested in a clean test tube. The hematocrit of the sample to be tested should not exceed 60%.
      3) Pipette 100 µL of the sample into the tube containing 40 µL of lysing agent. Rinse the pipette several times to mix the two fluids, until the pipette tip is no longer coated with intact red cells.
      4) Pipette 360 µL of crystal violet stain into the mixture and mix fluids by pipetting up and down several times. The final volume is now 500 µL.
   b. *For Platelets*
      1) Place a representative sample of the platelet in a clean test tube.
      2) Pipette 100 µL of the platelet sample into a clean test tube.
      3) Pipette 400 µL of crystal violet stain into the 100 µL of platelets and mix fluids by pipetting up and down several times. The final volume is now 500 µL.
2. Fit the hemocytometer with a coverslip and, using a pipette, load the mixture until the counting area is completely covered but not overflowing.
3. Cover the hemocytometer with a moist lid to prevent evaporation (a plastic petri dish into which a piece of damp filter paper has been placed works well) and let it rest undisturbed for 10 to 15 minutes, to allow the white cells to settle in the counting area of the chamber.
4. Remove the moist lid, place the hemocytometer on the microscope and, using a 20× objective, count the white cells present in the entire 50-µL volume of the counting chamber.
5. Calculate and record results.
   a. White cell concentration:

$$\text{leukocytes/µL} = (\text{cells counted}/50 \text{ µL}) \times 5$$
$$= \text{cells counted}/10$$

where 50 µL is the volume counted and 5 is the dilution factor resulting from the addition of lysing agent and stain.

b. Total white cell content of the leukocyte-reduced component:

$$\text{leukocytes/component} = \begin{array}{c}\text{leukocytes/µL} \times \\ 1000\,\text{µL/mL} \times \\ \text{volume in mL} \\ \text{of the component}\end{array}$$

6. Record the component's identity, the date, and the identity of the person performing the testing.

Notes

1. White cells deteriorate during refrigerated storage; counts on stored blood or red cell components may give inaccurate results.

2. Use of talc-free gloves is recommended because talc particles that contaminate the counting chamber can be misread as white cells.

3. Experience identifying crystal-violet-stained white cells can be obtained by examining samples from components that have not been leukocyte reduced.

4. The accuracy of the counting method can be validated from a reference sample with a high white cell content that has been quantified by another means. This reference sample can be used for serial dilutions in blood or a component that has been rendered extremely leukocyte reduced by two passages through a leukocyte reduction filter. Counts obtained on the serially diluted samples can be compared with the expected concentration derived by calculation.

5. This counting technique is not known to be accurate at concentrations lower than 1 white cell/µL.

References

1. Lutz P, Dzik WH. Large-volume hemocytometer chamber for accurate counting of white cells (WBCs) in WBC-reduced platelets; validation and application for quality control of WBC-reduced platelets prepared by apheresis and filtration. Transfusion 1993;33: 409-12.

2. Dzik WH, Szuflad P. Method for counting white cells in white cell-reduced red cell concentrates (letter). Transfusion 1993;33:272.

Appendices

Appendix 1. Normal Values in Adults

Determination	SI Units	Conventional Units
Alanine aminotransferase	4-36 U/L at 37 C	4-36 U/L at 37 C
Bilirubin, total	2-21 μmol/L	0.1-1.2 mg/dL
Haptoglobin	0.6-2.7 g/L	60-270 mg/dL
Hematocrit		
Males	0.40-0.54	40-54%
Females	0.38-0.47	38-47%
Hemoglobin		
Males	135-180 g/L	13.5-18.0 g/dL
Females	120-160 g/L	12.0-16.0 g/dL
Hemoglobin A_2	0.015-0.035 total Hb	1.5-3.5% total Hb
Hemoglobin F	0-0.01 total Hb	<1% total Hb
Hemoglobin (plasma)	5-50 mg/L	0.5-5.0 mg/dL
Immunoglobulins		
IgG	8.0-18.0 g/L	800-1801 mg/dL
IgA	1.1-5.6 g/L	113-563 mg/dL
IgM	0.5-2.2 g/L	54-222 mg/dL
IgD	5.0-30 mg/L	0.5-3.0 mg/dL
IgE	0.1-0.4 mg/L	0.01-0.04 mg/dL
Methemoglobin	<0.01 total Hb	<1% total Hb
Platelet count	$150\text{-}450 \times 10^9/\text{L}$	$150\text{-}450 \times 10^3/\mu\text{L}$
Red cells		
Males	$4.6\text{-}6.2 \times 10^{12}/\text{L}$	$4.6\text{-}6.2 \times 10^6/\mu\text{L}$
Females	$4.2\text{-}5.4 \times 10^{12}/\text{L}$	$4.2\text{-}5.4 \times 10^6/\mu\text{L}$
Reticulocyte count	$25\text{-}75 \times 10^9/\text{L}$	$25\text{-}75 \times 10^3/\mu\text{L}$
Viscosity, relative	1.4-1.8 × water	1.4-1.8 × water
White cells	$4.5\text{-}11.0 \times 10^9/\text{L}$	$4.5\text{-}11.0 \times 10^3/\mu\text{L}$

Appendix 2. Selected Normal Values in Children

		SI Units	Conventional Units
Bilirubin (total)			
Cord	Preterm	<30 mmol/L	<1.8 mg/dL
	Term	<30 mmol/L	<1.8 mg/dL
0-1 day	Preterm	<137 mmol/L	<8 mg/dL
	Term	<103 mmol/L	<6 mg/dL
1-2 days	Preterm	<205 mmol/L	<12 mg/dL
	Term	<137 mmol/L	<8 mg/dL
3-7 days	Preterm	<274 mmol/L	<16 mg/dL
	Term	<205 mmol/L	<12 mg/dL
7-30 days	Preterm	<205 mmol/L	<12 mg/dL
	Term	<120 mmol/L	<7 mg/dL
Thereafter	Preterm	<34 mmol/L	<2 mg/dL
	Term	<17 mmol/L	<1 mg/dL

	Hemoglobin	WBC	Platelets
26-30 weeks' gestation	11.0-15.8 g/dL	$1.7\text{-}7.1 \times 10^9$/L	180,000-327,000/μL
Term	13.5-19.5 g/dL	$9\text{-}30 \times 10^9$/L	192,000/μL (mean)
1-3 days	14.5-22.5 g/dL	$9.4\text{-}34 \times 10^9$/L	252,000/μL (mean)
2 weeks	13.4-19.8 g/dL	$5\text{-}20 \times 10^9$/L	
1 month	10.7-17.1 g/dL	$4\text{-}19.5 \times 10^9$/L	
2 months	9.4-13.0 g/dL		
6 months	11.1-14.1 g/dL	$6\text{-}17.5 \times 10^9$/L	
6 months-2 years	10.5-13.5 g/dL	$6\text{-}17 \times 10^9$/L	150,000-350,000/μL
2-6 years	11.5-13.5 g/dL	$5\text{-}15.5 \times 10^9$/L	150,000-350,000/μL
6-12 years	11.5-15.5 g/dL	$4.5\text{-}13.5 \times 10^9$/L	150,000-350,000/μL
12-18 years			
Male	13.0-16.9 g/dL	$4.5\text{-}13.5 \times 10^9$/L	150,000-350,000/μL
Female	12.0-16.0 g/dL	$4.5\text{-}13.5 \times 10^9$/L	150,000-350,000/μL

Appendix 2. Selected Normal Values in Children (cont'd)

	IgG		IgM		IgA	
Newborn	831-1231	mg/dL	6-16	mg/dL	<3	mg/dL
1-3 months	312-549	mg/dL	19-41	mg/dL	8-34	mg/dL
4-6 months	241-613	mg/dL	26-60	mg/dL	10-46	mg/dL
7-12 months	442-880	mg/dL	31-77	mg/dL	19-55	mg/dL
13-24 months	553-971	mg/dL	35-81	mg/dL	26-74	mg/dL
25-36 months	709-1075	mg/dL	42-80	mg/dL	34-108	mg/dL
3-5 years	701-1157	mg/dL	38-74	mg/dL	66-120	mg/dL
6-8 years	667-1179	mg/dL	40-80	mg/dL	79-169	mg/dL
9-11 years	889-1359	mg/dL	46-112	mg/dL	71-191	mg/dL
12-16 years	822-1070	mg/dL	39-79	mg/dL	85-211	mg/dL

Activated Partial Thromboplastin Time

Preterm	70 seconds
Full-term	45-65 seconds

Prothrombin Time

Preterm	12-21 seconds
Full-term	13-20 seconds

Reprinted with permission from The Harriet Lane Handbook. 15th ed. St. Louis, MO: Mosby, 2000.

Appendix 3. Typical Normal Values in Tests of Hemostasis and Coagulation (Adults)

Test	Normal Value
Activated partial thromboplastin time	25-35 seconds
Bleeding time	2-8 minutes
Coagulation factors	500-1500 U/L
Fibrin degradation products	<10 mg/L
Fibrinogen	2.0-4.0 g/L
Plasma D-dimers	<200 mg/L
Protein C	70-1400 U/L
Protein S (total)	70-1400 U/L
Prothrombin time	10-13 seconds
Thrombin time	17-25 seconds

Reprinted with permission from Henry JB. Clinical diagnosis and management by laboratory methods. 20th ed. Philadelphia: WB Saunders, 2001.

Appendix 4. Coagulation Factor Values in Platelet Concentrates

Factor/ Protein	Normal Range	Day 0	Day 1	Day 2	Day 3	Day 4	Day 5
II %	78-122	104	91-96	96	85-94	90	90
V %	47-153	78-98	69-78	50	36-47	28	24-35
VII %	51-168	108	93-117	88	80-103	75	72
VIII %	48-152	68-126	85-99	76	68-76	75	39-70
IX %	62-138	72-105	100-106	95	91-98	93	63-97
X %	58-142	66-101	93-94	92	85-88	84	60-83
XI %	52-148	91-111	106-108	103	96-98	101	86-110
XII %	46-126	117	107-112	116	106-123	123	131
C %	57-128	106	102	101	98	99	100
S %	83-167	95	75	61	40	32	31
Antithrombin %	88-126	103	99	101	102	103	97
Plasminogen %	60-140	140	133	126	122	124	117
Fibrinogen mg/dL	198-434	217-308	278-313	310	265-323	302	221-299
Ristocetin cofactor %	50-150	106	124	125	133	116	127

Note: Coagulation factor % = 100 x coagulation factor units/mL.

Reproduced with permission from Brecher ME, ed. Collected questions and answers. 6th ed. Bethesda, MD: AABB, 2000.

Appendix 5. Approximate Normal Values for Red Cell, Plasma, and Blood Volumes

	Infant[1]		Adult[2]	
	Premature	Term Birth at 72 hours	Male	Female
Red Cell Volume mL/kg	50	40	26	24
Plasma Volume mL/kg	58	47	40	36
Blood Volume mL/kg	108	87	66	60

The adult values should be modified to correct for:
1. Below age 18: increase values by 10%.
2. Weight loss:
   a. Marked loss within 6 months—calculations made at original weight.
   b. Gradual loss over a longer time—calculations made at present weight and raised 10% to 15%.
3. Obese and short: values are reduced by 10%.
4. Elderly: values are reduced by 10%.
5. Pregnancy[3]:

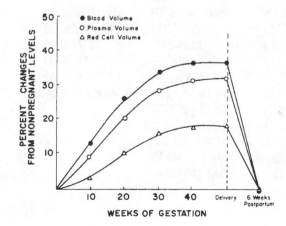

WEEKS OF GESTATION

Estimation of Body Surface Area[4]:

$$BSA(m^2) = \sqrt{\frac{Ht(cm) \times Wt(kg)}{3600}} \text{ or } \sqrt{\frac{Ht(in) \times Wt(lb)}{3131}}$$

Blood Volume (BV)[5]:
   BV = 2740 mL/m^2—males
   BV = 2370 mL/m^2—females

Hematocrit[6]:
   Venous hematocrit = H_v (blood obtained by vein or finger puncture)
   Whole-body hematocrit = H_B
   $$H_B = (Hv) \times (0.91)$$

References
1. Miller D. Normal values and examination of the blood: Perinatal period, infancy, childhood and adolescence. In: Miller DR, Baehner RL, McMillan CW, Miller LP, eds. Blood diseases of infancy and childhood. St. Louis: C.V. Mosby, 1984:21,22.
2. Albert SN. Blood volume. Springfield, IL: Charles C. Thomas, 1963:26.
3. Peck TM, Arias F. Hematologic changes associated with pregnancy. Clin Obstet Gynecol 1979;22:788.
4. Mosteller RD. Simplified calculation of body-surface area. N Engl J Med 1987;317:1098.
5. Shoemaker WC. Fluids and electrolytes in the acutely ill adult. In: Shoemaker WC, Ayres S, Grenvik A, et al, eds. Textbook of critical care. 2nd ed. Philadelphia: WB Saunders Co., 1989:1130.
6. Mollison PL, Englefriet CP, Contreras M. Blood transfusion in clinical medicine. 9th ed. Oxford: Blackwell Scientific Publications, 1993.

Appendix 6. Blood Group Antigens Assigned to Systems

In 1980, the International Society of Blood Transfusion (ISBT) formed a Working Party on Terminology for Red Cell Surface Antigens. The task of this group was to devise a uniform nomenclature that would be both eye- and machine-readable. The numeric system proposed by this group was not intended to replace traditional terminology but, instead, to enable communication using computer systems where numbers are necessary. ISBT terminology uses uppercase letters and Arabic numbers for system and antigen codes. Each system, collection, or series of antigens is given a number (eg, ABO system = 001), and each antigen within the system is given a number (eg, A = 001, B = 002). Sinistral zeros may be omitted. Thus, in ISBT terminology, the A antigen would be written using computer code as 001001 or 1.1, or using the system symbol, as ABO1.

Periodically, the Working Party meets to update assignment of antigens to systems, collections, and series. The table below lists the blood group systems and the antigens assigned to those systems. Other red cell antigens are assigned to collections and to series of high- and low-incidence antigens. Although all terms in the table are acceptable, the *Technical Manual* and *TRANSFUSION* choose to use traditional terminology in most cases. Further information on blood group terminology, which antigens are assigned to the collections, and the series of high- and low-incidence antigens can be found in the references.

System (ISBT Symbol/Number)	Antigen (ISBT Number)			
ABO (ABO/001)	A(ABO1)			
	B (ABO2)			
	A,B (ABO3)			
	A_1 (ABO4)			
MNSs or MNS or MN (MNS/002)	M (MNS1)	M^e (MNS13)	Dantu (MNS25)	ERIK (MNS37)
	N (MNS2)	Mt^a (MNS14)	Hop (MNS26)	Os^a (MNS38)
	S (MNS3)	St^a (MNS15)	Nob (MNS27)	ENEP (MNS39)
	s (MNS4)	Ri^a (MNS16)	En^a (MNS28)	ENEH (MNS40)
	U (MNS5)	Cl^a (MNS17)	ENKT (MNS29)	HAG (MNS41)
	He (MNS6)	Ny^a (MNS18)	'N' (MNS30)	ENAV (MNS42)
	Mi^a (MNS7)	Hut (MNS19)	Or (MNS31)	MARS (MNS43)
	M^c (MNS8)	Hil (MNS20)	Dane (MNS32)	
	Vw (MNS9)	M^v (MNS21)	TSEN (MNS33)	
	Mur (MNS10)	Far (MNS22)	MINY (MNS34)	
	M^g (MNS11)	s^D (MNS23)	MUT (MNS35)	
	Vr (MNS12)	Mit (MNS24)	SAT (MNS36)	
P (P/003)	P_1 (P1)			

Appendix 6. Blood Group Antigens Assigned to Systems (cont'd)

System (ISBT Symbol/Number)	Antigen (ISBT Number)			
Rh (RH/004)	D (RH1)	Hr_0 (RH17)	hr^B (RH31)	Nou (RH44)
	C (RH2)	Hr (RH18)	Rh32 (RH32)	Riv (RH45)
	E (RH3)	hr^S (RH19)	Rh33 (RH33)	Sec (RH46)
	c (RH4)	VS (RH20)	Hr^B (RH34)	Dav (RH47)
	e (RH5)	C^G (RH21)	Rh35 (RH35)	JAL (RH48)
	f (RH6)	CE (RH22)	Be^a (RH36)	STEM (RH49)
	Ce (RH7)	D^W (RH23)	Evans (RH37)	FPTT (RH50)
	C^W (RH8)	c-like (RH26)	Rh39 (RH39)	MAR (RH51)
	C^X (RH9)	cE (RH27)	Tar (RH40)	BARC (RH52)
	V (RH10)	hr^H (RH28)	Rh41 (RH41)	JAHK (RH53)
	E^W (RH11)	Rh29 (RH29)	Rh42 (RH42)	DAK (RH54)
	G (RH12)	Go^a (RH30)	Crawford (RH43)	LOCR (RH55)
				CENR (RH56)
Lutheran (LU/005)	Lu^a (LU1)	Lu6 (LU6)	Lu12 (LU12)	Au^a (LU18)
	Lu^b (LU2)	Lu7 (LU7)	Lu13 (LU13)	Au^b (LU19)
	Lu3 (LU3)	Lu8 (LU8)	Lu14 (LU14)	Lu20 (LU20)
	Lu4 (LU4)	Lu9 (LU9)	Lu16 (LU16)	Lu21 (LU21)
	Lu5 (LU5)	Lu11 (LU11)	Lu17 (LU17)	
Kell (KEL/006)	K (KEL1)	Ul^a (KEL10)	K18 (KEL18)	VLAN (KEL25)
	k (KEL2)	K11 (KEL11)	K19 (KEL19)	TOU (KEL26)
	Kp^a (KEL3)	K12 (KEL12)	Km (KEL20)	RAZ (KEL27)
	Kp^b (KEL4)	K13 (KEL13)	Kp^c (KEL21)	VONG (KEL28)
	Ku (KEL5)	K14 (KEL14)	K22 (KEL22)	
	Js^a (KEL6)	K16 (KEL16)	K23 (KEL23)	
	Js^b (KEL7)	Wk^a (KEL17)	K24 (KEL24)	
Lewis (LE/007)	Le^a (LE1)	Le^{bH} (LE4)		
	Le^b (LE2)	ALe^b (LE5)		
	Le^{ab} (LE3)	BLe^b (LE6)		
Duffy (FY/008)	Fy^a (FY1)	Fy4 (FY4)		
	Fy^b (FY2)	Fy5 (FY5)		
	Fy3 (FY3)	Fy6 (FY6)		
Kidd (JK/009)	Jk^a (JK1)			
	Jk^b (JK2)			
	Jk3 (JK3)			

(cont'd)

Appendix 6. Blood Group Antigens Assigned to Systems (cont'd)

System (ISBT Symbol/Number)	Antigen (ISBT Number)			
Diego (DI/010)	Diᵃ (DI1) Diᵇ (DI2) Wrᵃ (DI3) Wrᵇ (DI4) Wdᵃ (DI5) Rbᵃ (DI6)	WARR (DI7) ELO (DI8) Wu (DI9) Bpᵃ (DI10) Moᵃ (DI11) Hgᵃ (DI12)	Vgᵃ (DI13) Swᵃ (DI14) BOW (DI15) NFLD (DI16) Jnᵃ (DI17) KREP (DI18) Trᵃ (DI19)*	Frᵃ (DI20) SW1 (DI21)
Yt or Cartwright (YT/011)	Ytᵃ (YT1) Ytᵇ (YT2)			
Xg (XG/012)	Xgᵃ (XG1)	CD99 (XG2)		
Scianna (SC/013)	Sc1 (SC1) Sc2 (SC2) Sc3 (SC3)	Rd (SC4) STAR (SC5)		
Dombrock (DO/014)	Doᵃ (DO1) Doᵇ (DO2) Gyᵃ (DO3) Hy (DO4) Joᵃ (DO5)			
Colton (CO/015)	Coᵃ (CO1) Coᵇ (CO2) Co3 (CO3)			
LW or Landsteiner-Wiener (LW/016)	LWᵃ (LW5) LWᵃᵇ (LW6) LWᵇ (LW7)			
Chido/Rodgers (CH/RG /017)	Ch1 (CH/RG1) Ch2 (CH/RG2) Ch3 (CH/RG3) Ch4 (CH/RG4) Ch5 (CH/RG5) Ch6 (CH/RG6) WH (CH/RG7)	Rg1 (CH/RG11) Rg2 (CH/RG12)		
H (H/018)	H (H1)			
Kx (XK/019)	Kx (XK1)			

Appendix 6. Blood Group Antigens Assigned to Systems (cont'd)

System (ISBT Symbol/Number)	Antigen (ISBT Number)			
Gerbich (GE/020)	Ge2 (GE2) Ge3 (GE3) Ge4 (GE4)	Wb (GE5) Ls^a (GE6) An^a (GE7)	Dh^a (GE8) GEIS (GE9)	
Cromer (CR/021)	Cr^a (CROM1) Tc^a (CROM2) Tc^b (CROM3) Tc^c (CROM4)	Dr^a (CROM5) Es^a (CROM6) IFC (CROM7) WES^a (CROM8)	WES^b (CROM9) UMC (CROM10) GUTI (CROM11) SERF (CROM12)	ZENA (CROM13)
Knops (KN/022)	Kn^a (KN1) Kn^b (KN2)	McC^a (KN3) Sl^a (KN4)	Yk^a (KN5) McC^b (KN6)	Sl2 (KN7) Sl3 (KN8)*
Indian (IN/023)	In^a (IN1) In^b (IN2)			
Ok (OK/024)	Ok^a (OK1)			
Raph (RAPH/025)	MER2 (RAPH1)			
JMH or John Milton Hagen (JMH/026)	JMH (JMH1)			
I (I/027)	I (I1)			
Globoside (GLOB/028)	P (GLOB1)			
GIL (GIL/029)	GIL (GIL1)			

*Provisional.

Daniels GL, Anstee DJ, Cartron JP, et al. International Society of Blood Transfusion working party on terminology for red cell surface antigens. Vox Sang 2001;80:193-6.

Daniels GL, Fletcher A, Garratty G, et al. Blood group terminology 2004. From the ISBT committee on terminology for red cell surface antigens. Vox Sang 2004;87:304-16.

Garratty G, Dzik W, Issitt PD, et al. Terminology for blood group antigens and genes—historical origins and guidelines in the new millennium. Transfusion 2000;40:477-89.

Issitt PD, Anstee DJ. Applied blood group serology. 4th ed. Durham, NC: Montgomery Scientific, 1998.

Appendix 7. Examples of Gene, Antigen, and Phenotype Terms

System	Genes	Antigens	Phenotypes
ABO	$A\ A^1\ A^2\ B$	A A$_1$ A$_2$ B	A A$_1$ A$_2$ B
Rh	$D\ C\ E\ c\ e$	D C E c e	D+C+E–c+e+
MN	$M\ N\ S\ s$	M N S s	M+N+S–s+
P	$P1$	P$_1$	P1+ P1–
Lewis	$Le\ le$	Le^a Le^b	Le(a+)Le(a–b+)
Kell	$K\ k\ Kp^a\ Js^a$	K k Kp^a Js^a	K–k+Kp(a+)Js(a–)
Kell	$K^1\ K^2\ K^3$	K1 K2 K3	K:–1,2,–3
Scianna	$Sc^1\ Sc^2\ Sc$	Sc1 Sc2	Sc:–1,–2,–3
Kidd	$Jk^a\ Jk^b\ Jk^3$	Jk^a Jk^b Jk3	Jk(a+)Jk(a+b+)Jk:3

Modified from:

Denomme G, Lomas-Francis C, Storry J, Reid ME. Approaches to blood group molecular genotyping and its applications. In: Stowell C, Dzik W, eds. Emerging diagnostic and therapeutic technologies in transfusion medicine. Bethesda, MD: AABB Press, 2003:95-129.

Garratty G, Dzik W, Issitt PD, et al. Terminology for blood group antigens and genes—historical origins and guidelines in the new millennium. Transfusion 2000;40:477-89.

Zelinski T. Chromosomal localization of human blood group genes. In: Silberstein LE, ed. Molecular and functional aspects of blood group antigens. Bethesda, MD: AABB, 1995:41-73.

Appendix 8. Examples of Correct and Incorrect Terminology*

Term Description	Correct Terminology	Incorrect Terminology
Phenotype	Fy(a+)	Fy^{a+}, Fy$^{(a+)}$, Fya$^{(+)}$, Fy^a+, Fya(+), Duffy^a+, Duffy^a-positive
Phenotype	Fy(a+b–)	Fy$^{a+b–}$, Fy$^{(a+b–)}$, Fy^a(+)^b(–), Fy$^{a(+)b(–)}$
Antibody	Anti-Fy^a	Anti Fy^a, Anti-Duffy
Antigen	K	Kell (name of system)
Antibody	Anti-k	Anti-Cellano
Phenotype	K:1, K:–1	K1+, K:1+, K(1), K:(1), K1–, K:1–, K1-negative
Phenotypes	A Rh+, B Rh–	A+ (means positive for A antigen) B– (means negative for B antigen)
Phenotype	M+N–	M(+), MM (implies unproved genotype)
Phenotype	Rh:–1,–2,–3,4,5	Rh:–1,–2,–3,+4,+5 Rh:1–,2–,3–,+4,+5+

Note: The examples shown may not represent the only correct terminologies. In the Rh system, for example, use of CDE terminology is also acceptable and is more commonly used. The example demonstrates the correct usage if numeric terminology is used.

*Issitt L. Blood group nomenclature. In: Blood groups: Refresher and updates. Bethesda, MD: AABB, 1995.

Appendix 9. Distribution of ABO/Rh Phenotypes by Race or Ethnicity*

Race or Ethnicity	Number	Phenotype Distribution (%)[†]							
		O Rh+	O Rh−	A Rh+	A Rh−	B Rh+	B Rh−	AB Rh+	AB Rh−
White non-Hispanic	2,215,623	37.2	8.0	33.0	6.8	9.1	1.8	3.4	0.7
Hispanic[‡]	259,233	52.6	3.9	28.7	2.4	9.2	0.7	2.3	0.2
Black non-Hispanic	236,050	46.6	3.6	24.0	1.9	18.4	1.3	4.0	0.3
Asian[§]	126,780	39.0	0.7	27.3	0.5	25.0	0.4	7.0	0.1
North American Indian	19,664	50.0	4.7	31.3	3.8	7.0	0.9	2.2	0.3
All donors	3,086,215	39.8	6.9	31.5	5.6	10.6	1.6	3.5	0.6

*Used with permission from Garratty G, Glynn SA, McEntire R, et al for the Retrovirus Epidemiology Donor Study. ABO and Rh(D) phenotype frequencies of different racial/ethnic groups in the United States. Transfusion 2004;44:703-6.

[†]Percentages may not add up to 100.0% because of rounding.

[‡]Hispanic includes Mexican (68.8%), Puerto Rican (5.0%), Cuban (1.6%), and other Hispanic donors (24.6%).

[§]Asian includes Chinese (29.8%), Filipino (24.1%), Indian (13.8%), Japanese (12.7%), Korean (12.5%), and Vietnamese (7.1%) donors.

Appendix 10. Suggested Quality Control Performance Intervals

Equipment and Reagents	Frequency
I. Refrigerators/Freezers/Platelet Incubators	
A. Refrigerators	
1. Recorder	Daily
2. Manual temperature	Daily
3. Alarm system board (if applicable)	Daily
4. Temperature charts (review daily)	Weekly
5. Alarm activation	Quarterly
B. Freezers	
1. Recorder	Daily
2. Manual temperature	Daily
3. Alarm system board (if applicable)	Daily
4. Temperature charts (review daily)	Weekly
5. Alarm activation	Quarterly
C. Platelet incubators	
1. Recorder	Daily
2. Manual temperature	Daily
3. Temperature charts (review daily)	Weekly
4. Alarm activation	Quarterly
D. Ambient platelet storage area	Every 4 hours
II. Laboratory Equipment	
A. Centrifuges/cell washers	
1. Speed	Quarterly
2. Timer	Quarterly
3. Function	Yearly
4. Tube fill level (serologic)	Day of use
5. Saline fill volume (serologic)	Weekly
6. Volume of antihuman globulin dispensed (if applicable)	Monthly
7. Temperature check (refrigerated centrifuge)	Day of use
8. Temperature verification (refrigerated centrifuge)	Monthly
B. Heating blocks/Waterbaths/View boxes	
1. Temperature	Day of use
2. Quadrant/area checks	Periodically
C. Component thawing devices	Day of use
D. pH meters	Day of use
E. Blood irradiators	
1. Calibration	Yearly
2. Turntable (visual each time of use)	Yearly
3. Timer	Monthly/quarterly
4. Source decay	Dependent on source type
5. Leak test	Twice yearly
6. Dose delivery check (with indicator)	Each irradiator use
7. Dose delivery verification	
a. Cesium-137	Yearly
b. Cobalt-60	Twice yearly
c. Other source	As specified by manufacturer

Appendix 10. Suggested Quality Control Performance Intervals (cont'd)

Equipment and Reagents	Frequency
F. Thermometers (vs NIST-certified or traceable)	
1. Liquid-in-glass	Yearly
2. Electronic	Monthly
G. Timers/clocks	Yearly
H. Pipette recalibration	Yearly
I. Sterile connecting device	
1. Weld check	Each use
2. Function	Yearly
J. Blood warmers	
1. Effluent temperature	Quarterly
2. Heater temperature	Quarterly
3. Alarm activation	Quarterly
III. Blood Collection Equipment	
A. Whole blood equipment	
1. Agitators	Day of use
2. Balances/scales	Day of use
3. Gram weight (vs NIST-certified)	Yearly
B. Microhematocrit centrifuge	
1. Centrifuge timer check	Quarterly
2. Calibration	Yearly
C. Cell counters/hemoglobinometers	Day of use
D. Blood pressure cuffs	Periodically
E. Apheresis equipment	
Checklist requirements	As specified by the manufacturer
IV. Reagents	
A. Red cells	Day of use
B. Antisera	Day of use
C. Antiglobulin serum	Day of use
D. Transfusion-transmissible disease marker testing	Each test run
V. Miscellaneous	
A. Copper sulfate specific gravity	Day of use
B. Shipping containers for blood transport (usually at temperature extremes)	Twice yearly

Note: The frequencies listed above are suggested intervals, not requirements. For any new piece of equipment, installation, operational, and process qualification must be performed. After the equipment has been suitably qualified for use, ongoing quality control (QC) testing should be performed. Depending upon the operational and process qualification methodology, the ongoing QC may initially be performed at a greater frequency than one ultimately wishes to use. Once a track record of appropriate in-range QC results has been established (either during equipment qualification or the ongoing QC), the frequency of testing can be reduced, but, at a minimum, the frequency must comply with the manufacturer's suggested intervals. If no such guidance is provided by the manufacturer, the intervals given in this table would be appropriate to use.

Appendix 11. Directory of Organizations

AABB
8101 Glenbrook Road
Bethesda, MD 20814-2749
(301) 907-6977
FAX: (301) 907-6895
www.aabb.org

American Association of Tissue Banks (AATB)
1320 Old Chain Bridge Road, Suite 450
McLean, VA 22101
(703) 827-9582
FAX: (703) 356-2198
www.aatb.org

American Medical Association (AMA)
515 N. State Street
Chicago, IL 60610
(800) 621-8335
www.ama-assn.org

American Red Cross National Headquarters (ARC)
2025 E Street, NW
Washington, DC 20006
(202) 303-4498
Disaster Assistance: (866) 438-4636
www.redcross.org

American Society for Apheresis (ASFA)
570 West 7th Avenue, Suite 402
Vancouver, BC, Canada V5Z 1B3
(604) 484-2851
FAX: (604) 874-4378
www.apheresis.org

American Society for Clinical Pathology (ASCP)
2100 West Harrison Street
Chicago, IL 60612-3798
(312) 738-1336
Outside Illinois: (800) 621-4142
FAX: (312) 738-1619
www.ascp.org

American Society for Histocompatibility
   and Immunogenetics (ASHI)
15000 Commerce Parkway, Suite C
Mount Laurel, NJ 08054
(856) 638-0428
FAX: (856) 439-0525
www.ashi-hla.org

American Society of Anesthesiologists (ASA)
520 N. Northwest Highway
Park Ridge, IL 60068-2573
(847) 825-5586
FAX: (847) 825-1692
www.asahq.org

American Society of Hematology (ASH)
1900 M Street, NW, Suite 200
Washington, DC 20036
(202) 776-0544
FAX: (202) 776-0545
www.hematology.org

America's Blood Centers (ABC)
725 15th Street, NW
Suite 700, The Folger Building
Washington, DC 20005
(202) 393-5725
FAX: (202) 393-1282
www.americasblood.org

Armed Services Blood Program Office (ASBPO)
5109 Leesburg Pike, Suite 698
Falls Church, VA 22041-3258
(703) 681-8024
FAX: (703) 681-7541
www.tricare.osd.mil/asbpo

Association of Donor Recruitment Professionals
   (ADRP)
P.O. Box 540524
Grand Prairie, TX 75054-0524
www.adrp.org

College of American Pathologists (CAP)
325 Waukegan Road
Northfield, IL 60093-2750
(800) 323-4040
FAX: (847) 832-8000
www.cap.org

Foundation for the Accreditation of Cellular Therapy
   (FACT)
University of Nebraska Medical Center
986065 Nebraska Medical Center
Omaha, NE 68198-6065
(402) 559-1950
FAX: (402) 559-1951
www.factwebsite.org

ICCBBA, Inc.
204 St. Charles Way, Unit 179E
York, PA 17402
(717) 845-4790
FAX: (717) 845-9727
www.iccbba.com

Appendix 11. Directory of Organizations (cont'd)

International Society for Cellular Therapy (ISCT)
570 West 7th Avenue, Suite 402
Vancouver, BC, Canada V5Z 1B3
(604) 874-4366
FAX: (604) 874-4378
www.celltherapy.org

International Society of Blood Transfusion (ISBT)
Central Office
C/O Jan van Goyenkade 11
1075 HP Amsterdam
The Netherlands
+ 31 (0) 20 679 3411
FAX: + 31 (0) 20 673 7306
www.isbt-web.org

Joint Commission on Accreditation of Healthcare
    Organizations (JCAHO)
One Renaissance Boulevard
Oakbrook Terrace, IL 60181
(630) 792-5000
FAX: (630) 792-5005
www.jcaho.org

National Hemophilia Foundation (NHF)
116 West 32nd Street, 11th Floor
New York, NY 10001
(212) 328-3700
FAX: (212) 328-3777
www.hemophilia.org

National Marrow Donor Program (NMDP)
3001 Broadway Street NE, Suite 500
Minneapolis, MN 55413-1753
(800) 627-7692
Outside the US: (612) 627-5800
www.marrow.org

Plasma Protein Therapeutics Association (PPTA)
147 Old Solomons Island Road, Suite 100
Annapolis, MD 21401
(410) 263-8296
FAX: (410) 263-2298
www.plasmainfo.org

United Network for Organ Sharing (UNOS)
700 North 4th Street
P.O. Box 2484
Richmond, VA 23218
(804) 782-4800
FAX: (804) 782-4817
www.unos.org

Note: Contact information changes rapidly. Therefore, the data listed above may not be current for the entire life of this publication.

Appendix 12. Resources for Safety Information

Centers for Disease Control and Prevention (CDC)
Office of Health and Safety, Biosafety Branch
Mail Stop F-05
1600 Clifton Road
Atlanta, GA 30333
(404) 639-2453
FAX: (404) 639-2294
www.cdc.gov

Clinical and Laboratory Standards Institute (CLSI)
940 West Valley Road, Suite 1400
Wayne, PA 19087-1898
(610) 688-0100
FAX: (610) 688-0700
www.clsi.org

Department of Transportation (DOT)
Office of Hazardous Materials Standards
Research and Special Programs Administration
DHM-10
400 7th Street, SW
Washington, DC 20590-0001
(202) 366-8553
FAX: (202) 366-3012
www.dot.gov

Environmental Protection Agency (EPA)
Chemical Emergency Preparedness and Prevention
    Office (5104A)
1200 Pennsylvania Avenue, NW
Washington, DC 20460
(800) 424-9346
In Washington, DC metropolitan area: (703) 412-9810
www.epa.gov

Environmental Protection Agency (EPA)
Office of Solid Waste (5305W)
1200 Pennsylvania Avenue, NW
Washington, DC 20460
(800) 424-9346
www.epa.gov/osw

Food and Drug Administration (FDA)
Center for Biologics Evaluation and Research
Division of Blood Applications, HFM-370
1401 Rockville Pike
Rockville, MD 20852-1448
(301) 827-3524
FAX: (301) 827-3535
www.fda.gov/cbcr

International Air Transport Association (IATA)
1776 K Street, NW, Suite 400
Washington, DC 20006
(202) 293-9292
FAX: (202) 293-8448
www.iata.org

International Civil Aviation Organization (ICAO)
999 University Street
Montreal, Quebec
Canada H3C 5H7
(514) 954-8220
FAX: (514) 954-6376
www.icao.int

National Fire Protection Association (NFPA)
1 Batterymarch Park
Quincy, MA 02169-7471
(617) 770-3000
FAX: (617) 770-0700
www.nfpa.org

National Institute for Occupational Safety and
    Health (NIOSH)
Education and Information Division
4676 Columbia Parkway
Cincinnati, OH 45226-1998
(800) 356-4674
Outside the US: (513) 533-8328
Clinicians' Post-Exposure Prophylaxis Hotline:
    (888) 448-4911
FAX: (513) 533-8588
www.cdc.gov/niosh

National Institutes of Health (NIH)
Division of Safety
Building 13, Room 3K04
Bethesda, MD 20892
(301) 496-2346
FAX: (301) 402-0313
www.nih.gov

Nuclear Regulatory Commission (NRC)
Office of Public Affairs
Washington, DC 20555
(800) 368-5642
In Washington, DC metropolitan area: (301) 415-8200
FAX: (301) 415-2234
www.nrc.gov

Appendix 12. Resources for Safety Information (cont'd)

Occupational Safety and Health Administration (OSHA)
Office of Communications
Room N-3647
200 Constitution Avenue, NW
Washington, DC 20210
(202) 693-1999
Workplace safety and health-related questions:
    (800) 321-6742
www.osha.gov

US Postal Service (USPS)
Headquarters, Room 9301
475 L'Enfant Plaza, SW
Washington, DC 20260
(800) 275-8777
www.usps.com

Note: Contact information changes rapidly. Therefore, the data listed above may not be current for the entire life of this publication.

Index

Page numbers in italics refer to tabular or illustrative material.